THESE ARE THE VOYAGES

ALSO BY MARC CUSHMAN

These are the Voyages — TOS: Season Two

These are the Voyages — TOS: Season Three

I SPY: A History and Episode Guide of the Groundbreaking Television Series

THESE ARE THE VOYAGES
TOS: SEASON ONE

Marc Cushman

with Susan Osborn

foreword by John D.F. Black and Mary Black

Jacobs/Brown Press
San Diego, California

LIBRARY OF CONGRESS CATALOGUING-IN-PUBLICATION DATA
Cushman, Marc
These Are the Voyages – TOS: Season One /
Marc Cushman, with Susan Osborn; with a foreword by John D.F. Black and Mary Black;
First Edition edited by Jon Zilber and Dylan Otto Kryder, with Judith Bleses
Revised Edition edited by George A. Brozak and Mark Alfred,
with Thomas C. Tucker
Publishers: Robert Jacobs and Matthew Williams Brown
p.   cm.
Includes bibliographical reference and index

ISBN 978-0-9892381-0-6 (hard)
ISBN 978-0-9892381-2-0 (soft)
ISBN 978-0-9892381-3-7 (ebook)
First Edition print run … August 2013
Revised Edition print run … December 2013

Library of Congress Control Number: 2013940946
©2013 Marc Cushman. All rights reserved

This book is a work of journalism, protected under the First Amendment, and is not endorsed, sponsored, or affiliated with CBS Studios Inc. or the "Star Trek®" franchise. The *Star Trek®* trademarks, logos, and related names are owned by CBS Studios Inc. and are used under "fair use" guidelines.

No part of this book may be reproduced or transmitted in any form or by any means, electronic or mechanical, including photocopying or recording, or by any information storage and retrieval system, without permission in writing from the publisher.

Cover design: Susan Osborn, Leo Sopicki and Gerald Gurian
Interior Design: Marc Cushman, Susan Osborn and Gerald Gurian
Back photo of author: Mike Hayward Photography

Manufactured in the United States of America

Jacobs/Brown Press
An imprint of Jacobs/Brown Media Group, LLC
San Diego, California
www.JacobsBrownMediaGroup.com

To Gene Roddenberry and Robert H. Justman
for their encouragement and invaluable help in providing the documents needed
for this telling of the *Star Trek* story.

To Dorothy C. Fontana
for her extra efforts in supplying me with the information and further connections
to make much of what follows possible.

To John D.F. Black and Mary Stilwell-Black
for their friendship and candidness in regard to their *Star Trek* memories.

Acknowledgments

Beyond Gene Roddenberry and Robert H. Justman, who guided this project through its early research stages, dating back to 1982, and Dorothy Fontana, John D.F. Black and Mary Black, my appreciation to those who gave further encouragement and guidance and support:

For all her help going through the *Star Trek* show files at the UCLA Performing Arts Library (since absorbed into the UCLA Special Collections Library), my gratitude to Lauren Buisson.

For locating the Nielsen ratings for the original broadcasts of *ST:TOS*, I am indebted to Kate Barnett at Nielsen Media Services.

A special thank you to those who kindly granted interviews: Barbara Anderson, Jean Lisette Aroeste, Emily Banks, Hagan Beggs, John D.F. Black, Mary Black, Bill Blackburn, Robert Brown, Judy Burns, Marvin Chomsky, Paul Comi, Joe D'Agosta, Leslie Dalton, Win de Lugo, James Doohan, John M. Dwyer, Harlan Ellison, John Erman, Dorothy C. Fontana, Michael Forest, David Frankham, Ben Freidberger, Lisa Freidberger, Gerald Fried, David Gerrold, Clint Howard, Bruce Hyde, George Clayton Johnson, Robert H. Justman, Stephen Kandel, Sean Kenney, Tanya Lemani, Gary Lockwood, Barbara "BarBra" Luna, Don Mankiewicz, Bruce Mars, Don Marshall, Tasha "Arlene" Martel, Richard Matheson, Vincent McEveety, Lee Meriwether, Lawrence Montaigne, Sean Morgan, Stewart Moss, Joyce Muskat, Julie Newmar, Leonard Nimoy, France Nuyen, Leslie Parrish, Eddie Paskey, Roger Perry, Ande Richardson, Gene Roddenberry, Rod Roddenberry, Joseph Sargent, Ralph Senensky, Peter Sloman, Louise Sorel, Norman Spinrad, Malachi Throne, Tralane, Bjo Trimble, Beverly Washburn, Andrea Weaver, Grace Lee Whitney, William Windom, John Winston, and Celeste Yarnell.

Many of those who helped to make the original *Star Trek* are sadly no longer with us. In an effort to include their voices in this documentation, I relied on hundreds of newspaper and magazine articles, as well as dozens of books. A full list of these sources can be found in the bibliography, but I wish to give special mention here to the following books and their authors:

Beam Me Up, Scotty by James Doohan with Peter David. *Beyond Uhura: Star Trek and Other Memories* by Nichelle Nichols. *The City on the Edge of Forever* by Harlan Ellison. *Eighty Odd Years in Hollywood* by John Meredyth Lucas. *From Sawdust to Stardust: The Biography of DeForest Kelley* by Terry Lee Rioux. *Gene Roddenberry: The Last Conversation* by Yvonne Fern. *Gene Roddenberry: The Myth and the Man Behind Star Trek* by Joel Engel. *Great Birds of the Galaxy* by Edward Gross and Mark A. Altman. *I Am Not Spock* and *I Am Spock* by Leonard Nimoy. *Inside Star Trek: The Real Story* by Herbert F. Solow and Robert H. Justman. *The Longest Trek: My Tour of the Galaxy* by Grace Lee Whitney with Jim Denney. *The Making of Star Trek* by Stephen E. Whitfield and Gene Roddenberry. *The Music of Star Trek,* by Jeff Bond. *On the Good Ship Enterprise: My 15 Years with Star Trek* by Bjo Trimble. *Science Fiction Television Series* by Mark Phillips and Frank Garcia. *Shatner: Where No Man ...* by William Shatner, Sondra Marshak and Myrna Culbreath. *The Star Trek Compendium* by Allan Asherman. *Star Trek Creator* by David Alexander. *The Star Trek Interview Book* by Allan Asherman. *Star Trek Memories* by William Shatner with Chris Kreski. *To the Stars: The Autobiography of George Takei* by George Takei. *Trek Classics* by Edward Gross. *The Trouble with Tribbles* and the *The World of Star Trek* by David Gerrold.

For those who have either shared in the decades of work or have given their support and encouragement in other meaningful ways:

Mark Alfred, Barbara Asaro, Paul Barry, Wayne Beachley, Andrew Beirne, Brian Beirne, Judith and Tony Bleses, George A. Brozak, Shay Cranfield, Mike Crate, Dawn Cushman, Druanne Cushman, Steven Dai Watkins-Cushman, Kathleen Dougherty, Curtis Fox, Melody Fox, David Furlano, Karen Glass, Gerald Gurian, Bonnie Hill, Gerald Hill, Joan Furlano, Dylan Otto Kryder, Bernie Kulchin, Linda J. LaRosa, Jon Laxton, Kathy Marshall, Tom McClane, Larra Morris, Alex Nava, Susan Osborn, Ian Peters, David-Mark Peterson, Mark Phillips, Jim Plaster, Patti Plaster, Bill and Mikki Jo Resto, Jake and Patricia Satin-Jacobs, Ruth Anson-Sowby, Paul Stuiber, Jeff Szalay, Paula Taylor, Thomas C. Tucker, Gary Werchak, Eric Zabiegalski, Michael Zabiegalski, and Jon Zilber.

May you all live long and prosper.

TABLE OF CONTENTS

Foreword / Preface / Author's Note	xi
01: The Creator	1
02: To Boldly Pitch	23
03: Designing *Star Trek*	35
04: Test Flight -- Filming *The Cage*	61
05: Double or Nothing – A Second Pilot	73
06: Episode 1: *Where No Man Has Gone Before*	89
07: The Calm Before the Storm	107
08: Episode 2: *The Corbomite Maneuver*	132
09: Episode 3: *Mudd's Women*	153
10: Episode 4: *The Enemy Within*	168
11: Daniels Leaves His Marc / Episode 5: *The Man Trap*	186
12: Episode 6: *The Naked Time*	206
13: Episode 7: *Charlie X*	220
14: Episode 8: *Balance of Terror*	236
15: Episode 9: *What Are Little Girls Made Of?*	253
16: Episode 10: *Dagger of the Mind*	270
17: Enter Gene L. Coon / Episode 11: *Miri*	284
18: Deadlines, Breakdowns, and Replacements	302
19: America Meets *Star Trek*	319
20: Episode 12: *The Conscience of the King*	327
21: Episode 13: *The Galileo Seven*	346
22: Episode 14: *Court Martial*	363
23: Episodes 15 & 16: *The Menagerie, Parts 1 & 2*	385
24: Mid-Season 1966	401
25: Episode 17: *Shore Leave*	420
26: Episode 18: *The Squire of Gothos*	441
27: Joseph Pevney into the Arena / Episode 19: *Arena*	453
28: Episode 20: *The Alternative Factor*	471
29: Episode 21: *Tomorrow Is Yesterday*	487
30: Episode 22: *The Return of the Archons*	499
31: Episode 23: *Space Seed*	512
32: Episode 24: *A Taste of Armageddon*	527
33: D.C. Joins the Staff / Episode 25: *This Side of Paradise*	538
34: Episode 26: *The Devil in the Dark*	556
35: A Back Order of Three / Episode 27: *Errand of Mercy*	571
36: Episode 28: *The City on the Edge of Forever*	583
37: Episode 29: *Operation: Annihilate!*	607
38: Ratings, Reactions, Repeats, and Rewards	618
Appendix / Season One Quick Reference	630
Bibliography	633
Quote Index	642
Memos / Letters Index	655

FOREWORD

Why *Star Trek*?

Has there ever been anything like the *Star Trek* phenomenon? Not in our lifetime.

Has anyone ever offered an explanation of what caused it to explode like that meteor over Russia in February 2013, becoming so deeply meaningful to millions, maybe billions, of people? There's been no explanation so far, not one that we can recognize as the full and real answer.

Whatever we're watching, whatever we're reading ... Bang, there it is! *Star Trek*!

We'll be listening to a news show. The panel will be using phrases like "the latest iteration" and "fiscal consequences," then one of the experts decides to reference *Star Trek* to illustrate a problem and a second expert proposes a solution, using another *Star Trek* reference.

A travel show on PBS presents Paris, its museums, restaurants ... and a charming hotel where the show's host steps into a small, vintage elevator and announces "Beam me up, Scotty."

Central characters in comic strips identify themselves as Trekkers and expound lengthily on the subject, as do central characters in comedy series like *The Big Bang Theory* and *Family Guy*.

Pundit-comedians, such as Stephen Colbert and Jon Stewart, make the idiom of *Star Trek* part of their own idiom as though the language invented nearly fifty years ago had been taught them in a university classroom, not from a television screen.

Maureen Dowd, in her *New York Times* column -- *The New York Times*, for God's sake! -- uses the plot of "The Naked Time" to make a political point.

When we left the show, we pretty much believed that was the last time that *Star Trek* would be any part of our everyday life. Then, when it was cancelled after three seasons, we were certain it was no longer anything to be reckoned with. We were not alone in that conviction.

When it all started, nobody – *nobody* – in Building 9 at Desilu had the slightest clue how gigantic *Star Trek* would become. The hope that everybody in Building 9 and on Stages 9 and 10 had in the spring of 1966 -- the *"Oh, whoopee, we've got a real hit!"* kind of hope -- was that the series would go five seasons on NBC, hence the Enterprise's "five year mission" that Captain Kirk's voice intoned at the start of each episode. The significance of *five*? At that time, if a series managed to hold on for five years, building up a package of 130 episodes, it was an easy sell to syndication where the big money came from ... a nice, neat expectation, one that was achievable, not grandiose or unrealistic.

We'd all do our jobs, we'd do them well -- in fact, we set ourselves to do them *very* well -- and we could expect the work we'd done on this new series would serve to fill out our resumes for future work.

There was good reason to be optimistic:

- The writers who'd signed on for the first group of episodes -- among them giants in the science fiction field -- had committed themselves to bring their best possible work to *Star Trek*. The lead actors, Bill Shatner and Leonard Nimoy, were gifted, not merely solid. "Solid actor in the lead" usually means that a series had to settle for someone who was attractive, well-trained and only moderately interesting. Bill and Leonard were many, *many* notches above "solid."

- Bob Justman was so reliable that he might have been a perfectly-tuned robot -- a robot with a dry sense of humor.

- The intense dedication extended through the company, from the editor Fabien Tordjmann to our art director, Matt Jefferies, to ... everyone.

And Gene Roddenberry? Gene was the *leader*. There was never a moment when Gene showed the slightest degree of hesitance or uncertainty. He was committed to that vision he had of what the series should be, of what direction each scene and segment should take, and he never wavered. Like a general -- Patton comes to mind -- he knew his plan and nothing would stand in its way.

All of us marched together, our eyes on that distant star.

As spring 1966 was turning into summer 1966, it wasn't that difficult to put in an occasional 9 a.m to 2 a.m. workday. Not when you're young, you're happy in your work and you've been set up in an office that Desilu had newly carpeted, newly painted and equipped with the *first real copier that most of us had ever had access to!*

9 a.m. to 2 a.m. Seventeen hours. From this distance, it sounds like relentless, intense work. It was. You're like that frog in the water ... you've been put in a pot ... the pot's been put on a stove ... you're paddling around, not noticing that the water is changing from cool to lukewarm to warm to ...

Looking back, the whole experience seems less like the frog getting gradually poached and more like the frog locked inside a pressure cooker.

Could that be the answer to Why *Star Trek*? ... why *Star Trek* has its never-ending energy?

Maybe all that stress and urgency and agita threw itself into the very soul of the series, making it what it has become for so many. The clashing of egos, like flint on steel ... did it create that spark?

Or maybe some kind of magnetic lines of force converged, creating a new universe on film, opening up a world that so many needed to have ... filled now with devices that parallel those that appeared on *Star Trek*, like cell phones and Kindle and the internet ... the miniskirt that Grace Lee Whitney wore ... and even her swirly hairstyle which shows up now and then. The crew of the Enterprise would set their weapons to stun, not kill. Now we have tasers. Stretching it a bit: Spock, the perfect nerd. appeared in 1966 and not too long after came the emergence of Steve Jobs.

Whatever the next fifty years holds for *Star Trek*, the book that follows these two pages does put forth the complete, truthful and conscientious narrative of the *Star Trek* phenomenon. The facts Marc Cushman has so meticulously assembled -- they can stand as a Bible for *Star Trek* true believers.

And answer, for *Star Trek* non-believers, that question ... Why *Star Trek*?

John D. F. Black and Mary Black
May, 2013

PREFACE

Toward the end of 1966, my fellow fifth graders at Hebo Elementary School had fallen in love with a new TV series called *Star Trek*. I remember the first time I heard about it -- on a Thursday, just a few minutes before the end of the school day. Mrs. Ruff, our teacher, was about to assign homework when nearly every kid in the class let out a collective groan. Now, no fifth grader likes homework, but I had never heard a disheartening sound like this after the mere mention of it. And then Mrs. Ruff said, "I know. It's *Star Trek* night." It was an odd sounding combination of two words, greeted by a knowing murmur, then her adding, "All right, no homework tonight." A cheer went up. I felt like cheering, too. Hey, no homework. But because of what...something called a star trek?

After the bell rang and we headed into the hall, I asked a friend what a star trek was. He looked at me as if I were from another planet. In a way, I suppose I was.

Most of the students and teachers at Hebo Elementary lived in or around the town, which was deep in the heart of a dairy community near Tillamook, Oregon, and were able to watch the three television stations transmitting out of Portland, 100 miles away. On our family farm, the antenna my father placed on a hill behind the house only picked up the ABC and CBS affiliates. Except for during a month or two in the summer when its signal penetrated the tree covered mountain tops, KGW, Channel 8, the NBC broadcaster, was nothing more than a snowy picture with a lot of static. My three older sisters were just as curious and frustrated as I was. You see, all the students and teachers at the local high school had been talking about it, too.

During the remainder of 1966 and early '67, Thursdays continued to be designated as "no homework night," and my fellow students kept buzzing about this *Star Trek* show. I'd ask them to tell me about it and, in answering, I noticed something strange -- these 11 and 12 year olds from this cow town weren't just talking about story plot but something much deeper. There seemed to be little morality lessons in each episode, something akin to Aesop's Fables, but with, they said, "A really 'boss' space ship and a cool guy with pointed ears." Mrs. Ruff would even use the storylines of these episodes as springboards into what we were studying.

On June 15, 1967, *Star Trek* finally beamed into our house. The reception on Channel 8 was sub-standard but we could at least make out these men in futuristic military-type attire who were moving about in caves deep in the belly of a planet, hunting a creature that was killing the miners and tunneling through solid rock. We were captivated. And then the channel faded out. We waited with great anxiety hoping the picture and sound would return. Eventually it did, somewhat. And this is how it went the first time I saw "The Devil in the Dark."

Over the following weeks, the signal was stronger and we were able to see additional episodes in spotty, flickering black and white. The end of each had a profound effect on all of us as the show's writers used stories about the future to comment on issues of the day.

1967 was also the year I discovered my calling -- to write for television. There were a few TV series that helped ignite this passion in me, but no other show came close to sparking my imagination or seeming to have as much to say. *Star Trek* guided me as I practiced writing scripts, and grew from teenager to young adult.

By 1982, I had relocated to Los Angeles and was working as a writer for a small production company that supplied programming to local TV. My boss wanted to do a one-hour special on the *Star Trek* phenomenon. The series was still airing five nights a week in most cities; the conventions were annual events throughout America; and *Star Trek: The Motion Picture* had been the big box office hit of 1980, with *Star Trek II: The Wrath of Khan* soon to hit the theaters. A phone call was made and I was off to Paramount Pictures to interview Gene Roddenberry.

Gene was warm and gracious. I went from nervous to calm in a matter of minutes. He talked to me about *Star Trek* for over an hour then had Susan Sackett, his personal assistant, take me around the lot to various storage rooms where props, art department sketches and other artifacts were kept. I was allowed to take anything I wanted on the honor system. Susan also gave me every script from the series to copy and then return. She was not only helpful but remarkably trusting.

A few weeks later, after I had roughed out a script for *These Are the Voyages* -- as we were then calling it -- and arranged for a second interview session with Gene, our *Star Trek* special was suddenly off. Paramount decided a show of this type should be owned by the studio, which led to *Leonard Nimoy's Star Trek Memories* (1983). As it happened, I was with Gene in his office when the news came. I will never forget his look of profound disappointment, with a trace of betrayal. *Star Trek* had already been wrested away from him -- he was merely serving as a consultant on *The Wrath of Khan* -- and now the video program that was supposed to be about him and the series he created was going to be about Nimoy and the series he starred in. Gene grew silent for several seconds as he stared off into space, and then said, "Well, you can always do it as a book. And screw them."

On the drive home, I wondered how long a project such as this would take if done properly. A year? Two? Three? I was busy trying to establish myself in television and, at the same time, holding down a day job. My commitment to writing a book on *Star Trek* was still a long ways down the road.

I didn't see Gene for several years. Then, in the fall of 1987, he was back on top with *Star Trek: The Next Generation*. I sent him a letter of congratulations and asked if he would allow me to pitch some story ideas. He was as gracious as always and invited me in. One of the stories I pitched would become the episode "Sarek." We also talked about that book I might one day write. Gene asked how it would differ from Stephen Whitfield's *The Making of Star Trek*, from 1968, or David Gerrold's two books from 1973, *The World of Star Trek* and *The Trouble with Tribbles*. I explained that the Whitfield book, written when the series was still in production, and to which Gene had contributed, only covered the first two seasons and, therefore, was an incomplete account of the series. Nor did it focus on the making of the individual episodes. Gerrold's *The World of Star Trek* was more of a long-form essay examining the popularity and assessing the series as a whole. His other book, *The Trouble with Tribbles*, while offering an in-depth look at the writing of that episode, dealt with no others. My approach would be to focus in great detail on the creative process behind the writing of all the episodes, as well as the scripts that never made it before the camera. Gene suggested I not limit myself to just "the writing." He said, "Of course, it all starts with the script, but writing science fiction for television is just as much about understanding what can and cannot be done in front of the camera and in post production as it is dreaming up stories. We had no shortage of ideas; the problem was finding affordable ways in which to tell them."

Gene recommended I go through the massive show files that he and *Star Trek* associate producer Robert Justman had safe-guarded for nearly two decades. "You'll find your book in those files," he said. "Making *Star Trek* was more work, compromise and sacrifice than any one could imagine…unless they had been there."

And there lay the key. I would have to build a time portal through which the reader could transport back to the years 1964 through 1969 so that they *could* be there. Sadly, building time portals can take what seems like forever.

Gene's health started failing him shortly after this. By the time "Sarek" was made, in the third season (with Peter Beagle handling the teleplay), Gene had already scaled back his involvement with the series. One year later, in 1991, he left us.

During the next decade, many of those who worked on the first *Star Trek* were publishing books. Yet none of these took a good hard look at the making of the "Classic 79." Why was each story chosen? Who contributed what to which script? What compromises had to be made in developing these stories and making the productions affordable? What difficulties were encountered while producing them? Which did the creative staff consider their successes and which did they see as their failures, and why?

With each new book I read, it seemed the history of *Star Trek* was becoming more, well, reinvented, and I became more determined to make the commitment to spend two or three years, or whatever it took, writing the type of book *I'd* want to read. My agent liked the idea of an all-out "biography" of a landmark television series but, with all those other books on *Star Trek* crowding the marketplace, he suggested I find another subject.

It was at this time that I met Robert Culp, who said that he and Bill Cosby were both confused as to why no one had ever written a book on their series from the 1960s -- *I Spy*. That show had, in a sense, changed the face of TV. *I Spy* was the first series to cast a white actor and black actor on equal status, and made possible the first instance of a Black winning an Emmy -- three years in a row for Bill Cosby as Best Lead in a Drama -- and it was also the first series to film around the world, ushering in the technology to make that achievement possible. It certainly deserved a book and I approached the project much as I had wanted to for *Star Trek* -- treating the show as flesh and blood, giving it and its makers a proper biography. The *I Spy* book was published in 2007 by McFarland & Company to positive reviews, and this motivated me to get back to work on the one about *Star Trek*.

Dorothy Fontana, *Star Trek*'s talented top writer and Script Editor, granted three separate interviews and connected me with many others from the first series. Robert Justman, the nuts-and-bolts producer, proved to be a great friend to this project as well. He welcomed me into his home on several occasions during the last year of his life as he battled Parkinson's disease, talking with me, providing me with many essential documents, and doing as Gene had -- insisting that I utilize the show files they had loaned to the UCLA Performing Arts Library. "We all have failing memories," he said. "Those documents are not susceptible to such disorders."

Gene and Bob were right, the show files were stained with the blood, sweat and tears that had gone into the making of each of the episodes and the many aborted stories and scripts. With every document I transcribed and every interview I conducted, my manuscript swelled in size. After connecting with a publisher, it was decided that this book would, in fact, be presented in three volumes, one devoted to each season of the original *Star Trek*.

Between researching, interviewing, writing, and editing, this trilogy on the first *Star Trek* has taken six years of my life, spread over 30, and I've loved every minute of it. With this first volume, and the two soon to follow, I hope you will enjoy taking this journey through time to witness the making of *Star Trek: The Original Series* as much as I have.

Marc Cushman, February 2013.

AUTHOR'S NOTE

In the pages that follow, many behind-the-scenes details about the inspiration and production of the *Star Trek* series and individual episodes are shared with the public for the first time. This recounting is drawn from a variety of sources, including Desilu and Paramount archives (the *Star Trek* show files stored in the UCLA Performing Arts Special Collections), the ratings reports from A.C. Nielsen Media, the archived papers of many of the individuals involved, newspaper and magazine articles from the 1960s, personal interviews, and my own synthesis of bits of stories told by different people at different times, as published in a wide variety of outlets. Contextual information about the history and state of the television industry before and during the *Star Trek* era is drawn from public sources.

In regard to the ratings reports from A.C. Nielsen, the manner in which the information was presented varied as a result of source and date. Nielsen had multiple ways of gauging audience numbers, from its overnight 12-city Trendex reports, to the 27-city or 30-city reports that arrived a week later, to the national surveys which came a week after that, and factored in rural areas, to periodic demographics reports. Some of these would estimate the audience numbers by ratings points, others by audience share, or by estimates of households watching, while others would cite two or more of these statistics. The complete significance of the Nielsen numbering systems from the 1960s may be difficult to interpret -- even for those whom this author spoke to who currently work at Nielsen Media Services. In order to determine the audience share for independent stations and give a full picture of the division of the ratings-pie, I subtracted the share assigned by Nielsen to NBC, CBS, and ABC, thereby arriving at the percentage remaining for independent stations. One thing is clear from all of these reports: which network programs for any given time slot came in at first, second and third place. *Star Trek*'s placement, after more than four decades of misleading folklore, may surprise you.

The picture images presented on the front and back cover, and within this book, came from numerous sources, including vintage magazines, NBC publicity pictures for *Star Trek* from the 1960s, Lincoln Enterprises film trims (sold to the fans through Gene Roddenberry's mail order service in the late 1960s and early 1970s), and which were then restored by private collectors, and, for non-*Star Trek* images, numerous news and internet sources. In regard to the restored film trims, photo caption credits acknowledge the individual, group, or fan website which contributed the image to this project. On the few instances when two fan sites either claimed credit for the restoration of an image or legal justification to contribute the image to this work, both sites have been listed.

After the first edition of this book was sent to print in June, 2013, and issued in August of that year, additional documents and images became available to this author, as well as a handful of new interviews. Some errors were also found in regard to copy editing. Therefore, this revised and expanded version of *These Are the Voyages – TOS: Season One* is being issued. My thanks for the assistance of the fans (and new friends) who felt that it was important to make this book as accurate and consistent as possible.

1

The Creator

He would ultimately become a pilot and a policeman, survive two grisly airplane crashes, change the course of network television and become an idol to countless fans of his visionary writing and ideas. But before any of that, Gene Roddenberry had a different plan for his life: He wanted to be a modern-day Jonathan Swift, the Irish poet and political pamphleteer who today is remembered mostly as a satirist.

Roddenberry admired Swift's ability to imagine new places and convey meaningful themes, saying: "I always enjoyed Jonathan Swift, the lands he went to and the characters he invented. It always seemed to me the type of writing I was doing was like what Swift did." (145-23)

In 1726, Swift wrote *Travels into Several Remote Nations of the World, in Four Parts. By Lemuel Gulliver, First a Surgeon, and then a Captain of Several Ships*, today known simply as *Gulliver's Travels*. Most people only remember the land of the Lilliputians, but the seafarer also encountered giants, ghosts, immortals and other fantastic creatures, often using parables to make a moral or political point. Roddenberry recalled how impressed he was with Swift's ability to tackle hot issues of his day by disguising them in the trappings of far-off alien places and societies. "Swift," he said, "used his characters to point out stupidities in our own system of thinking." (145-23)

With *Star Trek*, Roddenberry followed Swift in commenting on a similar list of issues: war, racism, over-population, slave labor and even prostitution. The influence is easy to spot -- Roddenberry intended it that way. He *wanted* to be compared to Swift. His super-charged ambitions pushed him to be something more than a word-slinger for hire; he was

Inscription refers to *Daily Variety* review. Roddenberry wrote: "Greatest writing compliment ever received – '333 Montgomery Street' review which accused me of stealing the dialogue from [courtroom trial] records."

driven to be regarded as a writer who had important things to say -- things that influenced positive change, both in his professional field and in society. Swift, presumably, wouldn't have minded the comparison -- his epitaph includes the challenge "Go forth, Voyager, and copy, if you can, this vigorous... Champion of Liberty."

To most fans of *Star Trek*, Roddenberry is a hero. A genius. A man with a vision. A humanitarian. A writer and producer of uncompromising ethics. The "Creator." Many marveled at his imagination and moral integrity. But like Swift, Roddenberry is not without his critics. They chastise him as a writer whose material vacillated between liberal and "jingoistic dogma," with sexist overtones, romantic naiveté and preachy dialogue. Among those who worked closely with Roddenberry, some proclaimed him to be self-glorifying, controlling and even mediocre.

Critical opinions will remain divided, but the many documents that have survived from the original *Star Trek* give evidence to Roddenberry's quick fluid mind, boundless creativity, and keen instinct for drama. They also tell us that like any good character in fiction, this creator was not perfect. Perfection, after all, would be dull.

***

Eugene Wesley Roddenberry was born in El Paso, Texas on August 19, 1921, though he was always called "Gene" to distinguish him from his father of the same name.

Papa Eugene, a native of Georgia, had been dirt poor and was a self-taught man. At 17, he lied about his age to join the Army and serve in World War I. While stationed in Texas, he married a local girl named Caroline Golemon. Two years after the birth of their son, Eugene left the military and moved his family to Los Angeles, where he became a policeman.

The Roddenberrys settled in Highland Park, a middle-class neighborhood that was predominantly white, but quickly changing as L.A. was becoming a multicultural metropolis. Eugene, the Southerner, the former dough boy, the "street beat" cop, had trouble adapting. Gene Roddenberry himself referred to his father as a man who was driven by fits of anger and, due to his upbringing in the Florida-Georgia backcountry, prejudice.

Roddenberry was determined not to be influenced by his father's negative side and sought to emulate the positives. He said, "[My father] was a good beat cop. I think [he] was very often embarrassed with what the police did in those days.... I guess many of my beliefs about ordinary people and what they can do come out of respect for my father." (145-23)

Roddenberry also attributed to his quiet father many aspects of his own ability to imagine the future, saying, "He was advanced beyond his time. Once he took me out to the front yard of our Monte Vista Street house and said, 'Gene, someday they'll rip out whole blocks of the city and put gigantic highways through here.' He was talking about the freeways that I later saw being built. He said this to me in the 1930s." (145-23)

The first freeway in Los Angeles -- the Arroyo Parkway (now The Pasadena Freeway) -- was completed in 1941.

At the time the Hollywood Freeway opened in 1968, Roddenberry received a letter which highlighted his father's knack for seeing things to come. He recalled, "Two elderly ladies wrote from Jacksonville, Florida when the original series was on NBC. They had watched *Star Trek*, saw my name, and wrote that they could have predicted that I would have done something like *Star Trek* because I had talked of such futuristic things when they had met me on my way to Europe to fight in World War I. They thought they had discovered my father and what he was doing long after he came back from the Great War. They thought I was my father.... To have them say about my father -- that he held such thoughts when they knew him -- was exciting.... It made me proud that, in spite of not being formally educated, he had dreamed such dreams." (145-23)

The Roddenberry clan grew with the arrival of Bob and then Doris. Eugene allowed his wife, a devout Baptist, to put the fear of God into the kids. Roddenberry told writer David Alexander, "She took us to church every Sunday, but my father didn't go…. I didn't really take religion that seriously. It was obvious to me, almost from the first, that there were certain things that really needed explaining and thinking on, but why bother about them?" (145-23)

Organized religion shocked young Roddenberry. On one trip to church, he was appalled when his Bible-thumping pastor described communion as consuming the flesh and blood of Christ. As he watched fellow parishioners stuff bread into their mouths -- bread that represented the body of Jesus -- and wash it down with the Son of God's blood in the form of red grape juice, the theme of many *Star Trek* scripts was born: question authority; do not pray to false gods, and any god interpreted by man is likely to be false.

Future *Star Trek* collaborator Robert H. Justman said, "The kind of organized religion that infuriated Gene was exploitive. Human beings exploit. Human beings are the only species on Earth that I know of who kill their own kind. Constantly." (94-6)

Although Roddenberry was becoming increasingly aware of mankind's frailties, he wanted to believe the future would see humankind choosing right over wrong. This was not an attitude later manufactured for the press; Roddenberry was a true Utopian. And these high hopes for the future had started at a young age.

As a boy, Gene Roddenberry was an avid reader, checking out three or four books from the library at a time. He also discovered the pulps, including magazines that catered to science fiction fans, like *Amazing Stories* and *Astounding*. The former was the brainchild of Hugo Gernsback, the man who first put the words "science" and "fiction" together (although he preferred the term "scientifiction"). The latter, *Astounding*, has been credited with ushering in the Golden Era of science fiction in 1939 with the discovery of A.E. Van Vogt, Isaac Asimov, Robert Heinlein and Theodore Sturgeon. In 1966, Roddenberry would invite all four authors to write for *Star Trek*. Two of them – Van Vogt and Sturgeon – did. Asimov wanted to but never quite found the time. Heinlein passed.

Roddenberry at L.A.C.C. (Courtesy of Gerald Gurian)

Roddenberry loved the radio, too, especially adventure shows such as *The Lone Ranger*, fantastic fare like *The Green Hornet*, and mysteries like *The Shadow*. With these influences, he discovered a passion to write. Mrs. Virginia Church, Roddenberry's English teacher and a published writer, recognized the teen's talent and a flair for storytelling. She encouraged him to keep writing and continue with his education.

Following high school, the only school the family could afford was the free Los Angeles City College. It was on a bus ride to L.A.C.C. where Roddenberry met an attractive blonde, two years his junior. Her name was Eileen Anita Rexroat. They were soon dating.

With Eileen by his side, Roddenberry believed he could shoot for the stars, so he enrolled in flight school. To appease his dad, he also focused on police studies. Two years later, his education was interrupted. The military needed pilots. Within days after the Japanese attack on Pearl Harbor, he was inducted into the Army Air Corps. Prior to shipping out, on June 20, 1942, he married Eileen Rexroat.

Captain Gene Roddenberry, USAF
(Courtesy of Gerald Gurian)

Roddenberry was only 20 when he received his officer's commission as a second lieutenant and assigned to Bellows Field, Hawaii where he joined the 394th Squadron. By January 1943, at age 21, he was flying B-17 bombers on combat missions out of Espiritu Santo Island, Guadalcanal. It was there, on August 2, that a B-17 piloted by Roddenberry crashed. The plane lost altitude on take-off, plummeted back to the runway, then skidded to a stop. Two members of the crew stationed in the nose of the plane perished. Seven others escaped the fire that consumed the wreckage. Army investigation found the crash to be the result of a mechanical failure. Roddenberry's record remained clean and he soon transferred back to the States where, ironically, he served as a crash investigator.

After the war, Roddenberry was discharged from the military and took a job as a junior pilot for Pan Am, which was breaking new ground in world airline service with the first around-the-world air route in 1947. On the night of June 18, 1947, he was off-duty and returning home on Pan Am Flight 121, the Eclipse, departing from Karachi, India. While flying over Syria, an engine burst into flames and the plane crashed in the darkened desert, killing seven of the nine flight crew members, including both pilots. Seven of the 26 passengers also perished. Roddenberry was the highest in rank of the surviving Pan Am employees on the scene. Despite suffering a pair of broken ribs, he took charge of the crash site, quickly getting survivors off the burning plane, tending to the injured and orchestrating the efforts that led them out of hostile territory to their safe rescue.

As the survivor of two harrowing plane crashes, with wife Eileen and now baby daughter Darleen to consider, Roddenberry decided it was time to change his occupation and move the family to Los Angeles where they took up temporary residence with his parents. During the first few months there, he made money as a salesman, but his short term goal was to follow in his father's footsteps into police work.

In February 1949, Gene Roddenberry took the oath as a policeman with the LAPD. He served first as a patrol officer, then as a traffic cop. Interviewed by David Alexander, he later reflected, "I was much more a macho-type person. I was still accepting things from my childhood as necessary and part of reality -- how men related to women, etcetera.... As a dramatist doing *Star Trek*, I have had a chance to sort those things out and say to myself, 'Jesus, that was a stupid attitude I had about this or that.'... But I had many saving graces, too.... I did not like violence for violence sake [in entertainment]. I had many female traits, which is certainly a part of any whole man or human. I wasn't part of the crowd that sat around on the sidelines and made fun of people. I always had great respect for people -- even those with different ideas.... [And] I hated animals to be hurt." (145-23)

During his seven years on the force, Roddenberry only used his gun once, to spare an injured dog from further suffering after being hit by a car.

Los Angeles Chief of Police William H. Parker, who had been Eugene Roddenberry's sergeant, took the younger Roddenberry under his wing. Knowing of the patrolman's growing interest in writing, Parker transferred him to Public Affairs where he wrote press releases and more. Roddenberry admitted, "I was Parker's speechwriter, writing his philosophical beliefs. I had to justify for him many of the things he did. These were things of rare honesty. I was close to him in the days when he dreamed of building a better police department and when he was engaged in putting his dreams into action." (145-23)

Parker was a visionary. He reinvented the LAPD into a highly mobile and rigidly trained force to reckon with. It was Parker's idea to hire Marine drill instructors and implement the paramilitary police model that would bring esteem to his department, as well as notoriety. Within law enforcement circles, Parker's LAPD gained a reputation for being "the finest in the world," but to many in Los Angeles, particularly those among the youth and minority groups, he was seen as a political boss who abused his power.

"It was only when he forgot he was a philosopher and began to think he was God that he got into trouble," Roddenberry said. "As his student, I have gotten into trouble the same way." (145-23)

***

In the early 1950s, television was just establishing itself in Los Angeles. In its first few years, TV programming originated almost exclusively from New York. The live shows, such as anthology series, transmitted their one-hour productions from the East Coast, as did the half-hour comedies and the variety and contestant shows. Los Angeles contributed the filmed series, with *The Lone Ranger* being the first western, *Dragnet* the first cop show, and *I Love Lucy* the first sitcom, all shot on film. As a result of this booming industry, production companies with little experience were sprouting up all around Hollywood, and they needed writers. Jack Webb's Mark VII Productions was one such company.

Producing the radio version of *Dragnet* and its TV counterpart required 80 scripts a year. Webb needed true stories from the files of the LAPD, so he sent an offer to the Public Affairs division to pay $100 for any police cases that could be used on his series. In 1951 this was very good money for a cop pulling in only $400 a month. In today's economy it equates to a $900 bonus, added to his $3,500 monthly paycheck from the city. All that was required was one page, typed, giving Webb "just the facts" of a real-life police investigation and its outcome.

Word quickly passed from one detective to the next to send their best stories to Roddenberry in Public Affairs where he would write the cases up and submit them to Webb. For each story *Dragnet* bought, the $100 prize was split down the middle. Soon Roddenberry was making enough money to consider pursuing a future in television. He was not alone. Don Ingalls, also assigned to Public Affairs, would follow Roddenberry into television as a writer-producer. The two would remain friends, with Roddenberry working for Ingalls on *Whiplash* and Ingalls working for Roddenberry on *Star Trek*.

The Public Affairs division also enabled Roddenberry to work as a technical consultant on Hollywood-produced cop shows. TV was seen as a great propaganda tool and Chief Parker wanted to ensure that television's version of the men in blue was portrayed in a proper and positive manner. This pushed the door open even further for Roddenberry to pursue a full-time career in television.

Following *Dragnet*'s lead in seeking the endorsement and cooperation of the LAPD was *Mr. District Attorney*, from Ziv Television Programs. While forgotten today, *Mr. District Attorney* deserves at least a footnote in history -- this was where Gene Roddenberry got his first real job in television.

Frederic William Ziv, head and namesake of the company, remembered, "A very large police officer in full uniform -- badge, whistle and gun -- was on the set for several days, reading scripts and giving advice. Finally, he looked at Jon Epstein [head of the Story Department] and said, 'I can write scripts as good as this.'" (197)

Roddenberry was invited to make good on his boast and send in a story idea in outline form. Along with the treatment, he wrote Epstein:

> Dear John [sic]: This is it! MR. DISTRICT ATTORNEY finally has a story tailored to TV's every need. If you don't like this you should go back to, you'll pardon the expression, Longuyland [Long Island]. P.S. This story is of current interest because gambling operations are currently giving [our] industry a headache. Its [sic] been in the news recently.

Epstein managed to forgive Roddenberry's slap to the face of his show and paid the cocky LA cop $700 to write a script. "Defense Plant Gambling" was dated March, 2, 1954. The pseudonym on the title page was Robert Wesley, a name Roddenberry later resurrected for a character in a *Star Trek* episode ("The Ultimate Computer"). The nom de plume was necessary because members of the LAPD weren't supposed to moonlight as television writers. And thus Roddenberry's career in TV was born -- with good timing, bluster, and an unexpected opportunity mixed with a little bit of rule-bending.

Roddenberry quickly followed with another *Mr. Distract Attorney* episode, "Wife Killer," in April 1954. It was an ironic title. Just as his dreams of becoming a working writer were being realized, his marriage was falling apart. The birth of a second daughter, Dawn, only delayed the inevitable. Eileen wanted her husband, newly promoted to sergeant, to forget writing and stay focused on a stable career in law enforcement. She wouldn't get her wish.

In 1955, Roddenberry sold four more scripts to *Mr. District Attorney* and submitted a story idea to another Ziv show -- *Science Fiction Theater*. Regarding the treatment for "The Transporter," he wrote, in part:

> The proposed story is of the invention of "The Transporter," a device which is television, smellovision, soundvision all rolled into one. A device which creates an artificial world for the user, capable of duplicating delight, sensation, contentment, adventure -- all beyond the reach of the ordinary person living the ordinary life. With it you can voyage to far-off lands, argue with Socrates, earn and spend a million dollars, or lay Marilyn Monroe. Take your choice. And this is the story of the inventor who, after

> achieving this miracle, suddenly realizes that a commercial, greedy, sometimes inhuman world would take over his miracle. And it might be used as they have used the miracle of radio, television, the motion pictures -- with more devastating results.... It could create wants and desires for which the world would destroy itself -- a dying race sitting at their "transporters." (145-7)

Science Fiction Theater passed, believing the story too expensive to film. Nine years later, Roddenberry resurrected the transporter in a different form for the first *Star Trek* pilot, "The Cage." That episode also used the theme of this earlier treatment, giving the Talosians the ability to duplicate delight, sensation, contentment and adventure, and show how they themselves would become a dying race, living vicariously through others.

The rejection of "The Transporter" was but a modest speed bump. As 1955 progressed, so did Roddenberry the writer, selling three scripts to the newest Ziv entry, the durable *Highway Patrol*.

At this time, Roddenberry took another step forward. With Lawrence Cruickshank on board as his agent, Roddenberry could pursue writing assignments beyond Ziv, beginning with a second stab at science fiction. This time, he wrote a full teleplay with the emphasis on character over sci-fi gadgets. The anthology series *Four Star Playhouse* bought and filmed the script, then sat on it for a year before shopping the property as part of a syndication package and selling it under a variety of banners to different markets. In California, "The Secret Weapon of 117" (AKA "The Secret Defense of 117") aired as an episode of *Chevron Hall of Stars*. In other parts of the United States, it was slotted into weekly anthology series, such as *Stage 7*, sponsored by U.S. Steel.

Roddenberry said, "In those days, Four Star [Productions]... considered it one of those odd things that happened and it never occurred to them that science fiction might have a life of its own. U.S. Steel wanted it, too [in addition to Chevron], and everyone was startled that an interesting story could be made out of science fiction elements." (145-26)

Roddenberry's episode starred Ricardo Montalban, who would later appear as Khan on *Star Trek*. The story dealt with a pair of aliens who had taken human form to spy on mankind. Becoming man and woman, however, caused great distraction for the pair with all the newfound emotions and temptations they felt. They ultimately abandoned their mission and their former kind, choosing to stay on Earth as imperfect human beings. If this sounds familiar to *Star Trek* fans, elements of the story appeared in the episode "By Any Other Name."

Daily Variety's review from March 1956 said:

> A tongue-in-cheek science-fictioner which takes off on a romantic comedy tangent, this *Chevron* proves a gay little romp with sharp philosophical overtones. It also marks the maiden "telepie" [*Variety* lingo for "teleplay"] effort of a promising scripter, Robert Wesley, which is the nom de video of an L.A. cop -- oops -- policeman.

It would be another eight years before "Wesley" had a chance to write science fiction again, being kept from it by a whirlwind of writing assignments for an assortment of TV cops and cowboys, in addition to writing for a real cop -- the Chief of the LAPD.

In 1956, Roddenberry wrote two more scripts for *Highway Patrol* and a couple for another Ziv hit, *I Led Three Lives*, which followed the exploits of an undercover FBI agent battling Communism in America. Ziv also put him to work on *West Point*, with a staggering fourteen script assignments over two years. One of these jobs was to finish a teleplay started by Sam Rolfe, who left the show when he sold a series of his own: *Have Gun - Will Travel*. Rolfe appreciated Roddenberry's handling of the script and the two men became friends.

In May 1956, as Roddenberry struggled to balance his television commitments with his fulltime LAPD job, he sent a letter to newfound literary friend and mentor Erle Stanley Gardner, the creator of *Perry Mason*. He talked of the important things in life -- "freedom to create, explore, travel, plus a comfortable income and some [professional] challenge" -- and how he saw few of these things happening if he remained on the force. He wrote:

> Although the challenge can be found in police work, not much else is there. During the past seven years... I've learned a big part of what the job teaches -- and the remaining education at a cost of 23 more years doesn't look like a good investment.... The thing that tipped the scale in favor of writing was, of course, the recent success of several scripts which has led to a number of top-paying assignments. Am working on two pilots now, continuing on *West Point*, which goes on a national hook-up this fall. ZIV's head of production was quoted in *The Reporter* the other day naming me as their top writer -- this and other things still have me amazed and grateful. (145-7)

Roddenberry resigned from the LAPD on June 7, 1956. Two weeks later, agent Lawrence Cruikshank arranged a meeting at CBS where his client pitched one of the two pilot ideas he'd mentioned to Gardner. From the series proposal, dated June 20:

> "Hawaii Passage" is a series of stories which take place mainly aboard an ocean liner, a cruise ship which travels between the mainland and Hawaii and possibly other Pacific ports.... The continuing main characters in the series of stories, outside of the ship itself, are the ship's captain, purser, and/or deck-officer. The stories are of a general anthology nature. They will concern passengers and the ship personnel, separately or in combination. (145-7)

1957, now a full time TV writer

CBS passed on the proposal (ABC would buy a comedy take on this 21 years later from producer Aaron Spelling, called *The Love Boat*).

With his time no longer split between two opposing careers, Roddenberry became even more prolific. In 1957, Ziv paid him to write a pair of pilot scripts based on in-house ideas for new series. One was "Junior Executive," which went nowhere; the other, "Coastal Security," was later reworked into what became a modest success called *Harbor Command*. The busy production house also assigned him two script jobs for a new series making its move from radio to TV. The short-lived *Dr. Christian* premiered in October.

Roddenberry worked for other production companies as well, taking four script assignments on a new western, *Boots and Saddles*. One episode featured DeForest Kelley and

James Doohan in prominent roles. Then Roddenberry reconnected with an influential friend and producer -- Sam Rolfe.

In 1957, *Have Gun - Will Travel* was beginning a long run on CBS. Star Richard Boone, a big name in television at the time, ensured good ratings from the outset. Show-runner Rolfe welcomed Roddenberry with five script assignments for the series' freshman season, beginning a long professional relationship between the two.

This rapid rise in Roddenberry's stature soon brought him an assignment writing his first hour-long script, "So Short a Season," for the NBC anthology, *Kaiser Aluminum Hour*. At year's end, he was paid to write two more pilot scripts: "Threshold," for an independent production company, which was set at the United States Air Force Academy; and, for Screen Gems, the newly-formed television arm of Columbia Pictures, a western called "The Man from Texas." While neither made it to series, the assignments exemplified Roddenberry's newfound prestige. He had sold more than two dozen scripts in a single year.

In 1958, as Roddenberry continued to write for *Have Gun - Will Travel*, he did a favor for Don Ingalls, his friend from the LAPD. Ingalls left the force to become a newspaper columnist, but also had his eye on television. Roddenberry passed a "spec script" written by Ingalls to the producer of *Harbor Command*, which led to a few assignments. Now Ingalls had a spec ready for *Have Gun*. Roddenberry connected him with Sam Rolfe, who was so impressed by both Ingalls' personality and abilities that the near-novice writer was given a job as the series' new associate producer. The ambitious Roddenberry took notice.

In November 1958, one of Roddenberry's *Have Gun - Will Travel* scripts, "Helen of Abajinian," won a Writers Guild Award in the Best Western category. This improved the odds for him to achieve what Sam Rolfe had -- to create and run a series of his own. He tried with another pilot script for Screen Gems: "Sam Houston," which was about the 19th century statesman, politician, and soldier. This also failed to find a sponsor. Undaunted, he wrote a pilot script based on his own idea: "The Man from Lloyds," dramatizing the cases of an insurance investigator. Screen Gems was not interested, so Roddenberry didn't get paid for the work. Next, he pitched a series idea to CBS. "Foot Beat" was about a cop walking a beat in Manhattan. The network passed.

More work came with a new Screen Gems series, *Jefferson Drum*, about a newspaper editor in a lawless frontier town. Roddenberry was given three assignments. In all, he sold 11 scripts in 1958. But Roddenberry was suddenly feeling "written-out." Looking for help, he sent a letter to his mentor, Erle Stanley Gardner:

> Dear Earl [sic]: Help! As you once advised (and the wisdom becomes more apparent every day), writers have a way of going stale. The battery runs down. You said you had a system of recharging which you were holding until I said I needed it. I need it.

Gardner advised Roddenberry to pursue other interests outside of writing, explaining that those activities would create experiences that could enrich his work. In time, the interests and activities Roddenberry chose to pursue would end his marriage.

1959 brought another half-dozen *Have Gun - Will Travel* assignments, courtesy of Sam Rolfe and Don Ingalls. And there was a new customer: Four Star and its latest series for ABC, *The Detectives*, starring Robert Taylor. Roddenberry picked up two assignments there. But his sights were now focused more than ever on getting a series of his own. To this end, he returned to Screen Gems, on assignment to turn "Foot Beat" into a pilot called "The Big

Walk." In March 1959, ABC announced that the series was on its fall schedule for Tuesdays 10:30 - 11 p.m. It seemed that Roddenberry was about to have his first series as a creator be broadcast. Five weeks later, Jack Hellman reported for *Daily Variety*:

> [Advertisers] are generally agreed that never in their experience has there been such an aggravating season of changes in the lineup of network shows. Overnight programs are moved around and what was scheduled yesterday doesn't hold good for tomorrow.... We have before us a list of 30 such shows, mostly half-hour, and any network exec who can tell at this time where they'll end up deserves a special Emmy.... Let the ad men try to figure out just where such shows as "The Big Walk" will land in the schedule.

"The Big Walk" was shuffled around, penciled in and then erased, and then penciled in again. One upside from all the shuffling: Roddenberry was getting noticed. On June 2, 1959, *Daily Variety* reported:

> Writer Gene Roddenberry, whose "The Big Walk" telefilm package at Screen Gems found a sponsor but no time slot, is one of the unusual breed of scripter who lived his stuff. "Big Walk" is about a cop on the beat, which Roddenberry was.

During the same month as this near miss, Roddenberry was presented with an unlikely second award -- at the American Baptists Convention. For his work on *Have Gun - Will Travel*, he was acknowledged as one of a handful of writers who were "consistently identifying themselves with the Christian way of life on radio and television." He later said, "I used religion several times in *Have Gun - Will Travel*. Once in a penitentiary, where a pastor was trying to keep a fellow from being hung, I wrote that the pastor grabbed a hacksaw blade, was cut by it, and was bleeding. I had him make some comment about blood and salvation. It's not that I actually believed in blood and salvation being connected, but that was the way the audience believed and I can remember going out of my way not to deal directly with what my thoughts were for several reasons.... I had learned early in school that the world was a cruel and difficult place, so I learned to cover myself. Perhaps I was consciously dishonest. Yes, I was, but I knew that a certain amount of dishonesty about such things covered you." (145-23)

As a result of the award from the American Baptists Convention, John M. Gunn, producer of the Christian television program *Frontiers of Faith*, contacted Roddenberry in regard to a series he wanted to launch dealing with "the modern application of the Christian ethic." Preoccupied with "The Big Walk" at the time, Roddenberry wrote back:

> Waited a week before answering you in the expectation that some [of the other series] might cancel out or fold, but the situation just got more grim.... "The Beat Cop" thing became "The Big Walk" which sold to L & M, was set to go ABC Sunday night following *Maverick*, then was cancelled out last moment on a policy decision to go all-western. Ah well... at least it may come alive again this winter but, frankly, I've become disenchanted with it now. (145-7)

The "grim" situation was about to get back on an upward trajectory.

In December 1959, the Hollywood trades reported that Gene Roddenberry and Don Ingalls had come together to produce a new western anthology series called *The Weapon*, in association with *Zane Grey Theatre* producer Hal Hudson. A pilot was made and aired as an episode of *Zane Grey*, but the series never materialized. A short time later, Roddenberry received a better offer. *Daily Variety* broke the news, reporting that he had been "inked to an exclusive writer-producer pact by Screen Gems," with his serving to "develop new properties for the company, as well as function as producer on 'Nightstick' [the new title for 'The Big Walk'], should it be sold for the following season."

***

Roddenberry, Kelley and Jake Ehrlich, "333 Montgomery Street"

At Screen Gems, a new pilot called "333 Montgomery Street" was moving forward. William Dozier, West Coast Vice President of Screen Gems, made the announcement on December 16, 1959 that, besides pursuing an effort to get a series out of "The Big Walk," the studio was planning to have a script written based on San Francisco criminal attorney Jake Ehrlich's book *Never Plead Guilty*. Roddenberry was assigned the job and finished the script quickly before the writers' strike started in mid-January, 1960. He then spent the remainder of the month working not as a writer but as a producer, preparing production under the watchful eye of studio executive Robert Sparks. Dozier and Sparks recommended he hire DeForest Kelley for the lead role based on attorney Ehrlich. Familiar with the actor, and having liked him in the *Boots and Saddles* episode he had written two years earlier, Roddenberry happily obliged.

In late January 1960, as the production of "333 Montgomery Street" shifted from the streets of San Francisco to the sound stages of Los Angeles, Roddenberry responded to another correspondence from Christian TV producer John Gunn, writing:

> I'm still involved in winding up the show I produced in San Francisco last week, and it looks like another ten days or two weeks before we get it into the can. Which means it would be at least that long before I could prepare any sort of story line for your approval.

Roddenberry didn't really want the job. In another letter to Gunn, from March, he continued to procrastinate, writing:

> Unfortunately, despite the continuing strike [January 16 to June 10], Screen Gems has elected to put my agreement with them into immediate effect, a marriage which includes a clause similar to the one my wife insisted upon some nineteen years ago. So, for better or worse, I'm bound-up exclusively theirs. For a year, anyway.

"333 Montgomery Street" aired in June 1960 as an episode of the anthology series

Alcoa Goodyear Theatre. The critic for *Daily Variety*, finding the half-hour to have "polish and gleam," wrote:

> Best aspect of Gene Roddenberry's script was the establishment of the central character -- and the lines given him to speak in court, unless they were verbatim out of Ehrlich's memoirs.

Despite the praise, the series did not sell to a sponsor.

Throughout the spring of 1960, as the writers' strike continued, so did Roddenberry's hefty $100,000 producer's salary from Screen Gems, which allowed him plenty of time to tinker with new projects, writing them now and turning them in later when the strike was over. "Kapu" was an action-adventure set in the Hawaiian islands, circa 1800; "Freelance" featured a mystery-writer playing amateur detective (think *Murder She Wrote*); "The Centurion" was a Roman Empire saga with an Army commander as the lead; and "Caravan" was described by Roddenberry as a "*Sea Hunt* type action-adventure utilizing the mysterious desert instead of the mysterious sea." None of the properties found a sponsor.

As the strike -- and the abundant free time -- dragged on, Roddenberry gained notoriety within the television industry by serving as a panelist on what the Writers Guild called "a unique and provocative inquiry." The June meeting presented by the Guild followed its Annual Television-Radio Writers Awards show. The "Television on Trial" panel consisted of TV producers Roddenberry and Peter Kortner (*Studio One* and *Playhouse 90*), *LA Times* entertainment writer Cecil Smith, Federal Communications Commissioner Ted Meyers, ABC exec Selig Seligman and, representing the advertising agency of Batten, Barton, Durstine & Osborn, ad man Bud Stefan. Larry Tubelle for *Daily Variety* observed:

> In response to Roddenberry's contention that the FCC, since it was set up to protect the public interest in this area, has every right to discipline a network for permitting "an obvious falsehood that harms the nation," [FCC man] Meyers expressed "doubt that the Commission would take a step to interfere with the internal content of a program that did not violate the law." ... Roddenberry's plea capped a sustained barrage of examples of sponsor interference in program content, and several sharp exchanges in which [ABC's] Seligman -- whose views brought audience hissing on a few occasions -- and [ad man] Stefan more or less lined up against [producers] Roddenberry, Kortner and [*Times* writer] Smith on a number of ticklish, inflammatory issues. Roddenberry's basic beef was with "the tremendous number of taboos" a writer must contend with. He cited, at the outset, a 22-point sponsor's edict to which he, as a writer, had to conform, and questioned their origin and basis. Such taboos, he noted [included] a major edict in which it was decided that "no Negroes were ever to be seen" on the *Riverboat* series, thus inaccurately depicting 1860 life on the Mississippi to the American public. This condition, Roddenberry heatedly maintained, was "ridiculous and damned near criminal."

Tubelle further quoted Roddenberry as saying:

> Is our nation, this priceless commodity, best served by [prestige] programs being exclusively tailored to sell soap and toothpaste? Even lesser shows should not be warped and changed to sell product.... For sponsors to twist facts to sell a product is wrong -- it should be prohibited by the FCC.

Gene Roddenberry's name was now familiar to all the studio heads and network chiefs. Notoriety can jumpstart a career in entertainment. In time, it can also end one. But

Roddenberry's stature now seemed strong enough to survive his controversial opinions.

After working together on "333 Montgomery Street," Robert Sparks felt Roddenberry needed more experience in production. The moment the strike ended, Sparks arranged for him to get a crash course in producing with a project started under Screen Gems show-runner Paul Harrison. *Wrangler*, a new western set to fill in as a summer replacement for the *Tennessee Ernie Ford Show* on NBC, would be a co-venture with Paramount Pictures, a novice in television, and Hollis Productions, a new company setup by Charles Irving, who had produced live soap operas in New York. With an order for 13 episodes, *Wrangler* was to be shot outdoors on videotape, and the industry was watching this experiment closely to see just how inexpensively and fast a primetime action-oriented series could be made. On June 29, Bob Chandler of *Variety* reported:

> Thus far, the all-tape series, such as they are, have been restricted to interiors, and consequently have had the same limitations, insofar as action is concerned, as live programs.... *Wrangler* involves action by its very nature -- it's a western.... The implications could be enormous, provided the shows work out.

On July 6, one day before *Wrangler* was scheduled to premiere on NBC, *Variety* reported that things were going badly and the network had cut the order back from 13 episodes to 11. According to the trade:

> Four tapes of the cowpoke skein are in the can, and apparently the network and JWT [the ad agency] have seen them all [and this] reportedly doesn't please the agency.... First of the four segments was taped in "film technique," but the director didn't tape enough covering footage, so that it's almost impossible to edit. Second segment was taped okay, in live sequence, but NBC continuity & acceptance insisted on deletion of a couple of scenes. Hollis [Productions] said this was impossible, that in shooting it "live style," such deletions would require complete re-doing of the entire scenes involved, at prohibitive cost. It claimed NBC should have posted a continuity man [network rep] on set instead of after-the-fact editing.

The finger-pointing had already begun and NBC postponed the premiere of *Wrangler* by two weeks. The order for episodes, in turn, was reduced again, from eleven to nine. On July 27, *Variety* reported that NBC, ad agency J. Walter Thompson and sponsor Ford Motors were united in their disappointment over the series, but would reluctantly go forward since there was not enough time to find a substitution for the time slot.

Wrangler made it on the air, but with its order slashed to six episodes. *Daily Variety* reviewed the first of these on August 8, saying it was "just another western that plods over the same old trails" and the "script of Gene Roddenberry played it safe without any attempts at striking a new note." Two days later, the weekly edition of *Variety* chimed in, saying:

> *Wrangler* doesn't answer many questions as to the future of tape, unfortunately. Overall, the opening show was so poor as to obviate some of the plus aspects of the cost comparison between tape and film.... The trouble with the show lay primarily in the creative end. A sometimes confusing script by Gene Roddenberry and a completely confusing job of direction by David Lowell Rich were mainly responsible.

KTLA unit manager Stretch Adler, involved in the project with the station's videotape mobile production unit, later said, "*Wrangler* was a debacle from beginning to end.

It was done by amateurs who had no knowledge of what they were doing." (1a)

Because Roddenberry, one of those amateurs, was working under Paul Harrison, he escaped blame. It had, however, been an eye-opening education as to what can and often will go wrong in television.

On December 20, 1960, with his Screen Gems contract in its final months and concerned it wouldn't be renewed, Roddenberry wrote to Bill Dozier:

> At a party the other evening, someone asked why nothing has ever been done with Michener's book *Tales of the South Pacific*. I was about to reply, mentioning the stage play, the motion picture, and Twentieth-Century's television series. Then it struck me that this was a hell of a good question. One single short story from the book has been used. Over and over again. And it was the weakest and most undramatic story of the entire book.... The bulk of this great book, one of the all-time best sellers, is a collection of unusually well-written, small and varied tales of Pacific war camp life. As you know, it is not a collection of war stories. Rather, it tells of the old Tonkinese woman who sold souvenir shrunken human heads, of the savage whose dream was to parachute from an airplane, of heat itch, of bootlegging, of the admiral who caught his zipper in his underwear, of the weird escapades planned to relieve their endless waiting, of gigantic poker and crap games and their humorous aftermaths.... In short, I am suggesting a half-hour, network-quality television series unlike anything which has been done. The title: "The Wild Blue." Not *Tales of the South Pacific*; no deal [needed] with Michener, but involving the same area of story, emphasizing quiet, ordinary and identifiable men caught up in the extraordinary background furnished by this most romantic, bizarre, and flavor-filled backwash of World War II. (145-7)

Just as "Hawaii Passage" could have been *The Love Boat* some 21 years before that ship sailed, this new concept contained the same framework to later be choppered in as *M*A*S*H*. Dozier, knowing a potential hit when he read one, extended Roddenberry's contract by six months, with a new provision: He could now also write for outside shows.

With his income from Screen Gems secured, Roddenberry took his time delivering pages on the series' proposal, instead grabbing several fast-paying script jobs around town. He accepted more writing assignments from *Have Gun - Will Travel*, including an episode directed by Robert Butler, who would later direct for *Star Trek*. He also wrote three scripts for old friend Don Ingalls, who was now serving as story consultant on *Whiplash*, a new western filming in Australia. One of Roddenberry's scripts was chosen to be the network premiere episode.

Finally, on May 5, five months after getting the go-ahead to further develop "The Wild Blue" and the contract extension that went with it, Roddenberry followed up with Bill Dozier, writing:

> Keeping you posted on things -- am in the process of delivering to Bill Sackheim a very detailed sales presentation and format on the World War II Pacific Campaign series.... Have written a memo to [agent] Cruikshank, explaining why I began this project at such a late date in my contract -- specifying the guarantees you have agreed to afford me. He has also been made aware of my cordial relationship with you and my desire for a separation agreement which will see that friendship has not impaired in any way. (145-7)

Sackheim, who Roddenberry mentioned in his letter, was a writer/producer at Screen Gems who had worked on such series as *Playhouse 90* and *Alcoa Theatre*. He felt Roddenberry's series proposal needed work, and a better title. On May 17, upon receiving the revised material from Sackheim, Roddenberry wrote Dozier:

> Have in my hand the mimeographed presentation of "APO 923," dated May 15, 1961, which will go to New York. Wanted you to know I am pleased it credits Bill Sackheim for his part in designing this presentation. (145-7)

Roddenberry's choice of the words "his part in designing this presentation" were calculated -- "designing" not "creating." In a letter to his agent, he said:

> Now, to the subject of the property "APO 923" -- before the decision to leave Screen Gems occurred, I selected Bill Sackheim as the Executive Producer with whom to work on this project. It was a happy choice, we see pretty much eye to eye on the project, both of us have great enthusiasm for it. When the Exodus question arose, I told Dozier I would go ahead with this project only if certain agreements and protections were agreed upon.

Among those terms, Roddenberry wanted "exclusive billing as series creator" and to be guaranteed full royalties per his Screen Gems contract.

As for that new title ("APO" stands for "Army Post Office"), Sackheim was thinking along the same lines as author Richard Hooker did several years later when he wrote *M*A*S*H* (an acronym for "Mobile Army Surgical Hospital").

With his contract ended, Roddenberry found more money at Screen Gems with a pair of assignments for the studio's new private detective show, *Shannon*, produced by Robert Sparks, and one of his scripts was chosen to open the series' one-year syndicated run.

Roddenberry expanded his footprint, working outside of Screen Gems with a script assignment for an hour-long series *Target: The Corrupters*. His script was heavily rewritten and the "teleplay" credit ended up going to staffer Harry Essex, leaving Roddenberry with only a "story by" acknowledgement and diminished residuals. It was a bitter pill to swallow, one that would leave him hesitant to add his name to other writers' scripts that he rewrote in the future, even when there was little left of the original material.

Meanwhile, news continued to trickle in regarding the two pilot scripts he had left behind at Screen Gems. On November 22, *Variety* reported that the studio planned to film the "APO 923" pilot. The December 19 issue added that CBS would finance and William Sackheim would produce. Roddenberry was listed as "head writer." By the first days of January, the cast had been set with three up-and-coming actors: Ralph Taeger, Pat Harrington, Jr. and James Stacy. CBS programming executive Oscar Katz was hot on the property and, in early February, told *Daily Variety* the series would offer "a different kind of war story." But on February 26, the trade reported that *Perry Mason*, the network's powerhouse lawyer series, would exit Saturday to make room for the return of Jackie Gleason, with *Perry Mason* landing in the Thursday night spot reserved for "APO 923." This second series by Roddenberry to be bought by a network, suffered the same fate as the first: it was never to be heard from again.

One last pilot -- and potential Screen Gems series for Roddenberry -- also started in 1961 and carried over into early 1962, was "Defiance County." This final project for the studio would ultimately create bad blood -- not between Roddenberry and Screen Gems, or

Roddenberry and CBS, but between Roddenberry and his mentor, Erle Stanley Gardner.

On November 11, 1961, *Daily Variety* announced that Screen Gems was planning to film the pilot. In the same report, Paisano Productions, the makers of TV's *Perry Mason*, was reported as planning one of its own pilots, based on *Doug Selby*, a well-known property of Erle Stanley Gardner's with nine novels published between 1939 and 1949 (beginning with *The D.A. Calls It Murder* and ending with *The D.A. Breaks an Egg*). The title character was a young and somewhat inexperienced rural area district attorney. Roddenberry's "Defiance County" also involved a young and somewhat inexperienced rural area D.A. Another coincidence: CBS was the network with whom Paisano Productions -- and, therefore, Gardner -- had their relationship. Because of *Mason*, the production company believed it had a handshake deal with the network regarding a TV version of *Selby*.

In the December 19 issue of *Daily Variety*, Dave Kaufman reported that Paisano had to hold up pilot plans on "Douglass Selby" (the title given to the TV version of *Doug Selby*). In the same issue, a different columnist reported that CBS would be financing "Defiance County" for Screen Gems. It didn't take a sharp legal mind like Perry Mason to figure this one out. Jackson Gillis, the story editor on *Perry Mason*, got a hold of a copy of Roddenberry's script, then reported to his boss, producer Gail Patrick Jackson:

> I certainly think the script comes close to [our proposed series], since *Selby* has been in wide circulation for a very long time.... For considering how long the Gardner books have been sitting on CBS desks, I'd say they've certainly violated something here! (73a)

Recalling how Roddenberry and Dozier united to make a TV version of James Michener's *Tales of the South Pacific* without involving or paying Michener, it takes little imagination to see that they might think to do the same with Gardner's *Doug Selby*. They certainly had opportunity to know about the book series -- Bill Dozier had once been Gardner's literary agent, and Roddenberry was Gardner's friend and, in a sense, student.

Roddenberry later said, "I don't think for a moment that I am the grand knight in shining armor, forever courageous. I've seen my moments of cowardice and my moments of confusion. I keep trying to improve these situations, but I don't allow myself to be swept away because I would be swept away by a lie. I allow myself to forgive myself and like myself even though I lie. I keep hoping and working for a better Gene Roddenberry." (145-23)

When Gardner learned of Roddenberry's latest creation, he referred the matter to his attorney, who then contacted Screen Gems' legal counsel. According to writer David Alexander, there exist notes in the Gardner Archives that document how the famed author's lawyer told the studio's lawyer, "I thought you ought to know you're starting a show which is very comparable to a show Paisano owns."

On February 9, Roddenberry wrote Gardner:

> I have created a format and written a pilot film, produced last month and now in cutting stage, which has as its central character a prosecuting attorney in a Midwestern town. Not an entirely new idea, I suppose; understand several other studios have tried similar things, but my hope was to come up with something rich in mid-America flavor, capturing the spirit of a portion of our country neglected by those who see drama as strictly East or West Coast big cities.... Again, making no claim for particular "freshness" in concept, the format, character and pilot story were wholly

my original creation.... At about the time the show was being produced, the Screen Gems attorney called me to say he just received a telephone call from a lawyer representing Paisan [sic] Productions or Mrs. Jackson there (exactly which was unclear), claiming my show a copy of a property owned by yourself. The implication was, referring to our friendship of long standing, that I had somehow gained access to your files or had been told of your creation in this area and had rushed into production with my own version.... As with you, I am tremendously proud of my reputation and I certainly did not want any rumors affecting it flying around this strange little town. (145-7)

Gardner, having been a practicing attorney before turning to writing courtroom dramas, knew a thing or two about how lawyers talked and wrote letters. He sent Roddenberry's correspondence to his attorney, along with a note, saying:

This letter is very friendly and informal, yet has everything in it. It could well have been plotted by an attorney and then paraphrased. (70a)

On March 9, Gardner wrote Roddenberry:

I was, of course, disappointed when CBS elected not to proceed further with my property *Doug Selby*. However, on the basis of all the information that we have, I am not taking the position that either you or Bill Dozier, or Screen Gems has committed any actionable wrong. (70a)

Roddenberry fired back on March 15:

I was not writing for Wm Dozier, or for Screen Gems. I was not asking what legal position you were taking. A thief is a thief, "actionable" or not. Either I stole something from you and my latest letter is a lie -- or neither is true.... I can't very well find out who's fucking who without a straight answer from you. (145-7)

On April 2, Gardner wrote Roddenberry:

I never said you stole anything, I never said you copied anything, I never accused you of anything which was unethical. I never authorized anyone to represent me in making any such statement to anyone. (145-7)

Roddenberry responded in a calmer tone on April 29, telling Gardner:

Am happy to accept the fact that your phrase "no actionable wrong" was something said in the haste of diction [sic], carrying no special meaning. (70a)

After that, aside from a change of address card sent from Roddenberry to Gardner, there is no indication of any further correspondences between the two men.

"Defiance County" was filmed in January and, in February, scored by George Duning (later to write music for *Star Trek*). By April, CBS passed on the series and the pilot was never aired. Roddenberry was four for four (with "The Big Walk," "333 Montgomery Street," "APO 923" and now "Defiance County") at not being able to take a pilot to series.

Roddenberry, while gaining nothing, lost a valuable mentor in Erle Stanley Garner.

***

During 1962, Roddenberry returned to the world of freelancing. His goal was to get another development deal but, until that happened, he was determined to make a comfortable living and keep a high profile. His first step was an obvious one: more work at *Have Gun -*

Will Travel. He also sold a script to the highly regarded hour-long detective series *The Naked City*, followed by another hour-long, *G.E. True*, produced and hosted by Jack Webb, the first man to give him a job in Hollywood. A third hour-long script was placed with the popular medical drama *Dr. Kildare*, starring Richard Chamberlain. It was here Roddenberry made an important connection: Norman Felton, a producer who would soon greatly advance his career.

After a short period of rest -- the production hiatus from February through April when no one is buying scripts except for pilots -- Roddenberry returned again to *Have Gun - Will Travel* to write five more scripts for its final season. The last of those, "The Savages," his 24th teleplay there, made him the writer to have the most scripts produced for the series.

The *Dr. Kildare* episode Roddenberry had written several months earlier had since aired, and now producer Norman Felton was calling. Felton later said, "Writers write scripts for episodic television, then the show is made and nobody tells them that the script was good. They just tell them what was wrong with it or that they should make it better. I wanted to tell him that I liked it, that I thought it was good." (58bb)

Roddenberry was quick to respond to Felton's praise and asked if he could pitch an idea for a new series. Felton knew Roddenberry had credentials as a producer and a meeting was arranged. It went well and, after tidying up the proposal, Felton took it to MGM, the studio that produced *Dr. Kildare*. Development money was advanced for Roddenberry to write a teleplay. The title on his first draft script from October, 1962 was "The Lieutenant."

NBC press photo, Gary Lockwood in *The Lieutenant* (MGM, 1963)

MGM believed it had a winner in *The Lieutenant* as a potential series and decided not to seek network money to make a pilot. Instead, the studio chose to finance the pilot itself and hoped to start a bidding war by screening it for all three networks simultaneously. By early February 1963, the pilot had been shown to the networks. As quickly and easily as MGM had predicted, a deal was made. On February 7, NBC announced that it had bought the series for the fall TV season. Norman Felton would serve as Executive Producer, and Roddenberry, now 42, would produce. In just nine years, he had gone from aspiring writer to professional tele-scribe, to in-demand freelancer, to contracted developer for a television production company, to writer-producer with the biggest studio in Hollywood.

MGM did more than merely screen the pilot for the networks. *Daily Variety*, on April 3, 1963, reported:

> [Norman Felton and Gene Roddenberry] just returned from Quantico, VA, where they screened pilot for U.S. Marine Corps officials. Producers noted full cooperation of Marines has been assured, including permission to film portions of normal base activity, using Marine personnel in backgrounds. Pilot was shot

at Camp Pendleton.

The Lieutenant, a peacetime look at the United States Marine Corps, portraying human drama in a military setting, premiered on NBC on a Saturday night in September of 1963. Gary Lockwood, later to be the top guest star in the second *Star Trek* pilot, played title character Lieutenant William Rice. Robert Vaughn, one year shy of being cast by Norman Felton for *The Man from U.N.C.L.E.*, played Lockwood's superior.

Although Roddenberry had written the original pilot, he chose to re-edit the film so it could be scheduled later, and then selected another writer's script to kick-off the series. *Variety* reviewed the starter, saying:

> Like all TV series that are based on a profession (medicine, law, teaching, etc.) the success of *The Lieutenant* will depend to a large degree on (1) whether military careerism with its special conflicts can sustain mass interest on a weekly basis, and (2) the plausibility of the dramatic situations that arise. The debut of Gene Roddenberry's video brainchild showed some promise on the first count, but struck out on the second with the premiere script. Clearly, the new series can't afford to be just a potboiler when it's up against Jackie Gleason and the popular *Hootenanny*.

The reviewer liked the star of the show but not his fictional character, writing:

> Lockwood has the looks, a special pensive quality and the basic acting ability to arrest the public fancy as a new TV star; but the character he portrays will have to give off more heroic magic than he did in the initial chapter.... [Premiere] show seemed to have as its purpose an explanation of why there can be no fraternizing between officers and enlisted men in the military [a recurring theme for Captain Kirk in *Star Trek*].... The script grew hard to believe before it got very far.... Ed Waters script was flawed too by stilted dialog, and the story had trouble overcoming the artificiality of the opening scene.

Roddenberry could not blame Ed Waters for the dialogue; he himself had rewritten the script extensively without credit. But, even after suffering a bloody nose in front of boss Felton, MGM and NBC, the novice show-runner rebounded quickly when the Nielsen ratings came in. On October 23, *Variety* announced the surprise news: "NBC's Saturday night *Lieutenant* [is] taking the count away from Jackie Gleason and Phil Silvers [on CBS]."

Roddenberry quickly gained status as a reliable producer and began a relationship with numerous writers, directors, technicians and performers who later returned for *Star Trek*. Among the writers were Paul Schneider, Art Wallace, and Lee Erwin. The directors later to land on *Star Trek* included James Goldstone, Vincent McEveety, Marc Daniels, Robert Gist, Michael O'Herlihy, and Robert Butler. Among the actors who were soon to be space bound: Gary Lockwood, Majel Barrett, Leonard Nimoy, Nichelle Nichols, Walter Koenig, James Gregory, Michael Strong, Don Marshall, Ricardo Montalban, Madlyn Rhue, Leslie Parrish, and Barbara Babcock. Another new member of Roddenberry's inner circle was a young casting director who would later make many talent discoveries for *Star Trek*: Joe D'Agosta.

D'Agosta was, in a sense, a discovery himself -- of Gene Roddenberry's. D'Agosta recalled: "I was just an 'extra' clerk then, checking in extras at MGM. The casting director on *The Lieutenant* got sick and I was asked if I thought I could fill in for a couple weeks. I immediately said yes, knowing I knew *nothing*. I had been an actor for five years in the theater, so I would bring in people that had never worked in television; they just worked in the little theaters around town. The thing that sold Gene Roddenberry on me is he insisted on military haircuts for all his actors because they were marines. The other casting director was lazy about getting actors to cut their hair -- they were TV actors, after all; they worked a lot, they didn't want to change their look. But my actors didn't worry about that, so I made sure everyone came in with military haircuts, even if I had to sit in the barber shop with them. I remember doing that with Dennis Hopper, telling the barber, 'Take a little more off,' and Dennis saying, 'Oh no; really?' And I'm saying, 'Yup, take more off.' Gene was impressed that he didn't have to worry about military haircuts on his actors anymore, so he fired the other guy and kept me." (43)

It was during the production of *The Lieutenant* when Roddenberry first gained a reputation as a producer compulsively driven to alter the work of other writers. He said: "Scripts aren't written, but rewritten." (145)

As a result of all the rewriting, some of the writers who worked on *The Lieutenant* complained to executive producer Felton, and, of the 27 scripts Roddenberry bought for the series, he burned through 19 different writers.

Gary Lockwood saw Roddenberry as a good "fix-it man" (MGM-TV, 1963)

Gary Lockwood, as the series' star, was allowed to see the first draft scripts as well as the final drafts. He was satisfied that Roddenberry improved the quality, saying "One of the things that I thought was good about him is that when he got hold of a story, or when there was something that was not quite working correctly, he could fix it. He was a real good 'fix-it man.' His name should have been Gene 'Bondo' Roddenberry. If you're familiar with cars, you know that Bondo fixes everything." (109)

The directors of the series seemed destined to fail Roddenberry, as well. In *The Lieutenant*'s one-year run, 17 different directors came and went through the revolving doors of the production office. These directors were not getting the exact performance Roddenberry wanted from his series' lead. Lockwood said, "Roddenberry was a terrific guy; I liked him. But he was untrustworthy in that he would always bullshit me. You know, if there was a problem with a script, but he wanted it that way, he'd say it was for the network. If he wanted me to play the part different, it was because of the director. But *he* was the one trying to get the directors to loosen me up; make me smile and do all kinds of boyish things. And it's not my style. And I'd go to him and say, 'I'll do it if there's a reason. But, if there's no reason I'm not going to walk around grinning all the time. I find it silly.'" (109)

As the series progressed, trouble began for Roddenberry with backlot talk about his extra-curricular activities. Majel Barrett and Nichelle Nichols, two female guest performers, later admitted that romance bloomed with the producer as a result of appearing on his series. Roddenberry later said, "I have an active love of females." (145-23)

Even before any of the lovers went public, the rumors were rampant and quite a few made it back to the network. It was a touchy subject in 1963, so much so that executives at MGM and NBC were nervously *not* seeing, *not* hearing and, except behind closed doors, *not* speaking about these matters. Regardless, Roddenberry was assumed guilty with "one strike" against him. Then came "Strike Two."

Roddenberry was gaining a reputation for fighting authority. One incident would jeopardize *The Lieutenant*. Exteriors for the series were filmed at Camp Pendleton, a Marine training facility an hour-and-a-half's drive south from Hollywood. The location was provided for free, as were military vehicles, uniforms, weaponry and countless extras played by actual soldiers. The only thing the Pentagon expected in return was a series that portrayed the Marine Corps in a favorable light. It was a win-win situation, but Roddenberry was looking to push the envelope.

Roddenberry's opinions regarding abuse of authority and discrimination based on religion, race or creed were well known. Now he wanted to tell the adult-type stories that episodic television instinctively avoided. To accomplish this, he put into production an episode called "To Set It Right," concerning a black Marine who, without apparent provocation, attacks a white member of the platoon. As the story later reveals, the two men had known one another from high school where the white teenager often joined with other racists to gang up on the black teen.

Cast in the episode were Dennis Hopper as the white bigot, Don Marshall as the black Marine who learned to hate back, and Nichelle Nichols as his wife. Marshall said, "That was a chancy episode. But you had Gene Roddenberry, and he was such an honest man and would come straight from the heart. And he had seen so much in the world and resented discrimination and things like that. He didn't run away from the issues like other producers did. Gene would go straight at it. I felt really good about being part of that." (113b)

Don Marshall and Dennis Hopper in "To Set It Right" episode of *The Lieutenant* (MGM TV, 1963)

This episode was not so much about entertaining, but about making a statement: prejudice begets prejudice. But the Pentagon's position was that racial problems did not exist in the Armed Forces -- especially TV's Armed Forces. Regardless, Roddenberry chose to go forward with the controversial story and suddenly Camp Pendleton was no longer available for production of the series. Norman Felton said, "It was this story that lost us the cooperation of the Pentagon." (58a)

Cast and crew returned to Los Angeles and resumed filming on the MGM backlot. To make up for the loss of Marine extras, Roddenberry recruited two former Marine drill instructors to whip a small army of bit players into fighting shape. Through economic rewriting and frugal spending, *The Lieutenant* finished its order of 29 episodes. But losing the support of the military took much of the shine off the armor of the series in the eyes of NBC and the network refused to air the episode that had kicked up so much negative attention, prompting Roddenberry to say, "My problem was not the Marine Corps; it was NBC, who turned down the show flat…. There was only one thing I could do, I went to the NAACP and they lowered the boom on NBC." (145-11)

The NAACP, a civil rights watchdog, supported the story about the domino effect of racial prejudice. Pressure was put on the network to air the controversial segment. NBC caved, but this proved to be "Strike Three." Gene Roddenberry had won the battle ... but lost the war. Despite satisfactory ratings, *The Lieutenant* was cancelled.

***

Before the final episode of *The Lieutenant* finished filming, Roddenberry presented Norman Felton with a proposal for a science fiction series called *Star Trek*. He described it as "*Wagon Train* to the stars."

Felton was not interested. *Wagon Train* was fine. For a series like that, Hollywood had plenty of what it needed -- replicated covered wagons, horses and western gear. *Wagon Train* could be done relatively inexpensively. But, when placed in the future, new worlds had to be envisioned and constructed week in and week out. Spaceships had to be designed, built, and subjected to expensive, time-consuming photographic effects. And then there were costumes, futuristic hair styles and all those gadgets.

There was another reason to say "no." Like elephants, studios never forget. Robert Justman later said "They passed on [*Star Trek*] having had experience with Gene and not wanting anymore." (94-2)

Roddenberry said, "I was chafing increasingly at the commercial censorship on television, which was very strong in those days. You really couldn't talk about anything you cared to talk about. [So] I decided I was going to leave TV... unless I could find some way to write about what I wanted to." (145-11)

Roddenberry was intent on taking a page from Jonathan Swift. He felt, given the oppressive nature of the American television, he could only produce the stories he wanted to tell by setting them in a far-off context. He later said, "[Swift] wanted to write satire on *his* time and went to Lilliput in his story to do just that. He could talk about insane prime ministers and crooked kings and all of that. It was this wonderful thing. Children could read it as a fairy tale, an adventure, and as they got older they'd recognize it for what it really is…. It seemed to me that perhaps, if I wanted to talk about sex, religion, politics, make some comments against Vietnam and so on, that if I had similar situations involving these subjects happening on other planets to little green people, indeed it might get by." (145-11)

Determined that this new series concept was the only way to tell stories about hot-topics, Roddenberry turned down an offer from Ivan Tors to produce the pilot film for *Daktari*. He now had a greater mission: to sell *Star Trek*.

2

To Boldly Pitch

> **Star Trek**
>
> Created by: GENE RODDENBERRY
> FIRST DRAFT
> March 11, 1964
>
> STAR TREK is...
>
> A one-hour dramatic television series.
>
> Action - Adventure - Science Fiction.
>
> The first such concept with strong central lead characters plus other continuing regulars.
>
> And while maintaining a familiar central location and regular cast, explores an anthology-like range of exciting human experience. For example, as varied as ...
>
> THE NEXT CAGE. The desperation of our series lead, caged and on exhibition like an animal, then offered a mate.
>
> THE DAY CHARLIE BECAME GOD. The accidental occurrence of infinite power to do all things, in the hands of a very finite man.
>
> PRESIDENT CAPONE. A parallel world, Chicago ten years after Al Capone won and imposed gangland statutes upon the nation.
>
> TO SKIN A TYRANNOSAURUS. A modern man reduced to a sling and a club in a world 1,000,000 B.C.
>
> THE WOMEN. Duplicating a page from the "Old West"; hanky-panky aboard with a cargo of women destined for a far-off colony.
>
> THE COMING. Alien people in an alien society, but something disturbingly familiar about the quiet dignity of one who is being condemned to crucifixion.
>
> (See later pages for more)

Star Trek **series proposal, dated March 11, 1964
(By permission of Gene Roddenberry)**

One of *Star Trek*'s first supporters was Alden Schwimmer, Roddenberry's agent at Ashley-Famous. Confident there was a market for good science fiction on TV, Schwimmer suggested Roddenberry commit his ideas to paper.

Roddenberry's original vision for *Star Trek* was shaped with a strong emphasis on character, drama and bold ideas. One such inspiration was the 1956 film *Forbidden Planet*, a futuristic telling of *The Tempest*, the classic play by William Shakespeare (who knew a little something about character, drama and bold ideas). Another influence was *Space Cadet*, a juvenile novel written by sci-fi master Robert Heinlein and published in 1948. Roddenberry said, "*Space Cadet* is a very humane book. It deals with not only the problems of science -- about space travel and technology and so on -- but of the need we have to act in a conscious responsible manner with all this technology.... That book had such profound influence on me... there are so many, many ideas that [Heinlein and I] shared. He wrote many of them down before I did, but they were -- have always been -- in my heart." (145-2)

Paraphrasing a section of Heinlein's book, Roddenberry interpreted the positive theme of *Space Cadet* this way: "I welcome you to our fellowship. You come from many lands, some from other planets. You are of various colors and creeds, yet you must and shall become a band of brothers." (145-2)

23

Roddenberry wanted *Star Trek* to emulate those types of characters and themes. Dated March 11, 1964, the 16-page proposal offered this premise: "*Star Trek* is a one-hour dramatic television series; action / adventure / science-fiction; the first such concept with strong central lead characters…"

Dorothy Fontana, Roddenberry's secretary at the time, may have been the first person to read the written proposal for *Star Trek*. She said, "There was nothing like it on television at that time. It had lots of possibilities and you could see the stories. They'd begin to pop into your mind automatically." (64-2)

Watching the first 16 episodes of the series and looking through the script assignments that Roddenberry gave out and compulsively reworked, one can see he stayed true to this promise. "Drama" was the key element, followed by "action" and "adventure" and, only then, "science fiction." The episode "Court Martial" was, in a sense, *The Caine Mutiny* transplanted into outer space. "The Conscience of the King" offered a Shakespearean play set on a starship. "Balance of Terror" was essentially a restaging of the World War II submarine movies *The Enemy Below* and *Run Silent, Run Deep*. "Charlie X" provided a study of the dangerous combination of adolescent immaturity and power. Roddenberry wanted an open format that allowed for a vast array of stories, all with human conflict at their core. He would tell his writers not to get overwhelmed with the enormity and the foreignness of science fiction, and explained in the *Star Trek* Writers' Guide: "Joe Friday doesn't stop to explain how his gun works when he pulls it from the holster." The gadgets should not take center stage; the stories would instead revolve around the characters.

Captain Robert April (later renamed Christopher Pike, and finally James T. Kirk) was described as a 34-year-old space-age incarnation of C.S. Forester's Captain Horatio Hornblower: "Colorfully complex, capable of action and decision which can verge on the heroic -- but who lives a continual battle with self-doubt and the loneliness of command." Hornblower's sense of duty and drive to succeed rendered the darker aspects of his character undetectable to his crew. To them he was a hero, a man to be revered and followed. But Hornblower suffered from his extreme ambition and was an emotional prisoner on his own ship during its long sea voyages.

A character named Number One was also in the proposal. She was described as "a mysterious female, slim and dark, expressionless, cool, one of those women who will always look the same between years 20 and 50." To be more specific: actress Majel Barrett, Roddenberry's lover.

The ship's doctor, Phillip Boyce, 51, nicknamed "Bones," was drawn as "humorously cynical... enjoys his own weaknesses; [and is] the Captain's only real confidant." Roddenberry knew veteran actor DeForest Kelley from their association together on the pilot film "333 Montgomery Street" and the part was meant to be his from the start.

Mr. Spock was First Lieutenant, the Captain's right-hand man. He was described as "satanic looking with semi-pointed ears, probably half-Martian, with a red complexion."

On another page of the proposal was that famous comparison: "*Star Trek* is a *Wagon Train* concept -- built around characters that travel to worlds 'similar' to our own and meet the action-adventure-drama which becomes our stories."

Interviewed for this book, Harlan Ellison (who would write for the series' first season), said Roddenberry got the idea for his famous *Star Trek* pitch line from a renowned associate. "He got '*Wagon Train* to the stars' from Sam Peeples. That's what Gene said to me. They were at dinner and Sam Peeples, of course, was a fount of ideas, and Gene said something or other about wanting to do a space show and Sam said, 'Yeah? Why don't you do *Wagon Train* to the stars?' And when Gene started shopping it around, that's how he presented it." (58)

The overriding mission for the "space cruiser" of the future was to explore "Class M planets" with atmospheres similar to Earth. The "Class M" mandate made *Star Trek* affordable. Roddenberry wrote:

> The "Parallel World" concept makes production practical via the use of available "Earth" casting, sets, locations, costuming, and it means simply that our stories deal with plant and animal life, plus people, quite similar to that on Earth.

The wording was important. The studio heads and network executives needed to be convinced that a show like *Star Trek* could be made within the limited budgets allocated to episodic TV. In 1964 those budgets were quite small, rarely higher than $150,000 per show.

"Parallel Worlds" also meant Jonathan Swift-type stories, the ones Roddenberry had always admired. He wrote:

> Social evolution will also have interesting points of similarity with ours. There will be differences, of course, ranging from the subtle to the boldly dramatic, out of which comes much of our color and excitement. And, of course, none of this prevents an occasional "far out" tale thrown in for surprise and change of pace.

In order to draw a mass audience, *Star Trek* had to appeal to more than just science fiction enthusiasts. Television viewers needed to relate to the characters on the series and identify with the surroundings, so in Roddenberry's proposal the geography was already well in place. The vessel used to transport us into the dramatic stories, with the registry of "United Space Ship," was the Yorktown, later to be re-christened Enterprise. It was described as 190,000 gross tons, carrying a crew of 203 and able to travel beyond the speed of light, thanks to its "space-warp" drive. The mission of the U.S.S. Yorktown was set for five years.

John D.F. Black, who would later help write the opening title narration for the series, said, "There was a reason for it being five years. Sure, the Navy -- and this, in a sense, was the U.S. Navy in space -- will send you on a tour of duty, but not for five years. Truth is Gene was hoping the show would last five years! If you could get five seasons done, you were assured a long run in syndication." (17)

Besides drawing parallels to *Wagon Train* (which ran eight seasons), Roddenberry also used *Gunsmoke* in his presentation for making comparisons. That series -- the granddaddy of all TV westerns -- ran for an unprecedented 20 consecutive years. Roddenberry wrote:

> As with *Gunsmoke*'s Dodge City, we may never get around to exploring every cabin, department and cranny of our cruiser. The point being -- it is a whole community in which we can anytime take our camera down a passageway and find a guest star or secondary character who can propel us into a story.

Roddenberry was already thinking about budgetary constraints by proposing "the bottle show" -- an episode requiring only the use of the existing primary sets. He wrote:

> Now and then, a story will take place exclusively on the Yorktown, i.e., such as the tale of a strange "intelligence" which has made its way aboard and is working to take over the minds of certain key crewmen [such as in "And the Children Shall Lead" and "Day of the Dove"]; or the transportation of a person

or a material which poses a mounting jeopardy to the ship and our characters [as in "Charlie X," "The Conscience of the King" and "Space Seed"].

The Yorktown's orders -- and the type of stories to be told -- were broken into three categories: 1) Earth security; 2) scientific investigation; and 3) any required assistance "to the several Earth colonies, and the enforcement of appropriate statutes affecting such Federated commerce vessels and traders." The wording "Federated commerce vessels" would set the foundation for later nomenclature that helped to frame key concepts of the series. Gene Coon, the writer/producer to follow Roddenberry onto the series, would later coin "The United Federation of Planets." As to the physical shape of the ship, Roddenberry summed it up simply as having "a slight naval flavor."

The series' proposal also contained two dozen story synopses, many of which were destined to become *Star Trek* episodes.

After Norman Felton and MGM passed on the *Star Trek* proposal, it became Alden Schwimmer's job to find a buyer. Conveniently, his boss, Ted Ashley, had just negotiated the unusual deal to make Ashley-Famous the representatives for Desilu Productions, and Desilu needed television properties.

***

Lucille Ball may not have been a sci-fi buff, or even understood the magnitude of what she was endorsing, but the reluctant TV mogul played a major role in launching the Enterprise. In an indirect way, it all happened because Desi loved Lucy and the two wanted to spend more time together.

In the late 1930s, Lucille Ball was getting top billing in B-films. A few years later, she was the lead in modestly-budgeted main features, including *Too Many Girls*. It was during the making of this movie that she met the love of her life: Desi Arnaz. He was an extroverted Cuban band leader with steady work in club engagements who had also found success as an MGM contract player with lead roles in movies like *Cuban Pete* and *Holiday in Havana*. Thanks to a studio "loan out," he was given a supporting role in RKO's *Too Many Girls* and an opportunity to meet its star. By the end of the production, Desi and the leading lady were romantically involved. Shortly after, they were married.

As Lucy's film career heated up, so did her radio series *My Favorite Husband*, in which she and Richard Denning played a married couple, proving that opposites could attract. By 1950, CBS wanted to move *My Favorite Husband* to television. Lucy was reluctant -- she was still doing well on the big screen, cast opposite Bob Hope in the hits *Sorrowful Jones* (1949) and *Fancy Pants* (1950), and it seemed unlikely that TV could boost her career. But it was possible that it could be a healthy move for her marriage.

Lucy and Desi had been struggling to find time together. Lucy's work kept her on a soundstage in Hollywood while Desi's work had him in nightclubs all across the country. When the two found time together at Desilu -- the name of their *ranchito* in Chatsworth -- their reunions were marred by quarreling. Lucy suspected Desi was being unfaithful while on the road and his temper did not tolerate such accusations. Now the tension in Lucy's real life gave her an idea to turn off-screen drama into an on-air comedy. She told CBS that she would do the television series, provided Desi was cast to play her husband. To prove to the network that a widespread audience could embrace the real life mixed-couple, Desi and Lucy formed Desilu Productions and embarked on a summer vaudeville tour. They were a hit and *My Favorite Husband* was immediately earmarked to become *I Love Lucy*. There was still one last hurdle to clear: Desi and Lucy needed to find a way to originate the show from Hollywood, California. They were told it was not possible.

TV History 101: The cheapest way to do television series in the early 1950s was to broadcast live from New York, then delay the programs for the West Coast through the technical wizardry of kinescope -- a crude procedure in which television programs were literally filmed off a TV set at the network's studio on the West Coast where the East Coast live-feed was monitored. This film was then rushed through processing and aired three hours after the East Coast broadcast. But in these early analog days, making a film of a video picture resulted in greatly diminished picture and sound quality.

Desi had a better idea. He had watched the way live sitcoms from New York, such as *The Honeymooners*, were being shot before studio audiences with three video cameras running at once, each aimed at a range of wide and close-up shots. His idea was to use the same approach but substitute film cameras for those which fed out a live video signal. By shooting the script in its actual chronology, filming before a live audience remained feasible and, unlike the editing of feature films, the post-production requirements could be greatly reduced since the program had been filmed in sequence. With two copies of the edited half-hour film, one on each coast, both East and West would be able to air first-generation masters. Although the net production cost would be considerably higher, Desilu was offering to cover this -- in exchange for an unknown commodity that Desi called "rerun rights." To the network men's thinking, CBS was giving up nothing and gaining everything.

I Love Lucy went on the air in October 1951, produced by Desilu Productions. After six months, it was a Top 10 hit. Six months later, it was the No. 1 rated show on television. Suddenly, other TV producers came knocking at Desilu's door hoping the production company would share its magic formula with them. For the fall of 1952, Eve Arden and *Our Miss Brooks* went from radio to TV, and Desilu was paid to do the moving. The following year, *The Danny Thomas Show* began production and, one year after that, *December Bride* became the third concurrent hit Desilu was hired to film for outside production companies.

Desi Arnaz had proven he could produce series, now he wanted to own them too. Over the next few years, Desilu retained ownership of the series that resulted from the pilots it produced. *Line Up*, in the mode of *Dragnet*, premiered in the Top 20 and enjoyed a six year run; *Whirlybirds*, a half-hour action series about a helicopter service, stayed air bound for three seasons, and *The Untouchables*, Desilu's first hour-long series, became the production company's biggest hit not to feature Lucille Ball. Fueled by this success, Desi and Lucy decided to get into the studio business.

By 1957, with over 200 filmed episodes in the can and *I Love Lucy* still at the top of the prime time ratings, the CBS executives saw there was indeed a market for that thing Desi called "reruns." The network wanted the rights back and a deal was quickly made. Desi sold the *I Love Lucy* rerun rights to CBS for a cool million and then set out to buy a studio, ending Desilu's need to rent space and materials.

RKO, one of the top motion picture factories from the 1930s, the maker of the Fred Astaire/Ginger Rogers musicals, plus classics such as *King Kong* and *Citizen Kane*, had fallen on hard times and was up for sale. There were three facilities: one in Hollywood adjacent to Paramount Pictures and two in nearby Culver City, which included a large backlot filled with western towns, Army barracks, an Arabian fortress, and even the remains of Tara, the mansion from *Gone with the Wind*. The buyout cost was $6,000,000, with Desi and Lucy using the money from CBS as a down payment. For this price, they got all physical assets, including 26 sound stages, 457 furnished offices, camera equipment, and lighting equipment, Essentially, anything and everything they needed to produce television and film, and that included the headaches.

Desi Arnaz and Lucille Ball were now indisputable TV moguls.

Over the next few years, Desilu Studios rented out its facilities, its equipment and its personnel to over a dozen network TV series including such hits as *The Andy Griffith Show*, *The Dick Van Dyke Show*, *The Real McCoys*, *My Favorite Martian*, *The Ann Sothern Show*, *My Three Sons*, *Wyatt Earp*, *Lassie*, *Ben Casey* and *The Millionaire*. But as the 1950s came to a close, the pressures of producing and starring in a hit series, as well as running a studio, had taken its toll on Desi. His drinking increased, as did his infidelity, and in 1960 Lucille Ball shocked the world by filing for divorce. *I Love Lucy*, or *The Desi-Lucy Hour* as it was being called in its eighth season, would be no more ... except in reruns.

Lucy and Desi, studio moguls (Courtesy of Gerald Gurian)

Although their marriage was over, the couple remained tied through their mutual ownership of a studio. Desi ran Desilu while Lucy concentrated on acting, including work on stage and films. In 1962, Desi beckoned Lucy to return to weekly TV and to the CBS Monday night schedule. The new series was called *The Lucy Show*. Desi directed the pilot and served as executive producer.

All seemed well again, until November 9, 1962, when *Daily Variety* broke the news that television's "oldest partnership ended yesterday when Lucille Ball bought out Desi Arnaz's stock interest in Desilu Productions, Inc. for a sum estimated at $3,000,000." As part of the deal, Desi also relinquished his position as executive producer of *The Lucy Show*. The official word from him: "I quit the business because it got to be a monster. At the beginning, it was fun. But when you are in charge of three studios, with 3,000 people and 35 soundstages working all the time, the fun is long gone." (6)

The real story was darker. After a few stays in the hospital, Desi was diagnosed as an alcoholic. He no longer wanted to come in to work, so Lucy reluctantly became the boss.

During the first year that Lucy ran Desilu, *The Untouchables* was cancelled. Two new studio properties -- *Glynis* and *The Greatest Show on Earth* -- failed to find an audience and, lasting only one season each, ended up costing the studio money instead of making it. Suddenly, the only current series Desilu owned was *The Lucy Show*, beginning its third season and already looking tired. And then the exodus began. Madelyn Martin and Bob Carroll, Jr., long time *I Love Lucy* writers who had guided the first two seasons of *The Lucy*

Show, departed, as did executive producer Elliot Lewis, producer-creator-writer Cy Howard, and Desilu Vice President in Charge of Production, Jerry Thorpe.

Fred Ball, Lucy's brother and a Desilu employee, said, "When Desi left, everybody was apprehensive. There was so much at stake for everybody. The whole structure, because of Desi's absence, started to break down and deteriorate." (8)

The legend "Filmed at Desilu" was still featured in the end credits of a dozen current network series. And, as a rental facility, Desilu appeared to be doing fine. But in reality the financial forecast was bleak. In that first year without Desi, the studio lost over $650,000. That would be like losing $5 million in 2013, a huge hit for a "ma and pa production house" that had experienced rapid growth and was suddenly drowning in red ink. Lucy needed help. It would come from an unlikely source: CBS.

Hollywood's lone female studio mogul, circa 1964 (Desilu publicity photo).

The Columbia Broadcasting System had a vested interest in Lucille Ball, so any problem that Lucy had was also a problem for William Paley, the founder and owner of the network. Paley was determined to see Lucy and her studio stabilized. Ed Holly, Paley's top Financial Officer, was the first CBS man sent to Desilu's rescue. Next, Paley found someone to oversee the running of the entire facility.

Oscar Katz, like Holly, was a network man. He was highly regarded by the brass at CBS and served as Vice President of Network Programs. In 1963, with the blessing -- and even some arm-twisting -- of the CBS top dog, Katz resigned his position at the network and packed his bags for California. The task awaiting him: run the studio, unburden Lucy and try to appease the "old guard," Desilu's less-than-happy Board of Directors. *Variety* said it best: "His job is to restore Desilu's place in the sun as supplier of network prime-time merchandise, the studio's only such series now being the one starring the ex-network man's boss."

Katz had a challenge ahead, but he wouldn't face it alone.

Herbert F. Solow, a young network executive, soon came on board as Katz's right hand man. Katz knew Solow from CBS, where the latter had served as the head of Daytime Programs. Solow also had worked for NBC at the network's Burbank offices, as the Director of Daytime Programs. In April 1964, Lucy's instruction to Katz and Solow was simple: "Get some shows for the studio." (9-2)

***

Alden Schwimmer arranged for meetings between Desilu's two new execs and a pair of his favorite clients, the spacey Gene Roddenberry and the more down-to-earth Bruce

Geller. Geller was easy for Katz and Solow to "get." He was a Yale graduate, a political liberal and the son of a New York State Judge. He had just finished producing the last season of *Rawhide*, had served as a writer on numerous westerns, including *The Rifleman* and *Have Gun - Will Travel*, and his idea for a series was appealing to the studio men: a spy show called *Mission: Impossible*.

Roddenberry was a different story. Dorothy Fontana once remarked, "Somebody said you could dress Gene in a tailored suit and five minutes later he'd look like a saggy, baggy elephant." (64-2)

John D.F. Black said, "Gene's suits *always* came with stains." (17)

Mary Black, who worked at *Star Trek* as John D.F.'s assistant/secretary, added, "Bruce Geller, who had his office upstairs, came in and said he had one question: 'Did G.R. buy his suits with the cigarette ashes already on them?'" (17a)

Solow's first impression of Roddenberry was "this tall, unkempt person [who] recently learned to dress himself but hadn't yet quite gotten the knack." (161-3)

Then Roddenberry, a "mumbling exotic," according to Solow, handed the Desilu exec a piece of paper with a crumpled corner -- his abbreviated presentation for *Star Trek*. What followed was the "pitch," which Solow remembered as being awkward. The former network man thought Roddenberry was the most ineffective pitchman for a series he had ever met in the television business. He later said:

> The one thing I thought was really very, very good that Gene had done was to make science fiction familiar to an audience by handling it like the United States Navy. It invited the audience into something they knew about. They knew the terms like "Captain" and "Admiral," "starboard," "port" and the U.S.S. Yorktown, which later became the Enterprise. Also, I think I said "yes" because Desilu was down in the depths and needed shows that would quickly make Desilu important again. I didn't think that would happen if we did normal, average shows. That's why I ended up, my first year, developing both *Star Trek* and *Mission: Impossible*. (161-5)

Solow offered Roddenberry a contract. The next task was to find a network for *Star Trek*. The best bet was ABC because the "alphabet network" was targeting kids. But ABC already had a sci-fi series called *The Outer Limits* and, for the fall of 1964, a series set onboard a futuristic atomic submarine. *Star Trek* had been pre-empted by Irwin Allen and *Voyage to the Bottom of the Sea*. The next best bet was CBS, which had tried its hand at science fiction only once, with *The Twilight Zone*, just ending a five-year run. Katz had a relationship with the network, as did Lucy, and Lucy's current series was a hit. William Paley's people would not refuse a meeting.

Oscar Katz accompanied Roddenberry to the CBS pitch meeting and recalled the mood as being not only formal but "frosty." He said, "We were in a dining room with six or seven executives, one of whom questioned us rather closely about what we were going to do with the show. We answered his questions and it turned out that his interest was due to the fact that they were developing a science fiction show of their own." (96-1)

Roddenberry seethed over it for years, ranting, "You S.O.B.s, if you wanted technical advice and help, hire me and pay me for it! It's like calling a doctor and having him analyze you for two hours and then telling him, 'Thank you very much for pinpointing what's wrong, I've decided to go to another doctor for treatment.'" (145-4)

Roddenberry's loss was Irwin Allen's gain. He had caught the eye of CBS first with *Lost in Space* and was now two for two.

Herb Solow, not present at the CBS meeting, was brought up to speed afterwards. Based on his assessment of Roddenberry as a public speaker, he was certain that the writer who didn't know how to dress had nervously mumbled his way through the meeting, pushing his "*Wagon Train* to the stars business."

Roddenberry defended his pitch to this author, saying, "You know how I said that -- that '*Wagon Train* to the stars' thing. It was about finding a means for *them* to see that it wasn't that impossible to tell those kinds of stories. Technically, of course, we had challenges -- more than any other series, certainly. But the first thing to get them to see was that the stories we would tell could appeal to a broad television audience. If a family can watch a western, a story set a hundred years in the past, why not something a hundred years in the future, or two hundred years in the future? And that is the primary thing they [the network] are going to think about; are going to question -- can this appeal to a mass audience, meaning, a broad audience. Not just men, not just women, not just teenagers, not just those crazy science fiction people, but a broad enough audience to have 15, 20 million households tuning in. So I made those comparisons, intentionally so." (145)

Regardless of the intentions, the execution is equally important. Robert Justman said, "When Gene [first] attempted to get *Star Trek* on the air, he didn't succeed. In part because he was, at times, almost tongue tied. He didn't learn to be glib and didn't learn to be voluble until sometime after we began the series and he became accustomed to dealing with the press and with others than himself." (94-2)

Solow not only lacked confidence in Roddenberry but in Katz. He felt "there wasn't a nicer or brighter man than Oscar Katz." But nice and bright didn't always get the job done. Oscar didn't speak the local language -- West Coast TV-speak; West Coast TV-attitude.

Losing CBS represented a major blow. Lucy's clout with William Paley was of no use to *Star Trek* now. Once a network says "no," the answer never changes. Licking his wounds, Katz agreed to stay in the background and turn *Star Trek* over to Herb Solow. In a time before the existence of Fox, or HBO and Showtime, or TNT, A&E and SyFy (aka Sci-Fi Channel), there was only one place left to go and that was Solow's old turf: NBC. Herb Solow later said he spent a great deal of time with Roddenberry, grooming him and helping to develop the perfect pitch for NBC. One month later, in May of 1964, he arranged to meet with his former boss, Grant Tinker, Vice-President of West Coast Programming, and Jerry Stanley, NBC Program Development Vice President.

The odds against Desilu were monumental. NBC and *Star Trek* were an impossible match. In 20 years of broadcasting, the network had never aired anything even remotely resembling science fiction. After all, this was the network of Bob Hope, Andy Williams, Mitch Miller and *The Bell Telephone Hour*. In most science fiction, there is a beast, a demon, a monstrous alien. In the story of *Star Trek*, according to Gene Roddenberry, the monster was always NBC.

It is ironic Gene Roddenberry would see television networks as unreasoning monsters. After all, *Star Trek* didn't tell standard monster stories. In the classic episode "The Devil in the Dark," the Horta, a tunnel-boring silicon-based creature, turned out to be anything but a monster. It was a mother and she was protecting her children. In 1968, Roddenberry said, "What's been wrong with science fiction in television and motion pictures for years is that whenever a monster was used, the tendency was to say, 'Ah, ha! Let's have a big one that comes out, attacks and kills everyone.' Nobody ever asked 'Why?' In any other story, if something attacks -- a bear, a man or whatever -- the author is expected to explain,

'Here is why it is the way it is, here are the things that led it to do this, here is what it wants.'" (142-2)

Yet the criticism he often voiced against NBC signaled a lack of understanding or effort to co-exist with the network beast, only to hate and fight it. The beast, then, hated and fought back.

Jerry Colonna and Bob Hope, pitchmen for a network
(NBC publicity photo, 1940)

***

Every beast has a back-story.

The National Broadcasting Company had been America's first radio network, beginning operation in 1926. General Electric and Westinghouse, both manufacturers of radios, and American Telephone and Telegraph -- better known as AT&T -- got together with an unlikely fourth partner, the United Fruit Company, and set up the Radio Corporation of America (RCA). This entity focused on the manufacturing of radios and records. Shortly after that, NBC was formed as a means of selling more RCA radio receivers and promoting the company's record albums.

CBS -- the Columbia Broadcasting System -- soon followed, started by Columbia Records, later sold to William Paley, a Philadelphia-based cigar manufacturer. But NBC dwarfed CBS in those early days and actually had two separate radio networks -- NBC "red" for entertainment programs, and NBC "blue" for news. Each consisted of five company-owned stations, plus numerous affiliates spread across the nation. In 1944, the U.S. government and its Federal Communications Commission shook up the network with a ruling that, while NBC could have two different networks, RCA would not be allowed to own ten broadcast stations -- only five, the same limit that had been set for CBS. The radio pioneer was given a matter of months to rid itself of 50% of its holdings. NBC "blue" was quickly put on the market. The buyer, for $8 million dollars, was Edward Noble, owner of Life Savers candy and the Rexall drugstore chain. The new network, brought to life at the sacrifice of NBC "blue," was called the American Broadcasting Company, or, more simply, ABC.

In the mid-1940s, television sets had begun being manufactured and sold in the U.S. DuMont Laboratories, founded by Allan DuMont, was aggressively devoted to the advancement, manufacturing and the marketing of those TVs, and also interested in the transmission of television signal. The DuMont Television Network, in fact, was the first to receive a television broadcast license from the FCC. NBC came next and both began their historic broadcasting at very nearly the same moment: the fall of 1946. Two years later CBS got into the game, as did the less powerful ABC. And now there were four.

Between 1948 and 1950, NBC continued to grow. Among the stars under contract, making the short walk from NBC radio to NBC TV, were Bob Hope, Jack Benny, Milton Berle, Sid Caesar, Robert Montgomery, William Bendix, Groucho Marx, and Kukla, Fran & Ollie. CBS had plenty of stars of its own. DuMont and ABC, however, were struggling to compete. For ABC, it all came down to size. The radio network that was created out of a piece of NBC's hide had far fewer affiliates than either NBC or CBS. DuMont's situation was worse. With no radio holdings, the TV pioneer had no stars under contract and that meant the network had less leverage to entice the independent television stations across America. As a result, DuMont was forced to go dark in 1955. Its parent company, the television set manufacturer, would also close shop.

By 1956, with the addition of hits such as *Gunsmoke*, *The $64,000 Question*, *Alfred Hitchcock Presents*, *I've Got A Secret*, *Lassie*, *The Honeymooners* and *The Phil Silvers Show*, CBS became America's No. 1 network. It remained so for 20 consecutive seasons. NBC had dropped to No. 2, but it had a plan -- or at least an agenda.

RCA wanted to market color TV sets. The company had been working on the design for years and, on November 22, 1953, used its experimental "compatible color" system for the broadcast of an episode of the *Colgate Comedy Hour*. A month later, on December 23, as a Christmas present to parent corporation RCA, NBC aired "The Big Little Jesus," an episode of the network's most popular series, *Dragnet*, which had been filmed in Technicolor. On September 7, 1957, for a special colorcast of *Your Hit Parade*, the animated NBC peacock made its debut with the immortal words heard for the first time: "The following program is brought to you in living color ... on NBC." In 1959, NBC began delivering color each and every week for series such as *The Perry Como Show* and *Bonanza*.

Despite the status -- or gimmick -- of being America's first color network, NBC's audience wasn't growing and to the peacock's embarrassment, ABC's audience *was*. The "Alphabet Network" had aimed low with their programming and the strategy was paying off. Inexpensive black-and-white westerns for the kids and shows with teen appeal had elevated ABC into second place. TV, after all, belonged to the baby-boomers. CBS had figured this out, too, and strived to find programming that appealed to the young and the old alike -- shows the entire family could watch together. This left NBC with a stagnating audience despite its pioneering technology. The majority of the network's series were now in color, yet in many ways these shows were the least colorful ones on the air. *The Perry Como Show* was on NBC. So were *The Dinah Shore Show, This Is Your Life, Sing Along With Mitch* and *The Bell Telephone Hour*. Despite the star power, they weren't bringing in the numbers to match the other networks.

By 1964, the year Gene Roddenberry began shopping *Star Trek*, the once mighty National Broadcasting Company was in the ratings basement. According to A.C. Nielsen, of the 20 highest-rated prime time series on all three networks, NBC had only three. CBS was commanding $50,000 per prime-time minute from their advertisers. ABC was getting $45,000. NBC could only collect $41,000. When Gene Roddenberry and Herb Solow entered the offices of NBC Burbank in May of 1964, they knew they had at least one thing in their favor: the network was as desperate as they were.

***

During the meeting with Jerry Stanley and Grant Tinker, Roddenberry, according to Herb Solow, did exactly as Solow suggested. He looked like a younger version of Albert Einstein -- strange, brilliant and hard to figure out. He purposely didn't offer any more information than needed, nor did he elaborate on how *Star Trek* could be better than filmed sci-fi of the past because it wouldn't be telling conventional monster stories. And he didn't compare *Star Trek* to *Wagon Train*. What he did was present the material he and Solow had prepared and then do one of the hardest things to do in a pitch -- stay quiet and wait.

Roddenberry later said, "Herb had worked within that system. He understood the mentality; that strategy of sitting and smiling and saying very little, and putting your opponent in the hot seat, like in a game of poker. Thirty years doing this and I still don't understand why it has to be that way. But it was that way at CBS when we presented *Star Trek* there. Oscar [Katz] had come from CBS, but from the East Coast. And things like that did make a difference at that time. So, it helped that Herb was there when we went to NBC [Burbank]. He had worked out of that office. He was friendly with Grant and Jerry. And that's what we needed at that moment." (145)

Solow had the inside track, knowing that in four months NBC would be premiering *The Man from U.N.C.L.E.*, a series unlike anything the network had aired before -- a series intended to appeal to teenagers and cash-in on the spy craze sweeping the country due to the recent big screen success of James Bond. Also in development, *I Spy*, an espionage show that would travel the world and co-star a "Negro." It would be hip, unconventional and extravagant. There was more. Like *Flipper*, a series for the kids about a boy and his pet dolphin, and *Daniel Boone*, a *Davy Crockett* rip-off which went so far as to feature the actor who played Crockett for Disney and ABC: Fess Parker.

Solow knew how to do the dance. NBC had never done business with the CBS golden girl, but now had an opportunity to partner up with the No. 1 star of America's No. 1 network. He also knew that these cool, confident-looking men in tailor-made business suits had a collective bellyache from CBS and ABC kicking their butts. *Star Trek*, he insisted, was nothing like anything tried before -- a space show for adults as well as for kids. Unlike *Lost in Space*, where the Jupiter II was scheduled to crash land in Episode Three and remain planet-bound for the remainder of its first season, this new space show would actually *stay* in space. Above all else, *Star Trek* would be in living color.

Then Solow did what executives with ice water in their veins are so good at: he stared at Jerry Stanley and Grant Tinker. Stanley and Tinker stared back. Roddenberry stared at the ceiling. The pitch for *Star Trek* had turned into a staring contest. NBC blinked first. It was a small blink, but a blink nonetheless. The network men agreed to take the first step: a check was written for "script development." Jerry Stanley later said, "It was Herb's tenacity and Herb's presentation that sold the series." (166)

3

Designing *Star Trek*

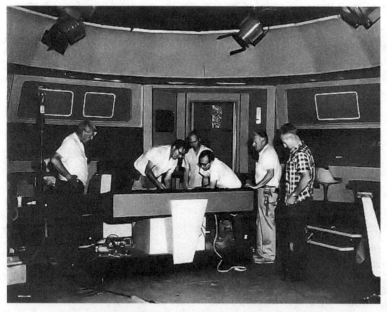
The spending starts here (Courtesy of Gerald Gurian)

In May, 1964, NBC put up $20,000. Roddenberry was to develop three stories for the pilot, then write a script based on the network's favorite. He immediately got busy -- not writing, but getting a crash course in science fiction. Samuel Peeples, a sci-fi enthusiast, was his first call. Roddenberry and Peeples had competed for a Writers Guild Award years earlier. Roddenberry's *Have Gun - Will Travel* script "Helen of Abajinian" had been nominated, as had Peeples' "The Bounty Hunter," for *Wanted: Dead or Alive*. Roddenberry won, but the two met and said they had actually voted for one another. It was the polite thing to say, true or not.

Peeples later said, "I thought [the idea for *Star Trek*] was fascinating and fun because [Gene] was going to try to do what I considered to be science fiction, which is not often done in Hollywood. Most so-called science fiction movies are horror plays. Gene actually had an idea, a plan, a dream of making a genuine science fiction series that would be very much like the better science fiction magazines." (136-3)

Peeples loved science fiction. But, while his head may have been in the stars, his feet were planted firmly in the good earth of the American frontier. He created five TV western series (*The Tall Man*, *Frontier Circus*, *The Legend of Jesse James*, *Custer* and *Lancer*) and was a staff writer on *Overland Trail*, *The Rough Riders* and *The Texan*. Harlan Ellison's recollection that Roddenberry said he got the phrasing "*Wagon Train* to the stars" from Peeples seems quite plausible.

Peeples remembered having drinks with Roddenberry and "just shooting a lot of bull" about the possibilities of the series. He felt that Roddenberry had done his research, conveying knowledge of numerous scientific theories including the paradoxes involved in faster-than-light travel. Peeples loaned him a couple science fiction books, and Roddenberry soaked it all up. Peeples also recommended other writers to check out. Among them: Robert Bloch (*Psycho*), Theodore Sturgeon (*More Than Human*), Richard Matheson (*The Twilight Zone* and *I Am Legend*), Jerry Sohl (*The Twilight Zone* and *The Outer Limits*) and Fredric Brown (*What Mad Universe*), all of whom would become involved with the series.

Jerry Sohl had his first meeting with Roddenberry at Nickodell Restaurant on Melrose Avenue, a studio hangout for Desilu employees and those of its next door neighbor, Paramount Pictures. Sohl said, "I found him to be amiable and easy to talk to. He didn't seem to know an awful lot about science fiction and he confessed that he didn't. That's why I was there. He was going to pick my brains and, quite frankly, find out what I thought of this series that he had in mind and whether I'd be available as a writer." (160-1)

Roddenberry asked Sohl to recommend other writers. He came up with some names that Peeples hadn't. New on the list: George Clayton Johnson, who Sohl met while working for *The Twilight Zone*, and Harlan Ellison, whom he knew from *The Outer Limits*.

There were others who gave Roddenberry valuable input. Harvey Lynn, a physicist from the RAND Corporation, was contacted in June to act as a technical consultant. This was a feather in Roddenberry's cap. RAND, generally cited as the very first scientific "think tank," was established in 1946 by the United States Army Air Corps (the acronym RAND stood for Research and Development). Roddenberry's instructions to Lynn, from a June 30, 1964 letter: "Keep [*Star Trek*] enough in accord with the laws of physics that scientists can enjoy the program, too."

Now that his support team was in place, Roddenberry started writing.

The first treatment was "The Cage," with a first draft from June 25, 1964, and revised versions dated June 29 and July 8. The story dealt with hypnotic suggestion and mental illusion. Forbidden sex was also part of the mix.

The second story treatment was "Visit to Paradise," from July 20, 1964. This was later used as the basis for a first season episode: "The Return of the Archons." In the story, Roddenberry attacked both authority and conformity. He wrote:

> Archon is anything but a paradise. What can be seen on the street, the happy friendliness and tranquility, masks despair, dullness, almost a living death. There are no police, no crime, no jails, because the slightest infraction is stamped out ruthlessly by The Lawgivers.

Writer Joel Engel (*Gene Roddenberry: the Myth and the Man behind Star Trek*) said, "This would be the first of what would be several *Star Trek* episodes in which man searches for God, finds Him, debunks Him, and lives more happily afterward -- or kills Him off metaphorically, thus improving mankind's well-being." (58b)

Christopher Knopf, a friend of Roddenberry's and a fellow TV writer, said, "Gene seemed to distrust high authority -- people in power. He liked to tweak authority, as opposed to just nailing them and going to war. That was his way of bringing them down. Just tweak them." Looking for a silver lining to this gray cloud, Knopf also noted that Roddenberry "seemed to have a great affection for people in low places." (101a)

Those low places were the inspiration of the third story submitted to NBC. "The Women," from July 23, 1964, was eventually filmed as "Mudd's Women.". For this earlier version, the antagonist of the story was a con artist named Harry Patton (later renamed Harcourt Fenton Mudd), a scoundrel practicing the trade of "wiving settlers," or, more simply put: interstellar prostitution. Roddenberry was trying to sneak a sex story past the network.

By the end of July, "The Cage" was selected to be developed into a screenplay. NBC had made an unusual and calculating choice in selecting this particular story. If filmed, it would require more optical effects than the others. It would also pose a greater challenge in makeup, costuming and set design. This was more than a pilot, it was a test. If Roddenberry and Desilu were going to prove themselves, they had to do so with the most impossible of the three concepts.

Roddenberry immediately went back to Sam Peeples, who was proud of his collection of science fiction magazines, later boasting it was "probably one of the most complete around." Roddenberry photographed many of the covers and discussed with Peeples every element of what he hoped to accomplish with *Star Trek*. At the same time, Desilu assigned him a small staff, including a graphic artist and a set designer.

***

Rolland "Bud" Brooks, Desilu's supervising art director, arrived at work one day to find *Star Trek* dumped in his lap. It was a giant leap from *The Lucy Show* and *Ben Casey* (the latter being a series that, while not owned by the studio, was filmed on the Desilu lot). Brooks said, "I was sitting there thinking, 'My God, we gotta come up with a lot of stuff here'... and I thought of Matt." (22-1)

Walter "Matt" Jefferies was fascinated by flight. He had joined the Army Air Corps during World War II and flew combat missions over Europe and North Africa. After the war, he became an illustrator for the Library of Congress, as well as a freelance artist for various magazines. In 1957, Jefferies was hired by Warner Brothers as a technical consultant and unofficial set designer for *Bombers B-52*. The movie was a success and Jefferies was given more work by the studio.

Because he proved he knew a great deal about airplanes, someone at Warner Bros. decided he must also

Matt Jefferies (Courtesy of Gerald Gurian)

know a great deal about sharks -- they were both grey, after all. And so Jefferies found himself designing a 20-foot mechanical, man-swallowing shark for *The Old Man and the Sea*. Work at MGM followed, where Jefferies designed the ship interiors and models for *The Wreck of the Mary Deare*. Then, because some felt the inside of a sea ship was not that far away from the interior of a space ship, Jefferies was put to work on *Men Into Space*, a science fiction series produced by Ziv. It premiered on CBS in 1959 and lasted one year. From the low rent offices of Ziv, Jefferies was lured to Desilu for *The Untouchables*, followed by *Ben Casey*. His title, finally: set designer. The illustrator who thought he was taking a single job on a film to help recreate the interior of a B-52 had now spent seven years designing everything from planes to moon bases to prohibition-era breweries.

Interviewed in 1968 for the fanzine *Inside Star Trek*, issue 4, Jefferies said, "At that point, [my wife and I] took a month off and went to the East Coast to visit the family. [We] came back and I couldn't find my equipment. My little cubicle was empty. So I went to Bud Brooks' office and said, 'Where's the next *Casey* script?' and he said, 'You're not on the show anymore.' It served me right for taking a month's vacation."

Jefferies was wrong in thinking he had been fired. He had actually been given a promotion ... of a sort. He remembered Brooks saying with mischievous glee, "Your stuff is in the big drafting room... and there's a man coming in this morning by the name of

Roddenberry to do a space show." (91-9)

Brooks had already told Roddenberry that Jefferies flew B-17 bombers in the war, which led to a bond between the two men. Jefferies said, "When he came in, we re-fought World War II for about 20 minutes, and then he told me what he wanted. Actually, about all he said that would help me along was several 'don'ts,' such as, 'no flames, no fins, no rockets.' And one 'do,' -- 'Make it look like it's got power.' And then he walked out." (91-6)

As a member of the Aviation Space Writers Association, Jefferies was able to amass a large collection of designs from NASA and the defense industry. He also viewed episodes of *Buck Rogers* and *Flash Gordon* to see their vision of intergalactic space craft, and quickly decided: "This is what we will *not* do!" (91-5)

Pato Guzman, the second man on the team, was a talented Desilu set designer. He had been under-challenged with his duties on *The Lucy Show* and immediately demonstrated abilities far greater than previously believed. Guzman's time on *Star Trek* was brief but his contributions influenced much to come.

Regarding the direction they were given, in a 1968 interview, Jefferies said, "Roddenberry insisted everything be believable. We had to base it all on fairly solid scientific concepts, project it into the future and try to visualize what the fourth, fifth or tenth generation of present-day equipment would be like. So, working within those limits, Pato and I sat down and began to sketch out ideas. When we had about two walls covered with sketches, we called Roddenberry in and he looked them over. *Damn it, but he can be irritating.* He liked only a piece of this one or a small part of that one, but none of our ideas had what he was really looking for. So we did 20-some more designs, using the few elements he had said he liked." (91-4)

Again Roddenberry was called in. This time he brought along people from the sales department, the production office, and Harvey Lynn from the RAND Corporation. Again the designs were narrowed down to four or five that included something/anything that he and his entourage liked. Then Jefferies and Guzman started the process all over again.

One thing had to change: that the spaceship would land on planets. Roddenberry later said, "Land a ship 14 stories tall on a planet surface every week? Not only would it have blown our entire weekly budget but just suggesting it probably would have ruined my reputation in the industry *forever*. This is one of many instances where a compromise forced us into creative thought and actually improved what we planned to do. The fact that we didn't have the budget forced us into conceiving the transporter device – 'Beam them down to the planet' -- which allowed us to be well into the story by page two." (145-4)

On July 24, with "Enterprise" now chosen as the name of the ship, Roddenberry sent a memo to Pato Guzman, telling him:

> More and more I see the need for some sort of interesting electronic computing machine designed into the U.S.S. Enterprise, perhaps on the bridge itself. It will be an information device out of which [Captain] April and his crew can quickly and interestingly extract information on the registry of other space vessels, space flight plans for other ships, information on individuals and planets and civilizations, etc. This should not only speed up our storytelling but could be visually interesting.

A follow-up note from Roddenberry suggested that the computer should talk. It hardly seems like an innovative idea now with Siri and other speech gadgets in our pockets. But in 1964, this was a concept that could only come from a daydreamer in a wrinkled suit. Another memo from Roddenberry to Guzman, dated August 25, stated:

It seems to me likely that design of controls, dials, instruments, etc., aboard our spaceship, particularly the complex "three dimensional" ones which our scientist friends insist would be there, necessitates we locate some hopefully near-genius gadgeteer and electrician and jack-of-all-trades here at Desilu who can augment our speculation and sketching with some idea of what he can accomplish with batteries, lights, wires, plastic, etc.

The near-genius gadgeteer was Joe Lombardi, who had been handling the special effects for *My Favorite Martian*.

Another August 25 letter from Roddenberry -- to Kellam de Forest, a second technical advisor, this time courtesy of Desilu -- said:

We are dangerously near the time we must settle on a shape and configuration for our spaceship of the future... but are running into considerable difficulty in settling on that design.

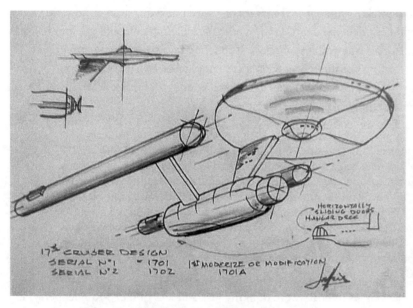

Early sketch of U.S.S. Enterprise by Matt Jefferies
(Courtesy of Bob Olsen)

Jefferies remembered, "I decided that whatever we came up with had to be instantly recognizable. The habitat part, I felt, ideally, should be a ball, but it got too awkward to play with. It just didn't look like it would get out of first gear, much less the speeds [Gene] was talking about. So it gradually got flattened. I was trying to stay away from a saucer because the UFOs, or flying saucers, were old hat. But it did gradually turn into a saucer.... I felt if [Gene] was going to get some sort of fantastic performance out of the thing, there would have to be very powerful engines of some kind or other, even to the point they might be dangerous to be around. I said, 'Well, we better get 'em away from the main hull.'" (91-1)

Eventually Jefferies came up with a design he was happy with, and said, "We knocked out a small model and went to Solow and Gene and Mr. Katz, and some of the others from the network came in that day. I pulled the model out. We had put a little hook in the top of it with a string, but I was holding it [from] underneath. It was made out of balsa wood, except for the two engine pods, which were stock birch dowels, which are much heavier than the other wood. I held it up and Gene took it by the string and it immediately flopped upside down. He liked that better. *I didn't*. That was one of our biggest arguments." (91)

Jefferies finally won the fight, but later lamented, "When the show hit the air, it was on the cover of *TV Guide* -- printed *upside down!*" (91)

Well, not exactly. The upside-down Enterprise was actually featured on the cover of a TV supplement magazine carried in numerous newspapers right before the premiere of the series. Three years later, *TV Guide* did get it wrong and did print the Enterprise upside-down, not on its cover but for a Close Up listings (in 1969, for "The Tholian Web").

Regarding the identifying imprint of NCC, Jefferies had very specific reasons for his choices. The letter "N," under international aviation agreements, designated registration within the United States. "CC" (or "CCCC") identified aircraft from the Soviet Union. Jefferies, believing that a venture of this magnitude would have to be the result of a United Earth, wanted the letters combined. Roddenberry agreed. As for "1701," Jefferies didn't want to use any numerals on the spaceship that would be hard to read at a distance and therefore eliminated threes, fours, sixes, eights and nines.

How the ship looked on the outside was only part of the work to be completed. Concerning the bridge design, Jefferies said, "It was pretty well established with the model that the thing was going to be a full circle. From there, it became a question of how we were going to make it, how it could come apart, [and] where the cameraman could get into it." (91)

Desilu, meanwhile, was sweating bullets. Roddenberry, in 1968, mocking his employers, said, "The studio's attitude was 'Come on, baby, what's so difficult about designing a spaceship? You take a cigar shape, put some windows on it, now there you've got it. Let's get on to the next thing.'" (145-4)

Taking offense to the comment, Herb Solow later wrote:

> As Gene completed the first draft pilot script, he unfortunately became overly protective of his new baby. I cautioned Gene that having good reason at times was no excuse to continually cast blame, especially when dealing with people who had a lot to do with the future of the series and his ultimate survival. He didn't listen. He didn't want to. And, as the series' development progressed, his behavior foreshadowed a continuing rocky future for Gene Roddenberry and *Star Trek*.... Gene and I met with NBC to get their script comments. He took offense at most of them, at times unnecessarily so. Some ideas were really good. (161-3)

Solow's former bosses at NBC were thinking less and less of Gene Roddenberry. It would build over time, but "Strike Three" was already in the making.

Meanwhile, the ideas were indeed flowing in from all directions. On September 14, 1964, Harvey Lynn wrote to Roddenberry:

> To accommodate smaller shuttles, taxis and tugs, I visualize the Enterprise having something like a bomb bay. When a ship is to be docked, the doors open.

This idea was incorporated into the design of the ship. Lynn received no credit -- just a $50 weekly check. Another suggestion from Lynn involved the ship's weaponry. The RAND man pointed out that "Laser," which stood for Light Amplification Stimulation Emission Radiation, and "Maser," with the "M" standing for Microwave, were already in use in 1964. He asked Roddenberry:

> Don't you think it likely that they will have a new name? A new name will also serve to silence critics who will contend that a Laser cannon will not whip up dust [as portrayed in the script for "The Cage"] and will not need to be dug-in.

Eventually a new acronym surfaced – "phaser," standing for <u>Ph</u>oton-<u>ma</u>s<u>er</u>. This word born of fiction can be found today in most dictionaries.

Roddenberry acknowledged Lynn's contributions on September 16, writing:

Dear Harvey: Have your comments on "The Cage" and find them very thoughtful and helpful. Am already making script changes which reflect them.

On September 24:

Dear Harvey: Enclosed the revised draft of the *Star Trek* pilot. Reference your comments on September 14 and you'll note we've taken out the whole 'docking' procedure. Will hold your suggestion here for future stories which involve it.... Most of your suggestions are reflected in this new version.... Any point you feel strongly about, please feel free to continue arguing.

Roddenberry finished his first draft screenplay on October 6 and submitted it to NBC. The network wanted changes, resulting in three more drafts, dated October 10, November 16 and November 20 but, based on the strength of the first draft, gave the "okay" to proceed with filming. The production was scheduled for late November and early December, the start date little more than a month away. At the same time, CBS had ordered a script for Bruce Geller's proposed series, *Mission: Impossible*, and all indications were that a pilot film would follow. Suddenly, Desilu had two impossible missions to deal with: one in name and the other in almost all other regards.

According to Herb Solow, Lucille Ball thought *Star Trek* was going to be a show about USO performers visiting troops stationed in faraway lands. Some say she had been referring to it as "that South Seas show." Now, with an order for a pilot, Solow had to set Lucy straight. *Star Trek* was not about movie stars trekking off to do good deeds with Bob Hope; it was about outer space. Lucy was speechless. The Desilu Board of Directors was not.

Questions were fired at Solow. Questions were fired at Katz. How much were these "far out" pilots going to cost the studio? No one liked the answers. The pilot films would cost more than the networks were willing to pay. Far more. If the pilots sold, the studio, in producing the series, would continue losing money, week in and week out.

How Money Is Made In TV 101: In the 1960s, when a network bought into producing a series, what they actually paid was a licensing fee that only covered about two-thirds of the cost of the production. If the show did well, the network would pay additional money -- typically half of the original fee -- to air repeats of selected episodes. Then, for these episodes at least, the studio would break even. Their profits came from overseas sales. Later, if the series stayed in production long enough to generate 100 or more episodes, further profits could be reaped from syndicated reruns. But for series that stayed on the air less than three years, the studio almost always lost money. Too many money-losing duds and a studio could go out of business. This basic business model is still the dominant structure today, although series now need to survive for four years or more, since fewer episodes are produced for each season.

Desilu studio man Ed Holly said, "We had two properties that were both tremendous; we were highly enthused about them. But, as we got more and more into the pilot-preparation stage, it was becoming more and more obvious that the executive producers of each show -- Gene Roddenberry and Bruce Geller -- were inflexible on making compromises that would enable the shows to be produced on an economically sound basis. According to our estimates, we would lose $65,000 per episode on each series [nearly $500,000 in 2013]. We didn't have the financial strength to afford that type of show. And we recommended to Lucy and the board that we do not do the pilots, much less the series. I told Lucy, 'If we do these and are unfortunate enough to sell them as series, we're going to have to sell the company and go bankrupt.'" (84)

Katz and Solow felt differently. They had done what Lucy asked -- they found TV properties the studio could own. Yes, there were risks. And yes, there would be red ink. Desilu would lose money at first. For years, even. But these two series had the potential of becoming hits. And that meant reruns. And foreign sales. And merchandising.

The advice from Katz and Solow struck a chord with Lucy. She may have initially misunderstood the *Star Trek* concept, but TV's "wacky redhead," known for playing a character that always had a harebrained scheme up her sleeve, had learned well from Desi Arnaz. He had been called crazy many times by industry insiders, but always proved his critics wrong.

Ed Holly admitted, "One of the biggest decisions that had to be made was when [Lucy] went against my recommendation and Argyle Nelson's [Desilu's general manager in charge of production] that had to do with *Star Trek* and *Mission: Impossible*. If it were not for Lucy, there would be no *Star Trek* today." (84)

***

Roddenberry faced a daunting challenge with the script for "The Cage": design a universe filled with diverse individuals and alien creatures, all the while providing the reader of the script (or viewer on the show) with enough information to comprehend the technology of the futuristic times -- without ever letting the gadgetry get in the way of the story. It was certainly harder than writing *Bonanza*.

When the final draft script was presented to cast and crew, some were confused. They didn't have the advantage of seeing what *Star Trek* would look like. They couldn't know the ship's abilities (or limits). They couldn't conjure up an image of the bridge, or a transporter device capable of turning a human into sparkling dots, then reassembling that flesh and blood at a different location.

Gene Coon, who would become an essential creative force in *Star Trek*, already had an appreciation of the TV miracle the team had pulled off when he was interviewed in 1968, a mere four years after *Star Trek*'s inception. From that relatively fresh vantage point, he observed: "Gene [Roddenberry] created a totally new universe. He invented a starship, which works, by the way, and is a logical progression from what we know today. He created customs, morals, modes of speaking, a complete technology. We have a very rigid technology on this show. We know how fast we can go. We know what we use for fuel. We know what our weapons will do. And Gene invented all these things. He did a monumental job of creation. He created an entire galaxy and an entire rule book for operating within that galaxy, with very specific laws governing behavior, manners, customs, as well as science and technology. Now that's a hell of a job. He didn't create a show. This was a massive, titanic job of creation. One of the most impressive feats of its kind that I've ever seen." (36a)

Of course Roddenberry had a lot of help. But he must be credited with assembling the team, inspiring the team, pushing and pulling at the team, deciding which ideas to use and which to discard. He then melded it all together to create the screenplay for "The Cage."

It was a herculean task, so much so that it flew right over the heads of many involved. Morris Chapnick, assigned by Herb Solow to be Roddenberry's assistant, said, "I have to say... I don't know diddly from science fiction. I am sure there are many other worlds out in the sky somewhere, but I don't think in those terms.... Some of the stuff Gene does... I don't understand it... I read this thing, and I don't know anything about outer space, but the wagon train to the stars -- *that* I understand." (31a)

It's easy to underestimate how profound and holistic Roddenberry's vision of the techscape of the future was. By today's standards, the available technology of 1964 was downright primitive. Doors did not open automatically when we approached them. The first handheld calculator was still in the future, as were microwave ovens and cell phones. 1964 was a year before most Americans had even heard of a place called Vietnam, five years before man walked on the moon, 25 years before anyone ever surfed the Internet. Phone had a curly cord, and the new innovation of "touchtone" dialing was merely a year old. Even the television sets that viewers watched would be considered positively prehistoric today. Most TVs were black-and-white models, and the majority of those sets had no remote control. There was no cable or satellite; rabbit ears and roof-top antennas were the norm. The world looked, and was, different.

***

Roddenberry needed collaborators. His *Star Trek* script wrote a new language: warp drive, hailing frequencies, mental illusion, thought control, and green-skinned sex-driven dancing girls from a place called Orion. How was he going to find someone imaginative and daring enough to direct?

James Goldstone, a well-regarded TV director, was offered the job. Roddenberry knew him from *The Lieutenant*. Solow, on behalf of Desilu, approved of the choice. So did the network. But Goldstone had a "scheduling conflict." A man with no reputation could find one at *Star Trek*. An established reputation, however, could be ruined with a job like this. The search continued.

Solow asked around to see who was on the network's A-list. He asked: "Who's new? Who's hot? Who's talented? Who won't step on toes?"

Robert Butler was the name Solow came up with. Like Goldstone, Roddenberry knew the 36-year-old Butler from *The Lieutenant*, where he had directed two episodes. One of Butler's first directing jobs was for *Have Gun - Will Travel*, with a script written by Roddenberry. Other recent television credits included multiple assignments on *Stoney Burke*, *The Fugitive*, and Desilu's *The Untouchables* and *Ben Casey*. (Not yet on his resume, but in his future: directing for *I Spy* as well as the pilot and numerous episodes for the Emmy-winning *Hill Street Blues*. He would also create *Remington Steele*, for which he also directed and produced.) Roddenberry and Solow were taking no chances. They wanted the best they could get -- or at least, the best they could afford, who was also available on short notice and willing to take on a headache like *Star Trek*.

Despite having directed two episodes of *The Twilight Zone*, Butler was no great fan of science fiction. He later said, "I read the script, and I was doubtful.... I thought, 'This is just a palette of science fiction.' Everything in science fiction that I knew of was dragged into this pilot. The beautiful young woman who's really an old hag, etc. -- all the chestnuts were in the pilot. And I read it and remember talking to my wife about it and saying, 'This thing is too nuts; it's just crazy. I don't know whether to do this' -- being young and pure. And she said, 'Aah, why don't you do it?' So I did." (26-3)

Among other things, Butler wanted to change the title. Decades later, he admitted, "At that time, without the brainwash of the show becoming a massive hit, I remember *Star Trek* sounded kind of inert and boring to me, whereas 'Star Track,' I thought, had a bigger vista to it. But Gene was not in the mood to receive any such input." (26-1)

Roddenberry wanted a director, not a co-creator. Butler said, "I remember thinking that Gene was too far into it. Too close to it. So I just gave up." (26-2)

Or, rather, gave in.

Next, Roddenberry and Butler needed a cinematographer. The problem was, the official "pilot season" fell between March and May. Desilu had entered the game late. By November, both the new series and the older ones that had gotten their network "pick up" were well into production. All the best people -- almost all the people worth having -- were unavailable. Almost, but not all.

William E. Snyder, 62, was on hiatus from Walt Disney Studios where he was signed to a contract. Snyder was a three-time Academy Award nominee for Best Cinematographer in the 1940s (*Aloma of the South Seas*, *The Loves of Carmen* and *Jolson Sings Again*). His film credits also included a movie that received no nominations of any kind: the 1954 cult sci-fi monster bash *Creature from the Black Lagoon*. He had also photographed *Moon Pilot*, a 1962 Disney space comedy, and this gave him the credentials Roddenberry was looking for. Disney, as a favor to NBC, the home of *Walt Disney's Wonderful World of Color*, agreed to loan Snyder out, making him a key *Star Trek* player -- as director of photography.

For the position of associate producer, Roddenberry turned to James Goldstone for advice. Even though Goldstone declined the invitation to direct, he did introduce a second key player to *Star Trek* -- one, who in time, would become among the most important.

***

Herb Solow and Bob Justman
(Used by permission of Robert H. Justman)

Robert H. Justman had been in show business for 14 years, working his way up from production assistant to associate producer. Before that, he dealt in farm produce.

"I had been buying and selling fruit," said Justman, in his last interview, given for this book. "That was my father's business -- wholesale fruit. But World War II saved me from that. Not right away. I'd been sitting around waiting to get called in for service. And it got to be the summer of 1944 and still no call. So I went into the draft board and I said to them, 'How come you haven't called me yet?' The guy said, 'You don't have to serve; we have plenty of guys like you,' meaning, guys they didn't think they wanted. I had been found to be 4F because my eyesight was so bad. I said, 'But I want to go.' I raised so much hell that they agreed to re-examine me. There were a bunch of near naked guys getting examined in this large room and some doctors who were sitting behind a table, saying, 'Take off your clothes, go to this room, go to that room, go to that other room.' So I went to 'that other room,' and was re-classified A1-Specialist, which meant I finally went overseas, into the Pacific, as a radio operator on a destroyer escort. My ears, as they found out, were fine." (94-1)

After the war, Justman returned to Los Angeles to attend college. "I went to UCLA for a couple of years but, in that time, I hadn't learned anything I hadn't already known from my high school education in New York, so I ended up doing what my father wanted me to do

-- going to work in his firm. He sent me to Texas, then back to California, then out to various other places around the West, and I wasn't liking it at all. Most of these places had no culture, like Imperial Valley, with the temperatures at 110° and 115°. So, after doing my rounds one time, after I had made a lot of money for the company, I decided it was time to quit. I woke up one morning in Phoenix and said, 'Today's the day.'" (94-1)

A family friend had been working at Motion Picture Center on Cahuenga Boulevard in Hollywood (the facility where *I Love Lucy* would soon film its premiere season), and offered Justman a job as a production assistant on the latest Joe Palooka boxing picture -- 1950's *Joe Palooka in the Squared City*. Justman later said, "As word spread that I could do my job, and do a few other people's jobs while doing my job, I was seen as being someone in demand, and went from production to production to production." (94-1)

These were B-pictures, such as 1951's *The Groom Wore Spurs*, 1952's *Red Planet Mars,* and 1953's *Abbott and Costello Meet Captain Kidd*. Justman said, "I did have a great career as a production assistant. So much so that I finally priced myself out of the production assistant business. I started at 50 bucks a week and I was up to $150 and then $175, which was more than a second assistant director made in those days. So I took the next step and *became* a second assistant." (94-1)

The only way a P.A. gets to be a second assistant director is by proving himself invaluable. Justman did this in no time and found himself in the Screen Directors Guild union as a second assistant in television for the 1953 sitcoms *Life of Riley* and *The Loretta Young Show*. The second assistant's job is to prepare the set for the director, making sure all crew and cast members are present and ready to do their jobs. But the goal of every second assistant is to get to be first assistant.

Justman said, "After a couple years, I wrote to the Director's Guild and asked for a hearing. They agreed to hear my case, knowing full well that the only way you could make a move from second to first assistant director was if you inherited the job, or if you had been nominated by a major studio, and the studios were only entitled to nominate one person a year. Well, the Navy didn't want me in 1944 and the Screen Directors Guild didn't want me in '54, but I'd changed the Navy's minds so I figured I might be able to change the minds of those on the assistant director's counsel. I had worked with a number of these people who were on the board, including Bob Aldrich. I went before them and pleaded my case. And, with fair dramatics, I said, 'I will not use the Taft-Hartley Law to get into the Guild; I will get in on my own merits or not at all.'" (94-1)

The Taft-Hartley Labor Law, also referred to as the "slave labor law," was enacted by Congress in 1947 to protect workers from having to work too many hours for too little pay. Justman was making a joke, but this hardly seemed the place for it. He remembered, "They said, 'Wait outside, please.' I went outside and closed the door and sat there in my best suit and regretted what I had told them when I was in there. And I said, 'Asshole, why did you have to do that to yourself?' I figured that all was lost. After about 20 minutes, the door opened to the Board Room and I was brought inside to be given the bad news. Bob Aldrich got up from his chair, stuck out his hand and said, 'Welcome, brother.' Feeling I had behaved a bit like an asshole before, I remember thinking, 'I hope I'm not expected to behave this way too often.' And that's how it all started. I went from feature to feature to feature.

"There were a number of memorable films, and some not so memorable. I worked with people like William Wellman [on *Blood Alley*, starring John Wayne], Lewis Milestone [on *Mutiny on the Bounty*, with Marlon Brando] and Allan Miner [on *The Way Back*, with

Anthony Quinn]. And I did a number of films with Bob Aldrich [including *Apache*, starring Burt Lancaster]. We had a great time together." (94-1)

Daily Variety in 1956 reported one such great time:

> Actors really put their hearts into it on the set of the Robert Aldrich production *The Fragile Fox* yesterday [renamed *Attack* when released later that year]. In a scene calling for Yank soldiers to browbeat a captured Nazi soldier, the Nazi bit was enacted by Robert Justman, first assistant director on the film -- the man responsible for all the early morning calls.

Justman was also in great demand in television. He was so appreciated on *The Adventures of Superman* that he not only worked as A.D. but also, at the same time, as associate producer. This new position was greater than the title implied. Today, the screen credit more accurately reads "producer" or "line producer." Justman's job was to beg, borrow and steal to keep the show running with too small a budget, too short a schedule, and too lean a staff. And he did this 39 times a season.

After two years of wearing two hats and feeling exhausted, he removed one hat, then left the series and returned to being just an A.D., for *My Friend Flicka*. At this time, Justman hooked up with fellow A.D.s Leon Chooluck and Leonard Shapiro and, in association with the Screen Directors Guild, formed the "Assistant Directors Roundtable" to survey and analyze problems pertinent to that aspect of film production. Within a few years, the roundtable was an official branch of the SDG, with Justman as Vice President.

In 1958, MGM hired Justman to exclusively work for its various television series. That year, he served as assistant director on *Northwest Passage* and *The Thin Man*. The following year, he continued with these shows and was assigned a third, *Phillip Marlowe*. In 1960, MGM rewarded Justman for his hard work with more hard work, naming him "Production Liaison Executive" for TV's *National Velvet* and, in 1961, the same post for *Dr. Kildare* and *Father of the Bride*, simultaneously. Other series Justman involved himself with during his tenure as Production Executive were *The Islanders*, *Outlaws*, *Cain's Hundred*, *Stoney Burke*, and *The Outer Limits*. For the latter, he also became associate producer.

When Roddenberry was looking to staff his *Star Trek* pilot, *The Outer Limits* -- the only series in 1964 dealing with science fiction and its requirements, such as specialty makeup, strange costuming, props, sets, effects and eerie music -- had just been cancelled in the middle of its second year. Taking James Goldstone's recommendation, Roddenberry contacted Justman, offering him the chance to line-produce "The Cage." Justman was tempted but didn't feel knowledgeable enough in the area of optical effects to accept the position. He did, however, agree to work in the capacity of A.D. and recommended someone else as associate producer; someone more experienced whom he had met on *The Outer Limits*.

***

Byron Haskin was 65 and had a long list of screen accomplishments. A cinematographer from the silent era of motions pictures, Haskin had also helped with the development of sound for film. In 1934, he shifted his professional emphasis to special effects. In this area, he was nominated for three Academy Awards, winning one for Technical Achievement in 1939. Haskin then proceeded to add "director" to his resume. In 1950, he helmed Disney's first live-action feature, *Treasure Island*. Three years later, he began a long and rewarding association with producer George Pal and entered the realm of science fiction, directing 1953's *The War of the Worlds*. More science fiction followed with *Conquest of*

Space, *From the Earth to the Moon* and the cult classic *Robinson Crusoe on Mars*. Immediately following *Crusoe*, Haskin directed three episodes for *The Outer Limits*, including "Demon with a Glass Hand," scripted by Harlan Ellison. Now, with *Limits* folding, Haskin agreed to meet with Roddenberry.

Running into Justman on the Desilu lot, and not knowing who had recommended him for the job, Haskin commented to his friend, "I'm gonna see some guy with a really weird name, Rodenberg or Rosenberry... or whatever. I don't know. Probably another rank amateur who doesn't know diddly and wants me to save his ass." (94-8)

Haskin, impressed by the rank amateur's concept and commitment to quality, agreed to join the team and save "Rosenberry's" ass. It would be a stormy union -- just one of many.

***

Matt Jefferies and Pato Guzman, designated as production designer and art director, respectively, were already deep into their work. Before filming of the pilot could begin, Guzman, homesick for his native country, returned to Chile. It was another tough break for *Star Trek*. All the competent set designers were already otherwise engaged ... almost all.

Franz Bachelin, 68, was old enough to have served as a German fighter pilot in World War I. He was also old enough to have been designing film sets in Hollywood since 1937. Among the jobs he tackled: the POW camp sets of *Stalag 17*, the fantastic worlds of *The Magic Sword* and the inner world of *Journey to the Center of the Earth* (for which he received an Academy Award nomination). Now Bachelin wanted to retire, which is why he was home on the day Byron Haskin called. Bachelin was told this last job would be fun, a mere month's work, and then back to retirement well in time for the holidays. He took the bait. By doing so, the old pro with the German accent would take everything he had learned in the past and turn it upside down. Literally.

Roddenberry was fond of telling the story of how the foliage brought to dress the alien planet set was just too earthlike. He complained. Different and more exotic plants were located. He complained some more. The trees, bushes and flowers still looked like they had come from Earth. Completely frustrated with the situation, Roddenberry pulled one of the plants from its pot, turned it upside down and shoved it back into the soil, roots sticking up. "*There*," he said. "Now *there's* an alien plant!" (145-4)

It was pure Roddenberry -- fighting the system, standing alone, showing his well-meaning but ignorant colleagues the right path to the future. It made a great story. It also made veteran professionals like Franz Bachelin and Byron Haskin grind their teeth.

***

One crew member who clicked with Roddenberry from the start was the man behind the yet-to-be-seen *Star Trek* mini-skirts. William Ware Theiss, at 33, had done his time without screen credits as an apprentice in motion picture wardrobe departments, including a six-month stint at Universal working on films such as *Spartacus* and *The Pink Panther*. In 1964, Theiss was still toiling without credit, this time as an assistant costumer for Screen Gems. One series was a sci-fi sitcom about a Martian living on Earth.

Interviewed in 1968 for *Inside Star Trek*, issue 6, Theiss said, "On *My Favorite Martian*, I came in contact with Ray Bradbury's production secretary and was offered the job of costume designer for 'The World of Ray Bradbury,' three one-act plays. One of these was an adaptation of his famous short story, 'The Veldt,' which offered a marvelous opportunity to do lavish futuristic costumes.... As a result... a smart alec secretary whom I had met while at Universal -- D.C. Fontana -- called me to the attention of Gene Roddenberry."

Fontana said, "A friend introduced us, and we thought alike about many things. I knew he was gay, of course, but we were really good friends. Gene was muttering about costumes again, and I said, 'I have a friend who does costuming.'" (64-4)

Fate smiled on *Star Trek*. Theiss would prove to be the perfect man for the job. Among other innovations, he had a theory that the sexuality of a woman had less to do with the amount of skin exposed and more to do with the likelihood of her clothing slipping off. He said, "Clothes, since the mid-19th-century, have become less and less bulky, cumbersome, protective -- both physically and morally -- and headed faster and faster apparently into complete nudity. This does not mean clothes of the future will be non-existent or that people in the future will be nude, [but] I can only deduce the future will bring literally thousands of style changes and nudity will be one of them." (172-3)

Roddenberry liked the cut of Theiss's out-of-this-world fashion sense, reflected in the scanty attire worn by a green-skinned dancing girl. The distinctive gold and blue velour shirts started here, as well. The RCA color TV-friendly red shirts had yet to be introduced.

This new *Star Trek* universe required more than spaceship designs and futuristic wardrobe. There would also be gadgets -- and creatures. Again, the sudden demise of *The Outer Limits* became a blessing for *Star Trek*.

Wah Chang (Courtesy of Gerald Gurian)

Wah Chang, at 46, had already designed masks and headdresses for many films, including *The King and I* and *Cleopatra*. Chang started making monsters in 1953 for *Cat Women of the Moon*. For that "classic," he created and operated a spider puppet. In 1960, he designed the title object in George Pal's *The Time Machine*. In 1963 and '64, he was making strange creatures for *The Outer Limits*, some of which would, with slight modifications, turn up on *Star Trek*. Among his contributions to "The Cage" were the huge rubber heads of the Talosians, complete with pulsating veins, as well as the now famous flip-open communicator and tricorder.

Also added at this time was Fred Phillips, *Star Trek*'s primary makeup artist. He was 56 and had worked on *The Wizard of Oz*. He was "second chair" then, but "first chair" in TV, where he shared the chores with John Chambers on 49 episodes of *The Outer Limits*.

With these additions, Roddenberry was able to turn his attention toward the cast.

***

Joe D'Agosta, who handled casting for *The Lieutenant*, had just accepted a job at Twentieth Century Fox. *Star Trek* looked better to him but he couldn't throw away a weekly paycheck for a job that might only last a few weeks. D'Agosta recalled, "Gene suggested we do it on the phone. I would tell his assistant who to call in and they'd come in and then Gene would call me and we'd work out the selections. And when it was over, he actually sent me a check for $750. That was big money for me!" (43-4)

For the Captain, now named Christopher Pike, Roddenberry wanted Lloyd Bridges, best known for the *Sea Hunt* series. When offered the part, Roddenberry recalled Bridges saying, "Gene, I like you, but I've seen science fiction and I don't want to be within a hundred miles of it." (145-11)

Bridges hadn't just seen science fiction; he had been burned by it. In October 1962, *Daily Variety* reviewed *The Lloyd Bridges Show*, where the star played a newspaperman who gets involved in various adventures, including, for the episode being scrutinized by the trade magazine, becoming an astronaut and landing on a strange planet. The tale was co-written by Barry Trivers, later to write for *Star Trek*. The critic slammed the episode, calling it "sluggish... overlong... preachy." Less than two years had passed and Bridges was not anxious to be shot into outer space again.

More names on the list were Peter Graves, Rod Taylor, Mike Connors, George Segal, Efrem Zimbalist, Jr., Warren Stevens and William Shatner, among others. After NBC had their say, a short list appeared with just three names: Patrick O'Neal, James Coburn and Jeffrey Hunter. Robert Butler said, "I did not know Jeff [Hunter], and I thought he was probably a good, chiseled hero for this type of part. He was an extremely pleasant, centered guy, and maybe decent and nice to a fault.... I remember thinking, 'God, he's handsome,' and this was sadly the opinion of him at the time. When one is trying to bring reality into an unreal situation, that usually isn't a wise thing to do -- to hire a somewhat perfect looking actor. You should find someone who seems more natural and more 'real.'" (26-2)

Jeffrey Hunter, at 37, was more than handsome, he was a movie star. Hunter's rise to fame started when he was signed by Twentieth Century Fox in 1950. In the first four years of his contract, he was prominently featured in nine films, moving up in the cast until he hit the lead for 1953's *Sailor of the King*. Hunter's breakout role came in 1956 in John Ford's western classic *The Searchers*, where he took second billing to John Wayne. He also had second billing that year in *The Proud Ones*, under Robert Ryan, and *A Kiss Before Dying*, under another young actor the studio was pushing -- Robert Wagner.

In 1957, Hunter led the cast for *The Way to the Gold* and *Count Five and Die*, and accepted second billing in a much bigger movie, *The Last Hurrah*, under Spencer Tracy and again directed by John Ford. Hunter worked a third time for Ford, in 1960, this time as lead for the well-received *The Trials of Sergeant Rutledge*. In the same year, he topped the cast a second and third time, for the film noir *Key Witness* and, to rave reviews, *Hell to Eternity*.

Hunter took a big chance with his career in 1961 when he played Jesus in the Biblical epic *King of Kings*. In the November 9 edition of *Variety* that year, the headline on the front page read, "Jeffrey Hunter Sees Playing Savior Start, Not End of Big Acting Roles." *Kings*' director Nicholas Ray said, "Today, a career depends entirely on performance and the importance of the picture -- not on the character portrayed. Smart money is convinced that Hunter will become great box-office after he is seen as Christ." *Variety* called the movie "carefully, reverently and beautifully made" and said of its star:

> Foremost among the players must be Jeffrey Hunter as the Savior. Did he not carry conviction one may only imagine the embarrassment. But he does come remarkably close to being ideal.... Hunter's blue orbs and auburn bob (wig, of course) are strikingly pictorial.

Hunter had the lead in 1961's *Man-Trap* and 1962's *No Man Is an Island*. A year later he was asked to star in a one-hour TV series. In a move that surprised Hollywood, he accepted the offer from Jack Webb, currently head of Warner Brothers Television.

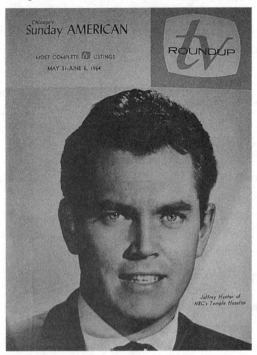

Jeffrey Hunter as Temple Houston

The studio purportedly deemed the expensive pilot film as "too good" for TV and it was released to the big screens as *The Man from Galveston*. In truth, Jack Webb found it too light in tone and ordered the series to take a more serious route -- like *Dragnet*.

NBC, with a hole in its fall schedule, wanted the series – now called *Temple Houston* -- sooner than was realistically possible. On July 4, 1965, Hunter told J.D. Spiro of *The Milwaukee Journal* that the series represented a "disappointing experience" for him. He complained, "We had no time to prepare for it. I was notified on July 17 to be ready to start August 7 for an October air date."

Then the network moved that first air date further forward to September. This not only meant rushing the production even more, but it required a great sacrifice from Hunter. On July 24, *Variety* reported:

> Jeffrey Hunter out of star role in John Ford's *The Long Flight* at WB, due to Warners preempting him for its *Temple Houston* teleseries which goes into immediate production.

Hunter said, "It was done so fast that the writers never got a chance to know what it was all about. We all wanted to follow the line indicated by the pilot film, which we thought would make a charming series. NBC, however, favored making it serious." (86a)

Temple Houston premiered to poor reviews. *Variety* said that the first episode:

> ... tried to mix many elements in the old "oater" [western] form, but came out with neither a fast-paced actioner nor an absorbing, if slowly developed, character study... it was a ho-hum outing, hardly the series which might spell the turn in WB's fortunes on network TV, which is low at this point.

Hunter said, "[A]fter 13 episodes, the ratings were rather low and Warners switched to tongue-in-cheek comedy, something on the order of *Maverick*." (86a)

On December 16, *Daily Variety* reviewed the retooled *Houston*, saying:

> Changing formats in midseason is a risky business, particularly for a film series because once the change is made the company is more or less stuck with it. NBC-TV and Warner Bros. switched the format of *Temple Houston* from a straightaway oater to comedy-oater, and the mélange is a poor one, judging from the first entry.

The disappointing experience would soon end. Hunter later lamented, "We wound it up after 26 episodes." (86a)

Just one year later, perhaps fearing his initial failure in television had hurt his chances to reclaim big screen status, Hunter agreed to make another pilot and signed on as Captain of the Enterprise.

The next biggest role in "The Cage" was Vina, the human crash survivor on Talos IV who is being used by the Talosians to lure Captain Pike into a life of imprisonment. On October 30, Roddenberry sent a memo to Herb Solow and others notifying them of actresses who had responded favorably to playing the character. Anne Francis, Barbara Eden, Piper Laurie, Yvette Mimieux, Susan Oliver, Dyan Cannon, Yvonne Craig and Suzanne Pleshette were all available. According to Roddenberry's notes, all could dance. The big question then: which one would look best painted green.

Susan Oliver, at 32, had been a frequent TV guest player, often appearing on *Playhouse 90*, *Wagon Train*, *The Fugitive* and *The Twilight Zone*. Roddenberry remembered her from a 1957 episode of *The Kaiser Aluminum Hour* he had written, as well as *Wrangler*, that short-lived series which put him in the producer's chair.

Oliver gained attention on a national level in 1964 when her character on the popular night time soap *Peyton Place* was killed off. Months later, after finishing a lengthy film assignment, she was eager to leave for a vacation, but Roddenberry wanted her and asked Oscar Katz to see what he could do.

Susan Oliver with Bill Cosby and Robert Culp from *I Spy* (Courtesy of Three F Productions)

Katz said, "Although I'm usually not that charming with women, I talked her into taking the part. Part of the appeal was that it was going to be very easy -- she could knock it off 'just like that.'" (96-1)

Katz snapped his fingers. The job, of course, would be anything but.

To play the ship's doctor, Roddenberry wanted DeForest Kelley. Robert Butler didn't, and later said, "I'm not really proud of this, but I was against DeForest. I guess I felt that he was more of a 'heavy.' I remember Gene stood up for DeForest to the end, but ultimately he backed me and went with John Hoyt." (26-2)

John Hoyt, like Kelley, was a familiar face on television and in films. He had never been a star, or even a regular on a popular series, but he had appeared in hundreds of productions. He was professional, reliable and likeable, but not the face Roddenberry pictured as belonging to the ship's doctor. The elder actor would have a tough job in proving himself.

Also cast for "The Cage": Peter Duryea, at 25, was picked to play Navigator Tyler. He was well recognized in television, not so much because of the work he had done but because he was the spitting image of his father, Dan Duryea, a well-regarded character actor.

Laurel Goodwin, 22, won the role of Yeoman Colt. A child model, she had begun her acting career only two years before and already had a pair of films out which gave her prominent billing and exposure: as one of the "Girls" in the Elvis Presley sex-romp *Girls!*

Girls! Girls! and as the daughter of Jackie Gleason in *Papa's Delicate Condition*.

Meg Wyllie, 47, was made up to play "The Keeper," a hairless alien man. Director Butler had the idea that it might be interesting to create an "anti-sexuality" for these aliens who had given up all physical sensation in favor of intellectual pursuits. Roddenberry loved the idea; it was an inventive and daring choice. It was also Butler's idea to cast Wyllie. He had directed her before during her career in television, which included repeat appearances on *Perry Mason* and *Wagon Train*.

Also wanted for the pilot was Malachi Throne, on TV since 1959, including a 1964 episode of *The Outer Limits* that starred William Shatner. Throne said, "They called me in and said 'What do you want to play?' I said 'I want to play Spock.' They said, 'Well, we have Leonard.' They offered me the part of the doctor, but I had just read a book by Paul Fix, *The Third Man through the Door*."

Meg Wyllie, center, as The Keeper in Desilu publicity still (Courtesy of Gerald Gurian)

Throne was hesitant to play the "third man," a term referring to the character who follows the hero and the hero's sidekick into the action, typically winding up as comic relief. Author Paul Fix, who was an expert on such roles (he had played Marshal Micah Torrance in *The Rifleman*), would later enter the *Star Trek* universe as, you may have guessed, the third man through the door (as the doctor in "Where No Man Has Gone Before").

Throne said, "I decided that I didn't want to be third man through the door. I turned them down and said I was late for the unemployment line. And when they picked themselves up off the floor, they said, 'Well, we want you to do something.' I said, 'I want to do something, but the only thing I can think of right now would be to do the voice of the Talosian.' I was able to pitch my voice up real high, and demonstrated that. And they said, 'How much do you want?' Without even thinking of contacting my agent, I said, 'I'll let you know in a minute.' I called my wife and I said, 'How much was that chair in Sloan's window? You want it?' And she told me, and I told them I'd do it for the price of the chair. It was a wonderful chair -- a big, old, green velvet wing chair. And it lasted a long time." (173-2)

Although not as big a role in terms of lines or storyline, the part of Mister Spock was in many ways the second-most important character in "The Cage." Gary Lockwood remembered, "After *The Lieutenant* was off the air, Roddenberry invited me to his house for a meal. Afterwards, we were standing out on his terrace overlooking the city of L.A., both sort of drunk, and, out of nowhere, he started telling me about *Star Trek*. He says, 'Hey, I wanted to ask you a question. I got this character and I think he's going to be named Spock, and he's an alien traveling with this group of Earth guys in this ship, going through the universe. I'm gonna have him be very intelligent and relaxed and cool, and maybe green or something. Do you have any advice as to who I should get to play that guy?' And I said, 'So he's kind of a strange looking dude and he's going to be a little different than others? Well, you know, there was a guy in one of our shows, a Jewish guy, and he was really good, but he had kind of a strange face, and he had one of those names -- the kind that Jewish guys get teased about because their mother named them a funny name, like... *Leonard*.' And he knew immediately -- the way he looked and sounded when he said, '*Nimoy*.' And I said, 'Yeah, that's the guy. *That guy*. He would be great as your character.'" (109-3)

A few days later, Dorothy Fontana read Roddenberry's proposal for *Star Trek*. She asked him, "I have only one question, who's going to play Mr. Spock?" Roddenberry handed Fontana an eight-by-ten glossy from his desk. She recognized Nimoy from his one-time appearance in *The Lieutenant*. When it was time to cast the pilot, however, other actors had to be considered. NBC wanted a say -- and a star. Herb Solow wanted a say, too. And so did Robert Butler. Despite the director's opposition to DeForest Kelley playing the doctor, he and the network liked the idea of the well-regarded character actor in a different role on *Star Trek*.

Kelley recalled: "Gene called me and asked me to have lunch with him; he wanted to talk to me about something. So we had lunch and he started to explain to me about this project he was embarking on. He described the character, this alien with the ears, and asked me how I felt about playing it... and I said, 'No, Gene, really, I don't want to do it.'" (98-1)

To appease his director, and the studio and network, Roddenberry went after another well-known face in movies and TV. "I was offered the role of Mr. Spock, but I turned it down" said Martin Landau. "I felt the emotional range of the character was too limiting. And I didn't want to be locked into playing a character like that, week after week." (104a)

A few months later, Joe D'Agosta was able to get Landau to say yes to playing the role of Rolland Hand, master-of-disguise-turned-spy, on *Mission: Impossible*. With Kelley and Landau out of the picture, Roddenberry was free to bring his first choice on board. And it turned out to be the only logical one.

***

Leonard Nimoy was 33 and had been acting for 15 years. His first role of any merit was in a 1952 low-budget boxing film. *Daily Variety*, for its April 17 review, said:

> *Kid Monk Baroni* is a fair prize-ring yarn for the [double bill] market... and serves to introduce a young actor named Leonard Nimoy in the title role. He is a capable "juve" who merits attention.... Nimoy delivers a good account of himself both in the ring and out.

The following year, Nimoy played his first alien in a sci-fi cheapie, *Zombie of the Stratosphere*. He married actress Sandra Zober in 1954, and then a hitch in the Army during the Korean War interrupted his attempt at an acting career. He later said, "When I got out of the Army, I knew I wouldn't be returning to a flourishing career.... My first job after I left the service in December 1955 was driving a cab for three months. I also sold life insurance, acted as a soda jerk at Wil Wright's ice cream parlor, and held all kinds of odd jobs. I wanted to return to being an actor, but it was very difficult to get an opportunity to act. Agents would take one look at me and shake their heads. Some said brutally, 'You're not handsome enough.'" (128-20)

In addition to the odd jobs, small roles in television helped to provide for Nimoy and his wife. He appeared more than once on *Highway Patrol*, *West Point* and *Dragnet*, all series where Roddenberry worked as a writer. In 1958, hoping for more artful acting jobs, Nimoy began studying with Jeff Corey at his actors' workshop.

Nimoy said, "[Corey] cast me with Paul Mazursky and Michael Forest in *Deathwatch* by [the French writer and political activist] Jean Genet. We did the play in a coffeehouse on Cosmo Alley, off of Vine Street. Because Genet had never been produced on the West Coast, and there was this intrigue about this exotic writer, the industry people came." (128-24)

Nimoy with Michael Forest (later to play Apollo in *Star Trek*), from *Deathwatch* (1966, Altra Films Int.)

Cosmo Alley [aka Cosmo's Alley] had 140 seats. The director was Vic Morrow, famous as the switchblade wielding punk from *Blackboard Jungle* and well-regarded as an actor in films, television and on stage, as well as a director for the stage. Morrow had played the lead role of Jules Lefrank one year earlier for the play's U.S. premiere in New York City. Now he had written and was preparing to direct an adaptation of the play for the Hollywood stage, and followed Corey's recommendation to cast Nimoy as Lefrank.

In an interview from the time, Nimoy said, "The entire story takes place in a French prison with three men in one cell. One of them is a killer -- which means he is tops in this milieu. Therefore, the man I play, and the third inmate, a homosexual, are always struggling for the killer's friendship. They want to be identified with him." (128-23)

The killer was played by Michael Forest, a future *Star Trek* guest star (Apollo in "Who Mourns for Adonais?"). Paul Mazursky had the role of Maurice, the homosexual. In February 1960, *Daily Variety* reviewed the play, saying:

> An actor's play and a stunning exercise in emotions.... Vic Morrow handles his cast with swift, exciting touches, drawing sharp portraits and blending the sympathy and derangement with the interest of careful conniving. The cast is excellent... their work, in single passages and together, has strength and sinew. As actors, they know they are playing flaming characters, and they make a good deal of the sharp dialog furnished in a fine translation.... The off-beat play is bound to cause talk, particularly among the *avant garde*, and Cosmo's Alley should be loaded with cats for its indefinite run.

Nimoy said, "The *L.A. Times* referred to it as a 'miasma of homosexuality.' Of course, everybody wanted to see this." (128-24)

On March 18, after eight weeks of standing room only at Cosmo Alley, and with reservations stretching into mid April, *Deathwatch* moved to the bigger Players' Ring Gallery Theatre, where it enjoyed a long run. Nimoy told a 1960s tabloid, "I owe a lot to that play. Many people from the industry saw me in it and I was lucky enough to get great reviews.

After that, I worked more regularly." (128-23)

Nimoy made multiple appearances on *Sea Hunt*, *Wagon Train*, *The Virginian* and *Gunsmoke*. He even did a *Twilight Zone*. With a fair visibility factor, he began substituting for Jeff Corey as the coach of an actors' workshop in Hollywood and, in early 1963, started his own workshop.

Daily Variety took notice in its "Legit Bits" column on January 9, reporting that Nimoy was opening a weekend repertoire theater -- The Leonard Nimoy Studio --- where he would direct both classic and original plays. A few weeks later, on February 1, the same trade reported that singer Bobby Vee, who had recently sold over three million records with his hits "Take Good Care of My Baby," "Devil or Angel," and "The Night Has a Thousand Eyes," was turning to acting, with Nimoy as his coach.

With all the press, Nimoy was being considered for bigger roles on television, and getting cast on hit series, including *Perry Mason*, *Dr. Kildare* and, in two episodes, *The Outer Limits*. He worked on Roddenberry's *The Lieutenant* and buddy Vic Morrow got him two jobs on his hit series, *Combat!*, where the star was also directing.

It was at this time that the two friends decided to produce *Deathwatch* as an art house movie. They agreed to jointly produce, with Morrow directing and Nimoy starring. The latter reprised his role from the Hollywood stage production along with Michael Forest and Paul Mazursky. Filmed in early 1964, but held from release for two years, *Daily Variety* reviewed *Deathwatch*, saying:

> Picture is remarkable in that it was shot on a limited budget -- $120,000.... Forest and Mazursky both give fine performances in respective parts as the king of the prison inmates and a weak homosexual.... Nimoy, who coproduced the film with Morrow, is excellent as the 'outsider' not quite accepted by prison society, even though he has withstood extreme tortures in solitary confinement.

Gerald Fried, a third man who was *Star Trek* bound (besides Nimoy and Forest), wrote the score.

By mid-1964, Nimoy had over 50 TV episodes and films to his credit, but he was still struggling and needed a break-through role. It was clear Mr. Spock could bring him what he wanted, but as Jeffrey Hunter had found with the misfired *Temple Houston*, the wrong TV series could also do an acting career irrevocable harm.

Nimoy said, "I wasn't sure about doing the role because one of the first things [Gene] said was this was going to be an alien, 'a rather bizarre, exotic character, and he's going to wear pointed ears and have some other strange makeup which has yet to be determined.' And, not knowing the caliber the series was going to be or the caliber of the character, I had some reservations, because I had a rather serious acting career in the works and I didn't want to be playing the fool." (128-26)

***

The final character cast was the ship's second in command, Number One. Roddenberry had someone in mind from the very day he wrote the part: Majel Barrett. They had met when he was producing pilots for Screen Gems and, as an aspiring actress, she was making the rounds to casting calls. She made an impression on Roddenberry, even though he had no roles that suited her. In 1963, he did, and cast her in an episode of *The Lieutenant*. It was then that the two became lovers. Just as *Star Trek* was getting ready to launch, Roddenberry's marriage was disintegrating.

The stress on the marriage had started much earlier. Sam Rolfe, Roddenberry's former boss on *Have Gun - Will Travel*, put it bluntly: "Eileen hated Gene's writing career." Rolfe and his wife, while socializing with the Roddenberrys, had seen firsthand the change in the couple's relationship. Rolfe said, "She loved the money -- all the perks -- but she couldn't keep up with it. She never understood it. She once told my wife, 'I wish he had never started writing.' She didn't comprehend the society in which he was moving. Eileen is of the world that is more natural, more Middle America. So, increasingly, she got left out of it." (146)

Gary Lockwood saw this as well. He sensed that there was no common ground in the lifestyles the two Roddenberrys wanted to pursue. They had, he observed, "an incredible home up in the hills, in Mandeville Canyon," but he also noticed how his producer's wife seemed to be out of place: "He had a very proper wife -- she was very attractive but appeared to be a rather straight-laced type." (109-3)

Robert Justman said, "I think she feared the sort of life that Gene was getting into. She feared for their marriage, for their family, for their financial future. The people that Gene was now associating with represented an industry that disgusted her and threatened her. That, I think, is what made her cold." (94-5)

Justman also felt that Roddenberry had become somewhat cruel to his wife, saying, "From time to time, he would make remarks in front of her and I would feel terribly embarrassed. There was a lot of heartbreak for her, because he would mess around." (94-5)

Roddenberry did little to disguise his affairs. Majel Barrett, his primary romantic interest, lived near Desilu. This had been arranged so that she could be close to her lover. Justman said, "Gene made no bones about the fact that he was keeping Majel. He even invited me over one evening to the apartment for drinks -- you know, sort of a party. I said, 'Gene, I don't want to know about it.' I tried to talk him out of continuing their relationship. She was his mistress. I was afraid that someone might find out. Little did I know that he enjoyed that sort of illicitness." (94-5)

"Let's face it, Gene played around a lot after that," Sam Rolfe said of one of the consequences of Roddenberry's move from TV writer to TV producer. "He had all these openings, and he took them." (146)

Headshot used by Majel Barrett when she met Roddenberry (*L.A. Times* file photo)

Majel Barrett was Roddenberry's fantasy girl come true -- dark, mysterious, intellectual, sensual. But NBC would want a marquee player for such an important part as Number One, and Barrett was mostly unknown -- except to those who worked with Roddenberry. Now he relentlessly pushed the issue with Solow. "You'll like her, Herb," he insisted. 'She's solid." (161-3)

Solow tried to sell Barrett to the network. He looked for a spin. He told them that the producer believed in the actress's ability, but he mostly tried to sell them on the idea that, because Barrett was a new face on television, she would add believability to the role. NBC's Jerry Stanley and Grant Tinker were no fools. Solow remembered them exchanging looks, then Stanley saying, "Christ, Herb, this is madness. She's his girlfriend. I remember her hanging around Gene's office at MGM when he was doing *The Lieutenant* for us." (161-3)

Solow believed the NBC execs resented being put in such an awkward position, but Tinker and Stanley didn't want to rock the boat with Roddenberry -- at least not on this point. In television, you choose your battles and there were plenty of bigger ones ahead. So NBC blinked again, and Barrett became TV's first woman to serve in outer space and, more importantly, in a position of command. Roddenberry had gotten his way. Or so it seemed. For those at the network who were keeping score, this was already "Strike Four."

Roddenberry wasn't worried about the disapproval of others. In his affection for Barrett, he was blind to the negative thinking. Robert Justman said, "Gene loved [Majel]. He loved her and he was proud of her.... He would light up when she was around." (94-6)

And Roddenberry didn't have to wait long to light up. Test footage needed to be shot of the green dancing girl. Barrett agreed to do it for free. Justman recalled that she was a good sport and allowed herself to be covered with various shades of "bilious green makeup," then would stand near naked in front of a neutral background as a series of test films were made.

It's a famous *Star Trek* story now. The day after the test shots were made, the footage was screened. Barrett looked normal, and quite in the pink. Fred Phillips was told to mix more green into his makeup. More footage was shot. The results were very nearly the same. In the flesh, Barrett had been extremely green, yet once the film had been returned from the lab, she merely looked like a woman who was somewhat seasick. Another test was scheduled. The makeup was made greener still. Then the footage was returned from the lab. Still not green enough; still very nearly a normal-but-not-very-healthy-looking Caucasian woman. This tale is not folklore. Fred Phillips, quoted in 1968 while working on *Star Trek*, said, "We did this three days in a row. We had her so green you couldn't believe it, and she still kept coming back pink!" (142-2)

Eventually the mystery was unraveled. The lab technicians, believing the green was a mistake, had been color-correcting the film to return Barrett's skin to as close to normal as possible. Who, after all, would paint a woman green?

It was an innocent time. People looked alike back then. Same skin, same hair, same clothes. Only the Beatles looked different and it had only been nine months since they first landed in America from another world -- England. For the moment, *Star Trek* was charting unknown waters.

***

The race to begin production continued. Matt Jefferies focused on working out all the details concerning the bridge, while Franz Bachelin proceeded to design the rest of the sets for the pilot. The location was Desilu Culver City Studio, stages 14, 15 and 16. The bridge alone took six weeks and, in 1964 money, a whopping $60,000 to construct.

Meanwhile, back on the Desilu-Gower Street lot, Fred Phillips was asked to try his hand at creating the pointed ears. Already busy trying to come up with an acceptable solution for Spock's makeup, primarily that reddish complexion described in the script, Phillips passed the ear job on to Lee Greenway, a Desilu makeup artist.

This idea of red-toned skin, by the way, was quickly vetoed in favor of a yellowish hue. Red, on the black-and-white television sets most Americans owned at this time, came off looking dark and muddy. Yellow, however, would lighten Spock's face, giving him a paler appearance than his Earthling comrades. Buster Keaton and Stan Laurel had proven decades earlier that a pale complexion in photography helped enhance deadpan expressions.

Nimoy, with reddish complexion, poses for makeup test alongside an actress resembling Susan Oliver, her wearing an early prototype for the Star Fleet uniform (Courtesy William Krewson)

Greenway had been told there was no time or money to build the ears properly and, for the first "test," he had to come up with a "down and dirty" version. Nimoy, already nervous about his Spock role, was appalled. In an interview for this book, he said, "I was called in to one of the soundstages where they were shooting *The Lucy Show*. And Lee Greenway tried to patch on some kind of a rough mock up of what they thought my ears might look like. He did it with *papier-mache* and glue and what-have-you. It was looking pretty bad. Herb Solow stuck his head in the door and saw what was going on and jokingly said over his shoulder to Gene Roddenberry, 'Gene, this poor guy needs help.' And my heart sank. I thought, 'My God, I'm so trepidatious about this whole ear issue and the first thing I hear is a joke about it. They stood me in front of a video camera on the Lucy set and shot some footage. I hope it's been destroyed. It was dreadful." (128)

Roddenberry, during the time *Star Trek* was in production, said, "As always happens with high-spirited crew, they began making jokes about 'Pixie' and 'Jackrabbit.' Now, Leonard is a very serious actor, and these remarks finally began to get to him. So one day Leonard came into my office, sat down, and began to explain his doubts about the 'Pointed Ears' role. He explained his desire to be known as a serious actor, the hopes and dreams he had for the future. This Spock part was beginning to look to him like he'd be playing a freak with ears. He wound up saying, 'I've decided I don't want the part.' Well, after all that we had gone through, and with only a few days left before shooting, and I'm certain Spock can be a meaningful and challenging role, now comes the problem of talking Leonard out of this. We must have argued for at least half an hour." (145-4)

Around this time, Nimoy confided to a reporter, "Playing some monster or freak can be the kiss of death for an actor, and this emotionless guy with pointy ears from another planet didn't appeal to me.... [Gene and I] talked it over and agreed that I wouldn't just be a walking computer who gives scientific data. I trusted Roddenberry's tastes." (128-17)

Nimoy agreed to tolerate more experimentation. But someone else was needed to come up with the now famous Vulcan ears. Many sources wrongly credit famed Hollywood makeup artist and prosthetics maker John Chambers with the creation. Chambers himself fueled the rumor mill when he admitted to a reporter: "Fred brought me a set of ear molds but they had been damaged so I couldn't use those... I had to remake the whole thing. The molds I devised were technically functional.... I devised molds that you could get nice ears out of." (31-1)

From this, it was easy to assume that Chambers was there from the first day. To set the record straight, Leonard Nimoy told this author: "The next thing I hear, I was to go to the studio to meet Freddy Phillips, who was going to be the makeup man on the show. Freddy sat me down in a chair and pulled out a set of ears that had been made from a mold of my ears by this time, put them on, and he hated them. I wasn't that sophisticated in this area at that time, but he told me the material they were made out of was rough and would never match the look of human skin. And it was 'goo' material for things like creature faces and creature heads and creature feet, and had been made in fact by a company that Desilu had contracted to do appliance work for creatures for the show. He complained to the management that these wouldn't work, and they said, 'Well, work with the company that we're working with because they're being paid. The contract includes Leonard's ears, so just work with them until they get it right.' Well, we tried two or three more times, back to the studio and back to the company and then back to the studio, over a period of two or three weeks, and they came back just unacceptable as far as anyone was concerned." (128)

Roddenberry said, "We had to try a lot of different types of ears on Leonard to get the right ones, ones that looked real. We had them too big, too flat, too pointed and so forth." (145-4)

Nimoy said, "The problem was that contract. To have them made by an outside appliance maker who really knew how to do them was going to cost -- can you believe this? -- about $600. So, the last time out, Freddy worked with them and put plaster on, and did all kinds of things to them. It was just totally frustrating. He finally took them off of my ears, and called a man at MGM named Charlie Schram. I never will forget this. Charlie Schram was the *head* of the makeup department at MGM." (128)

Phillips knew Schram from *The Wizard of Oz*, the first major motion picture to use foam latex prosthetics on a large scale. Phillips handled the more humanlike characters, while Schram took on the outrageous ones, including Bert Lahr's Cowardly Lion, which required orange-toned makeup, false eyebrows, whiskers, fur, a bald cap, a wig with rubber ears, and other rubber appliances. He also saw to the hooked rubber nose, warts and all, for Margaret Hamilton's Wicked Witch.

Nimoy recalled, "Freddy said, 'Charlie, I need a favor. I've got a guy who has to wear a pair of devilish ears and I need them by Friday.' Then Freddy hung up and said, 'Come with me.' We got into his car and drove to MGM, on the spot. We went to this guy's department, he laid me on a slab and made a mold of my ears and on Friday morning, or whatever the day was -- I'm saying Friday -- but whatever day it was, in the morning when we were to begin shooting the first pilot, the ears arrived and of course they were perfect because Charlie Schram knew exactly what to do and he used the right kind of material.

"Now the story goes a little bit further. Freddy put them on me and he was satisfied. He did my eyebrows and my hair was already cut appropriately. I walked out on the stage where Bob Justman took a look at me. He was concerned how my ears stood out a little bit farther from my skull, and when Freddy put these extensions on, it accentuated the problem, so my ears were out there sort of flapping in the wind. Bobby Justman said, 'I wonder if we can do something to pin those ears back.' We go back in the makeup department. Freddy put some glue behind my ears, gluing my ears back to my skull so I had a very compact, very tight, clean look. And that was finally the way it was done, except for one minor modification. After that day, Freddy used a piece of what we called 'two-face tape' -- tape that sticks on both sides. He put a little piece of that on my skull and pressed the ear against it. And that's the way the ears were finally accomplished. From that point on, Freddy used the mold Charlie Schram had made. Each day he'd make them at home, overnight, until he got so overloaded with work that he couldn't do it anymore and he turned the making over to John Chambers. John had more of a reputation around town because he had done a lot of prosthetics work and was known for it so people assumed that he had done the job. Which he did -- he made ears -- but not until Charlie Schram and Freddy Phillips came up with it." (128)

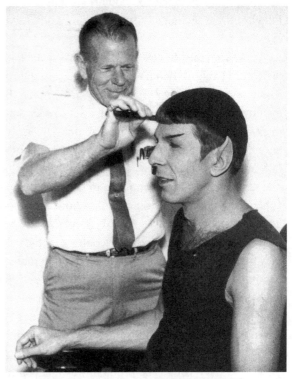

According to Nimoy, Fred Phillips created the look of the Vulcan (Courtesy of Gerald Gurian)

***

One other phase of the production had to be arranged: choosing who would handle the innovative and complex photographic effects.

The Howard Anderson Company, an optical effects house in business since the 1920s and recently passed from father to sons Darrell and Howard, Jr., was now providing photographic effects for B-movies such as *Phantom from Space*, *Invasion of the Saucer Men* and *12 to the Moon*. Anderson was a tenant on the Desilu lot and it was a short walk to the *Star Trek* offices. Better still, the Anderson brothers had a close association with the studio, having created the opening animated title sequence for *I Love Lucy* on a tight deadline.

Howard Anderson, Jr. and Darrell Anderson were enthusiastic and confident they could deliver. On August 24, 1964, Roddenberry sent a memo to Argyle Nelson, head of Desilu Business Affairs, saying:

> I am delighted Anderson and others find the project interesting and fascinating. It will take a lot of cooperation and creative thinking to bring this in exciting and on budget.

The Andersons had no idea of the challenge awaiting them.

4

Test Flight – Filming "The Cage"

Friday, November 27, 1964. It was the day after Thanksgiving. America was into its ninth month of Beatlemania, but "Leader of the Pack" by The Shangri-Las was the song getting the highest amount of airplay on U.S. radio stations. The most watched TV shows the night before were *Bewitched* and *My Three Sons* on ABC, followed by *The Munsters* on CBS. The Ford Mustang had been introduced a couple months earlier with a sticker price of $2,395, and you could fill the tank for 30 cents a gallon. A first class stamp cost a nickel. And principal photography commenced at Desilu-Culver on "The Cage."

The interior of the Enterprise had been built at great expense into Stage 16 -- a gigantic space for a gigantic spaceship. But the stage had gone mostly unused for years. Desilu was a TV company and this was a big screen movie stage, built for epic silent films by Cecil B. DeMille, including 1927's *King of Kings*. DeMille needed space to tell his story of Christ. He did not need quiet. *Star Trek* needed both.

The scene between Captain Pike and Dr. Boyce in the Captain's quarters

Susan Oliver in Desilu publicity photo taken during the filming of "The Cage"
(Courtesy of Gerald Gurian)

was first up, to be followed by all transporter room scenes as well as those in the ship's corridors and in the briefing room. On paper, it seemed an achievable goal for one day of filming. In reality, the production company didn't even come close.

Sound issues began immediately. The first delay came from pigeons that had nested in the ancient rafters above. With the commotion below, and heat rising from the bright lights, the pigeons became anxious and tended to coo whenever Jeffrey Hunter or John Hoyt delivered their lines. Unhappy pigeons soon made for unhappy actors.

A member of the lighting crew was sent into the rafters to scare the cooing birds. He did as he was told – he waved his arms and yelled. The terrified pigeons took flight and proceeded to fly into beams, into scaffolding, into crew people, and into hot lights. Robert Justman urgently yelled for the electricians to turn off the big stage lights and for the ground crew to open the giant stage doors. The hope was the pigeons would fly toward daylight and escape the madhouse that was *Star Trek*. Many did. Many others, unaware of the fate awaiting them, flew in from outside. The mayhem continued. Finally, Justman hatched the

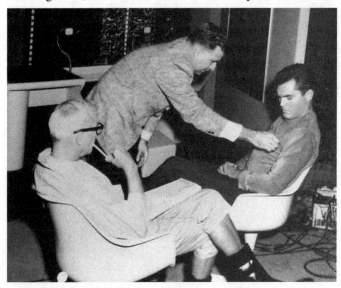

Day 1: Roddenberry with two unhappy actors (John Hoyt and Jeffrey Hunter) waiting for "quiet on the set." (Courtesy of Gerald Gurian)

idea to scatter bits of bread, birdseed and even Cracker Jack on to the studio street outside. It worked and the pigeons were lured away from the soundstage. All that was needed now was a stage hand to guard the doors, making sure only people and no birds came or went … with the exception of the big alien bird planned for the upcoming menagerie scene.

Day 2, Monday, November 30, the company was supposed to be on Stage 15 to film the spectacular bridge set. But with the production schedule already compromised, the bridge would have to wait. Work continued as they labored over the briefing room scene, then into the ship's corridors.

Day 3, Tuesday, December 1. The company was still on Stage 16 finishing work that had been planned for only one day, while trying not to lose all hope. In retrospect, these scenes which spanned three days were among the easiest in the production. On this day, work took place in the transporter room for the first stab at camera tie-down shots needed for the post production work to create the dazzling never-before-seen effect of "beaming."

Day 2, Scene 50H, Take 1 (Courtesy of Gerald Gurian)

Days 4 and 5, Wednesday and Thursday. Cast and crew finally moved to Stage 15 and began filming on the bridge. This was supposed to take one-and-a-quarter days. It took two.

Director Robert Butler was not happy. He later complained, "I remember pleading to get some vertical structures in the bridge, because that was just too 'clean' for me. I [tried] like hell to shake up that bridge, and it fell on heavily deaf ears…. Anytime I get into a 'clean' situation, I start grinding my teeth. And *Star Trek* was a 'clean' situation." (26-2)

Production designer Matt Jefferies had other concerns regarding the bridge. In 1968, while still working on *Star Trek*, he explained his challenges, saying, "The split level bridge was not part of the original idea. I did not like it and, in many ways, I do not now. There is much to be said for it pictorially, in terms of people movement and picture composition. But the split level design limits the type of camera shots you can do. Another problem is the high noise level in the bridge." (91-4)

**Day 5, a second day on the bridge - Scene 9C, Take 3
(Courtesy of Gerald Gurian)**

The bridge was designed to include eight "wild" sections. That meant it could be moved to allow different lighting and a greater variety of camera angles. But "wild" sections with split levels are problematic, with connecting portions loosening through wear and then emitting noise whenever a cast member walked on them. Squeaks. Groans.

The soundtrack suffered further because of the water and sewer pipes that ran along the walls. Money had been saved many decades earlier when a second wall had not been placed between the lavatories and the stage. In the silent film era, there was no need for this. Now, whenever a faucet was turned on or a toilet flushed, the sound was picked up by the sensitive microphones. Filming would stop. Then, after the old pipes settled down, it would begin again. Then another flush. And another delay. In desperation, a red light was put into the bathroom so visitors would know not to flush when the camera was rolling. They flushed anyway. Robert Justman commented, "When you gotta go, you gotta go…. My director was getting just a smidgen agitated… So toilet monitors were deployed outside the stage lavatories. No one was allowed in until each new shot was over. Sometimes the shots took a long time. What one doesn't do for art." (94-8)

To add to the squeaks, groans and flushes, friction was growing on the set. Butler was not thrilled with the results he was getting from cinematographer Bill Snyder, who, as cinematographers will, was calling the shots more than the director. Butler, who wanted the dark and moody script for "The Cage" to be filmed in a dark and moody visual style, grumbled, "I remember thinking that when Bill Snyder shot it, he made it too pretty. I can accurately say that I was in a situation that made me less than comfortable." (26-2)

Roddenberry and Haskin, meanwhile, were mixing as well as oil and water. The associate producer, who had directed sci-fi movies and critically acclaimed episodes of *The Outer Limits*, was now taking orders from a man who had far less experience than him. Having recommended Haskin, assistant director Robert Justman was often cast as the reluctant peacemaker. But there was little he could do. Haskin didn't respect Roddenberry, and Roddenberry didn't like being disrespected.

Day 6, Friday. Production was now two and a half days behind. The company remained on Stage 15, having moved over to the "Ext. Orion Courtyard" set. Robert Butler's next challenge was over the controversial scene where Susan Oliver, wearing little more than green paint, did her sexy dance for Jeffrey Hunter. He complained, "I remember my reaction was, 'Oh God, those costumes, and that belly dancer; are we doing Victor Mature all over again?'" (He was referring to that actor's roles in such exotic and campy films as *Samson and Delilah*). Butler added, "I thought, 'Dare we?' Generally I was wincing and wondering if we were going to get away with that." (26-2)

Day 6. Fred Phillips touches up Susan Oliver with more green body makeup (Courtesy of Gerald Gurian)

Susan Oliver remembered, "The usual easy 'Hi Suse' [sic] banter was gone. The guys stood back and stared or averted their eyes as though it were immoral to look at such a woman. There seemed almost to be a sense of their whispering, 'Wow, Susan's not such a nice girl after all; she's maybe wild; evil.' Even before the dance began and I was just standing demurely to the side, this feeling was in the air. Gene had touched on something dark in man's unconscious; one could imagine doing things with a green mate that he would never dare with one of his own color." (132)

"Take 1. Action!" Oliver remembered thinking the crew were whispering, "Wow, Susan's not such a nice girl after all."

Sound problems continued. Stage 16 was not the only one that lacked soundproofing. Stage 15 was just as big and just as noisy. While the company filmed on Stage 15, there was construction next door. Dialogue had to be recorded between the roar of power saws and pounding hammers.

Days 7, 8 and 9, Monday, Tuesday and Wednesday. The company moved back to Stage 16 where the Enterprise had been replaced with the inhospitable surface of Talos IV. The beam down of the rescue party was filmed, then their journey along the ravine, Spock's fascination over the "musical plants," and the discovery of the spaceship wreckage and crash survivors. This barren, dusty alien world was more to director Butler's liking. There was nothing even remotely "clean" about the scenery. There was nothing easy about it either.

Bob Justman recalled the set was encircled by a huge backing that had been painted to simulate the sky of an alien world. Director of Photography Bill Snyder and his gaffer, Bob Campbell, spent two days trying to pre-light the massive background with its unearthly sky. Campbell finally complained to Justman, "No matter how much light we throw on it, it's never enough. The damn backing just soaks it all up." Thirty years later, Justman could still hear Campbell's next words: "You can kiss your f…..g shooting schedule goodbye."

The massive Desilu-Culver Stage 16, and the surface of Talos IV (Courtesy of Gerald Gurian)

Actually, they already had.

Work resumed on the infertile surface of Talos IV. The scenes filmed included Pike accompanying Vina to see the mystery behind her survival and that of the other stranded space travelers, then the "Rocky Knoll" where a portal opens and Pike is abducted by the Talosians, followed by the sequence where Number One and her rescue party use a laser cannon to try to blast apart the doors of the portal. Next, the scene where the "lift" brings Pike, Vina, Number One and Yeoman Colt to the surface for the final confrontation with The Keeper.

Day 10, Thursday. The final days on this expansive planet set turned out to be the hardest. The "Camera Tie-down" shots of Vina as she ages was supposed to take half a day. It ended up taking almost a full one.

For the aging of Vina, a special brace was built to hold Susan Oliver's head immobile and was hidden from view by her hair and neck. Footage was rolled in the camera, approximately 15 seconds worth. Then Fred Phillips whisked Oliver away to alter her makeup, making her older, uglier. Then back into the brace, with more film exposed. Another 15 seconds. Then back into the makeup chair. The ordeal took more than half of the day. Oliver was going well beyond the call of duty, well beyond the "snap of a finger" she had been led to expect. She politely added, "It was a process that required a great deal of patience." (132)

"I knew that she would not be kindly disposed towards me," said Oscar Katz, who had promised the actress an easy shoot. "And so I had to forgo my usual visit to the set on the first day of shooting. I'd made it a habit to attend the first day of shooting of a pilot to show that the head of the studio was with them. On *Star Trek*, I stayed away religiously even though it was just a 15 minute ride away from my office." (96)

**Susan Oliver dares Oscar Katz to show his face
(Courtesy of Gerald Gurian)**

As the production went over schedule, Oliver realized she would have to sacrifice her vacation to Hawaii. Each day she asked where Katz was. The joke behind the question became so apparent that shooting stopped as Oliver posed for a photographer, holding signs with the legend "OSCAR WHERE ARE YOU?" The photograph was sent to Katz. He still didn't show. More pictures were taken -- a new one each day -- with other cast members holding the sign. And still no Katz.

At the end of Day 10, the company moved back to Stage 15 to work on a new set -- the underground living areas of Talos IV -- for scenes where The Keeper and two other Talosians watch a monitor depicting images of the Enterprise crew on the planet's surface and Pike in his jail cell. It was the first easy shot Butler and his crew had taken.

**Day 11. Robert Butler reluctantly films a scene with "the killer fowl," to be deleted
(Courtesy of Gerald Gurian and Fred Walder)**

Day 11, Friday. A short move across the cavernous stage took the company to the "Int. Menagerie-Cage" set. Among the sequences filmed, Pike awakening to find he is a prisoner, then seeing an "Anthropoid Spider" and a "Humanoid Bird" in other "cages." Robert Butler hid his displeasure from the cast and crew by grinding his teeth. He later said, "I remember there was some chicken -- some killer fowl -- being locked in some cell somewhere, and I'm talking to this stuntman -- it's crazy, me talking to this Janos Prohaska, [who was] Hungarian or something... [saying], 'Janos, okay that's good, baby, now try this.' And there's this big chicken -- this killer chicken -- or some equivalent. I mean, it was nuts." (26-3)

Most of the film of the "killer fowl" was left on the editing room floor, although the great bird of the galaxy appeared briefly as part of the creature menagerie.

As work progressed on this day, leaving behind the Humanoid Bird creature, the Talosians entered and communicated with Pike. He threw himself against the transparent wall to the amusement of his captors, the veins in their heads wiggling as they sent thoughts to one another. Bob Justman was the man crouching below the camera's frame and squeezing a rubber bulb which forced air through a plastic tube running inside Meg Wyllie's gown. The tube also ran up the back of her neck and into the oversized head where the spurts of air manipulated the pulsating veins, all to the rhythm of The Keeper's dialogue being read out loud by script clerk George Rutter.

Day 11, Stage 15. Note the open ceiling and lights at the top of shot (Matt Jefferies collection; courtesy of Gerald Gurian)

The refined Meg Wyllie said, "I had never played such a role nor had such a makeup job applied to me. The base was an old-fashioned rubber bathing cap -- the type with a chin strap.... Upon the cap, a rubber substance was placed. When that was set, the special effects people finished the skull -- placing the blood vessels and covering them. The makeup was not comfortable -- my ears especially suffered being so confined under the cap." (195)

Filming "The Cage," Day 9 of production, Scene 45, Take 2, with Meg Wyllie (Courtesy of Gerald Gurian)

Wyllie's instructions were to play the part with "dignity and control." She remembered, "A mental, rather than physical, approach was needed to concentrate on the words I was saying. The pulsing in the veins in my skull and very little facial expression were to be the only visible effects of my thought transfers.... I was most intrigued." (195)

Despite the challenges, the hard work and the sacrifice, Wyllie found the mood to be surprisingly light. She said, "We were encouraged daily by Gene Roddenberry's visits to the set. It was an enthusiastic company enjoying their work." (195)

Jeffrey Hunter was also enthusiastic, especially concerning the potential of the series. In an interview with Joan Schmitt for the *Los Angeles Citizen News*, he said, "We run into pre-historic worlds, contemporary societies, and civilizations far more developed than our own. It's a great format because the writers will have a free hand -- they can have us land on a monster-infested planet or deal in human relations involving the large number of people who live together on this gigantic ship."

Filming at Desilu 40 Acres for the fight with the "Neanderthal Creature" (Courtesy of Gerald Gurian)

Later in the day on December 11, scenes were filmed where Pike paces in his cage seeking a way out, questioning Vina about how to hide his thoughts from the Talosians. Finally, Vina reacts to being inflicted with excruciating pain and disappears.

Days 12 and 13, Monday and Tuesday -- the company held at four days behind. This was the only exterior work, with filming on Desilu 40 Acres behind Stage 15 and 16. The scene where Pike and Vina run toward the "Rigel Fortress" was photographed to be used for a matte shot, sharing the film frame with a brilliant painting by Albert Whitlock of the giant fortress looming in the distance. Next, inside the courtyard of the fortress for Pike's fight with the "Neanderthal Creature." It was supposed to take one day. It, of course, took two.

Days 14 and 15, Wednesday and Thursday. The company returned to Stage 15 for two additional days in Pike's cell. First up: the scene where Pike tries strangling The Keeper, which then transforms into some form of alien beast. Next, Pike's journey in and out of a place listed on the schedule as "Hell-Fire." After this, Pike is joined in his cell by Number One and Yeoman Colt, the women The Keeper has selected for Pike to breed with. Last to be filmed: the scene where Pike uses the phaser to blast a hole in the transparent wall, allowing all to escape.

Roddenberry inspects a model of the U.S.S. Enterprise while on location at Desilu 40 Acres, before approving the making of the 11 foot 2 inch version (Courtesy of Gerald Gurian)

Day 16, Friday, December 18, 1964. The ping-ponging company had moved back to Stage 16 for scenes in the darkened stone maze of corridors where Pike again encounters the green skinned Orion dancing girl. In many ways, the production had been hell, so it only seemed appropriate that Jeffrey Hunter was agonizing in the "Hell-Fire" pit. Finally, ending on a happier note was the "Parkland" set, portions of which would be combined with another matte painting by Albert Whitlock, this time of a modern Earth city in the distance. The final scene filmed was the picnic between Pike and Vina. There was a touch of irony in making the picnic the last scene. The production had been anything but.

"That's a wrap!" Susan Oliver, Gene Roddenberry, Robert Butler and Robert Justman at end of shoot
(Courtesy of Gerald Gurian)

The pilot had taken 16 days to film, not 11. It had also gone well over budget.

"We spent more on those sets than any studio in television had ever spent before," Roddenberry boasted in 1968. "I think probably we spent more than even any motion picture had ever spent in building a spaceship up until that time. On several occasions the studio got very upset about the mounting costs, but fortunately Herb Solow went to bat for us. He believed in us and helped us, and that was a great help." (145-4)

Truth be known, Solow was not pleased. As the liaison between the studio and the network, how could he be? The Desilu bean counters were mortified. And the NBC men, skeptical to begin with, would certainly factor in the final tally before making their decision whether or not to order the series. It was a bad situation and the biggest bills had yet to hit the studio accountants' desks -- those tied to the costly post production phase. The biggest ticket item -- the Enterprise -- had yet to even be delivered for filming. And it was long overdue.

***

Work on the starship began in October. Based on Jefferies' detailed drawings, Richard Datin, a model builder, fashioned a three-foot version of the Enterprise from wood. It took two weeks. His prototype was sent to Darrell Anderson in early November. An 11-foot, two-inch version of the ship was still needed for filming, and time was running out. To expedite construction, Datin took his smaller model and the plans to Volmer Jensen at Production Model Shop, located in Burbank. Jensen immediately assigned the construction to two employees: Mel Keyes and Vernon Sion. Datin supervised the building and did the detail work, including decals.

According to Datin's job notes, it took 350 hours over a span of six weeks to make the big model. It weighed 220 pounds. The cost, prior to installing lights, was roughly $3,000 ($22,600 in 2013). The lights were actually an afterthought. This addition resulted in another 300 hours of labor and kept the model from being delivered until mid-December, as the pilot was wrapping. Datin recalled, "Roddenberry had said he didn't want any lights at all. But then he got the idea of running lights on the port and starboard sides of the saucer section, so we put those on. He liked those running lights so much that he wanted even more lights here and there. But he ran out of money. I believed in him and the series idea, and so I added some [lighted] windows, *gratis*." (46)

Volmer Jensen's Production Model Shop, Burbank, CA, December 1964
(Courtesy of Gerald Gurian)

Matt Jefferies lamented, "The most difficult thing about doing the show was that we did not have today's materials to play with. Even fiberglass molding and that kind of stuff was still relatively new and there weren't many people around who could do it. Nowadays you've got all kinds of wide-eyed plastics and molding stuff. None of that was available to us then." (91-2)

The model Datin built was mounted on a metal pole, elevated off the floor in a stationary position. Behind it was a "blue screen." The camera did the moving.

The Howard Anderson Company also provided other optical effects needed for the pilot, including the transporter effect. For this, Anderson turned a slow-motion camera upside down and photographed shiny grains of aluminum powder as they were dropped between the camera and a black background.

Editing came next. Leo Shreve was put in charge of the team. He had worked as a film editor in television on *Maverick* and, on the big screen, with *Voyage to the Prehistoric Planet*. The cutting of "The Cage" would take close to a month.

Then came the music. Roddenberry had prepared a wish-list of composers. They were Les Baxter, Elmer Bernstein, Alexander Courage, Dominic Frontiere, Jerry Goldsmith, Lalo Schifrin and John Williams. It was an impressive Who's Who. Baxter was the leader of a big band and had numerous popular hits. Bernstein's most famous movie score was *The Magnificent Seven*. Courage had recently scored the Connie Francis big screen hit *Follow the Boys* and, for television, episodes of *Voyage to the Bottom of the Sea*. Frontiere had provided the ominous music for *The Outer Limits*. Goldsmith wrote the eerie theme to TV's *Thriller* series, plus composed the scores for recent big screen big events such as *Seven Days in May* and *Lilies of the Field* (he would later score five of the *Star Trek* motion pictures). Schifrin would compose the music for *Mission: Impossible*. And Williams would soon do the theme for *Lost in Space*, with *Star Wars* in his future.

The man who got the job: Alexander "Sandy" Courage. William Hatch, Lucille Ball's musical director, made the recommendation to Roddenberry. Courage recalled, "Rodenberry told me, 'Listen, I don't want any of this goddamned funny-sounding space science fiction music. I want adventure music.'" (37-1)

***

Roddenberry and company had done a spectacular job, but good work does not come cheap. Post-production costs factored in, the pilot, which had been budgeted at a very expensive $452,000, ended up costing $616,000, or $4.6 million in 2013 -- a staggering amount for a single TV program in 1964. Roddenberry later said, "Yes, it was an abnormal amount to spend on a pilot. But they had to realize that we were building the interior of a spaceship, doing complex opticals of ships in flight and transporter effects and so forth. All props had to be built from scratch; all costumes had to be designed from scratch. To be honest, I don't think the 'powers that be' at the studio were aware of how much we were spending until after it was spent. But we spent it making a good product." (145-4)

Roddenberry trusted that time would prove him right concerning the worthiness of his expensive venture. What he didn't know was that excessive spending and derogatory comments about the "powers that be" would, for a very long period of his professional life, take him out of the game.

As for the film he directed, Robert Butler remained pessimistic, saying, "I thought to myself, 'Well, if they understand it, great, but wow, we should have made it easier for them.' It would just have been negative to have said that to Gene at that point because he just wasn't entertaining other thoughts. I was still thinking, 'I hope they understand it, because it's a difficult trip to get from A to Z in a straight line on that particular story.'" (26-2)

The story, despite Butler's harsh words, had just enough cliché and familiarity in the characters to help the audience "get" who they are right away. With an equal amount of unexpected elements and strong central themes, the writing came off as fresh -- and still does, half a century later.

The screen story plays by the rules: a character with a problem (the ship's captain), tired, guilt-ridden, needing to take a break, reassesses his life and priorities. He is already dealing with inner conflict before the antagonists of the story go to work on him.

Like any good script, there is a message. Vina says it to Pike: "They've found it's a trap. Like a narcotic. When dreams become more important than reality, you give up travel, building, creating; you even forget how to repair the machines left behind by your ancestors. You just sit, living and reliving other lives in the thought records left behind. Or ... probe the minds of zoo specimens."

The underlying theme is clear: Man is not meant to be completely unburdened. We need our challenges and setbacks to keep us pushing forward. Pike says: "You either live life, bruises and all ... or you turn your back on it and start dying."

Vina's sadness is profound. She lives life alone, without the companionship of her own species. The terror she experiences day in and day out, including the risk of being raped and murdered by the image of a savage Kalar warrior, is best conveyed when she says, "They keep at you and at you, year after year, probing, looking for weakness, and tricking ... and punishing ... and they've won. They own me." A frightening moment, both then and now, comes when we see how the Talosians go about trying to own Pike, as he screams in agony, on his knees in boiling water and brimstone, with flames lapping at him from all directions.

Susan Oliver in publicity shot
(Matt Jefferies collection; courtesy of Gerald Gurian)

In another line from the script, Vina says of the Talosians, "Since their minds can reach anywhere, most are like cocoons or larvae now. They just sit and let the thought records of some specimen live for them. Some of them hardly move, except to take the blue protein drink once a day. And there are only a few machines left to make that."

This gives us further clarification as to the motives behind the actions of the Talosians -- they need to breed humans so they will have an endless supply of servants.

Finally, there is the horror of seeing Vina as she truly is. After the disturbing transformation, she tells Pike, "They found me ... in the wreckage ... dying, a lump of flesh. They fixed me. Everything works. But they had no guide for putting me back together."

With all that works in "The Cage," the script broods and lacks humor -- as does the Captain. As a stand-alone film, "The Cage" is superb. As the template for a continuing series, it lacks a certain something -- primarily, the energy, the wit and the swagger of William Shatner as Captain James T. Kirk.

***

The *Star Trek* pilot was delivered in February 1965, almost ten months after NBC had first expressed interest. Nothing like this had ever been seen. NBC execs in attendance were stunned. Herb Solow reported, "The best screening I ever had for network executives was running the first *Star Trek* pilot for Mort [Werner], Grant [Tinker], Jerry [Stanley] and the others. They were blown away with the production, the scope of the film, the music, the whole physicality and feeling of the film." (161-3)

Stories have been told they even applauded. Then they rejected it.

5

Double or Nothing: A Second Pilot

Back to the drawing board
(NBC publicity photo courtesy of Gerald Gurian)

The official word on NBC's rejection of the *Star Trek* pilot: "too cerebral." For decades, that word was the only one ever mentioned. Roddenberry would be cheered and applauded every time he recalled the story for a crowd of adoring fans. "The Cage" was too smart, too good for TV, too misunderstood by those who should have known better. During a speaking engagement at Rochester Institute of Technology in 1976, he said, "The first pilot was rejected on the basis of being too intellectual for you slobs out in the television audience. It did go on to win the international Hugo Award, but I suppose many things turned down by networks win awards."

Actually, they don't. Nor had this one. Something else achieved that honor -- an offshoot of "The Cage," combining new footage with old to create a story within a story. That hybrid -- "The Menagerie" -- would become a footnote in the history of both science fiction and of the television medium. But why ruin a good story over technicalities?

In truth, the "cerebral" nature of "The Cage" was not the only concern. From *Inside Star Trek: The Real Story*, Herb Solow and Robert Justman joined together to lay out the case from NBC's perspective -- the network was very uncomfortable with the "eroticism" seen in the pilot and what that ingredient "foreshadowed for the ensuing series." Solow and Justman felt the network's knowledge of Roddenberry's attitude concerning sex and his illicit but not-so-secret relationships with a couple of wannabe starlets didn't help. The NBC sales department was concerned with the Mr. Spock character, fearing he would be seen as "demonic" by Bible Belt affiliate station owners *and* by important advertisers. Furthermore, Solow said NBC was not happy with some of the casting. The network supported the idea of a woman in a leading role, as proven in recent series starring Juliet Prowse, Barbara Eden, Shirley Booth, Barbara Stanwyck and Loretta Young, but it had reservations concerning Majel Barrett's abilities to "carry" the show as its costar. They were not saying she lacked talent, merely that she did not have star potential.

In 1968, even while *Star Trek* was still in the middle of its NBC run, Roddenberry would go on record for the first of many times claiming the network had a problem with the Enterprise's racial mix and, for this reason, wanted cast changes made. But just as *Star Trek* was getting its network debut, NBC seemed to be very much in favor of interracial casting, as demonstrated by a 1966 memo from Mort Werner sent to all the network's program providers. Werner had requested that the producers continue to make strides in this area. In particular, he praised Sheldon Leonard's *I Spy* project, with its mix of white (Culp) and black (Cosby). The interracial casting of *Star Trek* was not the source of NBC's jitters, nor was the caliber of the production in question.

Oscar Katz said, "[NBC just] didn't like the type of story we told. I think they selected [this pilot] to test Desilu on the hardest kind of story to produce because of the reputation Desilu had. Then, when they saw it, they were satisfied that Desilu was able to produce quality material, but it was the wrong kind of episode to take around to advertising agencies and sell. It was too off the beaten path." (96-1)

Roddenberry understood this and said, "I should have ended it with a fistfight between the hero and the villain if I wanted it on television." (145-4)

In a way, Oscar Katz corroborated this view: "I asked NBC, 'Why are you turning this down?' and was told, 'We can't sell it from this show, it's too atypical.' I said, 'But you guys *picked* this one. I gave you choices.' [Mort Werner] said, 'I know we did and, because of that, we're going to give you an order for a second pilot.'" (96-1)

It was an encouraging word but not yet official.

On February 8, 1965, Roddenberry wrote to his agent Alden Schwimmer at Ashley-Famous Agency:

> Am writing this without yet hearing anything definite on *Star Trek*. Whichever way this project goes, sale or no sale, the weekly problem of earning a living continues. Although *Star Trek* has been expensive for Desilu, it has been perhaps even more expensive to me individually in that I have continued putting week after week into the project far beyond normal production and post-production schedules. No complaints on that score but it is a fact I must see some immediate income either from Desilu or from somewhere else.

One project Roddenberry talked about in his letter to Schwimmer was "Assignment 100," a TV pilot script that would later evolve into the *Star Trek* episode "Assignment: Earth," and a second pilot script for a TV version of the western *High Noon*.

On February 12, Roddenberry again wrote to Schwimmer:

> Have just talked to Oscar Katz in New York about present indefinite sales status of *Star Trek*. I felt that all sides had been heard from but me and I owed it to Oscar that he understood my feelings clearly.... Whether or not this was the right story for a sale, it was definitely a right one for ironing out successfully a thousand how, when and whats of television science fiction. It did that job superbly and has us firmly in position to be the first who has ever successfully made TV series science fiction for a mass audience level and yet with a chance for quality and network prestige too.... We have an opportunity, like *Gulliver's Travels* of a century or more ago, to combine spectacle-excitement for a mass group along with meaningful drama and something of substance and pride.... This particular story, whatever its other merits, was an ideal vehicle for proving this point to ourselves. And if the network wants to be partners in such ventures as these, they have to share some of the pain, responsibility and risk of this type of planning. Or they can have copies of other shows, or parallels, breaking no new ground, without any pain or risk at all.

Roddenberry was hoping Mort Werner was going to make good on his word and order a second pilot, even though such a thing had never before been done. The wait was tormenting. Concerned that some of his key personnel might be lured away by other job offers, Roddenberry put his time to good use and began writing letters in hopes of keeping his highly talented team assembled.

On March 5, he wrote to Matt Jefferies, head of the Art Department, and responsible for designing the Enterprise inside and out:

> Dear Matt: I've owed you this letter of gratitude for some time. Actually, I've been waiting in the hope that the future of *Star Trek* would firm up and this letter could include a call on your services. We'll let you know the moment anything definite happens... In the meantime, would like to go on record that your combination of creative imagination and practical set design is entertaining and much of the reputation of the production for class and quality was due to your hard work. Working with you was a rare pleasure for me. Sincerely yours, Gene Roddenberry.

He was also hoping Desilu would agree to partner up with the network and gamble further. On March 19, he sent a note to Jeffrey Hunter, saying:

> Strangely enough, network interest continues and it sometimes seems they're caught in the dilemma of being a little afraid to do something this unusual and equally afraid of letting it drop and get away from them. Good. I like to see executives tormented.

The true intent of the note was not to disrespect the "suits" -- that was just Roddenberry having fun -- but to invite Hunter for a screening of the pilot at Desilu.

After filming had ended, Hunter talked enthusiastically about "The Cage." In a story for the *Los Angeles Citizen News*, on January 30, 1965, Joan Schmitt quoted him as saying, "The thing that intrigues me most about the show is it's actually based on the RAND Corporation's projection of things to come.... It will almost be like getting a look into the future, and some of the predictions will surely come true in our life-time."

Hunter could not have known how right he was. The coming of the PC, the Internet, the cell phone, Bluetooth, the sensor-operated automatic opening doors, the MRI and CAT-scan, and even CDs, DVDs and e-books were all envisioned on *Star Trek* first.

But Hunter's contract called for his participation in one pilot, not two. There had never been two pilots made for any series, so there had been no reason to specify such a provision. If the pilot sold, Hunter would be locked into a "five-year mission." If the pilot did not sell, he was free to pursue other interests. It had been a standard arrangement. But it was already becoming clear that there would be nothing standard about *Star Trek*. For *Star Trek: The Inside Story*, Herb Solow wrote:

> In the eyes of the television world, *Star Trek* was already a failure. Gene and I waited in the Desilu projection room for [Hunter] to arrive. He never did. Arriving in his stead was actress Sandy Bartlett -- Mrs. Jeffrey Hunter. As the end credits rolled and the lights came up, Jeff Hunter's wife gave us our answer: "This is not the kind of show Jeff wants to do. And besides, it wouldn't be good for his career. Jeff Hunter is a movie star." (161-3)

Also present at the screening was actor John Hoyt, who played Dr. Boyce, the ship's wise and fatherly medical officer. He, too, was underwhelmed and said, "It was really a dog. They spent too much time on unimportant scenes. They had Susan

Oliver all painted green, doing a long dance. People at the screening departed in silence afterwards and no one thought *Star Trek* would come to anything." (86)

Oscar Katz said, "Business Affairs negotiated with Jeffrey Hunter and we all thought it was the usual actor/network situation -- they don't want to do it for reason XYZ, and it's a device for getting the price up. We kept increasing the price and he kept saying no. One day I said, 'What's with Jeffrey Hunter?' and I was told he just won't do it at any price. Finally I said, 'Tell Jeffrey Hunter to get lost.'" (96-2)

A short while later, after the trade papers starting talking of a second *Star Trek* pilot, Hunter told J.D. Spiro for his *Milwaukee Journal* report, "I was asked to do it, but, had I accepted, I would have been tied up much longer than I care to be.... I love doing motion pictures and expect to be as busy as I want to be in them."

Sadly, Jeffrey Hunter's fortunes changed for the worse. By the late 1960s, he was dividing his time between "guest star" appearances on shows like *Love, American Style* and low-budget films shot outside of the country. In 1969, after completing *Super Colt 38*, a quickie western filmed in Mexico, Hunter suffered a series of minor strokes. A fall after one stroke resulted in trauma to the head, which led to his untimely death. He was only 42.

***

History was about to be made. On Friday, March 26, 1965, NBC officially ordered a second pilot. There was one condition: the budget was set at $216,000, a staggering $400,000 less than the first time around. NBC justified this by citing that the sets were now built, the spaceship constructed, the costumes woven and the gadgets hatched; the next go-round should be a cheaper ride. Bottom line: The network wanted to see if Roddenberry and Desilu could deliver *Star Trek* close to the normal budget of a 60-minute drama.

There was also a "request" from the network to shake up the cast. Roddenberry himself had decided not to bring back John Hoyt as the doctor. When the smoke cleared, only Mr. Spock made the cut, despite NBC's reservations. Roddenberry shared the story often. "The network told me to get rid of Number One, the woman first lieutenant, and also to get rid of 'the Martian fellow.'... I knew I couldn't keep both, so I gave the stoicism of the female officer to Spock, and married the actress who played Number One. Thank God it wasn't the other way around."

Majel Barrett recalled, "[Gene] sat down with me and said that he knew this was going to break my heart. The network had given him orders to get rid of the characters Number One and Spock. Then he explained to me that he could probably fight to save one character, but not both. He told me about how badly he wanted to keep Spock and how important that character could become to the series. He tried to be very nice about it, and he also said, 'We'll work you into it. Somehow or other, you'll be in the show.' And I just sunk. I had wanted the role so badly, and it was everything I'd wished for.... I mean, Gene wrote it for me, for God's sake. So being let go was devastating." (10-3)

There was one other concern from the network. Solow remembered being told by a friend at NBC, "And one more thing, for God's sake, no more scantily-clad green dancing girls with the bumps and grinds, okay?" (161-3)

Surprisingly, Desilu agreed to co-finance a second pilot. Despite the massive monetary loss with "The Cage," the old guard was not ready to do battle with Lucy. And Lucy was still determined that her studio needed to own prime-time real estate. Everything was at stake. According to Joseph Sorokin, a Desilu sound editor who worked on "The Cage," Roddenberry was well aware of the risks. Sorokin said, "I'll never forget, after I found out that we were going to do the second pilot, I was talking with Roddenberry one night and he said to me, 'Joe, I'm either going to make Desilu or break Desilu.'" (162)

***

NBC took steps to be certain the second pilot would have *the write stuff*, authorizing money for three scripts this time, of which only one would be produced.

Samuel Peeples, who helped Roddenberry so much during the development of "The Cage," was assigned one of the three, given the catalog number of "ST-2" -- Story Treatment #2 ("The Cage" had been ST-1). ST-2 would become "Where No Man Has Gone Before," which dealt with the intellectual concept of what to do when a pair of crew members become altered into godlike creatures. In light of the problems NBC had with the overly (and overtly) intellectual theme of "The Cage," this new story seemed risky.

The second script -- Roddenberry's -- appeared to be a safer bet. "The Omega Glory" (aka ST-3) was an action/adventure story about a parallel world ravished by a nuclear conflict, with an upside-down look at the clashes between a mutated Western culture and the remnants of a Communist Asian society. It even had a fistfight toward the end, as well as a flag-waving grand finale.

Roddenberry's choice for a writer to develop the third script was Stephen Kandel, who had solid credentials in television. He was not a science fiction writer *per se*, but Roddenberry had read a script he'd written for an unsold pilot about UFOs. As Kandel recalled, "'Stranger in Our Midst' dealt with a UFO carrying refugees from another world. They were undocumented aliens -- immigrants. And the problem -- the thing that made it interesting to Gene, I think -- was they had different strengths and weaknesses than human beings, but they were able to blend in to our culture." (95)

Roddenberry was familiar with Kandel's reputation for coming up with material the networks liked. The two met and discussed story ideas, leading to the April 22, 1965 treatment of "Warrior World." Kandel said, "It was about a planet where combat created a sort of a regency existence. The crew of the Enterprise found itself caught up in this highly hierarchal villagerized [sic] world where everybody was excessively polite because a breach in manners would lead to deadly combat. The problem was not to offend and thereby create an interstellar incident. But, of course, they *did* offend and this led to a great deal of individual combat." (95)

Roddenberry wrote to Kandel on April 26, saying:

> An interesting outline, certainly full of action, but perhaps weighed too heavy in the direction of a feudal-Roman world and a bit too lightly in story and motivated character.

Kandel responded with revised outlines on April 28 and May 7 before the decision was made to have him switch stories to one of Roddenberry's ideas -- "The Women" -- about that rascally space trader who, in reality, is a pimp traveling through the cosmos with a cargo of prostitutes. Roddenberry had already tried to interest NBC in this story as a contender for the first pilot. Perhaps the network would like it better this time with a different writer, a different title, and different names for the characters. The only name that did not get changed was Mr. Spock. The new title, now catalogued as ST-4, was "Mudd's Women." In light of NBC's misgivings about the sexual content of "The Cage," this was another odd choice.

In late May, as the three script assignments were being farmed-out, it was decided the new Captain of the Enterprise would be named Kirk. Jack Lord was approached first. He had been gaining attention in television with high profile guest appearances and had received rave notices for his turn as CIA agent Felix Leiter in the first James Bond movie, 1962's *Dr. No*. Next, ABC snatched him up to play a modern day rodeo rider in the 1962-63 series *Stoney Burke*. The series didn't hit, but the buzz around Hollywood was that Lord's star was on the rise (a 12-year stint as Steve McGarrett on *Hawaii Five-0* would soon prove this to be true).

Roddenberry wanted Lord to play Kirk. But, according to numerous *Star Trek* insiders, the actor demanded a hefty ownership of the series and co-producer status, something Roddenberry was not going to let happen. Dorothy Fontana said Roddenberry quipped, "Jack takes his [last] name too seriously." (64)

Lord was out. And then, by a quirk of fate known as a sudden TV cancellation, the man destined to play Kirk became available.

***

William Shatner, 1959

Born in Montreal on March 22, 1931, William Shatner was trained in the Shakespearean classics. His first work in television, however, was light years away from the Bard -- a guest role in 1953 on *Space Command*, a sci-fi series produced in Canada, followed by a semi-recurring role in 1954 on the Canadian Broadcasting Company's version of *Howdy Doody* as Ranger Bob. One year later, he made two appearances on the CBC anthology series *Encounter*. In one he played the title character in a production of Herman Melville's "Billy Budd," supported by Basil Rathbone and Patrick Macnee.

Television and radio helped pay the bills, but Shatner's heart was on the stage -- and in the hands of fellow "legit" performer Gloria Rand. The two were married on August 12, 1956. Two days later, Shatner got an unexpected break. Christopher Plummer took ill while playing the title role in the Stratford (Ontario) Shakespeare Festival production of *Henry V*. With Plummer in the hospital suffering from kidney trouble, Shatner, who played a lesser role and was also Plummer's understudy, was advanced to the lead. Plummer soon returned, but his understudy was already on the road to bigger things.

Several weeks later, Shatner was in New York and appearing in "Mr. Finchley Versus the Bomb," a live television presentation of *Kaiser Aluminum Hour*, written by Rod Serling. A second *Kaiser* show, "Gwyneth," paired Shatner with future *Star Trek* guest star Joanne Linville.

Shatner and wife Gloria ping-ponged between New York City and Canada for the next six months. In his homeland, he appeared in a stage production of *Oedipus Rex*, which CBC broadcast in January 1957. America picked up the live feed and presented it as an episode of *Omnibus*. New York casting agents caught the program and, one month later, Shatner was back in the Big Apple for the first of three live plays on *Kraft Theatre*, followed by the first of five appearances on the prestigious *Studio One*. The second and third of these

Studio One shows made up TV's first two-part episode: "The Defender," starring Ralph Bellamy as a defense attorney and Shatner as his son and aide. Steve McQueen costarred as their troubled client.

Positive reviews and a big TV audience for "The Defender" brought Shatner to the attention of Hollywood. He was flown to California one month later to star in his first filmed program, *Alfred Hitchcock Presents*. A few days after that he was auditioning for a plum role in the upcoming big-budget film *The Brothers Karamazov*. MGM was offering Shatner not only a standout part but an actor-friendly contract. He would be allowed to pick his own projects from scripts offered by the studio and, until finding one he liked, he could appear in non-Hollywood television productions and stage plays.

Brothers Karamazov was released in February 1958 to positive reviews and strong box office. Yul Brynner and Richard Basehart played two of the brothers, Shatner the third. The reviewer for *Variety* wrote:

> William Shatner has the difficult task of portraying youthful male goodness and he does it with such gentle candor it is effective.

While waiting for MGM to find a suitable follow-up project, Shatner returned to live TV, appearing on series such as *Suspicion* and *Climax*, as well as three episodes of *U.S. Steel Hour*. In June, he gained attention with a standout role on the prestigious *Playhouse 90* in the episode "A Town Has Turned to Dust" -- the second time he performed a script written by a pre-*Twilight Zone* Rod Serling. *Daily Variety* said:

> William Shatner exhibits a good deal of self-control in a role that might have been butchered by a lesser actor, giving a very fine performance.

And yet still no script from MGM that made an impression on the serious young actor.

At the end of August, the Shatners welcomed the first of three daughters, Leslie. The pressure on dad to make more money was heating up. He later told a tabloid writer, "We were always broke in New York. I did more live television than many actors, but you didn't get paid very much for those live shows… so that the amount of money I received was just enough to pay the rent on a small apartment and to pay for our groceries. We were never ahead." (166-19)

With director Joshua Logan and France Nuyen for *The World of Suzie Wong* (AP photo)

A bump in pay came when Shatner was offered the male lead (opposite future *Star Trek* guest star France Nuyen) in a big Broadway event: *The World of Suzie Wong*. The play dramatized a love affair between an American artist (Shatner) and a Chinese prostitute (Nuyen), set in a Hong Kong brothel. But to take the role, Shatner had to sign a one-year contract, and that meant buying off his agreement with MGM. He later said, "Purchasing my contract cost me more money than I made in my first ten years of acting. I left MGM because the play I read was a beautiful poetic play. By the time *Suzie Wong* reached Broadway, it was nothing but a story of a Chinese prostitute and I was nothing but a male dancer supporting a ballerina." (166-17)

France Nuyen with Shatner on stage in 1959

Shatner may have had his regrets, but the play nonetheless gave him a chance to shine. During a trial run in Boston, *Daily Variety* summed *Suzie Wong* up as "a world of shock to the Hub [that] is so highly censorable it's inflammable, but it looks like a surefire hit." The critic added:

> It needs a sign, 'For Adults Only,' for this is truly strong fare spelling sex from opening curtain to finale of the two-act, 12-scene drama.... William Shatner is great as Robert Lomax, the artist torn by his love for the Chinese girl whose "work" disturbs him, but not her.

Six weeks later, with *Suzie Wong* on Broadway, the critic for *Weekly Variety*, also impressed by the play, said, "Shatner is engaging as the confused but steadfast artist."

France Nuyen said, "Bill was obviously an experienced actor and he was the one in charge, as far as I was concerned." (129-1)

Suzie Wong was a hit, and kept Shatner off television for nearly all of 1959. Once free, he bounced back onto the airwaves in December with an episode of *Hallmark Hall of Fame* and "The Indestructible Mr. Gore," a presentation of *The Sunday Showcase*. Regarding the latter, *Daily Variety* said the television play "had great strength in its theme, and a fine performance from William Shatner as the blind lawyer setting out to make a place in the world for himself." The play was written by Gore Vidal about his own grandfather, Thomas P. Gore, who served as a U.S. Senator. The review continued:

> Shatner turned in a brilliantly distinctive and believable performance as Gore, not only from the physical standpoint of making the blindness believable, but from the construction of a characterization of a strong and determined personality that rang true at every turn.

At this time, Shatner was offered a pair of TV pilots, both placing him in the primary supporting role. The first was based on the successful two-part *Studio One* presentation of "The Defender" in which he had appeared. He turned it down in favor of the second: "Nero Wolfe." *The Defenders*, as the series version was called, with E.G. Marshall taking over for Ralph Bellamy and Robert Reed for Shatner, made it onto the fall 1960 CBS schedule for the start of a four-year run. "Nero Wolfe" didn't go beyond pilot film and never aired.

In 1960, taking what at the time seemed to be bad advice, Shatner turned down lead roles in two more TV pilots: *Dr. Kildare* and *Checkmate*. The former made a star of Richard Chamberlain when it began a five-year run on NBC; the latter did very nearly the same for Doug McClure, staying on CBS for two seasons. Regardless, Shatner was all over the dial.

Typical of his high visibility, in a single month, Shatner had six prominent roles in five different series, including *The Twilight Zone* ("Nick of Time," written by future *Trek* scripter Richard Matheson) and *Alcoa Presents* (also known as *One Step Beyond* and directed by John Newland, who would also travel to *Star Trek*). In October, he was on the big screen for the lead in *The Explosive Generation*, as a high school teacher dealing with his student's curiosity concerning sex.

Publicity photo with Shatner and Patricia Breslin in *The Twilight Zone* "Nick of Time" (Courtesy of Gerald Gurian)

Nineteen sixty-one opened well with "The Hungry Glass" and "The Grim Reaper," a pair of memorable episodes for the *Thriller* series, hosted by Boris Karloff. Following his unforgettable death scene by the Reaper's sickle, Shatner reported to work for the filming of one of the year's top-grossing films, *Judgment at Nuremberg*.

Shatner in "The Grim Reaper" on NBC's *Thriller* (1961)

Making a film is not as all-consuming as work on the stage or in television, and Shatner kept himself busy writing a script for one of the TV series he had turned down. In March 1961, *Daily Variety* reported:

> William Shatner, actor presently in *Judgment*, doesn't believe in breaks between scenes. He makes his own breaks. Between scenes Shatner scripted a teleplay, "The Button Down Break" and has sold it to the *Checkmate* series as a seg. What now? Shatner also has got himself cast in a lead role in

his teleplay.

Work on *Judgment*, however, stretched into the end of May, causing him to miss the filming of the *Checkmate* episode, with Tony Randall taking his place. Once *Nuremberg* wrapped, Shatner immediately accepted a guest star role in an episode of one of the series he had turned down -- *The Defenders*. Also cast, future *Trek* guest star Joanne Linville, her second time opposite him. Shatner would do four more *Defenders* over the next couple years, always as top guest.

In June, the Shatners welcomed their second daughter, Lisabeth. Starting in September, proud dad was back on the stage as the lead for *A Shot in the Dark* (playing the precursor to the role that, in the Blake Edwards film of the same name, would go to Peter Sellers after much campy rewriting). For its out-of-town warm-up in New Haven, *Weekly Variety* said:

> *A Shot in the Dark* is a sure-fire hit, a must-see that has bubbling good humor, sparkling dialog, bright staging and outstanding performances.

The trade wrote that Shatner "impresses favorably." Hitting Broadway in October, *Daily Variety* added:

> William Shatner is credible and engaging as the dedicated magistrate who risks his legal career in pushing through with the investigation of a murder case.

That same week, *Judgment at Nuremberg* opened in movie houses to sensational reviews and brisk business. Critics praised Shatner but, with all the famous faces around him, including Spencer Tracy, Burt Lancaster, Richard Widmark, Marlene Dietrich, Maximilian Schell, Judy Garland and Montgomery Clift, he was not to find movie stardom ... yet.

Shatner left *A Shot in the Dark* in September 1962, at the end of his one-year contract. He then dropped in on *Dr. Kildare* and did the first of two top spots on *The Naked City*, plus the first of two on *The Doctors and Nurses*. In January 1963, he was on the big screen as the star of *The Intruder*. *Weekly Variety* wrote:

> Roger and Gene Corman's *The Intruder* comes to grips with a controversial contemporary issue -- integration, and those who would defy the law of the land -- in an adult, intelligent and arresting manner.... Shatner, a fine young actor who deserves to be seen on the [big] screen more frequently, masterfully plays the bigot.

For his work, Shatner won the Best Actor award in the second annual Peace Film Festival, held in Los Alamos, New Mexico.

Two months after the release of *The Intruder*, in March 1963, *Dick Powell Theatre* aired a pilot called "Colossus" starring Shatner and future *Star Trek* guest star Robert Brown. Brown said, "That was supposed to be a series. Dick Powell was going to take it to New York; it was all set to go. And he died before he got onto the plane. But the *Dick Powell Theatre* put the pilot on and it got some phenomenal reviews. If that had sold, Shatner might not have been able to do *Star Trek*." (24-1)

In September and October, with the fall TV season, Shatner was seen in five consecutive episodes of *77 Sunset Strip* as a recurring character, more segments of *The Doctors and Nurses, Alfred Hitchcock, The Defenders,* and a second trip into *The Twilight Zone*, with the famous "Nightmare at 20,000 Feet," again written by Richard Matheson. He also made appearances in episodes of *Channing, Route 66* and *Arrest and Trial*, the latter a precursor of *Law and Order*, with series' lead Roger Perry, later to be top guest on a *Star*

Trek.

Shatner was working relentlessly, gaining attention and respect. He was also earning a fair wage now that episodes of TV series were filmed and repeated rather than aired only once as a live broadcast. But being a professional guest star does not make for a secure future. He later said, "Sooner or later your string of luck is going to give out, and

Shatner's second trip into *The Twilight Zone* for "Nightmare at 20,000 Feet" (1963)

then, if you haven't saved any money, you're in trouble." (166-19)

Reconsidering the pluses and minuses of having his own series, Shatner decided in favor of the steady pay a series could offer. His agent at Ashley-Famous put the word out. In November 1963, Shatner traveled to Utah for the title role in the expensive "Alexander the Great" TV pilot, working under Selig J. Seligman, the creator/producer responsible for the hit ABC series *Combat!* It was big, it was splashy, it was expensive -- and it was a joke. Even its dynamic star admitted that this "Alexander the Great" lacked greatness, and was little more than "*Combat!* in drag." (156-8)

Although a TV series was proving elusive, the successful film roles continued. On the heels of "Alexander the Great," Shatner flew off to appear in the MGM motion picture *The Outrage*, starring Paul Newman. Next up in 1964: the Shatners had their third daughter, Melanie.

ABC gets Shatner in space first, for "Cold Hands, Warm Heart" on *The Outer Limits* (1964, UA TV)

Meanwhile, dad was on the wish-list in the offices of Desilu and NBC regarding casting for the Captain of the Enterprise. Unaware that this thing called *Star Trek* was even considering him, the busy actor took a prominent guest role in *Burke's Law*, followed by an episode of *The Outer Limits* ("Cold Hands, Warm Heart"), as an astronaut who returns from a trip to Venus with unexplainable problems. That episode also featured yet more *Star Trek* foreshadowing, with actor Malachi Throne alongside Shatner in the cast.

In November, Shatner appeared with Leonard Nimoy in an episode of *The Man from U.N.C.L.E.* for director Joseph Sargent (later to direct the *Star Trek* episode "The Corbomite Maneuver"). In December, he appeared on *Bob Hope Presents the Chrysler Theater*. Already in the can for airing in January 1965, his fifth top-billed guest stint on *The Defenders*, this time with yet another future *Star Trek* guest performer: Madlyn Rhue. He was now also filming his first series, *For the People*, for a mid-season premiere in January.

Dwight Newton, writing for the San Francisco Examiner on January 31, said:

> *For the People*, to put it bluntly, is an aggressive, hard hitting CBS drama series designed for the express purpose of knocking *Bonanza*'s block off. It premieres tonight at 9.... Ever since Ben Cartwright and his sons came riding across the Sunday night sagebrush they have inflicted a terrible whipping on the rival CBS ratings. Everybody has failed against them, especially Judy Garland. This time CBS is coming out fighting mad with a fighting mad show. *For the People* is a reverse switch on *The Defenders* and produced by the same cagey opportunist, Herbert Brodkin. *The Defenders* defends people suspected of crime, *For the People* prosecutes -- sometimes savagely and ruthlessly. The hero is a high strong, opinionated assistant district attorney portrayed by William Shatner.... *The Defenders* and Perry Mason labor to protect the innocent. This fellow isn't interested in the innocent. His objective is to prosecute law breakers and get convictions. Will this "hard line" approach lure viewers? CBS thinks it is worth a good and expensive gamble.

The network took ads out in *TV Guide* and newspaper TV sections across the country, telling us:

> Drama with a bullet's speed and impact as William Shatner stars in Herbert Brodkin's bitingly different new series about crime and justice and the law. FOR THE PEOPLE.

On February 2, *Daily Variety* said:

> William Shatner, a youngster with looks and talent... whose dedication to the job is admirable... is the main prop of the series and should hold up his end with the proper support and meaty stories.

The following day, the critic for *Weekly Variety* added:

> In *For the People*, producer Herb Brodkin has come up with a series which crackles with reality, which focuses on people caught in the storm of crime, and which grabs and holds viewer attention.... William Shatner appealingly [plays] the young assistant district attorney, pinched by a strain of impracticability. He [is] the young man out to become a hero, chopped down to human proportions by outside forces.... It's a pity that this midseason hour-long replacement is up against NBC-TV's *Bonanza* powerhouse. Judging from the pre-em, it deserves a better chance to vie in the network sun.

Terrence O'Flaherty of the *San Francisco Chronicle* called Shatner "a big new star." Rick Du Brow of United Press International, wrote, "William Shatner is real hero material and a strong actor, a young veteran." Win Fanning, for the *Pittsburgh Post-Gazette*, said, "Shatner is a handsome, exceptionally capable actor who manages to convey exactly the right balance between dedication and the facts of life." And Hank Grant, for *Hollywood Review*, added:

Shatner is an unusually fine actor who makes his role a living thing. When he portrays anguish for instance, it's not scenery-chewing, but the real emotion.

Despite the good notices, the ratings were not supportive. *For the People*, scheduled not only against *Bonanza* but opposite the popular *ABC Sunday Night Movie*, was off the air by May after just 13 episodes. Shatner felt the failure had to do with more than strong competition. He told Dave Kaufman of *Daily Variety*, "We preached too much. We dealt with subjects such as drug addiction, abortion, crime-in-the-streets, and people don't want to see these on a week-to-week basis." (166-12)

Once again, Roddenberry's bad fortune -- trying to shoot a pilot while the entire TV industry was already in production for the coming fall -- turned out to be good timing. Within days of losing his first series, Ashley-Famous called Shatner with news that he was wanted for the lead in a science fiction pilot. Being a sci-fi enthusiast, Shatner was happy to meet with Roddenberry, who arranged for a screening of "The Cage." Shatner later said, "I remember as I watched it I was impressed by a number of things -- the green girl, and Leonard, and Majel Barrett as Number One, and I thought it was extremely innovative and extremely inventive." (156-8)

Finally, Roddenberry had found someone who liked his green-skinned dancing girl. With this, the two men bonded. Producer and actor then discussed how the new Captain should be portrayed. By the end of the day, Shatner agreed to play James Kirk. He was 34. Just as *For the People* was leaving the CBS prime time schedule, on May 4, 1965, *Daily Variety* reported:

> NBC-TV has okayed production of a second seg of *Star Trek*, hour-long sci-fi series, and William Shatner will replace Jeffrey Hunter as the lead in this projected series. Web [*Variety*-speak for network] has also okayed three more scripts and is interested in *Trek* for a mid-season or 1966-67 start.

"As an actor, Bill was of a higher echelon, and hiring him was really a coup," casting director Joe D'Agosta said. "Everything he was doing, whether it was on stage, on film or on television, was highly prestigious. I couldn't believe we got him." (43-2)

Bob Justman added, "Gene was very happy that he was able to get Bill Shatner. I had worked with Bill on *The Outer Limits* and he had a good reputation in television. He was someone to be reckoned with and we certainly understood that he was a more accomplished actor than Jeff Hunter was, and he gave us more dimension.... [Hunter] didn't run the gamut of emotions that Bill Shatner could do.... [Shatner] had enormous technical abilities to do different things and he gave the captain a terrific personality. He embodied what Gene had in mind, which was a flawed hero, or the hero who considers himself to be flawed. Captain Horatio Hornblower." (94-14)

Shatner's deal for the pilot was $10,000 (comparable to $75,000 in 2013) plus a contractual guarantee that, should the pilot go to series, he would receive profit sharing -- the same arrangement Jack Lord had asked for, but not as "Lordly" a chunk.

***

The captain was on board. However, the science officer was considering jumping ship. Like the character of Spock, Leonard Nimoy was experiencing great internal conflict. After the ordeal of making the "The Cage" and the embarrassment over the makeup, he again feared that playing such a character on weekly TV could hurt his career. Like Jeffrey Hunter, Nimoy's contract allowed for an escape clause. If a series had been ordered, he would have been stuck. But he wasn't obligated to appear in a second trial run.

Nimoy visited his friend Vic Morrow to discuss the dilemma. Because of Morrow's attention-grabbing debut as a young hoodlum in *Blackboard Jungle*, followed by numerous other bad guy roles in popular films like *King Creole* (making trouble for Elvis Presley) and *Cimarron* (shooting it out with Glenn Ford), he knew all too well what it meant to be typecast. It took a concentrated effort between Morrow and his agent to change this, which meant turning down roles, working less and holding out for the parts which might reestablish him as something other than a villain. It was a gamble and took more than a few years to play out, but now the role of Sgt. Chip Saunders on the hit series *Combat!* had made Morrow famous as a brooding hero.

Morrow considered his friend's problem and then advised Nimoy to take a chance, to do the second pilot and commit to the series. If *Star Trek* even sold, it was likely to be cancelled in a year or less, and with all the makeup Nimoy would be wearing it was unlikely he would be recognized as the actor who had played that strange alien on a short-lived TV series. All he really had to worry about was if *Star Trek* was a hit.

With Nimoy's new contract, Spock would now be a more important character in the series -- not merely the ship's Science Officer (as in "The Cage") but also First Officer, taking over that position from the departing Number One. The promotion also came with a raise -- for the pilot, anyway, his paycheck would be $2,500. The extra money was certainly a factor in Nimoy's decision. "I was raised in a tenement neighborhood where you couldn't have a dog," he said for a 1967 *TV Guide* article. He added, "The first time I bought a house, I bought a dog." (128-21)

***

With the two series' leads locked in, Roddenberry set about assembling his production people. James Goldstone, 33 at this time, was already slated to direct. He had met Roddenberry on *Highway Patrol*. Other notches on his director's chair included dramas in nearly every locale: drama in the courtroom (*Perry Mason*), drama in the West (*Rawhide*), drama on wheels (*Route 66*), drama on the run (*The Fugitive*), drama with monsters (*The Outer Limits*) and, working under producer Roddenberry, drama at a boot camp (*The Lieutenant*). Now he would add a notch for "drama in space."

Goldstone said, "There had been several problems with 'The Cage.' One of them was that it cost so much money and the other was that it took so long to shoot. One of the requisites put on the second pilot was to shoot it in eight days, which would then prove that a weekly series could be done in six or seven days.... The other requisite was that NBC very much wanted something that could be 'commercial' against the police shows and all the other action things that were then on television. [This] was not so much a pilot as it was an example of how we could go on a weekly level." (75-3)

Next, Roddenberry needed a line producer, and it would not be Byron Haskin. Robert Justman had been his first choice for "The Cage" and remained so now. Goldstone, the one who had recommended Justman to Roddenberry in the first place, also wanted him.

This time, knowing that a post-effects company was already in place, Justman agreed to take the more demanding job of associate producer. He said, "I imagine the reason I worked as frequently in television as I did was because I occasionally said no. I tried to never accept a position I was not ready for; not when I knew of someone who was better suited for it. This is why I turned down associate producer on the first pilot. And this is why Gene was so sure he had to have me doing that very job in the second pilot. Sometimes playing hard to get can work out, especially when you're not so sure you want it to work out. It was going to be a great deal of work. I knew that going in. And I was right." (94-1)

Stepping in as assistant director was Greg Peters, who knew Justman from *The Outer Limits*. He was now an employee of Desilu and assistant director on *The Lucy Show*, and would become an important behind-the-scenes *Star Trek* production person, eventually advancing to Justman's job as associate producer. Eddie Paskey, who was soon to join the cast, and referencing Peters' resemblance to an iconic advertising character, said, "We used to call Greg 'Mister Clean.' He was a big man, I mean probably 6'3, and he had a shaved head. He was intimidating to look at, but a very sweet guy." (135-2)

George Merhoff came aboard, replacing Bob Campbell as gaffer. Merhoff would become very important to the series, in charge of the lighting unit for every episode produced and helping to create the look for *Star Trek* under the direction of the cinematographer. Prior to this he had only worked as a lighting assistant, known as a "grip." In that capacity, he served Alfred Hitchcock on *Psycho*.

Robert Dawn, hired to temporarily replace Fred Phillips, who had a scheduling conflict, was the new head of makeup. Dawn had also worked on Hitchcock's *Psycho*, as well as the famous director's *Marnie* and TV's *Thriller*. His Mister Spock had a look more extreme than the one Phillips designed, with Spock's eyebrows swept sharply upward and his shorter bangs adding to the stark, alien look of his face. Dawn also added more yellow to Spock's complexion.

Matt Jefferies, the man who built the Enterprise inside and out was back, "Refurbishing, redesigning, and restructuring." He said, "The bulk of the sets from the first pilot were set up so that they could only be shot from one angle. We had to broaden those aspects, so that if the second pilot sold, the same sets could work for the series.... That's when we made them 'wild,' but we also had to add more to them, so that they could be shot from a number of different directions. What [is enough] for a pilot is far from adequate for a series. There had been so much money spent, we knew that if it sold they wouldn't give us anything with which to build additional sets, so we had to make sure the things would work series-wise when we did the second pilot." (91-7)

Bill Snyder, the director of photography on "The Cage," had returned to his chores at Disney and would not be available as cinematographer, so Robert Justman immediately checked with the cameramen's union for a replacement. He was told that the "list was empty" and there were no qualified lead cameraman available. When given this news, Herb Solow was mortified. How was he going to call Mort Werner at NBC and tell him Desilu had so little clout that it couldn't even find a qualified director of photography in all of Hollywood to shoot their pilot for the network?

Before that call could be made, James Goldstone came to the rescue, again. He knew of someone who was no longer on the union's active list but would be well worth having. He explained, "I wanted a real old pro, since we were doing some radical things with color, attempting some things that were not conventional. I wanted a cameraman who could deal with depth and things of that kind." (75-2)

Solow, Roddenberry and Justman knew nothing about the "old pro" Goldstone called in to meet with them. They expected he would bring in his resume. He didn't. They expected he would be in his 40s or 50s. He wasn't. In fact, the 69-year-old had recently retired. They expected he knew TV production, but, when asked what shows he had worked on, he said he hadn't. When asked what experience he did have, the humble reply was, "I did a little thing called *Gone with the Wind*."

Ernest Haller had been filming movies since the 1920s, including *Captain Blood* with Errol Flynn, *Dark Victory* with Bette Davis and, much later, *Rebel Without a Cause* with James Dean. Haller had been nominated for the Academy Award for Best Cinematography six times, for *Jezebel* (1938), *All This and Heaven Too* (1940), *Mildred Pierce* (1945), *The Flame and the Arrow* (1950), *Whatever Happened to Baby Jane?* (1962), *Lilies of the Field* (1963) and that "little thing" called *Gone with the Wind*, in 1939, for which he took home the Oscar.

Solow, Roddenberry and Justman could never have expected someone of Haller's status would nonchalantly wander into Desilu, willing to come out of retirement to shoot a mere TV pilot. But he did, as a favor to James Goldstone. The grey-haired Director of Photography who had never done television was hired on the spot. Haller couldn't have known it, but he was about to go where no cinematographer had gone before.

6

Episode 1: WHERE NO MAN HAS GONE BEFORE
Written by Samuel A. Peeples
(with Gene Roddenberry, uncredited)
Directed by James Goldstone

NBC press release, issued August 31, 1966:

Sally Kellerman with William Shatner in NBC press photo (Courtesy of Gerald Gurian)

> Gary Lockwood and Sally Kellerman are guest stars in the story of two spacecraft crew members who are transformed into superior beings following a collision in space on the NBC Television Network colorcast of *Star Trek* Thursday, Sept. 22. Co-starring regulars in this episode, "Where No Man Has Gone Before," are William Shatner as Captain James Kirk and Leonard Nimoy as Mr. Spock. As the first manned spacecraft to venture beyond the limits of the Earth's galaxy, the U.S.S. Enterprise is severely damaged after passing through the totally strange and unfamiliar elements of an outer galaxy. Not until the craft makes its way to a friendly planet for repairs is it revealed that Lt. Commander Mitchell (Lockwood) and psychiatrist Elizabeth Dehner (Miss Kellerman) are possessed of powers of a master race after their exposure to the new atmosphere.

Mr. Spock becomes convinced that the Captain's friend, Mitchell, and Dr. Dehner -- both of whom possess abnormally high ESP ratings and are rapidly mutating into something more than mere human beings – are increasingly becoming a threat to ship and crew. His recommendation to a resistant Kirk: abandon them on a desolate planet and try to escape the danger they present before it is too late.

In 1966, there was much concern over the ultimate power that was in the hands of a few ambitious men. The episode's true message lies in a line of Kirk's: "Beware a god with human frailties."

SOUND BITES

- *Kirk, to Elizabeth Dehner:* "You were a psychiatrist. You know the ugly, savage things we all keep buried -- the things none of us dare expose. But he'll dare! Who can stop him? He doesn't care. Did you hear him joke about compassion? Above all else, a 'god' needs compassion!"

- *Sulu, attempting to gauge Mitchell's intellectual growth:* "Do the math. It's like having a penny, doubling it every day. In a month, you'd be a millionaire."

- *Kirk, to Spock:* "Will you try for one minute to feel? At least act like you have a heart? We're talking about Gary.... Dr. Dehner feels he isn't that dangerous. What makes you right and a trained psychiatrist wrong?" *Spock:* "Because she 'feels.' I don't."

- *Gary Mitchell:* "You should have killed me while you could, James. Command *and* compassion are a fool's game.... Time to pray, Captain. Pray to me."

ASSESSMENT

"Where No Man Has Gone Before" is filled with mystery, terror, a personal conflict and an immensely difficult decision for the protagonist -- Captain Kirk. It gives us a physical confrontation between good and evil, as two men who were once like brothers do battle to the death. Writing, direction, acting, music, sets and cinematography all rate high -- especially for a TV production from this era.

THE STORY BEHIND THE STORY

Script Timeline
Samuel Peeples' story outline, "Esper," ST #2: First week of April 1965.
Peeples' revised story outline, "Star Prime": Second week of April, 1965.
Peeples' 1st Draft teleplay, now "Where No Man Has Gone Before":
Late April 1965.
Peeples' 2nd Draft teleplay (listed as Rev. 1st Draft): May 27, 1965.
Gene Roddenberry's rewrite (Mimeo Department "Yellow Cover" 1st Draft):
June 16, 1965.
Roddenberry's second rewrite (Final Draft teleplay): June 26, 1965.
Roddenberry's third rewrite (Rev. Final Draft teleplay): July 8, 1965.
Additional page revisions by Roddenberry: July 12, 14 & 15, 1965.

Sam Peeples turned in his story outline, "Esper," at the start of April 1965. Roddenberry was enthusiastic about the outline, although it was light-years away from what would eventually be filmed. He wrote to Herb Solow:

> The idea of character change in the guest star "Esper" is most interesting. His change from decent, kind, very human individual into massive power and evil could be exciting drama.... Equally exciting, and certainly right down the line with what all believe is necessary in this next episode, is the factor of immediate peril to our captain and his ship... and almost from the first page of our script we recognize giant risk and danger. (GR2-1)

At this stage in the development of the story, the character identified as Esper was not a member of the Enterprise crew, nor a friend of Captain James Kirk. He was a member of a remote Earth colony who, once he started mutating, was held prisoner by the colonists. A landing party from the Enterprise takes him into custody. There is no trip beyond the realm of the galaxy, no damage to the ship, no abandoning Esper on a planet devoid of life, no big climactic fistfight between the brave Captain and a man who believes himself a god.

Roddenberry's note to Solow continued:

> Although obviously there are motivations, story direction, and other things yet to be worked out, the story line seems to have the potential of being direct and excitingly dramatic, a straight-lined growth of powerful peril and danger to our lead and his ship, leading to a head-to-head conflict between

the captain and the guest star, and yet containing meaningful themes and points of view which should lift it far out of the ordinary. A tale of <u>absolute power corrupting absolutely</u>. (GR2-1)

Roddenberry worked out the story elements with Peeples before having him revise the outline, delivered during the second week of April -- this one with the working title "Star Prime." It was a substantial overhaul and now more in line with the story to be filmed. The character of Esper had been changed to Lt. Mitchell, a member of the Enterprise crew with a high "esper" rating. Also present in this new version of the story was Dr. Elizabeth Dehner, who becomes involved with Mitchell.

A few days later, Roddenberry wrote to Peeples suggesting many changes and specifically asking that Dehner be portrayed as "something less than a 'swinger,'" that she be "a little overly intelligent and inhibited." Roddenberry's verdict of the story, even before the requested changes: "A hell of an exciting outline." (GR2-2)

Excitement notwithstanding, more changes were made before Peeples proceeded to script. One thing the writer was proud to take credit for was the title. He said, "That title is *mine*. That was the original title of the very first copy of the very first version of the story that was submitted to Gene Roddenberry." (136-1)

The *Star Trek* show files are more precise than Peeples' memory. It was actually on the third version of the story -- the first draft teleplay -- when the epic title initially appeared.

The script arrived on April 27, 1965. Roddenberry immediately wrote Herb Solow:

> Sam Peeples has written an interesting script and delivers it with his usual remarkable speed. You'll note in the copy we made for you that he understands the *Star Trek* format and makes excellent use of our main continuing characters and of the ship. And, with a couple of possible exceptions which we should study and analyze, it promises a show which could be made on budget. (GR2-3)

Herb Solow took credit for a change in the next draft: the idea of the Captain's log. Having read *Gulliver's Travels* in college, Solow admired how the fantastic storytelling was documented as if in a journal. He made a recommendation to Roddenberry that the Captain's log entries could quickly clue in the viewer as to events having already taken place, eliminating the need for numerous pages of "boring exposition." Solow remembered kicking the idea around with Roddenberry, who then "accepted the concept." (161-3)

Sam Peeples said Roddenberry brought the idea to him with no mention of Solow's contribution. He recalled that "G.R." dropped by his house for a few drinks, after which they discussed the concept of the Captain's log entry serving as a mechanism to advance and accelerate the narrative for each story.

Peeples' revised first draft, dated May 27, 1965, included the Captain's log, but it did not yet include a "stardate." One of Kirk's voiceover entries begins, "Captain's Log, Report 197." Peeples remembered the conversation with Roddenberry that brought about the signature stardate. He said, "We tried to set up a system that would be unidentifiable unless you knew how we did it. So the stardate on Earth would be one thing, but the stardate on Alpha Centauri would be different. We thought this was hilarious, because everyone would say, 'How come this date is before that date when this show is *after* that show?' The answer was, because you were in a different sector of the universe." (136-1)

Other differences in Peeples' revised draft from the filmed pilot: Spock is the one who knew and worked with Mitchell for years, not Kirk. Kirk liked Mitchell but was not as close as in the aired version, and there was no talk of shared history, including Mitchell having once saved the Captain's life. There is no decision as to whether or not to maroon Mitchell on Delta Vega, nor is there even a Delta Vega. Lt. Kelso is killed by Mitchell, but on the Enterprise, not on a barren planet. The body count is higher, with other crewmen also being killed, strangled by power cables. Mitchell is never forced to leave the Enterprise but, instead, uses his mental powers to divert the ship to an unnamed planet to which he and Elizabeth Dehner transport themselves. Kirk regains control of the ship, then, armed with a "laser rifle," follows them to the planet. Mitchell throws "blue flames" at Kirk, as well as "a gale-force of wind." When Kirk counterattacks, Mitchell is so weakened by the onslaught of energy barbs flying his way from Elizabeth Dehner that he tumbles over the side of a cliff. Kirk offers Mitchell a hand, but the latter is too weak to hang on and plummets to his death.

Sam Peeples later said, "One thing that was put in that I didn't particularly like was the fight at the end. Although I thought it was staged very well, I was opposed to it because I felt that an all-powerful man like Mitchell would not have to resort to physical violence. Gene wanted this physical action at the end of the script, and that's the way it worked out." (136-3)

Roddenberry, knowing what NBC wanted, wrote to Solow:

> It is believed imperative that the final climactic scene, the ultimate battle between the captain and the Esper, be reduced to a <u>physical encounter</u>. (GR2-3)

During the first week in June, Peeples' revised draft of "Where No Man Has Gone Before" and Roddenberry's second draft of "The Omega Glory" were sent to NBC. The first draft of "Mudd's Women" had been delivered to Desilu, but Kandel's obligatory revision had been delayed due to the writer becoming ill.

Solow didn't want to wait. He had read the first try at "Mudd's Women" and, while finding it to be "well written" and "fun," felt strongly that it was completely wrong as a potential pilot. He also believed "The Omega Glory" was a poor contender, later saying that the script "wasn't very good." (161-3)

That left "Where No Man Has Gone Before," the winner by default. On June 10, Solow informed Roddenberry, with a "cc" to the Desilu Board of Directors, that NBC had chosen Samuel Peeples' work over that of *Star Trek*'s creator. For the sake of Roddenberry's pride, he wrote to all concerned:

> From a writing point of view, I must say NBC preferred "The Omega Glory." However, from the point of view of doing a more straight-line adventure show, they felt that the Peeples' script, as a finished film, would better complement the first pilot and would also show the two different ranges in which the series can go. As you know, this is also <u>our</u> feeling. (HS2)

Solow later said that NBC most certainly did *not* prefer "The Omega Glory" from a writing point of view. He had included the lie in his letter only to help Roddenberry save face.

Solow's letter continued:

> NBC has, however, inquired as to what would happen should they much prefer Steve Kandel's script, "Mudd's Women," to Sam Peeples' script. I have told them, that after a reading of the first draft of the Steve Kandel script, it would still be our recommendation that we do Sam Peeples' script, as "Mudd's Women" is a little too light and frothy and would not be a good example of the overall series.... I would appreciate, therefore, Gene, if you would put the Peeples' script into production. I have made NBC aware of the fact that you will be polishing the script yourself. (HS2)

Roddenberry responded to Solow, with a "cc" to all the higher-ups:

> As I have said before, no sensitivity here at all over which script they choose and this office is now proceeding full speed into casting and preparation. And with enthusiasm. Our aim is to make an episode which will sell *Star Trek*. (GR2-4)

James Goldstone, who Roddenberry wanted as director of the first pilot, agreed this time to beam aboard. Regarding Peeples' revised first draft, and the "Elizabeth-Mitchell relationship," Goldstone wrote Roddenberry:

> Need to dramatize Elizabeth's active hostility toward Mitchell in the opening section so that, when the combination of his physical acts and the ESP influence takes over, she has both an internal and external conflict which can have sexual manifestations and thereby help to humanize both characters... or am I being too personal when I suggest that sex has both external and internal conflicts implicit? (JG2-1)

Donald Bays, speaking on behalf of NBC, opposed this idea. After reading a first take on the exchange, where Mitchell refers to the aloof Dr. Elizabeth Dehner as "frigid," Bays wrote Roddenberry:

> The sexual connotation of the word "Frigid" precludes its use with reference to Elizabeth. It is suggested that another word conveying her chilly exterior be found. (DB2)

Roddenberry removed "frigid" and replaced it with "Walking freezer unit." He would also do as Goldstone suggested and turn up the steam between the two espers. But Bays had other concerns, and told Roddenberry:

> As written, the strangulation of the two crewmen is unacceptable. A suggested alternate is that we see the cables rise behind the men and move toward them. Later scenes will reveal that the men have been strangled, but we have avoided showing the act of strangulation. [Further] it is suggested that we only see one crewman. (DB2)

Roddenberry met Bays halfway. He reduced the body count from Lt. Kelso and two crewmen to just Kelso. And while showing the cable encircling Kelso's neck and tightening down on his throat, he had the scene end sooner, before becoming overly graphic.

Regarding the big finale, as Mitchell and Dehner hurl energy bolts at one another, Bays wrote:

> In as much as this scene of violence includes a woman, please exercise great caution and restraint in the clash between Elizabeth and Mitchell. Avoid having her "lifted and smashed back against the rocks, crumpling, broken." It is suggested she simply slump to the ground after having been unable to withstand the force of Mitchell's power. (DB2)

Roddenberry made the change. This would save money and time in production. Regarding Kirk slugging it out with the weakened "god," Bays wrote:

> Please exercise caution on the fight between Kirk and Mitchell. Eliminate the kick to the groin and any other similar brutality. The fight must be as brief as possible and rely on wrestling rather than toe-to-toe slugging. Caution on make-up, if used....The overall violence, however novel, must be handled with restraint and even diminished wherever possible in order to make the episode acceptable for broadcast. (DB2)

Roddenberry took out the kick to the groin. The rest stayed as originally written -- quite graphic for TV of this era.

Roddenberry finished his version of the script on June 16, 1965, designated "Yellow Cover First Draft" -- the first to be sent to the mimeo department and formatted to where each page would translate to roughly a minute of screen time. In an era before word processors and desktop printers and copiers became commonplace, this was not a trivial matter.

James Goldstone read the script that day, and came up with the eerie and effective moment in which Kirk, on the bridge, is monitoring Mitchell in sickbay as he reads a book on a video screen, flashing through the pages of a book faster and faster. Goldstone wrote:

> Suggest Mitchell "knows" Kirk is there without possibility of seeing or hearing. Suggest we use this haunting method of mutation when we can -- starting here in this way and building in whatever frightening ways we can throughout. (JG2-3)

Roddenberry continued rewriting the script, with revised pages clearing his typewriter on June 26 and July 8, 12, 14 and 15, the last coming just four days prior to the start of principal photography. Many highlights of the filmed episode -- the friendship between Kirk and Mitchell, the Captain's difficult decision to strand Mitchell on Delta Vega, the grave that Mitchell opens up in the ground for Kirk, and Mitchell's death, tumbling into that grave as Kirk uses a phaser rifle beam to dislodge a massive rock from a cliff above, which then falls on top of Mitchell, crushing and entombing him -- were all added by Roddenberry, without credit.

Pre-Production
Mid-June through Early July, 1965.
Cast rehearsals, in office: July 15, 1965; on set: July 16.

Joe D'Agosta returned to help with the casting. With a storyline concerning two Enterprise officers gaining mental power and becoming godlike, Roddenberry and D'Agosta knew exactly who they wanted to play one of the two -- the story's antagonist, Lt. Gary Mitchell. James Goldstone, having given direction in the past to the actor they hoped to get, was in complete agreement.

Gary Lockwood was 28 and well acquainted with both Roddenberry and D'Agosta. He had, after all, played the lead in *The Lieutenant*. A veteran on TV series such as *Twelve O'clock High* and *Gunsmoke*, he had also popped up in strong supporting roles in motion pictures, including the fanciful *The Magic Sword* and an Elvis Presley vehicle, *It Happened at the World's Fair.*

Lockwood recalled,

Anne Helm with Gary Lockwood in
The Magic Sword (1962, UA)

"Roddenberry said, 'I made one pilot and it went to New York and there's problems, but this one will have more action, and it will have *you*.' I told him I couldn't do it. I had just gotten the new Kubrick job (*2001: A Space Odyssey*), and I was getting ready to go to England and do this big movie. He said, 'I'd really like you to do it, this character *is* you.' And, you know, he'd been good to me, so I said 'yes.'" (109-3)

The timing worked out. *2001* was set to begin filming later in 1965 (nearly two and a half years before it would finally be released). Lockwood was signed for "Where No Man Has Gone Before" on June 29, 1965, with three guarantees: 1) "Top Guest Star Billing," 2) top guest star rate of $5,000, and 3) that he would not be late for the start of *2001*.

Sally Kellerman, hired to play Dr. Elizabeth Dehner, was also 28. She had been working regularly in television since 1960 with prominent guest spots on dozens of series, including two turns each on *Ben Casey*, *Twelve O'clock High* and *The Outer Limits*. Kellerman signed her contract on July 9, 1965 with a guarantee of $3,000 and "Second Position Guest Star Status." She would later be nominated for an Oscar as "Hot-Lips" Houlihan in the film version of *M*A*S*H*.

**Paul Fix in *To Kill a Mockingbird*
(1962, Universal International Pictures)**

For the ship's doctor, Roddenberry again suggested DeForest Kelley. And, again, he allowed his director to talk him out of this choice. Goldstone had someone else in mind.

Paul Fix won the role of Dr. Mark Piper, the "third man" in the *Star Trek* regular cast. Fix was another familiar face from TV. At 64, he had close to 300 credits in television and films, including the recurring role of Sheriff Micah Torrance, the third cast member on TV's popular *Rifleman*. Fix had often accepted third billing, prompting him to write *Third Man through the Door*, the book that, ironically, influenced Malachi Throne to turn down the very same role on *Star Trek* -- back when the character was named Dr. Phillip Boyce, in "The Cage." The fixed price for Fix was $1,250.

Paul Carr, 31, was booked to play the ship's helmsman, the ill-fated Lee Kelso. Carr already had 100 TV and film appearances behind him, including multiple trips to *Twelve O'clock High*, *Voyage to the Bottom of the Sea* and *The Virginian*. He would make history, of a sort, by being the first member of the starship Enterprise to die in the line of duty. For this he was paid $1,500, very good money in 1964.

Andrea Dromm was the young, pretty model hired to play Yeoman Smith. The 23-year-old was brand new on the scene in Hollywood but had achieved national recognition as a top New York model with a pair of successful TV and print ad campaigns. She was the perky stewardess in a 1963 National Airlines commercial who exclaimed, "Is that any way to run an airline? You bet it is!" The following year, as a Clairol girl, she appeared in their "Summer

Blonde" TV spots. Her contract for the pilot was for $450, covering four days work.

Lloyd Haynes, 31, an African-American making his television debut, played Communications Officer Lt. Alden. He was present on the bridge, but little more. Roddenberry expected the character could become worthy of attention if and when there was a series. For now, Haynes had a couple lines of dialogue and a half-dozen "reaction shots." For this he was paid $400.

Rounding out the cast, Roddenberry and Peeples had written in two new characters, both having the potential of becoming recurring roles. One was the ship's engineer.

James Doohan, 35, with over 100 TV and film credits, first journeyed into science fiction in 1952 for an episode of *Tales of Tomorrow*. In 1953 Doohan spent a TV season playing Phil Mitchell on a cheapie syndicated serial *Space Command*, and made appearances on *The Twilight Zone*, *The Outer Limits* and two episodes of the brand new *Voyage to the Bottom of the Sea*. It was James Goldstone's idea to bring Doohan in for a reading.

"I was asked to come and read one Saturday morning," Doohan said in 1968, for fanzine *Inside Star Trek,* issue 5. "I had met the director of the pilot about ten days before and I had done some accents for him. I didn't get that job, but he wanted me to read for the *Star Trek* people. So I sat down there and did about five or six different accents."

Doohan recalled how Roddenberry had asked him which accent he thought best fit the part of engineer. "Well, if you want an engineer," Doohan responded, "it had better be a Scotsman, because, in my experience, Scotsmen are the best. They've invented so many things, especially to do with ships." (52-1)

Andrea Dromm with Shatner
(NBC publicity still; courtesy of Gerald Gurian)

James Doohan in NBC Publicity photo
for second pilot (Courtesy of Gerald Gurian)

Roddenberry agreed to Doohan's choice for the accent. He even allowed Doohan to name his character -- Montgomery Scott. Doohan's agent named his price -- $750.

In Hollywood, when it rains, it pours. Days later, Doohan was offered regular work back at *Voyage to the Bottom of the Sea*, this time to play the Chief of the Seaview (replacing character actor Henry Kulky, who passed away toward the end of the first season). But, having just committed to a long-shot called *Star Trek*, Doohan had to say "no" to producer

Irwin Allen.

The other new character added into the script: astrophysicist, Sulu.

George Takei, 28, began his life as an actor when he answered an ad to do the English dubbing for several characters in a Japanese movie being prepared for U.S. release. It was called *Gigantis: the Fire Monster*. The following year, he repeated the task for *Rodan: the Flying Monster*.

"I was kind of lucky," Takei said in 1968, for *Inside Star Trek*, # 8. "Many people complain about being of minority groups and so forth. But I think the very fact that I have this face opened a lot of doors for me at a time when it wouldn't have opened for other people."

Among the ethnic types Takei was cast for: parts on *Hawaiian Eye*, *I Spy* and "Made in Japan," for *Playhouse 90*.

Nimoy with Takei for NBC publicity photo taken for the second pilot (Courtesy of Gerald Gurian)

Takei remembered his first meeting at *Star Trek* vividly. All he knew then was that a producer from Desilu had called his agent about the casting of a pilot. He showed up at the production offices and was greeted by Dorothy Fontana, who he remembered as having a "soft, welcoming smile," which he much appreciated. Takei, you see, was nervous. Although he had been keeping busy as a guest actor, this was the first time he had been considered for a recurring role in a series.

Takei's first impression of Roddenberry: "A large, genial man who rose up from behind a desk and came forward to greet me with the affability of a country squire.... I instantly liked this man. He was unlike any other producer I had ever met -- spontaneous, unaffected." (171-4)

Takei was also immediately taken with Roddenberry's vision for *Star Trek*, saying, "In his disarmingly amiable way, he had me dazzled. I was swept away, not just by the images, but by his soaring ideals." (171-4)

For his new job soaring through the stars, Takei received $375. Cast and crew were now ready to go "Where No Man Has Gone Before."

Production Diary
Filmed July 19, 20, 21, 22, 23, 26, 27, 28 & 29 (½ day), 1965
(Planned as a 7 day production; took 8 ½ days; total cost $355,000).

Monday, July 19, 1965. The day the second pilot began filming, "(I Can't Get No) Satisfaction" by the Rolling Stones was the most played song on U.S. radio stations. The *Mary Poppins* soundtrack had top spot on the LP charts. The week's highest rated TV show aired the night before -- *Bonanza* on NBC. And Gene Roddenberry received two telegrams. The first was from Robert Butler, director of "The Cage," reading, "Good luck today. I hope all goes well... *and it sells.*" The second, from Oscar Katz and Herb Solow, read, "Do us a favor and make it good this time."

July 20, 1965, Day 2 of filming, and the first day Shatner sat in the command chair, for Scene 104, Take 1 (Courtesy of Gerald Gurian)

Filming began at 8 a.m. on Stage 15 at Desilu Culver City, the same stage where Enterprise sets had been shot for "The Cage." The actors, of course, arrived much earlier, for makeup, breakfast and rehearsal. Shatner's call time was 6:30 a.m. Nimoy had to be there by six for his ear-job. And this is how it would be every day the *Star Trek* series was filmed.

First up were scenes in the rec room, where Kirk and Spock play a game of three-dimensional chess and give a little back-story on the pointed-eared half-human. Next, while the rec room was being transformed into the briefing room, the company moved to the corridors for all the scripted scenes in these areas. Transporter room sequences followed, including beaming a drugged Gary Mitchell down to Delta Vega. Shooting then moved to the transformed briefing room where Kirk holds a meeting with staff heads and argues the fate of Mitchell with Spock. It had been a productive day. At 6:55 p.m., the camera stopped rolling and the cast was released to have their makeup removed and turn in their wardrobe, while the production crew "wrapped" the set.

Day 2, Tuesday, July 20: Shooting began in the turbolift elevator, moving onto the bridge. All of Day 3 and part of Day 4 were also spent here on what was certainly one of the most spectacular sets in 1960s TV.

In the latter half of Day 4 and for the first half of Day 5 the action moved to sickbay, where the world gets its first glimpse of an e-book (as Gary Mitchell reads from a video screen), then to Stage 17 for the "Int. Delta Vega Control Room" set.

With production already starting to fall behind, the company was struck by an attack of "killer bees."

High above the actors, among the seldom-used catwalks of the ancient soundstage, a colony of wasps had nested in the eaves. The hot lights irritated the

Day 2. The new Captain ... between takes (Courtesy of Gerald Gurian)

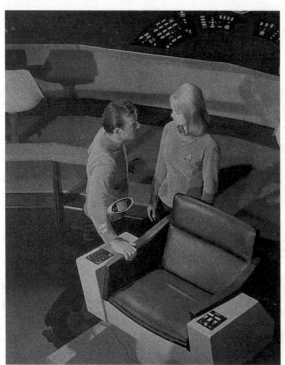

Still photographer shot taken of Shatner with Andrea Dromm from the wasp infested catwalks (Courtesy of Gerald Gurian)

temperamental insects, causing them to swarm. Shatner was stung first, on the eyelid. The area around his eye swelled to "softball-sized proportions." Fortunately, this was Friday; he had until Monday for the swelling to subside. Makeup hid the rest.

It was reported Sally Kellerman was also hit, but not in her face. "Luckily, all her shots that day were done standing," Justman quipped. "Even though the sting must have hurt, to her credit, she never complained -- not even when she sat down." (94-8)

On Day 6, Monday, July 26, the wasps were gone but another "casualty" would strike the Delta Vega control room set with the strangulation of Lt. Kelso. Paul Carr, playing Kelso, said, "I was very angry that I was going to be killed. I wanted to be on that show... there was that wonderful feeling that I was on a winner. I really liked it." (30)

With makeup covering Shatner's swollen eyelid, the company moved onto the "Int. Delta Vega Security Area" set. For the first scene, as Mitchell threatens Kirk and Spock from inside his cell, standing beside them is the yet-to-be-named character played by Eddie Paskey. It was the first of 59 *Star Trek* appearances for Paskey, who served as Shatner's stand-in for the lighting set-ups, making him one of only five cast members (along with Shatner, Nimoy, Doohan and Takei) to go from pilot to series.

Paskey recalled, "Greg Peters remembered me from *The Lucy Show*, where I had done some bit parts, and a few other Desilu things, and he got me onto the second pilot. It was just a non-speaking role, nothing major, but I walked onto the set and there was Paul Fix, an old fixture in TV. And Gary Lockwood, who'd just had a series. And William Shatner, of course, I recognized. So it was kinda neat, me being a real novice and I'm on the same set with these people. And there was this little thing going on because Sally Kellerman wasn't wearing a bra under her uniform, and it was pretty apparent. I remember someone from the network was there, frowning about that. But this was well into the production, too late to really do anything about it, so they finally decided to let it go and we got the shot." (135-2)

Later that day, the company had a brief stay on the "Ext. Planet & Lithium Plant Beam Down Area." In post-production, this would serve as a matte shot to be combined with Albert Whitlock's impressive painting of the futuristically eerie Lithium Cracking Station on Delta Vega.

Whitlock, 50, had started in the 1930s, working for Alfred Hitchcock, and stayed with him for the rest of the director's films, providing matte paintings, creating miniatures and designing special effects. He also worked extensively for Disney. Whitlock and his eight-man team were responsible for all of *Star Trek*'s matte paintings, including the fortress on

Rigel VII, as seen in "The Cage."

With Day 7 came additional shots in the maximum security area as Elizabeth Dehner transforms from human to godlike and Kirk and Spock are zapped unconscious.

This was Kellerman's first day wearing the silver contact lenses. Lockwood had already worn them for days and his eyes were suffering. Today, with computer generated imaging (CGI), turning eyes to silver is child's play, but 1965 was a different story. Robert Justman had found only a handful of optometry suppliers still making old fashioned sclera lenses (which covered the entire exposed eyeball) and none of these corporate firms were willing to create the silver lenses needed for Gary Lockwood and Sally Kellerman. Should something go wrong, a lawsuit could follow. However, one of the contact lens makers did give Justman the name of a competitor -- an independent lens maker who was cantankerous enough to consider the job. Justman remembered John Roberts as a "gruff" old-school pro who liked a challenge. Roberts' solution was to crumple tinfoil and laminate it between two layers of lenses. A small pinprick in the foil would allow the actors to see. That was the theory, anyway.

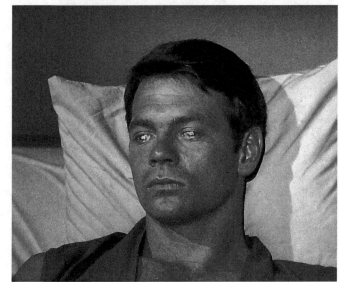

Gary Lockwood enduring the silver contact lenses (Lincoln Enterprises film trim, courtesy of Gerald Gurian)

The lenses were thick. Keeping them in the eyes for long amounts of time caused heat to build up, creating immense discomfort for the person wearing them. Sally Kellerman managed fairly well, having worn regular contact lenses for years and only wearing the specialty lenses for two days. Lockwood was a different story.

"Gary couldn't stand it," Kellerman said. "He'd have them in for one second and he'd scream 'Get these lenses out of my eyes!'" (97-1)

Lockwood said, "It was the most miserable six days of my life. I'm not exaggerating. I couldn't wear those silver lenses very long. After five or six minutes, I'd say, 'You have to take them out!' And I'm kind of a tough cowboy guy, but my eyes just become so irritated after a period of time. It was the worst." (109-3)

Beyond the discomfort, the lenses were hard to see through. Lockwood admitted, "I was almost a little embarrassed, because I never saw any of what we were doing. I mean, I had these eye lenses in, and I did everything by rote. And I thought, 'How is this going to come out?'" (109-3)

A widely shared bit of *Star Trek* lore claims Lockwood could only see who was standing before him by tilting his head back and looking down his nose, and that this pose inadvertently added to the godlike presence of his character. It did add to the character, but Lockwood told this author it had nothing to do with the lenses.

"Tilting my head was a selection that I made to show arrogance," he said. "Think about it. You want to show arrogance, you don't bow your head; you raise your head up.

There's certain things a human being recognizes in other human beings that influence what we think of them. That posture implies a sense of superiority; arrogance." (109-3)

Later on Day 7, only Shatner, Kellerman and a suffering Lockwood were needed as the company moved onto the massive Ext. Planet set, with Ext. Planet Locales 1, 2 and 3. Since this was filmed at the spacious Culver City facility and not in Hollywood where the remainder of the series was shot, Delta Vega's surface has a more impressive scale than the worlds the Enterprise would visit in the future. The soundstage, built in the era of Hollywood's silent pictures, was immense.

By Day 8, Goldstone and company were shooting beyond the schedule, spending Desilu money which had not been earmarked for this venture, and it was now apparent filming would roll into a ninth day of production. This alone could provide enough reason for the old guard at the studio to override Lucille Ball and refuse the series, even if the network wanted it. Therefore, the shooting pace was increased to an unheard of 30 camera set-ups for the day. Justman recalled, "It was astounding to move so quickly. But we had to do it because Desilu was a cheap outfit. I remember we were going crazy trying to finish." (94-4)

NBC publicity photo taken on Day 8 of production
(Courtesy of Gerald Gurian)

The previous seven days, production began at 8 a.m. and wrapped between 6:30 and 7:10 p.m.. At 7:10 on the eighth day the end was nowhere in sight. The big climactic fight between Kirk and Mitchell was only at the halfway mark. Shatner and Lockwood made a good show of it. Stuntman Hal Needham stood in for Lockwood during the more elaborate punches, falls, and throws. Paul Baxley, who would work often for *Star Trek*, did the same for Shatner.

The fight, despite instruction to the contrary from NBC's Donald Bay, was brutal. Sand and Styrofoam got kicked around to the point where it covered the dolly tracks laid out for the camera, causing further delays. Goldstone remembered, "We had a 40- or-50-foot dolly shot, and we only had one [stage hand] walking in front of the dolly, sweeping the Styrofoam out from under the wheels. But he could only get one side or the other." (75-2)

Some say the man with the broom suddenly had a helper -- Lucille Ball. As the stunned crew watched Lucy sweeping, she finally broke the silence and said, "What do I have to do to get you to finish?!" (94-8)

Whether the Lucy story was true of not, it is a fact that the camera rolled until 9:37 p.m. By the time makeup had been removed, costumes sent to the cleaners and the stage wrapped, it was past 10. Most involved had just put in a 17-hour day.

Day 9, Thursday, July 29, 1965. With no actors needed, Goldstone and the production unit returned for "camera tie-down shots" on the bridge, the transporter room, sickbay, the Delta Vega central control room and various Ext. Planet locales. These shots were to be used in conjunction with the camera footage that included the actors, getting materialized, dematerialized or zapped, by the optical effects team.

At 4:17 p.m., the director finally called out, "That's a wrap," meaning the crew was free to continue working, wrapping up the wires and securing the set.

Post-Production
Delivered to editing July 30, 1965. Music Score recorded November 29, 1965.
Cleared post / shipped to NBC: January, 1966.

The pilot was far from being finished. The studio's anxiety increased over the time Roddenberry and his post-production team took to film the photographic effects, create matte shots, then edit and score the film -- a staggering five months.

Alexander Courage, who wrote and conducted the score for "The Cage," returned to perform the same duties here. He explained the genesis for the theme music, saying, "I based the [theme] on an old Hebridean tune from the outer islands of Scotland. I wanted something that had a long, long feel to it, and I wanted to put it over a fast-moving accompaniment to get the adventure and the speed and so forth. There was an old song called 'Beyond the Blue Horizon' -- they used to play a double-time accompaniment to it, while this thing was singing over the top, so that's what I really wanted to do. I wanted to make all of the scales go way out, and I wanted the intervals to be long, and I wanted to have a kind of exotic feel to it." (37-4)

Jack Cookerly, a musician who contributed to the recording sessions, said, "I developed the first electronic guitar [special electronic effects], of all things. Nobody knew what it was but Sandy had heard it and I'd shown him some of the things it could do so he wanted to use it on the score, and that gave it a quite different sound. You have six synthesizers, one for each string, and you can make various different sounds on any string -- you can have the string tone or something like a trumpet or a flute or make it play an octave higher and it could make some strange sounds that you can't make on a keyboard." (35a)

Regarding the "sonar pings" heard at the outset of the main titles, an early version of the synthesizer was used. Cookerly called it his "magic box." He said, "I made it out of a Hammond organ, took it all apart, and then it had all new parts in it and made all kinds of strange sounds. It was almost a mechanical sound, almost sound effects, and Sandy Courage wrote something, and the instrument had a melodic purpose in the score but as it changed it became more like a sound effect." (35a)

Fried Steiner, later to be hired to alternate writing the scores for episodes with Courage and composer Gerald Fried, said, "I was quite shocked when I first heard it, because I thought it was nothing that I had conceived of, and it wasn't well received at first, because it was such a sort of a far-out idea. But of course, subsequently, you know, it's become a standard." (168-1)

Darrell Anderson, busy running the front office of the Anderson Company, left much of the post work on *Star Trek* to his brother Howard, who brought in long-time Warner Brothers cartoon animator Lloyd Vaughan to create the various phaser blasts, lightning bolts and force field glows. Lloyd's brother Boyd designed and executed the title sequences. Bob Ryder photographed the Enterprise and other stellar properties. Gary Crandall was the key optical camera operator, one of his contributions being the filming of the transporter effects. And Lou Cusley was key grip, the man in charge of assembling tracking systems and dollies. This was the Howard Anderson Company team for this pilot and future episodes of *Star Trek* -- a small but talented group of technicians who worked long, hard hours and invented optical effect techniques that were used for years to come.

Howard Anderson Company filming the large model on January 23, 1965
(Courtesy of Gerald Gurian)

Anderson designed and realized the composited images that made up the highly dimensional multi-layered field of stars coming toward the camera, a giant step forward from the flat star fields used in most sci-fi space shows. Howard Anderson, Jr. said, "[The moving stars] were just as much, or probably more, trouble and took more experimenting than any of the rest of the problems that were presented to us with doing *Star Trek*. I don't think anybody had seen moving stars before, or stars moving at the speed of light. We tried everything, but as soon as anything moved close to camera, of course, [the] stars looked like meatballs.... We finally evolved a method, [but it] took us a long, long time. It was a toughie." (2-1)

Anderson remembered the filming of the Enterprise as being the major challenge. "We had to constantly stop shooting after a short while because the lights would heat up the ship. We'd turn the lights on and get our exposure levels and balance our arc lights to illuminate the main body of the ship and then we'd turn the ship's lights off until they cooled down. Then we'd turn them on and shoot some shots all in one pass." (2-2)

James Goldstone scoffed: "We planned the opticals with Howard Anderson, and he was a wonderful talent, but I'll go to my grave complaining about optical effects. They never look exactly the way you want them to, you can't hold on them for too long in a shot, and you're forced to wait for them to come back from the lab. I made my cut of the episode, then I re-cut it with Gene, and we were *still* waiting for the damned opticals. By the time they arrived I was working on [the TV series] *Iron Horse* and I had to come back at night to the cutting room to look at them." (75-1)

Besides the various detailed Enterprise flybys, transporter effects and matte shots, the Anderson brothers created the rainbow barrier at the edge of the galaxy, force field effects, phaser rifle beams and the lightning bolts Lockwood and Kellerman threw at one another. It was a tall order for 1965. The total bill came to $17,400 (130 grand in 2013).

John Foley replaced Leo Shreve as editor. A Desilu man, he had cut episodes for *The*

Untouchables, *The Lucy Show* and, right after this job, the pilot for *Mission: Impossible*.

Alexander Courage returned to handle the score. Roddenberry had been ecstatic over the music Courage created for the first pilot, and wrote to him on March 3, 1965:

> Dear Sandy: The reaction to the music you composed and directed for *Star Trek* has been so universally outstanding that I thought I owed you this letter. What we have had is not just an occasional compliment but rather consistent praise. You successfully avoided all of the stylizations and other traps of past and present [science fiction]; in short, you did really outstanding work. You've made a lot of admirers and friends during this job.

Release / Reaction

**The original, unaired opening to Act 1, as it appeared in the pilot film
(Courtesy of Gerald Gurian)**

"I was very happy with it," James Goldstone said. "I was very proud of the work we were able to do. We, being Gene especially, Bobby Justman, and the main actors who later became the main stars. It was a very collaborative effort." (75-3)

Goldstone also gave mention to Matt Jefferies and Bill Theiss, saying, "The whole [look of the] picture was really designed by Matt Jefferies.... The costuming concept: we brought Theiss in, and the whole velour look was 'the thing' that had just started that week. You didn't see shadows on it, you didn't see wrinkles in it, and it had a sense of ease, comfort, and practicality." (75-2)

Gary Lockwood was less sure they had hit the bull's-eye when filming finished. He said, "Look, you come to work, and this is a scene where you become god-like. There isn't any manual on that. I mean, there isn't some book. How does one play god? And I remember at the time being a little bit embarrassed, thinking, 'How is this going to be, me becoming this kind of weird god?' I wasn't seeing it -- *literally*. I was acting in the dark. And then one day Roddenberry saw me in Beverly Hills and he said, 'I'm sending a car for you, because I know that you won't watch our show and I'm going to have you see it at the studio.' So, when I saw *Star Trek*, I was alone in a room. Can you imagine -- watching it on a big screen, in a screening room by yourself? And I thought it came out better than in my head. My attitude was, 'Okay, this is pretty cool.' I wasn't embarrassed anymore." (109-3)

Leonard Nimoy couldn't predict the series' future but he was convinced something magical had happened in regard to the development of the character he played, directly as a result of the interaction between him and Shatner. He said, "I really thought that there was a chemistry between us that made a lot of sense. I didn't know where I was with Jeff Hunter. I was floundering when working with him. Jeff was playing Captain Pike as a very thoughtful, kind of worried, kind of angst-ridden nice guy thinking his way through a problem, and I, as Spock, couldn't find a space.... [Bill] brought with him a great deal of zest and passion. [His] Captain Kirk was a swashbuckling Errol Flynn type of hero; he played the role with a great deal of energy and élan, and wasn't afraid to take chances.... That energy was vital for the show and made it possible for me to finally find a niche for my role." (128-13)

"Where No Man Has Gone Before" was finally delivered to NBC just after New Year's Day, 1966. The final damages: The mandated seven production days turned into nine, a one-month post-production schedule stretched into five, the estimated cost of $216,000 became a very real cost of $355,000. Regardless of NBC's decision, the Board of Directors who served the president of Desilu wanted to end *Star Trek* right then and there.

***

Regardless of Desilu's concerns, "Where No Man Has Gone Before" would make it onto the air over NBC, twice. For its first broadcast, Joan Crosby reviewed the episode on September 22, 1966 for the syndicated column *TV Scout*. Among the newspapers to carry the review was the *Appleton Post-Crescent*, serving Appleton, Wisconsin. Crosby wrote:

> *Star Trek* runs its pilot tonight, a fine piece of science fiction. This show that has some excellent scenes and ponders what happens when man tries to play God. Gary Lockwood and Sally Kellerman guest star. Lockwood is an old friend of William Shatner who, after a collision in deep space, develops strange powers and eyes that look like they are made of shiny silver. Shatner, searching for clues as to what destroyed a spaceship 200 years earlier, concludes that it was a strange being like Lockwood, who must now obviously be destroyed. But how? And can he do it in time?

Steven H. Scheuer reviewed it for his syndicated *TV Key Previews*. Among the newspapers to carry the review was the *Galveston Daily News*, in Galveston, Texas. Scheuer wrote:

> The kids and science fiction fans will enjoy this yarn about an incident that occurs aboard the super-spacecraft Enterprise, in which one of the crew is transformed into a mutation with limitless powers. Gary Lockwood plays the almost super-being with assist from the makeup man -- silver contact lenses that give him a strange, eerie quality.

And then came the ratings. "Where No Man Has Gone Before" won or tied for first position in its time slot.

RATINGS / Nielsen 30-Market report for Thursday, Sept. 22, 1966:

8:30 - 9 p.m., 58.9% households using TVs.	Rating:	Share:
NBC: *Star Trek* (first half)	**20.0**	**33.3%**
ABC: *The Tammy Grimes Show*	14.7	24.5%
CBS: *My Three Sons*	18.9	31.5%
Independent stations:	8.8	10.7%

9 - 9:30 p.m., 60.1% households using TVs.
NBC:	*Star Trek* (second half)	19.4	31.0%
ABC:	***Bewitched***	**19.9**	**31.8%**
CBS:	*CBS Thursday Night Movie* (start)	19.1	30.5%
Independent stations:		10.0	6.71%

According to A.C. Nielsen, *Star Trek* was the clear winner from 8:30 to 9 p.m. From 9 to 9:30 p.m., the race was too close to call, with all three networks within a fraction of a ratings point of one another. (For the ratings reports for the second airing, see Chapter 38.)

7

The Calm Before the Storm

After posing for this publicity shot, Shatner returned to work for other networks and studios
(Courtesy of Gerald Gurian)

Between July 1965 and February 1966, while waiting to learn if there would be a *Star Trek*, William Shatner had the lead guest star role in segments of *Twelve O'clock High*, *The Fugitive*, *The Big Valley*, *Bob Hope Presents the Chrysler Theatre* and *Gunsmoke*. He also accepted a limited recurring role in *Dr. Kildare*, prominently featured in six episodes as Dr. Carl Noyes.

Leonard Nimoy had supporting roles in *The Virginian*, *Combat!*, *A Man Called Shenandoah*, *Daniel Boone*, *Get Smart*, *Gunsmoke* and, once a distributor had finally been secured, *Death Watch*, the art house film he starred in and co-produced with Vic Morrow.

George Takei found himself 11 acting assignments between July and February, including a role in the same episode of *Bob Hope Presents the Chrysler Theatre* that William Shatner appeared in. While on the set, Takei enthusiastically approached Shatner to say hello. It took the lead guest star a moment to remember the bit player. After all, Takei had appeared in only two scenes with Shatner in "Where No Man Has Gone Before" and the filming had taken place several months earlier. It was a polite exchange but Takei was disappointed that he had made so little impression on the man he hoped to call "Captain."

James Doohan also stayed busy. He appeared on *A Man Called Shenandoah*, *Bewitched*, *Blue Light*, *Laredo*, *The Man from U.N.C.L.E.*, *The Virginian*, and twice each on *The F.B.I.* and *The Fugitive*. And he had a recurring role on *Peyton Place*, and appeared in a feature film - *Scalplock*.

Roddenberry, too, was busy. Desilu put him to work producing a pair of pilots -- one he cared about, the other, according to Herb Solow, he did not.

The important one to Roddenberry was "Police Story," which he also wrote. It starred future *Star Trek* players Steve Ihnat, Grace Lee Whitney, DeForest Kelley and Malachi Throne. The director was Vincent McEveety, who had worked on *The Lieutenant* and who would also journey into *Star Trek*. Malachi Throne said, "It was unfortunate that it didn't go because it was one of the first police stories, and, since Gene had that background, it had an authenticity about it that the others didn't quite have." (173-2)

The second pilot, "The Long Hunt of April Savage," had been created and written by Sam Rolfe, Roddenberry's former boss and friend from *Have Gun -- Will Travel*. In the lead was Robert Lansing, who would be brought back for a *Star Trek* episode ("Assignment: Earth"). Otherwise, Solow said, Roddenberry didn't take to the assignment. The Desilu exec claimed Roddenberry was "coasting along" and "halfheartedly producing" Rolfe's pilot and believed his only interest was in picking up a paycheck.

Dorothy Fontana, Roddenberry's secretary during this period, said, "Bullshit. Sam Rolfe was a long-time friend of Gene Roddenberry's. He [Gene] was happy to be able to help on 'The Long Hunt of April Savage' project when Sam had to be in England to work on another project. [Sam] trusted Roddenberry to produce his pilot for him." (64-4b)

The harsh criticism from Solow does seem unwarranted considering that the pilot was successful. After seeing it, ABC ordered a series and placed it on the network's fall schedule. The series ended up not making the cut, but this was clearly not a result of Roddenberry's production work.

Also, contrary to accusations made by Roddenberry's unauthorized biographer Joel Engel that the two men had a serious falling out over "April Savage," Rolfe and Roddenberry remained friends and Rolfe even received a pair of writing assignments on future Roddenberry series -- one for *Star Trek: the Next Generation*, the other for *Star Trek: Deep Space Nine*.

Even if not between Roddenberry and Rolfe, there was some bad blood to arise as a result of the filming of "The Long Hunt of April Savage." Robert Justman, who was working on the production as associate producer, remembered the incident. While filming near Big Bear Lake, a network man named Harve Bennett dropped by the location. This irritated Roddenberry, who ordered Justman to throw the meddling ABC junior executive off the set. Bennett would return into Roddenberry's life 15 years later to take *Star Trek* away from its creator and become producer of the big screen movie series, starting with *Star Trek II: The Wrath of Khan*. A line from that movie offers an apt commentary on the relationship: "Revenge is a dish best served cold."

***

In late February, 1966, "good news" arrived at Desilu: CBS wanted *Mission: Impossible*, NBC wanted *Star Trek*, and ABC wanted *April Savage*. All three series were to premiere in the fall. It had been an expensive gamble for the studio. Desilu produced 22 pilots in 1964 and 1965 and only three were "picked up." And of these three, two were shows that many at the studio didn't even want.

Desilu suddenly had a new agenda: terminate Oscar Katz, the executive responsible for all the failed pilots and -- worse -- the two potentially expensive hour-long ones which succeeded. The headline in the March 9, 1966 issue of *Variety* read, "Oscar Katz Calls Quits at Desilu." In a statement, Katz cited "personal reasons" compelling him to move on to, as *Variety* told it, "other projects in other areas." Katz said he had asked for and received his contractual release. The *Variety* story also noted that Herb Solow would supervise the production of the new series. The new Vice President of Programs later said, "Oscar Katz was my boss, but his relationship with Lucy [Ball] and the board soured as they realized Oscar's lack of studio experience made him only a titular chief operating officer." (161-3)

The second item in the studio's agenda: convince Lucy to keep the half-hour western *April Savage* and, because of her relationship with CBS, perhaps go forward with the potentially costly *Mission: Impossible*, but to let go of *Star Trek*, a series whose costs could sink the studio.

A board meeting was called. Financial VP Edwin Holly told Lucy she couldn't afford all of these atypical series. Production VP Argyle Nelson agreed. One witness to the meeting said Nelson called Bruce Geller "that crazy college kid" and Roddenberry "that crazy ex-cop." Fred Ball, Lucy's brother, believed that real estate was the way to go. Buy hotels, not starships. Business Affairs VP Bernard Weitzman was the only Desilu executive Herb Solow remembered as being pro-*Star Trek*.

The meeting was going badly. But Lucy was determined to follow Desi's plan for the studio. She listened to all the griping, then turned away from the naysayers and gave Solow a nod of her head.

That was all *Star Trek* needed. A nod from Lucille Ball.

On March, 2, 1966, *Daily Variety* printed the "First Round" fall schedules for the three networks. NBC had picked Thursday at 8:30 p.m. for *Star Trek*. On this rough draft of the primetime schedules, ABC had slated *April Savage*. This would later change, with *Savage* dropped in favor of *The Tammy Grimes Show,* the latter to be partnered with *Bewitched* as ABC's competition against *Star Trek*.

On March 6, 1966, both *Star Trek* and *Mission: Impossible* were assigned space at the Desilu's Hollywood facility, where studio heads could closely monitor their progress -- or lack of it. Filming on that lot for the fall were the half-hour sitcoms *The Lucy Show*, *The Andy Griffith Show*, *Gomer Pyle U.S.M.C.*, *My Three Sons*, *Hogan's Heroes*, *Family Affair*, *That Girl* and *Hey Landlord*. Also shooting at the Hollywood facility: *Lassie*, *Rango* and, when it was in town, *I Spy*. And then there was *Mannix*, a new pilot to be owned by the studio and produced by Bruce Geller. It was going to be a tight fit but Herb Solow arranged for *Star Trek* and *Mission: Impossible* to each get a pair of soundstages and 10 office spaces for their staffs.

***

The *Star Trek* staff was going to have to hit the pavement running. NBC was starting their new season a week early and needed the premiere episode of *Star Trek* ready in the first days in September. The network also wanted to preview a handful of episodes for audience testing to help it choose which would lead off the series. The deadline for the delivery of these was set for mid-August, just five months away.

Robert Justman stayed on as associate producer, Morris Chapnick as Roddenberry's production assistant, Matt Jefferies as the Art Director, George Merhoff on lighting, William Theiss on wardrobe, Wah Chang with gadgets and monsters, Howard Anderson Company at work on photographic effects, and Harvey Lynn of the RAND Corporation, as well as De Forest Research, to read scripts and provide technical notes.

Kellam de Forest worked with all the Desilu shows, but none as hard as he did with *Star Trek*. He and his staff would search through story outlines and scripts for anything remotely wrong. And they did this in a world without the Internet. Their tools: books, magazines, newspapers, phone directories, government reports, private reports, any kind of reports. Herb Solow later commented, "Kellam had a field day with *Star Trek* because Kellam believed everything -- *everything* -- must be accurate!" (161-3)

De Forest, born in 1926, had originally tried for a career as a TV writer, selling a few stories to westerns such as *Yancy Derringer* and *The Adventures of Jim Bowie*.

Pete Sloman, who was working as a file clerk at De Forest Research, and would later be promoted to take over *Star Trek*, said, "Kellam had majored in history at Yale. And when he got out he wanted to get into television, but he didn't know what to do because he had no background in anything that was something that television might be interested in. And then he was doing some sort of historical research and the producers of *Profiles in Courage* went to him. [President] Kennedy had allowed the use of his book [*Profiles in Courage*] as something to be dramatized, if it was historically accurate. And so they got the idea that Kellam de Forest, as a history major and somebody who was really very fast with history, could provide the historical background for what they wanted to do, which he did, and that's how he got into the field. This was in the late 1950s, so that was when Kellam started doing this. He got space at Desilu Studios, right next to the old prop department. We worked on *The Lucy Show*; *Mission: Impossible, Hogan's Heroes, Mannix, I Spy*; all kinds of stuff. At one point, we were doing close to two dozen shows. And Kellam did some of the very first *Star Trek* episodes. He did the pilot and maybe a few others. But Kellam was not a scientifically oriented person and, in time, would be looking for others, such as myself and Joan Pearce, to take on *Star Trek*." (158a)

Joe D'Agosta, who had unofficially helped with booking talent before, was Roddenberry's only choice as casting director. D'Agosta remembered, "Gene found out from Herb Solow, who was running Desilu, that they needed a new head of casting for the studio, and he sold him on the idea that it should be me." (43-4)

Solow checked in with the producers of the other two studio owned series -- *The Lucy Show* and *Mission: Impossible* -- to get their approval. D'Agosta recalled, "I'd worked for Bruce [Geller] on *Rawhide*, and he said, 'There's nobody else.' But my main interview was with Gary Morton [*Mister* Lucille Ball], because Lucy had to approve me. And she sat in the corner, sort of in the dark, while Gary interviewed me and she observed from an observation point. And, at one point, she said, 'Here's all I want to know -- Lucy is...' -- she talked about herself in the third person -- '... a big-boned person and needs strong men to make her look feminine.' And I said, 'Well, that's cool; I could do that.' Then I said, 'Can I ask *you* a question? How do you feel about women or girls that are prettier than you?' She hesitated, then looked at me and said, 'Bring 'em on. I'll eat 'em alive.' And I got the job." (43-4)

Since D'Agosta would be hiring actors for three series, he was able to offer multiple appearance deals, which kept costs down. He said, "The only rate you're locked into is scale. And most actors that you hire are 'working actors,' so they're getting more than scale. So I came up with a two or three picture contract -- or understanding -- with the actors. I'd make a deal and say, 'Okay, instead of paying $1,500, I'll give you $1,000 [per appearance] and guarantee two or three shows. And, as long as I was above scale, I could make any kind of deal I wanted." (43-4)

Dorothy Fontana remained as Roddenberry's secretary. She would also write scripts. No one knew it yet but *Star Trek* had found one of its guiding lights.

***

Dorothy Catherine Fontana grew up outside of Paterson, New Jersey. Her house was on an acre of land, where her father built a brooder coop and a small one-level building for the raising of chickens and rabbits during the hard New Jersey winters. Fontana said, "Our neighbors raised chickens, ducks, donkeys, etc., but it was (then) a typical suburban town – just a tad more rural than city." (64-4b)

Fontana spent her time reading from a very early age, and wanting to write. She said, "As I got older, when I was in the seventh and eighth grades, I was writing stories that were adventures with scary elements that featured all my friends and me." (64-2)

After college, Fontana went job hunting and spotted an ad for the New York offices of Screen Gems. The company's president, Ralph Cohn, nephew of Columbia Pictures' Harry Cohn, was looking for a secretary. Fontana was persistent in calling until she was finally granted an interview. Cohn, impressed by Fontana's skills as well as her spunk, put her to work. Fontana remembered, "The first time a television script crossed my desk, I said, 'I can do this.' That's when I got really interested in writing for television." (64-2)

D.C. Fontana, circa 1960s
(Courtesy of Dorothy Fontana)

Once Fontana realized that the main suppliers of programming for TV were relocating to Los Angeles, she also decided to make the move. Landing in LA in 1959, she learned that Revue Studios, the maker of *Alfred Hitchcock Presents*, *Wagon Train* and *Leave It to Beaver*, needed typists. It was a nowhere job for most but, once inside the studio system, Fontana kept a watchful eye on the job postings. One was for a western called *Overland Trail*. The producer needed a secretary, and that brought Fontana to Samuel Peeples. He became more than a boss; he was also a mentor.

Peeples knew Fontana wanted to write. When she showed him a treatment she had written for *Overland Trail*, he agreed to give it a read. She later said, "He didn't like the first story I turned in. But he did tell me to keep trying." (64-2)

Peeples' next series, *The Tall Man*, was a western based on the relationship and adventures of Pat Garrett and Billy the Kid. Fontana was still Peeples' secretary by day and writing treatments by night. The next story she handed to her boss made the grade. Peeples bought the story, but then handed it off to a seasoned TV writer to flesh out into a teleplay. Fontana was given a few hundred dollars -- the going price then for providing the storyline for a half-hour episode -- and a "story by" credit. It was a start.

A short time later, Fontana tried again, and again was given only the money and credit for contributing a story to the series; someone else got the bigger paycheck and the bigger acknowledgment that came with writing the script. When Fontana turned in a third treatment that Peeples liked, she hesitated in accepting the standard deal. She told him, "I seem to know the show now, why not let me have a shot at a script?" (64-2)

Peeples liked Fontana's confidence and told her to start writing. That first script was credited to Dorothy C. Fontana. Peeples had no qualms about associating a woman writer with his shoot-'em-up series, but others would.

"I was being turned down for interviews," she recalled. "They were saying, 'Oh, well, I don't think a woman can write this show.' And it would be a *western*. And I'd say, 'But I've got six credits on westerns. Why don't you think I can write this?'" (64-2)

The answer was always the same: writers for television came with first names like Gene, Sam, and Rod -- not Dorothy. And so the pen name of D.C. Fontana was born.

With the pseudonym now on the title page, Fontana was able to sell a spec script entitled "Did Your Mother Come from Ireland, Ben Casey?" to *Ben Casey*. It was her first hour-long teleplay -- a character-driven story which blended comedy and drama, much like some of her best future work on *Star Trek*.

Also new to the *Star Trek* team was John D.F. Black, hired to serve as a second associate producer. Justman, the other associate producer, was in charge of production. Black would focus on scripts.

***

John Black grew up in Pittsburgh, Pennsylvania in the late 1930s. He recalled, "I got my first taste of show business at three years old when someone pushed me up on stage at the Charm House -- a nightclub in Pittsburgh -- and had me sing 'The Music Goes Round and Round,' all the way through! The audience threw money but I didn't have an appreciation for what it was. I just knew they were throwing something at me and I didn't like it. So I threw it back." (17)

Black hadn't found his calling yet. That would come later.

"I lived next door to Bob Gerstrich, who wrote for *The Fat Man* radio series [1945-1951; Dashiell Hammett's follow-up to *The Thin Man* series]. I used to love the *The Fat Man*. I'd been listening for a couple years and, when I was in the third or fourth grade, I finally couldn't stand it anymore -- I couldn't resist the temptation -- and I said, 'If I write something down will you read it,' and he said, 'Sure.' So I wrote it on a yellow pad; he read it, and he loved it. He said, 'You're a writer.' And he said, 'Here's five dollars.' I got five bucks for ten storylines! That was a lot of money back then for someone that age [about $60 in 2013], so, as far as I was concerned, that made me a professional." (17)

Now a professional name was needed. John D. Black's signature came next.

Black had been born and raised Catholic, and baptized John Donald. In his early teens, while going through Confirmation, he chose his second middle name – Francis. When asked about the double middle initials, he would usually just say, "The D.F. really stands for 'Damn Fool.'" (17)

While Black was in high school there was an opening on a radio program called *The Sponsor Show* with The Carnegie Library System out of Pittsburgh. Black recalled, "I went in as a kid actor from high school. And they said, 'Oh no, we need a writer. Can you write?' And I said, 'Sure. I've written *Fat Man*.' So I wrote maybe five or six shows for the Carnegie Library. And then they made me a director, and then they made me a producer. So that's where it began." (17)

After completing a hitch in the Army, as a Military Policeman, Black surrendered to his call of pursuing a career as a writer and moved to California. He said, "I was working for *The Los Angeles Times* selling classified ads and I got a call to go see a film producer named Boris Petroff. I went to see him and asked, 'What kind of an ad would you like?' He said, 'I want an ad for a writer.' And I said, 'You can save yourself a lot of money and hire me. I'm a writer.' So we talked story and concept and all of that for a little while and I ended up doing a picture for him called *The Unearthly*, starring John Carradine." (17)

It was hardly a prestigious start. *Variety*'s review of *The Unearthly* for its July 3, 1957 issue, read:

> The mad doctor bit again. There's nothing to recommend this one beyond its cheapness. Fodder for a very unsophisticated audience.

However, what *The Unearthly* got in bad reviews was made up for at the box office, as part of a "hook in the kids" double feature with the sci-fi film *Beginning of the End*. A full page ad in the June 26 issue of *Variety* boasted:

> IT'S JUST BEGINNING! BEST SCIENCE-FICTION OPENING OF <u>ALL</u> TIME! BEST OPENING OF YEAR OF <u>ALL</u> PICTURES!

With a hit picture on his resume, Black soon found work in television, often writing for *Lawman*, *Mr. Novak* and *Laredo*, as well as occasional scripts for *The Virginian*, *The Fugitive* and *The Untouchables*. In 1962, the industry was abuzz for "Survival," a gripping episode Black wrote for *Combat!* Viewers and critics alike were stunned by the dark, graphic story where Sgt. Chip Saunders (Vic Morrow), with severely burned hands and in shock, tries to evade German patrols and find his way back to the American lines. *Daily Variety* called it "a shocker... a taut, stirring drama... clutching in its suspense and projecting the nobility of raw courage against overwhelming odds." *The Washington Post* said, "We will be hearing more about Vic Morrow and 'Survival' when Emmy nominations roll around." While Black missed his Emmy nod for this teleplay, the edgy material helped Morrow win his well-deserved nomination as Best Actor in a series.

John D.F. Black, in his home office – a two-car garage
(Courtesy of Mary Black)

Gene Roddenberry met John D.F. on March 24, 1966 at a Writers Guild award show where the latter had just won for a *Mr. Novak* script. Black said, "I wasn't into science fiction. If I hadn't won the Writers Guild award that year, I wouldn't have been invited to his house after the awards for a drink. So we went. I had my father and my mother with me, and an actor friend, Jimmy Goodman [later to be cast in *Star Trek* as Lt. Farrell in three episodes]. And Harlan [Ellison] was there; he was invited also." (17)

Mary Stilwell, the future Mrs. John Black
(Courtesy of Mary Black)

Mary Stilwell, later to be Mary Black, John D.F.'s constant companion, was there, too. She remembered, "Harlan did most of the talking. He and John had just won, and everyone was just absolutely floating. It was like we were drunk without drinking, although we did drink a bit. Gene had a bar in his home and we seemed to spend a good part of the night around that. And Gene and his wife were terrific hosts. They were extremely pleasant, but nothing was said about John coming to work on *Star Trek*, other than maybe doing a script assignment. And Harlan had an assignment on the show as well." (17a)

"No writers were there other than Harlan and me," John D.F. said. "Then, a couple days later, my agent called, Roddenberry had made an offer for me to work on *Star Trek*. When I talked to Roddenberry, he told me he had had a problem with *The Lieutenant*, and the problem was that he rewrote some things and the writers didn't like him. The writers liked me, and he wanted me on his show, as Executive Story Consultant *and* Associate Producer."

Mary Black added, "He also stated, with John in that job he'd be able to direct the writers so that a lot of rewriting wouldn't really be necessary. It was sort of a dream thing at that time; it was going to be this wonderful series where writers actually wrote." (17a)

John Black was allowed to pick his own secretary and he wanted Mary by his side. She said, "I had been in the Media Department at Foote, Cone and Belding [ad agency], so I typed well, but I never thought of myself as a secretary. I had done research, critiquing, public relations, trying to figure out how to get *Variety* to notice something, just a general mishmash of what needed to be done. But that was part of what a wonderful place it was; Roddenberry said, 'Sure, anything you want,' ... *other than the private bathroom*." (17a)

Robert Justman had the private bath. John D.F. Black said, with a smile, "The reason why Bob Justman had the private bathroom is because he got there first. And that's the only reason." (17)

***

Several others joined the series at this time.

Greg Peters, after working in an unofficial capacity as assistant director on "Where No Man Has Gone Before," was instated as the full-time A.D. He had performed this job well on the 1965 picture *Harlow* and, more recently, on *The Lucy Show*. His involvement freed Justman to concentrate on his demanding producing chores.

Irving Feinberg was brought in to build props. The 58-year-old was a property master at Desilu. He was now being asked to make things he had never

Jim Rugg (on the left), with Irving Feinberg, in 1968
(*Inside Star Trek*, **issue 4**)

even dreamt of. Matt Jefferies and Wah Chang designed some, but most -- especially the smaller ones -- came from Feinberg. Cast and crew would christen the props "Feinbergers."

Jim Rugg, 46, became *Star Trek*'s special effects wizard. His experience came from numerous TV series and movies such as *Mary Poppins*. Matt Jefferies dubbed Jim Rugg's inventions as "Ruggisms." Among the various Ruggisms were blinking lights, flying sparks, and explosions. A few of those explosions resulted in some injuries on set, including ones involving the series' leads.

Star Trek also needed a new cinematographer, someone able to imitate the look achieved by Ernest Heller for the second pilot. Roddenberry wanted Harry Stradling, Jr., *Gunsmoke*'s director of photography, but it was unlikely the busy DP would leave a secure by-the-numbers job on a hit western for a massive headache like *Star Trek*, which, by the way, could only guarantee five months of employment. Roddenberry nonetheless had Justman call Stradling ... and then call again ... and again. After several more attempts, the elusive cinematographer's dad dropped by the *Star Trek* offices.

Father Harry Stradling, Sr., a famed feature film cameraman, had won two Academy Awards for Best Cinematography on *My Fair Lady* and *The Picture of Dorian Gray*, with 12 additional Oscar nominations in that category, including one for *A Streetcar Named Desire*. He told Justman that his boy was absolutely *not* interested. Then he suggested someone who would be.

***

Jerry Finnerman during first season production (Courtesy of Gerald Gurian)

Jerry Finnerman, Harry Stradling, Sr.'s godson, was 34. He had been working in TV as assistant camera operator with his father, Perry Finnerman, a director of photography at Warner Bros.. The elder Finnerman was only 56 when, while filming an episode of *Maverick*, suffered a heart attack. Young Jerry was assisting at the time and stood by helplessly as he watched his father die.

Harry Sr. helped get his distraught godson back to work by adding Finnerman to his crew and, in time, advancing him to the position of camera operator for *My Fair Lady*, followed by Cary Grant's last movie, *Walk, Don't Run*.

Finnerman later said, "The interesting thing is, in our profession, we have three basic steps.... The 'Assistant' [camera operator] -- he follows the focus, he threads the camera, he cleans the camera, he puts the filters in if the director of photography asks for it.... [Then] the 'camera operator' sits behind the camera, turns the wheels and composes the shot.... [and then] the director of photography creates the vision of the show." (63-3)

Stradling, one such visionary, believed Finnerman had the gift as well, and expressed this to Justman. The opinion of an Oscar winning cinematographer carries weight. The opinion of an in-demand director does, too. James Goldstone, who continued to be a guiding force for *Star Trek*, told Justman he had seen Finnerman's work as a member of a camera unit and was also confident the kid had the right stuff. Justman was sold.

Roddenberry's reply to Justman: "If you want him, *I* want him." (94-8)

Finnerman recalled, "So I get a call from *Star Trek* and am asked to come over for an interview. And I went over and I met with Gene Roddenberry and Herb Solow and Bob Justman and they said, 'What would you do if we gave you the series?'" (63-3)

Roddenberry had explained to Finnerman how he would be lighting and photographing the inside of a giant space ship and the landscapes of alien worlds. The man with no prior experience as a DP loved the concept and the potential for painting with light, but he also had concerns.

"I said, 'Well, I'd like to,' but, in the meantime, in the back of my head, I'm saying, you know, 'I'm only just a little bit over 30. If I don't make it, if they fire me, I'll have to sit for six months or a year, because I'm out of classification -- because that's the way it was if you worked as a cinematographer for 30 days and then you dropped back. You had to stay back for a year.... And Harry was going to do *Funny Girl*, with William Wyler... and I wanted to very much operate on that picture. William Wyler was one of my favorite directors, and I wanted to work with [Barbra] Streisand, and, you know, I felt very good with Stradling, because operating a camera anybody can do. It's not hard." (63-3)

Finnerman wasn't being offered a contract with *Star Trek*. He wasn't even guaranteed more than a couple weeks' work. What he was offered was a chance to prove himself -- with one episode -- and, depending on the picture he delivered, perhaps more week-by-week assignments spanning five months (the time it would take to film a half-season's worth of episodes). Unable to decide, he called his mentor and boss. Stradling assured Finnerman that he would do well and convinced him to take the job. No one knew it yet but *Star Trek* had just hired itself an undiscovered genius -- a cinematographer who, on his very first day of work, would do something no one else had yet done in television: elevate a color TV show to the look of a feature film.

***

Finally, there was NBC's contribution to the creative staff. The title is Network Production Manager. The job is to oversee every aspect of the making of a series and to be sure that everything is to the absolute liking of the network. Stan Robertson was NBC's choice to watch Roddenberry and his people like a hawk.

Stanley G. Robertson

Stanley G. Robertson was born November 20, 1925. He was visually handicapped and had 14 eye surgeries by the time he was 20. Despite his difficulties seeing, Robertson read constantly. And he also had a passion for writing. He graduated from Los Angeles City College in 1949 and shortly thereafter went to work as a reporter for *The Los Angeles Sentinel*, the leading African-American newspaper in the city. Two years later, Robertson accepted a job at *Ebony* magazine as an associate editor. In 1954 he left *Ebony* to study telecommunications at the University of Southern California, then, in 1957, embarked on a new career with NBC. Despite his college degree, Robertson started at the bottom, as a page. Both ambitious and efficient, he steadily climbed his way up the ladder and eventually landed a job in the network's music clearance department. By the mid-1960s, Robertson was transferred from New York to Los Angeles where NBC-Burbank was experiencing growing pains. He was now 40 and was in the right place at the right time for the next step in his career. The network needed production managers, each to be assigned a handful of series to oversee. Robertson applied for one of the positions, at the very time *Star Trek* was added to the schedule. He got the job to manage the series no one else in the department seemed to want.

Roddenberry met with Robertson and was duly impressed. He liked the sharp junior network man because, primarily, Robertson didn't resemble a network man. Being black and having once worked as a writer, Roddenberry felt Robertson would "get" what *Star Trek* and

DeForest Kelley, 1947 headshot

its interracial cast was all about. Before long, however, the two men would be at odds.

***

On March 22, 1966, Ed Perlstein of Desilu Business Affairs sent a certified letter to William Shatner, reading, "Dear Bill: This is to advise you that the *Star Trek* series has been sold and that we intend to commence production on or about May 23, 1966, and that we require your service on or about that date."

It was exceptionally good news -- albeit expressed in a very understated way. Leonard Nimoy was sent a similar letter of this type, as was George Takei. No one else who appeared in the second pilot film was. Roddenberry, after discussions with both the studio financial officers and the network, had decided to make some cast changes, including that of the ship's doctor.

DeForest Kelley, born in Atlanta, Georgia, got a taste for show business when singing in the choir of a Baptist church where his father was minister. It was a strict upbringing, with Kelley describing his father's sermons as "Earthquakes of fire and brimstone," then adding, "My father believed sincerely that smoking, drinking, dancing, going to the movies were all sinful." (98-15)

At 17, Kelley was itching to smoke, drink, dance and go to the movies. He was also yearning to get out of Georgia. He travelled to California to visit an uncle in Long Beach and this led to a decision to give up his earlier notion of one day becoming, ironically, a doctor. He now preferred to be an actor. Kelley gave his father the bad news, later saying, "When I told him I had decided to become an actor, he was sure my soul was lost forever. I was going straight to hell." (98-1a)

While day-lighting at menial jobs, including short-order cook, janitor and hospital orderly, Kelley took stage work where he could find it. He also studied film making at the Long Beach Cinema Club.

In 1941, William Meiklejohn, Paramount's head of casting, was searching for an unknown to play a baby-faced killer in a new movie, and this led to several meetings with Kelley. Meiklejohn seemed set not only on signing the young actor to the sizable role but also a studio contract. Kelley remembered, "While I was waiting for the producer in his office, I happened to glance over at his desk. There I saw a slip of paper and a penciled line through my name. Underneath was written another name -- Alan Ladd. The picture was *This Gun for Hire* and it made Ladd a star, and I went back to Long Beach." (98-15)

At the end of November, Kelley was cast as the lead in the Long Beach Playhouse's production of *Skylark*. Also in the cast was a young actress named Carolyn Dowling. The two became friends, then sweethearts, beginning a lifelong romance.

On December 7, life in America changed with the attack on Pearl Harbor. The Community Playhouse did its part in the war effort, cancelling further performances of *Skylark* and heading out to entertain the troops. Kelley stayed behind. With many of his friends being drafted, he had decided to enlist in the Army Air Corps. After basic training, and because of his ability as an actor to speak clearly and calmly, he was assigned to work as a control tower operator at Roswell Air Base in New Mexico. In early January 1945, he was transferred to the 18th Army Air Force Base Unit, also known as the First Motion Picture Unit, located at the Hal Roach Studios in Hollywood. There he would aid in the making of military training films. Also stationed at "Camp Roach" was George Reeves, later to be TV's *Superman*. Kelley and Reeves became good friends and appeared together in numerous short-subject films, such as *How to Clean Your Gun* and *How to Act if Captured*, as well as countless Armed Forces radio broadcasts. Another film featuring Reeves and Kelley, made for the Navy, was the 40-minute *Time to Kill*, released to theaters in 1945 on the bottom-half of a double bill. Bill Meiklejohn saw it and was reminded of the contract he had almost given Kelley four years before.

Within a month, on August 15, the nation celebrated V-J Day, marking the end of the war. Three weeks later, Kelley and Carolyn Dowling married. Kelley requested his Army discharge and, just before the orders came through, he got some surprising news. He said, "I was sitting on a bunk when a telegram came through from Bill Meiklejohn at Paramount and it said, 'We're prepared to offer you a seven-year contract,' and I almost fell off my bunk." (981b)

He later quipped, "I had to join the Army to make a Navy picture to become an actor." (98-14)

Kelley was discharged in January 1946, and soon after signed with Paramount. The contract was for one year, with the studio having the option to renew six more times. The starting pay was $150 per week -- nearly $2,000 today. Kelley was making excellent money to spend most of his day studying film technique at the Paramount Acting School.

Two months later, Kelley stepped before the cameras to make his first Paramount movie, sharing the lead with Paul Kelly in *Fear in the Night*. He played a young man who dreams he commits murder and then wakes to find it may be true. By December, Kelley was filming a second movie: *Variety Girl*. One day before Christmas, before *Fear in the Night* had even been released, Paramount renewed his contract and raised him up to $200 a week. While celebrating the renewal at a party, Kelley, as a lark, had his fortune told by a palm reader. Despite the promising start in Hollywood, he was told nothing of real importance would happen in his career until he was past 40. Kelley later told *TV Guide*, "I was prepared to hear about how marvelous I'd be. Instead I got what turned out to be a very prophetic statement." (98-15)

In February 1947, *Daily Variety* called *Fear in the Night* "one of the better features of the year." *Motion Picture Daily* said, "Guaranteed to raise the short hairs on the nape of your neck." *Boxoffice* called it, "A definite standout." *Weekly Variety* said, "It's a good psychological melodrama unfolded at fast clip and will please the whodunit-and-how fans.... DeForest Kelley is good as bewildered man."

Kelley had every reason to believe he was on the road to stardom. His second Paramount picture, the extravagant *Variety Girl*, with a storyline involving a "nameless waif" getting discovered by a talent scout (Kelley) and signed to a Hollywood contract, was out in October. *Variety* said, "DeForest Kelley looms as a good new juvenile potential." The problem for him was that *Variety Girl* was an all-star event and had dozens of the studio's biggest marquee names appearing as themselves. Even with a prominent role and a nod from Hollywood's top trade paper, all the famous faces making cameos -- Bing Crosby, Bob Hope, Gary Cooper, Alan Ladd, William Holden, Barbara Stanwyk, Veronica Lake, Dorothy

Lamour, and Burt Lancaster -- kept Kelley's face from making a memorable impression. A short time later, he told a reporter, "The other day I met actor John Lund near the studio, and he cracked, 'De, they sure must have been worried about your acting, putting in all those stars to help you out.' He sure had me there, didn't he?" (98-1a)

Kelley's fortunes were about to change. The big Hollywood studios were rethinking their long-standing policies of signing promising young talent and training them to be stars. Kelley remarked, "The way they are laying people off these days makes one stop and think. At one time, they had 30 young actors [at Paramount], but now I'm one of three newcomers left. So I'm not buying any Beverly Hills mansions. In fact, there is an automobile salesman's job waiting, just in case." (98-1a)

A short time later, Kelley was informed that Paramount would not be renewing his contract.

As a free agent, he quickly picked up sixth billing in *Cannon City*, a factual depiction of a large-scale breakout from Colorado State Prison that was a hot news story six months earlier. Next, some TV work trickled in, including three episodes of *The Lone Ranger*, with Kelley playing a rancher, then a sheriff, then a doctor. He also found himself small roles on several of the anthologies of the day, but the jobs were few and far between. He later quipped, "There was a time when I was ready to change my name to DeForest Lawn." (98-15)

With the minor paychecks that went along with TV work from this period, the Kelleys were barely able to afford their one-bedroom apartment. Fortunately, an old friend was now writing and directing for *You Are There*, a half-hour series hosted by Walter Cronkite which took viewers back in time, in the form of live news reports with Cronkite interviewing the participants of historical events. In Kelley's first appearance, he played a Union officer in "The Capture of John Wilkes Booth." He stepped back into history eight more times over the next few years. He also won small roles in shows that would find their way into syndicated reruns, earning him much-needed residual payments from shows such as *Gunsmoke*, *Zane Grey Theater* and *The Millionaire*. In an episode of *Science Fiction Theatre*, entitled "Y.O.R.D.," which *Daily Variety* called, "One of the better [in] the series... a well-done yarn about space ships from another planet, magnetic waves, etc.," Kelley was mentioned for his good performance. For "Inside Out," a second episode of *Your Favorite Story*, Kelley had the lead as an American correspondent held prisoner behind the Iron Curtain. A month later, for "Storm Signal" on *Studio 57*, the trade paper's critic wrote "DeForest Kelley is okay in his appearance as the meanie." The "meanie" roles were starting to come his way and this, more than anything else, would bring him financial security.

"When I was much younger and just starting out I thought that I had to have success," Kelley told a tabloid writer while doing *Star Trek*. "It meant glamour and stardom. But I soon learned that I *was* a success almost from the very beginning. For one thing I had Carolyn, my wife.... For another, I was doing just what I wanted to do -- *act*.... When I got a role -- big or small -- I had the chance to create a living, believable human being out of a one-dimensional character who had previously only existed in a few lines in a script." (98-13)

In 1956, with another appearance on *You Are There*, Kelley was cast as another meanie, this time Ike Clanton, in a news-style video report on the "Gunfight at the O.K. Corral." This in itself got him back onto the big screen, in an A-picture, no less. At the time of the *You Are There* episode's airing, film producer Hal Wallis was preparing a big-budget movie about the famous gunfight to star Burt Lancaster and Kirk Douglas. Paul Nathan, a casting director, wrote to Wallis, "For Ike Clanton you saw on TV and liked DeForest Kelly

[sic], and when you catch your breath, I want to bring him in." Wallis had been so taken by Kelley's Ike Clanton that he wanted him to play the same part in the big screen treatment. But another producer noticed Kelley in that TV role and had just cast him in the big screen western *Tension at Table Rock*, playing the heavy. With a scheduling conflict, someone else had to be hired to play Clanton, but Wallis was sold on Kelley being in the cast and offered him a smaller part that could be shot later in the production. He would play Morgan Earp to Lancaster's Wyatt Earp.

DeForest Kelley, western villain

Kelley was injured during the filming of *O.K. Corral*. He later said, "I was doing a scene with Kirk Douglas. We were approaching the corral and the shooting starts, and we jump into this ditch.... I was carrying this rifle, and when I jumped into the ditch, I fell the wrong way and the rifle jammed my ribs.... I awakened with Burt Lancaster sitting there with a brass spittoon, and I was throwing up." (98-1)

Kelley had hit the big time, with a movie star holding his head as he vomited.

In 1957, Kelley was back on the big screen in the epic three-hour long *Raintree County*, as a Confederate Officer who gallops into battle against star Montgomery Clift and his Union soldier colleague Lee Marvin. Mustached and looking both gallant and dashing, Kelley is shot from a charging stallion and captured by the Yankees. Later, he kills Marvin and then is killed by Clift in a scene that is both compelling and tragic.

On the small screen in 1957 and 1958, Kelley had more than two dozen guest spots, including episodes of *Steve Canyon*, *M Squad*, *The Adventures of Jim Bowie*, and *Boots and Saddles* (in an episode written by Gene Roddenberry). He also had the lead in "Kill and Run," an episode of *The Web*, playing a police detective trying to prove a juvenile (James Darren) was innocent of a hit-and-run accident that killed a young girl. *Daily Variety* said, "Kelley is especially good as the cop, with scruples as well as brains."

Kelley was also back on the big screen in 1958 in another well-received A-picture, *The Law of Jake Wade*, starring Robert Taylor and Richard Widmark. Of the film's star, the *Variety* critic wrote:

> Widmark is the more interesting of the two men, he is thoroughly amoral, but such an engaging villain that when he is finally shot you are sorry to see him go.

Kelley later said, "If I do say so, I'm quite a good heavy. Maybe not as good as Richard Widmark -- when Widmark turns nasty, it's like looking into the face of death -- but [I'm] still pretty good." He credited his inspiration to a small-town Georgia sheriff he knew as a kid, recalling, "He had the look of a cobra. He talked very quietly, and before doing some act of cruelty, his lips would purse into a thin, mean smile." (98-15)

Kelley worked with Widmark again the following year, for *Warlock*, which co-starred Henry Fonda and Anthony Quinn.

Back on TV, he made the rounds on all the westerns, making trouble for good guys Robert Culp (*Trackdown*), Steve McQueen (*Wanted: Dead or Alive*), Clint Eastwood (*Rawhide*), Peter Breck (*The Black Saddle*), Henry Fonda (*The Deputy*), Richard Boone (*Have Gun -- Will Travel*), Lorne Green and Pernell Roberts (*Bonanza*), Dale Robertson (*Tales of Wells Fargo*), Gene Barry (*Bat Masterson*), and Darren McGavin (this time on *Riverboat*). Other stopovers on westerns of the day included *Stagecoach West*, *Lawman*, and *Two Faces West*.

In a letter Carolyn Kelley wrote to a friend from this time, she said:

> Seems all westerns this year. This last week was not a western but he shot someone even in that one. I don't know how anyone so sweet could act so mean; he is just a good actor. (98-1)

With all these high profile guest shots, Kelley was now a very familiar face in television. William Dozier and Robert Sparks of Screen Gems were well aware of his recognition factor and believed he might do well to play Jake Ehrlich, the San Francisco defense attorney who had written a dozen books on law and served as the model for Erle Stanley Gardner's *Perry Mason*. A pilot film based on Ehrlich was about to be made and the Screen Gems men recommended Kelley to the writer/producer they had on the assignment. The actor recalled, "I walked up this little flight of stairs and [into] a tiny office with a desk, and here was this bear of a man sitting there. So we had a long talk about this particular show, and [he] told me... 'We have no trouble with you. We'll take you to San Francisco and have you meet Jake Ehrlich -- who you're going to portray -- this famous criminal lawyer.'" (98-1c)

The bear of a man was Gene Roddenberry. The pilot was "333 Montgomery Street." Roddenberry of course was familiar with Kelley, who had acted in an episode the former had written for *Boots and Saddles*, as well as having been featured prominently in so many other TV programs and films. Ehrlich knew who he was, too, and sent a telegram on February 5 inviting the Screen Gems people to a cocktail party at his apartment at 333 Montgomery Street, in San Francisco, saying that he was particularly interested in meeting "the menacing heavy who is to portray me -- DeForest Kelley." (57a)

The pilot film "333 Montgomery Street" received a test airing as an episode of *Alcoa Theatre*. The critic for *Daily Variety*, on June 15, 1960, praised the production in general, then, regarding its star, wrote:

> A strong argument which may weigh in favor of a series is the central character as delineated by DeForest Kelley; he makes him human and creditable out of court and vivid when defending a client.

The critic for the *New York Journal-American*, on June 24, asked, "How can it miss? Not nearly as dreadful as most TV trash."

Regardless, the pilot failed to sell as a series. Kelley remarked, "Like everything Gene did, it was ahead of its time. I was defending a guy who was guilty, and I got him off, and the networks didn't like that." (98-1c)

For 1963, Kelley was given fourth billing in the big-screen western *Gunfight at Comanche Street*, starring Audie Murphy. Back on TV, among other series: another episode of *Laramie*, then a pair of 90-minute *Virginian*s. In 1964 and 1965, he was back in the movie houses in the westerns *Apache Uprising*, starring Rory Calhoun and Jane Russell, *Black*

Spurs, again under Calhoun, and *Town Tamer*, starring Dana Andrews. After nearly two decades of playing mostly cowboy bad guys, Kelley said, "I thoroughly enjoyed those years. I liked westerns for two reasons: First, it took the actor outside. They were all very physical at that time and not limited to a stage. Second, they paid my rent an awful lot." (98-12)

Also in 1965, Kelley was in *Marriage on the Rocks*, starring Frank Sinatra, Dean Martin and Deborah Kerr. He got sixth billing and the privilege to work alongside screen legend Bette Davis in 1964's *Where Love Has Gone*. The critic for *Variety* said, "DeForest Kelley impresses as an unscrupulous art critic." He was also making a second pilot film for Gene Roddenberry. Steve Ihnat, later to guest star in *Star Trek*, had the lead in this one, supported by Kelley and Grace Lee Whitney, also to go to *Star Trek*. A two-hour TV movie was produced, which later aired on NBC after the decision was made not to go to series. According to Roddenberry, who always pictured Kelley as the doctor for the U.S.S. Enterprise, the victory to come from "Police Story" was how it changed NBC's perception of the actor. Once the network, the studio, and his *Star Trek* colleagues got a look at the former heavy in the role as a doctor-like police coroner, they finally agreed he would make a good fit for McCoy.

Kelley told Ruth Berman, from the set of *Star Trek*, for the fanzine *Inside Star Trek*, "I was never a science fiction buff, although one of my very favorite shows was *The Twilight Zone*. I was an avid fan... but, at the time, it seemed that I couldn't connect with it.... I had been mostly involved in westerns, not as a choice, but something I fell into, in playing 'heavies.' It was making me a very comfortable living, and I had just about figured, 'Well, this is the way I'm going to go.'" (98-3)

Shatner said, "I remember being in the office at *Star Trek* with De and Bob Justman that first day. I recognized him from *Raintree County*, and I was an admirer of his work." (156-6)

Nimoy said, "I remember meeting him and was delighted because I knew his work and I knew the role he was going to play and I felt very good about it. I thought he was a very good choice." (128-9)

Doohan said, "I was very glad that Gene brought DeForest on board. In terms of acting... DeForest was far superior to the man who played the doctor in the [second] pilot." (52-6)

Kelley, 46 at the time, was guaranteed only seven episodes of *Star Trek*'s initial order of 16, at $850 each. He recalled telling this to his wife. Carolyn remained encouraging and pointed out that those seven shows would pay the mortgage for a couple months. Kelley responded, "I just hope it goes seven." (98-1)

***

Grace Lee Whitney came on board as Janice Rand, the Captain's Yeoman. She was 35. A former stage dancer with more than three dozen credits in television and film, she had recently played a lead role in "Controlled Experiment," the only comedy episode produced for *The Outer Limits*. Whitney first met Roddenberry on *The Lieutenant*. Charmed by the pretty blonde, he cast her as the female lead in "Police Story." And that led to *Star Trek*.

"When Gene beamed me aboard, I was thrilled," Whitney said much later. "I didn't fully realize it at the time, but my life had just taken a sharp turn in a totally new direction." (183-2)

The sharp turn brought a fair amount of rumors.

Whitney in pilot for Jeffrey Hunter's series, *Temple Houston* (1963, Warner Bros.)

"The suggestion that Gene Roddenberry put me in *Star Trek* because of a 'previous personal relationship' is flatly false," Whitney insisted. "I never had a romantic relationship with Gene Roddenberry before *Star Trek*, during *Star Trek*, or after *Star Trek*. Did Gene make passes at me? You better believe he did! Passes, innuendoes, double-entendres, the whole nine yards. But I wanted to keep our relationship on a professional basis." (183-2)

Whitney remembered Roddenberry's description of Janice Rand. She would be as *Gunsmoke*'s Miss Kitty was to Matt Dillon. The Marshal could always talk his problems over with his favorite saloon girl; she knew him better than anyone else. That was the relationship Roddenberry wanted Rand and Kirk to have. The Captain could confide in her, be warmed by her and secretly love her. But he would never openly admit his deeper feelings, not even to himself. Roddenberry told her, "Because of your duty, you can never openly express your attraction toward him. There will always be an undercurrent of suppressed sexuality between you that will come out in very subtle ways. You're to be as beautiful as you can be and as efficient as you can be, and you are to love the captain." (183-2)

Whitney saw a contradiction with the instructions Roddenberry gave her. She was to be as beautiful as she could be and bring forward an undercurrent of sexuality, but do so while wearing a somewhat loose gold turtleneck uniform top and black pants -- as the women onboard the Enterprise had in both pilots, and as she was dressed for all the early publicity photos. She said, "I told Gene, 'You're covering up my best part -- my dancers' legs! Rand should wear a skirt -- a short one!' He loved the idea, but it wasn't *his* idea, or Bill Theiss' idea, although it *was* their idea as to how short that short skirt turned out. Nichelle used to let her skirt sneak up a bit while she sat at the communications station. That was no accident. She wasn't going to be 'out-legged' by me." (183-6)

Whitney's contract promised her seven out of the first 16, at $750 each.

***

James Montgomery Doohan, at 46 in 1966, enjoyed working as an actor, but did not define himself or his life by his many guest performances. For the June 1968 issue of *TV Star Parade*, Doohan told writer Roger Elwood, "Acting can be an escape from life for some individuals but not for me. I was never attracted to acting until after the war. I was going to be a dentist in fact." (52-8)

Doohan's father had worked as a dentist, as well as a pharmacist and veterinarian.

James Doohan in "Hail to the Chief" on *Voyage to the Bottom of the Sea* (1964, 20th Century Fox)

But Doohan's decision to follow in his father's professional footsteps changed when he realized his talents lay elsewhere. He said, "One night, I heard a radio broadcast and I told myself I could do as well as any of the people in it. So my determination grew from that moment on. However, for some, acting is an escape from the problems of reality into the fantasy world of a make-believe character." (52-8)

Not for Doohan; he had never been one to seek escape. His nature was to hit the challenges of life head on. One such challenge came in the form of the Second World War, when Doohan was only 18. He said, "I volunteered for the Army. Even though I was on the young side, I was accepted and began as a gunner in the artillery section, advancing to captain [in the Royal Canadian Artillery].... I was the first guy to hit the beach during the D-Day invasion of Normandy. It was at 11:30 at night. I was in charge of the fifth boat of my company. There I was, racing ashore -- only to be wounded very badly, at least badly enough to be sent back to England and hospitalized." (52-8)

Doohan had been sprayed by bullets from a German machine gun. He'd been hit four times in the leg, as well as having the middle finger of his right hand shot off. A potential lethal hit to the chest was deflected by a metal cigarette case in his shirt pocket, a life-saving gift from his brother.

Doohan did not let these wounds keep him from the job at hand. He returned to serving the war effort as an observation pilot, stationed out of Cambridge, England.

Those who knew Doohan were not only struck by his daring, but by his ethics and inherent kindness. His nature is well represented in a story he told writer Roger Elwood regarding his upbringing in British Columbia, Canada. He said, "One of the greatest things I recall was the absolute freedom, especially the freedom I had, of running with my dogs, just going off and being with them and the bright clear sky and the pure air. It was marvelous, simply unforgettable!... I had to leave the dogs and the horses behind. That was a large part of the reason why I felt so low and despondent. They were my companions; my friends." (52-8)

Leslie Parrish, who worked with Doohan in the *Star Trek* episode "Who Mourns for Adonais," said, "Jimmy Doohan was a truly beautiful soul, very much like the character everyone loved in *Star Trek* -- warm, caring, loyal, devoted! My relationship with him in the show is still with me: we had very warm feelings for each other and I saw that Scotty was ready to put his life on the line to defend me when I came under the spell of Apollo [in the *Star Trek* story]. It's impossible not to love a man like that.... Ah -- what a sweetie he was!!!" (134a)

After the war, Doohan studied acting during a two-year scholarship to New York's famed Neighborhood Playhouse, whose alumni included Gregory Peck, Steve McQueen, Dustin Hoffman, James Caan, Robert Duvall, Grace Kelly and, also *Star Trek* bound, Walter

Koenig. Doohan quickly gained a reputation for his ability to tackle different dialects, including that of a Scotsman.

Doohan married in 1949, at age 29, to Janet Young. They had four children during their 15-year marriage, which ended one year shy of his first *Star Trek*.

Doohan had created the character of Montgomery Scott, a name he chose, for "Where No Man Has Gone Before." He was happy that the pilot had sold and said, "I thought, 'Oh great, I have a running job here.'" (52-1)

Leslie Parrish said, "Over the years, as I watched casting choices, I was amazed at casting directors' abilities to read character. They nailed Scotty with Jimmy! Can you think of one other man who could have played that role believably with such childlike innocence and genuine love for his spaceship and his captain and crew?" (134a)

If Doohan hadn't been willing to stand up to life's challenges, however, Scotty never would have made it back into space. The contract was for nine shows, but a few days after signing, he received a letter from Gene Roddenberry. In his memoirs, *Beam Me Up, Scotty*, Doohan recalled it reading, "Thanks very much, but we don't really think we're going to need an engineer." (52-1)

Roddenberry was nowhere near that crass, but the end result would have been the same. The actual letter from April 11, 1966 read:

> Dear Jim: As you probably know, *Star Trek* will be on the air this coming September. Due to changes in format, budget structure and character concepts, we cannot pick up a number of options, including yours. But we do hope that "Engineering Officer Scott" will reappear in future stories and hope we will be fortunate enough to find you interested and available at that time. Let me thank you for your important contribution in the making of the *Star Trek* pilot. As mentioned many times before, I value your talent and ability highly and it will always be a particular pleasure for me when we are able to work together.

Doohan was remarkably busy making the rounds as a guest performer. He didn't need *Star Trek*. But he wanted it.

"There's a danger [in doing a series] in that you can get typed," Doohan said. "If the show hits and the role is [that] noticeable, they may never again see you as being anyone other than that one character.... All right, but at the same time you can only count on so many years at finding guest work. Sooner or later that runs its course. So it comes down to whether or not the role in a series is worth the gamble. I saw the potential of science fiction, if it was done properly, and I saw the potential of this role -- the engineer; the Scotsman. I felt it was worth fighting for. And any good Scotsman is not afraid of a proper fight." (52)

Doohan called his agent, who went to Roddenberry and Solow. A compromise was made. Doohan was given a new contract for five out of 13 shows, with a salary of $850 each.

With this, there was only one final series regular to lock in.

George Takei had just turned 29. His character was changed from astrophysicist to helmsman. According to Takei, Roddenberry said the network people liked the idea of an interracial cast and had expressed interest in making Sulu more visible. His contract also promised seven of the first 16. His pay rate: $600 per episode.

***

Star Trek had an order for 16 episodes. One of these, the second pilot, was in the can.

Fifteen to go.

The scripts for "The Omega Glory" and "Mudd's Women," ST-3 and 4, respectively, were on hand. ST-3, Roddenberry's script, at the insistence of Stan Robertson, was put aside in hopes of finding better material. Roddenberry received his first slap in the face from the man he had approved to be NBC's production manager to *Star Trek*.

The search for the better material began. A screening of the second pilot was arranged at Desilu for March 7, 1966, with six more screenings to follow. Members of the Writers Guild were invited. Of those who showed up, only a handful stayed until the end. Freelance writers of this time were looking for a few weeks' work for a few thousand dollars, not something that would entail a crash course about life in a whole new universe. Every writer in town knew how to tell stories about cops, doctors and cowboys. Something like *Star Trek* required far more work.

"The problem is most writers have no scientific background whatsoever," said Stephen Kandel. "They were English majors; they never took physics, so science fiction scared them. The language scared them. The concept scared them. Gene Roddenberry scared them. He was talking about a series that accepted the fact that interstellar space is essentially airless, but distances are really substantial, that other cultures can truly be alien, that the kind of life you meet is modified by planetary distances. That was very daunting to a lot of writers." (95-1)

But some writers like a challenge. A few stepped forward, with a few more on each of the subsequent screening days. Some were science fiction authors with little or no experience in television. For them, *Star Trek* was a new toy to play with. Some were TV writers looking for a quick job and a fast buck, ignorant as to how much work writing for Gene Roddenberry and *Star Trek* would be. Only a few of the interested writers had a background in both science fiction and screenwriting, and shows like *Lost in Space* could hardly prepare them for *Star Trek*. Nor could TV anthologies like *The Twilight Zone* and *The Outer Limits*, where the writers were free to dream up their own characters and not be restricted by the rules of someone else's universe.

Roddenberry was gambling with each story assignment he gave out. He knew many would not make the cut, so during March and April, to satisfy the order for 16 scripts, he assigned 21 story treatments.

***

The job now was to build Disneyland on a County Fair budget. The sets for the Enterprise had to be relocated to Desilu Hollywood where the interior of the starship, including the elaborate bridge set, was reassembled on Gower Street Stage 9. With Jim Rugg now a part of the team, each "wild" section of the bridge was wired separately. This way, when the bridge was pulled apart to allow for camera movement, all the panels and display screens would still blink and flash.

Sickbay received a makeover, as well. Jefferies, with Rugg's help, outfitted each bed with a medical monitoring device. The briefing room, the transporter room, the ship's corridors and the Captain's quarters were also given a sprucing up. And there would be a new set for engineering, although it wouldn't come about until a specific episode called for it ("The Enemy Within").

Star Trek fan Kay Anderson, the editor of *ST-Phile*, one of the earliest fanzines, was given a tour of Desilu stages 9 and 10. She shared her observations in a pair of 1968 articles, describing how Stage 9 was entered by "negotiating a tangle of bicycles and tugging open a large, thick, heavy door equipped with the sort of handle one sees on meat lockers." Inside, Anderson observed that the sickbay sets were closest to the front door. Beyond that, "the enormous area" seemed "like a cave." The ceiling was crisscrossed with "beams and girders, conduits and air conditioner ducts, and dripping stalactites of chains suspending lights and positioning the walls of the sets." The walls of the building were thickly insulated and curtains of sound-deadening material also hung from the ceiling, causing any noise from within to have "a curiously remote, muffled quality." The floor of the "cavernous room" was cluttered with sets, props, equipment and people. Once past sickbay, Anderson wandered down a corridor -- the hallways of the Enterprise -- which led to the other sets, and also provided easy access to the entire complex and the makeup and dressing rooms. Just past the lower part of the "Jefferies tube" – named after Matt Jefferies -- the corridor ended and gave way to the engineering set.

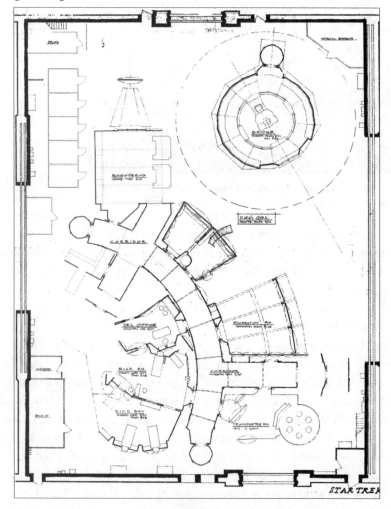

Stage 9, Season One layout:
Ship's corridors run bottom center to middle left.
Stacked left of corridor, from bottom: sickbay, exam room/McCoy's office, the brig and the elevator.
To the right, bottom up: transporter room, side corridor, briefing room, Captain's quarters, guest quarters, side corridor, and engineering.
The bridge is top right. Note the indoor dressing trailers, upper left.
Makeup room is bottom left.
(Courtesy of Bob Olsen and Gerald Gurian)

"They had a thing about the size of a car port that was basically the engineering section," said George Clayton Johnson, who visited the stages when writing for the series. "It was all artificially foreshortened in layers so that, if you stood in front of it and looked into it, you got an optical illusion of looking down through a vast area. But it was all a forced perspective. It didn't take up a lot of space, but it was an incredible thing to look at." (93-1)

Bottom left of production still reveals a wedge of the bridge that has been removed to make room for the camera setup
(Courtesy of Gerald Gurian)

As for the bridge, Anderson described it as, "A large set, circular when completely assembled, cut into wedges like slices of a pie." (2a)

"It was very, very weird," said George Clayton Johnson. "They had it all on wheels so that they could take sections out like a segment of pie. They could whip out a wall and stick a camera in there and shoot the bridge. Then they would put that wall back in place and take another segment of the pie out and reposition the camera. So, they were able to move the cameras pretty freely because they had made the bridge in six or eight fairly large chunks that were light enough to move and that would clamp back together. It was really quite ingenious to watch." (93-1)

"It was gorgeous," Stephen Kandel said. "It was beautiful. It was like a film set that somebody had stolen for a TV episode. And the cast, of course, was in awe of the set." (95-1)

George Clayton Johnson was interested in the lights on the bridge. He had often watched television shows and movies being filmed but had never seen anything like this. He said, "The crew would cut holes in one piece of plywood and cut holes in another piece of plywood so that, when you slid one board past the other, some holes would coincide. Then they'd have colored lights behind these pieces of plywood, and you got this blinking light array on the wall screens and the control consoles. And it really, really looked good.... And those sliding doors were operated by people. So, when the actors approached the damn thing, *whip,* it would come open. Then they'd go through and, *whap,* the door would go back. Just outside of range of the cameras, there were a couple of guys shoving this stuff back and forth." (93-1)

"There always had to be a man to operate," said Jim Rugg. "The doors were tied together with cables and one actually opens the other.... A nice piece of sound editing in there gives you the illusion of a machine." (147)

In 1966, this was better than Disneyland.

The planet set on Stage 10 was a sight to be appreciated, as well. Kay Anderson described it as "enormous... probably 3,000 feet square and 75 or 80 feet to the ceiling." (2a)

Jerry Finnerman said, "The stage was huge, and it had a white 'cyc' [cyclorama] on it -- a canvas covering all around the set. And that was the 'planet set.'" (63-3)

The thinking was to paint backgrounds on the canvas, such as mountain ranges, skies, and clouds, as had been done in the two pilots, and had been done in motion pictures and television since the beginning of both mediums. But Robert Justman and Jerry Finnerman decided to keep the backgrounds white. That way, planet skies could be created by merely directing high-powered lights with different colored

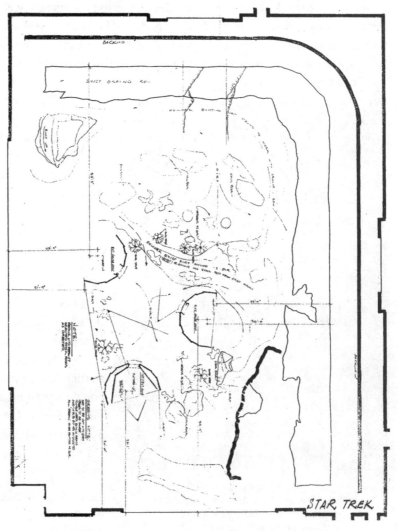

Desilu Stage 10, the permanent home of alien worlds
(Courtesy Bob Olsen)

"gels" toward the walls. Easier, faster and cheaper than paint. More effective, too. Finnerman remembered that he was the one who approached Roddenberry, saying, "'Wouldn't it be nice to put color on the lamps. So, if you're on an evil set, or planet, you can have a hot red sky, which shows evil. Or, if you're on a love planet... light it to be pink.'... And he said, 'Well, shoot a test.... You get the colors that you want and I'll look at them.'... So... we had people and the rocks and the sand, and I lit the set and I put color on the lamps on the cyc. I had no idea what it would look like until I put them on. And it was gorgeous. I remember I used a combination of red/yellow; I used magenta; I went with the pinks; I went with the beautiful blue/green for, like, a night planet." (63-3)

"I thought it was just gorgeous," said George Clayton Johnson of the colored skies. "I was completely astonished." (93-1)

Kay Anderson, also astonished, wrote, "The walls are made of the same sort of material home movie screens are made of, and onto them the alien-hued skies were projected." (2a)

Below the skies, a forced perspective was created, allowing for a range of mini-mountains to encircle the set on three sides. Anderson commented, "Near the walls are horizons of mountain ranges with walkways behind them, so visitors are often presented with the curious spectacle of curious heads peering at them from over the edge of the world." (2a)

On hand were tons of dirt and sand, as well as artificial rocks and even, when needed, a body of water.

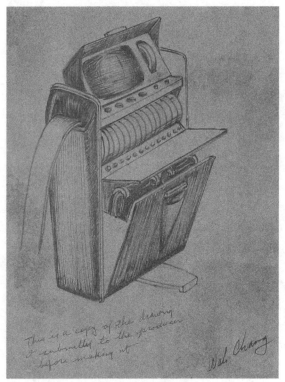

Wah Chang wrote:
"This is a copy of the drawing I submitted to the producer before making it."
(Courtesy of William Krewson)

The opposite side of the stage was left open and therefore available for the building of additional sets, such as caverns, alien buildings or spaceships and, once someone was willing to pay for it, the shuttlecraft.

Meanwhile, having already designed the flip-open communicator (which Martin Cooper -- the creator of the first handheld cell phone -- would later cite as his inspiration), Wah Chang kept busy dreaming up the tricorder and the phaser pistol. Nothing rented. Everything invented.

Roddenberry, meanwhile, was starting to see missed opportunities for potential personal revenue, prompting him to write to his agent, Alden Schwimmer at Ashley Famous Agency. On April 25, 1966, a bitter Roddenberry wrote:

Have just completed sketching out for our art people a rather unique three-stage phaser hand weapon-pistol-rifle, one convertible into another. Not only do they meet *Star Trek*'s dramatic requirements but also they are adaptable for the toy market in which each device when added to the other does something different, new lighting effects plus new sounds plus new sighting potential.... Have also invented a "tricorder" device for our female Yeoman, again basically for dramatic uses on our show but also with female child's toy potential, a device which acts sort of as a portable secretary-recording-photographic unit capable of taking down any information the Captain wishes at any time he is away from his bridge.... Also have spent a considerable amount of time working with our costumer, improving the basic design -- items which also have considerable sales potential. And without depreciating the work of any of our talented people involved, these are all items on which I have had to come up with the basic conception.... The point of all this, Alden, is that I am finding myself required to come up with inventions and designs far beyond what we earlier thought necessary and far beyond what any show creator-producer should be expected to provide. I absolutely am not content to see Desilu and others getting profit-loss statements on the entire show. Admittedly, *Star Trek* is a very special thing and requires a special kind of inventiveness, perhaps also a special kind of "unity" from one person. But however it is sliced, I find myself necessarily becoming a toy-costume-etc. creator and inventor and going far beyond what any of us conceived necessary when we set up the original contract.... The point of this all is that I am not at all happy with these provisions in this contract. They are one-sided, unfair, and each day become more demonstrably so.... I have mentioned this to Herb Solow.

William Theiss modified the uniforms. The high collars were now gone. Per Grace Lee Whitney's suggestion, the women's pant suits were replaced with eye-catching mini-skirts and high black boots. Shatner was pleased to report, "*Star Trek*, to the appreciation of all the men on the set and, in fact, all around the world, would boast the shortest skirts on women of any regular series on television." (156-2)

But changes and additions cost money, and little was set aside for this. These costs would have to come out of monies allocated for the production of individual episodes.

With a per-show budget of $193,500, *Star Trek* would compete with the globe-trotting *I Spy* for the title of Most Expensive Series on Television during the 1966-67 season.

The salaries were coming in high. As the series' star, William Shatner was contracted to appear in every episode, at $5,000 per show. For the first five repeats, he would receive further payment equal to 20 percent of his original salary... if there were any repeats. And he would also be a limited partner, receiving 20 percent of the series' net profits... again, should there be any. Finally, he was guaranteed a raise of $500 per episode for each year that the show stayed on the air.

Like Shatner, Nimoy was to be in every episode produced. Billed as "co-star," his pay was $1,250 per show. For reruns, he'd receive SAG scale plus 10 percent.

Salaries for DeForest Kelley, Grace Lee Whitney, George Takei, and James Doohan were all absurdly cheap by today's standards, but in line with the money being spent on TV in 1966. Roddenberry's salary as creator and producer, was set at $3,000 per episode. John D.F. Black, carrying two separate titles as both associate producer and story editor, was banking $1,725 per episode. Robert Justman as the second associate producer, was earning $1,115. Even these prices were a fraction of what is paid today for the same jobs, inflation already factored in. It was a different world, one *Star Trek* would have much to do with changing.

Even with the modest salaries, *Star Trek* was budgeted above nearly all other series on television at this time. Desilu's board of directors remained cynical. Lucille Ball, however, projected strength and confidence. Frequent memos from Herb Solow to Lucy and her worrisome board, assuring all that the development of *Star Trek* was progressing smoothly and close to being on budget, provided Lucy with much needed comfort. As production neared, on April 19, 1966, she wrote to Solow:

> Dear Herb: I don't want to forget to tell you how much I appreciate your memos to me. They are very helpful, and I understand most appreciated by everyone at the studio. Be talking to you soon. Love, Lucy.

The first episode to be filmed was "The Corbomite Maneuver," with production scheduled to begin on May 24, 1966. All systems were go.

8

Episode 2: THE CORBOMITE MANEUVER
Written by Jerry Sohl
(with Gene Roddenberry, uncredited)
Directed by Joseph Sargent

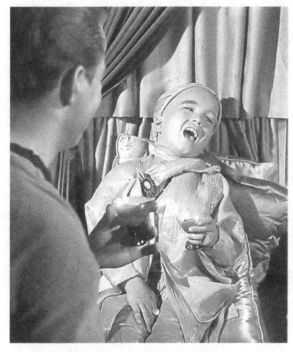

Outtake with Shatner and Clint Howard (Lincoln Enterprises film trim courtesy of Gerald Gurian)

NBC press release, issued October 18, 1966:

Accused of trespassing in a foreign galaxy, the USS Enterprise engages in an eerie mid-space confrontation with the flagship vessel of an alien civilization, in "The Corbomite Maneuver" on the NBC Television Network colorcast of *Star Trek* Thursday Nov. 10.... When it becomes obvious that the enemy vessel is vastly superior in size and weaponry, Captain James Kirk (William Shatner) vainly resorts to evasive tactics, only to have his craft rendered powerless by his adversary, Captain Balok (Clint Howard). A battle of wits ensues between the two spacecraft commanders when Kirk angrily defies a surrender ultimatum in a desperate ruse to gain time.

The penalty for trespassing in this area of space is death, and the helpless Captain Kirk is only given 10 minutes to prepare his crew for execution. With those precious few minutes ticking away, tension on the bridge mounts, taking an especially high toll on Lt. Bailey, a young officer who Dr. McCoy feels Kirk promoted too quickly.

This is not Man against Beast, as first glance at the face of Balok's grotesque alter ego might have us believe. Kirk says it while addressing his crew over the intercom: "You know the greatest danger facing us is ourselves -- an irrational fear of the unknown. But there is no such thing as the unknown. There are only things temporarily hidden, temporarily not understood. In most cases, we have found that intelligence capable of a civilization is capable of understanding peaceful gestures.... All decks stand by, Captain out."

SOUND BITES

- *Dr. McCoy, talking to himself:* "If I jumped every time a light came on around here, I'd end up talking to myself."
- *Lt. Bailey:* "Raising my voice back there doesn't mean I was scared or couldn't do my job. It means I happen to have a human thing called an adrenaline [sic] gland." *Mr. Spock:*

"It does sound most inconvenient. Have you considered having it removed?"

- *Bailey:* "We've got phaser weapons. I vote we blast it!" *Kirk:* "I'll keep that in mind, Mister Bailey, when this becomes a democracy."

- *Mr. Spock:* "Has it occurred to you that there's a certain inefficiency in constantly questioning me on things you've already made up your mind about?" *Kirk:* "It gives me emotional security."

- *Bailey:* "I don't understand this at all. Spock's wasting time; everyone else just sitting around. Somebody's got to do something! What do they want from us? Let's find out what they want us to do!" *Kirk:* "They want us to lose our heads..." *Bailey:* "We've got only eight minutes left!" *Sulu:* "Seven minutes and forty-one seconds." *Bailey:* "He's doing a countdown!"

- *Mr. Spock:* "I regret not having learned more about this Balok. In some manner he was reminiscent of my father." *Scott:* "Then, may Heaven have helped your mother."

ASSESSMENT

The cleverness of this script lies in the scope of its back-story. The space buoy the Enterprise first encounters – that "cube in space" -- is the "fly paper" which lures us into this well-constructed tale. Like the game of chess -- or poker -- played out by the two captains, each move in this story reveals a new layer, enriched with surprise. And the surprises are wonderful: the Enterprise being confronted by the grandness of Balok's mother ship as it dwarfs the Earth vessel; meeting the real Balok, a man who physically resembles a child; and then discovering this strange alien's true intent.

A soon-to-be recurring theme of *Star Trek* -- that mankind is worthwhile even though we humans are flawed -- is already in place. And those flawed humans make for great conflict. Bailey's gradual breakdown is superbly played, as he withdraws into shock and loses the ability to relate to his colleagues. Kirk is in the hot seat, all eyes on him, and one pair flashing disapproval. McCoy enjoys the privilege of being the only one on board who can needle the Captain, and then that teasing turns serious as the Doc challenges Kirk about his judgment, his intent, and even his weight. When being ribbed about the pretty yeoman, Kirk admits that he already has a woman in his life -- her name is the Enterprise. Kirk only has love for her.

The characters, fleshed out and three-dimensional as the sector of space they intrude upon, carry the story. With so much going for it, "Corbomite" doesn't need fast pacing or a variety of sets. Like a tautly written stage play, our attention is held fast.

THE STORY BEHIND THE STORY

Script Timeline
Jerry Sohl's story outline, ST #6, "Danger Zone": Late March 1966.
Sohl's revised outline, gratis, now entitled "The Corbomite Maneuver":
April 4, 1966.
Gene Roddenberry's revised story outline: April 7, 1966.
Sohl's 1st Draft teleplay: April 21, 1966.
Sohl's 2nd Draft teleplay: April 29, 1966.
Sohl's gratis script polish (Mimeo Department "Yellow Cover 1st Draft"):
May 3, 1966.
Gene Roddenberry's first rewrite (Final Draft teleplay): May 9, 1966.
Roddenberry second rewrite (Rev. Final Draft teleplay): May 12, 1966.

Roddenberry's third rewrite (2nd Rev. Final Draft teleplay): May 20, 1966.
Additional page revisions by Roddenberry: May 23 & 25, 1966.

"The Corbomite Maneuver" was designed to introduce us to the crew of the Enterprise and their ship. William Shatner said, "We couldn't have asked for an easier maiden voyage, and for that reason it was hoped that this simple, self-contained story would allow us to ease ourselves into the rigors of weekly shooting." (156-8)

Jerry Sohl provided the not-as-simple-as-it-seemed premise. The 51-year-old was best known and respected for his popular science fiction novels, such as *Costigan's Needle* and *The Mars Monopoly*. He had already written for *The Twilight Zone* and *The Outer Limits* and, with less artistic respect, cheap monster films for the big screen.

Daily Variety called 1965's *Die, Monster, Die* "a routine sci-fi horror... slowly paced in scripting and direction." For 1966's *Monster of Terror*, which the trade labeled as another "routine horror pic," the critic wrote, "Jerry Sohl's screenplay hasn't much nerve to it." Sohl didn't even bother taking a writing credit for the 1966 Japanese horror, *Frankenstein Conquers the World*.

Roddenberry, having befriended Sohl while researching and writing the *Star Trek* pilots, was determined to make him one of the series' first writers. Sohl was invited to Desilu for the initial screening of "Where No Man Has Gone Before" on March 7, 1966, the first of seven such private play dates. Also in attendance that day, and given *Star Trek* writing assignments: John D.F. Black, Lee Erwin, Don Ingalls, Stephen Kandel, Adrian Spies and renowned science fiction author A.E. van Vogt.

As for the story's origin, Sohl recalled, "I was thinking, suppose you ran across a cube in space. A cube is so damn finitive [sic] and so square and so unlike nature, that you know right away it represents intelligent life. 'What is it doing there?' It's like an electronic warning system at the frontier." (160-2)

Sohl's outline from March 1966 was called "Danger Zone." It was rough, of course. Many of the characters of the series, as well as the technology of the Enterprise, were still on the drawing boards. Sohl was paid for the outline and then rewrote it for free, with a title change to "The Corbomite Maneuver," now emphasizing the bluff Kirk plays to save his ship. Upon reading this draft, associate producer Robert Justman wrote to Roddenberry:

> For the most part am greatly pleased with Jerry Sohl's revised outline.... He has done everything that we discussed together last time we met and has tightened up the story considerably so that it really works. (RJ2-1)

Justman couldn't help but be pleased this first time out. More than 90% of the story stayed on the Enterprise and most of that on the bridge. This was a show *Star Trek* could certainly afford to make.

Stan Robertson at the network had mixed feelings, writing Roddenberry:

> The story snares our attention right from the top and builds for three-and-a-half acts to a pinnacle... and then goes downhill in the final few critical moments. (SR2-1)

Robertson was right. In this version, after the Enterprise breaks free of Balok's smaller secondary ship, the seemingly unconscious alien Commander, a normal-sized humanoid, is brought aboard and rushed to sickbay. This is the final test of Kirk's crew by Balok -- to see what they will do once he appears helpless. Their humanitarian goodwill impresses him and he accepts their friendship. This ending lacked the cleverness that was yet to come.

A new draft of the outline was quickly written by Roddenberry, this one containing the spin at the end -- Balok now described as an adult alien resembling a human child. Jerry Sohl approved of the change, later saying, "They added the fellow at the end, which was like so many of my novels, where a little kid is behind the whole thing. That tickled Gene Roddenberry. And Robert Justman was taken by the whole thing." (160-2)

For this new ending, however, it is Kirk and McCoy alone who beam over to Balok's ship to make the discovery. There was no Lt. Bailey subplot at this stage.

Matt Jefferies, reading the outlines with an eye toward set construction and seeing the ship's interior described as both spacious and very alien, shot Roddenberry a note warning that "several weeks may be required" to design and build such a set. (MJ2)

Bill Theiss, looking the outlines over with a different eye -- toward costuming needs -- was immediately struck by another problem. Balok -- *the real Balok* -- is seen on the Enterprise viewing screen delivering his threats... or, at least, his head and shoulders are seen. Later, we meet and see all of him, with the hope for a surprise reveal that he is actually quite a tiny fellow. Hearing that they were thinking of hiring a child to play this part, Theiss wrote Roddenberry:

> One of the main characteristics of a child in relation to an adult is the head of a child is proportionally larger in relation to the body, e.g., the width of the shoulders. If Balok is indeed played by a child actor... and if you show any of the neck and shoulders in the scene [on the Enterprise viewing screen], you run the risk of tipping the hat that he is indeed smaller than the average human. (BT2)

Star Trek had a good staff. And they had many unique problems to solve.

Sohl delivered his first draft teleplay on April 21. Justman, still uncharacteristically happy, wrote:

> I am quite pleased with this screenplay. Although the amount and type of post-production opticals contained within the body of the script are almost staggering, the show itself would seem to be economically feasible.... On Page 5 I don't think it's necessary for us to have the device of the brash young officer who has been taking everybody on board the ship with the old shell game. I think that Kirk can develop his own bluffing maneuver with the previous spark triggering him. Later on in Act II, I think that when the Enterprise is touched by the strong sensor beams, instead of the ship plummeting into a vortex, we could have it suddenly come to a dead stop. This would save us some very expensive miniature shooting. (RJ2-2)

After reading the memo from Bill Theiss, Justman suggested Balok be played by "a midget or dwarf," not a child. Having read Matt Jefferies memo about the interior of Balok's ship, he made the suggestion that it should be scaled down and kept on Stage 9, perhaps as a redress of the Enterprise briefing room. To sell this idea, he wrote:

> Having a set this size would tend to make the small size of Balok all the more impressive.... I am tempted to consider this show as either our first or second to be produced. I am beginning to feel a little better. (RJ2-2)

With the staff notes in hand, Sohl did his obligatory rewrite, turning in his 2nd Draft on April 29. Proving to be a team player, he agreed to wait on receiving his final paycheck until after NBC's reaction to the script was known.

Stan Robertson was not as pleased as Robert Justman had been. He wrote to John D.F. Black:

> Generally, this script lacks interest, enthusiasm and suspense until we are so far along in it that it is doubtful if we will be able to hold our audience that long. It seems as though the writer has unsuccessfully come to grips with what appears to be, at this point, one of the major obstacles which our writers must overcome -- the utilization of the "gadgets" of our series without making the "things" more predominate than the basic story we are telling. (ST2-2)

Robertson also suggested a solution regarding the casting of Balok and how not to "tip the hat" as to his true size. He wrote:

> As to the "problem" of using the small actor to portray Balok... you might consider using the physical features of a large actor... when he is shown on screen. However, when we actually meet him in person, at this time we could see that he is a "Michael Dunn" type person. (ST2-2)

The Oscar-nominated actor Michael Dunn would later appear in *Star Trek* ("Plato's Stepchildren"), but Sohl took Robertson's suggestion in a different direction. With his final script polish -- a free rewrite -- from May 3, Balok now had a frightening "puppet" avatar whose image would be seen on the Enterprise's viewing screen.

In all, Jerry Sohl did three drafts of his screenplay. He later said, "Bob Justman and Gene Roddenberry and I went over 'The Corbomite Maneuver' with a fine-tooth comb to determine whether or not the things that were in it were things that we really wanted to use from that point on." (160-3)

Not all felt the teeth of the comb were fine enough. Sohl's last handling of the script is a somewhat disappointing read. The plot points are all there but the "character" of the filmed episode -- the diverse personalities and conflicts, and dialogue that feels both natural and alternates between clever and edgy -- is not yet in place. Also absent: Spock's speculation that the cube they have encountered is "flypaper"; his suggestion that Bailey consider having his adrenal gland removed; that Spock thinks Balok, in some ways, resembles his father, and Scott's reaction to this.

Also missing, McCoy talking to himself about how he would *start talking to himself* if he jumped every time a light flashed on and off; Janice Rand heating up coffee by zapping it with a phaser; the dietary salad of "green leafs" that McCoy has her bring to Kirk, irritating the Captain so. Even pivotal moments such as Kirk's realization that this is not a game of chess but one of poker, and Bailey's meltdown on the bridge, are nowhere in sight.

Bailey still doesn't make the trip to Balok's ship (the Fesarius) and he is not the navigation officer. Instead, he sits at the communications station -- which means there is no Uhura. It was Gene Roddenberry's series of rewrites, beginning with the May 9 Final Draft, which brought much of the life and conflict into "The Corbomite Maneuver," as well as the character of Uhura.

"Of course there was much rewriting," Roddenberry said in a conversation with this author in 1982. "There was very little to go by at this point for our writers, other than the pilots, and much was changing. But Jerry brought in a wonderful story and premise. With something like this, a producer can immediately see the potentials with establishing the characteristics of the series' regulars. Much like in a wartime movie about a submarine being pursued and depth charges dropped, these men are trapped together; looking to the captain to make the right choices, certain that this is the end. You can build on that." (145)

The next look NBC got of the script was with Roddenberry's May 12 revised final draft. Stan Robertson immediately saw the difference and wrote back:

> The humanitarian qualities and character development in this draft are excellent. Kirk grows more and more and becomes a more believable and "live" person through his relationship with the young officer, Bailey, Dr. McCoy and Balok. Sulu's character begins to grow also, and we get a closer insight into Spock. (ST2-3)

Beyond this, Robertson still had reservations. This was the first "bottle show," with nearly the entire plot playing out on board the Enterprise. The story took the time needed to bring the Enterprise to life for anyone watching for the first time -- and this wasn't what Robertson wanted to see. His letter continued:

> Although there is a very decided improvement in this draft... on paper, at least, our story still seems to drag somewhat.... We realize that in a series of this nature it is most important to give reality and believability to the tools we must live with. However, except for "science fiction buffs" in our audience, which it is logical to assume will be in the minority, the broad segment of our viewers will be attracted to our stories by the action-adventure and dramatic qualities they contain. Technical data or details should, we would think, never interfere with or replace any of the above mentioned ingredients. (ST2-3)

Roddenberry wanted to play it slow, following Kirk from room to room, down corridors and up and down in an elevator to establish the immense scope of the Enterprise so that it could be better appreciated later when this giant Earth vessel is dwarfed by the much bigger alien ship. He also wanted to establish the characters, the chain of command, and the science as to what does work, what doesn't work, and why. In a different and more innocent time when audiences weren't well versed in science fiction, he believed it was important to establish a feeling of the world of *Star Trek*.

Stan Robertson either possessed the impatience of the average American of 40 years hence, or had a premonition as to how that impatience would manifest itself in the TV audience of his distant tomorrows. His opinions would influence the further development of *Star Trek* -- whether for good or bad depends on one's tastes.

In an attempt to appease Robertson, Roddenberry tinkered with the script further, creating a 2nd Revised Final Draft on May 20, with additional page revisions on May 23 and 25, immediately following something seldom done in the making of dramatic episodic TV -- a full day of rehearsing.

Pre-Production
May 16-20, 1966 and, for rehearsal, May 23, 1966 (6 days prep).

Joseph Sargent was hired to direct. At 41, he was well regarded in both television and on the stage. Typical of many of the trade reviews given for his TV assignments, *Daily Variety* said of a 1964 episode of *Kentucky Jones*:

> Direction by Joseph Sargent has real quality, with a keen eye for the values contained in the script, and is equally fine in his delineation of characters.

That same year, for his Los Angeles stage production of *The Bald Soprano*, the trade said:

> [With] Joseph Sargent's sensitive but free-flowing direction, the overall production is superb. Sargent paces his collection of stalwart performers to draw ethereal projections but still maintain a basic reality that gives them credulity.

On the little screen, among his many credits, Sargent had directed 14 episodes of

Lassie, 11 for *The Man from U.N.C.L.E.* and seven for *Gunsmoke*. He also had experience with William Shatner, giving him direction in an episode of *The Fugitive*. In Sargent's future, the 1967 pilot episode for *The Invaders*, the Hugo nominated 1970 sci-fi film, *Colossus: The Forbin Project*, the critically acclaimed 1974 big screen feature *The Taking of Pelham One Two Three*, and both an Emmy and a Director's Guild of America (DGA) Award for "The Marcus-Nelson Murders," the 1972 pilot for *Kojak*.

John D.F. Black recalled, "I knew Joe from *Novak*, and I called him. I said, 'Joe, it's the first episode, it's important, we need you.' And that's all you had to say to Joe, that you needed him. He called his agent who called us and said, 'Okay, you got him.'" (17)

Of his introduction to *Star Trek*, Sargent said, "I read the script and it was fascinating. And I saw where Gene was going with the concept of it, which was to do with making some social commentary on what was going on in the world. It was something to identify with if you certainly went past all the razzmatazz and discovered that contemporary issues were coming sneakily at you from different angles." (151)

Sargent made a significant contribution to *Star Trek* -- it was his idea to put a black woman on the bridge as the communications officer. Even though Lloyd Haynes, an African-American who would later be the star of TV's *Room 222*, had sat at that station in the second pilot, the script described the new character as white and male.

"I suddenly became conscious of the fact that we had a good representation -- a good diversity in virtually all ethnic areas -- except black people," Sargent said. "There wasn't a black actor in the group and I gingerly, *and obsessively*, approached Gene. And he immediately agreed that there *had* to be a Black on the bridge." (151)

When Sargent made the suggestion, Joe D'Agosta remembered, "I said to Gene, 'What about Nichelle?' He said, 'Yeah, let's get her.' There was no hesitation; no question at all." (43-4)

Nichelle Nichols between takes during briefing room scene on Day 6 of production (Courtesy of Gerald Gurian)

Nichelle Nichols, 31, was a fairly new face in TV. On stage, Nichols was a dancer and singer and had appeared in *Porgy and Bess*. Joe D'Agosta was responsible for her television acting debut, for the racially-charged episode of *The Lieutenant* that ruffled the NBC peacock's feathers so badly and contributed to the cancellation of the series. He recalled, "I had seen Nichelle and a fella named Don Marshall do a scene in an acting class that I was in, so I brought them in for an audition. They didn't have SAG cards; they had never done film or television. But they soon would get them, because we hired them on the spot for the lead in that episode." (43)

Roddenberry and D'Agosta were both impressed by Nichols' performance on *The Lieutenant*. D'Agosta did not know that Roddenberry and Nichols had had an affair; he merely recalled her as cooperative, reliable and talented. To Roddenberry's credit, he was determined not to allow his past relationship with Nichols influence the casting decision; he left that up to Sargent.

Nichols was on a tour of European nightclubs when she received an urgent message from her agent saying to return home immediately, that an audition had been arranged and she was being considered for a series that would commence production in one week. Nichols hurriedly flew back to Los Angeles and drove herself to Desilu for an interview with the unnamed producer of something called *Star Trek*. She didn't discover her former lover was involved until she walked into the production office. Joseph Sargent was there, as were Bob Justman, Joe D'Agosta and Eddie Milkis. And then she saw Roddenberry. Nichols remembered saying, "Why, Mr. R, what are you doing here?" and that Roddenberry answered with a grin, "Oh, I've got a little something to do with this." (127-2)

Nichols had three competitors for the role. Mittie Lawrence and Ena Hartman were early in their TV and film careers and happy to take the consolation prize – appearing in the background, one as "Crew Woman," the other as "Crew Woman #2." The third candidate was Gloria Calomee, who turned down the offer for a "walk on," but did well for herself in the 1960s and 1970s on TV. Nichols was the standout in Sargent eyes. He said, "When she read and showed the kind of class that I was looking for, it all came together." (151)

The communications officer's name came about when Roddenberry and Sargent noticed a book Nichols was reading while sitting in the waiting room. It was about a real life African woman named "Uhuru," translating to "freedom." Roddenberry liked the idea but felt the name would be easier to pronounce if given an "a" at the end instead of the "u," and Uhura was born. It was Roddenberry's third rewrite, dated May 20, 1966, just four days before the start of principal photography, which had the first reference to the character.

While given no guarantee as to how many episodes she would appear in, Nichols was paid well for her time -- $1,000 flat rate per episode. Within a few weeks, Desilu would be rethinking this deal (see Pre-Production, "Mudd's Women").

Anthony Call as Mister Bailey
(Lincoln Enterprises film trim courtesy of Gerald Gurian)

As for the pivotal role of Junior Navigations Officer Dave Bailey, six young actors were considered. One, Bruce Mars, was also put in the background of this episode, as "Crew Man #1." He'd get more out of his audition than that, returning in a few months to play a substantial guest role as the rascally Finnegan in "Shore Leave." Also in consideration for Bailey was Stewart Moss. Joe D'Agosta saved him for the plum role as Joe Tormolen, the crewman with the itchy nose and sweaty hands who kills himself with a butter knife in "The Naked Time."

Anthony "Tony" Call was the winner. He had appeared on an episode of Jeffrey Hunter's series *Temple Houston*, as well as *The Twilight Zone*, *Lost in Space* and *Combat!* He was 25.

Walker Edmiston, who worked for decades in television and film providing hundreds of voices for cartoons and TV commercials, was the voice of the childlike Balok. In Los Angeles, Edmiston had his own self-titled Saturday morning kiddie show.

Clint Howard in his second series with co-star, the bear, from *Gentle Ben* (Ivan Tors Productions, 1967)

Ted Cassidy -- Lurch from *The Addams Family* -- provided the voice of Balok's ominous alter ego. What we saw on camera -- that face that not even a mother could love -- was designed by Wah Chang.

Clint Howard, as little Balok, was seven. He already had many TV and film credits, including appearances on *The Andy Griffith Show* as Opie Taylor's friend Leon (Ronny Howard -- "Opie" -- was Clint's real-life big brother) and as a cast member for one season on the series *The Baileys of Balboa*. A starring role in TV's *Gentle Ben*, under a bear and Dennis Weaver, was still two years away.

The bridge stations were manned by many soon-to-be-familiar faces on *Star Trek*.

William Blackburn, with light brown hair and wearing gold, made his first of 59 appearances. He was the lighting stand-in for DeForest Kelley.

Bill Blackburn at navigation station (left), where he would sit for many of his 59 appearances (Unaired film trim courtesy of Gerald Gurian)

Frank De Vinci, with dark hair and a blue top, has his first of 44. He stood in for Leonard Nimoy as the sets were lit. It was decided early on that sprinkling in familiar faces among the crewmen would help to maintain believability, and these three, being needed on set every day, were the obvious choices.

Eddie Paskey, William Shatner's stand-in for lighting set-ups, returned for his second of 59 appearances. He's the one with brown hair and wearing a red uniform top.

Paskey recalled, "Greg Peters, the series' A.D., called and asked if I wanted to be on the show as Bill's stand-in, and I said 'Yeah!' I'd only been in the business for maybe a year, but I had seen some of what stand-ins did and I thought, 'Jeez, you know, this would be kinda fun.' Plus it was a steady income, with my wife and I raising two kids at the time. On the very first show we did, which was 'The Corbomite Maneuver,' Greg told me, 'I want you to get up there in that seat,' which was the seat on the bridge that became mine -- Scotty's engineering area. They got me a red shirt like the Engineering crew wore, which stood out pretty good, and Greg says, 'That's going to be your spot.' So Greg was the instigator of me being in almost every show, because I was always sitting there at the console, at that station." (135-2)

Before production began, first-time director of photography Jerry Finnerman had a talk with his mentor, Harry Stradling, Sr.. Finnerman had screened the pilot and felt it looked "a little lush." He later said, "In those days, NBC and, I presume, all of the networks felt better if everything was bright and bubbly. But this wasn't that kind of show." (63-1)

"Bright and bubbly," the result of flat *over*-lighting where everything in the picture is bathed in equally balanced light, translated to a sharper, cleaner broadcast image. Of the three networks, NBC was especially fond of this approach, with its series from this period beaming across America looking sharp but lacking visual texture and mood, so much so that filmed prime time series often looked more like video-taped daytime soap operas.

Finnerman, who had great admiration for Harry Stradling, Sr., wanted to recreate the look his former boss had achieved with *The Picture of Dorian Gray*. He said, "I loved it and wondered how he accomplished those beautiful half-tones. And he told me, 'Jerry, when you take the lights down so far that they scare you, that's when it'll look beautiful, that's when you get the half-tones'.... So we went into those definitions, the types of things like people turning into shadow, the goods and the bads, the darks and the lights, the message being in the story *and* the photography." (63-1)

Finnerman who, following his mentor's advice, had quit Stradling's crew and thereby lost a chance to serve as camera operator on *Funny Girl*, excitedly threw himself into the pre-production stage for the only *Star Trek* episode he was guaranteed. If his cinematic vision for *Star Trek* worked, he would get more episodes -- perhaps the entire season. And then excitement turned to anxiety.

Finnerman recalled, "They gave me the first show and I prepped this show, and two nights before the show was going to start, I went to Herb Solow -- who was a wonderful man; very soft spoken -- and I said, 'You'd better get somebody else.' And he said, 'My God, what's wrong; are you sick?' I told him my problems; I knew I was going to fail and, if I failed, I would have to drop back [to camera operator in the cameraman's union] and, if I dropped back... Harry would be doing *Funny Girl* and I wouldn't be doing anything....

"He never raised his voice, but he raised his voice this time, and he said, 'You're worried about a *year*? How would you like it to never work in Hollywood again?... I went out on a limb for you.... And I know you'll do well. So you'd better be here and be ready to go the first day of shooting.'" (63-3)

Finnerman would be on set that first day. As he recalled it, he would also often be in the men's bathroom, sick.

Monday, May 23, 1966, was designated as a rehearsal day. In television, only situation comedies have rehearsals, or "table reads," where the cast sit around a large conference table and read through the script together with the producer, director and writers watching, making notes for possible changes in dialogue. Joseph Sargent had insisted a table reading take place for the first *Star Trek*. He later said, "It's shocking how it's so much part of the film culture where rehearsals have always been looked upon as unnecessary, because you're shooting out of sequence with your people, and it would cost money, and all the lame excuses that studio's producers can come up with to avoid rehearsing. They ignore the fact that without rehearsals you *are* wasting money, in front of a paid crew, in the middle of a production. I would never ever approach a film without some kind of rehearsal and I always made that clear in my contract." (151)

John D.F. Black said, "We agreed to give him a rehearsal day because it was a new company -- everyone wasn't settled in yet. There were new people around, both in the cast and on the crew, and he wanted everybody there for a rehearsal. It's much like a dress rehearsal. I was there, and it went beautifully." (17)

Production Diary
Filmed May 24, 25, 26, 27, 31, June 1 & 2 (1/2 day), 1966
(Planned as 6 day production; finishing 1/2 day behind; total cost: $190,430).

Tuesday, May 24, 1966. The No. 1 song on U.S. radio was "Monday, Monday" by The Mamas and the Papas. CBS had the top rated TV program from the night before -- Desilu's own *The Lucy Show*. The Broadway play *Mame* was opening for the first of 1508 performances at the Winter Garden Theater. And this was kickoff day for production on *Star Trek*, the original series.

Gene Roddenberry sent a memo to his production staff first thing in the morning, telling them:

> On this first day of production, I think it wise we establish certain routines of value to us during the shooting year:
> 1. Assistant director should convey to my office, or in my absence to the office concerned, at noon and at late afternoon before our office closes, a simple verbal report of pages completed and any problems or information pertinent.
> 2. John D.F. Black should establish a routine of visiting the set once morning and afternoon, establishing that the tenor and mood of the scenes being photographed are generally in keeping with the script and our discussions with the director. If this is found not to be the case, he and I should confer on the subject immediately.
> 3. None of the above is meant to replace or supersede R. Justman's normal production responsibilities and routines.
> 4. Cameramen and script supervisor have been alerted to flash this office should the director depart appreciably from dialogue, characterization, etc. In my absence or unavailability, John D.F. Black will handle the matter as appears best.
> 5. Notification from set of deviation from production planning and routine will be handled by R. Justman.
> 6. Where possible, in order to insulate us from actor problems and maintain our friendly relationship with cast, complaints from actors, unusual or special requests from them, etc., should be passed on to Morris Chapnick of Herb Solow's office....
> In short, for best efficiency and a minimum of anguish, let us of the *Star Trek* staff start along with the show and the crew with a planned routine and division of responsibility which will have us all drinking champagne and feeling smug a year from now.

This was not Roddenberry's first time around the block; not his first series; not, for that matter, his first war.

The first scene on schedule was Kirk's physical in sickbay, accompanied by the verbal sparring with Dr. McCoy. It was also when Roddenberry's meticulous plan went to hell.

DeForest Kelley recalled, "Gene Roddenberry came down to the set, called the crew to attention, gathered everybody around and made a speech on what we were embarking on, the dedication that had gone into the show, and that he wished it to continue with everyone who was involved -- himself, and everybody from the stars to the man who sweeps the floor." (98-6)

After the pep talk, Kelley said Roddenberry took him aside and asked that he remove the ring he wore -- the ring that had belonged to his deceased mother. Kelley remembered, "Roddenberry said 'no jewelry.' I said, 'No jewelry, no DeForest.'" (98-1)

Roddenberry, not always willing to bend, relented.

As for the first scene, Kelley said, "[Gene] had this thing all laid out in the medical lab, giving Bill a physical examination. I said something about, 'I'm a doctor, not a moon shuttle conductor...' and that was the first scene shot in the series." (98-6)

For this, William Shatner agreed to allow his chest to be shaved. Shatner, with a moderate amount of hair on his body, did not fit into Roddenberry's idea that men of the future would have little or no body hair.

The scenes in Kirk's quarters came next, again with McCoy, and introducing Yeoman Janice Rand who, per McCoy's instructions, brings Kirk his dietary salad. Of this, NBC's John Kubichan had instructed:

> Please avoid playing this sequence in any manner which might suggest the relationship between Kirk and Janice is anything more intimate than that of Captain and Yeoman. (BS2)

William Theiss was given full credit from Grace Lee Whitney for Rand's hair ... but Whitney came up with the mini (Courtesy of Gerald Gurian)

Kubichan, one of the network's watchdogs for programming and censorship issues, knowing that Roddenberry was pushing for sexual tension between these two characters, felt it inappropriate for a ship's captain to flirt with a subordinate. Roddenberry and Sargent went for the sexual tension anyway. With Rand's miniskirt -- the shortest to be seen on TV -- it was hard to take it any other way.

William Theiss designed -- or rather built -- the wig Yeoman Rand wore. Grace Lee Whitney said, "They put a cone on my head, and put the blonde hair [from two separate wigs] on it, and tried to find different ways of weaving it. It was really her signature. Without that hair I am practically unrecognizable. That hair put me on the map.... But that was Bill Theiss all the way. A genius." (183-3)

Theiss had also rethought the look of the uniforms -- with that "mini" Grace Lee Whitney dared him and Roddenberry to allow her character to wear, and now with the addition of the third primary uniform color, joining the gold and the blue. While Uhura -- for this episode and the next -- was clad in gold, Rand, like Scotty, got an upgrade to the more RCA color TV-friendly red. Bill Theiss said, "The colors were chosen purely for technical reasons. We tried to find three colors for the shirts that would be as different from each other as possible, in black-and-white as well as color.... I think the uniforms' greatest asset is their simplicity." (172-2)

And then the company moved to the spectacular -- for its time and medium -- bridge set. George Takei, for his book *To the Stars*, recalled:

> What commanded all eyes and pulled them like some gravitational force to the blazingly lit center of the set was the single most compelling presence there, the unmistakable star of the production, William Shatner. Everything seemed to revolve around him. The camera crew, the light crew, the sound crew were all converged on him. And Shatner fully occupied the epicenter. He commanded the hub of all activity on the set. He radiated energy and a boundless joy in his position. He shouted his opinions out to the director; he sprang up, demonstrating his ideas; he laughed and joked and bounced his wit off the crew. He beamed out an infectious, expansively joyous life force.

Joseph Sargent took his last shot at 6:45 p.m., one half-hour into union overtime.

Day 2, Wednesday -- the first of four days on the bridge, with more of that "infectious, expansively joyous life force" of which George Takei spoke. Leonard Nimoy, however, was not projecting the same energy and sense of pleasure. He recalled that Joseph Sargent helped him to "break through" and "realize exactly who the Vulcan

Camera tie-down set up for matte shot to include alien spacecraft, to be added during post (Courtesy of Gerald Gurian)

was." Spock was supposed to stare at the giant alien space ship growing on the view screen. His spoken reaction was a single word, for the first time: "Fascinating."

Nimoy remembered, "I just didn't have a handle on how to say it. I was still somewhat in 'first officer' mode, but it didn't seem appropriate to shout such a word out. Everyone was reacting in character -- humanly, of course -- but I couldn't figure out how the Vulcan would respond or how the word should come out." (128-3)

Sargent said, "Leonard came up to me and he was ready to quit. He said, 'Joe, I can't take this. I'm an actor and I don't know how to play a character that has no emotion.' As an actor, he was trained to work for an emotional element in his character, and he felt there wasn't any. Having been trained myself as an actor, I knew exactly what was bothering him. Fortunately, I was able to make a virtue out of something that, for him, seemed awfully negative, and I convinced him that having so-called 'no emotion' was just an external aspect of the character's element. It didn't have anything to do with the richness of his intellectuality. He was merely able to conquer the emotional distortions that can interfere with reasoning." (151)

Nimoy remembered, "The director gave me a brilliant note which said: 'Be different. Be the scientist. Be detached. See it as something that's a curiosity rather than a threat.' I said, 'Fascinating.' Well, a big chunk of the character was born right there." (128-18)

Nimoy was not the only one who very nearly quit. Sargent remembered how Jerry Finnerman still wanted to jump ship. Even with the production schedule this relaxed, spending more time on a single set than any other episode, Finnerman was overwhelmed by the pressure of running the camera and lighting units -- an immense responsibility for anyone, especially someone who had never done it before.

Finnerman later said, "The director of photography -- the cinematographer -- creates the look of the show. They create the dimension; they tell a story with their lights, hopefully not overpowering the story so much that you're looking at the photography and not the story. I've always considered cinematographers like composers. You get a real good one on a real good story and you're listening to Wagner, Tchaikovsky, or Beethoven. You know, people get that emotional feeling. It's more than just putting the lighting on a face. Anybody can do that. But it takes a special breed to be a good director of photography." (63-3)

Finnerman just wasn't sure he was of that breed, and admitted, "I used to get very nervous. And Bob Justman would accompany me to the men's bathroom when I regurgitated, and tell me how good I was. Really.... It's terrible to talk about, but I was *that* nervous... being so young." (63-3)

Justman stood by Finnerman as the green cinematographer lost his breakfast and lunch. And Sargent gave Finnerman pep talks as a counterpoint to Herb Solow's threat that he might never work in Hollywood again. All could see the talent their novice cinematographer was bringing to the series, the textures and moods TV lighting rarely saw.

"I would describe it as classic black-and-white photography of the '40s," Finnerman said. "I never thought of it as television. I thought of it as theatrical. If I'd thought of it as television I would have just come in and taken a light and lit *everything*. That wasn't what they wanted and it wasn't what I wanted.... So, when you look at *Star Trek*, even today, you're gonna say, 'Hey, that looks like a feature.' And it was lit that way." (63-3)

Nichelle Nichols (behind DeForest Kelley), staying in good spirits after a trip to the hospital (Courtesy of Gerald Gurian)

Fortunately, Finnerman stayed. His work was brilliant, even though his nerves were frayed. He later said, "That continued through my lifespan, unfortunately. I used to get awfully nervous.... But I never regurgitated after that." (63-3)

The second day's production stopped at 6:50 p.m.

Day 3, Thursday, began with a bang ... on the highway. Production notes reveal Nichelle Nichols had been involved in an "auto accident" on her way to the studio and was "sent to hospital for stitches in lip (inner), returned to work at 9:50 a.m." Nichols' call time for makeup had been 6:30 a.m.

Sargent started filming at 8 a.m., shooting around Nichols until she made it to the set at 9:50. He took his last shot at 7:15 (a full hour into overtime pay for the crew).

On *The CBS Evening News with Walter Cronkite* this night, America saw startling still images of a Buddhist monk setting himself on fire in front of the U.S. consulate earlier that day, in Hue, South Vietnam.

Day 4, Friday. Another full day on the bridge set, with filming stopping at 7:10 p.m. and the set wrapped by 7:30.

Monday, May 30. While the stage was dark for Memorial Day, the U.S. launched Surveyor 1 to the moon, and 300 U.S. warplanes bombed North Vietnam.

Day 5, Tuesday. On the fifth day of production, as work continued on the bridge, seven-year old Clint Howard was brought in for makeup tests. He remembered, "They asked me -- or, actually, they asked my dad -- if I might be willing to shave my head bald. And I didn't think that was a good idea at all. I didn't want to go to school bald, didn't want to be that kid with the shaved head; I didn't want any part of that. Neither did my dad, because I was a working actor and that would take me out of the running for parts for a couple months. So we said 'no' on the shave. Then they said, 'Okay, we can put a bald cap on him.' And I remember really vividly going in and sitting in the makeup chair and the one fella, you know, the main guy, the old guy with white hair [Fred Phillips], fitted me for the bald cap. He was really nice. They were all nice. It took the whole afternoon, because they wanted to do a test, to make sure they could get it to look good. And it looked great." (85)

James Doohan said of Howard in his Balok makeup, "I had never seen anyone as strange as he." (52-1)

Meanwhile, the grownups continued filming until 6:50 p.m., followed by the removal of makeup and wrapping the set.

Day 6, Wednesday. Work continued for the first half of the day on the bridge set, and then the company moved to the briefing room. Later, this set was redressed for the interior of Balok's ship.

Clint Howard said, "I certainly appreciated the whole sort of spaceship fantasy thing of being on the Enterprise. I certainly thought it was cool. I had my dad take some snapshots of me sitting in the captain's chair. But, even at that age, I understood I had a job to do. I knew I was playing a 400-year-old little alien who ran this giant spaceship all by himself. And I knew that I was curious and that I had the power over the Enterprise.

Day 6: Kelley and Shatner waiting "Action!"
(Courtesy of Gerald Gurian)

"They called me on the set and William Shatner seemed very professional -- everybody did. I liked the costume, I was having fun, and the people were all nice. Of course, they never told me right out of the box that they were going to replace my dialogue, and, in fact, what I remember them telling me is they were going to run my voice through this new-fangled gizmo called a synthesizer. They were going to synthesize my voice and then stretch it and bend it and make it like an alien." (85)

"Clint was a darling kid," Joseph Sargent said. "But he didn't have quite the treble or the vocabulary at seven that took care of the kind of authoritarian cadence that was necessary." (151)

Howard had no problem with his voice being replaced. It was something else that worried him. He said, "You know, I did have issues with the 'tranya.' Because, the prop man, when he wheeled his cart over and we were getting ready to shoot, showed me and my dad what 'tranya' was, and it was pink grapefruit juice. And I've never had a taste for pink grapefruit juice. Even today, I'd be choking it down. It just bothers me. But by God it was pink grapefruit juice. And I asked my dad, 'Can't they put some grape juice or apple juice in the canister? Does it have to be pink grapefruit juice?' And I remember my dad looking at me and he said, 'You're gonna drink the grapefruit juice and you're gonna like it.' So, as you see in the scene, when I swallow it, I let out this overblown reaction, like a little kid drinking liquor. Because that's what it tasted like to me." (85)

Howard took his last sip of tranya and filming stopped at 7:10 p.m.

Day 7, Thursday, June 2, 1966. Even with all the action taking place on a single stage, Joseph Sargent had fallen behind, delaying the start of the next scheduled production ("Mudd's Women") by a half day. He took his last shots in the transporter room.

At 1 p.m., "The Corbomite Maneuver" wrapped. Robert Justman, keeping production notes at the time, wrote, "One-half day over -- shot extra camera but blew it on unnecessary setups."

John D.F. Black recalled, "On that night of the first shoot, I was coming from the stage and I saw Shatner sitting on the rear fender of a car across from my office. And we talked a bit. He said, 'What am I going to do, Johnny?' And I said, 'What do you mean, pal?' And he said, 'Well, if it doesn't work ... It's just so damned important to us.' And I said, 'No, no, it's going to work. It's going to be fine.' And he said, 'I hope so,' and walked away." (17)

On that last night, DeForest Kelley said to Roddenberry, "This is going to be the biggest hit or the biggest miss God ever made." (98-1)

Then the editors and musicians, not God, took over.

The other Balok takes a cigarette break. The brand, according to John D.F. Black: Pall Mall, unfiltered
(Courtesy of Mary Black)

Post-Production
June 3 through October 31, 1966. Music score recorded on September 20, 1966.

Robert Swanson was chosen to head the first of three editing teams alternating *Star Trek* episodes. Prior to this he was busy on the Desilu lot, having served as the lead cutter of episodes for *The Untouchables*. Swanson was also a top editor on the prestigious *Playhouse 90*. Justman remembered Swanson "worked quickly with great confidence."

NBC requested that Swanson remove a scene from the edited film. In Act 1, when Kirk tells Spock over the intercom that he'll go to his quarters and change clothes before coming to the bridge, the Captain finds newly-assigned Yeoman Rand waiting for him, with clean clothes laid out. Kirk is learning about the job specifications of a "Captain's Yeoman."

Deleted scene from the Captain's quarters
(Color image available on startrekhistory.com and startrekpropauthority.com)

Composer Fred Steiner was 43 and had already provided music for, among other series, *The Wild, Wild West, Gunsmoke* and *The Twilight Zone*. He was also the writer of the haunting theme to *Perry Mason*. He recorded the score for "The Corbomite Maneuver" more than three-and-a-half months *after* the episode was sent into editing. Even at this late date, Steiner was conducting his orchestra blind, still without optical effects to project on a screen to show him or anyone else what the alien spaceships might look like.

"Fred Steiner was kind of like the John Williams of his time," Robert Justman said. "Broad, sweeping themes, a very melodramatic style of music. My first choice, always, unless there was a particular reason, was Fred, who caught the inner being of *Star Trek*." (94-9)

Steiner created several variations of a theme for the Enterprise, to be heard whenever we see the Enterprise in space; a signature, of a sort, representing the personality of the ship itself. He also created a theme for Captain Kirk. In an article Steiner wrote in 1982 for the Library of Congress concerning the music of *Star Trek*, he said, "It is played by French horns, an orchestral color which lends the theme a noble, almost Wagnerian quality, somewhat tinged with melancholy. It expressed what I saw as the mythic hero, dual personality of the Enterprise leader -- a strong, resourceful, dependable man who also has a softer, more vulnerable side and who is, at times, a solitary, lonely figure." (168-1)

Because of the demands of editing a one-hour science fiction series, with post-visual and sound effects slowing the process to a crawl, three weeks were planned for each episode. This one, jam-packed with what a memo from Justman warned to be "staggering" optical effects, took much longer.

The Howard Anderson Company, with the work being handled by Howard

Anderson, Jr. and his brother Darrell, had been given the challenge of figuring out how to have the mammoth Enterprise dwarfed by a spaceship a hundred times bigger, and to create a smaller ship to tow the Enterprise. And a space buoy to block its way. And to conjure up more starship flybys, and transporter effects, and phaser effects, and explosions in space. And the Andersons were running into immense problems (detailed later).

The Howard Anderson Co. prepares to film "the cube," 7/12/66 (Courtesy of Gerald Gurian)

The total cost for the optical effects, once all the problems were resolved and all the delays had passed, topped off at $17,317. This was roughly 10% of the episode's total budget and over $4,000 more than what Desilu had allocated for photographic effects on a per-episode basis. This time, Justman was able to rob Peter to pay Paul -- the extra money needed for the opticals came from the savings of making this a "bottle show."

"The Corbomite Maneuver" cost $190,430, which was $3,070 under *Star Trek*'s initial first season per-episode studio allowance of $193,500, creating a cash surplus to draw from on future episodes. It would be needed.

Despite *Star Trek* being one of the most expensive series on television in 1966, an inflation-adjusted budget of $1.35 million would not cover a show like this today. In 2013, a typical prime-time one-hour drama cost $3 to $3.5 million, with science fiction being on the higher end.

Release / Reactions
Premiere air date: 11/10/66. NBC repeat broadcast: 5/11/67.

Gene Roddenberry said he wanted to premiere the series with this episode, but NBC preferred a "planet show" to be first up. A compromise was made on August 4, a month and four days before the scheduled premiere: "The Man Trap" (the fifth episode filmed) would go first, followed by "The Corbomite Maneuver." On August 12, three months after work on the optical effects had begun and, with nothing yet delivered, "Corbomite" was pushed back to be the sixth episode to air. On August 23, it was pushed back again, to be the eighth. On October 12, with those challenging photographic effects still undelivered, the broadcast schedule was adjusted one more time, placing "Corbomite" where it finally did air, as Episode No. 10.

Each episode of *Star Trek* experienced a long and turbulent journey, from inception, to story and script development, followed by pre-production, production, and post-production (including film editing, sound editing, insertion of optical effects, titles and, finally scoring). After all of this, the real battle had to be fought with the broadcast, and the immediate response through reviews, letters from the audience and, most importantly, the ratings.

The Nielsen National ratings reports were a crucial scorecard for the networks. These nightly reports indicated several things, including how many televisions were powered on that evening, what percentage were tuned in to each of the major networks or a local independent station, and what the net ratings were for each show. Nielsen provided data for each half-hour segment, so for an hour-long program one can determine how well a program held the attention of those who tuned in from the start.

RATINGS / Nielsen 30-Market report for Thursday, October 10, 1966:

8:30 - 9 p.m., with 61.3% of U.S. TVs in use.	Rating:	Share:
NBC: *Star Trek* (first half)	15.9	25.9%
ABC: ***The Dating Game***	**19.2**	**31.3%**
CBS: *My Three Sons*	16.5	26.9%
Local independent stations:	11.0	15.9%

9 - 9:30 p.m., with 63.3% of U.S. TVs in use.		
NBC: *Star Trek* (second half)	16.4	25.9%
ABC: ***Bewitched***	**21.4**	**33.8%**
CBS: *Thursday Night Movie*	18.9	29.9%
Local independent stations:	8.9	10.4%

The numbers from Nielsen for this first "regular" episode produced would seem to support the 45-year old myth that *Star Trek* failed in the ratings. However, as revealed in the ratings reports for episodes that were shot later but aired earlier, *Star Trek* had already come in at No. 1 on more than a few of its previous weeks by the time "The Corbomite Maneuver" went out as NBC broadcast episode No. 10. On most weeks, *Star Trek* earned a respectable second place entry against formidable competition.

According to Nielsen, at 8:30 p.m., *My Three Sons*, considered a success by its network (CBS), was less than one ratings' point ahead of *Star Trek*. The new prime-time version of *The Dating Game* was the surprise top-rated show this night, due to one of its "celebrity date specials."

At 9 p.m., *Bewitched*, ABC's most popular series, took the lead. CBS's big gun, its *Thursday Night Movie*, was a strong second with the television premiere of Otto Preminger's 1964 political intrigue *Advise and Consent*, and its all-star cast that included Henry Fonda, Charles Laughton, Don Murray, Gene Tierney, and Peter Lawford. Even with a third-best showing, *Star Trek* hung on to roughly a 26% of the TV sets running in America from start to finish. Today, this kind of ratings performance would be considered an immense success.

Another nose-counting service, Home Testing Institute, with its TVQ report for *Broadcasting* magazine, conducted a national survey during this month in 1966, asking participants what their favorite new show was. *Star Trek* came in No. 1. When ranking all prime-time series, both new and old, the survey results placed *Star Trek* at No. 2, just under *Bonanza*, as the most liked series on television.

Many of those who missed the first airing caught the summer repeat.

RATINGS / Nielsen 30-Market report for Thursday, May 11, 1967:

8:30 - 9 p.m., with 56.4% of U.S. TVs in use.	Rating:	Share:
NBC: *Star Trek* (first half)	15.1	26.8%
ABC: ***Bewitched***	**19.2**	**34.0%**
CBS: *My Three Sons*	13.8	24.5%
Local independent stations:	9.7	14.7%

9 - 9:30 p.m., with 60.6% of U.S. TVs in use.

NBC:	*Star Trek* (second half)	18.0	29.7%
ABC:	*That Girl*	17.4	28.7%
CBS:	**Thursday Night Movie**	**19.6**	**32.3%**
Local independent stations:		7.9	9.3%

At 8:30 p.m., the rerun of "The Corbomite Maneuver" was in second position. *My Three Sons* came in third.

At 9:00 p.m., the winner was *The CBS Thursday Night Movie* showing of 1964's *Love Has Many Faces*, with Lana Turner and Cliff Robertson. *Star Trek* held onto its No. 2 standing. *That Girl*, in no danger of being cancelled by ABC, was at No. 3.

"The Corbomite Maneuver" was a hit with critics and fans. After its encore airing, it received a nomination as Best Science Fiction Presentation of the Year, at the 1967 Hugo Awards -- sci-fi's version of the Oscar, Emmy, and Peabody all rolled into one (details later).

From the Mailbag

A sampling from the letters received -- and stored in the *Star Trek* show files -- from the week after "The Corbomite Maneuver" first aired:

> Dear Sir, I'm sure you have lots of fan mail to answer, so I won't take long. I want to tell you how realistic your show is. It's interesting and in every scene you have a plot. My favorite actors are Spock, Captain, Scotty, Baily [sic]. I would like to have a color photo of the beautiful ship, the "Enterprise." It's the most amazing ship I've ever seen. So please, please send me a color photo. And, please, will you try to send me Spock and Captain and Scotty's autographs. Sincerely, Your Best Friend and Fan. David. K. (Hampton, Virginia).

> Dear sirs: Perhaps I'm mistaken, but there has never been, in my opinion, a more excellent series of adult science fiction. The stories are plausible, the characters are well portrayed in depth, and the special effects are exciting. Sam W. (Kansas City, Missouri)

> Dear Gene: When I saw you last I didn't get a chance to tell you how much I liked "The Corbomite Maneuver" and -- even if I do say it! -- it was the best so far. I hear a lot of nice things about *Star Trek* -- some of the kids even say it's the "in" show! -- and I hope they aren't just saying that because they know I have written for you.... The show looks great and I am chafing at the bit to do something more for it. Need anybody to empty wastebaskets or anything? Warmest regards, Jerry [Sohl].

Memories

Jerry Sohl said, "I thought it turned out very well, with considerable drama and incident.... I was highly pleased." (160-2)

Nimoy, in 1996, said, "Re-watching 'The Corbomite Maneuver' recently, I was struck by the wonderful sense of camaraderie on the bridge between the characters, as the crew awaited possible death during the countdown. The chemistry between the characters was there from the very start." (128-3)

Aftermath

Clint Howard recalled, "Around the time I was 18, I went in for an audition with George Lucas. It may have been for *Star Wars*. And I was nervous, because I knew who

George was -- Ron [Howard] had worked for him in *American Graffiti*, and I knew he was a big time director. So I went into his office and sitting right off of the main desk was Francis Coppola. And I thought, 'Gee, wow, Francis!' It was pretty impressive with Francis Coppola over there, and George Lucas over here, looking me right in the eye. And the first thing George says is, 'Commander Balok, Corbomite Maneuver!' And I was stunned. This was just a dozen years after the series, so there hadn't been any DVDs; there probably hadn't been any video tapes. I mean, George had probably just seen the episode in reruns about a dozen times. But he knew me; he knew that I played Commander Balok; and he knew the name of the episode. And that just shows you, ultimately, what an impact *Star Trek* had." (85)

In 2010, at the *Rally to Restore Sanity and/or Fear*, Jon Stewart used the imaginary threat of "Corbomite" in bottled water to illustrate how media figures create and magnify fears in the public, then said, "You just got scared by something that is not real!"

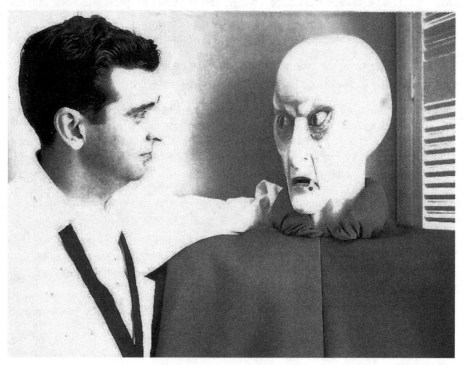

John D.F. Black and his pal, Balok
(Courtesy of Mary Black)

9

Episode 3: MUDD'S WOMEN
Teleplay by Stephen Kandel
(with John D.F. Black & Gene Roddenberry, uncredited)
Story by Gene Roddenberry
Directed by Harvey Hart

From *TV Guide*, October 8, 1966 issue:

> The Enterprise intercepts a spaceship commanded by a wily scoundrel, Capt. Harry Mudd, a convicted smuggler, whose only cargo is three stunning women.

Publicity photo: Maggie Thrett, Nimoy, Susan Denberg, Shatner and Karen Steele (Courtesy Gerald Gurian)

Intended to be sold as wives to wealthy but lonely space settlers, the women have an alluring effect on the male members of the crew, so much so Captain Kirk and his officers believe some unknown element is at play. One woman in particular, Eve, has even been causing the unflappable Kirk to lose his cool. But Kirk has little time to solve the mystery -- the energy of the ship's engines, diminished after a chase through space and the rescue of Leo Walsh (AKA Harcourt Fenton Mudd) and his "cargo," has placed the Captain in a compromising position: Deal with Harry Mudd on the rogue's terms or run the risk of never making it back to safe harbor. Kirk's only hope is to convince Ben Childress, the leader of three lonely miners on the otherwise unpopulated and inhospitable planet Rigel VII, to sell him the energy source his drained ship needs -- the "lithium" crystals they mine. But Childress has already struck a deal with Mudd -- Kirk will receive no help from the miners unless they get the women and Mudd is freed.

The theme: Outer beauty is a product of inner beauty and peace of mind; confidence and self-worth *will* change how a person is perceived by others. As for drug use: Belief in one's self must come from within, not from a bottle of pills.

SOUND BITES

- *Kirk, surprised by the women:* "Is this your crew, Captain?" *Mudd:* "Well, no, Captain. This is me cargo."

- Mudd, to Spock: "You're part Vulcanian, aren't you? Then a pretty face doesn't affect you. Not unless you want it to."

- Mudd: "You're a hard-nosed one, Captain." *Kirk:* "And you're a liar, Mr. Walsh. I think we both understand each other."

- Engineer Scott: "That jackass Walsh not only wrecked his own vessel but in saving his skin we..." *Kirk:* "If it makes you feel better, Engineer, that's one jackass we're going to see skinned."

- Eve, flirting: "I read once that a commander has to act like a paragon of virtue. I never met a paragon." *Kirk, nearly speechless:* "Neither have I."

- Mudd: "Ship's captains are already married to their vessels, Evie. You'll see, the first time you come between him and his ship."

- Eve: "Is this the kind of wife you want, Ben? Not someone to help you, not a wife to cook and sew and cry and need, but this kind. Selfish, vain, useless. Is this what you really want?"

- Kirk: "There's only one kind of woman..." *Mudd:* "Or man, for that matter..." *Kirk:* "You either believe in yourself or you don't."

ASSESSMENT

"Mudd's Women" glides effortlessly between drama and humor. Adding to the fun is watching Spock bend a pointed ear to observe the weaknesses of the human condition, allowing us to see ourselves through the eyes of this curious alien.

There are many tense moments at the outset of the story, as the "lithium circuits" blow and eerie quiet and darkness envelop the ship. And then the ship is suddenly years away from home instead of mere months.

As the story enters its final act, there are some inconsistencies. Why does Ben Childress' living quarters look so much different inside than out? A cylindrical metal pre-fab hut suddenly becomes something more in line with a cave. The furnishings aren't fabricated but appear made of wood -- on a planet that is clearly devoid of trees. Wouldn't Ben have goggles and a particle mask handy for his trips outdoors? How can Eve's final transformation from drab to beautiful be explained? She took no drug, yet her eyelashes suddenly grow, her lips somehow are coated in sparkling lip gloss and her hair miraculously becomes styled.

Despite the nitpicking, "Mudd's Women" is well deserving of its classic status. The crisp writing and the story's profound message are bolstered by top-notch performances and stylish direction. Encouraged by director Harvey Hart, Jerry Finnerman's lighting is filled with those picturesque half-tones he longed to create.

THE STORY BEHIND THE STORY

Script Timeline

Gene Roddenberry's story premise, from his series proposal: March 11, 1964.
Roddenberry's story outline, "The Women": July 20, 1964.
Roddenberry's revised outline: July 23, 1964.
Stephen Kandel's 1st Draft teleplay, based on Roddenberry's outline, now
"Mudd's Women," ST #4: May 1965.
Kandel's 2nd Draft teleplay: June 1965.
John D.F. Black's rewrite, his 1st Draft teleplay: May 17, 1966.
Black's script polish (Mimeo Department "Yellow Cover 1st Draft"):
May 23, 1966.

Gene Roddenberry's rewrite (Final Draft teleplay): May 26, 1966.
Additional page revisions by Roddenberry: May 31, June 2 & 6, 1966.

Gene Roddenberry's story outline, "The Women," was one of three he wrote for NBC to choose from when planning the first pilot. The others were "Landru's Paradise," later to be made as "The Return of the Archons," and the one the network picked, "The Cage." The story in Roddenberry's early drafts served as a blueprint for what was finally filmed except for one important fixture -- there is no Harry Mudd. That character came from Stephen Kandel.

NBC wanted to see three full screenplays by three different writers to choose from for the second pilot. Roddenberry wrote "The Omega Glory" and Sam Peeples wrote "Where No Man Has Gone Before." The third script went to Kandel, who was not a science fiction writer but knew how to deliver scripts that network executives liked.

Stephen Kandel had started in television with half-hour shows such as *Sea Hunt* (for which he wrote 14 episodes) and *The Millionaire*, and then advanced to hour-long formats with *Burke's Law*, *The Wild, Wild West*, *I Spy* and, in the tradition of lovable con men like Harry Mudd, 12 assignments on *The Rogues* (with David Niven and Charles Boyer). By 1964, the studios were eyeing him as a possible show runner and paying him to develop TV pilot scripts, including one at Screen Gems to star Vince Edwards of *Ben Casey* fame. Roddenberry, who'd also developed pilots for Screen Gems, read an unproduced script by Kandel -- the writer's first foray into the science fiction genre -- and was duly impressed. The two men met and kicked around ideas.

Kandel enjoyed brainstorming with Roddenberry, saying, "I liked Gene a lot. He was fun to talk to because he liked to spin ideas. So, we had a good time.... He was always full of tremendous amounts of enthusiasm." (95-1)

The concept which intrigued Roddenberry most was "Warrior World," for which Kandel wrote a treatment, followed by a story outline. The somewhat violent and potentially costly tale was not working out, so Roddenberry asked Kandel to consider swapping stories and trying his hand at turning "The Women" into a teleplay. Since NBC had already seen and passed on Roddenberry's outline, the story would need some major retooling.

The biggest hurdle in getting "The Women" on TV was its subject -- prostitution and drugs were hardly the type of thing NBC wanted in the prime time schedule. Helping the network to swallow the bitter pills was Kandel's addition of the flamboyant, conniving Harry Mudd into Roddenberry's story of "hookers in space." Kandel said, "I originally had the idea of a kind of a traveling salesman and con man -- the medicine salesman in *The Wizard of Oz* that ends up as the Wizard; an interstellar con man hustling whatever he can hustle; a lighthearted, cheerful, song-and-dance man version of a pimp." (95-1)

Portrait of a con man - Harry Mudd – a discarded film frame revealing a blank monitor screen (Courtesy of Gerald Gurian)

155

The slight-of-hand trick worked. Mudd effectively distracted the otherwise worrisome NBC censors from the hot topic issues at play in the story.

"We are talking about television in a primeval state," said Kandel. "There was always something that was too hot to handle. We thought in a science fiction setting it was possible to do some stories that you couldn't do in a street crime drama. So we treated this as if it were the American West, you know, 'mail order brides.' What else could you call them? We took it from there." (95-1)

Kandel wrote two drafts of his "Mudd's Women" script in 1965 when it was still an underdog contender for the second pilot film. Now that *Star Trek* was a series with an immediate need for scripts, it seemed sensible to resurrect one that had already been developed to some extent. But Kandel was preparing to produce a series of his own -- *Iron Horse* for ABC, which he co-created with *Star Trek* director James Goldstone -- and was not available to do the additional drafts of the script needed to incorporate new cast members and format changes.

Jack Guss, a TV writer who had recently served as script editor for 26 episodes of the one-hour dramatic series *Channing*, was offered the assignment. Roddenberry sent Guss a copy of Kandel's revised first draft. Unaware that the script was based on a story by the show's creator, Guss wrote back:

> I read "Mudd's Women" and consider the idea of this script beneath the challenge and breadth of the show's concept as I visualize it from the pilot and my conversation with you.... Apart from any intricate weaknesses in the script it is not the strongest kind of action-adventure entry this early in the season.... To me, the theme is cloying and naïve and I find the resolution predictable.... There is no serious conflict between Kirk and Mudd or Kirk and Eve or Kirk and Childress.... The story has no focal point. (JG3)

Roddenberry took "Mudd's Women" away from Guss and invited the writer to pitch a concept of his own. Guss received a story assignment, but this was "cut off" without proceeding to script. His association with *Star Trek* started and ended with equal abruptness.

Regardless of who would do the rewrite, Robert Justman was concerned over the number of characters in the script and suggested that Mudd's women, as well as the miners who barter for them, be cut back from five each to four or, even better, three. The script needed to be cut back as well, from 75 pages to 65. And Justman felt many other things needed to go. He wrote Roddenberry:

> You get me a horned koala creature that has been trained and won't excrete on the actor's shoulder, and I will be pleased to use it in the show.... On page 55, we see Benton riding a digging machine toward his cabin. Let's eliminate this device right now. (RJ3-1)

Benton was one of the miners. The horned koala creature belonged to Mudd -- a sci-fi take on the parrot perched on a pirate's shoulder. Otherwise, Justman liked much of what he read, writing:

> I believe that by the use of judicious script editing, we can have a damn fine show out of this story. (RJ3-1)

Roddenberry was rewriting "The Corbomite Maneuver," so "Mudd's Women" was handed to *Star Trek*'s brand new script editor who was just moving his things into the office. Roddenberry's April 18 memo to John D.F. Black read:

> I think the only intelligent course is for you to take this on as an early project,

giving it whatever time you can kick free from the more regular and routine tasks. No answer necessary now -- we can discuss after you've had time to settle in. (GR3-1)

Black's regular and routine tasks, as soon discovered, were massive. He had to educate himself on all of Roddenberry's ideas concerning the format of the series and nuances of its characters, its ship, its universe, sit in on story development meetings, read each draft of the story outlines and treatments as they came in, plus all the memos filled with comments from Roddenberry, Justman, NBC and De Forest Research, and then write memos filled with comments of his own, plus two original scripts and rewrite at least two other scripts started by other writers. He also had to write a pair of scripts in order to fulfill a prior commitment.

Mary Black recalled, "John had been working for Universal -- on *Run for Your Life* and *Laredo* -- and part of the contract with Desilu was that he was allowed to work on those projects, to finish them up, while he was beginning his work at *Star Trek*. That's part of why we were working until two in the morning during much of that time." (17a)

Despite the work load, and the overlapping deadlines, Black's first stab at "Mudd" hit Roddenberry's and Justman's desks on May 18, just four weeks after he had been asked to take the project on. Mudd's women now numbered at four.

Robert Justman, suggesting an idea that would stick, wrote:

> It might be interesting to have someone other than Mister Spock in the Transporter Room when Harry Mudd and the girls first arrive. Later, in the beginning of Act 1, therefore, the four women could have some effect upon the person who is there to escort them to the Captain's quarters. And they would be in close proximity inside the elevator and this might be some way of getting a little fun in a little earlier. (RJ3-2)

The final shooting script placed McCoy and Scott in the transporter room with Mr. Spock, allowing him to see the immediate reaction the others had to "the girls." It was a delightful moment, as was the trip down the corridors and the "close proximity inside the elevator" with their escort. Credit Black for picking Spock as the escort and giving Harry Mudd the line about a pretty face not turning the head of "this one," the "Vulcanian." Credit director Harvey Hart for the "push in" on Spock's face, revealing the dark anguish that tells us Mudd's statement is not necessarily true.

Justman's note, and concerns, continued:

> We have the girls being transformed from ugly old crows to beautiful young chicks. I'm still plenty worried about being able to convince the audience that this change works. (RJ3-2)

In closing, worrying over the condition of all the outlines and scripts he was reading, and aware of a production schedule hungry for material, Justman said:

> I feel, unless Gene has strong reasons to the contrary, that we must go with this script on the second show to be shot. And we cannot delay any longer. The decision must be made. (RJ3-2)

Roddenberry's long memo to Black began:

> A good script, excellent dialogue and characterizations; enjoyed reading it. But I do think our 8:30 time slot and NBC's continued emphasis on a need for action-adventure requires that we hypo [inject excitement into] the story wherever possible; explore ways which might increase the mystery and suspense elements. (GR3-3)

Roddenberry didn't like that Black followed Stephen Kandel's lead in having Mudd and his women beam onto the Enterprise at the outset. He told his executive story consultant:

> Suppose our teaser began at the point where a vessel -- out of visual sight -- has been picked up on the ship's instruments and is trying to escape. It refuses communication, has no register beam.... The Enterprise instruments show the mysterious vessel tries to super-power its way to escape. Then we see a slight -- inexpensive -- flare-up of the moving dot on the Enterprise viewing screen, then the dot is no longer visible. The vessel has overloaded, blown its engines, and now Kirk is worried that the mysterious vessel is drifting into certain destruction in a meteor belt. In other words, we extract during the teaser all the juice of the element, leaving Mudd and his women to serve as an additional dramatic element in Act 1. (GR3-3)

In this one memo, dictated quickly and late at night over a cocktail or two, Roddenberry had given John Black nearly everything seen in the filmed teaser segment ... except for one plot point. His next sentence took care of that.

> Now, strain of a decision on Kirk, i.e., super-load -- or whatever term -- his own vessel in order to extend the Enterprise deflector beam far out into space to protect the other vessel. Also play at this same time frantic efforts to contact it, frantic efforts to establish Transporter Room contact so its occupants can be removed before destruction -- all this against increasing warnings by the proper control stations that the Enterprise is overloading. (GR3-3)

The teaser was mapped out. Roddenberry's memo continued, walking Black through the early stages of Act 1:

> The Enterprise power fails at an unexpected point -- the lithium crystal circuits.... A flare-up on the ship's screen in the distance ahead of us, one meteoroid has gotten through the Enterprise's fading deflector screen. The mysterious vessel is beginning to explode; break up. At this same moment, word from the Transporter Room that they've locked onto the bridge; are bringing in the Captain of the other vessel... where we first look at Harry Mudd -- and the "cargo" arrives -- Mudd's women. (GR3-3)

It only took Black five days to hand in his rewrite, sent to the mimeo department and designated as the "Yellow Cover" First Draft script -- first to be sent to NBC; first to be circulated to the series' department head; first to be leaked to the cast.

Black's rewrite received guarded praise from Justman, although he didn't care for the changes Roddenberry had asked for and said so in his next memo to both.

> I feel that this is a much better version than we had previously.... [But] I don't think the teaser is what we really need in this show. I don't think it has a strong enough hook. To tell you the truth, I still think our teaser ought to end with the arrival of Mudd's Women on board the Enterprise and I really do feel that the first six, seven or eight pages of this version really do not get us into the story soon enough. (RJ3-3)

Roddenberry liked Justman's frankness, but many of the latter's ideas concerning this script were ignored. Case in point: Justman said:

> I would like to see Ben finally say that he _does_ want Eve as she is, and vice versa. I have a feeling that we may have left this fact unresolved for the audience. I'd just like to see Ben finally crumble and admit that he has been wrong and indicate strongly how much he wants Eve. (RJ3-3)

This change was made, but only after Eve transformed back to beautiful, thereby losing the whole point of Justman's recommendation.

At this point, Roddenberry had taken over, completing his rewrite -- the Final Draft from May 26, with additional revised pages arriving on June 2 and 6. His rewrite here, as with many of the early and formative scripts, was substantial. Wounded writers could -- and would -- complain, but a close comparison of first draft and final draft scripts clearly demonstrate the transformation from something better suited for an anthology series to something that was, by its nature and its execution, *Star Trek*.

Stephen Kandel understood this and, with no trace of animosity in his voice, later said, "Oh, Gene rewrote. He loved to meddle. No script was ever finished." (95-1)

Roddenberry had rewritten the script for "The Corbomite Maneuver" even more so than that of "Mudd's Women," but did not ask to share in the screen credit with Jerry Sohl, whose notoriety as a science fiction author was an asset to *Star Trek*. Kandel, although a respected TV writer, did not bring such status to the new series, so on June 3, 1966, while still in the thick of the rewriting, Roddenberry petitioned the Writers Guild of America for a change in the writers' credits on "Mudd's Women." He believed that his and Black's contributions went beyond the call of duty of producer and script editor and warranted both acknowledgement and compensation. In his letter to the WGA, he wrote, "The writing credit we propose is as follows: Story by Gene Roddenberry; Teleplay by Stephen Kandel, John D.F. Black and Gene Roddenberry."

The Guild believed the many script changes Roddenberry and Black made were in accordance with their positions as the series' writing staff, which both were well compensated for. On June 31, Roddenberry's request was denied. He would get the "story by" credit; Kandel alone was credited for the teleplay.

Roddenberry said, "Steve came up with that character. It was my story, but that was his character. By the time we filmed it, John Black and I had rewritten most of the dialogue and moved a lot of the action around. But that character of Harry Mudd was still a significant influence in everything we did; all those changes. And that was probably what the Arbitration Board was looking at." (145-12)

All the rewriting made for a better script, a better episode and a better impression on NBC's Stan Robertson, who was surprisingly supportive of this potentially controversial material. Of Roddenberry's Final Draft script, Robertson wrote:

> This has the makings of a very charming and somewhat different story for us, more so than anything we've attempted so far. Harry Mudd comes alive as one of those unforgettable characters who illuminate our lives and our literature -- a lovable scoundrel. (SR3)

With so many troublesome *Star Trek* story outlines and scripts arriving on his desk, Robertson delighted in reading one which held his interest and, in the end, left him feeling moved. He continued:

> There is a definition and motivation among our principals. One can easily understand and sympathize with the human emotions and feelings which exude from the women and the companion-starved miners they are paired with. As far as our regulars are concerned, they take on more dimension and we are exposed to newer facets of their personalities. Good dialogue and interplay between Kirk and Spock as there is between Kirk and Mudd. (SR3)

Nonetheless, Robertson also had misgivings. Echoing Robert Justman's opinion that the story was taking too long to kick into gear, he told Roddenberry that too much time was spent explaining "gadgetry and use of instruments" and that this sort of thing was of "little interest to the development of the plot." He complained:

> It seems that all of the teaser and much of Act 1 is spent in <u>establishing</u> rather than <u>saying</u>.... We have to start like a sprinter rather than a distance man. (SR3)

Robertson, like Kandel, then Black, then Justman, preferred to meet Mudd's women in the teaser. Regardless, there was no time for further debating. "Mudd's Women" began filming the same day Robertson's memo arrived at Desilu.

Pre-Production
May 24-31 and June 1, 1966 (6 days prep).

Harvey Hart, 37, was chosen to direct. Having begun in Hollywood as an actor, Hart had recently directed episodes for *Alfred Hitchcock Presents, Laredo* and *The Wild, Wild West*. James Doohan took direction from Hart in the 1965 film *Bus Riley's Back in Town*, which also featured Kim Darby (who would play the title character in *Star Trek*'s upcoming episode "Miri").

Jerry Finnerman, despite the raw nerves he experienced during "The Corbomite Maneuver," was back in charge of the camera and lighting units. He said, "They'd given me one show and then would decide [whether] to give me another one. I'm on ["The Corbomite Maneuver"] a week and Herb Solow comes down with Roddenberry, and they say... 'We don't know what you're doing, but we love it. And we'd like to sign you to a contract.' Well, in those days, nobody had a contract; the days of the contract were gone. But they said, 'We'll give you a three-year contract.' I think it was starting at $800 [per week]; the next year it would be $900; and then the following year a thousand. So, I talked to Harry [Stradling] and he said, 'That's fine... I'm going to get you my agent; he'll make all the deals and anything that goes on he'll handle it.' So, in one week, I had a three-year contract." (63-3)

Roger C. Carmel, at 33, was the obvious choice to play Harcourt Fenton Mudd. He had been successfully making the rounds on television, gaining more attention with each appearance, including multiple turns on *The Naked City*, *The Man from U.N.C.L.E.* and *I Spy*.

Joe D'Agosta said of Carmel, "He was working all over town; he was a well-known flamboyant character. He was just one of those great interesting actors with a lovable, joyful kind of personality, a bigger than life kind of character. He was the right person for that role and, when you look at his contribution, maybe the *only* person for that role." (43-4)

Steven Kandel said, "I was immensely happy. I thought he was terrific. Roger Carmel was perfect." (95-1)

Robert Culp and Roger C. Carmel in an episode of *I Spy* (Courtesy of Three F Productions)

John D.F. Black said, "I liked Roger C. Carmel. He was a sweetheart. And I loved him in 'Mudd's Women.' I thought he was charmingly large. He played the character so broadly, but he was good at it." (17)

Karen Steele in *Ride Lonesome* (1959, Columbia Pictures)

Susan Denberg in NBC publicity photo (Courtesy of Bob Olsen)

Carmel said, "You [saw] how they dressed me in many of the roles I played at that time. Not the best fitting clothing. But this character was like a tailor made suit for me. The moment I read the script, I knew how to play him. And that was met by complete support when I stepped in front of the camera, by Harvey Hart and the cast. It was an absolute joy." (29)

Yeoman Rand was in the earlier drafts of the script, but was written out, more because of budget concerns than anything else. This actually helped the story by enabling Kirk to better interact with Mudd's women and allowing the three alluring females to have little competition.

Karen Steele, the sympathetic Eve, was 35. A former model and cover girl, she was prominently featured in 1955's Academy Award winning Best Picture *Marty*, then had the female lead in numerous B-pictures, such as 1956's *The Sharkfighters* (under Victor Mature), 1957's *Bailout at 43,000* (under John Payne) and 1959's *Ride Lonesome* (under Randolph Scott). She also had the top female spot in the 1960's mob-pic *Rise and Fall of Legs Diamond*.

Susan Denberg, as Magda, the one with the short blonde Dippity-do hair-style, originated from Poland, moving to America to become a Las Vegas chorus girl. TV and film roles followed. Immediately after working here and prior to the first broadcast of "Mudd's Women," Denberg appeared in the August 1966 issue of *Playboy*.

Doohan recalled, "Susan Denberg appeared as a centerfold playmate of the month. When they were shooting the sequences where we're supposed to be ogling the women, I didn't consider that an acting challenge. I looked at her and thought, Wooooeeee." (52-1)

Denberg had a co-starring role in 1967's *Frankenstein Created Woman* before fleeing the Hollywood fast life for the safe refuge of Poland and a non-show-business future.

Maggie Thrett, the dark-haired Ruth, had appeared in an episode of *The Wild, Wild West* with future *Star Trek* guest star William Campbell ("The Squire of Gothos" and "The Trouble with Tribbles"). She also made her feature film debut this same year in *Dimension 5*, a sci-fi starring the Enterprise's former captain, Jeffrey Hunter.

Science fiction writer Harlan Ellison, working in the offices at this time on his script for the upcoming "The City on the Edge of Forever," found Thrett to be the most alluring of Mudd's women. Mary Black recalled, "Harlan came into John's office after one of his many visits to the set and announced to John that he had 'really hooked up' with 'Maggie Treat.' And John started laughing and said, 'Harlan, her name is not Maggie Treat; her name is Maggie Thrett.' And Harlan says, 'Well, it just goes to show you the difference between you and me. To you, she's a threat; to me she's a treat.'" (17a)

Wardrobe designer William Theiss, who made sure these women's dangerous curves were highly noticeable, had a theory about sexy clothing. He believed nothing could be more titillating than a dress that appears as if, at any moment, it might slip an inch out of place and reveal something the network censors would panic over. Ruth's dress design in particular, with that diagonal slit traveling from shoulder to the underside of one breast and then to her waistline, is a very early and classic example of Theiss' almost-too-hot-for-TV designs.

William Shatner said, "Somehow Gene always showed up for the fittings to make his own design adjustments. He'd like to add his two cents. 'A little less here,' he'd ask Bill [Theiss], 'A little shorter there.' Gene's two cents added up to skimpier costumes, and skimpier costumes kept Bill's budget in check." (156-2)

John D.F. Black said, "The basic problem we had with 'Mudd's Women' was not the script so much as the wardrobe, as designed, and getting it past the censors. It was a very overtly sex-oriented piece." (17-4)

In all, 20 actresses tried out for the roles of Mudd's women, nearly all of which already had or would have successful careers in front of the camera. Among them, Phyllis Davis, who went on to appear as Beatrice Travis in 69 episodes of *Vegas*, Gayle Hunnicutt, who played the recurring character of Vanessa Beaumont in *Dallas*, and Donna Michelle, the May 1964 cover girl for *Playboy* magazine.

Gene Dynarski, playing Ben Childress, was 33. His credits included *Ben Casey* and *The Big Valley*. A reliable character performer, Dynarski would work steadily in television and return to the various *Star Trek* series more than once.

Jim Goodwin, on TV from 1961 to 1979, and having small roles prior to this on series such as *Surfside 6* and *Combat!*, made his first of three visits to *Star Trek* as Lt. John Farrell, courtesy of his friend, John D.F. Black.

Majel Barrett was an excellent choice for the mechanically dispassionate voice of the Enterprise's computer. Bitter over her losing the

Gene Dynarski as Ben Childress
(Unaired film trim courtesy of Gerald Gurian)

plum role of the ship's first officer, "Number One," Roddenberry kept his promise to Barrett and found a way to bring her back on board. It was to *Star Trek*'s benefit.

Nichelle Nichols almost didn't make the cut. Regarding her being hired for this episode, Roddenberry wrote to Joe D'Agosta:

> In this episode we actually need a Communications Officer for only two or three lines. Eventually, we must discuss the whole Nichelle Nichols deal -- the present "one-shot thousand dollars" being clearly double our budget. In the meantime, after first getting an estimate of days from the A.D., we must decide whether to use Nichelle in "Mudd's Women" or get a cheaper alternate. All things being equal, of course it would pay us to use her and have familiar faces in these early shows. (GR3-2)

And they did.

Production Diary
Filmed June 2 (1/2 day), 3, 6, 7, 8, 9, 10 & 13, 1966
(Planned as 7 day production; finishing 1/2 day behind; total cost: $198,534).

Holding to the approved per-episode budget can be a life-or-death matter for a series. The associate producer typically shoulders the lion's share of this burden, although the producer, executive producer, episode director, network and studio execs also play key roles. The key driver is the number of days budgeted for production, which will factor in the cost of cast, crew, equipment and locations, etc.. In some instances, the post-production costs -- especially, in this case, optical effects -- can tilt the balance between making or breaking the budget.

"Mudd's Women" was given a seven-day filming schedule instead of the usual six. Cast and crew were still learning their way around and this script required the company's first visit to Stage 10 for the planet sets.

Thursday, June 2, 1966. *What Now My Love* by Herb Alpert and the Tijuana Brass was the top selling record album in America. "When a Man Loves a Woman," by Percy Sledge, was gaining the most radio play for the second week, keeping "A Groovy Kind of Love" by the Mindbenders out of the top spot. The previous night, ABC was the most watched network from 7:30 with *Batman* before the younger viewers switched over to CBS at 8 p.m. for the last half of *Lost in Space*, followed by *The Beverly Hillbillies*, *Green Acres*, and *Gomer Pyle, U.S.M.C.* The adults took over after that and made *I Spy* on NBC the ratings winner from 10 to 11 p.m. The new day brought news that Surveyor 1 was Earth's first spacecraft to make a soft landing on the moon. And *Star Trek* clapped slate for "Mudd's Women."

Production started at noon, four hours late due to delays finishing "The Corbomite Maneuver." On this day, filming took place only on the bridge set until 7 p.m., 40 minutes into overtime.

Day 2, Friday. Another full day on the bridge set, and another late night with Hart capturing his last camera shot at 7:50 p.m., then releasing the cast for makeup removal and the crew to wrap the set. It had been an especially long day for William Shatner, who had been running a temperature.

Day 3, Monday, June 6, began where Day 2 was supposed to end, in the transporter room for the introduction of Mudd's women. Here, cinematographer Jerry Finnerman started the use of soft-focus photography on *Star Trek*. This technique became standard practice for many of the female guest stars. If an alluring look was called for, the soft focus lens was used.

Next came the scenes in Kirk's quarters, followed by the turbolift and ship's corridors. Harvey Hart's determination to use elaborate camera setups throughout the production resulted in delay on these sets and work had to be carried over into the following morning. Hart surrendered the camera to the studio "time keeper" at 7:24 p.m., more than an hour into overtime.

"That was quite a thing, being so early in the history of that show," Roger C. Carmel said. "That was one of the first episodes they made. But all of them seemed well aware of who their characters were. Leonard may still have been trying to find himself, although you would never know it from watching. But Bill Shatner and the others had no hesitation in the way they approached the scenes. Now, Leonard tried to remain in character throughout, but Bill had no problem in stepping back and forth from portraying Kirk as the lonely, somewhat stern leader and then, once the camera stopped, being the life of the party. And I don't remember many wasted takes. He'd have us laughing one minute, then the director would call 'Action,' and there he was, the grim-faced Captain. Remarkable discipline to do that." (29)

Day 4, Tuesday. Hart's shots were striking and the performances were finely tuned -- but striking and fine tuning require extra care and time, things a television shooting schedule does not typically allow. Filming in Kirk's quarters, followed by the ship's corridors and ending with the turbolift elevator, kept the camera rolling one hour into overtime at 7:15 p.m.

Day 6. Karen Steele, as Eve, going through Venus drug withdrawal
(Unaired film trim courtesy Gerald Gurian)

Day 5, Wednesday. The company filmed all the sickbay and briefing room sequences. With the camera rolling until 7:18, the union crew happily earned another full hour's worth of time-and-a-half. The actors, working for a flat rate, were just getting tired.

Day 6, Thursday, was supposed to begin on Stage 10 for planet scenes but the crew remained on the Enterprise, finishing up scenes in Mudd's quarters before making the move out of Stage 9 at 3:50 p.m. The first work on Stage 10 was the dwelling used by Ben Childress. There was a reason it was so cave-like,

despite the modern looking exterior (to be filmed the next day). This design idea can be traced back to a Bob Justman memo, reading:

> Due to the climatic conditions which prevail on the surface of this planet, perhaps we would be wise in establishing that any living quarters that the prospectors use are below ground.... I know if I were one of those prospectors I would attempt to do something of this sort to get out of the way of the wind. (RJ3-1)

It seemed a good idea, but when Matt Jefferies added a window into the underground lair, and director Hart asked that sand be blown into the living quarters whenever the insulated door opened, the illusion went straight to hell.

Hart took his last shot at 7 p.m.

Friday, June 10. It was now Day 7 and the end was not yet in sight. Filming included the final shots in Ben's dwelling, followed by a move to the inhospitable planet surface. Both took place on Stage 10, where the innovative look of *Star Trek* planets was born.

Jerry Finnerman recalled, "I talked to [Bob Justman] and Gene Roddenberry and said, 'Wouldn't it be nice for each planet to have a different atmosphere? Who's to say that Planet 17 isn't purple or orange or magenta?' And they really liked that idea. So we would cut gels for these huge 10k lights on the sets and each week we would have a different color.... We were doing each episode in only six days [and] I found I could change the sets literally by changing colors. So I asked them to keep all the sets neutral. Then I would go in and, if I wanted the sets red or green or blue, I would just do it with the lights on the walls." (63-1)

Nimoy and Shatner on Stage 10 during production Day 7
(Courtesy of Gerald Gurian)

It was a big time-saver and one of the series' many visual signatures. But, contrary to Finnerman's recollections, some episodes took longer than six days. This was into its eighth.

Later in the day, Kirk, Spock and Mudd beam down to the inhospitable surface of Rigel VII and the approach to the exterior of Ben Childress' hut was filmed. In this scene, they do not go into the modern pre-fab hut but appear to go down a ramp or stairway leading below the small building -- exploring the cave-like interior. Unfortunately, this action is only seen -- almost undetectably -- in the distance. Jefferies had gone to the trouble to build a ramp to the sub-chamber door but Hart didn't show it.

Filming stopped at 6:50 p.m., Hart's best day yet, only 30 minutes into overtime. However, while screening dailies, the producers discovered Hart had been doing a little trick called "camera cutting" -- he was calling for unusual camera angles while shooting sequences of dialogue and leaving out the "singles," those much needed close-ups of each actor which later could be used to reshape or shorten the scenes.

John Black said, "That was his technique – cutting in the camera. He did the same thing on an episode of *Laredo* I'd written, and I'd had problems with him there. He camera cut everything!" (17)

To Hart's credit, the staging of his shots and blocking of the performers was quite

Day 8, Stage 10 (Courtesy of Gerald Gurian)

intriguing, more in line with a feature film than an assembly line TV episode. But, television being television, the producers could not risk encountering problems assembling one or more of the scenes after a production wrapped. Therefore, the company resumed work on "Mudd's Women" the following day.

Day 8, Monday, June 13, 1966. Filming continued in Ben's dwelling for additional "camera coverage," then the company moved back to the stormy surface of Rigel and, with a 3:45 p.m. move to Stage 9, returned to Mudd's guest quarters on the Enterprise. Bob Justman's production notes documented how Hart, despite his excellent work, sabotaged his own chances of returning to *Star Trek*. The associate producer wrote:

> One day over -- too much rehearsal -- elaborate setups -- camera cutting -- difficult to trim.

In television, good work does not always ensure more work. Hart would not return.

Post-Production
June 14 through October 31, 1966. Music score recorded on September 7, 1966.

Bruce Schoengarth, 47, was hired to run the second editing team, alternating with Robert Swanson and his staff, and a third team yet to be assembled. Described as "quiet and accomplished" by Justman, Schoengarth had been a "lead cutter" for *Lassie* and *Ben Casey*.

Fred Steiner, who set "The Corbomite Maneuver" to music, continued to define the sound of *Star Trek* with his score for "Mudd's Women." One week before Steiner recorded his tracks, composer Alexander Courage helped out by providing the music for this episode's preview trailer. *Star Trek* was backed up on its delivery of episodes, with many arriving at NBC just days before broadcast. Courage was asked to score the trailer quickly, since it was scheduled to air one week before the actual episode. His sultry trombone music, reminiscent of David Rose's early 1960's No. 1 hit "The Stripper," worked so well that it was also used in the actual episode as Mudd's women parade down the ship's corridor.

The Westheimer Company, the second of five optical houses to work on *Star Trek*, was rushed in at the last minute to cover for Howard and Darrell Anderson who were completely over their heads with "The Corbomite Maneuver."

Owner Joseph Westheimer had studied optical effects under Byron Haskin, Roddenberry's right-hand-man for "The Cage." Westheimer set up his own shop in 1958, with his first client being *The Twilight Zone*. The results of Wertheimer's work, especially the meteor storm, are impressive.

All shots of the Enterprise, however, are lifted from the first two pilots and what the Andersons had finished so far for "Corbomite." Those asteroids Westheimer created, along with the flare-up of Mudd's ship, the transporter effects, and a glowing Venus drug in the palm of Eve's hand, cost Desilu $10,530, a considerably smaller bill than the one being tallied by the Andersons for "The Corbomite Maneuver."

Even with this savings, "Mudd's Women" came in over budget. Due to overtime -- 82 crew and stage hours instead of the allotted 72 -- this episode topped out at $198,534, more than $6,000 over. Adjust for inflation and we can better appreciate the hit to Desilu: total cost of $1.4 million, going $43,000 over budget.

Release / Reactions
Premiere air date: 10/11/66. NBC repeat broadcast: 5/4/67.

When Stephen Kandel first saw "Mudd's Women," his immediate impression was, "I thought it was terrific. They really pulled it off. And I thought those special effects were excellent for their time. I was delighted." (95-1)

Jerry Stanley, NBC Manager of Film Programs, recalled, "One of the problems we had was in trying to talk [Roddenberry] out of some of his sexual fantasies that would come to life in the scripts. Some of the scenes he would describe were totally unacceptable." (166)

John D.F. Black said, "GR got away with murder with the network. The girls' outfits -- my God, you couldn't do that on television back then. But he took the network on, and he brought it to a standstill, and he won -- every time!" (17)

Shatner said, "As for the drug angle, well, it's possible the network executives weren't aware of what was going on. That NBC allowed 'Mudd's Women' to be produced at all is still a minor miracle." (156-2)

RATINGS / Nielsen 30-Market report for Thursday, October 13, 1966:

8:30 - 9 p.m., with 60.5% of U.S. TVs in use.	Rating:	Share:
NBC: *Star Trek* (first half)	**19.0**	**31.4%**
ABC: *The Dating Game*	17.3	28.6%
CBS: *My Three Sons*	17.4	28.8%
Local independent stations:	7.7	11.2%

9 - 9:30 p.m., with 60.4% of U.S. TVs in use.		
NBC: *Star Trek* (second half)	**19.0**	**31.5%**
ABC: *Bewitched*	18.2	30.1%
CBS: *Thursday Night Movie*	**19.0**	**31.5%**
Local independent stations:	6.2	6.9%

From 8:30 to 9 p.m., *Star Trek* was No. 1. From 9:00 to 9:30, it tied for the top spot with *The Victors*, a 1963 war film on CBS starring George Hamilton and George Peppard. *Bewitched*, one of ABC's biggest hits, came in third this night.

The numbers were equally impressive when NBC repeated the episode.

RATINGS / Nielsen 30-City report for Thursday, May 4, 1967:

8:30 - 9 p.m., with 57.5% of U.S. TVs in use.	Rating:	Share:
NBC: *Star Trek* (first half)	17.1	29.7%
ABC: *Bewitched*	**17.6**	**30.6%**
CBS: *My Three Sons*	12.5	21.7%
Local independent stations:	12.0	18.2%

9 - 9:30 p.m., with 53.9% of U.S. TVs in use.		
NBC: *Star Trek* (second half)	**20.5**	**32.1%**
ABC: *That Girl*	14.9	23.3%
CBS: *Thursday Night Movie*	16.9	26.4%
Local independent stations:	13.4	18.2%

The same week *TV Guide* ran an article about how "dreamy" Mr. Spock was, *Star Trek*, with a repeat of "Mudd's Women," tied or beat its competition during the hour run. At 8:30, the lead that ABC's red-hot *Bewitched* held over *Star Trek* was merely a single ratings' point. At 9 p.m., with CBS offering the world premiere made-for-TV movie *The Crucible*, starring George C. Scott, *Star Trek* was the clear winner.

Harry Mudd caught on fast, first with NBC's Stan Robertson, then with the viewing audience. The lovable scoundrel would return.

Episode 4: THE ENEMY WITHIN
Written by Richard Matheson
(with Gene Roddenberry, uncredited)
Directed by Leo Penn

NBC press release, September 13, 1966:

Publicity photo of the first attempted rape on NBC (Courtesy of Gerald Gurian)

> A malfunction in the Transporter Room of the USS Enterprise turns Captain Kirk (William Shatner) into a Jekyll-and-Hyde, in "The Enemy Within" on *Star Trek* NBC Television Network colorcast of Thursday, Oct. 6....While being "beamed" aboard his spacecraft from another planet in what is normally a routine operation, the commander is the victim of an electrical failure that literally transforms him into two "Captain Kirks." The Enterprise is threatened with complete chaos when the two personalities, identical in appearance but opposites in behavior and intellect, vie in a nightmarish conflict for control of the ship.

Lt. Sulu and a landing party, meanwhile, are stranded on a barren world where the nighttime temperatures drop so low as to make survival impossible. With the transporter out, the officers of the Enterprise are unable to depend on their captain and are running out of time to find a way to save the men left behind.

The theme: Being a leader requires a melding of one's bad as well as their good.

SOUND BITES

- *Mr. Spock, to Kirk:* "You can't afford the luxury of being anything less than perfect. If you do, they lose faith, and you lose command."

- *Spock:* "Being split in two halves is no theory with me, doctor. I have a human half, you see, as well as an alien half, submerged, constantly at war with each other. Personal experience, Doctor, I survive it because my intelligence wins over both, makes them live together."

- *Kirk's evil duplicate, to Yeoman Rand:* "You're too beautiful to ignore. Too much woman. We've both been pretending too long."

- *Kirk:* "I have to take him back into myself. I can't survive without him. I don't want to take him back. He's like an animal... and yet it's me!"

- *Dr. McCoy, to Kirk:* "We all have our darker side, we need it... men, women, all of us need both halves... it's half our humanity... it's not really ugly, it's human. God forbid I should have to agree with Spock, but he was right. Without the negative half you wouldn't be the captain. The strength of command is mostly in him.... The mental discipline to keep it under control, that he gets from you."

- *Kirk:* "I've seen a part of myself no man should ever see."

ASSESSMENT

Every ingredient for a good -- if not great -- hour of dramatic TV is here: conflict, a difficult life and death decision, self-revelation, a bold statement, and a ticking clock.

A better opponent could not be found for Kirk than Kirk himself. Spock says it best: "It is apparent that, however different in temperament, this double has your knowledge of the ship, its crew, its devices." Kirk is literally fighting himself and, therefore, the protagonist *and* the antagonist are one and the same.

"The Enemy Within" is an important episode in the evolution of *Star Trek* and serves to further define the series' two leads. We see the guts of Kirk on display, both his good and bad. The "Evil Kirk" lives within the captain of the Enterprise and is the monster of this story. As for Spock, he is given a chance to explain his mixed heritage and confess to the difficult challenges presented by his hybrid makeup.

"Enemy" also introduces the Kirk-Spock-McCoy triangle, with Spock and McCoy playing a game of tug-o-war and the Captain serving as the rope. This episode helped to solidify the differences and establish the feud between Spock and McCoy. The first instance may be the most telling, when Spock says, "For once I agree with you, Doctor."

And it was this script that inadvertently resulted in the creation of the "Spock Neck Pinch," as the writers and cast soon named it, although fans would identify it as the Vulcan Nerve Pinch.

With these attributes, "The Enemy Within" is, nonetheless, flawed. There are a few production goofs that can be spotted without even trying, and one must wonder why they don't use a shuttlecraft to rescue the crewmen stranded on the planet. Finally, it is here that we are treated to the first example in *Star Trek* of William Shatner going a bit over the top. This is not only a tale of two Kirks but a tale with two Shatners. An argument can be made for the exuberant performance regarding the "Evil Kirk." An argument can also be made that director Leo Penn should have said, "Bring it down a notch, Bill."

For the attempted rape scene, however, Shatner is right on his mark, and so is Penn. The violent encounter is frighteningly real and extremely daring. It still raises an eyebrow today. In 1966, it was shocking.

THE STORY BEHIND THE STORY

Script Timeline
Richard Matheson's story outline, ST #14: April 4, 1966.
Matheson's revised story outline, gratis: April 22, 1966.
Matheson's 1st Draft teleplay: April 25, 1966.
Matheson's gratis rewrite (Revised 1st Draft teleplay): May 19, 1966.
Matheson's 2nd Draft teleplay: May 31, 1966.
John D.F. Black's script polish (Mimeo Department "Yellow Cover 1st Draft"):
June 6, 1966.
Gene Roddenberry's rewrite (Final Draft teleplay): June 8, 1966.
Additional page revisions by Roddenberry: June 11 & 15, 1966.

A script penned by Richard Matheson gave Roddenberry bragging rights among the science fiction community. Matheson had frequently written for *The Twilight Zone*, including "Nightmare at 20,000 Feet," starring William Shatner. On the big screen, Matheson wrote *The Incredible Shrinking Man* -- based on his own book -- and *The Last Man on Earth*, a screen adaption of his sci-fi horror novel *I Am Legend*. He also adapted Jules Verne to the big screen, in the space opera *Master of the World,* as well as the short stories and poems of Edgar Allan Poe for filmmaker Roger Corman, including *House of Usher*, *Tales of Terror*, *The Pit and the Pendulum*, and *The Raven*.

Of his playful body of work, and specifically concerning *The Raven*, *Daily Variety* wrote:

> The Richard Matheson screenplay is a skillful, imaginative narrative of what comes to pass when there comes a rapping at magician Vincent Price's chamber-door by a raven -- who else but Peter Lorre, a fellow magician transformed by another sorcerer, Boris Karloff.

By 1964, Matheson was scripting tongue-in-cheek horror films for American-International -- such as *The Comedy of Terror*, again teaming Price, Lorre and Karloff, and 1965's *Die! Die! My Darling!* Right before this *Star Trek* assignment, he scripted "Time of Flight" for *Bob Hope Chrysler Theatre*. *Daily Variety* called it "a scary combo of private-eye-tough-guy and sci-fi, well-written by Richard Matheson."

In years to come, Matheson would write the screenplays for *The Night Stalker, Somewhere in Time* -- and Steven Spielberg's cult TV hit, *Duel*.

Matheson's introduction to *Star Trek* came with an invitation from Roddenberry and Desilu to attend one of the studio screenings of "Where No Man Has Gone Before." He dropped in for the second of these on March 8. In the room with him were future *Star Trek* writers George Clayton Johnson ("The Man Trap"), Paul Schneider ("Balance of Terror" and "The Squire of Gothos"), Oliver Crawford ("The Galileo Seven" and "Let That Be Your Last Battlefield"), John Kneubuhl ("Bread and Circuses"), and Meyer Dolinsky ("Plato's Stepchildren").

Matheson returned to see the pilot a second time on March 16 (with a handful of other writers who would unsuccessfully try to get their material produced). He said, "I think Gene's idea was to get all the science fiction writers in the TV and film business to write for the show. But I'm not so sure that worked out the way he had hoped." (116a)

As for the inspiration behind the story, Matheson said, "I had just looked at *Dr. Jekyll and Mr. Hyde* and immediately saw the potential of using that transporter device for separating the two sides of a person's character. Having an accident with that offered a good way to study the alternative personality. And it was part of my original concept that he [Kirk] needed that negative element in his personality in order to be a good captain. I think, probably, we're all mixtures of good and bad. If any one of us was all good, we'd be boring. And leaders have to have that drive and that ambition." (116a)

Despite Matheson's impressive credentials, the creative team at *Star Trek* had mixed feelings about his April 4, 1966 story outline. In an interoffice memorandum to John D.F. Black and Robert Justman, Roddenberry immediately pointed out the upside, telling his associate producers, "I think this could be a tour-de-force for Bill." There was no question Shatner would love it, but Roddenberry worried, "Wonder if the NBC censors will allow an attempted rape scene?" (GR4-1)

The scene was rendered all the more brutal by Matheson's description of Kirk's alter ego. As the "Evil Kirk" wanders the ship, he doesn't just swill Saurian brandy, he gets downright drunk. He is more barbaric, more reckless, and far less cunning than what was ultimately depicted on screen.

It was important to Matheson that the attempted rape be included. It wasn't part of his story outline merely for exploitation purposes, but to enable Kirk's bad side to take the place of the obligatory science fiction monster. He said, "What else could we show about this side of the Captain that would be more frightening?" (116a)

Attacking and beating a human being, which Kirk's bad side certainly does, was not enough. A grizzly bear will do that out of instinct. But molestation goes beyond mere survival. It is calculated, even perversely hedonistic. It is the dark side of humanity.

Absent in this first version is the subplot -- that ticking clock -- where the "landing party" is stranded on the planet, sure to perish if Kirk can't pull himself together in time. Sensing something vital was missing but not sure what, Roddenberry shared with his staff:

> Generally, I feel we have a good story here, but I think it may get dull if we let Kirk sit around probing his soul and consulting the doctor about the meaning of all this. (GR4-1)

Robert Justman did not want the outline sent to NBC. He argued:

> This story idea certainly seems to have value to me, but I think in its present form it is rather messy and over-convoluted.... I think we need a revised outline from Mr. Matheson. (RJ4-1)

Mr. Matheson was agreeable and revised his outline at no charge, turning in version #2 on April 22. The Yeoman being attacked by Kirk was now identified as Rand. Little else had changed. Later that day, Justman wrote to Black, "How do you feel about this story now? I must confess that I am *not* enthused." (RJ4-2)

John D.F., however, was. Realizing he was in the minority, his memo to Roddenberry said:

> Without meaning to sound facetious, I still like the story; have nothing but confidence in Matheson's being able to handle it. (JDFB4-1)

The encouraging word was a moot point. Roddenberry, desperate for scripts and not wanting to alienate someone of Richard Matheson's status, had already given the go-ahead for him to write his teleplay -- even before hearing from NBC regarding the concept.

Matheson's first draft script hit Roddenberry's desk on April 25. New to the story now, at Roddenberry's insistence, was the subplot dealing with the men left behind on the planet. The leader of those men was not Sulu but a crewman named North.

"I was a little disappointed that Roddenberry built in a necessity to have a 'B-story' about the members of his crew stuck on the planet," Matheson admitted. "I can see why he did it, because 'B-stories' seemed to be a very regular occurrence in television in those days, and maybe still are. But I wanted to concentrate on Bill Shatner's performance, because he was so good. I had more for him to do in that way. I used to go out of my way to watch Bill Shatner on TV. He was in two of *The Twilight Zone* episodes I wrote and he was wonderful in both of them -- a very dynamic actor. I didn't write the script the way I did to challenge him. I wrote it to make it as good as I could. But I was confident Bill could do it." (116a)

Matheson reluctantly added in the B-story, taking care not to let it dominate the tale -- one he believed had enough drama in it already. With all of Kirk's inner angst, creating an outside problem for him to deal with felt artificial to Matheson. Roddenberry disagreed, believing that the men stranded on the planet not only put pressure on Kirk and created an urgency for him to resolve his problems, but tested the Captain, better illustrating the point Matheson wanted to make about the human quality required to make a command decision.

Robert Justman wrote to his colleagues:

> This scene in Janice's Quarters with Kirk's Double [is] going to be a very tough scene to handle censorship-wise.... Also know you this, that every time we have to show the animal knocked out, it's going to cost us a hundred dollars for a veterinarian and an injection. This, in addition to the cost of rental of the animals and trainer's fees.... [A]fter leaving the dispensary, the Double goes to Kirk's cabin and puts more medicated cream over the scratches. Why does he do this? At this time, both Kirk and his double have scratches on their faces. Incidentally, please order me a jar of this cream. (RJ4-2)

Bill Theiss, looking for costuming ideas, was first to respond to the script, but his memo had nothing to do with wardrobe. Theiss, having worked on the sci-fi sitcom *My Favorite Martian*, warned Roddenberry:

> At John D.F. Black's suggestion I am apprising you of the fact that *My Favorite Martian* did a show in which Ray Walston split into three -- negative, positive, and *undecided*; and another show in which he split into two -- much more to the point of this script, in which the wild half went 'tom-catting' off with [actress] Joyce Jameson and the sober side kept trying to get back together. (BT4)

Roddenberry didn't care about concepts made silly by *My Favorite Martian* and turned his attention to writing a long letter to Richard Matheson, outlining numerous deep changes he wanted to see in the script. Near the top of the list was the depiction of Dr. McCoy. Matheson had been writing the role for Dr. Piper, the character played by Paul Fix in the second pilot film, the only example of *Star Trek* to be seen. Roddenberry wrote:

> You should have now a copy of the mimeo Writers Information on the ship's doctor. You will find a cynical "H.L. Mencken" quality which will be most helpful in your script which <u>does</u> use the Doctor considerably. (GR4-2)

Roddenberry also didn't like how Matheson played Kirk's double as being so primal that he was incapable of being deceitful. He wrote:

> Suggest some caution in portraying him too animalistic. Let's keep in mind that even this negative side of Kirk would have our Captain's intelligence and thus even the most evil things would be done with considerable cleverness. This should help the general blocking of the story too, since the more shrewd and cunning this double, the more of a threat he poses. If he just went drunkenly bumbling around, we'd begin to wonder after a while why our well-trained crew hasn't been able to apprehend him more easily.... The more I review this aspect, the surer it seems that the double should not be drunk. Let him drink, but does he have to be out and out drunk to be evil? (GR4-2)

An important addition to the story was made at this time, with the idea coming from Roddenberry. He told Matheson:

> Suggest early in the script, certainly early in Act II, we should begin to suggest that the real Kirk has been changed by all this too. Deprived of the negative side... he must begin to lose some of the strength that positive-negative gives a man. Decisiveness would be one of the first things he'd have trouble with. And he would probably have some difficulty making decisions that endangered others, i.e., the men left down on the planet surface. If his alter-ego is bad and disdainful of the life and safety of others, the real Kirk would possibly be *over-*

conscious of the safety and comfort of others. <u>Important</u>, however, his intelligence would tell him something is wrong and he would struggle against all of this.... In other words, this allows us to display the problems the real Kirk is fighting, but keeping him something of a hero figure even in this strange state since he will be making a valiant fight to stay in command of himself. (GR4-2)

Roddenberry also suggested that Kirk not allow himself the prerogative of letting the crew in on his dilemma. He knew from his own experience in the military that, in order to lead, a leader can never be seen as weak in the eyes of his subordinates. This would be one more weight on the strained shoulders of the tormented Captain.

These suggestions and others like them infused the story and character elements with the concepts and themes that elevate "The Enemy Within" to classic status. It was no longer just an outer space version of *Dr. Jekyll and Mr. Hyde*.

This was a sizable rewrite to be ordered from a freelancer who had already provided two story outlines before going to script, especially since this rewrite was being provided for free. As such, it was regarded as a Revised First Draft, instead of a 2nd Draft, so Matheson still had one final version he was contractually obligated to deliver and, finally, be compensated for. Gene Roddenberry, as all the *Star Trek* writers would learn, was a perfectionist who lived by the credo, "Scripts aren't written, they're rewritten."

Matheson later said, "Roddenberry had a specific attitude toward the writing of the show. It had to be maintained or he wasn't satisfied. Rod Serling, on the other hand, was very open-minded. I mean, he was a writer himself. I guess Roddenberry was a writer, too, but Rod did not have any compulsion to impose his own way of thinking on the other writers. He did *his* scripts for *The Twilight Zone* as social commentary, which Chuck Beaumont and I never did, and he never said anything about that. He let ours be different." (116a)

Of course *The Twilight Zone* was an anthology series with no recurring characters or sets, an entirely different kettle of fish.

It wasn't until Roddenberry sent his letter to Matheson that NBC, still unaware that a script had been written, finally responded to the story outline. Jon Kubichan, speaking for Broadcast Standards, gave his okay to "go to script" with one very big stipulation that:

> [T]he scenes between Janice and Kirk's double be tempered in such a means as to make them acceptable both to NBC and the NAB [National Association of Broadcasters] Code. (JK4)

The next day, Stan Robertson, also having only read the revised story outline, told Roddenberry:

> Our primary concern with this outline in its present form is... the effect upon the viewer that Kirk's "alter ego," as outlined here, might have. (ST4-1)

Matheson's revised first draft teleplay, meanwhile, was already underway. When delivered on May 19, Roddenberry seemed somewhat content. His memo to John Black and Robert Justman said:

> Like this story very much. Dick has done a good job and it should make a good episode. With some "hypoing" of the perils, both emotional and physical, with some thought and work on increasing the moments of suspense, it could become an <u>outstanding</u> episode. (GR4-3)

One aspect that Roddenberry felt needed "hypoing" was the character of McCoy. He felt that the yet-to-be-seen ship's doctor was portrayed too much like *Gunsmoke*'s "Doc" instead of like "H.L. Mencken, the curmudgeon, the sharp-tongued individual," and that the dialogue written for McCoy did not have enough "bite." Roddenberry also felt Matheson was not utilizing the Spock-McCoy relationship as established in the sample scripts provided, and had not understood "that the two men don't get along too well." (GR4-3)

He told Black and Justman:

> As written now, despite Dick's well-known ability at dialogue, many scenes in this script lack the spice and excitement of <u>individual strong personalities</u> and the conflict of distinct and separate ideas and attitudes on life, medicine, discipline, etc. Too often they are simple exchanges of information, admittedly well done, but without the excitement which sharply defined personalities and attitudes can bring.... Not complaining, understand.... Sure, it is not everything we want, certainly not everything Matheson can do, but it's still one of the best first drafts we've gotten in. (GR4-3)

Except that this particular "first" draft was Matheson's second.

Justman too felt there was still much work to do. The same day Roddenberry's memo hit, he wrote a long one of his own, complaining to John Black:

> On the first page of the teaser, do we need to establish sixteen crew members down on the surface of the planet? Five lives are important too. Sixteen lives are more than I feel we can afford for this segment.... On page 45, McCoy's second speech is schmucko. I don't think "half of Kirk's cellular structure is missing" or "half his blood." I just think the poor fella is emotionally deprived.... Someday I hope to be able to write memos that are full of sweetness and light, and optimism, and faith and hope and charity and all the other chozzerai -- Yiddish for "crap" -- that I have been unable to corral up to now. I really do like to be a happy individual. Maybe I'm in the wrong business? Maybe I'll just raise chickens. (RJ4-3)

John D.F. was less critical and becoming bothered that Roddenberry "couldn't keep his hands off the scripts," especially when those scripts had been written by sci-fi legends like Jerry Sohl and Richard Matheson. He later said, "In [Matheson's] case... he really wanted to make his own fight with GR, and *could* do it. He was a professional. I know he had a talk about the final draft in GR's office. I was there. He understood what the show was. He knew what we were doing. He tuned in immediately. So it was difficult for GR to make any kind of real arguments about structure. He had some bitches about where the story turned here and there, but, by and large, ['The Enemy Within'] was one of the easy ones." (17-4)

Or perhaps not. Matheson was already on draft number three of his teleplay, to be turned in on May 31 with a clear message to Roddenberry. On the title page, he didn't type "2nd Draft," but, instead, sought closure with two simple words: "<u>Final Draft</u>."

Beyond the issues of screen credits and residuals, the magnitude of the work being done by the freelance writers on *Star Trek* was out of proportion to the money paid. The volume of the workload expected at *Star Trek* was unprecedented, with writers often receiving dozens of pages of notes from the producer on each and every draft, requiring more than mere script polishing but complete overhauling of their teleplays. What would be two weeks' work on most other shows almost always became -- for the same money -- a full month's work on *Star Trek*. This obsessive rewriting helped to make a TV classic but left in its wake many bruised egos, aborted writing assignments, and irreparably damaged producer/writer relationships.

With the new draft in hand, Robert Justman sent another lengthy memo to John Black concerning production problems in filming the script as written, as well as inconsistencies with ship's characters and the working of the Enterprise, as established in

"The Corbomite Maneuver" and "Mudd's Women." These included Matheson calling for doors on the ship to be ajar and a description of Kirk splashing his face with water while in his cabin. The doors on the Enterprise, of course, slide open and shut and would never be left ajar. As to splashing water onto the face, Justman wrote to Black, "We have no provisions for a bathroom _or_ a fire hydrant." He closed, writing:

> John, I think it is important enough, since this is supposedly our third show to shoot and we are starting our second one in the morning, that we get right to work on the revisions of this screenplay as fast as possible. I don't know if Dick Matheson will be able to accomplish everything we need done in the amount of time we have left to get it done.... This script is not too feasible in its present state and I don't think we have anything else that is more ready than this one. (RJ4-4)

Black rolled up his sleeves and did a script polish. He was careful to confine his changes to those that pertained to character traits of the series regulars and the workings of the Enterprise. He did not want to lose Richard Matheson's distinctive voice -- that certain something that stamped this work as coming from a science fiction master.

This latest draft, the mimeo department "Yellow Cover 1st Draft" dated June 6, was intended to go to NBC for approval. It never made it out of the producers' offices.

Roddenberry did a rewrite of his own two days later, creating the June 8 Final Draft. Among the changes, he replaced crewman North with helmsman Sulu as ranking officer among the men left behind, and put more emphasis on this B-story and more personal anguish onto the "good Kirk" over his inability to find a way to save his landing team. It was this draft that was the first to be sent to the network and be distributed to cast and crew.

Leonard Nimoy was enthusiastic about the script. Nonetheless, he had some issues, and it was here where Nimoy began giving script notes -- something seldom allowed for in television production of the time. His letter to Roddenberry began:

> Gene, I hope you won't mind my dropping some notes on "The Enemy Within." Generally, I feel it is the best material we have had so far, and I will not dwell on the things I like but rather on some of the areas which struck me as problematic. (LN4)

Among them, Nimoy was bothered by the antagonistic relationship between Spock and McCoy. He complained that it "borders on open hostility." He continued:

> Also, it comes at a time when the Captain is in trouble, and the bickering in scenes 18 and 19 reduces two military men to a pair of children arguing over who should do the errand for mommy. (LN4)

Time would prove Nimoy wrong; the fans of _Star Trek_ came to love the Spock/McCoy feud. For this story, in particular, the "bickering" helps to visualize much of Kirk's growing inner conflict. However, the character conflict in this draft of the script needed -- and would receive -- some refinement.

The next day, a memo arrived from Stan Robertson at NBC. He was perturbed over not having been shown the script until now. He wrote:

> Quite honestly, Gene, our approval of this script is given very reluctantly since we feel that the major point which we objected to in the outline is more prominently apparent in the script. And that is what the characterization of Kirk's "Alter Ego," as portrayed, might do to the viewer's image of our hero. (ST4-2)

Robertson recommended that the episode be pushed back on the NBC broadcast schedule so as to not alienate audience members tuning in for the first time.

Roddenberry made additional script changes, with revised pages coming in on June 11 and, even after production began, on June 15. It was Roddenberry who added the tidy conclusion to the confrontation on the bridge, with evil Kirk falling apart and seeking the embrace of the good Kirk. (In Matheson's script, Kirk had knocked his evil self out with a phaser set on stun.) Despite the screen credit (acknowledging only Matheson as the writer), the script was now a collaborative endeavor.

"I know he wasn't happy with the rewrite GR did on 'Enemy Within,' and he shouldn't have been," John D.F. Black said. "Matheson was a fine writer. I mean, he was *fine*. He knew screenwriting; he knew teleplay writing. He knew how to do it. And you could tell. Now, when you had somebody in there who didn't know their ass from a hole in the ground, okay, you got busy behind the typewriter. But, if somebody did know how to write, boy, you knew that right away. Mary would walk into the office and say, 'Wait until you read this. Wow!' And that was Matheson." (17)

Mary Black said, "You don't rewrite a good writer. You don't go fiddle with it, particularly when you've had a couple belts. You don't do that. You just don't. That's all. Period. Especially Matheson. He was a superb writer. I had more respect for him than almost anybody." (17a)

With the writing and rewriting of this episode, the dissention in the producers' offices had begun.

Pre-Production
June 7-10 and June 13, 1966 (5 days prep).

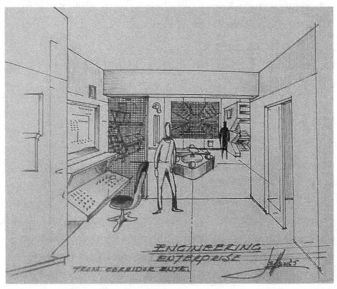

Matt Jefferies first sketch of the engineering section
(Courtesy of Gerald Gurian)

While planning the production, Bob Justman worried about the story's need to show more of the Enterprise than had been designed and built. He contacted Black and Roddenberry, writing:

We have the chase and fight in the "shadowy cavern of the power plant." A set of this sort would be extremely expensive to construct and would take up an enormous amount of room. And I know we don't have this sort of room on either of our two stages for this kind of set. (RJ4-2)

Roddenberry contacted Matt Jefferies, writing:

Much pleased with our Enterprise sets, Matt. Now, however, we shall shortly be getting two scripts which call for other Enterprise sets. Referring now specifically to the need for "Engineering Deck" or "Engine Room," we should definitely think in terms of creating an illusion of a room of considerable size. We've got a huge ship and I definitely feel the audience will ultimately be disappointed if they are not taken occasionally into a set or sets with some feeling of vastness. Some areas of considerable spaciousness would only be logical within a vessel of these dimensions. (GR4-4)

To accomplish this "illusion of room," Jefferies relied on forced perspective. The engineering deck, deceptive in its scale, was built into a corner of Stage 9.

Leo Penn, 44, was hired to direct. He was an actor-turned-director and had recently helmed episodes for *Voyage to the Bottom of the Sea*, *Lost in Space*, and *I Spy*. The series in which he was most appreciated were *Dr. Kildare*, where he directed seven episodes, and *Ben Casey*, where he was responsible for 19. He would later win an Emmy in 1973 for directing "Any Port in a Storm" for *Columbo*. He was also the dad of the future Academy Award winning actor and director Sean Penn.

No name guest stars were needed for this episode. Jim Goodwin was back for the second time as Lt. Farrell, the ship's Navigator. He would return again for "Miri."

Ed Madden played Fisher, who gets battered by a fall and then by the "Evil Kirk." Madden worked sporadically in the 1960s, showing up on *Gunsmoke* and *The Fugitive*, among other series. He also had been seen briefly in "The Cage" as "Enterprise Geologist."

Garland Thompson, 27 at this time, played the Transporter Crewman. Primarily a stage actor, he had also played a dancer in the film version of *South Pacific* and worked in television with a couple of stops at *Perry Mason* and other series. He would return as an Enterprise crewman again, for "Charlie X."

Production Diary
Filmed June 14, 15, 16, 17, 20, 21 & 22 (¾ day), 1966
(Planned as 6 day production; finishing ¾ day behind; total cost: $193,646).

Day 2, second day on the Transporter Room set
(Courtesy of Gerald Gurian)

Tuesday, June 14, 1966. Herb Alpert and the Tijuana Brass clung onto the Top Selling LP position in record stores with the *What Now My Love* album, for the fifth of eight weeks at the summit. Also in the Top 10, by the same band, *Whipped Cream and Other Delights*, at No. 3, and *Going Places*, at No. 5. While American teenagers were going through Beatlemania, their parents were on a Tijuana Brass kick. The kids, however, were controlling the radio. "Paint It Black" by the Rolling Stones was No. 1 on A.M. radio station turntables. Right under it, "Did You Ever Have to Make Up Your Mind" by The Lovin' Spoonful and, in third place, "I Am a Rock" by Simon & Garfunkel. In South Africa, anti-apartheid revolutionary Nelson Mandela was sentenced to life in prison. Also, this week, the U.S. Supreme Court passed the Miranda decision, requiring police to inform suspects of their rights. And "The Enemy Within" began filming.

Production started on Stage 10 with the planet-bound scenes. At half past noon, the company moved to Stage 9 for the first of the transporter room sequences. No one thought it odd that Kirk's command insignia was missing from his uniform. The insignia had been removed the night before when the shirt was sent in for cleaning, as it was done every day the shirt was worn. This day, however, someone neglected to sew the insignia back on. Cast and crew, wrongly assuming the omission was intentional and racing to beat the clock, went about their work without question.

Director Penn took his last shot at 6:45 p.m., leaving the second series of transporter room scenes for the next day.

Day 2, Wednesday. The scene with the odd little dog's arrival from the planet, and its transporter-generated vicious twin, was filmed. Next up: scenes in the corridors, then the turbolift elevator. The insignia was back on Kirk's shirt, thereby creating a continuity problem in the finished episode.

Penn worked the company until 7:12 p.m., at which point the crew

Day 2: Shatner and his body double, Don Eitner, prepare for a second camera take (Courtesy of Gerald Gurian)

began wrapping set while the cast had their makeup removed, with costumes sent to the cleaners. For most, the drive home started at 7:30 p.m., with a call time the next morning at 6:30 a.m.

Day 3, Thursday. Scenes were filmed in Kirk's quarters and on the bridge. The camera rolled until 6:55.

Day 4, Friday. Filming took place in sickbay and McCoy's office. It was here that William Shatner gave a hand to Grace Lee Whitney -- literally. During a sequence in McCoy's office, where Yeoman Rand confronts Kirk and tearfully accuses him of attacking her, Whitney was not sure how she was going to generate the needed emotion. She said, "When I had to do that scene, where I was crying, with tears running down my face, it was 20 minutes to 12 and everybody was on edge, thinking, 'Oh god, if this woman can't cut this scene, we're gonna be here through our entire lunch break.' So, at my close-up, I've got the tears coming down my face but I'm struggling to bring up the emotion, the confusion and the shock, and Bill comes up from behind the camera and smacks me right across the face to get me into character. Well, what it did was it just shocked me so much that I did the scene in one take." (183-6)

Whitney remembered, "The director yelled, 'Cut! Print it!' The cast and crew applauded, and Leonard gave me a hug. I looked at Bill, and he smiled at me and said,

'Beautiful!'" (183-2)

Despite Whitney's nailing it in one take, the crew worked late anyway. Penn didn't stop filming until 7:55 p.m.

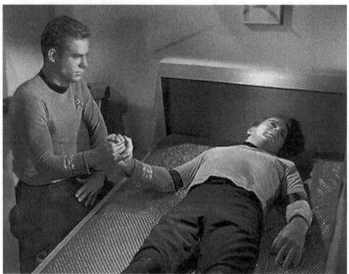

Shatner (on bed) and his double, Don Eitner, prior to split-screen process (Courtesy of Gerald Gurian)

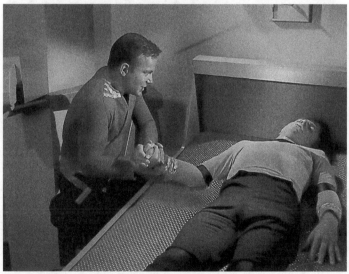

And the reverse, with Shatner now sitting and Eitner on the bed (Courtesy of William Krewson)

Day 5, Monday. Work continued in sickbay with the two Kirks. Putting the two together on screen would pose a new set of challenges. Jerry Finnerman said, "Oh, I remember that show.... They came to me... and they said, 'You have to shoot split-screen. You *have* to do it.'.... I said [to myself], 'What am I going to do?'" (63-3)

It is easy today -- it's all done digitally -- but not in 1966. Jerry Finnerman, 35 years after the fact, relived the terror of that day, saying, "I called my dear friend Lynn Dunn [of Film Effects of Hollywood]. He was probably the best special effects man around and a good friend of my father. I told him the situation, and he told me exactly what to do.... You take the camera and you get a soft matte line in the middle of the scene [dividing the set], where the actor can't go over that line or he'll be in the [opposite] shot.... And you have to block the camera off with a solid [black opal]... so one side of the screen is black; you can't see anything.... Then you had to send the film to the camera department and they had to notch it.... Then we got the film back... notched... we put it in the camera, and we shot the scene, and Bill played to the mirror off stage [or to a double]."

"'Cut!... Okay, do the other side.'... Now, they have to rewind that film to where the notch is. Meantime, the camera's all tied off -- locked off and braced -- and we have to take the black opal and bring it over on the other side of the lens so that what was black is now clear and the side that was clear is now black.... And Bill played to the mirror [or double], off screen, and he was good.... I was beside myself, because I figured it wouldn't work.... And I went home and I thought about it all night. I really did.... And we ran it the next day. Oh, I was so proud. I mean, I was really proud. That stuff just came out perfect. I have to thank Lynn Dunn for that; for telling me how to do it, or I would have been in bad shape." (63-3)

Don Eitner, holding hands with Shatner, hugging Shatner, sharing the long hours in creating all those split-screens with Shatner, said, "I never worked harder than I did on *Star Trek*. It was a very exciting schedule. I had to rehearse both 'characters'.... Bill [Shatner] even challenged some of the logic of the scenes in 'The Enemy Within.' Things were worked out and it turned out to be a terrific show.... Bill was very pleased with the results. The cast was very dedicated." (57b)

Day 6, Tuesday, June 21, was the planned final day of production. The company moved onto the new engineering set. This was when Leonard Nimoy made a move of his own to rectify what he perceived as a problem in the script. The stage direction said that Spock "lunges out from behind one of the generators and kayoes the double."

Nimoy recalled, "The scene jarred me when I first read it. It seemed more appropriate for the Old West than the 23rd Century." (128-3)

Near the time of this production, Nimoy told a newspaper writer, "Although we are essentially a humanistic show, the Enterprise is heavily armed and a lot of guns get shown. My way of avoiding participation in the violence was the Spock Pinch. I decided that Vulcans knew so much about the human anatomy that they could knock out an enemy just by pinching a nerve in the neck and the shoulders." (128-17)

Nimoy approached Leo Penn with his idea. Shatner had been listening in, so when Penn asked for a demonstration, he quickly volunteered to be the guinea pig. Nimoy recalled, "I applied pressure to the juncture of Bill's neck and shoulder, and he most convincingly fell into an 'unconscious' heap on the floor. Thus the famous neck pinch was born, in part because of Bill Shatner's talent for fainting on cue." (128-3)

The "pinch" stayed, but had not been cleared by the front office. Producers Roddenberry, Justman, and Black had no idea that Nimoy, Shatner and Penn had behind their backs made a substantial change to the character of Spock and the format of *Star Trek*. They found out the next day while viewing the dailies.

Roddenberry and his creative staff couldn't help but embrace the idea and immediately began looking for ways to use the pinch in future episodes. The gimmick was even given a name -- "The Famous Spock Neck Pinch." In time, the pinch became so commonplace that it was merely referred to by its initials, with a passage in the script often reading, "Spock applies the FSNP." Regardless of the acceptance, Nimoy had broken protocol and, before this episode saw the light of day, Roddenberry would make an attempt to pull the reins in.

Next on the schedule for Day 6 were sequences in the corridor outside Yeoman Rand's cabin and the attempted rape in her quarters. Grace Lee Whitney commented, "It's a violent, scary scene. Bill is a very physical actor and extremely strong. Because I had been on diet pills for so long, I was very light-weight and Bill picked me up like a twig and threw me around the room. We did endless takes on that scene -- and some of the retakes were due to the fact that my beehive wig wouldn't stay on through all that tossing and shaking. It took us the better part of the day." (183-2)

Whitney later added, "I was black and blue for weeks. Bill held me so tight that I had bruise marks with the imprints of his fingers on my arms -- for days!" (183-6)

The final set-up of production was scheduled for the briefing room, but it was 7 p.m.

and Leo Penn was more than 30 minutes into overtime. These last sequences had to wait until the next day, a *seventh* day of filming, delaying the start of *Star Trek*'s next episode.

Day 7, Wednesday, June 22, 1966. The camera followed Shatner as the vicious Kirk walked down the corridor, swilling Saurian Brandy. Also filmed: the tortured, passive Kirk, alone in the briefing room. Penn finished filming at 3:30 p.m., finally allowing director Marc Daniels to begin "The Man Trap."

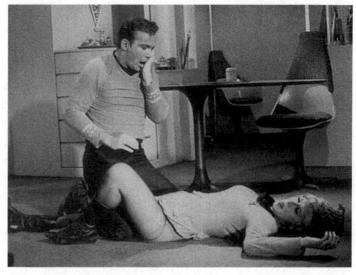

Publicity photo NBC was reluctant to issue, depicting the moment after Rand scratches Kirk's face (Courtesy of Gerald Gurian)

"It was a challenging show to do," Penn said. "We had to hire a photo double and it was particularly tough in the scenes where they [the two Kirks] had physical contact. You had to resort to shooting over the double's shoulder, switching them around and so on. It took time, but the results were worth it." (137)

The bean counters at Desilu disagreed. Robert Justman's explanation for Penn not being given work on *Star Trek* was because of daily overtime, and going six-eighths of a day over-schedule. Three episodes were in the can, and three directors (Sargent, Hart, and Penn) would not return.

"Television [directing is like] being a really good hooker," said Penn. "It's a one-night stand; you give it your best shot and do as well as you can under the circumstances." (137)

Post-Production
June 23 through September 26, 1966.
Music score recorded on September 14, 1966.

Fabien Tordjmann began as head of the third two-man editing team here. He later said, "I worked for Gene Roddenberry on *The Lieutenant* at MGM.... I did not yet have enough time in the union, so I couldn't do the [*Star Trek*] pilot, but the minute it sold they said, 'We want you,' which was very nice of them. In the meantime, I was going to do *The Monkees*. It was very different but I had to turn it down as I was committed to Gene." (176)

Dorothy Fontana said, "Fabien's team member was John Hanley, a lovely guy from Boston. It was really funny to listen to their debates back and forth – French versus Boston Irish – on the cutting. They were a great team!" (64-4b)

With this episode, Tordjmann and Hanley entered a most difficult race. Their challenge was to match the quality of the other two teams -- headed by the more experienced Bob Swanson and Bruce Schoengarth -- and meet the three week deadline given for each episode. Robert Justman described Tordjmann as "an excitable Frenchman, a rabid film buff" who was "enthusiastic and always ready to experiment." But for this first assignment, Justman felt Tordjmann was a bit too enthusiastic.

Inspired by Jerry Finnerman's expressive camera work, Richard Matheson's risqué story and William Shatner's sexually-charged performance, Tordjmann saw an opportunity to add a new dimension to American TV. Justman explained, "Fabien decided to enhance the story, utilizing an esoteric approach. However, the story had Shatner playing both Kirk and Kirk's evil alter-ego; it was already esoteric enough for the television screen. Using experimental editing techniques was, to put it mildly, counter-productive." (94-8)

There are a few brief instances left in the finished episode displaying Tordjmann's proposed "esoteric" approach. At one point, the good Kirk with Spock enters the turbolift. Just as the doors close, without the camera angle changing, there is an abrupt cut to the same shot with a bloody hand now in center screen. Then the evil Kirk steps into the shot and sucks the blood from his own hand. If left to Tordjmann's discretion, much of the episode would have been presented in this jolting fashion. Justman vetoed the idea.

"Bob Justman was very involved in the series, and I liked him very much," Tordjmann said. "He was wonderful. He was very tough in the beginning with me, but I was very resilient, and we developed a very good relationship." (176)

Regarding a second production goof in this episode, a mistake in filming had to be corrected in editing. During the climactic showdown between Kirk and his alter ego on the bridge, the scratch on his face suddenly jumps to the wrong cheek. The blame for this rests on the shoulders of director Leo Penn and cinematographer Jerry Finnerman. They "crossed the line" -- that is, they angled the camera wrong when they took this shot. To make the shot line-up properly with its corresponding reverse angle, the film had to be "flipped."

Roddenberry, of course, saw problems of this type first-hand while screening the rough cuts and would routinely send notes to the film editors asking for changes. He also sent notes to his actors.

On September 14, as "The Enemy Within" was being prepared for delivery to NBC and Roddenberry again watched the first instance of the Famous Spock Neck Pinch, he wrote Nimoy, explaining that while he appreciated a good idea, "obviously none of us want this to become a habit since it is precisely this type of thing which has destroyed the format and continuity of more than one television series." His letter continued:

> The time and pressure everyone on set is undergoing during actual photography does not permit the kind of in-depth analysis of scenes which is necessary when such changes are to be made. Most often, as you are well aware, they may seem to improve the specific scene being shot but create difficulties and surprises in the cutting room later when it is suddenly realized that key information -- seemingly unimportant at the time -- had been lost.... I'm sure you realize that I have little fear about the kind of professional changes which you come up with. But when one person makes a change, others who may be less capable are encouraged to stick in their oar, too, and you know what generally happens. (GR4-5)

Roddenberry's battles with Nimoy over control of the character of Spock were just beginning.

Sol Kaplan, hired to write the score, was next to join the post-production phase. The 46-year-old had been creating music in Hollywood since the 1940s, primarily for motion pictures, including the 1953 version of *Titanic* and the 1965 Richard Burton hit *The Spy Who Came in from the Cold*. Robert Justman, after hearing samples of the composer's work, said, "It appeared to me that Kaplan was not only very talented but he was cerebral; he wrote intelligent music." (94-9)

The Howard Anderson Company was assigned the job of supplying the optical effects, but, overwhelmed with too much work on too many episodes, was helped out by a second post production house, Film Effects of Hollywood. The latter billed *Star Trek* $4,000 for opticals and an additional $1,292 for "stage work" (miniatures and photography). The total, in 2013, equates to $38,200, with that bill coming in from only the secondary post effects provider.

The reason a shuttlecraft was not available to retrieve the landing party is that Desilu decided to defer construction of the life-size prop and its corresponding miniature until it was known if the series would be picked up for the balance of the season. This was a necessary decision. Even without a shuttlecraft, at a cost of $193,646, "Enemy" nudged above its studio-mandated allowance. Today this would be in excess of $1.4 million.

Release / Reaction
Only NBC air date: 10/6/66.

Stan Robertson at the network had worried over how the "Evil Kirk" might bother viewers tuning in for the first time and asked Roddenberry to push "Enemy" back in the broadcast schedule. But because the other shows in production had more time-consuming optical effects, the furthest it could be pushed would make it the fifth episode aired. For the night of October 6, 1966, there were no other episodes of *Star Trek* ready.

Syndicated entertainment columnist Joan Crosby reviewed "The Enemy Within" on October 1. 1966. Among the newspapers carrying her *TV Scout* column was the *Post Herald and Register,* out of Beckley, West Virginia. Crosby wrote:

> For a supposed futuristic spaceship traveling around the outer dimensions, the USS Enterprise must have been put together with wire and wax. This week there is a transporter malfunction and that's all writer Richard Matheson needed for his plot to transfer Captain Kirk (William Shatner) into a Jekyll and Hyde.

A.C. Nielsen counted the noses of those watching that night.

RATINGS / Nielsen 30-Market report for Thursday, October 6, 1966:

8:30 - 9 p.m., with 58% of U.S. TVs in use.	Rating:	Share:
NBC: *Star Trek* (first half)	17.3	29.8%
ABC: *The Dating Game*	15.4	26.6%
CBS: **My Three Sons**	**17.6**	**30.3%**
Local independent stations:	9.8	13.3%
9 - 9:30 p.m., with 63.3% of U.S. TVs in use.		
NBC: *Star Trek* (second half)	16.8	26.5%
ABC: *Bewitched*	17.8	28.1%
CBS: **Thursday Night Movie**	**23.1**	**36.5%**
Local independent stations:	7.8	8.9%

At 8:30 p.m., *Star Trek* was a strong second, a mere three-tenths of a rating point below *My Three Sons* on CBS, and beating ABC's *The Dating Game*. Thirty minutes later, following the attempted rape of the mini-skirted Yeoman Rand by the "Evil Kirk," *Star Trek* fell to No. 3, behind the family-viewing safe harbors of *Bewitched* and *The CBS Thursday Night Movie*. The "Tiffany Network" had brought out the big guns on this night with television's first offering of the 1961 favorite, *Breakfast at Tiffany's*, starring Audrey Hepburn and George Peppard.

Regardless of the competition, NBC's belief that the startling sexual assault on a yeoman by her captain was the reason for the mass exodus of viewer-ship and contributed to the decision to not give "Enemy" a network repeat broadcast.

On October 7, 1966, the day after "The Enemy Within" had its only NBC showing, Gene Coon (*Star Trek*'s new producer by that time) wrote to Fenton Coe, Director of Film Productions at NBC, requesting that the network stop correcting the color to make Spock appear to have "conventional flesh tones." He explained to Coe that people from Vulcan were supposed to be "yellow" and "the sallower, the better."

Despite the problems in getting this episode made, the continuity goofs, and the lack of a shuttlecraft, Roddenberry named "Enemy Within" as one of his 10 favorite episodes.

During an appearance on *The Mike Douglas Show* in 1968, William Shatner said "Enemy" was his favorite episode ... so far.

James Doohan commented, "A remarkably daring episode when you think about it. How many series, in one of their first half-dozen episodes, have an entire plotline involving the heroic lead's darkest rape fantasies? I thought Bill's performance was pretty okay in that one." (52-1)

Richard Matheson said, "I thought Bill Shatner was brilliant. I loved what he did. He carried the whole thing. I was a little sorry that Roddenberry put so much emphasis on the crew being stuck on the planet. It took so much time away from Bill. But I liked it, and I was very satisfied with the production value." (116a)

Grace Lee Whitney said, "I love 'The Enemy Within' because it gave me a chance to really react and act with Bill Shatner. I love it! I loved the whole concept of him breaking into two characters because that really was what Kirk and Rand were about. There were two sides of Kirk and two sides of Rand. Rand was there to be of service to him but she was also in love with him. But she knew she mustn't over-go the boundaries." (183-7)

Leo Penn said, "In every human being there's good and bad. Hopefully, the good is reachable.... That particular *Star Trek*... was personal. There was a personal tug-of-war that was -- *is* -- intriguing stuff.... I worked very intimately with them, hopefully in a stimulating way. It was give-and-take. William Shatner's a very good actor and gave a very good performance.... I had a good time on that show." (137)

"Leo Penn was fabulous," Grace Lee Whitney said. "We loved him. And all our directors were so excited to do *Star Trek*. It was something different for them. Something special." (183-6)

Despite the praise from Whitney, Penn was already out of the building and not to return. Nor was sci-fi master Richard Matheson.

Richard Matheson didn't write for *Star Trek* again. Or, more accurately, he didn't have his material produced for *Star Trek* again.

Gene Roddenberry, in a January 12, 1967 letter to Damon Knight, editor of the newsletter for the Science Fiction Writers of America, said that Matheson had been given an offer to take another assignment but, at that time, was unavailable. Many who knew Matheson -- members of the science fiction writing community -- believed the famed writer did not return to *Star Trek* because he was displeased about being rewritten to such a degree by Roddenberry.

Matheson stayed silent on the issue for decades, but, in an interview with this author, said, "I would have liked to have done more. I had some good ideas. I remember one where Kirk wakes up and the whole ship is empty. There were reasons for it all, of course, and a mystery for him to solve. But Bill Shatner suddenly being alone on this big ship was the basic idea, which I thought was intriguing. I sent that and some others in right after writing that first one. He [Roddenberry] just said no. I don't know what his reasons were. Maybe his reasons were he just didn't like me. Roddenberry had his own concept of what the series should be. He would try to influence the writing, but I just kept on doing my own thing. And my own thing happened to grate on him the wrong way." (116a)

From the Mailbag

A sample of the letters received (and placed into the *Star Trek* show files) the week following this episode's airing:

> Dear Mr. Roddenberry... I usually am not inspired enough to write "fan" letters, but felt compelled to do so in your case. Let me begin by saying that you and your associates are to be commended for having the courage to present a truly stimulating science fiction series -- undoubtedly the first of its type to deal adultly with the fantastic themes that have so long stimulated fans of this genre. There is nothing like it anywhere on television and you can rest assured that I will be watching every Thursday night I am available to do so.... Certainly Richard Matheson's scenario for the October 6 presentation was far and above the rest of your stories. He is a master and it showed in this single episode. Its theme was so eternal and thought-provoking -- the idea of each man possessing two sides. However, there was one single glaring error which so irritated me that I was forced to compromise my enjoyment somewhat. I found it most singular that the U.S.S. Enterprise does not carry aboard it any secondary craft. A comparable example would be "The Flying Sub" carried aboard The Seaview [in *Voyage to the Bottom of the Sea*]. I ask that you continue to bring us *Star Trek* and its intriguing concepts -- but that you do so in a manner that is acceptable. Good luck with future episodes. With sincerest regards, John Stanley, TV Editor, Sunday Datebook, *San Francisco Chronicle*.

And the reply:

> Dear John: I couldn't agree with you more. In fact, we have just completed an episode for which we built the exterior and interior of such a vessel and, since then, have used it still another time...." Gene Roddenberry.

Aftermath

While hosting *Saturday Night Live* on December 20, 1986, William Shatner made a notorious reference to this episode. In a comedy sketch Shatner, appearing as himself at a make-believe *Star Trek* convention and taking one too many questions from fans overly-devoted to the series, goes into a rant, telling the Trekkies to "get a life." Seeing how he has hurt their feelings, Shatner immediately backpedals and explains that what they just witnessed was a "recreation of the evil Captain Kirk from episode 37 [sic], 'The Enemy Within.'" The actors playing the fans perk up and shower Shatner with applause.

In the 2011 *Family Guy* episode "The Hand That Rocks the Wheelchair," baby Stewie accidentally creates an evil duplicate of himself. The homage to *Star Trek* includes lighting and music reminiscent of "The Enemy Within."

11

Daniels Leaves His Marc / "The Man Trap"

Marc Daniels was one of the series' most beloved directors. He would tie with Joseph Pevney (yet to join the series) at 14 episodes each, more than double that of any other director. Daniels was now preparing to take his first *Trek*. Lucille Ball knew and respected him, as did Roddenberry.

His credentials were certainly impressive. Daniels, like many directors from the early days of television, began as an actor on stage in New York, where he also studied at the American Academy of Dramatic Arts.

During World War II, Daniels saw two years of combat before being reassigned to assist on an Army-sponsored project intended to boost the morale of a nation: Irving Berlin's *This Is the Army*, made into a motion picture in 1943.

Back in New York in 1946, Daniels found work as an instructor with the American Theatre Wing, sponsored by the GI Bill. The Wing provided workshops for war veterans in theater, opera, radio, and the experimental medium the press was calling "tee-vee."

Marc Daniels (James Lind Library)

After a two-year internship, Daniels was given the opportunity to direct a new anthology series for CBS staged in New York. *Ford Television Theatre* premiered in October 1948. By January, it was a hit with the critics and building a loyal audience. For its presentation of "The Man Who Came to Dinner," *Variety* reported that the "direction by Marc Daniels of both the 'thesps' and cameras was standout." A few months later, the same trade reported:

> Television matured quite a few notches Monday night when the CBS hour-long *Ford Theatre* carried a video adaption of Moss Hart's "Light Up the Sky," which closed a few weeks back on Broadway.... As adapted to "tele"... and directed by Marc Daniels, with most of the Broadway legit cast intact, Hart's comedy of anguish and ecstasies came off as one of the TV treats of the season.

Daniels said at the time, "In doing the nine shows this year we were able to perfect our production technique to the point where we could do 'Light Up the Sky' in five days from the purchase of the property. This included adapting and preparing the script." (44-5)

Daniels was learning to think and direct fast, a talent which would benefit *Star Trek*.

In the fall of 1950, Daniels left *Ford Theatre* to direct *and* produce *Nash Airflyte Theater*, a 30-minute series. *Variety* said:

> With the flock of hour-long productions involved in a cooperative race for suitable properties, Daniels is exploring the short-story, one-act field for his

adaptations and has at his command a vast supply of heretofore untouched properties.... Here a good scripter has infinite possibilities to develop a play for the TV medium unfettered by previous treatment, or the ogre of cutting.

Daniels had now introduced another innovation: the 30-minute anthology -- a format later to be utilized so well in *Alfred Hitchcock Presents*, *One Step Beyond*, and *The Twilight Zone*.

In 1951, Daniels had a major hand in yet another innovation, one that would inadvertently lead to the funding for *Star Trek*. For the fall TV season, he collaborated with Desi Arnaz in developing the technique of utilizing three *film* cameras in front of a studio audience, making *I Love Lucy* the template for all sitcoms to come. For its October 17 review, *Variety* said:

> It's a slick blending of Hollywood and TV showmanship, for which much of the credit belongs to [cinematographer] Carl Freund on the camera masterminding and Marc Daniels on the direction.

Daniels stayed closely involved with *Lucy* during that first formative year, but on May 14, 1952, the same trade reported:

> *I Love Lucy* will be without the services of Marc Daniels next season. After he finishes off the last of the 38 [first season episodes], which he directed from the outset, he'll drop off the show because of money differences. Desilu Corp. refused to meet his demands for upped coin.

Daniels later said, "Maybe it was a stupid thing to do, but then we didn't know we were creating history. We were just doing a show." (44-7)

Five months after he resigned, the dispute was settled and Desilu hired him to direct the first season of a new sitcom, at double his previous price -- *I Married Joan* starred Joan Davis and Jim Backus. The critics and public loved the show. *Variety* in its review said, "Marc Daniels' direction saw to it that the film erupted with proper climaxes."

In the fall of 1953, Desi Arnaz moved Daniels to yet another sitcom, this time for *The Ray Bolger Show*. Bolger is best known today as the scarecrow from *The Wizard of Oz*. *Variety* said, "Marc Daniels again demonstrates his deft directorial touch." Daniels stayed long enough to get the show established, then resigned after filming his 13th episode. He had done much for Desilu, now he wanted to do for himself. One month later, NBC aired a special two-hour presentation of "Backbone of America." *Daily Variety* said:

> One of the literary events of television's brief but brilliant career flashed across the nation's screens last night and the "average" American family must've felt the warming influence of their own depiction.... Direction of Marc Daniels [was] well executed.

In 1960, Daniels directed a two-hour live presentation of *Mrs. Miniver* for CBS. *Daily Variety* deemed it to be "one of the more satisfactory attempts at TV remakes of screenplays this season.... Credit its success to the acting of Maureen O'Hara... and to the careful direction of Marc Daniels." Next, he directed the premiere episode of *The Chevy Mystery Show*. *Daily Variety* said, "Movement and positioning of the players was handled with adeptness and originality by director Marc Daniels," and credited him with getting the new series "off to a crisp start." He also directed "The Scarlet Pimpernel," an episode of *The DuPont Show of the Month*. The cast for this movie-length television presentation included William Shatner. The critic for *Variety* wrote:

Apart from the excellence of the physical production and the flawlessness of the performances, this "Pimpernel" had just the right touches and flavor to make an immensely enjoyable show.... Daniels handles a large cast with ease and fluidity, and his show clicked off with the pace of a racehorse.

Regarding 1961's *The Heiress*, *Variety* wrote, "Under the skillful directorial hands of Marc Daniels, the production had a swift, direct, pungent movement." Later in the year, another two-hour drama -- Laurence Olivier in *The Power and the Glory* -- brought more praise from the trade: "Marc Daniels' direction was sensitive." For this job, Daniels also received a Directors Guild Award nomination.

In 1962, Four Star Productions put Daniels under contract to direct *The Dick Powell Theatre* and to produce and direct pilot films for the studio. One, *Saints and Sinners*, created by Adrian Spies (later to write for *Star Trek*), and starring Nick Adams as a newspaper reporter, sold as a 30-minute drama, with Daniels as the resident director. Warren Stevens was in one episode and this meeting resulted in Daniels casting him for the *Star Trek* episode "By Any Other Name."

In 1963, Daniels created another TV event. On August 30, *Daily Variety* announced:

Marc Daniels has been signed to produce and direct a t-version [*Variety* slang for TV-version] of *The Advocate*, which will set a precedent when it beams performance on its Broadway opening night.... The director will take over a fully-rehearsed Broadway cast... and restage the play to meet the needs of a taped video presentation.

The big night was October 14. The critics were ecstatic. Eleanor Roberts of *The Boston Globe* wrote, "This was more than TV theatre. It was true theatre transplanted to the little box." Donald Kirkley of *The Baltimore Sun* wrote:

The TV direction of Marc Daniels left nothing to be desired. In style and content it was like something in the *Play of the Week* series, which remains the outstanding result of cooperation between stage people and the electronic medium. This is not surprising when one considers that Marc Daniels also was responsible for "A Month in the Country," one of the best of the P-W series.

Donald Mainwaring of *The Christian Science Monitor* wrote:

Congratulations are due all around. First to the Group W program department whose notion this was, and especially to the director of the television version, Marc Daniels, who can add this play with pride to an already large number of television successes.

Never resting on his laurels, Daniels kept busy for the remainder of 1963, directing the critically acclaimed one-hour drama *East Side/West Side*, starring George C. Scott, and Gene Roddenberry's *The Lieutenant* (the episode featuring Leonard Nimoy and Majel Barrett).

In 1964, he worked for *Burke's Law* and *The Man from U.N.C.L.E.* James Doohan was a guest player in the latter, less than a year away from *Star Trek*. Daniels also did several episodes of *Ben Casey*. Among the guest players were Susan Oliver, fresh off "The Cage" and *Star Trek*-bound Eddie Paskey. Also present was Alfred Ryder, whom Daniels would book for his first *Star Trek* assignment "The Man Trap."

For 1966, among other series, Daniels directed for *Mission: Impossible*, where he met guest player Barbara Luna, whom he would later cast in "Mirror, Mirror," for *Star Trek*.

During all of this, Marc Daniels had given direction to a sky full of movie stars: Bing

Crosby, Henry Fonda, David Niven, Ronald Reagan, Fredric March, Charles Boyer, Julie Harris, Joseph Cotten, and Boris Karloff, among so many others.

And Broadway stars like Paul Muni, Paul Mazursky, Farley Granger, Sammy Davis, Jr., and Zero Mostel.

TV stars who received direction from Daniels included series' leads James Arness, Elizabeth Montgomery, George C. Scott, Chuck Conners, Robert Cummings, Barbara Eden, Gene Barry, Robert Culp, Eddie Albert, Vince Edwards, Richard Chamberlain, Richard Crenna, Robert Lansing, Gary Lockwood, Robert Vaughn, and Patty Duke. And William Shatner ... and Lucy and Desi.

Daniels was now 54 and, as proven by his past, willing to take on a challenge. When his agent called with an offer from a chancy show like *Star Trek*, he naturally said "yes."

***

Episode 5: THE MAN TRAP
Written by George Clayton Johnson
(with Gene Roddenberry, uncredited)
(additional story elements by Lee Erwin, uncredited)
Directed by Marc Daniels

From *TV Guide*, September 8, 1966 issue:

> This science fiction series centers on the crew of the USS (United Space Ship) Enterprise as they travel on an extended space patrol. Tonight: the Enterprise stops on planet M113 for the annual medical checkup of archeologists Bob and Nancy Crater -- but Nancy doesn't seem to be herself.

Nancy is an old flame of Leonard McCoy, and the good doctor's eyes now seem to be clouded by past fondness. As Captain Kirk struggles with growing doubts concerning his Chief Medical Officer's judgment, a member of the landing party suddenly dies under mysterious circumstances. All McCoy can tell Kirk is that the crewman -- the first of many to die in this story -- had all the salt instantaneously depleted from his body.

NBC publicity photo
(Courtesy of Gerald Gurian)

Able to change its form and appear as various crew members, the chameleon-like alien "beams up" to a new feeding ground -- the Starship Enterprise.

"The Man Trap" is a study of loneliness. This is not a simple Man against Beast tale but more so Man against Himself. The message: the mind believes what it wants to; if not, the heart certainly will. And hang on to your salt.

SOUND BITES

- *Uhura:* "Tell me how your planet Vulcan looks on a lazy evening when the moon is full." *Mr. Spock:* "Vulcan has no moon, Miss Uhura." *Uhura:* "I am not surprised, Mr. Spock."

- *Kirk:* "You could learn something from Mister Spock, Doctor. Stop thinking with your glands."

- *Kirk, to Uhura:* "Keep a tight fix on us. If we let out a yell, I want an armed party down there before the echo dies."

ASSESSMENT

On the surface, "The Man Trap" appears to be a mere monster story. But the theme of loneliness is handled in a way not before seen on television. Only on an alien world with a ravenous creature that kills to survive and can change its form to take on the appearance of its past victims could the subject of love and loss of love be examined in such a unique way.

Because the monster takes on the image of "that one woman from his past," McCoy is distracted from his duty. Beyond this, Professor Crater lost his wife. He admits that he almost destroyed the creature when it killed Nancy. Had he given in to his impulse to kill, he would have been completely alone. Instead, he chose to allow the creature to replace the woman he had loved. "Nancy lives in my dreams," Crater says, "and it becomes her for me. It doesn't trick me. It needs love, too."

With this, "The Man Trap" is elevated above a standard monster tale.

There are many standout moments. The speech in the briefing room about the creature being the last of its kind, nearly extinct like the buffalo, is one. Another is Crater's confession that he has transferred the love for his wife to the creature, so much so that he cannot even pinpoint the exact date of his wife's death. "A year... or was it two?"

There are also some bad moments: the screeching plant in the botany lab that is clearly a man's hand wearing a fluffy pink glove, the tacky sci-fi type music on the soundtrack played whenever the creature lurks nearby, and a few unnatural lines of dialogue, courtesy of Mr. Roddenberry's rewrite, all to the chagrin of George Clayton Johnson. These include: "Go chase an asteroid," "Do you suppose he's gone space happy or something," and "May the great bird of the galaxy bless your planet."

These peeves aside, "The Man Trap" is a personal story for McCoy, and contains elements of mystery, suspense, horror and action-adventure. It provides us with a tour of the Enterprise and does a splendid job of introducing many of the main characters. And, to NBC's pleasure, it delivered on that bold speech made by Kirk at the start of each episode about exploring strange new worlds -- one reason why the network approved this as the lead-off episode for the series.

THE STORY BEHIND THE STORY

Script Timeline
Lee Erwin's story outline, ST #13, "The Man Trap": April 7, 1966.

*Erwin's revised story outline, gratis: April 15, 1966.
George C. Johnson's 1st Draft teleplay, based on Erwin's outline, now "Damsel with a Dulcimer": May 23, 1966.
Johnson's 2nd Draft teleplay: May 31, 1966.
Johnson's rewrite, gratis (Rev. 2nd Draft teleplay, now changed back to "The Man Trap"): June 8, 1966.
John D.F. Black's script polish (Mimeo Department "Yellow Cover 1st Draft"): June 13, 1966.
Gene Roddenberry's rewrite (Final Draft teleplay): June 16, 1966.
Additional page revisions by Roddenberry: June 17, 20 & 21, 1966.*

George Clayton Johnson, at 36, was a veteran writer of *The Twilight Zone*, contributing to eight episodes. Johnson had also written for *Route 66* and *Honey West*, and provided the story for Frank Sinatra's big screen hit *Ocean's 11*. In the near future, he would co-author the science fiction book *Logan's Run*, which spawned a movie and a short-lived TV series. And he acted once -- in *The Intruder*, a 1962 movie starring William Shatner.

John D.F. Black said, "I knew George for a long time. I knew George very well and I was glad he was on the show because I knew he could write. The only thing Mary and I could ever agree on about George's writing was that he wrote a soap opera, meaning with a touch of sentimentality." (17)

Johnson's first *Star Trek* assignment, "Chicago II," based on Roddenberry's idea about a planet patterned after Chicago of the 1920s and run by a crime syndicate, wasn't working out. After reading Johnson's treatment, Roddenberry wrote John D.F. Black:

> I feel this story lacks action. There is a lot of background and a lot of soul searching, but not much happening.... While well-written, and makes me want to keep him authoring for us, has too many points of similarities with other tales we've put to work. Therefore, rather than lose him... he and I are making a simple switch of stories. (GR5-1)

The premise for "Chicago II" would be resurrected and merged with a story by a freelance writer to become "A Piece of the Action." In the meantime, the new story selected for Johnson was another from Roddenberry's 1964 *Star Trek* series proposal. Johnson was the second writer to get a crack at it. Roddenberry first assigned "The Man Trap" to Lee Erwin, who had written an episode of *The Lieutenant*. Erwin delivered his outline about a salt-sucking vampire on April 8, 1966. Justman told Roddenberry:

> I don't think that we have enough story material in this outline to sustain an hour as it presently stands. I think it needs some more juice... perhaps we could find a way to get something *else* into the story. (RJ5-1)

The "something else" added into Erwin's free revised outline, dated April 15, gave the creature the ability to fool its intended victims with illusions. Justman wrote to Roddenberry that the revised outline was "a much cleaner and straighter story line." He said:

> The "apparition" gimmick in this story is extremely intriguing to me. However, I think we have to get some action into this prior to the end. (RJ5-2)

Stan Robertson at NBC wanted to see more action, too. But he also liked the idea, writing Roddenberry:

> The basic germ or idea for an excellent action-adventure story appears to be present in this very thin presentation. The idea of introducing an animal as a central antagonist in one of our stories is excellent.... [But] we would caution against making the animal so "far out" that its effectiveness is not believable....

Also, you might check the medical exactness of a person dying "instantaneously" as the result of having one or another of the body chemicals suddenly drained from his person. (SR5-1)

Roddenberry did, with De Forest Research. Since no person had ever had all of a particular vital chemical suddenly drained from his body, there was no way to say for sure how quickly death would occur. But it was deduced that death would likely occur, and would likely occur soon.

At this stage, the "animal" was never seen as anything other than a salt-sucking creature who could put its victims into a hypnotic trance. Justman wrote Roddenberry:

> I don't know what the grotesque biped should look like, or how we are to go about handling this creation. I might make a suggestion which goes in an entirely opposite direction. Perhaps the grotesque biped could be an extremely beautiful, but terrifying, young lady. Perhaps she could be something along the lines of the green dancing maiden we had in *Star Trek* pilot No. 1. Would you believe a blue dancing maiden? With orange hair? And plenty stacked? I'd like to be in on the casting of this part. (RJ5-2)

Roddenberry agreed that a sexy monster was intriguing, but Stan Robinson had already endorsed the idea of the protagonist being an "animal." The question: how to get both? George Clayton Johnson had the answer. He later said, "My very first *Twilight Zone*, 'The Four of Us Are Dying,' had to do with a person who could change his appearance. I figured something that worked once, and succeeded, could work again. So I started thinking in terms of a shape-changer and came up with the idea of 'the last of its kind' -- the idea that, at one time, there were three, four, five states completely covered by one herd of buffalo, tens of hundreds of thousands of these beasts, and now there are almost none of them left. What if there was only *one* left? That appealed to Gene -- that idea, the very last of its kind." (93-1)

Roddenberry was so enthusiastic about this idea, which now had a clear central theme, that he paid Erwin a "kill fee" of $345 (on top of the $655 he had already gotten for the first draft of his outline) and assigned the script to Johnson. Using Erwin's outline as a guide, which had been approved by NBC, Johnson inserted his shape-shifting element and went straight to teleplay. He said, "Well, off I went to try to write it, with John D.F. Black being sort of assigned to me as a story editor. And then I'm calling up John, saying, 'This isn't working for me. I don't understand it.' So, I went in and met with him, told him what I was doing, and he said, 'Ah-ha! You made your mistake by bringing the creature aboard the ship in Act III. It should be in Act I. That's what the whole thing is about -- *the creature*.' And I said, 'That's all very well and good, but you billed the show as exploring alien planets, other environments, so, really, there should be some action that takes place *on* the planet.' So, I worked out that part of the action involving Captain Kirk trying to capture Professor Crater -- the character who had been protecting the creature – on the planet." (93-1)

Johnson also came up with a new title for his first draft script, turned in on May 23: "Damsel with a Dulcimer." Mark Alfred, a fan of both *Star Trek* and English literature, explained the reference, saying, "Poet Samuel Taylor Coleridge wrote a poem in 1797, published in 1816, called 'Kubla Khan.' It was a wild vision in his imagination of the savage Khan's establishment of a 'pleasure dome.' But the last few lines of the poem changed gears to describe the Coleridge's poetic vision. The last stanza begins, 'A damsel with a dulcimer in a vision once I saw,' and says that if the writer could only reproduce her beauty and song, the world would go wild for it, and say that he was crazy for carrying on so…. [W]riter Johnson wanted to use this reference to Coleridge's poem to form a deeper resonance in the mind of a perceptive *Star Trek* viewer."

The day after Johnson's teleplay was received, Robert Justman wrote to John D.F. Black, saying, "This first draft is damn fine!" But Justman being Justman, there were numerous pages of suggestions and criticism. He wrote:

> I pose the musical question: where is the TEASER? Also, I think the script is plenty short. I only count about 56 ½ pages.... Would you believe a <u>wooden crate</u> and labelled [sic] medical supplies? I wouldn't. While I think of it, naturally most of the exteriors would have to be done on location. I think I know just the spot for our locations. Ask me nicely and I'll tell you.... [W]e will have to be careful in the way we handle the varying appearances of NANCY down on the planet. The audience should have no doubt what they are seeing is either Kirk's or McCoy's personalized representation of Nancy. We must not confuse the audience in any respect with regard to this point.... On Page 14, the audience discovers the dead body of DARNELL. I don't think that the audience should discover this before Kirk and McCoy. I think it's important that Kirk and McCoy find Darnell and react for the end of ACT I. Also, may I suggest that we ask writers not to write in such things as boom shots on location, or anything of that intricacy for the directors. I think the directors can get intricate enough all by themselves without any additional help from any of us.... I hope NBC does not feel that the script is too "cerebral." (RJ5-3)

NBC did. Stan Robertson told Roddenberry:

> Since the utilization of hallucinative, hypnotic vision, etc., are a strong part of the storyline in Pilot Number 1, we should minimize these tools. (SR5-1)

In this first stab at a teleplay, Johnson had depicted everything on the planet as an illusion, including the buildings. He was asked to tone this down, substantially. The only illusion remaining in his second draft script from May 31 was in how the creature chose to reveal itself to its intended victims.

Two days after delivery, Justman wrote John D.F. Black:

> Again, a very good draft by George Clayton Johnson. I shall not level anymore praise at him, but shall instead go to work and tear this draft apart as best I can. Nothing personal, mind you. (RJ5-4)

The memos and notes that the producers sent each other about the story outlines, scripts, and rewrites served a variety of purposes. They offered story critiques, as well as thoughts about how well the plots and characterizations fit the evolving gospel according to *Star Trek*. Another purpose of the notes was to scale the stories and roles to fit the budget and casting constraints. They also provided more than occasional dollops of wit, sarcasm and comedic relief from the never-ending stresses of production.

Justman was always very thorough and came up with more than a few pages of notes concerning things needing immediate correction. One such note had to do with Roddenberry's instructions to the writers to avoid putting the science fiction over the personal drama. Of this, he said:

> We establish a plant named "Beauregard." This bit is very amusing and quite science fiction. But are we telling science fiction stories or are we doing a television dramatic show? I'm not sure that the plant routine is out of place. I'm just not sure that it is <u>in</u> place in this story. (RJ5-4)

Roddenberry could have -- and possibly should have -- killed the Beauregard the Plant bit. But he allowed Johnson to leave it in, with the warning:

> One moving plant, okay. One which makes sounds, okay. But if we go much further, we'll get outlandish. (GR5-3)

Justman's notes continued:

> I understand that the various guises that Nancy appears in are to key off of whosoever is looking at her. And we should follow this method throughout the script. However, what does she look like when Crater looks at her? And he does exactly this on the top of page 7. (RJ5-4)

It was decided that the audience should *not* see what Crater sees. Showing us this would take away from the surprise at the end of the story when we do see the true appearance of the creature.

George Clayton Johnson did a free polish on his script and trimmed the scene back to have only one plant moving and making noises. And it *was* outlandish. In Johnson's defense, his description of "Sulu's zoo" is intriguing and, if budget, time and technical abilities allowed it to be brought to life as the writer envisioned, it would have been well worth doing. Example:

> In the center of the room -- obviously one of Sulu's prize pets -- is a large, undulating plant with a pansy-type face -- a plant that looks like a Pekingese dog. It is swaying with sentient life and gives off a CHIMING, MELODIC HUM, like a harmonium. As Janice enters, it senses her presence and leans toward her. Almost unconsciously she strokes it as one might stroke a friendly German shepherd. It CROONS MUSICALLY and ducks its head as though welcoming her touch.

A splendid idea, but there was no TV show from this period that could do something like this and not have it come off damn silly. And it *did* come off damn silly.

Another change Roddenberry requested:

> While I like the lilt of your revised title, suggest we consider "The Man Trap" is still a better 8:30 action-adventure slot heading for our show. I know what NBC is going to say. (GR5-3)

Johnson complained, "I was really disappointed when Gene put that title on it. I thought it trite and predictable and obvious - 'The Man Trap,' yeah, it's clever, it's hard-boiled, it's almost Dashiell Hammett-esque. 'Yeh, she was a man trap.' Whereas 'Damsel with a Dulcimer' was somehow trying to romanticize the dismal creature that was so depleted in her life substance that she looked like death, but she still had the power to look voluptuous or strong or intelligent by reading the minds and emotions and, I guess, the soul of these people that she met." (93-1)

Then again, would most audience members even know what "Damsel with a Dulcimer" meant?

Johnson's Revised 2nd Draft, always provided at no charge per Writers Guild of America guidelines, and his final handling of the script, was turned in on June 8. He had caught the voices of the characters better than any other freelancer so far. But, of course, with only the pilot film as a guide, he could not be expected to deliver a draft ready to go before the cameras. Bob Justman, desperate for another script to put into preproduction, responded two days later, writing John D.F. Black:

> I still find many of the previous points I made about this script unresolved so far as I'm concerned.... And the beginning of the TEASER in the Transporter Room, shouldn't the audience know where Kirk, McCoy and Darnell are going?

And shouldn't we see this Trio arrive on the surface of the planet?... I still feel there is an enormous problem concerned with what Nancy looks like when certain people are looking at her. And I don't think that this problem has been resolved yet. Especially at the end of the story, when Kirk and Spock and McCoy are in the throes of getting rid of Nancy, or whatever she is. How does Spock see her? Are we going to have to keep on jumping two or three different actresses back and forth within the same sequence, depending upon who is looking at her? If we do this, we can be shooting this show forever, because we will have to cover it for all looks. I think it would be best if Kirk and McCoy and Spock see Nancy as one physical representation. And Darnell sees her as the brassy blonde. I think we can easily believe that Kirk sees Nancy the same way that McCoy sees her physically. It is evident now that McCoy and Kirk have discussed Nancy prior to ever coming down on the planet. Kirk would know what she looks like. (RJ5-5)

Black disagreed. He felt that once it was established how each person saw her, the audience would not need to be reminded of this, unless Nancy allowed herself to be seen differently, and added an effective moment to the script where, after Kirk corrects McCoy, stating that Nancy is "a handsome woman," but hardly as young as McCoy believes he sees, Nancy allows the doctor to see her more realistically, as a woman past 40.

Justman continued:

On page 14, if I were Spock, I would kick Uhura's ass right off the ship.... Don't you think it is a bit too much on the nose for Yeoman Janice to enter the Transporter Room with a tray on which she has a bowl of nuts and a salt shaker? ... We will have to discuss with Gene our conception of what the Creature really looks like [at the end of the story], and how Nancy changes into this Creature. Also, how we are to create the Creature. The various visualizations of what the Creature is, cannot dissolve into each other, but will have to be some sort of optical ZAP EFFECT due to the difference in physical characteristics.... John, this is supposedly our next show after "The Enemy Within" and I feel it needs a lot of work - and right away. (RJ5-5)

Black did not agree that the script needed a lot of work, but he did do his contractually-obligated script polish. A nice in-joke added here for Nichelle Nichols, in consideration of how many times she said "Hailing frequencies open, Captain" in the first few episodes, was the line: "Mister Spock, I think if I hear that word again, I'll cry."

Black's rewrite, sent to the mimeo department and designated as the "Yellow Cover First Draft" was ready to send to NBC and *Star Trek*'s various department heads on June 13. As with the Yellow Cover draft of the previous episode's script, it never got to any of them.

George C. Johnson said, "Gene liked it, or claimed that he did. Then he hid it from me for a while and the next thing you know I got a copy of the final script and it had been rewritten -- *quite a bit*." (93-4)

Johnson felt Roddenberry's "tinkering" resulted in "downgrading the story." (93-2)

John Black agreed, believing that Johnson's story successfully dealt with humans' insatiable need for companionship. He said, "I don't remember what GR put in, but I do remember that he took out a lot of George's material. Again, we're back to 'it's a gift horse, leave its mouth alone.' There could have been a hell of a lot more art in *Star Trek* if GR kept his hands off the scripts." (17-4)

One scene Roddenberry tossed out was in the teaser Johnson wrote. McCoy is uncomfortable about being beamed down to the planet; he doesn't trust the transporter; he even suspects that it can somehow alter the personalities of the people using it. Roddenberry felt this scene was irrelevant to the story being told and delayed getting Kirk and McCoy to the planet. It also encroached on the premise of "The Enemy Within," being written by Richard Matheson. But the lost moment was too good to be lost forever, especially in light of what happens to Kirk in the Matheson story. McCoy's transporter phobia would be inserted into other episodes.

In George Clayton Johnson's final handling of the teleplay, we feel more for Crater and better appreciate his heartache over losing Nancy -- *twice* -- since Crater lives in Johnson's version. And we discover, as does Kirk, that Crater truly did care for the creature and does ache from the knowledge that the last one may now be dead. He has spent years digging among the ruins, finding the art and the music the creatures made, and he has lived with one and exchanged love with it. More was made of this relationship before Roddenberry's rewrite.

The tragedy built into the story actually works better with Crater living at the end; it helps us empathize more with the creature, since it is *not* so cold-hearted to callously discard and even feed upon its companion and protector -- and lover -- as Roddenberry has it do. We also get a stronger sense of its fear. When it impersonates McCoy, it tries harder to convey to Kirk and Spock that they don't have to kill "the creature" -- it has just been trying to survive and, now, by enabling it to nourish itself on salt from the ship stores, it would pose no further threat. But they argue with the "Unreal McCoy," telling him the creature cannot be trusted and that it might be the type of living being that, if fed regularly, can reproduce by fission, thereby posing a greater threat, especially with it being on a ship that can take it to any planet -- any grazing ground -- in the universe. Spock even compares it to a drug addict and says that, in the creature's eyes, "all of us are sweating heroin." The Unreal McCoy -- the creature -- realizing it cannot reason with them, slowly backs away, and then bolts for the turbolift, fleeing the bridge. It is truly terrified.

At the story's end, as Johnson played it, Crater tells Kirk he has decided to stay behind on the planet, alone, spending the remainder of his life searching for another of these remarkable creatures. Kirk's anguish is more profound than what we see in the filmed version. We sense from Johnson's writing that, with the danger now over, with Kirk thinking with a cooler head and realizing how wrong he was about Crater, he truly has taken some of the heartbroken man's anguish onto his own shoulders. He tells Spock, "I was just thinking about the buffalo."

Roddenberry left that line in but, with so much of the emotional aspects removed from the script, it had far less impact.

As for the elements John D.F. Black could not remember Roddenberry adding, there were many. The red ring-like markings on the faces of the dead came at this time. In Johnson's final draft, the body of each victim "glows with a phosphorescence." In Johnson's script, McCoy doesn't get reprimanded by Kirk in sickbay with the confrontational line, "How your lost love affects your vision doesn't interest me, Doctor! I've lost a man. I want to know what killed him." Those words, as well as the underlines, came courtesy of Gene Roddenberry's rewrite. In Johnson's version, it is Scotty who beams down to the planet with Kirk to search for Crater, not Spock. While the scene works just as well this way, there does seem to be a lack of Spock throughout much of the story. For that reason alone, the change helps. And, in Johnson's versions, Crater gives up when Kirk and Scott surround him. In Roddenberry's, Kirk hits Crater with a phaser stun beam, resulting in his groggy and slurred confession about his wife's death. Roddenberry also added the perfect final chill to this scene, when Kirk asks how long Nancy has been dead and Crater can't remember if it was "a year ... or was it two?"

One other change -- Roddenberry's idea to have the creature, while appearing as a black crewman, speak to Uhura in Swahili. De Forest Research provided the actual lines, for which the translation is, "How are you, friend. I think of you, beautiful lady. You should never know loneliness."

Leonard Nimoy's stand-in Frank da Vinci in make-up test for Roddenberry's red blotches (Courtesy of Fred Walder)

George Clayton Johnson and John D.F. Black have frequently expressed their belief that there could have been more to *Star Trek*, and in fact there *was* more to this *Star Trek*, before Roddenberry's rewrite. It really comes down to taste. In the end, despite some of the clunky lines of dialogue that Roddenberry added -- about chasing an asteroid, being space happy, and the Great Bird of the Galaxy -- and an ending which is more action-adventure and less tragic, the final shooting script smudged in Roddenberry's fingerprints is faithful to and certainly as good as the last draft by Johnson. But it is not better.

It was Roddenberry's version that was sent to NBC, and to good result. Stan Robertson was happy. Still bothered over "The Corbomite Maneuver," which he believed was a stagnant script, Robertson sent Roddenberry a back-handed compliment, writing:

> Dear Gene: This is a superior script because it contains one ingredient which we both realize must be an <u>essential element</u> in our series -- <u>interest</u>. "The Man Trap" locks our <u>interest</u> right from the beginning and, as each succeeding tangent of the plot is exposed, our <u>interest</u> grows and grows. And when we've told our story and there is no more, we are left with the same feeling a man has when he's savored something extra-special. A craving for more, whetted by an appetite which has been stimulated but not satisfied. If we can leave our viewers each week with a feeling of wanting more, we'll be home free! (ST5-2)

Roddenberry's rewrite -- his June 16 Final Draft, with additional page revisions from June 17, 18, 20 and 21 -- was more in line with what NBC was asking for, putting emphasis on action/adventure ... with a monster. Johnson's version had just a bit more heart.

Pre-Production
June 16-17 and June 20-21, 1966, and June 22, for ½ day (4 ½ days prep).

With Marc Daniels in the offices during the six days that Leo Penn filmed "The Enemy Within," preparation for "The Man Trap" began.

Jeanne Bal, at 38, was cast to play McCoy's former flame, Nancy Crater. Her work in TV began several years earlier with appearances on *Thriller*, among other series, and multiple episodes of *Perry Mason* and *Bachelor Father*. She also co-starred with William Demarest in a short-lived sitcom *Love and Marriage*.

Alfred Ryder, as Professor Crater, was a familiar face on TV and in films. He was 50 and, among a hundred jobs, he'd made two visits to *The Wild, Wild West* and one each to *The*

Outer Limits and *One Step Beyond*. He played the ghost of a Nazi U-boat captain on *Voyage to the Bottom of the Sea* and the leader of the alien invaders on *The Invaders*. Ryder was also a busy stage actor and director.

Michael Zaslow, 23, played Darnell, the first Enterprise crewman to die at the hands and suction cups of the Salt Vampire. He would return as a crewman with a different name (Jordan) for "I, Mudd." Zaslow was best known to daytime TV audiences and fans of the soaps where he enjoyed recurring roles on *Search for Tomorrow*, *Love Is a Many Splendored Thing*, and *One Life to Live*. His biggest success was as the villainous Roger Thorpe on *The Guiding Light* from 1971 to 1980. He received numerous Emmy nominations and one win -- for Thorpe. His on-screen death was voted the top scene in the series by fans when *The Guiding Light* celebrated its 50th anniversary. This prompted Thorpe being resurrected and Zaslow returning to the series for another long run -- 1989 through 1997. The gimmick: Thorpe had faked his death and was in hiding for nine years. Thorpe's "death" may have been bogus on *Light*, but Zaslow's character in "The Man Trap" did indeed die, and this was the first time McCoy exclaims the now famous line: "He's dead, Jim," regarding a crew member (he said "it's dead" in the previous episode – "The Enemy Within" – about a dog).

John Arndt played Sturgeon, the second of the three victims of the Salt Vampire on Planet M-113. Despite dying, Arndt, easy to spot with his distinctive looks, returned as a crewman in four more episodes. Arndt worked sporadically in TV for more than two decades. Joe D'Agosta also cast him in a two-part episode of *Mission: Impossible*.

Bruce Watson, 25, played Green, the third to die on the planet and the crewman whose appearance the creature uses while beaming aboard the Enterprise. Watson worked often in TV and films throughout the 1960s and '70s, including two appearances each on *Mission: Impossible*, *The Mod Squad*, and *Adam-12*.

The Salt Vampire required some creative casting. George C. Johnson said, "When I first saw the costume, it was in Robert Justman's office, laying over a chair. He said, 'This costume is not very tall, it's only about five feet. We've hired this little tiny dancer to fit inside of it.' And I'm saying, '*Oh no, Bob*,' because I had pictured something like a refugee from a concentration camp, kind of ashen-colored, hair all completely lifeless, gray skin, and tattered gunnysack clothing. I had seen it as something really, really pathetic to look upon, something really sad. And that, for me, had worked in the writing. So now, I'm being faced with this thing with all the teeth. But I must say, the way it photographed, really, the heart goes out to this thing." (93-1)

Wah Chang was the designer. Sandra Gimpel was the tiny dancer turned stunt performer in the Salt Vampire suit. Johnson said, "She was incredible. She got the whole spirit of the damn thing. For some weird reason, at the end of the show, the creature really *did* look sad. It had that haunted look, and you thought, 'Oh my God, it's like killing a helpless dog or something.'" (93-1)

While Johnson fretted over the salt vampire, Justman worried about the salt shaker called for in the script. Of this, he wrote to John Black:

> I think we had better discuss what a salt shaker of the future looks like. Do we have salt shakers a couple hundred years from now? And, if we do, do they look like what we have today? And if they don't, how can we let the audience know that this device *is* a salt shaker so that the audience will recognize it every time it comes up in the picture? Because it comes up a number of times. And they had better know it is a salt shaker or else we are in deep trouble. (RJ5-4)

It was *Star Trek*'s prop man Irving Feinberg's job to conjure up the salt shaker of the future. He scoured Los Angeles shops looking for the perfect salt-and-pepper set before finding a pair of oddly shaped Swedish chrome-plated shakers. Roddenberry, however, rejected them because, as Justman had worried, they looked too unusual to be recognized for what they were. Some sources say that, with the addition of a small rotating light in the top, Feinberg turned the shakers into McCoy's pocket scanners. If right, the doctor uses one in this episode while examining Crater. Others say that these salt shakers were converted into McCoy's laser scalpels, and that his medical scanner was fabricated out of aluminum with the grip coming from a Sears' Craftsman screwdriver handle.

So what did get used as the futuristic salt shakers? Word has it Feinberg found a set of cheap but stylized plastic ones at J.C. Penney that fit the bill fine.

Production Diary
Filmed June 22 (¼ day), 23, 24, 27, 28, 29 & 30 (¾ day), 1966
(6 day production; total cost: $185,401).

Daniels with Shatner and Jeanne Bal, filming in McCoy's Quarters on Day 3 (Courtesy of Gerald Gurian)

Wednesday, June 22, 1966. The Beatles had the No. 1 song on U.S. Top 40 stations with "Paperback Writer." Frank Sinatra was chasing them up the charts with "Strangers in the Night." You could hear both playing hourly from the A.M. radio in your new Ford Mustang convertible -- with a sticker price of $2,600. You could fill that car up for 32 cents a gallon and that got you a smiling service station attendant who would wash your windows, check your oil and add air to your tires. And the cast of *Star Trek* were arriving at Desilu to begin work on "The Man Trap."

Due to "The Enemy Within" finishing late, the start of production was delayed until 3:20 p.m. Marc Daniels, having waited patiently, jumped into four hours of filming on the bridge, keeping the company until 7:10, before releasing the cast to have their makeup removed and the crew to wrap set.

Day 2, Thursday. The first full day of production was also spent on the bridge, with the camera rolling between 8 a.m. and 6:50 p.m. Daniels was one-quarter day behind when he took his last shot. Two scenes had been postponed and would be filmed during production of the next episode -- "The Naked Time." One was the brief shot in the teaser, of Spock in the command chair and the unusual placement of Lt. Uhura and Lt. Leslie at the helm -- the plot for "The Naked Time" explaining why. With the addition of the Captain's log entry that opens the episode -- not in the shooting script, but written and recorded later -- Roddenberry felt the audience needed to see Spock on the bridge when Kirk refers to him. He was right.

Day 3, Friday, saw the filming of the many corridor shots, as well as the climactic ending in McCoy's quarters with Sandra Gimpel, the Salt Vampire. A nice touch of direction by Daniels, seen many times in the footage from this day, is how the creature, whether manifesting itself as Nancy, Green, or McCoy, has a tendency to put a hand to its mouth when trying to contemplate its next move, almost appearing to nervously suck on the knuckle of its index finger. This not only helps the audience realize that the character we're seeing is actually a doppelganger, it also conveys that this "monster" is a living thing that, like us, worries. After stopping the camera at 7 p.m., Daniels was one-third of a day behind.

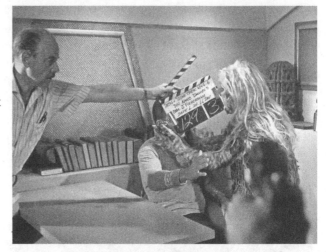

Day 3. Bill McGovern, with Shatner (hidden behind clapboard), and the Salt Vampire, Sandra Gimpel (Courtesy of Gerald Gurian)

Day 4, Monday, took the production crew into the botany lab, with that shrieking plant Robert Justman was not so sure belonged in this story, and looked more like a man's hand in a pink floral glove. The hand, by the way, belonged to Bob Baker, a famed maker of marionettes who had his own theater in downtown Los Angeles.

Next: the briefing room and then sickbay. It was here where we first see that Vulcans have green blood... almost. Marc Daniels said, "The green blood was my idea. If Spock was going to have a yellow complexion, he ought to have green blood." (44-2)

Day 4. Beauregard and Grace Lee Whitney (Unaired film trim courtesy of Gerald Gurian)

The green blood on Spock's forehead is very subdued and can easily be missed. There is even a little red mixed in. The film developing lab was again trying to right a wrong, as they had done with the green-skinned dancing girl from "The Cage." This time, their tinkering was allowed to get by. Daniels said, "I think Gene thought that idea [of green blood] was going too far." (44-2)

Daniels took his last shot at 7:15. He was back to being a quarter day behind.

Day 5, Tuesday, was spent on Stage 10 with the set for the "Interior Living Quarters" of Professor Crater and his "wife." Daniels had caught up to the original schedule and finished only 30 minutes late, at 6:45 p.m.

Day 6, Wednesday, was also spent on Stage 10, this time on the outdoors set. George

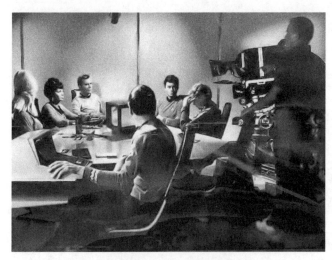

Day 4. Filming in the briefing room
(Courtesy of Gerald Gurian)

Bill McGovern, with slate, and the boxes and gummite
(Courtesy of Gerald Gurian)

C. Johnson had made some specific requests for the look of planet M113. His note read:

This is the only exterior set in the script and will be used a number of times so give me a real creepy alien environment here, please. It is a limited set and can be built on a stage for a grand effect.... The terrain is desert but let it be layered in great slab surfaces like tilted and heaped tiles. The few sparse growths jag up like drunken lightning. Come on, fellows. Nobody else has ever tried a green sky! [I] know this end of it is none of my business but if I was only interested in things that were my business I'd be a pretty dull fellow. (GCJ5)

Cinematographer Jerry Finnerman, with his colored gels, chose instead to give the desert planet a "dreamsicle" orange sky. Otherwise, Johnson got what he wanted in this regard -- no other science fiction production had ever presented an alien world with such a striking unearthly atmosphere. As for the ground and sparse vegetation, it didn't turn out exactly as Johnson had described, but he didn't mind. He later said, "The ancient ruins and all of that stuff that was there, that was just a corner of the sound stage. A bunch of boxes caked together to form a structure and then covered with gummite -- like you would for a swimming pool. They would take this wet concrete and spray it over the outside of these cardboard boxes to make this weird looking, broken up temple. And it really worked well against the painted sky." (93-1)

Daniels remained on schedule, although running a bit late in the evening with his last shot at 6:40 p.m.

Day 7, Thursday, June 30. Four more hours were spent on Stage 10, finishing sequences needed for the "Ext. Excavation" set before a noon time move back to Stage 9 to get additional camera coverage in the sickbay. Daniels wrapped at 2:55 p.m., essentially on schedule, considering his 3:30 p.m. start six production days prior.

Post-Production
July 1 through August 29, 1966.
Music score recorded on August 19, 1966.

Even though production had wrapped, the writing hadn't. Justman sent Roddenberry a memorandum, saying:

> After viewing "The Man Trap" with Sandy Courage this afternoon, I am of the opinion that we need narration for the opening of the teaser. The teaser starts out with a shot of the Enterprise orbiting about a planet and then we dissolve from that to an establishing shot of planet surface and then from that to a shot of Kirk and his companions materializing on the surface of that planet. These three shots take quite a bit of time on the screen. And since this is liable to be our first or second show on the air, I think it would be wise to establish where we are and what we are doing over these shots. (RJ5-7)

Roddenberry's response: "RJ, Agree. Am writing it."

Composer Alexander Courage, heralded by Roddenberry for his work on the two pilot films, strayed from the action-adventure-type music requested and turned in a moody and eerie score, gaining much of its flavor from electronic keyboards, electric violin and other techniques designed to give the music otherworldliness. Roddenberry hated it.

On August 24, with less than a week left before the NBC's delivery deadline, Roddenberry sent a letter to William Hatch, head of Desilu's Music Department. He wrote:

> The music for "The Man Trap" was most disappointing. It was ethereal, very science-fiction-ish, if not outright fantasy in quality, often very, very grating on the nerves, as it whined on and on. Was this a failure in communication? Or are we in trouble with a composer who will not, or is unable, to follow the expressed format directions of the producer? (GR5)

Of the series theme song, recorded the same day and also written by Courage, Roddenberry added:

> I like the theme. If the music had followed that direction, we would have been well off. (GR5-2)

Interviewed in 1982, Roddenberry said, "My feeling was this -- that for the first time on television, I was going to have situations and life forms that were totally unlike what the audience was accustomed to. And I thought, my God, I had better keep as many things as possible very understandable to my audience. I was afraid that if, on top of bizarre alien seascapes, I had *beep-beep-beep* music, then I would be in trouble. And so I wanted music that said adventure, courage, boldness -- all the things we talked about, as a matter of fact, in the opening words of, you know, 'To boldly go,' and so on…. I wanted very Earthlike, romantic music. Almost -- and I think I used the term with Sandy [Courage] -- *Captain Blood*; a seagoing feeling of adventure; human adventure. And he responded, and seemed to understand, and seemed to be enthusiastic to do it. Music, to me, is where the inner you – your guts and so on – come in contact with a show." (145-25)

Howard Anderson Company provided the optical effects. Of the first batch of episodes to be filmed, "The Man Trap" took the least amount of time in post -- two months instead of three to six. As it turned out, fewer new optical effects were needed for this episode than most and the cost for those was therefore kept on the low side -- only $8,680. The price paid in stress and sweat, however, was much higher -- with delays (detailed later) jeopardizing not just other photographic effects, but entire episodes.

Since it was now known that either this episode or "Charlie X" -- the only two episodes ready, other than the second pilot film -- would be the first to air, Roddenberry arranged for the opening title credit on both episodes to read "Created by Gene Roddenberry." After these two programs, and some pressure from the studio, his name did not appear in the opening title sequence ... until the next season, when this became the norm.

"The Man Trap" came in $8,099 under the studio per-episode allowance, for a total cost of $185,401.

Release / Reaction
Only NBC air date: 9/8/66.

The network premiere on September 8, 1966, was an anxious night for many of the series' writers. Richard Matheson and Jerry Sohl, with their wives, joined George Clayton Johnson at his home to watch the premiere. Also in attendance were Charles Beaumont, one of the regular writers for *The Twilight Zone*, and William F. Nolan, Johnson's collaborator on *Logan's Run*.

"I'm sitting there frozen with fear that it's going to turn out badly," said Johnson. "I have no idea what they've done with it. Even though I had watched them film parts of it, I had no idea how it would really fit together or how it would play. But I was vastly relieved when it was all over because I felt like I had my dignity. I had succeeded another time. And this was not going to be held against me the next time I go looking for work. I could talk about this." (93-1)

On the night *Star Trek* premiered, the series won its time slot across America hands down. The first word from A.C. Nielsen came in the form of the company's Trendex report -- an overnight phone survey conducted in 26 cities across the United States.

RATINGS / Nielsen 26-City Trendex report for Thursday, Sept. 8, 1966:

8:30 - 9 p.m.		Rating:	Share:
NBC:	*Star Trek* (first half)	**19.2**	**40.6%**
ABC:	*The Tammy Grimes Show*	14.7	31.1%
CBS:	*My Three Sons*	10.1	21.4%
Local independent stations:		No data	6.9%
9 - 9:30 p.m.			
NBC:	*Star Trek* (second half)	**20.4**	**40.6%**
ABC:	*Bewitched*	16.5	33.3%
CBS:	*Thursday Night Movie*	10.9	21.6%
Local independent stations:		No data	4.5%

For this early report, *Star Trek* pulled in over 40% of the total viewing audience between 8:30 and 9:30 p.m. The numbers improved once a more detailed National report could be analyzed.

RATINGS / Nielsen National report for Thursday, September 8, 1966:

8:30 - 9 p.m., with 54% of U.S. TVs in use.		Rating:	Share:
NBC:	*Star Trek* (first half)	**25.2**	**46.7%**
ABC:	*The Tammy Grimes Show*	14.1	26.1%
CBS:	*My Three Sons*	9.4	17.4%
Local independent stations:		No data	9.8%

9 - 9:30 p.m., with 57.3% of U.S. TVs in use.

NBC:	*Star Trek* (second half)	24.2	42.2%
ABC:	*Bewitched*	15.8	27.6%
CBS:	*Thursday Night Movie*	10.7	18.7%
Local independent stations:		No data	11.5%

At its peak, "The Man Trap" lured in just under 47% of all the TV sets playing across the United States.

Dorothy Fontana recalled, "The very first day after we were on the air, I went into the office, nine o'clock, same as always. First call that I got was from Leslie Nielsen, one of my heroes, because I love *Forbidden Planet*. He said, 'I would like to say that I saw the show last night and I thought it was great.'... So, the very first call was from an actor of a rather well-known science fiction movie who said, 'I loved it.'" (64-2)

And while the men at NBC also loved this episode, not everyone at *Star Trek* did. "The Man Trap," per Robert Justman's choice, was *not* given a network repeat.

Some reviews for "The Man Trap" were favorable, such as from Steven H. Scheuer, for his syndicated column, *TV Key Previews*. On September 8, 1966, Scheuer wrote:

> In the premiere episode, Jeanne Bal plays the wife of scientist Alfred Ryder, but there is a chameleon-like quality to her, so that everyone sees her differently. To one person, she is seen as a warm and lovely woman but to another, she is a brassy blonde. She can assume any shape and has a strange need for salt. When you see her in her actual form, well ... that is the kicker of a good science fiction plot.

Other reviewers were more critical, including the critic for *Daily Variety*, who, on September 9, wrote:

> The opener won't open up many new frequencies after this sampler. The vampire act of paralyzing victims by drawing salt out of their bodies is not very palatable.... [The cast] move around with directorial precision with only violence to provide the excitement and very little of that over the hour spread. It needs to be shaken up and given more life than death.... William Shatner and Leonard Nimoy are the good guys, who pass most of the time tracking down the phantom killer. For what they have to do they do well, but hardly impressive enough to vitalize the story line.

Syndicated columnist Rick du Brow filed his verdict on September 9, 1966 in, among other newspapers, the *San Mateo Times*, in San Mateo, California. He wrote:

> *Star Trek* is a new science fiction opus centered on a mammoth spaceship. It is so absurd that it is almost entertaining, what with its playboy bunny-type waitresses aboard ship. The premiere was a futuristic twist on the old vampire films. The villain was a creature able to change its shape to any human form and it required salt to survive and got it by helping itself to the body content of other people, leaving them very deceased. Tune in next week. Whee!

Clay Gowran, of *The Chicago Tribune*, turned his thumb down on September 9, writing:

> Gene Roddenberry vowed this science fiction hour would specialize in adult plots scripted by fine writers. From the premiere, he has considerable distance to go to attain that objective. We hope Roddenberry comes up with *saltier* material than this in the future [pun no doubt very well intended].

Lawrence Laurent, writing for *The Washington Post* on September 10, felt that

Shatner was "one of the finest actors around." He said that the series had been "produced with care and lots of money." But Laurent was less thrilled with the salt-sucking premise and ended his assessment with a touch of sarcasm, saying:

> [If audiences] can endure a creature that can assume any shape and has the power to paralyze and draw life from anyone, then, there's quality in this series.

Weekly Variety, on September 14, reported:

> Even within its sci-fi frame of reference it was an incredible and dreary mess of confusion and complexities at the kickoff. The interplanetary spaceship trudged on for a long hour with hardly any relief from violence, killing, hypnotic stuff and a distasteful, ugly monster.... By a generous stretch of the imagination, it could lure a small coterie of the small fry, though not happily time slotted in that direction. It's better suited to the Saturday morning kidvid bloc.... The performers are in there pitching, but the odds are against them in all departments -- script, direction and overall production. William Shatner, one of a star billed pair, has a good track record in TV and legit, but as the skipper of the Enterprise spaceship appears wooden, and uncertain about his function; same goes for Leonard Nimoy, costarred as Mr. Spock, so-called chief science officer whose bizarre hairdo (etc.) is a dilly.... A quota of decorative females, most of them in vague roles, are involved in the out-of-this-world shenanigans.

Ken Murphy, with a review carried in the *Waterloo Daily Courier*, Waterloo, Iowa, on September 25, 1966, said:

> *Star Trek* was a stupendous bore and therefore it will probably succeed. Its premier episode had horrible moments in the Dr. Jekyll and Mr. Hyde manner but the plot sequences bogged down in a maze of confusion, guaranteed to make reruns of the *Twilight Zone* look like Noel Coward's precious moonshine. To paraphrase Ring Lardner, it must be said that, although the script was embarrassing silly, the actors were inept.

Not all who watched were disappointed. The morning after *Star Trek*'s premiere, Roddenberry received a letter from a special fan:

> Dear Gene: Saw *Star Trek* last night and I thought it was just tremendous. It was one of the most exciting hours I've seen on television in a long time. Garry Morton [Lucille Ball's husband].

Memories

Marc Daniels said, "Right from the beginning, it was easy to see that the characters were extremely well drawn. There was some trial and error with the peripheral characters, but the main ones -- Kirk, Spock, and McCoy -- were excellent." (44-2)

George Clayton Johnson, regarding the legacy of "The Man Trap," said, "One of the things about that is it's the very first one America saw, so almost all the critical reaction to *Star Trek* came off that first show -- and the things that I read, the basic attitude of America's reviewers, was one of total bewilderment." (93-1)

Bewilderment, as we'll see, can be either good or bad.

Episode 6: THE NAKED TIME
Written by John D.F. Black
(with Gene Roddenberry, uncredited)
Directed by Marc Daniels

NBC press release, September 1, 1966:

> The space ship U.S.S. Enterprise faces imminent destruction when a strange sickness incapacitates the crew in "The Naked Time" on *Star Trek* Thursday, Sept. 29, NBC Television Network colorcast.... Co-starring regulars are William Shatner as Captain James Kirk and Leonard Nimoy as Mr. Spock.... A landing party returns to the Enterprise from another planet, unaware that they are bringing aboard a disease with which they have been contaminated and which soon spreads throughout the crew. As Dr. McCoy (DeForest Kelley) frantically seeks an antidote to stem the epidemic, the crew verges on mutiny which virtually paralyzes the huge craft.

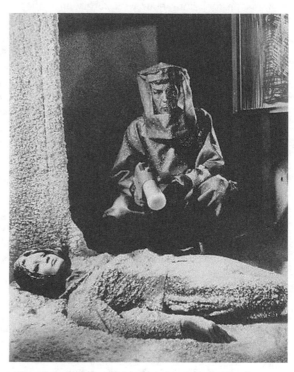

Day 2, a department store mannequin on the frozen "Observation Station" set, Stage 10 (NBC promotional photo courtesy of Gerald Gurian)

To compound the situation, due to an act of sabotage carried out by one of the inflicted, Lt. Kevin Riley, the ship is being pulled toward an unstable arctic world and inescapable destruction.

The theme tells us that we are not alone with our particular neurosis and that all humans repress certain dark emotions, often a damaged side that we dare not show. We are in good company, as we witness the principal *Star Trek* characters stripped bare and revealed with their insides out. There is no monster in this story. Or is there?

SOUND BITES

- *Joe Tormolen, to Sulu:* "Get off me! You don't outrank me and you don't have pointed ears! So just get off my neck!"

- *Sulu:* "I'll protect you, fair maiden." *Uhura:* "Sorry, neither."

- *Nurse Chapel:* "I'm in love with you, Mr. Spock... you... the human Mr. Spock... the Vulcan Mr. Spock. I see things... how honest you are... I know how you feel... you hide it, but you *do* have feelings. How we must hurt you... torture you. *You*... just as you are... I love you." *Spock:* "I'm sorry. I *am* sorry."

ASSESSMENT

This classic episode begins on a series of bad notes. The teaser is marred. First, there are those ridiculous looking environmental outfits. Since the hoods do not connect to the rest of the suits, they create no seal and, therefore, provide little protection. Next, Joe Tormolen, a trained officer picked to accompany Spock to investigate a strange occurrence at an isolated research station, lacks the good sense to keep his gloves on -- even when the room and all that he touches could be contaminated. Moments later, Spock tells Tormolen, "Be certain to touch nothing." Tormolen doesn't seem to "get" that he's already screwed up. And then Spock calls the ship, ending the teaser with the unforgivably melodramatic line, "It's like nothing we've dealt with before."

Once the awkward start is out of the way, "The Naked Time" has nothing to apologize for.

We hear a very loud ticking clock. The tension on the bridge and throughout the ship is unrelenting as the Enterprise spirals out-of-control toward a certain burn-up in the planet's atmosphere. Kirk is losing his command and nothing he does seems to help. This is his greatest challenge and nightmare. His crew, losing the ability to reason, is abandoning him.

Nurse Christine Chapel is seen first here, and confesses her hopeless love for Spock. She places her hand on his. The disease is transferred and, with Spock infected, Kirk loses his greatest asset: "The best first officer in the service."

Under the influence of the disease, Spock confesses to his stunned Captain: "My mother... I could never tell her I loved her... An Earth woman, living on a planet where love; emotion... [it's] bad taste." Of his relationship with Kirk, Spock says: "When I feel friendship for you, I'm ashamed."

Kirk crashes. He's been carrying the bug for a while but was too driven to let it overpower him. Now it comes to the surface with his own confession: "Love! You're better off without it! And I'll be better off without mine. This vessel. I give, she takes! She won't permit me *my* life; I have to live *hers*. Now I know why it's called *'she'*."

Darker still, Kirk speaks directly to the ship: "Never lose you... *never*."

"The Naked Time" tells a story that would be difficult for a drama set contemporaneously in the 1960s -- a fantastic disease, something that can only exist in the future worlds of science fiction, is the catalyst for an examination of subdued emotion, inner conflict, obsessive ambition and the loneliness of unanswered love.

THE STORY BEHIND THE STORY

Script Timeline
John D.F. Black's story outline, ST #9: April 4, 1966.
Black's 1st Draft teleplay: June 14, 1966.
Gene Roddenberry script polish (Revised 1st Draft teleplay): June 15, 1966.
Black's 2nd Draft teleplay: June 20, 1966.
Black's script polish (Mimeo Depart. "Yellow Cover 1st Draft"): June 23, 1966.
Gene Roddenberry's first rewrite (Final Draft teleplay): June 28, 1966.
Roddenberry's second rewrite (Rev. Final Draft teleplay): July 1, 1966.
Additional page revisions by Roddenberry: July 5 & August 11, 1966.

Star Trek associate producer/script editor John D.F. Black wrote the 1957 sci-fi horror movie *The Unearthly*. For TV, he was a regular contributor to many series, including *Laredo*, *The Untouchables* and *Mr. Novak*. It was a *Novak* script which won him a Writers

Guild award, and that led to Roddenberry pursuing him for *Star Trek*.

With "The Naked Time," Black saw the potential of the series' format and used his script to get the most out of the characters. He later said, "What I did, purely and simply, was take drunkenness and remove the slurs and staggers." (17-5)

There was one visual concept being kicked around between the creative staff members that was eliminated prior to the writing of the first draft script. Bill Theiss summed it up in a memo from April 18, 1966 to Gene Roddenberry:

> I had heard that the idea of the frozen corpses splitting open in this script had been scrapped. (BT6)

And, with this, NBC's Broadcast Standards (the censors) breathed a heavy sigh of relief.

As the story evolved from outline to script, the characters played a game of musical chairs. In Black's story outline, and also his first try at the script, it is McCoy and Scott that accompany Spock to the frozen outpost, not Joe Tormolen, as filmed. The three witness the results of the mayhem and return to the ship without incident. For this version, it's in the transporter room where we meet Tormolen, a member of the "decontamination section." It is his job to collect the environmental suits. He also wears one. It's here where he gets the urge to scratch his nose and, to do so, removes his glove, thereby becoming contaminated. We get to the same end, but Tormolen comes off as just a little less idiotic in this handling, since his breach in procedure happens on the Enterprise and not in a frozen madhouse where horrific and unexplainable events have occurred.

Something else that's very different in this version than in those to follow: Spock's breakdown happens in one of the ship's corridors, in front of numerous crew members, with Janice Rand calling out to the others, "He's crying!" And then the crying Spock is hurried away to sickbay where we see little of him until after a cure is found.

As he had done during the filming of "The Enemy Within," with the invention of the Vulcan Neck Pinch, Leonard Nimoy was again looking to help develop -- or perhaps protect -- his character. He told this author, "John Black and I had, I think, an unfortunate confrontation. On 'The Naked Time' script, there was originally written that an elevator door opens up in one of the corridors and Spock is there crying. And there's a guy going around with a paint brush, painting silly stuff on walls and so forth, and he comes up and paints a funny mustache on Spock's face. And Spock goes on crying. I said to John Black, 'I think we're missing an opportunity here. If Spock can get into a private space, then he can let out some of his interior strife, and we might learn something touching and interesting about him.' What I remember John saying was, 'No, it would spoil the rhythm of the piece.' Well, I thought strongly enough about it that I really did not want to do this painted face thing, so I went to Gene and I told him my idea. Then, a little while later, John came down to the set and said, 'Alright, tell me again what you have in mind.'" (128)

George Takei also wanted to have a hand in the development of his character. He recalled, "John D.F. Black was thinking of putting a Samurai sword in Sulu's hands. I told John... 'Sulu is a 23rd century guy. I'm a 20th century Asian-American, and I didn't grow up brandishing a Samurai sword. I was swept away by Errol Flynn and *The Adventures of Robin Hood*. What about putting a fencing foil in Sulu's hand?' He said, 'Great idea; do you fence?' I said, 'My favorite hobby.' I was lying, of course. But you never ask an actor whether he can or cannot do anything, because we are experts at *everything*. And, if we aren't, that night, we'll go out and become one." (171-2)

The one person Black expected to get notes from was Roddenberry, but Roddenberry chose to give his feedback in a different way, one which damaged his working relationship with Black. He did a script polish.

After only two months, John Black was becoming increasingly bothered watching Roddenberry overhaul material by renowned writers such as Jerry Sohl, Richard Matheson, George Clayton Johnson and, soon to come, Robert Bloch, all of whom Black believed displayed better talent at writing. He said, "I couldn't bear to see quality work changed to the point where the dialogue did not have the sharp edge that it had. And Roddenberry would use the word 'fast' at least once a page -- as in, 'We've got to get there *fast*.' I was watching too much good material getting screwed up and I couldn't take it." (17-4)

In fairness to Roddenberry, examination of his rewriting reveals the word "fast" used on an average of two times per script, not once per page -- and almost always in descriptive action, rarely in dialogue. In "The Man Trap," the one script from this period which does not clearly show improvement from Roddenberry's contributions, the dreaded adverb is used four times.

Defending his inclination to rewrite, Roddenberry said, "You understand, television series are a hungry thing; that's one way to look at it.... We didn't have big writing staffs back then, so there would be two of us... trying to do that; to feed this TV show.... Every show had a writer/producer, and he had someone, his 're-write man,' and you rode herd over all the stories and scripts that came in.... When you have something that is so different like *Star Trek* was, the creator has to be there, has to get it all set up, has to get the format set. Others can do more once everything is in place, but you have to establish that first.

"During those first shows, none of our writers knew what I wanted to do. Not fully. But I had this idea; I could see where to take it, who Kirk was, who Spock was. In that first year, I put everything on hold. You live for the show. Writers write; we do that. But no writer wants to write that much -- to risk your health like I did... sometimes still writing a particular script even as it was being photographed. They're waiting on the stage for these changes; or production needs them for the next week's show, to know what they will need in terms of the sets and so on. I'd find myself changing one script during the morning, another during the afternoon; maybe another at night, dictating changes for the next one to come up. That was my life that first year. I put the scripts out there [through Lincoln Enterprises, Roddenberry's merchandising business]; the First Drafts, the Final Drafts.... You can see the type of changes I made... and with each rewrite, the characterizations were more locked in." (145-12)

John Black said, "My deal with Roddenberry, by the by, was that neither he nor I would touch a script until the writer had finished his first draft, his second draft and his polish, or her polish [with regard to Dorothy]. When I delivered mine -- my first draft on 'The Naked Time' -- there were two or three scripts that were in on that day – Friday. I delivered it to Gene, on time, as I always did, then went home – six o'clock, seven o'clock. I came back on Monday and I was told that Gene had rewritten me over the weekend." (17)

Mary Black remembers, "I was hit with it first. John, throughout his career, has always been prone to work late and then sleep in. I don't have that schedule in my head, so I went in at nine and Dorothy came in to see me as I was setting up in my office, outside John's office, and she had pages in her hand and she didn't like what she was there to do at all. She said to me, 'Mary, GR rewrote John's script over the weekend and he wants all the secretaries to copy it.' I can still feel the way I felt then. John and I are Catholic; we're used to saying, 'Oh, that's what we're supposed to do? Alright, got it, I trust you.' And, honest to God, I tried. And I was not only given pages, I was also given a dictaphone machine so I could transcribe the notes GR had recorded. Now, the word is, he was drunk while he was doing it, and he could well have been, because he was very slurry. And the things that he had written across the lines on the pages were rather sloppy. And I kept trying to type these changes, but the sense I had at the time was that he was showing us, and saying, 'This is mine. *Mine*. And I'm going to prove to you that it is *mine*.' And, finally, I knew that I just couldn't do this with John's material, so I carried it back to Dorothy and said, 'Dorothy, I simply can't do this.' And Dorothy, to her credit, said, 'Mary, don't worry. I'll take care of it. I'll do it.' So Dorothy did get me out of that horrible situation. When John came in, I told him what had happened and I think he went straight over to GR's office." (17a)

John Black concurred, "Yeh. I was not gutless. I was ready for him. And I said, 'What the hell did you do to my script?' And he said, 'I made it better.'" (17)

Black told how he said, "For God's sake, Gene, I can maybe -- *maybe!* -- understand it for somebody who doesn't know the show. But I'm the Story Executive. I work here. I know the show. And you *know* I know it." (17-4)

Black remembered, "He gave me a 'that's the way it is and screw you' smile. Then he said he had a phone call he had to make to the network and he had a couple meetings that afternoon with Lucille Ball or somebody, and he said we'd talk about it another time. But that time never came about." (17)

"Well, there was a lot that had to change in that one," Roddenberry said in 1982 to this author. "This episode was going to lock in many character traits that would then come back in other episodes. You have to take extra care with a story like that. You know, these types of shows are going to be more important to the overall series because of what they tell us about our people -- our primary characters. So you have to get it right. Normally, I'd give written notes or we'd sit down and talk about it. Then more notes for the next draft, and so on. But with that script, I remember getting into the rewriting early. With a member of the staff, you may be able to take some shortcuts." (145-12)

Black felt Roddenberry's shortcut was disrespectful. He said, "I wasn't going to go for this. Solow came down, because he had heard what happened with Roddenberry. He said, 'What do you think?' And I said, 'I think it stinks.' First of all, it's illegal. The Writers Guild does not permit the script to be rewritten by a staff member before the writer gets to do a second draft. So I should have been able to do first draft, second draft, and polish. And that's what I did -- went back to work on it and ignored Gene's rewrite." (17)

Black's rewrite was dated June 20, 1966 draft. In the teaser for the new version, McCoy and Scott stay on the ship and Joe Tormolen makes the trip to the frigid scientific station on Psi 2000. The contamination now happens there, much as in the filmed episode, sans the melodramatic tag line about it being like nothing they've dealt with before.

Black, in accordance with his position as executive story editor, did his own polish, turned it in at the end of the day on June 23, mimeographed and distributed it to the staff the following day, Friday, June 24. Just as with the Yellow Cover drafts of "The Enemy Within" and "The Man Trap," it did not make it to NBC.

Roddenberry put his imprint on the script before circulating it to cast, crew, studio and the network. He later said, "That was a hell of a premise, but the script wasn't utilizing the characters to the degree that it could; taking full advantage of the inherent drama of seeing our people subjected to this condition. The rewriting took care of that. But I don't remember having a lot of time on that one. That script, as I recall, was very last minute. We needed the changes fast [sic!].... I don't think any writer is completely receptive to being rewritten. I've been on the other side of it and can certainly understand." (145-12)

Black has said many times that he was never a fan of Roddenberry's dialogue, believing it to lack subtlety. George Clayton Johnson echoed Black's feelings, saying of Roddenberry, "I thought that what he was doing to the work was, by and large, dumb. When I saw him doing to it John D.F.'s script, I said, 'I liked it better *before* you started fucking with it.'" (93-2)

An examination of the June 23/24 draft (Black's last) and the June 28, July 1 and July 5 drafts (Roddenberry's rewrites) does reveal some ham-fisted changes in dialogue, but there are also many positive additions to the script.

In the June 23/24 draft, it is Lt. Farrell, from "Mudd's Women" and "The Enemy Within," played by Black's friend Jim Goodwin, who takes over engineering and shuts down the engines. There is no Lt. Riley and therefore no "I'll Take You Home Again, Kathleen." Black had Farrell sing "Danny Boy."

In John Black's final script polish, Spock's meltdown had been moved from the ship's corridor to the briefing room, but there is no big moment between him and Kirk, no slapping Spock and no Spock backhanding Kirk and sending him reeling across the table. Nor does Kirk confess to loving the ship and understanding why it is called "she." His memorable line, "Never lose you," spoken to the Enterprise *is* in Black's last draft, but doesn't appear until the end of the story, on the bridge, as the ship escapes danger.

With his rewrite, Roddenberry reconsidered his objection to director Marc Daniels wanting to show Spock's blood as green. For the first time in the series, mention is made of the "green ice water" running through Spock's veins. And, yes, that unsubtle line about "like nothing we've dealt with before" was added to close out the teaser.

Another change involved the role of Nurse Ducheau, added to the script by Black both to assist McCoy in sickbay and to be one of the many conduits for spreading the disease. Roddenberry changed the name to the not-so-subtle angelic-sounding Christine Chapel and made much more of the character, with clear intent of casting Majel Barrett in the role.

Regarding this, Robert Justman and Herb Solow, from *Inside Star Trek: the Real Story*, wrote:

> [Gene] adapted the Nichelle Nichols non-recurring role manifestation [when he] created Nurse Christine Chapel. As Executive Producer, Gene would see to it that this "necessary" character would definitely recur. And since NBC hadn't liked the dark-haired Majel in the first pilot, the "series Majel" would be a blonde -- as if no one at NBC would notice. But they did.

While it can easily be argued that not all of the changes made to Black's script were for the better, Roddenberry's handling of "The Naked Time" helped to elevate an extremely good story and script to one which can be considered epic. Regardless, irreparable damage between producer and associate producer had occurred.

Mary Black said, "I think because we were so sour that mostly we it would have been so much better if 'that line' had been left in, or if 'that visual' had been left in, or 'where the hell did that line come from?,' like George calling Nichelle a 'fair maiden' and her saying, 'Sorry, neither,' which was put in by Gene Roddenberry afterwards. We were not good sports, and there's no point in pretending otherwise. We were gnashing our teeth." (17a)

Pre-Production
(no director prep days provided)

In May, Roddenberry had announced that he'd hired nine directors -- Joseph Sargent, Harvey Hart, Leo Penn, Marc Daniels, Bernard L. Kowalsky, Lawrence Dobkin, Vincent McEveety, James Goldstone, and Tom Gries, respectively, and they would direct the first nine episodes. It was now Kowalsky's turn.

Bernard Kowalsky was in great demand. He had served as producer for two popular series -- *Dick Powel Presents* and *Rawhide* -- and had just produced the pilot for *Rat Patrol*. Kowalsky was also a prolific director, and made points with Roddenberry when he directed the former's script for the premiere episode of the 1957 TV western *Boots and Saddles*.

With *Star Trek* falling behind schedule, the dates planned for "The Naked Time" now conflicted with the many other jobs Kowalsky had committed to, as the busy director juggled assignments on *The Monroes*, *Mission: Impossible*, and *Gunsmoke*. Frantic phone calls were made but no other director capable of taking on a challenging show like *Star Trek* was available on such short notice. So Marc Daniels was tapped to direct back-to-back episodes.

"I did two shows in a row, once," Daniels said. "It was craziness, but I did it. You usually get one day of preparation for every day that you shoot. And you had to spend those six days in preparation trying to solve these problems. You couldn't wait until you got to the set, starting to shoot, and say, 'Oh, gee, how are we going to do this?' because you'd never have gotten it done." (44-3)

In an amazing feat, Daniels prepared "The Naked Time" while filming "The Man Trap." Considering the anxiety the former script caused for some cast members, the calm and encouraging Daniels was the perfect choice.

Bruce Hyde, in the role of Kevin Riley, was 24. He had been appearing before the camera for only one year, with a guest spot on *The Trials of O'Brien* and a minor and brief recurring role in a few episodes of *Dr. Kildare*. Desilu had cast Hyde in a pilot film called *Dilby* and wanted to keep him close by in case the series was picked up. *Star Trek* casting director Joe D'Agosta was asked to find Hyde work. Marc Daniels approved.

Bruce Hyde recalled, "I had worked with Marc a year or so previously in a summer tour of a play by William Brown called *Linda Stone Is Brutal*. We had a great time with that tour, and Marc was very much a warm father figure to the young people in the cast. I loved Marc and having him as the director was a gift." (88-4)

Hyde would return for a prominent role in "The Conscience of the King" a few episodes down the line. But "The Naked Time," with Riley's maddening rendition of "I'll Take You Home Again, Kathleen," is Bruce Hyde's true shining moment.

As for the song, even though it is revered as an Irish ballad, it was actually written in America by an American, named Thomas P. Westendorf. Being 91 years old, the song was in the public domain and *Star Trek* did not have to pay to use it.

Stewart Moss as Joe Tormolen
(Unaired film trim courtesy of Gerald Gurian)

Stewart Moss, at 28, was cast as Joe Tormolen, the careless crewman with the itchy nose. With a background on the stage, Moss

212

had been working in TV for a few years with guest spots on *Perry Mason, Twelve O'clock High* and multiple episodes of *Hogan's Heroes*.

Moss said, "Joe [D'Agosta] was a personal friend. He called and told me he was casting a new TV 'sf' series which hadn't aired yet and there was a part in an upcoming show that I was right for. He mentioned the cast, and I was a big 'sf' fan at the time -- I had read everything Heinlein and Sturgeon and Asimov had written and so I said 'yes.'" (122-3)

Moss was among good company on the *Star Trek* set. He said, "I met Bill Shatner in '63 or '64. He had acted in a film short for a director, Richard Colla, who was my roommate at Yale Drama School. Colla invited Bill and his wife and myself and a date to his home for dinner with him and his wife -- a sort of wrap party. I remember Bill as affable, charming and self-deprecating... and he was married to a gorgeous woman aptly named Gloria. I did a two-part *Bonanza* with DeForest Kelley in late '64. It was a two-week shoot and I got to know De after he approached me and asked if I was a stage actor. He gave me a few tips on hitting marks and 'think it, don't just do it,' which were much appreciated. He was my favorite of all the *ST* regulars. Leonard I knew from casting calls. Quiet, withdrawn, odd." (122-3)

As for the familiar faces, the ever-present Eddie Paskey takes over the helm when Sulu abandons it. Frank Di Vinci takes over the navigation station after Riley exits. And Ron Veto helps a recovered Sulu from his bed in Sickbay.

Production Diary
Filmed June 30 (¼ day) and July 1, 5, 6, 7, 8 & 11 (1/2 day), 1966
(Planned as 6 day production, took only 5 ¾ days; total cost: $174,269).

Day 2. "Ice Station Star Trek" ... on planet Psi 2000 (Courtesy of Gerald Gurian)

Thursday, June 30, 1966. "Strangers in the Night" by Frank Sinatra was at the top of the pops pushing the Beatles' "Paperback Writer" down a notch to second place. Two big films out were writer/director/star Carl Reiner's *The Russians are Coming, The Russians are Coming* and *Nevada Smith*, starring Steve McQueen. You could see either for a buck. The median price for a new home was $14,000. The average annual wage was $7,000. And a true classic was about to begin shooting on the *Star Trek* stages.

Production was actually beginning a day early. Daniels had finished "The Man Trap" over three hours ahead of schedule and so, instead of waiting until 8 a.m. the next morning, he broke ground on "The Naked Time" at 3 p.m. on this Thursday. Shatner, Nimoy and Kelley, holdovers from "The Man Trap," were already there; guest performers Majel Barrett and Steward Moss had been called in with the hopes of an early start. Then the scenes with Joe Tormolen in sickbay were filmed.

Moss recalled, "When I read the script, I thought, 'This is going to be a challenge.' I knew it was moralistic to a degree. It was a message show. But it was in the context of a spaceship and the quest -- it was almost Homeric. And *Star Trek* wrote for actors. You would carry on for three or four pages. You would have something to do and a place to go, and there was an emotional arc. And that is why I was very much attracted to that particular script and that show. With *Star Trek*, you knew you had a part. It was a lot more fun for actors." (122-3)

Day 2. On Friday, the first official day of production, the company began working on Stage 10, filming the episode's teaser on the "Observation Station" set. Nimoy and Moss were the only actors needed, surrounded by mannequins filling in for the frozen station personnel.

Moss recalled, "I questioned Marc Daniels about whether a Star Fleet officer who probably had at least a PhD in engineering would be stupid enough to take his glove off in that situation. He said, "Of course not. But if you don't do it, we don't have a show." (122-3)

So Moss took off his glove.

At 11:15 a.m., cast and crew moved back to Stage 9 for more work in sickbay. Filming stopped at 6:45 p.m., nearly eleven hours after it had begun.

A three-day holiday weekend followed, with production resuming on Tuesday, still in sickbay, followed by a move to the transporter room and the recreation room, respectively. Stewart Moss had scenes on all three sets. He said, "Marc [Daniels] was one of those directors that I always liked, the type who doesn't pretend to know more than he knows. He gave me very little direction and, in my recollection, did not over-direct anybody in terms of their acting. He left you alone. I did go to him and I said, 'Listen, this prose is a little purple [exaggerated],' and he said, 'Stewart, just do what you're doing; it's very honest.'" (122-3)

Of the commotion in the recreation room, Moss said, "I killed myself with a butter knife. I think I was the only actor in the history of television who had died that way." (122-1)

Immediately following the stabbing, cast and crew moved to the bridge to shoot numerous sequences. Moss recalled, "My whole impression of it -- and maybe this was because of Marc [Daniels] -- was that you get on the set, you light it, you do it and you're done. Marc knew what he wanted and he was fast. After the scene where I'm struggling with the other two and fall on the knife, I remember lying on the floor, and I don't think I had even had a chance to get up yet, and he said, 'Cut! Gentleman, we're on the wrong set.' And they're all gone. And I thought, 'Well, I guess I did alright." (122-3)

All of Day 4 and most of Day 5 were spent on the bridge. Eddie Paskey, whose character Lt. Leslie took over for Sulu at the helm, only to have to be relieved when he too is infected by the disease, was given his first speaking part in *Star Trek*. He recalled, "I was to become, basically, kind of drunk, because the disease had infected me. Well, I was so nervous, I couldn't remember my lines. So Marc Daniels wrote them down in grease pencil on the top of the glass covering the helm. But, as they tried to get the shot, I became more and more nervous, and I got to the last line and I froze. And Lenny [Nimoy] reached over, hit a button on the helm and said the line for me. And a couple seconds later, Marc says, 'Cut, print!' And there was no condemnation of it; I was still accepted, I was still one of the guys; I just had a bad day. This is what made that *Star Trek* crew who they were. They were there to help each other." (135-2)

The next scene featured Sulu charging the bridge with a fencing foil. Paskey, sitting in Sulu's seat at the helm during the scene, said, "Rehearsal was just great, no problems. But when the director called 'Action!,' George came out of that damn elevator like he was shot from a cannon and started wielding that sword, and Bill backs up and says, 'Jesus Christ,

Takei running amok
(Courtesy of Gerald Gurian)

George, you're going to kill me with that damn thing.' And he almost did." (135-2)

Marc Daniels said, "I had to really physically restrain him. He got so excited that I was scared to death he was going to stab somebody -- not purposely, but he was getting too close. I took the sword away from him and had the end of it dulled down. George has a lot of enthusiasm." (44-3)

Shatner also had an opinion about -- and a memento from -- that performance: "George had always had a sword fighting fantasy. In shooting this sequence, he saw his dream about to come true. He attacked the scene -- *and me* -- with such gusto that I have a very small scar to prove what a wonderful swordsman he was." (156-8)

Takei denied that he was behaving in anything other than a professional way. What Daniels, Paskey, Shatner and the others saw, according to him, was his commitment to the character -- a performance.

After getting the last bridge shot, the company followed the bare-chested Sulu to the ship's corridors... for more sword play and "acting."

Filming didn't stop on Day 5 until 7:30 p.m. It had been a 13 to 14 hour work day for all involved.

On Friday, July 8, filming moved to the engineering set. Bruce Hyde recalled, "In those days I was a pretty uptight guy. And I played very tense, nervous characters.... I was used to acting on stage -- that's what I did most -- and when you did comedy on stage, you got laughs. And I remember the whole experience [of making 'The Naked Time'] being somewhat uncomfortable.... All the time I was doing that stuff in [Engineering], when I was singing and walking around and leaning on things, they would just ask me to improvise that, and I wasn't very loose.... I was doing all that stuff and nobody was laughing, and you can't tell if you're bombing or you're doing it right." (88-3)

Director Daniels helps Bruce Hyde loosen up
(Courtesy of Bruce Hyde)

**Day 6. Happier times between Shatner and Doohan
(Courtesy of Gerald Gurian)**

Stewart Moss said, "I don't remember my part as 'scary,' but I didn't have to do all the things that Bruce did. I mean, Bruce singing 'Take Me Home Again, Kathleen' for hours on end. I thought he was wonderful. I thought it was hysterical.... I think he stole the episode in spite of everyone getting to 'chew the scenery.'" (122-3)

After Hyde's emotional performance, it was Nimoy's turn to try hitting all the right emotional notes. Last up that day: his breakdown in the briefing room.

Nimoy recalled how Roddenberry and two of his production assistants came to the set to let it be known by their "silent, ominous presences" that the clock was being strictly watched and the scene had to be finished by 6:18 p.m. -- the preferred "wrap time," allowing the fast-moving camera crew to store away equipment, wrap up the cables and make room for the electricians to turn off the lights, all before overtime kicked in at 6:31. With this pressure, Nimoy recalled that he and Daniels had only one take to get it right.

"The clock ticked and the cameras rolled," Nimoy remembered, "and through some miracle or magic, the scene went as planned. We got a lovely take the first time out and, at precisely 6:18 p.m., we wrapped." (128-3)

It *was* a perfect take. But, contrary to Nimoy's recollection, the company wrapped his scene at 7:25 p.m., not 6:18. And this explains why Roddenberry and perhaps Robert Justman and Greg Peters were there, watching their watches.

The final shots from Monday, July 11, finished up the work in the briefing room, and this included the dramatic confrontation of Spock by Kirk, and the Captain's anguished admission of his obsessed love of a "she" called Enterprise. Daniels wrapped production at 1 p.m., and then, following a 60-minute lunch break, director Lawrence Dobkin took over to begin filming "Charlie X."

Post-Production
*July 12 through September 19, 1966.
Music score recorded on August 31, 1966.*

As with "The Man Trap," even after the filming was over, the rewriting was not. Revised script pages dated August 11 were needed to add in additional Captain's log entries. In this early period of the series' development, the creative staff worried that the Captain's log might become tiresome if overused and therefore mandated that it be utilized sparingly in the scripts. This line of thinking soon changed, due first to the needs of the editors, then to please the viewing audience once the series hit the air and viewer feedback began arriving -- by the mailbags.

The editor who requested the additional log entries was Bruce Schoengarth, with Team #2, on their second assignment, following "Mudd's Women."

Alexander Courage scored his fourth episode with "The Naked Time," this time jettisoning the sci-fi feel of the music for "The Man Trap." This new score, along with those being written by Fred Steiner, were instrumental in setting the tone for the series: action/adventure laced with romance and mystery. Lighter moments are also present, including a hint of an Irish melody for Lt. Riley, and a nod toward swashbuckling fanfare for Sulu. The best is saved for last, which the exciting music for the Enterprise's journey back through time provides.

The Howard Anderson Company handled the optical effects, including the planet spinning round and round on the bridge viewing screen, and that wild star journey back through time. But, due to a delivery deadline (this was the fourth episode to air), there was no time left to add in a phaser beam as Scotty burns through the bulkhead outside Engineering.

Because this was primarily a bottle show, the final cost of "The Naked Time" was kept to $174,269 ($1.3 million in 2013).

Release / Reaction
Premiere air date: September 29, 1966. NBC repeat broadcast: April 27, 1967.

"The Naked Time" was reviewed on September 29 1966 in the *Charleston Gazette*, out of Charleston, West Virginia. The uncredited reviewer wrote:

> *Star Trek*'s show tonight is tense as life aboard the starship Enterprise continues to be an eerie adventure with the unknown. The danger here takes the form of a communicable disease contracted while on a visit to another planet which drugs, disorients and even kills its victims. The imaginative skills involved in tracking down the cause and cure of the epidemic, together with the drama of keeping the victims from blowing up the ship in space, add up to a very tense and interesting hour.

RATINGS / Nielsen 30-Market report for Thursday, Sept. 29, 1966:

8:30 - 9 p.m., with 57.2% of U.S. TVs in use.	Rating:	Share:
NBC: *Star Trek* (first half)	**19.5**	**34.1%**
ABC: *The Tammy Grimes Show*	9.8	17.1%
CBS: *My Three Sons*	19.1	33.4%
Local independent stations:	9.8	15.4%
9 - 9:30 p.m., with 61% of U.S. TVs in use.		
NBC: *Star Trek* (second half)	**18.7**	**30.7%**
ABC: *Bewitched*	17.8	29.2%
CBS: *Thursday Night Movie*	18.5	30.3%
Local independent stations:	7.0	9.8%

Star Trek again won its time slot. More significant than beating *My Three Sons* and *The Tammy Grimes Show* at 8:30 p.m. was the victory at 9:00 p.m. over *Bewitched* and *The CBS Thursday Night Movie*. *Bewitched* came in third, just under the television premiere of *By Love Possessed*, starring Lana Turner, Jason Robards Jr., Efrem Zimbalist Jr., and George Hamilton.

Immediately following the first broadcast of "The Naked Time," Leonard Nimoy knew that this episode had an enormous effect on both the show's popularity and Spock's appeal. In 1968 he told a reporter, "Within two weeks after that show, my mail jumped from a few hundred letters to 10,000 a week. That scene got to a lot of people, and I knew what I had to play in the scripts that followed -- it solidified everything. I knew that we were not playing a man with no emotions, but a man who had great pride, who had learned to control his emotions and who would deny that he knew what emotions were. In a way, he was more human than anyone else on the ship." (128-17)

Star Trek's ratings remained strong through the repeat season, as further demonstrated by the second airing of this episode.

RATINGS / Nielsen 30-Market report for Thursday, April 27, 1967:

8:30 - 9 p.m., with 56.4% of U.S. TVs in use.	Rating:	Share:
NBC: *Star Trek* (first half)	16.6	29.4%
ABC: **Bewitched**	**17.1**	**30.3%**
CBS: *My Three Sons*	12.7	22.5%
Local independent stations:	11.7	17.8%
9 - 9:30 p.m., with 56.6% of U.S. TVs in use.		
NBC: *Star Trek* (second half)	16.0	28.3%
ABC: *That Girl*	14.3	25.3%
CBS: **Thursday Night Movie**	**19.1**	**33.7%**
Local independent stations:	9.8	12.7%

With the repeat of "The Naked Time," *Bewitched* grabbed the No. 1 spot at 8:30, but with less than a half ratings point lead over *Star Trek*. *My Three Sons*, still considered a hit at CBS and with many more seasons ahead of it, was a weak third. At 9 p.m., the winner was *The CBS Thursday Night Movie* with the television premiere of 1963's *Toys in the Attic*, starring Dean Martin and Geraldine Page, but *Star Trek*'s audience remained loyal and kept the repeat of "The Naked Time" in second place. *That Girl*, in its first of five seasons on ABC, settled for third.

From the Mailbag

Dated October 6, 1966, the week after the first airing of "The Naked Time":

> Dear Mr. Roddenberry... to begin with, I must say I enjoy your television program *Star Trek*, but I have one complaint. <u>All of the episodes are exciting</u>. I suppose that isn't really too bad, but if all the episodes are exciting, and there are no dull ones, the exciting ones start to become dull, and people stop watching. I wouldn't want that to happen. I want the show to go on for maybe 12 or 15 seasons but, if you use up all the good plots on the first season, it just can't last. Anonymous.

Memories

Bruce Hyde recalled, "It was a strange experience, being one of the first times I'd seen myself on film. At this point most of my acting experience was on the stage. So the *Star Trek* episodes were almost the first things I'd done that were actually going to be televised. This prospect would have excited me regardless of the role. It also scared me because of my inexperience.... I think what seemed unusual was the whole idea of doing sci-fi on TV. At this point TV sci-fi had been confined almost entirely to children's shows. So it wasn't a genre into which adult TV had ventured much." (88-4)

Stewart Moss said, "A few days after 'The Naked Time' aired, I got a note in the mail from the writer John D.F. Black, thanking me for making him look good. That was a first and a last for me. I was worried about my performance because I had some dialogue that

Shatner gets his revenge in this posed publicity shot (Courtesy of Gerald Gurian)

was a little much. I had asked Marc to make sure I didn't get too big. He assured me I was believable. Yet the note from John was very much appreciated." (122-3)

John Black said, "Stewart was marvelous. He's a fine actor. He was and I think he always stayed that way. He certainly deserved a note from me. An actor like that deserves a lot of notes of praise. He gave that role everything he had and everything it needed." (17)

Grace Lee Whitney remembered the excitement, both in making *Star Trek* and in watching it. She said, "If you could have seen us when *we* saw us -- when we saw the dailies after the first few shoots. I was so blown away; I couldn't imagine that we were so good together. All of us were so good together -- the crew *and* the cast. That's what made the show, the interaction between the crew and the actors -- the chemistry. It was rollin', let me tell you." (183-6)

Roddenberry said, "That was an important show, and another way of establishing who our people are. We had Jerry's story ['The Corbomite Maneuver'], how people reveal certain things about themselves when under pressure. They also do that when under the influence. So, a device like that, it's a good way to strip away a lot of things, show who is really in there. And much of that, what we were able to do there, comes back. What we learn about our Captain, and Mr. Spock and some of the others, is now part of the series. You don't lose sight of those character traits as you move forward." (145-12)

Aftermath

"The Naked Time" almost gave us double the nakedness -- it was actually intended to be a two-part episode. As presented, up until the final few minutes, we see Part 1. Part 2 was to deal with the Enterprise traveling back in time. That chapter of the story would have to wait (see "The Story Behind the Story" of "Tomorrow Is Yesterday").

This episode worked so well, in fact, that Roddenberry wanted to do a sequel. A treatment was written in May 1967 before the start of the second season, then it was put aside for 20 years -- eventually becoming "The Naked Now" for *Star Trek: the Next Generation.*

The "formula" used to jump-start the engines of the Enterprise and send the ship hurtling back in time was used again too, as Kirk foreshadows with the line: "One day we may risk it." That day would come, in Season Two's "Assignment: Earth."

George Takei named "The Naked Time" his favorite *Star Trek* episode. Gene Roddenberry put it on a list of his Top 10. William Shatner considered it to be "one terrific episode."

The sci-fi community agreed and this episode was nominated for a Hugo Award in 1967. The category was Best Filmed Science Fiction. This was the second *Star Trek* episode from Season One to receive a nomination -- the other being "The Corbomite Maneuver." And there would be a third (the winner will be revealed in a later chapter).

13

Episode 7: CHARLIE X
Teleplay by D.C. Fontana
Story by Gene Roddenberry
Directed by Lawrence Dobkin

From the October 10, 1966, issue of *TV Guide*:

> "Charlie X." Spock is suspicious of Charlie Evans. The 17-year-old says he was the sole survivor of a spaceship crash when he was three -- and that he managed to live completely on his own.

Charlie has a secret -- and a power. The awkward, shy teen may already be responsible for the destruction of a rescue ship and the deaths of its crew. Is the crew of the Enterprise next?

As with most *Star Trek*s, the beast is Man himself, fueled by his inherent weaknesses. Corruption of power, already examined in "Where No Man Has Gone Before," is back with a twist: beware a god who is going through puberty.

Robert Walker, Jr. and Grace Lee Whitney
in NBC publicity photo
(Courtesy of Gerald Gurian)

SOUND BITES

- *Charlie, to Yeoman Rand:* "The other girls on this ship... they all look like Tina.... You're the only one that looks like you. If I had the whole universe, I'd give it to you. When I see you... I feel like I'm hungry all over."

- *Kirk, to McCoy, about Charlie:* "He's a boy in a man's body, trying to be an adult with the adolescent in him getting in the way."

- *Charlie, to Kirk:* "Everything I do or say is wrong. I'm in the way... I don't know the rules... I don't know what I am or what I'm supposed to be... and I don't know why I hurt so much inside all the time.... It's like I'm wearing my insides outside!"

- *Kirk:* "Charlie, there are a million things in the universe that you can have... and another million things you can't have. There's no fun in facing that... but that's how things are." *Charlie:* "Then what am I going to do?" *Kirk:* "Hang on tight and survive. Everybody has to." *Charlie:* "You don't." *Kirk:* "Everybody, Charlie... me too."

- *Charlie, to Kirk, after Janice Rand vanishes:* "Growing up isn't so much. I'm not a man and I can do anything! You can't."

ASSESSMENT

A near perfect episode, "Charlie X" is a harmonious collaboration between Dorothy Fontana and Gene Roddenberry (his idea, her script, his script polish). The story relates the anxieties of adolescence in ways seldom achieved in film or television. At its core, and with its conclusion, this is a tragedy. Nothing conveys this more than Charlie's final moment, as the Thasians return to claim him and he pleads, "Please don't let them take me. *I can't even touch them*! They don't care... not about anything.... They don't love *anybody. Please...* I want to stay... stay... *stay...*"

This story reveals what can happen when power is placed into the hands of an emotionally immature person. Charlie is a victim of his upbringing. Blame his foster parents -- the Thasians.

THE STORY BEHIND THE STORY

Script Timeline
Gene Roddenberry's story premise in Star Trek series proposal:
March 11, 1964.
Roddenberry's story outline, "Charlie Is God": April 23, 1964.
Roddenberry's revised story outline: August 28, 1964.
Roddenberry's updated story outline (with new ship crew members),
now called "Charlie X": April 14. 1966.
Roddenberry's revised outline: April 23, 1966.
D. C. Fontana's outline, based on Roddenberry's story, ST #21:
April 27, 1966.
Fontana's revised outline, gratis: May 9, 1966.
Fontana's 1st Draft teleplay: June 6, 1966.
Fontana's 2nd Draft teleplay: June 27, 1966.
Mimeo Department reformatted "Yellow Cover 1st Draft" script:
June 30, 1966.
Gene Roddenberry's script polish (Final Draft teleplay):
July 5, 1966.
Additional page revisions by Roddenberry: July 11 & 13, 1966.

The kernel of "Charlie X" first appeared as a single paragraph in Roddenberry's 1964 *Star Trek* series' proposal. The title then: "The Day Charlie Became God." Roddenberry expanded on his idea for a story treatment, with the shorter title "Charlie Is God." The theme of the story would become familiar to fans of *Star Trek* -- that of absolute power corrupting absolutely. What made it unique was the story's unusual villain.

Roddenberry said, "We didn't tell conventional monster stories. The alien creatures who posed a threat to our people had reasons behind their actions. Well, teenagers have reasons for what they do, too. The danger there is that they are like a sort of volatile mix of ignorance and arrogance -- and insecurity -- like putting certain chemicals together and suddenly you have a highly unstable explosive.

"Children have a lack of morality in that morality is primarily a learned behavior. That's not to say children don't process traces of humanitarianism, but, for the most part, they have to be taught [right from wrong]. We are inherently reckless when we're young and not able to fully empathize with others -- people or animals or any living thing. Now you take an inexperienced person like that and give him the ability to 'think' someone out of existence and you have a real danger. You run the risk that if you reject this immature person -- deny him what he wants, tell him he's wrong about something, provoke him in any way -- he will more than likely use that power. Seeing it this way, if you're going to tell what some may call a monster story, what better [antagonist] than a teenager?" (145-12)

In a pair of story outlines written in April, 1966, utilizing the new cast of *Star Trek*, Roddenberry shortened the title of his unconventional monster tale to "Charlie X."

"You remember in the westerns," he explained, "and someone would say, 'Make your mark here.' And the prospector or ranch hand draws his 'X.' And you understood he had no formal education. Well, I think we explained it that Charlie learned to talk from playing back taped recordings on the wrecked ship. That's the way he explained it, anyway. But you have to wonder who would have taught him to read and write? The 'Charlie Is God' title gave too much away. Changing that to 'Charlie X' only told us that he is uneducated -- and uneducated at many things, [like] understanding people, knowing how to fit in, knowing how to control his temper." (145-12)

Roddenberry abandoned the concept after deciding it lacked the action/adventure elements NBC was looking for in each episode.

Dorothy Fontana, Roddenberry's 27-year-old secretary and part-time writer with a half dozen screen credits, felt differently and asked for a chance to develop the story. She found it easy to relate to the character of Charlie Evans, saying, "I had two teenage brothers at the time. I think it was an unconscious tapping of that, 'What would a teenager do?' I was kind of aware of the things that were frustrating them; things that were driving them." (64-2)

But Charlie Evans didn't have a normal upbringing, and his teenage angst was also beyond the norm. Fontana added, "Here's this kid who hasn't had any exposure to other humans, and I felt that this incredible humanity shock to him is a little like growing up. You're a child, then, suddenly, you're considered an adult. Plus you're starting to really appreciate but not understand the other sex. And he had not built up to that, where, at least, your average human child has had other human companionship, someone to talk to, someone they felt they could go to, whether it be a teacher or a parent or whatever. Charlie had none of that. So everything that landed on Charlie landed with both feet all at once. And he had no way to know how to deal with it, except to react in the way he was taught to survive." (64-1)

It was this deep understanding of the character that helped Fontana's story and script stand out. Charlie Evans, with all the terrible things he was capable of, was a character we cared about. Even with all the sci-fi tricks that surrounded him, the character never stopped being believable. And we believed that those on the Enterprise could both fear him and feel compassion for him.

Fontana's version, told in a story outline, was delivered to her bosses on April 27. Robert Justman wrote Roddenberry:

> A very good treatment. Clean, straight and to the point with interesting character development.... I really think it is fine. (RJ7-1)

With tongue firmly in cheek, he added:

> This guy, D.C. Fontana, shows definite promise as a writer and I would like to find out more about him. (RJ7-1)

One qualm Justman had with the story outline involved a recreational activity. He wrote to John D.F. Black and Gene Roddenberry:

> On page 5, in the Recreation Room sequence, Janice and Charlie play cards. Do people still play cards at this time in the future, and if they do, do the games and the cards still resemble what we know in our own present civilization? (RJ7-1)

Justman had a fair point, but the card game would stay. It was needed to establish an important plot point.

Stan Robertson had a qualm of his own, which had nothing to do with a deck of playing cards. He approved the story, but was not taken with its setting aboard the Enterprise. He called Roddenberry about this and then followed up with a memo, writing:

> Your point that we want our viewers to identify with the Starship and those who sail on it, as a western fan might come to be familiar with Dodge City and its various landmarks, colorful characters, etc., is an excellent one. We couldn't agree with you more.... Let's use our ship to its obvious advantages, but let's think of a good blend of on and off-board stories. (SR7-1)

Robertson pushed the point further. He telephoned again and told his idea of restaging the action away from the Enterprise to John D.F. Black. But in a memo to Roddenberry, Black said:

> The writer [Fontana] and I are mutually agreed that, should we move the story to a planet, we would weaken Kirk's involvement and dissipate the intrinsic drama that can only exist when the safety of the Enterprise is at stake. Further -- despite the size of the Enterprise, the characters in this piece are restricted to the confinement of the ship – "caged" -- a big plus. My own opinion is that the story would suffer should we acquiesce to Stan in this instance. (JDFB7)

Roddenberry's five-word response: "Agreed. Stay on the ship." (GR7-1)

Robertson tried a third time by calling Dorothy Fontana. She later said, "I was still a secretary. He called me and started giving me notes on the script. I just said, 'Thank you, Mr. Robertson,' and I went directly into Gene and said, 'Maybe this is the wrong attitude but I don't think Stan Robertson should be giving me notes on my script over the phone when he doesn't give them to anybody else.' Gene called him back and ripped him a new one. He said, 'You don't mess with my writers. You don't make comments to *my writers*. If you have notes from the network, you give them to me. But you do not call *my writers*.'" (64-2)

Fontana's first draft script arrived on June 6. Mary Black, who would read the scripts first before passing them on to John D.F., said, "I was so relieved when 'Charlie X' came in the first time, because I liked Dorothy so much. And I thought, 'Oh my God, if she's a rotten writer, this will be terrible.' And then the first draft came in and, oh, what a relief, she was a wonderful writer." (17a)

Justman was quick to write Roddenberry and Black, telling them:

> I feel it is very unusual to get a first draft screenplay in this good of shape.... Charlie is more fully resolved in this version and much more of a person than he was before. And I kind of hate to see him get zapped out of existence at the end of the show. (RJ7-3)

Roddenberry read through the comments from Black and Justman, and then wrote a memorandum of his own -- to Fontana:

> I agree with the other memo writers that it is an excellent first draft; would be very pleased if all of our writers performed as well the first time around.

It also appears to be done with a very common sense attitude toward budget and practical limitations of photographing *Star Trek*. It has the potential to make an excellent episode. (GR7-2)

But Roddenberry wanted some changes made before sending the script to NBC and going another round with Stan Robertson about the story's setting. His memo continued:

> The principal aim of this revision should be toward more excitement, a growing "unusualness" in Charlie, unwrapping the package of which he is, bit by bit, more and more... <u>indicating</u> at first the possibilities of danger here, then as Charlie grows frustrated, <u>showing</u> the danger that exists, a very steady build of tension and excitement toward our climactic moments which themselves mount higher and higher with each Act. (GR7-2)

It was Roddenberry's idea that, as he put it, "the Enterprise should become a hell ship." He elaborated:

> Why be content with a person zapped into disappearance here and there when the possibilities are almost limitless? (GR7-2)

One suggestion was that Charlie turn a crew member into a tiny bug, then steps on it. Another suggestion involved the series' protagonist, with Roddenberry writing:

> And now, most importantly, what about Captain Kirk? Frankly, I think you hit it much more closely with the supporting characters than with him. First of all, the <u>responsibility</u> to find an answer is totally his and no combination of impossibilities can relieve him of that primary chore. Like it or not, even to some extent wise or not, he has to take a stand against Charlie once he fully realizes what is going on. To do it by guile, without first attempting it by full confrontation, reduces Kirk in our eyes. (GR7-2)

Fontana's 2nd Draft, brimming with confrontation and an ounce less guile, was turned in on June 27. Kirk was more proactive, even when appearing near-powerless against superior alien beings. Fontana later said, "Kirk could not solve this problem. But I redeemed him and, at the age I was, it amazes me that I was smart enough to do it -- that I had him beg for Charlie. He pleaded for him... and I felt that *that* served dramatically, even though I had the aliens rescue the Enterprise." (64-2)

Fontana also added the scene in the recreation room where Uhura is described as entertaining off-duty crew members by singing a song. No other details were provided.

NBC's Stan Robertson wrote Roddenberry:

> All of the original problems, <u>except one</u>, which we felt were embodied in this story as first submitted have been taken care of in this fine draft.... <u>The exception</u> is the one thing with which we are most concerned at this point in the development of our series -- that is the confinement of our stories on board the U.S.S. Enterprise.... Without becoming involved in a rehash of all the dialogue which has passed between us on this point, we are very aware that the Enterprise, with all its lavishness, depth and grandeur, plus the imagination it took to construct it, is a definite plus as far as *Star Trek* is concerned. However, we are very aware of the dangers inherent in restricting any series of plots to the confines of only "four walls," regardless of how magnificent they are.... In the case of "Charlie X" and other stories not yet in production, give some serious thought to measures by which part or all of our dramas might be told by action away from the Enterprise, possibly on planets or scientific stations. (SR7-2)

Roddenberry ignored the request. He did, however, do a rewrite -- the final draft, dated July 5. Actor Jim Goodwin lost a job with these latest revisions. In all the previous drafts, Lt. Farrell was present at the helm. Roddenberry changed this to read nondescript "navigator."

The notes from Robert Justman continued. He told Roddenberry:

> Again, for a stronger ACT ending, I suggest that we end ACT III with the Disappearance of Janice.... On page 71 the Thasian materializes on the Bridge of the Enterprise. Does the Thasian have to be vaguely humanoid in form? Why not this time can't we go completely far out and have nothing that resembles anything humanoid? (RJ7-4)

Justman got the Act break he desired, but the Thasian, to better serve the production schedule and the budget, would remain humanoid in appearance, at least regarding his head, which was all we would see.

Regarding another change, Fontana remembered coming to work to find her scenes about the guilelessness of youth were now rewritten into a teenager's introduction to his raging hormones. Her reaction: "Sex always got into Gene's work." (64-2)

John Black said, "GR's habit was to put sex into everything. It drove Dorothy crazy because he did that to 'Charlie X.' He had to make it sexy." (17)

Charlie's pat on Yeoman Rand's rump was already in Fontana's script, as was his innocent question in the teaser: "Is that a girl?" The big change, really, was a shifting and sharpening of dialogue in the man-to-man talk Charlie is given by Kirk. Fontana had it come from McCoy. Roddenberry reassigned the task to the reluctant captain and incorporated in Charlie's admission of feeling sick all the time because of his hunger for Janice Rand.

"There is a good example as to why I wanted to do *Star Trek*," Roddenberry said. "You can take on subjects; say things that you can't say on other shows. Now that one, it could tell teenagers that they weren't alone with what they felt; with that confusion, wanting so much but not knowing how to go about getting it, and really, not even knowing why you want it. And where are you going to hear a father/son talk like that [between Kirk and Charlie]? Could *Father Knows Best* do it? Maybe, very much disguised, but not like this." (145-12)

Fontana later said, "I was trying to play on the naïveté and the innocence of the boy rather than his raging hormones, but, you know, that's the way the story went. And some of that went pretty well, I thought." (64-1)

It was in Roddenberry's draft where new lyrics to the traditional Scottish tune "Charlie Is My Darling" were added. Giving accompaniment to Uhura was Spock, picking at the Vulcan harp.

But most of Roddenberry's changes were confined to moving things around and tightening and rephrasing a few lines of dialogue. This was the least amount of work he had done on any script from this period. There was no question in anyone's minds that if the series were picked up for additional episodes, Fontana would be writing again ... and Gene Roddenberry might be looking for a new secretary.

Fontana thanked Roddenberry for letting her moonlight and demonstrate her abilities as a writer when it came time to submit the proposed screen credits to the Writers Guild. Just as with teleplays, per strict Guild rules, a producer cannot take "story credit" from a freelance writer without first proving that at least 51% of the story elements were his. Even though Fontana used Roddenberry's last outline more as a springboard into her own treatment and did not stay close to its structure, or the character of Charlie as originally envisioned, she nonetheless gave her boss full credit for the story. She said, "The Writers Guild actually called me and said, 'Technically, you are an outside writer, so this has to be arbitrated. Arbitration has to look at it. Are you sure you want to give him full story credit?' I said, 'Yeah, sure.' So I just took the tele-credit. But yes, I developed the story. If you look at the drafts, you can see it." (64-2)

Pre-Production:
July 1, July 5-8, 1966, and July 11, for ½ day
(5 ½ days prep).

Lawrence Dobkin, 46, was hired to direct. He was actually more an actor than a director with hundreds of credits in film and TV including 1955's *Illegal*, which also featured DeForest Kelley. He turned to directing in the 1950s for series such as *The Rifleman*, *The Donna Reed Show*, and *77 Sunset Strip*.

"I was in Europe, helping an old friend with a spaghetti western," he told Allan Asherman for *The Star Trek Interview Book*. "I was playing a villain, and helping to rewrite it as we shot it.... The arrangement to direct the eighth [*Star Trek*] episode was made through my agent sometime during the period when I was away, and he wired me and told me that I had to be home by a certain date. I got home two days late, as I recall, after being delayed in Spain." (49)

The casting of Charles Evans was *the* key element. This was one of the biggest and most important guest roles at this point in the series. Roddenberry had been hearing good things about Michael J. Pollard, who recently finished filming a surprisingly somber and touching episode of *Lost in Space*, and suggested him for the part. Casting director Joe D'Agosta had been thinking of Pollard, too, but for another upcoming episode -- "Miri." For "Charlie X," he had a bigger catch in mind.

Robert Walker Jr. as Ensign Pulver

Robert Walker Jr., at 26, was a product of show business. His parents were Hollywood leading man Robert Walker and movie queen Jennifer Jones. When his father died suddenly at age 32, Walker's mother remarried movie mogul David O. Selznick. After TV guest spots on *Route 66* and *The Naked City*, among others, Walker landed second billing in 1963's *The Hook*, just under Kirk Douglas. Also in '63, he had third billing in *The Company*, for which he received a Golden Globe award as Most Promising Newcomer. In 1964, he won a Theatre World Award for his back-to-back stand-out performances in the off-Broadway productions *I Knock at the Door* and *Pictures in the Hallway*. Then he took over a plum role from Jack Lemmon, as the title character in *Ensign Pulver*, the sequel to *Mister Roberts*. His top-billing placed him above co-star Walter Matthau. During all of this, Walker continued to make selected high profile appearances on television. Even though he was nine years older than the character, the role of

Charlie Evans appealed to him.

Joe D'Agosta said, "It's pretty amazing that we were able to get actors of a certain status, but *Star Trek* was an unusual show and I think it was recognizable to them as that right from the beginning. We were the only theatrical show on television. We had the costumes, yes, that's always part of it, but we also had current topics under the guise of science fiction. The scripts read theatrically, they read in such a way that they were very appealing to actors. They weren't getting the same thing from other shows." (43-4)

"When they talked about Charlie Evans, I welcomed it when they said young Robert Walker," Lawrence Dobkin said. "I don't remember if he was in to read or not because, as I say, I was a couple of days late by the time I showed up, and everybody was panicked.... When I came in, I had so much to do -- getting used to the effects team, the cameraman, the lighting design that one had to make room for, the resident cast and then digesting the storyline. I don't believe I got involved in the casting." (49)

"Robert Walker was a stroke of casting luck for *Star Trek*," Grace Lee Whitney said. "It's impossible to imagine anyone else in the role. He captured the perfect balance, projecting vulnerability, innocence and horrifying menace, all at the same time." (183-2)

Abraham Sofaer, at 70, played the Thasian. He had over a hundred film and TV credits, including an episode of *Have Gun -- Will Travel* written by Roddenberry. In the sci-fi genre from this period, Sofaer played the alien leader Arch in Harlan Ellison's "Demon with a Glass Hand" on *The Outer Limits*, and another alien leader, Sobram, in "The Flaming Planet," an episode of *Lost in Space*. He'd return to *Star Trek* in voice only for another superior alien being in "Spectre of the Gun."

Another guest player of a sort was Gene Roddenberry. He provided the voice of the chef who reports to Kirk that the meatloaf he put into the oven has come out as real Thanksgiving turkeys. At the time of the production, it was believed this episode would air on NBC right before Thanksgiving. However, due to other episodes being held up in post with more demanding needs for photographic effects, "Charlie" advanced in the schedule.

For the production, only Stage 9 was required, and only two new sets were needed: the ship's gym and the brig, both of which were reconfigurations of existing Enterprise sets.

Production Diary
Filmed July 11 (1/2 day),
12, 13, 14, 15, 18 & 19, 1966
(Planned as 6 day production; finished 1/2 day over;
total cost: $177,941).

July 11, 1966. "Hanky Panky" by Tommy James and the Shondells was the most played record in America, replacing "Paperback Writer" by the Beatles, who were touring the U.S. amidst protests to John Lennon's remark that he and his band mates were bigger with the teenagers than Jesus Christ. Among the top selling albums in record stores: *Wonderfulness* by Bill Cosby, the soundtracks to *Dr. Zhivago* and *The Sound of Music*, *Strangers in the Night* by Frank Sinatra, and three LPs from Herb Alpert and the Tijuana Brass – *Going Places*, *Whipped Cream and Other Delights* and, still at the top of the charts, *What Now My Love*. The Beatles, in support of their tour, were flying up the album charts with their new album, *Yesterday ... and Today*, while their last long-player, *Rubber Soul*, was still selling strong. And the *Star Trek* cast and crew were assembling to make another sci-fi classic.

Filming of "Charlie X" began immediately after lunch on Monday, July 11. The company had just completed "The Naked Time." Director Marc Daniels turned cast and crew over to Lawrence Dobkin, who stayed on Stage 9 and broke ground in sickbay with McCoy's physical exam of Charlie Evans. William Shatner, DeForest Kelley, and Robert Walker, Jr. were the only cast members needed on this short day, which concluded in Kirk's quarters with that man-to-man talk Roddenberry added to the script. Due to the late start, Dobkin was not held responsible for overtime with a 7 p.m. wrap (the actual "wrapping of the set" would extend the time-and-a-half pay to 7:20).

Day 2, Tuesday, July 12, saw the start of a major continuity mistake. In one of the ship's corridors, Charlie asks Kirk if he can tag along to the bridge. Kirk is wearing his regular uniform top. But seconds later as he and Charlie walk onto the bridge, Kirk is wearing his alternate tunic -- the one created for "The Enemy Within" to help differentiate between "good Kirk" and "bad Kirk." It was used during part of "Charlie X" to help convey the passing of time, as Charlie's attitude changes day by day. There is no real excuse for a blunder like this, but there are always reasons.

The corridor scene that was so crucially tied to the one on the bridge was to be filmed later on this same day, but Dobkin was falling behind and called for another 7 p.m. wrap, with the corridor sequences left undone. By the time he was able to get back to picking up the various unfinished scenes in the ship's corridors, it was a full week later -- Tuesday, July 19. The passing of so much time and the juggling of so many scenes, rethinking the schedule as they went along, resulted in the oversight. By the time the error was caught in editing, Robert Walker, Jr. was busy elsewhere and unable to return to reshoot the scene with Kirk in his proper uniform top. All that could be done was to hope no one would notice.

Day 3, Wednesday, saw the company still on the bridge. Shots taken this day included the climax where Kirk confronts Charlie and is sent to his knees in pain.

Eddie Paskey, as Shatner's lighting stand-in and usually present on the bridge as Lt. Leslie, recalled, "Part of a stand-in's job is to watch the actors as they rehearse their scene, seeing where they're gonna be going as they're delivering their lines. So we stand off camera and watch that rehearsal and then duplicate it while the main actors go and get their makeup freshened or study their lines. And then we take their place, standing in so that the cinematographer, his camera operator, the gaffer and his main electrician can work out the lighting set-ups and the camera moves.

NBC publicity photo of Eddie Paskey (Courtesy of Gerald Gurian)

"As I got to know Bill a little bit more, I saw that when he ended up on the ground in a fight or if he had some sort of pain going through him, you could almost depend on his face going to the camera for a full-on shot -- even though, when he rehearsed it, he didn't do it that way... because the camera hadn't been positioned yet. So George [Merhoff] and I, between the two of us, picked up on the fact that if he's gonna be down on his knees, in pain, that face is gonna go to the camera when it's shot. Sure enough, that's exactly what he did. Consequently, we'd try to second guess Bill so that he would get the best lighting he could.

And of course this made the shot go quicker, too, because they didn't have to change the lights in the middle of the scene and reshoot it." (135-2)

Paskey was appreciated by the lighting crew for helping come up with this time-saving innovation -- second guessing the series' lead. And the lighting crew rewarded him.

Typically, lighting crews merely ensure that a background extra like Paskey be visible, but gaffer George Merhoff went one step further. Paskey said, "George did a funny thing. After he had lit for what Bill was going to be doing, he would say, 'Eddie, where are you going to be in this scene?' I would show him and he would light me with a 'key light' and a 'back light,' which popped me out of the background. It was kinda neat because he didn't have to do that. I really respected him, and all the crew because you could see they all wanted to make the very best show that they could possibly make, and if I helped make their job easier as a stand-in, then all is well and good. But that was just his way of saying 'thanks.'" (135-2)

Day 3. Nimoy shows Shatner and Whitney where his eyes will be directed for an upcoming scene. Shatner believes the eye line for the ship's viewing screen should be lower (Courtesy of Gerald Gurian)

At the end of the scene, Charlie pleads for Kirk to not let the Thasians take him away, he wants to stay... stay... stay. By the time the last "stay" was spoken, it was 7:30 p.m.

Day 4 was spent in the recreation room filming, among other things, the chess game between Charlie and Spock, Charlie's efforts to impress Janice Rand with card tricks and Uhura's playful rendition of "Charlie Is My Darling." The wrap time, again, was late, at 7:30 p.m. Tired actors were dismissed to have their makeup removed. Tired crew began securing the set. It had

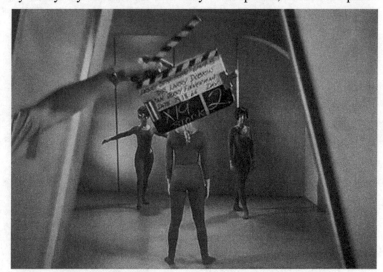

Day 6. A section of Stage 9 is converted into the ship's gym (Color image available at www.startrekhistory.com and www.startrekpropauthority.com)

been a 13-hour day by the time most left the studio.

Day 5, Friday, began in the transporter room for the teaser, and Charlie's innocent question, "Is that a girl?" Next up: Janice Rand's quarters where Charlie makes his "first crush" vanish and then uses his mental prowess to break Kirk's ribs and Spock's legs. Dobkin, meanwhile, was breaking the bank. He had fallen further behind in addition to wrapping later each day of production. Cast and crew were kept on stage this night filming until 7:45 p.m.

Day 6, Monday, took the company into the briefing room and the ship's gym for the scene where Kirk, stripped down to the waist, teaches Charlie the art of self-defense.

Mary Black recalled, "Bill [Shatner] was very at ease with himself other than that one time he had the attack of insecurity. I was on the set and there was a debate going on about whether or not Kirk should do the scene with the shirt on or off. And Roddenberry must have been away somewhere, so John was called to the set to help decide. Solow was there also, and he was the one who was engineering the discussion, trying to get Bill to do it without the shirt. Bill still had his top on and was talking about why Kirk would or wouldn't, and he turned to John and said, 'What's your opinion?' And John said, 'Well, let's see you do it with the shirt on.' And Bill did. 'Okay, now take the shirt off and let's see how it works.' And Bill took the shirt off and went through the moves again. And John decided to be a smart ass and he said, 'Let's do the audience a favor, Bill, and keep the shirt on.' Bill took it in good part and laughed." (17)

Shatner had been seen shirtless before, in "The Corbomite Maneuver" and "The Enemy Within," filmed more than a month earlier. But after two months of 13 hour workdays, less time to exercise and eating on the run, he had gained a few pounds. When posing,

Conflict on the set: Shatner preferring to keep his shirt on
(Courtesy of Gerald Gurian)

Solow wins – an unhappy Shatner strips to the waist
(NBC publicity photo)

230

and sucking in the gut, extra poundage can be hidden. Not so easily when doing an athletic scene.

After John Black left the set, Solow, determined that the viewing audience wanted to see the star bare-chested, even with an expanding mid-section, was able to reach Roddenberry by phone. Black's decision was overruled. The shirt came off and Shatner did the wrestling match with Charlie Evans, topless.

It was 7:08 p.m. when they stopped the roll.

Day 7 returned the company to the ship's corridors for scenes outside the brig. Other corridor scenes were shot, including one between Kirk and Charlie that Dobkin had failed to cover the previous Tuesday, cementing the continuity gaffe. The regular cast was then dismissed and the company moved back to the bridge, this time to film a camera tie-down shot of an empty wall, then Abraham Sofaer, whose wavering image would be superimposed before that wall. Dobkin didn't finish with Sofaer until 9:15 p.m. He was more than half a day late and, on all seven days of production, the studio lost a good chunk in overtime pay.

Dobkin later admitted that he was struggling with personal issues during the production. He said, "All the people in the cast were perturbed either by me or by the work. They had to be reassured by the producers that my personal problems of that period, the stress, weren't reflected in the film. And apparently they weren't." (49)

Robert Walker, Jr. was needed for all seven days. Grace Lee Whitney, struck by his devotion to creating and maintaining a character, remembered, "He wouldn't go near anybody while we were shooting because he didn't want to be friendly with us; he wanted to be 'method,' to stay in character even when he was *not* in character. I didn't understand it then, while we were doing it. You know, you never understand anything when you're doing it. But in hindsight, he didn't want to get close because Charlie was alienated from us." (183-6)

Whitney recalled, at the end of that last day, Walker did make it a point to let his fellow actors know how much he relished his time on *Star Trek* and how impressed he was with the caliber of work they had accomplished together.

"I thought he was excellent," Dorothy Fontana said. "He was a fine actor. A little old for it but he still looked young. When I saw the finished show, I thought, 'Gee, he did a really good job.' And he managed to pull off a lot of the things that were important to me." (64-2)

Lawrence Dobkin was struck by the entire cast. He later recalled, "The sense of cooperative effort was very, very strong. Shatner's ability to envision shots was evident even though he hadn't started directing yet." (49)

Despite the fond words, those "personal problems" Dobkin admitted to, and the resulting overtime, "Charlie X" was his only directing job on *Star Trek*. He did return, however, as an actor, playing Klingon Ambassador Kell, for "The Mind's Eye," an episode of *Star Trek: the Next Generation*.

Post-Production
July 20 through September 6, 1966.
Music Score recorded on August 29, 1966.

Fabien Tordjmann did the cutting -- his second *Star Trek* assignment, following "The Enemy Within." Among the notes Roddenberry gave after watching the first cut was to repeat the word "stay" in Charlie's final plea, adding reverb with each usage.

Fred Steiner scored his third episode of *Star Trek*. His work is exquisite. Of the 12 complete scores Steiner contributed to the series, "Charlie X" was his favorite.

Howard Anderson and Company struggled to supply the photo effects in a timely fashion. In fact, some were never completed.

Editor Tordjmann said, "The opticals would trickle in, but what we did was cut in the reactions to those effects that were still being completed, and when they came in we had to change very little." (176)

With "Charlie X" being needed as the second episode to air on NBC, there was no time to wait for some of the photographic effects. One that was passed over involved the cargo ship Antares, which the Enterprise sides up to. Even though it was called for in the script and is spoken of in Kirk's Captain's log, the Antares is a no show. A stock shot of the Enterprise was used instead.

Despite the overtime hours during filming, this "bottle show" only cost $177,941 ($1.3 million in 2013), coming in at $15,559 under the current Desilu per-episode allowance.

Release / Reaction
Premiere air date: 9/15/66. NBC repeat broadcast: 6/1/67.

NBC didn't want "Charlie X" to be the second episode to air but, other than the second pilot, "Where No Man Has Gone Before," which lacked several of the series' regular characters, there were no other episodes ready.

Three days before "Charlie X" aired, Stan Robertson wrote Roddenberry:

> "Charlie X" was, by anyone's standards, a most moving and memorable, sensitive portrait of a boy-man caught twixt never-never land of carefree puberty and responsible adulthood. It could just as easily have taken place in 1966 instead of the 200 years hence. I think that we are all in agreement that "Charlie X" was a class show but one which was at times slow and lacking in enough pace to sustain the interest of a large section of the audience. And, if our testing methods are of any value -- and we find that they are when evaluated in proper perspective – "Charlie X" suffered whenever we became involved in a long stretch of dialogue relating to Charlie's internal struggles to find himself, or whenever the members of our crew engaged in lengthy discussions attempting to understand him and his dilemma. (SR7-3)

Mixed reviewed from the TV critics seemed to support Robertson's assessment of this episode as having quality but being slow in pacing.

Syndicated columnist Steven H. Scheuer reviewed "Charlie X" for his column, *TV Key Previews*. Among the newspapers to carry his mostly positive words on September 15, 1966 was the *Lima News*, serving Lima, Ohio. Scheuer wrote:

> Space show addicts will get a second look at the elaborate starship Enterprise and its bewildering problems while researching life on other planets. This time the crew picks up a 17 year-old named Charlie, who spent 14 years alone on a strange planet -- the only one saved from the crash of his plane [sic]. How Charlie's innocence intrigues the crew until his more deadly talents emerge adds a puzzlement to the suspense in this moderately entertaining hour. Robert Walker Jr is quite convincing as Charlie.

Joan Crosby, for her *TV Scout* column, also reviewed "Charlie X." Among the newspapers printing her endorsement on September 15 was the *Free Lance Star*, serving Fredericksburg, Stafford, Spotsylvania, Orange, King George, and Culpeper regions in Virginia. Crosby wrote:

Following its sneak premiere episode of last week, *Star Trek* follows it up with another good episode, "Charlie X," with a good performance by Robert Walker as a young passenger who terrorizes the crew of the Enterprise.

The unnamed critic for the *TV Highlights*, carried in the *Milwaukee Journal*, out of Milwaukee, Wisconsin, on September 15, 1966, said:

> The Enterprise puts in [sic] at a raw, wild planet and picks up a nice young man who has been stranded there since birth, Charlie Evans (Robert Walker Jr.). But it turns out that Charlie is not such a darling after all when he suddenly displays the power to make things and people disappear. Some very good photographic tricks and the usual touch of weirdness tonight.

Canadian entertainment critic Don McLean, writing for the *Lethbridge Herald*, in Lethbridge, Alberta, voiced his opinion on September 16, 1966, saying:

> *Star Trek* is a wild combination of way-out mechanical advancement in space and it has a chance of high interest from the science fiction crowd. We've seen two episodes of this series so far and the difference in plots leads us to believe it has a good chance for success.

Jack Gould, of *The New York Times*, from his September 16, 1966 column, gave "Charlie X" a thumbs' down. He wrote:

> *Star Trek*, which NBC is presenting at 8:30 p.m. on Thursdays this season, makes it clear that life in space will probably be more traumatic than on Earth. A sick teenager who was never acquainted with terrestrial amenities ran amok last night on the master patrol ship. The accent was less on super-duper gadgetry usually associated with travel in the heavens than on astronautical soap opera that suffers from interminable flight drag. It was TV's first psychodrama in orbit.

Robertson had predicted "Charlie X" might start strong in the ratings but, unlike "The Man Trap," would lose many of its viewers before the hour had ended. The Nielsen overnight Trendex report (based on a national phone survey) seemed to prove him right.

RATINGS / Nielsen Trendex report for Thursday, Sept. 15, 1966:

8:30 - 9 p.m.:	Rating:	Share:
NBC: *Star Trek* (first half)	**19.1**	**35.9%**
ABC: *The Tammy Grimes Show*	11.9	22.4%
CBS: *My Three Sons*	19.2	36.0%
Local independent stations:	No data	5.7%
9 - 9:30 p.m.:		
NBC: *Star Trek* (second half)	12.3	22.8%
ABC: *Bewitched*	15.6	29.0%
CBS: *Thursday Night Movie*	**24.0**	**44.6%**
Local independent stations:	No data	3.6%

At 8:30 p.m., A.C. Nielsen shows that *Star Trek* was only one-tenth of a point under that of *My Three Sons*, a dead heat for the lead spot. At 9:00, *The CBS Thursday Night Movie* had the television premiere of *The Music Man*, starring Robert Preston and Shirley Jones, drawing nearly 45% of the America's TV households.

The Arbitron report (published in the September 19, 1966 issue of *Broadcast* magazine) placed *Star Trek* a little lower for the first half-hour, yet stronger for the second, very nearly tying with *Bewitched* for the second position.

RATINGS / Nielsen National report for Thursday, Sept. 15, 1966:

8:30 - 9 p.m.:	Rating:	Share:
NBC: *Star Trek* (first half)	**16.9**	**32%**
ABC: *The Tammy Grimes Show*	11.4	21%
CBS: *My Three Sons*	**18.1**	**34%**
Local independent stations:	No data	13%
9 - 9:30 p.m.:		
NBC: *Star Trek* (second half)	16.1	28%
ABC: *Bewitched*	16.6	29%
CBS: *Thursday Night Movie*	**20.7**	**36%**
Local independent stations:	No data	7%

According to this report, *Star Trek* delivered a hard blow to the season premiere of *Bewitched*. Just weeks earlier, *Bewitched* was ABC's highest-rated series and the seventh biggest audience grabber on television. Now with the airing of its first color episode, the National Arbitron rating service showed it missing the Top 20 altogether.

Was Robertson right that the audience numbers dropped at the half-way point of "Charlie X" because the episode lacked physical action, or was the shift in viewers a result of the CBS movie beginning at 9 O'clock?

But according to the October 16, 1966 issue of *The New York Times*, Nielsen's numbers showed that the 9 - 9:30 race was actually quite close. While *Star Trek* was faring better in cities than in rural areas, and while *Star Trek* still came in third, it had a much stronger 30% audience share. *Bewitched*, in second place, had 32%. And the margin for the big CBS movie, with 34%, was far more modest.

From the Mailbag:

Among the letters received the week after "Charlie X" first aired:

> Dear Mr. [sic] Fontana, I watched the first adventure you wrote called "Charlie X." I enjoyed it very much. It was real fantastic. I think *Star Trek* is even better than *Lost in Space*, because of the ideas and the special effects. I especially liked the way you wrote "Charlie X." I like the plot. Unsigned.

> Mr. Fontana, if it's not too much to ask, would you please send me a script [for] "Charlie X" so I can read it and study it, so in the future I can write scripts like you.... I am very interested in being a script writer. Carl W. (Chula Vista, California).

The reply to the latter letter:

> Dear Mr. W.: Thank you for your interest in *Star Trek*. I am, of course, very pleased you especially enjoyed "Charlie X." Unfortunately, the studio legal department does not allow us to send out scripts as samples. I would suggest, however, that you contact local universities which offer courses in television writing... or one of the local high schools which also have such courses in their night school classes.... I have enclosed for your information the publicity package made up on the show in the hope it will interest you. Sincerely, D.C. Fontana.

Two of many letters mailed in sharing the same sentiment:

> Dear Mr. Roddenberry... on Sept. 15 on *Star Trek*, a Negro girl sang a song to and about Mr. Spock. Due to the confusion at our house at the time, I was unable to catch all the words. Could you please send me the words to the song. Also, let's have more of Mr. Spock. He's sexy.... Thank you for your time & trouble." Pat S. (Northfield, Min).

> Dear Sir, I just love your new show - *Star Trek*! It's really Strasto!! (stratospheric!!). Last week, Sept. 15, a Yeoman sang a song about Spock. I loved it. Would you please send me the words. Thank you. Judy C. (Horseheeds, N.Y.)

The response sent to both Pat S. And Judy C.:

> Thank you for your letter[s]. We are naturally very pleased you enjoy *Star Trek*, and we hope you'll be able to come "aboard" often. Enclosed is a copy of the words of the song Nichelle Nichols sang on "Charlie X," as you requested. Sincerely, Gene Roddenberry, Executive Producer, *Star Trek*.

Memories

D.C. Fontana said, "I always liked that show. It felt really good for my first *Star Trek*." (64-2)

Grace Lee Whitney, in her book *The Longest Trek*, wrote, "['Charlie X' was] a beautiful episode -- gentle and sensitive in its treatment of a troubled, confused adolescent. When I opened the script for the first time, I was struck by what a tender, sensitive, yet powerful tale it was. The story wrings every emotion out of you -- fear, horror, sympathy, laughter. Seventeen-year-old Charlie Evans is easily the most frightening yet sympathetic character ever presented on television. To this day, it is one of my all-time favorites." (183-2)

Talking with this author, she added, "The whole first year of *Star Trek*, I believe, was made from the most fascinating scripts ever written. 'Charlie X,' I thought, was especially brilliant. But all of them -- all those scripts -- truly amazing." (183-6)

Lawrence Dobkin said, "Probably my best memory of *Star Trek* is all those people.... My god, what a talented bunch." (49)

Episode 8: BALANCE OF TERROR
Written by Paul Schneider
(with Gene Roddenberry, uncredited)
Directed by Vincent McEveety

TV CLOSE-UP GUIDE 7:30 ④⑥⑥ STAR TREK—Adventure

'Balance of Terror'

[COLOR] Responsibility weighs heavily on Captain Kirk, who must make a decision that could trigger a full-scale galactic war.

After a century of peace, the warlike Romulans have sent a powerful flagship to probe the earth's defenses. With three outposts already destroyed, Kirk knows that retreat will only invite further devastation. His alternative: counterattack.

Producer Gene Roddenberry created an abundance of special effects to heighten the visual impact of this episode. Vincent McEveety directed from a script by Paul Schneider. Kirk: William Shatner. Spock: Leonard Nimoy. McCoy: DeForest Kelley. (Rerun; 60 min.)

Guest Cast
Romulan Commander	Mark Lenard
Stiles	Paul Comi
Decius	Lawrence Montaigne
Centurion	John Warburton
Tomlinson	Stephen Mines

William Shatner

NBC press release, issued November 22, 1966:

> The USS Enterprise embarks on a fateful seek-and-destroy mission following a series of unprovoked attacks by the marauding flagship of an enemy power, in "Balance of Terror" on NBC Television Network's colorcast of *Star Trek*.... William Shatner and Leonard Nimoy co-star. Captain Kirk (Shatner) engages the hostile spacecraft in a furious mid-space battle but is forced to take quarter when the equally-powerful enemy, although suffering serious losses itself, inflicts heavy damage and injuries on the Enterprise. With most of their power and weaponry gone, Kirk and his wily adversary become locked in a suspenseful battle of wits as they maneuver for advantage. Mark Lenard portrays the commander of the enemy craft.

Complicating the matter for Kirk is that the Romulans have an uncanny resemblance to Vulcans. The Captain must now deal with issues of prejudice when one of his officers, navigator Lt. Stiles, suspects the half-human Spock of having split interests.

The theme involves an examination of bigotry, and how easily it spreads when one's enemy is different in appearance. Is it Man against Man ... or Man against Himself? Try both.

SOUND BITES

- *Kirk:* "I didn't quite hear that, Mister Stiles." *Stiles:* "Nothing, sir." *Kirk:* "Repeat it." *Stiles:* "I was suggesting Mister Spock can probably translate it for you." *Kirk:* "I assume you are complimenting Mister Spock on his ability to decode?" *Stiles:* "I wish I were sure, sir." *Kirk:* "Here's something you *can* be certain of, mister. Leave any bigotry in your quarters; there is no room for it on this bridge. Do I make myself clear?" *Stiles:* "You do, sir."

- *Dr. McCoy:* "Jim, attack begets attack; it doesn't stop war. Galactic war! Do you want that on your conscience?!"

ASSESSMENT

"Balance of Terror" offers thought-provoking entertainment, and two milestones for the series. This is our introduction to the Romulans, one of two recurring opponents of the Earth-led Federation (conceived to correspond to the enemies of 1966 America). This is also the first episode to deal directly with the issue of racial bigotry. In doing so, we learn more about Spock's background. Spock himself shares this information, saying, "If Romulans are an offshoot of my Vulcan blood, and I think this likely, then attack is even more imperative. Vulcan, like Earth, had its aggressive, colonizing period. Savage, even by Earth standards. If the Romulans retain this martial philosophy, then weakness is something we dare not show."

This episode provides a strong reminder of Roddenberry's inspiration for Kirk's character. Robert Justman said, "Captain Kirk was Hamlet, the flawed hero. Gene told me that, early on, he modeled him on Captain Horatio Hornblower and he had characteristics of Hamlet, who knows what he has to do but agonizes over it, *feels* -- as Hornblower did -- that he had to put on a brave front for the sake of his crew.... He wasn't strong enough, and yet he had to be strong because otherwise, they would have no one to protect them." (94-6)

The following passage of dialogue came from Roddenberry's script rewrite.

Kirk: "I look around that bridge and see the crew waiting for me to make the next move -- and, Bones, what if I'm wrong?" *McCoy:* "Captain..." *Kirk:* "I don't expect an answer, Bones." *McCoy:* "But I've got one. In this galaxy, there is a mathematical probability of three million Earth-type planets. And in all the universe, three million, million galaxies like this. But in all of that, and perhaps more, only one of each of us. Don't destroy the one named Kirk."

In a very subtle and effective way, "Balance of Terror" accomplished Roddenberry's aspiration to be the 1960s' equivalent to Jonathan Swift and to make commentary on current events through the actions of characters far in the future. One of the hottest disputes in 1966 involved the Demilitarized Zone dividing North and South Vietnam. The troops of North Vietnam continued to pour across the DMZ into the South, carrying out their military strikes, testing American defenses, then retreating to the safety of home. The actions of the Romulans in "Balance of Terror" were clearly designed to mimic the tactics of the Viet Cong of this era.

The episode is marred by a notable flaw: The Romulans speak English amongst themselves. NBC was not likely to agree to sub-titles, nor was there time or money to devise a language for the aliens.

THE STORY BEHIND THE STORY

Script Timeline
Paul Schneider's story outline, ST #18: April 14, 1966.
Schneider's revised story outlines, gratis: April 26 & 29, 1966.
Schneider's 1st Draft teleplay: May 20, 1966.
Schneider's 2nd Draft teleplay: June 3, 1966.
John D.F. Black's polish (Mimeo Department "Yellow Cover 1st Draft"):
June 21, 1966.
Black's script polish -- undesignated revised draft: July 2, 1966.
Gene Roddenberry's rewrite (Final Draft teleplay): July 14, 1966.
Roddenberry's second rewrite (Rev. Final Draft teleplay): July 18, 1966.
Additional page revisions by Roddenberry: July 19, 20, 21, 22 & 25, 1966.

Paul Schneider got his start writing *Mr. Magoo* cartoons. By 1966, at 42, he had numerous TV credits such as multiple episodes of *Bonanza* and Barbara Eden's first series, *How to Marry a Millionaire*. Roddenberry had hired Schneider to write a script for *The Lieutenant*. But science fiction was new terrain for the writer. It should come as little surprise then that Schneider's first *Star Trek* was a reworking of a non-science fiction property.

"Balance of Terror" is based on the 1957 movie *The Enemy Below*, in which the captain of an American destroyer (Robert Mitchum) pursues an elusive German submarine (with its skipper, played by Curd Jurgens). In that story, as the action alternates between the American ship and the U-boat, we get to know and respect both the captains who are very nearly equally matched and engaged in a deadly game of chess and we see the strain a prolonged encounter can take on the crew.

Roddenberry later said, "We had touched on that in ['The Corbomite Maneuver'] -- the conflicts that come from men confined together and in prolonged danger, as in submarine warfare. Then we added in the racial mistrust. The character elements came together without too much trouble. The problem was doing a war story [on a TV budget]." (145)

Schneider sent a note along with his first try at the epic sci-fi story outline, telling Roddenberry:

> It's long and full-blown, but I think it'll make a hell of a show. The only thing I feel uncertain about is the production areas. But I don't doubt that, if my concepts are too expensive, we can find ways around. Let me know. P.S. -- 31 pages means I enjoyed writing this one. Mostly. (PS8)

An outline is typically much shorter, but Schneider's enthusiasm led him to flesh the story out in greater detail and with added description. Roddenberry wasn't about to forward a 31-page treatment on to his overworked staff, or NBC, and wrote back to Schneider:

> We need a faster opening and a stronger hook. Suggest that we should already be somewhat mid-story, i.e. "tension on the bridge," as they seek a Romulan craft, which has violated the treaty and is somewhere out here in Earth's area of space.... Before we are more than a page or two into it, Kirk decides to go ahead with the wedding.... Then, as in the outline, just as they start to dress for the wedding, the enemy craft has been sighted. Teaser FADE-OUT. Now, opening ACT I, we can fill in more of the back story which otherwise would have slowed the teaser.... There are some very definite things we must do before sending to NBC. 1) Simplify much of the language. For example, in the dialogue there are a lot of words I can't even pronounce, much less understand. Also, we should make an effort to simplify some of our descriptions of weaponry, and force fields, and so on. These things are interesting and well-done, but they get awfully scientific and I think where

possible we'd be better off to use general descriptive phrases rather than science-fiction words – for example, instead of visual radar sweeps, we could much more simply say that the "bridge instruments register nothing out there yet." ... Not that any one description would foul us up, but the sum of it is a bit frightening – and leads to the next comment: 2) Let's come up with a clear-cut analysis of what the enemy ship can do and what our ship can do and devote an early paragraph to it, explaining in the simplest possible words. For example, I don't know if this is right, but we could state that the Enterprise has phaser weapons and the Romulan ship has these torpedo energy bolts; the Enterprise has one way of hiding, the enemy ship has another, etc. Also, when we get to the script, let's let the pictorial aspects of our story explain for us – in other words, an instrument lights up and begins to make an alerting sound and instead of getting into too many specifics of what it is and what it does, we simply have the man at the instrument inform the Captain that the enemy vessel is doing such and such, or is so far away, or whatever. Indicating this will work very well for us in the fact that I doubt if the motion picture audience in a submarine/destroyer tale really understands what sonar does and if the writer of that motion picture had had them talking about the technical aspects of it – and sonar does have its complexities too – the motion picture audience would have been lost.... It would be very interesting, and perhaps this is your intention, if we make it very clear that the Enterprise is out-weaponed by the enemy ship, but the problem of the enemy ship is that to use this terrific weapon means enormous expenditure of fuel. Thus, we get into a situation of Kirk guessing at the truth and taking huge risks to diminish the enemy's fuel supply, so that he finally gets the advantage. (GR8-1)

Roddenberry had Schneider tighten his outline, which the writer agreed to do at no charge, pruning 31 pages back to 23, with the new draft arriving on April 26. Roddenberry wrote to his staff:

There is an awful lot of production in this. This is Bob's area, and I'm sure he will have many comments. But I feel Paul has a fine action story here. If, as in *The Enemy Below*, this can be played primarily as a battle between Kirk and the commander of the other ship, we will have an excellent *Star Trek*. Certainly it gives a light on Kirk not shown in other stories we now have in work. Our main problem will be to cut down on all the production and concentrate on the men, if at all possible... cut down on the sci-fi technical and battle terms... keep it straight and simple -- a battle between two strong men of honor, each carrying out his duty, in which one must, sadly, lose. (GR8-2)

Robert Justman did as Roddenberry asked -- he looked the treatment over. Then he did as Roddenberry expected -- he got upset. Justman wrote back:

I must say that there are certain basic elements in this piece which will make it well-nigh impossible for us to produce it. Just the miniature and optical work alone can wipe us out. The physical special effects on board our ship and the other ship are an added burden to our costs. Also, we have a whole bunch of crewmen and principals on board the alien vessel.... They will all have to have extensive makeup time. This necessitates additional makeup personnel to handle same and also the cost of making all the additional ears to fit. It also entails haircuts, eyebrows, and the yellowish complexion. It also entails special wardrobe for these people.... Certainly the story itself is of classic proportions within the medium of film. But I must register strong objections to this project. It's a simple matter of just not being able to afford this kind of show. I hate to be negative, but I see no other way out. (RJ8-1)

To help save money and, at the same time, capture the feel of *The Enemy Below*,

Roddenberry and Schneider decided to give the Romulan ship the advantage of being elusive, as a submarine can be, and hatched the idea of the cloaking device. Matt Jefferies was thinking "submarine" as well when he submitted his set design -- the bridge of the enemy ship would be cramped and even have something resembling a periscope at its center.

To further capture the feel of a destroyer vs. submarine tale, Roddenberry and Schneider decided that in this episode the Enterprise's weaponry would be fired through a chain of command -- Kirk to helmsman, then passed on to the phaser control room -- just as a destroyer captain's orders would be relayed to an officer on the deck manning the depth charges. The Enterprise phasers are depicted here as energy blips instead of beams. The reason -- besides drawing another parallel, this time with that of a destroyer's depth charges -- is that Kirk has ordered the weapons be "set for proximity blast." In future episodes, the blips became photon torpedoes. Another nod to the destroyer/submarine parallel was to have the Romulans flush debris out of a weapons tube to simulate wreckage.

Another free rewrite from Schneider trimmed the outline further, and then Roddenberry sent this third draft to NBC. Stan Robertson responded, writing that "Balance of Terror" had "the potential of becoming an excellent action-adventure story." His letter continued:

> Since, in reality, this is a "war story," let's play it as one, utilizing all the cross-cutting, interwoven stories, mounting tension, battle scenes, camaraderie, human cameos, etc., which has been characteristic of the most successful of these types of dramas.... Let's not let the writer take the "easy way out" and turn this into a story in which the engagement between the two space ships becomes more dominant than the dramatic effects which they initiate. We all know that one of the major factors for *All Quiet on the Western Front* being considered a film classic is the effect and ravages of the war had on the people. More specific: we would suggest that you build in the story of the young people planning to be married in the midst of all this chaos. While some may consider this "corny," or in the vein of a "cliché," actually it is a very warm and human touch.... Interwoven with the scenes of battle and death, this love story should play well, particularly in view of the poignant twists at the end.... The relationship between our Captain Kirk and the captain of the alien ship should be played for all it is worth. The alien is a hero, just as much a hero and a dynamic man as is Kirk.... The point is very clear that, by enhancing our alien Captain and the courtesy and respect given him by Kirk, we are adding greater heroic proportion to our own star. (SR8-1)

Schneider turned in his first draft script on May 20. Four days later, Justman wrote John D.F. Black:

> This is a very exciting screenplay and was highly enjoyable for me to read, when I could forget my monetary problems. (RJ8-2)

Justman, being Justman, had several pages of notes regarding even a script that he found to be exciting and highly enjoyable to read. He told Black:

> In Scene 22, I find it hard to believe that Brenner [a character in this early version of the story] can put his hand on the wall and feel that the engines are putting out about half power. This is the U.S.S. Enterprise, not a ferryboat.... In Scene 25, Spock enters the Briefing Room. Where the hell was he at the beginning of this meeting?... On Page 25, for the first time we establish the interior of the Romulan Vessel and its occupants. Suggestion is hereby made that most of the Romulans wear helmets, which would appropriately mask the need for creating Spock-like ears. Certainly, we could get the parts for

Commander, Centurion and possibly Decius cast early enough, so that ear molds could be made. However, be quick to realize that this will involve a certain amount of money and fitting. (RJ8-2)

Despite monetary concerns, and a fair amount of nitpicking, the material and the handling of the Romulan Captain impressed Justman enough for him to add:

> I must say that the part of the Commander, as written, is unusually well developed. This is a very good characterization on the part of our author. (RJ8-2)

Schneider said, "It was a matter of developing a good Romanesque set of admirable antagonists that were worthy of Kirk. The Romulans [were] an extension of the Roman civilization, to the point of space travel." (154)

John D.F. Black said, "Paul was a known entity. When he came up with the Romulan characters, they were so wonderful -- I mean, they were full." (17)

Justman had another change he hoped to see before the script was developed further. He wrote:

> I suggest that before we submit this screenplay to NBC, we check over the "tag" sequence. As you know this is the burial sequence and might raise certain objections on the part of the Network to "Their ashes tendered full military honors." In any event... I think it would be nicer always when possible to end our show with a shot of the Enterprise zooming away into the distance as it heads toward next week's adventure and our beautiful original theme music swells up and grabs the hearts of one and all as they go back into the kitchen to get another can of beer. (RJ8-2)

Roddenberry agreed about dropping the scene (and perhaps the beer), but he liked ending the episode on a somber note, leading to the bookending scene that takes us back to where we started in the ship's chapel, as Kirk returns to console the bride-to-be, whose groom-to-be had perished in the conflict.

Roddenberry also wanted Schneider to find opportunities to reinforce the lead characters' personalities in the dialogue. He explained to the writer:

> The captain of the ship must maintain an image. To keep him from being stiff and lifeless and unlikeable, find ways in which the man "Jim" peeks out from behind the image. Three places in which this can be used: 1) when Kirk is alone or not being observed; 2) with McCoy -- he can level with the ship's doctor; 3) to some extent he can even talk to Spock because he respects Spock's intelligence, integrity, efficiency. Under enormous pressure, let Kirk slip and then he is sorry for letting it show.... We may want to show a little more on the nose the Captain's fatigue and agony at what they are doing. The lonely man in his stateroom -- possibly a McCoy-Kirk scene. Suggest playing this somewhere near script's middle, showing the Captain exhausted, heartsick, etc. Balance this against the hardness he must show on the bridge. Consider giving McCoy a point of view different from the Captain's since the doctor is a great humanist under his sharp surface. Articulate this in the Kirk-McCoy stateroom scene. (GR8-3)

Roddenberry could easily envision the scene -- he had written something very much like it once before, between Captain Pike and Dr. Boyce in "The Cage."

Schneider turned in his rewrite on June 3. Again, Justman was quick to do his job as the series' nuts-and-bolts producer, picking the script apart scene by scene, pointing out things that were too expensive and should therefore be dropped. He wrote John D.F. Black:

Scenes 50 & 60 will cost one million dollars for Anderson to shoot. Would you believe half a million? All kidding aside, it is scenes like this that cause me to say that this show is going to be immensely over budget. And that is after quite a bit of money saving on the part of you and Gene with regard to the story itself. This show just has money built into it and there is not too much that I can see that we can do about it at this time.... On Page 67, Scene 118, the Romulan ship is hit several times. Please take out any references to walls buckling. We have got enough effects and special construction in this as it is. The more I see of this show, the more I realize that it can bankrupt Desilu Studios all by itself. Just this one episode. (RJ8-3)

Roddenberry, impressed with the input from Justman, wrote back:

Agree with your comments almost completely. Want to try your hand at the script? (GR8-3)

Justman, who already had too much on his plate, declined. So Roddenberry had John Black do a polish. Of this, Black later said, "I remember that one was tough. We were dealing with the Romulans and the Spock relationship to them, and that was something that needed very special handling." (17-4)

After reading Black's script polish (the Mimeo Department Yellow Cover Draft from June 21), Stan Robertson wrote Roddenberry:

From a purely dramatic stand point, this may possibly be the classiest of the scripts we have received to date. It is very reminiscent of some of the classic "formulas" which have been guide points for those concerned with the art of creative writing, such as *The Enemy Below*. Particularly are the "humanistic aspects" of our protagonists, antagonists, and minor characters developed superbly in the script. The quality of Mr. Spock, Kirk's strength in the face of this quandary, the antagonism of Styles [sic] and his heroic death [he would live in the final draft], the warm "G.I. Joe" type relationship between the young crewmen and the scarred veteran [later dropped], and the poignant, bittersweet story of the newly-weds, are all excellent touches. (SR8-2)

Robertson did have critical notes, as well. His memo continued:

Our concern, Gene, as mentioned to you on the telephone today, does not at this stage involve the dramatic elements. They are all there. What we would question at this point would be the pacing and setting. 1) Pacing. Although this is a highly dramatic script, it appears that it is very slow in getting started and moving into the real meat of our story.... Again, as has been one of our continuing points of criticism, it seems as though the usage and interest in the gadgetry aboard the Enterprise stands in the way of story-telling. In short, our plot is made stationary [rather] than mobile at this point. 2) Setting. Another subject which has taken up a great deal of our discussions is our feeling that we do ourselves no good... by beginning each of our stories on board the Enterprise.... The need to move away from the ship as much as possible, doing stories which will be set on planets.... Since the action in this story takes place either on the Enterprise or on the Romulan spaceship, a suggestion would be that we begin our story with an attack by the Romulan vessel on station 4203. This would seem to us to serve several purposes. Among them would be that it would give us a different and exciting opening, which should be a great audience hook. Further, having this set up the Romulans, it would seem that what follows should be more powerful and meaningful. (SR8-2)

And then, as with the scripts to the seven episodes produced prior to this, Roddenberry did a rewrite of his own.

"Gene rewrote everything," said Justman. "But the original writers got the credit." (94-6)

Schneider appreciated the credit, but said, "It's painful to watch my stuff on TV. About the only thing I recognize is my name." (154)

One of the many changes Roddenberry made was with the dialogue Schneider wrote for that "Kirk-McCoy stateroom scene." As written, it was too obvious, with Kirk saying, "I'm a Starship Captain. This is a decision for diplomats, not one man! How can I decide if we risk starting a war -- risk millions of lives?" Roddenberry preferred the less direct approach, having Kirk tell McCoy, "I wish I was on a long sea voyage somewhere. Not too much deck tennis, no frantic dancing. And no responsibility." Then, after a pause, he asks, "Why me, Bones?"

Pre-Production
July 12-15 and July 18-19, 1966 (6 days prep).

Vincent McEveety was hired to direct. His resume included multiple episodes of *Rawhide*, *Branded*, and *Gunsmoke*. For the latter, he directed a whopping 45 episodes between 1965 and 1975. In 1959, he won the DGA Award (Directors Guild of America) for his direction of "The Scarface Mob," the pilot for *The Untouchables*. Roddenberry knew McEveety well -- he'd directed five episodes of *The Lieutenant*.

Regarding the preparation McEveety was given for this strange new series which hadn't even hit the air yet, he said, "They showed me the pilot, and I had a little advantage of seeing the sketches and some additional film they'd already shot with the miniature of the ship itself, and some effects that they had. They talked about it being like *The Enemy Below* while they were developing it, so that gave me a clear idea as to the approach. Other than technical aspects, the bridge of the space ship and one on a destroyer were not that different, any more than the enemy vessel and a submarine were that different. And racial bigotry is the same, whether it's a white military man in, say, Vietnam, not trusting a colleague of Asian descent or an Earth man not trusting a shipmate with pointed ears. It's the human aspects of the story that we relate to." (117-4)

Paul Comi, a prominent guest performer in this episode, considered McEveety to be "a very underrated director," adding, "He doesn't give you a whole lot of direction because he believes in you. He helps you find your own talent and gives you the confidence to find the answers within you." (35)

Comi, cast as Navigator Stiles, was 39. He worked often in TV, with multiple appearances on series such as *The Wild, Wild West, The Virginian, 12 O'clock High*, and *The Twilight Zone*. For the latter, he appeared in "People Are All Alike" with Susan Oliver (Vina, from "The Cage"). Prior to *Star Trek*, he played Deputy Johnny Evans for one season on the western *Two Faces West*. He had also worked for Gene Roddenberry, twice.

Paul Comi in "The Odyssey of Flight 33," one of three trips into *The Twilight Zone*

"Vincent McEveety was the one who called me in for that role," Comi said. "He had been an assistant director on an *Untouchables* episode I was in. Then directed me in an episode of *The Lieutenant*. He also cast me in a half-hour pilot Roddenberry had written ["Police Story"] as a somewhat retarded kid in a red cap who was working on the roofs of buildings and was mistaken for a shooter who also wore a red cap." (35-1)

McEveety also directed Comi in several episodes of *Rawhide* where the actor had a reoccurring role as a cowboy named Yo-Yo. The director knew that Comi had great range as a performer.

"It was McEveety who contacted my agent about doing *Star Trek*. But Roddenberry didn't think I would be right because he'd seen me play the retarded character. He said, 'I don't think he's strong enough to play Stiles.' And McEveety said, 'You don't know Paul.' So they arranged for me to meet Roddenberry. And he was really a lovely man. He was fantastic. We talked about writing, because I had written a sort of comedy super-hero script with a friend of mine from college. Roddenberry read it and told me he had never laughed so hard in his life. And that's how I got the job." (35-1)

John Warburton, Lawrence Montaigne (in helmet) and Mark Lenard (Unaired film trim courtesy of Gerald Gurian)

Mark Lenard was 41 when he stepped into *Star Trek* to play the Romulan Commander. Beginning in television in 1959 as a cast member in a pair of daytime soaps -- *Search for Tomorrow*, followed by *Another World* -- he soon moved into prime time for guest spots on numerous network series, often as villains.

McEveety said, "I liked Mark. He's a classic kind of heavy. He could do anything, I think, any kind of major heavy role, Shakespeare or anything like that. I think he was excellent for that part." (117-4)

This was the first of many *Star Trek*s for Lenard, even though the character he plays meets with a tragic but honorable end. He would appear next as Sarek in the classic second season entry, "Journey to Babel."

Lawrence Montaigne, playing the Romulan war hawk Decius, was 35. He worked often in front of the camera in character parts, and in much bigger parts than seen here. He was POW Hayes in charge of "Diversions" in *The Great Escape*. On TV series, he was featured well in episodes of *Dr. Kildare*, *The F.B.I.* and *The Fugitive*. He also appeared in "Cold Hands, Warm Heart," an episode of *The Outer Limits*, starring William Shatner and future *Star Trek* guest player Malachi Throne.

"When I went in for the audition with Roddenberry, I actually read for the part of the Commander," Montaigne recalled. "When I got home, my agent called and said, 'You didn't get the part, but they want you to play Decius.' Well, who the hell knew what that was? He says, 'He's the bad guy or something; but Mark Lenard is cast as the Commander.' Well,

Mark and I had just finished a show together and I thought it would be a lot of fun to work with Mark again, because he was a great guy. And that's why I took the smaller role -- because of Mark Lenard." (119a)

Montaigne would return to *Star Trek*, again wearing pointed ears, for the second season award-nominated "Amok Time."

Stephen Mines played Tomlinson, the weapons officer whose marriage is interrupted by the Romulan attack on an Earth outpost. He was a regular in a pair of daytime soaps right before this (*Paradise Bay* and *Days of Our Lives*) and a third (*As the World Turns*) immediately after.

Barbara Baldavin, the bride-to-be, would do better than her intended groom. She lived through the battle and returned to *Star Trek* in "Shore Leave" and "Turnabout Intruder." In real life, Baldavin was married to Joe D'Agosta, *Star Trek*'s head of casting.

D'Agosta said, "I never used my position to force her on anybody. In fact, just the opposite; I always resisted casting Barbara. But all of my producer and director friends, including Gene and Bruce [Geller], always encouraged me to hire her. All of these producers and directors seemed to have wives who were a little on the straight side, kinda just upright-types. Barbara was playful and sexy and fun. She was a guy's gal. So I'd make suggestions for parts, and they'd say, 'What about Barbara?' And I'd say, 'Look, are you sure you don't want to hire this one over here?' They'd say, 'No, let's just get Barbara.'

"She's held it against me to this day, saying, 'You always resisted hiring me!' And it's true, I suppose. It was always my producer friends who got her the jobs. In fact, Gene Roddenberry had a little crush on her. Just like mine with Sherry Jackson [who would appear in the upcoming 'What Are Little Girls Made Of?']." (43-4)

Sean Morgan, seen here as one of the crew members in the phaser control room, made his first of five appearances in *Star Trek*. He remembered, "Joe [D'Agosta] and his wife Barbara; we were all college mates together. I had done a whole bunch of stage work, as Joe had. So he had cast me in several shows he was working on, and *Star Trek* was just a natural thing to go in to." (120b)

John Warburton was 66 when he played The Centurion. His film and TV career spanned 1932 through 1978, including the hits *King Rat*, *Funny Girl*, and *Charlie Chan's Greatest Case*. On TV, he appeared 18 times on *Fireside Theatre* and dropped in eight times for *Judge Roy Bean*. The same year as his appearance in this *Star Trek*, he was featured

**Gary Walberg as Commander Hansen on Outpost 4
(Lincoln Enterprises film trim courtesy of Gerald Gurian)**

prominently in *The Wild Wild West* episode "The Night of the Brain."

Gary Walberg played the doomed officer on Outpost 4. The prolific actor had hundreds of TV and film credits spanning the 1950s, '60s, '70s, and '80s. Surrounding the filming of this episode of *Star Trek*, from 1965 through 1968, he was a regular on the primetime soap *Peyton Place* as Sgt. Edward Goddard. From 1970 through 1974, he played Speed, one of Oscar's and Felix's poker playing buddies on *The Odd Couple*, and, from 1976 through 1983, he appeared in 145 episodes of *Quincy, M.E.* as Lt. Frank Monahan.

McCoy continued to be well utilized by the writers. This was his seventh appearance in the series. His contract had been fulfilled. The next script to come down the chute had already been circulated to cast and crew and the character of McCoy was not present. DeForest Kelley, whose wife had said that seven episodes would pay the mortgage for a year, had no way of knowing if there would be seven more. Or even *one* more. They soon found there was no cause to worry.

Production Diary
Filmed July 20, 21, 22, 25, 26, 27 & 28 (1/2 day), 1966
(Planned as 6 day production; finished 1/2 day over; total cost: $236,150).

Frank Sinatra had the top selling record album in America with *Strangers in the Night*. At No. 2, The Beatles were breathing down Old Blue Eyes' neck with *Yesterday... and Today*. "Hanky Panky" by Tommy James and the Shondells remained the most played song on the radio. *The Red Skelton Hour* was normally the most watched Tuesday night TV show in the nation but, on this night, before the Wednesday morning production start on "Balance of Terror," the *Skelton Hour* was preempted by a variety special called "Hippodrome," where host "funny man" Woody Allen presented the dancing Kessler Twins, comedienne Libby Morris, a diversity of circus acts, including the aerialists Flying Armours, the motorcyclists Olaffs, magician Michael Allport and Jennifer, a boxing kangaroo, and, for the teenagers, vocal group Freddie and the Dreamers. On the news, and after a race riot in Cleveland, Ohio, Governor James Rhodes declared a state of emergency. And 50-year old Frank Sinatra, celebrating that top selling album, married 21-year old Mia Farrow. Oh, and American astronomer Carl Sagan turned 1000 billion seconds old.

For the second episode in a row, only Stage 9 was needed. New sets included the weapons room (a modification of engineering), a control room on the Earth outpost, the Romulan bridge, and a wedding chapel (a make-over of the briefing room).

Filming began Wednesday, July 20, 1966. The first four days, the company stayed on the bridge.

Paul Comi, present at the helm for this portion of the filming, expressed admiration of all three of *Star Trek*'s leads, saying, "My main impression of Leonard Nimoy was how serious he was. I almost got the feeling he already knew what was going to happen with *Star Trek*." (35)

Paul Comi, Eddie Paskey and George Takei
(Lincoln Enterprises film trim courtesy Gerald Gurian)

McEveety had the same impression, saying, "Leonard was a very good actor but, literally, no sense of humor. He was *always* in character. I got the impression he was always unhappy, too. I don't know why. I mean, once in a while he was pleasant, if the spirit moved him, but he couldn't just come on the set with a pleasant attitude. Bill [Shatner], on the other hand, always did, even though nobody would laugh at his jokes. He knew they weren't that funny, so he made fun of himself. It was that kind of thing. He's one of the few actors who may be full of himself -- because most of them are -- but has a sense of humor about it. You could tease him about it. And plenty of laughs… he's generally quite funny.

"I just think Bill's very enjoyable to work with and I liked him a lot. And yet when he got into character, he's as good as any actor around. Bill's a very, very, very good actor. And he's a gentleman; a total professional, there's no question about it. I never had any problem about that at all. And I think his best work, actually, with all the work I did with him over the years, was from *Star Trek*." (117-4)

Comi said, "William Shatner was much looser [than Nimoy]. He's very methodical in his acting style. His technique is visible when he acts, bringing a certain style to his work.... I was impressed with [DeForest Kelley's] portrayal of 'Bones.' His character is really one of the wonderful ones in *Star Trek*. The chemistry created by the three stars is attributable for much of *Star Trek*'s success. It was a brilliant job of casting." (35)

Grace Lee Whitney remembered this "bottle show" as being structured very much like a sci-fi stage play. She also acknowledged the importance of good chemistry between talented actors and the importance of a good captain. She said, "Bill was a rock. We bounced off him; everybody bounced off him. When I did a scene with Bill, I was compelled to be a good actor.… There was no way I could be bad if I was in a scene with Bill Shatner." (183-6)

McEveety shot until 6:50 the first day; 6:55 the second; 6:45 on the third. More than half the episode took place on the bridge. The company was on schedule.

Day 4, Monday, July 25. A few last shots on the bridge were taken, and then the company moved to the ship's chapel and phaser room. Sean Morgan, assigned to work in the phaser room, remembered his first impression of Stage 9, saying, "When I walked onto the set, I thought, 'My God, this is spectacular.' I mean, the size of it and all the gizmos and the flashing lights. At the time, it was really something. You did have a feeling -- at least I did, when I walked on there -- that I had somehow left Los Angeles, at least for a few hours, and I was somewhere else. You could obviously tell that there was a lot of money spent in comparison to what we were used to doing in television prior to that." (120b)

Barbara Baldavin knocked to the floor in the phaser control room
(Lincoln Enterprise film trim courtesy of Gerald Gurian)

Actors usually enjoy performing in death scenes. Stephen Mines, who played Tomlinson, had a different reaction, as the set filled with the colored gas that would take the life of his character. He said, "It was a terrible red powder that they fluffed into the air, and it damn near did kill me. It was very irritating and I could barely breathe. It stayed in my lungs for days afterward. It was probably something very innocuous, but I was coughing up pink and red stuff for a while." (119aa)

Camera rolled until 7:30.

Day 5, Tuesday. Filming took place in Kirk's quarters, the briefing room, sickbay and the ship's corridors. Also filmed, and still on Stage 9, was a section of the Enterprise dressed to appear as the blown apart communications center of Outpost 4. Jim Rugg gave the room a workout with plenty of sparks and smoke.

McEveety covered a great deal of ground, cutting camera at 7:20.

Day 6, Wednesday, July 27. The morning hours were spent filming in McCoy's office, and then the company moved to another section of Stage 9 where the Romulan bridge had been built.

Day 6. Romulans through "Coke bottle" lenses (Courtesy of Gerald Gurian)

Of the Romulan Bird-of-Prey's lighting and filming, Jerry Finnerman said, "Well, that was something. I have to tell you, when I left Warner Brothers, they gave me an old set of film filters that Ernie Haller had. Ernie Haller was a famous Cinematographer, like *Gone with the Wind* [and "Where No Man Has Gone Before"]. And you'd look through these filters and you couldn't see anything. Some of them looked like Coke bottles. I mean, they were curved and oblique.... And, on this particular episode, I put in so much color on the Klingons [sic] that I figured, 'Well, let's do something different; let's put these filters in.... And you'd look through the lens and you'd swear they were out of focus. But I knew Ernie Haller had used them, so they *couldn't* have been out of focus.... But they were pretty diffused. And it really gave it a weird look." (63-3)

Lawrence Montaigne, after playing the Romulan bad guy, said, "I'll be honest with you, most of us weren't overly excited about doing this. We had no idea what a *Star Trek* was. There was very little information available of what was going on. I was thinking, like, 'Oh God, I'm in a vacuum here.' But like I said, I was just happy to be working with Mark Lenard again." (119a)

Day 7, July 28, 1966. Work continued on the Romulan bridge. Production wrapped at 1:30 p.m., a half day over, but no one in the front office was complaining. Robert Justman said McEveety directed "Balance of Terror" with "great energy" and "style."

Post-Production
August 1 through December 5, 1966. Music score recorded on September 20, 1966.

Robert Swanson was back in the editor's chair with Team #1. He and his staff had cut the other *Star Trek* episode filmed to date, which required an abundance of interaction between actors and optical effects ("The Corbomite Maneuver," which The Anderson Company had yet to deliver).

Fred Steiner scored this, his fourth episode for the series, the same day as the music for "The Corbomite Maneuver." Steiner continued to conjure up memorable melodies creating a sense of tension, victory, defeat and, for the finale, sadness. And he continued to do all this while working blind, creating music to go along with images -- such as spaceships and plasma energy torpedoes -- that had yet to be seen.

Steiner also recorded a new version of the series theme song, to replace the more outer-spacey sounding one conducted by Alexander Courage. For this reboot, Steiner jettisoned the electric violin heard during the main title credits of "Where No Man Has Gone Before," "Mudd's Women," "The Enemy Within," "The Man Trap," "The Naked Time," "Charlie X," "What Are Little Girls Made Of?," "Dagger of the Mind," and "Miri," -- the first nine episodes to air on NBC -- in favor of a more traditional action-adventure arrangement, led by a prominent brass section. It would first be heard on "The Corbomite Maneuver," the tenth episode to broadcast over the network, as well as "Balance of Terror" and throughout the rest of the first season.

It was with "Balance of Terror" that Film Effects of Hollywood took over for The Howard Anderson Company as the primary supplier of photographic optical effects for *Star Trek*. The company had stepped in, without credit, to help out with "The Enemy Within" when Anderson fell behind. Now, with this episode, Film effects took the lead.

Linwood Dunn, the company's 62-year-old

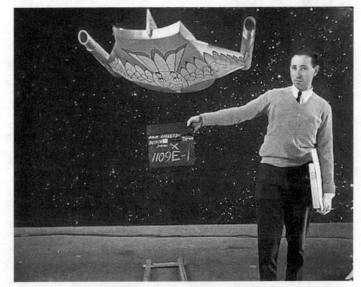

New frontiers in photo effects (Courtesy of Gerald Gurian)

owner, had shot optical photography for *King Kong* in 1933 and its much beloved 1949 bastard child, *Mighty Joe Young*. With offices on the RKO lot, Dunn was the man who filmed the famous RKO Pictures intro. Now those same offices were part of the Desilu studios complex and this allowed the 11-foot, 2-inch Enterprise to be shipped to Dunn whenever the Andersons weren't using it (his was the only other optical house to handle the valuable miniature).

The optical effects work is impressive for 1966. The new shots of the Enterprise moving through space surpassed anything yet provided by the Andersons. The Romulan Bird-of-Prey, debuting in this episode, was a detailed miniature, approximately a yard across, designed and built by Wah Chang over a two-week period. The miniature was delivered to

Film Effects to be painted and photographed. This, along with the weaponry fired by both the Romulan ship and the Enterprise, explosions in space and numerous viewing screen matte shots, catapulted the optical effects cost to $47,336 ($340,000 in 2013) -- higher than any other episode in the series. Just as worrisome to Robert Justman as the cash outlay was the time taken to create these effects.

On November 9, one month before the mandated NBC delivery date of "The Corbomite Maneuver," for which Justman had yet to see a single optical effect, he sent an anxious memo to his colleagues, pleading that the scripts be written to contain less need for optical photography. His warning:

> Right now I am concerned with making the Air Date on "Balance of Terror," which is supposed to air on December 15th, 1966. "Balance of Terror" finished shooting on July 28th, 1966. Need I say more?

"Balance of Terror" took over four months to clear post. Only "The Corbomite Maneuver" had taken longer -- a staggering five months.

With the new sets, and all those optical effects, the price tag for this episode far exceeded the studio allowance, topping off at $236,150 ($1.7 million in 2013). It was a hard hit, but all involved believed it a worthwhile expense ... except perhaps those who ran Desilu.

Release / Reaction
Premiere air date: 12/15/66. NBC repeat broadcast: 8/3/67.

Joan Crosby reviewed "Balance of Terror" for her syndicated entertainment column, *TV Scout*, on December 15, 1966. Among the newspapers to carry the review was the *Edwardsville Intelligencer,* in Edwardsville, Illinois. Crosby wrote:

> Viewers will find many modern-day parallels when watching tonight's drama. The weight of command lies heavily on Captain Kirk when he must decide whether or not to invade a neutral zone to fight a sometimes visible hostile spacecraft which has already destroyed some Earth outposts. It's an outer space version of the Cuban Missile crisis.

A.C. Nielsen wasn't interested in modern-day parallels, only nose counting.

RATINGS / Nielsen 30-Market report for Thursday, Dec. 15, 1966:

8:30 - 9 p.m., with 60% of U.S. TVs in use.	**Rating:**	**Share:**
NBC: *Star Trek* (first half)	16.8	28.0%
ABC: **The Dating Game**	**20.0**	**33.3%**
CBS: *My Three Sons*	16.3	27.2%
Local independent stations:	8.0	11.5%
9 - 9:30 p.m., with 62.7% of U.S. TVs in use.	**Rating:**	**Share:**
NBC: *Star Trek* (second half)	15.5	24.7%
ABC: **Bewitched**	**20.8**	**33.2%**
CBS: *Thursday Night Movie*	20.4	32.5%
Local independent stations:	7.9	9.6%

The Dating Game, having replaced *The Tammy Grimes Show* on ABC, was proving to be a prime-time hit, although its high ratings wouldn't last for long. *Star Trek*'s excellent "Balance of Terror" had to settle for second spot, a half a ratings point above the CBS staple *My Three Sons*. At 9:00, as ABC's top show, *Bewitched*, took the lead, CBS had the television premiere of the 1964 hit drama *Baby, the Rain Must Fall*, starring Steve McQueen,

Lee Remick and Don Murray. And this dropped *Star Trek* to third place.

When "Balance of Terror" came around for the second time on NBC, *TV Guide* awarded it the editor's pick -- a "CLOSE-UP" listing. Without McQueen on CBS this night, the Nielsens painted a much different picture.

RATINGS / Nielsen National report for Thursday, August 3, 1967:

8:30 - 9 p.m., with 42% of U.S. TVs in use.	Share:	Households:
NBC: *Star Trek* (first half)	32.0%	10,650,000
ABC: *Bewitched*	29.7%	8,620,000
CBS: *My Three Sons*	24.7%	7,300,000

9 - 9:30 p.m., with 47.5% of U.S. TVs in use.	Share:	Households:
NBC: *Star Trek* (second half)	31.6%	No data
ABC: *That Girl*	27.5%	No data
CBS: *Thursday Night Movie*	33.1%	No data

Star Trek won its time slot, against both its 8:30 p.m. competition and the 9 p.m. movie on CBS -- the television premiere of 1965's *Genghis Khan*, starring Omar Sharif in the title role, with Stephen Boyd, James Mason, Telly Savalas, and Eli Wallach.

During the summer months, with longer days, many American families on vacation and traveling, and the three U.S. networks filling their primetime schedules with repeats, the overall audience numbers were lower than during the other seasons of the year. Nonetheless, A.C. Nielsen estimated 10,650,000 households were watching *Star Trek* this week. On top of this, numerous trade sources (*Variety*, *The Hollywood Reporter*, and *Broadcasting* magazine) reported in the 1960s that *Star Trek* had an audience of roughly 20,000,000 people. These sources were estimating two people per household, and then factoring in Nielsen's estimate (to use this week as an example) of 10,650,000. These impressive numbers did not include families watching on NBC stations throughout Canada.

Vincent McEveety credited the success of "Balance of Terror" to strong characterizations -- particularly Kirk and the Romulan commander. He said, "They were very heroic characters pitted one against the other, and it dealt with the length to which people would go for their honor. It was a morality play, [and] terribly gripping." (117-1)

D.C. Fontana felt this was one of *Star Trek*'s "very best episodes," and Roddenberry placed it among his Top Ten.

From the Mailbag

Received December 12, 1966, the week following the premiere broadcast:

> Dear Mr. Roddenberry... Do you smoke Kools? I'm trying to because they help to sponsor *Star Trek*, but I must confess I do not care for menthol.... I shall watch repeats and re-runs so long as I am privileged to see them. When the day comes that the films are stored away, the only robbery I could ever seriously contemplate would be to rob those vaults to see even once again the beautiful, the vivid, the quixotic, chimerical *Star Trek*. Sincerely, Miss Sebie L.

Memories

John D.F. Black said, "Paul Schneider was a sweet man, and I liked his work. He was the father of the Romulans. Not Gene, not me, not anyone else -- but Paul Schneider. And when he came up with the Romulan characters, they were so wonderful -- I mean, they were full. I liked that script a lot." (17)

Stephen Mines, after dying in his first and only *Star Trek*, said, "When my son saw it, he said, 'What was Spock thinking? Why did he save that one jerk [Stiles] and leave you to die? Couldn't he have grabbed each of you under one arm?'? (119aa)

Lawrence Montaigne said, "I hadn't been watching it. My mother called and said, 'Hey, you're on television.' Well, I'll watch Mark Lenard read the phone book, so I switched it on. I was very pleased, I really was. I wasn't sure what *Star Trek* was about, but I remember it was enjoyable. And I thought I did an adequate job. But what I really liked was the interplay between me and Mark." (119a)

Mark Lenard said, "The Romulan Commander was one of the best roles I ever had on TV. At conventions, I used to say that the role of Spock's father [from 'Journey to Babel'] was the one I preferred because a big cheer would go up when I said that. I think it was because Sarek was part of the family. In many ways, I did enjoy that role, but I think the more demanding role and the better acting role was the Romulan Commander." (107-2)

Gene Roddenberry said, "That one worked very well. Mark Lenard did well, showing the different layers to that character. A man much like Kirk, but serving on the other side. The hardest thing about war [is] you're fighting for what you believe, fighting for your country, but so is the other guy. And one of you doesn't go home." (145)

Paul Comi, in 1990, recalled that, "I was teaching a class in acting at the University of Southern California recently and I was approached by a young man who told me how much he enjoyed my character on *Star Trek*. I mean, this kid could hardly have been born when 'Balance of Terror' was made. That amazes me." (35)

Pete Sloman, who covered this episode for De Forest Research, said, "I liked 'Balance of Terror.' I thought it was extremely well done. It was a rip-off of *The Enemy Below* – that sort of classic thing where you've got two guys trying to outwit one another – but I liked that one a lot." (158a)

Paul Schneider's final word from 1991: "['Balance of Terror'] holds up remarkably well." (154)

And Vincent McEveety's, from 2011: "That was another of my favorites. Wonderful writing. I like that show a lot." (117-4)

15

Episode 9: WHAT ARE LITTLE GIRLS MADE OF?
Written by Robert Bloch
(with Gene Roddenberry, uncredited)
Directed by James Goldstone

NBC's press release, September 28, 1966:

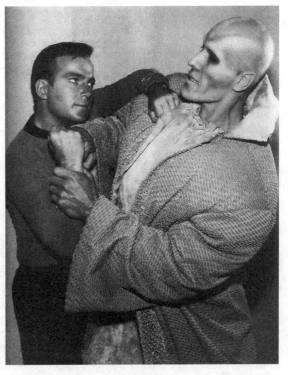

NBC publicity photo (Courtesy of Gerald Gurian)

> The search for a long-missing archaeologist leads the USS Enterprise to an underground colony of hostile and near-human robots, in "What Are Little Girls Made Of?" on NBC Television Network's colorcast of *Star Trek*, Thursday, Oct. 20.... Capt. James Kirk (William Shatner) locates scientist Roger Korby (Michael Strong) only to become a prisoner and guinea pig in a mad experiment to create a civilization of mechanical beings. Unable to cope with the unreasoning robots which Korby has at his command, Kirk realizes his only hope is Korby himself, but is stunned by a revelation about the long-lost scientist.

Korby's fiancée, ship's nurse Christine Chapel, must now decide where her true loyalties lie, with the man she loves or the Captain she serves under. To add to her confusion, Korby has manufactured a near perfect duplicate of Kirk... and a beautiful female android named Andrea.

The theme: the age-old battle of Man versus Machine ... and defining what is human.

SOUND BITES

- *Dr. Korby, about Andrea:* "Remarkable, isn't she? Notice the lifelike pigmentation, the variation in skin tones. The flesh has warmth. There's even a pulse, physical sensation..." *Nurse Chapel:* "How convenient." *Korby:* "You think I could love a machine?" *Chapel:* "Did you?"

- *Korby:* "Love can't exist at all when it's predictable. There must be imperfection -- moments to be lied to, worshiped, hated -- anger, fear. Andrea is incapable of that. She has no meaning for me. No emotional bond exists. She simply obeys orders."

- *Kirk, to his duplicate:* "Eating is a pleasure, sir. Unfortunately, one you will never know." *Kirk's duplicate:* "Perhaps. But I'll never starve, sir."

253

- *Korby:* "Can you imagine how life could be improved if we could do away with jealousy, greed, hate?" *Kirk:* "It can also be improved by eliminating love, tenderness, sentiment. The other side of the coin, Doctor."

ASSESSMENT

"What Are Little Girls Made Of?" is underrated. The writing is engaging, the direction stylish, the acting compelling. The photography and lighting combine together to create shadowy pictures textured and rich with drama. The sets, for their time, are impressive. And the theme -- that all-important statement -- rings clear as a bell. It speaks of what it is to be human and how our flesh is part of our being -- remove the biological elements in a person and the inner soul goes as cold as the arctic surface of Exo III.

We have a mad scientist. Korby says, "No one need ever die again! No disease, no deformities, even fear can be programmed away, replaced with joy! I sit here offering a practical heaven, a new paradise." But he is more than merely obsessed. He is less than human now, in denial and desperate to get back among the true living, and be accepted.

There are surprising and chilling moments. In one, the imposter Kirk tricks Nurse Chapel into divulging information about her loyalty. After she suggests that he eat something, he pushes a plate of food away and says, "Androids don't eat, Miss Chapel."

And there is tragedy. Korby had no choice but to trade his body for intellectual immortality. His flesh was dying. He chose to give up his physical being to preserve his mind. In the end, he pleads with Chapel, "It's still me, Christine. Roger. In this android frame... I'm the same as I was before... better... no death for me, ever. I'm the same! A direct transfer -- all of me! Wholly rational... human, but without a flaw!"

Even with all that works and all the effective elements, there are also some glaring omissions. Spock barely registers in this story. He is utilized less here than in any other episode. McCoy is absent -- for the first of only three times in the series. Scott, Sulu, Uhura and Rand are also missing. And our home in space, the Enterprise, is visited only briefly. There is no humor; there is no optimism. "Little Girls" may be classic drama, but the type that is often underappreciated: a tragedy. Add to this that the scenery -- with the exception of the shapely Sherry Jackson -- is cold and uninviting. At the end of the day, despite its plusses, less Spock, less McCoy, less Enterprise, and less hope, add up to ... less.

THE STORY BEHIND THE STORY

Script Timeline

Robert Bloch's story outline, ST #8: March 19, 1966.
Bloch's revised story outlines, gratis: March 28 & April 4, 1966.
Bloch's 1st Draft teleplay: April 12, 1966.
Bloch's Revised 1st Draft teleplay, gratis: April 26, 1966.
Bloch's 2nd Draft teleplay: May 6, 1966.
John D.F. Black's script polish (Mimeo Department "Yellow Cover 1st Draft"):
mid-May, 1966.
Black's second script polish ("Yellow Cover Rev. 1st Draft"): June 15, 1966.
Gene Roddenberry's rewrite (Final Draft teleplay): July 25, 1966.
Additional page revisions by Roddenberry: July 26, 1966.
Roddenberry's second rewrite (Rev. Final Draft teleplay): July 27, 1966.
Additional page revisions by Roddenberry:
July 30 & 31, Aug. 1 & 3, and Sept. 12, 1966.

Robert Bloch, a fan of author H.P. Lovecraft and the horror genre, had already, at age

49, written scores of short stories -- enough to fill 15 published volumes. He'd also written 11 novels, including *Psycho*, for which he won the Edgar Allan Poe Award and caught the eye of Alfred Hitchcock. Hitchcock, besides directing the famous movie based on Bloch's book, hired its writer to contribute scripts for *Alfred Hitchcock Presents*. Bloch also wrote for the macabre NBC series, *Thriller*, hosted by Boris Karloff.

Bloch attended a screening of "Where No Man Has Gone Before" at Desilu in March of 1966. He was intrigued by what he'd seen and, with his standing in the literary world, was immediately offered a chance to write for the series.

It may have been a case of "writer's Bloch," because the story Bloch pitched borrowed many elements from Lovecraft's 1936 novella, *At the Mountains of Madness*, among other stories. In *Madness*, explorers discover an ancient frozen city in the Antarctic built by aliens known as "Elder Things." As the exploration team goes deeper into the city of ice, they find underground caverns which lead them to learn the fate of "The Great Old Ones," who were killed off by the "Shoggoths," things they created to build the city and perform various tasks. Discovery turns to jeopardy when the explorers find that the Shoggoths still exist.

In Bloch's *Star Trek* story, the Antarctic was swapped out for an ancient glacial planet; the aliens known as "The Great Old Ones" were now merely "The Old Ones"; and the exploration team was now marooned scientists. The underground caverns remained but, instead of an ancient city, these catacombs housed ancient facilities with android-making equipment. Instead of Shoggoths, Bloch gave us Ruk, an android who, like the Shoggoths, killed off his makers.

The title came from the question and its answer found in an early 19th century nursery rhyme: "What are little girls made of? Sugar and spice and everything nice." However, the "people" we meet here, including the girl named Andrea, are made of very different ingredients.

Bloch was happy to be writing for *Star Trek*, just as Roddenberry was proud to have a writer of Bloch's stature. Bloch's pleasure was conveyed in the note he sent on March 19 accompanying his first try at a story outline. He cheerfully said:

> Crew to Captain: Mission accomplished -- I think. Standing by for further orders. Over. Robert Bloch. (RB9-1)

Bloch got further orders to revise his outline, twice, for no additional pay, before his captain felt comfortable sending it to NBC. The submission from Roddenberry to Stan Robertson came with an apologetic note, saying:

> This outline by Robert Bloch requires some revision but am sending it to you in this rough form since I'm anxious to get this particular writer to work before he accepts another assignment. (GR9-1)

It was a clear case of being more impressed by the writer than by the material. But how could Roddenberry ask someone of Bloch's stature to write a fourth draft of a story outline? At *Star Trek* -- as with all TV series -- the writer was only paid for the first draft of the outline, a pay rate set at $655. The second pay increment came when the writer was "advised to proceed to teleplay." That check was for $695, but Bloch had yet to receive this. That would require NBC's blessing.

Stan Robertson understood the importance of associating *Star Trek* with renowned authors of science fiction or its distant cousin, horror. His tempered reply said:

> We would again caution against the "too cerebral" approach. There appears, by this outline, to be a slight tendency to lean in that direction. (SR9-1)

The character of Margo -- later retooled as an Enterprise crew member and estranged fiancée of the missing Korby -- is portrayed as a wealthy woman who admired the scientist and therefore "hires" the Enterprise to go in search of him. Korby drugs Kirk with a glass of spiked wine, then makes an android replica of him, all done to keep the Captain from telling of the discoveries made of the android-making machine and its results -- the terrifying Ruk, the beautiful Andrea, and the somewhat average-looking Smith (later to be named Brown). When the fake Kirk beams to the ship, Spock's suspicions are aroused -- not because of anything the imposter says or does, but because he doesn't wear the phaser the real Kirk had beamed down with. In the end, Ruk is destroyed and Korby -- a flesh-and-blood mad scientist -- is mortally wounded in a fight with Kirk. Andrea, who is "feeling" upset that Korby was thinking of leaving with Margo, refuses to save him. Before dying, Korby pushes her and the duplicate Kirk into a force-field, causing them to disintegrate.

Even with the story in such an embryonic and seemingly unworkable state, Bloch received his orders to proceed to teleplay and was given that second check, for $695. Roddenberry also gave Bloch story notes. In an effort to strengthen characters and add more conflict, he wrote:

> You have more than a hint of past romance between Korby and Andrea. This is an excellent situation, productive of Margo-Andrea conflict, productive of Andrea motivations, etc. Do you see Korby as having sort of "programmed" Andrea to please? It's a lovely thought. (GR9-1)

Roddenberry also told Bloch that he and his staff were confused as to why Smith and Ruk were completely different types of beings. The solution: Make Ruk an android built by the Old Ones and Smith one that Korby built, made to look like a member of his team who had died. The beautiful and sexy Andrea needed no explaining. What man would not make an android to look like her?

Bloch, at this point, was still under the impression that writing for *Star Trek* would be quick, easy and fun. He jumped into the work, delivering his first draft script in only four days, on April 12, and, in doing so, picked up his third pay check -- this one for $1,800. That was the easy money -- a hefty check for a script that had merely been delivered; it had yet to be approved. The fourth and final increment -- this one for $1,350 - was the hard money. It wasn't paid until the delivery and *acceptance* of the writers' final draft (not to be confused with the producer's final draft, AKA the shooting script). If, in reading the writer's initial draft, it was felt that he had failed to properly and completely address any notes given regarding the story outline, he could be asked to revise it for free. If all went wrong, as it often did at *Star Trek*, this process of providing free script drafts could go on for a while, just as the process of providing free story outline drafts often did.

Robert Justman was the first to express his shock and disappointment over Bloch's script. His mammoth list of grievances to Roddenberry, in a memo that ran for several single-spaced pages, began:

> As you can see from the length of this memo, I am disturbed about this first draft screenplay.... [It] seems stilted and forced. The characterizations are cartoon and the dialogue does not make me happy at all. I feel that this script needs a good rewrite man. (RJ9-1)

Days later, Roddenberry hired himself a good rewrite man, adding John D.F. Black as a second associate producer for the series who would serve as "script doctor" for several episodes. But he had no intention of putting Black to work on this script, not yet. Robert Bloch's name was too great an asset for *Star Trek* to discard. Besides, John D.F. needed to start rewriting "Mudd's Women" while Roddenberry rewrote "The Corbomite Maneuver."

Roddenberry sent a memo to his two associate producers, candidly sharing:

> My feelings on the Robert Bloch script are rather mixed -- it seems a good craftsmanlike job but, at the same time, I feel that Bob has come nowhere near extracting and using the dramatics inherent in his basic story and characters. Even with skilled direction, it could easily become slow.... Although Bob's talent is obvious in this, I think it's up to us to challenge that talent into the more vigorous and suspenseful writing for which he is justly well known. (GR9-3)

Roddenberry then wrote to Robert Bloch. His challenge to the writer read, in part:

> Margo seems rather dumb about a lot of things. It seems to me she should be intelligent and aware. Kirk should not have to spend so much time answering questions which have obvious answers.... Margo does a lot of screaming and sobbing... the character should be made of stronger stuff.... Would the Enterprise be at the beck and call of an influential family? There should be a better reason for the Enterprise's trip and Margo aboard.... Can the wine glass and the drug potion business be eliminated? It seems so old, and it takes time, and Kirk can be disabled some other way. How about a fight with Ruk, which might put some action into this?... There ought to be something more significant about Kirk than the lack of a phaser pistol to indicate to Spock something is wrong. Perhaps his "lack of attitude"? (GR9-4)

Roddenberry's lengthy letter discussed how both Kirk and Dr. Korby came off "stilted," how Korby's motivation for abducting the Captain seemed unconvincing and confused, and how the Margo character, besides rather dumb, was devoid of believable motivation. He suggested:

> Let's consider what happens if Margo becomes Dr. Korby's wife. For one thing, it gives us a little better orchestration with Andrea. And it would give Margo strong proprietary interest in Korby and, I suspect, stronger emotion, suspicions and values to play.... Imagine any wife or flame, visiting her man who has been gone five years or so, finding a lovely young lab technician has been there with him all this time. Even though she later turns out to be an android, isn't it true that androids can be programmed for anything? An even darker and uglier suspicion -- since they are perfect in anything for which they are programmed, would a man want to take back a normally illogical, female-type wife with all her problems when he has had the satisfaction of a perfectly obedient creature? Or, perhaps he would; perhaps he has grown tired of perfection, but either way and <u>during all the stages of our story</u>, there would be some pretty exciting conflicts in it. And although the networks do protest that sex isn't really very important in life, they always seem most pleased when it becomes a source of story conflict. (GR9-4)

Bloch was asked to provide a free rewrite -- that TV industry freebie known as a Revised First Draft. He dropped off his second try at a teleplay six days later, on April 26. He included a note to Roddenberry, saying:

> Margo is now Mrs. Korby.... Ruk is still a golem because I feel we need him to illustrate to our audience the "blind" obedience type of android in contrast to the developed personalities of the other two. Also, he represents the physical side of Korby's menace.... I think you'll find Korby less stilted. (RB9-2)

As for Smith, he was now Brown -- still devoid of personality, intentionally so, but with a slightly less common name. Very slightly.

In a hurry to get something/anything in front of the cameras -- and it seemed like a race between "Little Girls" and "The Corbomite Maneuver" at this point -- Roddenberry had John D.F. Black send the script to NBC even though it clearly needed further rewriting.

Stan Robertson, in a backhanded compliment, wrote to Black:

> The first draft of this script was a vast improvement over the initial script of "The Corbomite Maneuver." Simply stated - things happened. People weren't waiting around for something to happen. (SR9-2)

In a different room at NBC Burbank, the feeling was less upbeat. Bloch was notorious for having written a 1962 episode of *Alfred Hitchcock Presents* -- "The Sorcerer's Apprentice" -- that was deemed by the series sponsor, Revlon, as "too gruesome" to air. CBS had to shelve the episode, with the network and studio, Universal, splitting the financial loss. NBC Broadcast Standards was determined this sort of thing would not happen on their watch.

Jon Kubichan and Jean Messerschmidt, two different arms of the network's B.S. (Broadcast Standards) Department, banded together, albeit in separate memos, sending multiple pages of concerns to Roddenberry and Black, including:

> Please avoid having Brown wear "a glassy grin" in death, and please also avoid other effects which might appear grotesque or shocking to the home viewer.... Caution on Kirk's use of the binding as a noose and Korby's subsequent choking, as this could be objectionable and must be handled correctly.... A general caution with regard to the embrace between Korby and Margo.... General cautions that the kisses throughout the script are kept within the bounds of television propriety. (BS9-1, 2 & 3)

John D.F. Black immediately wrote to Roddenberry:

> Gene: Have just received two pages of remarks on "What Are Little Girls Made Of?" from NBC. Holy Christ! Has anyone told them *Let's Pretend* has gone off the air? I have a feeling we'd better discuss this and lay hold of NBC in short order... by that I do not mean to imply "anything grotesque and shocking"... and, naturally, "embraces" are out. Gently and nicely yours, John D.F. (JDFB9)

Robert Bloch turned in his obligatory 2nd Draft on May 6. Justman, picking up on the ideas Roddenberry had contributed, wrote to John D.F. Black:

> On Pages 26, 28, 29 and 30, there are references by Korby and follow-ups by Andrea with regard to "pleasing" Captain Kirk. Disregarding my own personal opinion, may I play Devil's Advocate and raise the question of NBC's reaction to such a situation?... This is probably my shortest memo on the subject of the Robert Bloch story. I don't think it's because I have little fault to find with the script. It's just that it's Friday and I think I'm getting tired. (RJ9-3)

The question at this point was whether to have Robert Bloch do another free script polish or to hand the material off to another writer. Justman voiced his opinion to John D.F., saying:

> I recommend at least a dialogue re-write by someone else, because I still feel that the dialogue is stilted and unnatural. (RJ9-3)

And then the shit hit the fan. De Forest Research found similarities in Bloch's *Star Trek* story with three short stories he had written and sold to the genre periodical *Fantastic Adventures*. Bloch wasn't just borrowing from H.P. Lovecraft (which Kellam de Forest somehow missed), but he was also borrowing from himself, and from *Fantastic Adventures*, the holder of the copyrights. Numerous elements from his *Star Trek* script traced back to "Queen of Metal Men" from 1940, "Almost Human" from 1943, and "Comfort Me, My Robot" from 1954, the first being the most blatant. In that story, a scientific exploration team discovers a lost underground city beneath the ice, filled with machines and robots. They also encounter a beautiful young woman who, it turns out, is also a robot.

Roddenberry quickly wrote to Desilu Executive Herb Solow:

> [W]e're having some revisions done on the Bloch script. From the magazine stories sent you, I think it seems safe that Bloch could not be accused of stealing the story. At any rate, we intend to go ahead with the Bloch script as we are in need, unless we hear immediately to the contrary from you. (GR9-5)

A bigger problem came when Kellam de Forest discovered that the story for "What Are Little Girls Made Of?" also resembled a recent episode of *Voyage to the Bottom of the Sea*. His letter to Herb Solow said:

> There remains a danger and grounds for possible litigation in that Bloch's script and the *Voyage to the Bottom of the Sea* script contain similar elements, and these elements appear in the same order in both scripts. To avoid possible repercussions, one, preferably more, of the elements should be changed. (KDF9)

Solow compared the new script to the short stories, and to the script written for ABC's popular sci-fi show, then wrote Roddenberry:

> Gene, it is incumbent upon us to alter Robert Bloch's script along some important lines so as to avoid a lawsuit.... Though the Bloch stories do contain some of the elements in Bloch's script, the "important" elements of the script are not in the Bloch stories but are in the *Voyage to the Bottom of the Sea* script. Kellam's recommendation... some important factor in the Robert Bloch script be changed so as to importantly make a difference between the *Voyage* script.... [He] particularly recalls John Black's thought that perhaps the mad scientist can turn out to be an Android also. This, of course, would give a different twist to our show. (HS9)

That different twist, the big ending that made "What Are Little Girls Made Of?" pay off, had not been part of the story until now -- and was added only as a legal defense.

Since the solution was John D.F.'s idea, he was given the chore of adding it to the script, creating the "Yellow Cover First Draft" from mid May. Besides revealing Korby at the end of the story as an android, another change was made -- the character of Margo Korby became Nurse Christine Baker, who transfers aboard the Enterprise when she learns the ship will be patrolling in the area where her fiancé (Dr. Korby) was last known to be.

Stan Robertson's opinion about the material had now changed. He complained that the pacing of the script was slow, beginning with the teaser, which he told Roddenberry:

> ... needs to immediately grab the audience, establishing the fact that the Enterprise and our heroes are going on a mission which is not only a vital one, but one which will be hazardous.... We must establish jeopardy and conflict as soon as possible and keep our characters "moving" and "doing," rather than "sitting" and "discussing. (SR9-3)

Roddenberry had Black rework the script again and, as John D.F. had done when dealing with the other celebrated science fiction writers to visit *Star Trek*, he endeavored to honor the style of the story's original author. Beyond this, in his polish from June 15, 1966, the character of Christine Baker was changed to Christine Ducheaux, the same ship's nurse

Black had just written into his original script, "The Naked Time."

Roddenberry and Black had a falling out around this time regarding the former's rewrite of "The Naked Time." Roddenberry also felt Black had failed to sufficiently fix "What Are Little Girls Made Of?," still agreeing with Bob Justman that the script needed a "dialogue re-write by someone else." He therefore offered the "Little Girls" job to George Clayton Johnson, the writer of "The Man Trap."

Johnson recalled, "I was told that I should polish the script and improve the dialogue. So I started going through the Bloch script and, as far as I could see, there was nothing wrong with the dialogue -- it was very effective, it was strong, it was Dashiell Hammett.... So, I said to Gene, 'I'm sorry, but I can't do this the way you want to do it, because I would have to really take this thing apart and rebuild it.' And Gene said, 'No, no, no.'" (93-1)

Robert Bloch later said, "They called George in, asked him if he could make certain changes in it, and he flatly refused. He said, 'This is the script, it is cohesive, you can't tamper with it without absolutely altering everything in the story.' He said, 'Either you want this kind of story or you don't.'" (18-2)

Johnson added, "As a result, I got a demotion from being part of the team, from doing rewrites and polishes to being pushed back to just an outside writer." (93-1)

John D.F. Black, too, wanted the script left alone. He later said, "Robert Bloch is a writer with a phenomenal and enormous stature among science fiction writers. I respected him... I don't think I would have touched it. GR did." (17-4)

On July 25, just three days before the start of principal photography, Roddenberry turned in his first rewrite, calling it the Final Draft. On the afternoon of July 27, less than a day before filming was to start, he rewrote it again, now as a Revised Final Draft.

Roddenberry later said, "On a television schedule, when you have delivery dates, production dates, air dates, you don't often get the chance to put anything aside; to sleep on it.... Deadlines are what make you stop. It's not usually because you say 'this is as good as it can be.' It's because you run out of time." (145-12)

Among the changes: the further development of the female lead -- Nurse Christine Ducheaux. Majel Barrett had been eyeing this role for some time. Barrett said, "As the series was beginning to get organized, I got to look at all the scripts coming in. One of the first dozen was 'What Are Little Girls Made Of?' As I read it, I saw there was a character going out into space to search for her fiancé. By the time I'd finished the script, I was thinking, 'I can do this. I *know* I can do this.' So I went home and immediately bleached my hair. Next morning, I came into Gene's outer office and waited for him. When he got in, he walked by me, sort of half-smiled and grunted a 'hello.' But when he took a second look at me, he said, 'Majel?! Is that you?!' I said, 'Look, Gene, if I can fool you, I can surely fool NBC.' He said, 'Yeah, you're right.'" (10-3)

Roddenberry saw the character of the ship's nurse as being so selfless, kind and virtuous that she was quite nearly saintly, and he opted for a name change to Christine Chapel, a name play on the Sistine Chapel.

Roddenberry not only changed Christine Ducheaux to Christine Chapel in "Little Girls" but also in his rewrite of "The Naked Time," thereby establishing her as a recurring character. According to Herb Solow, when the network executives got their first glimpse of Nurse Chapel, NBC's Jerry Stanley yodeled, "Well, well -- look who's back." (161-3)

Robert Justman was not fond of the character of Chapel. At first, he blamed Barrett, believing her performance was at fault. Later, he realized that his problems had to do entirely with the writing. He explained, "Nurse Chapel was a wimpy, badly written, an ill-conceived character. In 'The Naked Time,' all she did was stand around and pine for Mister Spock, much the same as Yeoman Rand did for Captain Kirk. And, in 'Little Girls,' Nurse Chapel pined for her fiancé, mad scientist Dr. Korby." (94-8)

Even Barrett had issues with the character. She said, "I've never been a real aficionado of Nurse Chapel. I figured she was kind of weak and namby-pamby." (10-3)

Other changes Roddenberry made to the script involved the Third Act break -- the hook right before fading down and going to a commercial, often a cliff-hanger. Of this, he wrote Justman:

> You may note that the cliff hanger in the third act is a cliff hanger. You're welcome. (GR9-6)

Roddenberry had written the scene where Kirk hangs by his fingertips, dangling into the mouth of a bottomless pit, as the monstrous Ruk glares down.

Roddenberry continued to send in new pages, even as the episode filmed, telling Justman:

> Please note the following changes in the script affecting set items, not properly annotated on blue and pink pages because of late hour. Or maybe even green pages, I'm not sure at this moment. (GR9-6)

Gene Roddenberry had, without credit, rewritten nearly every script to film so far. The little joke in his last memo would soon be no joke at all. He was tired -- the type of tired that a good night's sleep will not take care of.

Pre-Production
July 20-22 and July 25-28, 1966 (6 ½ days prep).

Many of the recurring cast members had to sit this one out due to budget constraints. Before a single frame of film was shot, Justman categorized this episode as "intricate" and "difficult," two of the reasons why, as a favor to him and Roddenberry, director James Goldstone returned to *Star Trek*.

Goldstone, who directed the second pilot but had no desire to be associated with such a demanding series on a recurring basis, later said, "I got a panic call from Bobby Justman that whatever plans they had for the episode had turned into a big problem. Would I please help them out?... Largely out of affection for Gene and other people involved, I read the script. It was not like anything else I'd done, and it was not like the pilot in any way." (75-3)

Michael Strong, cast to play the tragic Dr. Korby, was 41. He was well acquainted with melodrama -- from 1957 through 1959, he was a regular on the daytime soap *The Edge of Night* and then in 1964 had a recurring role on *Peyton Place*. He worked often all around the dial

Michael Strong as Dr. Roger Korby

as a lead guest player, with multiple appearances on series such as *The Defenders* and *The*

Naked City. He'd also appeared in an episode of *The Lieutenant* where he made an impression on Roddenberry and Joe D'Agosta. In his future: a role in *Vanished*, a 1971 made-for-TV thriller, starring William Shatner.

Sherry Jackson, as Andrea, began working in front of the camera at age six. By the time she hit the ripe old age of seven, she had a recurring role as little Suzie Kettle in the popular *Ma and Pa Kettle* film series. Three years on at 10 she began a half-decade stint on *The Danny Thomas Show* as daughter Terry. Guest spots on TV shows such as *77 Sunset Strip*, *Lost in Space*, and *The Twilight Zone* followed. By the mid-1960s, she had blossomed and steamier roles were coming her way.

Joe D'Agosta met Jackson when he booked her for an episode of *The Lieutenant*. With her memorable 36-22-35 measurements, D'Agosta immediately thought to cast her here as Andrea, and later said, "I was madly in love with her. I never saw a figure like that in my life. And such a sweet face." (43-4)

Shatner with Sherry Jackson in NBC publicity photo (Courtesy of Gerald Gurian)

Sherry Jackson said, "I never thought anybody had a crush on me. I was very shy and never picked up the signals. I just couldn't believe that there were so many people that had crushes on me that I didn't even know. I didn't know anything about Joe D'Agosta having a crush on me. I never even picked up a cue. I just figured he was a happy man." (90-1)

Roddenberry was attracted to Jackson, too. And, again, she didn't pick up on the signals, but said, "I came in to see Gene Roddenberry several times before I got the part. I remember also the fittings of the costume, and meeting several times with him over that. He was a real perfectionist." (90-1)

And, as Roddenberry himself would admit, a bit of a flirt.

Ted Cassidy would be Ruk. Cassidy made his debut in front of the cameras in 1964 with two words: "You rang?" As Lurch, for TV's *The Addams Family*, the six-foot-nine former college basketball player gained national fame with those two syllables. When the series folded, Cassidy was immediately tapped to play a variety of off-beat and intimidating characters,

Ted Cassidy as Lurch in *The Addams Family* (ABC publicity photo)

including the slave to "The Thief from Outer Space" on *Lost in Space*. The Thief was none other than future *Star Trek* guest star Malachi Throne.

It was Robert Justman's idea to dress Cassidy in the long-flowing, heavily-padded outfit he wore. His memo on the subject stated:

> I still feel he [Ruk] should not be clad in a flesh-tight garment. A more voluminous getup will allow us to increase his size. (RJ9-3)

During the filming of this episode, Cassidy took time to provide the voice of the Bad Balok for "The Corbomite Maneuver." He would return to do the off-camera hissing for the Gorn in "Arena," and Roddenberry would cast Cassidy again, along with other *Star Trek* veterans, in a pair of 1970s pilots he wrote and produced: *Genesis II* and *Planet Earth*.

Majel Barrett may not have cared for the character of Chapel but her talents shine through with this performance, just as they did when she played Number One in "The Cage."

There were only three episodes of *Star Trek* to not feature Dr. McCoy. This was the first. The other two are "The Menagerie, Part 2" and "Errand of Mercy."

"I originally signed for seven out of 13 episodes," Kelley told *TV Star Parade* in 1967, "but Dr. McCoy was so popular they left him in and made me a regular. I just got lucky. The mail began to show a trend and my part was broadened." (98-11)

Stage 10 -- the planet stage -- needed substantial new set designs to create the caverns and the chambers to the underground complex seen in this episode. Dorothy Fontana recalled, "Matt Jefferies used to say that every week he had to build a new planet on Stage 10. It was true. Most of the time you really had to do some building in there and drag in dirt and drag out dirt, put down floors, and it really was a major thing just to design it, to build it and to then decorate it." (64-2)

Production Diary
Filmed July 28 (1/2 day) & 29, and August 1, 2, 3, 4, 5, 8 & 9 (1/2 day), 1966
(Planned as 6 day production, finishing 2 days over; total cost: $211,061).

Thursday, July 28, 1966, began a week where comedian Lenny Bruce died of a morphine overdose, and South Africa banned Beatles records due to John Lennon's infamous Jesus Christ statement. *Yesterday ... and Today* by The Beatles, nonetheless, was the top selling album. In the Bible Belt, some were buying the record just to burn it. "Wild Thing," by The Troggs, was the most played song on U.S. radio stations. *Batman* was not only a hit on TV but in the movie house where its big screen version, also starring Adam West and Burt Ward, was now the top box office attraction. Alfred Hitchcock's *Torn Curtain*, the previous week's No. 1

One can only wonder (and no one is talking) about the fashioning of the prop, and how it got past the censors

movie, came in second. Montgomery Clift, one of the top movie stars of the late 1940s and 1950s died of a heart attack. He was only 45. U.S. warplanes started bombing the demilitarized zone in Vietnam. And at Desilu Studios the *Star Trek* cast and crew embarked on a war of their own, called "What are Little Girls Made Of?"

Filming began immediately after lunch at 1:30 p.m., just as Gene Roddenberry was dropping his latest rewrite on Bob Justman's desk. Vincent McEveety had cast and crew finishing "Balance of Terror" in the morning, buying Roddenberry time to make his last-minute script changes. Now it was James Goldstone's turn to call the shots.

To help ease into what was expected to be a horrendous production, Goldstone spent this first day on Stage 9, filming the bridge. His last camera shot was taken at 7 p.m.

Day 2, Friday. More work on the bridge, followed by a move to the ship's corridors, then Kirk's quarters, and ending in the transporter room. The final shot here was Kirk and Christine Chapel beaming away to the planet. And all of this was done by 11:50 a.m.

While the cast took an early lunch, the production crew made the move to Stage 10 for what Matt Jefferies had envisioned as the caverns of Exo III. In an interview for fanzine *Inside Star Trek*, from 1968, while Jefferies was still building sets for the series, he said, "'What Are Little Girls Made Of?' was probably one of the toughest. It was a big set requiring a lot of tunnels and even a precipice of what was supposed to be rock, always a difficult material to reproduce."

Ted Cassidy (Ruk) joined the production this day as Goldstone filmed the scenes in the entranceway to the caverns -- that beam-down spot where Kirk loses his first red-shirted crewman, beginning a tradition on *Star Trek* of "wear red, you're dead." As the day progressed, filming pushed deeper into the cavernous sets, to the point where a second red-shirted crewman dies, thrown into a "bottomless" crevasse by Ruk.

Goldstone was a full day behind when he stopped filming at 7:04, more than 30 minutes into overtime.

Over the weekend, while cast and crew rested, Gene Roddenberry continued working, turning in another set of revised pages on Saturday, with more on Sunday and more still on Monday.

Day 3, Monday. At 8 a.m., work resumed on Stage 10. Kirk tumbled into the mouth of a bottomless pit for that cliffhanger Roddenberry was so

Day 3. Shatner and Barrett in the caverns Matt Jefferies built on Stage 10 (Courtesy of Gerald Gurian)

pleased with. Shatner did the stunt himself, hanging from a makeshift ledge. The crevasse, of course, wasn't bottomless; mattresses lined the stage floor several feet below the star in case he lost his grip. Work stopped a little past 7 p.m.

Day 4, Tuesday, began four days of filming on a set described as "Korby's study." Michael Strong and Sherry Jackson joined the production for the first of three-and-a-half days on set in Dr. Korby's underground study. They, as well as the other cast members, arrived that morning to find yet more script revisions. Roddenberry had turned in his final changes this day, both tightening and eliminating dialogue in an effort to help Goldstone catch up.

Sherry Jackson, recalling the challenges of being a sexy android, said, "To play that role, I had to really go within myself and say 'I'm half real and I'm half *not* real, but I have to appear real until a certain point in the story.' Each little nuance was very, very planned to create the role where I was slowly becoming human -- but not really knowing, and being confused. I worked hard in developing that character." (90)

Regarding the costume, Jackson said, "I was the one who designed the cut up the front of my pants leg so that it would elongate my legs. The three of us -- me, Gene and Bill Theiss -- designed the costume together. It was really an engineering feat. My body was the fulcrum, and those straps and everything was based on the fulcrum and everything worked off of that. So I had to let them know when it was too tight, when it hurt, when it was pulling too much, whatever. And then it was made out of stretch ski material -- the old fashion kind. Every day, at the end of the day, the straps would stretch out by about an inch, so Bill Theiss had to take them in. There were buttons on the back and he would shorten the straps to compensate for how they had stretched out." (90-1)

Jackson added, "Bill Theiss is a fantastic costumer. He came up with this concept of doing this crisscross deal, which meant I could not wear a bra because it would show in the back." (90)

At this time on network television, a woman could display a certain amount of cleavage in the front but no part of the breast could be seen

Untouched film with Shatner's body double (on right) before split screen effect (Courtesy of Gerald Gurian)

Rehearsal with director James Goldstone (on right), running lines with Shatner

And the composite shot, combining two separate camera takes of two Shatners (see "The Enemy Within" to read how this trick was achieved in 1966)

from the side or the underneath without fabric covering it. Jackson, with amused wonderment, said, "They had a censorship person on the set every day to make sure there was no side cleavage." (90)

Bill Theiss said, "I was prepared for and eagerly anticipated the storm over Sherry Jackson's costume.... There was a lot of noise and indignation about it at the time." (172-1 + 172-3)

To pacify the network Executive in Charge of Cleavage, Theiss used double-sided tape under the edges of the crisscrossing top to make certain that neither of Jackson's breasts peeked through. Taped up tight and under the watchful eye of NBC, Jackson strove to deliver the performance to which she had given so much thought. Of her acting, she admitted, "To overcome my costume was the *real* challenge." (90)

D'Agosta said, "I don't know if she was a great actress or not, but who cared? I just remember she was almost like a *Playboy* kind of interest, as Hugh Hefner would say, 'It's never just about the body, it's always more about the face.' But, yeah, of course the costume that Bill Theiss made for her didn't hurt." (43-4)

While all eyes on Sherry Jackson, her eyes were on nearly everything else. She said, "This was my second time doing a science fiction [after *Lost in Space*]. It was very, very interesting. I'm a very curious person, so I took in a lot of what was going on. I was always fascinated by the director, the camera, the lighting. For instance, I thought the set looked really tacky, but it photographed much better than it looked. That was the lighting. Jerry Finnerman was a brilliant cinematographer. So it was the lighting that made it work, because the set, when you were there in the middle of it, was just a bunch of cardboard. You didn't really get to see the controls when you watched it, but, up close, they were just black plastic things. Most of them didn't even move. And then the stalactites, oh my God, those were so phony. I mean, they look phony in the pictures now. There are pink. So imagine being there and seeing them!" (90-1)

By Friday, the seventh day of filming, with the company now in the underground corridors and into the "sleeping chamber," Goldstone was a day and a half behind.

All of Day 8 was spent on the sleeping chamber set, where Captain Kirk gets to kiss the first of many space babes (the attempted rape of Yeoman Rand by the Evil Kirk notwithstanding).

Sherry Jackson said, "I was a little nervous working with Shatner because I had heard that he was a New York actor from the theater, and I don't usually like actors like that, because often they don't translate well to the small screen. They do all this theatrical stuff. But the only theatrical thing that he really did was his voice. If you watch some of the episodes you'll see that he had learned diaphragmatic breathing. You'll see his diaphragms, which is near his navel, extending back and forth. Every time he would take a breath it would go out, and then come back in when he said his lines. From the side view it is kind of noticeable." (90-1)

Regarding the rest of the cast, Jackson said, "Michael Strong was also a New York actor. I don't know how I knew, but I could tell, because of how they used their voices. In the early days of theater, they didn't have any microphones, so they had to project their voices to the back roll. So that's how I could tell. But there was no attitude from him like many who came from the stage. He was all about doing his job; very professional; and he didn't have any airs about him. He was brilliant.

"Ted Cassidy was an absolute gentleman. I'd worry about him because I knew his heart was being strained all the time, and I knew that he would die an early death. It was hard for him to pick the people up and do those sorts of things. So I was really gentle with him. And he was a doll. He was very, very, very nice to me, and I really liked him a lot.

"Majel was professional, but she was kind of cool with me. I didn't know if that was because she was just being in character, or if that's the way she was. She didn't warm up to you, didn't try to, didn't say anything, just a cold person. Of course, she was involved with the producer, so she could do whatever she wanted. And their secret affair wasn't so secret. And then he was having another secret affair with Uhura. (laughing) He was a dirty old man, wasn't he? But he didn't do anything inappropriate with me in the costume fittings." (90-1)

Day 9. Celebrating the end of production. Note the penny--loafers on Shatner (Courtesy of Gerald Gurian)

An unprecedented ninth day of filming (eight full days, actually, spread over nine) was needed for the interior laboratory where Korby uses his android-making machine on Kirk. The NBC representative from Broadcast Standards stayed close by; this was the day Shatner lay on the spinning platform nearly naked, only his groin area covered by a part of the machinery. For this, as it had happened during the filming of "The Corbomite Maneuver," Shatner was subjected to a close shave. Sherry Jackson confided, "Mr. Roddenberry felt that Captain Kirk wouldn't be hairy." (90)

Jackson said that Shatner was not happy but remained professional and surrendered himself to the barber's razor.

Production wrapped at 12:25 p.m. Lunch was taken, followed by a move to Stage 9 to begin filming "Dagger of the Mind" under the direction of Vincent McEveety.

The filming of "Little Girls" took eight full days spread over nine and, including weekends, spanned a total of 13. No other episode in the series (excepting the pilot film) took as long. Goldstone was not blamed for the extra time or the cost overruns. Robert Justman's notes from the time of the production cited the problem as being a "bad script" which "GR rewrote as it was shot."

Even after production wrapped, the filming was not over. On September 1, as "Little Girls" was edited, Justman wrote to Greg Peters:

> We need an INSERT of Dr. Korby's body and Andrea's body in close embrace and the phaser pistol being fired. This means we shall have to get someone to fit into Dr. Korby's outfit and a girl to fit into Andrea's outfit.... It is important for us to get this shot, so that we can get this film together. (RJ9-4)

"This shot" was the moment when Korby pulls Andrea close, kisses her deeply and, during this embrace, presses on the trigger of the phaser weapon she holds between them. In the shot Goldstone had taken, as scripted, Korby does not press the trigger. The phaser fires accidentally when their bodies press together. Once again, an essential element in making this story pay off was an afterthought.

The close-up was needed ASAP, but the *Star Trek* sets had gone dark the day before and would stay that way for another two weeks during the Labor Day hiatus. Greg Peters anxiously waited until September 13, the first day of production on "The Conscience of the King," to get the vital two-second shot. Frank da Vinci, a background player in 44 episodes of *Star Trek* including the episode filming that day, wore Korby's outfit. Jeannie Malone, a bit player who appeared in the background of numerous *Star Trek*s, usually as a shapely Yeoman on the bridge, was the slender woman who squeezed into Andrea's getup.

Post-Production
August 10 through October 10, 1966. Music scored on September 20, 1966.

Frank Keller briefly joined the staff as the head of a fourth editing team. To help *Star Trek* catch up on its deliveries, Herb Solow overrode Desilu Post Production chief Bill Heath and allowed Justman, as a temporary emergency measure, to bring in the extra help.

In the cutting room, Keller was a big gun. Among his earlier credits were the pre-Emma Peel *Avengers* and a pair of Frank Sinatra movies: *Come Blow Your Horn* and *Pocketful of Miracles*, the latter earning him an Eddie nomination from the Film Editors Guild. Of his work here, the most impressive moment is the splicing involved in the sequence of shots that depict the spinning android-making machine.

The rewriting which continued through the production also continued through post-production. Additional Captain's Log entries and "wild track lines" -- dialogue that could be inserted into an audio track without requiring the addition of any new video material -- were added into several pages of the script, dated September 12. This is why Majel Barrett's voice, when Chapel tells the android Kirk to go ahead and eat his lunch, doesn't quite match in tone to her other lines from this scene, and why we only see her from the back when she says it. This line, along with a handful of others, was "looped" in during post.

Fred Steiner had a busy day on September 20, 1966 recording the scores for three episodes: "The Corbomite Maneuver," "Balance of Terror" and this, his fifth *Star Trek* assignment. "What Are Little Girls Made Of?" was actually considered to be a partial score, since Steiner utilized snatches of musical themes written by Alexander Courage. Of the new material, the charming "Andrea's Theme" would be successfully reused in "This Side of Paradise," while the menacing Ruk music, with its effective use of kettle drums, returned to great effect during moments of danger in many future episodes.

The Westheimer Company, with its second *Star Trek* assignment, tackled the optical effects. All views of the Enterprise and the planet as seen from space were stock shots. Transporter effects, matte shots and phaser blasts made up a good share of the new work. The biggest single effect, however, was a near-naked Kirk spinning on the android-making wheel. The tab for post effects came to $6,848.

By the time "What Are Little Girls Made Of?" was delivered to NBC, $211,061 had been spent. Three other episodes during this first season would cost more. "Balance of Terror," due to all the optical effects needed, was one. The others, to Bob Justman's horror, were yet to come. The first season deficit was now up to $19,432.

Release / Reaction

Premiere air date: 10/20/66. NBC repeat broadcast: 12/22/66.

Steven H. Scheuer reviewed "What Are Little Girls Made Of?" for his syndicated newspaper column, *TV Key Previews*. Among the papers to carry the review was the *Hartford Courant*, in Hartford, Connecticut. Scheuer wrote:

> Robots are all the thing this season and so Captain Kirk is up against them this time around. This is a well played production, with a good plot. Captain Kirk goes in search of long-missing scientist Roger Corby (Michael Strong). The search for this archeologist leads the Enterprise to Corby, only to find out that he is creating a master race of robots which Corby has at his command. He now thinks Kirk is just the thing he needs to add to his collection, so he takes Kirk prisoner. The android Ruk, incidentally, is played by Ted Cassidy, who lurched along to this role from his previous part as the butler on ABC's *The Addams Family*.

RATINGS / Nielsen 30-Market report for Thursday, October 20, 1966:

8:30 - 9 p.m., with 62.8% of U.S. TVs in use.	Rating:	Share:
NBC: *Star Trek* (first half)	17.3	27.5%
ABC: **The Dating Game**	**20.6**	**32.8%**
CBS: *My Three Sons*	17.7	28.2%
Local independent stations:	9.0	11.5%

9 -- 9:30 p.m., with 62.3% of U.S. TVs in use.	Rating:	Share:
NBC: *Star Trek* (second half)	18.4	29.5%
ABC: **Bewitched**	**19.7**	**31.6%**
CBS: *Thursday Night Movie*	18.2	29.2%
Local independent stations:	7.8	9.7%

At 8:30 p.m., ABC had the top spot with *The Dating Game*. The No. 2 position was too close to call with *My Three Sons* only a fraction of a ratings point above *Star Trek*. At 9 p.m., the situation reversed, with *Star Trek* besting the competition on CBS by an equally small margin and taking second place. The movie on CBS was the TV premiere of the 1960 drama *The Rat Race*, starring Tony Curtis and Debbie Reynolds.

From the Mailbox

Knowing that Roddenberry loved to tinker (in post-production as much as he did with the scripts), and aware of how desperately behind *Star Trek* was with its deliveries to NBC, Robert Justman sent his boss one last memo concerning this episode, on September 28, as he left for a short and well-deserved studio-mandated vacation to Hawaii. "RJ" wrote:

> Dear Gene: It is our intention to dub "Little Girls" next Monday, October 3, 1966. It is my intention that either you or Eddie Milkis should sit in on this dub. Please dub quickly and be willing to compromise. Hopefully, you will get this memo after I have left, so that no matter how mad you get at me for suggesting that you compromise more, you won't be able to do anything about it. Don't send me nasty wires. Remember, at this point in your career, you need me more than I need you. (RJ9-5)

Memories

Sherry Jackson fondly said, "Shatner was his sexy, charming self. If you'll notice when you're watching, when he's kissing me, and when we pull apart, not only is my lipstick off but my lips are swollen. He *really* kissed me!" (90)

16

Episode 10: DAGGER OF THE MIND
Written by Shimon Wincelberg (as S. Bar-David)
(with Gene Roddenberry, uncredited)
Directed by Vincent McEveety

NBC press release, issued October 17, 1966:

> An escapee from a penal colony on another planet triggers a USS Enterprise investigation of alleged maltreatment of prisoners, in "Dagger of the Mind" on NBC Television Network's colorcast of *Star Trek*, Thursday, Nov. 11.... The near-incoherent ramblings of Simon Van Gelder (Morgan Woodward), who secreted himself aboard the Enterprise in a cargo delivery from the prison, cannot be ignored by Captain James Kirk (William Shatner) despite his respect for the noted director of the colony, Dr. Tristan Adams (James Gregory). Accompanied by a medical aide, Dr. Helen Noel (Marianna Hill), Kirk goes inside the prison to learn the truth.

Marianna Hill as Dr. Helen Noel in NBC publicity photo (Courtesy of Gerald Gurian)

Once there, Kirk reluctantly begins to suspect that Adams, a renowned expert on the human mind, may have a new agenda of mind-control, which could push his staunch supporters, Kirk included, into madness.

This episode melds two recurring *Star Trek* themes: the threat posed by unintended consequences of science and technology and the corruption of power.

SOUND BITES

- *Mr. Spock:* "Interesting. You Earth people glorify organized violence for 40 centuries. But you imprison those who employ it privately." *Dr. McCoy:* "And, of course, your people found an answer." *Spock:* "We disposed with emotion, Doctor. Where there is no emotion, there is no motive for violence."

- *Simon Van Gelder:* "I want asylum." *Kirk:* "At gunpoint?"

- *Dr. Adams:* "May we never find space so vast, planets so cold, heart and mind so empty that we cannot fill them with love and warmth."

- *Kirk, to Dr. Adams:* "One of the advantages of being a captain, Doctor, is being able to ask for advice without necessarily having to take it."

- *McCoy:* "It's hard to believe that a man could die of loneliness." *Kirk:* "Not when you've sat in that room."

ASSESSMENT

"Dagger of the Mind" gives us a first look at the Vulcan mind-meld, which, like the Spock Neck Pinch, went on to become a fixture of the series.

While this may not make many fan's Top 10 lists of favorite *Star Trek* episodes, it is nonetheless well crafted, entertaining and delivers a thought-provoking statement at its conclusion regarding intolerable solitude. Adams is found dead, a classic depiction of the mad scientist who falls into his own torture machine. Dr. Helen Noel says, "The machine wasn't on high enough to kill." Having been subjected to Adams' neural neutralizer, Kirk has the answer. He tells her, "But he was alone. Can you imagine the mind emptied out by that thing... and without even a tormentor for company?"

THE STORY BEHIND THE STORY

Script Timeline

Shimon Wincelberg's story outline, ST #5: Mid March 1966.
Wincelberg's revised story outlines, gratis: March 30, 1966.
Wincelberg's 2nd Revised Story Outline, gratis: April 25, 1966.
Wincelberg's 3rd Revised Story Outline, gratis: May 2, 1966.
Wincelberg's 4th Revised Story Outline, gratis: May 9, 1966.
Wincelberg's 1st Draft teleplay: Early June 1966.
Wincelberg's 2nd Draft teleplay: June 23, 1966.
Wincelberg's script polish, gratis (Revised 2nd Draft): June 27, 1966.
John D.F. Black's polish (Mimeo Department "Yellow Cover 1st Draft"):
July 6, 1966.
Gene Roddenberry's rewrite ("Yellow Cover Revised 1st Draft"): July 22, 1966.
Additional page revisions by Roddenberry: July 30, 1966.
Roddenberry's second rewrite (Final Draft teleplay): July 31, 1966.
Additional page revisions by Roddenberry: August 2, 1966.
Roddenberry's third rewrite (Revised Final Draft teleplay): August 5, 1966.
Additional page revisions by Roddenberry: August 6, 8 & 9, 1966.

Shimon Wincelberg, 42, was a veteran of dozens of television series. He also wrote for the stage. One of his plays, *Kataki*, received rave reviews upon its opening in 1959. *The New York Daily News* called it "a powerful suspense play scented strongly with the sweet smell of success." *Time* magazine said that it "ticks with time-bomb suspense." And Radie Harris, in *The Hollywood Reporter*, wrote, "Hats off... to playwright Shimon Wincelberg."

Wincelberg was one of producer Irwin Allen's favorite TV scribes. He wrote "Jonah and the Whale," the second season kick-off episode of *Voyage to the Bottom of the Sea*, and could have been considered co-creator of *Lost in Space* had Allen wanted to share credit. Wincelberg wrote the pilot, which later had additional subplots added in and was expanded into five hour-long episodes launching and crash-landing the Jupiter II. He also wrote two additional early and formative episodes. Roddenberry knew him from *Have Gun -- Will Travel* where Wincelberg wrote nearly as many episodes as the former did. Roddenberry's tally was 24; Wincelberg: 22.

Wincelberg dropped by for the third screening of "Where No Man Has Gone Before" at Desilu on March 9 and was impressed. He was immediately invited to a pitch meeting. He remembered, "While I was waiting to meet Gene, his secretary [Dorothy Fontana] mentioned that some agents had the *nerve* to suggest writers who had worked for *Lost in Space*!" (186)

Roddenberry, desperate for writers who understood the needs of TV as well as science fiction, took Wincelberg's pitch, despite the *Lost in Space* connection. He liked the irony of a healer of mental illness becoming the transmitter of mental illness in his own right, through mind-control and psychological torture, and put Wincelberg on assignment. In fact, ST-5, "Dagger of the Mind," was the first story assigned after *Star Trek* emerged out of pilot mode. (The writing of "The Cage," "Where No Man Has Gone Before," "The Omega Glory" and "Mudd's Women" had all begun before the series was green-lighted.)

Wincelberg amused himself in coming up with the names for his characters. In his story outline, the head of the penal colony is Dr. Asgard. In Norse religion, Asgard translates to "enclosure of the gods" and was a place surrounded by walls where the gods lived. Dr. Asgard certainly thinks of himself as godlike, and he lives in a prison. One of the "reformed" inmates on Tantalus is named Lethe. She has clearly had her mind conditioned and selected memories suppressed by the not-so-good doctor's brain probe. In Greek mythology, Lethe is the "river of forgetfulness," one of the seven rivers that run through Hades.

Even the name of the penal colony has meaning. Again, the origin can be found in Greek mythology --Tantalus was the son of Zeus who, condemned for his crimes, was made to rule in the deepest part of the underworld, a place reserved for evildoers. Dr. Asgard, feeling unappreciated, believes he too has been condemned, and he rules in an underworld of his own making -- a mad house deep below the surface of Tantalus V.

The character name Simon Van Gelder had significance, as well. Shimon Wincelberg's daughter, author Bryna Kranzler, said, "Later on in his career, [my father] was somewhat less diplomatic, using a pseudonym for his work as well as naming villains in scripts after people who had pissed him off (though Dr. Van Gelder in 'Dagger of the Mind' was named after a family friend who told me at my father's funeral how honored he had been to have had his name be used for a character in the show. [My father] also had a murder committed, in another show, on Bryna Avenue, so that the studio would have to produce the street sign that I then got to keep. But his naming of villains didn't endear him to a lot of people in Hollywood." (103b)

Wincelberg also put great thought into the title he chose. "Dagger of the Mind" is from *Macbeth*. In Shakespeare's play, Macbeth is preparing to murder his king's children and thinks he sees a dagger in his hand then realizes it is only a figment of his imagination. His soliloquy, in part, reads: "Is this a dagger which I see before me?... I have thee not, and yet I see thee still. Art thou not, fatal vision, sensible to feeling as to sight? Or art thou but a dagger of the mind, a false creation proceeding from the heat-oppressed brain?"

The neural neutralizer is used to repress thoughts in the brains of its subjects, creating daggers in their minds and inflicting unbearable pain. The characters of Shakespeare are filled with self-torture, and so are those subjects of Dr. Asgard. This includes Kirk and his companion on the trip to the colony who, at this early stage in the development of the story, was Yeoman Janice Rand.

The story outline process was a long one. Wincelberg was paid for his first draft, then delivered four more drafts between late March and early May 1966 for no additional pay. Of the second try, Robert Justman wrote Roddenberry:

> I feel a tremendous discomfort trying to analyze this story outline. I think I'm being defeated by the mass of special effect type devices which may be cluttering up my understanding of the storyline. Now, if I'm getting cluttered up, perhaps others would too. Perhaps Shimon has let the science fiction technical aspects of *Star Trek*, or what he perhaps conceives to be *Star Trek*, supersede the value of straight dramatic instruction which he does so well. I don't think that

we're out to do "astounding science fiction" tales -- we're not a science fiction pulp magazine type show. (RJ10-1)

Indeed, Wincelberg's initial approach to the story had far greater science fiction flavor and certainly more sci-fi gimmicks than later versions. For instance, hypnosis is not used to access Van Gelder's inhibited mind as in later drafts, but instead the story outline calls for a "truth beam" device. Another device allows Asgard to look in on nightmarish things the inmates see in their "heat-oppressed minds," through a series of moving "pictures." One such picture brings to life the image of a girl about to be ravished by a monster.

Roddenberry sent Wincelberg a letter, telling him:

> The story needs simplification and straight-lining our pivotal character Asgard -- he, his past, his motivations, etc., must be built to be much stronger and more vividly believable.... There is no possible way to do this tale as presently indicated without going much over budget.... Suggestion -- eliminate practically all the special devices, except for a very simplified kind of "dagger of the mind" room in which we get our dramatic effect not out of strange devices so much as out of what they do to the characters in the room. (GR10-1)

Wincelberg ended up delivering four free rewrites of his story outline before Roddenberry felt that it -- that fifth draft -- was good enough to show to NBC. Of this, the network's Stan Robertson commented:

> In this storyline and in others received to date, it appears that we are leaning in a direction which could prove to give our stories a sameness which none of us want. One point is that possibly we are allowing too many of our "heavies" to fall into the area of "mad scientists," or those egomaniacs who seek to create a world to their own liking and tastes. It appears, at least from here, that these are the "expected heavies" one envisions when thinking of science fiction. Let's not fall into that trap! We'll leave that to those who have neither the originality nor the talents of you and your people. (SR10-1)

Robertson had just finished reading another *Star Trek* story with another mad scientist type -- Dr. Korby in "What Are Little Girls Made Of?" and, to a lesser degree, Professor Crater in "The Man Trap."

Robertson added:

> Another point is that we seem to be allowing a number of our stories to fall into the broad general realm in which things happen in the mind or the mental powers of our heroes, or their antagonists. This, too, seems to be one of the accepted devices of science fiction which may be overworked. (SR10-1)

Overall Robertson liked the story and approved having Wincelberg proceed to script.

Wincelberg's first draft teleplay hit the *Star Trek* offices in early June. Bob Justman sent Roddenberry a four-page memo dissecting the story, its plot points and character turns. After listing all that irked him -- and there was much -- Justman concluded:

> I'm sorry, Gene, but I detest most of the dialogue in this script and I find it difficult not to get very upset by it.... I know there is a germ of a good idea in this story. But that's all I feel we have with this screenplay. Just a germ of a good idea.... Please count to ten before you scream and come running in to disembowel me. I'm just a poor honest Associate Producer, and I call 'em as I see 'em. (RJ10-2)

Mary Stilwell, working as John D.F. Black's assistant (and later to become Mrs. John Black), had also given script notes. She recalled, "I read Shimon Wincelberg's first draft, and

I wrote up my comments, and it wasn't unusual for my comments to be a bit smart assed, indicating actual stuff that needed addressing but having a good time with it. Why not? They weren't meant for the writer to see – or anyone else, for that matter – only for John to see. One of the things I remember with my comments had to do with this character that had snuck on board the Enterprise and, after being captured, he was trying to kill himself by swallowing his own tongue. My comment was, 'I have been sitting here for the last ten minutes trying to swallow my own tongue, and it can't be done.' And that was the tone of practically everything I'd written with my notes. The meat of it was valid, but I didn't do it with a great deal of reverence.

"John was under time pressure and he said, 'I really haven't had time to read your notes; I'll look them over while in the meeting.' And he went into GR's office where Shimon Wincelberg was meeting with Gene." (17a)

John Black said, "Within a couple minutes of being in there, GR announces that he has to leave to go to a network meeting and he says, 'Ah what the hell, here's John's notes,' and he takes them out of my hand and passes them to Shimon Wincelberg." (17)

Black added, "He came into my office later and thanked me for being that frank and that honest. He told me I was right and went home to rewrite the story. Now that's not only a gentleman but that's an honest and dedicated writer." (17-4)

Wincelberg followed up with a letter to Black. On June 15, he wrote:

Dear JDFB – And here I thought, at last, an outlet for the moldering stacks of Noel Coward dialogue I've been keeping in the garage ever since "Have Gun" went under. Thanks for your notes, with all of which (almost) of course I agree. You have the knack, pitiably rare in your present calling, of knowing how to be brutal without being hostile. Which can only mean that, unlike the countless and forgotten others who have taken the great leap backwards, you still think of yourself as a writer. (Your inability to swallow your tongue, of course, is only another sad example of how the present generation of Americans has gone soft.) The rewrite is coming out so well, this time I not only won't apologize when I submit it, but I'll fight for every one of my brand-new, clean-cut, mathematically square, all American type jokes. (SW10-1)

Mary Black said, "Wincelberg took it in such good part, he sent a note, saying, 'You have a special capacity, John, for being brutal yet kind.' His response was so gentlemanlike and classy; I have to assume that he recognized that the notes respected the material even though they were flippant. I've had a handful of moments where I really was thrilled by the grace of someone in the business, and that was certainly one of them." (917a)

The following day, John D.F. Black wrote to Wincelberg:

Shimon… Received your note… And I thank you for maintaining a writer's perspective which, to my mind, allows for sometimes rough criticism without jumping to the conclusion that he is under attack when, in fact, it is his material under scrutiny. You are among the rarest of all birds, Shimon … a full grown man that writes. Again, I thank you … now write. JDFB (JDFB10)

Wincelberg's freebie Revised 1st Draft was delivered in early June. More notes came from all involved. Justman, regarding only one of more than a few dozen areas of contention, wrote:

Say that's a pretty clever routine with the junction box on Page 57…. Too bad that when Janice drops the piece of conduit across the power lines, only a few drops of metal are left. Janice is also an extremely capable character with her judo twists and quick-thinking. (RJ10-3)

At this stage in the script development, it was still Yeoman Janice Rand who accompanied Kirk to the penal colony.

Wincelberg turned in a 2nd Draft (June 23) and then a Revised 2nd Draft (June 27) before being told he had satisfactorily fulfilled his contract and was thereby given his final pay.

The script was still not considered good enough for NBC's eyes, however, and John D.F. Black did a polish -- the Yellow Cover First Draft version dated July 6 -- before sending it to the network.

NBC Broadcast Standards responded. Among the changes requested:

> Please try to find some other way for Van Gelder to subdue the crewman since the knee in the face would be considered brutal.... McCoy's injection of Van Gelder must not be shown on camera if a needle-type hypodermic is used.... Please delete the underlined in Janice's speech: "I'm a damned attractive female." (BS10-2)

Rodenberry did a rewrite of his own on July 22 -- his being designated as the Yellow Cover Revised 1st Draft. For this, the knee in the face was changed to a judo chop on the back of the neck. The injection was administered by McCoy's air-hypo. And Janice Rand's line about being a damn attractive female was stricken. Janice Rand was stricken as well and replaced by Dr. Helen Noel, a member of McCoy's medical staff.

Keeping with Wincelberg's playfulness in having hidden meaning behind the character's names, Roddenberry chose Noel, since we are told Kirk first met her at a Christmas party in the science lab ("Noel" being French for "Christmas"). Breaking with the gimmick, the bad doctor's name was changed when Bob Justman cautioned Roddenberry that some viewers might snicker at a name that brought to mind some form of backend protection. Asgard became Adams.

As for the removal of Yeoman Rand, the official reason was that the producers wanted to avoid showing Kirk becoming romantically and physically involved with her, thereby allowing the understated sexual tension between the characters to continue.

There were rumors on the set that suggested other reasons. Shatner's version: "Grace had become noticeably distracted, visibly ill and as a result her performances suffered terribly. By the time we were filming our tenth episode ['Dagger of the Mind'], Grace's condition had worsened to the point where her scenes were consciously being given to other characters or completely written out of the episodes." (156-8)

Whitney countered this, insisting, "Bob Justman, who was present when the decision was made to put Dr. Helen Noel in the place of Janice Rand, has told me that it was a creative decision, based on the needs of the storyline and the characters. It was *not* a reflection on me." (183-2)

Justman, somewhat guarded on the subject when interviewed for this book, nonetheless seemed to confirm Whitney's statement over that of Shatner's. He said, "I believe the removal of the character from any of the stories had to do with either the needs of the story -- and that would have come from Gene or John D.F. Black -- or for monetary concerns, which came from me, *constantly*." (94-1)

In this instance it was not a monetary issue, but Justman nonetheless had indirectly been the catalyst in getting Rand taken out and Noel instated. While reading one of the many drafts of this heavily rewritten script, he memo'd Roddenberry:

> On Page 39, I come to one of my more vehement objections to what I find in

this screenplay. My reaction to Page 39 and thereafter is that Kirk is an essentially stupid man for attempting to fool around with a machine that he knows nothing about. (RJ10-2)

It did seem foolish for Kirk to sit in the neural neutralizer chair and instruct a mere Yeoman to work the controls. However, with a trained medical professional at the switches and dials such as Dr. Helen Noel, the Captain's stupidity wasn't quite so blatant. It certainly made better sense that Kirk would request a specialist in psychology to accompany him to the penal colony. A Captain's Yeoman could hardly have provided him with the support, or given the story the conflict that this strong-willed female doctor could.

As for the suggestion Dr. Noel puts into Kirk's mind -- something left over from the last draft to feature Janice Rand, who secretly loves Kirk -- Justman wrote:

> We might have a slight censorship problem from NBC with regard to what fantasies Kirk imagines. (RJ10-2)

Roddenberry left the scene as written with Kirk carrying Noel to his quarters following the ship's Christmas festivities. Surprisingly, the only note NBC sent: "Avoid the open-mouth kiss." (BS10-2)

Grace Lee Whitney was not the only cast regular written into this script and then written out. Although it was nothing personal, Justman lost James Doohan a paycheck, too, telling Roddenberry:

> On Page 1, we establish Engineer Scott in the Transporter Room. We have a five-out-of-thirteen deal on Jimmy Doohan, and it costs us $850 every time we use him. For what he has to do in this story, we could get by with a bit actor in the Transporter Room, and the other place where he has a line could be given to someone else. (RJ10-2)

An important change to the script came about because of the memo from NBC's B.S. Department, one which would showcase Spock's telepathic abilities. In Wincelberg's earlier drafts, as well as John Black's script polish, there was little that was special about the interchange between McCoy, Spock, and Van Gelder in sickbay. Leonard Nimoy remembered his first look at the script, finding it to be a "dull, expository scene" in which Van Gelder gets interrogated at length. At one point, Van Gelder is hypnotized in order for McCoy and Spock to gain access to the secrets of his mind -- and it is Spock who does the hypnotizing. The Broadcast Standards Department was adamant that:

> In accordance with the precautions to avoid hypnotizing a viewer, the act of hypnotizing must be either out of context or done off-camera. Further, since you are portraying hypnotism as a legitimate medical tool, Van Gelder should be hypnotized by Dr. McCoy rather than Mr. Spock unless Mr. Spock can be established as being qualified in the use of this technique. (BS10-1)

To give Spock the needed qualification, Roddenberry came up with the Vulcan mind-meld -- something that would give Broadcast Standards no reason to fret about unintended effects on home viewers. Once again, an occasion when the difficult alliance between *Star Trek* and NBC brought about positive changes.

In all, Roddenberry did three substantial rewrites on the script, beginning with his July 22 Yellow Cover Revised 1st Draft, followed by the Final Draft from July 31 and the Revised Final Draft from August 5. He also contributed two sets of additional page revisions from August 8 and 9. With all the rewriting, it should come as no surprise that most of the words heard in the filmed episode were from Roddenberry's typewriter. The sharpness of both the dialogue and the characters are much to his credit.

One misstep, however, came about as a result of Roddenberry's hope for mankind. In the July 31 Final Draft, we get an explanation for Dr. Adams' illicit experimentation. In the only line of this explanation that survived, Adams says how he's been fortunate to have a pair such as Kirk and Van Gelder to experiment on. The lines that were to follow would have added greatly to the episode, if they had been allowed to stay. Kirk, being subjected to the neural neutralizer beam, blurts out, "For... what purpose, Doctor? I cannot understand a man of your... of your ..." He is unable to finish his sentence due to the pain from the neutralizer. Adams answers anyway, saying, "Of my reputation? Unfortunately, I have little else... except now, with this device, power. Power over minds and thus over everything that counts. The final great criterion.... And since I have it, I've decided to use it for myself... after all these years of doing things for others. Say I want a very comfortable old age... on my terms... and I am a most selective man." Kirk, struggling to remain conscious, yells back, "Unnecessary. Just... trust." Adams says, "Trust mankind to offer me my just reward? You're an optimist, Captain. In this work, I've learned too much about men's minds."

Roddenberry did not want this to be what lay in our future. He later admitted to this author that his hope for mankind was to overcome petty differences and emotions such as envy, jealousy, and greed. He would implement this idealism in *Star Trek: The Next Generation* during that series' first two years, until his health failed him and his replacements looked for ways to add in more conflict.

Roddenberry, of course, knew all about character conflict, as his internal memos repeatedly demonstrate, and he made certain the original *Star Trek* was filled to the brim with it. But he could not tolerate dialogue such as, "Trust mankind? You're an optimist, Captain. In this work, I've learned too much about men's minds." Under the gun, with filming of the episode already underway, he chose to strike the lines from his August 9 polish. The motivation behind Dr. Adams' actions, therefore, is never clearly presented.

***

Shimon Wincelberg had reason to think Roddenberry was enamored with his talent. After turning in his fourth draft script for "Dagger of the Mind," he was given a second assignment, and delivered two drafts of a story outline, "The Squaw." While awaiting verdict on "The Squaw," Wincelberg was put to work rewriting "The Galileo Seven," a problematic teleplay started by another writer. Then he saw Roddenberry's rewrite of "Dagger."

The bruised writer fired off a letter to Roddenberry, saying:

> Even though you have in many places improved the script, you have also [been] carried away by a healthy creative momentum [and] "improved" a lot of scenes which conceivably could have been left alone, if only to satisfy the poor writer's vanity.... [The] overall effect, on me, at least, is something of a morale-depressant.... [I] shall resume my labors on "Galileo" with hopefully undiminished enthusiasm as soon as I get my friendly neighborhood quack to Neural Neutralize the image of "Dagger" from my bleeding mind. (SW10-2)

Roddenberry scribbled across Wincelberg's letter two words: "F--k him!"

The sentiment was soon returned. A letter arrived from Ed Pearlstein, Desilu's legal aid. Wincelberg did not want to take credit -- or blame -- for the writing of "Dagger of the Mind." He had decided, instead, to use his pseudonym -- S. Bar-David.

"In those days, I was very stuffy about that sort of thing," he later said. "I had plays on Broadway and didn't want my name associated with lines of dialogue I wouldn't have written." (186)

As for the pseudonym, Wincelberg explained that Bar-David, in the Jewish culture, stood for "son of David," which he was, and the "S" was for "Shimon." (186)

The decision to use a pseudonym for his screen credit was a slap in the face to Roddenberry, especially since Wincelberg had allowed his real name to go on the screen more than once for *Lost in Space*.

Mary Black said, "We knew that GR was really upset about the pseudonym being used for the screen credit. I think he actually contacted the Guild and tried to fight it, although I don't know how he thought he could." (17a)

Roddenberry later said, "*Star Trek* gave a writer an opportunity to do something more [than other series at the time did]. Some were up to the challenge; others weren't. Some were threatened by it and would go back to *Lost in Space*." (145)

John D.F. Black said, "I thought his [Wincelberg's] title was one of the more artful and the concept was absolutely clean. If you think about it, it's really an intelligent concept and I wasn't sure it would work as *Trek*. But it got a little more 'commercial' as it went from first to second draft and, finally, [to] filmed episode." (17-4)

Pre-Production
July 2, August 1-5 and August 8, 1966, and August 9 for ½ day (7 ½ days prep).

Vincent McEveety, having pleased everyone with his handling of "Balance of Terror," returned to direct, and made suggestions for the casting.

James Gregory, hired to play Dr. Tristan Adams, was 54. A familiar face from television and film of this era, Gregory had been acting before the camera since 1948. He was a regular on a 1959 series *The Lawless Years* and appeared often on *Bonanza*, *Gunsmoke* and scores of others. He met Roddenberry on *The Lieutenant*, appearing in two episodes. Still in Gregory's future: his best known role, as the irascible Inspector Lugar in 49 episodes of *Barney Miller*.

Morgan Woodward, playing Dr. Simon Van Gelder, was 40. They loved him on TV westerns where he played a variety of dastardly characters, including eight on *Bonanza*, 12 on *Wagon Train* and 20 on *Gunsmoke*, usually working for his friend, director Vincent McEveety. Woodward was a regular on one of the many westerns he appeared in, with a supporting role as Deputy "Shotgun" Gibbs in *The Life and Legend of Wyatt* Earp from 1958 to 1961.

James Gregory in NBC publicity photo (Courtesy of Gerald Gurian)

McEveety said, "Morgan Woodward could play anything. The more demanding the role, the quicker I was to suggest him. He could play out of his head and you still wanted to like him. He got you to care. That's an actor." (117-4)

Marianna Hill in NBC publicity photo (Courtesy of Gerald Gurian)

Regarding the role, Woodward said, "When I heard a favorite director friend of mine wanted me, and when I read the script, I really wanted to do the part. I recognized it as a difficult part and, fortunately, my friend, the director, felt I could do it and I certainly wanted to show him I *could* do it." (192-2)

Marianna Hill, cast as Helen Noel, was 25. Hill had been on television since 1960, working prolifically, including a recurring role in Samuel Peeples' series *The Tall Man* and, with Leonard Nimoy, in "I, Robot," an episode of *The Outer Limits*. Justman knew her from an appearance on *Dr. Kildare*, one of the series he had worked on as an associate producer.

Production Diary
Filmed on August 9 (1/2 day), 10, 11, 12, 15, 16 & 17, 1966
(Planned as 6 day production; finished 1/2 day behind; total cost: $182,140).

Tuesday, August 9, 1966. CBS was the TV ratings winner the night before with Monday's three big series -- *The Lucy Show*, *The Andy Griffith Show*, and *I've Got a Secret*. The Lovin' Spoonful had the top radio song -- "Summer in the City," followed by "Lil' Red Riding Hood" by Sam the Sham & the Pharaohs. At No. 3, Napoleon XIV with the politically incorrect (before people used expressions like "politically incorrect") "They're Coming to Take Me Away, Ha-Haa!" The Beatles' *Yesterday ... and Today* album was in the middle of a six-week reign at No. 1. Lunar Orbiter 1 was launched by the United States. And Captain Kirk was leading the crew of *his* Enterprise on its tenth mission.

As with many episodes, filming began on the bridge set, allowing cast and crew to ease into the production. Work started at 1:30 p.m. after the completion of "What Are Little Girls Made Of," a lunch break and move from Stage 10 to 9. Director McEveety was allowed by the Desilu "timekeeper" to film until 7 p.m.. After wrapping the stage, the union crew had earned an hour of time-and-a-half pay.

Day 2. The majority of Wednesday was spent finishing scenes written for the bridge. Then the company moved to the transporter room. Only a few shots were taken before McEveety was asked to stop -- again at 7 p.m. sharp. Fortunately, he was on schedule.

Day 3, Thursday. Work in the transporter room continued as Simon Van Gelder sneaks aboard the Enterprise in a crate and knocks out the transporter chief with a judo chop. Next, to Spock's guarded amusement, Helen Noel makes the normally unflappable Kirk flappable with her flirtatious demeanor. Scenes in the corridors were then filmed, followed by a trip to Kirk's quarters for the soft focus fantasy sequence where the Captain carries Helen to his bed. A move to sickbay came next, with the camera rolling until 6:30 p.m.

Day 4, Friday. The morning hours in sickbay were spent filming Morgan Woodward's gut-wrenching performance. It took a day and a half to complete. He later said, "Vincent was terrific. He and his brother Bernie -- the McEveety brothers -- they were two of my favorite directors. I felt very comfortable with Vincent. I was hoping that if he thought I was going overboard that he would say, 'Whoa, whoa, whoa, calm down.' But he never did.

Afterwards, I came home and went to bed for a week. It took me a long time to get over all of that screaming and straining against the restraints. It was the most difficult part I ever did." (192-3)

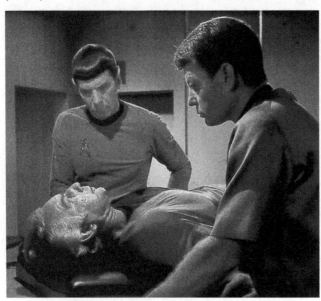

Day 4. Unaired shot from scene featuring Morgan Woodward (Courtesy of Gerald Gurian)

After a beaten Morgan Woodward left, the Tantalus main power chamber on Stage 9 was filmed, including a flash of an electrocution courtesy of special effects wizard Jim Rugg. The company moved to Stage 10 at 1:30 p.m. to begin the penal colony sequences including a scene Robert Justman was very much against. In one of his many memos concerning the script and the escalating cost of producing it, he wrote Roddenberry:

I strongly resent the fact that our people have to transport down on the exterior of the planet outside the prison for one-eighth of a page and we're never outside again and who can afford it? This would also call for a very expensive matte painting. Why can't they just transport down to the interior of Asgard's quarters and forget all the other chozzerai that occurs between the exterior and the first meeting with him? (RJ10-2)

Roddenberry liked the idea of showing the uninviting surface of the alien world, which explains why the penal colony is far underground. He knew Stan Robertson would like getting a glimpse of one of *Star Trek*'s "strange, new worlds" too, so the one-eighth page of "chozzerai" (studio Yiddish slang for "junk, stuff, expensive options") stayed. As for the expensive matte painting, a compromise was made. Albert Whitlock's stunning painting of the lithium-cracking station on Delta Vega from "Where No Man Has Gone Before" was recycled. A minor change was made, the upper level grid and towering tanks were airbrushed out, making the complex less industrial.

From here, Shatner and Hill stepped into the elevator, beginning Helen Noel's freefall into Kirk's arms. It was more chozzerai to Justman – an extra set to be built, another lighting and camera set-up. It was more excitement and sexual tension to Roddenberry. Roddenberry was right.

McEveety had covered a great deal of ground and was still on schedule when he took his last shot at 6:55 p.m.. The director and crew had found a comfortable rhythm, not exceeding 11 hours of filming on any of the days. Of course, even with an 11 hour shooting schedule, once prep time, including early morning makeup calls, wrapping set and stripping off makeup were factored in, many in the cast and crew had been at Desilu for 13 plus hours. And this was an easy day.

Day 5, Monday. On Stage 10, many of the sets used for "What Are Little Girls Made Of?" were modified for the underground Tantalus colony before being struck. The company filmed Dr. Adams' office and Kirk's guestroom, as well as Helen Noel's guestroom and, after Shatner departed for the day, Marianna Hill spent an hour crawling through the air ducts. By the time of her release, production had fallen a half day behind.

Day 7, Tuesday, August 17, began with filming the corridors of Tantalus, ending with sequences in the dreaded treatment room. Most of the day was spent in the latter set, this time with Shatner having to expose his inner torment from the effects of the neural neutralizer, and filming James Gregory's death scene. McEveety wrapped at 5:25 p.m., a half day behind, at which time the company made a fast move back to Stage 9 for retakes needed to finalize "The Naked Time."

McEveety was not blamed for running late. In Justman's production notes: "Too much material in script -- should have been trimmed." In other words, Gene Roddenberry was exhausted.

Post-Production
August 18 through October 24, 1966. Music score: Tracked.

Bruce Schoengarth and Editing Team #2 did the cutting. This was their third episode, following "Mudd's Women" and "The Naked Time."

Alexander Courage received credit for the score, even though no original music was written. For the first time in the series, the 50 minutes of edited film was augmented with "tracked music," combining various portions of scores for previous segments mixed with unused tracks by the various composers.

Music Editor Robert Raff said, "Gene Roddenberry and Robert Justman would sit in the projection room and ask me if we had material that would cover each episode. Looking at the picture we'd 'spot' the show each week. Gene was usually too busy, as I recall, so it was mostly Bob Justman and myself. The head of our music department would sit in, and the decision would be made whether we would track the show or score it." (143a)

Editor Bruce Schoengarth with Marianna Hill (Courtesy of Gerald Gurian)

When all the minutes of music were added up, Courage had composed the majority of the recycled score, constituting 51% or more, earning him the screen credit.

This was the third episode to feature optical effects supplied by the Westheimer Company. They were few and far between, since all shots of the Enterprise were harvested from the growing stockpile. And this was the final episode to feature Gene Roddenberry's name in the end credits as the sole producer. Another Gene, this one surnamed Coon, was already moving his personal items into one of the *Star Trek* offices.

By leveraging leftover sets from the previous episode and minimizing the need for optical effects, the tab for "Dagger of the Mind" was $182,140, several thousand dollars under the studio-mandated per-episode budget of $193,500.

Release / Reaction
Only NBC air date: 11/3/66.

Steven H. Scheuer reviewed "Dagger of the Mind" for his syndicated column, *TV Key Previews*. Among newspapers to carry the review on November 2, 1966, was *The News Journal*, serving Mansfield, Ohio. Scheuer wrote:

> This is an over-complicated but fairly interesting space age variation of the brainwashing theme. Captain Kirk finds his spaceship threatened by a violent escaped inmate from a penal colony on the planet Tantalus. Following the instincts of his top medical aide that foul play is afoot on Tantalus, Captain Kirk risks his sanity and his life to investigate the situation.

Joan Crosby reviewed the episode for her syndicated column *TV Scout*. Among the papers to carry her review, on November 3, 1966, was *The Monessen Valley* Independent, serving Monessen, Pennsylvania. Crosby wrote:

> A violent man comes aboard the Enterprise in a crate that is being transported from a penal colony run by Dr. Adams (James Gregory). Kirk, on advice of the ship's doctor, goes to the colony to investigate. While he and a psychiatrist (Marianna Hill) are there, the man on the spaceship keeps babbling about danger to Kirk and a horror machine called a "neural neutralizer." William Shatner comes through with another good dramatic performance tonight.

With "Dagger of the Mind," *Star Trek* won its time slot by a wide margin in the first Nielsen report based on a phone survey in numerous metropolitan areas.

RATINGS / Nielsen Trendex report for Thursday, November 3, 1966:

8:30 - 9 p.m.:		Rating:	Households:
NBC:	*Star Trek* (first half)	**24.3**	**13,340,000**
ABC:	*The Dating Game*	20.2	11,090,000
CBS:	*My Three Sons*	20.3	12,240,000

After a more detailed study of rural areas across America, a second report from Nielsen shifted the numbers in favor of the tastes of people living in smaller towns, putting *Star Trek* in a tie with *My Three Sons*, at No. 2, for the 8:30 to 9 p.m. spot.

RATINGS / Nielsen 30-Market report for Thursday, November 3, 1966:

8:30 - 9 p.m., with 63.5% of U.S. TVs in use.		Rating:	Share:
NBC:	*Star Trek* (first half)	17.5	27.6%
ABC:	**The Dating Game**	**20.2**	**31.8%**
CBS:	*My Three Sons*	17.5	27.6%
Local independent stations:		10.0	13.0%
9 - 9:30 p.m., with 64.5% of U.S. TVs in use.		**Rating:**	**Share:**
NBC:	*Star Trek* (second half)	16.6	25.7%
ABC:	**Bewitched**	**21.5**	**33.3%**
CBS:	*Thursday Night Movie*	18.7	29.0%
Local independent stations:		9.3	12.0%

The movie on CBS this night was Sidney Lumet's 1964 thriller *Fail-Safe*, starring Henry Fonda and Walter Matthau.

The shift in rankings makes it clear that those who lived in cities in the mid-1960s had a different perspective on the popularity of *Star Trek* than those in smaller communities; *Star Trek* was often the ratings-leader in major metropolitan areas.

Among those watching *Star Trek* in the cities was Morgan Woodward. He said, "When it first aired, I was watching and thought maybe I'd overdone it a bit. I'd done so many westerns and played so many villains, but never anything quite like this. Then my agent called and said, 'I didn't know you could do that!' I said, 'Well, I've been with you a few years, maybe you should pay more attention.' Vincent approved of everything I did and Gene Roddenberry liked it so much he nominated me for an Emmy with that performance. So I suppose my instincts were right in the first place." (192-3)

Grace Lee Whitney, who had read the Yellow Cover Draft of the script (which still included Yeoman Rand), and had been looking forward to filming this episode, remembered seeing the only network airing of "Dagger of the Mind." She said, "The hardest thing was to watch somebody else say my lines." (183-4)

"Dagger" was skipped over for a repeat showing on NBC.

From the Mailbag

Received shortly after the first broadcast:

> Dear Mr. Roddenberry: I know many *Star Trek* fans have probably asked about this but please make one exception. I would like to, along with two friends of mine who are just as crazy to be able to visit the set of *Star Trek* on a day of shooting, visit and be able to meet the cast and crew of the show! I know on a shooting day this is virtually impossible -- but I am a "fledgling" writer and I specialize in Science Fiction and am intrigued by your creation. Also, when it comes to *Star Trek*, boy do I get involved in the show. Mr. Shatner -- man am I crazy about him. I would like to meet you, Shatner, Nimoy -- I love his ears -- and see the set and meet others. Maybe you might even bother with letting me and my friends have lunch with the "stars" of the program. Please help me -- I've just got to see the set and I need help in writing sci-fiction!... Please let me know -- I'd really like to spend the day there and I wouldn't get in your way if I have a chair to sit in during the shooting. Thank you. Miss Gayle-Lynn G. (Sherman Oaks, California)

Memories

Despite the gut-wrenching performance he got from his friend Morgan Woodward, director McEveety said, "I don't remember liking that show a hell of a lot." (117-4)

In 2013, Woodward said, "My mind was made a vacuum by that Neural Neutralizer and I've never recovered." (192-3)

Aftermath

The 1998 *South Park* episode "Roger Ebert Should Lay Off the Fatty Foods" spoofed this episode. On a field trip to the local planetarium, the South Park kids are certain they will hate the experience until they watch the "star show." Suddenly they become planetarium enthusiasts, returning often and even volunteering to work there. The reason: The director of the planetarium -- *Dr. Adams* -- is brainwashing them with the star projector. School counselor Mr. Mackey (think McCoy) uses an ancient school counselor technique called a "mind meld" on a kid named Van Gelder, who had escaped from Dr. Adams. In a climactic showdown at the planetarium, the star projector is knocked over, resulting in Dr. Adams receiving a full blast of the mind controlling machine. With no one around to talk him through it, the evil doctor becomes a mindless shell.

17

Enter Gene L. Coon / "Miri"

"It is just impossible for one person to produce, write, and look over a show so extraordinarily complex as *Star Trek*," Roddenberry said. "What I became during the first half of the first year was full-time script rewriter, and you just cannot do that and, in addition, fulfill all producer functions." (145-9)

Roddenberry first called James Goldstone, director of "Where No Man Has Gone Before" and "What Are Little Girls Made Of?," who said, "Gene asked me if I would produce the series. I said, 'Gene, if I produced it, I'd have to *watch it*.'" (75-2)

The next invitation went to Sam Peeples, writer of "Where No Man Has Gone Before" and producer of the western series *Overland Trail* and *The Tall Man*, who later

Gene L. Coon, writer/producer

said, "I had to decline. I had two series of my own [in development] at 20th Century Fox -- *Custer* and *Lancer* -- so there was no way I could work with Gene." (136-3)

The third call went to Fred Freiberger. In Roddenberry's opinion, Freiberger had found the right mix for *The Wild, Wild West* one year earlier -- part western, part spy show and part science fiction. Freiberger later said, "I was going to Europe and I didn't want to cancel my trip. I told Gene that if the job was still available when I got back, in about six weeks, I'd love to do it. Well, it wasn't available." (68-4)

The fourth call went to another veteran of *The Wild, Wild West*. Robert Justman said, "Gene was fatigued and so was I. We both nearly didn't make it through the first season because of overwork. We were at our wit's end.... Honestly speaking, Gene Roddenberry would have died if he didn't have Gene Coon to do this." (94-7)

Gene L. Coon was born in Beatrice, Nebraska on January 7, 1924. After the family moved to Los Angeles, he attended Glendale Community College. In 1942, he enlisted in the United States Marine Corps and saw combat in the Pacific, then, after the war, he was stationed in occupied Japan and in China. Following his four-year hitch, Coon became a radio newsman and then a freelance writer, eventually relocating back to Los Angeles.

One of Coon's first credits as a screenwriter was 1957's *Man in the Shadows*, a contemporary western that starred Jeff Chandler and Orson Welles. That same year, he started writing for television with the Disney series *Zorro*. Script assignments soon followed for *Mr. Lucky*, *Bonanza*, *Wagon Train*, and countless others.

A prolific writer, Coon also squeezed in a couple of novels – 1962's *Meanwhile Back at the Front* and 1964's *The Short End (of the Stick)*, both dealing with the Korean War. Of the former, *The Los Angeles Herald-Examiner* raved, "First to give the Korean conflict the light touch [and] does so delightfully." *The Hollywood Reporter* felt it was "amply loaded with [enough] material for a hilarious motion picture." *The American News* said, "Author Coon has the best comic style since Hargrove." Marion Hargrove was well known for his popular humorous account of World War II, *See Here, Private Hargrove*. And *The New York Herald-Tribune* said:

> Gene Coon has everything going for him. Happily, he has sweetened his odds with the insight to recognize what was really going on, and the wit to express it pungently.

Coon also had a hand in the development of two hit series. The first was *McHale's Navy*, which was planned as a one-hour drama by Revue studios (soon to merge with Universal). The studio liked the concept but not the script. Coon had the idea to retool the show as a half-hour comedy. He was given credit for writing the pilot script and a second episode, but not for creating the series. The title and the general concept, although in a much different form, had already been in place, so that credit went to someone else.

When it premiered in October 1962, *McHale's Navy* was not only a hit in the ratings but with the critics. *Daily Variety* called it "an uproariously, zany, broad comedy with overtones of *Sgt. Bilko*." The trade's critic further noted:

> Gene L. Coon's sparkling teleplay provides a constant half-hour of laughs, not only in the situations but with its dialog which is far better than average.

The second series was also for Universal/Revue, designed to exploit the studio's *Frankenstein* movies by merging them with an unlikely source, another studio property, the long-running wholesome sitcom *The Donna Reed Show*. This outrageous idea was Coon's all the way, but his script was handed over to Bob Mosher and Joe Connelly, who had great success producing *Leave It to Beaver* for the studio. This time it was Coon's concept that got retooled and *The Munsters* was born. Coon was paid off and Mosher and Connelly took the "Created by" credit. Coon didn't seem terribly bothered. His passion was for writing, not producing.

"He loved to write," Coon's second wife Jackie Fernandez said. "He bounced out of bed in the morning at five or six o'clock, went straight to the writing room with his old beat up typewriter, and the cigarettes and pipes, and he just wrote his brains out until about 1:00. When he stopped, then *our* life took off. We just had fun for the rest of the day. I never once heard him complain about writing. It would have been unthinkable for him to be anything else but a writer." (60)

The studio did owe Coon a shot at producing, however, and assigned him to the 1964 midseason replacement series *Destry*, a one-hour western. When *Destry* failed to find an audience, Coon was imported to CBS to take the reins on its network-owned western-fantasy *The Wild, Wild West*, where he finished out the first season before being lured away from TV to write a pair of scripts for the big screen. One was for Warner Brothers -- *First to Fight*, about U.S. Marines in World War II -- and the other for Universal -- *The Killers*, where hit men played by Lee Marvin and Clu Gulager go gunning for Ronald Reagan, in his last film.

Back to working in television, the ever-prolific Coon tackled 11 script assignments in less than two years. These included a blending of comedy and science fiction for *My Favorite Martian*, an episode of *The F.B.I.*, six episodes of the hour-long western *Laredo*, and three poignant dramas for *Combat!*, including the gripping two-parter "Hills Are for Heroes," tautly directed by Leonard Nimoy's buddy and the series' star Vic Morrow.

"Coon was a sensitive, kind man -- once you got to know him well," Leonard Nimoy said. "But on the surface, he came across as a crusty James Cagney/Spencer Tracy type, the sort of guy you'd see cast as the tough 1940s newspaper editor." (128-3)

Robert Justman believed that Coon, based on appearance alone, would have made perfect casting for "the cold, cruel banker who forecloses on the widow's mortgage." From that first impression, Justman's gut feeling was *not* to like his new boss, something which early Justman-to-Coon memos indicate. But it didn't take long for that to change. Justman later admitted, "When I saw what he could write, I practically fell in love with the guy." (94-4)

John D.F. Black, whom Coon was to replace on *Star Trek*, only saw the "cold, cruel banker" side of the series' new "show runner." He said, "When I made it clear -- or when Mary and I made it clear -- that we were leaving, that's when Gene Coon was hired. He came in about three or four days before I left and I'm very glad he came in that late, because I really couldn't have handled him for two weeks." (17)

Concerning the changing of the guard, Mary Black added, "Gene Coon was clearly not burdened by undue sentimentality about the whole situation." (17a)

Dorothy Fontana saw a different Gene Coon entirely, saying, "Gene, no pun, was probably one of the most genial men I've ever met. He was rarely without a smile. I think he was just happy to have survived the Marines." (64-2)

Coon began as producer of *Star Trek* on August 8, 1966. His first task was to take over the rewriting of a script Roddenberry had approved and had since been struggling with.

***

Episode 11: MIRI
*Written by Adrian Spies
(with John D.F. Black & Gene L. Coon, uncredited)
Directed by Vincent McEveety*

NBC's October 4, 1966, press release:

**Kim Darby with Shatner, NBC publicity photo
(Courtesy of Gerald Gurian)**

The USS Enterprise discovers another "Earth" whose childlike inhabitants are victims of an abortive experiment to retard normal aging processes, in "Miri" on NBC Television Network's colorcast of *Star Trek*.... Captain James Kirk (William Shatner), Mr. Spock (Leonard Nimoy) and Dr. McCoy (DeForest Kelley) head a landing party to an uncharted planet, with the physical characteristics bearing an incredible resemblance to the Earth. They befriend Miri (Kim Darby), a disheveled and frightened young girl whose story of the failure of a mass youth experiment is questioned until their own lives are imperiled when they lose communication with the hovering spacecraft.

Miri, nearing puberty, soon develops a crush on Captain Kirk. She'll have her first love close at hand, for a short while anyway -- Kirk and his landing team cannot return to the ship; they are showing symptoms of having contracted the same infection that was responsible for eliminating the entire adult population of the planet.

As in *Lord of the Flies*, this episode takes a disturbing look at a culture run by children. The themes deal with modern society's obsession with youth and the inherent dangers in man's attempts to alter the forces of nature.

SOUND BITES

- *Yeoman Janice Rand:* "Eternal childhood, filled with play, no responsibility. It's almost like a dream." *Kirk:* "I wouldn't examine that dream too closely, Yeoman. It might not turn out to be very pretty."

- *Janice Rand, disfigured by the disease:* "Back on the ship I used to try to get you to look at my legs. Captain, look at my legs!"

- *Kirk, to the children:* "This is no game! The food is going! The time is going! There won't be anything left... not even *you*. Look at each other! Look at the blood on your hands! Is that what you want to be?"

ASSESSMENT

This was the second time members of the Enterprise crew were infected with a disease, the first being "The Naked Time." This time the disease lets us examine the price of humans attempting to prolong or drastically alter their lives. Even in the 1966 world, the scientific and medical communities were experimenting with cloning and the development of life-altering drugs. America, as with most Western cultures, had become youth-crazed. The divisions between the generations -- "the generation gap" -- seemed to be ripping America apart. "Miri," with its "Onlies" and "Grups," was another Swiftian way to place a lens on the changing times.

There are flaws. The chants of the kids, especially that "blah, blah, blah" business, becomes annoying; the blotches that vanish from McCoy's face -- although not a bad effect for the time -- could have been made to diminish more believably; and the parallel world the Enterprise encounters, that "another Earth," should have clouds in its atmosphere.

These points aside, "Miri" is entertaining and dramatically effective, with an intense and highly personal drama -- for Kirk, Rand, McCoy and, especially, Miri.

THE STORY BEHIND THE STORY

Script Timeline
Adrian Spies' Story Outline, ST #12: March 11, 1966.
Spies revised story outlines, gratis: April 5 & 11, 1966.
Staff polish of story outline: April 16, 1966.
Spies' 1st Draft teleplay: May 12, 1966.
Spies' rewrite, gratis (Revised 1st Draft teleplay): May 16, 1966.
Spies 2nd Draft teleplay: June 8, 1966.
John D.F. Black's rewrite (Mimeo Department "Yellow Cover 1st Draft"):
August 10, 1966.
Black's additional script polish (Final Draft teleplay): August 12, 1966.
Gene Coon's rewrite (Revised Final Draft teleplay): August 16, 1966.
Revisions by Coon and Roddenberry: Aug. 17, 18, 19 & 22, 1966.

Adrian Spies (pronounced "Spees"), 46 at this time, began as a reporter and feature writer for the *New York Mirror*. Once he made the move to television, Spies wrote for many of the prestigious anthology series from the 1950s, including *Dick Powell Theatre, Climax*, and *Studio One*. More than merely keeping busy in television, Spies was considered a "star" writer who was in great demand. And he was very well thought of by Desi Arnaz. Spies often wrote for *Desilu Playhouse*, and Arnaz honored him with an invitation to write an episode which would showcase the studio boss's dramatic acting ability. Of "So Tender, So Profane," *Daily Variety* said:

> In a momentous week, the veil was lifted on unseen phenomena, as far apart as heaven and earth. The Soviets let us see what the other side of the moon looked like and Desi Arnaz turned his serious side to the millions gathered around their sets Friday night. He acted rather than jollied.... He played the role with restraint and feeling, that of a Cuban factory worker forced against his wishes to reinstate in his society a sister who went wayward [played by future *Star Trek* guest star Barbara Luna].... Desi's every move was measured and tempered, yet it was he who gave the story by Adrian Spies its dramatic authority and sustained interest.

Spies wrote other high profile episodes of *Desilu Playhouse*. One, "Meeting At Appalachin," dramatized a 1957 fight between the law and racketeers in New York State. *Weekly Variety* reported that:

> The Desilu treatment of that confab was considered so hot that its telecasting was delayed until the completion of the conspiracy trial against participants. It was felt that the telecasting of Adrian Spies teleplay might prejudice the trial, which resulted in convictions and deportations of some of the participants.

After its airing, the reviewer for *Daily Variety* wrote:

Adrian Spies high-voltage teleplay... was a tense, gripping study of events leading up to and including that infamous crime conclave.

But Spies was not a science fiction writer. This was alien territory for him and, with "Miri," he was clearly borrowing from other sources. Consider this William Golding's *Lord of the Flies* meets Richard Matheson's *I Am Legend*, in search of the Fountain of Youth.

While the script for this episode was being written, Roddenberry told Dave Kaufman, of *Daily Variety*, that he believed:

> Kids reach their maturity at 12. As they reach maturity they go downhill. They are lovely and pure at 12.... Adrian Spies and I were talking about our kids, and out came a story by him on bacteriological warfare which kills all the adults on a planet. All the children escape this, and remain children forever. The kids are three centuries old when we come on their planet. This is how sci-fi should be done -- magnifying of a situation, and dramatize it. Sci-fi gives you selected magnification. (145-15)

Spies recalled, "When I went in to see Gene, I offered him the idea of a bunch of kids in this place where they are permanently young but are really very old. He said, 'You have to develop a language for these people.' I said, 'What the hell are you talking about?' He said, 'The kids would talk differently.' In that conversation, he made up the word 'grups' for grownups. I immediately liked it. That's an example of a creative producer at work. He had good ideas and good contributions. We worked out the story together." (164-2)

Roddenberry and Spies were in immediate agreement that Miri's world should be described as "another Earth." This allowed for contemporary Earth-like locations and clothing to be used, thereby saving money. It also explained the use of English as the children's language. And it was hoped this would better help the TV audience to empathize with the children -- contemporary American Earth children.

When Spies' story outline arrived in early April, Robert Justman wrote to Roddenberry:

> I like it very, very much.... I feel certain that we can find the sort of exterior sets we need for this show on the back lot at [Desilu] Culver. They certainly are in poor shape and would fit the story we have here. Also, I would suggest that wardrobe be contemporary to our century as we have it right now. (RJ11-1)

Justman was already counting the dollars he would be saving. Of course, even when Bob Justman liked something, he had a talent for finding problems. "Miri" promised one problem in particular. He wrote:

> Certainly, there will be some difficulties with regard to casting children in the parts called for. Hopefully, we will be shooting this show some time during the summer school vacation so that we can get the advantage of having six hours work with the kids instead of four. (RJ11-1)

Spies was asked for two more gratis drafts of his outline before it was sent to NBC in mid-April 1966. Stan Robertson seemed impressed. The mutual respect between *Star Trek*'s producer and NBC's Production Manager at this time was demonstrated in a correspondence from Roddenberry to Spies, reading: "Attached [is] a copy of the NBC program approval on 'Miri.' Ordinarily, I don't send these out, but we do seem to have in this Stan Robertson a fairly perceptive story reader." (GR11-1)

Among Robertson's comments, shared with Spies:

> The teaser gets under way quickly and splendidly, setting up the mystery and suspense well.... Act One presents a good opportunity to give further dimension to the character of Mr. Spock. It seems to us that the inclusion of Spock in the landing party selected to descend on Earth Number Two could be explained by a reference to his "unusual powers." He is an "unusual man" and we should remind our writers that anything they can do to play upon this and build this image in the minds of the viewer should be done. (SR11)

Leonard Nimoy once commented that he believed the bigger parts that came his way were a result of the audience reaction to "The Naked Time," first broadcast on September 29, 1966. But Stan Robertson's memo, dated April 15, nearly five months before *Star Trek*'s debut on NBC, gives credence to the network's recognition of the potential and importance of Spock.

Despite approval from Robertson, either Roddenberry or John D.F. Black did a polish of the outline, dated April 16, shoring up the story's structure before committing to Spies for the teleplay and the pay schedules associated with such.

After the first draft script arrived on May 12, and was given a quick free polish by Spies on May 16, the praise continued.

From Justman to Black:

> A very good first draft, to my way of thinking. Interesting characters and situations. (JR11-2)

From Black to Roddenberry: "No question about it, Adrian Spies writes." (JDFB11)
From Roddenberry to his staff:

> A good first draft, one of the best we've received, with the potential of being a most unusual and exciting episode.

Roddenberry nonetheless had issues, and added: "As normal in first scripts of a new series, lots of minor points to be corrected, some pulling and tugging necessary to bring the story and characters into line with where we are going." (GR11-2)

Among his concerns: Janice Rand was coming off too "chummy" with her captain. He suggested having the characters remain more professional, underlining the sexual tension.

Black had concerns, too, writing Roddenberry:

> Captain Kirk (his dialogue) is a bit spotty -- at times, very much our Kirk -- at other times, very much Jack Armstrong the All-American Boy -- and, at other times, a buddy-buddy with the crew, which I think is wrong for us..... Mr. Spock (his dialogue) at times borders very strongly on the "smart ass".... The entire relationship between Kirk and Janice is wrong -- far too chummy.... I also found that the inconsistency in Miri -- sometimes the child, sometimes the woman, needs some work....
>
> Not to open a can of peas, but, I question Spock's susceptibility to this condition -- since it is necessary to the story, I feel that somewhere we should explain that he is susceptible and why he is susceptible -- this needs only be in a line -- but what it could do for us is to prove the similarities between those of Planet Vulcan and the people of Earth....
>
> On pages twenty-eight and twenty-nine -- we now come to the major problem that [I] found in this script by way of <u>plotting</u>. As Mr. Spies wrote this, only Kirk had a communicator -- that just ain't so for us and, therefore, this beat doesn't work. I only have one suggestion as regards [to] a solution to this problem -- perhaps the entire company from the Enterprise could pursue the thief that stole Kirk's communicator -- have their path blocked by the mob of children ... jumping up and down ... making a game of blocking their path. When the urchins disappear, all the communicators are gone, as is Janice's tricorder....
>
> Page thirty-one -- and the remainder of the sequence that begins here -- found the "blah-blah-blah!" charming and beautifully-designed as a sequence....
>
> Page thirty-five -- we need a better tag-out line from Kirk than "Let's – start fighting back!" -- and less melodramatic....
>
> Page thirty-nine -- Mr. Spock does not drink coffee ... according to Leonard Nimoy....
>
> On page forty-seven -- at the top -- Janice's reference to her "legs" -- nice legs -- but the relationship is wrong for us.... And again on page forty-eight -- regarding their relationship -- "You'd end up being my guy" -- to Kirk? Huh-uh. And on page forty-nine -- the kiss is wrong -- the touch of a hand -- something less "passionate." I have nothing against passion, but we can't live with this kind of a beat in our other segments....
>
> In Act IV-- Am not sure how we're going to get away with the principal's office sequence and the attack on Kirk -- "children in jeopardy" taboo -- and all that jazz.... And Kirk's bloody face on page sixty-three -- it may keep them in line, but it won't make the air....
>
> Regarding the finish -- will have to leave some crew members behind to assist the children -- and there are other areas of the planet which would require an adult task force of medical aid to correct and disinfect the populace.... And thank God we're both immune to this disease, not having reached puberty yet. But I'm keeping an eye on Bob Justman. (JDFB11)

Justman had concerns regarding likely production problems in realizing what the script called for. As was becoming standard modus operandi, he had an axe to grind about too many sets, too many locations, too many opticals and too many guest players. He was still bothered by the ages of those guest players, writing to Roddenberry and Black:

> Naturally, we are going to have to work with children in this show. And, naturally, certain problems will arise. (JR11-2)

And the mix of children and violence:

> How come Kirk went to rescue Janice without taking Spock or McCoy? I still have the same fears about this sequence with the children. It is terribly brutal and terribly bloody. (JR11-2)

Spies believed he had fulfilled his contract with the delivery of his 2nd Draft teleplay dated June 8. Roddenberry didn't. He felt Spies was falling into the trap many of the other first time *Star Trek* writers had navigated toward: becoming overwhelmed by the grandness of it all. His letter to Spies began:

> Something's wrong. The premise is still one of the liveliest I've seen. There are wonderful moments of pathos and of meaning, moments delicate and delicious, and yet the execution does not live up to what is inherent in every page of the piece.... I thought you made an honest effort to consider our suggestions on the first draft. Unlike some of our fellow scribes, you are professional; you could not consciously give short change on a commitment if you tried. But, giving the same candor, I really don't see the revision we expected. (GR11-3)

Roddenberry asked Spies to think of Spock as a "half-Chinese scientist" and of Kirk as a "20th Century Naval Captain," the "central character upon which a series will rise or fall." The tricks and gadgets of science fiction could be added later. What was more important in a *Star Trek* script was that the drama, based on the characters, made sense -- and made sense to a 1966 television audience. Roddenberry continued:

> Does review of your script satisfy you that the job he [Kirk] is doing, his attitudes, the decisions we thrust upon him and his handling of them, are what you would have written in a non-sf script? (GR11-3)

Spies did -- or, at least, thought what he had written was good enough. Roddenberry had already gotten three drafts of the story outline and three drafts of the script from him. He now wanted to move on and take other writing assignments on series not so demanding as *Star Trek*, such as *Felony Squad*.

Roddenberry sent a letter to Spies' agent, writing:

> [Adrian] has worked very hard and given us a revised script. Fine, up to that point. But he has not done his homework, he has not read and digested the information sheets we have sent him, he has obviously not studied the other script we sent him for a sample so that he could properly use our sets, our people, our various characterizations, etc. Here's where I need your help. We are asking of the writer no more than any other new show asks or must have, i.e. study what is available on the lead character, his attitudes and methods, the secondary characters, the inter-relations, and those basic things you would have whether this was the beginning of a western, hospital drama, or cops and robbers [show].... Adrian has either "frozen up" in some imagined fear that "SF" is bigger than him, or he is simply using it as an excuse to avoid doing the homework every writer of a new series is expected to do, in fact commits himself to do. You've got to help us get this fact to him somehow.... At this point, we're not asking Adrian to write science fiction! We are asking him to give us quality in how he draws his characters, in making our regular people act and interact per our format with which he has been amply provided, to give them the "bite" of their individual styles, to have the Captain -- like Matt Dillon or Dr. Kildare even -- act like what he is, and above all, again forgetting science fiction, have everybody use at least simple 20th Century logic and common sense

in what they look for, what they comment on, what surprises them, how they protect themselves, and so on. For example, as you will see in the script, we are in an Earth-like city which stopped living some centuries ago. And yet, as they land there, no one comments on the strange ancient aspect of it. For God sakes, if Matt Dillon came upon an Indian village which had been deserted for even three or four years, he or Chester or someone would at least be aware of that fact, especially if it were an important story point as it is here. (GR11-4)

The strange abandoned city Roddenberry spoke of in his letter to Adrian Spies' agent. Note camera crewman Bill McGovern (bottom right) slating the shot (Courtesy of Gerald Gurian)

Roddenberry knew that, contractually, he didn't have a leg to stand on. As he admitted, Spies had addressed all the notes previously given with his official 2nd Draft; his <u>final</u> draft. He was entitled to all his pay and not required to do any further work. But, as Roddenberry wrote this letter on June 13, he was juggling rewrites, having just finished one on "Mudd's Women" on June 6, still working on "The Enemy Within" (finishing June 15) to be followed by "The Man Trap" (June 16 through 21), "The Naked Time" (June 28 through July 5), "Charlie X" (July 5 through July 13), "Balance of Terror," (July 14 through 25), "Dagger of the Mind" (July 22 through August 9) and, simultaneously, "What Are Little Girls Made Of?" (July 25 through August 3). How could he possibly make time for "Miri"?

Spies' agent was able to get his client and Roddenberry on the phone together. Roddenberry was a relentless debater when he believed he had a righteous cause. But Spies had the perfect out -- he had taken a script assignment on *Felony Squad* and was not available for *Star Trek* at this time.

Roddenberry waited a week and a half then sent Spies another letter, saying:

Hope you can find time now to accomplish this polish we badly need.... As much as we like the teleplay, we strongly believe a polish would resolve certain problems we feel strongly about. These are basically in areas of credulity and believability in what our characters do and say, consisting in how these trained, future-day astronauts would act in facing another space emergency, and in delineation of the characteristics. However lovely any tale we get, since we are not an anthology, we must have certain unities between this and the episodes which came before it and those after. It was an attempt to get these unities that lay behind many of our spoken or written points to you.... I avoid rehashing our last telephone conversation here, since we both have a certain feeling on this whole subject, have both expressed it, have come to an agreement without loss of personal or professional regard and affection. (GR11-4)

Spies response was to take a second *Felony Squad* assignment. He later said, "I think

Gene got mad at me about that, but we eventually patched things up." (164-1)

Roddenberry, not holding a grudge, later explained his technique, saying, "I'm -- for want of a better word -- crafty. I'm more likely to push too far -- to push a little over the edge to see if it works -- than not." (145-23)

John D.F. Black didn't see what all the fuss was about, saying, "The idea of 'Miri' was absolutely intriguing and fascinating, and it felt wonderful right from the get-go. It was there from the first draft and Adrian kept it there throughout. He was easy to work with because he was a consummate professional. What it would take ten minutes to say to somebody else, you could say to him in 30 seconds and he would have a clamp on it and know exactly what you meant. We were lucky to have him." (17-4)

With Spies gone, Black did his contractually-required polish, the Yellow Cover First Draft, dated August 10, and, at Roddenberry's insistence, a second polish, the Final Draft dated August 12.

Robert Justman was the first to speak, telling Roddenberry:

All in all, I feel that there is a worthwhile show in this effort. John has done a good job.... It will be expensive... but this is a change of pace kind of show and it is one of the ways we can get away from the Enterprise and onto a planet -- and I do believe that this is what our network wants us to deliver. (JR11-5)

Justman hoped for more script changes to assist him in tightening the episode's budget. NBC wanted changes, too. Jean Messerschmidt, the network's vigilant head of Broadcast Standards, wrote:

Page 9: Restraint is necessary here so the sight of the boy creature will not alarm or shock the viewer; please avoid the objectionably grotesque in general appearance and makeup.... Page 12: Caution on the sight of the dead boy creature; avoid seeing the open eyes.... Page 24: Please use restraint here and throughout the script to be sure the blemishes are not unnecessarily gruesome to the viewer.... Page 44: As above, caution on the sight of the dead girl creature.... Page 62: Caution here where Janice opens her uniform to check on the progress of the disease; avoid exposure which would embarrass or offend. (BS11)

And on and on.

John D.F. Black wouldn't be making further changes. His final draft was truly final -- the day of its delivery, Friday, August 12, was Black Friday at *Star Trek*. Black's contract was up and he would be leaving the series (more on this later). "Dagger of the Mind" was now in its fourth day of production, with two more days planned for the following week. "Miri" was scheduled to go before the cameras after that, bright and early on Wednesday morning, August 17. But the script needed a rewrite and Roddenberry didn't have another one left in him. Including "Miri," there were six episodes remaining in NBC's order of 16, and it was clear now that *Star Trek* needed a new producer.

Help arrived a few days earlier, which, as it would turn out for the planned filming of "Miri," was a few days too late. Gene Coon came into Desilu to sign a contract on Monday, August 8. He would take over as producer starting with the filming of "Miri," allowing Roddenberry to work a little less obsessively from the chair of the Executive Producer.

Coon spent the balance of the week getting a crash course on *Star Trek*, a series that had yet to broadcast a single episode. On the weekend, he did his rewrite of "Miri," bringing his cut-and-paste revised final draft in on Monday.

The overall structure and much of the dialogue was already in place, thanks to Black's latest polish. But in Black's draft, Miri knows her days are numbered right from the start. Jahn (Michael J. Pollard's character) knows he is close to becoming a victim of the disease, as well. Information comes to the landing party quickly and easily, especially in the first act. For example, when the landing party encounters Miri and she first refers to them as "grups," Spock asks, "What are they?" She immediately answers, "You should know -- you're all grups." She says she is afraid because grups always hurt others. Spock asks her what it is the grups do? She answers, "What did they ever do in their silly buildings?... Especially the science ones ... mixing things ... making pill things." She then tells them that the grups all died. McCoy asks, "The children didn't?" She says, "Of course, the onlies didn't die." Kirk and the others look confused and ask if the creature who attacked them outside was a grup. She says, "He became one.... You know, when things happen to an onlie ... the way it's starting to happen to me.... That's why I can't hang around with my friends anymore -- the minute one of us starts changing, the rest get ... afraid.... Like the boy outside ... I used to play with him.... Now, pretty soon, I'll be like him ... first, those awful marks on your skin ... then trying to hurt anybody you see."

It goes on like this. Too much, too soon, too few mysteries left to solve, resulting in too many redundant beats later. Miri even knows how long it's been since the grups died, and tells Kirk and company, "Three hundred years -- the onlies mark down all the hots and colds at a secret place." And now this is one more thing Kirk and his people don't need to figure out on their own.

This exchange of information through dialogue, mostly between Kirk and Miri, is much more effective in Coon's rewrite. This is not to say the writing is better -- Adrian Spies lived up to his reputation of being a gifted screenwriter, and John Black's polish gives Spies' script the *Star Trek* stamp -- but the drama is greater in Coon's reworking of the script, when Kirk forces Miri to admit that she has the disease, making her look at her own arm and see the beginning of a blemish, then pulling the sobbing girl to him and holding her tight. It is more endearing when he asks her, in a rhetorical question, if she ever wonders why she doesn't spend as much time with the other onlies, and then gives her the answer, telling her it is because she is becoming a woman. The Enterprise people are played smarter by having them figure out what the words "grups" and "onlies" mean on their own, instead of having Miri flat out tell them. Coon's rewrite is a prime example of small changes making big differences.

As proven again and again by the documents preserved in the series' files stored at UCLA, the *Star Trek* creative staff was obsessively driven to make every script -- every episode -- as good as they could possibly be, within the limits of time, budget and censorship.

Mimeographed copies of Coon's rewrite were distributed on Tuesday, August 16, the day before "Miri" was scheduled to begin principal photography -- at 1 p.m., since "Dagger of the Mind" was running a half day behind. It was enough of a rewrite to require network clearance, however, and production of "Miri" had to be pushed back. For the first time at *Star Trek*, cast and production crew were sent home for an unplanned paid holiday. Desilu Stages 9 and 10 went dark.

Pre-Production
(Director's prep: August 18 & 19; total 2 days)

Matt Jefferies and his people now had until Monday -- five days away, counting the weekend -- to build their sets for "Miri."

Tom Gries, who had produced the science fiction movie *Donovan's Brain* and also directed numerous episodes each of *Science Fiction Theater*, *Route 66*, and *Stoney Burke*, was the last of the nine directors Gene Roddenberry signed in early May to handle one *Star Trek* episode each. Gries had been slated for "Miri," but, as had been the case with Bernard Kowalsky during the period in which "The Naked Time" was planned and filmed, he had a scheduling conflict. The well-regarded director could not be blamed; it was *Star Trek* that had fallen behind, resulting in the changing of production dates. A decision was quickly made to hold Vincent McEveety over from "Dagger of the Mind," giving him only two days instead of the normal six for pre-production.

Gene Coon had until Monday to get notes from the network and feedback from Roddenberry and Justman and do the final polish of the script, with revised pages flying from his typewriter on August 17, 18 and, even as the cameras began to roll, on August 22.

McEveety said, "I thought it was a very involved script, and it was tough putting it together so quickly. I think they cast the quirky guy [Michael J. Pollard] unbeknownst to me, because they wanted to get him and they had to make a deal with him fast or lose him to another job. But Miri herself I was involved in. I just looked at film; she didn't come in to interview. She had decent film and we were in enough of a hurry, because I never met her personally until we began making it, which is why I had no way of knowing what to expect -- good and bad."

Kim Darby, in a captivating performance, was the shy, love-struck Miri. She was 18 playing 14. Starting in 1963, small roles on television quickly grew to substantial ones as she proved her abilities on *Dr. Kildare*, *Mr. Novak*, and *The Fugitive*. She moved to the big screen and worked with James Doohan in 1965's *Bus Riley's Back in Town*. In 1969, she would have second billing to John Wayne in *True Grit*, and would share top billing with William Shatner in *The People,* a 1972 sci-fi thriller.

Joe D'Agosta said, "Kim Darby was a real coup for us because she was an actress who could do very odd parts. Opposed to Sherry Jackson, who had *something else*, a kind of sexual heat that looked accessible, Darby delivered these victim-like characters with such ease.... Because it was *Star Trek*, and the nature of the show, the nature of the kinds of roles, we were able to get her interested." (43-1)

Michael J. Pollard, actor's headshot, circa 1966 (Courtesy of Gerald Gurian)

Michael J. Pollard, as Jahn, was 27 but was also playing 14. Pollard's big break came in 1958 when Bob Denver, who played beatnik Maynard G. Krebs in TV's *The Many Loves of Dobie Gillis*, was drafted into the Army. Pollard was brought in to replace Denver as Maynard's weird cousin Jerome Krebs. It was a short stay. Denver flunked out of the armed services as 4-F and returned to *Gillis*. Pollard's character was quickly written out, but the exposure helped catapult the oddball personality into other TV and film jobs. In 1965, Pollard played another teenager in "The Magic Mirror," a surprisingly somber and charming episode of *Lost in Space*. Next came a scene-stealing performance in Carl Reiner's big screen 1966 comedy *The Russians are Coming, the Russians are Coming*. And he was already being considered by Warren Beatty for a prominent role in the 1967 mega-hit *Bonnie &*

Clyde, for which he would receive a Golden Globe nomination and an Oscar nod, both in the category of Best Supporting Actor. (He was in good company; Gene Hackman was also nominated for Best Supporting Actor in that film.)

D'Agosta said, "Michael was one of a kind. You either loved him or hated him, because he was so, for the lack of a better term, quirky. Odd. But interesting; unique. He brought that same performance to every job he did." (43-4)

McEveety said, "When you're dealing with actors, any actors, you never know what you're going to come up with. I mean, they can be the sweetest guy in the world on screen and yet they're next to impossible when you meet them and attempt to work with them. He [Pollard] is a very quirky fellow. But, after a while, you don't care how quirky actors are as long as they hit their mark and remember their lines. In his case, he could play it any way he chose because that was the character that they [the writer/producers] envisioned. They wanted that quirkiness and that nuttiness. So it was a very strange take on the character, but by an actor who was absolutely professional." (117-4)

Cast as the "onlies": Darlene and Dawn Roddenberry were the ones on set who got to call Gene Roddenberry "daddy." Steven McEveety was the nephew of the director. Leslie and Lisabeth Shatner were the star's daughters. And Scott and Jonathan Whitney were the sons of Grace Lee Whitney.

Proud mother recalled, "Jonathan and Scott were 7 and 9. They were the kids who stole the communicators in the show, so we [the landing party] couldn't get back to the Enterprise. They sent a limo for all the kids, since their day would be shorter than ours. I was driving my Buick, and the kids were in front of me in the limo, and Jonathan and Scott were up in the back window waving at me as we were going down the freeway -- *at four in the morning*." (183-6)

The old-pro child actors in "Miri" included John Megna, the toothy "bop, bop on your head" kid. He was the brother of singer/actress Connie Stevens. If he looks familiar, watch 1962's *To Kill a Mockingbird*. In that movie, his character Dill was based on writer Harper Lee's childhood friend Truman Capote.

Phil Morris was the son of Greg Morris of *Mission: Impossible*. This Morris would return to *Star Trek* as Cadet Foster in *Star Trek III: The Search for Spock*, then as a Klingon Commander *and* a Ramata Klan warrior in two episodes of *Star Trek: Deep Space 9*, and as Lt. John Kelly in *Star Trek: Voyager*. Elsewhere, he played Grant Collier, the son of Barney Collier, the character his father played in *Mission: Impossible*, for that series' revival run from 1988 to 1990. But today he's best known for his role as the lawyer Jackie Chiles in several episodes of *Seinfeld*.

Ed McCready played Boy Creature in one of five *Star Trek* appearances. He would be seen again most noticeably, as the barber in "Specter of the Gun."

Jim Goodwin returned as Lt. Farrell, his third and final *Trek* appearance, this time sitting at communications. John D.F. Black had helped to get Goodman onto *Star Trek*, but now that Black was exiting, Lt. Farrell would lose his place on the bridge.

John Arndt was back, now as one of the two red-shirted security guards among the landing party. He was given the name Fields here, for one of his four *Star Trek* appearances. Prior to this, he played Sturgeon in "The Man Trap," one of the victims of the Salt Vampire.

David Ross joined the cast as "Security Guard 1," the other red-shirted crewman in the landing party. This was the first of eight appearances.

McEveety managed to complete his preparations by the end of Friday. When he returned to the studio on Monday morning, he had a leg in a cast, the result of a home accident (not a skiing accident as other sources have stated -- McEveety told this author he was accident prone and had never been skiing in his life). The accident-prone director proceeded to call the shots from a wheelchair.

Production Diary
Filmed August 22, 23, 24, 25, 26, 29 & 30, 1966
(Planned as 6 day production; finished 1 day behind; total cost: $206,815).

Aerial view of Desilu 40 Acres, Culver City, CA, circa 1966. Clockwise, from center: town of Mayberry (*The Andy Griffith Show*), Civil War era train station (*Gone With the Wind*), western street (*Rango*), Arabian village ("The Cage," "Errand of Mercy"), Camp Henderson (*Gomer Pyle, U.S.M.C.*), Stalog 13 (*Hogan's Heroes*), and farm set.

Monday, August 22, 1966. The Beatles arrived in New York City to play Shea Stadium before 44,000 screaming fans. *Yesterday ... and Today* was still top album in the nation. Lunar Orbiter 1, launched by the United States one week earlier, took the first photograph of Earth from the Moon. The space race, in full swing, saw the USSR launch Luna 11 to the Moon. And, on Stage 10, the *Star Trek* company launched something of its own -- "Miri," for scenes inside Miri's house, including the closet where she hid from Kirk and his crew. McEveety rolled film from 8 a.m. to 7:06 p.m., into overtime but ending on schedule.

Day 2. Tuesday was spent on Stage 9 where many of the Enterprise sets had been collapsed to make room for the interior of the laboratory and its surrounding corridors. No children were needed this day, only the series regulars with the two adults playing age 14.

Kim Darby recalled, "I was just 18 and it was the first time I didn't have to have a guardian or a teacher." (45a)

McEveety felt that he was cast in the role of Darby's "guardian," certainly more so than her director. He said, "While Michael J. Pollard was an absolute professional, the opposite was true of Kim Darby. She was extremely strange. She had a neurotic and very, very bipolar kind of personality. She'd do a scene and I was happy with her performance -- very happy, I thought she was wonderful in that respect -- and then she'd go off and cry like a baby afterwards. I'd never know why and, after a while, I didn't care. Total emotional nonsense." (117-4)

Perhaps, like the character she played, Darby was in love. She later admitted, "I always fell in love with my leading man." Admitting that Shatner was no exception, she added, "He was great to work with. He was extremely professional and right on target and he was completely there for me in [each] scene." (45a)

Shatner wasn't bothered by the schoolgirl crush aimed in his direction, but McEveety, responsible for keeping the production on schedule, had no time for such teenage behavior. He said, "Things like that would slow down the production, because we were trying to move so quickly and there was little time for actresses going off to have a good cry. We were trying to do these in six days, and those were impossible schedules. You worked very late at night and very hard to accomplish it. But she was really off the wall at that time. Getting that type of performance was not difficult because it seemed to be a natural for her. What was difficult was the way she reacted to everything." (117-4)

Filming stopped at 6:35, on schedule, despite the teardrops on set.

Day 3, Wednesday. The company traveled to Desilu Culver "40 Acres" for the exterior street sequences. Formerly "RKO 40 Acres" and situated in Culver City, the backlot once belonged to Selznick Studios and had been the location for the burning of Atlanta in *Gone with the Wind*, as well as the home of Tara, the Southern mansion. In 1966, it served Desilu well for the outdoor filming of numerous television series. Camp Henderson from *Gomer Pyle, U.S.M.C.* was

Nimoy, Shatner, Kelley, and Rand on the streets of Mayberry
(Color image available at www.startrekhistory.com and www.startrekprtopauthority.com)

located here, as was Stalag 13 from *Hogan's Heroes*. This was also the site of Mayberry, as seen in *The Andy Griffith Show*, and it is this location that serves as Miri's world. As the Enterprise landing party walk the streets of Mayberry, with buildings appearing abandoned and desolated, Sheriff Taylor's Court House can be seen in the background, as well as the town's bank and Floyd's barber shop.

Cast and crew filmed until 7:05, beating the summer sunset by half-an-hour.

Days 4 and 5 brought the company back to Desilu and Stage 9 for additional shooting in the government labs, this time with the children ... and a social worker to watch over them.

Lisabeth Shatner remembered the day she and her sister arrived for their first acting job. She said, "[Leslie] accompanied me to the makeup room to visit dad. When we walked into the room, he was sitting in the makeup chair, his back to us. We ran forward, excitedly, relieved to see his familiar outline. When he turned towards us, I caught a glimpse of his arm and saw the skin on the inside of his elbow was covered with a long, bluish-red scab! I blanched, and my dad burst out laughing, and told us to touch the sore. It was made of rubber. At that moment, I realized everything was 'pretend.' Once I understood, I relaxed." (155a)

The camera stopped rolling at 7:10 p.m., allowing the crew to wrap set before 8. Like most days, cast and crew had been working in excess of 12 hours.

Day 6. Monday brought the company back to Stage 10 where the classroom interiors and toy store had been built. The children and their social worker spent another six hours -- the maximum allowed by law -- on the set. McEveety, slowed by children, shot until 6 p.m., finishing three-quarters of a day behind.

Day 7. Tuesday, August 30 was the seventh full day of filming, again on Stage 10 for more sequences with the children. After the kids were sent home, the company moved back to Stage 9 to film the opening and ending of the episode on the ship's bridge, as well as the scenes featuring Lt. Farrell manning communications. There was a memo awaiting McEveety from Roddenberry. It said:

> The sound department tells us they are having considerable difficulty with footsteps on the bridge and throughout our vessel. Is it possible to rubber-sole or otherwise deaden the sound coming from the boots our people wear?

Whenever the camera angle did not reveal their feet, the sound men wanted Captain Kirk and Mister Spock to wear rubber booties over the real booties, in the interest of quiet.

McEveety wrapped production at 6:20 p.m., one day over. Robert Justman's production notes read: "One day over schedule -- children."

Vincent McEveety was pleased by the work. He said, "I think, if we have one obligation as so-called 'creative people' in this business, in the function of writing, producing and directing, it's to entertain. By entertain, I mean moving the audience. If you can move somebody, change somebody, give somebody a change of heart, have them look at something different than they may have in the past, provide some kind of introspection to themselves and have them walk away saying, 'Wow,' then I think you've done what you set out to do. I think 'Miri' fit it perfectly." (117-1)

Final appearance by Jim Goodwin as Lt. Farrell (Courtesy of Gerald Gurian)

Post-Production
August 31 through October 17, 1966. Music score: Tracked.

Ed McCready with Nimoy and Shatner, NBC publicity photo (Courtesy of Gerald Gurian)

Film Editor Fabien Tordjmann received high praise from Gene Roddenberry for this, his third *Star Trek* assignment. "Atta-boys" were also sent to Jack Hunsaker of the long-suffering sound department and music editors Joseph Soroken and Robert Raff, as well as Bill Heath, the post-production executive. The memo from Roddenberry to all involved read:

> The excellent post-production on "Miri," starting with the editing, and then through Sound, Music, and Dubbing, added immeasurably to the quality of the final product. The director, Vince McEveety, was particularly pleased and asked that his compliments be passed on to all who contributed. Thank you very much for this hard work and high creativity. (GR11-5)

Cinema Research Corporation was brought in to handle the opticals. This was already the fourth post optical house to contribute to the new series. The company had opened their doors in the early 1960s and just completed work on a small sci-fi film called *Wizards of Mars*. Other than presenting a cloudless planet Earth, the effects are excellent.

Included in the optical work was the series titles, and this was the last episode to list John D.F. Black as associate producer, even though he had already contributed to the next few scripts. Also in those titles, "Miri" marked the first listing of Gene L. Coon as producer.

The tab for Coon's first *Trek* was $206,815 ($1.5 million in 2013), over budget by more than 13 grand. The First Season deficit was now up to $21,387.

Release / Reaction
Premiere air date: 10/27/66. NBC repeat broadcast: 6/29/67.

Joan Crosby reviewed "Miri" for her column *TV Scout*. Among the newspapers carrying the review was the *Pittsburg Press*, in Pittsburg, Pennsylvania. Crosby wrote:

> *Star Trek* has a very frightening climatic scene with a bunch of children interested in killing Captain Kirk -- who is considered by the children to be "a grup" among their "onlies." The children are actually hundreds of years old, leftovers from an experiment from earlier times to prevent aging. Now, as the children reach puberty, they fall prey to a disease which causes advanced age and instant death. The disease soon attacks the Enterprise landing party, which has landed on the children's Earth-like planet, and they now have seven days in which to find an antidote.

October 27, 1966 was the night that the *Peanuts* TV special "It's the Great Pumpkin, Charlie Brown" premiered. Below is a sampling of two separate reports from A.C. Nielsen, the first counting households, the second factoring "ratings points," with an estimate of the percentage of U.S. TVs in use. From a vantage point of 47 years later, it is easy to expect that no other show was going to beat this particular "Charlie Brown" special in the ratings.

RATINGS / Nielsen National report for Thursday, October 27, 1966:

8:30 - 9 p.m.:	Share:	Households:
NBC: *Star Trek* (first half)	25.4%	12,350,000
ABC: *The Dating Game*	15.5%	8,510,000
CBS: **Great Pumpkin, Charlie Brown**	**49.0%**	**19,320,000**
9 - 9:30 p.m. (66.4% of U.S. TVs in use):	**Share:**	**Rating:**
NBC: *Star Trek* (second half)	28.3%	18.8
ABC: **Bewitched**	**31.9%**	**21.2**
CBS: *Thursday Night Movie*	31.2%	20.7
Local independent stations:	7.7%	No data

A.C. Nielsen believed over 19 million households tuned in for "It's the Great Pumpkin, Charlie Brown." *Star Trek* did respectable business, in second place and attracting over 12.3 million families of its own. When the *Peanuts* special cleared the air, a great deal of channel surfing raised *Star Trek*'s audience (from a 25.4% audience chare to one of 28.3%). More channel knobs were turned from CBS to the competition on ABC, however, resulting in a fairly close race, with a 3.3% spread between *Star Trek*, at the bottom, and *Bewitched* at the top. Snug in the middle was the movie on CBS: the television premiere of the 1961 comedy *All in a Night's Work*, starring Dean Martin, Shirley MacLaine, and Cliff Robertson.

Nielsen was not the only service counting noses.

Home Testing Institute, A.C. Nielsen's competitor, had a survey of its own called TVQ. For the month of October, which "Miri" closed out, TvQ prepared a Top 10 list and ranked *Star Trek* as being in a four-way tie for the fifth most popular series on TV, under *Bonanza*, *I Spy*, *Walt Disney*, and *Red Skelton*. The other three shows tied for fifth place were *Mission: Impossible*, *Family Affair* and the *NBC Saturday Night Movie*. *The Time Tunnel*, and *Gomer Pyle* were at nine and ten, respectively.

"Miri" was a well-liked *Star Trek* episode, not only by the fans, but by those responsible for making it. However, when ranking all of the episodes of *Star Trek* in a special November 1994 issue of *Entertainment Weekly*, the magazine's writers rightfully said: "The annoying 'Bonk, bonk on the head' kid should be sent to military school pronto!"

Memories

Adrian Spies commented, "['Miri'] looks good. It had a kind of sincerity to it. Gene was dealing with all the causes of the time in a very thoughtful and intelligent manner. I have only good things to say about *Trek* and my experience on it. I just wasn't into very much science fiction at that point." (164-1)

Vincent McEveety said, "A wonderful love story. It had touching performances. And it's another example how a good story can take place 200 years in the past or 200 years in the future, and the time frame doesn't matter as long as we are moved by the characters. 'Miri' was one of my absolute favorite films. I thought it was very special." (117-4)

18

Deadlines, Breakdowns, and Replacements

Grace Lee Whitney, shipping out
(NBC publicity photo, courtesy of Gerald Gurian)

August 28, 1966. Five episodes were left to produce for the initial order of 16. But following the completion of "Miri," *Star Trek* took a two-week break from filming. Shatner and Nimoy were needed to promote the premiere, now just a week away. Roddenberry and Justman, unbeknownst to their stars, were concerned that there might not be a premiere.

Virtually all aspects of *Star Trek* were behind schedule and over budget. Except for the second pilot, no episodes were ready to be turned over to NBC. The biggest bottleneck was the photographic effects. Nothing had been delivered.

This time bomb had started ticking back in April. As the series was preparing to film, a complex and fragile system for handling the post-production was devised. Bill Heath, Head of Post Production at Desilu, was the liaison between *Star Trek* and The Howard Anderson Company. His job: Make sure Roddenberry didn't go over budget (as he had with the pilot films) by keeping the editing and optical effects under control. The arrangement, as Heath worked it out, was that the Andersons had four weeks to create, photograph, process and tinker with the opticals needed for each episode. With as many as four episodes overlapping, this was an unworkable schedule, sure to dismantle the house of cards Heath had built.

Roddenberry was worried from the start. In the entire history of film production, the effects he needed had never before been produced on such a scale. As early as April 7, he wrote a memo to Robert Justman, intentionally sending copies to Herb Solow, the Howard Anderson Company and Bill Heath, saying:

> We are very concerned that even Anderson's <u>present</u> estimated time of four weeks to completion may put us in serious trouble in getting our first two or three shows finished in time to do the audience tests which NBC insists on.

Bill Heath was unconcerned.

By mid-June, the first assembly edit of "The Corbomite Maneuver" was delivered to the Andersons. By the first week of July, two more episodes had been delivered. The deadline for "Corbomite" to be completed and returned to the *Star Trek* production offices had already passed.

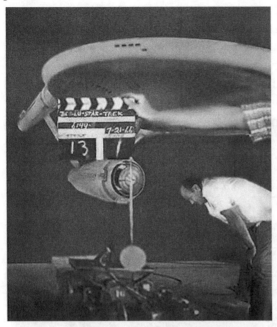

Filming the Enterprise one frame at a time at the Howard Anderson Company, 1966 (Courtesy of Gerald Gurian)

Sensing a lack of interest from Heath, Roddenberry recruited Justman to play the part of "The Mole." The associate producer/spy was dispatched to pay a friendly visit to Darrell Anderson and unofficially monitor how the work was progressing. Justman returned with grim news. He told Roddenberry how the Andersons had been struggling to create the photographic effects never seen before in movies and television. They were filming the stationary 11-foot, 2-inch Enterprise model in front of a blue screen by use of a camera dolly on metal tracks -- a camera that would inch toward the front of the ship, away from the back and, for flybys, dolly past it, sideways. It was a meticulously slow process.

"We had no motion control for the track," Howard Anderson, Jr. explained. "We [used] stop-motion [photography], *one frame at a time*." (2-2)

Motion was one problem. Lighting was another. Anderson recalled, "We had to constantly stop shooting after a short while because the lights would heat up the ship." (2-2)

Anderson and his team would turn the lights on to find their exposure levels and balance the giant arc lights to illuminate the main body of the ship, and then turn the lights off and

The slow hard work continues at the Howard Anderson Company (Courtesy of Gerald Gurian)

wait for the model to cool down. Twenty minutes later, the lights went back on, allowing a few frames of film to be exposed. And then the lights went off again. The model needed to cool. Anderson said, "It wasn't until later that someone developed fiber optics and 'cold lights' and other useful miniature lighting tools that are common today." (2-2)

Photographing the ship was only one part of the effect. In 1966, with no computers to streamline the job, the illusion of moving stars was created through the combination of three separate "star plates." One of these plates was stationary. A second would either move toward or away from the first plate -- and the camera -- creating an illusion of a closer star field moving at a slow speed. A third plate, which advanced toward the camera at a faster pace, was able to show a grouping of stars speeding by. All three backgrounds were then composited with the footage of the moving Enterprise. The slightest jiggle during one single shot would render an entire day's filming unusable.

The stage at the Howard Anderson Company. Note the tracks leading up to the 11-foot, 2-inch model of the Enterprise, using for dolly shots (Courtesy of Gerald Gurian)

Another month came and went. On July 14, with several episodes now delivered to the Andersons, Roddenberry had yet to see any completed work. The premiere of *Star Trek* was just seven weeks away. NBC needed the episodes sooner for inspection and advance test screening. Roddenberry sent another memo, this time to Darrell Anderson, writing:

> The purpose of this note is a friendly reminder that you and I have agreed that every basic stage and component of optical work will be shown to us for comment and approval. As such, if we should turn down a fully composited optical on which I have not had the opportunity to see the component parts, I would regretfully be placed in the position of having to refuse payment for the cost of making it.

A copy of this latest memo was again sent to Bill Heath. It was Heath's job to make sure the work was completed on schedule -- a schedule which had already been breached.

According to Justman, Anderson didn't respond. Heath, however, did. Justman said, "We were told not to worry. We were told the optical effects would be delivered with time to spare. Of course, there was no time to spare at the time we were told this. We pointed this out. And we were told not to worry." (94-1)

Also overdue was the footage needed for the opening title sequence. That triggered a domino effect of tardiness.

Hoping to be inspired by the amazing visuals, the Andersons were preparing, Roddenberry delayed writing the 30-second introduction needed for the opening title sequence. Alexander Courage was hoping to be inspired, too. He needed to compose the series theme music, but had no visuals to set his music to. He was also working on the score for "The Man Trap" and "The Naked Time" with no opticals to guide him. Fred Steiner needed to score "The Corbomite Maneuver" and "Mudd's Women," but he, too, had no effects to view.

Courage and Steiner proceeded as best they could. And, under increased pressure from Robert Justman, Roddenberry finally stopped waiting on Anderson, stopped rewriting scripts, and began sketching ideas for the narration needed for *Star Trek*'s title sequence. The soon to be famous intro was actually a collaboration between himself, John D.F. Black and, indirectly, Samuel A. Peeples. Roddenberry's first draft read:

> This is the adventure of the United Space Ship Enterprise. Assigned a five-year galaxy patrol, the bold crew of the giant starship explores the excitement of strange new worlds, uncharted civilizations and exotic people. These are its voyages and its adventures.

Later that day, Black did a rewrite:

> Space ... the final frontier. This is the story of the U.S.S. Enterprise. Its mission ... a five-year patrol to seek out and contact alien life ... to explore the infinite frontier of space ... where no man has gone before.

And with that, Sam Peeples had made his contribution, without even being in the room. He had written those last six words a year earlier.

On August 10, Roddenberry took a look at Black's version and then typed the three most famous sentences of his entire writing career (containing the most famous split infinitive in television history):

> Space ... the final frontier. These are the voyages of the starship Enterprise. Its five-year mission ... to explore strange new worlds ... to seek out new life and new civilizations ... to boldly go where no man has gone before.

William Shatner was immediately pulled from the set of "Dagger of the Mind" to record a voiceover. John D.F. Black dispelled other tales told by others of how Shatner managed to rush across the Desilu lot to the facility where the sound recordings were made and, without being short on breath, nail the opening narration in one take.

"We took him in a golf cart," Black said. "Bill was in good shape. But so was the golf cart. And it is true that he got it in one take. Except we didn't. There was a bump in the recording. So Bill did it a second time. And that was the one we used." (17)

On August 19, "Sandy" Courage was sent into a recording studio to conduct an orchestra, producing *Star Trek*'s opening and closing theme music as well as all the music for "The Man Trap." It was Courage's choice to use the eerie electric violin, featured so prominently in the score of "The Man Trap," for the opening title theme. At the recording session for "The Corbomite Maneuver," the tenth episode to air on NBC, the theme was rerecorded by Fred Steiner, and used for the balance of Season One.

Courage was still working blind. Fred Steiner worked blind, as well, while composing the excellent score for "Charlie X" a few days later, on August 29. He had only his imagination to rely on ... and a final draft shooting script.

The 12 foot, 2 inch model, lit for filming, on the Howard Anderson Company stage, Desilu lot (Courtesy Bob Olsen)

Roddenberry and Justman turned their focus back to The Howard Anderson Company. And, with *Star Trek* now less than three weeks away from its network premiere, Roddenberry's temper finally blew. It was the first time Solow had witnessed *Star Trek*'s creator in a fit of rage. He later described it as being a "sobering sight." (161-3)

Solow quickly called Heath; Heath quickly called Howard Anderson, Jr.; Anderson quickly arranged for a screening. Roddenberry and Justman were present, as was Darrell Anderson. Heath was not. Two minutes into the screening, it was all over. The *Star Trek* men had seen every foot of film the Andersons had shot. According to Justman, out of those two minutes there were, perhaps, "six good shots" and a few others that were "passable."

The lights in the screening room came up. Someone finally asked, "Where's the rest?" Justman remembered that Darrell Anderson began to shake and then jumped to his feet, shouting that *Star Trek* would never make its first air date. As tears came to his eyes, Anderson ran from the room. Roddenberry appeared to be in shock and remained still in his seat. Justman reacted differently. He chased after Anderson, who remained hysterical. He and his brother had been working day and night for months and all they had to show for their labors were two minutes of footage, most of which was dismal.

"By the time I caught up with him, he was weeping uncontrollably," Justman said. "I finally just grabbed hold of him and hugged him to me. I said, 'That's okay, Darrell, that's okay.'" (94-8)

That night Roddenberry and Justman slaved away at a Moviola, salvaging whatever scraps of film they could from the Andersons' two-and-a-half months of work. They also stole shots from the first two pilot films.

"We really put that main title together from nothing," Justman said. "Literally from garbage, trims and rejects." (94-8)

They also set aside enough footage of the Enterprise to satisfy the needs of "The Man Trap," the episode with which NBC had, as expected, opted to launch the series.

Justman said, "We got lucky, and we kind of disproved the old notion that you can't make a silk purse from a sow's ear. Still, this near disaster left Gene with a real hard-on against Bill Heath." (94-8)

The next day Darrell Anderson left for Palm Springs. He was in no condition to continue working. Justman later learned that this was his third nervous breakdown as a result of *Star Trek*. The first came during work on "The Cage." The second was a result of the long hours spent laboring over "Where No Man Has Gone Before," and the third, now, as a result of "The Corbomite Maneuver." Each time Darrell Anderson took on a job for *Star Trek*, he'd worked himself right into a hospital bed.

Things had to change. *Star Trek* needed another staff member -- someone to oversee the production and delivery of the optical effects, someone besides Bill Heath. The only person Roddenberry could think of who might be able and willing to help was Ed Milkis, an assistant film editor from *The Lieutenant*. Milkis remembered, "One afternoon [Gene] called and wanted to talk to me. I agreed to see him the next day and Gene said, 'No, no, I mean now! *Tonight!*'" (119-1)

Roddenberry offered Milkis a staff position to oversee all the effects that were so desperately needed. If he accepted, Milkis would receive the non-descriptive credit of Assistant to the Producer. He was reluctant. He was a film editor, not a post-production supervisor, and argued that he did not know how to manage people and supervise labs. Roddenberry's words were, "Yes, you do. You *do* know how to do it." (119-1)

Milkis, going where no editor had gone before, began his new job the next day.

"We were so under the gun," Milkis explained. "We worked out a routine of going to four different optical houses so that we could spread the work out and I was able to push each house to get the work done." (119-1)

The four competitors, now colleagues, were Film Effects of Hollywood, The Westheimer Company, Cinema Research, and The Howard Anderson Company. The Andersons and Linwood Dunn's Film Effects of Hollywood, the only two to handle the 11-foot, 2-inch Enterprise model, shared elements with each other and with the other two houses, allowing all to complete their *Star Trek* assignments. The house that provided the most new optical effects to an episode was given the screen credit. It was an unprecedented collaboration effort.

Robert Justman said, "Without Eddie Milkis we couldn't have gotten it done. He came along at just the right time. It was Gene and myself doing the show, and there was no staff. There was nothing. We were physically, emotionally and mentally exhausted by the time we were halfway through the first season." (94-17)

"The Man Trap" was finally delivered to NBC on August 29, 1966. The network quickly arranged a test screening and was pleased by the results. The programmers were assured they had chosen well for an episode to debut the series.

That same day, Fred Steiner was sent into the recording studio to lead an orchestra and provide the music for "Charlie X" -- the second regular episode to be scored and, two weeks later, to air.

Two days after that, Alexander Courage returned to score "The Naked Time," the fourth *Star Trek* to air, following the telecast of the second pilot, "Where No Man Has Gone Before," which NBC hadn't wanted to use due to casting and other changes made since it filmed in 1965. There was little choice now -- either the second pilot would air as the third episode or *Star Trek* would be missing from the schedule that night.

***

Scripts need conflict; writers don't.

Roddenberry and his team breathed a momentary sigh of relief. *Star Trek* would make its first four air dates. But the series was still seriously behind schedule and way over budget, and costs had just gone up with the addition of the new staff member. Adding further complications, the scripts for "Shore Leave" and "The City on the Edge of Forever" were far overdue. Renowned science fiction writer Theodore Sturgeon was at work on the first. The equally renowned (and notorious) Harlan Ellison was laboring over the second. Both men, while immensely talented, were not delivering pages at the speed *Star Trek* needed.

Another problem: John D.F. Black wanted out. The *Star Trek* associate producer and script editor, and his now-wife and then-secretary, Mary Black, told their side of the Roddenberry/Black fallout during interviews for this book. Black had given other interviews over the years and the message was consistent -- his four-month stay at *Star Trek* from mid-April to mid-August 1966 was a near-hellish experience.

Black had grown more disenchanted each week, believing Roddenberry's rewrites were damaging to many of the scripts. Black admired writers such as Jerry Sohl, Richard Matheson, George Clayton Johnson, and Robert Bloch. He felt Roddenberry displayed less talent than these men and should not be changing their words. Examination of the various drafts of the scripts for these episodes gives indication that some changes were for the better, some perhaps not, but, generally, it was more so a case of personal taste. Regardless, Black had other issues beyond the caliber of the rewriting. He later said, "I realized that there was no way that I could stay there. I gave the writers my word that they would get to do all their changes first, before we ever got to it. *Because GR told me I could say that.* And then he changed everybody's scripts. There wasn't a script he didn't screw with -- mine, Bob's, Richard's, George's, every script. And every time he did it, it became more and more clear to me that he was making my word bad. Every time I said to a writer, 'Hey, guy, you get to do it; this is a show for a writer; this is a writer's show,' he made my word bad. I was dealing with great writers, too -- Harlan Ellison, Ted Sturgeon, Richard Matheson, George C. Johnson, Bob Bloch. It made no sense." (17)

There were other problems. Mary Black said, "John and I put in long hours. Working until two in the morning was not unusual, because John would get caught on the set, and this and that, and any writing work had to be squeezed in. There was this one time where we had worked incredibly late -- it was at least two o'clock in the morning, it may have even been four o'clock. And then I drove home to the Valley, and then I got back at nine to start another day, and the whole time I was making that drive back to the studio, I was thinking, 'I hate you, Gene Roddenberry. I hate you, I hate you, I hate you.' And, I swear to God, I got back into the office and I was walking along the hall and G.R. was coming in the other direction and he said, 'Good morning, Mary. How are you?' And I smiled and I said, 'I'm fine.' And then I thought, 'What the hell?' But that's just what happened. I had to allow myself to think those thoughts, to say those words in my head, in order to face another day." (17a)

The straw that broke the camel's back, and Black's spirit, was when "GR" rewrote "The Naked Time." This was Black's baby, his first -- and only produced -- original script for the series. Being so closely involved with *Star Trek* and entrusted to rewrite other writers' scripts such as "Mudd's Women" and "Miri," Black believed he would be spared having his material reworked by Roddenberry.

"I could fight for the other writers," Black said, "and I always did. I'd go into G.R.'s office and sit across from him and tell him how I thought he had screwed someone's script up. Sometimes he'd listen, sometimes he wouldn't. Sometimes these meetings would last half-an-hour, sometimes for hours at a time. But he wasn't going to have that kind of a conversation with me over my script. He just changed it." (17)

Mary Black said, "Toward the end, the tension over the rewrites was filling the air. So, a few weeks before the exit, John and I had a conversation and decided that we were going to ask for the moon if we were to stay. We wanted Bob Justman's office, *with the bathroom*, we wanted a written promise from G.R. that he wouldn't do any rewriting unless such'n'such, we wanted a very inflated salary. I can't remember all of the goodies we asked for, but there were a lot." (17a)

John Black said, "We were prepared to say 'yes' if they were willing to give us the moon. Then we would stay. But we didn't expect them to, and they didn't. So it was a happy exit." (17)

Black's work for *Star Trek* ended with a rewrite on the "Miri" script and a first draft of the envelope script for "The Cage," allowing the pilot film to be repurposed to reflect the new cast members and other changes (see "The Menagerie"). Ironically, Black's title for his version of that script was "From the First Day to the Last." Both were delivered August 12.

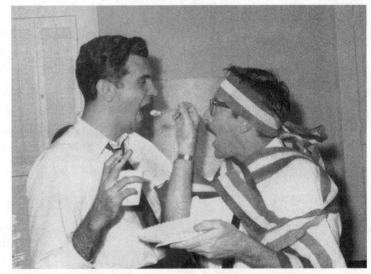

John D.F. Black and Robert Justman – a pleasant exit
(Courtesy of Mary Black)

Black's contract expired two days later on a Sunday.

Mary Black said, "One of us was quoted as saying that we opened a bottle of champagne that last day [Friday, August 10]. It was actually *two* bottles. That was great fun, because the usual inside staff was there – G.R., Majel, Dorothy, Sylvia [Bob Justman's secretary], Harlan Ellison. We had it in G.R.'s office and everybody was very amiable. And it was funny, because Harlan had no head for alcohol. And during the party, Harlan was on one of G.R.'s couches and he was slowly dozing off, just tilting more and more to the side. But it was a very pleasant party; a pleasant exit." (17a)

***

Exhaustion.

Robert Justman was the next to fall. He had been pushing himself beyond the limit, arriving at the studio at 5 a.m., not leaving until 7 or 8 p.m. Once home, he'd eat a quick dinner, then continue working by reading scripts and dictating memos. And he'd do this until he dropped.

"All of a sudden I found myself without the strength to carry on," Justman later acknowledged. "Everything hit me at once. My own inability to function more than 20 hours a day just kind of slammed into me." (94-4)

Justman experienced a breakdown one night while sitting at the dining table. "I was weeping. At the same time, I was trying not to make any noise, because I was embarrassed and ashamed of myself for being so weak as to give in to my emotion." (94-4)

Justman's wife Jackie, finding him in this state, poured a double scotch into her husband, then called Roddenberry and "read Gene the riot act."

Bob and Jackie Justman were sent to Hawaii for a week of R&R by Roddenberry. Awaiting them at the Hanalei Plantation Hotel was a telegram. It read:

DO NOT ACCEPT BILL HEATHS PHONE CALL WE CAN WORK IT OUT HERE. GENE RODDENBERRY.

Bill Heath had been only one of Justman's headaches -- concerning anything to do with the post production, especially the disaster over the photographic effects, or lack of them, which nearly kept *Star Trek* from making its first NBC air date ... or its second ... or its third.

One day later, on October 1, 1966, a new telegram arrived, reading:

DISREGARD LAST MESSAGE PERHAPS YOU HAD BETTER TALK TO HEATH. GENE RODDENBERRY.

And then another, on October 2:

URGENT WHAT DID YOU AND HEATH DECIDE. GENE RODDENBERRY.

Meanwhile, Roddenberry had told his entire staff not to take any calls from a frantic Bob Justman.

The work continued. Roddenberry said, "I don't think there is a person who has worked on this show who has not said to himself, 'I am taking a calculated risk with my health. I could die of a heart attack because of the strain of this work.'" (145-4)

William Shatner said, "A series starts off with a great idea and then time and fatigue affect everybody, so all everybody's trying to do is get the words out, to occupy 52 1/2 minutes of film time.... To do a halfway decent series is a Herculean task." (156-7)

Nimoy said, of that first season, "My days were beginning to blur together; working on a series is, to indulge in some Vulcan-like understatement, grueling." (128-3)

Nimoy's routine began at 5:30 a.m. so he could be in the makeup chair by 6:30.

From makeup, he was off to the rehearsal table and then, a short time later, standing before the cameras. Production was supposed to wrap by 6:20 p.m., but more often than not it went later. And then Nimoy went back into makeup to have the ears and eyebrow and yellow complexion removed. As for interviews with the press, reading fan letters, returning phone calls, and dealing with family matters and personal business, it all had to wait until night and weekends. And whenever a promotional appearance was arranged, it had to be scheduled for those too few days off, or holidays.

Interviewed for a March 1967 *TV Guide* article, Nimoy was asked how the exhausting workload impacted his personal life. He answered, "How do you make a marriage succeed in spite of the rigorous hours on *Star Trek*?... [It] has put my family and me on a stricter schedule than we ever had before. When I was freelancing, I'd often have a few days, sometimes a week or two between jobs. Don't get me wrong; I'm very grateful for the continuous work on *Star Trek*, but it has meant scheduling my time much more carefully. It has invaded some of my personal time." (128-21)

Sandra Nimoy said, "When you're married to an actor, you usually see quite a lot of him, but when he's in a series, you don't. This series has been a traumatic experience for me. It was very difficult at first, and it's still not easy." (128a)

"The first year was very hard work," DeForest Kelley said. "It almost killed us all." (98-8)

***

John D.F. Black, while at *Star Trek*, had been pulling double duty -- first, as one of the series associate producers, and second, as the show's story consultant and script editor. Gene Coon had taken his place with the upgraded title as "Producer." But Coon wanted help and therefore asked that someone else be designated as "Script Consultant."

Steven W. Carabatsos began working in TV just three years earlier when he placed a spec script with *Ben Casey*. That first sell ushered in a couple of additional assignments on *Casey*, and this led to a handful of script jobs with *The Big Valley*. A short tenure on the prime time soap *Peyton Place* followed. Carabatsos was off to an impressive start.

"It was an exciting time for me, because I was really just a kid, and this was a big opportunity," Carabatsos said. As for getting hired by *Star Trek*, he added, "My problem was that I didn't share the background; I didn't quite feel that I had the same preparation for it." (28-1)

Science fiction was not something Carabatsos was deeply interested in. Roddenberry and Coon were clearly taking a chance on their new script editor. Therefore, he was offered a contract for only 13 weeks, commencing on August 8, 1966, as Coon's had. If the series was renewed to finish the season, and things hadn't worked out with Carabatsos, he would be gone before the final episodes of Season One were shot.

***

Immediately after the filming of "Miri" in early September, Roddenberry met with Bob Justman, Herb Solow and Bernard Weitzman, Desilu's V.P. of Business Affairs. *Star Trek* was having money problems. The show now had a new producer whose salary was greater than John D.F. Black's had been, and the production staff increased with the additions of Eddie Milkis and Steven Carabatsos. Another new expense: DeForest Kelley's character of McCoy had worked out so well that he was wanted for nearly every episode produced from this point on.

Joe D'Agosta sent Roddenberry a memo on August 12, telling his boss:

> We have fulfilled our contractual guarantee of shows in this first cycle. DeForest has become enough of a valuable member of our group that I feel his contract should be re-negotiated so that we may have him for more days per show at an agreed salary.

Scotty, Sulu and Uhura were also working out well and wanted for more upcoming episodes. But Desilu was looking to reduce costs. Something, or someone, had to go. D'Agosta told Roddenberry:

> Grace [Whitney], for the most part, has cost us a lot of money for the little that we use her in each show. The character is one that if cast with a freelance player would cost less and would hold as much value. I suggest that we drop her option and use her on a "when needed and if available" freelance basis.

Roddenberry agreed that Yeoman Rand was dispensable. Whitney herself saw this coming and said, "They were starting to write me out of scripts because they thought that the relationship between Bill and I looked too close for him to then be able to cheat while away on other planets. They thought the audience would be upset with him if he cheated on Yeoman Rand, because there was clearly something going on between those two, even if not physical, but emotional." (183-6)

But she didn't suspect that the character would be taken out of *Star Trek* altogether. Nor did Robert Justman. He was against losing her and was surprised, as he saw it, that Roddenberry made no effort with Solow and Weitzman to fight for Grace Lee Whitney. Her agent got the news from Desilu Business Affairs. The contract would not be renewed. Yeoman Rand was not being written out, she would simply disappear.

Yeoman Rand from NBC publicity photo for "The Enemy Within," foreshadowing a traumatized Whitney from August 1966 (Courtesy of Gerald Gurian)

Whitney had been guaranteed only seven episodes and she had already filmed six. A final screen appearance in an episode of *Star Trek* would be so brief that few even noticed her presence. The official word: The character hadn't worked out. Rumors circulated that the actress hadn't worked out, either.

In her book, *The Longest Voyage*, Whitney gave a darker reason for her termination. Following the wrap party for "Miri," the actress accompanied an unnamed "studio executive" back to his office to discuss ideas he had concerning her character. Both had been drinking. The friendly get-together turned ugly. The executive wanted sex. Whitney wanted out. Her future with *Star Trek*, she believed, depended on what she did next. She gave in to the executive's demands. Days later, the call came from her agent -- she was being taken off the show. She later said, "I have always believed that the executive had me removed from *Star Trek* because he didn't want to be reminded of what he did to me that night. In other words, I was sacrificed on the altar of one man's lust and guilt." (183-2)

The curious handling of Yeoman Rand's last appearance in the series supports Whitney's suspicions. The actress' role for the next episode to film -- "The Conscience of the King" -- was downsized to a cameo, even though she was paid to be featured prominently.

At the time of her sacking, Whitney remembered DeForest Kelley and Leonard Nimoy being very "supportive," but they were powerless to keep her involved with the series. Even Roddenberry and Justman seemed lacking in the necessary clout. Whitney said, "Gene Roddenberry had told me that he let Rand go against his will. He did not want to let Rand go. He wanted to keep the [romantic] conflict [between Kirk and Rand] going…. Maybe I wouldn't have been in every episode but I wasn't contracted to be in every one of them anyway. Rand had a lot of strength and a lot of guts. I think her character could have been further developed." (183-7)

In a memo to Gene Coon, dated October 28, 1966, Roddenberry wrote:

> Bob Justman and I both think we should look for an opportunity to bring Grace Lee Whitney back as "Yeoman Rand" in some upcoming episode. We might discuss at that time the possibility of trying some slightly different hairdo, something more on the order of what she wore in 'Police Story.' It actually made her look much younger and softer.

But a certain power-that-be did not want this. Whitney was never asked to return.

***

Nichelle Nichols had survived the first cut. Despite this, for Nichols and her character, it had been a roller coaster ride.

Days before filming began on "The Corbomite Maneuver," a contract was quickly drawn up between Nichols and Desilu. Before it could be signed, the offer was just as quickly withdrawn. In her book, *Beyond Uhura*, Nichols cried "bigotry," writing:

> The network executives saw in the first script exactly what Gene meant when he said he was recasting one part and wanted to add a little "color" to the bridge. After having triumphed in the banishment of "Number One," the network men had a fit when they saw that not only was there now an important woman in the command crew and on the bridge, but a black one! When they realized that Uhura's involvement would be substantial and her lines went well beyond "Yes, Captain," they furiously issued Gene an ultimatum: "Get rid of her!"

It was a curious statement for Nichols to make. Her part in "that first script" was not *that* big. Nor was the part in the second script. Nichols often complained how she had little to do in those first shows other than say "Hailing frequencies open, Captain."

In all fairness to NBC, this was the network that had made history in 1965 by premiering *I Spy*, featuring Bill Cosby in a dramatic lead; the same network that Roddenberry himself admitted wanted to see Sulu, an Asian-American, featured more prominently on the bridge; the same network that didn't utter a single complaint about Lloyd Haynes, who was also black, being on the bridge for "Where No Man Has Gone Before"; the same network that assigned African-American Stan Robertson to serve in the vital position of Production Manager for *Star Trek*; and the same network that, at very near the moment Nichols was told her contract was cancelled, sent out a letter from the executive suite to all their series' producers encouraging increased hiring of non-white actors, with special emphasis on African-Americans.

**NBC: First with prominent interracial casting –
I Spy (Courtesy of 3 F Productions)**

Dated August 17, 1966, Mort Werner wrote about "NBC's longstanding policy of non-discrimination," and the "efforts in the past to assure that the programs broadcast on [their] facilities [be] a natural reflection of the role minorities in American life have met." He added, "We urge producers to cast Negroes," and he congratulated the producers who had extended themselves in that regard.

As for insinuations that the NBC men were sexist as well as racists, consider that, in the fall of 1965, this network gave America its first female spy and single working-girl -- Barbara Feldon in *Get Smart*, followed by Stephanie Powers in *The Girl from U.N.C.L.E.*

Regardless, NBC had nothing to do with the contracts that were negotiated between *Star Trek* and actors such as Nichelle Nichols -- only Desilu was involved in those dealings. But NBC's reputation had been tainted. Someone clearly had told Nichols that story about the network not wanting the character of "Number One" because she was female. The NBC men believed they knew who the instigator was – Gene Roddenberry.

The simple truth was that Nichols' contract rescindment came down to a matter of money. Roddenberry had been giving out contracts too freely, and now the studio was reining him in. He had promised Nichols $1,000 per episode. After only a couple episodes, those he answered to at Desilu, not NBC, were rethinking this handshake agreement. The episodes were coming in over budget and cuts had to be made. Nichols' salary, then, was reduced to $140 per day. If she was needed for all six or seven days required to shoot an episode, she'd make more money than with the previous arrangement.

"Gene kept on writing her in," Bob Justman stated, saying that Roddenberry would tell him, "Nichelle's great, and she's not that expensive. Someone else would cost a whole lot more." (94-8)

At the same time, Roddenberry was writing Majel Barrett back into the series and, in order to get away with this, turning up the heat on NBC by telling tales about how the network had rejected "Number One" on grounds of her gender.

"[Roddenberry] had conveniently forgotten that NBC execs, for both financial and moral reasons, had always favored a strong woman as a series star," Herb Solow insisted. "[NBC] just didn't want Majel. They resented having her forced upon them." (161-3)

This was now "Strike Six." In time, the network brass would strike back.

***

Like any good series creator/producer, Gene Roddenberry was doing all he could to build a buzz for *Star Trek*. For the June 7, 1966, issue of *Daily Variety*, he told staff writer Dave Kaufman, "There have been two types of sci-fi series -- about gadgetry, and fantasy. Rod Serling did a helluva good job on *Twilight Zone*, but basically it was a fantasy series. This is the first attempt to translate science fiction literature into TV. We have people stories. Too many series put gadgets first, people second. We put people first. Sci-fi in TV and pictures has usually consisted of monsters, or a gorilla destroying Tokyo."

Roddenberry boasted how he had nabbed such science fiction notables as Harlan Ellison, A.E. van Vogt, Ray Bradbury, Richard Matheson, Theodore Sturgeon, and Robert Bloch. He also talked about how he worked with RAND Corporation and CalTech in designing his spaceship, saying, "There is nothing about the ship that doesn't have its roots in science, that can't be done from what we know. It's practicable science; everything we do is possible by what we know today, therefore is believable. It's the most ambitious, difficult production ever attempted, because everything we do is new." (145-14)

And then Roddenberry got his first of many digs in against NBC, although a small and seemingly harmless one. Kaufman wrote that "the producer kids [that] they talked about doing a story about a planet populated only by ad agency and network people [but] rejected it because it was too unbelievable."

On June 19, for his syndicated newspaper column, Bob Mackenzie wrote, "We used to call it science fiction, but television producers are now calling it 'science fact.'" Quoting Roddenberry, Mackenzie wrote:

> If only one star in a billion is a sun, and only one sun in a billion has a planet with conditions similar to our Earth, then there is a minimum of three million worlds inhabited by living creatures.... *Star Trek* will concern the intergalactic meanderings of a giant space ship, "a huge star cruiser with displacement of 390,000 tons." This behemoth of the stratosphere contains a crew of 400 and is equipped with laboratories, libraries, offices and recreation rooms. It travels considerably faster than light, speeding between far-flung star systems to carry

out "scientific investigations, diplomatic courtesy calls, and enforcement of the laws that regulate Earth colonies."

Word was out: *Star Trek* was going to be bigger than the one-year-old *Lost in Space*.

For the July 15 issue of *Daily Variety*, Army Archerd quoted Roddenberry, saying, "Outer space is the new west." And then Roddenberry told how he was determined to not lower *Star Trek* to the expectations of children, but "to bring kids up to the level of the show." He added, "And this is a point under discussion right now with NBC." Indicating that the needs of a network and the assembly line approach used in cranking out episodes was counterproductive when striving for excellence, a fatigued Roddenberry said, "We're at the point of crisis in TV -- of how much we can do weekly and produce a quality show. 'Quality' is now the key word for a successful series." (145-15)

Echoing this quest for something that rose above the norm, Archerd told how William Shatner responded to being asked "How is your space show different than others?" The actor said, "We learn a lot." (166-13)

Cynthia Lowry for the *Indiana Evening Gazette*, on August 9, 1966, wrote, "Press agents for a new NBC entry *Star Trek* recently issued a release proclaiming that it was not, *definitely not*, science fiction, but 'real action-adventure in tomorrow's space age.'"

The second word was now out: Downplay the space stuff. NBC, the network that had never before touched science fiction, was doing everything in its power to camouflage *Star Trek* as being something else. In one notorious press release photo, the tops of Spock's pointed ears were airbrushed out, making him appear to be a very normal, quite human male of possibly Asian descent. Other pictures released of Spock were of him facing the camera, making his peculiar ears less apparent.

Pictures of William Shatner were more common, and the NBC boys were happy to promote the third most prominent cast member, that blonde space babe in the red miniskirt with go-go dancer boots ... who just got sacked.

Grace Lee Whitney struck a sexy pose for the August 28, 1966 cover of *TV Week*. The article inside declared, "NBC hopes the science fiction plots won't seem never-ending, and lays stress on the solid adventure approach."

NBC publicity photo airbrushed to give Spock human ears and eyebrows (Courtesy of Gerald Gurian)

Steven Carabatsos said, "They were extremely concerned about the program and how they were going to be perceived in it. Bill Shatner was a finely trained Canadian actor and didn't know what he was getting into. None of us did. Leonard Nimoy was especially concerned, although the Spock character worked out terrifically for him, the program and everyone involved. It could have gone the other way and been just as much an embarrassment." (28-1)

On August 21, the *Los Angeles Herald-Examiner*, in its television magazine, featured the first ever look at the starship Enterprise -- *printed upside down*. The mistake was understandable. Right side up or upside down, nothing like this strange spaceship had been seen before.

NBC was promoting Whitney more than Nimoy in early network publicity photos
(Courtesy Gerald Gurian)

For the first two weeks of September, the *Star Trek* sound stages remained dark. As cast members made themselves available to the press, Eddie Milkis used the time to catch up with the post-production. Gene Coon and Steven Carabatsos reviewed the episodes already filmed and stayed busy rewriting the five still to come. And Roddenberry, with Jerry Sohl, Harlan Ellison, Theodore Sturgeon, and Richard Matheson, traveled to Cleveland for Tricon, the world's largest science fiction convention at the time. It was there, on September 1, that he screened "Where No Man Has Gone Before." Also being shown, courtesy of 20th Century Fox, were the pilot for *The Time Tunnel* and a new film, *Fantastic Voyage*.

Roddenberry said, "I was nervous, particularly when I saw them watching other films that were shown before, and stomping and laughing." (145-9)

Jerry Sohl added, "There was what felt like 3000 people watching a new Irwin Allen show and, as soon as they saw his name, they started booing." (160-2)

But no one booed, stomped their feet or laughed while the *Star Trek* pilot was screened. The room was strangely silent. It remained that way even after the film ended and the lights came up.

Roddenberry reminisced, "I think I finally got to my feet and said, 'Is anybody going to say whether they liked it or not?,' and it was only afterward that the applause began. I remember calling up the studio and saying, 'I really think we may have something here,' and the studio's reaction was, 'Well, so a thousand goofs who go to science fiction conventions like it? That means nothing in television.'" (145-9)

The only studio man Roddenberry would have spoken to was Herb Solow, who had no recollection of saying anything of the sort. And he did not appreciate hearing Roddenberry tell such stories.

Two of the thousand "goofs" Roddenberry befriended at the convention were John and Bjo Trimble, who later proved instrumental in keeping *Star Trek* on NBC... for a while, anyway. The Trimbles were there to oversee the running of a futuristic fashion show. For the event, Roddenberry contributed a couple *Star Trek* uniforms and the costume worn by Sherry Jackson in "What Are Little Girls Made Of?"

Meanwhile, back in Hollywood, the pre-premiere publicity continued. Press releases were sent out; interviews were given.

Captain Kirk made the cover of the September 4 *St. Louis Post-Dispatch TV Magazine*. For the article, *Star Trek* was described as "television's first adult science fiction series." Pictured with Shatner were Nimoy, his Spock ears barely visible, and Grace Lee Whitney, win a gold pilot tunic, billed as the series' female lead.

Roddenberry received positive attention for himself in the *Chicago Tribune* on September 4, with the article "Pilot Turns Cop, Then TV Writer." The pilot/cop/TV writer said that he wished there was another way to categorize *Star Trek* other than calling it "science fiction," for the reason that "many people seem to equate science fiction with monster-who-gobbled-up-Tokyo sort of trash." He went on to tell writer Clay Gowran that the stories on *Star Trek* would focus on people rather than gadgetry, "although they may not always be people as we know them."

Shatner on cover of *TV Magazine*, Sept. 4, 1966, four days before premiere

On August 28, *TV Week*, a syndicated newspaper supplement, ran the article "*Star Trek* Resembles Space *Twilight Zone*." Shatner said, "We're not going to be like the children's show, *Lost in Space*, where characters battle villains in eerie costumes. We deal with human conflicts against a science fiction background." (166-11)

On September 7, one day before *Star Trek*'s NBC premiere, *Daily Variety* ran an interview with Shatner. He told correspondent Dave Kaufman, "We are science fiction, but as in all good sci-fi, human stories are told in futuristic terms.... *Batman* and *Lost in Space* zeroed in on a particular segment of the audience -- *the kids* -- and the proof they hit is their popularity. We are in a different timeslot, and will get an older audience. We are trying to provide action and excitement on one level and on another play a little conflict and character development. Our series has a more mature approach; it has jeopardy, romance, sentiment -- definite elements of entertainment.... If we make it, we will be setting a trend. In movies and TV, there is a cycle of anti-heroes. We are playing exactly opposite -- if nothing else, it's heroic." (166-12)

The week *Star Trek* premiered, NBC sprang for a quarter page ad in *TV Guide* and numerous leading newspapers. It featured Kirk and Spock, with Spock again looking more Asian than Vulcan, and a first look at the Enterprise, *right side up*. The copy read, "Welcome aboard the United Space Ship Enterprise. Where it goes, no program has ever gone before."

19

America Meets *Star Trek*

Half-page print ad taken out by NBC in *TV Guide* and numerous newspapers across the U.S. for the second episode to air, "Charlie X."

Dick Sargent as Tammy's uptight brother, and Grimes, disguised as an Arab Sheik, in *The Tammy Grimes Show* (ABC, 1966)

When *Star Trek* premiered on NBC, the official fall TV season had not yet begun. Even *TV Guide*'s Fall Preview issue was still a week away. But NBC had been running on-air promos for "sneak a peek at NBC week," a seven-day head-start on the traditional fall kick-off.

ABC's competition for *Star Trek* at 8:30 p.m. on Thursdays was *The Tammy Grimes Show*. Grimes was a star on Broadway, having won a Tony award for the lead in *The Unsinkable Molly Brown*. TV came calling and she was offered the role of Samantha Stevens in *Bewitched*. Certain the series would flop, Grimes turned the offer down. Two years later, after the surprise success of *Bewitched*, the unsinkable Tammy Grimes agreed to ABC's second series' offer, a half-hour sit-com presenting the feisty Broadway star as "a madcap heiress."

Star Trek, up against ABC's top show, *Bewitched*, with Elizabeth Montgomery, Dick York, and Agnes Moorehead (ABC, 1966)

And CBS's *My Three Sons*, with Fred MacMurray, William Demarest, and the boys.

Leading the charge on NBC: Fess Parker as *Daniel Boone* (1966) ...

Following *Tammy Grimes* at 9 p.m. was *Bewitched*, returning for its third season. The series was ABC's biggest hit and had become the second-highest rated show on television. Now it would be in color.

Scheduled for 8:30 on CBS was an old favorite: *My Three Sons*. The spirited comedy with a wholesome Disney feel starred Fred MacMurray as a widower raising three well-meaning but rowdy boys. *My Three Sons* had just finished the previous season as the fifteenth most watched series on television and was considered ideal programming for the "family hour." At 9 p.m. was *The CBS Thursday Night Movie*. Well before HBO, Showtime, and Netflix, prime-time movies were a huge draw, and one of the most popular was the Thursday movie on CBS.

TV insiders were predicting *Star Trek* would be lucky to survive the mid-season shakeup. To go beyond that, it needed a lot of help to stay afloat. In television, especially in the day before every TV came with a remote control, a series needed both a strong lead-in and a solid follow-up to keep its audience. *Star Trek* had neither.

The lead-in was *Daniel Boone*, starting its third year. The series had always done respectable business for NBC, but was not a ratings powerhouse. During the series' first year, the raccoon-capped pioneer lost out to CBS's ghoulish family, *The Munsters*. The following season, CBS's *Gilligan's Island* won the ratings race.

The NBC "help" on the back end was a new series called *The Hero*. Unknown funny guy Richard Mulligan (later to gain fame and collect Emmys on *Soap* and *Empty Nest*) played an actor cast as a TV western star who was afraid of horses, allergic to sagebrush, and all thumbs when it came to the fast draw, throwing a punch, kissing the pretty saloon girl, or anything else requiring coordination or guts. His exasperated "real life" wife on the series was Mariette Hartley. She too was years away from stardom.

If *Star Trek* was to succeed, it would have to do so on its own.

Roddenberry wanted "The Corbomite Maneuver" to open for the series, but it was held up in post-production. Of the episodes that were ready, the choices were limited to "Where No Man Has Gone Before" (the second pilot film), "Mudd's Women," "The Enemy Within," "The Man Trap," "The Naked Time" and "Charlie X." The choice was made by process of elimination:

1) With the second pilot, many of *Star Trek*'s key characters were not yet in place, particularly Dr. McCoy. Also missing was Janice Rand, who was featured in most of the network's advance publicity. Therefore, "Where No Man Has Gone Before" was not even in the running.

2) "Mudd's Women" was not on the negotiating table, either. Space hookers and the Venus Drug! It was surprising NBC even allowed the episode to get made.

... and covering the rear: Richard Mulligan as *The Hero* (NBC, 1966)

3) "The Enemy Within," that *Dr. Jekyll and Mr. Hyde* story in which a transporter mishap splits Kirk in two, exposing his hedonistic dark side, was hardly an appropriate choice for introducing the series and its hero to a television audience. Stan Robertson had already warned Roddenberry that this one would not be among the first to air.

4) "The Naked Time" was also out. A first look at Spock was challenging enough for the TV audience. Seeing him break down and cry was completely out of the question.

5) "Charlie X" was well-crafted, sensitive and effective, but deemed by the network to be a "slow-starter" leaning toward conflict on an intellectual level rather than tried-and-true physical action. Besides, thought the network, how many adult viewers were going to be interested in the sexual frustrations of an orphaned teenager?

6) "The Man Trap," then, was the winner by default.

The plan, as of August 4, 1966, was to lead off with "The Man Trap," followed by "The Corbomite Maneuver," provided the latter was even ready. Five days later, on August 9, as the progress (or lack thereof) with the demanding optical effects became better known, "Charlie X" replaced "Corbomite" in the schedule as episode No. 2. "Corbomite" was pushed back to Week 5. Three days later, with a revised list of air dates, it was pushed further, to position six. By August 23, it was listed as the eighth planned broadcast. And, by the time that list was revised a couple weeks later, "Corbomite" was delegated to the position of tenth to air. The sequencing of *Star Trek* episodes, during the first half of the first season, was based on availability more than any other factor.

America and Canada's sneak peek of *Star Trek* was "The Man Trap," the winner by default. The reviews were mixed.

Daily Variety, on September 8, warned:

> There had better be a hefty cargo of ["sci-fi buffs"] or the Nielsen samples may come up short. It's not for the common herd who prefer less cerebral exercises.

Weekly Variety, also on September 8, was equally discouraging, writing:

> *Star Trek* obviously solicits all-out suspension of disbelief, but it won't work.... The biggest guessing game is figuring out how this lowercase fantasia broke into the schedule.

On September 8, for his syndicated column, *TV Key Previews*, Steven H. Scheuer wrote:

> *Star Trek* is good science fiction, with great special effects, imaginative sets and a fine performance by William Shatner, who plays Captain James Kirk, commander of a spaceship on a five year tour of duty, checking in on galaxies and delivering supplies to space stations.

That same day, Hal Humphrey, for *The Los Angeles Times*, began his review with the stinging headline, "Stars Take a *Trek* into a Real Mess."

Percy Shain, for *The Boston Globe*, deemed it "too clumsily conceived and poorly developed to rate an A-1 effort."

Bob Williams of *The New York Post* said, "One may need something of a pointed head to get involved."

Ann Hodges, writing for *The Houston Chronicle*, dismissed "The Man Trap" as being a "disappointingly bizarre hour," adding, "Things better improve or this won't be a lengthy mission."

Taking the counter-point, Bill Ornstein of *The Hollywood Reporter* wrote, "There's quite a bit of tricks with gadgets that will please sci-fi buffs no end." He felt Marc Daniels directed with "an eye for building suspense." His conclusion: "*Star Trek* should be a winner."

Harry Harris, for *The Philadelphia Inquirer*, called the premiere a "suspenseful, puzzling and ultra-imaginative yarn."

The Indiana Evening Gazette called *Star Trek* "A good science fiction with great special effects."

Bill Irvin for *Chicago's American* proclaimed, "I LIKE THIS ONE!"

TV Guide, for its September 10 issue, took a tongue-in-cheek tone when its reviewer told America:

> [The ship's] officers and crew include representatives of every known race and gender, plus one startling character called Mr. Spock (Leonard Nimoy), who has pointy ears, slanty eyebrows and Beatles bangs, and turns out to be half-earthling, half-Vulcanian and all business (creatures from the planet Vulcanis [sic], as we all know, never display emotion). What these galaxy-trotters run into out there is even stranger to behold than spooky Spocky.

William E. Sarmento, for his syndicated Showtime column on September 13, wrote:

> *Star Trek* is for the science fiction crowd and although I am not a loyal member of that group, the first show of this series had me interested. It needs more action and spectacular gimmicks but *Star Trek* could make it.

Terrance O'Flaherty of *The San Francisco Chronicle*, on September 15, had an indecisive thumb. On the plus side, he was intrigued by the first episode, calling it a "breath-catcher" and considered Shatner "a capable man to have at the helm." On the negative was just about everything else.

Before the premiere, the network hadn't been pleased with Roddenberry. With the reviews leaning more toward the negative, some execs figured this as "Strike Seven." According to Herb Solow, "The day after the series premiered to mediocre reviews from around the country, NBC decided it wasn't totally happy with *Star Trek*." (161-3)

But then came the ratings.

***

**NBC promotional launch of *Star Trek*
(Courtesy of Gerald Gurian)**

In the 1960s, A.C. Nielsen delivered the gospel that the networks swore by. But there was an air of secrecy surrounding the gospels -- the ratings reports were not for public consumption. Nielsen would "loan" the survey documents to its customers -- NBC, CBS and ABC, who were very selective with whom the information was shared. Unlike today, those all-important life and death numbers for a television series were confidential. The theory was that if an actor, or producer for that matter, knew exactly how popular his show was, he would be all the more difficult to deal with. Time has proven this thinking correct. Consider how much more a star of a popular series is paid today compared to the 1960s. Shatner was a top-dollar star in 1966, but was only making $5,000 per episode. That would be comparable to around $35,000 in 2013, a paycheck that today's TV stars wouldn't even get out of bed for. (Try a quarter of a million dollars per episode ... or half a million ... or, in some special cases, a cool million.) Somewhere along the line the stars and their agents got smart, and the networks and the studios lost control. In *Star Trek*'s day, however, the power was still held in check by the networks, and NBC was not about to share it with Gene Roddenberry.

The reason behind all the misconceptions concerning *Star Trek*'s ratings has more to do with all the "strikes" tallied in these pages -- the history of Roddenberry versus the network men -- than perhaps anything else. Television networks are run by ego-driven people, and not all business decisions are based entirely on what is good for business. Some are more personal. Some are anything but logical.

Those ratings reports, which have not been examined since first prepared (1966-69), have been exhumed for this document. Much of the information presented here and elsewhere in this book has not been previously shared with the public. The truth is, *Star Trek* did far better in the ratings than NBC and 47 years of folklore would have us believe.

"The Man Trap" hit big in the ratings, drawing 46.7% of the TVs in use throughout America. The rating was a triumphant 25.2, compared to the 14.1 attributed to *The Tammy Grimes Show* and the 9.4 to *My Three Sons*. (Ratings reflect the total population of those watching, in the millions, while audience share reflects the percentage of TVs in use that evening, tuned to a particular show.)

Star Trek remained the clear winner at 9 p.m., as well. ABC's most popular series, *Bewitched*, drew a 15.8 rating. On *The CBS Thursday Night Movie* was *The Ladies Man*, starring Jerry Lewis. It only managed a 10.7. *Star Trek* towered above them with a 24.2 rating and 42.2% of the TV audience.

Lucille Ball was the first to congratulate Roddenberry and his team. Her letter read:

> Dear Gene and the rest of you hardworking people... Just heard the good news and want you to know how proud and happy I am. Looks like you really have a hit on your hands, and we all appreciate your efforts. Love, Lucy.

The following week, during the first half hour of "Charlie X," *Star Trek* tied for first place with *My Three Sons*. Both attracted a 36% share. *The Tammy Grimes Show* came in third with 22.4%.

One week later, short on available episodes, NBC opted to air "Where No Man Has Gone Before," even though there had been cast changes, costume changes, and changes to the Enterprise itself since the pilot was made. Within days, Nielsen pronounced *Star Trek* as No. 1 at 8:30, pulling a 19.9 rating and nearly 35% of the TV audience. *My Three Sons*, in second place, had 28%. The race at 9 p.m. was virtually a tie, with *Bewitched* drawing 31.8% of the viewing audience, *Star Trek* with 31%, and the CBS movie *Good Neighbor Sam*, a 1964 comedy starring Jack Lemmon, with 30.5%.

A deeper National study by A.C. Nielsen, combining the ratings for Week 2 and 3 (the first official two weeks of the new season, ignoring Week 1 -- the "Sneak a Peek" week), was reported by industry trade magazine *Variety* on October 12, 1966. The new report, ranking all 90 of the prime time series shown during that two-week period on NBC, CBS and ABC, representing a more intense study of smaller town and farm communities, improved the placement of series with rural appeal, such as *My Three Sons*. For this study, *Star Trek* was securely placed within the Top 40.

A.C. Nielsen National Report, covering September 12 - 25, 1966
(from *Variety* magazine, October 12, 1966):

Rank / Program:	Rating:	Rank / Program:	Rating:
1. *Sunday Night Movie* (ABC)	38.3	21. *Bewitched* (ABC)	19.8
2. *Green Acres* (CBS)	25.7	21. *Get Smart* (NBC)	19.8
3. *Rat Patrol* (ABC)	25.1	23. *Girl from U.N.C.L.E.* (NBC)	19.7
4. *Gomer Pyle, U.S.M.C.* (CBS)	24.9	24. *Friday Night Movie* (CBS)	19.5
4. *Bonanza* (NBC)	24.9	24. *Pruitts of Southampton* (ABC)	19.5
6. *Andy Griffith Show* (CBS)	24.6	24. *Tuesday Night Movie* (NBC)	19.5
7. *Saturday Night Movie* (NBC)	23.6	27. *Daktari* (CBS)	19.4
8. *Lucy Show* (CBS)	23.4	28. *Love on a Rooftop* (ABC)	19.3
9. *Red Skelton Show* (CBS)	23.3	29. *Lawrence Welk Show* (ABC)	19.1
10. *The Jackie Gleason Show* (CBS)	22.4	30. *Pistols 'n' Petticoats* (CBS)	18.9
10. *Beverly Hillbillies* (CBS)	22.4	**31. *Star Trek* (NBC)**	**18.7**
12. *My Three Sons* (CBS)	22.1	32. *Ed Sullivan Show* (CBS)	18.6
13. *Family Affair* (CBS)	21.4	32. *Peyton Place* (Wednesday) (ABC)	18.6
14. *The Virginian* (NBC)	21.2	34. *Batman* (Thursday) (ABC)	18.5
15. *Thursday Night Movie* (CBS)	20.8	34. *Hogan's Heroes* (CBS)	18.5
16. *Felony Squad* (ABC)	20.5	34. *Gunsmoke* (CBS)	18.5
17. *Man from U.N.C.L.E.* (NBC)	20.2	37. *It's About Time* (CBS)	18.3
17. *Occasional Wife* (NBC)	20.2	37. *Iron Horse* (ABC)	18.3
19. *Peyton Place* (Monday) (ABC)	20.1	39. *The Fugitive* (ABC)	18.2
19. *I Spy* (NBC)	20.1	40. *Lost in Space* (CBS)	18.1

A second report for this two-week period, this time a Trendex survey based on a National telephone poll conducted in 12 major cities, including New York, Los Angeles, and Chicago, also placed *Star Trek* into the Top 40, tied with the popular *Ed Sullivan Show* for the 33rd position.

Trendex Ratings, covering September 12 - 25, 1966
(from *Broadcasting* magazine, October 17, 1966):

Rank / Program:	Rating:	Rank / Program:	Rating:
1. Sunday Night Movie (ABC)	38.3	47. *The Big Valley* (ABC)	17.7
2. *Green Acres* (CBS)	25.7	48. *Dean Martin Show* (NBC)	17.6
3. *Rat Patrol* (ABC)	25.1	49. *T.H.E. Cat* (NBC)	17.5
4. *Bonanza* (NBC)	24.9	50. *The Man Who Never Was* (ABC)	17.3
4. *Gomer Pyle, U.S.M.C.* (CBS)	24.9	50. *Tarzan* (NBC)	17.3
6. *Andy Griffith Show* (CBS)	24.6	52. *Flipper* (NBC)	17.1
7. Saturday Night Movie (NBC)	23.6	52. *Road West* (NBC)	17.1
8. *Lucy Show* (CBS)	23.4	54. *Run, Buddy, Run* (CBS)	17.0
9. *Red Skelton Show* (CBS)	23.3	55. *The Monroes* (ABC)	16.9
10. *Beverly Hillbillies* (CBS)	22.4	55. *That Girl* (ABC)	16.9
10. *The Jackie Gleason Show* (CBS)	22.4	57. *Batman* (Wednesday) (ABC)	16.8
12. *My Three Sons* (CBS)	22.1	57. *Daniel Boone* (NBC)	16.8
13. *Family Affair* (CBS)	21.4	57. *Petticoat Junction* (CBS)	16.8
14. *The Virginian* (NBC)	21.2	57. *Run for Your Life* (NBC)	16.8
15. Thursday Night Movie (CBS)	20.8	61. *Gilligan's Island* (CBS)	16.7
16. *Felony Squad* (ABC)	20.5	62. *Jericho* (CBS)	16.5
17. *Man from U.N.C.L.E.* (NBC)	20.2	62. *The Rounders* (ABC)	16.5
17. *Occasional Wife* (NBC)	20.2	64. *Voyage to the Bottom of the Sea* (ABC)	16.3
19. *I Spy* (NBC)	20.1	65. *The Monkees* (NBC)	16.2
19. *Peyton Place* (Monday) (ABC)	20.1	66. *Time Tunnel* (ABC)	16.0
21. *Bewitched* (ABC)	19.8	67. *Jean Arthur Show* (CBS)	15.8
21. *Get Smart* (NBC)	19.8	68. *Mission: Impossible* (CBS)	15.5
23. *Girl from U.N.C.L.E.* (NBC)	19.7	69. *Walt Disney's World of Color* (NBC)	15.2
24. Friday Night Movie (CBS)	19.5	70. *Danny Kaye Show* (CBS)	15.1
24. *Pruitts of Southampton* (ABC)	19.5	70. *Hollywood Palace* (ABC)	15.1
24. Tuesday Night Movie (NBC)	19.5	70. *Please Don't Eat the Daisies* (NBC)	15.1
27. *Daktari* (CBS)	19.4	73. *Green Hornet* (ABC)	15.0
28. *Love on a Rooftop* (ABC)	19.3	74. *The Wild, Wild West* (CBS)	14.7
29. *Lawrence Welk Show* (ABC)	19.1	75. *Combat!* (ABC)	14.5
30. *Pistols 'n' Petticoats* (CBS)	18.9	75. *Laredo* (NBC)	14.5
31. *I Dream of Jeanie* (NBC)	18.8	77. *Andy Williams Show* (NBC)	14.4
31. Sunday Night Movie (ABC)	18.8	78. *Roger Miller Show* (NBC)	14.1
33. *Star Trek* (NBC)	**18.7**	79. *Hey, Landlord* (NBC)	13.7
33. *Ed Sullivan Show* (CBS)	18.7	80. *Milton Berle Show* (ABC)	13.4
35. *Peyton Place* (Wednesday) (ABC)	18.6	81. *The Hero* (NBC)	13.2
36. *Batman* (Thursday) (ABC)	18.5	82. *Candid Camera* (CBS)	12.8
36. *Gunsmoke* (CBS)	18.5	82. *Tammy Grimes Show* (ABC)	12.8
36. *Hogan's Heroes* (CBS)	18.5	83. *Hawk* (ABC)	12.7
39. *Iron Horse* (ABC)	18.3	84. *Shane* (ABC)	12.4
39. *It's About Time* (CBS)	18.3	85. *I've Got a Secret* (CBS)	12.3
41. *The Fugitive* (ABC)	18.2	86. *ABC Stage '67* (ABC)	12.2
42. *Lost in Space* (CBS)	18.1	87. *What's My Line* (CBS)	11.5
43. *Bob Hope Chrysler Theater* (NBC)	18.0	88. *12 O'clock High* (ABC)	11.1
44. *F Troop* (ABC)	17.8	89. *Garry Moore Show* (CBS)	10.9
44. *The F.B.I.* (ABC)	17.8	90. *CBS News Hour* (CBS)	7.6
44. *Lassie* (CBS)	17.8		

Both of the Nielsen National reports, the first based on daily "ratings logs" kept by "Nielsen Families," and the second based on a 12-city phone survey, placed *Star Trek* above many series considered to be hits of the day, such as *Gunsmoke*, *Hogan's Heroes*, *The Fugitive*, and *The Dean Martin Show*. *Star Trek* was also outperforming its sci-fi competitors *Lost in Space*, *Voyage to the Bottom of the Sea*, and *Time Tunnel*, and was a surprising 35 positions ahead of its sister show, *Mission: Impossible*.

Perhaps more significantly, *Bewitched*, which had averaged in at No. 7 out of 90 shows during the previous year in the same time slot and with the same competition from CBS, was now down to No. 21. The only change was with the competition from NBC -- from the western *Laredo* to *Star Trek*.

At this time, TvQ, the "Home Testing Institutes' qualitative report on television acceptance," conducted a survey of its own, ranking American's Top 20 favorite prime time shows. *Star Trek* made the list. In a separate survey, disclosed in the October 26, 1966 issue of *Daily Variety*, this time ranking the new favorite shows among men, all ages for the first few weeks of the new season, TvQ placed *Star Trek* at No. 2 out of 90.

For its fourth week on the air, with "The Naked Time," according to TvQ *Star Trek* won its time slot for the entire hour.

One week after this, with the airing of "The Enemy Within," A.C. Nielsen reported that *Star Trek* tied *My Three Sons* for the top spot between 8:30 and 9 p.m. on Thursday. With the attempted rape of Yeoman Rand by Captain Kirk, and the arrival of *Breakfast at Tiffany's* on CBS, the numbers dropped for the second half hour.

In its sixth ratings week, *Star Trek* was again looking strong according to Nielsen. "Mudd's Women" topped the 8:30 p.m. competition, which included *The Dating Game*, brought in by ABC to replace the underachieving *Tammy Grimes Show*. *Trek* had 31.4% of the TVs in use, leaving 28.8% for *My Three Sons* and 28.6% for *The Dating Game*. At 9 p.m., *Star Trek* tied *The CBS Thursday Night Movie*, up to a 31.5% share, besting *Bewitched*, which drew 30.1%.

Star Trek's victory was all the more impressive when considering the "help" it was given, with the lead-in of *Daniel Boone* and the back-end support of *The Hero*. On this week, typical of most weeks, *Daniel Boone* attracted a 14.4 rating for the network, which *Star Trek* then increased to a solid 19. Once *Trek* cleared the air, *The Hero* allowed those audience numbers to dwindle to a 10.9. Weeks earlier, with the Trendex report ranking the Top 90 series over a two-week period, *Daniel Boone*'s averages had it placed at number 57. *Star Trek* came in at 33. *The Hero*, in Nielsen's Bottom 10, was a grim 81. Another much-ballyhooed NBC show -- *The Dean Martin Show* -- was coming in at number 48. *Star Trek*, NBC's biggest Thursday night performer, had succeeded on its own.

Within days after the airing of "Mudd's Women," NBC made its decision. *Star Trek*, *Daniel Boone* and *The Dean Martin Show* were picked up for the remainder of the season. *The Hero* was cancelled. (It would vanish in eight weeks, replaced by a revival of an old NBC hit: *Dragnet*.) For the cast and crew of *Star Trek*, the success in the ratings race meant the race to produce the next batch of episodes was back in high gear.

Episode 12: THE CONSCIENCE OF THE KING
Written by Barry Trivers
(with Gene L. Coon, uncredited)
Directed by Gerd Oswald

Arnold Moss and Barbara Anderson,
NBC publicity photo (Courtesy of Gerald Gurian)

NBC press release, November 15, 1966:

The USS Enterprise provides passage for a stranded troupe of Shakespearean actors, one of whom plots the murder of Captain Kirk (William Shatner), in "The Conscience of the King" on the NBC Television Network colorcast of *Star Trek* on Dec. 8.... Although Kirk suspects that actor Anton Karidian (Arnold Moss) is actually a former notorious rebel leader, long-sought by authorities but now believed dead, there is insufficient proof to make an arrest. Meanwhile, Karidian's beautiful actress-daughter Lenore (Barbara Anderson) offers a special performance of *Hamlet* aboard ship as an expression of gratitude for being rescued. Kirk agrees, unaware he is setting the stage for a tragedy not in the script.

With the recent murder of Kirk's friend, Dr. Thomas Leighton, the Captain is one of only two surviving witnesses who might be able to identify the long-missing fugitive, Kodos the Executioner, who was responsible for the slaughter of 4,000 people. The other is Enterprise crewman Lt. Kevin Riley, and an attempt has now been made on his life.

This story has a unique hook: Shakespeare in space. The theme is one of vengeance, guilt, and self-punishment. Like the plays of Shakespeare, this is Man versus Himself every bit as much as it is Man versus Man.

SOUND BITES

- *Dr. McCoy:* "What if you decide he *is* Kodos? What then? Do you play God; carry his head through the corridors in triumph? That won't bring back the dead, Jim!" *Kirk:* "No. But they may rest easier."

- *Lenore:* "There is a stain of cruelty on your shining armor, Captain. You could have spared him.... You are like your ship. Powerful, and not human. There is no mercy in you." *Kirk:* "If he is Kodos, then I have already shown him more mercy than he deserves. If he isn't... then we'll put you ashore at Benicia... with no harm done." *Lenore:* "Who are you to say what harm is done?" *Kirk:* "Who do I have to be?"

- *Kirk:* "What were you 20 years ago?" *Karidian:* "Younger, captain. Much younger.... Blood thins. The body fails. One is eventually grateful for a failing memory."

ASSESSMENT

This is an episode of firsts and lasts. It's Yeoman Janice Rand's last appearance; it gives us the first mention of the shuttlecraft (and the observation deck that overlooks the flight deck); and we get our first and only explanation of the mood lighting on the Enterprise, designed to simulate day and night. It is also both the first and last time music was provided by composer Joseph Mullendore.

"The Conscience of the King" is an atypical *Star Trek*. Anyone looking for a fast-paced story with action, chills and out-of-this-world gadgetry will be disappointed. NBC certainly was. Others will find it to have profound depth and purpose.

The title is from *Hamlet*: "The play's the thing," Shakespeare wrote, "wherein I'll catch the conscience of the king." The script parallels Shakespeare's play in many ways: a leader struggles with his conscience; he is at risk of having his crimes exposed; and he has a daughter who goes mad with guilt.

In the teaser, the Karidian Company performs a scene from Shakespeare's *Macbeth*. Karidian, as Macbeth, murders King Duncan and utters, "Will all Neptune's great ocean wash this blood clean from my hand?" The role of the actor playing this tragic character of literature is a tragic character himself. He hides behind roles that force him to act out his anguish, and this goes to the heart of Shakespeare's writing -- characters engaged in obsessive self-examination. In this regard, Karidian is not alone. Tom Leighton, a witness to the 20-year-old slaughter on Tarsus IV, lives with the lingering images that haunt him. Leighton's wife Martha says, "He really died the first day those players arrived. Memory killed him, Jim. Do you suppose that survivors ever really recover from a tragedy?"

Kirk, like Captain Horatio Hornblower, is also prone to deep self-examination, but prefers to bury his suffering in the past. Early in the story, he tells Tom Leighton, "Kodos is dead. I'm satisfied with that. You've never let it out of your mind. Now it's become an obsession. It's over. Leave it that way. *He's dead*."

Despite his own advice, Kirk finds himself alone in the briefing room, revisiting a dark moment in his past with the help of the computer. Even before his friend is murdered, Kirk has begun his witch hunt.

Of her recently deceased husband, Martha Leighton says, "Twenty years and he still had nightmares -- I'd wake him and he'd tell me that he still heard the screams of the innocent -- the silence of the executed. Every dawn is a funeral. *That's* what killed my husband."

To create a parallel, writer Barry Trivers deliberately set the holocaust on Tarsus IV 20 years in Kirk's past; it was 20 years prior to this production when trials were conducted in Germany on charges of horrific crimes against humanity. Scores of Nazi officers took flight to avoid prosecution; there was even question as to whether Hitler had actually died. As "The Conscience of the King" was written and filmed, the scars from 20 years prior were still very much on the surface for all who witnessed the madness of the Nazi regime.

"The Conscience of the King" is purposeful drama with multiple levels of conflict for our protagonist -- Kirk – squared off against Leighton, against Karidian, against Lenore, against Spock and McCoy, against Riley, against himself. The episode may lack action, but the story does not lack conflict.

THE STORY BEHIND THE STORY

Script Timeline
Barry Trivers' story outline, ST #17: April 5, 1966.
Trivers' revised story outlines, gratis: April 13, 1966.
Trivers' 2nd Revised Story Outline, gratis: April 18, 1966.
Trivers' 1st Draft teleplay: May 9, 1966.
Trivers' Revised 1st Draft teleplay, gratis: May 12, 1966.
Trivers' 2nd Draft teleplay: June 8, 1966.
Trivers' Rev. 2nd Draft teleplay, gratis: July 11, 1966.
Steven Carabatsos script polish (Mimeo Depart.Yellow Cover 1st Draft):
August 11, 1966.
Gene Coon's rewrite (Final Draft teleplay): August 23, 1966.
Additional page revisions by Coon: August 25 & 30, 1966.
Coon's second rewrite (Rev. Final Draft teleplay): September 8, 1966.
Additional page revisions by Coon: Sept. 9, 12, 13, 14, 15, 19, 20 & 22, 1966.

Barry Trivers, an admirer of William Shakespeare and sensitive to the pain of those who witnessed the holocaust, was 59. He wrote the screenplays to nearly 40 movies from 1931 to 1951, most notably *The Flying Tigers*, starring John Wayne. Turning to television in the 1950s, Trivers frequently provided scripts for series as diverse as *The Millionaire*, *Have Gun - Will Travel*, and *Combat!* And Trivers had a commanding presence at the Writers Guild of America, where, in 1961, he shared responsibilities as Vice President with Christopher Knopf (another writer Roddenberry had his eye on for *Star Trek*). Like Roddenberry, John D.F. Black, and Knopf, Trivers had been the recipient of a WGA award. His came in 1962 for an episode of *The Naked City* with another title borrowed from Shakespeare: "The Fault in Our Stars."

Roddenberry was still the sole producer when the concept for this story was pitched and developed. Trivers stumbled at his first written attempt. His treatment from April 5, 1966, told us that the slaughter Kirk witnessed as a boy took place on Earth, which had been invaded by "an army of marauders" who "pillaged, burned, and murdered, waging Hitlerian war and, like Hitler, almost conquered the Earth." Trivers wrote how these marauders led by Karidian conducted "a program of extermination" and that one of the first victims was "Area Commander Kirk, Governor of a Province" -- James Kirk's father.

Roddenberry in no way wanted to depict such a bleak future for Earth. Nor did he want the parallel between Karidian and his forces to be so dead on with that of Hitler and his Nazi regime. Trivers was asked to reinvent his story.

The freebie revised story outline arrived on April 13. This time Trivers established the theme in the first sentence, writing, "Our story deals with the question: When does the search for Justice become a drive for Vengeance?" The back-story now had Kirk, as a boy, living with his father who headed up a research expedition at an Earth colony on an alien world. The colony is captured by "a group of revolutionaries led by Kodos." Again, Kirk's father is among those killed.

Bob Justman wrote to Roddenberry:

> There is a good story here, but it seems to take too long to get to it.... Throughout the whole story, I feel that we should be extremely careful in handling Kirk. His obsession with regard to Karidian has all the overtones of a personal vendetta. To an extent this vendetta damages his personal fitness for

command and must be carefully examined. (RJ12-1)

One day later, Roddenberry wrote to both Justman and John D.F. Black, saying:

> Mister Spock -- playing a solemn kind of Horatio -- warns against rashness in making any kind of charge unless Kirk is sure. But Kirk -- a kind of Hamlet -- is intent on learning the truth and punishing the villain. In other words, play the Hamlet theme with the exception that our Captain has not the Hamlet melancholia and vacillation. He must remain a man of strength and action.... Kirk is suddenly aware of the fact the ship is large and lonely for him -- he is a man who must, by position, have few friends and who must walk alone in many places. <u>There should be at least one attempt on his life</u> -- one that comes very close to succeeding. (GR12-1)

Roddenberry immediately vetoed the idea of Kirk witnessing the death of his own father, telling Black and Justman:

> The writer will be asked to eliminate the past murder of Captain James Kirk's father, substitute instead the murder of a very close friend, co-officer, or perhaps the killing of a beloved starship commander under whom Kirk earlier served.... But... not tying us down to an aspect of Kirk's close family past, creating something which may hem us in later. (GR12-1)

Trivers made the necessary changes, again at no charge, and turned in a second revised story outline on April 18. Roddenberry felt it was good enough to send to NBC. Stan Robertson, speaking for the network, responded:

> It would seem that this is an excellent piece for the writer to get his teeth into. This is a fine vehicle to further establish the character of Kirk, to show a deepening insight into both his human and heroic makeup. Also, for our other principal, Mr. Spock -- a man of cold reason, logic, and without emotion. The "chemistry" between the two, both men respecting and liking each other genuinely in a strong fashion, but neither really able to understand the other during the times of great stress. (SR12-1)

It was an idea from Stan Robertson that led to the attempted murder of Lt. Kevin Riley. Trivers had written in his outline that a crewmember was murdered. Robertson suggested:

> The death of the technician seems rather needless. You might consider the attempted murder of a person "mistaken" for Kirk.... Kirk's suspicion of the father could be made even more concrete by this act and his belief that there is a killer on the Starship.

With network approval, Trivers went to work on his teleplay. He delivered the first draft on May 9. Robert Justman checked in later that day, writing to John Black:

> I would like to state that I am about as close to being thrilled as I could ever be upon reading a first draft screenplay. (RJ12-2)

Of course, the script still had a long ways to go. More notes from all involved, funneled through and interpreted by Roddenberry, went to Trivers, to which he reluctantly yielded on numerous points. His free rewrite -- a Revised First Draft -- was dated May 12. John D.F. Black was first to respond, telling Roddenberry:

> Barry still labors under the false conviction that his original version of the script was a highly acceptable job.... However, he also bought your approach and explanation as to the reasons for changes in the story, structure, etc. (JDFB12-1)

More changes led to what Trivers thought would be his final handling of the script -- the official 2nd Draft of June 8. The attempt on Kirk's life that Roddenberry wanted was here but, as Trivers envisioned it, the threat came from a bomb planted in the Captain's quarters which, if triggered, would destroy the entire ship. Of this, Justman wrote to Black:

> I am completely befuddled by the explosion sequence.... I just don't get it. I understand the need for creating further hazard for Captain Kirk, but I don't believe that this is the way to get it.... If it would blow the ship up, it certainly isn't a good way to silence Captain Kirk. Well, yes, it is a good way to silence Captain Kirk, but it is also a good way to silence everyone else on board, including the person who planted the device in the first place. (RJ12-3)

Justman was sadly amused at how Trivers had Kirk run from his room, "screaming" to crew members in the corridor, "Fire in the hole [sic]!" Of this, he commented:

> The correct term is "Fire in the hold." Also, this line should be read by Captain Horatio Hornblower instead of Captain James Kirk.... Okay, so maybe I can believe that Lenore can gather like a cat and grab a phaser from a Guard's belt. But you don't think that Kirk is plenty stupid to advance on Lenore, knowing that she is psycho and wants to kill him anyhow? Also, why the hell does she shoot her father? (RJ12-3)

Justman also questioned whether there was truly a need for Yeoman Janice Rand in this story. From what he was reading, he felt there was not.

Later that day, Roddenberry dictated a letter to Barry Trivers. He began:

> It is good to get an honest rewrite. By that I mean, one doesn't necessarily have to agree with everything -- there can still be suggestions and comments for the polish, but it is refreshing to read a rewrite which is the author's full effort with no hanging back or dogging it. You don't shortchange, my friend... All in all, it begins to feel like a most exciting episode, even a memorable one. (GR12-2)

Déjà vu. The wording rings of Roddenberry's letter to Adrian Spies concerning needing yet another polish on the "Miri" script. That letter, in fact, was written only one day before this new one. Roddenberry was fishing from a different water hole, but for the same catch -- a free rewrite. He saw this script -- draft number three -- as representing a good starting point. In his 12-page memo, he asked for many changes in the areas of story, structure, characterization and dialogue. In other words, *everything*.

Roddenberry's main concern, as far as characterization was concerned, involved Mr. Spock. He told Trivers:

> Mr. Spock, frankly, has been a problem to all of us. We find ourselves blessed with one of the finest actors in town in Leonard Nimoy, and with a strange half-alien character who very well could be the hit of the year -- and yet we all keep missing on him, somehow. Only lately, working with him on stage and after hours in the office, have we begun to get a hint of where we should be going.... He pretends not to feel; is revolted by displays of emotion. We're finding our key in the word "pretend." Just as the Captain, in order to keep him identifiable and believable, where you must constantly give us the man peeking out from behind the image of the commander, we must have the half-human aspect of Spock constantly peeking out from behind his chosen image of imperturbable logic. (GR12-2)

Roddenberry disagreed with Justman about Janice Rand being unimportant to the story. But he did agree that she was under-utilized. While he was pleased that Trivers had

Rand interrupt Kirk and Lenore Karidian as they seem to be heading toward romance on the observation deck, he saw potential to create additional conflict by having Rand on the bridge when Lenore first calls on Kirk in hopes of securing passage for the Shakespearian troupe. He told Trivers:

> Would also suggest we might introduce Yeoman Janice Rand somewhere during this. She's too valuable and interesting a character, her womanly attitude about another woman -- however skillfully Janice hides them as she plays the cool, unemotional yeoman -- are too interesting to lose here. (GR12-2)

Trivers had added a plot point for this third version of the script whereby Kirk is not the only member of the Enterprise crew to have witnessed the executions conducted by Kodos. Lt. Daiken (later to be changed to Lt. Riley) was also a witness and an attempt is made to murder him while he is working the nightshift in engineering. As written here, however, Daiken is not alone but is with another crewman -- named Jeff -- who leaves the room briefly then returns to find Daiken has been poisoned. Roddenberry told Trivers:

> Our Communications Officer is Uhura, played by the charming Negro actress Nichelle Nichols, who is one of the great undiscovered singing talents around town. What would work well, and could make another memorable scene in this episode, is having Lieutenant Daiken alone in the scene, saving the cost of actor "Jeff".... We'll have our composer Sandy Courage give us a nice space ballad, couple it with the golden voice of our actress who plays Lieutenant Uhura [over the intercom], then, in the close of the song, instead of having to bring actor Jeff in, we'll have a glowing, happy Uhura ask her friend down below how he liked it, hear the choking sounds, him trying to ask for help; the body thud -- she gives the alarm. At the end of Act Two, *Star Trek* will come up against the CBS movie. Can we hypo this ending hook at all? Possibly would help if we have Daiken at this point seeming to be dying, and Doc and Spock stating that there is now only one man left who can identify Kodos -- <u>Captain Kirk</u>!

It was an idea that stuck, and played out just as Roddenberry had envisioned it. But 12 pages of notes filled with potentially good ideas was more work than Trivers was willing to deal with at this stage.

It was happening again; a writer had delivered three drafts of a story outline, was then given the go-ahead to use the structure established therein to create his teleplay, had done so, had revised his screenplay, had revised it again, and now wanted out.

Trivers balked at the request for a free polish just as Adrian Spies had. He went a step further -- he complained to his agent, especially making an issue of how long Roddenberry's memo to him had been.

A week later, Roddenberry sent Trivers another letter, telling him:

> Talked to your agent the other day... He quite understood my point that on a really bad script you can have short memos consisting of a lot of "I don't like it," "I don't believe it." "Bad dialogue," etc. It takes a great deal more to take a fine script and try to isolate a line or a small bit of action, to figure out why it's maybe a little bit off. (GR12-3)

After the praise came the guilt, as Roddenberry continued:

> [I] told him it should not be a rewrite, I don't want one, and if my suggestions about repositioning some scenes causes you great trouble and seems unfair, will be glad to do it myself, of course.... I may have let my enthusiasm for the script run away with me -- being more the <u>writer</u> than producer, saying to myself, "This is good, let's milk those fine moments, let's not take <u>any</u> chance that an

inconsistency will harm it," and so on. (GR12-3)

Then came the bribe. Roddenberry told Trivers:

> With what little script money I have available, am much more interested to getting you to work on some new stories. (GR12-3)

Translation: "If I pay you additional money on this first script, I won't be able to give you a new script assignment, which, in the end, will pay you much more."

Roddenberry would make good on his promise with a future writing assignment for Trivers (the unproduced "Portrait in Black and White"). For now, he wanted changes he forgot to ask for in the previous letter -- the letter that caused all the fuss. He continued:

> Can we milk the phaser danger more? See what you think.... Couldn't Kirk hit an alarm once he realizes what it is? Also, can't believe it'll blow up the "ship," since Lenore would then be killing her own father, too, even if she didn't care about herself. Blowing up the <u>deck</u> seems sufficient. (GR12-3)

Three more pages of additional notes followed. Trivers surrendered and wrote a fourth draft -- his second free one -- and sent the Revised 2nd Draft in on July 11. Following the lead of Richard Matheson and George Clayton Johnson, Trivers typed "<u>Final Draft</u>" on his script.

Was it worth all the arm twisting and a commitment now to give Barry Trivers a second script assignment? John D.F. Black answered that, writing Roddenberry:

> Gene: I have only one general comment to make regarding this script -- <u>all the dialogue</u> requires a deep examination and an extremely heavy rewrite. This, of course, implies that the character relationships are likewise -- primarily, they are two-dimensional at most -- more often than not, one-dimensional -- and totally without feeling. (JDFB12-2)

Black's memo cited dozens of examples of what he believed to be unacceptable dialogue and characterizations. One thing he had been noticing, in this script and with others, including a recent rewrite of "The Galileo Seven" by Shimon Wincelberg, was that whenever Kirk was troubled, he stopped eating. After being subjected to one too many of these not-so-dramatic beats, Black told Roddenberry:

> Page 15. Guess what? Dr. McCoy says, "Your food came back to the galley untouched. What's the matter with it?" It would appear that Dr. McCoy / Janice Rand / Barry Trivers / Shimon Wincelberg / Damn Near Everybody Else is more concerned with when Kirk eats than pretty near anything else. If it is at all possible to cut the food shtick, I think it would behoove us.... Page 18: Doc says, "It's just possible your appetite may improve now." And Kirk says, "Why do you say that?" And Doc says, "We now have *ham* on the menu." Question: Is this an Act ending? Another question: Does Shimon Wincelberg collaborate with Barry Trivers?... End Act 1. Thank God. (JDFB12-2)

As Black's seven pages of notes came to an end, he added:

> This script now counts about 70 pages. Presuming that all the inane flab is removed and the scenes are paced to size, I have the feeling we should be at least 20 pages short. (JDFB12-2)

Justman checked in the following day with five pages of his own peeves, including:

> None of our regulars seem to be saying things the way we're used to having them said. Nor are they doing things the way we're used to seeing them done. Everyone seems puppet-like in order to facilitate the constructional needs of the

script. (RJ12-4)

Fretting over the cost of converting script to film, Justman once again asked, "Do we need Yeoman Janice Rand in this show?" (RJ12-4)

It was now clear to the creative staff that there was no point in twisting Triver's arm for another rewrite. And this brought up several questions. First, how could writers of the caliber of Barry Trivers and Adrian Spies -- tried and true professionals -- keep missing so badly? Answer One: *Star Trek* had yet to beam into their living rooms; the writers were still, by and large, writing blind. Answer Two: the characters Gene Roddenberry created were unique and behaved and spoke in very specific ways. Was there really any character on any other show from this time that resembled Spock, or, for that matter, Kirk?

Or perhaps, in this case, it had to do entirely with the writer. John D.F. Black, normally an advocate for the show's writers and protective of their material, said, "Barry Trivers was a nice man... and he was very involved with the Writers Guild. But let's put it this way: he was more involved with the Writers Guild than the script he wrote for us." (17)

A more urgent question, then, was who would do the near "Page One" rewrite? It was the second week of August by this point. John Black was winding down with his final polish of "Miri" and first draft of "From the First Day to the Last." Roddenberry was hip deep during this week in finishing his rewriting of "What Are Little Girls Made Of?" and "Dagger of the Mind." The answer: two men who were brand new to *Star Trek* and barely knew the show: Gene L. Coon and Steven Carabatsos.

Carabatsos dealt with "Conscience" while Coon focused on a final rewrite of "Miri." Carabatsos sent his draft to the Mimeo Department for reformatting as the Yellow Cover 1st Draft, dated August 11. Justman sent Coon word before the end of the day -- Carabatsos hadn't gotten off to a good start. But Justman saw the potential for better work and told Coon:

> Kirk discovers the fact that Dr. Leighton has been killed. Do you think it would be more dramatic for Kirk to find Leighton's body, rather than to have someone else tell him about it?... What song does Uhura sing? I may be wrong, but I got the feeling that the Producer wanted Lt. Uhura to sing a song in this show. So therefore the writer wrote in "a song."... I find it difficult to believe the explosion sequence as written.... I find it difficult to believe that Sulu comes running in for one sequence in a whole show. In fact, I find it difficult to believe that anyone would come running into the Captain's cabin.... I ask, please, for Scene 102 to be written correctly so that each individual set is listed separately with its own Scene Number and what is happening within that scene number. This will give us a better idea as to the true length of this script and what we are supposed to do with it. (RJ12-5)

As for that song "the producer wanted," Roddenberry was at work writing -- not the song, but a memo -- to Wilbur Hatch, Desilu's Music Director. He explained to Hatch his reasons for needing to bother him to come up with something for Nichelle Nichols to sing. Roddenberry told how moments like this would help the audience to better identify with these characters from the future. He added:

> We've had considerable letters requesting more information on Uhura's "Spock and Charlie X" song, [which] reinforces this belief with both us and NBC. (GR12-4)

On the same day Coon received his first script notes from Robert Justman, he also received his first notes from Roddenberry -- six pages worth. One involved the tone of the material, with Roddenberry writing:

> While I do like Kirk-Spock-McCoy relaxation, family group dialogue, etc., we seem to get a little cute about it in the script. (GR12-5)

In time, this would become a major sore spot between the two Genes. Coon had both a talent and an inclination for writing warm and teasing dialogue between characters that have a history with one another, rich with elements of natural humor. Roddenberry had worked hard to set a much different tone for *Star Trek*. These were serious -- even brooding -- military men with a life and death job to do. Kirk might tease Spock in a very subtle manner. McCoy might do it more so, but Gene Roddenberry's *Star Trek* was not going to become light in nature, especially when dealing with the subject and the theme of episodes such as "The Conscience of the King." Regarding this, he wrote:

> Mr. Spock comes off a bit too much like a "buddy" in this script. While we have already played a strong personal relationship between Spock and Kirk, in the past we've always kept Spock a bit on the "stuffy" side, taking the curse off it by making it clear he <u>wants</u> to be very casual and human and friendly but his stoic nature fighting constantly against it. Then, when in moment of crises, Spock does resort to the familiar "Jim." We then understand it is indeed a big moment. We have a good actor in Leonard Nimoy, he does have the ability to play "stuffy" and computer-like and, at the same time, play the struggle of trying to be warm, if the dialogue and situation give him half a chance at it. Perhaps "stuffy" is the wrong word; the right term may be more on the order of "proud" or "formal." (GR12-5)

Roddenberry closed:

> Despite the length of my above memo, do not believe we are in great trouble on this script. We have a good story skeleton of an interesting melodrama. Something quite different from any of our other episodes. (GR12-5)

Perhaps not in great trouble, but, by referring to the fifth draft of a teleplay as "a good story skeleton," it was clear to everyone that they were at least in fair trouble.

After "Miri" wrapped, the *Star Trek* stages went dark for nine days for the Labor Day break, while the cast hit the road to promote the series' premiere on NBC. This allowed Gene Coon and Steven Carabatsos to further educate and immerse themselves in *Star Trek*, with additional screenings, more script reading and more rewriting.

Coon's first draft was the Final Draft, dated August 23, with revised pages from August 25 and 30. One thing added into the script at this time, for the benefit of Robert Justman and his stop-watch, was the lyric to that song Roddenberry had asked be performed. It was Gene Coon who proved to be a competent lyricist with the words to "Beyond Antares." The music was composed by Wilbur Hatch.

After reading the latest draft, Roddenberry memo'd Coon:

> I think it's going to make a good show. Seems to me the main thing it needs now is some hypo-ing of the characterizations and of the dramatic and melodramatic moments. (GR12-6)

In other words, once again, everything.

Coon delivered a new rewrite -- the Revised Final Draft, dated September 8. The character of Daiken was now changed to Kevin Riley. Yeoman Janice Rand's role in the story would dwindle with each new set of revisions from Coon, on September 9, 12, 13, 14, 15, 19 and 20, as the episode was filming. A final handful of page revisions arrived on September 22, after filming had concluded, adding in additional Captain's Log entries and "wild lines."

It was a good script now, but it would have been better if Coon had stopped rewriting it a few days before he did.

Pre-Production
September 6-9 and 12, 1966 (5 days prep).

Gerd Oswald was hired to direct. He was 46 and, just prior to World War II, had begun his show business career as an actor in Germany. Fleeing the Nazi regime, Oswald came to America and moved behind the camera, first as an assistant director on 1939's *Hitler -- Beast of Berlin*, then as a director in television for *Perry Mason*, *Rawhide*, and *The Fugitive*, among other series. He also had experience in science fiction with one episode of *Voyage to the Bottom of the Sea* and more directing assignments on *The Outer Limits* than anyone else -- 14, including "Soldier," written by Harlan Ellison, and "The Expanding Human," featuring James Doohan and future two-time *Star Trek* guest performer Skip Homeier. Oswald seemed a good fit for *Star Trek*.

Bruce Hyde, returning as Lt. Kevin Riley, said, "Gerd was a nice guy, good director, but very different from Marc Daniels. Gerd was also an actor and sometimes played Nazis, I believe; and there was this somewhat stiff Prussian quality to his personality." (88-4)

Hyde was making his second appearance as Lt. Kevin Riley. Because of his value to Desilu, with the pilot film for "Digby" still waiting on the network's verdict, Hyde was paid a generous salary -- in terms of 1966 TV wages for secondary guest players. He received a flat rate of $650 for three days work. The going rate for anyone else with his limited credentials would have been $300 to $450.

Arnold Moss was an obvious choice to play Anton Karidian, aka Kodos the Executioner. Moss was a Shakespearean stage actor who, in 1953, played King Lear on television. He also appeared as an array of Mexican banditos, Arab Sheiks, and American Indians. He was 56.

Anderson and Shatner, behind-the-scenes shot taken during filming (Courtesy of Gerald Gurian)

Barbara Anderson, the lovely but demented Lenore, was only 20. She said, "That was my first year in television. I was a stage actress. When I was a teenager I was doing Shakespeare, so I could handle parts like this even though I was so young. They hired Arnold and me because you can't fake that. You either had experience with it or you'd have trouble. The hard part was doing it for television instead of in a theater. I had to pull it in. The camera puts everyone in the front row. I wasn't fearful, but I was young and doing a new medium, and they are going so fast. I mean, my goodness, the speed in which they had to film." (1)

Anderson is best known for the work that immediately followed *Star Trek*, a four-year stint on *Ironside*, bringing her three Emmy nominations for Best Supporting Actress in a Drama. She won the trophy the third time out, in 1968. In 1972, she was reunited with William Shatner for "Cocaine," an episode of *Mission: Impossible*.

William Sargent played Dr. Tom Leighton. He worked often in television. The series he frequented the most: *The Twilight Zone*, *Alfred Hitchcock Presents*, *The Invaders* and *The F.B.I.*.

Natalie Norwich played Martha Leighton. She also was a regular on series TV, with numerous appearances on *Perry Mason*, *Dark Shadows*, and *Have Gun - Will Travel*. One of her seven guest spots on the latter was written by Gene Roddenberry.

Eddie Paskey was finally given a name for the character he played in so many episodes of *Star Trek*. He is stationed at the helm for this episode, and Kirk addresses him as Mr. Leslie.

For the first time, the guest players had a chance to see what they were walking into. *Star Trek*'s NBC premiere, "The Man Trap," aired Thursday night, September 8, four-and-a-half days before the start of production on "The Conscience of the King."

Production Diary
Filmed September 13, 14, 15, 16, 19, 20 & 21, 1966.
(Planned as 6 day production; running one day over; total cost: $184,859.)

Tuesday, September 13, 1966. *Bonnie and Clyde*, with Warren Beatty and Fay Donahue, remained the top film in U.S. movie houses. *The Monkees* TV series had premiered the night before on NBC. CBS was the ratings leader, however, with its popular comedy block of *Gilligan's Island*, *The Lucy Show*, *The Andy Griffith Show*, and *Family Affair*. Beatlemania was still going strong. The group had the No. 1 LP in the U.S. with *Revolver*. They also had *Yesterday ... and Today* and *Rubber Soul* sitting in the upper regions of the album charts; the No. 2 single: "Yellow Submarine" flipped by "Eleanor Rigby"; and, two weeks earlier, they had just wound-up their world tour in San Francisco's Candlestick Park. The most played song on American radio, however, was by The Supremes, with "You Can't Hurry Love," proving that Motown was flying high. And so was *Star Trek*. There was much conversation between cast and crew on the set this morning, having returned from a two-week break and with the series' network debut airing just days before. Early rating reports indicated the premiere episode had not only won its time slot but devastated the competition on ABC and CBS, capturing nearly half the TV sets running in America.

For many, work began before the sun rose. Barbara Anderson recalled, "I got in at 5 in the morning because we didn't have handheld blow dryers, so I had to go under a hair dryer and sit there for 45 minutes. And then makeup. So when working in TV, I always felt my day was 5 to 7. But I was young and it was good, and I was very lucky. I was working with some really good people." (1)

The only regular cast member needed this day was William Shatner, working with guests Anderson, William Sargent, Natalie Norwich, and several extras. Filming commenced on Stage 10 with the scenes in the Leighton home and the outdoor area where Kirk and Lenore discover the body of Thomas Leighton. Gerd Oswald made an impression on the producers this first day of his first *Star Trek*, finishing on schedule and on time.

Day 2, Wednesday. Arnold Moss joined the cast on Stage 10 for the shooting of the teaser in the theater (stage sequences only). At 11:45 a.m., the company moved to Stage 9 and the interior of Karidian's guest quarters. Again, Shatner was the only series' regular in front of the camera, although Grace Lee Whitney was on set, waiting for the observation deck scene that Oswald never got to. The director wrapped at 6:55 p.m., 35 minutes late and one-third of a day behind.

On Day 3, work resumed in Karidian's quarters, completing sequences scheduled for the previous day. The observation deck scene, now a day late, came next. Grace Lee Whitney was again present, on stage from 9:30 a.m. to 5:15 p.m., scheduled to appear with Shatner and Barbara Anderson. But the scene timed out long and Oswald was behind schedule. So a decision was made to eliminate Rand's involvement.

Day 3: Shatner and Anderson on the observation deck (NBC publicity photo, courtesy of Gerald Gurian)

As written, Rand enters the observation deck right after Lenore's risqué line, "And this ship, all this power, surging, throbbing, but under control. Are you like that, Captain?" Rand carries a duty roster. Kirk signs it, thanks her and she leaves, attempting not to react to what she has witnessed. The script tells us that Lenore "watches her go, somewhat amused," then says, "She's quite lovely." Kirk adds, "And very efficient." Lenore's woman's intuition has been alerted. She asks, "Tell me about the women in your world, Captain. Has the machine changed them? Made them ... just ... people, instead of women?" Kirk answers, "On this ship they have the same duties and functions as the men. They compete equally and get no special privileges. But they are still women."

Lenore says, "Especially those like the one who just left. So pretty. I'm afraid she didn't like me." Kirk says, "You're imagining things. Yeoman Rand is strictly business." Lenore teases, "How charming. Captain of a Starship... and to know so little about women. Still, I hardly blame her. You are an exceptional man, Captain." From here, Oswald resumed filming the scene as written.

Next, the company moved to the back stage area of the ship's theater -- a makeover of the gym used in "Charlie X." Bruce Hyde joined the cast, acting with Shatner, Arnold Moss, and Barbara Anderson. He later admitted, "I didn't like the confrontation scene with Shatner. When I said, 'He killed my mother and my father,' I sounded impossibly whiny. Ugh. I do like the milk-drinking bit, however." (88-4)

Also shot: the audience section of the theater on the planet for the teaser. William Sargent returned to put on that horrendous rubber mask and trade dialogue with Shatner.

Of the production, this day in particular, Barbara Anderson remembered the moody lighting, saying, "While doing that show, I broke out in a fever blister that ran from the top of my lip to the bottom of my nose. And that was catastrophic at that age. You really get crazy over it. That cinematographer [Jerry Finnerman] did a masterful job in hiding that. They would light my eyes to keep the focus off my mouth." (1)

Gerd Oswald later said, "The reason for that goes back to the fact that she is a little loony. That was done on purpose." (134)

Anderson countered, "The director may have said he was doing it to make me look crazy, but he mainly did that to hide my fever blister. And he could get away with it because she *was* literally crazy. The cameramen seem to be lighting for naturalism now, but in those years, on many shows such as *Star Trek*, you were protected with the wonderful key lights -- that wonderful lighting job the cameramen did." (1)

Overall, the lighting was kept dark. That was Finnerman's vision for the series and Oswald embraced the idea. He said, "The stage setting that I had was very dimly lit. Inevitably, I thought I would get away from the general bright lights because the storyline was so dark. To me, it was a dream -- the Shakespeare thing on another planet." (134)

As for her performance, Anderson added, "I thought the director was good in how he left me alone. And that's what you want -- the director to tell you what to do and then not get in the way. And I found him to be very helpful and very gentle, especially with that scene in the end, because that was all in one take. I remember them doing the master of that just once, and then covering it with various close-ups." (1)

Filming stopped at 7:07 p.m. The crew still had to wrap set and Nimoy had to have his makeup removed, but all were anxious to get home. In 1 hour and 23 minutes "Charlie X," the second *Star Trek* episode to air, would beam across Los Angeles on KNBC.

Day 4, Friday. Numerous extras were needed for the interior theater scenes, followed by sequences in the recreation room, including the scene where Nichelle Nichols delivered her second singing performance on *Star Trek*. Besides Shatner, Nichols was the only regular this day. Grace Lee Whitney had been scheduled, with Janice Rand appearing among the audience in the ship's theater. Her 10:30 a.m. makeup call was cancelled the day before when the revised script pages arrived. There was no reason to remove Rand from this scene. No money was saved; Whitney was paid a flat rate. It was beginning to appear that her character was deliberately being removed from the episode -- and the series.

When filming stopped at 6:50 p.m., the rec room sequences were incomplete. Oswald was now a full day behind.

Day 5, Monday. Work resumed in the rec room, completing the scenes started the previous Friday, and then to McCoy's office, followed by the darkly lit scenes in engineering where a lonely Lt. Riley mans his post -- "the milk-drinking bit" Bruce Hyde fondly remembered. DeForest Kelley and Leonard Nimoy were finally put to work this day, for their scene together in the doctor's office. Because the company was a full day behind, Shatner, Whitney, and Barbara Anderson, all scheduled to work in various bridge scenes, were given the day off.

On Day 6, Tuesday, Oswald was holding at one day behind, all day. Scenes in the transporter room and those on the bridge were shot.

Barbara Anderson recalled, "The bridge was kind of imposing. But it was sort of like being in a comic book -- a lot of fantasy, and yet very serious. And it was a very interesting, stressful time. This was perhaps the thirteenth episode of *Star Trek*, and they didn't know if they were going to get picked up. I mean, they weren't spending anything on costumes because they didn't know if the network was going to go forward or just drop it. A couple of my costumes were pasted on – *literally*! Bill Theiss was making them up as we went along. Oh my god was he inventive. It wasn't like I went in for fittings -- I didn't have fittings! The fittings were on the run. He flew the costumes in and then you'd walk on the set. And for that time those costumes were quite provocative. They were just hanging by a bobby pin. I remember it as, 'This is what we're going to do; this is where you are; walk down this aisle, do this, say this line, get across your intention and exit.' And the hardest thing I had to do was keep the costume on. But that's what made it so much fun and so creative. And so loose." (1)

Deleted scene showing the bridge crew watching the Shakespearean performance on the monitor screens (Courtesy of Gerald Gurian)

Noting the dress worn by Anderson during this day of production on the transporter room set and the bridge, she said, "I swear, I literally couldn't sit down in that. That was the thing Bill Theiss pinned onto my back and I had to stand up the whole time. And it was so short! I wasn't uncomfortable because it was revealing, I was uncomfortable in knowing that it may fall off if I did too many moves. That's why I moved so stiffly, taking the Captain's hand and slowly turning as if I were modeling a dress. That's exactly what it was like." (1)

This was Grace Lee Whitney's final day. With her part on the observation deck and the ship's theater cut, all that was left for her was to enter the bridge, see Kirk talking to Lenore as they barter a performance for a ride, and take notice while appearing to try *not* to take notice. Whitney confessed, "I vividly remember how horrible and humiliated I felt, going in to shoot that final six-second walk-on, knowing that my *Star Trek* career was already over." (183-2)

Day 7, Wednesday, September 21, was an extra day of production, and Oswald used every minute of it. Filmed on this day: scenes in the briefing room, Kirk's quarters, and additional work in the ship's corridors. Only Shatner, Nimoy, and Kelley were needed. Arnold Moss was originally scheduled to appear wandering the corridor late at night, haunted by his dreams, then, waking, he overhears McCoy and Spock talking about him. This should have been shot earlier in the week. But now, because of the delay, Moss had a

Nimoy and Kelley blow a "take" during scene in Kirk's quarters as Spock and McCoy confront the Captain (Film trim courtesy of Gerald Gurian)

scheduling conflict and could not be present. It was another good moment in the script which never made it onto the screen.

Filming wrapped at 7:15 p.m., a day late and an hour into overtime.

With the filming behind him, Gerd Oswald said, "Nimoy was the greatest. He's absolutely fantastic. Arnold Moss was excellent. The crew, everybody was fine, *except Shatner*, who I couldn't communicate with." (134)

Oswald was old-school and believed actors should play their scenes as the director told them to. Shatner, however, trusted his own instincts more, especially when it came to Kirk. Oswald said, "Those who come premeditated like Bill Shatner, there is no way you can direct them." (134)

Anderson had a different perspective. She said, "Bill Shatner was really great and made it fun. He had great humor, but he was very serious at that particular time, as well. I would suspect he knew that something might happen with his career because of that show. And they didn't know whether they were going to be dropped or picked up, so I'm sure that those thoughts were very present for him. But Bill would break character and use the humor as a release. He was a pleasure." (1)

Post-Production
September 22 through November 15, 1966.
Music score recorded November 2, 1966.

Frank Keller and special emergency Edit Team #4 were tapped for a second time, following their work on "What Are Little Girls Made Of?" This was Keller's only other *Star Trek*. In his future: Steve McQueen's mega-hit *Bullitt*, for which he won an Oscar.

Because the episode ran long, an entire scene taking place in Karidian's guest quarters between him and his daughter and substantial portions of several other scenes were cut. In the script, the missing Karidian/Lenore scene took place in between two scenes in Kirk's quarters -- one in which the Captain is confronted by McCoy and Spock and another in which Kirk and Spock search for the overloading phaser. Removing it resulted in an awkward transition bridging the two back-to-back scenes in Kirk's quarters.

During the post-production phase, Majel Barrett returned for the third time as the voice of the computer. As a result of this work, Roddenberry, sure that NBC might think he had given Barrett special treatment, wanted her vocal tones to be disguised more than they had before. The morning after "Conscience of the King" aired, he wrote to Eddie Milkis:

> I would like the *Star Trek* computer voice to be a little more metallic and machine-like than it came off last night. The toneless reading by the actress is right but we do need some kind of additional or better dubbing treatment on it. (GR12-10)

At this early stage of the series, Roddenberry was careful to always refer to Barrett as "the actress" rather than her name. This was, after all, a secret affair.

Composer Joseph Mullendore provided the haunting and beautiful score. He was 52 and had worked for Irwin Allen on *Voyage to the Bottom of the Sea* and *Lost in Space*. Feeling this atypical episode needed something different than what was in the *Star Trek* library, Gene Coon asked Desilu Music Department Head Wilbur Hatch if he could recommend anyone. Hatch had already commissioned Mullendore to compose a sloweddown version of the series theme, retooled here as cocktail music for the party where Kirk meets Lenore Karidian. One particular musical sequence, the "love theme" heard during the observation deck flirtation scene, would be recycled in future episodes.

When Lenore reveals that she has been murdering those who witnessed the executions ordered by Kodos, Mullendore provided a section of music played by a solo harp. He later said, "I remember when I was questioned about it. They said, 'This only has a harp in it.' And I said, 'That's right.' And it worked great." (123b)

"Joe Mullendore opened and closed in one," Robert Justman said. "I think he did a creditable job, but I was always hot to trot with Fred Steiner." (94-9)

The Westheimer Company was assigned the optical effects. There were few needed. All shots of the Enterprise were stock and the transporter was never used. Only a couple of matte shots (bridge viewing screen) and a phaser beam had to be created. As a result, "The Conscience of the King" had the lowest optical effects bill of any episode in the series, a paltry $3,036.

Despite having run a day late, the savings in post-production helped bring this episode in at $8,641 under the studio per-episode allowance, a total cost of $184,859. This won Oswald a second assignment -- the much maligned "The Alternative Factor."

Release / Reaction
Only NBC air date: 12/8/66.

Joan Crosby reviewed "The conscience of the King" for her syndicated column, TV Scout. Among the newspapers to carry the review on December 8, 1966 was the Oneonta Star, New York. Crosby wrote:

> This is an outer space "10 Little Indians" mystery that calls upon Shakespearian verse and Hitler's memory to aid to the drama and the terror of its plot. Actually, it is a simple tale of identifying a mass murderer 20 years after the fact, complicated by some violent and unexplained deaths of people who had witnessed the tragedy at the time. The possibility is that a great Shakespearian actor (Arnold Moss) is the same man who decades earlier had led a revolution and then, Hitler-like, decided who would live and die. Few people alive ever saw the rebel and two of three eye-witnesses are attacked, one fatally. The third person is Captain Kirk, who has little trouble analyzing his feelings towards the man's daughter (Barbara Anderson). For window dressing, there's also a troupe of space traveling Shakespearian actors who seem to be deeply involved somehow.

According to A.C. Nielsen ratings service, *Star Trek* started off strong but, by the halfway mark, many in the TV audience found the idea of Shakespeare in space to be less appealing than the bewitching twitching of Samantha Stevens' nose.

RATINGS / Nielsen National report for Thursday, Dec. 8, 1966:

8:30 - 9 p.m.:		**Households:**	**Share:**
NBC:	*Star Trek* (first half)	11,470,000	no data
ABC:	*The Dating Game*	10,870,000	no data
CBS:	***My Three Sons***	**12,680,000**	no data
9 - 9:30 p.m.:		Households:	Share:
NBC:	*Star Trek* (second half)	no data	24.2%
ABC:	***Bewitched***	**no data**	**39.1%**
CBS:	"The Glass Menagerie" (start)	no data	30.9%
Local independent stations:		no data	5.8%

At 8:30 p.m., *Star Trek* lagged behind *My Three Sons*, a rare occurrence, placing at

second position. With 11,470,000 households tuned in, Nielsen was estimating a total nose count of approximately 23 million.

Although a treasure to many, "The Conscience of the King" was not *Star Trek* for the masses. The coming attraction trailer and the description given by *TV Guide* and other television magazines and newspapers, indicating an episode that seemed more talk than action, warned many viewers away. For those who came, many tuned out at 9 p.m. for either *Bewitched* or the CBS special presentation of Tennessee Williams' *The Glass Menagerie*, starring Shirley Booth and Hal Holbrook.

While Stan Robertson and his colleagues at NBC were enthusiastic about the initial story outline and early drafts of the script, they were not excited about the realization of this highly dramatic but not-so-action/adventure-flavored episode. Nor were Roddenberry and Coon who, while liking the theme and many things inherent within the script and the production, agreed it was far too slow. Robert Justman agreed, and since he was the one in charge of putting together the rerun schedule, "Conscience" would not be given a repeat broadcast.

Many *Star Trek* fans were lukewarm to it as well, mostly because of the story's lack of action. But the more intellectual crowd seemed to embrace it.

The critics for *Entertainment Weekly*, in a 1995 issue devoted to *Star Trek*, deemed it "Shakespeare in a space suit -- and it's not a bad fit."

Ronald D. Moore, only two years old in 1966 but later to discover *Star Trek*, then be discovered by *Star Trek*, becoming a writer/producer for *Star Trek: The Next Generation, Star Trek: Deep Space Nine* and *Star Trek: Voyager*, named this as his favorite episode from the original series. Moore said, "I liked the Shakespearean overtures to the episode as well as the use of the plays themselves. And I absolutely loved Kirk in this episode -- a troubled man haunted by the shadows of the past, a man willing to lure Karidian to his ship under false pretenses, willing to do one of his more cold-blooded seductions, on Lenore, willing to fight with his two closest friends, and risk his entire command in the name of justice. Or was it vengeance? Kirk's aware of his own lack of objectivity, his own flaws to be in this hunt for a killer, but he cannot push the burden away and refuses to pull back from his quest to track down Kodos no matter what the cost.... The scene with Spock and McCoy in Kirk's quarters [confronting the Captain] is one of the series' highlights. The brooding tone and the morally ambiguous nature of the drama fascinated me and definitely influenced my thinking as to what *Trek* could and should be all about." (120a)

Matt Groening, creator of *The Simpsons*, named his recurring alien characters "Kodos" and "Kang" after the characters in this episode and the upcoming "Day of the Dove," respectively.

***

Star Trek said goodbye to two recurring characters here.

Bruce Hyde -- Lt. Kevin Riley -- walked away from acting shortly after this, later saying he was one of those in the 1960s youth movement to "tune in, turn on and drop out." Surviving the '60s, Hyde eventually tuned back in and became a teacher. Riley returned to the worlds of *Star Trek* for David Gerrold's 1980 novel *The Galactic Whirlpool*. Hyde said, "I thought it was great. [I] was honored to be selected by him as a subject." (88-2)

As for Yeoman Rand, the version of "The Conscience of the King" appearing in short story form for the first *Star Trek* paperback book in January 1967, kept her in the scene on the observation deck. Lt. Kevin Riley is not present in this version but, instead, Lt. Robert Daiken. The short story was adapted by James Blish from the August 25, 1966 version of the script, written before the order came down to lose Rand and change Daiken to Riley.

Grace Lee Whitney suffered greatly after being jettisoned from the Enterprise. She admitted, "It just about devastated me to be written-out. I really bottomed out after that. I was all the way down and it was very hard for me." (183-3)

Fans of *Star Trek* saw her once more in "Balance of Terror," which, having been delayed in post-production, followed "The Conscience of the King" on NBC.

With the help of her agent, Whitney rebounded briefly with guest starring roles in *Run for Your Life* and *Batman*, both from 1967, and *The Big Valley*, *Mannix*, *Cimarron Strip*, and *The Virginian*, all from 1968. By the start of the 1970s, she was emotionally at the bottom and the work stopped. To support herself, the former singer turned back to music. In 1976 she recorded "Disco Trekkin'". Alcoholism and sex addiction contributed to a further downward slide in her career and personal life. On the road to recovery in the 1980s, she returned to her career which included more appearances as Janice Rand in 1979's *Star Trek: the Motion Picture*, followed by *Star Trek III*, *IV* and *VI*, then back on the small screen for guest spots on *Star Trek: Voyager*, *Star Trek: New Voyages* and the video game *Star Trek: Of Gods and Men*. More music followed -- *Yeoman Rand Sings* in 1999, one year after Whitney's autobiography, *The Longest Trek: My Tour of the Galaxy*, was published.

From the Mailbag

Received the week after "The Conscience of the King" aired on NBC:

> Dear Mr. Roddenberry... As the man who brought [*Star Trek*] to reality, I think you deserve some well-earned praise. The writers are also doing a grand job. Each new episode somehow seems to surpass the previous one. I sit spell-bound from start to finish.... Whoever did the casting must have had a touch of genius; the actors are so right for their roles. Shatner, for his apt and very warm and human portrayal of Kirk; Nimoy, for his absolute touch of magic with Mr. Spock, an enigmatic alien from a culture that surpasses our own understanding. I dare say that Spock is one of the most well discussed characters ever to cross the TV screen. Somehow, with whoever I talk to, *Star Trek* comes up, and Mr. Spock provides some very interesting and speculative discussion. The character of Dr. McCoy is aptly done by Mr. Kelley, and I really enjoy the choice interplay of words that occur between him and Spock.... The crew of the Enterprise, comprised of all the nations and races of Earth working together in a joint effort, provides hope for the future of mankind. Wouldn't it be wonderful to be alive when these "fiction" stories of today become tomorrow's truths. Cheryl N. (Spokane, Washington, December 12, 1966).

> Dear Mr. Roddenberry... It is very evident that *Star Trek* is a labor of love. From the first episode the show has always been intelligently written, competently directed and well acted. I don't think such a standard could be maintained unless everyone connected with *Star Trek* cared very much about putting out the best effort. I hope that *Star Trek* wins the Emmy it deserves.... I enjoyed "The Conscience of the King"; it was nice to see Lt. Riley again. The previews for next week's show ["Balance of Terror"] were very interesting and I am looking forward to it. Sincerely yours. Mrs. Kay A. (Albuquerque, N.M., December 13, 1966).

Memories

Arnold Moss enjoyed playing Anton Karidian. He felt the episode was "well-written" and "beautifully directed." He also found it to be "credible." He said, "In a thing like *Star Trek*, where the whole premise is incredible, you must have something that's believable. Everything there was *quite* believable." (121)

Of her screen father, Barbara Anderson said, "Arnold Moss was a very lovely man. Came on and did his part, and he was such an important Shakespearean actor. He was just very nice with me; treated me very well." (1)

Director Oswald was fond of this episode as well, and the script that it grew from. He said, "The first one I did I liked very much. A very intriguing idea. A good story." (134)

The ghost of Lenore Karidian followed Barbara Anderson off the *Star Trek* set. Interviewed in 2013, Anderson explained, "A weird thing happened to me some time back in the 1980s. I was at a cocktail party and a man came up behind me and whispered, 'Hello, Lenore.' I turned around, but I had forgotten my character's name, and I said, 'I beg your pardon.' He said, 'Lenore Karidian. *Star Trek*.' And I thought, 'Oh my goodness, this is weird.' But he meant it as a lovely, sweet thing. He was a fan. You know, you go on and you forget your character's names, and you forget those lines, but over the years that show has been the thing people remember. I'm still receiving a ton of email, especially for *Star Trek*, and I don't know where it's showing, but they are writing in greater volume than usual, and it's surprising. I've moved enough to where I wouldn't expect people to know how to find me, so it's interesting that all these emails are now arriving. They send letters and photos for me to sign with return envelopes, and it's really very nice." (1)

Episode 13: THE GALILEO SEVEN
Teleplay by Oliver Crawford and Shimon Wincelberg (as S. Bar-David)
(with Gene L. Coon, uncredited)
Story by Oliver Crawford
Directed by Robert Gist

NBC publicity photo
(Courtesy of Gerald Gurian)

NBC press release, December 20, 1966:

The severely damaged shuttlecraft from the USS Enterprise threatens to become a tomb for its trapped crew after it crashes on a planet and loses contact with its mother ship, in "The Galileo Seven" on NBC Television Network's colorcast of *Star Trek* Jan. 5, 1967.... Marooned and under attack by ape-like creatures, a landing party with Dr. [sic] Spock (Leonard Nimoy) in charge faces imminent death when all communications are cut off. Meanwhile, in the orbiting Enterprise, Captain Kirk (William Shatner) must decide whether to continue the search or abandon his men to deliver emergency medical supplies to a plague-ridden planet some distance away.

Kirk's efforts to locate his missing shipmates have been hampered by a stellar occurrence in the region where the shuttlecraft Galileo was lost. The ship's sensory equipment is barely functioning. Adding to Kirk's dilemma is High Commissioner Ferris, traveling on the Enterprise with orders that the ship must soon leave the area.

Meanwhile, damage to the Galileo and limited fuel reserves have Spock calculating that two of the seven survivors must stay behind, facing almost certain death.

There are three layers of conflict here: Man versus Beast, Man versus Man, and Man versus Himself. As with "The Enemy Within," this is an examination of the requirements of command, with a look at the two sides of the human personality. This time, however, the case study is the hybrid half-human/half-Vulcan Mr. Spock.

SOUND BITES

- *McCoy:* "Mister Spock, life and death are seldom logical." *Spock:* "But attaining a desired goal always is, Doctor."
- *Lt. Boma, about Spock:* "Some minor damage was overlooked when they put his head together." *Dr. McCoy:* "Not his head, Mr. Boma. His heart."
- *Spock:* "Strange. Step by step I have done the correct and logical thing ... and yet ...

I seem to have miscalculated regarding them [and] inculcated resentment on your part. Impossible. The sum of the parts cannot be greater than the whole.... I may have been mistaken." *McCoy:* "Well, at least I lived long enough to hear that."

ASSESSMENT

"The Galileo Seven" provides an important stepping stone in the development and understanding of the character of Spock. The story is rich with conflict and filled with thrills and chills. There is even an analogy incorporated into the script for the benefit of Americans in 1967 (when this episode first aired) who didn't understand how a small and somewhat primitive nation like North Vietnam was holding its own against the might of the combined United States Armed Forces. Or, for that matter, why the North Vietnamese would even choose to continue to fight. Spock says, "When we demonstrated our superior weapons, by all accounts they should have fled." McCoy responds: "You mean they should have respected us?... Mr. Spock, respect is a rational process. Didn't it ever occur to you that they might react emotionally? With anger?"

Despite what works, the script has moments of being heavy-handed and much of the head-butting between the players is redundant -- Commissioner Ferris is a one-note character and the conflict on Kirk's bridge suffers from even more repetitiveness than the point-counterpoint debates in and around Spock's shuttlecraft.

As for the production, director Robert Gist guided the inconsistent material with an uneven hand. Some moments, and some camera shots, are inspired. However, watching the oversized spears clumsily heaved into the air, clearly by normal-size stage hands and not by giants, then falling yards shy from their targets, prompts snickers, not worry; the angling of the camera for the moment when the huge beast engulfs Gaetano's body only shows the creature to be smaller than otherwise depicted; and, perhaps worst of all, the papier-mâché boulder that pins Spock's leg appears to weigh half a pound.

When filming ended, the problems continued. The opticals were demanding and the end results added to the unevenness of the episode. Film Effects of Hollywood, which fared better with "Balance of Terror," struggled here. Many shots don't match the requirements of the script; for example, stars are actually seen flying past the Enterprise as it supposedly orbits the planet. Worse, at one point the stars are seen moving *through* the planet itself.

"The Galileo Seven" reached for the sky, but fell short on both budget and time needed to make it right. Regardless, even a flawed episode of the first *Star Trek* makes for superior TV. This one is worth a viewing ... perhaps two.

THE STORY BEHIND THE STORY

Script Timeline
Oliver Crawford's story outline, ST #16: April 1, 1966.
Crawford's revised story outline, gratis: April 7, 1966.
Crawford's 1st Draft teleplay: April 25, 1966.
Crawford's 2nd Draft teleplay: May 23, 1966.
Shimon Wincelberg's rewrite (Revised Draft): August 18, 1966.
Steven Carabatsos polish (Mimeo Department Yellow Cover 1st Draft):
September 1, 1966.
Gene Coon's rewrite (Yellow Cover Rev. 1st Draft): September 13, 1966.
Coon's second rewrite (Final Draft teleplay): September 15, 1966.
Additional page revisions by Coon: September 20, 22 & 27, 1966.

Oliver Crawford, with quite a bit of rewriting by others, provided the script. The former blacklisted writer, a victim of the 1950s Red Scare, had written for *The Wild, Wild West*, *Voyage to the Bottom of the Sea*, and *The Outer Limits*.

Crawford sold Roddenberry on the idea of doing a science fiction version of *Five Came Back*, a 1939 movie co-starring Lucille Ball in a rare dramatic role. For that film, a transatlantic flight is blown off course in a storm then crash-lands in a South American jungle known to be inhabited by headhunters. Repairs are attempted on the plane but, due to a lack of fuel, some of the 12 crash survivors may have to be left behind.

Crawford said, "Most of my approach as a writer had been to look to old movies and say, 'Gee, this would make a good western or a good detective story.'" (42-2)

Or, in this case, a good science fiction.

Crawford's first draft outline arrived on April Fools' Day. The joke didn't go over so well with Robert Justman. He quickly wrote to Roddenberry, listing the exorbitant costs that a story of this type would require, such as constructing a full size shuttlecraft mock-up (interior and exterior), constructing a shuttlecraft miniature, having the miniature take off from the Enterprise, crash landing on the planet, launching itself back into space, circling the planet, and then crashing again, this time exploding. There was one other thing that would add to the budget. Justman told Roddenberry:

> And last but not least, hospital care for Robert H. Justman who will no doubt undergo a nervous breakdown upon completion of a show with this sort of cost involved. (RJ13-1)

But Roddenberry liked the story which, at this point, had Kirk commanding the shuttlecraft and Spock remaining behind on the Enterprise with the ship's doctor (Dr. Piper, from "Where No Man Has Gone Before"). He wrote back to his associate producer:

> This story should work very well -- we don't have anything else remotely like it so far. I wonder, though, if it might be a little more complicated for Kirk if, instead of one of the yeoman being killed, it's the engineer. Then the situation is thrown squarely on Kirk's shoulders. A command pilot would be expected to know some kind of working knowledge of every section of his ship -- including engineering. Therefore, <u>Kirk</u> would have to repair the ship, making his responsibility even greater. (GR13-1)

At this point, in early April, it was Roddenberry's intention *not* to have James Doohan (as Engineer Scott) as a regular. Justman relented and wrote Roddenberry:

> I would suggest that instead of a foggy turbulence ahead of the Enterprise, there instead be an electro-magnetic disturbance whose dimensions the Enterprise is unable to determine at the present time and therefore sends out the scout craft. Therefore, when the scout craft is caught in the disturbance, it disappears from sight due to the fact that the Enterprise monitors are unable to track it due to interference with its instruments.... After Kirk finds Finney dead with a spear in his back, I think some more spears ought to be thrown in from off stage which force Kirk to rush back to the Galileo with this off-stage menace in close pursuit.... For reasons of economy, we had better not let Galileo crash land again, but instead set up our inter-cutting so that our people are transported out of the patrol craft just before it crashes and are transported, of course, back to the U.S.S. Enterprise. (RJ13-1)

As the "nuts-and-bolts" producer, in charge of realizing the scripted material, not writing it, Justman was not expected to give notes on a creative level. But, as this memo demonstrates -- as do so many others included in these pages -- Justman did make creative contributions. Many.

Crawford incorporated these and other ideas from Justman and Roddenberry into his story. He delivered a free revised story outline on April 7.

Matt Jefferies wrote Roddenberry:

> This [shuttlecraft] will require several working weeks to build; the cost of interior and exterior may perhaps be as much as $12,000. (MJ13)

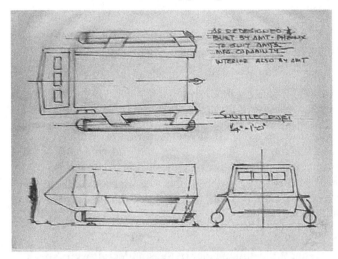

Shuttlecraft design sketches by Matt Jefferies which triggered Bob Justman's monetary concerns (Courtesy of Gerald Gurian)

It would actually be more -- in both time and dollars.

This didn't seem to matter. NBC's Stan Robertson was hooked from the start, writing to Roddenberry, "This is the action-adventure type story for which we are aiming." Robertson saw the potential of the dramatic elements, telling Roddenberry:

> The "command decision" of Captain Kirk to "ignite the remaining fuel in a brilliant retro-jet flare up" is a high dramatic point, but one in which it will be vitally important pictorially and audibly to show the weight and seriousness of the decision and the effect it has on Kirk. He took a calculated risk and won, but he could have lost -- his life and those of four subordinates. (SR13-1)

Roddenberry wrote Crawford:

> Dear Oliver: NBC was quite delighted with your outline and enthusiastic that you are quickly putting it into script form for us. (GR13-2)

Crawford finished his first draft script on April 25. It took Justman only one day to share his unhappiness, writing John D.F. Black, with a "cc" to Roddenberry:

> I don't think that the interior of the Galileo should show any scorching of friction-generated damage. There might be some showing on the exterior, but certainly not inside. If there was any inside, then our inhabitants would have been incinerated.... I'm beginning to get a little disturbed about the capabilities of the Enterprise. This is not the first script or story in which we have established the fact that the Enterprise is running out of fuel or doesn't have

sufficient power. I mean, what's the use of sending up an enormous ship like the Enterprise, when we discover that it drains the ship's power to an enormous extent when we start sending Landing Parties down through the Transporter Mechanism, I would have sent the Enterprise back to the drawing boards.... Allow me to iterate and reiterate, the optical and special effects are more than we can possibly afford for this segment. The construction of the Galileo exterior and interior itself is more than any one show can bear and will, of course, have to be amortized over a number of shows. (RJ13-2)

Justman had other issues, writing:

The dialogue is your problem, of course, but it <u>does</u> bother me. The shortness of the script is our common problem. (RJ13-2)

Justman's memo went on for three single-spaced pages, not as long or as bad as most to come from his office but certainly not upbeat. He did, however, make a suggestion as to how to lengthen the script -- by a page or so. He told Black:

To help the length of this story, perhaps we could have an added scene in which one of the landing parties which is transported down by Spock runs into trouble with these unknown inhabitants of this planet, loses a crew member and reports this upon transport back to the Enterprise. Certainly, this gives Spock further cause for worry, knowing that it is quite possible that Kirk and the others are actually on the surface of this planet. (RJ13-2)

This scene, like the others Justman had suggested, would be added to the script.

Roddenberry had ideas too. What if the commander of the shuttlecraft were Spock instead of Kirk? This would bring about greater conflict between shuttle commander and crew, and Kirk, back on the Enterprise, could experience great angst and self-torture over sending his men out in the first place. But this was a substantial change for a writer to be asked to make after two drafts of a story outline and one draft of the script had been written.

Once Crawford recovered from the shock, he did a "page one rewrite" -- a complete overhaul. The new version, dated May 23, had Spock in charge of the Galileo. It was also the first version to include the characters of McCoy and Scott; they were not yet part of the shuttle crew (as they would ultimately be) but instead remained on the Enterprise with Kirk. Also added to the bridge were helmsman Sulu and, from "The Corbomite Maneuver," navigator Bailey. High Commissioner Ferris had yet to be added to the story. The personal conflicts, both on ship and on the planet, were not fully realized.

The records kept by the writing staff labeled Crawford's 2nd Draft script as a "Revised First Draft," since it represented such a profound retooling of the story and would clearly require an additional polish from the writer. Crawford saw it differently. As it had happened with other freshmen writers on the series, Crawford typed "Final Draft" on this latest version of the script. His message to *Star Trek*: "No free rewrites; you want another draft, you pay for another draft."

Justman's reaction to the rewrite, again sent to John D.F. Black with "cc" to Roddenberry began on a deceptively good note. He said:

I think this screenplay is greatly improved over the previous draft.... Taking that as a blatant judgment, I will now get down to quite a few points which I think need correction in this version. (RJ13-3)

Those few points took five pages to convey. Some examples:

On page 19, Spock establishes the fact that they have ample food, water, and medical supplies for an indefinite stay. Why do they have this? And why do we have to make a point of it? Wouldn't it be better to establish the fact that we <u>don't</u> have enough for an indefinite stay?... On Page 49, Spock and Butler follow Swan's tracks to the edge of a deep crevice in the earth. It's going to be difficult for us to show a deep crevice in the earth. But it might be very effective for them to find Swan's body impaled with one of those big old spears.... On Page 66, we see the Galileo explode. I sure would like to avoid doing this. (RJ13-3)

The biggest challenge in realizing this episode remained in the making of the Galileo. Roddenberry had reluctantly done without a shuttlecraft for "The Enemy Within" but this new script, and the upcoming one for "The Menagerie," could not be produced without this essential -- and expensive -- "prop." Yet Desilu said no. Work on the script abruptly stopped and remained stalled for over two months. Then opportunity knocked.

In July, NBC had begun to run on-air previews of its new series for the fall. Glimpses of the magnificent Enterprise, as seen in the two pilot films, were now being beamed across America. Among those who caught sight of the unusual starship were the heads of AMT Corporation, a model kit manufacturer. Even though *Star Trek* had yet to premiere and there was no way of knowing whether it would last beyond 16 episodes, AMT wanted in.

Specialty car designer Gene Winfield, who helped make the Galileo, recalled, "When Desilu needed a shuttle, and AMT wanted the kit contract [for the Enterprise], they made a deal where AMT built and supplied the shuttle *free* to the series." (188)

The deal was closed on August 1, 1966, having been negotiated between Ed Perlstein of Desilu and Don Beebe of AMT. That same day, Robert Justman sent a memo to Roddenberry, saying:

[Perlstein] has made what I consider a very advantageous deal and has accomplished this at a time when everyone thought all was lost. (RJ13-4)

AMT got the exclusive model kit rights for the starship Enterprise in exchange for providing two full-sized shuttlecrafts, one for exterior filming and a second for the interior shots, plus a miniature of the shuttle to be used for creating the photographic effects.

Roddenberry turned his attention back to the script. It was felt Crawford's simplistic handling of the material was not making the most of the underlying plot. It was also felt Crawford's agent would rightfully want additional money for his client doing additional rewrites. A decision was made: If additional money were to be paid, someone other than Crawford should make the changes.

Shimon Wincelberg, having impressed Roddenberry with his initial handling of "Dagger of the Mind," was paid to add needed depth to the story. Crawford shrugged it off, saying, "They probably felt that I had run dry on the idea and came as far as I could." (42-2)

John D.F. Black later said, "Oliver Crawford was like Barry Trivers. His scripts were about half there. That's fair. And true. We had a lot of problems with his script. And they continued to have a lot of problems after I left." (17)

Wincelberg turned in his version of "Galileo Seven" on August 18, ten days after Gene Coon came on as *Star Trek*'s new front line producer. New in the script: High Commissioner Ferris, pestering Kirk to abandon the search for Spock and the crew of six. Also added: Yeoman Janice Rand, replacing "Yeoman Butler" as one of those six. Wincelberg also came up with the character names of Latimer, Boma, and Gaetano, taking away Finney, Guines, and Swan.

Stan Robertson remained supportive, writing:

> I like the idea of introducing Commissioner Ferris into the story. It gives us a link with Earth and the fact that there is a higher body to which Captain Kirk is responsible. (SR13-2)

Days after Wincelberg's script arrived, Justman directed his memo to Roddenberry, not the newly-instated Coon, saying:

> Have just finished reading Shimon Wincelberg's rewrite on "The Galileo Seven."... I am a little concerned about characterization in this show -- especially the characterization of regular performers such as Mr. Spock. They don't ring true. (RJ13-5)

Justman had many other issues, among which, to no big surprise, were monetary concerns. He wrote:

> In adding much excitement to this show, Shimon has also added many, many dollars. (RJ13-5)

After digesting Justman's eight pages of critical notes, Roddenberry told Coon:

> Agree this is an improvement over Oliver Crawford's in some areas -- in other areas I am quite disappointed. Suggest we should immediately decide whether to get some more work out of Wincelberg on this or to go into immediate rewrite of this ourselves. Most disappointing is that we have not developed a truly personal story of strong and believable conflicts between individuals. We had hoped that this might become a story of Mister Spock, always second in command in the past, getting full command here. Thus, this was to have been a story of Spock attempting now to apply cool and precise logic to a command situation. (GR13-3)

So far, on an emotional level, it wasn't coming across that way. A few days later, Roddenberry again wrote to Coon, saying:

> The three of us [including Justman] should sit down and get together on whether or not we can show the denizens or a denizen of this planet somewhere along the line. Dorothy had a suggestion about how Bob [Justman] once used seven-foot basketball players in another show for a similar premise and I thought it's worth discussions here, if only the use of one of them so that the audience will not feel cheated. (GR13-4)

Surprisingly, no draft of the script had yet called for the giant humanoid creatures to be seen. Only their giant spears gave indication as to their size.

To "meet budget," Roddenberry mandated that any "scenes involving transporter room, elevator and other sets will be deleted from script." (GR13-4)

Steven Carabatsos was given the task of polishing Wincelberg's script. He completed his script on August 31, constituting the Mimeo Department's Yellow Cover First Draft. Roddenberry rejected it as such and wanted it revised before sending to NBC. His memo the following day, to Coon, Justman and Carabatsos, included:

> Generally, Kirk is not under a lot of pressure on the Enterprise. Even the presence of Ferris does not create problems for Kirk. He has two days before he has to leave off the search. Let's put real pressure on Kirk -- cut the time available -- make delivery of medical supplies much more imperative -- put Ferris really on Kirk's neck -- and make Kirk's decisions tough ones -- keep him "alive" even when we're devoting more time to the others.... The "Spock in command and logic not serving him" theme has to be brought out. But Spock can't be entirely wrong or we wonder whether he is as good an officer as we've

established. Spock has to come out on top -- logically. And we have to counterpoint with Kirk doing the right things -- emotionally.... Dialogue throughout -- people do not talk this way.... I have a feeling "mists" [atmospheric effects] are going to cause Bob a great deal of pain.... Still cheating the audience when we only tell them, via Janice, the creatures are horrible. We'll have to face the fact we'll have to show at least a couple of them. (GR13-5)

Gene Coon took over the rewriting. His Yellow Cover *Revised* First Draft was completed on September 13, the third script he had now rewritten (following "Miri" and "The Conscience of the King"). The Grace Lee Whitney departure had since occurred and, with this draft, Janice Rand was replaced with Yeoman Mears. As Coon had done with "The Conscience of the King," the conflict between McCoy and Spock was amplified. He also injected humor into the story in the only place where it could be added -- at the very end.

It was this version that was sent to the network. And the network remained happy. Stan Robertson immediately wrote back, telling Roddenberry, not Coon:

I personally believe that this is the strongest *Star Trek* script that we have received to date. It seems to contain the ingredients and elements which we have been striving to interject into our stories since my association with the series. This is an appealing, exciting, action-adventure story with mounting tension, jeopardy, the alluring mystique of outer space, fine development and emotional conflict with a resolve which can only truly be described in trite terms -- it leaves me breathless.... I would strongly suggest that you and your colleagues make every effort to get this script into production as soon as possible so that it can be scheduled, depending naturally upon the filmed results, at the earliest. (SR13-2)

Another branch of NBC was less enthusiastic. Jean Messerschmidt from Broadcast Standards sent numerous notes. Among them:

Caution on the makeup used for Spock's wound as green blood may be somewhat jarring ... [and] ...Here and wherever else the creature appears, please use restraint so it is not unnecessarily alarming or gruesome. (NBC-BS13)

The green blood was so underplayed it never even registered. The creature, however, was shown with too little "restraint" and was considered to be "unnecessarily alarming and gruesome" to Messerschmidt. All shots featuring its face were edited out of the finalized episode before broadcast. And the shot revealing Latimer, lying face down with a giant spear protruding from his back, had to be covered over by additional "mists," added in post.

Pre-Production
Galileo design & construction: August/September, 1966.
Director's prep:
September 14-16 and 19-21, 1966 (6 days).

Auto designer Thomas Kellogg was asked to realize Matt Jefferies' plans for the Galileo. Gene Winfield of AMT's Speed and Custom Division, who had built the futuristic-looking Piranha car for *The Man from U.N.C.L.E.*, led a crew of specialty builders in the construction.

The first full-size shuttle, with a hollowed out interior and designed for exterior filming only, was made of plywood and fiberglass set onto a metal base. The second version, built for interior shots, had removable "wild sections" which could be separated, allowing better access for the camera. The work was done in August in Phoenix, Arizona. Coon flew

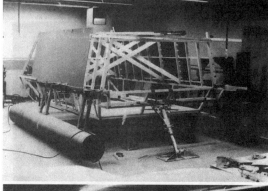

Matt Jefferies out at 7 a.m. on Monday, August 15 to inspect and report back as to the progress of the work. It was an economy flight. Jefferies returned that same afternoon at 4:40 p.m. with a positive report, and was rewarded with a first class ticket home.

Various versions of the Galileo were delivered to Desilu on September 12. The price tag was double what Matt Jefferies estimated -- $24,000, fully absorbed by AMT ($173,000 in 2013's economy).

Richard Datin, who built the Enterprise models, returned to design and build the model for the shuttle flight deck on the Enterprise. This miniature hangar bay was over ten feet long, more than six feet wide and six feet tall. The total cost: $2,100, charged to the episode's budget.

But, as with all the miniatures and optical effects photography, money was only half the concern. The other half was time. On September 9, after reading Carabatsos' polish of Wincelberg's rewrite of Crawford's script, Robert Justman finally wrote a memo directed to the series' new producer, and then proceeded to scold Coon:

In recent weeks I have been reading scripts and delivering memos with regard to the amount of Miniatures and Optical Effects contained therein. Please believe me when I say I am not trying to damage or cheapen the show by at times plaintively crying for certain effects to be eliminated from our show. Goodness knows, if we had time to get them in, I would be more than happy to go along with everything that we could possibly afford. However, I am going to make a prediction right now. Unless someone starts paying attention to what I say in my

Building the shuttle craft from AMT in Phoenix, AZ to Desilu Stage 10 (Courtesy of Gerald Gurian)

memos about Optical Effects, we are going to start missing Air Dates, one right after another. (RJ13-6)

The need for optical effects was scaled-back to some degree in the September 13 rewrite but, by the very nature and design of this story, Coon could only appease Justman to a point. "The Galileo Seven" would have to be one of the hard ones, and one of the slow ones, even though Stan Robertson was eager to push it forward in the schedule and air on NBC as soon as possible. *Star Trek*'s 13th produced episode would be its 17th to be broadcast.

Robert Gist, 42 when hired, was an actor-turned-director thanks to producer Blake Edwards. Gist was cast in the movie *Operation Petticoat* when he mentioned to Edwards that what he really wanted to do was direct. Edwards gave him that chance, for TV's *Peter Gunn*. Other credits included *The Naked City* and *The Twilight Zone*. Roddenberry met Gist when the latter directed an episode of *The Lieutenant*.

John Crawford, playing High Commissioner Ferris, had appeared with Leonard Nimoy in 1952's *Zombies of the Stratosphere* and DeForest Kelley in 1956's *The Man in the Grey Flannel Suit*. Among 100 plus TV credits: *Superman, The Lone Ranger, The Twilight Zone, My Favorite Martian, Batman, The Time Tunnel, Voyage to the Bottom of the Sea, The Wild, Wild West* and, 14 times, no less, on *Gunsmoke*. His favorite acting job was for *Lost in Space*, as Dr. Chronos in "Time Merchant," which he said he "really flipped over." (41)

Don Marshall, 30 when hired to play Lt. Boma, had his first big role in TV on Roddenberry's *The Lieutenant* with the controversial episode "To Set It Right," co-starring Dennis Hopper and Nichelle Nichols. With that exposure, he began working often, including multiple appearances on *Rawhide, Alfred Hitchcock Presents*, and *Bob Hope Presents the Chrysler Theatre*. Then the producers of *Daktari* wanted Marshall as a regular for the fall of 1966, and this, in an unusual turn, brought him back to Roddenberry.

"I didn't want to be a regular on *Daktari*," Marshall admitted. "As it turned out, I did three episodes but I really didn't even want to do one. My agent at the time said, 'Come on, these are my friends, do the pilot.' I said, 'But I'm playing second to Marshall Thompson and a cross-eyed lion. What will happen to me -- *my character*?' And he said, 'You don't have to sign a contract, so just do it.' So we did the pilot and no one said anything about a contract. But in the middle of the third episode, they came in and told me I had to sign one. I called my agent and he told me that if I didn't do it he'd blacklist me. My own agent! And then the work suddenly stopped coming. I called Gene and said, 'Can you check for me and see if I'm being blacklisted?' He called me the next day and said, 'Don, I'm afraid you are. Look, there's a one-day thing on *Mission: Impossible*. Go do that and get your name in the trades that you're working.' So I did it, and then Gene called and said, 'I got a part I want you to do.' And that was for 'The Galileo Seven.' Gene was right about getting my name in the trades, because, after I finished that show, then everybody was hiring me again." (113b)

Peter Marko, as the doomed Lt. Gaetano, had a short career in front of the camera. Among his handful of credits was "The Invisible Enemy," an episode of *The Outer Limits* where Marko, playing an astronaut, also dies at the hands of a sci-fi monster. That episode, incidentally, was written by *Star Trek* scribe Jerry Sohl.

Rees Vaughn, at 31, played Latimer, the first to die at the hands -- and spears -- of the giants. He had already made multiple appearances on *Alfred Hitchcock Presents, The Virginian,* and *12 O'Clock High*.

Phyllis Douglas, as Yeoman Mears, stepping in for the sacked Grace Lee Whitney, made her acting debut at age two in *Gone with the Wind* as little Bonnie Blue Butler. As a young adult she worked often in TV, including a pair of *Batman* episodes. She would return to *Star Trek* as Hippie Girl #2 in the notorious 1969 episode "The Way to Eden."

Robert "Big Buck" Maffei, who was seven feet one inch tall, was cast as the giant. He appeared in a handful of TV shows and small films, usually playing circus strongmen and the like, and had been in a pair of first season *Lost in Space* episodes as The Giant Cyclops.

Grant Woods, as Lt. Kelowitz, would be seen in two more *Star Trek*s: "Arena" and "This Side of Paradise."

David Ross (as Transporter Chief), Bill Blackman (with his first turn at the helm), Frank de Vinci, Eddie Paskey, and Ron Veto were all on the bridge, and were familiar faces on *Star Trek*; each would be seen in anywhere from 10 to 60 episodes.

Production Diary
Filmed September 22, 23, 26, 27, 28, 29 & 30, 1966
(Planned as 6 day production; finishing one day over; total cost: $232,690).

Unused camera angle of giant Buck Maffei revealing top of set in upper left corner (Courtesy of Gerald Gurian)

Production began Thursday, September 22, 1966. The Beatles continued to have the best selling album in the nation with *Revolver*. Otherwise, the over-30 crowd had a hold on the LP charts, with the soundtrack to *Dr. Zhivago* at No. 2, *Somewhere My Love* by Ray Conniff at No. 3, followed by the soundtrack to *The Sound of Music*, a pair of albums by Herb Alpert and the Tijuana Brass (*What Now My Love* and *Whipped Cream & Other Delights*), and Frank Sinatra with *Strangers in the Night*. The average cost of each was $3.99. On a tighter budget, the teenagers flocked to buy 45 rpm singles for 99 cents each, with "Cherish" by the Association in the top spot. A trip to the record store amounted to only pennies. You could fill your tank up for 32 cents a gallon. Or you could stay home and watch TV, as most Americans did the night before. NBC had the show with the highest audience share -- *I Spy*, pulling in 40.9% of the TV sets running in the 30-Markets area surveyed by A.C. Nielsen.

Filming of "the Galileo Seven" began on Stage 9 and the bridge set. Robert Gist worked half as quickly as hoped and was a half day behind when filming stopped at 7 p.m., barely allowing cast and crew time to get home for the 8:30 p.m. premiere of "Where No Man Has Gone Before," *Star Trek*'s third episode to air. They were not alone in watching. A.C. Nielsen championed *Star Trek* as winning its time slot, with 34.5% of the TV sets in use across the country. *My Three Sons*, in second place, delivered a 28.2 audience share for CBS. *Star Trek* had to settle for second position at 9 p.m., in a close race with ABC's hottest show, *Bewitched*, which put a spell on 31.8% of the TV households. *Star Trek* had 31.0%.

Day 2 picked up with the unfinished business from Thursday, and again was spent entirely on the bridge. At 7 p.m., when filming stopped, Gist was two-thirds of a day behind.

John Crawford had a dismal experience on *Star Trek*. William Shatner would direct him, telling him where to stand and limiting his ability to move about the bridge. He complained, "My friend Bob Gist was directing it. Now, sometimes Bob can be fun and sometimes he can be a pain. I think he was playing it safe, didn't want to make an enemy of the star because, after all, he might want to do one of these again.... It wasn't free and easy like all the things I did in *Lost and Space* where I could do any damn thing I wanted." (41)

But, then, wasn't that the problem with *Lost in Space*?

**Director Robert Gist's unique shot of bridge from above
(Courtesy of Gerald Gurian)**

Day 3, Monday, was supposed to start on Stage 10, but Gist still had unfinished business on the bridge as well as a short sequence in the transporter room where the commander of a search party reports to Kirk about giants living on the planet below. Finally, at 10:45 a.m., the company made the hour-long move to Stage 10 where sequences were shot on a set called "Ext. Rocks."

Don Marshall said, "On that show, Bob Gist was the director, and he was a former acting coach of mine. And I had left his class, because I had a problem with Bob -- he wanted everybody to be like James Dean. You know, all that fidgeting and turning your back and unsure and all of that. And he was asking me to play my character that way here, too. I said, 'Well, I'm playing an Astro-physicist, Bob. I can't play James Dean in this.' But in the first scene we shot, we'd found a dead crewman and Bob wanted me to be leaning against a rock, then turn around and respond when Leonard Nimoy does something, but like James Dean would. And I thought, 'I can't do this.' And Leonard Nimoy came to me and said, 'What's going on, Don?' He could tell I was down. And I said, 'I don't know if I should say anything to you but I'm playing an Astro-physicist and Bob wants me to play a James Dean-type character.' And Leonard says, 'Okay, Don, you go ahead and play it the way you want to play it and I'll handle the director.' I'd never heard that before, or since! It's like, 'Wow! Okay.' You talk about beautiful people -- that you could be working with someone and they're concerned about *you*, concerned about *your* character, and would give you the freedom to do the best work you knew how. It was just beautiful. I couldn't ask for anything better. And that's why the character came out so strong, really, because I felt free to do whatever it was that I needed to do. And the director just backed off. He didn't try to force me into doing anything of that sort after that, like leaning against the rock and being very withdrawn into myself." (113b)

Regarding the approach he used for the role of Lt. Boma, Marshall said, "It was a good part, and I felt I had to play this character as though he believed he was helping the rest of the crew, not just withdrawing into himself and thinking about himself, but fighting for the rest of them. So I just played that. And, with this character, if you notice, there was no shyness or hold back because of race or anything like that. You didn't get that a lot on TV at that time, where a black man could speak his mind to a white man without being regarded as out-of-line -- where race was not the issue and it was a different form of conflict between the characters. The argument there really was between myself and Spock as far as him not wanting to take the time to bury the dead was concerned. There was no color issue at all. It was not black against white. It wasn't even about bucking authority. It was about one person's beliefs versus another's and showing respect, including paying respect and acknowledging a loss. That was the message I got from it. And the thing that I saw was Gene Roddenberry and the other people on that show, like Leonard Nimoy, were greatly concerned about the show and about the people on it, and about how it depicted the future. There's so much beauty in that. They were there to help you with it, whatever it was. That's what my experience was." (113b)

This was also the first day that Buck Maffei stepped before cameras as the giant hairy beast. When Gist wrapped at 7 p.m., he was one-and-a-quarter days behind.

Day 4 continued on the "Ext. Rocks" set, then slowly progressed to scenes played outside the mockup Galileo, and then into a second mockup for interior filming.

Maffei returned during the exterior sequences for long shots, medium shots, and close-ups, although the close-ups would never see the light of a TV screen. Come 6:50 p.m. when Gist dismissed the cast, he had fallen one-and-a-half days behind.

Day 5, Wednesday, brought more filming among the rocks, and both interior and exterior of the Galileo. Don Marshall had never appeared in a science fiction series before and was unfamiliar with acting for post effects, such as holding perfectly still as he fired a "space gun" so animation could be added later. But he did not recall being overly aware of the surroundings or trickery, and said, "I came from the stage. So I trained that way. Whatever you do on the stage, that's it. The sets are all fake; it's all about the character in the middle of the room. So I wasn't worrying about how the phaser effects would come out or any of that, I was focused on what I was doing with my character. You don't play to the background, unless you have to do something with it, you play to the character in a particular situation. And that's all I've ever done, and that's the way that I look at it as to how it should be done. So I never worried about the rest of it. I figure, I'm going to attract your attention, anyway. I'd better. It's up to me to do my job, to keep people interested in the character. If I did that right, then it would all work out. And from what I saw, it all worked out." (113b)

No 'Big Buck' this day, but more big bucks were spent than the budget allowed for -- Gist quit at 7:12 p.m., an hour into overtime when the set was wrapped, and now one-and-three-quarters days behind.

Day 6 was spent inside the Galileo.

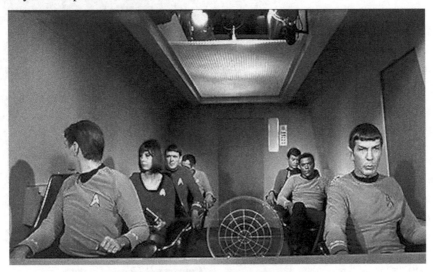

**Day 6: Interior shuttle with stage lights above
(Courtesy of Gerald Gurian)**

Scotty was very prominent in this episode, but most of James Doohan's acting was done from the floor. "I spent much of the episode on my belly with my face in the floorboard engineering system of the cramped shuttle," Doohan said. "The most memorable aspect of the episode for me was that it was the first opportunity I had to work closely with Leonard. We'd had scenes before, but it was the first time we worked just one-on-one. Leonard was easy to like from the get-go, as sincere, thorough and professional an actor as one could hope to work with." (52-1)

In the controlled environment of the shuttlecraft, Gist picked up some time. He stopped filming at 7:12 p.m., again a full hour into O.T. once the set was wrapped, with cast and crew rushing to make it home by 8:30 for the NBC premiere of "The Naked Time." A.C. Nielsen found it to be the top-rated show during its time period, with a 34.1 audience share.

By the end of Day 7, Friday. Gist was one day behind, having spent another full day inside the Galileo wrapping his first and last *Star Trek* assignment at 7:40 p.m.

Post-Production:
October 3 through December 13, 1966. Music score: tracked.

Bob Swanson and Edit Team #1 did not fare as well with their fourth *Trek* (following "The Corbomite Maneuver," "The Man Trap," and "Balance of Terror"). Perhaps Gist and Finnerman were to blame and Swanson and his team actually used the best shots available of those spears being heaved onto the exterior planet set and that papier-mâché rock pinning Spock against other papier-mâché rocks. Or maybe they were just trying to beat the clock.

Film Effects of Hollywood was in over its head with this assignment. The opticals were demanding and the results are inconsistent. But to the credit of Linwood Dunn and his team, the shots of the Galileo in space were deemed good enough to be seen in future episodes -- even with those "garbage mattes."

A garbage matte is a box or, in this case, a rectangular-shaped outline put around a model by the post lab to hide anything that was not intended to be seen -- like strings or wires. The viewers of the original broadcast did not see a visible border around the Galileo in flight. But in the 1980s, when the contrast levels were raised for the first remastering of *Star Trek* episodes, and now with the added clarity of DVD signals and HD TV, the garbage mattes, once hidden, are somewhat apparent.

For its time, with the technology available, "The Galileo Seven" was borderline-spectacular. It certainly wasn't cheap. The optical effects alone cost $20,655. And, at a total cost of $232,690, "Galileo" was one of the series more expensive outings, pushing the running first season deficit to $51,936.

Miniature of shuttle filmed against a projected star field (Courtesy of Gerald Gurian)

Release / Reaction:
Only NBC air date: 1/5/67.

The face only a mother could love and NBC would not allow to be seen (nixed publicity photo on left) and the one that replaced it (on right) (Both courtesy of Gerald Gurian)

Steven H. Scheuer reviewed "The Galileo Seven" for his syndicated column, *TV Key Previews*. Among the newspapers to carry the review on January 5, 1967 was the *Milwaukee Journal*, in Milwaukee, Wisconsin. Scheurer wrote:

> "The Galileo Seven." The Galileo is the shuttlecraft from the USS Enterprise which has dropped away from the mothership to investigate an Earth colony.

The "seven" are the seven crew members aboard the shuttlecraft, including Mr. Spock, who are marooned on a planet when the Galileo crashes. Unfortunately, the tiny planet is inhabited by grotesque creatures and it is entirely Mr. Spock's decision -- and Mr. Spock's show. Leonard Nimoy does his usual entrancing job as the spike-eared first officer.

Johnny Robinson reviewed the episode for his syndicated newspaper column, *Video Versions*, writing:

An exciting episode as the severely damaged shuttlecraft Galileo from the USS Enterprise threatens to become a tomb for its trapped crew after it crash-lands on a planet and loses all contact with its mothership. Marooned and under attack by ape-like creatures, the stranded party, with Dr. [sic] Spock (Leonard Nimoy) in charge, faces imminent death. Meanwhile, in the orbiting spaceship, Captain Kirk (William Shatner) must decide whether to continue the search or abandon his men and deliver emergency supplies to a plague-ridden planet some distance away.

The entertainment critic for *The Charleston Gazette*, in Charleston, West Virginia, wrote:

Recommended for tonight is this tale in which the personality of Dr. [sic] Spock (Leonard Nimoy) is put to a bitter test. Spock, born on a planet outside of Earth, adheres only to logic and is alien to all emotion. He insists on a logical solution to a problem that is totally beyond the realm of reason.

According to A.C. Nielsen, NBC should have stuck with the publicity picture that was more frightening.

RATINGS / Nielsen 30-Market report for Thursday, Jan. 5, 1967:

8:30 - 9 p.m., with 64.2% of U.S. TVs in use.	Rating:	Share:
NBC: *Star Trek* (first half)	16.7	26.0%
ABC: **The Dating Game**	**21.3**	**33.2%**
CBS: *My Three Sons*	17.9	27.9%
Local independent stations:	10.4	12.9%
9 - 9:30 p.m.:		
NBC: *Star Trek* (second half)	17.4	25.9%
ABC: *Bewitched*	19.5	29.1%
CBS: **Thursday Night Movie (start)**	**23.3**	**34.7%**
Local independent stations:	10.6	10.3%

The movie on CBS was the TV premiere of the 1951 adaption of Tennessee Williams' *Summer and Smoke*, starring Geraldine Page and Laurence Harvey.

The dip in the ratings for *Star Trek* weren't the only problem. "We had a failure," Leonard Nimoy said. "The Spock character had been so successful that somebody said, 'Let's do a show where Spock takes command of the vessel.' I had a tough time with it. I really appreciated the loss of the Kirk character for me to play against [and] to comment on. The Bill Shatner/Kirk performance was the energetic, driving [force] and Spock could kind of slipstream along and make comment and offer advice [and] give another point of view. Being put into a position of being the driving force -- the central character -- was very tough for me, and I perceived it as a failure." (128-2)

Regardless, Nimoy recalled this as representing a step in the evolution of Spock. He said, "Little by little I began to understand that it was possible to play the suppressed emotion and give the audience an occasional peek of the struggle of the character. I think it's a very human character. He's dealing with a very human problem. We're all living our lives trying to find a balance between emotion and logic. I think, for that reason, audiences identified with Spock." (128-4)

Don Marshall remembered watching the episode when it aired, and said, "The effects <u>were</u> great for their time. And the exterior of that shuttlecraft looked really good on TV. On the set, you know, it opened up and they could pull it apart to get different camera angles, so it was always half open as I was looking at it. There were the blinking lights and the buttons and so on, but it wasn't complete. Then I saw it on TV and it worked. Everything looked good. And, for me, the story worked because the characters worked." (113b)

We might have seen more of Lt. Boma in *Star Trek*. Marshall added, "They came back to me later on and asked me to become a recurring character. There were several scripts where they had written my character in." (113b)

But it was not to be.

Producer Irwin Allen saw Marshall playing a member of a shuttle crew in "The Galileo Seven" and immediately envisioned him as a member of another shuttle crew, for *Land of the Giants*. Marshall spent two seasons as one of that series' regulars.

Episode 14: COURT MARTIAL

Teleplay by Don Mankiewicz and Steven W. Carabatsos
(with Gene L. Coon, uncredited)
Story by Don Mankiewicz
Directed by Marc Daniels

Kirk about to go on trial, as Bill McGovern slates the shot
(Unaired film trim courtesy of Gerald Gurian)

NBC press release, January 16, 1966:

> Captain Kirk is charged with negligence and brought to trial following the disappearance and reported death of one of his officers, in "Court Martial" on the NBC Television Network colorcast of *Star Trek* on Feb. 2, 1967.... Investigation into the presumed death of Officer Finney (Richard Webb), who was lost during a hazardous assignment aboard the Enterprise, discloses evidence that Captain Kirk (William Shatner) may have perjured himself in his testimony regarding the incident. Kirk's case appears hopeless until a little-known fact in Finney's past is inadvertently revealed by his daughter.

The Captain's accuser: the Enterprise's own computer, which offers the damning visual evidence needed to convict Kirk. His primary advisory: Areel Shaw, the prosecutor at the court martial hearing and a former love. She offers further evidence to show that the late Ben Finney had a grudge against Kirk, which may prove motivation for the captain wanting

Finney off the ship. Kirk's only hope is an outdated defense lawyer who harbors a grudge of his own, against the mechanized and dispassionate world of computers.

The theme: The battle of Man versus Machine is a fallacy -- it is always Man against Man, for man is the machine's creator. The hook seemed irresistible: *The Caine Mutiny* in outer space.

SOUND BITES

- *Cogley, to the court:* "One might as well be a machine if he lets himself be handcuffed by a machine. A machine deals in facts, not justice!" *Commodore Stone:* "Very neat philosophy, Mr. Cogley. But you still haven't said why you desire the procedural change." *Cogley:* "Because I am against a machine pre-empting the ruling of this court -- a machine crucifying this fine man. And that is exactly what it is doing! Inexorably -- without feeling, remorse or concern. A machine has no conscience! This court has! I appeal to it!... I speak of rights. A machine has none. A man must."

- *Dr. McCoy:* "Mr. Spock, you're the most cold-blooded man I've ever known." *Spock:* "Why, thank you, Doctor."

ASSESSMENT

While the idea of doing a courtroom drama in outer space is interesting and "Court Martial" certainly has its moments, the overall execution is clumsy. The story, which went through too much rewriting by too many different writers (four in all, with a lot of string-pulling by a fifth) has plot holes and leaps of illogic. Consider the following:

- Jame, the daughter of Ben Finney, just happens to be on the nearest Starbase to where the Enterprise had been damaged and now orbits.
- The other officers visiting or assigned to the Starbase, all colleagues and/or peers of James Kirk, are surprisingly quick to assume his guilt. One must also wonder how word was leaked so quickly from Commodore Stone's office.
- One of Kirk's past loves, who just happens to be a Starfleet Prosecuting Attorney at this particular Starbase, also just happens to be assigned to nail him to the wall.
- We are told that the only man qualified for the job of defending Kirk is a cantankerous old-school lawyer named Samuel Cogley, who also just happens to be at the Starbase -- and is immediately available to take the case.
- The "white sound" device, which appears to be nothing more than a twentieth century microphone, is supposed to enable the ship's computer to amplify every sound on the ship but can also isolate and monitor only heartbeats, ignoring the voices and breathing and clanging about of those on board. Okay. But instead of merely throwing a switch to have the device ignore the sounds on the bridge, McCoy goes to the trouble -- and wastes the time -- to make the rounds and "mask" each person's heartbeat.
- One final peeve: During the fight on the engineering deck between Kirk and Finley, the use of stuntmen is painfully obvious.

Not all was bad. Worth noting:

- "Court Martial" provides our first of only two visits to a Starbase in the first series.
- This was the first time the nomenclature of "Starfleet" and "Starfleet Command" was used, courtesy of Gene Coon.
- The Starfleet dress uniform made its first appearance here.
- Starbase Commodore Stone was the highest ranking Black on *Star Trek*. Gene Roddenberry and Joe D'Agosta, as well as NBC, must be credited with taking bold steps in casting. *I Spy*, the first series to star a Black and a White opposite one another, was only one year old. It, too, was on NBC.
- The Albert Whitlock matte painting of Starbase 11 was, for its time, an eye-opener.
- There is a strong social statement in this story, relevant in 1967 when "Court Martial" first aired and even more so today. Cogley motions to a "table computer" -- the prototype for the PC -- and says, "I got one like this in my office. Contains all the precedents. A synthesis of every important legal decision since the beginning of time. Never use it.... Got my own system -- books, my young friend -- Books!"

It is hard to damn any work of fiction that has a clear theme and boldly makes a statement, and "Court Martial" certainly has its supporters. In conjunction with the theme, it is a unique story with a handful of engaging scenes, creating an episode the viewer wants to like, warts and all.

THE STORY BEHIND THE STORY

Script Timeline

Don Mankiewicz' outline, ST #23, "Court Martial on Starbase 811": May 3, 1966.
Mankiewicz' revised story outline, gratis: June 26, 1966.
Mankiewicz' 1st Draft teleplay: July 15, 1966.
Mankiewicz' Revised 1st Draft teleplay, gratis: Early August, 1966.
Mankiewicz' 2nd Draft teleplay: September 6, 1966.
Steven Carabatsos' rewrite (new 1st Draft, now "Court Martial"): Sept. 19, 1966.
Carabatsos' script polish (unspecified draft): September 21, 1966.
Mimeo Department's reformatted "Yellow Cover 1st Draft" teleplay: September 23, 1966.
Gene Coon's script polish (Final Draft teleplay): September 26, 1966.
Additional page revisions by Coon: Sept. 27 & 29 and Oct. 3, 1966.

Thanksgiving with the Mankiewicz clan must have been extraordinary. Don Mankiewicz was the son of legendary screenwriter Herman J. Mankiewicz, who shared an Academy Award with Orson Welles for co-writing *Citizen Kane*. His nephew, Joseph Mankiewicz, was the Oscar-winning writer/director who wrote the screenplays for *Guys and Dolls* and *All About Eve*. (Another nephew, Ben, not yet born, would become the co-host of the popular TCM movie channel.) Don had written for television series such as *The Naked City* and *12 O'clock High*, and was nominated for an Oscar of his own in 1959 for co-writing *I Want to Live*. He had never tried his hand at science fiction, but had provided six scripts for the supernatural series *One Step Beyond*. It didn't seem to matter to Roddenberry that Mankiewicz was a novice at sci-fi, or that he lived and worked out of Long Island, New York.

Between Herman, Joseph and Don, the Mankiewicz name represented a screenwriting dynasty that *Star Trek*, in these early days of looking for acceptance, would have trouble saying "no" to.

Don Mankiewicz was visiting Los Angeles and dropped by for one of the screenings of "Where No Man Has Gone Before" on the Desilu lot. A few days later, Roddenberry wrote to John D.F. Black:

> Met with Don, who had just seen the film and had not yet time to develop any ideas. Intend to talk on the telephone with him in the following days. I am told that Mankiewicz... is excellent and a fast worker when a good solid idea is given to him. Will proceed in that direction. (GR14-1)

Mankiewicz recalled, "My impression was that they needed what, in those days, would have been called a bottle show -- something that could be done very cheaply, that didn't require a lot of blowing up of anything. And I believe I suggested a courtroom show. I'd done many of those in the past, a novel and a screenplay. So I said, 'Why don't we do a court martial. Let's put Captain Kirk on trial.' And it would have to be a trial of that time. We're not going to bring in human characters if we can use electronic characters. So the witness against you would be a computerized device that can reveal everything that happened, and seems to nail him. So we started with that." (113-3)

One problem solved. Or perhaps not.

The outline for "Court Martial at Starbase 811," dated May 3, began a period of story and script development unlike any other on *Star Trek*. No story went through more changes than this, and, echoing Cogley's distrust of electronic media, there is more misinformation posted in cyberspace about the writing of "Court Martial" than any other episode.

Mankiewicz' not-too-costly courtroom story was anything but.

Kirk is suspected of creating a situation on the Enterprise which allegedly resulted in the death of Records Officer Finney, who had a grudge against the Captain due to a past disciplinary action. Finney's friend Farley, stationed on the bridge, is willing to lie under oath to bring down Kirk. The computer of the Enterprise, called IRRU (Information Reception and Retrieval Unit) has developed a personality and is fond of Finney, whose job it's been to maintain it, and IRRU doesn't like Kirk either, to the degree that it too is willing to lie on behalf of its friend. IRRU is actually the true culprit in the story since Finney is presumed dead and missing throughout much of it.

Finney's dad (Finney, Sr.), at Starbase 811, accuses Kirk of killing his son and does all he can to see the captain's hide is nailed to the courtroom wall. Additional irritants for Kirk are Prosecuting Attorney Shaw (a man in this version, not a former flame as in the episode), "Harbormaster" Sherek (later to get a name change to Stone), and numerous peers of Kirk's who are quick to assume his guilt. On Kirk's side: Spock and a father/son defense lawyer team, Cogley & Cogley (Samuel Cogley, Jr. and Samuel Cogley, Sr.). The latter Cogley, who begins the story as the second chair defense lawyer, is a throw-back to early 20th Century Earth and has a giant ax to grind against the computer age. The trial, then, pits men against machine.

The backstory has the Enterprise encountering a force field resulting in the "ship's mass" being "simply too great to maintain stability." Kirk has no choice but to "reduce the mass" by jettisoning the "after-cabin." But Farley, who is "Finney's bunkmate," tells a story that is different in one essential particular: according to him, Kirk hit the jettison button several seconds before the "breakup light" went on and "so altered the ship's characteristics that he caused the near breakup." In other words, Kirk either panicked or cold-bloodedly jettisoned the after-cabin to rid himself of Finney, who was sent tumbling into space where it is believed the discarded portion of the ship collided with an asteroid.

Cogley, Jr. quits as Kirk's attorney when he sees the computer log which supports Farley's story. He believes Kirk lied. Everyone else on the Starbase seems to agree and Kirk is thrown in jail before a verdict is even reached. Cogley, Sr. sticks with the Captain but finds opposition at every turn, from Farley, Shaw, Finney, Sr., IRRU the computer, Kirk's peers, and even Harbormaster Sherek, who is described as "a grouchy, elderly former flying officer, now grounded as overage and disposed to be prejudged against Kirk for the simple reason that Kirk still holds command-flight function." Stacking the deck even further against the Captain is modern justice 200 years hence, according to Mankiewicz, which presents evidence solely by computer.

Kirk is ready to give up. He is depicted as being in shock and for the most part waiting to be saved. Spock tries to save his captain, saying that IRRU is "this bundle of wires and impulses and tapes ... and is a liar!" Spock and Cogley, Sr. are able to show the court that IRRU had a high regard for Finney, who "fed it for so long a time" and therefore developed "a distaste for Kirk." But Spock and Cogley, Sr. are unable to get IRRU to admit that it has falsified evidence, nor can they even establish that it has "the ability to re-cut its tapes in order to tell that sort of lie."

Spock says, "_If_ Finney survived the impact of jettison; his new orbit _might_ have intersected with the asteroid, in which case, _if_ he survived the second impact, he _might_ still be alive on the asteroid." Cogley volunteers "an old rocket-jalopy" he owns. We are told that he is the only one who can "drive it," since "it has the galactic equivalent of a stick-shift."

Cogley and Spock help Kirk escape, then take the rocket-jalopy to the asteroid where it is believed Finney may be. They find him, rescue him, and bring him back to explain to the court what happened. Kirk is found innocent. IRRU, however, having "acquired judgment powers," is found to be useless as a guidance and log computer. But Cogley sees value in IRRU and decides it can help him with his pet project -- "a compendium of all the law in history, together with an argument for retaining human law, with such concepts as right to counsel, presumption of innocence, etc." However, Finney, Jr. is the only one IRRU will allow to be its operator. Finney, Jr., therefore, leaves Starfleet to work for Cogley in feeding data to IRRU.

And this -- with all its sets, new ships, and effects-laden space crusades -- was going to save _Star Trek_ money?

Robert Justman read the 10-page outline the day it arrived and, surprisingly, wrote to John D.F. Black, "I like the story idea very, very much." (RJ14-1)

Later memos from Justman helped to clarify what part of the story he was so taken with. It had nothing to do with the manner in which the events were told but the heart of the story underneath all the layers of convoluted plotting -- that Kirk's one true love, the Enterprise, with its electronic brain, IRRU, could turn on its captain and try to destroy him.

Justman's memo to Black continued:

> Sets, opticals and miniatures may be quite expensive in this show, but I <u>can't</u> deduce anything definitely from the outline. (RJ14-1)

Justman did attempt to wade through the clutter of the plot, telling Black, among other things:

> Due to the symmetry and construction of the Enterprise, I don't think that Kirk would have jettisoned an "after-cabin." Perhaps, since we don't ever have to see this, he could have jettisoned a sub-part or something to that effect.... Cogley suggests that they use his old rocket-jalopy for their escape. How about using the already-repaired U.S.S. Enterprise instead? That would solve various money problems that would arise otherwise.... In Act I, on Page 3, we are told that "almost all legal questions -- and certainly all questions of fact -- are now determined electronically." This bothers me because I felt that we were attempting to maintain our fight for humanity and against complete computerization within our show. (RJ14-1)

John D.F. Black also had issues with the story, and wrote Roddenberry:

> Mankiewicz has missed the boat with this idea. He gives us a story where all of Kirk's action, decision-making, thinking, etc., happened yesterday.... Kirk just stands around and reacts while everybody else does things.... Mankiewicz can do much better by us than what he has done. (JDFB14-1)

In a letter to Mankiewicz, Roddenberry took odds with the "pessimistic view of the future," writing:

> When you add up the following things, it is hard to have much feeling or respect for *Star Trek*'s century, the Earth, and the military service it represents. Things such as: a harbor master prejudiced against Kirk for the "simple" reason that Kirk still holds flight command; the use of a computer instead of reasoned judgment for legal questions; thus an implied assumption that computers are constantly photographing and recording all aspects of life, personal and professional; ugly antagonism from what seems an unreasoning group of individuals on the base, developing to almost physical violence; and the placing of a man of the rank of Starship Captain in jail even when a trial has not yet been concluded.... Not leaning on you, Don, but want you to see the direction in which the sum of all these things would be taking *Star Trek* as a series. (GR14-2)

Forty years later, Mankiewicz countered, "I didn't think it was pessimistic. What I did was I took their view of the [future], which was that everybody in this 'picture' was electronic. You did research by button, like you do today, to some extent; everybody was hooked on Google. But this guy -- the lawyer who was Elisha Cook, Jr., a very good actor -- he was the last person to have books. He looked things up, he pulled things down from the shelf, and they didn't know what he was doing. But he won the case. Yes, if you think that's a pessimistic view, that there would then be only one person with books, I think that's what Roddenberry meant." (113-2)

Not quite. Cogley, Sr. liking books was never even broached in Roddenberry's letter.

Mankiewicz later said, "I wanted to have a country lawyer; an 18th century lawyer that lives in the 23rd century -- or whatever century this was. I just wanted a man out of place, a guy who uses books. With a computer, you get abbreviated information, and you can't look back at it and make little underlines. There are unspeakable advantages in the just plain book. I've published three novels and I've always wanted them on paper. I don't want them displayed on somebody's computer." (113-3)

Mankiewicz revised his outline *gratis*, simplifying the story somewhat, eliminating a few of the cost factors and taking out the idea that man would be submissive to machines.

The revised outline, dated June 26, came with a letter from the writer, saying:

> This one, I think, meets your main objection to my earlier approach, since it casts no reflection on the nature of life in the future and -- to my eye, at least -- seems capable of developing within reasonable production costs. (DMM14)

Roddenberry agreed enough to advise Mankiewicz to proceed to teleplay. But, being as busy as he was with numerous other outlines and scripts, he neglected to get NBC's blessing; he hadn't even submitted the story outline in for network approval. Stan Robertson had no idea that a property called "Court Martial at Starbase 811" was being developed.

The first draft script from July 15 hit Roddenberry's desk on the 18th. John D.F. Black's reaction landed on the same spot hours later. It started well enough, with Black saying of Mankiewicz, "You know, this one writes. I think." (JDFB14-2)

Black liked the older Cogley character, for the most part, saying, "Cogley -- old-fashioned attorney -- is charming." But the character was too cartoonish for Black's liking, with him adding:

> Should be some feeling of the years having passed since Clarence Darrow could buy galoshes at the Emporium. In the time of the Enterprise, anyone who would take the pains to locate a gooseneck lamp and a shoe box to hold index cards would be a nut, loaded with affectations, or an antique collector. His words are fine, only his background is exaggerated. (JDFB14-2)

Black felt Finney, Jr. was "a louse." He didn't think a whole lot of Finney, Sr., either. And, while he liked IRRU, he believed the full potential of a computer that thinks freely and has feelings had yet to be realized.

Roddenberry worried the drama of a military court martial was being overshadowed by the gimmick of a vengeful computer.

Records show that Mankiewicz agreed to give *Star Trek* a free rewrite -- a Revised First Draft -- which he delivered in early August, just as Gene Coon and Steven Carabatsos were setting up their offices. Much had changed in the story, moving "Court Martial at Starbase 811" more in the direction of the "Court Martial" we would come to know.

Coon read the script, compared it to the previous version, then sent a memo to "all staff." He agreed with Black about Cogley being "a superb character, though perhaps just a shade too Clarence Darrow," but was bothered that "such a great character" had "nothing to do during the wrap-up!" He bemoaned:

> It seems a shame to have all these brilliant minds, augmented by such superb machinery, baffled and thrown into jeopardy and chaos and confusion by one small-time punk namely Finney. (GC14-1)

Comparing the scripts, Coon closed:

> I must confess that personally I liked the original idea... that the computer developed a personality, became jealous of Kirk and tried to destroy him by deliberately falsifying his own reports and logs and so on. (GC14-1)

But Roddenberry no longer cared for that approach. Coon would have to wait to get his computer with feeling -- as a humorous sub-story -- in "Tomorrow Is Yesterday."

There were many other differences in the new draft besides phasing out IRRU, such as elimination of the costly idea of the Enterprise being put into a space dock for major repairs. And Cogley, Jr. and Cogley, Sr. were now just plain Cogley.

The only problem in losing the son who was more computer-savvy was in understanding why Kirk entrusted his fate to a man who knows so little about those confounded machines. Robert Justman, in his next memo, wondered the same thing. He wrote:

> We do have a basis for a good show here. What it needs is some internal cleanliness and a cutting down of various costs which are inherent in the present version.... I find Finney, Sr. completely unbelievable and irrational in his vacillating behavior throughout this show. I also fail to find the Captain Kirk we have all come to know and love anywhere within these pages....Why does Kirk decide to trust his future to an old fogey like Cogley?... Kirk is a man who will take chances, but he must have a logical basis for doing same.... At one time many years ago, we had talked about having the culprit turning out to be IRRU and not a human being. Whatever happened to that concept?... Sumo's real name is Sulu.... On Page 63, Finney should not grab the tiller to steady the ship. He should instead pick up the reins that Sumo has dropped.... My feeling upon reading the last act, especially, was "this really isn't the end." Or I might better have made use of the first letter of each word in my last quotation. This would make the phrase read – "T.R.I.T.E." (RJ14-2)

Mankiewicz delivered his third draft script on September 6. The people at *Star Trek* considered it a 2nd Revised First Draft. Mankiewicz typed "Final Draft" on the front page. Regardless:

- The "after-cabin" was out, the "pod" was in;
- That "space-jalopy" more suitable as a prop in *Lost in Space* had been stricken;
- Base Commander Sherek was now Base Commodore Stone;
- Finney, Jr. was now merely Finney and not so much a "punk," since he was now older and an officer;
- Finney, Sr. had been replaced by Jamie (AKA Jame), the latter's daughter, named after Kirk since the two men used to be friends;
- The trial had an Act 4 move from the Starbase court to the briefing room of the Enterprise;
- It was now learned that Finney was hiding aboard ship instead of on some asteroid;
- A giant ear device was used to hear his heartbeat and locate him.

Mankiewicz said, "I added in that nice little bit about there's one person more on the ship than there's supposed to be. I said, 'white sound,' which was to record everybody's heartbeat and then you would remove, one by one, each beat until you've removed all the 29 heartbeats that were supposed to be on board. Then there would still be one. And this was all done by white sound. They said, 'What's white sound?' White sound is something I invented. I had no idea there really was such a thing." (113-3)

The next day, Justman wrote Coon, saying:

> First, I would like to suggest we shorten the title ["Court Martial on Starbase 811"] to something else if we possibly could. Second, I find that the script doesn't end in its present form. It just stops at the bottom of Page 73 and leaves me waiting for the rest of the script. I think we need an ending to the show.... In the Teaser, we introduce Jamie Finney, daughter of the missing man. Later on in the show, our Defense Attorney makes a point about what Jamie's motivation is and shows his suspicions. Is this supposed to be a red herring? We set up Jamie later on in the show as an object of suspicion and then never pay it off. I don't understand this.... Page 7: The whole Finney-Kirk-Jamie relationship, Jamie being named after Kirk -- and how old is our boy Kirk, anyway? -- will border on the maudlin if it gets out of hand. Suggest we get rid of it.... Page 7--11: What is Stone trying to do? Help Kirk or crucify him? He should have some definite attitude -- so far he has none.... Page 12: We start a sequence at a place entitled "Ext. Loading Area." Believe me, I raise extremely strong objection to playing this sequence in this particular place. You will have to shoot me before I will agree to let us do what is indicated here. (RJ14-3)

Justman's "just shoot me" notes continued for eight pages, including:

> Spock, Kirk and Janice [Rand] are all out of character.... Cogley certainly is a great lawyer to be able to go into court on a minute's notice like this.... Page 37: We finally bring McCoy into the story. If we're to use him, let's use him well and throughout.... Page 42: Why this attitude on Jamie's part? Where's she been for 20 pages?... Page 47: This act is very long. There are no exciting scenes in it. It's dull -- D-U-L-L.... At the bottom of page 62A, I don't know whether we need a huge "ear" or that sort of horn-auditory device. If we have the experiment adjourned at the bottom of Page 62A from the Briefing Room to the Bridge, we can listen to heartbeats over the Library-computer System [instead].... Page 64-66: I really don't know if we can sell the pulse-beat eliminator, etc. It's a little easy. Besides, I thought the whole story was supposed to be IRRU as the heavy, somehow acquiring independence of thought and deliberately trying to get rid of Kirk -- so the ship is Kirk's enemy and he has to trick it into giving itself away. Do we need to bother with Finney at all? Why?... We do not even refer to the computer as IRRU any longer. Sherek has been changed to Stone. There is no Farley in the script -- and [this] is therefore slightly confusing.... We've come from a man-computer struggle which was the original premise to a real "mellerdramer [sic]," and it's to our disadvantage. I think there will have to be a rewrite on this -- a major overhaul. I don't know if Don can give us any more since he seems married to Finney and that jazz. How about Steve [Carabatsos] taking a great big crack at it? (RJ14-3)

Justman was unaware that IRRU had been jettisoned at Roddenberry's request and the subject on the matter was closed.

Roddenberry later said, "*Star Trek* was action-adventure. It was human conflict. And, if done properly, it was these things before it was science fiction. There was a wonderful premise underneath all the layers of gimmickry in that story and I decided the best thing to do was strip it down. As it was, you couldn't see the forest through all the trees with all the sci-fi that was cluttering it up. A military court martial in the year 2180 [sic] had the potential of being far more interesting and dramatic than the gimmick of a computer out for blood." (145)

But Roddenberry, who had asked for that major change, also didn't care for how things were turning out. He wrote to Coon:

> Our only chance for action-adventure in this script is to throw out about fifty-percent of it as it presently stands, concentrate on: a) action in the court martial, and b) action aboard the ship as Kirk fights to prove he's not a liar.... Our teaser should begin right on the Board of Inquiry and we should see on the viewing screen of the room a scene from the ship's computer tape which "proves" that Kirk is lying. Seems to me, then, that the teaser hook is the board chairman adjourning the inquiry and announcing that a court martial will be convened. (GR14-3)

As shown in this memo, it was Roddenberry's idea to work in the video recording of the action on the bridge. A good add, but, if leading off with this, what would sustain the other 48 or so minutes? Roddenberry had ideas about that, too, and wrote:

> Contrasting with the stern jeopardy of the court martial, I'd like to see some of the life ashore -- women, recreation rooms, drinks, relaxation, et cetera.... Suggest we consider dropping Kirk's quarters and other Enterprise locations -- other than the bridge -- and concentrate on a change of pace and change of scenery by redressing our sets and playing these things down on Base 811. One of the things this show can do for us is give us this change of pace and faces and activities. Let's think of Base 811 as something more than just a maintenance station. (GR14-3)

Roddenberry's writers' instincts had been on the mark with many of the scripts produced so far, but how were changes of this type going to accomplish his goal of adding more "action-adventure in this script"?

He continued:

> Janice Rand is completely out of place in her role. If we have someone working closely with Kirk, it should be Spock.... Far too much talk when we should be seeing other things too. A good example of this is Spock's chess game. Wouldn't it be much better to be with him, savor his surprise as he beats the computer in the game? (GR14-3)

This was another good scene to make the episode which sprung from the fertile mind of Gene Roddenberry, but, again, hardly action-adventure.

Roddenberry closed:

> There are so many comments to make on this script that this memo could run pages. Rather, would suggest we meet on it and generally agree that this needs a major, major rewrite. (GR14-3)

Mankiewicz was not available for a major, major rewrite. He later said, "I had to stop working on that script for personal reasons, I was having marital difficulties. So I just left. So Steve Carabatsos, who I never met by the way, finished it off and did a wonderful job. But if I had stayed, I could have done what Steve did and maybe more." (113-3)

A few days later, Roddenberry wrote Matt Jeffries:

> Let's have a discussion, "re" the design and dressing for the court martial room

in the "Base 811" script. Reason -- it appears we will need a nearly identical room in the Pilot #1 envelope story ["The Menagerie"]. We might as well get a two-for-one bargain. (GR14-4)

Now there was another reason to push the problematic "Court Martial on Star Base 811" script toward production -- a two-for-one bargain.

"I don't know what the condition of the story was: good, bad or whatever," said Steven Carabatsos. "Gene Coon just said, 'Why don't you take this and write a different story? Do a court-martial, do this anachronistic lawyer defending Jim Kirk against a murder charge, but do it differently from what's here.' And that's what I did, resulting in pretty much a brand new script." (28-1)

In terms of story, the script that was "pretty much a brand new script" was not, but it did include some changes, including:

- Shaw, the prosecutor, was now given a first name, Areel, and a gender change to female;
- Janice Rand was taken out and replaced by a nondescript female Yeoman;
- McCoy got an earlier entrance into the story, doing what Rand had previously done and delivering the damning taped evidence in the teaser;
- The "ear" device was now something slightly less silly.

In another regard, it was seemingly a brand new script -- nearly all the dialogue had been changed. Carabatsos also did as Justman had requested -- he shortened the title.

And one last change -- Carabatsos now shared the writing credit with Mankiewicz.

"He's certainly entitled to his credit," Mankiewicz said. "There's no question that he made a substantive contribution to the teleplay, although I suppose the story is pretty much the way I laid it out." (113-1)

The Carabatsos draft arrived on September 19. Roddenberry sent more notes to Coon, writing:

> This script offers but does not take advantage of some great opportunities to explore our leading character, his status as a starship commander. The script is also our first opportunity to see him off his vessel and in contact with his peers. At present, he wanders around like everyone else, very little feeling of his special status, the pomp and ceremony and color of his position....The more we understand that a starship captain's position is rare and considerable, the more we understand the threat to Kirk's career and sympathize with our captain. Command is a lonely, highly dramatic, and potentially highly entertaining aspect of our leading man.... The greater this position of command, the greater the concurrent risks. (GR14-5)

As the creator, Roddenberry remained the primary caretaker for his principle characters, Kirk in particular. In his mind, Steven Carabatsos was playing Kirk as anything but Horatio Hornblower. The Captain was too friendly with too many members of his crew too much of the time. Roddenberry wanted these moments to be kept to a minimum in order to give them greater impact when used. His memo continued:

> When we play him on a chatty "first name" basis with his crew, he invariably comes off weak and a poor commander. On the other hand, when we play his role as ship's captain to the fullest, the occasionally under-the-correct-

circumstances-go-to-a-first-name-basis, this moment has impact and significance. (GR14-5)

Carabatsos did a polish on his script, creating the Yellow Cover First Draft, adding in greater emphases on Kirk's part to remain dignified throughout the ordeal, to stand tall in the face of accusations and ridicule, and, in accord with his rank, to guard against showing his anguish. To convey Kirk's human side, Carabatsos put more emphasis on his past involvement with Areel Shaw, which also added to the final indignity the Captain must rise above when he learns that his former love will be leading the charge against him.

This version of "Court Martial" was the first believed worthy enough to send to Kellam de Forest Research for a technical review. Among the notes sent back by de Forest's assistant, Joan Pierce, was the objection to having McCoy (instead of Rand) deliver the computer log to Stone:

> McCoy, as medical officer, would have nothing to do with the computer log. It would have been Finney's jurisdiction. Since Finney is "dead," the handling of such a log would be Spock's job. Also, legally, the evidence that this is "The Tape" must come from Spock since it is he who can testify first hand as to its authenticity. This scene should be Spock's. (KDF14-1)

McCoy lost his early entrance. The moment in the teaser was given to Spock.

De Forest Research had many more notes. In the script, it is said that Cogley "wears a rumpled business suit that might be more appropriate in Cleveland, 1950." Despite all the memos back and forth over this issue, the bothersome depiction of Cogley had somehow remained. Pierce got it stricken from the script, and did so by embarrassing the producers:

> Since *Star Trek* presupposes a future date in which all clothing will have changed, the use of a rumpled business suit appears grossly anachronistic. Such usage would be comparable to an attorney today wearing the garb of George Washington. (KDF14-1)

Gene Coon did a script polish of his own, creating the September 26 Final Draft. And this was the first version of "Court Martial" -- be it outline or script -- to go to NBC. And NBC was not happy.

Coon received an unpleasant call from Stan Robertson the next day, followed one day later with the longest memo the Network Production Manager had yet to send to *Star Trek*. It began:

> Just for the record, Gene, I would like to state again how disturbed we here were to receive [this] script so close to its production date, without even having received an outline or been privy to the discussions which resulted in it being commissioned. I realize that this script was put in motion prior to your association with *Star Trek*... however, so that there is no confusion or misunderstanding regarding future procedures in this area, I am requesting that you advise all of your colleagues of the dangers, as we discussed, which are inherent in commissioning a story without first attaining network approval. (SR14)

Robertson's upset also had to do with what he believed were serious problems in the script. He continued:

> This is the type of a teleplay about which, quite honestly, Gene, I have strong reservations. Granted, Don Mankiewicz is an outstanding writer and Steven Carabatsos has apparently done a splendid job of tightening his original script. We have to look no farther than *The Caine Mutiny* court martial to champion the

point that there is indeed high drama and great emotional conflict when you delve into a military-oriented personality and attempt to humble that strong mind and body for errors of judgment, unprofessional conduct or mental degeneration in a time of stress. Even in view of all the above, one is not strongly convinced that this episode, as presently scripted, is visual enough to hold the interest of our mass viewing audience. As we discussed, this is probably one of the most "cerebral" scripts that we have received to date. This is not to demean the writing, *per se*, at all. It's quality. But it's also very weighty and some of the dialogue, particularly those portions in which we examine the crux of our story -- can an emotional man be more fallible than an unemotional, logical machine -- is very preachy. Also, some of the philosophy as spewed by the old defense council, Cogley, is magnificent but, again, it's very cerebral and verbose.... Adding to the points mentioned above, is the fact that our entire story is confined within the interior setting of Planet 811 or aboard the Enterprise and that, save for our climax in Act IV, is completely devoid of physical action. The point is that people stand around and discuss philosophies and ethics rather than moving and doing. Because of the lateness of our receiving this script, any suggestions we might offer at this point are probably more academic than practical. (SR14)

Coon's script polish, dated September 29, focused on finessing dialogue, de-muddling the muddle and *not* adding in new scenes. One more polish came on October 3, the day more notes arrived from Broadcast Standards, again resulting in a few lines of dialogue being changed. The episode had started filming that morning.

Time had run out and the buck had been passed. "Court Martial" was now in the hands of director and cast.

Pre-Production
September 26-30, 1966 (5 days)

Marc Daniels, who many believed to be *Star Trek*'s touchstone, returned for his third directing assignment. He had little to suggest regarding the script, but did have some thoughts about casting.

The African-Canadian actor Percy Rodrigues was hired to play Commodore Stone. Rodrigues had a commanding presence on the small screen and often found roles that were unique and inspiring for black viewers. He played a doctor on *Ben Casey*, a Sheriff on *The Fugitive*, an African leader on *The Man from U.N.C.L.E.*, a debonair assassin on *The Wild, Wild West*, and now Commodore Stone, a Starbase commander.

Joan Marshall played Areel Shaw. She was one of the leads on TV's *Bold Venture* series in 1959 and often worked for Warner Brothers in that studio's crank-'em-out shows -- *Maverick*, *Bronco*, *Surfside 6*, *Hawaiian Eye*, and *77 Sunset Strip*. Gene Coon knew her. She was cast in the pilot film he had a hand in making -- *The Munsters*, as Herman's wife Phoebe (to be renamed Lily). Fearing Phoebe Munster was too much like Carolyn

Percy Rodriguez as Dr. Harry Miles in *Peyton Place* (ABC, 1968)

Jones' Morticia Addams on *The Addams Family*, Marshall was replaced for the series with Yvonne de Carlo.

Don Mankiewicz said, "I liked everybody in that show [but] I thought the girl was physically wrong. I would have preferred something other than a blonde. She gave a good performance, but, when I conceived the relationship, I saw her as a brunette, and so I always saw her that way." (113-3)

Richard Webb, the vengeful Ben Finney, was a 1950's TV icon, of a sort. He played the title character in *Captain Midnight*. He was 39 then, 50 here.

Joan Marshall in *The Munsters* pilot film (Revue TV, 1964)

Elisha Cook, Jr., 1940s film noir tough guy (Warner Bros. publicity photo)

Elisha Cook, Jr. was more to the liking of Mankiewicz. Cook, hired to play the old-school attorney Samuel Cogley, had over 200 screen appearances, including working with Bogart in both *The Big Sleep* and *The Maltese Falcon*. He had taken direction from Howard Hawks, John Huston, and George Stevens. And now Marc Daniels.

Winston "Win" De Lugo played the hostile officer named Timothy in the Starbase lounge. De Lugo was a stage actor having his first try at TV (thanks to Joe D'Agosta's tendency to hire actors he knew from the theater). D'Agosta also booked De Lugo to appear in an episode of *Mission: Impossible* at this time.

De Lugo was astounded by nearly every aspect of his first TV experience. He said, "They gave me a trailer, which really surprised me -- a trailer *indoors*. They had them lined up in the back of the soundstage. And my name was on a card slot by the door. I had never gotten anything like that doing Off-Broadway or Summer Stock. And 'Bones' came up and rapped on my door, and he's looking up at me and reporting about whether it was going to be five minutes or whatever, and asking if there was anything I needed. He made me about as comfortable as I could be. I couldn't believe it! I thought, 'When they realize I'm just a nobody from New York, they'll call security and drag me out of here.'" (47)

Hagan Beggs played Lt. Hansen on the bridge, and would do likewise in the next episode to film. From Canada, he had worked with and become friends with James Doohan in their homeland. He also knew Shatner, although the two had yet to work together. Beggs said, "I think it was a coincidence, quite honestly, that I knew someone in the cast. But it was only when I did *Star Trek* that I really hooked up with him again. It came about by my agent at that time sending me out to see about that role. It wasn't a case of Doohan saying you gotta see this Canadian guy." (12-1)

And Majel Barrett, the voice of the ship's computer, was now also the voice of the Starbase computer.

Production Diary
Filmed October 3, 4, 5, 6, 7, 10 & 11 (1/3 day), 1966
(Planned as 6 day production, running 1/3 day over; total cost: $175,182).

Production began on Monday, October 3, 1966. During this week, LSD was declared illegal in the U.S. Ironically, the Beatles' LSD inspired album *Revolver* remained at the top of the LP charts. "Cherish" by the Association was still No. 1 on the radio. Top at the box office: *Fantastic Voyage* and *Who's Afraid of Virginia Woolf?* The previous night, on *The Ed Sullivan Show*: Connie Francis sang a show tunes medley, Jimmy Durante did a song and dance routine, The Four Seasons performed their latest record, "I've Got You Under My Skin," and Ed introduced a new act called Jim Henson's Muppets. And then, with the start of the new day, Captain Kirk went on trial.

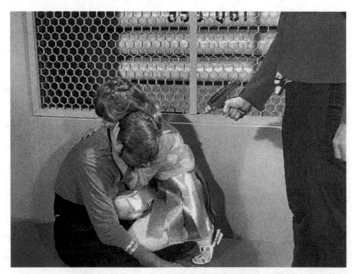

Deleted scene: Jame Finney comforts her father
(from startrekhistory.com and startrekpropauthority.com)

The location for Monday was Stage 9, with scenes in Commodore Stone's office, followed by the Enterprise briefing room. The studio representative asked Daniels to stop filming at 6:36, allowing the set to wrapped by 7 p.m.

Day 2, Tuesday, was also spent on Stage 9, with the company filming Kirk's guest quarters on the Starbase, followed by the Enterprise engineering set for Kirk and Finney's confrontation. The start of the fight scene, with stuntmen Troy Melton as Finney and Chuck Clow as Kirk, was started this day but only half-fought when Daniels stopped filming at 6:45 p.m., one-quarter day behind.

Day 3 saw the completion of the climactic fight. Daniels was overly cautious with actors for stunt sequences. He utilized Melton and Clow to the point that he couldn't hide from the camera that it wasn't Shatner and Webb.

Also shot, but left out of the finalized episode, was a scene where Cogley returns to the ship with Jame. She convinces her father to tell Kirk how he sabotaged the ship, so the damage can be undone. In the edited film, this scene was replaced by an additional Captain's Log voiceover to speed things along as Kirk climbs into the area referred to in the series as the Jefferies Tube (named after Matt Jefferies).

Next came scenes on the ship's bridge, which marked the first day for Hagan Beggs, playing Lt. Hansen. He recalled, "The bridge set was amazing. I had, of course, been on television sets and film sets before, but I must say it certainly was extremely different and I was just amazed by it. Quite honestly, it was like a kid looking at a bank of instruments. The design and all the detail was really something. And it didn't bother me at all that there were ropes being pulled by guys behind the doors; it still looked pretty damn fantastic. In that period, at that time, I was quite awed by it. An incredible set." (12-1)

This was light years from Beggs' last TV job on *Hogan's Heroes*. He said, "We'd get a shot, then step off so they could pull a different section [of the bridge] out and have us come back for a different camera angle. And there was a funny thing that happened where the doors wouldn't open on cue and someone would walk into them. There was a lot of orchestration involved in working on that set. So there were mistakes made, as to be expected, and retakes of things, because someone would yell, 'The door hasn't opened! It hasn't opened! Cut! Cut! Cut!' So here I am sitting at a desk [helm console] and told, 'Okay, shake violently now! We're into crashing mode!' And the actors would shake like crazy. We physically were shaking ourselves. I did like Marc [Daniels]. I found him very affable and very friendly guy. He was very pleasant, but had to also be very aware of the time, of course. It was a tight schedule." (12-1)

Cameras stopped rolling at 7:10 p.m. Daniels held at a quarter-day behind.

Day 4, Thursday, was spent entirely on the bridge, including the scene where McCoy uses that "white sound" device.

Despite the marginal material and substandard prop, moods were generally good. In this morning's *Daily Variety* word had leaked from NBC -- *Star Trek* was being picked up for at least another 10 episodes, promising a full season of no less than 26. The official notification was still a week away.

The last "Court Martial" shots taken this day were completed at 6:06 p.m., but the company continued filming with a pickup shot for "Dagger of the Mind" until 7:05. Half an hour was spent wrapping gear and removing makeup from Leonard Nimoy, giving cast and crew just enough time to make it home for the 8:30 premiere of "The Enemy Within" -- the fifth episode to air.

Win De Lugo as Timothy
(Courtesy of Paul Stuiber)

Day 5, Friday, had the company on Stage 10, filming the two Interior Officer's Lounge scenes. Winston De Lugo, playing his role as the hostile Starfleet officer, continued to be surprised by his first TV experience. When called to set, he found none of the preparation he was accustomed to in the theater world. This was television. And time was money. De Lugo recalled, "Marc Daniels says, 'Win, you stand here. Now, all the guys in the red shirts are your crew. You're the same as Kirk; a commander of a Starship and you're meeting him at this bar far out in space.' Well, I didn't know any of this; I didn't have the whole script; I just had my pages. But it was clear that my character is trying to intimidate Kirk. Of course, years later, they put out these trading cards and there's one of me and it says I'm a lieutenant. Well, a lieutenant can't talk to a captain like that! But I thought that Marc knew a little more about it than I did. So I did as he told me.

"Anyway, Shatner comes in and we do a rehearsal, and I was surprised how small he is compared to me. And he says, 'Timothy,' and starts to say something about the old gang at the Academy, and then, as he looks up at me, he calls, 'Cut!' He calls it. And he just reaches out and grabs Marc Daniels and pulls him over and whispers to him. And then Marc says, 'Alright, we're going to take a break. Relax; go to your trailers. We have to make some changes here.' When they called me back, I see they've changed the set around a little and all of a sudden there's a number of bar stools. And Marc says, 'Win, you sit here.' I'm thinking, 'Okay, I get it; I'm too tall.'" (47)

A few days after this incident, *TV Guide* published an article on Shatner, who was quoted as saying, "I've gotten a great insight into the omnipotence of the series lead. Everybody does his best not to upset the *star*. It's an almost unique position few in the entertainment world achieve... It's like absolute power." (166-14)

De Lugo added, "And so we start with Shatner's stuff first -- we're shooting over my shoulder at him, and he's now standing and I'm sitting. And the scene starts and, as things are going along, his eyes start filling up with water. And he calls, 'Cut!' And he calls, 'Makeup!' And he goes off behind somewhere. And then he comes back and we do that part of the scene again. And his eyes fill up with water again. And, 'Cut!' And he goes behind the set again. And I imagine the girl is back there dabbing his eyes. The third time, I thought, 'Well, things are always in threes, so this has got to be the last time.' But it wasn't. It happened four times. And this was the kind of scene where we had to hold each other's gaze, because my character is just inches away from throwing a punch at this guy. And then he asked for a minute and he disappeared somewhere." (47)

De Lugo knew nothing of the immense demands on Shatner as the star of the series and the relentless work load that came with that title. He couldn't know that Shatner's average work day was over 12 hours long, five days a week, with weekends spent reading scripts, all the while trying to squeeze in a moment here and there with his two daughters and struggling to hold together a marriage that was in the process of collapsing.

Near the time this episode was filming, Shatner told a magazine writer, "I hope that since my wife Gloria and I are reasonably intelligent people, things can be worked out. But we are having difficulties. Even under ideal circumstances, a couple nearly always has some marital problems. When you add to ordinary circumstances the stress and strain of doing a show that occupies almost all your time, you have extraordinary problems." (166-19)

Win De Lugo was witnessing the indestructible Captain Kirk with tears in his eyes.

"He was gone only a brief amount of time," De Lugo said. "How he recomposed himself, or what he did so fast, was beyond me. But it went absolutely beautifully after that. He was so cool and composed. He was like a different guy. Except that when he finished his camera shot, he walks away. And he's walking across the soundstage quite rapidly, and I said to Marc, 'Where the fuck is he going?' And, with that, Shatner opened the iron door and *bam*, he was out and gone. And Marc said to me, 'Don't worry about him; I'll work with you.' Being a naive New York actor, I'm thinking, 'Oh great,' because the director knows more about this than the actors do. He probably really studied this script.

"Well, they moved the camera around to get my shot -- and this camera was huge, a big round cylinder looking at me -- and Marc slips his arms around one side of the camera and he wiggles his fingers and says, 'Win, look at my hand.' And I look at his hand, and he says, 'Action!' "Well, I'll tell you, all my stage work didn't prepare me for that! – Saying my lines to five wiggling fingers!" (47)

De Lugo said his lines. Daniels called, 'Cut! Print it! We're moving on!" De Lugo remembered leaving as he had arrived, in a state of awe.

Hagan Beggs confirms that Shatner was not his normal self during production of this episode and the next, although he was less bothered over it. He said, "My friend was really Jimmy Doohan. I had a pleasant relationship with Spock and Bones. Very nice, very comfortable. Shatner less so, but he was very professional. He just didn't seem to get involved with us too much. He sort of did his work and then disappeared back into his dressing room. At the time, I felt, 'Well, no wonder, he has a shitload of stuff to learn. He has to stay focused.' But, in my opinion, he was slightly focused and separate from the rest of the cast who were more inclined to sort of stick around a bit or chit chat. He didn't. As soon as his scene was over, he'd go, 'Thank you,' and he'd head right to his dressing room." (12-1)

Marc Daniels was determined to catch up and pushed through the dialogue as quickly as possible -- too quickly, in fact. An example of how rushed production can adversely affect the performance from an otherwise competent actor is apparent in this scene. Notice how uncomfortable DeForest Kelley looks when with Joan Marshall in the Starbase cocktail bar. It almost appears as though someone gave Kelley a gentle shove to get him to cross to Marshal. Once there, Kelley froze, awkwardly, said his lines, terribly, and then, with complete woodenness, ushered Marshall out of frame. This was the result of an actor ill at ease with the "blocking" of a director in a hurry who was telling him how to play his role -- and perhaps wiggling fingers at him. Kelley was given only one take. It went badly. And then Daniels called, "Cut! Print! We're on the wrong set!" The company quickly moved on to the courtroom to begin what was scheduled for two days of work. Daniels was determined to get it covered in one-and-a-half.

Day 5. Joan Marshall during the trial sequence
(Courtesy of Gerald Gurian)

"There were a lot of great directors on *Star Trek*," Jerry Finnerman said. "And there were some that got a little pushy. I had one guy, he gave me a shot, and before we even got a light in he was screaming, 'Are you ready? Are you ready?' That doesn't make you feel good.... But I always stuck up for what I believed in." (63-3)

Finnerman admitted that Daniels was a "good director" but tended to come across as "a little grumpy." He said that they often "clashed" because Daniels pushed him more than any other directors on the series.

Last shot was taken at 7:06. Daniels was still one-quarter day behind.

Day 6, Monday. Daniels shot from 8 a.m. to 7 p.m. on the court set but was unable to pick up that quarter day, thereby delaying the start of the next episode set to film on Tuesday. Phone calls were made, schedules were changed.

Marc Daniels later said, "While we were making 'Court Martial' we all felt, 'Oh God, this is a dog, let's get it over with as best we can.'... Part of the problem was that it didn't have much action in it. Also, Elisha Cook couldn't remember his lines. When you're on a six-day schedule, trying to [stay on] time, and you've got to keep stopping and going back, it drives everyone crazy. You've got a courtroom scene and you're photographing him one line at a time because he can't remember two." (44-3)

Elisha Cook said, "People enjoy [my performance in] *Star Trek*, but for me it was another fast TV job. I didn't think I was very good." (36aa)

**Elisha Cook, flubbing a line
(from blooper reel, courtesy of Gerald Gurian)**

Day 7, Tuesday, continued with the shooting of one line at a time. Daniels only brought back Shatner, Nimoy, Kelley, Marshall, and Cook, spending the morning picking up close ups, which meant more finger wiggling. The last shot was taken by 11:30 a.m. Fifteen minutes later, Daniels, having had no prep days, began filming "The Menagerie."

Post-Production
October 12 through November 29, 1966. Music score: tracked.

Bruce Schoengarth and Edit Team #2 were assigned the cutting, following their work on "Mudd's Women," "The Naked Time" and "Dagger of the Mind."

Watching the dailies, Coon felt the first half of the episode moved too slowly. Stan Robertson had been right about it needing those flashbacks. To help the pacing, Coon instructed Schoengarth to juggle certain scenes and add more punch to the front end of the show. This caused yet more problems, among them Kirk's uniform changing from standard top to collarless top, again and again. The rearranging of scenes also resulted in some logic-defying character turns, including Jame's back-and-forth feelings about Kirk, and Cogley having confidence in the case, then not, then having it again. These were not turns of the characters, merely the editors.

One dialogue sequence cut from the script at the last minute, very nearly as it was being filmed, would have helped to better understand Jame's change of attitude. She is waiting for Kirk outside his quarters on the Starbase. She apologizes for her emotion-fueled accusations from earlier. She asks, "What are you going to do now? I mean, you're not going to stand trial?" Kirk says, "You've been talking to Commodore Stone, haven't you? And he convinced you to try to get me to take the easy way out." Jame says, "He didn't convince me of anything. He told me there was a chance this could be settled without a trial. I just want you to know, if you do decide to, well, to transfer to ground duty instead of standing trial, I won't make trouble." The script tells us, "Kirk looks at her -- at the simple, vulnerable trust in her eyes. He takes her hand." He then says, "Jame, I'll tell you something I don't believe I could say to any other human being. What they believe I did is a lie.... But... for the first time in my life that I can remember, I'm afraid. The bridge of a ship -- that's my world, my strength. Jame, they can take away my command permanently. And if they do that, they take away my life." She pleads, "Then don't let them! Don't ask for a trial. Let a year, or two, or three go by. This will be forgotten; they'll give you another ship." Kirk is adamant, and says, "No, Jame. They don't forget. They never forget.... And you wouldn't forget, would you? In the back of your mind, there'd always be that suspicion: Did he kill my father?... That's true, isn't it, Jame?" The following action reads: "Her eyes well up with tears. She looks away. Kirk moves abruptly and quickly to the door." The scene ends with Kirk exiting into his quarters, unable to speak further. And Jame crying.

Roddenberry decided that the powerful scene should be rewritten. He felt that Kirk would not reveal his inner feelings to anyone other than McCoy or perhaps Spock, and never to this degree even with them. Rather than modifying the dialogue, Coon, under pressure and running out of time, threw the scene out.

Another bad cut, this one from the editing sessions themselves, was not showing Cogley's return to the Enterprise with Jame. In *Star Trek 2*, the second paperback book for Bantam, published in February 1968, author James Blish based his short story version of "Court Martial" on the Final Draft screenplay and not the mutilated episode. For his story, Jame boards the Enterprise with Cogley and confronts her father. And it works.

Don Mankiewicz flinched when he saw the edited version. He said, "The other failure of this episode was entirely my fault. If I had been able to stay with it, I think I would have found a way to do it without the off-screen narration. When you're doing off-screen narration in a show, you're saying and admitting to the public that we have to go back. Don't say what happened, show it happening. In my version, you saw the daughter come onto the ship and talk her father out of trying to destroy it. But they ended up using the narration instead." (113-3)

While no new music was composed for "Court Martial," an unused Joseph Mullendore track from "The Conscience of the King" is heard here, an alternate slowed-down version of the series theme as Kirk talks with Areel Shaw in the Starbase bar and lounge. Mullendore's other slowed-down variation of the theme, his cocktail music rendition, which did make its way into "Conscience of the King," is resurrected here for the earlier bar scene, when McCoy meets Shaw.

Due to all the rewriting, with the abandonment of the space-jalopy vehicle and the trip to an asteroid, the story that had the potential of busting the bank at Desilu turned out to be a bargain ... from a bean-counter's point of view, anyway. The bill from Film Effects of Hollywood amounted to only $5,798, for matte shots and a transporter effect. As a result, the episode Robert Justman feared would be one of the most expensive of the season turned out to be one of the least.

"Court Martial" was made for 17 grand less than the studio's per-episode allowance. The episode's total cost of $175,182 helped to drop the first season deficit to $33,618.

Release / Reaction
Only NBC air date: 2/2/67.

Steven H. Scheuer reviewed "Court Martial" for his syndicated entertainment column, *TV Key Previews*. Among the newspapers to carry the review on February 2, 1967 was the *Pittsburg Post-Gazette*, in Pittsburg, Pennsylvania. Scheuer wrote:

> A thoroughly absorbing and credible space-age tale tonight that explores the inevitable man vs. machine conflict. Captain Kirk has been court martialed on a charge of negligence and causing the death of one of his officers on the evidence

made available by the ship's computer. How the infallible machine is proven to indeed be fallible will hold your interest through-out this drama.

Audience reaction from the 1967 airing of "Court Martial" was quite positive. Many viewers were favorably responsive to the idea of a military trial in outer space, and to the inherent drama a story of this type brings to the screen. The ratings were also rewarding.

RATINGS / Nielsen 30-Market report for Thursday, February 2, 1967:

8:30 - 9 p.m., with 67.4% of U.S. TVs in use.	Rating:	Share:
NBC: *Star Trek* (first half)	18.7	27.7%
ABC: **Bewitched**	**22.2**	**32.9%**
CBS: *My Three Sons*	16.9	25.1%
Local independent stations:	10.5	14.3%
9 - 9:30 p.m., with 67.1% of U.S. TVs in use.		
NBC: **Star Trek (second half)**	**19.7**	**29.4%**
ABC: *Love on a Rooftop*	19.6	29.2%
CBS: *Thursday Night Movie* (start)	17.4	26.7%
Local independent stations:	11.0	14.7%

For the second week in a row (based on the broadcast schedule), and the seventh time so far, *Star Trek* won part or all of its time slot. *The CBS Thursday Night Movie*, premiering the 1961 comedy *The Pleasure of His Company*, starring Fred Astaire and Debbie Reynolds, came in third.

Win de Lugo said, "We all thought it was a dead dog. And when I watched it, I was cringing, because I know Shatner's not there in the scene when the camera is on me and I don't have human eyeballs to look at and to react to. So I don't know what kind of look's going to be on my face. But I was okay with it. I thought, 'Thank God, I escaped!'" (47)

Despite the numbers from A.C. Nielsen and mostly positive feedback from letter writers, many of those responsible for making *Star Trek* were not fans of this episode and when the repeat season came, Robert Justman chose to pass "Court Martial" over.

From the Mailbag

Received the week after "Court Martial" first aired:

> Dear William [Shatner], "The Court Martial" was extra-super tremendously great!!!! You are the ideal person to play our friendly neighborhood heroic Captain Kirk. Man, the list of honors they rattled off at your court martial was very impressive. You wouldn't think that such a genius would be having a court martial. I didn't mean that sarcastically. You, Leonard Nimoy, DeForest Kelley, and everyone else connected with *Star Trek* are geniuses!! Thank you for being you!!! Ellen H.

> Dear Sirs... As a rule our family is not prone to writing fan letters, but we feel that in respect to the overall excellence of *Star Trek* we would like to express our gratitude and appreciation for the enjoyable entertainment it provides. That your writers, technical directors, members of your staff, crew, and cast have so realistically and meticulously prepared and presented week after week of excellent entertainment is indeed a tribute to their individual and collective talents.... Further, the ethnic backgrounds represented within the cast are exactly as they should be, for it will require the best of all Earth to achieve in fact what you are presenting as today's fiction. We hope the above will serve as one small voice expressing a sincere desire for a long and highly successful run of *Star*

Trek. Respectfully, Mr. & Mrs. Robert G. & family.

Dear Gene Roddenberry... in all sincerity, I like best your "Court Martial." It may be significant that it had fewer gimmicks than the others in the series, a thoroughly believable motivation for characters, and an intensely interesting story and denouement. Aside from the space ship angle, it could have happened in the very near future.... I'm rooting for you in your effort to put on an adult s-f series. Best, Phillip Jose Farmer.

(Farmer was a highly respected and successful science fiction author who, at this time, was interested in writing for *Star Trek*.)

Memories

Win De Lugo didn't stay upset at Shatner for long. He said, "We all used to hang out at the Raincheck on Santa Monica. That was where all the actors got together. And this was, like, a month-and-a-half later, and Shatner sent a drink over and invited me to his table to make up for that day. He was with a date, and he really amazed me, because, in making the introductions, he told the girl what he had done to me on the set of *Star Trek*. I was really bowled over that he was so open and forthcoming. He didn't try to hide anything. And then he apologized for it and shook my hand. That was pretty classy." (47)

Don Mankiewicz said, "I was very pleased with it. I didn't care for how the end was changed, losing the daughter and adding in the narration. It's just that the show was so good that I would have liked to have seen that part done differently." (113-3)

Marc Daniels remembered the feeling on the set when "Court Martial" wrapped, said, "We all felt, 'Thank God that's over with.'" (44-3)

Episodes 15 & 16: THE MENAGERIE, Parts 1 & 2
Written by Gene Roddenberry
(additional story elements by John D.F. Black, uncredited)
Directed by Marc Daniels

TV Guide listing, November 12, 1966 issue:

> In the first of a two-part story, Spock inexplicably abducts crippled Captain Pike, the Enterprise's former commander, locks the spaceship on a course for the only forbidden planet in the galaxy -- and then turns himself in for court-martial.

TV Guide listing, November 19, 1966 issue:

> Conclusion of a two-part story. Science officer Spock conducts his defense against a mutiny charge. Using the weird communication method of the planet Talos IV, Spock offers a startling re-enactment of his former commander's visit to the forbidden world.

Spock on trial, with Nimoy, Shatner and Malachi Throne
(Unaired film trim courtesy of Gerald Gurian)

It is learned that Pike had once been held in captivity by the mentally-advanced Talosians, who penetrated the Captain's thoughts and used his memories to create vivid hallucinations, forcing him to experience the most pleasurable and traumatic moments from his conscious and subconscious mind. As these images from Talos IV are received by the Enterprise, Kirk's problem is to discover the reason for his First Officer's uncharacteristic actions, and unravel the mystery of Pike's past.

Roddenberry's sly agenda with the original story of "The Cage" that forms the core of "The Menagerie" was a commentary on modern man's tendency to live vicariously through television and movies, as well as the erosion of the human spirit as a result of non-activity. His message: Live and let live -- not through others, but through one's own personal adventures.

With the wraparound material -- the envelope script – we were given a counterpoint: Live and let die, honoring an individual's freedom to choose when, where, and how.

SOUND BITES

- *Commodore Mendez:* "His wheelchair is constructed to respond to his brain waves; he can turn it, move backwards and forward slightly... Through the flashing light he can say 'yes' or 'no'... But that's it, Jim! That's as much as the poor devil can do. Inside, his mind is as active as yours or mine. But it's imprisoned inside a useless, vegetating body. He's kept alive, mechanically, with a battery driven heart."

- *Dr. McCoy:* "Blast medicine anyway!... That man can think any thought we can, hope, love, dream as much as we can -- but he can't reach out and no one can reach in!"

- *McCoy:* "Jim, forgetting how well we both know Spock, just the fact he's a Vulcan means he's incapable of falsehood..." *Kirk:* "You're forgetting that Spock is half-human."

- *Talosian Keeper, to Kirk:* "Captain Pike has an illusion, and you have reality. May you find your way as pleasant."

ASSESSMENT

"The Menagerie" constitutes an amazing and unparalleled creative work, most notably to the credit of writer/producer Gene Roddenberry, director Marc Daniels, and film editor Robert Swanson. With precious little time and resources, these three, with the support of the entire *Star Trek* team, pulled off a near-miracle and created one of the series most highly regarded episodes.

If the primary element of any good story is to present a character with a problem, then "The Menagerie" gives us a conflict four times over: Spock and Kirk have conflict with one another, and even inner conflict with themselves, as do Vina and Pike in the story-within-a-story. This one is about friendship. It is also about the quality and dignity of life.

THE STORY BEHIND THE STORY

Script Timeline

John D.F. Black's 1st Draft teleplay, "From the First Day to the Last":
August 12, 1966.
Gene Roddenberry's 1st Draft teleplay, "The Menagerie": September 21, 1966.
Roddenberry's 2nd Draft teleplay (Mimeo Department reformatted
"Yellow Cover 1st Draft"): October 3, 1966.
Roddenberry's revised teleplay (Final Draft): October 7, 1966.
Coon's script polish (Revised Final Draft teleplay): October 10, 1966.
Additional page revisions by Roddenberry or Coon: October 13, 14 & 17, 1966.

On March 6, 1966, Desilu received notification from NBC that the series had sold and was given an order for 16 episodes. The studio heads took a few days to decide if they wanted to proceed with the costly venture. At the end of the week, with a "go" from Desilu, Roddenberry gave out the first four story assignments: "Dagger of the Mind," "The Corbomite Maneuver," "The City on the Edge of Forever," and "What Are Little Girls Made Of?" Then, just days later, on March 14, he sent a memo to Herb Solow suggesting that "The Cage" be incorporated into a two-part episode, melding old footage and cast with new. He made the argument that this would not only save the studio money but, more importantly, would insure that *Star Trek* not fall behind in its production schedule and risk missing its air date commitments.

It was surprisingly early in the game for Roddenberry to be so sure that a move such as this would be needed. His real motivation for making the suggestion was to bring to the airwaves a work of which he was immensely proud.

NBC had already agreed that "Where No Man Has Gone Before," despite further cast changes made since it had filmed, could be one of the 16 episodes ordered. Now the network would consider letting "The Cage" be another.

Two days later, on March 16, "The Cage" went off to Stan Robertson. Like the others at the network, he was impressed by its scope, with production values that far exceeded anything produced for television in the past. He was quick to embrace the idea.

Even without a story outline to serve as a blueprint, NBC agreed to this unique proposal on March 21. "The Cage" could be used as one of the 16 episodes, with two caveats: 1) It would be combined with a companion story featuring the current cast members, comprising close to 50% of the material to be seen in the two-part episode, and 2) that the network would only pay for one of those two episodes. NBC, after all, had already contributed a fair amount of money into the making of "The Cage."

Desilu was not happy. If the studio went along with Roddenberry's proposal, it would be forfeiting $100,000 in revenue from the network, with the order for newly produced episodes decreasing from 15 to 14. On the other hand, if the companion episode -- that "envelope story" -- could be produced for the budget of a single new episode, the studio would save itself $92,000 in deficit financing by not having to make that 15th new episode.

The day after NBC agreed to the proposal, Roddenberry wrote to Mickey Rubin, the Financial Executive at Desilu. He appealed to the studio to accept the deal, stating that he believed the series would not be able to produce and deliver 15 new episodes in time to meet all air dates, but they might be able to produce and deliver 14. Rubin slept on it, uneasily, and then sent word the next day that Desilu reluctantly agreed to the network's terms.

It was an early victory for Roddenberry, and then the project was immediately put onto the back burner. He had suddenly found himself far too busy rewriting scripts to make time for creating the needed envelope story -- a teleplay which would clearly require intricate planning and structuring in order to properly utilize the bulk of the first pilot while, at the same time, incorporating a new storyline worthy of a marriage with the old. He asked John D.F. Black to take on the headache as his second *Star Trek* assignment, just as soon as he was finished rewriting "Mudd's Women."

Starting May 23, 1966, Black focused on finding a suitable structure for an envelope script that could solve the puzzle he'd been given. He ran his ideas past Roddenberry, then broke ground on his script, "From the First Day to the Last," on Friday, May 27, spending the weekend roughing out the better part of a first draft, then abandoned it for an urgently needed rewrite of "The Enemy Within," followed by the writing of a story outline, then three script drafts of "The Naked Time." More work followed for Black, with script polishing of "The Man Trap," "Balance of Terror," "What Are Little Girls Made Of?," "Charlie X," "Dagger of the Mind," and "Miri," before he could turn full attention back to the envelope script.

A memo from Robert Justman in late July, 1966, advised Roddenberry and Black:

> The most important thing I can say about the "Envelope" is that we must shoot it as the last of our commitments for the first batch of shows to be delivered to NBC. This means that we should start shooting the "Envelope" portion of this effort approximately October 7, 1966. It would be directed by Marc Daniels and should shoot no more than a total of four days.

Justman understood that the point of creating a two-part episode by combining "The Cage" with new wrap-around footage was to help *Star Trek* catch up in production, and also reduce the deficit spending. The new footage, therefore, would need to be shot in four days in order to make this goal possible. Having just done the near impossible in directing "The Man Trap" and "The Naked Time" combined in less than 12 days, with no preparation time for the latter episode, Marc Daniels seemed the best choice for the directing chore ... provided the "envelope" was written with economics in mind.

Black delivered his first draft teleplay of "From the First Day to the Last" on August 12, just two days before his contract with *Star Trek* as associate producer/story consultant was due to run out. He had one last obligation -- to provide a script polish of this final assignment.

Roddenberry did not give any notes to Black for his second original teleplay. Nor did he ask for a rewrite. Instead, notification was sent out on August 17 that Black's assignment was to be cut off at first draft.

Roddenberry now had Gene Coon on the front line, backed by Steven Carabatsos, to handle the rewriting of scripts and the assigning of further story outlines, allowing him to take the time to do the envelope script himself and, he felt, do it better than Black had.

While Roddenberry worked on the script, Robert Justman got a sinking feeling in his gut. On September 14, he wrote to Ed Perlstein at Desilu Legal, asking:

> Is there liable to be any hang-up with cast members that were used in the original pilot? Are we going to be able to use the original pilot as a two-parter in this series? Does Jeff Hunter's original contract allow for this sort of contingency? Perhaps you ought to check it out with his agent. I don't want to have Gene write an envelope to make this pilot into a two-parter, have us shoot the envelope section and then discover that we can't use the [original] film at all because of various contractual difficulties. (RJ15)

Remarkably, no one had thought about this until now. Of course, no one had ever tried anything like this before.

Seven days later, while Perlstein was still trying to work out the specifics concerning how the footage from "The Cage" could be used, Roddenberry turned in his first draft teleplay for Part 1 of "The Menagerie," certain he had not borrowed from Black's script, at least not to any consequence. Perlstein compared the two scripts and half agreed, making John Black an offer of $750 on September 28, provided he sign a document stating that he had been fully compensated and that he had not been asked to do any work beyond the expected duties of the series' executive story consultant.

Black's radar antenna went up. Not trusting Roddenberry, he filed a complaint with the Writers Guild of America, which automatically mandated that the Arbitration Board compare the two scripts and come to a determination of its own as to whether "From the First Day to the Last" and "The Menagerie" were in fact one and the same, or that the latter was based on the former.

Herb Solow, meanwhile, sent Roddenberry's first draft to Grant Schloss and Jerry Stanley at NBC, telling them:

> Folks – Here's part one of the two-part episode explaining what we are doing with the 1st pilot that you kindly financed. Script pt [sic] two ready soon – as you know – should Jeff Hunter's wife won't [sic] agree to let him appear in any envelope, Roddenberry has come up with an interesting device to treat Pike [sic] Character (Hunter) as having been injured beyond recognition – this so the actor can play the part. The whole affair is surrounded by newly produced footage featuring our trustworthy Enterprise crew -- thus we have two sets of actors in one episode. The only carryover is Leonard Nimoy!

Roddenberry continued working and, on October 3, had his second draft ready. He ran this version through the Mimeo Department, which put it into yellow covers and sent it to the network and to De Forest Research for review. Two days later, Stan Robertson at NBC responded, writing:

> This is a very creditable job of integrating the footage from our Pilot #1 with an original story by you, the screen results of which should make two exciting *Star Trek* episodes. We are very pleased that you have written in Mr. Spock as the primary character since, as you know, he is emerging as one of the definite "pluses" in the series. (SR15)

Roddenberry collected his notes from all concerned and did a third draft. Time was very quickly running out.

On October 7, Bob Justman found two things on his desk -- a Final Draft of "The Menagerie" and a memo, saying:

> An indication of my vast sincere regard for you, I leave behind while I am on vacation in the High Desert some fifty or sixty pages of sheer genius. Read and weep as did Alexander when he beheld the glories of Egypt. Humbly, GR.

While Roddenberry vacationed, Gene Coon did a polish of the script, armed with a heavily annotated copy of the Final Draft by Herb Solow. And this constituted a Revised Final Draft from October 10. Roddenberry returned from his short break and then, either by his typewriter or Coon's, or both, additional revised pages were put into the script, from October 13, 14, and 17, the last being the day filming began.

As for the complaint John D.F. Black made with the Writers Guild, he believed his original teleplay was proof enough of the origin of the new story and did not bother to file a statement on his own behalf. Roddenberry did submit a statement. He said that the idea for the envelope episode was his alone. What little of Black's scene descriptions and dialogue which remained was a contribution made in accordance to his position as the executive story consultant.

The Guild compared the two scripts. With no statement from Black, there could be no dispute to Roddenberry's claims to have been the sole idea man. And, since the approach to writing out those ideas was so different, as documented by two very different scripts, the Arbitration Board ruled in favor of Roddenberry.

Roddenberry believed the Board decision was correct, saying, "I had the idea of Mr. Spock breaking with regulations and taking his former captain aboard the Enterprise, even against the wishes of that former captain. Then, that he would have to take command of the Enterprise in Kirk's absence and that he would set course for the forbidden world. That was mine.

"But it was also always important to keep Kirk at the center of the story. With the Captain's log, it was set up that our *Star Trek* stories were told to us *by* Kirk. When a particular episode appears to be a Spock story, it is as much a Kirk story. And that had to be the case with this one. Why has Spock done this? Why would an officer as loyal to his captain as Mr. Spock is do this to him -- *to Kirk*? And how can Kirk get to the bottom of this and stop this from happening, if, in fact, it should be stopped. That's Kirk's part of the story, which is important.

"Spock's end is in how he will delay this. What can we invent to justify Mr. Spock, a loyal officer and a friend to the captain, being, for this one time, an adversary? But also redeeming himself at the end of the story? And that redemption comes in knowing he would do this for his current captain, too. He would risk his career and life for Kirk, as we see him do for Pike. So this is what I had. This and that idea of a shipboard trial where we see Captain Pike's side of it -- 'The Cage.'

"I discussed these ideas with John and handed it off to him. He gave it an honest try, but I didn't care for the mechanics of his story. This takes us here; this takes us there. So I went back to what I had and rewrote it. Completely." (145)

Black's complaint in 1966, and for over four decades to follow, has to do with his belief that the broad story points -- what little the two scripts have in common -- were his invention, not Roddenberry's. He said, "I never again trusted blindly in the process. I never again trusted that the truth would win out by itself." (17-1)

Pre-Production
(no director prep days)

To use the footage from "The Cage" a new deal had to be struck with the director and performers from that original pilot. The footage was, after all, being exploited in a context other than originally intended.

Robert Butler, who directed the pilot, was offered the job of expanding it into a two-part episode. He said, "Gene shelved the first pilot and wrote it as Enterprise history -- what had happened with the craft with the previous commander and all that stuff.... He called me and asked me if I wanted to direct the material around it so it would be a full two-hours by me, and I said, 'No thanks, I've been there, good luck.'" (26-3)

Even four decades later, with the legendary status *Star Trek* had achieved, Butler could not see any value in his work on "The Cage" or the series it helped to launch. He said, "I don't get it.... To me, it's too preposterous, too clean, and it's too wordy. Now, *Twilight Zone* was preposterous and wordy, but it was in black and white, it was a half-an-hour... They're about the same size, aren't they -- in our television history -- *Twilight Zone* and *Star Trek*? And I can get *Twilight Zone* because they're just good yarns, but I don't honestly get *Star Trek*.... People love it -- I'm not going to argue that -- but, for my tastes, it seems too square-jawed, too heroic. I don't know; I'm mystified." (26-3)

A deal was worked out where Butler took sole credit for "The Menagerie, Part 2," since the footage from "The Cage" dominated that segment. Marc Daniels, hired to shoot the new footage, received sole credit for directing "The Menagerie, Part 1," which leaned more toward the new scenes.

On October 18, Ed Perlstein wrote to Shirley Stahnke at Desilu Business Affairs that he had closed a deal to pay Jeffrey Hunter $5,000, Majel Barrett $750, Peter Duryea $750, John Hoyt $750, and Adam Roarke (who played the minor role of Chief Garrison) $600, in consideration for granting permission to allow their scenes from "The Cage" to be used in the two-part episode. But it wasn't until November 14, after the end of production and just days before the broadcast of "The Menagerie" that Perlstein wrote to Stahnke, saying he had finally secured permission from the few holdouts -- Meg Wylie, Clegg Hoyt, Ed Maddan, Georgie Schmidt, and Serena Sand for an undisclosed amount. And he was fighting Leonard Nimoy, who wanted $1,250 for use of his footage from the original pilot.

The way Nimoy and his agent looked at it, the actor was getting cheated out of an episode, getting paid for only one new *Star Trek* instead of two. The way Desilu saw it, Nimoy had already been paid for "The Cage," therefore already been paid for the first of the two parts. Desilu was the winner in this round of what was becoming a growing *Star-Trek*-versus-Leonard Nimoy saga.

Malachi Throne, who had provided the voice of the Keeper in "The Cage," would now appear on screen as Starfleet Commodore José Mendez.

Throne had continued to gain status in Hollywood and, at 37, was a guest star in great demand. Besides having previously worked with William Shatner in *The Outer Limits* episode "Cold Hands, Warm Heart," Throne had a recurring role in several episodes of *Ben Casey*, and recent multiple appearances on *Rawhide*, *Mr. Novak*, *The Fugitive*, and *The Big Valley*. Within a few months of this, he appeared as a murderous double-agent on *I Spy*, a madman obsessed with ruling the Earth on *The Wild, Wild West*, the ghost of Blackbeard the pirate on *Voyage to the Bottom of the Sea*, the evil Falseface on *Batman*, and the Thief in "The Thief from Outer Space" on *Lost In Space*.

Malachi Throne with Robert Wagner on *It Takes a Thief* (Universal TV, 1967)

"Oh God, I loved that part," Throne said of the Thief. "Oh was I ever chewing up the scenery! Irwin Allen just let me do any piece of shtick that I wanted, and I had them all. It was fun landing those jobs and going from one show to another. As a performer, you felt worthwhile that you were capable of shifting gears whenever it was called for. And there was little time for rehearsal, so you were working on your toes all the time. It's not the same thing as in the theater where you've had three or four weeks to come up with something. In TV, you had to come up with something right away. You just had to move right in." (173-2)

One year after his appearance here, Throne moved right in for a co-starring role with Robert Wagner in *It Takes a Thief*, a series produced by Gene Coon.

Julie Parrish was Miss Piper. She was 26 and had found a career in acting after winning a national modeling contest for which Jerry Lewis was the judge. Lewis subsequently cast Parrish in two of his early 1960s films. Frequent work on television followed, including a part opposite Jeffrey Hunter in his series *Temple Houston*.

Majel Barrett had dual roles here -- as Number One in the flashback segments and as the Voice of the Enterprise computer for the trial sequences.

Hagan Beggs made his second and final appearance as helmsman Lt. Hansen (last seen in "Court Martial"). He is in operational command of the ship when Spock hijacks the Enterprise to Talos IV. Beggs said, "When talking to Roddenberry, he was a very easy guy to talk to. And he had a very nice eloquence about expressing this idea of his that things can be so different -- different from what was on television at the time, and different from how many saw the future as possibly being." (12-1)

John D.F. Black was almost called back to active duty on *Star Trek* -- not as associate producer or story consultant but as an actor. Mary Black said, 'Dorothy [Fontana] called and said that they had this really fun idea. Because John's eyes matched the eyes of Jeffrey Hunter -- and they couldn't find another actor who had the right eyes, and they were so sure John's did -- they wanted him to come in and sit in the wheelchair and be Captain Pike, *with lots of makeup on*." (17a)

John Black said, "Both of us immediately had the attitude that *that* wouldn't be very much fun. I didn't hesitate at all in turning it down." (17)

The search for the right set of blue eyes continued.

Sean Kenney was 24 and new to TV when offered the chance to "sit in" for the former Enterprise captain. Kenney had auditioned for Casting Director Joseph D'Agosta and then, one week later, was called back to Desilu to meet with Roddenberry. For his memoir, *Captain Pike Found Alive!*, Kenney wrote, "I sat facing his desk and noticed my casting photo was lying there…. At first [Gene] talked about the show's concept and the fact that he had been looking for a lead actor to play the role of a former Starship Captain…. As I sat down, Gene got

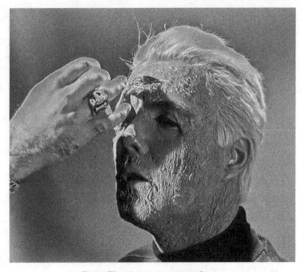

**Sean Kenney gets a touch-up
(Courtesy of Gerald Gurian)**

up and walked around me holding my casting photo in his hand. Continuing, he said that the lead character, Pike, had been severely injured in a training accident and was unable to speak or move any body parts."

Roddenberry explained to Kenney that he would only be able to communicate to the other actors and the camera by beeping. Kenney remembered thinking, "I'm the lead actor but no lines and all I do is beep, beep, for yes or no, hmm…"

Roddenberry continued, "You have a strong resemblance to an actor named Jeff Hunter, who is unfortunately filming a movie in Spain and is not available for the role. You're sure you don't have any allergies to latex makeup which will be used extensively on your face? It'll be the same makeup reconstructed every day for at least a week."

Kenney added, "Even if Gene had said, 'And we're going to starve you for those eight days,' I would have said, 'Sure, no problem.' Later, on the set, I actually felt like I was being starved. I had to eat all of my meals through a straw due to the heavy makeup restrictions." (100-3)

Kenney, rewarded for his suffering, would return for a pair of *Star Trek* episodes with no latex makeup needed -- to play Lt. DePaul in "Arena" and "A Taste of Armageddon."

Production Diary
*Filmed October 11 (two-thirds of a day), 12, 13, 14, 17 & 18, 1966
(Planned as 6 day production, only took 5 & 2/3 days; total cost: $220,953).*

Filming began mid-morning on Tuesday, October 11, after Marc Daniels took his last shots on "Court Martial." Those final sequences were from Stage 10, the Starbase courtroom set. The company quickly made the move to Stage 9 and the bridge for the start of production on "The Menagerie." Daniels covered all the bridge sequences needed for both Parts 1 and 2, then moved to the transporter room, then even made it into the Starbase Commander's Office to begin shooting with guest star Malachi Throne.

Of his first day on the set, Throne said, "I had a terrible time initially in the makeup; I didn't want them to cut my sideburns. In those days you had long sideburns, and they wanted to cut them in a peculiar angle. Oh, I objected to them so much, but to no avail. It was a funny thing. It was hilarious. But that started me off. And then when I got on the set, it was interesting because it <u>was</u> another world. You didn't quite have the familiarity with the furniture, with the ambiance. It was very interesting trying to adapt. You had to present a sense of seeming comfortable, as if you were in familiar surroundings, as if you were in your own living room. And you had to do this while wearing those costumes with no pockets to put your hands in, and you couldn't smoke a cigarette if you wanted to -- all the usual kind of tricks that actors use were not available to you. But you didn't want to just casually walk through this thing; you wanted to relate to it in a specific way. That was what Leonard was willing to do, and all of them. It was quite extraordinary of them to be able to do that, because it was a bit of a conflict to seem normal within that environment." (173-2)

**Day 3: The beam down site - this wall on Stage 10
(Courtesy of Gerald Gurian)**

**The end results: a composite shot now including Albert Whitlock's
matte painting of the Starbase
(Unaired film trim courtesy of Gerald Gurian)**

Day 2, Wednesday, continued with the scenes in the Base Commander's office, then on to Spock's quarters, where Sean Kenney joined the cast as the horribly disfigured Captain Pike. He said, "They had to dye my hair white, which I wasn't too happy about. I had never worked with extensive makeup before and it was a scary time when Fred Phillips wanted to perfect the makeup by making a life mask. They applied Plaster of Paris to my face with only two little rubber hoses in my nostrils for breathing.... My face hardened up like a rock and suddenly I wondered whether I was going to breathe or not.... The appliances were very tight around the face. Eating was very difficult, so my lunches were taken through a straw, consisting of soups and mush... It was quite an experience." (100-1)

For *Captain Pike Found Alive!*, Kenney elaborated: "Being a guest star on a show with no lines and unable to speak to any of the actors and crew [due to the makeup] had an interesting twist to it. After a few hours and not adding to anyone's conversation, you become a very keen listener and you also become like part of the set --

invisible. You start to hear interesting anecdotes coming out of certain people and you develop a keen insight into their personalities. I got an ear full!

"I soon realized that, yes, Bill Shatner was not well liked and in fact he was disliked. But then again, his role was the Captain of the ship and he took his role seriously, on and off the set. I didn't have any personal confrontations with him but he was known to thoroughly chafe the various directors on the show during filming. Shatner was from Montreal, Canada and a trained stage actor who used his voice effectively to bark out orders." (100-3)"

Next, a move back to Stage 10 for Shatner and Throne in the shuttlecraft. All this and Daniels managed to wrap at 6:42 -- less than a half hour into overtime.

"Tie-down" composite shot using footage from "The Cage"
(Unaired film trim courtesy of Gerald Gurian)

On Day 3, the company remained on Stage 10, beginning with the "Int. Base Mall Hospital Corridor," and on to "Pike's Hospital Room." Also shot this day, the beam down area against a small portion of a white brick wall with empty stage beyond, to be used for the matte shot showing the entire Starbase complex looming over them in the distance. A move back to Stage 9 took the company to the "Starbase Computer Center," not hard to spot as a redress of Engineering, and then into the "Hearing Room." It was 6:45 p.m. when Daniels took his last shot of the day.

Later, the 8:30 p.m. premiere of "Mudd's Women" on NBC -- *Star Trek*'s sixth broadcast episode. And everyone was watching. The *Star Trek* cast and crew were quickly becoming a family, much more so than on nearly any other series. This was due, in part, to the extra hard work and long hours put into the making of every episode, but also because of the excitement generated over being part of such a unique series. America was watching, too. *Star Trek*, with "Mudd's Women," won its time slot for NBC at 8:30 p.m., with a 31.4 audience share.

Days 4, 5 and 6 were all spent in the Hearing Room. It was a long three days for Sean Kenney under all that makeup and taking his meals through a straw. He said, "Most of the feeling had to come through my eyes, especially due to

Malachi Throne reacting to Shatner's onset antics, and trying to get a smile out of Nimoy
(Courtesy of Gerald Gurian)

the fact that they would tie the corners of my eyes down with scotch mending tape and give me an aged look." (100-1)

Malachi Throne, taking it all in, said, "It was hard to get a smile out of Leonard when he was in character. Of course, with Leonard, it's hard to get a smile out of him anyway. He *does* have a sense of humor, and a good one at that, but when he works he is very serious. Leonard was Spock. Now Shatner was the opposite. And I'm sure that was a relief from the severity of his character. Bill was fun, but he was also forthright and adamant about everything, because that was his character. And poor Sean -- Sean was stuck in the box." (173)

On these days, Daniels wrapped at 7:15, 6:55 and 7:06 p.m., respectively, anywhere from 35 to 60 minutes into overtime.

Sean Kenney recalled, "On the last day of the shoot Gene Roddenberry came up to me and congratulated me for my terrific 'emoting job.' Then he surprised me by offering a re-occurring role as Lt. De Paul, the ship's first helmsman. That's when De Paul was born. He said that I had put up with a lot and he wanted to reward my tenacity and good spirit." (100-3)

With the very organized and frugal -- and, according to Jerry Finnerman, "pushy" -- Marc Daniels directing, the new scenes for both Parts 1 and 2 of "The Menagerie" were completed in only five and two-thirds days. And this was accomplished with Daniels having no prep time. The front office was singing his praises.

Post-Production
October 19 through November 9, 1966. Music score: tracked.

The race was not yet over. Part 1 would have to be ready to air on NBC in less than a month if *Star Trek* was going to honor its air dates. The series had fallen that far behind. Less than four weeks were available to edit, to create all the needed photographic effects, and to dub the episode. Up to now, the shortest amount of time it had taken to push an episode through all these phases of post-production was six weeks for "Charlie X." The second-fastest delivery was "The Man Trap." As a result, these were the first two episodes to air. The longest time it had taken, so far -- and these two hadn't even made it all the way through the process yet -- was for "The Corbomite Maneuver," which would end up spanning nearly five months, and "Balance of Terror," requiring over four months. NBC was being kept in the dark as to how dismal the situation was at *Star Trek*, but the studio knew -- and there wasn't a single person at Desilu who believed "The Menagerie, Part 1" would make its air date.

Robert Justman was a nonbeliever, as well, but on October 21, 1966, in a memo to Roddenberry, he expressed a degree of hopefulness. He wrote:

> Believe it or not, what I am about to outline may sound improbable, but it is certainly not impossible. I do believe that the very clever and energetic, but highly overworked, Mr. Swanson may have a rough cut on Part 1 of "The Menagerie" ready sometime tomorrow. You will remember that we received the last of the dailies on this show yesterday. (RJ15-1)

Robert Swanson was pushing Editing Team #1 to make a rough cut in only two days. It needed to happen that quickly for Eddie Milkis and his post-production people to have time to do their end of the work. Justman was hoping against hope that this might happen.

To help the cause, Justman made his case to Roddenberry to stay clear. He wrote:

> This [will] get us "dupes" back sometime on Tuesday, October 25th, and thereupon our sound effects and music editors [can] start building up the reels

for dubbing the following Monday. To meet this schedule, it is, of course, necessary that we condition ourselves to making only the editorial changes that are really inherently necessary in this film. I think we should discuss the broad, important areas with Bob Swanson and then give him the picture back and let him run with it. (RJ15-1)

Justman didn't want the editing team to be hampered with too many last minute notes from the producers. He feared that the "very clever and energetic but highly overworked" Mr. Swanson was close to a collapse. His letter to Roddenberry pleaded:

Every little piece in this puzzle of how to get 'The Menagerie' on the air in time is interlocking with some other piece. If one piece doesn't fit in at the right time, at the right place, I think we will never be able to complete the puzzle. I tell you now, oh Great Bird, that this is a once-in-a-lifetime situation. I don't think any of us could stand sweating out a problem like this again without going completely crackers. (RJ15-1)

It was a line of dialogue Roddenberry had written into "The Man Trap" that had the staff now teasingly calling him "The Great Bird of the Galaxy." Justman was hoping his memo would keep Roddenberry away from the editing room and allow Swanson to complete his attempt at a miracle -- but his words fell on deaf ears. There was more at stake than making an air date. Roddenberry hadn't taken shortcuts while making "The Cage," his unaired masterpiece, and he wouldn't allow shortcuts to be taken now as "The Cage" was resurrected as one-half of "The Menagerie."

In another memo, Justman strongly recommended Roddenberry give his notes for Part 1 to Swanson's assistant editor Donald Rode, thereby leaving Swanson in the edit room continuing to work on Part 2. Justman explained the need for doing it, writing:

I hope you are sitting down when you read this memo... because he [Swanson] intends to have a rough cut of Part 2 ready this coming Monday. Unbelievable, but true. That's the fastest cutting job I have even heard of. If the cutting quality on this show is commensurate with the speed quality, it will be the greatest Editorial effort of all time. In any event, he deserves a medal. Regards, Bob, Small Bird of the Galaxy. (RJ15-2)

Roddenberry went straight to Swanson anyway. He wasn't going to risk his editing instructions losing anything in the translation. Swanson silently tolerated the "help." He worked through the weekend and late into the night, cutting Part 2 while at the same time re-cutting Part 1. Amazingly, he made the Monday delivery.

Roddenberry thanked Swanson and all involved with a memo directed to "Bill Heath, cc to Bob Swanson, Eddie Milkis, and all else [sound/music/dubbing]." He wrote:

Getting "Menagerie Parts I & II" out in the time accomplished was a major team effort by all the production people involved. The quality was excellent; these shows should go a long way toward helping ST during this critical Nielsen Rating period. We want to thank all of you for the hard work involved. (GR16-1)

Swanson had done a first-rate job, and it was right of Roddenberry to compliment him in front of his post-production bosses and peers. But the job, and the additional demands he put on Swanson, had taken its toll. By the time the thank you memo was circulated, Robert Swanson had quit.

Film Effects of Hollywood did the optical work, and did it quickly. Out of necessity, the music was tracked.

The race was won, but at a high cost. Besides losing Bob Swanson, Desilu spent

$220,953 for the new footage, and forfeited $110,000 in licensing fees from NBC. But the studio nonetheless came out ahead, financially. If two episodes (at $193,500 each) had a combined budget allowance of $387,000, and making the two-part "Menagerie" only cost $220,953, then, even after forfeiting $110,000 in licensing fees, *Star Trek* was ahead by $56,044. Applying this against the season-to-date deficit of $33,618, that I.O.U. note from Gene Roddenberry to Desilu would be forgiven, leaving *Star Trek* with a cash surplus of $22,426 to be applied toward future episodes.

This money would be spent almost immediately. The studio allowance for each episode was about to drop substantially.

Release / Reaction
Premiere air dates: 11/17 and 11/24/66. NBC repeat broadcast: 5/18 and 5/25/67.

Steven H. Scheuer and his *TV Key* staff reviewed "The Menagerie, Part 1" on November 17, 1966. Among the papers to carry Scheuer's column was the *St. Joseph Gazette*, in St. Joseph, Missouri. *TV Key* said:

> This is a bit off-beat, even for this series, but it is imaginative enough to hold the attention of fans. Of all things, Captain Kirk's trusted aide, Mr. Spock, shakes up the Captain and everyone connected with the space research program by re-routing the path of the USS Enterprise to the forbidden planet of Talos IV. Spock's unprecedented behavior is compounded by his insistence of being court-martialed until it becomes clear he has a story he wants unfolded and recorded for the record.

The question then: would "off-beat" translate into good ratings or bad? A.C. Nielsen provided their opinion based on a national survey.

RATINGS / Nielsen 30-Market report for Thursday, Nov. 17, 1966:

8:30 - 9 p.m., with 61.7% of U.S. TVs in use.	Rating:	Share:
NBC: *Star Trek* (first half)	18.0	29.2%
ABC: **The Dating Game**	**19.4**	**31.4%**
CBS: *My Three Sons*	16.9	27.4%
Local independent stations:	9.4	12.0%

9 - 9:30 p.m., with 66.1% of U.S. TVs in use.		
NBC: *Star Trek* (second half)	18.7	28.3%
ABC: *Bewitched*	18.5	28.0%
CBS: **Thursday Night Movie** (start)	**21.9**	**33.1%**
Local independent stations:	9.5	10.6%

The Dating Game, taking over for *The Tammy Grimes Show*, was a surprise hit and nosed ahead to win the top spot for ABC at 8:30. *Star Trek* followed at No. 2. At 9 p.m., *Star Trek* retained its hold on second place, ahead of *Bewitched*. The big gun on CBS, and the time period winner: the six-time Academy Award nominee and two-time Oscar winner *The Country Girl*, starring Bing Crosby, Grace Kelly, and William Holden.

Scheuer reviewed "The Menagerie, Part II" for the syndicated *TV Key Previews* a week later, writing:

> "Menagerie, Part II." This is by far the best *Star Trek* story to date and concludes tonight with Mr. Spock behaving in an increasingly un-Venusian [sic] manner. As the USS Enterprise continues to zone on Talos IV, the forbidden planet, Spock's court martial for mutiny continues. He forces the court to watch a re-enactment of Captain Pike's former insubordination. It's a weird, strange

show with Jeff Hunter doing an excellent job as the radiated and completely helpless Captain Pike, who now functions like a binary computer, with "yes" and "no" electrical replies from his wheelchair. The sequences of Hunter as Pike, 13 years ago, looking like himself, are part of the original pilot for *Star Trek*, in which Hunter was to be the star. Susan Oliver co-stars here as Vina. Be warned: some of the punishment scenes are a bit too much for the kids.

It was a testament to the good casting (of Sean Kenney to play the older Christopher Pike) that Scheuer, along with many others, believed it was Jeffrey Hunter under all that makeup.

Scheuer was not alone in liking Part 1 enough to come back for Part 2, and then loving Part 2 enough to keep watching, even with *Bewitched* starting at the halfway point of *Star Trek*. The ratings survey from Nielsen gave evidence to this.

RATINGS / Nielsen 30-Market report for Thursday, Nov. 24, 1966:

8:30 - 9 p.m., with 53.3% of U.S. TVs in use.		Rating:	Share:
NBC:	*Star Trek* (first half)	17.7	33.8%
ABC:	**The Dating Game**	**17.8**	**34.0%**
CBS:	*NFL Football*	10.0	19.1%
Local independent stations:		9.8	13.1%
9 - 9:30 p.m., with 52.9% of U.S. TVs in use.			
NBC:	*Star Trek* (second half)	**18.6**	**35.2%**
ABC:	*Bewitched*	14.9	28.2%
CBS:	*Thursday Night Movie* (start)	13.8	26.1%
Local independent stations:		14.7	10.5%

On Thanksgiving night 1966, "The Menagerie, Part 2" tied for first place at the start of the broadcast and was the clear ratings winner by the end of the hour. Doing little business for CBS, in the days before NFL football was an obsession in America, were the Cleveland Browns and the Dallas Cowboys facing off for the Eastern Division title. Following the game on CBS, a 1963 effects-driven look at Greek mythology, the cult classic *Jason and the Argonauts*, was trampled by the competition.

Two weeks after this, on December 7, 1966, Herb Solow wrote Roddenberry:

> Nielsen Company does a special research sample of the ratings in color set homes only. I have been advised that *Star Trek* is the highest-rated color show in its time period, beating *My Three Sons*, *Bewitched*, *Dating Game* and the *CBS Thursday Night Movie*. It's NBC's feeling that while other high-rated color shows, such as *Bob Hope*, *Bonanza* and *Dean Martin* score well due mainly to the star value within the show [Hope and Martin] or the longevity of the program [*Bonanza*], *Star Trek* derives much of its color rating from the magnificent technical quality of the show from the basic concept, design, photography and effects. You're all to be congratulated on the fine work. (HS16)

In the very immediate future, "The Menagerie," Part 1 and Part 2, combined together to create a feature-length production, was nominated for the Hugo Award, in the category of Best Science Fiction Presentation for the year of 1966. Among its competition were two other *Star Trek* episodes. (Stay tuned for the winner.)

For the December 1991 issue of *Cinefantastique* magazine celebrating *Star Trek's* 25th anniversary, critic Thomas Doherty selected a baker's dozen of the original series' best. At No. 3 was "The Menagerie," for which Doherty wrote, "The final farewell is a joyful metaphor for the liberating escapism of science fiction fantasy. Like the viewer, locked in a chair, Pike is free to roam the galaxy in his mind."

From the Mailbag

Letters received immediately following the airing of the two parts of "The Menagerie":

> Dear Sir, I enjoy *Star Trek* very much and I don't mean to try to tell you how to run the program, but, speaking for many teenaged girls here in Virginia, <u>please let Mr. Spock do more leading parts</u>. Patricia L. (Hampton, Virginia).

> Dear Mr. Roddenberry, I would like to say that I enjoy that wonderful program of your's, *Star Trek*. That is one of my favorite shows now, whereas, at its debut, I doubted that it could be anything spectacular. I'm glad I decided to give it a chance. The name got me intrigued [and] I love Mr. Spock. He is the greatest thing to hit TV since Illya [of *The Man from U.N.C.L.E.*]. Please don't change Mr. Spock!!!!! They began to change Illya. I don't like him as much now. But Spock should always be the same. Please! You wouldn't change his personality, would you? I'd probably die if you did. Anyway, I wouldn't like him as much, and that would leave me even less to live for, wouldn't it? May L. (San Gabriel, California).

> Gentlemen, I have been a science fiction reader for twelve years, and I am a confirmed follower of your program *Star Trek*. As one who has seen all the juvenile, mediocre hack-work that has been called science fiction on television, I feel that only *Star Trek* presently offers stories that are adult, intelligent and are not directed at a dismally low I.Q. level. I feel that this, in itself, is remarkable, since there are so few television shows of any nature that seem designed for an adult, aware audience.... I trust that everything will be done to retain this valuable and engrossing series. Thank you for your time in reading this. Mike D. (Newark, N.J.).

> Dear Mr. Roddenberry, judging from the glimpses we had of the original cast on the two-parter, the present cast is far superior, especially "Dr. McCoy," and Shatner, who is usually very good indeed, except when he is self-consciously grim. Mrs. Dan W. (Syracuse, N.Y).

And from November 29, 1966, five days after Part 2 was broadcast, from Gene Roddenberry to his assistant, Morris Chapnick:

> Dear Morris: Who writes up those idiotic one-line story descriptions which purport to explain the episode of the evening in the local TV section of newspapers? Can we do anything about them? Ours usually have been running something like, "The Enterprise runs into a situation which creates a few problems and it is eventually solved." Last week, [regarding Spock's trial in "The Menagerie"] the description had it as <u>Captain Kirk</u> who was being court martialed, and even the description of that was completely wrong!

Memories

Hagan Beggs recalled, "Gene brought me in to his office after we finished shooting and said, 'Everything is fine with your work but I'm making a change in the helmsman; I think I need to spread this out a bit more. So thank you very much, but I want to try to make it bigger -- I think it's got great possibilities.' I said, 'Okay,' and went on to do some other shows, and didn't think much about it. But it wasn't until a few years later, when the show was gaining renewed popularity in reruns, that I even thought I should put it back on my resume as being involved. I'd always felt slightly embarrassed because I'm thinking, 'My God, I'm literally sitting at a board pushing a couple of levers and people are giving me this great credit for being on this show, you know.' Yes, I did take the captain's chair at one point, but didn't see my part as being that important. In time, I became awakened to how popular this show was and how much it meant to so many people. It's phenomenal. Where it has all gone is totally amazing. It's by default that I'm luckily in the iconic grouping, and it was simply, honest to God, by me just being there. Because what I had to do was pretty simple." (12-1)

Sean Kenney said, "It was a thrill to be in the show -- it was my first film job and I received top feature billing in the credits. It took them almost five hours to apply the makeup daily so I guess they figured top feature credit was the least they could do to compensate for all the restructuring to my anatomy and reward my patience." (100-1)

In another interview, 44 years after playing the crippled and disfigured Captain Pike, Kenney said, "I think 'The Menagerie' was so ahead of its time. I'm proud of it because the story said so much and it was taken so -- how shall I say -- emotionally by so many people. Here was a guy, Captain Pike, who was almost the first physically challenged person anyone saw on TV in a major part. He was in a wheelchair; couldn't talk. I meet people now [in wheelchairs] who roll up to me and say, 'When I saw that show I thought, what if I lost my voice? I've only lost my legs.' It was a really profound episode and touched so many people." (100-2)

24

Mid-Season 1966

William Shatner, star of the starship ...
pre-Spockmania

In an interview dated September 30, Clay Gowran of *The Chicago Tribune* quoted William Shatner saying that "The Man Trap," NBC's premiere episode, was "a disappointment." Shatner was attempting damage control. Gowran was the critic who said Gene Roddenberry had considerable distance to go to attain his objective that *Star Trek* would specialize in adult plots scripted by fine writers. His damning review held Roddenberry personally accountable for the perceived failure. So *Star Trek*'s creator sent in his heroic captain to smooth things over. Shatner told Gowran, "It wasn't the strongest show we could have had. The program which was to have been our opener ["The Corbomite Maneuver"], which properly introduced all the characters and told a good story, couldn't be ready in time."

Roddenberry was spreading the same message. In a September 28 letter to TV columnist Hal Humphrey at *The Los Angeles Times*, he wrote, "As you know... our optical house gave us severe problems just before going on the air and we were not able to open with the particular shows I had selected. Actually, the first several were planned for mid-season episodes. In the end it may not have hurt us since we now can follow up with increasingly stronger shows. But who knows? I never could figure television anyway."

Even the people who thought they could figure television had trouble explaining the effect *Star Trek* was having on its audience. The critics, for the most part, may have panned the premiere installment, but the ratings had been phenomenal. Within weeks, it was clear that this was not just another TV show.

Daily Variety, in its September 14 issue, took notice of the interracial cast. *I Spy* had led the way one year before. Now staff writer Les Brown, under the headline, "Television Off to the 'Races': Previews Reveal the Racial Mix," wrote:

> ABC and NBC offered an unusual night of television last Thursday (8), not just because both were "previewing" new programs but because for the better part of primetime's three and a half hours they depicted a multiracial world instead of the usual Caucasian one. There was only one half hour at 9:30 p.m., when NBC had *The Hero* and ABC had *That Girl*, that the tint medium reverted back to lily white.... It is doubtful that any entertainment values were lost -- anywhere in the country -- from Tarzan having a Negro friend (Rockne Tarkington) and a little Mexican boy to look after (Manuel Padilla, Jr.); from Hawk being a full-blooded Iroquois working alongside a young Negro detective (Wayne Grice); or the

spaceship Enterprise in *Star Trek* having on its permanent manifest a Negro woman (Nichelle Nichols) and an Oriental (George Takei). The real significance of the casting is that in every case the role has no specific race designation and might just as readily be played by an Anglo-Saxon.

The interracial cast was only one of the unique aspects of *Star Trek*.

Dorothy Fontana said, "First week we got some mail. Second week we got a bag of mail. After that we started getting bags of mail to the point where the Mail Room literally couldn't handle it. Pretty soon the actors couldn't even answer it. They had to have mail services taking care of their mail for them. So, the mail was telling us that there were fans out there and they were not fans writing to say 'send me a picture,' they were writing to make comment on the show. And they were intelligent comments. We had a great audience." (64-2)

And so began the buzz.

The September 21, 1966, headline in *The Los Angeles Times* read: "*Star Trek* a Costly Sci-fi Epic." Staff writer Don Page described the series as "one of the most expensive and elaborate productions in the history of television." It was a point NBC wanted driven home. Mr. Page was especially impressed with the bridge of the Enterprise, writing, "If the show happens to fail television, they could easily turn the set into a tourist attraction."

Universal Studios Theme Park would do just that 22 years later.

In the letters section of *TV Guide* on November 5, 1966, Andrew Porter, the Assistant Editor for *Fantasy and Science Fiction Magazine*, wrote that Irwin Allen, with *The Time Tunnel*, was only "interested in creating a series which will sell him as a producer and sell the sponsor's product." Porter praised Roddenberry and *Star Trek* for taking a very different approach by "appealing to the intelligence of the viewer."

On November 13, 1966, Marion Purcelli of *The Chicago Tribune*, looking for another angle, wrote, "The most way-out fashion design for women to come along in months is the miniskirt, and that's exactly the look designer Bill Theiss has created for *Star Trek*."

Theiss did not invent the mini. That had happened in England one month earlier. But *Star Trek*'s hemlines were clearly at the forefront of the event, and the shortest to date.

William Shatner, for a newspaper article syndicated during October 1966, said, "All the plots have a basis in human experience or fact and all the equipment is authentic. The stories will be an extension of human experience in a different environment."

The mini first beams across America
(Courtesy of Gerald Gurian)

That same day, for the TV magazine of the *Boston Sunday Herald*, Shatner said, "If Shakespeare were alive today, he'd be doing science fiction. It would challenge that great imagination of his."

For a syndicated article picked up by the *Boston Sunday Herald* for its December

18th TV magazine, the headline read, "Shatner Catches a Big Wave." The star explained, "You have to catch a wave just as it crests. Last year I did a courtroom show -- *For the People*. It lasted only 13 weeks. Everyone liked the show but our timing was wrong. We were too late with a lawyer show, with message drama. We missed the cresting of lawyer shows when audiences were fascinated by them."

Shatner felt he was now on the right show at the right time. Explaining that *Star Trek* was aimed at adult science fiction fans, he said, "We're the first real science-fiction show and I honestly think it will be the biggest new series on television. It's exciting adventure but more important to me it has quality, in the filming and in the writing." (166-16)

While A.C. Nielsen did not rank *Star Trek* as the biggest among new shows, TvQ did. Shatner's prediction, according to Home Testing Institute, had come true.

As series' lead and primary spokesman, Shatner was showered with plenty of positive press. In the March 12, 1967 issue of the *San Francisco Examiner and Chronicle*, John Stanley presented an article entitled "Captain Kirk, A Man of Tomorrow." He wrote:

> Roddenberry's promise last summer that "we're taking the weirdest stuff and making it as believable as possible" has been realized. Even the main character -- James T. Kirk -- has become a "futuristic" personality as portrayed by William Shatner. Because Shatner has labored to make him a well-fleshed individual, Kirk has emerged as a firm symbol of authority who makes mind-boggling decisions with the calm efficiency and certainty of a man accustomed to moving through space at 186,000 miles per second.

Shatner told Stanley, "Because there has been nothing comparable to *Star Trek* in the history of television fantasies, we have had no precedent to follow. Thus we have established our own formula as we progressed."

Writer Michael Fessier, Jr., for *TV Guide* on October 13, 1966, also put the spotlight on Shatner. The article was called "No One Ever Upsets the Star," and Fessier, having witnessed the filming of "The Naked Time," described how Shatner and Nimoy planned out the moment when Kirk confronts the emotionally devastated Spock in the briefing room. Kirk was to slap him, repeatedly, and then Spock was to strike back. As a dare, Nimoy suggested Captain Kirk "fly backward over the table, *like a hero*," and to satisfy the needs of a closely positioned camera, Shatner did, without the aid of a stuntman. But the hero was receiving less attention than expected.

By mid October, the tide was changing. The TV magazine with the article on *Star Trek* that included Shatner's line about Shakespeare did not use a picture of Captain Kirk for its cover, but one of Mr. Spock, alone. Only a few weeks after hitting the airwaves, a new and very unexpected phenomenon was making itself known. It would soon be given a name: Spockmania.

***

A letter printed in *TV Guide* from October 1966 read, "Hooray for the guy with the ears and eyebrows on *Star Trek*. At last, someone who is really different... or sort of."

Frank Judge, for the *Boston Sunday Herald* on October 23, 1966, observed, "While Shatner gets top billing, Leonard Nimoy is piling up mountains of fan mail of his own."

Mr. Spock was again featured solo on a magazine cover, this time for the January 6, 1967 issue of *TV Showtime*. The caption: "Romantic Image with Pointed Ears." For the article entitled "New Breed of TV Hero," Tom Weigel wrote:

> TV viewers -- especially the teen variety -- [find] Nimoy an intriguing new variation of the cool, hard-to-rattle hero. *Trek*'s actual star is William Shatner, traditionally handsome fellow, who has all but been ignored by fans in their current predilection for the offbeat hero.

Syndicated columnist Bob MacKenzie added fuel to the co-star fire on February 10, 1967, writing:

> For reasons mysterious to me, in a show that should by rights be dominated by the broad-shoulders and anthropoid jaw of William Shatner, the titular hero, Leonard Nimoy gets most of the attention. The attention comes not only from teenagers, who are naturally drawn to strange heroes, but from grown ladies with husbands and children. One letter I received recently was from a local wife and mother who assured that Nimoy "can park his space-ship in my garage anytime." That touching sentiment was followed soon by a message from another indigenous hausfrau who claimed that Nimoy is "enchanting to look at."... that Nimoy "presents a challenge to women because he plays hard to get." Nimoy's character is supposed to be devoid of emotion; he is simply not interested in love and related activities. Is this a clue to the secret of male sex appeal in these anxious times? Total indifference?... On the other hand, maybe it's the pointy ears after all.

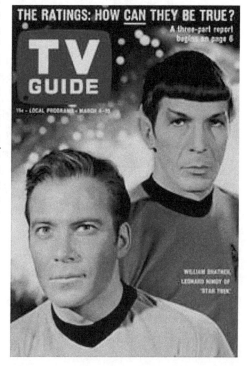

TV Guide featured *Star Trek* on its cover for the March 4, 1967 issue. For the picture, Spock stood behind Kirk. For the article, however, Nimoy stepped to the forefront. The lead-off line read, "Product of Two Worlds: Leonard Nimoy, as the hybrid Mr. Spock, has made it big in outer space." Writer Leslie Raddatz took note that the bulk of Nimoy's fan mail came from teenagers. Nimoy's explanation: "The kids dig the fact that Spock is cool." Roddenberry added, "We're all imprisoned within ourselves. We're all aliens on this strange planet. So people find identification with Spock." Nimoy understood this. He told Raddatz, "I don't want to play a creature or a computer. Spock gives me a chance to say some things about the human race."

Charles Witbeck, writing for *The Los Angeles Herald-Examiner* on April 16, 1967, declared, "A stone-faced man with pointed ears and bangs has tickled the kids and saved NBC's science fiction series *Star Trek* from oblivion on Thursday nights."

Isaac Asimov returned to *TV Guide* on April 29, 1967 to pen an article entitled "Mr. Spock Is Dreamy!" Asimov's 12-year-old daughter gave her father the article's title. She had said, "I think that Mr. Spock is dreamy -- he's *so* smart," prompting Asimov to write:

> The not-quite-human thinking machine may be starting a new trend in sex appeal. A revolution of incalculable importance is sweeping America, thanks to *Star Trek*, which, in its noble and successful effort to present good science fiction to the American public, has also presented everyone with an astonishing revelation.... [And] here I had been watching *Star Trek* since its inception because I like it, because it's well-done, because it is exciting, because it says things, subtly and neatly, that are difficult to say in "straight" drama, and because science fiction, properly presented, is the type of literature most appropriate to our generation. But it hadn't occurred to me that Mr. Spock was sexy. I had never realized that such a thing was possible; that girls palpitate over the way one eyebrow goes up a fraction; that they squeal with passion when a little smile quirks his lip. And all because he's *smart*?!

For "Girls All Want to Touch the Ears," a *New York Times* article, Nimoy said, "[T]here must be something very sexual about it. I tell you, frankly, I've never had more female attention on a set before. And get this -- they all want to touch the ears!" (128-17)

It was a phenomenon that baffled TV insiders and intellectuals all across America. It also baffled William Shatner.

Casting Director Joe D'Agosta said, "Everybody talked about Spock, and Leonard Nimoy, because he was so interesting. He was the guy that everybody gave all the credit to, all the accolades, writing about, 'Wow, this Leonard Nimoy *is* the show!' But Bill was the secret weapon on that show, because Bill got reams of dialogue and he'd give it excitement. And all Leonard did was raise his eyebrow and say, 'That's illogical.' It *was* illogical. Understandable, but illogical. Shatner was the energy." (43-4)

***

Gene Roddenberry was never afraid of a fight. One wouldn't expect the former WWII Air Force pilot, turned Pan Am pilot, turned Los Angeles Police Officer, who then advanced in the ranks to LAPD Sergeant, to hesitate to defend his honor, or his place in line. NBC had been fighting him, and would continue to do so. As would the studio. As would *Star Trek* insiders, such as John D.F. Black, Shimon Wincelberg, George Clayton Johnson, and, soon to come, Jerry Sohl and Harlan Ellison, among others.

For the November 26, 1966 issue of *TV Guide*, famed scientist and science fiction writer Isaac Asimov took on the makers of TV sci-fi with an article entitled "What Are a Few Galaxies Among Friends?" Asimov was having a good time pointing out the scientific implausibilities of Irwin Allen's three prime time series, *Voyage to the Bottom of the Sea*,

Lost in Space and *Time Tunnel*. He also had a few laughs at the expense of *It's About Time*. And then came *Star Trek*. Asimov was most kind, merely devoting a single paragraph of his four page article to Roddenberry's show. He wrote:

> In an episode of *Star Trek* (which seems to have the best technical assistance of the current crop) a mysterious gaseous cloud is sighted "one-half light-year outside the Galaxy." But the Galaxy doesn't have a sharp edge. The stars just get fewer and fewer and trail off. To speak of anything being one-half light-year outside the Galaxy is like saying a house is one-half yard outside the Mississippi Basin.

Three days later – on November 29 – Roddenberry fired off a letter to Asimov that was every bit as long as the former's *TV Guide* article. He wrote, in part:

> Dear Isaac.... In all friendliness, and with sincere thanks for the hundreds of wonderful hours of reading you have given me, it does seem to me that your article overlooked entirely the practical, factual and scientific problems involved in getting a television show on the air and keeping it there. Television deserves much criticism, not just SF alone but all of it, but that criticism should be aimed, not shot-gunned. For example, *Star Trek* almost did not get on the air because it refused to do a juvenile science fiction, because it refused to put a "Lassie" aboard the space ship, and because it insisted on hiring Dick Matheson, Harlan Ellison, A.E. van Vogt, Phil Farmer, and so on. (Not all of these came through since TV scripting is a highly difficult specialty, but many of them did.)....
> In the specific comment you made about *Star Trek*, the mysterious cloud being "one-half light-year outside the Galaxy," I agree certainly that this was stated badly, but on the other hand, it got past a Rand Corporation physicist who is hired by us to review all of our stories and scripts, and further, got past Kellam de Forest Research who is also hired to do the same job. And, needless to say, it got past me....
> We do spend several hundred dollars a week to guarantee scientific accuracy. And several hundred more dollars a week to guarantee other forms of accuracy, logical progressions, etc. Before going into production we made up a "Writer's Guide" covering many of these things and we send out new pages, amendments, lists of terminology, excerpts of science articles, etc., to our writers continually. And to our directors. And specific science information to our actors depending on the job they portray. Despite all of this we do make mistakes and will probably continue to make them. The reason -- Thursday has an annoying way of coming up once a week, and five working days an episode is a crushing burden, an impossible one. The wonder of it is not that we make mistakes, but that we are able to turn out once a week science fiction which is (if we are to believe SF writers and fans who are writing us in increasing numbers) the first true SF series ever made on television. We like to think this is what we are trying to do, and trying with considerable pride. And I suppose with considerable touchiness when we believe we are criticized unfairly or as in the case of your article, damned with faint praise. Quoting Ted Sturgeon who made his first script attempt with us (and now seems firmly established as a contributor to good television), getting *Star Trek* on the air was impossible, putting out a program like this on a TV budget is impossible, reaching the necessary mass audience without alienating the select SF audience is impossible, not succumbing to network pressure to "juvenilize" the show is impossible, keeping it on the air is impossible. We've done all of these things. Perhaps someone else could have done it better, but no one else did....
> Again, if we are to believe our letters (now mounting into the thousands), we are reaching a vast number of people who never before understood SF or enjoyed it. We are, in fact, making fans -- making future purchasers of SF magazines and

novels, making future box office receipts for SF films. We are, I sincerely hope, making new purchasers of "The Foundation" novels, *I, Robot*, *The Rest of the Robots*, and other of your excellent work. We, and I personally, in our own way and beset with the strange problems of this mass communications media, work as proudly and as hard as any other SF writer in this land....

If mention was to be made of SF in television, we deserved much better. And, as much as I admire you in your work, I felt an obligation to reply. And, I believe, the public deserves a more definitive article on all this. Perhaps *TV Guide* is not the marketplace for it, but if you ever care to throw the Asimov mind and wit toward a definitive TV piece, please count on us for facts, figures, sample budgets, practical production examples, and samples of scripts from rough story to the usual multitude of drafts, samples of mass media "pressure," and whatever else we can give you. Sincerely yours, Gene Roddenberry.

And, with this, a friendship was formed. Asimov even considered writing a script for *Star Trek*.

***

As early as the start of June 1966, over two months before Gene Coon came to *Star Trek*, Roddenberry was desperate for more help. His battles with many of the show's writers he hired -- TV writers unable to deal with the demands of science fiction or science fiction writers unable to deal with the demands of TV -- were wearing him down. Stan Robertson at NBC was unhappy with many of the story outlines coming from Roddenberry's office and was now becoming more and more critical.

On June 2 Roddenberry, weary from relentless work and impossibly long days, fired back at Robertson, writing:

> Keep in mind that the frantic nature of getting a show on the road precludes the kind of attention to outline which we'd like to give. We have to take certain calculated risks that an outlined general direction, plus our comments to the writer, will result in first draft scripts containing something more near what we need. Much of the problem, I'm sure you're aware, comes out of the totally unrealistic and impractical start date new shows get from networks. I sometimes wonder if people outside a working production office really realize the stupendous day and night effort required in preparing a new show for the camera, finding the writers, discussing ideas, sending stories back for revisions, re-revising, pleading, threatening, and at the same time casting, laying out sets, designing costumes, and so on, ad infinitum. We should have started, at the bare minimum, a full month earlier. We didn't. Okay, we'll make it anyway. But some of the niceties of story blocking and progression and communication have to be lost, some risks taken, in order to do it. It's not good business, it's not even fair to the people involved, but who am I to doubt that this is the best of all possible worlds? Okay? Cordially, Gene Roddenberry.

Roddenberry's disdain for the network was growing. In a letter to his agent, Alden Schwimmer, he wrote:

> There seems to be a popular delusion that networks do people a favor by buying shows. I happen to think the truth is somewhat nearer the other direction -- that a man who creates a format and offers integrity and a large hunk of his life in producing it, offers much more than networks or advertisers can give in return. Therefore, it logically follows, that side has a right to some terms too.

It was a fair criticism, but not criticism NBC was going to appreciate hearing -- that the network was being over-demanding, unhelpful and, with giving insufficient time and funding, doing very nearly everything possible to sabotage the very quality it demanded from its series producers. This salvo may very well have been "Strike Eight."

While Roddenberry battled his celebrity writers, and the network, associate producer Robert Justman continued to fight his seemingly losing battle over trying to meet higher production expectations with insufficient funding to realize them. The arrival of Gene Coon as the new first chair producer did nothing to help with Justman's concerns, including the mandated air dates that he was certain would not be met.

Optical effects were still proving to be the main cause for delays. On October 19, 1966, Justman wrote to Roddenberry, with a "cc" to Coon, Eddie Milkis, and Herb Solow, saying that Lin Dunn and his company Film Effects of Hollywood was *Star Trek*'s new primary supplier of its post-production miniatures and opticals. The Howard Anderson Company, for the time being, was out. The Westheimer Company was being kept as a secondary supplier, designated to taking care of the trailer optical work and end titles. Justman told all concerned:

> In this way, Lin Dunn's outfit will be free to concentrate upon the major Opticals and Miniatures. And, at the same time, we will have a secondary supplier who is familiar with the show in case we need to get bailed out again as we have had to be with Anderson Company. The Westheimer Company knows how to do our phaser animations and our Materialization Effects, and well equipped to handle Mattes and various other types of Opticals. I feel, as you do, that we must never let ourselves get in the position again of having all our eggs in one basket.

The guarded optimism was short-lived. Less than two weeks later, on October 13, Justman wrote to Ed Milkis about the optical photography needed to complete "Balance of Terror" and "The Galileo Seven." His discouraging memo to Milkis read:

> We have supplied Lin Dunn with the large model of the Enterprise, the small model of the Enterprise, the Romulan Vessel Miniature, the Shuttlecraft Miniature, and the Interior Hangar Deck from which the shuttlecraft takes off and lands. Every day when I come to the office I expect to get a call to go to the projection room where I would be deluged with reel upon reel of Miniature Photography for compositing. I go home every night and I am sure that I have not received this phone call. Please tell me that the sinking feeling I have in my stomach is self-engendered and not backed up by any facts that you know of. Having been burned before, I am writing this memo in order to get myself down on record.

More than three weeks passed and Justman still had nothing to look at from Lin Dunn and Film Effects of Hollywood. On November 11, he went above Milkis and wrote directly to Herb Solow, saying, "I hope and pray that we are not being faced with another 'Anderson situation.'"

Justman asked Solow to ask Bill Heath to make arrangements for Joe Westheimer to pick up more *Star Trek* shows, just in case. On the same day, Justman wrote to Gene Coon, pleading for him to make the necessary changes to the new batch of scripts in order to scale back on the optical effects needed for upcoming episodes.

As this latest problem presented itself, the *Star Trek* staff were hoping for a miracle. And then they got one.

On December 1, 1966, *Star Trek* was pre-empted by a Jack Benny special. "The Menagerie, Part 1" and "Part 2" had bought a week's worth of breathing room. Jack Benny bought the series another week. But that was still one week short.

There would be no new episode ready for December 29th. On that night, a repeat of "What Are Little Girls Made Of?" was substituted into the NBC schedule. The network was not happy. ABC and CBS would have new programs to run. *Star Trek* was bound to take a hit with A.C. Nielsen. And it did.

Up against first-run competition, the repeat of "What Are Little Girls Made Of?" was the lowest rated *Star Trek* episode of the first season. When aired several weeks earlier, "Little Girls" beat the *CBS Thursday Night Movie* in a close race. That night, at its peak, *Star Trek* drew 29.5% of the TVs in use. This week, for the unplanned rerun, the best it could do was a third place ranking and a 22.5% audience share.

Failing to make delivery of a required first run episode was an unprecedented breach of contract as well as trust in the eyes of NBC. And since Gene Roddenberry was the Executive Producer, the man at the desk where the buck stops, this was "Strike Nine."

***

The pressure on *Star Trek*'s producers was not letting up. Immediately following the mid-season pick-up, Roddenberry, Coon and Justman received word that Desilu was cutting *Star Trek*'s budget. The money for each episode was reduced from $193,500 to $185,000. The dark predictions made by the Old Guard to Lucille Ball about *Star Trek* and *Mission: Impossible* bankrupting Desilu were becoming a very real possibility.

With money concerns on everyone's minds, Theodore Sturgeon's "Shore Leave" was rushed through a series of rewrites. It was too big, too fantastic, too expensive. Harlan Ellison's "The City on the Edge of Forever" was nearly ready... or so the *Star Trek* producers were told by the writer. But it too required location production, as well as specialty sets and numerous extras, and it too would clearly exceed the budget and therefore needed further rewriting.

It has been speculated over the decades in newspaper and magazine articles, books, on the internet, and at various meeting spots for the fans of *Star Trek*, that there were very few discards from the story and script assignments given out by Roddenberry and Coon. To the contrary, there were many.

The series' creative team was learning that most TV writers could not handle a series as intricate as *Star Trek*. Most science fiction writers, with concepts too big to fit inside a small screen, were striking out too. The list of casualties, all with *Star Trek* money lining their pockets, was growing. Gene Roddenberry was the first name on the list.

ST-3, Roddenberry's "The Omega Glory," was paid for, only to be put on the shelf per the request of NBC. Stan Robertson didn't like the script, nor did Herb Solow, nor did Roddenberry's right-hand man, Robert Justman.

ST-10, "The Machine That Went Too Far," the tenth *Star Trek* story assignment given out by Roddenberry, along with the $655 that paid for it, went to sci-fi master A.E. van Vogt. With 20 science fiction novels and seven collections of short stories, van Vogt was one of three well-known genre authors who tried in vain on many occasions to be part of *Star Trek* (the other two being Robert Sheckley and Philip Jose Farmer). Roddenberry wanted van Vogt badly. Like Jerry Sohl, Richard Matheson, George Clayton Johnson, Robert Bloch, Theodore Sturgeon, and Harlan Ellison, van Vogt offered instant status to a new-fangled science fiction series with a reputation yet to make. But his concepts were either too strange, too risqué, too expensive or just too unlike *Star Trek* to be realized. This one, about an android that attempts to take over the Enterprise, would get a makeover and be paid for again, as "Machines Are Better," which, perhaps by coincidence, resembled certain aspects of a yet-to-come Gene Roddenberry premise for a second season entry: "I, Mudd." Roddenberry was entitled to borrow from van Vogt -- he had paid for the privilege, *twice*.

ST-11, "Chicago II," one of Roddenberry's ideas, was the first writing assignment given to *Twilight Zone* veteran George Clayton Johnson. Down the road, the concept would help influence the retooling of another writer's story and become the delightful second season entry, "A Piece of the Action." At this point, however, it wasn't coming together and so Roddenberry chose to kill "Chicago II" and assign Mr. Johnson to "The Man Trap" instead.

ST-15, "Alien Spirit" came from Norman Katkov, the writer of a dozen or so episodes for *Wanted: Dead or Alive* and a dozen or so for *Ben Casey*, including "A Cardinal Act of Mercy," which was nominated for a WGA award in 1964. "Alien Spirit" was a story that hinted at a 1958 cult sci-fi monster flick called *It: The Terror from Beyond Space*. The movie was about an alien creature that stows away on an Earth rocket ship and begins killing the crew, one by one, chasing them from one level to the next of the cigar-shaped space vehicle. Katkov changed the rocket to the Starship Enterprise and then opted for an invisible beast, capable of trashing rooms and tossing crewmembers through the air. After getting a look at the treatment, Roddenberry and his staff deemed the story too violent, too expensive, too impossible … at least, for 1966 network TV.

ST-19 was an untitled story by Jack Guss, who had served as an associate producer and script consultant on *Channing*, a 1964 series about life on a college campus. Roddenberry offered "Mudd's Women" to Guss for rewriting when Stephen Kandel became unavailable. Guss lost that assignment after voicing his uncomplimentary opinion of the story, not knowing it was Roddenberry's brainchild. Guss was invited to come up with an idea of his own, which Roddenberry then had an uncomplimentary opinion of, and the assignment was promptly cut off, so quickly in fact that no one on the *Star Trek* staff other than Roddenberry recalled seeing it and no trace of it remains in the series' show files.

ST-20, "Journey to Reolite," by Alfred Brenner, a veteran writer of *Ben Casey* and numerous 1950s anthology series, had Kirk assigned the mission of transporting the uncouth leader of the planet Acrid and his entourage to their neighboring planet Reolite for peace talks. The Acrids are described as harsh and militaristic. Those of Reolite are democratic, free, humanistic, and highly civilized. The Acrid leader, Hugo, and his mistress, Galatea, have a rare "life-giving drug" to use as a peace offering to the Reolites. It also works as an aphrodisiac.

On April 18, 1966, Justman wrote to Roddenberry and Black:

> Gentlemen: I find one really interesting idea in this story treatment. And that is of "The Galatea Syndrome" -- the thought of having a very beautiful, seductive, and highly unsophisticated female creature on board the Enterprise -- free to work her wiles -- a most engrossing sort of situation. Most everything else in the outline bothers me. Kirk does not act like Kirk; he is subject to sudden rages and also to weaknesses of the flesh that would panic NBC right out of its skull.

After listing everything in the story he didn't like, Justman added:

Why am I getting so emotional about this story? John D.F. Black is with us now. Let him become emotional.

John D.F. Black's memo trailed Justman's by two days. He said:

Personally, I've got nothing against sex/*Born Yesterday*/*Pygmalion*/comic books/eroticism/24 page outlines/etc. However... I hate this version of all of them.

The story assignment was cut off. Two years later, a variation of this story was resurrected by Roddenberry and used as the basis of "Elaan of Troyius."

ST-22, "Return to Eden" by Alvin Boretz, a writer for *The Defenders* and WGA award nominee, was good enough to evolve from a May 9 story outline to a May 23 revised story outline. Shortly after the second draft arrived, Roddenberry told Dave Kaufman of *Daily Variety*, "We have a story going to a planet with automated people, where it is so perfected there is no crime, no hunger, no illness, no choice, the climate is always the same. But the people are like zombies, it's a computerized society. They find what is Utopia for such a society is sterile." (145-15)

In a memo to Robert Justman, Roddenberry described the premise as:

[A] shore leave story in which the accumulated boredoms, fatigues, dissentions, male needs, etc., come to a head with our continuing characters... The shore leave planet will have something of a Shangri-La aspect with many temptations... "Eden" is a trap, a sort of death. When mankind, or a particular man stops growing, he begins dying.

Robert Justman, in a May 9 memo, said, "I detect a complete absence of action in this story." John D.F. Black called it "the Boretz version of Hilton's *Lost Horizon*." He was bothered by more than a lack of action, and told Roddenberry, "I think the Boretz piece is awful." And that ended that.

ST-25, "Rites to Fertility," was from Robert Sheckley, known for dozens of science fiction short stories and, at this time, three novels. His idea placed a crewman in an airlock where a portal closes on his hand, tearing his environmental suit and cutting his skin. McCoy, during an examination, observes that the crewman's skin "has hardened to a coarse, brown texture; the fingers are rigid, almost twig-like; each nail has turned into a soft, green leaf." In other words, the poor man had begun a metamorphosis into a vegetable. Worse, what is happening to him happens to others and the Enterprise becomes a plague ship filled with walking, talking foliage. Spock, who appears to be immune, beams down to a nearby planet in search of answers and, hopefully, a cure. Once there, he encounters a primitive Indian-like race that worships the trees and longs for the day when they can become one with their gods and to root among the forest. They are reluctant to share information as to how the crew can counteract the changing of flesh to soft wood until Spock explains to them, "Earth people do not consider turning into a plant to be an acceptable form of immortality."

On May 11, Justman wrote to Black:

The amount of sets, type of sets, cost of construction of such sets, construction of special effects and movable creatures, and physical special effects concerned with the operation of these elements, pretty well puts this story, as it stands right now, completely out of reach for us.... We also cannot have Bob Justman having a nervous breakdown. My doctor tells me that we cannot afford to make this show.

Justman's doctor was right and Sheckley was asked to come up with something else.

ST-27, "Sisters in Space," was a second chance for Sheckley. In his June 14 outline, the Enterprise encounters the hulk of its sister ship, the S.S. Saratoga, missing for five years. Kirk, Scotty, Sulu, Rand, and a pair of crewmen beam over to the derelict ship. There, they discover cage compartments in the lower hold where the crew had kept living specimens collected from various alien planets. They also discover that the cages have been torn open, "steel twisted like putty, steel bulkheads ripped the way a baling hook would bite through plywood." It becomes clear that something was taken onboard, turned on the crew and proved impossible to control. The damage it wrought is horrifying and then one of the Enterprise men (a non-regular) is heard screaming. When the rest of the boarding party reach him, he is dead, having been ripped limb from limb. In addition to its enormous strength, the creature is a sort of chameleon. It can change color, blending in with backgrounds. Sheckley wrote, "Now, as chips of metal fly across the room like shrapnel, the creature clawing its way out of the cage, it suddenly becomes visible." Then Robert Justman had a near-heart attack.

John D.F. Black spoke for Justman, writing to Roddenberry, "Too expensive," then adding:

> As a premise, the lost and drifting Enterprise-class space vessel holds promise -- when it has a monster aboard.... The question is, is Sheckley the writer to do it? From this version of this yarn, the question is a genuine question... I'm not sure at all.

The story also resembled Norman Katkov's "Alien Spirit." And, like "Spirit," it too was cut off.

ST-28, "Portrait in Black and White," one of Roddenberry's story concepts from the *Star Trek* series proposal, was given to Barry Trivers for devolvement. Roddenberry had promised Trivers another assignment in exchange for a fourth rewrite of his script for "The Conscience of the King." This was it.

"Portrait of Black and White" was a parallel world story, this one resembling the "Ole Plantation Days" of the South but turned upside down with white savages shipped and auctioned at slave marts run by blacks.

Robert Justman cringed when he saw Barry Trivers' story outline. On August 15, he wrote to Gene Coon:

> Since Gene Roddenberry assigned it, I assume that this story is what he was after.... Personally speaking, I am not sure about this property. There is more here than meets the eye. Allegories are fine and the allegoric cause as depicted in this show is naturally very close to many people's hearts. Certainly it is to mine. However, I wonder if we aren't starting to lose sight of the fact that we are supposedly making an "entertainment" show.

On August 23, after a retooled outline arrived, Justman spoke again, this time writing directly to Roddenberry, saying:

> We have several problems in this proposed outline... [including] a reference to sending a young girl to a "breeding farm" -- which I think NBC would strike immediately – [and] quite a lot of bloodshed indicated. We may have a lot of beautiful words and philosophies here [but] can we afford to spend pages on preaching?... Isn't a Negro Lincoln really a bit much?... I would suggest that this present draft be submitted to NBC immediately, prior to ordering a script. I am

afraid that this allegorical treatment will get resentment from all sides if it is ever shown on the air.... Secondly, again, we have a parallel world situation. I am afraid that someday the audience might get tired of seeing the same old ploy used again.... Thirdly, this show in its present form would be enormously expensive to handle.

But Roddenberry liked these Jonathan Swift-type parallel world stories. He had his heart set on "Black and White." He was also irked over NBC, Desilu, and his staff not rallying behind another of his parallel world situations – "The Omega Glory" -- and so, on August 24, he spanked Justman with a deliberate "cc" to Coon, writing:

Agreed that aspects of this tale, if improperly handled, could bring the white and the black power advocates down on us with a vengeance.... On the other hand, we could be in trouble with someone on any dynamic theme, i.e., union labors, peace-war, utopia-individuality, etc. This theme, if handled intelligently, and it is our duty as producers to see that it is handled intelligently, can be highly provocative, entertaining, and a revealing exercise in dramatic truths, making points via its "sf" approach that never could be made in a non-sf approach.... I can give you 37 reasons why every story we have ever received started out as illogical, tasteless, too expensive, etc.... Half of the job is, of course, in pointing out the above. The other half is in seeking replacements for these points, things we can do and should do to make it into the kind of script we will all be proud of.

In case Coon didn't get the point, Roddenberry fired off an August 24 memo to him too, writing:

Trivers is showing in this story outline opportunities for surprise, suspense, action, and physical jeopardy. With a little reworking, a little straightening out, and a little attention to milking the delightful and unusual parallels out of it, we should have an excellent script.

Two days later Stan Robertson spoke for the network. The rejection was short and not sweet. "We believe that this story does not fit into the *Star Trek* concept." Period.

Roddenberry had fought NBC before over his right as a writer/producer to do a program about the very black and white issue of racial prejudice. That episode of *The Lieutenant* had resulted in the end of the series. But Roddenberry remained undaunted and, on September 1, he wrote Barry Trivers:

There are political and moral attitudes in this story that only rarely have writers been able to attempt in television. Networks have either killed such stories or masqueraded them behind the Indian/Cowboy conflict. We are delighted that *Star Trek* will have the chance to go in, without the kiss of death, or the masquerade, and raise the points with honesty and dramatic impact. But let's make sure we don't panic NBC. Barry, we want to do this show.... What we want to emphasize is not the political conflict, but the melodrama of Kirk captured... thrown into physical jeopardy... emotionally moved to act and react... the advancing armies... the strangeness of Kirk being considered and treated like an inferior, etc.

Trivers wrote his script. Of the first draft on September 28, Gene Coon received memos from Steven Carabatsos and, indications are, Dorothy Fontana in an unofficial capacity. In part, their combined feedback stated:

All the dialogue is dreadful. None of our characters are in character. Kirk does absolutely nothing... nor does Spock. Action is pretty nil... what there is, is poorly conceived and possibly in violation of NBC Broadcast Standards code (i.e. shooting of women and children). Much of the script is (a) dull, (b) platitudinous, (c) preachy and/or (d) offensive....

This is a delicate and highly touchy subject with them... especially with Stan. Jean Messerschmidt has already requested that I send her two copies of the first draft, rather than her usual one, because higher authorities in NBC will be reading it....

I am really upset by this one as it stands, and I can hardly wait to see what Robert J. has to say when he reads it, if he can speak at all, that is, since this subject is also a sensitive area with him.

Justman had plenty to say later that day, writing Coon:

This piece will have to be totally overhauled... restructured, rewritten. You know what we had to go through the last time on a piece Barry wrote ["The Conscience of the King"]. With this one, I strongly feel you will have to completely redo the final draft that Barry turns in if you are to have any chance at all of getting NBC to even consider it.... Dialogue is "unspeakable." Mostly I strongly object to the Negro masters and the slaves using minstrel show accents and pronunciations. A Southern accent might be all right, but I think we should go for as straight a speech patterns as we can get so as not to insult the intelligence of our actors and our audience -- or Stan Robertson.

Coon worked with the script, as did Roddenberry, but neither ever won support from NBC over the controversial material. If Roddenberry had proceeded to produce "Portrait in Black and White," it would never have been aired. Both he and Coon had ignored the most important rule of the Jonathan Swift technique to making commentary on current political and social stigmas -- disguise it enough to get past the censors.

ST-29, "Rock-A-Bye Baby, and Die," with story outline from August 2, 1966, was George Clayton Johnson's third *Star Trek* assignment (following "Chicago II" and "The Man Trap"). Roddenberry was intrigued by Johnson's pitch and even contributed story points to the idea of the Enterprise being infused with an entity that is an alien child. Johnson's treatment displayed a rare talent for telling unusual stories, sadly to be soon lost to *Star Trek*.

Johnson wrote:

The ship in space, hurtling toward Minerva – a planet: To pick up two ruthless criminals. They have been judged criminally deranged and must be taken to a hospital planet. Several persons have been badly wounded apprehending the two and a starship doctor is needed.

Abruptly, a glowing speck on the view screens, swift, radiant, headed toward the ship on a collision course. Evasive action. The speck follows. Pressor beams. Phaser weapons. All fail to destroy the tiny hunk of matter. All hands brace for impact. The ship rocks savagely as the tiny sock of matter hits it.

Close on the communications console: a switch flips up on its own accord. All hands react to a strange sound that reverberates throughout the ship. The sound of a baby squalling!

A search of the ship reveals no baby. Instead, there is evidence to assume the ship is alive! The glowing speck of matter was an entity, a soul -- trying to be born -- to become -- to exist. It found a host -- the complex circuitry of the ship. There seems to be no way to separate the entity from the ship. To Mr. Spock it is a scientific marvel. To Kirk it is a responsibility -- something to take back to Earth for the experts to examine. To Dr. McCoy it is a nuisance -- something that stands between himself and his patients on Minerva. To Uhura, the ship is frightening. Her switchboard is the baby's voice. The crying disturbs her.

Kirk puts Spock and Scott to work to locate the offending circuits. Spock's advice: Save the ship at any cost. The complication: There is evidence that the "baby" is growing at an accelerated rate. In the first five minutes the ship had apparently aged one year. It is beginning to explore its body and environment -- working doors, the propulsion system. It is developing an awareness of itself.

And that was only the first of five pages. The big events, and big effects needed to convey those events, were in the pages to come.

Bob Justman was also intrigued, but had many concerns, and wrote to Gene Coon:

> Here it is, late on a Friday night, and I am about to take my life in my hands and give you some comments on some story material. The story idea of this outline is personally very intriguing to me, but it is also practically straight "Sci-Fi" rather than *Star Trek*. I think it would make a very interesting half-hour *Twilight Zone*.... Money-wise, we are in what I would characterize as a bit of a bind. Plenty Optical and Special Effects and other things which I am too tired to remember right now. In fact, that's all I'm going to say right now.

Coon was also worried the story was too farfetched for *Star Trek* and wanted to make substantial changes. George Clayton Johnson did not appreciate Coon's ideas and later said, "Here I am expecting [Roddenberry] to say, 'Go ahead,' and, instead, he's saying, 'Here's my new producer.' And the new producer is saying, 'I don't like the humanness of the little boy at the end of the story; I would like it to be an alien *thing* -- like he is merely a robot. For me, what you have is a fantasy.' And I'm saying, 'Gene, the *whole show* is a fantasy! Tell me the science that the transporter is based upon.' He looked baffled. I said, 'The whole damn thing is made up, Gene. Why are you wanting to change this for no real good reason?' So, we argued about it.... In the course of all this, I said to Roddenberry, 'Look, you have a dog in this fight, too. You and I, collectively, made this story that this guy [Gene Coon] is about to change, so you ought to have an opinion here.' And he said, 'George, I make it a policy that when I'm hiring somebody else to produce the show that this other person is going to have full authority and I don't feel it is my place to interfere.' I thought, 'What a chicken way to deal with it.' I was hideously offended by that. I was watching Gene [Roddenberry] backing away from me in terms of any moral responsibility or even, indeed, his personhood as a man. I said, 'No, Gene, I'm going to buy this back from you. There's a clause in the contract. Read it. It says, if I send you back every dollar you sent me, that severs the bond between us. It's in the contract, and I'll send you your check.'" (93-1)

Johnson bought his story back. It remains unproduced to this day. And the writer of the first *Star Trek* to air would trek no more.

ST #31, "The Squaw," which took Spock to "Vulcan 801," a cluster of planets to which he traces his ancestry, was the story Shimon Wincelberg wanted to do after "Dagger of the Mind." The ship's scanners pick up ancient space debris from Starship Pioneer XIX, missing for 60 years. Spock, leading a patrol to search the nearest planet for any trace that there may have been survivors, encounters a population of "savage Vulcans." The landing party is attacked and all but Spock are killed. Because he looks like the attackers, Spock is taken back to their camp. Only one of the Vulcans there speaks English. Her name is "Missie," and she befriends Spock. Missie is the Squaw.

Meanwhile, Kirk beams down to search for Spock and finds the dead landing party members, their bodies pierced by arrows. He and his team are then attacked by "*non* Vulcan cowboys." They are captured and taken to a western-type town called Fort Antrim. These cowboys are the descendants of the survivors of the Starship Pioneer, and have modeled their culture after a book one of the original survivors brought with him, called "Astounding Western Romances." It is "a pulp book of the lowest type" and has been used by "the settlers" as a combination encyclopedia, Bible, and history book. We soon discover that the Vulcans who lived on this planet were once gentle un-warlike people, but "The Good Book" told the descendents that the pointed-eared aliens were savages. Decades of hostilities have since contributed to the Vulcans now behaving as such.

Spock, meanwhile, has been deemed a "half-breed" by his Vulcan captors. They consider killing him, but Missie convinces them that they should cast him out and let the settlers deal with him. This leads to Spock finding Kirk and the Enterprise men, and all making their getaway from this distorted page from America's old west.

The story outline made it through two drafts, on July 15 and 28, before Wincelberg was sidetracked into rewriting "The Galileo Seven." The falling out between him and Roddenberry (over the latter's rewriting of "Dagger of the Mind") resulted in the early death of "The Squaw." Robert Justman, estimating the cost factor of doing such a story, was greatly relieved.

ST-32, "An Accident of Love," was assigned to Allan Balter and William Woodfield, a writing team responsible for many episodes of *Voyage to the Bottom of the Sea* and *Lost in Space*. The only hearts broken by this *Star Trek* love story, though, were those of the two writers... when their assignment was abruptly cut off, and, like Jack Guss's story (ST-19), done so without a trace.

ST-37, "Dreadnaught," by Alf Harris, a new writer on the scene, is a phantom among *Star Trek* stories. It came and went without a trace left in the show's files.

There were also unsolicited submissions (treatments *Star Trek* did not request and, with one exception, did not pay for).

Philip Jose Farmer, one of those three famed sci-fi authors who weren't quick to take "no" for an answer, sent in numerous story ideas during *Star Trek*'s first season. "Mere Shadows" came in on March 22, 1966, nearly six months before the series even premiered. The story has a woman rescued from a wrecked prospecting ship, and then falling in love with Kirk. Heartsick over his lack of interest, she arms herself with a phaser, takes over engineering, and sets the Enterprise hurling through space at speeds never before attempted. This causes the ship to break through "the skin of the universe" and become trapped in a space void.

Something like this would be tried in 1968 with "Is There in Truth no Beauty?" but, in 1966, the optical effects available could not even begin to satisfy a story of this type.

"Image of the Beast," submitted five days later by Farmer, had Kirk and a landing party beaming down into the middle of a vast desert on a barren planet, at the site of the wreck of an immense alien space ship. The Enterprise men search the ghost vessel, and then begin experiencing memory losses and strange hallucinations. We learn that, during one blackout, they had devices implanted into their skulls, allowing communication from the telepathic aliens.

Once again, costs were prohibitive. And NBC would never go for something this cerebral.

"The Uncoiler," from April Fools' Day 1966, was a third try from Farmer. This time, responding to a distress call from an uninhabited world, the men of the Enterprise encounter a long-bearded old man, clothed in rags, living deep in the jungle. They also find the wreck of his small spaceship, the ruins of an ancient city, and a statue of an idol allegedly worshipped by the long dead alien race. The old man refuses to be rescued unless Kirk agrees to beam the statue of the alien idol back to the Enterprise. Kirk relents.

Back on the ship, Kirk becomes confused and experiences memory lapses. Then Spock starts forgetting things. The ship's two top officers are having on-again-off-again amnesia. The cause: aliens called the Zaltots, who have transformed their minds into the statue. This statue had communicated to the old man to call for help and to have it taken aboard the rescue ship so that the Zaltots could then be transported to heavily populated planets in order to live vicariously through others. The Zaltots are referred to as "electronic vampires" and, during the 48-hour period needed for the complete "encoding and transferring" to take over a human's mind, Kirk and Spock write notes to one another whenever they get an idea and before they forget it. And these notes help them to find a means to exorcise the aliens from their minds.

The *Star Trek* people requested, and paid for, a second draft outline, dated April 5. John D.F. Black's final word on it to Roddenberry, from April 22, 1966, "I agree with you, it just doesn't make it."

"The Rebels Unthawed," Farmer's last effort of the year, from May, was considered too much like "Space Seed," a story in development at that time.

"Sleeping Beauty" was an outline sent in "on spec" from Robert Bloch after he finished his share of the work on "What Are Little Girls Made Of?" His new story involved a 21st Century "gangster" who puts himself into suspended animation to avoid being prosecuted for crimes. Bloch had it that the gangster is found and revived by the crew of the Enterprise. Gene Coon immediately nixed that idea. The premise, again, was in conflict with "Space Seed," that other sleeping beauty story in the works.

Other writers tried to make a sale to *Star Trek* but came up short with their "pitch sessions." (Since these pitches never advanced to outline, there is no documentation as to the storylines.)

Dean Reisner, who wrote an *Outer Limits* and would go on to write the screenplays for numerous Clint Eastwood movies including *Coogan's Bluff*, *Play Misty for Me*, and *Dirty Harry*, took his shot on March 15, 1966.

Theodore Aspen, a New York playwright who worked often for *Ben Casey*, tried on March 22.

Preston Wood, who had written for *The Wild, Wild West* and *Bonanza*, gave his pitch on April 8.

Arnold Perl, who wrote for *The Naked City* and was the Executive Producer for George C. Scott's 1963 series *East Side/West Side*, tried April 22.

Also from April, 1966 (exact dates unknown):

Albert Reubin, who knew Roddenberry from *Have Gun -- Will Travel*, for which the former wrote and produced, and would go on to write the screenplay for *The Seven-Ups* and write and produce for *Kojak*;

Chester Krumholz, another *Ben Casey* writer;

George Bellak, who wrote for *The Trials of O'Brien*;

Earl Hamner Jr., who had written eight scripts for *The Twilight Zone*, and would go on to create and produce *The Waltons* and *Falcon Crest*;

And Frederik Pohl, a prolific science fiction writer with 15 novels and nearly 100 short stories to his credit, as well as serving for 10 years as the editor of *Galaxy* magazine.

William Shatner wanted a writing assignment, too. Roddenberry, speaking with Michael Fessier for an October 1966 article in *TV Guide*, said of Shatner, "He came in and said, 'I have a few comments about this script,' and I thought, 'Oh no.'" But Shatner surprised Roddenberry, who told the *TV Guide* writer, "I have never had more intelligent suggestions and we used all of them." And then Shatner handed Roddenberry a story he had written. Roddenberry said, "He wouldn't let me take it home to read. He insisted on reading it right there. So I fortified myself with a scotch and prepared to suffer. But the story flowed and was so damn poetic I caught myself wishing I could write that well." Roddenberry passed the story -- and perhaps the buck -- to Coon who, either not liking the idea or not liking the idea of letting one of his actors also write for the show, said "no."

"I've submitted three scripts for the series," Shatner said for an article syndicated to numerous newspapers in October, 1966. None had been assigned an ST number. Shatner, like Kirk, never one to give up easily, added, "I also want very much to direct and I've been promised, if the series continues, I can do so."

There is no evidence of these three scripts in the *Star Trek* show files, but one treatment, "The Web of Death," dated April 29, 1966, and credited to William Shatner, has survived. In the story, the Enterprise comes upon its sister ship, the U.S.S. Momentous, at a dead stop near a planet. There is no life on board, but Kirk and an away team do discover the crew's uniforms, lying about the ship, even draped over chairs, all empty. All food is gone from the ship, as well, and holes have been pierced in the outer hull. As the Enterprise crew investigates, they find the reason for the holes, the missing food stocks, and the empty uniforms – a giant, ravenous spider in space.

***

Of the shift in power from Roddenberry to Coon, the former said, "I had no choice.... The only way I could get people like Gene Coon to come in and produce -- and I needed a producer, more helping hands -- was to become executive producer. I had to get some extra people in any way I could." (145-3)

The new system was now in place.

William Shatner said, "Gene Coon had more to do with the infusion of life into *Star Trek* than any other single person.... Gene Coon set the tenor of the show. [Roddenberry] was more in the background." (156-1)

Not completely so, as the interoffice memos shared here will continue to indicate. But Roddenberry, feeling exhausted, was certainly ready to let Coon lead the charge.

Robert Justman said, "Gene Coon was a brilliant find. You couldn't get anyone better." (94-7)

David Gerrold, a future *Star Trek* writer who signed on during Coon's watch, said, "When Gene L. Coon first came on board, you start getting things like the Prime Directive and a lot of the stuff that was later identified as the noble parts of *Star Trek*. Gene L. Coon created that noble image that everyone gives Roddenberry the most credit for." (73-4)

Shatner said, "Gene Coon created many of the basic conceptional points. The

Klingons, the Organian Peace Treaty and the Prime Directive were all conceived by Coon." (156-8)

Coon also added more humor to the characters, perhaps an even more important contribution. David Gerrold noted, "[W]hen Gene L. Coon took over, the characters locked into place very tightly and crisply." (73-4)

Dorothy Fontana added, "The humor between the characters began to become more and more developed, particularly the Spock and McCoy relationship became a lot more fun. It evolved into what it ultimately became, a basic friendship. Gene Coon led the way on that." (64-11)

Shatner said, "Coon's brand of humor always grew organically from within the characters. Captain Kirk never slipped on a banana peel for a laugh, we never put Spock in drag, instead, Coon felt that *Star Trek*'s humorous moments could be used to deepen our characters and the relationships between them." (156-8)

"The show was pretty straightforward in the beginning," Dorothy Fontana echoed. "But then we realized that any time we'd give the characters something humorous to play with, the show really sparkled." (64-2)

Coon had needed a few weeks to get up to speed. But now, with the next group of episodes, that sparkle -- the magic of Gene Coon -- was about to make itself known.

Episode 17: SHORE LEAVE
Written by Theodore Sturgeon
(with Gene L. Coon and Gene Roddenberry, uncredited)
Directed by Robert Sparr

7:30 ⑥ ⑭ STAR TREK—Adventure

[COLOR] In deep space, the USS Enterprise makes a rest-and-recreation stop that proves anything but restful.

Captain Kirk has selected an apparently ideal site for his crew's much-needed furloughs, yet there is something wrong.

The advance party sights storybook characters, living persons from their own pasts and a host of other strange objects. Even the superlogical Mr. Spock is mystified.

Robert Spaar directed from a script by Theodore Sturgeon. Kirk: William Shatner. Spock: Leonard Nimoy. McCoy: DeForest Kelley. Sulu: George Takei. (Rerun; 60 min.)

Guest Cast
Tonia Barrows ....Emily Banks
Caretaker ....Oliver McGowan
Rodriguez ....Perry Lopez
Finnegan ....Bruce Mars
Ruth ....Shirley Bonne

William Shatner and Leonard Nimoy

NBC press release issued December 6, 1966:

> While searching for a suitable rest area in which members of the USS Enterprise crew may take much needed furloughs, a landing party discovers an eerie fantasyland, in "Shore Leave" on NBC Television Network's colorcast of *Star Trek* on Thursday, Dec. 29.... At first more bemused than frightened by the amusement-park atmosphere of the supposedly uninhabited planet, Captain Kirk (William Shatner) sees no immediate menace to his ship and crew. However, the strange land soon poses a serious threat when Kirk's scouting party disappears and his ship's power source is lost.

In this wonderland, McCoy sees a girl named Alice being followed by a giant talking rabbit. Sulu, who likes collecting antique weapons, finds a revolver, fully loaded, and is chased by a Samurai warrior wielding a sword. Lt. Rodriguez and Specialist Angela Martine-Teller are chased by a World War II-era fighter plane on a strafing run. Yeoman Tonia Barrows, who believes in fairy tales and storybook romance, sees and is attacked by Don Juan, prompting McCoy, who believes in chivalry, to come to her defense, then they see, and are attacked by, a knight in armor on a stallion. And Kirk, who fondly remembers the days at Starfleet Academy before he carried so much weight on his shoulders, meets and receives a sock on the jaw from an old upper-classmate and practical jokester named Finnegan, and a different type of smack, this time to the heart, from Ruth, the girl he left behind.

The hook: Dreams and nightmares sleep side by side, so be careful what you think about while on a world where wishes do come true.

SOUND BITES

- *Spock, to Kirk, about Kirk:* "He's becoming irritable and quarrelsome, but he refuses to take rest and rehabilitation. Now, he has that right, but..." *Kirk, interrupting:* "That crewman's right ends where the safety of the ship begins. That man will go ashore on my orders. What's his name?" *Spock:* "James Kirk. Enjoy yourself, Captain."

- *Yeoman Barrows, to McCoy, as she changes her clothes:* "Don't peek." *McCoy:* "My dear girl, I am a doctor. When I peek, it's in the line of duty."

- *Spock:* "All we know for certain is that they act exactly like the real thing. Just as pleasant... or as deadly."

- *Spock:* "On my planet, to rest is to rest; to cease using energy. To me, it is quite illogical to run up and down on green grass using energy instead of saving it."

- *Kirk:* "The more complex the mind, the greater the need for the simplicity of play."

ASSESSMENT

Theodore Sturgeon's very original screenplay plays like a roller coaster ride, seamlessly winding its way through dips and peaks, with an abundance of thrills along the way. While the fantasy elements of the story may have been too fantastic for NBC's liking (see The Story Behind the Story), "Shore Leave" gave the network exactly what Roddenberry had promised -- a planet show with action *and* adventure.

We meet Ruth, Kirk's first love. Thanks to on-the-mark acting choices by William Shatner, Kirk appears intoxicated with feelings of both fondness and heartache. The mere presence of Ruth, her touch and scent, both comfort and torment him. Note how quickly the mood of the episode shifts. Credit the hauntingly beautiful music of Gerald Fried and the stunned and reflective look on Shatner's face for making Kirk's reunion with Ruth such a memorable one.

Equally emotional: the death of Dr. McCoy. Another superb acting choice on the part of William Shatner. The script called for: "PUSH IN EXTREMELY RAPID ON Kirk's reaction -- pure horror." Shatner, instead, gave us a tortured expression as Kirk is overwhelmed with grief to the point of appearing physically ill. The combinations of strong performances by Nimoy, Takei, and guest star Emily Banks create a scene that is as heartfelt as it is gripping. Few watching back in December, 1966, could have guessed that in the world of science fiction anything is possible and McCoy might return from the dead. DeForest Kelley was not listed in the opening credits at this point. He was presented as a supporting character, which, as had happened with Yeoman Janice Rand, can suddenly go away. When this episode first aired, the shock and the remorse of witnessing the death of Dr. McCoy was intense. It was very clear just how vital McCoy -- and DeForest Kelley -- had become.

Angela Martine-Taylor also dies in this story. And she too is "repaired." Due to a lack of camera coverage from director Robert Sparr, you'll need to watch closely, but she does return to Rodriguez's side for the final moment of the episode.

The fight between Kirk and Finnegan is noteworthy. The choreography and stunt work are as good as television got from this era. One can feel both Kirk's determination and physical exhaustion. Gerald Fried's score speeds up and then slows to a crawl, in perfect sync with the energy of the fight and the fatigue of the combatants.

Adding to all of this, the scenery, for a 1966 television series with a budget just reduced to $187,000 per episode (although "Shore Leave" went over by $12,000), is unparalleled. The story takes on a dreamlike effect as the eerie backdrop of this strange world changes from lush and tropical to barren and harsh, and as characters from the subconscious mind pop in and out of the surreal existence.

Moments like these elevate "Shore Leave" into the stratosphere of *TOS*'s very best.

THE STORY BEHIND THE STORY

Script Timeline
Theodore Sturgeon's story outline, ST #24, "Shore Leave": May 10, 1966.
Sturgeon's revised outlines, gratis: May 17, 1966.
Sturgeon's 2nd Revised Story Outline, gratis: May 23, 1966.
Sturgeon's 1st Draft teleplay: early June 1966.
Sturgeon's rewrite, gratis (Rev. 1st Draft teleplay; now called "Finagle's Planet"): June 20, 1966.
Sturgeon's 2nd Draft teleplay, title changed back to "Shore Leave": September 9, 1966.
Gene Coon's polish (Mimeo Department Reformatted "Yellow Cover 1st Draft"): October 3, 1966.
Coon's second script polish (Final Draft teleplay): October 14, 1966.
Additional page revisions by Coon: October 17, 1966.
Gene Roddenberry's emergency "rough step outline": October 18, 1966.
Rushed revised script pages from Roddenberry: October 19, 20 & 21, 1966.

The basic idea for "Shore Leave" is in Gene Roddenberry's March 1964 series proposal. Roddenberry handed the clever but vague concept off to Theodore Sturgeon who, at 48, was a science fiction legend known for his books, including *More Than Human* (1953) and *The Cosmic Rape* (1958).

Roddenberry, thrilled to have Sturgeon on his team, later reflected, "Up until then, he had always been a writer of great novels. Someone said to him, 'Ted, I understand that you are doing *Star Trek* now. Don't you know that 90% of everything on television is crap?' Ted rose up grandly and said, 'Ninety percent of *everything* is crap.'" (145-23)

Sturgeon's "story treatment," more like an abbreviated and somewhat disjointed short story, arrived May 10, 1966. Robert Justman got a look at it seven days later and was appalled. He wrote to John D.F. Black:

> What are we going to do about this story? Having just finished a memo on Harlan Ellison's story, I am in no condition to go through this one yet. (RJ17-1)

He didn't have to. The next day something more resembling a proper screen outline arrived from the TV novice (dated May 17, received May 18). Justman's memo to Black listed many things that could not be done in the real world of 1966 television, including:

> Why does McCoy's body have to disappear? If it does have to disappear, why does it have to disappear in a method that Ted outlines -- "The top of a nearby rock pops up, two mechanical arms snake out, gather up the body, swiftly and smoothly they lift it to the top of the rock and disappear with it. The top of the rock slams shut. (RJ17-2)

The scene was more effective as filmed, with McCoy's body moved but without seeing how or to where. This created a greater sense of mystery. The idea came from Roddenberry, who wrote to Sturgeon:

> Enjoyable outline to read. Without wanting to seem to stroke my long gray TV beard, and with no claims to a crystal ball, it seems to me that this script is one of those which has to be either an Academy Award nominee or totally impossible. With that in mind, Ted, I intend to be as critical as possible at this stage. (GR17-1)

Roddenberry's list of criticisms was extensive, including:

> Let's lose the mechanical arms taking McCoy's body. Let's just simply have it disappear. Mechanical arms are very expensive. (GR17-1)

More importantly for Roddenberry was the handling of the series' protagonist. He told Sturgeon:

> Create a story for Captain Kirk and intertwine it through the somewhat fragmented series of episodes which now exists. (GR17-1)

Roddenberry's notes continued for three pages, ending with a lecture defining a story -- the need for a character to have something happen or not happen. All else is window dressing.

Sturgeon didn't seem to take offense ... yet. His revised outline, for no pay, was dated May 23.

Besides having a different date, and that there were no mechanical arms dragging McCoy into a hollowed out rock on the top of a hill, the famed writer failed to address very nearly any of the notes given. In this treatment, we still see McCoy's body removed, although in a different manner than before, this time by Finagle (later to be named Finnegan). And it still required immense optical effects, as did so many other elements of the story.

Roddenberry, in a hurry to get scripts written, sent this embryonic, problematic version of "Shore Leave" through to NBC.

Days later, Stan Robertson sent one of his longer memos to Roddenberry, writing, in part:

> Frankly, I am disappointed with the written-out results of the story which I felt had such high promise when you verbalized it to me.... The idea is a good one but the writer seems to have gone far afield and come up with something, at least in the outline stage, less than dramatically sensational and which is not *Star Trek* as we all have envisioned. Primarily -- and I don't mean even to suggest that I am lecturing on the fundamentals of writing to two such talented people as you and the excellent writer of this story -- we seem to have lost sight of the foundation of any story. <u>The premise</u>. What are we trying to say here? What is the reason for this tale?... This is <u>not</u> Captain Kirk's story, nor a story in which he is an integral part. As we have stressed and must continue to stress, we <u>must</u> involve our star in our dramas as much as possible. We've got to make him a living, breathing, important, identifiable person to our viewers. He's got to be our Sandy Koufax -- the guy we build a Pennant-winning team around.... This is more a series of cameos than one continuing drama. The touches and the gimmicks are good -- the rabbit, Alice in Wonderland, the knight, etc. -- but after awhile they lose their interest and shock value and diminish into mere unrelated twists of a writer's fertile imagination. There is little suspense, tension, jeopardy, and real conflict established. Excepting for the "death" of Dr. McCoy, all else is rather meaningless and not of much value. There is not enough warmth and human feeling. As we have discussed, these are necessary ingredients of our stories and <u>cannot</u> be overlooked and ignored.... In summary, Gene, we would say that this story leaves the reader with the observation: "Okay, now tell me a story." There is just not enough "dramatic meat" to sink

your teeth into; not enough characterization to really give a darn about what happens to the people involved. (SR17-1)

Roddenberry responded with a long memo of his own, beginning:

Agree with your comments on "Shore Leave." The problem here is this was the second outline draft from the writer -- we had the choice of either sending him to script with instructions on what to add to it or forgetting the thing altogether. (GR12-2)

Roddenberry assured Robertson that he had already expressed very much the same comments to Sturgeon and was confident that all would be well when the script arrived. It wasn't.

The next delivery from Sturgeon was neither fish nor fowl -- an odd mix of outline and script. Roddenberry sent further notes -- *many further notes* -- beginning with the warning:

At the close of this you will no longer be a virgin.... The scatter-gun novelist technique confuses [my staff], and upsets me because dozens of people come pounding at my door. (GR17-2)

It also upset Roddenberry that too many of the gimmicks in the "script" seemed to be telegraphed ahead, meaning that one could see them coming. Of this, he told Sturgeon:

Maybe it's that I don't like the audience, or maybe I love them, but I like to keep the bastards off balance with the unexpected happening every two or three pages. (GR17-3)

After another two pages of criticism, Roddenberry, keeping Sturgeon off balance, closed, "You're lovely, inventive, wonderful. Now be commercial." (GR17-3)

Sturgeon fired off an indignant letter to Roddenberry, saying:

Something I want to get off my chest, and also something I think will save you time in your future comments to me.... This has to do with your off-handed use of the adjective "novelistic" during the defloration.... I am by bent and training a communicator... therefore touch me not with the brush so strikingly tarred by so many of my colleagues. (TS17-1)

Clearly, Sturgeon had heard the complaints from "colleagues" who felt they had been tarred by Roddenberry's criticism and requests for free rewrites.

Roddenberry's rebuttal:

Dear Ted, where did I tar you and with what brush? You say you're communicating; I think I'm communicating... but somebody ain't reading the communications.... A script, unlike a -- dare I mention the word? -- novel, is only the beginning of communicating with the audience. It does not, in fact, even reach an audience -- other than that audience of unseen technicians mentioned in your "defloration," i.e., the men who convert script descriptions into sets, costumes, optical effects, makeup, hair styles, sound, etc. The term "novelist's scattergun technique," whether aptly or correctly used, or not, was a request that description and direction passages in your script be broken down into shots and camera angles which specify "what," "how many," and "how much," the specifics so necessary to planning and budgeting television episodes. (GR17-4)

Roddenberry's letter crossed in the mail with a new version of Sturgeon's script. It arrived in two parts -- the first two acts dated June 17, the second two from June 20. Only a TV novice would think to send in his script piecemeal. And only a novice to the media would arbitrarily change the title -- "Shore Leave" was now "Finagle's Planet."

With the second half of the script was a short note from Sturgeon. He had read Roddenberry's letter by this point and, having cooled off, attempted to make nice. He wrote:

> In order to stay on top of this script, Gene, I have revised my personal plans. Though I am returning to New York on Wednesday, the 22nd, I shall be back here on Monday the 27th and will, if you like, work in your offices beginning the 28th. Yours as ever, a lot, Sturgeon. (TS17-2)

Robert Justman's mood, however, hadn't changed. In his latest memo to John D.F. Black, the only compliment he could muster concerned the mere germ of the idea behind the script. All else dealt with the impossible aspects of the written material which, for him, still did not resemble a proper TV script. He complained:

> Incidentally, is Ted Sturgeon going to direct and photograph this property? He sure has written it as if he is going to. When we get a rewrite on this show, and we are going to need one desperately, I suggest that all his "writer's asides" to the reader be deleted. Let's leave it up to the Director and the Cameraman as to how the shooting of the show is going to be handled. And let's leave it up to the rest of us as to how certain Special Effects are going to be created for the show. This will also give us a much more realistic script length. There are pages and pages of scene description, notations to the various departments, and Popular-Mechanics-type instructions to sundry persons, which really have no place in a Teleplay. (RJ17-4)

John D.F. Black later said, "My favorite part of the job was also the toughest part of the job, which was dealing with the writers. The intimidation of sitting down with Theodore Sturgeon, who was, at that time, the most anthologized writer in the English language -- at least, as far as I was told, (and) I didn't know science fiction... but I believed it. The man was an adorable human being, but his mind was absolutely incredible.... We came to the conclusion that he was somebody from outer space. He was just visiting here. He could talk, he could speak the language, he could do everything like any other human being. But he wasn't. So that was wonderful and, at the same time, it was terrifying." (17-3)

Justman found Sturgeon to be wonderful -- and frustrating. His wrote Black:

> As presently written, I'm sure you realize that this show is inordinately expensive. Most of the show will have to be shot on location, and there are piles and piles of extras and actors and wardrobe and other chozzerai that we need to review rather carefully. Also, the set construction as written is enough for a number of shows. And the Special Effects -- hoo-hoo-hoo!... I refer you to scene 132. You may have guessed that I intend to make a big change in this scene, if at all possible. I know it's nice for Finagle to lead a horse with McCoy's body across a saddle straight into the interior of a rock wall. But boy it sure as hell doesn't do anything to advance the story and it sure as hell does something to advance my psychiatrist bills.... You may have been able to determine that I have had problems with this show. Well, that's right. (RJ17-4)

Roddenberry, if nothing else, was happy about the peace offering sent by Sturgeon and sent one of his own, writing back to the author:

> Let me start this by saying how impressed I am at the attitude with which you approach all this. It is most trying for any writer to adopt himself to the terribly arbitrary rules of the current television form, and for one of your stature and success it must seem doubly annoying at times. (GR17-5)

Roddenberry had concerns as well -- nine single-spaced pages worth, beginning with the title. Of this, he wrote:

> "Finagle's Planet" seems to give too much emphasis to the character "Finagle," when actually our aim is to explore Kirk in more depth than this single character out of his past can provide. (GR17-5)

This still was not a Kirk story, despite all the hinting and pleading from Roddenberry and Stan Robertson. And the script remained episodic, with the various imaginative elements not properly pulled together and laid squarely on the shoulders of the series' lead.

Roddenberry's bad news letter to Sturgeon closed:

> My feeling is that very little of this first draft can be saved. It needs an almost complete rewrite. (GR17-5)

Sturgeon did his contractually required rewrite -- his third draft of the script, delivering most of the pages on September 8, with the balance the following day. Robert Justman delivered all of his criticism on the same day, this time directed to *Star Trek*'s new producer -- Gene L. Coon -- writing:

> Because of the way the screenplay is constructed, I am not sure whether we have sufficient length at the present time. There is [still] an awful lot of camera direction and scene description, which may affect the page count to our detriment. (RJ17-5)

As for the Alice in Wonderland scene, and the way it was presented in this script, Justman told Coon:

> If we attempt to put someone in a large rabbit suit, it will look like someone in a large rabbit suit. (RJ17-5)

And it did.

Janice Rand was still in this script. Of this, Justman wrote:

> I would suggest that we cast Rand's part as a Yeoman, but bring in someone new for this episode. Also, is it me or do I detect that the Yeoman becomes much too personal with Kirk in this sequence? (RJ17-5)

She did. In the next draft, by Coon, Rand was taken out, a new Yeoman put in her place, and the "much too personal" business was now between her and McCoy.

Justman continued:

> We establish the fact that Sulu shoots a police revolver six times. Later on in the script you will discover that Kirk, using the same pistol, fires at a mounted knight in armor five times. This would make the revolver an eleven-shooter. I can just see the letters we'll get from numerous members of the National Rifle Association when they see this show. (RJ17-5)

Coon removed a few of the shots. Sulu fires the gun four times; later Kirk shoots it three times. That many shots were needed for proper pacing in the running and charging sequences. It was one shot too many but the way Coon figured it, the same powers that created the gun could create an extra bullet if needed.

There was much more Justman didn't like. He wrote:

> I think all dialogue and usage of such terms such as "Roger," "Wilco," "over and out," etc., should be gone over and brought up to date with the terminology we have established in the series. (RJ17-5)

Roger that. Coon made the changes.

Justman continued:

> Bailey sees a full-grown Bengal Tiger. Whatever beast he sees, he will have to see it in CUTAWAY. Unless, of course, you want to screw around working with a full-grown Bengal tiger on location or on stage. In which case, include me out. (RJ17-5)

Bailey was changed to Rodriguez. Other than that, Coon *did* want to screw around with a full-grown Bengal tiger on location. Justman would be proven right -- it went terribly wrong (see "Production Diary").

Sturgeon was still determined to show the workings of the factory underground, where all the manifestations of the crew's fantasies were brought to life. Justman was equally determined that this would not happen, and wrote:

> I definitely feel we cannot afford to build the set as indicated. Couldn't we just DISSOLVE IN the Custodian on location and have done with the enormous expense of building the special rock set and all the special effects routines needed to operate it? (RJ17-5)

This too would be changed by Coon.

Kellam de Forest gave notes, as well. He was adamant that this planet could not look as described, which was devoid of both animals and insects. He wrote:

> Lush and complete vegetation is ecologically impossible without insect life. (KDF17)

Coon changed a couple lines of dialogue. The planet was now devoid of only "animal life." De Forest continued:

> The "White Knight" is currently an advertising gimmick of AJAX. To avoid commercial identification and possible derogation, suggest White Knight used not be similar to White Knight of the commercials, e.g. have him on a black horse. (KDF17)

The White Knight, then, became the Black Knight. Not only was his horse changed from white to black but so were his staff and much of the body armor he wore. At this time, Coon was not about to debate the issue -- Ajax was a much more powerful force in television than *Star Trek*.

Roddenberry had notes for Coon, too, writing:

> I like the fantasy of this show. We don't have anything else like it. LET'S DO IT -- with revisions.... We wind up the script very quickly - all the answers pat. But there are strings dangling -- Ruth for one. And... Finnegan for another. Kirk is [still] not so active in this show -- except he keeps getting beat up by Finnegan. I'd like to see him moving and doing and solving.... Why are all these pleasant fancies by our people getting to be pretty darn destructive to them? Is this our Theme?...Why is Kirk taking all this time over fighting with Finnegan? What about Ruth -- wouldn't he rather wrestle with her? What is Kirk proving with Finnegan anyway? He keeps getting clobbered by the guy. (GR17-6)

Roddenberry and Coon put their heads together, came up with answers they both liked -- Kirk wants to get back to Ruth and he *will* get back to Ruth, but Finnegan teases him with riddles and seems to have answers and this keeps our Captain chasing after him. And while Kirk does take a beating from Finnegan, in the end it is Kirk who beats the tar out of his fantasy, something he always wanted to do. As for the theme, it was sharpened to make the statement that fantasies *can* prove to be harmful if not kept in check. And this would now be revealed in the end.

Coon took a turn at the writing, with the Yellow Cover 1st Draft from October 3 and the Final Draft from October 14, with revised pages dated October 17.

Stan Robertson read Coon's handling of the script. Many of the NBC man's previous reservations had been resolved but one still remained. In a phone call to Roddenberry, not Coon, Robertson expressed his concerns over the more fantastic elements of the story. To receive network acceptance, those elements had to be toned down.

Roddenberry agreed to the terms. There was just one problem: he forgot to tell Coon.

Pre-Production
October 11-14 & 17-18, 1966 (6 days prep).

While the rewriting process continued, Robert Justman was arranging locations for "Shore Leave." This was only the second episode to shoot on location rather than on a soundstage ("Miri" being the first). The primary site was Africa USA, a wildlife preserve 40 miles north of Los Angeles. The secondary location, Vasquez Rocks, was less than a half-hour's drive from the first. Both properties were owned and operated by Ralph Helfer, a highly proficient animal trainer for film and TV, and his wife Toni.

Robert Sparr, hired to direct, had begun his career on TV's *Lassie*. He then moved to Warner Bros. where he was assigned episodes of *Cheyenne*, *Bronco*, *77 Sunset Strip*, and *Hawaiian Eye*. He was also a film editor, having cut several episodes of *The Wild, Wild West* in 1965, as well as directing for that series. In 1966, he proved good at fast-paced action sequences with *The Rat Patrol*.

Joe D'Agosta, with input from Sparr, booked the supporting cast.

Emily Banks on *Bewitched* (Screen Gems Television, 1972) (From cosmicduckling.com)

Emily Banks, selected to play Yeoman Tonia Barrows, began taking modeling jobs to help pay the tuition for her schooling in Boston. Business Administration was her planned vocation, but those modeling jobs brought unexpected dividends. In 1960, Banks won the title of "Miss Rheingold" and appeared in advertisements for the beer maker, and that led to steady work in both print and TV ads. She said, "I was living in New York by then. I guess I had the right look for that time. I did, like, 16 Alcoa [vinyl flooring] commercials -- 'Dancing through your kitchen' -- and about 17 or 18 Salem [cigarettes] commercials. I did Pepsodent [toothpaste] and every Proctor and Gamble thing you could imagine. I used to get hired to do some of the new fashions, too, when they would do a showing, because they wanted an All-American Girl. Eventually, I had to leave New York because I had 38 commercials on the air and I was so saturated that I couldn't do anymore. So, I came out here and signed with Universal in '66." (9a)

Universal got its money out of Banks, putting her to work in five productions in a single year, including *The Plainsman*, starring Don Murray, and *Gunfight in Abilene*, with second billing to lead Bobby Darin (and a screenplay by *Star Trek*'s John D.F. Black).

Once free of her studio contract, Banks picked a slew of Los Angeles TV ads before getting a reading at *Star Trek*. She said, "I came in for an audition and all I got to see were just a couple pages of the script. I really didn't know anything about the show, and I knew nothing about the script; I just knew my part; that I was supposed to be Dr. McCoy's love interest. I read with Joe D'Agosta [who did McCoy's lines]. He was a doll, and so nice. Gene Roddenberry and Gene Coon were there, and I remember that I didn't have to go back for a second reading. I knew I got the job." (9a)

Bruce Mars as a rascal named Finnegan
(Unaired film trim courtesy of Gerald Gurian)

Bruce Mars, in the second of three turns on *Star Trek*, played Finnegan. He said, "I came from New York, as every other actor did, where I'd appeared in summer stock and off Broadway things, then showed up in California with those credits behind me and a few numbers for people to call. And for some reason, the karma was good and I went to work now and then, in between starving and trying to feed my dog. I'd known Joe D'Agosta from when he was casting *Rawhide* and we just hit it off and he gave me a little role there. He was a super, super guy. We kept in touch and he got me the meeting at *Star Trek*." (113a)

Mars tried out for the role of Lt. Bailey in "The Corbomite Maneuver" but director Joseph Sargent preferred Anthony Call for that part. To help keep Mars and his dog from starving, D'Agosta gave the struggling actor a day's work as a background extra playing a crewman. D'Agosta was determined to find something worthy of Mars' talents. "And then up came this character," Mars recalled, "and Joe said, 'Come on in; do a reading for this.' So I went in and just nailed that baby. And I got the job right on the spot." (113a)

Mars did indeed nail Finnegan, and D'Agosta would bring him back as a bewildered 20th Century New York City cop in the second-season episode "Assignment: Earth."

Oliver McGowan, the Caretaker, was 59. He had over 100 filmed appearances between 1957 and 1970, usually as doctors, military officers, sheriffs, and governors.

Perry Lopez, as Esteban Rodriguez, was 35. He would amass around 100 credits in both film and on TV, starting in 1954. Along with *Zorro* and *Wagon Train*, he had noticeable parts in features such as 1962's *Taras Bulba*. From here, he went on to play the prominent role of Lt. Escobar in *Chinatown* and its sequel, *The Two Jakes*.

Barbara Baldavin first played Angela Martine, the grieving bride-to-be in "Balance of Terror." This time, she is the one who dies -- at least, temporarily. After being repaired by the Caretaker, her real-life husband, Joe D'Agosta, booked her in two more *Star Trek* episodes ("Space Seed" and "Turnabout Intruder").

Shirley Bonne, as Ruth, was older than 20, the age Kirk remembered his former flame to have been. Bonne was actually 31. She made the rounds on TV between 1960 and '69, with stops including *That Girl* and *Mannix*.

Production Diary
Filmed October 19, 20, 21, 24, 25, 26 & 27, 1966
(Planned 6 day production, ran one day over; total cost: $199,654).

As the production dates approached, Roddenberry, having suffered from a bout of exhaustion, took a break. He left behind a memo telling Gene Coon how Stan Robertson felt the script still leaned too much toward fantasy and wanted a few of the more fantastic sequences reined in. In his haste to leave for his own shore leave, Roddenberry failed to have the memo delivered to Coon.

Production began on Wednesday, October 19, 1966. Roddenberry returned from his R & R that morning and found the memo he intended for Coon still on his own desk. A copy of the shooting script was next to it. In the opening teaser, as it had been in all the previous drafts, was the giant white rabbit ... who can tell time ... and who can talk. "Oh my paws and whiskers! I shall be late!"

As cell phones, or their equivalent, were still just props on *Star Trek*, Roddenberry high-tailed it for Africa USA, over an hour's drive from Desilu. William Shatner recalled, "I can still remember him roaring up to our production vehicles in a cloud of dust." (156-8)

It was too late to nix the talking white rabbit -- that had been the first sequence filmed this day -- but other story elements from Theodore Sturgeon's fertile imagination were soon altered. Roddenberry found a shady tree and began rewriting the script on a yellow legal pad. The changes had to be driven to Desilu for typing, copying by the mimeo department, and then driven back to location. Fax machines, like cell phones, were also still in the future.

"I recall we had a lot of script problems," George Takei said. "There was one point where we actually shut down production and waited for the rewrites to be driven out. I had my running shoes, so I went out and got a good run in. Some people took their shirts off and worked on their suntan. But once the pages arrived, we had to do quick study." (171-1)

Also on location this day, William Shatner, DeForest Kelley, Emily Banks, Percy Lopez, Barbara Baldavin, and Bruce Mars, all for sequences in the lush "Ext. Glade #1" area. Emily Banks said, "I still hadn't seen any more of the script until I got out to [Africa USA]; that's when I started to see more pages and I asked, 'Oh, what is this?' and 'What is that?' I hadn't had much exposure to this sort of show, and had yet to see any episodes. But my part made sense; the love interest with McCoy. And he was just a doll. I really loved working with him -- such a nice man and a real gentleman." (9a)

Bruce Mars recalled, "Theodore Sturgeon had written the Finnegan character so he was a little nasty and moody, and I read that thing and I thought, 'This could be better. I'd like to make this guy fun, not nasty but just a bit annoying and bring him to life in a fun way.' And so I had a good talk with Bob Sparr and he said, 'You'll have to go a little higher to make those kind of changes.'" (113a)

This meant Mars would have to run his ideas by one of the producers, something that was not likely to happen.

"Little did I know that there were a lot of problems with the way the script was written," Mars said. "So, I'll be darned, but on that first day out on location, there's our boss [Roddenberry] sitting there on the set rewriting everything. And Theodore Sturgeon shows up too, and I introduced myself and he looked me over and said, 'Yeah, you could be that Irish rascal.' We talked a little bit and I said, 'I've got a couple ideas for the character, which Bob Sparr liked,' and I gave Sturgeon my ideas about making Finnegan a bit more charming, more playful. And he said, 'You know what, do it.' So Gene Roddenberry was sitting under a big tree and one of the sound men said, 'Good God, Gene is rewriting the whole script.' I said, 'You're kidding, what's up?' He said, 'Well, there have been some complications with the network and he's rewriting all these sequences for the next two days.' So I went up and said, 'Mr. Roddenberry, my God, I know you're a writer, but you're rewriting everything we're doing today?' He said, 'Yeah, and I'm going to make Finnegan more important in this. I just got a feeling that character is going to light up things.' So I told him my idea about the character, and said, 'I'm ready, and I'm athletic and coordinated and I want to do all the fight stuff myself.' He said, 'Well, we do have a stunt man that will take part in that. But there will be plenty in there for you to do.' And he fleshed the fight out and added all those scenes in that made it so much better." (113a)

As for that scene already shot with a girl named Alice and a giant white rabbit, Bill Blackburn, seen frequently on *Star Trek* in nonspeaking parts, including often sitting at the helm as the navigation officer, was chosen to be the man in the rabbit suit. He later blamed this job for giving him a lifelong case of claustrophobia, saying, "Bill Theiss always sewed *everything* on. No matter what it was, he sewed it. I never had claustrophobia before, but we were out on location, and it was warm, and I could only see out of the mouth. They didn't have any screening where my eyes would have seen it, so I had to tilt my head back to see out of the rabbits' mouth.... I had this mask on for about 45 minutes while Bill was sewing, because he wanted to blend this thing in from underneath. And when they put the bowtie on, it not only closed off my air but it closed off where I could see. And *it* hit. It was like a feeling that I never had before. I said, 'Bill, can I get out of this -- *Now*!' And I heard, 'Oh, just a few more minutes.' And then there were a few more minutes, and then a few more, and then, finally, I ripped the whole head off. It didn't wreck the suit, but the head came completely off. And I said, 'I can't put this on like this unless you have a way in which I can lift it up.' And he grumbled, and one of the ladies with him said, 'I can put Velcro on it.' And I thought, 'Well, why didn't you think of that in the first place!' And so they put Velcro on it. But that was me in that suit. [Laughing] That was my big claim to fame." (17a)

**Day 2, with Emily Banks and DeForest Kelley
(Unaired film trim courtesy of Gerald Gurian)**

On Day 2, Thursday, filming continued on the "Ext. Glade" location for the attack of Don Juan and the Black Knight. For this, Leonard Nimoy joined the cast for McCoy's death scene and the gunning down of the knight. Next, Kirk chasing Finnegan. Mars recalled, "Everybody was worrying about the budget and how long the filming was taking, and Bob Sparr says, 'Hey, listen, Bruce, we're losing light and I want to do everything in one take.' And so we only had one shot at a lot of that stuff, with Shatner chasing me -- one take, one take, and one take. We just nailed it. I of course had my fingers crossed and everything, but I knew the character; I had him down. And so it all worked out

431

and it really helped them to catch up a little bit." (113a)

There were problems, of course. Mars, despite being athletic and having played semi-pro baseball, twisted his ankle. He said, "It started to swell up pretty bad and I didn't take off the boot. If I had, I would have been dead. So, we continued shooting and, with all that action that was needed, my mind just rose above it, even though I could hardly walk. And when all the shooting was over, my foot was black and blue." (113a)

Mars was driven back to Hollywood and taken to Citizens Emergency Hospital for x-rays and treatment. As a result, the shooting schedule went through yet another of many revisions.

**Day 2. Bill McGovern slates a shot at Africa USA
(from startrekhistory.com and startrekpropauthority.com)**

Filming continued without Mars until 9 p.m. with large arc lights being used to simulate daylight for the remaining close angle shots. Many in the cast and all of the crew were unable to make it home for the premiere of "What Are Little Girls Made Of?," the seventh episode to air on NBC.

Day 3, Friday. More filming in the area of "Ext. Glade #1" took place, filming the airplane strafing scene and the tag scene featuring the Caretaker and his "Two Beauties." Emily Banks said, "I remember one thing, there was the lovely older gentleman who was the caretaker of the planet. He was such a nice man; so gracious and so handsome, but he had this one line that he kept forgetting. And they'd do it again. And then they'd do it again. And when I finally saw it, he had started to say the line and you could see he was starting to forget it, but the way it came out of him, when he caught up with the line, it looked absolutely like stunning acting. His expression was just so precious." (9a)

Also shot this day: the scene with the tiger which Robert Justman was so against.

William Shatner, unlike Justman, saw no need for concern and was even hot on the idea of Kirk wrestling the cat. He felt the action sequence would be good for the episode ... until he saw the 150 pound animal tearing into its midday snack -- a chunk of uncooked meat on a large bone just about the size of a man's thigh. And then the tiger got loose.

"I'll never forget it," said Bill Blackburn. "One of the grips was carrying a reflector and he tripped and, all of a sudden, that tiger just went berserk. The tiger had a chain around its neck, but the chain came off from whatever base it was attached to." (17a)

Eddie Paskey, Shatner's stand-in for the lighting set-ups, wasn't about to stand in against a tiger. He remembered, "Bill was like six feet from this thing when the chain came off and, of course, everybody went nuts." (135-2)

"In my mind's eye, I see Shatner jumping on top of the big prop box," Blackburn added. "Everybody else was, like, transfixed; they didn't know whether to run or not. And then the trainer came running in and got hold of the chain. It was one of those things that could have been really bad." (17a)

Shatner recalled, "Instantly my testicles rose up into my Adam's apple and the ignorant machismo that had been pulsing so heartily through my veins was replaced by sheer abject terror. I stood there trying not to look too horrified as I gracefully backed down [from the idea of wrestling the tiger], 'for the good of the show.'" (156-8)

At mid-day, the company made a move to the "Upper Lake" for the scene featuring Sulu finding the handgun and target practicing, and multiple camera dolly shots of Kirk and others running along the path. These later sequences required the laying of track so the large heavy camera and the men who operated it could be mounted on a rail platform and glide along, "tracking" Kirk and those who trailed behind as he ran toward the source of the gun shots. It is an elaborate type of shot and takes hours to set up and execute.

Emily Banks said, "I didn't realize that I was going to be running around with legs hanging out [from the uniform] and shoulders hanging out [from the torn tunic]. But I do remember I did a lot of running. There was a *lot* of running. And I remember thinking on the first couple days, 'They don't want an actress, they want an athlete!' I was exhausted, and we kept running and running." (9a)

Bruce Mars said, "We did do a lot of running and jumping. And Emily Banks did too. She was running back and forth with Shatner for the camera. And I saw her a few times just huffing and puffing afterwards. But so cooperative. She never complained." (113a)

Of her running partner, Banks said, "Bill's a lovely man; very talented; very calm. In fact, *everybody* was very calm, despite the pace of the work. It was just very easy to work with them. Everybody couldn't have been more helpful. We had a good time." (9a)

It was 7 p.m. and already dark for over an hour when the company turned off their daylight-simulating lights and wrapped for the night.

Day 4, Monday, October 24. Work continued around and near the Upper Lake, as Kirk chasing Finnegan (with Bruce Mars' ankle having sufficiently healed) toward the rock area, and McCoy and Yeoman Barrows finding the storybook gown. After this, the company packed up and drove to Vasquez Rocks for the first of many visits. Work began late in the day for the scene where Kirk meets the image of his former flame, Ruth. The big "HMI" arc lights were again brought in to simulate daylight as the company continued shooting an hour into darkness, stopping at 7 p.m.

Day 5, Tuesday. Spock's beam down at Vasquez Rocks was filmed, as well as more with the Tiger (now kept on a chain -- a chain even the camera could see), and Finnegan baiting Kirk to follow him further into the area of the giant jagged rocks. Bruce Mars recalled, "Bob Sparr said to me, 'Hey, Bruce, are you afraid of heights?' And I don't like heights! So I said, 'Well ... why? What's up?' And he said, 'Do you see this big rock up there -- it's about five stories high and I'd love you on top of that baiting on our captain.' And I said, 'Holy mackerel, that's way up there! What's the shot?' He says, 'We're going to shoot at you from below, you up there jumping up and down and waving your hands and everything.' I said, 'Okay,' even though it wasn't anywhere near being okay, and I went up the back of the rocks and stepped out on there. It was made all the more difficult because they had those high-heeled boots which weren't really grabbing on the rock surface. So I'm out there and Bob Sparr is yelling up at me, 'Alright, move forward! Forward!' And, man, I was freaking out!

And he was yelling up, "Forward! Forward! Come on Bruce, move forward! Now jump up and down and wave your arms!' Man, that was wild." (113a)

Also filmed, the start of the epic Kirk/Finnegan fight.

Day 6, Wednesday. The company had expected to be back at the studio for Day 6, but Robert Sparr, suffering through all the last minute rewriting, laying track for numerous dolly shots, and chasing daylight, had by this point fallen a full day behind. Nearly all of this day was spent shooting the balance of the fight between Kirk and Finnegan.

Bruce Mars recalled, "Bob told me that Gene Roddenberry wanted the fight expanded, that he felt it would be good for the show and make a great visual of me and the captain fighting. So he said, 'Bruce, make it rough and tumble.' I really enjoyed Shatner in that. We talked about the fight, and with Bob Sparr about working out some ballet moves -- 'This will happen here and this will happen there, and the stuntman will do this, and you will do that.' Shatner was very nice to me, asking me what I was doing and what I wanted to do. You never really know what to expect -- incredible arrogance or whatever -- but I remember

Day 6: With sun setting and temperatures dropping, Nimoy and Shatner rehearse dialogue for post Kirk/Finnegan fight scene (Courtesy of Gerald Gurian)

thinking, 'This guy's a really good guy.' And he made sure I had a couple good scenes during the fight. He'd say, 'Let's do this and let's do that' and, 'Ah no, the camera should be here not there,' and he would go talk to Bob Sparr about it. So he got me some good moments and I have nothing to say but good things about him." (113a)

Shatner, barely covered by his torn tunic, braves the cold (Courtesy of Gerald Gurian)

It may very well have been the best-staged fight shot for TV. Paul Baxley and Vince Deadrick subbed for Shatner and Mars, respectively, for the more brutal punches and flips.

Bruce Mars said, "I thought it was great. And something that spoke well of Bob Sparr is he was always taking the time to talk to Jerry Finnerman. He'd tell Jerry his ideas, but if

Jerry had an idea that sounded right, he'd do it. He'd sign off on it and let Jerry do it the way he wanted. And I thought that was terrific to see a director and a cinematographer in such good sync." (113a)

So much time was put into the fight, in fact, that there was precious little time to shoot the other scene that had to be completed this final day on location -- Sulu's encounter with the Samurai Warrior.

George Takei said, "I remember us losing the sun. That scene where the Samurai soldier leaps out -- that was supposed to be daylight. The beginning part we shot in daylight, and we had to match it. We were shooting that at nine o'clock at night. They brought in all of the lights they could to try and simulate daylight. It was really tense." (171-1)

The location phase of the filming finally wrapped a bit earlier than Takei recalled, but still well into darkness at 8 p.m.

Day 7, Thursday, October 27, was spent in safe harbor, on Desilu Stage 9, for scenes on the bridge and in Kirk's quarters. Emily Banks continued to be featured prominently with the series regulars in a role that many believed might become a recurring one. The last shot for "Shore Leave" was taken by 5:52 p.m. And, finally, that was a wrap, allowing cast and crew to make it home in time for NBC's first airing of "Miri" -- broadcast episode #8.

Post-Production
October 28 to December 6, 1966. Music score recorded on December 2, 1966.

There was magic in the editing room, too. Fabien Tordjmann and Editing Team #3 excelled at piecing this episode together.

"I was fascinated with 'Shore Leave' because they talked of being in a place where all your wishes are fulfilled," Tordjmann said. "They shot with two cameras, and the director was Robert Sparr, a wonderful man." (176)

That five-minute fight between Kirk and Finnegan, alone, is a masterwork. And it was Tordjmann's idea to let Finnegan pop in and out of the scenery at Vasquez Rocks, helping compensate for inconsistencies in the filming and, at the same time, present the dreamlike structure of the story.

Bruce Mars said, "We went back into the studio and did some wild lines for audio – with the laughing and yelling, that maybe didn't catch so good out at Vasquez Rocks." (113a)

"[They] didn't have time to finish the sequence where the man [Finnegan] is taunting Kirk," Tordjmann said. "I didn't know how to put that thing together. It was really a problem, and 20 minutes before the first screening I decided how to do it -- to literally have him popping in everywhere, taunting Kirk and talking to him over Kirk's shoulder.... The guy runs, Kirk turns around, and he goes somewhere else. I had to put them all in, but it was really wild.... And they loved it. They kept it that way." (176)

It was also Tordjmann's idea to do something different with the Enterprise, and this is the only episode where the ship is shown orbiting a planet from right to left. The reason the large model could only be filmed from the left was that the right side had access points for the electrical wiring. To achieve the effect seen here, the film had to be flipped. On screen for an instant and unapparent unless closely scrutinized, the numbers on the nacelles are reversed.

The Westheimer Company handled the Photographic Effects, including coloring the shore leave planet in a strikingly rich green.

Gerald Fried, 38, was hired to score the unusual episode. The composer had been writing music for television and films since the early 1950s, including a pair of movies directed by Stanley Kubrick -- *The Killing* and *Paths of Glory*. On TV, he was a frequent contributor to series as diverse as *The Man from U.N.C.L.E.*, *Mission: Impossible*, and *Gilligan's Island*.

Fried said, "It was Bob Justman with whom I dealt. I met Gene Roddenberry maybe twice. Now, this was before they handed us DVDs of the work, so we had only one or two shots at watching the edited episode. In a day or two, the music editor would send us timing notes down to a tenth or even a hundredth of a second. And that's in front of us. There's every start and stop of dialogue; every pause over a second is indicated by the music editor. So it's pretty much all there in front of us. We know it's going to be a crunch of a schedule, and we're used to it, and it's kind of exciting. And, yeah, the fact that it was so varied was a lot of fun. That episode was right up my alley." (69-5)

Fried recalled his inspiration for the fight between Kirk and Finnegan, saying, "Here's this Irish tough kid who tormented Captain Kirk in college. I thought, what could be more exciting and stimulating than an Irish jig? But you can't make it too danceable, that would be ludicrous. So I thought, let me take the feeling of an Irish jig and put it in some kind of symphonic setting. And so, instead of playing your ordinary battle music, make it an Irish jig battle music. So that was the feeling and thinking behind that one. I just followed them with all the starts and stops. That's why we had timing notes. A minute and seventeen and two-thirds seconds, they rest; Kirk slips on the rock here at a minute and twenty-three and nine-tenths seconds." (63-5)

Justman, in a letter to Coon, said:

> The music was delightful. Gerald Fried truly found the right notes and tempo for the moments between Kirk and Ruth, and also for the epic Kirk-Finnegan fight.... In its own way, the action sequence between Kirk and Finnegan rivals the very famous fist fight in *The Quiet Man*. (RJ17-6)

Fried later said, "Bob Justman actually told me that the fight music rivaled the music in *The Quiet Man* after the scoring session, which pleased me no end." (63-5)

The music accompanying Kirk's reunion with Ruth, as Justman pointed out, was also immensely effective. The hauntingly beautiful love theme would later be used to great effect in "This Side of Paradise" and "The Apple."

In 2011, Gerald Fried said, "I get letters from all over the world, including references to that theme (Ruth's love theme)." (63-5)

After only two viewings of the episode, and less than a week to compose the music using only timing notes, Fried's score was recorded and laid onto the completed episode. There could be no further manipulating.

Fried said, "They were under such pressure to go on to the next episode that once it was scored they didn't touch the print." (63-5)

Justman liked all the post audio in "Shore Leave," and made a point of telling this to Coon as well in his lengthy letter, saying:

> The use of the tinklybell sound as a planet background noise was a very good thought for this show. It was different and additionally gives a touch of magic to the proceedings. (RJ17-6)

Justman told Coon that he was "particularly impressed" with the work of Bruce Mars and Emily Banks, as Finnegan and Yeoman Barrows. He felt that Barrows, in particular, came off as a person that people would like to see again, and the rapport between her and McCoy should be explored in future episodes. Coon was not in agreement. He felt the flirtation between her character and McCoy, as directed by Sparr, had gone a bit far. If Yeoman Barrows returned, the implied relationship would have to be dealt with. The easy solution: Emily Banks was not offered further work. Bruce Mars would be – for Season Two's "Assignment: Earth."

Justman's letter to Coon ended:

> I think that "Shore Leave" was probably the most entertaining *Star Trek* show we have produced to date. I am probably alone in my opinion, but I am telling the truth as I see it. (RJ17-6)

It needed to be the most entertaining *Star Trek* show produced to date. It cost enough. With the reduced budget from Desilu, down to $185,000 per episode from $193,500, episodes such as "Shore Leave" would be few and far between. This one came in at $199,654 ($1.5 million today). The series' cash surplus -- thanks to the savings that came from transforming "The Cage" into "The Menagerie" -- had now dwindled to $7,772.

On the very day Sparr was wrapping, Roddenberry was rightfully covering his and Coon's asses with NBC. Along with the Revised Final Draft of the script, the one written *after* the start of filming, he sent a cover letter to Stan Robertson. It said:

> Perhaps there is some "I never break my word" ego behind this, but I would appreciate your reading over carefully this final version of "Shore Leave." You may recall I promised you this would not be an "illusion" show. It isn't now. No one was at fault, certainly not Gene Coon. In his gradual switch-over to taking the reins of more and more of the producing, this was one item about [this] particular show we never did get around to discussing. And, as you know, I was on vacation.... The final rewrite I did was accomplished while the show was actually being shot, at considerable risk and hazard to our budget and schedule. I felt I owed it to NBC and to you. (GR17-6)

It was a valiant attempt, but the talking white rabbit opener was going to have jaws dropping at NBC Burbank.

Roddenberry would survive. Others, sadly, did not.

Despite the excellent direction, Robert Sparr had fallen out of favor with some. Bruce Mars shared, "I know there were some grumbles. Some of the actors weren't thrilled with Bob Sparr and how he handled things, but, boy, I loved him. I thought he did a great job. He knew what he wanted to shoot. But he must have rubbed a few of them the wrong way with some of his shots. I remember they laid two sets of track for different dolly shots to have Shatner running after me. I wouldn't say there was friction, but I could feel an undercurrent there that perhaps [taking the time to shoot with the dolly and making Shatner do all that running] was just over the top." (113a)

In his post-production letter to Gene Coon, Bob Justman argued:

> Although I realize that a great deal of effort went into the cutting of this film, I am of the opinion that Robert Sparr did a superlative job. I realize that I am probably alone in my opinion, but I think that the conception of his shots and the motion and energy he created in his depiction of the exterior scenes was a truly creative achievement. Notwithstanding the fact that Bill Shatner and some of the other actors found much fault with Bob Sparr's abilities as a director of actors, his overall filmic judgment has definitely come through in this show. Perhaps he did not give lip service to the egos of our series' regulars, but Bob Sparr really cared about what he was doing and I, for one, am sorry that circumstances [are making] it impossible for us to bring him back. (RJ17-6)

Justman was right. Sparr would not return. Sadly, the director was killed in a small plane crash three years later when scouting locations with *Star Trek* cinematographer Jerry Finnerman. The pilot was also killed. Only Finnerman, severely injured, survived.

Release / Reaction:
Premiere air date: 12/29/66. NBC repeat broadcast: 6/8/67.

RATINGS / Nielsen 30-Market report for Thursday, Dec. 29, 1966:

8:30 - 9 p.m., with 60.7% U.S. TVs in use:		Rating:	Share:
NBC:	*Star Trek* (first half)	17.6	29.0%
ABC:	**The Dating Game**	**20.1**	**33.1%**
CBS:	*My Three Sons*	16.0	26.4%
Independent stations:		8.3	11.5%
9 - 9:30 p.m., with 61.3% of U.S. TVs in use:			
NBC:	*Star Trek* (second half)	**20.0**	**32.6%**
ABC:	*Bewitched*	19.9	32.5%
CBS:	*Thursday Night Movie* (start)	15.1	24.6%
Independent stations:		8.2	10.3%

During the first half-hour of "Shore Leave," *Star Trek* placed a strong second to *The Dating Game*. With the second half, *Trek* was No. 1, snagging nearly 33% of the total television viewing audience. *The CBS Thursday Night Movie*, in third place, was 1962's *Five Finger Exercise*, starring Rosalind Russell and Maximilian Schell.

For its repeat airing on NBC, on June 8, 1967, "Shore Leave" was the second *Star Trek* episode to be given the spotlight of a *TV Guide* half-page "CLOSE-UP" listing.

TV Guide was not alone in giving this episode complimentary mention for its encore network broadcast. Joan Crosby, for her syndicated column, *TV Scout*, had passed "Shore Leave" over for review the first time ... but was singing its praises come the summer. Among the newspapers to run Crosby's review on June 8, 1967 was the *Times Daily*, Nashville, in Tennessee. Crosby wrote:

> "Shore Leave." The pick of the programs tonight is this imaginative Star Trek episode, where the crew finds a paradise planet where dreams and sometimes nightmares literally come true. It begins when Dr. McCoy sees the White Rabbit and Alice. Then Kirk sees Finnegan, the practical joker and the bane of his days as a plebe. Others in the shore party see Don Juan, a Samurai warrior, wild animals, and a black knight, who proves deadly.

The positive press translated to a stronger audience share when A.C. Nielsen did its nose counting.

RATINGS / Nielsen National report for Thursday, June 8, 1967:

8:30 - 9 p.m.:		Share:	Households:
NBC:	**Star Trek (first half)**	**31.4%**	**10,980,000**
ABC:	*Bewitched*	30.7%	8,730,000
CBS:	*My Three Sons*	28.7%	8,180,000
Independent station		9.2%	No data
9 - 9:30 p.m.:		Share:	Households:
NBC:	*Star Trek* (second half)	**32.7%**	No data
ABC:	*That Girl*	29.0%	No data
CBS:	*Thursday Night Movie* (start)	23.3%	No data
Independent stations:		15.0%	No data

According to Nielsen, the repeat of "Shore Leave" won its time slot. The CBS movie was 1962's *Damn the Defiant!*, starring Alec Guinness. Despite the tendency in America for families to hit the road for their summer vacations, thereby reducing the number of households tuning in, Nielsen's estimate of 10,980,000 families watching (factoring an average of two people watching in each household) gave this rerun of *Star Trek* an audience of nearly 22 million. And this did not count those viewing it over NBC's affiliate stations in Canada, where *Star Trek* had achieved "hit" status.

Aftermath

The amusement planet would be visited again for an episode of *Star Trek: the Animated Series*. In "Once Upon a Planet," cartoon drawings allowed for some of Theodore Sturgeon's original concepts to be realized, such as the mechanical arms that rise up from trap doors.

Entertainment Weekly, in its 1995 special issue devoted to *Star Trek*, ranked this episode as being the 17th best from the original series, with the comment: "Someone was toking Romulan reefer when this one got made -- but it holds up surprisingly well."

This author agrees with Robert Justman -- "Shore Leave" rates higher than No. 17. This is among *Star Trek*'s very best.

One final footnote: In January, 1969, Los Angeles was hit by a torrential storm, flooding Ralph Helfer's Africa USA. Most of the animals perished and mudslides rendered the location unusable for future filming. The Helfers moved away and the destroyed ranch remained unoccupied until 1987 when actress and animal advocate Tippi Hedren purchased the land to be used as an animal preserve, which she christened "Shambala."

From the Mailbag

Received the week after the initial airing of "Shore Leave":

> Dear Mr. Roddenberry: Any list of compliments about your show and its stars would run volumes, so, in the interest of brevity, I will simply say *Star Trek* is the grooviest! And my family never misses it. My girl friends and I are mostly in love with the three stars. [But] what happened to Grace Lee Whitney as Yeoman Rand? We all enjoyed Janice very much and hope that nobody has assigned the Captain a new yeoman…. My girlfriends and myself, firm believers in intelligent life on other planets, have spent so much time thinking about and discussing the various things mentioned in the course of *Star Trek* that I think we've come up with a new school of philosophy -- Futurism, perhaps, but I think "Galacticism" has a nicer ring. Miss Robin Y. (La Habra, California).

To Whom It May Concern, What happened to Yeoman Rand?! (Several)

While far from the truth, the official response went like this:

> Grace Lee Whitney left *Star Trek* in order to be able to accept a greater variety of roles. She has since appeared in episodes of many television shows… Perhaps Yeoman Rand is still on board the Enterprise and happens not to be on duty when adventures happen, or perhaps she decided there was no point to competing with the Enterprise for Kirk's affections and transferred out. Ruth Berman, for *Star Trek*.

Memories

Bruce Mars said, "I loved those guys. God, it was so much fun. It was great on the set. DeForest Kelley was extremely nice, asking me how I was and if I had worked in New York, and so on. Nimoy was a little removed, very contained, not outgoing. He was "the guy" -- he was Spock. But he was nice when you would talk to him. And he nailed that character; he really had that down." (113a)

Emily Banks said, "They said something about bringing me back, but then they never did anything about it. So that was that. And I didn't see it right away, because I normally didn't look at anything that I did. But then, about 25 years ago [late 1980s], one of my husband's best friend's sons called and said, "Emily, you're on *Star Trek*! You're on one of the classics!' I said, 'Yeah.' And he said, 'No, no, this is one of the *classics* of the classics!' And I said, 'I don't know what you're talking about.' He said, 'Well, there are considered, like, six *classic* classics, and you're on one!' He was flabbergasted. And I thought, 'You know, maybe I'd better take a look.' And then, shortly after that, my godmother and her son came out for Christmas and he brought me the episode [just released on VHS]. And so I had a chance to sit down and look at it. And I thought, 'This is good! I really like it.'" (9a)

Episode 18: THE SQUIRE OF GOTHOS
Written by Paul Schneider
(with Gene L. Coon, uncredited)
Directed by Don McDougall

From *TV Guide*, January 7, 1967:

The Enterprise crew become playthings in the hands of Trelane, a powerful being who is using his human visitors as toys.

Kirk, who Trelane sees as a leader among predators, must barter for the release of ship and crew. The price: his own life.

"The Squire of Gothos" presents a study of human behavior, through the eyes of a self-gratifying, narcissistic alien child. The writer later acknowledged that this was a subtle anti-war story, mocking prejudice, aggressiveness, territorialism, and violence by seeing these negative human characteristics mimicked by an immature boy wanting to play soldier.

NBC publicity photo (Courtesy of Gerald Gurian)

SOUND BITES

- *Trelane:* "I cannot tell you how it delights me -- having visitors from the very planet that I've made my hobby!... Yes, I've been looking in on the doings of your lively little Earth.... There is so much I'd like to learn about you: your feelings about war; killing; conquest -- that sort of thing. You know, you're one of the few predator species that preys even on itself!" *Kirk:* "Our missions are peaceful -- not for conquest. And we battle only when we have no choice." *Trelane:* "That's the 'official' story, eh?"

- *Spock, to Trelane:* "I object to you. I object to intellect without reason. I object to power without constructive purpose." *Trelane:* "Why, Mr. Spock, you do have a saving grace, after all -- you're ill-mannered! The human half of you, no doubt?"

ASSESSMENT

"The Squire of Gothos" is fast-paced entertainment, both clever and surprising.

Star Trek often examined the human experience. Usually, this allowed us to see ourselves through the alien eyes of Mr. Spock. Here, we are confronted with the dark and violent past humans have to live down. Trelane sees us as killers, and this intrigues him. In

441

the end, Kirk demonstrates that mankind is capable of greater things than our detractors would believe.

This is the magic of *Star Trek*. In the turbulent 1960s, Americans, and especially America's youth, were desperate for a sign that we could survive and, more so, that there was reason for us to do so. Kirk was the spokesman as *Star Trek* repeatedly made the positive argument in favor of man.

The kids could have fun watching this, too. And they did.

THE STORY BEHIND THE STORY

Script Timeline
Paul Schneider's story outline, ST #30: August 11, 1966.
Schneider's 1st Draft teleplay: October 11, 1966.
Schneider's 2nd Draft teleplay: October 18, 1966.
Staff script polish (Mimeo Department reformatted "Yellow Cover 1st Draft"):
October 26, 1966.
Gene Coon's script polish (Final Draft teleplay): October, 26, 1966.
Additional page revisions by Coon: October 28 & 31 and November 1, 1966.

Writer Paul Schneider, on his follow-up writing assignment to "Balance of Terror," was nervous about this tale, which he described as "science-fantasy." Other series he had written for, such as *Ben Casey*, *Mr. Novak*, and *The Big Valley*, used conventional means of storytelling. Not this. And he was also late in delivering.

Schneider had been tardy before, when getting his first assignment to the *Star Trek* offices -- his epic 32-page story outline for "Balance of Terror." Mary Black recalled, "He was a little late in delivering. Not very late like Harlan [Ellison], but a little late. I had known what it was like to cover for John [D.F. Black] when he was a little late, so I was very familiar with the quality of the voice a writer uses when he's making an excuse. And Paul Schneider came with the most outrageous story. He told me to tell John about how he wasn't going to be able to bring the script in for another day or so. He said he was on his way in with it and then the tire of his car blew, and he was changing the tire, and the tire rolled down the hill, and he had to chase it, and ... well, it was really a wonderful story, except, as I said, I was so familiar how John sounded when he was making one up that I knew Paul was making this up. He was a very nice, *nice man*, but he wasn't a great liar. When I mentioned it to John, he said, 'So his dog ate his homework.' It's in the nature of writers that they're not good liars when it comes to their reasons for being late delivering." (17a)

John D.F. Black added, "I liked his work. He was a sweet man, and his work was good. But he was always late." (17)

Things hadn't changed since "Balance of Terror." Along with the outline for "Squire of Gothos," Schneider sent an apologetic letter to Gene Coon, saying:

> I think I understand now why I took so long with this story: because I had to work up the nerve to do it the way I felt it had to be done -- which is the wild way. And that it is, all right -- the wildest one I've ever attempted.... I feel the story has a "dash" to it which should make for good visuals and some toothsome character stuff. Also room for more than a pinch of comedy -- and a guaranteed-flabbergasting mystery, with a resolution just this side of conceivable.... I think I have something pretty damn good here. (PS18)

Schneider borrowed from a classic for the ending. He later admitted, "The biggest problem was coming up with a climax. How do you end something like that? So [I] used the climax of *The Most Dangerous Game*." (154)

The famous short story by Richard Connell involves a big-game hunter who, bored with tracking conventional prey, decides to go after a human. The story was adapted into a successful movie, remade twice, and imitated often.

In a memo to Coon, Robert Justman wrote:

> Paul Schneider was right. This story is science-fantasy. I leave it up to you whether you think this is the kind of story we want to do on *Star Trek*. Personally speaking, I rather like the idea. (RJ18-1)

For Justman, liking a concept and being able to afford to realize it were two very different and highly contrasting matters. He worried:

> If we intend to go ahead with this story, we will have to do something with regard to the costs of making it. I have a 12-page outline in my possession and I have dollar signs marked all over most of the pages.... Miniature and special effect opticals; location shooting with formal gardens, fountain, flowery vines, abbeys, towers, ruins, arbors and bowers, topiary hedges, mazes, archways, stately mansions; rich, darkly-furnished rooms, a great sumptuous library-dining room; weirdo costumes and wardrobing; plenty of extras and speaking parts; Enterprise attempting to avoid huge asteroid; materializations of gallows in a room; vanishing rooms and instead finding ourselves in a garden maze; a chase in an Arcadian Forest with stones and branches, gardening covering, all appearing and then disappearing... and then Bob Justman disappearing. (RJ18-1)

Someone else seemed to have disappeared. There was very little Spock in this treatment. Justman wrote:

> Our viewing audience seems to like Mister Spock. I feel as though we should give our audience what they like. If they want more of Mister Spock, we should give them more of Mister Spock. (RJ18-1)

Roddenberry shared his thoughts the next day. His note to Coon:

> Seems to me we have an interesting story here, one which could convert into an exciting script -- assuming Paul is willing to trim it into production size. He must find excitement and entertainment more in the characterizations and situations, less in opticals, costumes, and expensive sets.... Suggest we get back to the point of the original story premise, i.e., *The Most Dangerous Game*. "Gothos" is an avid sportsman, has trophies of the hunts in his drawing room -- the stuffed examples being a sort of "lizard man," a hairy Neanderthal type but with huge brain sac, etc. Perhaps some of these can be heads slightly altered from creatures we have done in past shows.... Only slowly do we begin to realize that Gothos has waited, perhaps for centuries, for an Earth ship to pass within his reach. He's heard of Man, has been fascinated by the schizophrenic bi-sexual homo-sapien creature; wonders if Man is as dangerous as other creatures he has hunted.... Plenty of action and adventure, and if we can avoid the fantasy elements, we also will have good action adventure in the "sf" vein. By all means, let's sit down with R. Justman and have a "round table" on this one. (GR18-1)

The meeting went well and Schneider was sent straight to script, the First Draft arriving on October 1. Unaware of the two-week-old Grace Lee Whitney termination, Schneider included the character of Janice Rand in his script. She would have been the pretty blonde yeoman who is the subject of attention and mock jealousy between Kirk and Trelane.

Coon was very pleased with Schneider's script, Justman less so. In his memo to Coon, Justman wrote:

> You were right, "The Squire of Gothos" is a damn good first draft. However, I think it needs more work than you do. (RJ18-2)

Justman had a plethora of notes, ranging from things he didn't like, things that made no sense to him, and things he merely needed clarified in order to carry out his job of realizing the production. He told Coon:

> On page 13, we have the "marbleized forms of Sulu and Kirk" available for this sequence. Naturally, we will have to make a mold of these two people some time beforehand and I don't feel that they necessarily have to match their positions when they disappeared on board the Enterprise. Also, what does the word "marbleized" signify? Does it mean that Kirk and Sulu look as if they are made out of marble? If so, how do we make the transition from this to real life Kirk and Sulu unfreeze?

The solution: forget the molds, forget using those molds to create statues of Kirk and Sulu that appeared to be made from marble, and forget transitioning from those forms to real life Kirk and Sulu. Instead, just place the actors under a key light with a green gel giving them a deathlike appearance, have them freeze, tell them not even to breathe, then, on cue, flip the colored light off and have the frozen actors come to life. For good measure, add in a sound effect. Money saved; time saved.

Notes came in from other staff members, including Steven Carabatsos and, having been invited to give notes in an unofficial capacity, Dorothy Fontana.

One wrote: "Respectfully submit Spock <u>would</u> go along with the landing party." (STAFF8-1)

Coon tried it this way with the next draft, and then changed it back. He preferred having Trelane come aboard the Enterprise, angry at Spock for having beamed the landing party up just when he was having so much fun with them. "You will see to his punishment," Trelane says to Kirk. "On the contrary," Kirk answers, "I commend his action." The next line was written as perfectly as William Campbell delivered it, staring coldly at Spock, saying: "But -- I -- don't -- like -- him."

One staffer wrote: "I think the German bit with Jaeger is too much." (STAFF18-1)

The reference was to Trelane clicking his heals and "stomping in cadence," bellowing, "Und Offizier Jaeger, der deutsche soldat nein? Eins, zwei, drei, vier!!"

Translation: "And Officer Jaeger, you're a German soldier, no? One, two, three, four!"

Coon liked "the German bit" and left it in.

Another staff note: "I think we can do without the reference to Uhura's color." (STAFF18-1)

Trelane's line: "A Nubian prize? Taken no doubt in one of your raids of conquest, eh, Captain?" Shatner, with a subtle sigh, ad-libbed, "No doubt." Coon liked it. The audience would too.

And another note:

> I don't even like the little bit of *Most Dangerous Game* Paul got around to putting in. Kirk ought to have some way to really fight back. Also, he oughta clobber the hell out of Trelane -- somehow. And then have Trelane not want to play anymore -- yell for help from Mom and Dad. Let's have more of Kirk doing things -- being our hero. He talks a great fight, but let's have him save himself. <u>Please</u>. (STAFF18-1)

Coon allowed Kirk to make a better fight of it, and even break Trelane's sword in the end, sending the alien child into a tirade.

Schneider delivered his 2nd Draft script one week later. Two days after that, Coon did a quick polish and created the October 21 Yellow Cover First Draft for NBC's eyes -- the network's first look at the material.

It had been a very fast process -- the episode was scheduled to begin production in seven days. But as had happened with "Court Martial," no one thought of keeping NBC in the loop. Coon, upon taking over as producer, assumed Roddenberry would still deal with the network directly. Roddenberry, tired of butting heads with the NBC suits, expected Coon to handle it. As a result of the lack of communication, and the wrong assumptions, Roddenberry and Coon collectively dropped the ball with a heavy thump.

NBC Production Manager Stan Robertson was rightfully irked. He wrote Coon:

> We understand the "errors" which led to our receiving this script a week before its planned shooting date without ever having received an outline, however, in the future, I would remind you, as we discussed, of the inherent danger apparent in this occurring again. (SR18)

Robertson didn't like how Trelane was portrayed in a "farcical" manner instead of one that was "serious." He didn't think much of *The Most Dangerous Game* homage, either, saying:

> In its present form, I think that the hunt and chase scene between Trelane and Kirk is somewhat overdone and duplicates sequences which, from here, appeared in other *Star Trek* episodes. (SR18)

Robertson was thinking of Kirk tracking and fighting Gary Mitchell in "Where No Man Has Gone Before" and chasing and fighting Finnegan in "Shore Leave." Trelane hunting Kirk was certainly a different kettle of fish but, to Robertson's thinking, still fish.

Knowing this episode would likely be televised within weeks of "The Menagerie" and "Court Martial," Robertson bemoaned:

> Remembering our scheduling problems, I would remind you again that this script contains the third "trial sequence" which has been contained in recently received material. (SR18)

And Robertson was not amused by the story's end. Of this, he said:

> The climax of this story seems to be a little weak and unbelievable.... I doubt very seriously if the audience will either buy or completely understand what we are trying to say here. (SR18)

That punch line that Robertson disliked was the icing on the cake. Kirk discovers Trelane, the all-powerful alien man, is but a mere boy. Starting with Paul Schneider's idea, and ending with Gene Coon's final script polish, it was a pure Coonism, with an astonished Kirk watching as Trelane's mother -- the pulsating light in the sky -- scolds her spoiled child, saying, "If you cannot take proper care of your pets, you cannot have them at all." And the spoiled child whining, "But I was winning! I was winning!... I never have any fun!" And then the stern voice of his father, scolding, "Stop this nonsense! At once! Or you won't be able to make any more planets!"

On this occasion, Stan Robertson had underestimated the audience. The irony was rich, the surprise a delight. But, because of the NBC man's concerns, Gene Coon did one further script polish -- the Final Draft from October 26 -- snipping out a few things and clarifying a few others.

Robertson seemed a little less irked. Not so for Justman. His next memo hit Coon's desk in less than 24 hours, complaining:

> Gene, I am going to carp again about Opticals. I know in my bones that we are in deep trouble with this show. And you may be able to detect from the tone of this memo that I am pissed off to beat the band. Not necessarily about this show, but what has been happening on the previous show and the one before that. I'll have to fill you in later on what happened at a little after 7 o'clock when I got a call from Location, but suffice it to say I am beginning to have fears that I have to sit personally on every God-damn shooting hour of this show. And if I have to, then this whole setup is incorrect. The time to ensure our getting as good a show for the money and in as decent amount of days and hours as possible is <u>prior</u> to shooting. (RJ18-3)

The 7 p.m. phone call from the day before concerned the final day of filming at Vasquez Rocks for "Shore Leave," as director Sparr failed to film the elephant that had been paid for, and failed to get any shots of the tiger -- the one that terrorized cast and crew – without the chain around its neck now clearly visible to the camera, and was, at that moment, trying to get his last daylight locations shots in the pitch black of an October night ... with the final shot finally taken at 8 p.m.

Justman hadn't completely lost his sense of humor. He added:

> If we transport McCoy, Jaeger and DeSalle down to the surface of Gothos in the orange space suits that we used in "The Naked Time," then the audience will take a full half hour to stop laughing from what our people look like. Perhaps I am jumping to conclusions because yesterday I saw Bill Theiss showing you one of those orange suits as I passed by. Please, <u>please</u> do <u>not</u> go with those outfits. (RJ18-3)

Coon took a look at the teaser from "The Naked Time." After he stopped laughing, he changed the script to indicate that the landing party would *not* wear environmental suits but would instead don oxygen masks.

Pre-Production
(Director's prep: two days -- October 26 & 27)

William Campbell in 1955 Universal-International publicity photo

Don McDougall, who had directed 26 episodes of *The Roy Rogers Show*, 20 of Johnny Weissmuller's *Jungle Jim*, 39 of Robert Culp's *Trackdown*, 20 of Steve McQueen's *Wanted: Dead or Alive*, and 31 of *Bonanza*, was brought in for his only *Star Trek*.

For Trelane, McDougall and casting director Joe D'Agosta wanted Roddy McDowall. Gene Coon had someone else in mind -- William Campbell, who appeared in an episode he produced for *The Wild, Wild West*.

Campbell, 39 at this time, had been gaining attention with prominent billing in big screen hits like *Escape from Fort Bravo*, *Man Without a Star*, *Backlash*, and *Love Me Tender*.

He was known for playing contemporary punks and thugs, not flamboyant characters teetering between malicious intimidation and comical innocence. Regardless, after reading the script, Campbell knew he could handle the part.

"It was a fantastic character," Campbell said. "It would be very easy for any actor who had any training to play the Squire of Gothos. The character was so well written and, of course, it *was* the show." (27-2)

After Campbell recited only a few lines of dialogue to Don McDougall and Joe D'Agosta, Roddy McDowall was out and Campbell was told to report to wardrobe.

Richard Carlyle, as Lt. Karl Jaeger, was 46. He had appeared over a hundred times before the camera and had his own short-lived series, *Crime Photographer*, in 1951.

Venita Wolf, making her television acting debut as Yeoman Teresa Ross, the one replacing Yeoman Rand in this episode, was a model and a former beauty contest winner. Following this, she was featured as the cover girl on the July 1967 issue of *Playboy* magazine. And then she married a wealthy nightclub owner and left show business.

Michael Barrier made three appearances on *Star Trek* as Lt. Vincent DeSalle. This was the first. He would return for "This Side of Paradise" and "Catspaw."

Barbara Babcock, 29, provided the voice of Trelene's mother. She returned for more voiceover work in "Assignment: Earth," "The Tholian Web" and "The Lights of Zetar." Also for *Star Trek*: prominent on-camera roles in "A Taste of Armageddon," and "Plato's Stepchildren." Her most famous role was 15 years away -- as Grace Gardner on a future NBC show, *Hill Street Blues*, for which she would win an Emmy.

Model Venita Wolf poses with Shatner for NBC publicity photo (Courtesy of Gerald Gurian)

James Doohan said he made a dual appearance in this episode -- on camera and on the soundtrack. Some sources credit the voice of Trelane's father as belonging to Barton LaRue, and for good reason -- it sounds remarkably like LaRue. The often-employed voice actor would indeed work for *Star Trek*, in four upcoming episodes. But, this time, the producers may have looked closer to home. That would also give them an excuse to allow Doohan to appear in "Squire."

Robert Justman, trying to balance the budget, had been protesting this. He sent word to Coon:

> James Doohan plays Engineer Scott. I have not seen the schedule yet, but I doubt that he works more than one or two days at the most. For that amount of work he will receive $850? (RJ17-3)

Figure $6,135 in 2013. So Doohan told this author he did double duty to earn his pay.

He dropped the Scottish accent, a good amount of reverb was added, and he did a first rate impression of Barton LaRue.

Eddie Paskey, as Lt. Leslie, got his first turn in the command chair. Watch for him -- he vacates the seat and makes way for Kirk after the Captain returns to the ship toward the end of Act 3.

Production Diary
Filmed October 28 & 31 and November 1, 2, 3, 4 & 7, 1966
(Planned as 6 day production, finishing one day late; total cost: $194,573).

Friday, October 28, 1966. You couldn't go anywhere without hearing "96 Tears" by Question Mark & the Mysterians, the top playing record on U.S. radio stations. The two biggest selling record albums in the Nation were The Supremes with *Supremes A' Go-Go* and The Beatles with *Revolver*. Ten bucks would get you both albums and the "96 Tears" 45, and pay for the gas driving to the record store, too. But if you worked at McDonalds, you were only making minimum wage, which was $1.25 per hour. Those two record albums and one single would cost you an entire day's pay.

Hitting newsstands this day: the cover of *Life* magazine had the grisly image of a badly-wounded American soldier, fallen in a muddy field in Vietnam and being comforted by his grief-stricken comrades. Along with the latest death tolls in Vietnam, the morning papers were reporting that both China and the USSR had just exploded nuclear bombs in separate "tests." Humanity seemed on the brink of annihilation and, the night before, NBC premiered "Miri," a story about the end of Western civilization as we knew it ... on a new series called *Star Trek*. The production company was now commencing the filming of an episode that would be less dark but every bit as poignant. Work took place on Stage 9 in the transporter room, followed by the bridge set. Director Don McDougall finished at 6:45 p.m., already a quarter-day behind.

Day 2, Monday, was spent entirely on the bridge. William Campbell joined the cast this day for Trelane's visit to the Enterprise. McDougall wrapped at 7 p.m., now one-third of a day behind.

Day 3, Tuesday. The company was on Stage 10, "Int. Trelane's Drawing Room." Paul Schneider recalled, "I was very excited that they built a whole special set for it; a totally round set, which was then

A distant relative to the Salt Vampire from "The Man Trap" on display in Trelane's drawing room (Courtesy of Gerald Gurian)

kind of a new concept in itself. If you look at the episode, you'll see that the camera goes all the way around." (154)

Matt Jefferies was proud of this unique set, more so than any other he designed for the series' first season. The company would spend a total of three and a half days here. On this day, McDougall took his last shot at 7:10 p.m. He was now a half-day behind.

On Days 4 and 5, Wednesday and Thursday -- work continued in the drawing room. Venita Wolf and Nichelle Nichols joined the cast during these two days. Scenes shot included the one where Uhura plays the harpsichord. The song was "Roses from the South," by Johann Strauss, Jr.

By the end of Thursday, the director had fallen further behind -- now by three-quarters of a day; his final shot taken at 7:30 p.m.. After wrapping the set, anyone wanting to get home in time to watch the premiere of "Dagger of the Mind," the seventh episode of *Star Trek* to air, had at best 30 minutes to make the drive and warm up their color RCA.

On Day 6, Friday, McDougall took his last shots in Trelane's drawing room proper, then had a section of the room redecorated to include the judge's bench and the lighting trick that cast the shadow of a gallows noose on the wall.

William Campbell recalled that Gene Coon proved to be "awfully fair" over a dispute during filming. The problem occurred when a wig Campbell was to wear arrived. The Squire was to be dressed as an old world English barrister who pronounces judgment on Kirk.

Day 6: Jerry Finnerman's "lighting gags" puts a surreal noose on the wall
(Unaired film trim courtesy of Gerald Gurian)

"They started that scene late in the day," Campbell said. "They called for the wig, and the makeup person comes over and puts [it] on and I look like an old Shirley Temple. It was a French period wig, very curly and full. I immediately told them, 'You've got the wrong wig.' And I remember Bill [Shatner] had been working his blank off, and he came over and said, 'What difference does it make? Nobody's going to know that.' I said, 'It *does* make a difference to me. It's not only a difference in the acting that I would do, but it isn't right.'" (27-2)

Don McDougall was put in the awkward position of taking sides with either the star of the series or a mere guest performer. McDougall chose *not* to have an opinion.

Next, Gene Coon was called to the set. Campbell said, "Gene didn't take two seconds to say, 'Campbell's right; get another wig; go to another sequence' -- which is exactly what we did, and it didn't hold up anything. That's the kind of guy he was. He was very sensitive about the quality of the show [and] how it was done." (27-8)

That other sequence was the beam down of McCoy, DeSalle, and Jaeger in the woodsy area outside Trelane's castle. The company then returned to Trelane's drawing room for the mock trial scene, this time with a proper wig for William Campbell.

McDougall stopped filming at 6:52, now a full day behind.

Day 7, Monday, November 7. The exterior of the castle was used for the final day of production on Stage 10. This was where the re-enactment of *The Most Dangerous Game* took place. William Shatner, being chased by the sword-wielding Campbell, had a stuntman to take the falls for him. Campbell did not, since Trelane had no planned falls. Campbell, however, thought it would be a good idea if his character also went to the ground at some point. There was a problem. The "ground" on a sound stage, no matter what else it appears to be, is made of concrete. Campbell's shoulder popped out of joint, resulting in a further delay in production as a doctor was called to the set to pop the shoulder back into place. And this resulted in the unplanned seventh day of filming not wrapping until 7:15 p.m.

Despite steering clear of the argument between Campbell and Shatner, and doing a first rate job at directing, McDougall was not invited back.

Post-Production
November 11 to December 20, 1966. Music score: tracked.

Bruce Schoengarth and Edit Team #2, following the difficult chore of splicing together and resequencing scenes from "Court Martial," had a less problematic assignment this time out.

The music was effectively recycled from past episodes. A nice touch on the part of sound editor Doug Grindstaff was adding in a music cue from "The Man Trap" just as McCoy gets a look at the Salt Vampire on display in Trelane's drawing room. It was same cue used in the former episode whenever the creature, in the guise of a crew member of the Enterprise, lurked about the ship.

Film Effects of Hollywood was the primary supplier of the photographic effects, including those of the planet Gothos chasing the Enterprise through space. It was not a perfect job. Some stars can be seen bleeding through the planet as it comes at the Enterprise on the main view screen. One effect called for in the script could not be accomplished. When Kirk fights Trelane at the end, he knocks the saber from Trelane's hand, picks it up and slashes at his tormentor. The script instructed: "CLOSE ON TRELANE. The saber blow cuts right through him, without leaving a sign of the passage. Frozen with surprise and frustration, Kirk stares at him." Director McDougall had shot the sequence properly, shooting with a tied down camera for a split screen process. One shot had the two men facing one another. Shatner begins his swing of the saber. In the next shot, Campbell steps out of the shot while Shatner, standing in the same position, slashes the sword through thin air. Combining two shots like that with today's technical tools is a snap. In 1966, they were not able to make the sword pass through Trelane's body properly and, instead, chose to have him pop out of the scene as the saber slashes out, then pop back in. Broadcast Standards breathed a sigh of relief. This was one of the shots called for in the script which had concerned them as being too jarring for the tastes of the NBC viewing audience.

The final price tag was $194,573. This was $9,573 over the Studio's new reduced per-episode allowance. The cash surplus was gone. The deficit was back, at $1,801.

Release / Reaction:
Premiere air date: 1/12/67. NBC repeat broadcast: 6/22/67.

Steven H. Scheuer reviewed "The Squire of Gothos" for his syndicated *TV Key Previews* column. Among the newspapers carrying the review on January 12, 1967, was the *Milwaukee Journal*, in Milwaukee, Wisconsin. Quickly becoming a *Star Trek* fan, Scheuer wrote:

> This is a weird and well-conceived episode, as usual. The uncharted deserted planet of Gothos actually turns out to be a handsome Victorian country manor,

complete with harpsichord playing Trelane (William Campbell). Trelane is a hunter in the tradition of a country squire and he is put out when Kirk, Spock, and scientist Carl Jaeger (Richard Carlyle) do not find his little ways amusing. They quickly become the foxes and Trelane the hunter.

Scheuer, in fact, was becoming so enamored with *Star Trek* that he wrote a second review for another column, this one carried by the *Pittsburg Post-Gazette*, in Pittsburg, Pennsylvania. Scheuer told his readers:

> This is a highly imaginative space adventure written by Paul Schneider. The Enterprise encounters a planet, unknown to science, that harbors a remarkable fanatic who plays games with people and history, the way a child might play with toys. How Captain Kirk escapes from the madman's power after an hour of sophisticated and hair-raising adventures, will hold you glued to your television set.

Scheuer was right about the gluing to one's TV. According to A.C. Nielsen, *Star Trek* was a strong second place for the first half-hour, then saw its audience share rise for the second half.

RATINGS / Nielsen 30-Market report for Thursday, January 12, 1967:

8:30 - 9 p.m. (62.9% of U.S. TVs in use):	Rating:	Share:
NBC: *Star Trek* (first half)	18.6	29.6%
ABC: **Bewitched**	**21.3**	**34.7%**
CBS: *My Three Sons*	16.4	26.1%
Independent stations:	7.3	9.6%
9 - 9:30 p.m. (66.8% of U.S. TVs in use):		
NBC: *Star Trek* (second half)	21.1	31.6%
ABC: *Love On A Rooftop*	15.4	23.1%
CBS: **Thursday Night Movie** (start)	**25.1**	**37.6%**
Independent stations:	7.7	7.7%

"The Squire of Gothos" grabbed a strong second place for the entire hour, with the latter half attracting 32% of the TV audience. The big winner: *The CBS Thursday Night Movie*'s television premiere of *A Summer Place*. The 1959 film with Richard Egan, Sandra Dee, and Troy Donahue had spawned a No. 1 Billboard hit -- "Theme from a Summer Place."

Stan Robertson had fretted over whether "The Squire of Gothos" would be accepted and understood by the viewing audience. There had been no reason to worry. The episode, and the character of Trelane, proved to be immensely popular.

From the Mailbag

Received the week following the first airing of "The Squire of Gothos":

> Dear Mr. Roddenberry, I would like to tell you how very, very much I enjoy *Star Trek*. As a science-fiction buff from way back, I had almost despaired of ever seeing anything on TV that was not meant for children -- and not very bright children, at that. I sincerely hope your program will be continued next year. If not, I think I'll kill all my present bras, and never buy another living one! With very warm wishes for your program and for you, personally. Edna Z. (Reno, Nevada).

(One of *Star Trek*'s sponsors at this time was Playtex, for their " living bra" campaign.)

The reply:

> Dear Mrs. Z., thank you for your delightful letter. Your first paragraph did provide our laugh of the day. Sincerely, Gene Roddenberry, Executive Producer, *Star Trek*.

Memories

William Campbell said, "In my lifetime, I met maybe five people I found impossible to dislike, and, strangely enough, two of those were on *Star Trek*: DeForest Kelley and Gene Coon." (27-1)

As for the episode itself, Campbell said, "It was just a great role. It was sensational. I'll never forget it." (27-2)

27

Joseph Pevney into the "Arena"

Rock Hudson, Cyd Charisse and Joseph Pevney, *Twilight of the Gods* (1958, Universal-International)

Director Joseph Pevney was brought to *Star Trek* by Gene Coon, who knew him from when both worked at Universal Studios. In time, Pevney would tie with Marc Daniels for directing the most *Star Trek* episodes -- 14 each.

Pevney, like Daniels, began as a stage actor in New York. What he really wanted to do was direct, and he got his chance in 1942 with *Let Freedom Sing*, a musical revue on Broadway, starring Mitzi Green. The play closed after only two weeks but was not a total loss -- Pevney and Green married, beginning a 30-year union which led to four children and only ended as a result of Mitzi's untimely death at 49.

Pevney returned to acting on Broadway in November 1942 with a plum role in *Counselor-at-Law*, starring Paul Muni. When the play closed, he went off to "fight" World War II -- as a staff sergeant in the Army Signal Corps, where he staged revues for the troops.

In January 1946, Pevney was back on Broadway, in *Home of the Brave*, for a prominent role as a shell-shocked soldier. *Variety* said, "Play, written by an ex-GI, has several ex-GIs in the cast, notably its leads, Joseph Pevney and Alan Baxter, so that it carries conviction." Pevney was praised for showing "restrained poignancy."

Soon Pevney was on the big screen and had fourth billing in the film noir *Nocturne* as Ned "Fingers" Ford, a wise-cracking nightclub pianist suspected of murder by "hardboiled detective" George Raft. Next came *Body and Soul*, which *Daily Variety* declared a "can't miss." Besides praising star John Garfield, the trade said, "There's more good thesping by Joseph Pevney." Pevney registered strongly in three more noirs: *The Street with No Name*, *Outside the Wall*, and *Thieves' Highway*. During this time, he studied the mechanics of making films and continued to make connections. By August 1949, Universal-International Pictures signed him to a contract to direct low-budget B-pictures.

Pevney's first directorial assignment, *Shakedown*, starring Howard Duff, was released in August 1950. *Daily Variety* took note of "the fine direction of Joe Pevney." Two months later, the same trade stated that *Undercover Girl*, his second film, was "directed at a fast and suspenseful pace." Pevney had passed the test.

Universal-International put out four more of Pevney's movies in 1951, a pace that taught the director to shoot film fast enough for TV. *Air Cadets*, with Rock Hudson came in

February. In the cast was Charles Drake, whom Pevney hired 16 years later for "The Deadly Years" on *Star Trek*. After that was *Iron Man*, with up-and-comer Jeff Chandler, whom the director would work with on six different movie projects. *Daily Variety* graded the fight picture as "realistic and carefully worked out" and stated that "Joseph Pevney in his direction [is] achieving a ringing note of authenticity." Weeks later, Pevney had a western on the big screen with *The Lady from Texas*. *Variety* said, "Joseph Pevney directed most capably to bring warmth and plenty of humor."

The studio, now trusting its young contract director with higher-priced properties, promoted him to handling movies designed to top a double bill. Pevney's sixth picture, *The Strange Door*, with Charles Laughton and Boris Karloff, introduced him to the horror genre. *Variety* wrote, "Direction of Joseph Pevney helps sustain the yarn's somber mood and suspense." Universal squeezed five movies out of Pevney for release in 1952. The first, and a clear step up, was *Meet Danny Wilson*, starring Frank Sinatra. *Daily Variety* called it "bright drama, with comedy and songs... aided by slick and fast direction supplied by Joseph Pevney."

For 1953, Universal served up three movies by Pevney, including *Desert Legion*, an Alan Ladd "swashbuckler." Pevney had three more movies out in 1954. Of *Yankee Pasha*, already his 14th feature, *Daily Variety* wrote, "Joseph Pevney's direction guides it along." Only a month later, Universal and Pevney had Shelley Winters, at a slender 32, in the exploitation piece *Playgirl*. By year's end, the director was on loan to Paramount for the Dean Martin/Jerry Lewis comedy *Three Ring Circus*. *Daily Variety* cited:

> Production values... through locationing with the Clyde Beatty Circus are given lush definition by the VV [VistaVision] cameras, which director Joseph Pevney uses to fine advantage in effectively catching the antics of the stars.

Back at Universal-International for a January 1955 release, Pevney took on *Six Bridges to Cross*, a cops-and-robbers melodrama with Tony Curtis, followed by a pair of Jeff Chandler movies. Celia Lovsky was in the cast of one. Pevney would later put her in *Star Trek*'s "Amok Time."

In 1956, Universal released *Away All Boats*. This marked Pevney's fifth turn with Chandler, and introduced the director to Keith Andres, whom he would later cast for *Star Trek* in "The Apple." *Cargo Crossing*, with Peter Lorre in the cast, came next. It was Pevney's 21st feature in just seven years.

With 1957 came *Istanbul*, starring Errol Flynn, followed by Pevney's biggest hit to date -- *Tammy and the Bachelor*. *Daily Variety* raved:

> Director Joseph Pevney shrewdly underlines Miss [Debbie] Reynolds' indomitable artlessness, without falling into the pitfall of over-sentimentality.

Less than a month later, Pevney had Tony Curtis for the third time in *The Midnight Story*. *Daily Variety* said:

> Pevney makes excellent use of San Francisco locations... which adds atmospherically to the overall scene, and [the] feel of the Italian quarter and its people are particularly caught in his helming.

In July, Universal put out Pevney's 25th directorial assignment -- James Cagney as Lon Chaney in *The Man of a Thousand Faces*. *Daily Variety* raved:

> Director Joseph Pevney gets the most out of the heart-tugging scenes, and this is undoubtedly his best directorial credit to date.

In 1958, Rock Hudson starred in *Twilight for the Gods*, followed by another loan-out, this time from Universal to MGM for *Torpedo Run*, starring Glenn Ford. *Daily Variety* said, "Director Joseph Pevney unfolds the screenplay at a suspenseful pace."

At this point in his career, there seemed little reason for Pevney to go into television. But the studio system of keeping actors and directors under contract was coming to an end, as had his 10-year contract with Universal. While waiting for a worthy film offer to come along, he dabbled in television by shooting two pilot films. One -- a science fiction for CBS, *Destination Space* -- didn't sell. The other -- a jazzy P.I. show designed to top *Peter Gunn* -- did. *Staccato* presented John Cassavetes as a former jazz musician turned private eye who makes his home base in New York's Greenwich Village.

Pevney got back to the big screen for December 1959 with a big hit -- Warner Bros.' *Cash McCall*, starring James Garner and Natalie Wood. The studio, delighted over the box office returns, assigned its director to a second project, for 1960. *The Crowded Sky* was crowded with WB contract players, such as Dana Andrews, Rhonda Fleming, Efrem Zimbalist, Jr., Anne Francis, and Troy Donahue. Also in 1960, Pevney made time to helm several episodes of *Wagon Train*. One featured William Schallert, whom he would hire for *Star Trek*'s "The Trouble with Tribbles."

In 1961, Warner Bros. had Pevney back for a third turn -- the director's 31st feature film. *Portrait of a Mobster* starred Vic Morrow and Leslie Parrish, the latter destined for a plumb *Star Trek* role ("Who Mourns for Adonais?"). Also in the cast was Ken Lynch; Pevney would put him in the *Star Trek* episode "The Devil in the Dark."

1962 and 1963 were prolific years for Pevney in television. He directed numerous episodes of *The New Breed*, starring Leslie Nielsen, with three guest players destined for *Star Trek*: James Doohan, Joanne Linville, and Bobby Clark. He reunited with Loretta Young for episodes of her new series -- *The New Loretta Young Show* -- where he met series regular Beverly Washburn, whom he would cast in "The Deadly Years" for *Star Trek*. He also directed for *Ben Casey*, *Alfred Hitchcock Presents* (including one featuring a guest player named Walter Koenig, whom Pevney was responsible for casting in *Star Trek* as Ensign Chekov), and the pilot and first 13 episodes for *Going My Way*, starring Gene Kelly.

In 1964, Pevney took on nine more episodes of *Wagon Train* and eleven episodes of the kooky TV version of Universal's Frankenstein franchise, *The Munsters*. This was where Pevney met Gene Coon, who had a hand in developing that series.

In 1965, Pevney directed future *Star Trek* guest Kathryn Hays ("The Empath") in an *Alfred Hitchcock Presents*, and, for *Kraft Suspense Theatre*, Stanley Adams, whom he cast for *Star Trek*'s "The Trouble with Tribbles."

Just prior to Coon's invitation to join *Star Trek*, Pevney directed a slew of TV shows, including episodes of *Gunsmoke*, *The Big Valley*, *Bewitched*, *Twelve O'clock High*, *Pistols 'n' Petticoats*, and *The Legend of Jesse James* (with an episode featuring Jeffrey Hunter, the former Captain of the Enterprise). Pevney also stopped off at *The Fugitive*, with guest player Arlene Martel, whom he would put into the *Star Trek* episode "Amok Time"; and *T.H.E. Cat*, where he met a visiting Theodore Marcuse, and would remember him for a standout role in *Trek*'s "Catspaw."

During his career, Pevney directed countless movie stars, including Dean Martin and Jerry Lewis, Errol Flynn, Alan Ladd, James Cagney, Gene Kelly, Frank Sinatra, Charles Laughton, Boris Karloff, Jeff Chandler, Tony Curtis, Rock Hudson, Glenn Ford, James Garner, Rod Steiger, George Seagal, Ryan O'Neal, Jeffrey Hunter, Peter Fonda, Natalie

Wood, Debbie Reynolds, Loretta Young, Barbara Stanwyck, Fay Wray, Joan Crawford, and Jane Russell.

He also directed many of the biggest stars in TV, including James Arness, Ward Bond, Robert Horton, Robert Fuller, Raymond Burr, John Forsythe, Lee J. Cobb, Lee Majors, John Cassavetes, Lorne Green, Michael Landon, Vic Morrow, Lloyd Bridges, David Janssen, Vince Edwards, Peter Falk, Paul Burke, William Windom, Leslie Nielsen, Walter Brennan, Brian Keith, Ernest Borgnine, Efrem Zimbalist, Jr., Richard Basehart, Don Rickles, Anne Francis, Katherine Ross, Elizabeth Montgomery, Agnes Moorehead, and Linda Evans.

And now he was about to give direction to a man in a rubber lizard costume out at Vasquez Rocks.

***

Episode 19: ARENA
Teleplay by Gene L. Coon
Story by Fredric Brown
Directed by Joseph Pevney

From *TV Guide*, July 1, 1967:

Famous battle between the Gorn and Kirk
(Unaired film trim courtesy of Gerald Gurian)

> The fate of the Enterprise hinges on the outcome of a personal duel between Captain Kirk and the lizard-like commander of an alien spaceship. On a barren asteroid, the unarmed Kirk must rely on his ingenuity to defeat his powerful adversary.

> The enemy is the Gorn. A space chase leads both the alien vessel and the pursuing Enterprise into an uncharted solar system, the home of the Metrons. There is a penalty for bringing a mission of violence to the doorstep of the superior Metrons: the captain of each ship must face off, pitted in hand-to-hand mortal combat. The prize for the winner: the destruction of his enemy's ship.

"Arena" offers an examination of prejudice and mercy. And *Star Trek* tricks us again. What appears on the surface to be a Man versus Beast tale is really Man versus Himself. Humankind, represented by James Kirk, is being tested.

SOUND BITES

- *The Metron:* "We have analyzed you, and have learned that your violent tendencies are inherent. So be it. We will control them. We will resolve your conflict in the way most suited to your limited mentalities."

- *McCoy:* "We appeal to you in the name of civilization! Put an end to this!" *The*

Metron: "Your violent intent and actions demonstrate that you are *not* civilized."

- *Kirk, to the Metrons:* "No, I won't kill him -- do you hear?! You'll have to get your entertainment someplace else!"

- *The Metron, to Kirk:* "By sparing your helpless enemy, who would surely have killed you, you demonstrated the advanced trait of mercy ... something we hardly expected. We feel there may be hope for your kind. You will not be destroyed. It would not be ... civilized.... Perhaps, in several thousand years, your people and mine shall meet to reach an agreement. You are still half savage ... but there is hope."

- *Kirk:* "We're a most promising species, Mr. Spock ... as predators go. Did you know that?" *Spock:* "I have frequently had my doubts." *Kirk:* "I don't. Not anymore. Maybe in a thousand years we'll be able to prove it."

ASSESSMENT

NBC got what they most wanted: a planet show ... with a monster. Gene Coon's brisk and colorful script pleased the network and delighted the fans. And Coon proved himself a writer who could both entertain and educate. Here, Kirk is taught an important lesson regarding his own prejudice. And, as Kirk learns, so do we. Watch for the change, as the Captain bent on revenge, having admitted to a "natural revulsion to reptiles," learns empathy and comes away from the battle certain of one thing, that he is not qualified to judge the actions of these creatures, nor dispense justice.

"Arena" has not aged as well as other *Star Trek* episodes. The Gorn mask, so startling in 1966, will conjure up very little fear today. And the ominous voice of the Gorn commander (provided by Ted Cassidy, the seven-foot-two-inch actor who played Lurch on *The Addams Family*) will ring more melodramatic than menacing in the ears of today's somewhat jaded and desensitized television audience. But, if you can watch this episode from within the context of the 1960s, "Arena" remains exciting, stirring, memorable, and poignant.

THE STORY BEHIND THE STORY

Script Timeline
Gene Coon's story outline, ST #39: October 10, 1966.
Coon's 1st Draft teleplay: October 13, 1966.
Coon's 2nd Draft teleplay (Mimeo Department "Yellow Cover 1st Draft"):
October 18, 1966.
Coon's Final Draft teleplay: October 28, 1966.
Coon's Revised Final Draft teleplay: November 3, 1966.
Additional page revisions by Coon: November 4, 7, 8, 10 & 15.

Gene Coon, for his first two months at *Star Trek*, had been far too busy rewriting scripts started by others to contribute original material of his own. By October, he had good reason to believe it would be less work to write something new rather than continue to fuss over inherently problematic stories purchased before the series was even on the air.

Coon's story outline for "Arena" was dashed off and sent to NBC in one day -- October 10, 1966 -- which was also the day Coon, with Roddenberry out of the office, did his script polish on "The Menagerie." Coon always dazzled his colleagues with his speed as a writer and, very nearly as often, by the quality of what came from his typewriter.

NBC's Stan Robertson was among those dazzled. He wrote back:

I think this is one of the really superior *Star Trek* story outlines we have received to date. This is action-adventure at its exciting best. (SR19)

In this early telling of the story, once Kirk vanishes from the Enterprise at the end of Act II, the Enterprise itself seems to vanish ... from the story, at least. Robertson told Coon:

> My only concern is that in Acts III and IV, Kirk and the Gorn are on camera most of the time. Even though the action is very thrilling, I'm of the belief that this could become repetitious to the viewer and result in a large tune-out. (SR19)

Robertson suggested Coon find a way to "cross-cut" from the action on the planet to the inherent action on The Enterprise. It was a good idea, but came too late to be incorporated into the First Draft script. Coon was so sure of his story that he wrote the First Draft faster than Robertson could read and respond to the outline.

Robert Justman remembered and often spoke of how Gene Coon wrote the script in a single weekend. Actually, he did it during the work week. The story outline popped into existence on a Monday; the First Draft teleplay was finished three days later, on Thursday. As Coon typed "FADE OUT," however, the feedback on the outline began flooding in. Stan Robertson's high praise came first, but, later that same day, the clearance notes from Kellam de Forest landed on Coon's desk. And then all hell broke loose.

Gene Coon's first original story for *Star Trek* was anything but original. The new producer had apparently forgotten that he once read a short story by science fiction author Fredric Brown, also called "Arena," first published in *Astounding* magazine in 1944. Pete Sloman at Kellam de Forest Research spotted the resemblance immediately, beginning with the title, and then followed by:

> 1) Aliens attacking earth colonies; 2) Imminent battle between Earth and aliens; 3) Intervention of third, highly advanced intelligence; 4) Instant transportation of Earthman and Alien, unarmed, to "arena" on an asteroid; 5) Single combat to determine which race survives; 6) The quality of mercy being the decisive factor in the outcome.... It is our opinion that Coon's "Arena" is substantively similar to the copyrighted story "Arena" by Fredric Brown, and the airing of a screenplay from this outline without purchase of the Brown story could be actionable. (KDF19)

Sloman said, "There were occasional rip-offs. I remember that 'Arena' was a rip off down to the title. And anybody who knows science fiction knows Fredric Brown's work. It's possible they didn't. It seemed to me that so few people on that show knew about classic American science fiction, but it would be hard to imagine that case was coincidental. Even so, we had virtually no idea what was going on over at the production office because our job was so specialized and we were so insulated from NBC or the production company or anybody else. So we just got the results of what everybody was freaking out over." (158a)

And there was a great deal of "freaking out." The disclosing of this particular "rip-off" caused great embarrassment for Coon, with his first *Star Trek* story, which had not only been accepted by NBC but trumpeted by Stan Robertson.

Desilu Legal switched into high gear and contacted Fredric Brown's agent, who then took the matter up with his celebrated client.

Bjo Trimble, who Gene Roddenberry had befriended at Tricon in September 1966, said, "Fred Brown was very surprised to be contacted by Desilu. He talked to me about it at a science fiction convention. They asked him, 'How would you like to write something for *Star Trek*.' And he said, 'Well, maybe, but I've never written anything for TV before.' And they said, 'Well, actually, you have.'" (177-8)

Brown was open to the idea but wanted to see the script before agreeing to sell the film rights to his story.

Coon got busy rewriting.

Other elements in the script did not happen as a result of subconscious plagiarism. A more deliberate design was at play here. The Metrons were named after "Metatron," an angel in Judaism. In Greek, the word translates to "instrument of change." Cestus III, the name of the outpost, was taken from the Latin word Cestus, meaning a form of boxing glove worn by gladiators in the arena.

Coon's revised script -- his second draft -- was sent off to be reformatted by the Mimeo Department and designated as the Yellow Cover 1st Draft, dated October 18. It was cleaner, but Coon still hadn't figured out a satisfactory way to address Stan Robertson's earlier criticism -- that the last half of the story, limited to the action on the planetoid as Kirk fights the Gorn captain, could become redundant for a TV audience. Coon tried to stimulate the action by adding a voiceover -- a sort of extended Captain's Log, clueing the audience in on Kirk's thinking, his concerns, and how he figures out a way to perhaps win the battle.

It was Gene Roddenberry who finally found the means to alternate between Kirk's story and the ones of those left behind on the Enterprise. Roddenberry's memo to Coon opened and ended on very positive notes:

> Like it very much; it certainly is very exciting.... Excellent ending. I think it is an excellent draft, very much what the series needs. (GR19)

In between the praise were many concerns, including:

> Bob will no doubt have some comments on the cost of providing a ruined colony. We may have to be inventive here. (GR19)

As for the structure problems, including the one noted by Stan Robertson, Roddenberry wrote:

> [Regarding] Kirk's voiceover during battle -- obvious why you had to go this direction. Good voiceover; well handled. But let's discuss a couple other possibilities, i.e., a) the Gorn can speak English after some effort, b) Kirk and the Gorn try to communicate, fail, but attempt breaks up some of the possible monotony of voiceover, c) the Enterprise bridge personnel are shown the battle on the screen and their spoken comments, their excited suggestions to the unhearing Captain far below, does what our voiceover has been doing for us. (GR18)

Robert Justman had notes for Coon, as well, writing:

> As I started to bring out the other day, having had some experience with ambulatory creatures [on *The Outer Limits*], you must realize that whatever creature we use with a stunt man inside of it will necessarily have a certain limitation as to physical movement. For instance, undoubtedly the creature won't be able to move faster than a normal walking pace, and that only for a very short distance.... Another problem that I have had in the past... is that when you see one of these creatures full figure, it is apparent that there is a man inside no matter how clever you have been in disguising it.... In scenes 80, 81 and 82, Kirk delivers some Narration over action. I think this would be a good time to sell in dialogue the fact that the injury caused by the rock striking his leg has slowed him down to such an extent, that he is doubly vulnerable to the Gorn. His mobility has been cut down quite a bit and he certainly cannot get around with sufficient speed to continually escape the Gorn. (RJ19)

NBC Broadcast Standards had their own notes. Jean Messerschmidt wrote:

> Page 1: Please keep to a minimum the number of bodies seen in the destroyed area. Page 2: Caution on the makeup used on the wounded Lt. Harold [the survivor of the alien attack], so that his injuries are not unduly alarming. Page 3: Caution on the death by ray of the Security Guard, so that his disintegration is not grotesque. Page 15: I assume Dr. McCoy will be using your air-hiss device for the injection; if the needle-type is used, please do not show this on camera. Page 28: Please use restraint when filming the results of the sudden stop [of the Enterprise] so that the action of being thrown to the floor and the pain is not unnecessarily alarming. Page 32: Please make sure there is nothing offensive in the Gorn's appearance. Page 46: I realize the necessity of establishing that the spear cannot penetrate the Gorn's hide, but please be especially cautious when filming this sequence. (NBC B.S. 19-1)

The body count was reduced; the radiation burns on Lt. Harold toned-down; and Kirk's attempt to penetrate the Gorn's hide with a spear was struck from the script. As for the "death by ray" that frightened Jean Messerschmidt, the script played it like this: "EXT. ANGLE ON LANG AMONG RUINS, slithering forward, his phaser ready, careful. He comes around a pile of rubble, looks out, reacts in what is plainly shock and revulsion. He picks up his communicator, flips it open. Alarm and distaste are written all over his face. He says, 'Lang to Captain!... I see them! Captain, they're...' As he says his last word, a ray SLASHES INTO FRAME, catching him squarely. He throws up his hands, freezes, glows red, disappears." Coon took all this out and replaced it with a line of dialogue from Crewman Kelowitz, reporting to Kirk, "They got Lang, sir."

These changes, among others, constituted Coon's Final Draft script, from October 28. He had wanted to make an impression on Fredric Brown. This was the draft sent to the famed writer.

Brown liked what he read and a deal was made on November 2, giving the sci-fi author both money and screen credit, as "story by."

Later that day, more notes arrived from the ever-fastidious Kellam de Forest (or his staffers, Joan Pearce and Peter Sloman). And this meant more changes for Coon's script. Regarding the two space vessels being forced to stop suddenly, de Forest Research said:

> The stresses of a sudden stop in space from warp speed would cause the ship to disintegrate. Any object inside the ship that was not a part of the structure, including the crewmen, would continue traveling at warp speeds right through the hull. These are the "impossible" things that should be commented on. (KDF19-2)

Concerning Kirk's makeshift cannon, described in the script as "a hollow shaft about three feet long, three or four inches across the mouth," with Kirk "thrashing his arm down it," de Forest wrote:

> It would be difficult for Mr. Shatner to get his arm down a tube of this size. Suggest he poke inside with another stick.... That this primitive cannon would fire and not blow up would be more believable if Kirk did something to strengthen the bamboo tube, either binding sticks to the outside, or slipping two pieces together, or inside the other. (KDF19-2)

There were many more notes -- many pages worth -- not uncommon from de Forest Research. Coon went along with the ideas about the cannon. He had Kirk wrap it in vines to help shore up the makeshift weapon. And then he had the cannon blow up anyway, knocking Kirk back and momentarily stunning him, as it sends out a blast of diamond missiles into the

Gorn. But Coon wasn't going to lose his "sudden stop" in space. Sulu reports the situation, saying, "It's impossible." Kirk goes one further, telling Sulu, "From Warp 8? Have you lost your mind?" As far as Coon was concerned, that was enough -- impossible for us to understand and accomplish, not so for the Metrons.

Two sets of page revisions soon followed, as "Arena" sped toward production, passing by many other scripts which had been in development for months. This was the shortest trek that any episode in the series had taken from story outline to final shooting script. And the results were outstanding.

Under Gene Coon's guidance, *Star Trek* was rapidly becoming faster-paced. Coon felt that *Star Trek* could remain adult and, at the same time, be a bit more fun. Care, however, was still taken to keep the series believable. To this end, it was agreed among the creative staff that the Gorn would not speak English. Instead, to honor a suggestion made by Roddenberry, a translator device was introduced to allow the two combatants to communicate.

"Arena" was the first episode to refer to the Earth space alliance as the "Federation," a contribution from Coon. The script for the upcoming "A Taste of Armageddon," having been around for a while and going through various revisions by Coon, would be more specific, identifying the alliance as The United Federation of Planets. "Arena" was also the episode which introduced the photon torpedoes, another Gene Coon invention.

Pre-Production
October 28 & October 31, and November 1-4 & November 7, 1966 (7 days prep).

"Joseph Pevney was an ex-actor turned director," Robert Justman shared. "Some former actors became good directors; some former actors became directorial hacks. Pevney was the former. [He was] more than just 'good.' *He directed 'Arena.'*" (94-8)

Bill Blackburn, one of the men to take a turn inside the Gorn suit, said, "My favorite director, who I absolutely adored, was Joe Pevney. He was outgoing, and kind of typical 'old show business.' He was fun. And he wasn't a 'yeller.'" (17a)

Jerry Finnerman had great respect and fondness for Pevney, as well. But his first impression, and the beginning of their association with one another, was not good. Finnerman said, "The first time I met Joe he said to me, *in front of Production*, 'How fast are you?' I said, 'I don't know.' And he said, 'Well, I'm fast, and we're going to get this show done on schedule.' Like the cameraman is holding it up! Okay. So I thought, 'I'll get this sonofabitch.'" (63-3)

Finnerman was becoming more confident and less willing to be intimidated. After his recent experience with Marc Daniels on "Court Martial" and "The Menagerie," where the director struck Finnerman as "pushy," *Star Trek*'s gifted Director of Photography was determined not to be pushed around.

Ted Cassidy, hired to provide the voice of the Gorn, had also been the voice of Balok's alter-ego in "The Corbomite Maneuver." He was seen in "What Are Little Girls Made Of?" as Ruk.

Vic Perrin provided the voice for the Metron. This was his first job with *Star Trek*, although many sources wrongly credit him as being involved in two previous episodes. Gene Coon and Joe D'Agosta knew exactly who they wanted: Perrin -- the "Control Voice" from *The Outer Limits*. Perrin later returned to do more voiceover work for *Star Trek* ("The Changeling") and appeared on camera in "Mirror, Mirror."

Carole Shelyne played the boyish-looking Metron. She was working regularly on *Shindig!*, and followed this with a recurring role as Fanny on *Here Come the Brides*. *Star Trek* had cast a woman to play an alien man before, in "The Cage," looping in a male voice. It worked again here -- beautifully.

Jerry Ayres, 30, played Ensign O'Herlihy, the crewman in the red shirt who dies on the planet, the result of a disintegration beam. He would be resurrected to play Ensign Rizzo in "Obsession," where he again donned a red shirt and, again, perished.

**Carole Shelyne as a Metron male
(Unaired film trim courtesy of Gerald Gurian)**

Grant Woods, 34, was the blue-shirted member of the landing party. This was his second of three episodes. Woods and his character Kelowitz were last seen in "The Galileo Seven." Still ahead: "This Side of Paradise."

Tom Troupe, at 38, played Lt. Harold (also referred to as Lt. Hadley in early drafts of the script), the sole survivor of the attack on Cestus III. Troupe worked often on television. He had just played doctors for episodes of *Ben Casey*, *Dr. Kildare* and *The Fugitive*, as well as a medic on *Combat!*

**Sean Kenney (sitting) as Lt. DePaul
(Unaired film trim courtesy of Gerald Gurian)**

Sean Kenney, who resembled Jeffrey Hunter enough to win the role as the crippled Captain Pike in "The Menagerie," made his first of two appearances as Lt. DePaul, the navigator on the bridge. Next for DePaul: "A Taste of Armageddon."

Wah Chang, responsible for the monsters on *The Outer Limits*, designed the Gorn costume.

Stuntman Bobby Clark began his relationship with *Star Trek* here, as the man who spent the most time in the Gorn suit (Gary Combs alternated, with Bill Blackburn taking a few brief turns for pickup shots). Of the casting, Joe Pevney said, "I talked Roddenberry into using a stuntman. An actor would have been worn out in nothing flat, and I would not have been able to get enough footage without building a fan into the suit. I said, 'We'd better get a guy accustomed to roughing it out there,' somebody who would be able to go without water for the length of time in order to get enough footage, or we'd be stopping all the time to allow someone to put the suit on and take it off, over and over." (141-3)

Bobby Clark remembered, "Joe Pevney called me and he says, 'Bobby, I got a good job for you. Are you busy such and such?' I says, 'No, I'm just working on the ranch here.' He says, 'Good. It's really a nice part; you don't have a whole lot of dialogue in it but it requires some physical stuff that I know you're capable of doing, so I want you to go to Desilu and go to the wardrobe man and he'll handle you for the costume.' I said, 'Well, what am I suppose to do in this?' And he says, 'I

Another Wah Chang contribution to *Star Trek* -- the Gorn (Courtesy of Gerald Gurian)

don't have time to tell you now; just go and get into your wardrobe.' And that was it. So I go to Desilu and into wardrobe and I said, 'I'm Bobby Clark and I'm here for a fitting for *Star Trek*, whatever that is.' And the guy there says, 'Okay, yeah, we're expecting you, Bobby. Go into dressing room whatever number.' So I go in and there is a curtain to close behind me, which I do, and there's a rack, which is suppose to have my wardrobe on it. And there's all this strange stuff on it but nothing that I can see that I'm suppose to put on, so I yelled out, 'Hey, there's no wardrobe in here for me!' The guy yells back, 'It should be in there, Bobby.' I yell out, 'There's no wardrobe in here' So he comes in and points to the stuff on the rack and says, '*That's* your wardrobe.' I said, 'Oh my God, what is it?' He says, 'It says here on our sheet that you're doing the Gorn.' I says, 'The Gorn? What's a Gorn?' He says, 'It's that thing in front of you.' Well, how was I to know; I'd never watched *Star Trek*. I watched the shows I was doing -- westerns! So I put it on, which was no easy thing. It was all rubber. It was a base wet suit and then they put all those muscles and shit on top of it, and then the gauntlets for the hands and the big feet on top of tennis shoes. The feet were maybe 16, 17 inches long. And then a tunic went on, and the hood over that. If I wanted to see down I'd have to lower my head, because I could only see what was right in front of me. Well, I suppose that's why Joe Pevney didn't have time to tell me what the part was." (31e)

Production Diary
Filmed November 8, 9, 10, 11, 14 & 15, 1966
(6 day production; total cost: $197,586).

Production began on November 8, 1966, a Tuesday. This was election day across America. Edward W. Brooke, a Republican from Massachusetts, became the first Black elected to the United States Senate. And movie actor Ronald Reagan was elected as Governor of California. The two top selling albums in record stores were the soundtrack to *Dr. Zhivago* and the début of The Monkees. Songs getting the most radio play across the Nation were "Last Train to Clarksville," by the Monkees, "96 Tears," by Question Mark & the Mysterians, and "Poor Side of Town," by Johnny Rivers. *The Monkees* TV series was a winner, too, according to A.C. Nielsen. It held the top-spot for its time period on NBC the night before, grabbing 31.4% of the TVs in use across the country. The big winners for that Monday night, however, were Desilu's own Lucille Ball, who's *Lucy Show* attracted a 43.1 audience share at 9 p.m., and Barbara Stanwyck, over at ABC, whose one-hour western, *The Big Valley*, had the 10 to 11 p.m. slot locked up, with a 43.4 audience share, at its peak. Odds were most of the *Star Trek* cast and crew were "hitting the hay" before *The Big Valley* cleared the air. They all had an early morning call.

Makeup went to work at 6:15 a.m. The lighting and camera crew were on set a little past 7. Filming started at 8. Joseph Pevney chose to do the easy stuff first, starting with the bridge set on Stage 9. There were many sequences to film, including that sudden stop in space that Broadcast Standards was worried might alarm the audience.

Pevney, having been offered a $500 bonus if he could stay on schedule and finish the demanding episode in just six days, was determined to hit the field running. And this resulted in him bruising Jerry Finnerman's ego when he told the young cinematographer in front of his entire crew that this episode would stay on schedule and the camera/lighting department was not going to slow things down.

Bobby Clark said, "I worked with Joe Pevney on westerns before then, and Joe and I got along very well. But he could get a little nasty with the cameramen if he wasn't getting what he wanted." (31e)

Jerry Finnerman said, "So, we go into the first shot, and we started to get the people in. They're not even in makeup [and only] half-dressed.... And I said, 'Joe, you want a little light to work with?' And he said, 'That would be nice.' So, I had a 10k over there [a large stage lamp used to flood a set with light]. It wasn't my style, but I said, 'Let me hit this light.' So, we hit the light.... And Joe rehearsed them, and he said [to me], 'Well, that's your shot.' And these guys aren't even in wardrobe, and I said, 'Ready.' And he said, 'What?' And I said, 'Ready.' So, I did this for about half a day, and he took me aside and said, 'Hey, you know, I like you. Let's be friends. Let's not go through this.' And I said, 'Okay. But I'm fast.' And he said, 'I know you are. Just calm yourself down.'... Joe and I were good friends after that.... Joe Pevney was a good director." (63-3)

As Finnerman and Pevney were figuring out how not to push each others' buttons, Sean Kenney was cautiously pushing some buttons of his own. Stationed at the helm as Lt. DePaul, Kenney recalled, "When I sat at the console and pressed the buttons, sometimes they would get so hot my fingers would stick to the melting plastic. This was before the days of low-voltage bulbs. I couldn't yell out; I would just have to pull my fingers off as quickly as I could and hope the camera didn't pick it up." (100)

Even though Pevney was new to the series, he got everything he needed, and then some, and wrapped early, at 5:25 p.m.

Day 2 took the *Star Trek* company back to Vasquez Rocks. William Shatner, along with Bill Blackburn (standing in for Shatner's regular lighting stand-in, Eddie Paskey), and stuntmen Gary Combs and Dick Dial, along with Pevney and the production crew, left Desilu at 6 a.m. for the hour-plus drive to the location. Bobby Clark said, "I lived in Saugus then – and that was only seven miles from Vasquez Rocks, so I just went out there and met up with them." (31e)

Clark had been given instructions about how to approach his role, and they had nothing to do with acting. He remembered, "After I had my fitting, a couple days before the shoot, I get a call from the wardrobe guy and he says, 'Bobby, do you drink a lot of coffee in the morning?' I said, 'Not a lot, but I do drink coffee.' He says, 'Good. Drink a little coffee; don't drink a whole lot of coffee. And, if you can, we'd appreciate it if you could go to the bathroom before you get into that suit. We'd rather not take you out any sooner than we have to.' They told me this because the bottom part of the wetsuit came up to here [the rib bone], and there were no zippers and I had to cornstarch my ass off to get into the costume. You can imagine what it was like to have to pee." (31e)

Clark relieved himself and Pevney began filming promptly at 8, shooting Kirk's first encounter with the Gorn, and many of the scripted action sequences to follow.

Being November, it was nippy at Vasquez Rocks and Shatner wore thermal underwear under his costume. If you look close, you can see the sleeves of the long-johns peeking through the sleeves of his Star Fleet uniform. The men who took turns inside the thick rubber hide of the Gorn did not find the climate to be as cool.

Bobby Clark said, "We started very early in the morning and we worked until the sun went down.... And you figure you have about three and a half to four inches of rubber on top of the wetsuit, so, hot, yes, it was very, very hot. Not excruciating because... the director would call us in when he's ready to shoot, then we'd put the head back on, zip up the tunic, then I'd go down and do whatever I had to do for the shot. And, as soon as he gets the shot, he says, 'cut'... and I can walk away, go to what I

Bobby Clark, minus the Gorn head and with black makeup around his mouth, takes a break and chats with a member of the wardrobe department (Courtesy of Bobby Clark)

called my 'perch,' where I had to stand on a ladder because I couldn't sit down. But then the wardrobe man would take the head off and unzip the tunic and he could unzip the top of the wet suit, and I'm cool to go.... As for makeup... I did have makeup. I had makeup all around my mouth and my nose and that whole area because when the Gorn made his 'Aarrgghh' noise, the mouth opened up and you could see in there, and they had to paint me black." (31d)

Clark had an alternate. Gary Combs, a young stuntman who was temporarily out of work due to an injury, was given the less demanding shots in the rubber suit as a favor from Pevney.

Bill Blackburn, one of *Star Trek*'s most visible extras, went invisible this time. Said Blackburn, "What I loved about *Star Trek* was that every time I went in to work, I never knew what I was going to do. If I wasn't going to be on the bridge, then I'd be doing something else -- like playing the Gorn. I didn't do the stunts; I did the close ups." (17b)

Shatner's stunt double for the flips and falls was Dick Dial.

Bobby Clark said, "I'd stay in that rubber costume from morning until lunch. I could take the top off at lunch, but I couldn't take the bottom off. It'd be too rough to get back into it. When I had to relieve myself, the hardest part was getting up to the 'honey wagon' and going up them friggin' five steps with those feet on. And then you get in and try to close the door! The feet were too big. And there was no fly in that damn suit. I'd have to go in there and pull the bottom part -- all fitted on that wet suit -- from the rib cage down to here, just enough so I could pee. Then I'd go back to the set. Fortunately, I had a stand-in [Blackburn] there for me while they planned the shots and lit the shots. I could rest during those times, in the shade, with the head off, up against my ladder. And when they were ready to shoot, I'd come down and go to my spot and the director would tell me, 'Alright, in this shot, Bobby, it's going to consist of you coming after Kirk, but remember that you're moving very slowly because you're reptilian.'" (31e)

Of his sparring partner, Clark said, "Shatner's always good to work with. He had done a lot of other things before *Star Trek*, so he knew what he was doing. But I'm not a bonafide actor; I'm a stuntman, so I'm doing physical stuff with him; not lines of dialogue. And we got those scenes shot pretty fast. We'd talk. We weren't pals, but we would talk. I give him credit -- the man worked hard." (31e)

Behind-the-scenes picture taken by a member of the wardrobe department of Bobby Clark as the Gorn in his full glory (Courtesy of Bobby Clark)

Despite the short November day, Pevney covered 34 scenes -- 9 pages of script. He stayed on schedule and wrapped at 4:45 p.m., just as the sun dipped below the horizon. The company packed up and arrived back at Desilu at 6 p.m. Shatner and the crew were thrilled. The producers were flabbergasted.

On Day 3, Thursday, November 10, Shatner and guest performer Carole Shelyne reported to makeup at 5:15 a.m. Along with the three stunt performers, Shatner's stand-in, and the production crew, they departed Desilu at 6:30 a.m. Filming at Vasquez Rocks again began promptly at 8. Pevney captured 53 scenes this time, and covered 10 pages of script. Remarkably, he was still on schedule when he called for a wrap at 4:30

Shatner and Clark discuss a fight sequence about to be filmed (Courtesy of Bobby Clark)

p.m., beating darkness by half an hour. Again, cast and crew were returned to the studio by 6 p.m., allowing Shatner to make it home in time to catch the long-delayed premiere of "The

Corbomite Maneuver" on NBC at 8:30 p.m.

Day 4. Leonard Nimoy, DeForest Kelley, Tom Troupe, James Farley, Jerry Agers, and Grant Woods joined Shatner, Dick Dial, and Eddie Paskey at Vasquez Rocks for the filming in the old fort, both modernized and battled-scarred by the art department.

Behind-the-scenes shots taken by Eddie Paskey (Courtesy of Gerald Gurian)

The fort at Cestus III, located at the foot of the jagged rocks, was originally constructed by Screen Gems in the mid-1950s for *Tales of the 77th Bengal Lancers*, a television series which followed the exploits of a British Calvary unit stationed in 19th century India. The staggering cost, back then, in 1956 dollars: $117,843.

Day 4: The fort at Vasquez Rocks (Courtesy of Gerald Gurian)

Eddie Paskey said, "Anytime you go on location, it is hard, but, for me, Vasquez Rocks was a treat. I mean, here I am in the middle of a set that's history -- that fort that looked like it was out of *Beau Geste*. And Vasquez Rocks, where I saw Roy Rogers and Gene Autry riding on TV, and remember from *Death Valley Days* when I was watching as a boy back in Harrington, Delaware. You get kinda taken up with all the history. And I'm thinking, 'I'm part of this now; I've been here with *these* people.' No, I didn't mind going on location at all." (135-2)

Portions of the episode's teaser were filmed, along with the attack on Cestus III for Act I. Pevney covered 15 scenes and 10 pages of script, shooting past sundown, using the large arc lights to simulate daylight for selected close up shots at the tail end of the day, wrapping at 6:15 p.m. Cast and crew made it back to Desilu at 7:20 p.m., but not all were in

Final day of production, back home on Stage 9 (Unaired film trim courtesy of Gerald Gurian)

good working condition. Both Shatner and Nimoy had fallen victim to the explosive charges set by Jim Rugg. The booms, bigger than expected, resulted in permanent ear damage. The condition, known as tinnitus, causes a constant ringing in the ear.

Day 5, Monday, saw a second day's work on the bridge set on Stage 9. The remarkable Joseph Pevney covered 22 camera set-ups and nearly 12 pages of script.

Day 6, Tuesday, November 15. Pevney spent the morning hours on the bridge, and the afternoon in the transporter room and, lastly, Kirk's quarters. He wrapped the ambitious and difficult production on schedule and budget.

Post-Production
November 16, 1966 to January 10, 1967. Music score: tracked.

Fabien Tordjmann and Edit Team #3 handled the cutting. Explaining the process, Tordjmann told Allan Asherman for *The Star Trek Interview Book*, "We'd talk with the director, then we'd talk to the producer, and they'd tell us what they wanted to do with it, and of course we'd have to consider the film being shot, because a lot of imponderables happened during the time of the shooting. New things happen -- acting is different, lines are changed. So we'd put it together and then we'd look at it with the director, and I believe also with the producer, and the director would work with us to try to make our work as close to his vision as possible. The director would leave and we would show it to the producer again, and he would try to adjust it to his vision, too. So it was a compromise. And sometimes we'd also fight for something we'd think was right. We were usually closer to the director, because we had the same type of background; however, the producer and the network have the last words, so at times we had to make some changes. Gene Roddenberry, Bob Justman, Eddie Milkis, and Gene Coon all had some wonderful ideas and we all worked together to achieve the best possible results in the amount of time allotted to us. So it's really a collaboration." (176)

"Arena" introduced a sound effect to be used often in future *Star Trek*s. Sound editing supervisor Jack Finlay said, "The photon torpedo sound, the 'twang,' came from *War of the Worlds*, and was obtained by striking a stretched length of cable. This was used with another effect over it to create a 'popping' type of sound." (62)

The Westheimer Company earned its money providing the photo effects, including the series' first use of the photon torpedoes, plus the transporter effects, a crewman being zapped away by a death ray, the fading in and out of the Metron, and the colorful array of signals seen on the viewing screen when the "control voice" speaks. Using stock shots of the Enterprise in flight and in orbit kept the cost down. The final bill: a manageable $6,931.

The budget for this ambitious episode was set higher by the producers than the norm, at $197,086. As a reward for getting it all done in six days -- an amazing feat -- Joseph Pevney was paid the $500 bonus, bringing the final cost to $197,586.

Release / Reaction
Premiere air date: 1/19/67. NBC repeat broadcast: 7/6/67.

Joan Crosby reviewed "Arena" for her syndicated *TV Scout* column. Among the newspapers to carry the review on January 19, 1967 was the *Edwardsville Intelligencer*, serving Edwardsville, Illinois. Crosby said:

> *Star Trek* has a visual outing in which William Shatner finds himself all alone on a planet, being tracked down by a Gorn, a monstrous being, with the outcome of their eventual battle being the safety of the Enterprise. There are some preliminaries before we come to all of this but be patient, because the end of the show, and the message of mercy that it contains, is good science fiction stuff.

And then came the ratings.

RATINGS / Nielsen 30-Market report for Thursday, January 19, 1967:

8:30 - 9 p.m., 65.3% of U.S. TVs in use.		Rating:	Share:
NBC:	*Star Trek* (first half)	17.4	26.6%
ABC:	***Bewitched***	**25.4**	**38.9%**
CBS:	*My Three Sons*	15.8	24.2%
Independent stations:		8.9	10.3%
9 - 9:30 p.m., 66.2% of U.S. TVs in use.			
NBC:	*Star Trek* (second half)	20.9	31.6%
ABC:	*Love On A Rooftop*	18.5	27.9%
CBS:	***Thursday Night Movie*** (start)	**21.6**	**32.6%**
Independent stations:		8.7	7.9%

According to A.C. Nielsen, over 30% of the TV sets playing in America were tuned in to see the outcome of Kirk's battle with a lizard creature. But many in the audience had missed the first half hour. *Bewitched*, a perfect show to attract and entertain younger viewers, dominated the 8:30 to 9 p.m. period this night. At 9 p.m., *Star Trek*'s numbers improved, just a single ratings point behind *The CBS Thursday Night Movie*, a first run showing of *My Geisha*, a 1961 comedy starring Shirley MacLaine, Edward G. Robinson, and Bob Cummings.

***

"Arena" is a *Star Trek* classic. In the December 1991 issue of *Cinefantastique*, writer/critic Thomas Doherty picked "Arena" as the fourth best episode from the original series.

A footnote about the foothills: Six years after this production, the State of California acquired Vasquez Rocks (from Ralph Helfer, who also owned this property) and designated it a public park. Concerned that the crumbling structures and high walls of the fort might pose a threat to park visitors, it was demolished.

From the Mailbag

Received the week after "Arena" first aired on NBC:

> Dear Mr. Roddenberry: Some time ago, during the summer, the networks started announcing their new shows for the Fall Season. Most were the same, with kids' shows, movies, and spy series, but I noticed a new and different attraction -- *Star Trek*. I have been reading space books, both fact and fiction, for about three years and naturally was very enthusiastic about your new show. I decided after watching the previews it might be well worth my time to watch it -- It was! I am still very excited about it, especially Mr. Spock. I firmly believe in his philosophy in that everything should be approached logically in space or on earth.... I do hope *Star Trek* will be on next season, for my 8th grade friends and I enjoy it very much! John H. (Burbank, California).

> Dear Mr. Nimoy: First, thank you for the picture. I consider receiving it an honor which I certainly didn't expect.... I'll continue to watch *Star Trek*, admire your performance as Mr. Spock, wish that the chess games hadn't been eliminated, and consider what a great opportunity someone's smart crack about Mr. Spock's musical instrument would be for him to say something about "logical mathematical progressions." Jessica M. (University of Washington, Seattle, WA.)

Memories

William Shatner complained, "There was one show, I've forgotten the name of it, which somebody said to the director, if you bring the show in in five days [sic], you'll get $500 extra. And it was a show I was mostly alone in. I did fourteen pages of dialogue in one day. The average was nine or ten pages a day, but I did *fourteen*. The show came in on time, the director got the 500 bucks and I didn't even get a thank-you." (156-9)

More *Star Trek* folklore to believe or dispel -- Frederic Brown's short story and Gene Coon's teleplay get merged into a novelette by Bantam Books, circa mid 1970s ... or is it fan art from the Internet?

28

Episode 20: THE ALTERNATIVE FACTOR
Written by Don Ingalls
(with Gene L. Coon and/or Steven Carabatsos, uncredited)
Directed by Gerd Oswald

NBC press release from January 12, 1967:

Shatner with Robert Brown for NBC publicity photo (Courtesy of Gerald Gurian)

Robert Brown guest-stars in a dual role in "The Alternative Factor," a drama involving two strange men from an uncharted planet who threaten destruction of the universe on NBC Television Network's colorcast of *Star Trek* Thursday, Feb. 2.... A landing party under the command of Capt. James Kirk (William Shatner) encounters Lazarus (Brown), an embattled and desperate man who begs assistance in his defense against an enemy (Brown) who he claims to be insane. When Kirk is reluctant, Lazarus makes an incredible claim of being the only man who can prevent the impending total destruction of civilization.

Lazarus appears human. His behavior is erratic, as are the effects of the energy source which is opening a door between our universe, one of positive matter, and an alternative universe, where existence is based on anti-matter. Allowing the twain to meet will cause the instant annihilation of each.

"The Alternative Factor" is a study in madness, obsession, and self-sacrifice. And, as almost always on *Star Trek*, a Man versus Beast story is at its core Man versus Himself.

SOUND BITES

- *Kirk:* "Sometimes pain can drive a man harder than pleasure."
- *Spock:* "Madness has no purpose. No reason. But it could have a goal."
- *Kirk:* "So you're the terrible thing? The hideous, murdering monster?" *Lazarus #2:* "Yes, Captain. Or *he* is. It depends on your point of view."
- *Kirk:* "You'll be trapped forever with a raging madman at your throat." *Lazarus #2:* "Is it such a large price to pay for the safety of two universes?"

ASSESSMENT

With "The Alternative Factor," we are treated to a recurring *Star Trek* theme, how the needs of the many outweigh the needs of the few ... or the one. It would be said later, in those very words, in *Star Trek II: the Wrath of Khan*. It is said here by a mournful Kirk, regarding the "good Lazarus." When all the madness has finally ended, a drained Kirk sits in his command chair and says, "How would it be ... to be trapped forever with a raging madman at your throat ... until time itself comes to a stop ... for eternity. How would it be?" Spock points out, "But the universe is safe, Captain." Kirk softly replies, "Yes ... for you and me. But what of Lazarus?"

And what of "The Alternative Factor"? This *Trek* is an awkward mix of good and bad. Problems during the final scripting phase and production were to blame. Cast and crew endeavored to maintain *Star Trek*'s high standard, but too much around them was going wrong. The profound message at the story's end is a plus, as is Robert Brown's performance as Larzarus #2 -- the good Lazarus. But even the stage-trained Brown suffers from the unevenness of the writing and direction as he and his "opposite" meet to do battle -- lunging, wrestling, falling off rock formations, one, two, three times, which is two times too many. Lazarus #1 -- the crazy one -- is both written and played with little subtlety. And this is the Lazarus who has most of the screen time. There are also continuity errors, such as the stringy beard on Lazarus, which goes from thick to thin and then to thick again. And the very cerebral and, at times, convoluted plot never connects enough to fully engage the viewer.

This well-meaning story reached for the stars ... and, more often than not, came up with dust.

But even lesser TOS is still a trek worth taking. As Robert Justman would later say, "I loved them all." And that meant he also loved "The Alternative Factor."

THE STORY BEHIND THE STORY

Script Timeline
Don Ingalls' story outline, ST #34: August 29, 1966.
Ingalls' revised outline, gratis: September 12, 1966.
Ingalls' 2nd Revised Story Outline, gratis: September 14, 1966.
Ingalls' 1st Draft teleplay: October 14, 1966.
Ingalls' 2nd Draft teleplay (Mimeo Department "Yellow Cover 1st Draft"):
November 7, 1966.
Script polish by Gene Coon or Steven Carabatsos (Final Draft teleplay):
November 11, 1966.
Coon's rewrite (Rev. Final Draft teleplay): November 14, 1966.
Additional page revisions by Coon and/or Carabatsos:
November 15, 16 & 18, 1966.

Don Ingalls was a former cop and a friend of Gene Roddenberry. He was also one of Roddenberry's peers, having worked as both a writer and then producer on *Have Gun - Will Travel*. Ingalls continued to work as a writer/producer in television on the western *Whiplash*, where he farmed script work out to Roddenberry, and then on to *The Travels of Jaimie McPheeters*, *The Virginian*, *12 O'clock High*, and *Honey West*.

Roddenberry wanted his friend to write for *Star Trek* and approved the pitch concerning a man's obsessive hunt for his other self (a self that exists in an alternate universe based in anti-matter) and Kirk's efforts to solve the mystery regarding the hunter and the lookalike hunted, thereby preventing universal annihilation.

The story outline, in which the Enterprise crew encounter Lazarus "shipwrecked" on a planet devoid of humanoid life, arrived on August 29, 1966. Ingalls, in his treatment, wrote:

> [Lazarus] is an interplanetary hunter. His game? A creature -- a humanoid monster that destroyed his civilization on a far distant planet. He is dedicated now to destroying the destroyer. Underlying the surface likeableness, the twisted grin, the deep blue eyes that look sadly into yours, is the visible memory of his horror, fighting up from the depths within him. The sympathies of Captain Kirk and the others go out to him.... Especially attracted and sympathetic is Charlene Masters, a pretty space chemist, nearly thirty and never before having met a man who might become more important to her than her test tubes and her formulas.... To the Enterprise crewman, Lazarus is a swashbuckling, tragic figure with hair on his chest and a chip on his shoulder and a girth of arm and chest to slay a dragon! He is a natural leader who infuses the young crewmen with a lust for the hunt and, like the harpooners and mariners of a bygone age clustered about their Ahab, so they find themselves mustering to the siren call to the hunt of this fantastic anachronism of a man.

The passionate writing, while confusing the producers, nonetheless seduced them into keeping the assignment alive -- just as Lazarus confused and seduced the crew of the Enterprise into keeping his quest alive.

Gene Coon, in a four-page memo to Roddenberry, was careful to be gentle in his criticism concerning this well-written but otherwise underdeveloped outline. He said:

> This outline is so sketchy that we have no specific idea of what kind of action, story line, movement, motivation we are in for.... Don't misunderstand this memo. I love the idea of Ahab pursuing the whale, which turns out to be himself. I love the idea of alternate worlds, of the stepping from dimension to dimension. It is simply that there are many things in this outline which must be explained and resolved <u>before</u> we go to screenplay. (GC20-1)

Justman, also writing to Roddenberry, since Roddenberry had given out the assignment, said:

> I have just read this story premise. I am extremely confused. I have just read Gene Coon's memo on the premise. I agree with everything he says. I find that he seems less confused than I do. I congratulate him. (RJ20-1)

Roddenberry agreed, and wrote back to Coon:

> I am in a state of confusion over the whole story and not quite sure who is doing what to who. But I <u>am</u> sure Kirk is not doing much to resolve the story.... Don is rather vague about a good many sections of the action and progression in this story. Recommend he come back with a more explicit and definitive version. (GR20-1)

A revised story outline arrived on September 12, *gratis*. Ingalls was resisting making the changes asked for. In trying to retain the magnetism Lazarus #1 had over Lt. Charlene Masters, and over Kirk and his crew, Ingalls was not putting in the negative personality traits needed to differentiate between this Lazarus and his anti-matter self -- the "good Lazarus." Both were on a mission, both were charismatic, both looked alike, both spoke alike and, adding to the confusion, Ingalls often neglected to add "#1" or "#2" to the character's name.

Roddenberry wrote to Coon:

> I still cannot easily follow Lazarus "good" and Lazarus "bad" and who's really

where. The audience has to know who's who and who's where at all times -- as we found in "The Enemy Within." (GR20-2)

The bigger problem remained that the lead character in *Star Trek* was not the lead character in this story. Roddenberry continued:

> Kirk is leading another search party. This is all he seems to do in this story. Let's get him really involved. There has got to be some jeopardy and danger to our people. So far we've just been walking through this piece. (GR20-2)

Ingalls' second free rewrite, from September 14, attempted to put more Kirk into the story -- double the Kirk, in fact. In this version, there were now two Kirks, with the "door" between Universes 1 and 2 swinging open far enough for Kirk to meet his own alternate self.

Coon liked the addition and sent the retooled story outline to NBC. Stan Robertson, however, was not keen on this new gimmick, which he saw as being an *old* gimmick. Kirk had already met a duplicate of himself in "What Are Little Girls Made Of?" and "The Enemy Within." Otherwise, Robertson was very optimistic about what he described as "a very fine story outline," writing Coon:

> If the writer of this outline, Don Ingalls, instills the same exciting elements and sheer beauty of writing into the screenplay as are contained in this treatment, this should make for a fine *Star Trek* episode. (SR20-1)

Lazarus, or Don Ingalls, had just seduced Stan Robertson and thereby recruited another follower.

Justman, taking the counterpoint, dropped Coon a memo the next day, which was one day too late. He wrote:

> I have ambivalent feelings about the Story Treatment. I enjoyed the Teaser and part of the First Act and found it very intriguing. The mystery of Lazarus and what he is doing on that little planet and the start of the relationship between him and the girl are somewhat compelling. However, as we begin to find out more about the story and about Lazarus, I find my interest waning rather rapidly. Also, the more we know about Lazarus and his counterpart, the more confusing the story becomes to me.... I see that you have already put Mr. Ingalls to work on a First Draft screenplay. Therefore, I will reserve any further comment until he turns in this draft. (RJ20-2)

With NBC's approval, Ingalls had been sent to script, although told not to play the idea of Kirk meeting Kirk.

The First Draft teleplay, dated October 14, arrived on the 17th. The duplicate Kirk was out and, in his place, a stronger romance between Lazarus #1 and Lt. Charlene Masters, someone he could woo and then use to gain access to the energy source of the ship's dilithium crystals.

In the scene where Masters and Lazarus #1 meet, she is in the recreation room, sitting alone. Sulu notices a sad expression on her face and approaches. He asks, "Lonely?" She invites him to join her, but her attention quickly shifts to a man who enters -- a man she has never seen before. He is the type of man a woman of her era might rarely have a chance to meet, a throwback to a more romantic time -- a rugged, driven man. When Sulu, in an attempt to flirt, asks what she is doing "in a place like this," Masters replies, "Waiting for someone like ... you." But her eyes are clearly focused on Lazarus. Ingalls writes:

> Her eyes have never left Lazarus and there is that almost imperceptible something in her manner that comes alive when a woman sees <u>the</u> man approach

her. ANGLE WIDENS as Lazarus reaches their table. He looks at Charlene and, for the first time, he smiles. A small, gentle little smile, softening the hawk-like features.

In another scene, Lazarus #1 is again with Masters. The script reads: "She stares at him, a strange look in her eyes. He stares at her. Then, softly, he tells her, 'I have moved through eternity to find you. You know that, don't you? When we first saw each other ... you must have felt it.' She says, 'You were like a wounded eagle.' He says, 'An eagle looks a long time for his mate ... and, once he finds her, he never leaves her. I have looked a long time.' He pulls her close. She draws back for a moment, but his force, though gentle, is relentless. He tells her, 'You have no idea what it's like ... eternity unrolling before you ... and to be alone, through all time ... and then I saw you.' Hungrily, he sweeps her into his arms and kisses her. For a moment she resists...and then she melts.... He says, 'I knew it the moment I saw you. You belong to me. It is as inevitable as my struggle.... Charlene... I can't be alone any more. When the Enterprise leaves here, I will stay. I want you to stay with me.'"

Later, Lazarus #1 tells her, "With your love, and help, I can end this terrible quest, then live a real life again, anywhere you say, together, the two of us."

Masters conspires to help Lazarus. She sets the fire in the department of the engineering deck where she is assigned -- the dilithium recharging station -- creating a smokescreen so Lazarus can steal the crystals. She even travels to the planet where his "inter-dimensional ship" is located, then accompanies him into the "corridor" separating the two universes. As she becomes trapped with him, she discovers too late that he is mad.

Kirk's personal stake in the story is hinged on his need to solve the mystery of the hunter and the hunted, save Masters from herself, and *not* save Lazarus from himself, thereby preventing the annihilation of two universes. To do this, Kirk enters the corridor and encounters Lazarus #2 -- the "good" Lazarus -- hard at work on a means to close the doorway for all time. He tells Kirk that he will catch Lazarus #1 when he enters, preventing him from making it through to the other end, and, at the same time, buying Kirk the time he needs to find Masters and pull her from the corridor. Kirk does so, and then uses the ship's phasers to destroy the inter-dimensional ship and seal the doorway for all eternity. The ending is poignant. Lazarus #2, a man Kirk had looked-up to, will spend eternity at the hands of a raving madman, for the good of two universes. The other, damned to the same fate, is Lazarus #1, the man Charlene Masters had loved despite his self-torture.

Robert Justman, now believing he was able to follow who was who, liked the positive/negative tragedy in space and wrote to Coon, "I must admit, I'm rather intrigued by this property." (RJ20-3)

Justman's intrigue soon turned to trepidation. He continued:

> On page 4, I get to my first major hang-up with the show. Lazarus' strange-looking spacecraft. As you may be aware, Gene, the Shuttlecraft exterior and interior mockups that we have probably cost well over $30,000. Unless we can find a way to re-use the Shuttlecraft for this show, we are going to end up with a pretty cheap-looking Spacecraft for Mr. Lazarus because we can't afford to spend $30,000, or even $5,000 for this exterior and interior set. (RJ20-3)

Roddenberry was also satisfied. Kirk was more proactive. A non-regular was still the central focus, but this had been done before with "Charlie X" and had worked. With the right actor playing Lazarus, as it had happened when Robert Walker Jr. was cast as Charlie, the story could very well succeed.

Roddenberry knew who the right actor was. He suggested John Drew Barrymore for the role. Barrymore, a gifted and somewhat offbeat performer, was the son of famed stage actor John Barrymore and film legend Dolores Costello. Where John Drew went, free publicity followed.

A few days later, Bob Justman wrote to his colleagues, suggesting that the "corridor" which separates the universe of matter from that of anti-matter could be created through the use of reverse polarity, turning a positive image into a negative one, allowing white to turn to black and black to white -- an effect which, in its simplicity, served as a metaphor for the story being told, where good is bad and bad is good. It was also an effect Justman knew *Star Trek* could afford, and one which would be effective on both black-and-white and color TVs.

Ingalls turned in his 2nd Draft teleplay on November 7. The story, for the most part, seemed to work; the writing was certainly fluid and dramatic, enough so for Coon to tell Ingalls he had fulfilled his contract. This version of the script was sent to John Drew Barrymore and succeeded at interesting the actor into playing Lazarus ... and Lazarus #2.

Now that Barrymore was locked in, attention turned back to the script for additional polishing by the staff. Four things needed to be accomplished: 1) the dialogue required finessing so that the recurring characters sounded more like themselves; 2) the technology on the Enterprise had to be faithful to what was already established in the series; 3) greater emphasis had to be made to create a difference in the personalities between Lazarus #1 and Lazarus #2 to prevent audience confusion, something Ingalls had been reluctant to do; and 4) Lt. Masters could no longer betray her captain. This last change came about because of a memo from Roddenberry to Coon.

Roddenberry wrote:

> In both "Space Seed" and this story, we have a crew woman madly in love with a brawny guest star and flipping our whole gang into a real mess because she is in love. Isn't that really pretty selfish, which is not to say that women in love *don't* do strange, stupid and/or selfish things ... but do they have to do them in two of our scripts? (GR20-2)

Roddenberry wasn't suggesting "The Alternative Factor," first to film, be altered. His criticism had more to do with "Space Seed" using the same plot device. Regardless, one had to be changed.

To Coon's thinking, the betrayal element was more essential for "Space Seed." With "The Alternative Factor," the story elements which intrigued him the most had to do with the idea of an obsessed hunter hunting himself, and the villain being of *our* universe -- the positive side -- and the one who is willing to sacrifice his life for the good of all being from the negative side. This amused him. He also liked how Kirk slowly came to realize he was dealing with two different men -- one sane, one mad -- each stepping back and forth between two incompatible worlds. Finally, he was taken by the tragic example of self-sacrifice, by Lazarus #2, and the burden on Kirk's shoulders in allowing the sane one to give up his life in such a horrific manner. And all of this could stay.

The changes were made for the November 11 Final Draft, likely by Steven Carabatsos.

Coon had underestimated the importance of the romance in the story. By taking out passages of dialogue where Lazarus admits to Charlene Masters that he is growing weary of the chase, and is in fact lonely, the audience has less reason to empathize with the character.

The burden was now on the shoulders of John Drew Barrymore to make a crazy man seem somehow appealing.

Pre-Production ... and more rewriting
November 8-11 and 14 & 15, 1966 (6 days total).

John Drew Barrymore (1960s publicity photo)

Gerd Oswald, the man who directed more episodes of *The Outer Limits* than anyone else, and who had pleased the producers with his handling of "The Conscience of the King," was brought back for his second *Star Trek* assignment.

John Drew Barrymore, now signed to play Lazarus, had more going for him than his legendary family name -- he had achieved stardom in his own right. This Barrymore had shared the lead on the big screen with Steve McQueen in 1958's *Never Love a Stranger*, and with Julie London in 1959's *Night of the Quarter Moon*. He then traveled to Italy to top the bill in numerous films there, such as 1960's *I'll See You in Hell* and, as Ulysses, opposite Steve Reeves' Hercules, in 1961's *The Trojan Wars*. Between films in the early and mid-Sixties, Barrymore was always given choice television guest star roles, in series such as *Gunsmoke*, *Rawhide*, *The Wild, Wild West*, and now, tentatively, *Star Trek*.

Janet MacLachlan (casting department photos)

For the part of Lt. Charlene Masters, Joe D'Agosta and Gerd Oswald liked the idea of hiring an up-and-coming black actress -- Janet MacLachlan. She would soon take the lead guest spot, as a love interest for Bill Cosby, in a 1967 Emmy-winning episode of *I Spy*, then go on to receive second billing in a racially-charged movie, *Halls of Anger*, well above newcomer Jeff Bridges, and play the on-screen wife of star Jim Brown in ... *tick... tick...*

tick.... But in 1966, MacLachlan was mostly known for her work on the stage. She had yet to achieve any standout recognition on television, so there was no real name value in hiring her, only color value. If Barrymore didn't bring the press to *Star Trek*, television's first interracial love affair certainly would.

For her casting call, MacLachlan wore a wig, but it was decided for the episode to go with the more natural short Afro hairstyle. Ande Richardson-Kindryd, secretary for Gene Coon, felt it was a small but important step in Black civil rights. She said, "At that time, black women were all wearing wigs. And my mother had made me swear that I would always wear a wig to work because I should not ever let them see my natural hair. It was just too radical."

Kindryd remembered seeing MacLachlan on the *Star Trek* stages, and said, "It was very courageous that she wore her hair in an Afro at that time. Most network TV shows wouldn't have had her do that. But the people at *Star Trek* thought in those terms -- individual rights; personal choices. It was a very freeing environment, and a very positive message. So now I knew I was finally at a place where I felt that we had a chance to be – *we*, being black people. I took off my wig and stuck my head under a water tap and combed out my Afro and went back to work. I sat down at my desk and no one ever said a word to me and I knew I was at a place where I belonged, that this was home and I was with good people." (144a)

But the attitudes within the *Star Trek* buildings and stages were not representative of all of America in 1966, and the domino effect which took most of the good out of "The Alternative Factor," began first with Coon's decision to trim back some of the romance, now intensified with the casting of Janet MacLachlan to play opposite John Drew Barrymore. It was still one year before the release of the controversial *Guess Who's Coming to Dinner?*, in which black Sidney Poitier and white Katherine Houghton fight for their right to be married -- and win. As NBC became aware of the casting, the network programmers expressed misgivings. Even with the success of *I Spy* and its equal-status casting of Robert Culp and Bill Cosby, and the love story in "The Alternative Factor" now pushed into the background, many were nonetheless wondering how the affiliates in the South might react to this interracial pairing. With only a few days left before the start of production, Gene Coon began receiving off-the-record phone calls suggesting that either Janet MacLachlan be replaced with a white actress or that the script be changed to remove the remaining scenes depicting sexual or romantic interest between Lazarus #1 and Charlene Masters. The simplest solution would have been to pay MacLachlan a "kill fee" with the promise of future work. Coon, however, zigged when he should have zagged.

With Coon's November 14th Revised Final Draft, the last traces of the love story were removed. Lazarus #1 had lost all his charismatic traits and, because of this, was now intolerably annoying. The character of Charlene Masters, no longer a chemist but instead a member of engineering, became pointless. She was left with so little to do that one has to wonder why she is even in the story, representing the engineering section in place of Scotty.

With filming due to start in two days, the new script was sent to the director and the regular cast members. John Drew Barrymore was not scheduled to work that first day of filming. For the moment, he was unaware of the drastic story changes.

Production Diary
Filmed November 16, 17, 18, 21, 22, 23 & 25, 1966
(Planned as a 6 day production, finishing one day over; total cost: $210,879).

Wednesday, November 16, 1966. The morning papers were filled with pictures of an historic event from the day before -- after accomplishing the longest and most successful spacewalk to date, astronauts James Lovell and Buzz Aldrin returned safely to Earth with the splashdown of Gemini XII. The four most popular songs awaiting them on the radio were "Poor Side of Town" by Johnny Rivers, The Beach Boys' "Good Vibrations," The Supremes' "You Keep Me Hanging On," and "Last Train to Clarksville" by The Monkees. America's teens, in fact, had a sudden case of Monkeemania. The "pre-fab four," as the press was calling them, had the No. 1 album in the nation and their TV show was on its way to winning an Emmy as Best Comedy. However, as popular as the pop music sitcom was, *Star Trek*'s ratings were higher. And out of 90 primetime TV series, the two that received the most fan mail by far were *The Monkees* and *Star Trek*, neck and neck. The top movies people were willing to pay $1 to see were *Way... Way Out*, with Jerry Lewis, *Madam X*, starring Lana Turner, *Spinout*, an action-romance vehicle for Elvis Presley, *The Professionals*, a western starring Burt Lancaster and Lee Marvin, and the risqué *Penelope*, with sexy Natalie Wood in the title role. All five films took a one-week turn as box office champ in the period spanning the final writing, the preproduction, and the filming of "The Alternative Factor."

Principal photography commenced on Stage 9 for the bridge scenes that did not involve Lazarus. Janet MacLachlan was present, and given a blue uniform to wear. This was the first of many mistakes -- although a relatively minor one. Lt. Masters was originally written as a chemist; as a member of the medical or science departments, so she would have worn blue. But with the change in the script that had her assigned to engineering, red should have been her new color. Someone forgot to clue-in the wardrobe department.

Oswald covered 23 scenes and more than 10 pages of script, wrapping at 6:50 p.m., 30 minutes into overtime but otherwise on schedule. All seemed well ... at least, on set. It was a different story in the producer's office.

Earlier in the day, a memo from Stan Robertson arrived. It said nothing about the casting but, instead, focused on a plot device used in the script. Robertson wrote:

> This will confirm our telephone conversation of yesterday, in which I again voiced objections to this script which has as its premise another "duplicate character."... We have gone over this point many times in the past, Gene, and it appears as though we are only continuing to perpetuate the "sameness" which has been one of the continuing criticisms of our series. (SR20-2)

This was a curious note to send to Coon on the first day of production. Robertson had previously approved "this very fine story," duplicate character included. But, now, as the cameras were rolling, he was making it clear that NBC could refuse to air "The Alternative Factor." And that meant NBC would not have to pay for the episode. The network had found its out.

Within hours, director Gerd Oswald, finishing work on the set, received new script pages for the next day. He later said, "The script was so complicated, it was even hard to interpret for some of us deeply involved with it." (134)

John Drew Barrymore was visiting wardrobe on this day for final costume fittings. Before leaving, he was given the revised script. And then he quit the production.

In a memo from the next day to Herb Solow, Joe D'Agosta wrote:

> Between 4 and 5 p.m., [Barrymore] sent word that he did not want to do the role and refused to accept a work call for filming the following morning, November 17. With the cooperation of his agent and lawyer, I told him that he was committed and had to report to work. Mr. Barrymore then became unavailable and out of reach. His reasons were that the script changes had altered his

character. (JDA20)

D.C. Fontana recalled, "They recast the lead with Robert Brown at eleven o'clock at night, and that poor man had to be on set with makeup and costume the next morning, with the script he had just read the night before. Talk about lack of rehearsal." (64-2)

Brown remembered differently. He believed his preparation time was even shorter.

Robert Brown was 38 when he was tossed a live hand grenade called "The Alternative Factor." Prior to this, he worked often on the stage, including shows on Broadway. In 1958, he snagged a prominent role in the sci-fi movie *The Flame Barrier*. In television, Brown found notable guest spots on series such as *Perry Mason*, *Wagon Train*, and *Bonanza*. In 1962, he starred with William Shatner in the unsold TV pilot called "Colossus." Still in his future, top billing in *Here Come the Brides*, above Trekker Mark Lenard and future heartthrobs Bobby Sherman and David Soul.

Day 2, Thursday. Robert Brown remembered it well. He said, "I got a call on my birthday [November 17] and it was from Roddenberry. Shatner and I had gotten along really well while making 'Colossus,' and Roddenberry said, 'Shatner gave me your number; I hope you don't mind me calling.' I didn't know who Roddenberry was. I didn't know what *Star Trek* was. It had just started and I hadn't seen it. But he knew that I lived out in the Malibu colony and he said, 'Listen, it will take you about an hour to get here. Can you come out?' So I drove in and Roddenberry greeted me and said, 'You just follow me back to makeup and don't worry, we'll find a place for you to live near the studio.' I said, 'What are you talking about?' He said, 'Well, you got the part. Shatner says you can handle it. So, after I called you, my office called your agent to talk about the script.' I said, 'What script? I haven't heard anything about it. I'm not familiar with this show or the genre, so I don't think so. Thanks, but no.' He said, 'Listen, you're an actor, you're from the theater, you can do this. Look, I'll tell you what we'll do -- I've got a contract with Shatner that says nobody can get more money than he does, but I'll arrange something. We'll pay you what he makes and I'll put in a little extra myself. But you can't tell him or else I'll sue you.' And then he reached in his pocket and gave me five dollars. He said, 'Here.' And then he arranged for a motel near the lot. Since I was living so far away from the studio, and with the schedule being what it was from the first shot of the day to the last shot of the night, they didn't think I'd be able to manage the trip. They were right. It was an hour and a half each way, at least. I would never have gotten any sleep." (24-1)

Brown took the five bucks and reported to makeup. He said, "Luckily the costume Barrymore was going to wear fit me. And then the nice guy who did the ears – [Fred Phillips] the head of the makeup department -- said 'We'll give you a special who-knows-what kind of a look. Barrymore didn't have that, but man I'll do it for you.' And out came the beard." (24-1)

For this day, in his scenes on the bridge followed by sickbay and the transporter room, Brown's beard was thin, although not yet completely sparse. This would soon change.

With all the confusion, care normally shown in the making of *Star Trek* was now nowhere in sight. For a scene in the transporter room, Lazarus knocks out the transporter technician and beams himself to the planet. One must wonder where he learned to operate the transporter. One must also wonder why the Technician seems fine and dandy a minute later when Kirk races in and asks to be beamed down. Blame the writers(s) and the director. The scene description merely reads: "INT. TRANSPORTER ROOM. Kirk standing on a plate, the technician, recovered now, standing by." Shouldn't Coon have at least written into the script that the technician is rubbing his sore neck where Lazarus gave him a judo chop? Shouldn't Oswald have directed it this way, regardless of whether it was so indicated in the script? Never before on the series had a writer and a director shown such sloppiness in this regard.

When Oswald wrapped at 7 p.m., he was one-half day behind.

"The Menagerie, Part 1" was on NBC that night, as the 11th broadcast episode.

Day 3. On Friday, the company finished the scenes intended for the previous day -- sequences on the bridge and in the ship's corridors. Fortunately, on this day, Brown's beard matched from the day before. Again, that would soon change.

The scenes in the alternate engineering set were planned to come next but Oswald barely got started on this before calling for a wrap at 7:15 p.m., a full hour into overtime.

Brown said, "They broke the rules concerning their timing. They were shooting late every day. So I didn't get home during that whole time except for the weekend." (24-1)

Day 4. Come Monday, filming took place in an area of engineering identified in the script as "Lithium Crystal Recharging Section." This information was supposed to go on the door outside. The sloppiness continued and the sign by the door merely read "Engineering," adding to the confusion. Why does engineering suddenly not look like engineering? And where is Scotty?

As the day progressed, the company moved to the recreation room, followed by a move to sickbay. Again, on the plus side, the beard looked the same and the cast were holding well at learning the new dialogue coming down from the producer's office. But the work was exhausting.

Brown vividly recalled, "I was living a nightmare because I was playing catch-up. I was being pushed and chased every day. A lot of times they wouldn't do reverse shots; they'd just do over-the-shoulder angles, because they were so late. They knew they'd be going into overtime and they couldn't afford it. And all this rushing created an uncomfortable feeling. Not from Shatner. He couldn't have been better. And the rest of the cast was a nice group ... except for the morose man with the ears. And the director was always rushing and pushing me. And he said he was going to call SAG and tell them that I was not a good actor if I couldn't speed up with all this strange dialogue they were handing me. And I tell you I was going day and night." (24-1)

Vasquez Rocks

Oswald wrapped at 6:50 p.m.

Day 5 took the company to Vasquez Rocks for the third time. All of the scenes featuring Lazarus shaking a fist at the sky, bellowing about wanting to kill the beast, and tumbling off rock formations injuring himself repeatedly, were filmed.

Brown remembered, "Working out at Vasquez Rocks was actually the easiest part of the shoot. They had to take time to set the camera up and light everything just right, so there was time to study the script and plan things out; planning for the rocks – which ones I would climb and how to land on a mattress. Watching the cameramen do what they do was quite special. It was tougher being at the studio." (24-1)

While the lighting and camera crew excelled with their work on location, makeup did a horrible job with Brown's fake beard. It was much thicker than in any of the scenes shot on stage. This had nothing to do with whether it was Lazarus #1 or #2; the beard was the same for both, completely wrong considering what we had seen before.

Brown said, "The great makeup guy had a couple understudies -- other people who were dispatched out to location and onto the set at times, who were just sticking it on. And I was looking at the lines. I never had a minute to think about anything but

Picture taken by Eddie Paskey - on location at Vasquez Rocks (Courtesy Gerald Gurian)

'What am I supposed to say.' And I didn't really have any clue what those words meant, with the description of the stars and the different universes." (24-1)

No one else had time to notice the beard either. Oswald, for one, was busy watching the house of cards known as a TV production schedule fall down around him. He was only able to cover four pages of script this day and, plunged into darkness at 5:20 p.m., ended three-quarters of a day behind.

"Gerd was kind of an old-fashioned director," Dorothy Fontana said. "The script wasn't *that* bad. It was kind of a mish-mash. It didn't help that the actor was being thrown into a difficult situation. And then the director had problems. 'Conscience of the King' was all indoors, it was all on the set.

Shatner freezes for the post optical effect to be added later (Unaired film trim courtesy of Gerald Gurian)

This one was sort of splattered all over the landscape, and it was a more difficult show to do." (64-2)

Day 6. The company returned to Vasquez Rocks for a second day of location production, this time at and around the "time ship." Shatner and Brown were again needed, along with their stunt doubles, Gary Combs and Al Wyatt. Nimoy/Spock led the Security Detachment, comprising of Bill Blackburn, Tom Lupo, Ron Veto, Vince Calenti, and Frank da Vinci. The beard that arrived this day for Robert Brown was again the thick one.

The sloppiness and illogic continued. One must wonder why Kirk fights Lazarus #1 alone, when Spock and a security team are standing several feet away, watching. The answer: Roddenberry wanted Kirk to do more, to be the hero, and this was the best Don Ingalls and Steven Carabatsos and Gene L. Coon, with their various script drafts, and Gerd Oswald, with his direction, could come up with.

Again, Oswald wrapped at 5:20, having taken his last shots on close up, where artificial day light could be shined in the direction of the actors from the giant arc lights. The last scene intended to be filmed on location -- the Alternate Universe -- was never even started.

Day 7 -- an extra, unplanned day of production, back at the studio. Kirk's journey into the alternate universe was filmed where he meets the "good Lazarus," working on his time ship. Knowing Oswald was nearly a full day behind, Jefferies and the Art Department had spent the previous day preparing a section of Stage 10 to pass for the area where the time ship had come to rest. This actually turned out to be more effective, since the sky and the surroundings could be painted differently with the huge stage lights. The direction is better here, as is the beard.

Also filmed this day, also on Stage 10, were the sequences in the "negative/magnetic corridor." For these effects-driven scenes, Brown wore a fluorescent colored outfit in a blackened room with, as he described it, "black lights on a tilting stage that [they] jostled while the camera rotated around." (24)

Kirk in the "negative/magnetic corridor," before post-production (Courtesy of Gerald Gurian)

It was badly done. It seemed as if the director had tossed in the towel by this point. Compare the approach taken in the filming to the description of the action in the script. When Kirk enters the corridor, the script tells us:

> Kirk is spinning through the terrible white and black and slow motion terror! Grabbing at space that comes off in fluffy hunks of nothing! Suspenseful beats of falling, twisting, then: THE SHIMMERING AGAIN -- EVERYTHING FADES, THEN BRIGHTENS!

We got the black and white, and the slow motion and, in the end, Kirk falling. Otherwise, he just slowly runs up the corridor, then turns and slowly runs down the corridor, then turns and slowly falls on his stomach.

When Lazarus #1 and #2 have their final fight, the script tells us that they are "locked in mortal combat." The descriptive passage continues:

> One of them leaps away, clawing at the walls, trying to escape. The other Lazarus leaps on him, pulls him back, and they fall away together ... the two of them facing eternity ... and we HEAR A SOUL-SHATTERING HOWL OF ANGUISH.

What we got was a negative image of Robert Brown and a stunt man wrestling.

Oswald took his last mediocre shot at 5:30 p.m., and, finally, the production from hell was over -- at least, the writing and filming of it.

Post-Production
November 28, 1966 to January 24, 1967. Music score: tracked.

James D. Ballas, who had been the assistant editor to Robert Swanson, was now running Editing Team #1 (Swanson having resigned after completing "The Menagerie"). Ballas had an impressive resumé -- prior to this, he was nominated for an Emmy in 1961 for his work on *Ben Casey*.

With too short a script, due to the removal of the love story, many redundant beats were played up, involving the maddening Lazarus on the planet, with all his running, shouting, shaking his fists, and falling from rocks.

Film Effects of Hollywood provided the majority of the post opticals, including the "winking out" effect. As described in the script:

> There is a terrible GRINDING sound. At the same moment the entire ship becomes TRANSPARENT. We can see the stars through the ship. All personnel are thrown from their seats, and there is a high wild noise of STATIC, as if some vast interference has ripped through the entire universe.

This would, of course, have been better than what we got -- a transparency of the galaxy superimposed over the shot of the bridge, pushing in and pulling out. The fault lies with the writers more than the post-effects house. They were placing themselves and their written material at the mercy of what was not technically possible in 1966.

In the end, inconsistent writing and direction, blaring action music, and the cheesy photo effects, only contributed to a long list of reasons why this episode should have been pushed back in the production schedule, allowing for further story development and planning.

Robert Brown recalled, "Apparently, if I hadn't taken the role, they were going to scrap the episode and start filming another one right away." (24)

That would have been the better option.

"The Alternative Factor" cost $210, 879 to make, $25,879 over the per-episode allowance provided for by the Studio. The First Season deficit was now up to $46,266.

***

There was one last fight surrounding this production.

On November 21, 1966, "The Alternative Factor" was in its fourth day of filming and it was clear to all involved that the end results would be disastrous. Herb Solow, writing to Bernie Weitzman, a Desilu Business Affairs Executive, said:

> I think it is incumbent upon us to bring every action possible against Mr. Barrymore. The tangible damage he has done to us in terms of dollars is something we can calculate. The intangible damage he has done to us in terms of the resultant picture is impossible to calculate. We have had to bring in a replacement actor in the middle of the night; we have had to force actors into scenes without sufficient rehearsals, etc. If we did not take every action possible, we would be acting in a most selfish manner in that we would be condoning this type of activity that possibly would be felt by other producers as this specific actor and possibly others flex their pseudo-creative muscles and cause damage within our industry. (HS20)

Desilu filed a complaint with the Screen Actors Guild. A hearing took place on

January 4, 1967. Joe D'Agosta, Robert Justman, and Herb Solow attended. Karl Malden headed the Hearing Board, consisting of Charlton Heston, Ricardo Montalban, Jeanette Nolan, and Donald Randolph.

Joe D'Agosta recalled, "Ricardo, yeah, we were kind of friends with him, because he had done the show or was going to do the show, so he was an ally. Charlton Heston, I remember, really worked to see if we were just being bad-ass producers; he wanted to make sure that the guy deserved some reprimand. I remember he was being very fair to Barrymore, but ended up agreeing with us." (43-4)

The headline on the front page of the January 16, 1967, issue of *Daily Variety* proclaimed, "John Drew Barrymore Reprimanded by SAG for Balking at *Star* Role." Barrymore was found "guilty of conduct unbecoming a member" of the Screen Actors Guild. He was fined $1,500 (think $10,500 in 2013) and his SAG card was suspended for six months, preventing him from working. Quoted in the trade paper, Roddenberry said, "We didn't understand his reasons. He didn't like script changes, but there weren't any which affected his part." (145-16)

Like hell.

D'Agosta said, "Poor guy. I wish we hadn't done that now. But we were bent on making an example of him because it was such an unprofessional move, as far as we were concerned, as a whole, anyway. It may have been Gene -- or Herb Solow, I think -- whose ire was up and Bob Justman and me joined in concert with him. I'm just sorry it had to happen." (43-4)

Over the next decade, the handsome actor with the famous name continued his downward spiral into failing mental and physical health. The Barrymore legacy continued, however, through his children: John Blyth Barrymore and Drew Barrymore.

Release / Reaction
Only NBC air date: 3/30/67.

The degree of the "intangible damage" to "The Alternative Factor" that Herb Solow spoke of would soon be known. The episode was planned to air on February 2, 1967. NBC sent out a publicity picture to help promote the "event," but mistakenly identified Robert Brown as John Drew Barrymore. The network PR men caught their mistake and, along with the press release describing the episode (printed at the outset of this chapter), ran a disclaimer that said:

> ATTENTION: PHOTO DESK AND TV EDITORS -- The caption to a picture on the above *Star Trek* episode mailed in the NBC Feature Photo Service dated 1/6/67, incorrectly identified Robert Brown as John Drew Barrymore, who is not in the cast.

Not everyone saw the announcement and many newspapers ran the picture, identifying Brown as Barrymore. The ad was wrong in more ways than one -- as it turned out, "The Alternative Factor" did not air that Thursday night after all. Once the episode cleared post and Robert Justman and the NBC programmers got a chance to take a look at it, all were in agreement that it should be pushed back to the end of the season. "Court Martial," another episode that disappointed the producers and had been planned for a delayed airing, was pulled forward to fill the slot on February 2. "Alternative," the 20th episode filmed, was rescheduled to be the last to air in the first season. The late delivery of the final two episodes produced, however, resulted in another schedule re-adjustment. "Alternative" may not have been ready for prime time, but it aired nonetheless, as Broadcast Episode No. 27.

Joan Crosby reviewed "The Alternative Factor" for her syndicated column *TV Scout*. Among newspapers to carry the review on March 30, 1967 was the *Syracuse Herald Journal*, in Syracuse, New York. Crosby wrote:

> The crew of the starship Enterprise is puzzled by very strange happenings tonight on *Star Trek*, but their puzzlement will be nothing compared to the viewers of this strange, confused episode. It's something about a black hole in the universe, matter and anti-matter, a mysterious humanoid and a man who apparently can heal himself, just like a lizard. Robert Brown, who has a good acting opportunity here, does a good job in the guest spot and there are some nice, weird, and good special effects, including slow-motion negative stuff that is fun to watch.

Crosby was kind. A.C. Nielsen was, too, during *Star Trek*'s first half-hour. The mass exodus of viewers took place shortly thereafter.

RATINGS / Nielsen National report, Thursday, March 30, 1967:

8:30 - 9 p.m., 61.8% of U.S. TVs in use.		Share:	Households watching:
NBC:	*Star Trek* (first half)	No data	13,180,000
ABC:	**Bewitched**	No data	**14,000,000**
CBS:	*My Three Sons*	No data	11,200,000
Independent stations:		No data	No data

9 - 9:30 p.m., 61.8% of U.S. TVs in use.		Share:	Households watching:
NBC:	*Star Trek* (second half)	28.1%	No data
ABC:	*Love on a Rooftop*	30.7%	No data
CBS:	**Thursday Night Movie** (start)	31.4%	**No data**
Independent stations:		9.8%	No data

"The Alternative Factor" started a strong second-place, but at the halfway point of what Joan Crosby called "this strange, confused episode" a sizable chunk of the audience tuned-out to watch either the CBS movie *Underworld, U.S.A.*, starring Cliff Robertson, or ABC's sitcom *Love on a Rooftop*.

No one needed to take a hint from Nielsen Media Research. Robert Justman had no problem convincing the network not to give this episode a repeat broadcast.

Memories

Robert Brown, in 2013, said, "It was really a remarkable experience. I had no idea, nor did anyone, that this was going to be such a hot property. Like any show, *Star Trek* was a bunch of actors talking about what they were going to do next. They had no idea that this would last a lifetime. I was under the gun while shooting that. But it turned out that the public liked me in that show. I'm getting fan mail to this day – from all over the world." (24-1)

Episode 21: TOMORROW IS YESTERDAY
Written by D.C. Fontana
Directed by Michael O'Herlihy

NBC December 28, 1966 press release:

A malfunction causes the USS Enterprise to be returned in time to the late 1960s and into an Earth orbit, where it is sighted as a UFO by a U.S. Air Force jet in "Tomorrow is Yesterday" on NBC Television Network colorcast of *Star Trek*.... Since their confrontation with the Air Force jet is due strictly to an accidental warping of time and space, Captain Kirk (William Shatner) and Mr. Spock (Leonard Nimoy) agree that it is imperative to erase any recorded data on the sighting lest the normal course of the Earth's events be altered. While the jet pilot, Captain Christopher (Roger Perry) is held incommunicado aboard the Enterprise, a landing party transports to Earth in an attempt to retrieve the records.

Takei and Shatner flub a take on *Star Trek*'s first semi-comical episode (Courtesy of Gerald Gurian)

Struggling to find a way to get his own people home, Kirk now has the future of two more to worry about -- that of Captain Christopher and Christopher's unborn son, which history says will grow up to make essential contributions to Earth's space program.

The theme is similar to that of *It's a Wonderful Life*. Jimmy Stewart's character didn't realize how one person's life could impact others, and even dramatically influence the world -- until a miracle opened his eyes. "Tomorrow Is Yesterday" brings along a few miracles of its own.

SOUND BITES

- *Captain Christopher, to Kirk, unaware of Spock's presence:* "I never have believed in little green men." *Spock, making his presence known:* "Neither have I."

- *Spock, explaining why the computer flirts with Kirk:* "We had to put in at Cygnet 814 for general repair and maintenance. Cygnet 814 is a planet dominated by women. They seemed to feel the Enterprise computer system lacked a personality, so they gave it one -- female, of course."

- *Kirk:* "Now you're sounding like Spock." *McCoy:* "If you're going to get nasty, I'm going to leave."

- *Christopher, to Kirk:* "Maybe I can't go home, but neither can you. You're just as much a prisoner in time as I am."

- USAF Colonel Fellini, interrogating Kirk: "I'm going to lock you up for two hundred years." *Kirk:* "That ought to be just about right."

ASSESSMENT

As with many episodes of *Star Trek*, "Tomorrow Is Yesterday" is, at its core, a celebration of life. Captain Christopher is a jet age cog in a wheel. But, as we discover, even a cog can keep the wheels of progress moving in a unique and positive way.

The cleverness of D.C. Fontana's story is richly layered. The concept of having a 1960s contemporary man receive a guided tour of the Enterprise, and for us to see the wonderment that is *Star Trek* through his eyes, struck a chord with the fans. The comedy, including the sexy computer voice flirting with Kirk, was inspired. It is the humor, and the interaction between guest players and regulars, which elevate this episode to classic status.

The passing of time, however, has left its marks on "Tomorrow Is Yesterday," rendering it a flawed classic. There are a handful of questionable plot-points, mostly with regard to science. The idea of our crew being able to beam two 20th Century men home, with split-second precision, while the Enterprise is hurtling through space and time and shaking apart at the seams is hard to fathom. Not helping are the photographic effects. We are supposed to believe the Enterprise is accelerating into a slingshot effect around the sun. What we see is the ship sitting in space, vibrating.

James Doohan, 30 years into the future, said, "The special effects -- shaking the ship slightly, that sort of thing -- seem primitive compared to what you see nowadays. But back then we were cutting edge and the viewership was willing to take a good deal on faith -- as opposed to today's far more literal-minded fans, who scrutinize every effect and hold it up to the highest standard." (52-1)

Dorothy Fontana, 40 years into the future, said, "The effects weren't the best. I mean, they were as good as we could get at the time on the budget we had. We had to have it pretty fast. We had to have it reasonably cheap. So some of that suffered, no question about it. But I'm proud of the fact that the stories pretty-well hold up. The acting pretty well holds up, as does the directing. The intent of the stories comes across and I think the relationships -- especially between Kirk, Spock and McCoy -- were always there. It was in the scripts. It was on the stage. And all the other stuff, well, we just had to hope that it played -- that it all worked for us." (64-3)

Unlike a good wine, the technical aspects of "Tomorrow Is Yesterday" have not necessarily aged well. But even a bottle of cheap port can contribute to a good time, if one can appreciate the year it was corked. By 1966 standards, this is a delightful installment of *Star Trek*. Taken as that, it remains delightful, now and forever more.

THE STORY BEHIND THE STORY:

Script Timeline
D.C. Fontana's story outline, ST #38: October 3, 1966.
Fontana's revised outline, gratis: October 13, 1966.
Fontana's 1st Draft teleplay: October 31, 1966.
Fontana's 2nd Draft teleplay (Mimeo Department "Yellow Cover 1st Draft"):
November 9, 1966.
Gene Coon's script polish (Final Draft teleplay): November 21, 1966.
Additional page revisions by Coon: November 22 and December 1, 1966.

Dorothy Fontana contributed her second script to the series, and it would be the second episode in a row to be produced from material that sped through the normally slow and painfully laborious process of outline to revised outline to various revised teleplays. This one came together with very nearly the same ease and speed as "Arena" and matched that episode's great success. The reason: Gene Coon wrote one, Dorothy Fontana the other. The lesson wasn't lost on Executive Producer, Producer, and Associate Producer. Nor was it lost on the writer. It was during this time that Fontana made the decision to go from full-time-secretary/part-time-writer to full-time writer.

Fontana recalled, "I had done the teleplay for 'Charlie X' and I was in the middle of writing ['Tomorrow Is Yesterday']... and I came to the conclusion that I just didn't want to be a secretary anymore. And I said to myself, 'I think I'll give it a try. I've got some money in the bank, and even if I don't sell *anything*, I'll be okay, and at least I'll have tried.' Actually, I was kind of hoping that Gene might let me write some more *Star Trek*s. So I gave my three weeks' notice and I said, 'Gene, I love working for you, but I really want to write. You know I've been working for this all my life, I have to give it my best shot.' And Gene could appreciate that ambition because, at one point, he had to face a very similar decision in regard to leaving the police force. So, he survived, but he *did* hate losing a good secretary." (64-16)

The initial premise for this episode, a mere germ of an idea, was intended to be Part 2 of "The Naked Time."

"['Tomorrow Is Yesterday'] actually spring-boarded off John D.F. Black," Fontana said. "There *was* a plan to do a Part 2, but that never happened. John left the series and, as a result, 'The Naked Time' was just sort of out there. It was a contained episode. It didn't need any more. But there was the idea of going back in time. And I suggested doing it." (64-1)

Fontana was immediately struck by the dramatic and comedic potential of a story that would transport the Enterprise to modern day Earth -- *our* Earth -- and have it regarded as a UFO.

Robert Justman also had been struck by the dramatic and comedic potential of this type of story -- six months earlier. On April 12, 1966, even predating the first draft of "The Naked Time, Part 1," Justman sent a memo to Roddenberry suggesting a story idea for the series. He wrote:

> The Enterprise is returning to Earth. There is a malfunction of the ship's machinery with regard to its time warp capabilities. The Enterprise does arrive back at Earth, but this is Earth of 1966 and not of their time. The Enterprise is sighted and is identified as a UFO. Kirk begins to see, by breaking through time, he is starting off a whole sequence of events which will affect the history and civilization of our planet in future years. Perhaps it will turn out that he and Spock and the Enterprise and its crew will therefore never really exist in the future. Thereupon, the problem arrives as to how they are to go back and change what they have already set in motion. (RJ21-1)

With the arrival of D.C. Fontana's treatment for "Tomorrow Is Yesterday," and then, one month later, a full screenplay, Justman was convinced he had sparked the story by his memo. On December 1, he wrote another memo to Roddenberry, this time asking to be compensated for the story. He wouldn't be.

"Gene gave Bob neither credit nor payment for the story," Herb Solow said. "In fact, he never even thanked him." (161-3)

"At the time, I was disappointed," Justman said. "I knew that he had come up with a number of story ideas for the show, 'springboards' as we called them. He claimed that he wouldn't get paid for them; they were part of his duties as the creator of the show. Since I was part of the management team, I rationalized that if Gene could do it, *gratis*, then so could I. At that time, I had no idea that Gene *would* receive extra money from the studio for this 'extra work.'" (94-8)

Then again, perhaps this was not a case of denying credit where it was rightfully due -- a common occurrence in television production. Perhaps it was a case of a different sort of common occurrence in TV -- two creative people thinking along the same lines.

"Bob Justman swears he wrote a memo suggesting this very story," said D.C. Fontana. "I never saw the memo. I came up with it on my own." (64-1)

NBC's Stan Robertson didn't care who the idea came from -- he liked it. His enthusiastic letter to Gene Coon read:

> The writer of this story should be commended for a very exciting and intriguing submission, one which falls into a general area which we have for some time suggested that you investigate. (SR21-1)

Robertson wanted one change. Fontana's story, at this point, opened on the Enterprise, dealing with "the destruction of an external force." Robertson felt this duplicated other stories he had received recently and preferred beginning things at the air base, where a "scramble alert has been issued due to the sighting of a UFO." (SR21-1)

A Revised Story Outline was created on October 13 to incorporate the wishes of the NBC man. This draft was shown to Justman. He responded to Coon, voicing numerous concerns, then saying:

> I kind of hate to keep on trying to pick holes in this treatment, but the holes are there and there are plenty of them. There is nothing at all wrong with the essential dramatic situation in this story. In fact, it is rather a very good dramatic situation. However, the audience must be able to believe this dramatic situation. If there are as many flaws in the credibility as I fear there are, we are going to have big trouble. (RJ21-2)

Coon relayed Justman's concerns to Fontana and instructed her to go to script.

When the First Draft teleplay arrived on November 1 (script dated October 21), Justman, putting aside his suspicions regarding the story's origin and any past reservations over the outline, expressed only praise. In a memo to Coon, with cc to Fontana, he said:

> Fellows, you do understand that if we are going to scramble planes in STOCK, they are going to be planes that we are familiar with today. They will be planes whose capability is, say, somewhere up to 60,000 or perhaps 70,000 feet. This is still within the atmosphere limits of the Earth, and there is still daylight up there – we are not in inky blackness at that altitude. Therefore, when we discover the Enterprise at the end of the teaser, IT WOULD NECESSARILY HAVE TO BE WITHIN THE ATMOSPHERE LIMITS OF THE Earth and we would have to composite a shot of the Enterprise against a sky background. If the Enterprise were at an altitude of this sort, it would clearly be visible from the Earth, due to its enormous size. I might suggest that we establish the fact in dialogue in the TEASER that the Enterprise appear over the Earth and be picked up on the radar, which indicates that it is over a large body of water, such as the Atlantic or Pacific. In this way we should get away with saying that it could not be discerned from a ground installation. (RJ21-2)

Justman's criticisms were mild, however, and he added:

> This is a very good First Draft screenplay by the mysterious D.C. Fontana. Its construction is solid and logical and there are some very interesting situations

contained within this work. (RJ21-2)

Justman took his praise one step farther, writing a second memo, this time to Roddenberry. He told his boss:

> I would like to state that a new day has dawned. Never in all her yesterdays or her tomorrows will D.C. Fontana ever again approach the quality inherent in "Tomorrow Is Yesterday."... I feel it's about time we started getting more scripts like "Tomorrow Is Yesterday." (RJ21-3)

With this story, Coon's presence is clear, supporting Fontana's inclination to add humor to a series that, just a short while before, had been played completely straight. With Fontana writing, and Coon polishing, it was now comedy relief, roasted to perfection. This was *Star Trek*'s first semi-comical episode.

One clever addition was the idea of the flirtatious computer, which had gotten a personality overhaul during a visit to a planet governed by women. Coon had liked the computer becoming emotional in the early drafts of "Court Martial," but, with Fontana, saw it presented in a much more lively fashion here.

Justman, however, wasn't so sure the comedy worked, or was even needed. With a dash of his own humor, he wrote to Coon:

> I would like to request that we don't show my memo to the writer of this screenplay. I would appreciate it if Mr. Roddenberry would ask his secretary to make sure that the memo does not fall into the hands of the writer. I guess now it is time to open up a can of peas.... Although the whacked-up Computer Voice routine is quite amusing by itself, I seriously doubt that it has a value for us in this type of story. The story we are attempting to tell here should be completely credible to our audience. I think, therefore, that this amusing side-play tends to distract from the believability of our tale. (RJ21-2)

Coon disagreed. The "whacked-up" Computer Voice stayed. And thank God for that.

Fontana delivered a Second Draft teleplay, dated November 9. Justman didn't have any major issues to pick on, so he instead picked on minor ones. Among those, he told Coon:

> As a father and a man, I invite your attention to Scene 70. Christian says, "A boy. I'm going to have a boy." I think he would rather say, "A son. I'm going to have a son." Boy goes with man goes with woman goes with girl. Son goes with father goes with mother goes with daughter. No man of my acquaintance has ever said that he is going to have a boy. And, anyhow, our program is directed toward a mass heterosexual-type audience. (RJ21-5)

The change was made.

New information was added to the series "bible" as a result of this script: there are 12 starships in the fleet, and the other 11 are identical in design and size to the Enterprise.

Pre-Production
November 17-18, 21-23, and 25, 1966 (6 days).

Director Michael O'Herlihy was new to the series. He was 47 and had cut his teeth as a director for Warner Bros. with their factory-produced series *Maverick*, *Bronco*, and *77 Sunset Strip*. Roddenberry knew O'Herlihy from *The Lieutenant*, where he called the shots on one episode.

Roger Perry, who played Captain John Christopher, was a prominent guest star on TV. He had already been the co-star of two series -- 1960's *Harrington & Son* and 1963's *Arrest and Trial*. He had also taken the lead in smaller films, such as 1966's *T.H.E.Cat*.

Roger Perry and Georgine Darcy in *Harrington and Son* **(ABC publicity photo)**

Regarding *Star Trek*, Perry said, "It had never happened to me this way before, or since, but I went in to Desilu and there was nobody in the office except the secretary, and she said, 'You can go right in.' So I walked in and there was Michael O'Herlihy, sitting alone in the room behind the desk. We talked for maybe, *maybe* five minutes, and he said, 'Okay, you'll do, we'll see you on the set.' That was it. *Star Trek* was the easiest interview I ever had." (139-1)

As for the script he was given, Perry added, "I thought it was a good part and the twist was interesting about how when you go back in time you can change history. That whole concept was a little strange to me at the time because I wasn't a great sci-fi fan, so I'd never heard that theory before, about a time warp and trying to not change what would be the future, so I found it to be kind of interesting. And that whole concept about the son being born -- I remember thinking right away that that was a damn good scene. My son at the time was about seven or eight years old, so that whole subject kind of struck a chord with me." (139-1)

Ed Peck, 49, played the humorless Colonel Fellini. He'd starred in his own short-lived series in 1951, playing the title character of *Major Dell Conway of the Flying Tigers*.

John Winston made his first of 11 appearances as Transporter Chief Kyle. Joe D'Agosta had met the young actor while working in the theater. Winston said, "It never occurred to me when Joe D'Agosta called that it would be more than one job. I'd never heard of *Star Trek* at that point. I was of the stage; that's where I worked, that's where I got my best roles. For this, I simply went in as an actor, made sure I was there on time, got into makeup and then waited until the director wanted me. I just said, 'What do you want me to do with the lines,' then one, two, three. When you're a bit actor here in Hollywood, invariably the director doesn't want any more from you than to say those lines. Don't blow it so they don't have to do another take; do it right the first time and let them get on with it." (189a)

Winston didn't blow it. He brought more to the role than he gives himself credit for. Others recognized his contribution and he would often return.

Majel Barrett got to add a personality to the ship's computer. Hearing the machine flirt with Kirk is a delight. Credit Fontana. Credit Coon. But don't forget to credit Barrett. The naughtiness in her voice is priceless.

Production Diary
Filmed November 28, 29, 30 and December 1, 2 & 5, 1966
(6 day production; total cost: $178,629).

Production began on Monday, November 28, 1966, following the four-day Thanksgiving holiday weekend (although the *Star Trek* company worked the day after Thanksgiving struggling to finish "The Alternative Factor"). *Star Trek* was the ratings winner on Thanksgiving night at 8:30, with Part 2 of "The Menagerie" nosing ahead of the NFL game on CBS (the Cleveland Browns / Dallas Cowboys). At 9 p.m., *Star Trek* stayed in the top-spot, with 35.2% of the TVs in the country tuned-in. ABC's *Bewitched*, came in second, with 28.2%. The big news story breaking that day: "Mystery Killer Smog Kills 400 in New York City." It remains unexplained to this day. The big event over the weekend in movie houses was *The Bible: In the Beginning*, an epic production from Dino De Laurentiis, casting Michael Parks as Adam and Italian actress Ulla Bergryd as Eve, supported by Richard Harris (as Cain), John Huston (as Noah), George C. Scott (as Abraham), and Peter O'Toole (as the Three Angels). Americans were eating it up, sending the movie to No. 1 at the box office for this and three more weeks to come. Helping to balance things out, "You Keep Me Hanging On," by the Supremes, was the most played song on the radio, with The Beach Boys' "Good Vibrations" hot on its tail. The Monkees had the top selling album in record shops. And a bare-chested Ron Ely, as Tarzan, had the cover of *TV Guide*. As William Shatner, Leonard Nimoy, and Roger Perry studied the script for "Tomorrow Is Yesterday" on Sunday night, NBC's *The Andy Williams Show* had Carl Reiner and Mel Brooks performing their classic "2000-year-old-man" skit.

Principal photography began at 8 a.m. on Monday, on Stage 9, for the majority of the sequences on the ship's bridge -- portions of which were in dire need of repair. The small screens above Spock's and Uhura's stations, and elsewhere, appear battered -- they looked more like the abused props they were, rather than the advanced technology they were supposed to suggest. Six months of separating and moving sections of the bridge set around for various camera angles was taking its toll. When the footage was screened for the producers, a mandate was immediately issued to replace the artwork in the screens. We would see an improvement in the following episode.

Of his first day on the bridge, Roger Perry said, "I thought the sets were terrific. I wasn't quite used to that in television, certainly not on the *Harrington* set and *Arrest and Trial*. I'd never seen anything like that." (139-1)

And Perry was among familiar faces. He said, "I knew who Shatner was. The first time I'd seen him was in *The Brothers Karamazov*. And I had seen Leonard in an independent movie that year, kind of a deep, dark subject, one of those intense movies [*Deathwatch*], and I told him when I got on set that I thought he was really terrific in that." (139-1)

Day 2 brought more shooting on the bridge, followed by a trip to the transporter room. Perry said, "I was constantly amazed by how easy it was for Leonard to say all those highly-technical, complicated lines." (139)

Day 3. The company filmed in the ship's corridors, turbo-lift elevator, sickbay, and Kirk's quarters. O'Herlihy was staying on schedule. Roger Perry said, "Those six day schedules weren't a problem for me at all. It had been like that with the other shows I worked on, so you just know to come to the set knowing your part and being prepared to get it in one or two takes.

Day 3: Captain Christopher takes an elevator to the bridge (Unaired film trim courtesy of Gerald Gurian)

Michael was good to work with but I don't remember a whole lot of feedback. He was an actor's director, meaning he would let you do what you felt was right. Later, you may worry about whether you did it right or not, and I certainly did, but if the director doesn't say anything, you move on." (139-1)

Day 4 saw additional filming in Kirk's quarters, followed by the briefing room scenes and ending in engineering. During the sequence when the Enterprise is straining to get back to her own time, Scott, in engineering, is shown thrown against the background grid, cllutching onto it to stay on his feet. Doohan later said, "It was such a dynamic-looking shot that they wound up using it in other episodes, such as 'The Doomsday Machine.'" (52-1)

On this Thursday night, *Star Trek* had its first preemption on NBC, for Jack Benny.

Day 5 production took place on Stage 10, with the filming of the scenes in the "ADC Corridor" and "Int. ADC Records Section," followed by "Int. Security Office."

Day 6, Monday, December 6. The company remained on Stage 10, filming on the sets identified as "Int. Jet Cockpit" and "Int. Jet Mockup," both against a blue screen, plus "Int. ADC Photo Lab," "Int. ADC Dark Room," and "Int. Radar Room." The Radar Room scene, from the episode's teaser, failed to realize the written material. An Air Force radar room with one man sitting at a scope and an officer at a desk seems underwhelming and unbelievable, even for 1966. Fontana's script described it differently, with the written "action" telling us:

> At first we only see the Technician leaning forward intently, a dim glow reflecting back against his face. Then CAMERA PULLS BACK TO REVEAL he is bent over a radar scope. We will not see anything distinctly in the background in the way of equipment or personnel -- the room is too dim for that. But there is the HUM of gentle "conversation" of ELECTRONIC DEVICES going about their work. The Technician stiffens suddenly, staring at his o.s. [off-screen] screen in puzzlement and surprise. He studies it a brief second longer, then turns in his chair quickly. He says, "Captain!" An AIR FORCE CAPTAIN appears from the dark b.g. [background], coming quickly to stand beside the Technician.

Fontana had gone to great detail to explain how, with lighting, a small area could be presented and believed to be part of something much larger. Sadly, no one else seemed to share the importance of her vision.

Regarding his last day with the company, Roger Perry said, "I was talking to Bones [DeForest Kelley] about my shirt and I said, 'I kinda like this, I wonder if I can take it home.' And he said, 'Well, they frown upon that. But you could probably just stick it into your bag and nobody's going to say anything.' Guess what? I didn't. Looking back now, with all *Star Trek* has become, I wish I had." (139-1)

Michael O'Herlihy finished on schedule and on budget. Everyone -- cast, crew, network, and (a few weeks later) fans -- was thrilled by the results.

O'Herlihy later admitted how he had been immediately drawn to the material, and to the characters. Oblivious to the contributions from Fontana, Justman and Coon, he attributed the success of the series, and the episode he directed, entirely to his friend Gene Roddenberry, saying, "The one thing I did like is that Gene Roddenberry went into the realm of science-fiction, but he didn't go too far too often. You have a story to tell and you must tell it with as much honesty as you possibly can, that this *did* in fact happen. You can't say, 'This only happened because we're making science-fiction.' You must consider that this is the way people live. I don't think that human nature has ever changed or that it ever will. One of the reasons that *Star Trek* became so successful was that Gene Roddenberry instinctively kept the people human. It's always a question of search and conflict that makes good drama." (131-1)

Roddenberry returned the compliment. On January 31, 1967, he sent a letter to O'Herlihy, writing:

> Forgive me for not getting in touch with you immediately to tell you how much I enjoyed and appreciated the outstanding job of direction you did on "Tomorrow Is Yesterday." Again, as always, the O'Herlihy touch to any script is something extra. (GR21)

O'Herlihy was asked to direct again but turned down the offer in order to do a Disney western called *Smith!* He later said, "*Star Trek*, in those days, was just another bloody show. It was a six-day show with fellows in funny pajamas... I thought *Smith!* would be a better career move." (131-1)

Smith! bombed.

Post-Production
December 6, 1966 through January 17, 1967. Music score: tracked.

Footage of the 11-foot, 2-inch model climbing from the Earth's atmosphere, which was shot by the Howard Anderson Co. but, sadly, left unused (Courtesy of Gerald Gurian)

Bruce Schoengarth and Edit Team #2 did the cutting. This was their sixth of 14 *Star Trek* assignments, following three classics ("Mudd's Women," "The Naked Time," and "The Squire of Gothos"), one run-of-the-mill entry ("Dagger of the Mind") and one – according to its director, Marc Daniels, in a word – "dog" ("Court Martial").

The Westheimer Co. was brought in when the Howard Anderson Company failed to make their delivery dates. Westheimer, then, was responsible for the substandard opticals. The transporter effects were fine, and it was nice that someone put clouds around the Earth from shots lifted from "Miri." But the Enterprise, as seen in Earth's atmosphere, were created using only the smaller ship model, the only one Westheimer had access to. And it shows.

Regardless, Robert Justman was thrilled. First, the price tag was low -- only $8,760; second, the effects and therefore the episode were delivered quickly, allowing for early scheduling on NBC. On January 6, as Justman watched the delivered optical elements inserted into a nearly finalized cut of the episode, and knowing he would be able to ship "Tomorrow Is Yesterday" off to NBC in 10 days, he wrote Westheimer:

Dear Joe: I would like to take this opportunity to express my personal thanks to you and all the fellows at The Westheimer Company for the superb work that has been turned out on behalf of *Star Trek*. The quality of your Opticals and Titles seems to improve week by week. The courtesy and cooperation you furnish to us here at Desilu goes beyond description. Warmest personal regards.

Justman was mostly pleased that the optical effects were delivered. The Howard Anderson Company had been working on the photographic effects, also, with the 11-foot, 2-inch model of the Enterprise but, sadly, were unable to deliver in time.

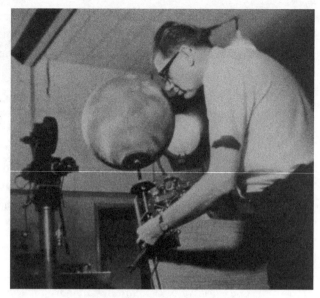
Joseph Westheimer filming a rotating planet
(Courtesy of Gerald Gurian)

At $178,629, this was one of the cheaper ones. The first season deficit dipped a bit, down to $39,895.

Release / Reaction
Premiere air date: 1/26/67. NBC repeat broadcast: 7/13/67.

"Tomorrow Is Yesterday" first aired on Thursday, January 26, 1967, the night before the deadly fire during the testing of Apollo One, which claimed the lives of astronauts Gus Grissom, Ed White, and Roger Chaffee.

Watching the episode, Roger Perry said, "I thought it was done well, shot well. It was a good episode. When I watched it, being self-critical, I felt I could have done just a little bit more -- reacted a bit more to what I was seeing. I thought, 'Should I have done more when I beamed up?'"

Fans will tell Perry his reactions were spot on.

Joan Crosby reviewed "Tomorrow is Yesterday" is for syndicated column TV Scout. Among newspapers to carry her column was the Edwardsville Intelligencer, in Edwardsville, Illinois. Crosby wrote:

Star Trek has a cleverly worked-out episode tonight with several touches of humor. The USS Enterprise gets caught in a time-space warp or whatever it is that they always make up on these shows, which is the excuse used by the writers to place a UFO in the 1960s, which, indeed, is now our spaceship, the Enterprise. A jet spots the space craft hovering over the Earth, gives chase, and the pilot ends up aboard the starship but he poses a terrible problem. He now knows too much about the future to be allowed to return to the past. Also, the photographed tapes of his mission must be retrieved from Earth. It's an interesting problem and an interesting solution.

Steven H. Scheuer reviewed the episode for his syndicated *TV Key Previews* column. Among newspapers to carry Scheuer's assessment was *The Meriden Journal*, in Meriden, Ohio. He wrote:

Imaginative and engaging space-age nonsense tonight that puts the starship Enterprise into a wholly untenable position. Jolted out of its time sphere by an accidental brush with a star, the spaceship finds itself planted smack into the year 1960, interfering with an approaching jet plane from Earth and taking the jet pilot prisoner. How Captain Kirk and his crew get out of this mess takes some tall doing, but script writer D.C. Fontana rides it all out with a smile.

A.C. Nielsen Media Research declared "Tomorrow Is Yesterday" a winner, too.

RATINGS / Nielsen 30-Market report for Thursday, January 26, 1967:

8:30 - 9 p.m., 66.2% of U.S. TVs in use:	Rating:	Share:
NBC: *Star Trek* (first half)	18.3	27.7%
ABC: *Bewitched*	**22.6**	**34.2%**
CBS: *My Three Sons*	18.0	27.3%
Independent stations:	10.5	10.8%

9 - 9:30 p.m., 63.9% of U.S. TVs in use:		
NBC: *Star Trek* (second half)	**20.6**	**32.2%**
ABC: *Love On A Rooftop*	19.0	29.7%
CBS: *Thursday Night Movie* (start)	17.0	26.6%
Independent stations:	10.1	11.5%

"Tomorrow Is Yesterday" started in second place, and then claimed the No. 1 spot at 9 p.m., above the movie on CBS -- the television premiere of 1964's *Behold a Pale Horse*, starring Gregory Peck, Anthony Quinn, and Omar Sharif, which trotted in for CBS in last place.

The slingshot-around-the-sun technique, having worked here, was used again by the crew of the Enterprise in *Star Trek IV: The Voyage Home*.

From the Mailbag

Received the week after "Tomorrow Is Yesterday" first aired:

> Gentlemen... As one who supports in some small way the business you serve, I know you are interested in my opinion of the presentation of *Star Trek* from January 26 on KRON TV 4. I like it very much because, 1) William Shatner is an excellent actor; 2) The show has a good set of writers and special effects engineers; 3) I am an astronomer and I think it is commendable the way you try to make this series more believable by building the show around facts. Brian J. (Woodacre, CA).

> Dear Mr. Roddenberry, unfortunately I did not get to catch the name of the writer of last week's episode in which the Enterprise, flung back in time, became a UFO in the Earth skies of today. This script was masterful! Among the delights, it finally allowed a bit of charming humor into the Captain's hitherto grim life. You *must* retain that female computer. Captain Kirk looks so engaging and exasperating when she calls him "dear." *This* is a writer! I hope he [sic] is doing, or has done, more work for you. Anonymous (Inglewood, California).

> Dear Mr. Roddenberry, I am overjoyed at being able to see *Star Trek*.... On the whole, the program is consistently good -- well-written and well-acted. Two excellent programs come to mind immediately: the one in which inhabitants of a planet visited by the Enterprise are Earth children whose aging processes have

been slowed down phenomenally ["Miri"] ... and the one in which the transporter malfunctions and two "Capt. Kirks" come back to the ship, each only a part of the real man ["The Enemy Within"].... When you stick more to human values than to mere gadgetry, you succeed more fully.... The best episode so far -- "Tomorrow is Yesterday." I enjoyed it so much partly because it was humorous, and thus Shatner and Nimoy were more believable in the situation, and partly because the time warp mix-up was such an ingenious explanation of UFOs.... Best of luck with the season. Mrs. D. W. (Syracuse, N.Y.)

Roddenberry's reply:

Dear Mrs. W.: We cannot guarantee perfection in every episode, what with all the time and budget pressures of television, but you may be sure we will keep trying to please you. Thank you, and we hope that you and your family will continue to watch *Star Trek* and find enjoyment in it. Yours truly, Gene Roddenberry, Executive Producer, *Star Trek*.

Memories

D.C. Fontana said, "That was a fun show to write, and it was an easy one to write. It is one of my favorite episodes. What I liked about it best was that everything that Kirk does -- which is by the book, exactly the right thing to do -- is the *wrong* thing to do ... until about the middle of the episode, and then he starts pulling it together and makes it right. But I had a chance to have a little fun with it, particularly with Kirk, because you knew Shatner could play comedy." (64-1)

Director Michael O'Herlihy said, "I rather liked the script. I'm not a science-fiction fan, but even I could relate to it and understand it. I enjoyed it very much." (131-1)

DeForest Kelley said, "I had hardly anything to do in ['Tomorrow Is Yesterday']... I was very light in it, but I thought it was one of the best." (98-9)

Roger Perry said, "The show is a classic, and for good reason." (139)

Episode 22: THE RETURN OF THE ARCHONS
Teleplay by Boris Sobelman
(with Gene Roddenberry and Gene Coon, uncredited)
Story by Gene Roddenberry
Directed by Joseph Pevney

From *TV Guide*, February 4, 1967:

> Kirk's search for survivors of a long-missing starship leads the Captain to a society where visitors are treated like infection -- which must be absorbed or destroyed.

Return to the streets of Mayberry for "Return of the Archons" (Courtesy of Gerald Gurian)

The mysterious leader of Beta III is Landru. He is both revered and feared by his subjects, a society which offers a curious paradox of its own. The zombie-like people are orderly by day, but become hedonistic and violent during an annual nighttime event called "festival." And now some of Kirk's crew have crossed over, turning on their Captain and becoming "one with the body."

The theme deals with Gene Roddenberry's belief that all men are driven by their egos and/or fears, and no one man possesses the wisdom, be it in the name of religion or government, to rightly control the will of others. Spock says it to Kirk: "This is a society organized on the physiological concept -- one body, maintained and controlled by the ones known as Lawgivers, directed by one brain."

Taking it one step further, this episode attempts to demonstrate what can go wrong when a society submits to the unconditional rule of something less than a human.

SOUND BITES

- *Landru:* "You have come as destroyers. You bring an infection.... You come to a world without hate, without conflict, without fear. No war, no disease, no crimes, none of the old evils. Landru seeks tranquility, peace for all, the universal good.... You will be absorbed."

- *Spock:* "All is indeed peace and tranquility -- the peace of a factory, the tranquility of the machine -- all parts working in unison.... This entire society is a machine's idea of perfection. Peace and harmony ..." *Kirk:* "And no soul."

- *Kirk, to Marplon and Reger, the leaders of the resistance:* "You said you wanted freedom; it's time you learned that freedom is never a gift -- it has to be earned."

- *Landru, losing its battle of wits with Kirk:* "I am Landru! I am he! All that he was, I am. His experience, his knowledge." *Kirk:* "But not his wisdom. He may have programmed you, but he could not have given you his soul. You are a machine.... Without individual freedom of choice there is no creativity. Without creativity there is no life. The Body dies! The fault is yours!"

- *Spock:* "How often mankind has wished for a world as peaceful and secure as the one Landru provided." *Kirk:* "And we never got it. Just lucky, I guess."

ASSESSMENT

"The Return of the Archons" has much going for it. The writing is engaging, there is mystery, discovery and revelation. For its time, the direction and production values are impressive. And Roddenberry's beloved *Gulliver's Travels* template provides a vehicle for the story's hidden political agenda.

In 1966 and 1967, with the Vietnam war raging in Asia and the Cold War still very much a part of the political climate, the world was divided between Western and Eastern, Communists and Capitalists and, in America, the Hawks and the Doves. "Archons" let *Star Trek* make a statement about life under the Communists' system, where individual freedom was stifled in favor of the good of the party, or, in this case, "the body."

Another concern -- for Roddenberry and others -- was that as technology advances faster than man's wisdom, the very machines built to serve man will one day kill the human spirit. The concerns voiced here are still relevant today.

"Archons" marked the first time that Mr. Scott, still referred to as Engineering Officer, commands the bridge. And this episode, courtesy of a script polish by Gene Coon, introduced the Prime Directive of non-interference. Coon even built-in a loophole, that the policy only applies to living, growing cultures. This was also the first episode to bring forth what would soon be a *Star Trek* formula show: the landing party is captured while the Enterprise is attacked, forcing Kirk and his away team to gain their own freedom as well as saving the ship. And this was the first time we saw Kirk out-think a machine by using logic, or illogic, driving his opponent out of its mechanical mind. What soon became *Star Trek* clichés were, in this instance, unique and effective.

THE STORY BEHIND THE STORY

Script Timeline

Gene Roddenberry's premise, "The Perfect World": March 11, 1964.
Roddenberry's story outline "Paradise XML," July 20, 1964.
Roddenberry's revised story outline, "Landru's Paradise": July 22, 1964.
Boris Sobelman's story outline, ST #33, "The Return of the Archons":
August 18, 1966.
Sobelman's revised outline, gratis, August 29, 1966.
Gene L. Coon's revised outline: September 14, 1966.
Sobelman's 1st Draft teleplay: October 11, 1966.
Sobelman's 2nd Draft teleplay: October 24, 1966.
Steven Carabatsos' polish ("Yellow Cover 1st Draft"): November 1, 1966.
Gene Coon script polish (Final Draft teleplay): November 10, 1966.
Gene Roddenberry polish (Rev. Final Draft teleplay): November 29, 1966.
Additional page revisions by Roddenberry and/or Coon:
November 30 and December 1, 2, 5 & 7, 1966.

Gene Roddenberry came up with the concept for "The Return of the Archons." It was in his 1964 series proposal as a story synopsis, called "The Perfect World." His first try at a story outline, "Paradise XML," from July 20, 1964, was a contender for the first *Star Trek* pilot film. Two days later, with his second draft outline, Roddenberry changed the title to "Landru's Paradise." It was sent to NBC and passed over for "The Cage."

Freelance writer Boris Sobelman picked it up from there. He worked in television throughout the 1960s, providing scripts for *Thriller* and *Alfred Hitchcock Presents*. In 1966, the same year Sobelman wrote this *Star Trek*, he concocted episodes of *The Girl from U.N.C.L.E.*, *The Man from U.N.C.L.E.*, and *Run for Your Life*. He had also just been nominated for a Writers Guild award for a *Dr. Kildare* script.

When Sobelman asked to see the series "bible" and a sample script, Roddenberry also provided a copy of his own outline for "Landru's Paradise." Sobelman took the hint and requested to build the story into a teleplay with a new title, also supplied by Roddenberry. The name "Archons" came from a debating club that Roddenberry belonged to during his time at Los Angeles City College. It was taken from the Greek word "archon," meaning a ruler or a leader.

By the time Sobelman's story outline was turned in, on August 19, 1966 (dated August 18), Gene Coon was in the middle of his first week as *Star Trek*'s new producer. Robert Justman responded to the material first, writing to Coon:

> I find myself well pleased with the story idea contained within Sobelman's outline. As usual, I find the contemplated production beyond our means, money-wise. (RJ22-1)

Illustrating how different Sobelman's telling of the story was from what would eventually make it to the TV screen, Justman wrote:

> On Page 19, we discover that Landru is really a robot. His head flies off! Why does Landru have to be a robot? On the other hand, do we need Landru? Suppose that Landru turns out to be the computer that controls the civilization? If you don't like this idea, how about having Landru [as] a human being? (RJ22-1)

Coon opted for the computer idea.

Justman had another issue with this story that he otherwise found himself "well pleased with." His memo continued:

> I might caution you that we are starting to get an awful lot of shows that have a parallel world type of feeling to them. It seems that more and more often we get a story in which our audience will be able to recognize similar cultures to what we have already undergone. You will find this particularly in Trivers' story called "Portrait of Black and White." (RJ22-1)

It was a moot point -- or perhaps a mute one. Both that story and this one were Roddenberry's ideas and Roddenberry had made it a point in his series proposal to say that *Star Trek* would make use of parallel world themes and locals to help the audience identify with these places, and make production possible on a TV budget.

Roddenberry, however, had some issues with Sobelman's take on his original story, writing to Gene Coon:

> Am a little afraid of the number of sets Sobelman is suggesting. When I wrote my original of this – "Visit to Paradise" [sic], loaned to Sobelman -- I visualized using our backlot small village for the main part of the story. (GR22-1)

The backlot would be used -- not the outdoor village set Roddenberry had visualized, but the outdoor early Americana town set. Coon saw to this change and asked Sobelman to chip away at the number of sets needed, to be reflected in a revised story outline.

Sobelman sent in his new outline, *gratis*, on August 29. Of this, Justman wrote Coon:

> I would like to again repeat that I think the original idea of this story is a gas to me. The idea that each individual is one cell of the complete organism is really a very original and daring conception. I wish I had thought of it. Boris needs a big pat on the back for this idea. (RJ22-2)

Sobelman was taking a pat that rightfully should have landed on another's back. Justman was unaware that the story he was so enthralled with had been given to the writer by Roddenberry. Sobelman had neglected to add Roddenberry's name to the cover page, an oversight which would not go unnoticed by the latter.

Justman still worried that the story, as told, was too costly. In one scene, he wrote how Sobelman called for the Lawgivers to use a "triple-barreled optical beam-shooting device and blast away at a couple [of] people." This would be downgraded to the hollow-tube staffs the Lawgivers carried which emit a brief sparkle and puff of smoke, thereby saving money that would be spent on post animation. At the end of the story, Sobelman wanted Landru -- the computer -- to disintegrate. Justman told Coon:

> I would suggest that when the computer finally gives up the ghost, it does not disintegrate. But we can let it shoot out a bunch of sparks and smoke and come to a screeching halt and all its lights would die away and it would be silent. And I would be happy. (RJ22-2)

Somewhat happy, anyway. Justman felt the ending -- Kirk outwitting a machine and causing it to self-destruct -- was a bit much and not in keeping with the tone of the overall story. But he had heard that Coon, now in his third week on the job, hadn't known what to make of his sarcasm in his previous memos. So Justman held his punches for the first five pages of his six-page memorandum. At the end, concerning the self-destructing computer, he wrote:

> I know that NBC has a policy against portraying suicide. But I don't think that they would mind too much, as long as this is a computer that commits suicide and not a real person. <u>This was a sarcastic remark....</u> I hope you have enjoyed this memo as much as I have enjoyed dictating it. I feel it is one of my kindlier efforts in this regard. As you no doubt have read, I have made a conscious effort to be kind and not write my usual mean, nasty comments. Gently, Bob. (RJ22-2)

Coon wrote a six-page memo of his own, to Boris Sobelman. He appreciated the freebie draft, and told Sobelman:

> Thanks for your rewrite. It is a much more direct storyline, cleaner and a little cheaper -- not enough, perhaps, but maybe this memo can take care of that. With this, I suggest you can go into screenplay, keeping these suggestions in mind and working them into the script whenever possible. (GC22)

Among the suggestions, Coon wanted Sobelman to prune back on the speaking parts, and wrote, "I am appalled by a script with more than fifteen speakers." And there were still too many opticals, prompting Coon to say:

> I would point out that even such a simple and prosaic matter as our regulars firing their phasers calls for animation, which is expensive, and so we don't go around firing our phasers at any old thing; only when it is important and

> unavoidable.... We have done an awful lot of shows which refer to an artificial magnetic force around a planet, which may be responsible for snatching a spaceship and, if not dragging it down, at least freezing it in orbit. We will have to live with something like this from time to time, but let us try to come up with something fresher -- call it a mechanically stimulated gravitation, or a direct dimensional warp field, or some other fancy double-talk -- but not to make it sound like somebody's down there with a large electrified horseshoe, pointing it at our ship and throwing everything into tumult. (GC22)

Those "awful lot of shows" Coon referred to included the tractor beams used to freeze the Enterprise in "The Corbomite Maneuver," the mysterious energy field from a planet which drains the Enterprise of power in "Shore Leave," the unidentified energy source which paralyzes the ship in "Arena," and the planetary defense batteries which open fire on the Enterprise in the upcoming "A Taste of Armageddon."

The solution was a "heat beam" that causes the Enterprise to channel all its power to the shields, resulting in a decaying orbit -- and in Scotty's memorable line "You've got to cut them off, Mr. Spock, or we'll cook one way or another."

Some of the more effective and eerie moments in the episode came about as a result of an idea from Coon, who told Sobelman:

> Throughout the script I think it is terribly important that we know that each person on this planet is a member of The Body and acts in concert with his fellows. I strongly suggest that when our people arrive in town we see the people of the town, those few we can afford, reacting in concert as though there is some unspoken communication between them.... To sum up, write cheap, think cheap, be cheap, a minimum of speaking parts, a minimum of extras, a minimum of optical effects and animation. Keeping these points in mind, I see no reason why this can't be a good, exciting show. (GC22)

But it wouldn't be cheap. Regardless, there would be no backing out. Stan Robertson, at the network, liked this one and, writing to Roddenberry, not Coon, said:

> This is a splendid idea which, with proper direction and handling, has the promise of being one of the outstanding episodes in our series. (SR22)

Robertson was pleased that the premise was reminiscent of George Orwell's *1984* and Romain Rolland's *The Revolt of the Machines*. He told Roddenberry:

> I find it very intriguing that the underlying point here, which cannot be minimized, is one which our contemporary society must come to grips with: that is, the dangers inherent in a culture when it becomes too computerized and its most basic needs, emotions, and functions can be "programmed." (SR22)

In closing, Robertson cautioned Roddenberry not to allow the story to become too "cerebral."

Coon quickly covered up for himself and Roddenberry and wrote a third draft of the story outline, dated September 14, incorporating in the notes from the network, which he then sent to Sobelman as a guide for the script he was already writing.

When the screenplay arrived on October 11, Robert Justman gave it a thumbs down. In a memo to Coon and Roddenberry, he said:

> Generally, dialogue is not good and is uncharacteristic of our people. No action on the parts of Kirk and Spock for three-quarters of the script. The drama of this piece must be punched up -- involve our people in real jeopardy.... I am confused. Also bored. When are we going to stop talking and start doing?

(RJ22-3)

More notes to Coon, from Steven Carabatsos or perhaps Dorothy Fontana (the "staff" memo did not identify the sender), took sympathy with *Star Trek*'s overworked associate producer. The unnamed staffer told Coon:

> The opening scene has a mob of people in it that will have Bob J. shrieking....
> Do we need so many lawgivers? I ask in the name of Robert H. Justman.
> (STAFF22)

Sobelman was given more notes and further requests to prune back on speaking parts, extras, and opticals. His October 24 Second Draft script addressed enough of these notes for Coon to dismiss the writer as having fulfilled his contract.

The script was handed-off to Steven Carabatsos for a polish, making the *Star Trek* characters sound more like the *Star Trek* characters. This draft, the Mimeo Department's Yellow Cover 1st Draft, from November 1, was sent to de Forest Research and shared with the series' Department Heads and cast, but not given to NBC. In this version, Sulu still had a much bigger part. After being absorbed by the Lawgivers, we see him under observation in sickbay and then, phaser in hand, taking over the bridge, attempting to carry out the will of Landru by forcing the ship to enter the planet's atmosphere.

There was no sense in sending this draft to the network. Robert Justman made that clear, writing to Coon:

> I suggest that once Stan Robertson reads this and "Power Play" [a new script from Jerry Sohl, later to become "This Side of Paradise"], he will say -- with a good deal of justification -- that they have a close parallel.... Suggest we lose the business of Sulu running amuck, being strapped down, not himself, etc. It parallels "The Naked Time" and "Naked Time" was much better. Also, we have him being taken over by spores in "Power Play" in much the same manner. His nerve ends ought to be shot to a frazzle by this time. Can we involve someone else -- Scott maybe? Jim Doohan could do it very nicely.... We are also getting into the interference with an alien society business again -- how do we justify destroying it? (RJ22-3)

In another memo, Justman told Coon:

> What did Bilar do to Reger's daughter? I only ask because I feel sure that NBC will ask.... If we must see an orgy out in the street, we should only see a small portion of the orgy and let the audience create the rest of it in its mind. (RJ22-4)

The passages in the script that worried Justman so, knowing they would worry NBC, told how Bilar, with his shirt ripped open and carrying a club, runs up to Tula with an "exultant look on his face." He yells at her to come with him, beats away the Enterprise men who try to intervene, then takes her. Later, as Kirk watches the mayhem from the upstairs window of the boarding house, the script describes what he sees as:

> Two men are flailing away at one another with clubs. Another man chases a half-clad, screaming woman across the street, and they vanish in an alley. Several people lie motionless in the street. Up the street further there is a small riot, as eight or ten people fight wildly among themselves. A fire burns in the middle of the street. There is much screaming, yelling, crashing of glass.

Later still, after the festival ends, Reger is "holding the bloody, bedraggled figure of Tula, who is sobbing hysterically." He tells his daughter, "It's alright now, child. It's over for another year."

While the filmed episode depicted much of this action, it would have to be sneaked past Broadcast Standards, and that meant cooling down the script.

There were other problems. Justman's memo to Coon continued:

> I am now reading pages 29 and 30 and I am getting heartsick. We're running into masses of people to outfit and wardrobe, which will cost a bloody fortune. And we are running into enormous Phaser animation costs. I do fear that we will have to change our conception of this part of the script. I swear to you that we cannot afford these costs. If it ends up that we have to throw the money we've spent on this screenplay out the window, then we will still be better off than if we attempt to make this particular episode in anything approaching the state it is in right now. I have to make a guess and say that this show in its present state has got to cost somewhere around $230,000. So, that means we either have to junk this script, or slash, slash, slash. (RJ22-4)

Even with further slashing, the final price tag proved Justman right. His cost estimates were not far off the mark.

Justman finished his bad news memo to Coon, writing:

> We need a strong TEASER and TEASER ending. We need a strong Second Act ending. We need a strong Tag scene. We need a show we can shoot <u>pretty soon</u>. (RJ22-4)

Coon did a script polish of his own -- the Final Draft from November 10. This one went to NBC. As Justman had predicted, the network had grave concerns over what he had deemed as "the orgy." Broadcast Standards wrote:

> Please use restraint when filming the festival, do not over-sensationalize and make certain there is no brutality. Particular care is needed when Bilar hits Lindstrom with a club [and] please make certain the "half-clad" woman is clad enough not to embarrass or offend. (BS22)

Roddenberry read this draft of the script, as well. He had no new notes but he did have a request -- of Desilu Legal. His memo to Ed Pearlstein, in part, stated:

> The script by Boris Sobelman entitled "The Return of the Archons" is taken from a written story which I gave him to read. Although he strayed away from my story on a couple of points, he keeps coming back to it.... I definitely want to put in for credit and I'm a little surprised that Sobelman has never offered proper story credit on any of his drafts. (GR22-2)

Roddenberry, knowing his name would end up on this script, took the time to do a polish of his own -- the November 29 Revised Final Draft, tightening the action and removing some redundant beats.

Pre-Production
November 28-30 & December 1-2 & 5, 1966 (6 days).

To address Stan Robertson's wish that the production have "proper direction and handling," Joseph Pevney returned to the series. He kept "Arena" on both schedule and budget, while rendering it grand in scope.

To fill up the town, and bring about the festival, "Return of the Archons" required more guest players and extras than any episode filmed so far. Only one would top it: "The City on the Edge of Forever."

Harry Townes played Reger, the owner of the boarding house and the first of the three leaders of the resistance we meet. He was 52 and had close to 200 credits in TV and film, including multiple appearances on *The Twilight Zone*, *Thriller*, *Alfred Hitchcock Presents*, and *The Wild, Wild West*.

Torin Thatcher played Marplum, the third leader of the resistance -- the inside man. He was 61. Starting in 1952, he appeared in roughly 200 roles for TV and films. One year before this, he was the title character in "The Space Trader," an episode of *Lost in Space*.

Harry Townes and Torin Thatcher
(Unaired film trip Courtesy of Gerald Gurian)

Jon Lormer, seen as Tamar, the timid elder killed by the Lawgivers, appeared in three episodes of *Star Trek*. He was one of the crash survivors in "The Cage." Later, he returned as the elderly man who gave us the title of "For the World is Hollow and I Have Touched the Sky." In that episode, he also drops dead, again the victim of a computer controlling a society.

Morgan Farley, at 78, played the hostile Hacon. He had been working steadily in front of the camera since the 1920s. He would return to *Star Trek*, unrecognizable, as a Tribal Elder in "The Omega Glory."

Brioni Farrell, 21, played Tula. She was new on TV, but already getting roles in *The Man from U.N.C.L.E.*, *The Wild, Wild West*, and *Bonanza*.

Christopher "Karl" Held, at 35, played Lindstrom, a key member of the landing party. He worked often in TV, including as a regular on several series. Among those, and prior to this, he spent a year on *Perry Mason*. Two decades down the road, he'd enjoy a longer stay on *Falcon Crest*.

Sean Morgan and his character Lt. O'Neil, the one being chased with Sulu in the teaser and later absorbed by The Body, had already appeared in "Balance of Terror." He would return for other episodes, most prominently in "The Ultimate Computer" and "The Tholian Web."

Charles Macauley, 39, was a versatile actor. He was unrecognizable as the man who played Landru from his next role on *Star Trek*, as Jaris in "Wolf in the Fold." From the same year, he took on an entirely different look and persona, as a frightening Nazi assassin for "Child Out of Time," a startling episode of *I Spy*.

Lev Mailer, as Bilar, the reveler who calls out "Festival, festival!" and presumably rapes Tula, began working in television here. He would return to *Star Trek* for "Patterns of Force."

Eddie Paskey, here as a member of the landing party and disguised enough to also play a member of The Body, was already making his 19th out of 59 appearances on the series. Also with the landing party was David Ross, making his third of nine appearances.

Bobby Clark, last "seen" as the Gorn in "Arena," had his only speaking role in the series when he leapt through a window and, like the character of Bilar, cried out "Festival! Festival!" A frequent stunt performer on *Star Trek* who often doubled for Shatner, Clark would be seen later as one of the evil Chekov's henchmen in "Mirror, Mirror."

Production Diary
Filmed December 6, 7, 8, 9, 12, 13 & 14, 1966
(Planned as 6 day production; running one day over; cost: $210,793).

Return to 40 Acres (Courtesy of Gerald Gurian; also on the internet courtesy Tom Redlaw, and also startrekhistory.com)

Tuesday, December 6, 1966. *The Monkees* had the top-selling album in America. "Good Vibrations" by The Beach Boys was the most played song on radio stations. The U.S. and the U.S.S.R. prepared to sign a treaty to prohibit nuclear weapons in outer space. And production began on "Return of the Archons."

Filming took place on Stage 9 and the bridge set. The viewing screens above the various control stations had been replaced after looking so worn and crumpled in the last few episodes, especially in "Tomorrow is Yesterday."

Next to film: the sequence in the transporter room, where a freshly absorbed and very tranquil Mr. Sulu beams up from planet Beta III. The third set of the day was a temporary one, for which many of the Enterprise sets had been collapsed to make room. The filming here in the "Interior Dungeon Cell" had to be left unfinished so that Desilu's Culver City backlot could be used during the two days in which the town of Mayberry was not needed for *The Andy Griffith Show*.

Day 1, filming on Stage 9
(Unaired film trim courtesy of Gerald Gurian)

On Day 2, the company returned for its second visit to Desilu 40 Acres. The first day was a long one, filming all the daylight scenes on the streets prior to the start of Festival, and then the violence of the festival itself, both in daylight and at night.

507

Lev Mailer, playing Bilar, recalled, "People were walking on a 'beat.' I was so nervous, I couldn't do it. And Joe Pevney, the director, came over and he took me by the hand and he said, 'Now, walk with me.' He walked me across the street [at the required pace and beat] to sort of settle me down. And then I was fine." (112)

There was a curious continuity error regarding Mailer's performance. He explained, "They said, 'Oh, this is going to be New England, circa late 19th Century. I said, 'So you want a little bit of old New England, 'A-yah, come for festival, a-yah-a.' And they said, 'Oh, yeah, sure.' But, of course, when I finally saw the program, I'm the only one with an accent. Everybody else is just doing it straight." (112)

After dark, Joseph Pevney found a way around the censors. The eerie shadow of a man attacking a woman projected onto the wall of a building during the nighttime portion of Festival was more than an effective directorial touch. In 1967, a physical confrontation bordering on rape could not be shown on TV. Pevney not only snuck it by NBC Broadcast Standards by only showing it in giant shadow form, but he added greatly to the stylistic nature of the episode.

On Day 3, the first shot taken was from the same position as the last from the night before -- Kirk's P.O.V. of the town's main street -- but this time in daylight as the clock on the tower strikes 6 a.m. and the revelers suddenly become peaceful and, looking quite drained from their night of madness, go back to their normal zombie-like state. The clock tower itself was built specifically for this episode. Nearby, on this same piece of real estate in 1966 was the Marine base used in *Gomer Pyle, U.S.M.C.* and the German concentration camp from *Hogan's Heroes*.

The same Desilu 40 Acres street in 1966 being used for *The Andy Griffith Show* (above) and *Star Trek* (below) (www.retroweb.com_40Acres)

The remainder of the day, until sunset, was spent filming Kirk and his team making their way through the post-festival streets, including the scene where they are surrounded and stoned by the zombie-like crowds. Pevney wrapped early enough for cast and crew to make it home in time to see "The Conscience of the King" for its only NBC airing.

On Day 4, shooting resumed on Stage 9 and the special dungeon set. The script called for Spock to administer the "Famous Spock Neck Pinch" on one of the Lawgivers. But since he had already done this more than once in the episode, and the blocking Pevney had planned for this scene would make it difficult for Nimoy to position himself properly for this, Spock had to improvise -- by slugging one of the Lawgivers. Kirk's reaction was an ad lib, courtesy of Shatner: "Isn't that a bit old fashioned?"

Next came filming in two temporary sets on Stage 9 -- the interior of the absorption chamber and the interior of the upstairs room in the boarding house. For the final sequences, we see how Spock sleeps -- with his eyes open. This, too, was not in the script. Nimoy got the idea during the filming.

On Day 5, Monday, the company worked on Stage 10 for the interior Subterranean Chamber where the landing party first encounter Landru, followed by interior "Main Room/Vestibule" of the Boarding House.

Day 6. The scene in the hallway leading to the Hall of Audiences was filmed, followed by Kirk and Spock's second encounter with the projection of Landru, this time in the Hall of Audiences.

Day 5, Stage 10, "Main Room/Vestibule" of Boarding House (Unaired film trim courtesy of Gerald Gurian)

By Day 7, the production was running late. Work continued in the Hall of Audiences, now with the opened wall revealing the computer complex, and the filming of Kirk and Spock's battle of wits with Landru the machine.

And, finally, one full day over schedule, Pevney called for a wrap.

Post-Production
December 15, 1966 through January 31, 1967. Music Score: Tracked.

Fabien Tordjmann and Edit Team #3 did the cutting. This was their sixth episode, following "The Enemy Within," "Charlie X," "Miri," "Shore Leave," and "Arena." Not a bad apple in the bunch.

Film Effects of Hollywood handled the Optical Effects, including all those animated phaser blasts that Coon lectured Boris Sobelman about. The cost, just for the animated phaser beams: $8,000.

With a seventh day of production, including all the location work needed, extra set construction, and dozens of extra performers, "Archons" became one of the more expensive *Star Trek* episodes. That big supporting cast that worried both Justman and Coon cost the series $28,395. The sets, dressings, wardrobe and props ran more than $32,000 alone. The total cost: $210,793 ($1.5 million in 2013).

Release / Reaction
Premiere air date: 2/9/67. NBC repeat broadcast: 7/27/67.

Joan Crosby reviewed "Return of the Archons" for her TV Scout syndicated column. Among newspapers to share Crosby's assessment on February 9, 1967 was the Pulaski Southwest Times, Virginia. Crosby said:

> *Star Trek* has an interesting look at the ultimate worship of a computerized society. William Shatner and Leonard Nimoy land on a planet where the people dress in homespun and have an orgy when the red hour strikes and worship Landru. It's a mysterious, intriguing episode to watch and it does make some good points about the futility of life in a soul-less society.

All's well that ends well, according to A.C. Nielsen.

RATINGS / Nielsen National report for Thursday, February 9, 1967:

8:30 - 9 p.m., 65.9% of U.S. TVs in use.		**Rating:**	**Share:**
NBC:	*Star Trek* (first half)	18.4	27.9%
ABC:	***Bewitched***	**20.2**	**30.7%**
CBS:	*My Three Sons*	19.7	29.9%
Independent stations:		11.1	11.5%
9 - 9:30 p.m., 66.4% of U.S. TVs in use.			
NBC:	*Star Trek* (second half)	20.2	30.4%
ABC:	*Love on a Rooftop*	15.7	23.6%
CBS:	***Thursday Night Movie*** (start)	**25.4**	**38.3%**
Independent stations:		8.2	7.7%

Star Trek trailed as the third place entry in a close race during the first half-hour. *My Three Sons* bested it, but only slightly, with 29.9% to *Star Trek*'s 27.9%. *Bewitched* had the lead with 30.7% of the total audience. There are no losers when a race is this close. At 9 p.m., the television premiere of 1963's *The Caretaker* on CBS, a drama starring Robert Stack, Joan Crawford, and Robert Vaughn, took the lead, with *Star Trek* in second position.

From the Mailbag

> Dear Mr. Roddenberry... I bought a Playtex bra today so that I could include the label in a letter to the manufacturer in which I praised *Star Trek*, and when it gets a little darker, I'm going to go and tear the sheet of paper they paste on the window of a new car off a Plymouth at a car lot and enclose it in a letter to Chrysler Corporation saying I bought a Plymouth because I like your show.... Your series is the best thing that has been done on television in the much-abused name of science fiction.... *Star Trek* gets much very favorable discussion among fans and we would all go to darn near any length to keep it on the air.... Not that I think you care for my carefully considered opinion all that much, but I am going to award you a weekly letter-of-comment in the interest of increasing your volume of fan mail by even that small amount.... You have a very fine show and I hope you have many seasons of success. Very truly yours. Kay A. (Albuquerque, New Mexico).

The reply:

> Dear Miss A. ... On the contrary, your considered opinion is most cared for and much appreciated by all of us here on the *Star Trek* staff.... Although we certainly do appreciate our weekly checks and hope eventually to make a profit on our efforts, *Star Trek* has also been very much a "labor of love."... We hope

to continue to please you and merit your loyalty to the show.... Sincerely Yours. Gene Roddenberry, Executive Producer, *Star Trek*.

Aftermath

Boris Sobelman, with help from Carabatsos, Coon and Roddenberry, had put plenty of drama on the screen with "The Return of the Archons." There was also a little drama behind the scenes regarding the names on the script. Roddenberry got the story credit he demanded and deserved, and the paycheck that went along with it. Sobelman, who neglected to add Roddenberry's name to the script in the first place, never returned to *Star Trek*.

In early 1968, the script was nominated for a Writers Guild Award as Best Screenplay, One Hour Drama. It was a good script but certainly not the best of the *Star Trek* episodes aired during 1967. The reason the Guild singled this one out over all others: it was the only script shown to them that year, sent in by Roddenberry. Years later, *Star Trek*'s creator told *TV Guide* "Archons" was one of his 10 favorite episodes from the original series.

Memories

Karl Held, who played Lindstrom, said, "*Star Trek* was a well-done and imaginative series. The premise made for good stories, and they were realized by the writers." (78a)

31

Episode 23: SPACE SEED
(Incorrectly listed in many sources as Production #24)
Teleplay by Gene L. Coon and Carey Wilbur
(with Gene Roddenberry and Gene L. Coon, uncredited)
Story by Carey Wilbur
Directed by Marc Daniel

Filming the Enterprise's encounter with the Botany Bay on the stage of Film Effects of Hollywood (Courtesy of Gerald Gurian)

From the NBC press release, issued on January 26, 1967:

> Ricardo Montalban guest-stars as the survivor of a tyrannical super race in 'Space Seed,' a drama in which Captain Kirk (William Shatner) and his crew are unwitting accomplices to an attempt to seize world power, on NBC Television Network's colorcast of *Star Trek*.... Found aboard an ancient and foundering cargo vessel with his body in a state of suspended animation, Khan (Montalban) is allowed to convalesce on the USS Enterprise. Suspicious of Khan's true identity, Kirk and Mr. Spock (Leonard Nimoy) soon determine their "patient" is one of a group of scientifically-bred super-beings bent on world domination, and put him under guard. With the aid of a sympathetic crew member, Marla (Madlyn Rhue), who has fallen in love with him, Khan escapes, wrests command of the Enterprise and threatens the entire ship's complement with execution.

"Space Seed" is a study of human ambition and loyalty. It also explores power as an aphrodisiac.

SOUND BITES

- *Spock:* "I fail to understand why it always gives you pleasure to see me proven wrong." *Kirk:* "An emotional Earth weakness of mine."

- *McCoy, referring to the transporter:* "I signed aboard this ship to practice medicine, not to have my atoms scattered back and forth across space by this gadget."

- *Spock, regarding Khan:* "The scientist behind [eugenics] had overlooked one fact. Superior ability breeds superior ambition."

- *Khan:* "You're an excellent tactician, Captain. You let your second-in-command attack, while you sit and watch for weakness." *Kirk:* "You have a tendency to express ideas in military terms, Mister Khan. This is a social occasion." *Khan:* "It has been said that social occasions are only warfare concealed."

- *Khan:* "I am in fact surprised how little improvement there has been in human evolution. There has been technical advance, but how little man himself has changed. It appears we will do well in your century. Very well. Did you have any other questions?" *Kirk:* "Thank you. They've all been answered."

- *Scott:* "It's a shame for a good Scotsman to admit it, but I'm not up on Milton." *Kirk:* "The statement Lucifer made when he fell into the pit: 'It is better to rule in hell than serve in heaven.'"

ASSESSMENT

This is a smartly-written script and, overall, a well-made and effective episode. The positive/negative dynamic between Ricardo Montalban and William Shatner was still electric a decade and a half later when their characters again clashed, this time on the big screen, in *Star Trek II: The Wrath of Khan*.

Despite its attributes, "Space Seed" does break with the pattern of very nearly all other *Star Trek* episodes. It projects a bleak future for mankind, in the 1990s anyway -- one filled with war and despair -- a future well-within the lifetimes of many who were watching when "Space Seed" first aired in February 1967. Time has proven the terrible events predicted in this episode for the late 20th Century wrong -- or at least that their timing was off. Strange and dismal happenings of the new millennium, more coming with each year, indicate that the dark ages talked about in "Space Seed" could yet be just around the corner.

Two minor blemishes: The awkward fight scene in engineering is reminiscent of the one in "Court Martial," also staged by director Marc Daniels; and the chauvinistic attitudes of Khan, combined with the passiveness of Lt. Marla McGivers, are either believed or dismissed, depending on the tastes and beliefs of individual audience members.

THE STORY BEHIND THE STORY

Script Timeline
Carey Wilbur's story outline, ST #35, "Botany Bay": August 29, 1966.
Wilbur's revised outline, gratis, now "Space Seed": September 1, 1966.
Wilbur's 1st Draft teleplay: October 26, 1966.
Wilbur's 2nd Draft teleplay: Early December, 1966.
Gene Coon's rewrite (Mimeo Department "Yellow Cover 1st Draft"):
December 7, 1966.
Coon's script polish (Final Draft teleplay): December 9, 1966.
Coon's further script polish (Rev. Final Draft teleplay): December 12, 1966.

Gene Roddenberry's rewrite (2nd Rev. Final Draft teleplay):
December 13, 1966.

Carey Wilbur was 50 when he did his share of the writing on "Space Seed." His screen credits went back to 1948 for *Studio One*, with stops in between at *Captain Video* and *Robin Hood*. He had even written for Jeffrey Hunter's series, *Temple Houston*; one of his two contributions to that show was badly panned by *Daily Variety*, which said:

> Carey Wilbur's script, "Fracas at Kiowa Flats," was not a good one, [with] the humor belabored and downright silly at times. It was an inane yarn.

The trade also savaged an episode of *Schlitz Playhouse of Stars*, saying:

> Somewhere in scripter Carey Wilbur's typewriter there may have been the germ of a good idea, but it got lost between the keys. Consequently, his "Whale on the Beach" comes across with no more sincerity than the papier mache whale washed up on [the] sand.

Roddenberry probably hadn't read these reviews, and might not have cared anyway -- every TV writer got a bad review from the trades now and then, Roddenberry included. What mattered was that "GR" knew Wilbur and liked him. The two had worked together briefly on a 1950s Ziv production *Harbormaster*, where Wilbur served as Story Editor. During the same period Wilbur wrote for *Star Trek*, he sold scripts to Irwin Allen for *The Time Tunnel* and *Lost in Space*. To Wilbur, science fiction shows were interchangeable.

"Hell, the plot for 'Space Seed' came from an old *Captain Video* I did," he admitted. "We did some very far out things on that show, including the popular idea of people being transported in space while in suspended animation." (184-1)

Elements of the plot for "Space Seed" can also be found in the first few episodes of *Lost in Space*, where Wilbur was working one year earlier. The space family Robinson is frozen, their breathing and heart rates slowed, thereby reducing aging while their space ship makes the long journey to Alpha Centauri. Wilbur's *Star Trek* story also involves space travelers put into suspended animation. Something goes wrong with this ship and it too is lost in space ... only to be found by the Enterprise two centuries later.

The new element -- the real point of the story -- is that these space travelers are criminals, discarded much the same way misfits from England back in the 1700s and early 1800s were exiled to Australia. The space ship is even named after the landing place of the first convicts to set shore in Australia: Botany Bay.

(Contrary to popular belief, and the rewriting of history presented in this episode by Wilbur, Coon, and Roddenberry, there never was a penal colony at Botany Bay. After landing there, the British soldiers in charge of the convicts soon discovered the area to be unsuitable for colonization and made their way to Port Jackson, which then became the first permanent European settlement in Australia.)

For his story, Wilbur chose the name Harold Ericsson for the leader of the convicts, describing him as a "Nordic superman." "Second Communications Officer" Marla McGivers falls for Ericsson and helps him to revive the rest of the convicts on the damaged sleeper ship so they can commandeer the Enterprise.

Wilbur's story outline, dated August 29, was 18 pages long. Three days later, before anyone at *Star Trek* had a chance to respond or even read it, he turned in a revised draft, adding three pages of additional plot points.

Coon was enthusiastic ... at first. He wrote to Wilbur:

> This is one of the best outlines, in my opinion, that we have received, certainly the best since I have been on the job. (GC23-1)

Coon had only been on the job for two weeks. Robert Justman had been reading outlines and scripts for more than six months now and was less enthusiastic. Four days after Coon's complimentary letter to Wilbur, Justman told his new producer boss:

> As presently written, [this] is incredibly expensive and difficult. There is more financial retribution inherent in this story treatment than in the original story treatment for "The City on the Edge of Forever." When are we going to get back to the original idea of *Star Trek*, which is essentially a series about people in dramatic situations and conflicts? When are we going to do another "Charlie X"? When are we going to do another "Naked Time"? Yes, the basic story idea here is extremely fascinating. It is also very much science-fiction. It is very much "astounding science-fiction." It is at times very Buck-Rogerish. Very much akin to *Flash Gordon* at times. We need <u>people</u> stories. (RJ23-1)

Justman signed his memo, "Ming the Merciless," the villain from *Flash Gordon*. Coon ran the numbers with his production staff, and then sent Wilbur the bad news.

> Carey, quite a few people have talked to me about your outline and, while they all agree that it is a fine story, and would make a whale of a script, they are, to a man, all frightened by its potential cost. (GC23-2)

Among other notes, Coon tried to help Wilbur with the characterizations. He wrote:

> And don't understand Marla. She should be a strong woman, though a little fuzzy in the head when it comes to historical novels and ancient Viking warriors or conquistadors. She is giving up an important career for love… in fact, she actually turns traitor for love. Technically speaking, by helping Ericsson in his capture of the ship, she is engaging in mutiny, and could be strung from the nearest asteroid by her neck, or whatever they do to mutineers in that far-off time. So she is much in love… and Ericsson would also be in love with her. It is Kirk's great understanding of people which allows him, so to speak, to let Marla off the hook after what she has done.

Some notes were more difficult to give than others. This was the part of the job Gene Coon dreaded. In his letter, which lasted several pages, he asked Wilbur to cut many of the scenes requiring optical effects, elaborate sets, and space suits. With a mix of embarrassment and humility, he wrote:

> The inevitable question, which you are allowed to ask, is why and how are we doing a science-fiction series without allowing for any science-fiction. We lie a lot, for one thing. We cheat a lot, for another. (GC23-2)

On the same day, Coon wrote a letter to Mary Dorfman of the Writers Guild of America. The tone, as in the letter sent to Wilbur, betrayed his disdain for certain aspects of being a TV producer. It began:

> I seem to find myself producing *Star Trek* and, in the course of so doing, I have bought a story from Carey Wilbur, entitled "Space Seed," which deals very roughly with persons traveling through space in a state of suspended animation. Since buying this story from Carey, I have discovered in our files another story entitled "The Rebels Unthawed," apparently written, if I may use the word, by one Philip Jose Farmer. This story was submitted to us unsolicited and was not purchased. It bears a vague resemblance to the Carey Wilbur story insofar as it deals with the discovery of persons on board a space ship in a state of suspended animation. (GC23-3)

Coon's letter was the first line of defense against possible litigation from Farmer, the sci-fi author with no TV experience but with whom Roddenberry had been corresponding.

Better news arrived a few days later from NBC. Stan Robertson liked the story outline for "Space Seed." And he was now acknowledging Gene Coon, writing to the new producer directly rather than to Roddenberry. Robertson gushed:

> The author of this storyline, Carey Wilbur, seems to have, at least in the initial presentation, come up with a most exciting *Star Trek* episode. There is an exciting blend of past Earth history -- the similarity of the plot with the colonization of Australia; [plus] a current problem of our contemporary society -- over-population; and a believable and interesting, if not novel, science fiction gimmick -- the revitalization of people several hundred years after their normal span of life. (SR23)

Robertson did not complain that "Space Seed" was in a sense a bottle show, since, at this stage, to the horror of Robert Justman, much of the action took place on the sleeper ship and even out in the vacuum of space.

When Wilbur's First Draft script arrived, Justman fired off a new memo to Coon, Roddenberry, and Carabatsos, warning, "Gird your loins, gentlemen. You are about to get another long memo from Constant Reader" (the sign-off often used by the acerbic writer Dorothy Parker). Several pages later, after noting one or more problems on nearly every page of the script, Justman wrote:

> What the hell is Systems Officer Marla McGivers doing on the Bridge in Scene 2? What is all this schtick about her humming a song and all the other jazz that occurs on the first page of this screenplay? I don't believe it and I really don't like it either.... Why does Kirk have to be asleep in Scene 4? If Uhura gives Kirk the message that the signal is originating from the "Coal Sack" [the name of the ship they encounter], then why does Kirk ask for a heading and range on the signal? Why does Kirk tell Uhura to alert all decks? Why is this signal considered to be dangerous by the writer? My feeling is that this TEASER as written is fake. It doesn't establish anything, least of all jeopardy to the Enterprise and its crew. Also, the TEASER is too short. Also, where is Mister Spock?... Spock's last speech on page 4 is definitely not Spockian. Mister Sulu's first speech on page 5 and Kirk's answer are, I feel, entirely out of place. Sulu wouldn't venture a remark about Mister Spock's spirit breaking and Kirk would not pick him up on it and tell Sulu that it wouldn't hurt to shake Spock up a little.... As you may know, escape velocity is the velocity an object needs to escape the gravitational pull of a planet or other body. Therefore, Sulu's speech about "escape velocity" is not applicable in this case. There is no standard escape velocity that can be used as a yardstick throughout space. I also find no need for Yeoman Rand in this script and even if there were a need, she would not be the one to announce action stations over the ship's intercom.... For some strange reason I find that Scene 17 irritates me no end. (RJ23-2)

And this was only the first page of Justman's six-page memorandum. He continued:

> Gee whiz, fellows, I suppose I could go on forever giving you instance after instance of bad dialogue or unbelievable situations in this script. So, therefore, I will hit the rest of them as fast as I can in the few minutes remaining to me before I run out of energy.... Please don't let Kirk and Ericsson fight with phasers guns on Pages 60 and 61. They will not only rip the ship to shreds, but they will rip the budget to shreds. (RJ23-2)

Justman closed:

> I'm sorry that I have been so caustic in my analysis with regard to this script -- but I just don't have the time to be kindly. This script needs an enormous amount of work if we are going to be able to salvage it. (RJ23-2)

Justman was not alone in disliking Wilber's teleplay. The staff memo, which did not identify if the sender was Stephen Carabatsos, still working as Script Consultant, or Dorothy Fontana, who had been giving notes in an unofficial capacity, was highly negative. Among the damning remarks:

> This story starts much too slowly and plods in other spots. All our regular characters are out of character, especially Kirk and Spock. Kirk has no command presence, no strength. He stands around a lot. In fact, almost all our people stand around a lot. Marla's attitudes and the "love story" with Ericsson are unbelievable and the payoff is mellerdramer [sic]...not *Star Trek*. (Staff23)

Later that day, Coon wrote to Carey Wilbur:

> We have quite a bit of work to do on this script. Part of it is because of the unfamiliarity with what is possible or probable in standard operating procedure on our ship, and part of it is due to just flat missing the mark here and there.... The character of Ericsson just does not come off as the heroic, gigantic, conquistadorian figure I think we need. In some aspects he comes off almost as a small time thug, almost a punk, who would have no chance of taking over the Enterprise, and couldn't even conceive of a grand decision, which is, I believe, hacking out a place for himself in this world of the future.... The second major flaw we have going for us is in the character and action of Marla McGivers. As it is, she takes a look at the unconscious Ericsson and decides she loves him. It is imperative that we establish first that she, too, is a person out of her time. She yearns for the ancient heroic, the grand, the days when men were men, and all that jazz. And she has not known love in this modern age. She has never found a man of the stature she requires -- the great conquistador, the hero, the flamboyant world-shaking giant of a man, a la Ayn Rand. (GC23-4)

Ayn Rand, the popular writer of the 1950s, wrote many stories about women falling for domineering men. One such man in one of Rand's early novels, *The Little Street*, was Danny Renahan, whom the author described as "a man with no regard whatever for all that society holds sacred, and with a consciousness all his own... A man who really stands alone, in action and in soul." In other words: Ericsson/Khan.

Part of the problem regarding Marla McGivers was that Wilbur made her Uhura's alternate as ship's Communication Officer. Coon would later change this and have her be the ship's historian, a crew member in love with the past, and its men, and whose input is so rarely needed that Kirk can't even get her name right.

Coon's dense letter, clocking in at 13 single-spaced pages, listed all the problems he and his staff had come up with in the 66-page screenplay.

Wilbur accepted the feedback and harsh criticism well and, in early December, turned in his Second Draft. The improvements were far and few between.

Gene Roddenberry had much to say to Gene Coon over Wilbur's rewrite. In a lengthy memo, Roddenberry called it "A deceptive script," then elaborated:

> At first reading, it seems clean, straight-lined, an orderly progression of ideas and emotions. But actually its entire underpinning is weak -- fixable, however, if we take a long hard look at the shaky logic supporting the whole story, replace it with believable ideas. (GR23-1)

At the center of the shaky logic was the very seed of Wilbur's story -- that Earth's misfits would be frozen and shot into space. Beginning with a reference to the sleeper ship named Botany Bay, Roddenberry wrote:

> This concept, sounding romantic, may have gotten us into trouble. For example -- it is hard to believe the world of the 1990s sending men off to a penal colony in the stars. Romantic, but impractical. No "advanced" world of the 1990s would do this; no barbaric or dark ages world of the 1990s would spend the hundreds of millions required to do it, when a simpler expedient for a barbaric world would be simply to put the men to death. So the entire concept is rather shaky to start with. (GR23-1)

And then there were what Wilbur described as "The Dark Ages of the 1990s." Roddenberry wrote:

> This may be a possible key to making this story believable. Let's say the Earth, during the 1990s, was catapulted into a kind of "dark ages." Let's further say that it's this period that, instead of being involved with criminals and criminal deportees, was a period of crime and the criminals being glorified. It's not that impossible -- criminality, from one philosophical viewpoint, was glorified in the age of chivalry. So, following that line of logic, let's say that a "society" of super-criminals, highly intelligent, intellectually and physically daring, believing in the purity of violence in war and conquest, took advantage of atomic war and catastrophe and rose to control the Earth. This could, in fact, be Ericsson and his men. Think of it in terms of Hitler and his cohorts in the black -- from their point of view -- days of 1945. Had space travel been practical at that time, Hitler and his crew might well have decided upon the "suicide" of leaving this world.... At any rate, this could be the background of Ericsson and his crew -- a dangerous group in the extreme. As such, they offer much more jeopardy to the Enterprise than merely a group of common criminals usually rounded up and deported. (GR23-1)

As he had done many times before, in one memo -- and, in this instance, in only two paragraphs -- Roddenberry completely reinvented a story, from something that might have worked on *Lost in Space* to something that *did* work on *Star Trek*.

But there was much more than the back story that Roddenberry felt needed to be changed -- the characters of Ericsson and McGivers annoyed the hell out of him. Roddenberry continued:

> This script is an example of how illogical, unmotivated antagonists and protagonists can reduce science fiction to "space pirates." (GR23-1)

Lt. McGivers especially bothered him. He told Coon:

> Marla is so sophomoric, I doubt if any of us could stand her even today ... except, possibly, as an extremely shapely immoral actress, of which, unfortunately, due to gross negligence on the part of the casting department, we get too few of on this series. (GR23-1)

Roddenberry was also disturbed with how Kirk was portrayed. In Wilbur's script, Kirk avoids making a decision about whether to revive Ericsson's frozen shipmates. Roddenberry told Coon:

> Worse than any of the preceding, our Starship Commander must wait on "higher command" to make a quite ordinary and human decision whether or not to revive a group of people who are presently in suspended animation. God help us if we've come no further than this in three more centuries! In fact, God help us

if the Captain of the cruiser, U.S.S. Los Angeles, would wait for higher
command in the Pentagon or State Department to make a simple decision like
that.... There seems to be a compulsion among writers to picture the future as
totally computerized, inhumanly authoritarian, and coldly big-brotherish. I know
none of us want to go that direction, but God help *Star Trek* if our writers push
us that-a-way. (GR23-1)

Roddenberry closed:

This is really getting to be a Robert Justman-type memo, isn't it?... I have more
comments, but I've run out of tape. (GR23-1)

Carey Wilbur was not asked to do a third draft of his script, as badly as a third draft was needed. Someone else would inherit that job: Gene Coon.

Following the directions set forth in Roddenberry's memo, Coon did a major overhaul of the story, generating the Yellow Cover First Draft from December 7. Harold Ericsson was now John Ericsson, who is revealed to really be Ragner Thorwald, a major participant in "The First World Tyranny" of the 1990s. Coon didn't show his script to anyone. He slept on it for two nights then on December 9 came in with a Final Draft -- tighter, cheaper, and sharper. This version never made it out of his office, either. A few days later, Coon had rewritten himself again, and now had a Revised Final Draft, dated December 12. He felt confident enough to send this one to de Forest Research, NBC, all *Star Trek* department heads including Justman, and to Roddenberry.

All seemed happy ... except Justman ... and Roddenberry. Twenty-four hours later, Roddenberry had rewritten the script himself -- a 2nd Revised Final Draft. In this draft, Ericsson finally became Khan.

Of the Final, Final, Final Draft, Bob Justman sent word to Roddenberry:

I would like to state that I find it well nigh incredible that you managed to do
this complete rewrite in the space of one single night. And I also find it
practically astounding that you have managed to clean up the story and
streamline it into its present shootable condition. (RJ23-3)

One element Roddenberry had added disturbed Justman, who wrote:

Although I find that Khan's badgering Marla in scene 56 is a very clever device
to get her to finally capitulate, I feel that I must object strongly to having him
shove her down on the floor. I feel that perhaps we should discuss this more
fully. Also, I'm still not quite in a position to accept Marla's final capitulation to
Khan. (RJ23-3)

With this draft, Roddenberry listed himself as first writer, followed by Gene Coon. Wilbur's name did not even appear on the title page. However, by the time the episode was aired, Gene Coon was listed as top writer, followed by Wilbur, who was also given a separate "story by" credit. This time, Roddenberry's name was absent. A higher source had spoken. On January 6, 1967, the Writers Guild of America turned its thumb down to a request by Roddenberry to share the credit and payments for the script. Robert Justman, if asked, would have argued this point adamantly.

If Roddenberry's name was omitted, he was in good company. Khan and Kirk both make reference to John Milton. The 17th Century English poet wrote the epic poem *Paradise Lost*, in 10 books (later expanded into 12), chronicling the temptation of Adam and Eve by Satan, and their expulsion from the Garden of Eden. Milton received no story credit, either.

Pre-Production
December 6-9 & 12-14, 1966 (7 days).

Ricardo Montalban poses for the cover of *Life* magazine, November 21, 1949 issue

Director Marc Daniels, after the crowning success of directing "The Menagerie," returned for his sixth episode of *Star Trek*. Despite his weakness at staging action sequences, Daniels remained a favorite of the producers.

"During a drought, you pray for rain," said Robert Justman. "During the first year of *Star Trek*, we prayed for Marc Daniels." (94-8)

Ricardo Montalban, everyone's first choice to play Khan, was already a star. The 45-year-old had had top billing in films since 1947, usually as Latin-lover types. In fact, he was the male lead in a movie called *Latin Lovers*, from 1953, exchanging dialogue and kisses with Lana Turner. On the stage, in 1958's *Jamaica*, he was nominated for a Tony award as Best Actor in a Musical. Roddenberry knew Montalban from their association in a 1956 sci-fi project for the *Chevron Hall of Stars*: "The Secret Weapon of 117" [wrongly listed on imdb.com and other internet sites as "The Secret Defense of 117"]. Montalban worked for Roddenberry again in an episode of *The Lieutenant*.

Joe D'Agosta said, "Ricardo was one of those people we all knew in Hollywood, because he was a movie star and just beginning to do television. We scored with a higher caliber actor than we expected." (43-1)

Madlyn Rhue, at 31, played Lt. Marla McGivers. A well liked TV guest-star, she had been on television since 1957 and would work with Montalban on three occasions, first in a 1960 episode of *Bonanza*, then here, and ending with a 1982 episode of *Fantasy Island*. She also frequented many of the same series Montalban did, with appearances on either side of this *Star Trek* on *I Spy* (1966) and *The Wild, Wild West* (1967). And she too appeared on Roddenberry's *The Lieutenant*.

Montalban with Madlyn Rhue during Day 4 of the production (Unaired film trim, courtesy of Gerald Gurian)

Blaisdell Makee, 34, played Lt. Spinelli, taking Sulu's place in this story. He returned to *Star Trek* for the 1967 episode "The Changeling," as Lt. Singh (no relation to Khan Noonien Singh).

John Winston, in his second of 11 turns as Lt. Kyle, is knocked out by Khan.

James Doohan, and his Scotty, continued to gain stature. NBC was as pleased with Doohan and his character as the producers were and all were looking for ways to involve Mr. Scott in more episodes and to greater significance. After commanding the bridge for the first time in the previous episode, Mr. Scott is now included among the top officers attending the formal dinner with Khan. Other than Kirk, Spock and McCoy, Mr. Scott is the only other one to wear a dress uniform. Also included at the table is Mr. Leslie (Eddie Paskey), who had sat in the Captain's chair in the past, but, as designated by the lack of formal attire, is now outranked by Mr. Scott.

Production Diary
Filmed December 15, 16, 19, 20, 21 & 22, 1966
(6 day production; total cost: $197,262).

Day 3: Scene 54, Take 2, December 19, 1966
(Courtesy of Gerald Gurian)

Thursday, December 15, 1966. The day *Star Trek* began filming the classic "Space Seed," Walt Disney died. He was 65. During the last months of his life, he saw the Disney studio's *Robin Crusoe, U.S.M.*, starring Dick Van Dyke, become the fifth top grossing film of 1966. And *The Wonderful World of Walt Disney*, for which he had served as host, placed at No. 19 for the season. Brand new in the movie houses (only one week old) and already a box office champ was *A Man for All Seasons*. The two most played songs on the radio seemed ages apart -- "Winchester Cathedral," by the New Vaudeville Band, and "Mellow Yellow," by Donavan. Big James Arness, as Matt Dillon, had the cover of *TV Guide* for the sixth of 12 times. *Gunsmoke* was in the middle of a 20-year run. And in a few days, CBS would premiere Dr. Suess' *How the Grinch Stole Christmas,* destined to repeat annually for four-and-a-half decades to come, and counting ... small potatoes compared to the amount of times "Space Seed" would repeat around the country ... and the world.

For the production, Stage 9 got a workout. The bridge, two crewman's quarters, sickbay, the transporter room, the briefing room, (plus a redress of the briefing room as a wardroom), the main engineering room, and the corridors were all used. A new addition was also needed for sickbay: the decompression chamber. Stage 10 was needed only for the Botany Bay sleeper ship set.

Filming began on the bridge. Daniels covered 10 pages of script, 15 numbered scenes in all. He wrapped at 5:55 p.m., allowing cast and crew to make it home in time for "Balance of Terror" on NBC -- the 14th episode to air.

On Day 2, Daniels finished on the bridge, and then continued filming in McCoy's office, followed by sickbay, where Khan holds a knife to the doctor's throat. Twenty-one scenes, and 11 pages of script later, Daniels wrapped at 7:20 p.m., well into overtime but otherwise on schedule.

On Day 3, Monday, Daniels covered the action and dialogue in Marla McGivers' quarters, the wardroom and, after a quick re-dress, the briefing room scene.

**Day 4, for a redress of the Briefing Room
(Courtesy of Gerald Gurian)**

On Day 4, more shots were taken in the briefing room, followed by Khan's quarters, and finishing in the corridor as Khan breaks out of his room and attacks the guard.

Marc Daniels said, "Part of the problem in 'Space Seed' was trying to visualize Khan's tremendous power -- where he could turn out a finger and turn somebody upside down. That was difficult, but we got away with it thanks to stunt people and judicious cutting." (44-2)

Day 5. All other corridor scenes were shot, as well as scenes outside sickbay, by the elevator, and outside Marla McGivers' quarters. The latter was meant to give us our introduction to McGivers, where she interacts with another crew member (and friend), Angela Martine (Barbara Baldavin), who was previously seen in "Balance of Terror" and "Shore Leave." Martine tells McGivers of a crewman interested in asking her out. McGivers is not interested in any man who doesn't have the spine to do the asking himself. Later, this insight to McGivers' character helps us to understand her immediate attraction to a man such as Khan. Due to time constraints, however, this very worthwhile scene was left on the editing room floor.

The transporter room came next, followed by a move to engineering for the fight between Khan and Kirk. Of this, James Doohan commented, "The fight scene in engineering, while nicely choreographed, made extensive and, unfortunately, very obvious use of Bill's stunt double, Gary Combs. Stuntmen are most effective in quick cuts, but Combs was on screen for relatively lengthy sequences, with Bill only in tight close-ups." (52-1)

Day 6. The company was on Stage 10 filming the scenes inside the Botany Bay. Some of them never made the final cut. Dorothy Fontana revealed, "Jean Messerschmidt [of NBC Broadcast Standards] was very hard-nosed about the outfits on the people who had been awakened. And, if you look at the finished show, there are some of those people in the foreground who are talking to Khan, and others in the background that have just come out of cold-storage, if you will, and are stretching and bending. Well, those outfits were quite skimpy and we had deliberately hired dancers and gymnasts who had great bodies so that they could wear these costumes and look great. Jean insisted that a whole lot of that be cut -- as much as possible. The costumes were pretty revealing, and she said, 'No!'" (64-3)

Next came a move to Stage 9 for a set built earlier that morning -- the decompression chamber.

Moods were good when cast and crew, having taken the last shots for "Space Seed," left the set that evening. Jerry Finnerman explained the feeling, saying, "That was a very strong show, especially for the schedule we had." (63-3)

Daniels had finished on schedule, and early enough for everyone to make it home for the repeat broadcast of "What Are Little Girls Made Of?" which was

Day 6: Slating the shot where a weakened Kirk crawls from the decompression chamber (Courtesy of Gerald Gurian)

taking the place of "Shore Leave" that night, as the latter episode was late getting to NBC. For many involved with *Star Trek*, this was their first chance to see "Little Girls." When it aired the first time, several weeks earlier, the company was running late, stuck out of town at Vasquez Rocks filming (ironically) "Shore Leave."

Post-Production
December 23, 1966 through February 5, 1967. Music Score: Tracked.

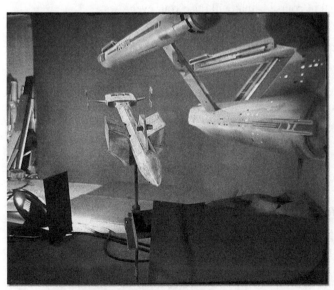
Two giant miniatures -- state of the art for 1966
(Courtesy of Gerald Gurian)

James D. Ballas, former editing assistant to Robert Swanson, was not blamed for his first go-round as lead editor on "The Alternative Factor," and returned, now the permanent head of Edit Team #1.

The Westheimer Co. received screen credit for the optical effects, including matte shots (images on viewing screens) and transporter shimmers. But the primary optical effects, those of the Enterprise encountering the S.S. Botany Bay, were taken by Film Effects of Hollywood, without credit.

Designer Matt Jefferies, who came up with the Enterprise, inside and out, also designed the model of the Botany Bay. In 1968, for fanzine *Inside Star Trek,* #4, Jefferies said, "The Botany Bay was actually designed *before* the Enterprise. It was a little idea that

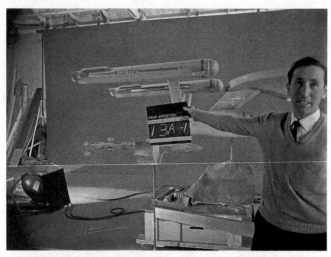

Filming the miniatures on the Film Effects of Hollywood stage, 1966 (Courtesy of Gerald Gurian)

popped up and was labeled 'antique space freighter.'"

Star Trek once again spent more than its near-impossible episode allowance of $185,000. "Space Seed," despite being primarily a bottle show, actually cost $197,262. Most of the overrun was due to the cost of building and photographing the Botany Bay miniature, and the design and construction of the interior of the sleeper ship. The running deficit was now up to $77,950.

Release / Reaction
Premiere air date: 2/16/67. NBC repeat broadcast: 8/24/67.

Steven H. Scheuer reviewed "Space Seed" for the syndicated *TV Key Previews* column. Among newspapers to carry the review on February 16, 1967 was the *Evening Independent*, in St. Petersburg, Florida. Scheuer said:

> A highly imaginative tale about a 20th century spaceship lost on its own star trek for hundreds of years. Its discovery confounds the men of the Enterprise. What makes this drama particularly interesting is its commentary on the scientific know-how of the late 1990s and the kind of world it bred. Tune in for a bit of anticipated history -- fictional of course -- that will raise your eyebrows nevertheless.

Joan Crosby weighed in for her syndicated *TV Scout* column. Among newspapers to spread the word was the *Pittsburg Press*, in Pittsburg, Pennsylvania. Crosby said:

> This is a good piece of science fiction tonight. Ricardo Montalban is very good as the leader of a large group on a "sleeper ship" of the 1990s. He is discovered by the Enterprise crew and is brought back from a state of suspended animation. He turns out to be a perfect specimen in every way -- he soon sends Earth historian Madlyn Rhue into a tizzy.

Excellent reviews; average ratings.

RATINGS / Nielsen National report for Thursday, February 16, 1967:

8:30 - 9 p.m., with 67.8% of U.S. TVs in use.	**Households:**	**Share:**
NBC: *Star Trek* (first half)	13,120,000	no data
ABC: **Bewitched**	**14,440,000**	**no data**
CBS: *My Three Sons*	12,790,000	no data
Independent stations:	no data	no data

9 - 9:30 p.m., with 67.9% of U.S. TVs in use.	**Households:**	**Share:**
NBC: *Star Trek* (second half)	no data	28.0%
ABC: *Love on a Rooftop*	no data	30.7%
CBS: **Thursday Night Movie** (start)	**no data**	**35.5%**
Independent stations:	no data	5.8%

At 8:30 p.m., *Star Trek* held a respectable second position. At 9 p.m., even with this excellent episode, the numbers turned downward with the arrival of the *Thursday Night Movie* on CBS -- the 1961 Western *One-Eyed Jacks*, starring Marlon Brando.

***

From the beginning, it was clear that "Space Seed" would be a special episode. Sound editor Douglas Grindstaff recalled, "'Space Seed' was one of my favorites.... We won the Golden Reel Award given by the M.P.S.E. [Motion Picture Sound Editors] on that particular episode." (76-1)

Audio effects and editing were essential to *Star Trek*. Sound Editing supervisor Jack Finlay said, "In those days the major studios wouldn't give you what you wanted if you wanted it for television production. I called a friend over at Paramount and got some stuff from *War of the Worlds* [the photon torpedo effect].... I got that stuff, and whatever else I could scrounge from around the town. I went to libraries and got every possible thing that might work to put together. I ran those sounds backwards, slowed them down, and did whatever I had to do to them so they would work for us." (62)

Second in charge in the sound department was Joseph Sorokin. He recalled, "I obtained all the sound effects from the Air Force Library... some of these sounds are rather hokey and corny now, but you have to view them in the context of the past. At the time that we were putting *Star Trek* together, the existing sound effects were like something out of *Flash Gordon* or *Buck Rogers*. So we had to come up with something else. Authenticity was very important to Gene Roddenberry." (162)

Sound editor Grindstaff explained, "Every room aboard the ship had a sound, and every planet had a sound. It was a monumental thing. Gene Roddenberry once told me to think like a painter -- he wanted a 'painted' sound, which I'll never forget." (76-2)

***

After leaving Khan and his followers on an uninhabited world, Spock suggests it would be interesting "in a hundred years" to see what crop has sprung up from the seed they have planted. A line in an earlier draft of the script, not in the filmed episode, has Kirk say that he hopes the crop won't "spring right out of the ground" and come looking for them. It took 16 years, not a hundred for Khan's return, in *Star Trek II: The Wrath of Khan*.

Entertainment Weekly picked "Space Seed" as the second best *Star Trek* ever made. "Seed" also made sci-fi magazine *Cinefantastique*'s Top Ten list for *Star Trek*'s all-time best.

From the Mailbag

Received shortly after the first airing of "Space Seed":

> Dear Gene, that episode of *Star Trek* with Ricardo Montalban was, in my estimation, the show's finest hour. Warmest regards, Jerry (Sohl).

And, in response to a letter from Miss D. Jones in Berkeley, California:

> My Dear Miss Jones: Thank you for your kind letter concerning our sponsorship of *Star Trek*. Our official position is that it is a good program with good ratings. As a personal opinion, I think it is the <u>best</u> program on the air and perhaps the best program over the last five years. It is practically the only program I ever

watch. I hope you will continue to watch it. I know I will. Maybe with you working on the West Coast and me endorsing it on the East Coast, we can build it into a run-away success. -- Edward E. Permelee, Assistant Director of Advertising Services, Bristol-Myer Company, New York.

Memories

Ricardo Montalban said, "I thought the character of Khan was wonderful.... He was an overly ambitious man that had dimension. Sometimes when you read a villain, he's a villain through and through, but this man had facets. He was genetically engineered with mental and physical superiority and it's only natural that he uses that superiority and wants to conquer. On the other hand, he falls in love. He takes his girl as his wife when he goes into exile. It was a love that was very real; it humanized the character for me." (120-1)

DeForest Kelley said, "I enjoyed working with Ricardo the best [of all of *Star Trek*'s guest stars]. I was privileged. He is a marvelous actor." (98-1)

Montalban said, "It was a very happy company and everybody was very cordial; very nice. All the regulars were wonderful to me, most helpful, and I loved it.... I thought [the script] was well-written, it had an interesting concept, and I was delighted it was offered to me." (120-1)

Jerry Finnerman said, "That was a wonderful show.... I mean, this show was so good that they made a feature out of it, which was a big-time feature.... And, if you realize it, you take a show like that, where there's hardly any action -- very little action; mostly dialogue -- but you never get tired of it.... Now, if you can hold people with that dialogue for what, 48 minutes, isn't that wonderful? I mean, we had strong shows, and that just goes to show you how strong the writing was.... And that's the way most of our shows were." (63-3)

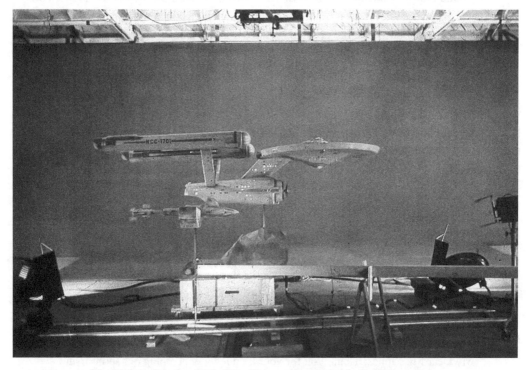

**The 11-foot, 2-inch model of the Enterprise, alongside the Botany Bay,
with blue screen behind, at Film Effects of Hollywood, 1966
(Courtesy of Gerald Gurian)**

32

Episode 24: A TASTE OF ARMAGEDDON
(Incorrectly listed in all other sources as Production #23)
Teleplay by Robert Hamner and Gene L. Coon
Story by Robert Hamner
Directed by Joseph Pevney

**David Opatoshu in deleted scene
(Courtesy of Gerald Gurian)**

NBC's January 30, 1967, press release announced:

David Opatoshu guest-stars as the ruler of a seemingly peaceful space nation whose reluctance toward establishment of diplomatic relations draws Captain Kirk (William Shatner) into the center of an interplanetary war, in "A Taste of Armageddon" on the NBC Television Network colorcast of *Star Trek*.... The unexplained hostility of leader Anan 7 (Opatoshu) baffles Kirk who is denied permission to deliver Ambassador Fox (Gene Lyons) to the planet Eminar [sic] for a top-level diplomatic conference. Kirk and Mr. Spock (Leonard Nimoy) decide to investigate and soon find themselves prisoners of war in a simulated but deadly conflict between two planets.

As in "The Return of the Archons," we witness the pitfalls of man submitting to machine. New here: a "disguised" anti-war statement.

SOUND BITES

- *Kirk:* "Disease, suffering, hardship -- that's what war is all about. That's what makes it a thing to be avoided. But you've made it neat and painless -- so neat and painless, you've had no reason to stop it. And you've had it for *five hundred years*!"

- *Anan 7, to Kirk:* "Once in orbit around our planet, your ship became a legitimate target. It has been classified destroyed by a tri-cobalt satellite explosion. All persons aboard your ship have twenty-four hours to report to our disintegration chambers."

- *Spock, distracting a guard with a deadpan lie:* "Sir, there is a multi-legged creature crawling on your shoulder."

- *Kirk:* "I've given you back the horrors of war. The Vendikans will now assume you have abandoned your agreement and are preparing for a real war, with real weapons.... The next attack they launch will do a lot more than count up numbers on a computer. It will destroy cities; devastate your planet. You'll want to retaliate, of course. If I were you, I'd start making bombs.... Yes, councilman, you've got a real war on your hands. You can either wage it, with real weapons, or you might consider the alternatives. Put an end to it. Make peace!" *Anan 7:* "There can be no peace! Don't you see -- we've admitted it to ourselves! We're a killer species." *Kirk:* "All right, it's instinctive. But the instinct can be fought. We're human beings, with the blood of a million savage years on our hands. But we can stop it! We can admit we're killers, but we're not going to kill today. That's all it takes -- knowing that you're not going to kill today."

ASSESSMENT

"A Taste of Armageddon" is well-regarded, despite looking rather dated, more so than most other episodes of the original series. The sets and costumes on Eminiar 7 are reminiscent of those seen in the old *Buck Rogers* serials. Adding to the problem, writer Robert Hamner and even Gene Coon, who made significant changes to the script, displayed a fondness for exclamation points in their dialogue, contributing to the melodramatic delivery of many of the speeches. The combined result makes a look into the future seem more like a trip into the past. That disclaimer aside, this story had profound purpose when it first aired and remains insightful to this day.

In 1966, when this episode was conceived, napalm was being dropped in Vietnam in an effort to burn the Viet Cong from the jungles, while the men dropping the bombs never had to see the faces of their victims ... or hear their screams. War had become impersonal. In "A Taste of Armageddon" we encounter a world in which individual significance is so unappreciated that characters have names like Anan 7, Mea 3, and Sar 6. Even the planet is identified with a number. It is the seventh world in this system called Eminiar.

Mea 3 tells Kirk that she has been declared a casualty and must report to a disintegration chamber. He asks, "Is that all it means to you? You just report -- and die?" She answers, "Don't you see, if I refuse to report, and others refuse, then Vendikar would have no choice but to launch real weapons. We would have to do the same, to defend ourselves. More than people would die then. Our civilization would be destroyed! Surely you can see that ours is the better way."

With this, the script offers an abstract but clear comparison to our world of 1966. At that time in America, the first of the draft-dodgers were fleeing to Canada. They were refusing to "report." Those loyal to the U.S. government's policies saw this as a threat, believing one resister would lead to hundreds, then to thousands, causing the downfall of a system. In this regard, the political agenda of "A Taste of Armageddon" is apparent.

Some things to watch for:
- "The Federation" had previously been mentioned in "Arena." The organization's full name, "The United Federation of Planets," is revealed in this episode, again courtesy of Mr. Coon.
- This is the second time that a soon-to-be familiar formula was used: landing party in trouble; ship under fire and unable to help; Kirk must save all (first used in "The Return of the Archons").
- We previously saw Spock's ability to perform the Vulcan mind-meld (from "Dagger of the Mind"). Here we learn he can also use "inception" to plant ideas into the minds of others. This device would be used again in "By Any Other Name" and "The Omega Glory."

THE STORY BEHIND THE STORY

Script Timeline
Robert Hamner's story outline, ST #36: September 12, 1966.
Hamner's revised outline, gratis: September 23, 1966.
Hamner's 2nd Revised Story Outline, gratis: September 26, 1966.
Hamner's 3rd Revised Story Outline, gratis: September 28, 1966.
Staff revised story outline: Early October 1966.
Hamner's 1st Draft teleplay: October 17, 1966.
Hamner's 2nd Draft teleplay: November 9, 1966.
Steven Carabatsos' script polish (Mimeo Department
"Yellow Cover 1st Draft"): November 23, 1966.
Carabatsos' second script polish (Final Draft teleplay): November 28, 1966.
Gene Coon's rewrite (Rev. Final Draft teleplay): December 12, 1966.
Additional page revisions by Coon: December 15 & 21, 1966.

In the Bible, Armageddon is where the last decisive battle between the forces of good and evil will be fought before Judgment Day. Writer Robert Hamner believed that if man didn't soon change his evil ways, Armageddon might be just around the corner.

"At the time, the military was developing neutron bombs," Hamner said. "These were designed to kill people without harming the buildings. It was like big business going to war. 'Don't destroy the factories, just kill the workers!' I thought it would be terrible if a neutron bomb were developed. It would take all the devastation out of war and just leave death.... That was the whole idea of the script when I walked into Gene Coon's office." (78)

Hamner, at 38, was very much in-demand. He had already written for *The Fugitive*, *The Wild, Wild West*, and *Voyage to the Bottom of the Sea*. One year before this, like Roddenberry and Coon, he was a writer/producer. His series: *A Man Called Shenandoah* (taking over for Fred Freidberger, later to produce *Star Trek*).

Robert Hamner's original outline and screenplay called for very different staging than the filmed episode. Damaged by a meteor storm, the Enterprise heads to nearby Eminiar 7 to make repairs, but is refused permission to approach. With no other options, Kirk ignores the warnings and transports down to search for the mineral elements needed to repair his ship. The landing team, which includes Yeoman Janice Rand, materializes in a rural area with a large modern city looming in the distance. An anti-gravity "bubble car," carrying representatives from the government, approaches. The Eminiar officials, who had warned the Enterprise people to stay away, have now relented, treating them with courtesy and giving assistance, hoping to quickly send them on their way. While a search is made for the needed raw materials, Kirk is invited to visit the city and meet Anan 7 and the ruling council. The city that Hamner describes is something out of *Metropolis*. It is grand, futuristic and very alien. And we spend much time in it --- not inside buildings but out on the streets. It is further established that the computers and machines do everything for the people.

While visiting the city, Kirk meets Mea 3, the daughter of Anan 7. A romance brews between her and Kirk. When Eminiar 7 is attacked and Mea 3 is classified a war casualty, Kirk is determined to keep her from reporting to a disintegration chamber. For this reason, he argues with the rulers about the foolishness of their virtual-reality computer-generated war, and then sabotages the computer system, saving Mea 3 and forcing the people of Eminiar to seek peace or face the horrors of a real war. Kirk then returns to the Enterprise, bidding farewell to Mea 3 and leaving her and her people to work out their troubles with their enemies ... or perish.

Coon wrote to Robert Hamner:

> Your entire idea, Kirk's philosophy, that this war goes on only because it is so neat and clean and non-destructive, is intriguing and exciting ... as is Kirk's hypothesis that making war horrible again would bring about peace. (GC24)

Hamner had told Coon that he felt his own treatment lacked action. Coon responded:

> You are right about one thing. We have too little action in the body of the story. I think Kirk, as a fugitive from the anti-matter stations, must be pursued, captured, escape, get into fights, and so on, in the process of gathering his forces. Don't forget that Kirk has a strong military force, and many weapons, on board the Enterprise. I think the thing to do here is have Kirk on the surface of the planet at the time when the authorities on the surface stop the systems of the Enterprise. All systems would be unworkable except routine communications, for we would want Kirk to be able to talk to those aboard ship to establish the danger of the Enterprise's condition, and so on. (GC24)

Coon had issues with some elements within the story. Regarding budget, he told Hamner:

> Do not stage the barrage of meteorites on the Enterprise. Too expensive -- a big horrible optical. Pick up the Enterprise *after* a meteor shower, as the ship limps, badly injured, toward [the planet].... We must not -- repeat NOT -- have scenes laid on the city streets. This would mean total set construction of the sort restricted only to multi-million dollar movies. Interiors we can do, long distance matte shots we can do, but we cannot have our principals walk down a street which is obviously of design and construction far ahead of ours. (GC24)

Coon also had problems with the way Hamner depicted the people of Eminiar. If played as written, how could a man such as Kirk be attracted to a person such as Mea 3. More importantly, how could a 1967 television audience get the references to the Vietnam war if the society depicted was so alien to our own? Coon told Hamner:

> Please do not have the computers and machines doing everything for the people of this culture. Have them used to a great extent, but at all times under the complete control of the people.... These should be vital people, well in control of the situation. (GC24)

Coon was left cold by the story's resolve. Of this, he wrote:

> The problem -- the main problem -- with this story as presently outlined is that Kirk really accomplishes nothing, wreaks no changes, gives us no solutions. Why not let him be the big hero? By threatening to bring down the total war in all its horror upon them -- a seemingly inhuman thing to do -- he is in effect insuring the coming of peace and the settlement of the long dispute. (GC24)

Kirk's agenda, as written, was clouded. His motivation seemed to be primarily driven by love -- a love he would have to abandon in the end, anyway.

Coon was not about to send the outline, as written, to NBC. He told Hamner:

> Okay, Robert, I think we're close. But there are, of course, some things in this we cannot do, and some areas I think can be improved. (GC24)

Hamner turned in three more drafts of his story outline, at no charge, with an eye toward reining in the costs, providing Kirk with better motivation and endowing the story with a more satisfying resolve.

Robert Justman, well-aware that there were major cost concerns, nonetheless embraced the story, writing to Coon:

> I find myself extremely intrigued by this idea.... I am very eager to read a First Draft screenplay on this. (RJ24-1)

Stan Robertson at NBC was also impressed. He wrote to Coon:

> This story idea has all of the ingredients to be developed into one of our more outstanding *Star Trek* teleplays. The writer shows great logical imagination in setting up this alien society; and, in doing so, isn't he subtly, almost by osmosis, getting across to the viewers a very weighty message without being overly cerebral? The point he sinks home, of course, is a very strong plea for the abolition of war. (SR24)

This story, like "The Return of the Archons," was what Robertson wanted to see on *Star Trek* -- planet stories with oodles of action and adventure and, as a bonus, a profound message conveyed without grandstanding. He told Coon:

> I would suggest that all of us who are so vitally concerned with telling action-adventure stories which have some substance carefully analyze this storyline and use it as a guide as to how we can achieve our goals and not short-change the creative heights we've set, to come up with something which is truly distinctive for television. (SR24)

But *Star Trek*'s budget could not afford such stories produced on a regular basis. Creative thinking and further deep cuts would have to be implemented.

Hamner's First Draft script arrived on October 17. After running the numbers, Robert Justman wrote to Coon:

> I can see why NBC is so happy with it. If I were the Network, I'd like to have a script like this all the time for our show. My only problem is, liking it doesn't mean that I feel we can afford to make it. (RJ24-3)

In a barrage of interoffice memos, Roddenberry, Coon, Justman, and Carabatsos began making suggestions as to how to chip away at the pricier parts of Hamner's story. One wrote:

> I wonder if [the meteor shower] is valid. We have established the Enterprise has a meteor deflector shield [in "Mudd's Women"]. This would have to be a helluva storm to damage us this badly.... Can we find some other way to damage the ship, if we must? Why are we always damaging the Enterprise anyway? (STAFF24)

The meteor shower was eliminated and the character of Ambassador Fox was introduced. The ship was now on a diplomatic mission with orders to make contact and establish an alliance at any cost.

Another wrote:

> Generally, there are too many extras and explosions, too many sets to be constructed, too many "futuristic city" mattes to lay-in ... to say nothing of that futuristic bubble-car. (STAFF24)

The Eminiar city became smaller still, represented primarily by a series of corridors and windowless rooms; the explosions were downsized; and the bubble-car was stricken entirely.

Another on the staff asked, "Why do we need Janice Rand in this script?" (STAFF24)

They didn't. Rand's part was reassigned to a character named Yeoman Tamula. The extras were reduced, as were many of the speaking parts.

Another wrote:

We have Kirk being a do-gooder for the benefit of a whole society -- which we said we didn't want. (STAFF24)

Someone else had a solution, and wrote:

Kirk and landing party are among those "killed" in the attack. Now they are ordered to report to the anti-matter machines to extinguish themselves... and Kirk ain't about to go. Escape and be hunted. And away we go on an action story. (STAFF24)

The change was made. Kirk and his landing party weren't declared casualties but, instead, the entire crew of the Enterprise was. Now Kirk was fighting for the lives of over 400 of his people. There was nothing to run away from; only something to beat.

Hamner was sent back to his typewriter. His Second Draft script arrived on November 9. Much still needed to change and it was clear to Coon those changes had to be handled in-house. Steven Carabatsos was assigned the job, his final task as the series' Script Editor.

Carabatsos' rewrite -- the Yellow Cover First Draft -- hit Coon's desk on November 23. After some discussions between producer and rewriter, Carabatsos did a polish, designated as the November 28 Final Draft.

Of this, Bob Justman wrote:

I think Steve has done a good job in converting this show into an action piece. Let me digress.... I wouldn't want Steve to get the idea that I dislike this screenplay, because I do like it very much.... My only problem is liking it doesn't mean that I feel we can afford to make it in its present form.... I am normally rather calm, but the amount of action fights and stunts called for in this show and the extensive nature of them causes me to lose my cool.... I do think we have established the fact that our Enterprise people are not to interfere with the culture of any civilization they come across. Since Kirk must necessarily interfere with the culture of this planet, it would be best if he was forced to interfere with it. He should not, therefore, start to do anything to change the course of this planet's civilization until the Enterprise and its crew are declared casualties of the war with the other planet. At that time, he can then proceed to take effective steps to save the ship and crew.... I am not exactly sure that I am going to end up liking the girl in this story. After all, who is she supposed to be in love with? Is she supposed to be in love with the fellow from the planet, or with Captain Kirk? If she is in love with the fellow from the planet, then what in hell is she doing screwing around with Captain Kirk? I think she may end up a two-timing little tramp. And Kirk is not too much better. He's kind of a snake in the grass with the girl. (RJ24-3)

Coon knew he would have to do a rewrite of his own, but was in the middle of giving "Space Seed" a makeover with his various drafts coming in on December 7 and 9, and the morning of the 12th. As Coon put that script to bed, he finally had time to read the latest memo from Justman, telling him that it would take eight to nine days to film "A Taste of Armageddon" based on the most recent draft by Steven Carabatsos. And production was supposed to begin in just three days. A quick decision was made to push "Armageddon" back in the production schedule and place "Space Seed" in front of it. The production numbering, however, was not changed, resulting in many other sources listing "Armageddon" as having been filmed first.

Justman breathed a sigh of relief, hoping the delay would result in the script being "trimmed down to size." (RJ24-4)

Amazingly, before the end of the same day that Gene Coon finished his final rewrite of "Space Seed," he did a major overhaul of "A Taste of Armageddon," his Revised Final Draft script, also dated December 12, 1966.

"To the best of my recollection," said Dorothy Fontana, "it was Gene Coon who wrote the speech at the end that man has a reputation as a killer, but you get up every morning and say 'I'm not going to kill today.'" (64-11)

Director Joseph Pevney concurred, saying, "The final speech from Bill, the demand for peace and not giving up human lives to a computer, was rewritten several times until we got it the way we wanted. Gene Coon rewrote the script and it was quite powerful." (141-3)

Coon turned in two sets of page revisions, on December 15 and 21. These script changes, along with his massive one-day rewrite from December 12, were of such significance that the Writers Guild Arbitration Board determined Coon should receive a co-writing credit in second position to Robert Hamner. The latter received a separate credit for his original story.

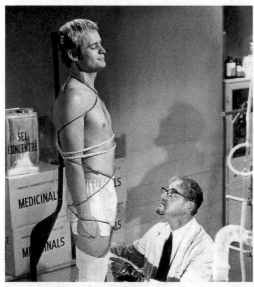

David McCallum is all tied up by David Opatoshu in a 1965 episode of *The Man from U.N.C.L.E.* (MGM TV)

Pre-Production
December 15-16 & 19-23, 1966 (7 days).

Joseph Pevney was chosen to direct this potentially difficult episode -- but this was not a back-to-back assignment for Pevney on the heels of "The Return of the Archons" as previous sources have indicated.

David Opatoshu, 48, played Anan 7. He tackled hundreds of acting roles between 1948 and 1991. In the early days of television, he kept busy on the prestigious dramatic anthology series, including frequent appearances on *Studio One*, *Philco Television Playhouse* and *Alfred Hitchcock Presents*.

He also appeared in multiple episodes of *Dr. Kildare*.

Barbara Babcock, 29 when cast as Mea 3, had worked for *Star Trek* once before, providing the voice of Trelane's mother in "The Squire of Gothos." Her voice would be heard again in "Assignment: Earth" and "The Tholian Web." The future Emmy Award winner would be seen in *Star Trek* again, in "Plato's Stepchildren."

Gene Lyons, who played Ambassador Fox, was 45. He worked often in television during the 1950s and 1960s. *Studio One*, *Kraft Television Theatre*, and *Goodyear Television Playhouse* were among the series on

Barbara Babcock in the 1960s

which he made multiple appearances.

James Doohan continued to rise in favor with both the producers and the network. This episode marks Mr. Scott's second turn at commanding the bridge. He is still identified as Chief Engineer, not Lieutenant Commander, as in later episodes. But his status had clearly changed with the one-two-three punches of "The Return of the Archons," "Space Seed," and now "A Taste of Armageddon."

Miko Mayama had played Yeoman Tamula once before, in "The Return of the Archons." She returns here to take the place of the departed Yeoman Janice Rand.

Gene Lyons as Commissioner Dennis Randall on *Ironside* **from 1967 through 1974 (Universal TV)**

David L. Ross was back for a third appearance as security officer Lt. Galloway, this time with dialogue. He says, "Get in line."

Sean Kenney, sitting in the helmsman's chair, made his fourth and final appearance in the series as Lt. DuPaul (previously seen in "Arena"). Kenney also played the crippled Christopher Pike in Parts 1 and 2 of "The Menagerie."

Bill Blackburn mans the navigation station -- his 13th appearance so far.

And Majel Barrett continued as the voice of the ship's computer. This time, per the wishes of Gene Roddenberry, the voice sounded a bit more mechanical.

Production Diary
Filmed December 27, 28, 29, 30 and January 3 & 4, 1967
(6 day production; total cost: $194,108).

Production began on Tuesday, December 27, after a four-day Christmas break. *Murderers' Row*, the second of four Matt Helm movies starring Dean Martin, was an unlikely holiday hit, knocking *A Man for All Seasons* out of the top box office position. The most watched TV shows from the night before were *The Lucy Show* and *The Andy Griffith Show*, on CBS, followed by *Iron Horse* and *Peyton Place*, on ABC. The songs getting the most radio play across the nation were "Snoopy vs. the Red Barron" by The Royal Guardsmen, "Winchester Cathedral" by The New Vaudeville Band and, about to hit the top of the charts, "I'm a Believer" by the Monkees. The "Pre-Fab Four" weren't monkeying around in the record stores, either. They had the top selling album.

Filming of "A Taste of Armageddon" started with the bridge scenes on Stage 9.

On Day 2, the company finished on the bridge, then moved to Stage 10 to film in the corridor area near the Eminiar council room. Matt Jefferies had been working to create the world of Eminiar 7 on a shoestring budget. He was happy with the results, but acknowledged that the most difficult aspect of his job was "compromise."

"Usually what we wind up with is only a small part of what I would like to see," he said in 1968. "But you have to go with the material you have available, the capabilities of the people working for you, time, money; bend for the lighting man, bend for the cameraman, for the director. The most difficult thing is to come up with something you visualized that is on budget and will work best for the company. Frequently, when we get up there to shoot, there's not a lot left of the original concept." (91-9)

On Day 3, Pevney did additional filming in the Eminiar corridor areas built on Stage 10, including the sector with the disintegration machine and the area outside the detention quarters. This was one of the areas where Gene Coon's rewrite helped to save money. In the script, where a second disintegration chamber is established, Coon wrote:

> Since all these corridors are identical, and since this, an advanced civilization, uses building modules, there is no reason this cannot be the same disintegration chamber we used before, with perhaps minor dressing changes in the immediate vicinity.

When the chamber is destroyed, Coon's script told Pevney:

> There is no reason why this cannot be a SECOND CAMERA SHOT, from a different angle, of the first disintegrator being destroyed.

A shot from Stage 10 (above) combined with a matte painting of the futuristic city, painted by Albert Whitlock (below) (Courtesy of Gerald Gurian)

The suggestions not only saved money but time, allowing cast and crew to make it home in time for the premiere broadcast of "Shore Leave." A.C. Nielsen declared it the ratings winner at 9 p.m., by a nose, with *Star Trek* attracted a 32.6 audience share, compared to 32.5 for ABC's top-rated show, *Bewitched*.

On Day 4, Friday, December 30, work resumed on Stage 10. The scenes in the "Detention Quarters" were filmed, followed by the materialization area -- a section of white wall built in front of a giant blue screen to be used for the matte painting of the Eminiar city. Last up: Anan 7's quarters.

The company had three days off, given a Monday holiday as part of the New Year's weekend.

Day 5, Tuesday, January 3, 1967. When cast and crew returned in the new year, work continued on Stage 10 for the interior of the Council Chamber and the computer room where the mathematical war is staged. Pevney got a little sloppy here, in a scene where Anan 7 calls the Enterprise and pretends to be Kirk. The script made it clear that Anan 7 was not a voice mimic. The passage in Coon's Revised Final Draft read:

> Anan is sitting at a table, speaking into a device with a mike on one side and a speaker on the other ... as he holds Kirk's communicator before the speaker. It is a voice duplicating machine and when he speaks, the voice is that of Kirk.

Sadly, the way this scene was shot, the voice duplicating machine is not recognizable as such, and even though Pevney had Jerry Finnerman pan from a small electronic unit over to Anan 7 holding Kirk's communicator and speaking, it merely appears that the Eminiar leader was an impressionist worthy of an appearance on *The Ed Sullivan Show*.

Day 6, Wednesday, January 4 -- a full day continuing filming the scenes in the Eminiar council room. Pevney, amazingly, finished on schedule.

Post-Production
January 5 through February 14, 1967. Music score: Tracked.

Bruce Schoengarth and Edit Team #2 did the cutting. This was Schoengarth's eighth episode. Past work included the excellent "The Naked Time."

The music was recycled from previous episodes.

Film Effects of Hollywood handled the photographic effects, including the matte shot placing the landing party in a courtyard with the Eminiar city looming in the background. All shots of the Enterprise, however, were created using stock footage.

The show Robert Justman feared would take eight to nine days to film had, thanks to a great deal of rewriting and painful compromises, finished in six. The price tag, however, was a bit on the high side due to the construction required on Stage 10. The final toll: $196,486. The series' deficit was now $89,436.

Release / Reaction:
Premiere air date: 2/23/67. NBC repeat broadcast: 7/20/67.

RATINGS / Nielsen National report for Thursday, February 23, 1967:

8:30 - 9 p.m., 67.4% of U.S. TVs in use.		Share:	Households:
NBC:	*Star Trek* (first half)	29.8%	13,670,000
ABC:	***Bewitched***	**38.6%**	**15,540,000**
CBS:	*My Three Sons*	24.5%	10,160,000
Independent stations:		7.1%	-

9 - 9:30 p.m., 66.7% of U.S. TVs in use.		Share:	Households:
NBC:	*Star Trek* (second half)	30.2%	no data
ABC:	*Love on a Rooftop*	28.0%	no data
CBS:	***Thursday Night Movie*** (start)	**36.7%**	no data
Independent stations:		5.1%	no data

"A Taste of Armageddon" held at second place for the entire hour. On CBS at 9 p.m. was the television premiere of the 1962 Robert Wise film *Two for the Seesaw*, starring Robert Mitchum and Shirley MacLaine.

***

"A Taste of Armageddon" was a well-received episode and solidified the tradition of Kirk mounting his soapbox in the name of humankind, something Coon and then Roddenberry had him do, to a lesser extent, in "Arena" and "The Return of the Archons."

David Opatoshu remembered the significance of "A Taste of Armageddon," saying, "I was very excited about it. It made a social comment that was very important, showing the madness of people playing war with computers. I read the script and said, 'By all means, I would *love* to do the part.' You can say so many things that are taboo, all in the name of science-fiction and fantasy. And you can write about social problems without being stigmatized." (133)

Barbara Babcock recalled, "It's one of the more philosophical episodes. And since this was filmed in '67, we were still at war with Vietnam, and that issue was paramount. For me, doing those episodes [this and "Plato's Stepchildren"] was a thrill because they really were trying to keep up with the latest developments." (7)

Sean Kenney recently said, "'A Taste of Armageddon' was about two civilizations battling, where they thought they were humane to destroy each other just by walking everyone who had to die into a destruction chamber. You bring that script out now, on any show, and it'd be lauded as so futuristic. But we did it almost 44 years ago. That's my argument -- that good things always survive." (100-2)

George Takei said, "*Star Trek* was about the only show that was infusing and enriching the television medium with pertinence, substance, and contemporary relevance. *Star Trek*, by using science-fiction as a metaphor, was reflecting the reality of the times in a medium that was characterized by the chairman of the FCC as 'the vast wasteland.'" (171-2)

From the Mailbag

Received after the first airing of "A Taste of Armageddon":

> Dear Mr. Roddenberry: Quite sincerely and honestly, I am flabbergasted by reports that the show is "weak," or any implication it is "unpopular." I live in rural Indiana and I assure you the show is popular with both children and adults, from everyone from Den Mothers to draftsmen to housewives who read Gothic novels. Isn't there any way to throttle those arbitrary few thousand robots who determine Nielsen ratings? Their ratings do not, by God, reflect *Star Trek*'s ratings in this section of the boondocks. Sincerely, Juanita C., Hartford City, Indiana.

But, as documented here, A.C. Nielsen – as well as its rival, TvQ – showed *Star Trek* to be doing strong business on Thursday nights, both in the boonies as well as, and even more so, in the big cities. The Den Mothers and draftsman and housewives who read Gothic novels in Hartford City, Indiana were right -- as NBC's top-rated Thursday night show, *Star Trek* was deserving of hit status, something its broadcast carrier was refusing to acknowledge. The reason for all the misinformation, and the threats of cancelation, were complex. Gene Roddenberry had many strikes against him at this point at the network. Stay tuned.

D.C. Joins the Staff / "This Side of Paradise"

As the stories Roddenberry assigned began arriving, many were proving to be unsuitable. *Star Trek* was in danger of running short on scripts. Coon would give out six additional assignments in December, all to writers who had proven themselves reliable. One assignment each went to Paul Schneider (ST 40, "Tomorrow the Universe"), Theodore Sturgeon (ST 41, "Amok Time"), Steven Carabatsos (ST 42, "Operation: Destroy"), and Dorothy Fontana (ST 43, "Friday's Child"). The final two Coon assigned to himself (ST 44, "The Devil in the Dark" and ST 45, "Errand of Mercy").

Steven Carabatsos' contract as Story Editor was for 13 episodes, ending with "A Taste of Armageddon." Carabatsos later admitted that he was not a fan of science fiction and had far less exposure to the genre than series' writers and sci-fi enthusiasts such as Samuel Peeples, Jerry Sohl, Harlan Ellison, Richard Matheson, George C. Johnson, and Theodore Sturgeon. Not to mention Gene Roddenberry and Gene L. Coon.

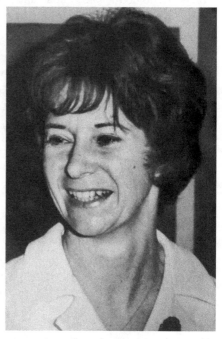

D.C. Fontana
(Courtesy of Gerald Gurian)

For Carabatsos, *Star Trek* was no better or worse than the other series he had worked on -- like *Peyton Place*. He said, "The honest fact is that when it was first on, to me... it was just another show. Granted, because of all the famous science-fiction writers involved there was a sense of something else, a sense of more going on, but you have to understand, nobody knew what we had there. *Nobody* had any idea.... [*Star Trek*] didn't light up the stars." (28-1)

Roddenberry would argue that. Most who worked on the series did feel that *Star Trek* was lighting up the stars. Not Carabatsos. Twenty-five years after leaving the series, he said "It beats the hell out of me why the show has gone on the way it has." (28-1)

Carabatsos had one last contractual obligation -- write an original script (he had been given co-writing credit for "Court Martial," which was a rewrite). He didn't have a storyline his bosses liked, so Roddenberry gave him one. Carabatsos went home to work on "Operation -- Destroy!" and left an empty office in the *Star Trek* building. Roddenberry, Justman, and Coon already knew who they wanted to put behind the desk in that room.

Dorothy Fontana's gamble -- resigning as Roddenberry's secretary to become a full-fledged screenwriter -- had paid off. Now her former boss had nothing to lose in offering her a shot at being on staff. Nonetheless, for 1966, it was a bold move. Fontana later said, "To have a woman story editor on an action-adventure show... *That* was unheard of." (64-2)

Fontana brought much to the table. The two scripts she had already contributed, "Charlie X" and "Tomorrow Is Yesterday," were among the series' least problematic. They required less rewriting and were two of the least-expensive episodes filmed. And Fontana, unlike Carabatsos, embraced science fiction. She had watched *The Twilight Zone* and *The Outer Limits* faithfully and admitted to loving Byron Haskin's movie *Robinson Crusoe on Mars*, as well as *Forbidden Planet*, the 1956 film that in many ways played like an episode of *Star Trek*. Perhaps, just as importantly, she loathed *Lost in Space*.

Fontana had something else going for her. Along with a passion for writing, a story editor must know how to work within the system, to listen to the producers, to listen to the network, to understand budgets, and to know what is and is not possible in production. A story editor has to have a level of practical professionalism that many creative-minded people -- science-fiction-minded people, especially -- do not possess.

Fontana explained, "I had dealt with the scripts all the time and had my own opinions about them. I just never put [those thoughts] down on paper, although I spoke to Gene [Roddenberry] and Gene Coon secretly about the shows they were doing." (64-17)

Those conversations and her two original screenplays showed the two Genes that Fontana understood *Star Trek* as well as they did. She recalled, "Gene came to me and said, 'We have a script that's not working and we'd like you to do a rewrite on it. And, if you can do a fast rewrite that satisfies the network and the studio, then I'll invite you to join us as story editor.'" (64-1)

It was an offer a struggling writer who just quit her day job could not refuse. Fontana said, "Okay." What she was handed would become "This Side of Paradise."

***

Episode 25: THIS SIDE OF PARADISE

Teleplay by D.C. Fontana
Story by Nathan Butler (Jerry Sohl) and D.C. Fontana
Directed by Ralph Senensky

NBC press release, March 2, 1967:

NBC publicity photo - Nimoy with Ireland

Jill Ireland guest-stars as Leila, the first woman with whom the normally unemotional Mr. Spock (Leonard Nimoy) falls in love following the discovery of a drug-like plant, in "This Side of Paradise" on NBC Television Network's colorcast of *Star Trek* Thursday, March 2. Expecting to find no sign of life on the planet Omicron Ceti III, which has been bombarded by deadly space rays, Captain Kirk (William Shatner) is amazed when his landing party is greeted by botanist Leila (Miss Ireland) and colony ruler Sandoval (Frank Overton). Apparently unaware of the danger that surrounds them, the group rejects Kirk's evacuation order. Before Kirk realizes the entire settlement is infected by a plant which induces a false sense of security and happiness, his own crew is similarly infected, including Spock, whose romance with the stunning Leila leads him to open defiance of his captain.

"This Side of Paradise" offers an examination of duty and responsibility, the dangers of repressed emotions, and a warning for the growing drug culture of the 1960s.

SOUND BITES

- *Leila, to Spock:* "There was always a place in your heart where no one could come. There was only a face you allow people to see -- only one side you would allow them to know." *Spock:* "Emotions are alien to me." *Leila:* "Someone else might believe that -- your shipmates, your captain -- but not me."

- *Kirk:* "No wants or needs? We weren't meant for that, any of us. Man stagnates if he has no ambition, no desire to be more than he is."

- *Kirk, after his crew abandons him:* "I'm beginning to realize just how big this ship is ... and how quiet."

- *Kirk, goading Spock:* "All right, you mutinous, disloyal, computerized half-breed, we'll see about you deserting my ship.... What makes you think you're a man? You're an overgrown jack rabbit, an elf with a hyperactive thyroid.... You belong in a circus, Spock, not a starship! Right next to the dog-faced boy!"

- *Kirk, after succeeding in provoking Spock to experience anger:* "It's not every first officer who gets to belt his captain ... several times."

- *Sandoval:* "We don't need you. Not as a doctor." *McCoy:* "Oh, no? Would you like to see how fast I can put you in the hospital?"

- *Spock:* "I have little to say about it, Captain. Except that for the first time in my life, I was happy."

ASSESSMENT

This is *Star Trek* at its best: science fiction blended with surprising humor and gut-wrenching drama, seamlessly interwoven through purposeful writing and inspired direction.

"This Side of Paradise," at its core, is a heavily-disguised anti-drug statement. When made in 1967, a large segment of America's youth were choosing to turn on and tune out -- and this desertion of America's young left the straight and sober feeling betrayed and abandoned, much like the lonely, brooding captain of the Enterprise.

In the earlier episode "The Naked Time," Spock experienced emotion, but it was painful. Here he admits, for the first time in his life, he is happy. He grins from ear to pointed ear, hangs upside down in a tree, laughs and gazes at the sky, imagining dragons in the clouds. And he feels love. These are stirring and unforgettable images. Equally burned into the memory, Spock's display of surprise, hurt, and then homicidal fury, as Kirk verbally attacks him. And, finally, the terrible sadness when he realizes that his ability to experience love and to laugh was merely temporary.

"This Side of Paradise" is a story about Spock. But it also rings strong for Leila Kalomi and Elias Sandoval. The audience is taken by her sadness, when Leila says to Spock: "I have lost you, haven't I? Not just you, but all of it. The spores too... I've lost them too. And this is for *my* good?" And then Sandoval, with his somber realization: "We've done nothing here. No progress; no accomplishments. Three years *wasted.... Three precious years!*"

But "Paradise," as with all *Star Trek* stories, is primarily about Kirk. The Captain spoke of his loneliness in "The Naked Time," how his life was obsessively devoted to a "she" known as the Enterprise. Now we discover the depth to his inner torment. Without its heart and soul -- her crew -- Kirk's beautiful ship is not whole. The Captain has never looked lonelier than when he steps onto the deserted bridge. Even when presented with a chance for paradise, the tormented Kirk is too driven and too tortured for the spores to take hold.

There is more. We see Dr. McCoy unburdened by duty and the determination to live his life for others. There was a hint of his Southern roots in "Shore Leave," but no hinting around here.

It is rare, and certainly special, when a one-hour drama, restricted by the format of a continuing series, can service so many characters this effectively.

THE STORY BEHIND THE STORY

Script Timeline

Jerry Sohl's treatment, ST-26, "Sandoval's Planet": June 15, 1966.
Sohl's revised story outline, gratis, "Power Play": July 15, 1966.
Sohl's second revised outline, gratis: August 9, 1966.
Sohl's 1st Draft script, "The Way of the Spores": September 1, 1966.
Sohl's 2nd Draft script: October 11, 1966.
Sohl's script polish, gratis (Rev. 2nd Draft): October 16, 1966.
D.C. Fontana's story outline, now "This Side of Paradise": Nov. 16, 1966.
Fontana's 1st Draft script: December 7, 1966.
Fontana's 2nd Draft script (also Mimeo Department "Yellow Cover" 1st Draft): December 11, 1966.
Gene Coon's script polish (Final Draft): December 15, 1966.
Coon's second script polish (Rev. Final Draft): December 28, 1966.
Additional page revisions by Coon: December 30, 1966 & January 4, 1967.

Jerry Sohl, having written "The Corbomite Maneuver," returned for a second *Star Trek*, by invitation of Gene Roddenberry. Of his pitch to Roddenberry, Sohl said, "Spores, as you know, are inanimate up until the point when they are mixed with water or with anything else, then they come alive.... So I had the idea that these things could be consumed by someone and, as a result, the whole character chemistry of that person could change to a nice, peaceful and loving person." (160-4)

"The Naked Time" showed us what could happen if everyone on the Enterprise were drunk. Sohl took it a step further. He said, "It was a psychedelic kind of thing. A lot of that was going on at the time. The premise of the thing was that everyone on the Enterprise takes LSD. What would happen?" (160-2)

Roddenberry put Sohl on assignment. His story, first called "Sandoval's Planet," then "Power Play," then "The Way of the Spores," had Sulu, not Spock, falling in love. And the spores were at the bottom of a well, described as "thousands of puffballs, varicolored and luminescent and moving about."

Robert Justman was the first to react to the June 15, 1966 story outline for "Sandoval's Planet." He wrote Roddenberry:

> I have just read Jerry Sohl's treatment. I have to confess to you that I ended up very confused. I can't seem to make any sense out of the story. And I think all the sub-stories only tend to confuse the issue. I don't know which story is the main line of the treatment. (RJ25-1)

One element Justman *did* find of interest was the spores. Even while physically separated from one another, they were somehow connected and part of a larger organism -- a living, sensing, growing being. Presented in a very different manner, it was the idea he was most fond of in "The Return of the Archons," that all of Landru's people were a part of The Body. In his memo to Roddenberry, Justman wrote:

> That to me, that idea, is the marvelous idea contained within Jerry's treatment. <u>There</u> is the intriguing concept for us to play around with. (RJ25-1)

Sohl was asked to revise his outline for free, which he did, twice, turning in a second draft on July 15 and a third on August 9, the latter being the first to go to NBC. The title now was "Power Play."

Stan Robertson, at the network, had mixed feelings. He wrote Roddenberry:

> Again, Gene, we have another example of "something" infiltrating into the bodies of our crewmen or into our ship, threatening the lives of our heroes and the destruction of their ship. In "The Naked Time" we called it a "virus." This time it is a "spore." In other stories, we've given "it" various names and varying components and attributes. And the result is a "sameness." (SR25)

As for those "other stories," Robertson was remembering:

- "Miri," in which the landing party is infected with, and dying from, a man-made disease;
- "The Return of the Archons," in which Sulu has been absorbed by Landru and, in early drafts of the story and script, takes over the bridge and tries to pilot the ship into the planet's atmosphere for a burn-up;
- The unproduced "Rites of Fertility," in which the crew begin turning into plants.

It may seem from here, in 2013, that Robertson was being too critical. But he had his eye on the reviews from various TV critics, and some of them were being that critical. Regarding "The Naked Time," when it had its network premiere, entertainment critic Don McLean, writing in the *Lethbridge Herald*, Alberta, Canada, said:

> It now appears that *Star Trek* may be settling into a rut early on -- the same type of premise has been used in two of its three stories so far. Mind over matter may become a reality but right now it is pretty way out. Even the monster in the premiere episode, that changed into a chameleon, was more believable but probably *Star Trek* isn't supposed to be believable.

On the same day Robertson wrote to Roddenberry, Justman wrote to Coon, who was setting up his office at *Star Trek*. He told the new producer:

> Since this would no doubt be one of our shows that goes after a pickup from NBC, we shall have to be careful with regard to costs. It is Herb's stated intention that we will bring in the next batch of shows for $185,000 or less. This show, on the surface of it, is greatly <u>over</u> budget. (RJ25-2)

With Roddenberry pulling back from his producer responsibilities, and Coon just starting to find his way at *Star Trek*, Sohl was advised to go to script with few notes other than, as always, to keep it cheap.

The First Draft script arrived on September 1. A collection of the staff notes, from Roddenberry, Justman and Carabatsos, told of many concerns. One wrote:

> The dialogue is miserable -- and there is a lack of characterization. We keep losing sight of people, like Sandoval and Leila, then dragging them in by the heels when we need them. Recommend cutting and trimming, since the script is long now -- straight-line the action and have Kirk acting like the trained ship's

captain we know he is. (STAFF25-1)

Justman wrote:

> Matt Jefferies is going to have to come up with some plants that we can have work and have them shoot spores when necessary. However, when we have the effect several times in the script of the spores actually floating around, I am a bit of a loss as to how to handle this effect. (RJ25-3)

Of Sohl's Second Draft, now called "The Way of the Spores," the notes from the staff included:

> This is better than it was, certainly more straight-line and logical. The dialogue has also sharpened. One specific request: <u>Change the title!</u> (STAFF25-2)

Sohl did a free polish, dated October 16, but neglected to change the title. In fact, he neglected to change anything of consequence. So Roddenberry and Coon collectively decided to change the writer.

Dorothy Fontana recalled: "I looked at [the script] and thought about it, and there were two problems. One, the love interest was for Sulu. Nothing wrong with George Takei, and I really like George, but he wasn't one of the heavy-weight stars of the show and, if you're going to have a love story, you're going to have to have it with one of *them*. And, with the spores, you could make it Spock, and you can make it a very emotional story, harking back a little to 'The Naked Time.' 'What will happen when Spock is out of control?' Only, this time, in terms of love.

"The other thing that was wrong with it was that the spores, which were the infection, were in a cave, and they kind of fumbled and bounced up and down like ping-pong balls. And the answer to that was, '*Don't go into the cave*!' So, by making them part of a plant that was all over the planet, anybody could be infected at any time. Everybody was at risk." (64-1)

With Fontana's rewrite, she had passed Roddenberry's test and *Star Trek* found its new story editor. And, with her script, Fontana added elements to the *Star Trek* bible. We knew before that Spock's mother was a human, his father Vulcan. Now it is established that his mother is a teacher, his father an ambassador. We will meet both in "Journey to Babel," also written by Fontana.

Robert Justman was ecstatic. He wrote to Coon:

> As usual, a shootable and well-constructed First Draft from the mysterious D.C. Fontana. (RJ25-4)

In fact, Justman's memo lasted only three pages, unusually slight from him. He closed:

> You will note that [this memo] is quite short. That means that I am quite happy. (RJ23-4)

Fontana, too, was happy, saying, "The fact that Spock not just disobeys an order from Kirk, but totally disregards it -- '*Not interested*' -- that was a lot of fun." (64-1)

Leonard Nimoy was less sure. Recalling a conversation with Fontana, he said, "I told her, 'It makes me nervous to hear you even talk about such a thing. I feel I've finally gotten a good grip on the character and I don't want to lose what we have.' The Vulcan was firmly established in my mind -- and the audience's -- as a cool, distant character, and the very phrase 'Spock love story' seemed oxymoronic." (128-3)

Jerry Sohl would have objected too, if he had known of the changes. On December 12, 1966, a day or two after Fontana turned in her Second Draft script, Sohl wrote to Roddenberry:

> And how's "The Way of the Spores"? I hope you shoot it. Since I haven't received any revised pages, I have the uneasy feeling it might have been put on a shelf somewhere. No -- sob! -- no. Say it isn't so. (JS25-1)

Roddenberry delayed saying anything. He knew "Spores" was going to be made, but with a different title, different authorship, and an entirely different approach.

Meanwhile, Gene Coon was so pleased with Fontana's Second Draft script that he declared it to be the official staff Yellow Cover First Draft and, without changing a word, distributed it to all Department Heads and sent a copy to de Forest Research.

Kellam de Forest had fewer peeves than usual, but did challenge the idea that a high degree of radiation bombarding the planet, as it had been described thus far, could accomplish what the story needed -- the destruction of living tissue, thereby, over a period of time, killing people and animals, but not killing insects and vegetation. He told Coon:

> The general term "living tissue" would include all the plant life, as well as the animal life on the planet. Suggest dialogue indicate the radiation destroys the red blood cells and bone-marrow, which is more in line with the damage known that radiation causes and could conceivably not affect the vegetation. (KDF25)

Coon felt he had a better idea. For his December 15 Final Draft, the word "radiation" was stricken from the script and replaced by "Berthold rays." Spock explains, "Berthold rays are such a recent discovery we do not yet have full knowledge of their nature. It is known that living *animal* tissue disintegrates under exposure after periods as brief as seventy-two hours.... A planet's atmosphere would cut some of the effects, but any sustained exposure would mean death." It was explanation enough to satisfy de Forest. NBC was also satisfied and approved the script on December 19.

Later that day, Roddenberry finally wrote to Jerry Sohl, trying to lay the blame on the network. His letter read, in part:

> We did a rewrite on "The Way of the Spores." You probably got a copy of it by now. Much of the reason had to do with Network pressure on this and that. I don't think your script was hurt by the rewrite at all -- in fact, I wouldn't let it be. But with the end of the year coming up and with a second year of *Star Trek* soon to be decided, it is important we bend with NBC when it doesn't actually hurt the show. (GR25-1)

As Sohl read Fontana's "This Side of Paradise," he saw very little of his original material -- so little, in fact, that he not only lost the teleplay credit but had to share the "story by" credit. One of *Star Trek*'s first writers and staunchest supporters was feeling deeply betrayed. He would respond and vent his anger, but not for several days, after "This Side of Paradise" had begun filming.

Pre-Production:
December 27-30, 1966 & January 3-4, 1967 (total 6 days prep).

Ralph Senensky, new to *Star Trek*, was hired to direct. Senensky began in television during the early 1960s. He proved his abilities on *The Naked City*, *The Fugitive*, *Twelve O'clock High*, and *The Wild, Wild West*, where he worked for Gene Coon.

It was Coon's idea to bring Senensky to *Star Trek*, and had him screen several episodes, which did not include the recently produced and semi-comical "Tomorrow Is Yesterday." Senensky saw nothing resembling comedy in the episodes he was shown. To the contrary, the series struck him as very dark, which is why he was pleased when, for his first *Trek*, he was offered "The Devil in the Dark." Struck by the story, its theme, and its visual possibilities, Senensky immediately knew how to approach the somber material. And then the script was taken away and given to Joseph Pevney to direct. In its place, Senensky was assigned "This Side of Paradise." Back then, before the experience of making it, seeing it, and witnessing its enduring popularity, Senensky admitted, "I have to say I was disappointed. 'The Devil in the Dark' was a strange, eerie script, where 'This Side of Paradise' seemed almost like a modern love story." (155-5)

Jill Ireland on location with *Star Trek* (NBC publicity pix courtesy of Gerald Gurian)

Jill Ireland was 30 when she played Leila Kalomi, the girl from Spock's past. She had been a regular for one year in the 1966 TV version of *Shane*, and had appeared in five episodes of *The Man from U.N.C.L.E.* with real-life husband David McCallum. After *Star Trek*, and after McCallum, Ireland's acting career prospered through numerous big screen co-starring roles with second hubby Charles Bronson in *The Mechanic*, *The Valachi Papers*, and *Death Wish II*.

Ireland had been watching *Star Trek*. She had recently seen "What Are Little Girls Made Of?" and came to the series a little worried. In 1968, Bill Theiss admitted, "When I first met Jill Ireland, she was a little uneasy about me. I didn't find out until later it was because she had seen Sherry Jackson's costume, and she was afraid I was going to do something as revealing on her. She could have carried it well, but the script would have been ill-served by anything as revealing." (172-4)

While the clothing was not stirring, Ireland's performance was. Dorothy Fontana said, "Jill Ireland, as Leila Kalomi, was exquisite." (64-13)

Ralph Senensky said, "Jill Ireland and I had not worked together but, of course, I'd heard of her. I didn't cast her, since I was so busy looking for a location. But Frank Overton I'd done four shows with on *12 O'Clock High*. A wonderful, wonderful actor, and a very nice man." (155-6)

Grant Woods, following appearances in "The Galileo Seven" and "Arena," returned for the third and final time as crewman Kelowitz. He had also been seen in additional first season episodes, as an extra. A short time after this Woods lost his life in a motorcycle accident.

Michael Barrier was back for a second turn as Lt. DeSalle, having been featured prominently in "The Squire of Gothos." Barrier and his character DeSalle would return, to command the bridge in "Catspaw."

Frank Overton, cast as Elias Sandoval, had nearly a hundred appearances in films and television, including multiple turns on *The Twilight Zone*, *Wagon Train*, and *Bonanza*, and a recurring role for three seasons on *12 O'clock High* as an Army Air Corp Major. On the big screen, among many classic films, Overton played Sheriff Heck Tate in *To Kill a Mockingbird*. Less than six months after filming "This Side of Paradise," and just weeks after it aired, Frank Overton died of a heart attack. He was 48.

As for those meddling plants and their projectile spores, something like them had been seen before. "Specimen Unknown," a 1964 episode of *The Outer Limits*, also had alien plants that shot spores. Wah Chang created them. He created the ones seen here, too.

Frank Overton as Elias Sandoval
(Unaired film clip courtesy of Gerald Gurian)

The next hurdle to clear was to find some place to represent the settlement on Omicron Ceti III. Senensky said, "Our big thing was to find the location. There wasn't the time or money to build anything, so we had to use something that was already built. The only place was the Disney Ranch, which was totally wrong, unless you use some creative imagination that they had gone to the past for their inspiration." (155-6)

Golden Oak Ranch, owned by Walt Disney Productions, was the home of *Swamp Fox* and *Zorro*. Located near Santa Clarita, a couple hours' drive from Hollywood, it was close to Vasquez Rocks and Africa USA, which the *Star Trek* company had recently visited. Golden Oak hardly looked futuristic.

With the revised script pages, dated December 28, Sandoval says to Kirk, "I think you'll find our settlement interesting. Our philosophy is a simple one -- that men should return to the less complicated life. We have very few mechanical things here; no vehicles, no weapons.... We have harmony here; complete peace."

Production Diary
Filmed January 5, 6, 9, 10, 11, 12 & 13, 1967
(Planned as 6 day production, finishing one day over; total cost: $171,681).

Filming began on Thursday, January 5, 1967 -- the same day "The Galileo Seven," the 17th episode to air, had its only network broadcast.

This was the week Carl Wilson of the Beach Boys was indicted for draft evasion. Jack Ruby, the assassin who killed Lee Harvey Oswald after Oswald allegedly assassinated President John Kennedy, died at age 55 from cancer at Parkland Hospital, Dallas, Texas. This was the same place where Kennedy had been pronounced dead, and Oswald also had died. "I'm a Believer" from The Monkees was still No. 1 on the radio, and would stay there long enough to become the top selling single of 1967. "Snoopy vs. the Red Barron" sat underneath it at No 2 for the second of four weeks. The Monkees had the best-selling LP in the nation, too. Being kept out of the top spot and stuck at No. 2 for six weeks was the new one from Herb Alpert and the Tijuana Brass – *S.R.O.* CBS was top-dog for most of the night before the filming of "This Side of Paradise" began. *Lost in Space* did the network well from 7:30 to 8:30 p.m., followed by *The Beverly Hillbillies*, *Green Acres*, and *Gomer Pyle, U.S.M.C.* At 10 p.m., the majority of Americans watching TV switched channels, to NBC, where *I Spy* secured 37.6% of the total viewing audience before it cleared the air at 11 p.m. You could watch any of these shows in color on a new Magnavox console TV for $400.

Day 2: At Golden Oak Ranch with Bill McGovern slating, Michael Barrier to his immediate right, and Frank Overton on far right (Courtesy of Gerald Gurian)

The shooting schedule for "This Side of Paradise" provided for three days at Golden Oak, to cover nearly a third of the script. Senensky remembered, "The first two days went swimmingly. We completed over eight pages each day, were right on schedule, and all seemed as if I was filming a rustic love story.... Then came the third day. We reported to the ranch as usual, in the dark, so that we could be ready to film with the first light of day. But before the first light got to us, the news did that Jill Ireland would NOT be reporting to the location; it was feared that she had the measles." (155-5)

This was Monday. Ireland had fallen ill over the weekend and was scheduled to see a doctor later in the day.

Senensky added, "We then went to work, completing all the scenes at the ranch that did not include her; after which we packed up, moved back to the studio and finished the day filming on the Enterprise." (155-5)

The remaining scenes for that day would be shot in the interior of Kirk's quarters, where only Shatner was required. Meanwhile, frantic phone calls were made to bring in cast members now needed for Tuesday.

On Day 4, Tuesday, the bridge scenes were filmed, including those in which Kirk is the only one left on the Enterprise. Fontana had written a hell of a scene for Shatner to play. She learned well from Roddenberry and understood the character. She knew Kirk would be the last to give in to the spores. He was too driven, too content with his life to turn himself over to drink, or drugs, or women (in the long term), or spores. He would first have to be broken. And being so alone on the ship he loves, discovering that it is an empty love without the people who share the vessel with him, very nearly does break him.

For the Final Draft screenplay, Fontana, with a little finessing from Coon, wrote of Kirk:

> He needs people. And there ain't nobody there but those damn computers.... Kirk moves down to his command chair, folds into it. He holds a moment, listening to the monotonous HUM and CHATTER of the instruments around him, then he abruptly flips a switch on his panel.

Kirk says, "Engineering... Scotty?... Biochemistry lab?... Security?... This is the Captain. Is there anyone aboard?"

The descriptive passage continues:

> He waits. He didn't expect an answer.... He sinks, slumped and defeated.... As

Kirk sits, head down, the pod plants erupt suddenly beside him. The drift of spores settles around Kirk.... A moment, and there seems to be no effect. Then Kirk raises his head slowly. CAMERA MOVES IN TO CLOSER SHOT. Kirk's face has an infinite peace and tranquility. He has been taken over.

Director Senensky said, "The scene with Shatner alone on the bridge -- he's wonderful!" (155-6)

Fontana knew Kirk couldn't really leave the Enterprise. He would die first. For the next scene, she wrote:

Beneath the peace imposed upon him by the spores is a surging, driving need to keep this job of his ... this life ... this self-made hell of command.

As Kirk makes his way to the transporter room, in a brief scene cut from the episode, Fontana wrote how he moves through the corridor, "every foot of it beloved by him ... the great ship ... empty, deserted ... but his one love."

In the transporter room, the script reads:

Conflict within him now ... against the building transporter SOUND and LIGHTS. He should enter the chamber, but he cannot. Instead he turns off the console quickly, the LIGHTS and SOUND DYING.

Kirk shouts his next lines: "No! ... I ... can't ... leave ... you!"

Gene Coon changed this last part, just slightly, feeling it rang too much like Kirk's confession of "Never lose you," from "The Naked Time." But whether one reads Fontana's final handling of the script or Coon's polish, "This Side of Paradise" is stirring. This script, like so many others from the original *Star Trek*, is in a league of its own. A comparison with the writing of other contemporaneous series -- or with later series, for that matter -- helps to explain the enduring popularity of *Star Trek* for nearly a half century (and counting). These scripts, based on a strong original series concept and well-drawn characters, were among the best writing television has ever known.

Of his first day on Stage 9, Senensky said, "They [the standing sets] were exciting, the bridge in particular. There was all the electrical hookups; the blinking lights, and, of course, Jerry Finnerman was just brilliant with the lighting he added. But that was Desilu. That year, Herb Solow was the head of production and there was a different way of thinking than what came later with Paramount. You had *Star Trek* and *Mission: Impossible*, starting at the same time, and both were big shows. If they had started a year later with Paramount, they would not have looked like that." (155-5)

As filming continued in the corridors, with more bad news for Kirk as he confronts those abandoning his ship and tells Lt. Leslie (Eddie Paskey), "This is mutiny, Mister!," and Leslie responds, "Yes, sir, it is."

Good news arrived concerning the condition of Jill Ireland. The measles turned out to be something less serious and she would be able to return to finish her work.

Days 5 and 6, Wednesday and Thursday, were spent at Desilu, with Ireland back in the cast. Scenes filmed included the one between Leila and Spock in the transporter room on Stage 9, followed by a move to Stage 10 for the interior of the ranch house on Omicron Ceti III. At the end of the sixth day, "The Squire of Gothos" -- the 18th episode of *Star Trek* to run on NBC -- had its first broadcast.

**Jill Ireland rejoins the cast on Day 5
(Unaired film trim courtesy of Gerald Gurian)**

**Nimoy and Ireland hanging in the trees at Bronson Canyon for NBC publicity photo
(Courtesy of Gerald Gurian)**

Day 7, Friday, January 13, 1967 -- an extra day added onto the production -- was intended for a return to Golden Oak Ranch for pick up shots with Ireland. But the ranch was unable to accommodate the schedule change. Another location had to be found, and quickly -- one that would match the look of Golden Oak and be available on the only day the company could film with Ireland.

Senensky said. "The fortunate thing for us was that all of the scenes that involved buildings at the ranch had been completed." (155-5)

After numerous frantic phone calls, Justman was able to book nearby Bronson Canyon on the south edge of Griffith Park, in the Hollywood Hills. Of course, Bronson Canyon bore no resemblance to Golden Oak Ranch. There were no oaks, nor was there anything golden, or even remotely green. Bronson Canyon was, and is, basically a rock pit with caves. The location, in fact, was a former quarry operated by The Union Rock Company at the turn of the last century which extracted the rock needed to pave the streets of early boomtown Los Angeles.

Senensky marveled, "I was amazed then, and now, inching toward a half a century later. I am still in awe of those studio magicians who in answer to a request for a 'garden' in the middle of a pristine green landscape [in the middle of a rock pile] could fulfill my request." (155-5)

Among other scenes filmed here were those in which Spock gets hit by the spores and, as a result, falls head-over-heels in love ... literally. Of the famous tree scene, Leonard Nimoy remained uneasy and later said, "Even after we began shooting the episode, I found it both scary and liberating to emote as Spock. How would fans react to seeing the cool, rational Vulcan literally swinging from a tree?" (128-3)

That business on the tree, that head-over-heels playfulness, was improvised. Senensky said, "The scene was all set up and ready to shoot with Kirk and Spock meeting in the center of a field. Jerry Finnerman had lit it, and we did a run-through, and it was just dull.... They were just standing there facing each other. Nothing was working. Something said to me, 'I've got to do something more than that.' Right out of camera range I saw a tree with a strange limb and I asked Jerry if I could change the setup, which I seldom do, and he said, 'Of course.' So we went over and had Spock hang from that tree. Well, they loved it. And I remember there was a lovely response to the comedy element that Shatner brought into his performance." (155-3)

"This Side of Paradise" finished one day behind. Since a key cast member had fallen ill, production insurance paid for the overage, sparing Desilu the financial hit.

Post Production
Available for editing: January 16, 1967. Music score: tracked.

James Ballas and Edit Team #1 handled the cutting, and the Westheimer Company provided the matte shots and materialization effects.

As "This Side of Paradise" was being edited, anyone who came to see the dailies, or was witness to the film being cut together, knew they were seeing something special. Moments of this episode were as dramatic as anything *Star Trek* had presented, with intense conflict and emotional angst, yet other portions were carefree and unexpectedly funny. It was a rare blending of dark and light. On the heels of "Tomorrow Is Yesterday," it served as the template for some of *Star Trek*'s most beloved episodes, thanks to Dorothy Fontana and Gene Coon.

Ralph Senensky, who had felt disappointed when Robert Justman switched scripts on him, later said, "As it worked out, 'This Side of Paradise' was the better show for me to be doing my first time out. And, quite frankly, I probably did the show better than anybody else directing for them could have done it." (155-6)

Curiously, some of *Star Trek*'s best episodes were also among the least expensive to make. "The Corbomite Maneuver," "The Naked Time," "Charlie X," and "Tomorrow Is Yesterday" were all brought in under budget. And, even with location filming and the cost of an extra day of production, "This Side of Paradise" was brought in under the studio allowance. With a total cost of only $171,681, the first season deficit was down to $76,117.

Release / Reaction
Premiere air date: 3/2/67. NBC repeat broadcast: 8/10/67.

Steven H. Scheuer reviewed "This Side of Paradise" for his *TV Key Preview* column. Among newspapers to carry his assessment, on February 25, 1967, was the *Free Lance Star*, serving the cities of Fredericksburg, Stafford, Spotsylvania, Orange, King George, and the Culpeper region, in Virginia. Scheuer wrote:

> Mr. Spock, the guy with the slanted eyebrows and weird ears, who also gets more mail from women than Captain Kirk or anybody else aboard the Enterprise, finally has a romance. The girl (Jill Ireland) is a member of a planet colony who is unaware that she and all of the other settlers are under the influence of a drug-like planet. Don't worry, girls -- this is just a one-episode affair for Mr. Spock and he will be back in circulation next week.

A.C. Nielsen offered an estimate for the number of households tuned in during the 8:30 to 9 p.m. period. This was followed by a percentage ranking for the three networks and, grouped together, all independent stations, from the 9 to 9:30 period. Data not disclosed on this particular report was the audience share estimates covering 8:30 to 9 p.m., and the estimated households watching from 9 to 9:30 p.m.

RATINGS / Nielsen National report, Thursday, March 2, 1967:

8:30 - 9 p.m., 67.4% of U.S. TVs in use.		**Households watching:**
NBC:	*Star Trek* (first half)	12,900,000
ABC:	**Bewitched**	**13,830,000**
CBS:	*My Three Sons*	12,080,000

9 - 9:30 p.m., 66.7% of U.S. TVs in use.		**Audience share:**
NBC:	*Star Trek* (second half)	29.1%
ABC:	*Love on a Rooftop*	26.0%
CBS:	**Thursday Night Movie (start)**	**33.6%**
Independent stations:		11.3%

Star Trek placed second for its entire hour. The movie on CBS was the 1963 comedy-musical *Bye Bye Birdie*, starring Dick Van Dyke, Janet Leigh, Ann-Margaret, and Paul Lynde. ABC's *Love on a Rooftop* trailed in third position.

For its repeat broadcast on NBC, "This Side of Paradise" was one of four episodes from *Star Trek*'s first season to be given a half-page *TV Guide* CLOSE-UP.

 8:30 ❸ ⓬ ㉑ **STAR TREK—Adventure**

[COLOR] On the planet Omicron-Ceti 3, Kirk seeks an antidote to paradise.
 The colonists on the planet enjoy an idyllic existence. They have been infected by spores that produce a strange disease: perfect physical health and complete peace of mind.
 Under the influence of the spores, the crew deserts the Enterprise. Even Mr. Spock is not immune. For the first time in his life, the unemotional Vulcan falls in love.
 Kirk, for some reason, remains unaffected, and he must find out why if he expects to return his mutinous crew to normalcy.
 Ralph Senensky directed from a script by D. C. Fontana. Kirk: William Shatner. Spock: Leonard Nimoy. McCoy: DeForest Kelley. Sulu: George Takei. Uhura: Nichelle Nichols. (Rerun; 60 min.)
Guest Cast
Elias Sandoval .... Frank Overton
Leila .... Jill Ireland

Leonard Nimoy and Jill Ireland

At the time "This Side of Paradise" was repeated, the *Free Lance Star*, in Virginia, had switched from carrying Steven H. Scheuer's syndicated review column to that of Joan Crosby's *TV Scout*. For her August 10, 1967 column, Crosby wrote:

> Love comes to Mr. Spock tonight, the normally unemotional one, when he falls in love with the beautiful Leila (Jill Ireland) on the planet Omicron Ceti III. It happens when he discovers a drug-like planet, where the population is devoted to a life of leisure and they seem awfully happy and peaceful on a planet which has been bombarded by deadly space rays. The colony is ruled by Sandoval (Frank Overton) and his snappy botanist assistant, Leila (Ireland). Before you can say "poppy drug," the whole starship crew becomes indolent and falsely secure, including Spock. Of course, it would take spores to do the trick of

making Spock fall in love with Leila, although she has some power of her own. All of this, of course, is pretty upsetting to Captain Kirk. This episode of the far-out series, far out in many more ways than just outer space, is a repeat.

A *TV Guide* "pick" was always a boost to a show's ratings, even during the summer months when Americans travelling on summer vacations left fewer people parked in front of their TVs. Note the difference in estimated households for this second report compared to the first from March:

RATINGS / Nielsen National report, Thursday, Aug. 10, 1967:

8:30 - 9 p.m.:		Households watching:
NBC:	*Star Trek* (first half)	**9,610,000**
ABC:	*Bewitched*	8,510,000
CBS:	*My Three Sons*	8,340,000

9 - 9:30 p.m.:		Audience share:
NBC:	*Star Trek* (second half)	26.4%
ABC:	*That Girl*	25.0%
CBS:	*Thursday Night Movie* (start)	**39.0%**

Star Trek won its time slot from 8:30 to 9 p.m., and then settled into second place at 9 p.m., with the start of 1963's *Lilies of the Field*, featuring Sidney Poitier in an Oscar-winning role.

***

Entertainment Weekly also liked the episode. The magazine picked this as the eighth best *Trek* of all time.

Putting aside any qualms he had during the production, Leonard Nimoy liked "This Side of Paradise," too. He picked it as among his half-dozen favorites.

Jerry Sohl, however, was determined not to like it, and expressed his hurt in many ways. First, he called his science fiction pals who had also written for *Star Trek*, comparing experiences and seeing that many were disgruntled over being severely rewritten by "a TV guy" named Roddenberry. Convinced that he and his colleagues had been "used" by a member of "the Hollywood crowd," Sohl refused to allow his name -- one of those feathers in Gene Roddenberry's cap -- to be further exploited and insisted his screen credit read Nathan Butler.

Harlan Ellison, still on board with *Star Trek*, was bothered by this action and the rumblings from his fellow sci-fi elites. He went public with his opinions, blasting Sohl and the others in the November 1966 issue of the SFWA (Science Fiction Writers Association) newsletter.

In early January 1967, Sohl fired back with a letter of his own. Addressed to Damon Knight, editor of the newsletter, Sohl wrote:

> [Gene Roddenberry] needed science fiction writers to get a feeling about science fiction for his show, to flesh out the stories and characters, so to speak. He paid for them. He got them. They gave him their all. When his show was off and running, Roddenberry didn't need them anymore. He'd got what he wanted. Now the hacks could get on with it.... The fact that Roddenberry has turned his back on us all is unfortunate and disappointing, for we all thought Roddenberry was of a different caliber.... We did our best -- Richard Matheson, Robert Bloch, Theodore Sturgeon, A.E. van Vogt, myself, and others. Perhaps Harlan Ellison

and Gene Roddenberry find that disappointing. I do not. (JS25-2)

A week later, Roddenberry sent a private letter to his friend Frederik Pohl, editor for *Galaxy* magazine, writing:

> I would not know how to give a writer better treatment than we gave Jerry. He had all the privileges of a member of the production staff... True, in the beginning of *Star Trek* he was kind enough to give us names of people he considered good possibilities as writers. In return, I worked very hard with him in explaining and demonstrating what I conceived to be necessary television technique for a SF show. I even rewrote his first script completely, refused to put in for credit -- and residuals -- and I have never mentioned this rewrite to a soul, giving Jerry full credit. One of the things that irritates Harlan [Ellison] is the fact that Jerry Sohl's great outburst of indignation was not based upon any unfairness toward him but on the simple fact we considered his second script pretty bad, felt that a rewrite did not improve it, finally had to assign it to another writer. The other writer did turn in a shootable script and the Writers Guild of America Arbitration Committee, which read all versions of the script, awarded credit to that other writer. Then, and only then, came Sohl's blast at us for violating the purity of SF and the personal blast at me for "using" SF writers and casting them aside when finished. A bit unfair. (GR25-3)

A month passed. Sohl had cooled down. He sent Roddenberry a short but sweet peace offering, writing:

> Dear Gene: That episode of *Star Trek* with Ricardo Montalban ["Space Seed"] was, in my estimation, the show's finest hour. Warmest Regards, Jerry. (JS25-3)

Roddenberry responded, but not necessarily warmly. His letter read, in its entirety:

> Dear Jerry: Thank you for your comments on the *Star Trek* episode "Space Seed," starring Ricardo Montalban. Comments on individual episodes are always helpful and always appreciated. Yours Truly, Gene Roddenberry, Executive Producer, *Star Trek*. (GR25-4)

There was no mistaking the tone. Someone was going to have to instigate a conversation and try to repair the damage. Sohl, knowing he had fired the first shot, now knew he would have to swallow his pride. His letter to Roddenberry, a few days later, attempted to explain his side of the misunderstanding. He wrote:

> I had submitted "The Way of the Spores" final draft on October 16, hearing only from Gene L. Coon, who said, "It's an excellent rewrite," and later said there would be some minor revisions. When I had come in to see you, you were busy... [and] said I should come back in a couple weeks. Even then I sensed something was wrong. So I phoned. I never received a return call. After a few days, I called again. Once again there was no return call. So I wrote to you on December 12, and I said I felt left out and I asked how "The Way of the Spores" was doing. The next day I received a copy of 'This Side of Paradise' by D.C. Fontana.... As a creative person I guess I can be as unstable as most, if not more so. I was hurt.... I started calling around among science fiction writer friends to ask them if they knew what was going on. One of them who had written a script for the show said that he was disgusted with the way he was treated and would never again write for the show. Another s-f writer who had written for the show said that he did not like your cavalier treatment of him and that he would never work for you again. Ordinarily I would disregard such remarks as just sour grapes or the reactions of neurotic writers, or perhaps they might be rationalizations to cover their own inadequacies. But it fit in with what I thought was an emerging pattern.... I felt somehow used. (JS25-4)

Sohl added that much of his confusion and hurt came about as a result of Harlan Ellison's "tirade" in the SFWA newsletter. He believed Ellison was speaking on behalf of Roddenberry, accusing Richard Matheson, George Clayton Johnson, and himself of being "leeches" who were trying to "grab a few bucks from those [TV] schmucks." Sohl couldn't understand how Roddenberry, his newfound TV friend, could think such things after all the help he had given *Star Trek* in the early days, recommending writers for the series, and helping to flesh-out the characters and premise with his "Corbomite Maneuver" script. And so he reacted as he did, and now he was sorry. Sohl closed his letter, writing:

> I have been guilty of not being patient, of not being trusting. I have been judging instead of loving. For all of that all I can ask is your forgiveness. Love, Jerry. (JS25-4)

Roddenberry wasn't feeling forgiving, or loving. He wrote back:

> Let me correct a few misconceptions. Firstly, Harlan does not speak for me. *Star Trek* has not "reverted to Hollywood hacks." I have never produced a show using "hacks" nor do I ever intend to.... Reference your assistance during the early stages of *Star Trek*, I am most grateful for it. However, let's not create any legends between ourselves that you introduced me to science fiction. I had been a fan of that field of literature since the 1930s, written one of televisions early SF scripts ["The Secret Weapon of 117"], and had the *Star Trek* format and first pilot conceived and executed before we met. Understand, this is not to diminish the value of your friendly and even enthusiastic cooperation. There is, however, one damage which has not been repaired. In the article printed in SFWA you intimated that I am a liar and a cheat. Or, at least, so a number of people interpreted it. I feel that you owe it to me and to yourself to find some way in that same publication to correct that "infamous letter" as you describe it. Sincerely yours, Gene Roddenberry. (GR25-5)

Sohl attempted to clean up the matter with the Science Fiction Writers Association. Roddenberry, smarting over the accusations that the science fiction writers having written for *Star Trek* so far would never return, attempted some damage control of his own, writing to SFWA newsletter editor Damon Knight:

> Incidentally, Harlan [Ellison] can hardly be characterized as a leech, since we have not even shot his show yet. We intend to before the season is out and, liking it very much, we will undoubtedly want to sign him for further scripts should we go to a second season. Ted Sturgeon has already been signed for a second. Robert Bloch and Richard Matheson have received offers from us and we are waiting until they get some free time. We have contacted Lester del Rey, Poul Anderson, Isaac Asimov, Norman Spinrad, and others, soliciting ideas for stories, although we are bought-up for this particular television season. We are hoping to heavily use such talent should we go to a second year. (GR25-2)

The second assignment Roddenberry referred to for Theodore Sturgeon, planned for the end of the first season, was "Amok Time." Norman Spinrad would respond and send in an idea, although not the one that eventually was purchased and developed into "The Doomsday Machine." Bloch would return to write for *Star Trek* again ("Catspaw" and "Wolf in the Fold"). Richard Matheson came in for a pitch but didn't stir interest in his idea. The others would pass.

As for Jerry Sohl, he remained estranged from Roddenberry for over a year. He would get a chance to write for *Star Trek* again, but not until the halfway point of Season Three, and that experience would not go well (see "Whom Gods Destroy").

From the Mailbag

Sent out 11 days after the completion of filming of "The Side of Paradise":

> Dear Ralph: I would like to have you know how much I enjoyed the work that we did together on "This Side of Paradise." It was not only a special Spock experience, but it was special for me as well in that I felt safe in the hands of a capable and sensitive director. Unfortunately, a rare experience in TV. I sincerely hope that we will spend much more time working together on sound stages and locations in the future. Many, many thanks. Sincerely, Leonard Nimoy. (January 24, 1967).

Received the week after "This Side of Paradise" aired:

> To Whom It May Concern... As part of this country's vast viewing audience, we would like to commend you on putting forth such fine, creative, entertainment as *Star Trek*. It is indeed one of the finer shows on television. However, we also feel that, as a viewer, it is our duty to make several comments on the offering for Thursday, March 2nd. Like many other viewers, we seem to especially like the Mr. Spock character in the series. He lacks the conceited, smug, and egocentric attitude that we find in certain other characters on the show. Unfortunately, his image was disastrously ruined on the March 2nd offering. With no regard for quality, the script writer changed Mr. Spock into a kind, sentimental, and (if you'll pardon the expression), "mushy" human.... We don't wish to sound crude or vehement in our criticism, but we must demand a digression from things of this sort in the future lest it provoke your large Thursday night audience into desertion. The National Association for the Betterment of Television Viewing.

> Mr. Gene Roddenberry, well thank goodness, it finally happened!! I've been waiting since September for my hero to blow his cool and, after watching "This Side of Paradise" last night, I can see it was all worth waiting for. They almost had to use a net to get me back down out of the clouds this morning. That episode generated more excitement around our office than the time Pat Boone took his first drink.... I hope, when next season rolls around, we can look forward to seeing that great big hunk of stoic sex appeal getting another girl to romance (however briefly). I really don't think one mental lapse per season would be too much to ask. He looks so divinely handsome when he smiles; I hope you will let him do that once in a while, too. Mrs. Beverly C. (Toledo, Ohio).

Memories

Jerry Finnerman, as impressed with Senensky as Senensky was with him, said, "'This Side of Paradise'... was a well-directed show.... I thought he [Ralph] did a wonderful job at directing the women [Jill Ireland here; Elinor Donahue and Diana Muldaur in future episodes], and he had a sensitivity. And he wouldn't compromise, either. I liked that about him." (63-3)

Ralph Senensky said, "'This Side of Paradise' has to do with love, the ability to love and the themes that go beyond the confines of the space genre in which it was written.... I've always loved that last line ... where Spock says, 'For the first time in my life, I was happy.' That pulls on the heart and it makes a universal statement, which TV or movies too seldom make today." (155-2)

Dorothy Fontana said, "I love it. I thought it worked out really well. And NBC liked it *very much*. And Gene liked it *very much*. So I got to be Story Editor." (64-2)

Episode 26: THE DEVIL IN THE DARK
Written by Gene L. Coon
Directed by Joseph Pevney

NBC's press release, February 14, 1967:

A distress call from a mining station on an ore-rich planet leads the Enterprise crew to an encounter with a space creature who has been thwarting delivery of critically-needed metals, in "The Devil in the Dark" on the NBC Television Network colorcast of *Star Trek*.... Captain Kirk (William Shatner) and Mr. Spock (Leonard Nimoy) join Chief Engineer Vandenburg [sic] (Ken Lynch) of the planet outpost Janus VI in a desperate attempt to stem the harassment of their important mining operation by Horta, a strange and apparently indestructible life-form. While tracking Horta through a maze of subterranean shafts, the men are isolated during a cave-in and Kirk finds himself face-to-face with the creature.

Nimoy mind melds with the Horta
(Unaired film frame courtesy of Gerald Gurian)

The Horta, who is capable of moving through solid rock, kills without warning and, seemingly, without purpose. Now it has taken components needed to keep the life support systems on Janus VI working, forcing Kirk and the miners to race against a ticking clock as they search for the missing equipment.

As with "Arena," this story offers a study of bigotry and fear, and gives challenge to the meaning of "monster."

SOUND BITES

- *Kirk, after the Horta attempts to communicate:* "'No kill I.' What is that? A plea for us not to kill it? Or a promise that it won't kill us?"
- *Vandenberg:* "That thing has killed 50 of my men!" *Kirk:* "And you've killed thousands of her children!... Those round silicon nodules you've been collecting and destroying are eggs.... She's intelligent, peaceful and mild. She had no objection to sharing the planet with you people ... until you broke into the nursery and started destroying her eggs. Then she fought back in the only way she could -- as any mother would, when her children

were endangered."

- *McCoy, after Kirk tells him to help the Horta:* "I'm a doctor, not a bricklayer." *Kirk:* "You're a healer, there's a patient -- that's an order."

- *Spock:* "The Mother Horta said to me that our appearance is revolting, but she thought she could get used to it." *McCoy:* "Oh? She didn't happen to make any comments about those ears, did she?" *Spock:* "I did get the impression she thought they were the most attractive human characteristic of all. I didn't have the heart to tell her that only I..." *Kirk:* "She really liked those ears, did she?" *Spock:* "The Horta is a remarkably sensitive and intelligent creature, with impeccable taste." *Kirk:* "Because she approved of you?" *Spock:* "Really, Captain, my modesty..." *Kirk, interrupting:* "Does not merit close examination."

ASSESSMENT

"The Devil in the Dark" represents a rare and early instance in science fiction where a monster is transformed from a thing to be feared to, unexpectedly, an object of Kirk's (and the viewer's) empathy. An exceptional moment in Gene Coon's script comes when Spock is in telepathic contact with the Horta. The scene itself, depending on one's tastes and patience, plays either as brilliant or overly long and somewhat silly, but the cleverness is in the words Coon has the Horta choose when describing its enemies -- the humans. Vandenberg and his men have already called the Horta a "devil" and repeatedly referred to it as a "monster." In turn, the Horta accuses the humans of being both "devils" and "monsters."

Once again, Jonathan Swift had been effectively channeled through a writer/producer of *Star Trek*, albeit a different Gene. The humans and the Horta, seeing one another as killers and thereby blinded by prejudice and fear, are determined to annihilate the other. They could have just as easily been written as Americans and Russians; or blacks and whites; or Republicans and Democrats; or, even, male versus female ... except NBC would have never put the show on the air, not in 1967, anyway. Flesh-and-blood people versus a silicon-and-rock creature, however, were completely acceptable for the American airwaves of this era. This episode broke new ground, enlightened its audience, and is rightfully considered to be a classic.

Nonetheless, "The Devil in the Dark" is dated and flawed. It is claustrophobic. The smooth stage floors in these tunnels are a distraction. The matte painting of the underground complex is so clearly a drawing that it draws attention to itself, as do the absurdly simplistic charts and maps that decorate Vandenberg's office.

Beyond the cosmetics, there is sloppiness in the plotting and execution: the illogic of Chief Vandenberg, after losing 50 men to the "monster," to continue to post sentries deep in the tunnels, not in pairs but on their own, each to become yet another victim; or why these miners have no replacement parts for their "antique" 20-year-old fission power reactor and its circulating pump, which, if it breaks, will result in the death of all on the planet long before help can possibly arrive; or how Vandenberg's men, who fear the Horta, are, in the end, willing to charge it manned only with clubs. The Enterprise crew doesn't behave any more sensibly. Knowing 50 men have died, Kirk allows his security team to go in search of the creature, and even splits them up, leaving one man searching alone to be the next to die. And Kirk and Spock hold a portion of the recently severed hide of the Horta in their bare hands, without Spock even taking a tricorder reading first to be sure it is not covered in the corrosive acid which has already killed numerous men and burned holes through metal and solid rock. It strains credulity to imagine how this immensely heavy rock-creature, which we only see scurry across the stage floor, can leap into the air and pounce on a man twice its own height, or clear its way through a hole it made in a wall when that hole doesn't even reach to the ground ... or how it makes off with the circulatory pump, without hands, without pockets, without a buggy.

"The Devil in the Dark," while an important episode with a profound message, is far from perfect. But, with thought-provoking material such as this, who needs perfection?

THE STORY BEHIND THE STORY

Script Timelines
Gene Coon's story outline, ST #44: November 29, 1966.
Coon's revised outline, gratis. December 5, 1966.
Coon's 1st Draft script: December 19, 1966.
Coon's Second Draft script (Final Draft): December 22, 1966.
Script page revisions from Coon: January 16, 1967.

Janos Prohaska, with *Star Trek* from 1964 through 1968 as both maker and wearer of monster costumes

"The Devil in the Dark" came about as a result of a Hungarian immigrant turned Hollywood stuntman who began his career dressed as apes in the circus. Janos "James" Prohaska had an arrangement with *Star Trek* -- if he came up with a creature the producers liked, they would not only rent it from him but would also pay him to be the man inside the horrible thing.

In the January 25, 1969, issue of *TV Guide*, Prohaska explained, "First TV series I do is *Riverboat*... it is about a traveling circus, and I played the chimp. But then I got type-roled. People keep telling me, 'Thank you, we don't need no chimps today.' Then Ivan Tors put me in *Man and the Challenge*. I played a gorilla, and I saw they needed a bear, so I make bear. Then when monster shows start, I start to make monsters."

Regarding the Horta, Prohaska used a similar looking alien for "The Probe," the last episode of *The Outer Limits*. After some alterations, and hidden inside the costume, Gene Coon recalled Prohaska crawling into his office to make a presentation. Dorothy Fontana remembers it happening outdoors.

"Janos asked Gene Roddenberry, Gene Coon, Justman (and I was included) to look at his proposal OUTSIDE THE OFFICE BUILDING IN THE STUDIO STREET. He had backed off a bit to hide the 'blob creature,' but he brought it up to us as we stood in the street." (64-4b)

Robert Justman said, "Suddenly, the blob skittered around the corner, making straight for us. Then it stopped, curiously, backed away, and rotated in place." (94-8)

Fontana added, "The 'creature' backed and bobbed a bit, then ran up, paused, and left a skeletal chicken 'drop' in the street as it skittered off."

Justman and Coon said it was a large egg-like object that the creature left behind.

Roddenberry claimed it was not, that the idea for the egg came later.

Justman said he was "dumbfounded." He had watched this thing give birth.

Fontana said, "We loved it – Janos got up and turned to us as we stood in the street – and the Horta was born." (64-4b)

Interviewed in the late 1960s, Coon, said, "I fell in love with it, [then] put a hold on the delightful glob and sat down and wrote 'The Devil in the Dark' in four days."

Knowing Coon, the script probably *was* written in four days. But even a producer for *Star Trek* had to play by the rules and work within the system. A treatment came first.

Roddenberry remembered the origin of "The Devil in the Dark" -- or, at least, the part about the egg -- differently. "Let me tell you about 'The Devil in the Dark'," he said. "[Gene Coon] had written an episode that had a planet in it where miners were mining things, and [he] had created something that I didn't like. It was a story of them discovering large nodules, and [he] just made them valuable, because they had some chemical composition or something we needed.... It was basically a story of... greed.... And I said, 'Gene, I don't like your story.... I would like the story much better if these nodules were created by creatures, and they were eggs.'... And he said, 'Jesus, Gene, that's a marvelous idea!'" (145-2)

One thing certainly different in the first story outline as opposed to the episode was its beginning. The Enterprise does not respond to an emergency call from the miners on Janus VI but, instead, limps its way to the mineral-rich planet, damaged by a meteor storm and needing materials to make repairs (a plot device not dissimilar to that used in "Mudd's Women" and, more recently, in the early drafts of "A Taste of Armageddon"). Upon arriving at Janus VI, Kirk discovers there is no salvation for him and the Enterprise; the mining operation has been shut down, due to the attacks of the Horta. The stakes for Kirk, therefore, are greater, and much more personal.

Robert Justman kept his memo to Coon short but, even when writing to the show's lead producer, this associate producer was determined to point out the problem areas. He wrote:

> I find a few similarities to "Mudd's Women" in this show, especially in the beginning. I am sure that there is no problem taking care of this minor thing (that's a joke).... For what it's worth, we have established the fact that our phaser pistols can zap into nothingness non-life forms, such as cabinets, rocks, machinery and budgets. Therefore, there may be some slight problem explaining why phasers can't take care of silicon-based forms.... I find it slightly hard to believe that the Enterprise carries about a supply of ready-mixed concrete, but I could believe that they would send down a hundred-weight of human gall stones. (RJ26)

Otherwise, Justman was very enthusiastic regarding Coon's "latest creation," and wrote, "Am very pleased. *Please write the screenplay quickly*." (RJ26)

Still waiting for a shootable draft of Harlan Ellison's "The City on the Edge of Forever," Barry Trivers' "Portrait of Black & White," and Paul Schneider's "Tomorrow the Universe," or any draft at all of Theodore Sturgeon's "Amok Time," all in various stages of development (or non-development), Justman was desperate for something/anything to schedule for production.

Coon, needing NBC approval before advancing to screenplay, chose to take one more day and revise his outline first. Regarding the set-up for the story, which Coon rather fancied as-is, he ignored Justman's note and left it for Stan Robertson to accept or reject.

Upon reading the revised outline, Robertson echoed Justman's thinking, saying:

Excellent story, Gene, however... I think we should find a different opening since this one is somewhat similar to the others we have had. Other than that, the remainder of the story is totally different than anything we have had to date. Good luck on the script. (SR26)

It was everything Robertson had been asking for -- a planet show, with a monster, and a message. And now, pleasing Robertson even more, the story would begin on a planet and not with a shot of the Enterprise -- a device the NBC man argued was becoming redundant. This, in fact, was only the second story to begin away from the Enterprise (the other being "The Conscience of the King").

Coon begrudgingly jettisoned the idea of the Enterprise damaged in a meteor storm and needing repair. The urgency now had to do with the "pergium" mined on Janus VI desperately needed on a dozen other planets to maintain life support systems.

Coon wrote his first and second draft teleplays in December, within days of one another. There was a secret behind his speed at the typewriter. Coon's secretary, Ande Richardson-Kindryd, said, "He liked amphetamines. And that really contributed to him grinding his teeth and being grim-looking. He was under a lot of pressure a lot of the time. But that was how he was able to write "The Devil in the Dark" so fast." (144a)

With such an urgent need for a new script to go before the cameras, Coon's first draft of "Devil," dated December 19, was immediately bound in yellow covers and designated as the staff-generated First Draft teleplay, even though no one else on the staff -- neither Roddenberry nor Fontana -- had laid a typewriter key on it.

Something different in this version, as opposed to the final shooting script, is that the Horta steals a "control rod" from the reactor, not a "circulating pump." Coon had done his homework in learning that a control rod was, and still is, used in a nuclear reactor to control the rate of fission of uranium and plutonium, thereby preventing a power generator from becoming a nuclear bomb. In this draft of the script, the theft of the control rod by the Horta creates an immediate danger of an explosion that will kill all the humans on the planet and leave the Enterprise crew nowhere to escape to once the damaged ship is unable to maintain a safe orbit. Coon's ticking clock was a loud one.

De Forest Research, however, had issues with the plot contrivances. Among the coverage notes sent to Coon by Joan Pearce at De Forest Research:

> If the Horta is intelligent and understands the operation of the reactor, it seems unlikely that she would steal a [control] rod, thereby risking an explosion which might kill her and destroy many eggs. It would be more likely that she would shut down the reactor and then steal a part, thereby making the environment unlivable for the humans without endangering herself or the eggs. (KDF26)

Pearce was right and Coon's next draft changed the control rod to a circulation pump. In doing so, the ticking clock was somewhat muted. And the change did nothing to help with the problem as to why neither the miners nor the Enterprise have no replacement parts for the reactor. The explanation that the fission reactor is 20 years old, therefore too much of an antique to repair, seems foolish. It was a contrivance that served the story, but made no real sense -- something seldom seen in *Star Trek*.

Also from Joan Pearce:

> There have been serious scientific investigations of the possibility of intelligent life based on a silicon chemical cycle. Silicon is one element capable of building the complicated molecules necessary for life processes. But silicon-based life could only develop and be sustained under conditions of extreme heat -- perhaps

an environment comparable to that prevailing on the planet Mercury. It could not possibly exist in the oxygen atmosphere. In the presence of oxygen, the silicon compounds would undergo spontaneous chemical transformation -- that is, they would burn. (KDF26)

Coon did not have the luxury of time to completely rethink his story or put it through a major overhaul. Justman was standing on his desk, waiting for a shooting draft. So he instigated a compromise -- he added in a few lines of dialogue. McCoy says, "Silicon based life is physiologically almost impossible. Especially in an oxygen atmosphere." Spock retorts, "May I point out, doctor, the atmosphere in these caverns is artificially created to support our form of life. It may be the creature can exist for brief periods in such an atmosphere before retreating to its own environment." McCoy -- speaking on behalf of Joan Pearce and de Forest Research -- says, "I still think you're imagining things." Kirk -- making Gene Coon's argument to Pearce -- interjects, "You may be right, Bones. But it's something to go on."

Believability factor aside, Gene Coon, with his first two scripts (the other being "Arena") had redefined the Starship Enterprise's mission. Herb Solow said, "*Star Trek* was a series that dealt with non-human characters [being] treated as human beings. At first, before we hired Gene Coon, we did have episodes where, when we landed on a planet, if Captain Kirk didn't like the people, he'd shoot them. Coon came in and said, 'Hold it. Why do we do that? Why don't we go in and find out what *they* want, why they're there? Maybe they have the right to be there and we don't.'... I really think that doing that was an amazing approach to television, back then, in the mid '60s. And I think the audience found it." (161-4)

In this respect, "The Devil in the Dark" demonstrates how Coon would have handled "The Man Trap," another story about "the last of its kind." In the latter, Kirk is determined to destroy the monster. In "Devil," Kirk cools down faster and seems more interested in discovering why this "creature" has been killing.

David Gerrold, whose script "The Trouble with Tribbles" was filmed in Season Two, said, "I would have to point to 'The Devil in the Dark' as being the best episode Gene L. Coon ever wrote, because it really gets to the heart of what *Star Trek* was. Here you have a menace, but once you understand what the creature is and why it's doing what it does, it's not really a menace at all. We end up learning more about appropriate behavior for ourselves out of learning to be compassionate, tolerant, understanding. To me, in many ways, Gene L. Coon was the heart and soul of *Star Trek*." (73-4)

Roddenberry liked "Devil in the Dark" enough to want some credit, too, saying, "Gene Coon and I, we thought on the same lines, constantly, and that was all part of the *Star Trek* tradition of our attitude toward other races. Up until that time, we hadn't really decided what our point of view on other races would be.... [That episode] laid out the whole rule of treatment of others. This was really putting together a series, and beginning to state what the series was." (145-2)

Coon handled his own rewriting, creating a Final Draft screenplay on December 22, followed by various page revisions on December 28 and January 6, and even on January 16, the day filming began. A final set of revised pages came on January 18, when the production schedule would be rocked by the death of William Shatner's father. Scenes originally written for the briefing room on the Enterprise had to be changed to work in Vandenberg's office on Janus VI, in the interest of saving time.

Fontana confirmed that "The Devil in the Dark" was a rare case at *Star Trek* where the writer credited on the screen was actually the only one to work on the script. "Nobody touched that one," she said. "I had no input on it whatsoever. It was Gene Coon all the way. If he conferred with Roddenberry about it, I don't know about it. Gene just did that, and I thought it was a great script." (64-3)

Classic episode status notwithstanding, the script actually reads better than the episode plays. Some elements which could have been very effective were either not filmed or not included in the final edit. In the script, it is clear that the Horta is watching the humans, especially Kirk and Spock. It recognizes Kirk is in command by the way he points and speaks to the other humans who nod and appear to comply with his wishes. The Horta, therefore, targets Kirk and arranges for the cave-in that forces the leader of the humans into a showdown. Also made clear in the script, the creature quickly learns that Spock's tricorder is not its friend, and that the device can somehow detect when it is hiding nearby. When the creature hears the tricorder sound, it scurries away. The only story element of this type that made it into the episode was when the Horta, after being injured, knows the phaser is its enemy and cowers each time Kirk points the weapon in its direction. But in the filmed episode, it is not made clear why the Horta does not flee at this moment. The script, however, tells us explicitly: "The Horta holds its ground, facing Kirk and his phaser, risking further injury and perhaps death, to protect its eggs."

Pre-Production
December 27-30, 1966 & January 3-4, 1967 (total 6 days prep).

"The Devil in the Dark" was supposed to be episode 25, followed on the production schedule by "This Side of Paradise." And that's how it has been listed in perhaps every published or posted account, as well as in the home video/DVD sequencing. The official records say differently. Matt Jefferies needed more time to design the special sets required, while Coon and Justman needed more time too, to make a switch in directors.

"The first script I was sent was 'The Devil in the Dark,'" said Ralph Senensky. "I went back to Iowa for Christmas and, while I was there, they sent me out 'This Side of Paradise.' At the time I was very disappointed because I liked 'The Devil in the Dark' better." (155-3)

Senensky was a newcomer to *Star Trek* and, as "Devil" entered into its planning stages, Coon and Justman got nervous. Joseph Pevney, they believed, was far better suited for the ambitious production.

Ken Lynch as Chief Engineer Vandenberg (Unaired film frame courtesy of Gerald Gurian)

Pevney kept getting tough assignments. The results here, as with Pevney's previous assignment, "A Taste of Armageddon," are mixed. There are nice touches, like the shots of the Horta sliding through tunnels, leaving behind a cloud of steam from the corrosive elements. Other moments, including some questionable acting choices, the lighting and photography of the matte paintings, the set design, costuming, and even the geography of the holes made by the Horta, all things in which a director gives input, could and should have been better.

Ken Lynch, 46, was Chief Engineer Vandenberg. He worked prolifically in TV and films throughout the 1950s, '60s, and '70s, with more than 200 appearances. Described as "the perfect Irish cop," he often played the role, including recurring roles on four different series: *The Plainclothesman* from 1949, *Checkmate* from 1961, *Arrest & Trial* from 1964, and *Honey West* from 1966, the latter filming at the same time as this episode.

Barry Russo, here as Security Chief Giotto, had acted in a 1958 episode of *Have Gun - Will Travel* written by Gene Roddenberry. Often billed as John Duke, he was a prominent guest player in dozens of TV series including *The Outer Limits*. For two seasons, just prior to *Star Trek*, he was a regular in a soap called *The Young Marrieds*. Russo, whose performance is spot-on, returned to play Commodore Robert Wesley in "The Ultimate Computer."

Brad Weston, cast as Appel, the only miner to see the creature and live, had also acted in a *Have Gun - Will Travel* written by Roddenberry. It was one of his many appearances on that series. He was also often seen in *77 Sunset Strip* and *The Virginian*.

Barry Russo as Chief Giotto. Brad Weston is to his left (Unaired film frame courtesy of Gerald Gurian)

Roddenberry took notice of Appel and sent a memo to Joe D'Agosta, saying:

> In "The Devil in the Dark" I saw a young "Fess Parker" type character; I think his name was Weston... who was sort of a second in command of the miners... with the heavy set of hair. I'm interested in him; can we talk about his background and ability? (GR26-2)

Roddenberry was already thinking about adding a younger male actor to the regular cast in the hopes of strengthening *Star Trek*'s teen appeal. Weston, in time, would be supplanted by Walter Koenig and his portrayal of Ensign Pavel Chekov.

Bill Elliot, as Schmitter, "burned to a crisp" in the teaser, was 43 and had acted in Roddenberry's *The Lieutenant*. He often appeared in *Alfred Hitchcock Presents* and, from the same time period as "The Devil in the Dark," *Mission: Impossible*.

Production Diary
Filmed January 16, 17, 18, 19, 23, 24 & 25, 1967
(Planned as 6 day production; ran one day over; total cost: $188,439)

Principal photography began on Monday, January 16, 1967, the day after the first Super Bowl, where the Green Bay Packers, led by quarterback Bart Starr, beat the Kansas City Chiefs, 35-10. Later in the evening, on the *Ed Sullivan Show*, Mick Jagger had to substitute a line in the title of the band's new single from "Let's Spend the Night Together" to "let's spend some time together." When the ratings came in, despite the censorship, Sullivan and the Stones commanded 44.5% of the total television audience. In the movie houses, *The Sand Pebbles*, starring Steve McQueen, was top film. The Monkees still held the top-selling album in the record stores, as well as the song being played the most on U.S. radio stations, with the Neil Diamond composition, "I'm a Believer."

Unaired film trim showing the caverns built into Stage 10. Note the smooth floors, to become an issue between Roddenberry and Coon (Courtesy of Gerald Gurian)

Filming for "The Devil in the Dark" began on Stage 10, which had been dressed at great expense to be a maze of caverns, augmented with tube-like tunnels made by the Horta. This gave "Devil in the Dark" a unique look. It also gave the production company many problems with which to contend.

Joseph Pevney said, "The primary problem was photographing the Horta. We had to put a glistening on it, a kind of sheen, to make it stand away from the walls, because everything was the same color. Then, we exaggerated its motion as it moved so that the audience would be sure to see it." (141-1)

Despite this, Pevney was off to a good start, staying on schedule Monday, as well as Tuesday, still among the tunnels, although finishing late each night. On Tuesday he filmed until 7:38 p.m.

Day 3, Wednesday, January 18. Filming continued at a brisk pace during the morning hours, but was suddenly interrupted by sad news. William Shatner received a phone call on the set from his mother -- his father had died unexpectedly while in Florida.

Leonard Nimoy recalled, "The producers told him to go ahead and leave, that they were making immediate arrangements to get him on the plane. But Bill just shook his head and gritted his teeth and said, 'No, we're right in the middle of a scene and I'm going to finish it before I walk off the set.' De Kelley and I both said, 'It's okay, just leave, Bill. Just go.' But Bill was determined to finish the scene, though the tension on the set was almost unbearable as we all helplessly watched him struggle to get it done. It was a tough, emotional afternoon; there was really nothing we could do for him except remain close by." (128-3)

The flight Shatner was able to book wouldn't leave Los Angeles until that evening, and he preferred to stay busy, working. He later admitted, "At that moment in time, the pain was awful.... All through the scene, I kept having trouble with a particular line. My emotion was getting in the way, making me forget.... The one thing that I recall perfectly and that I'll never forget is the closeness that my friend Leonard had toward me. Not just emotionally, but physically as well. I mean, I've seen film of elephants that support the sick and the dying with their bodies, and Leonard somehow seemed physically close to me.... Our cinematographer, Jerry Finnerman, whose father had also recently passed away, stayed close, too. And together, they kind of herded around me, assuring me that there were people close by in case I wanted to talk or just needed a friend." (156-8)

Pevney said, "Shatner was very shaken then, and Leonard was very good to him at that point; he was with him all the time, and able to give him great comfort." (141-2)

Curiously, just as Kirk only confided his feelings to McCoy, or Spock, and kept his inner torment hidden from the crew, Shatner chose not to discuss his sadness with many on the set. Kirk would stay strong in front of his crew, and Shatner did the same in front of his. Eddie Paskey said, "We were doing the scene where Bill has us in the Security detail all lined-up in the caverns, and I was there, and I know Billy Blackburn was in there, and the other regular stand-ins, with some extras. We were basically lined-up, getting our orders from the Captain, telling us what he expected from us. I didn't know at the time that his father had just passed away, and, as far as I knew, no one else on the set knew it. When he went out the door, I think it was Mike Glick, the Assistant Director, who informed us all what had been happening with Bill; that he was on his way to the airport, and I just thought, 'Wow, here he is working his butt off for the good of the show, even though, personally, he knew his father had just passed away. That spoke to his character, and who Bill Shatner really is. I have a lot of respect for that. I'll never forget it; he did a great job." (135-2)

Day 4: Eddie Paskey (photographed from the back) with Nimoy, carrying on in Shatner's absence (Courtesy of Gerald Gurian)

Nimoy added, "Finally, Bill finished the scene and left, then we went on to shoot the scene where Spock approaches the Horta in order to make mental contact with it. Kirk is supposed to be standing and watching during this time. We wound up filming across the back of Bill's double [Eddie Paskey], so that we got the wide master shot, then the shot of me with the Horta. Later, when Bill returned, we got some close-ups of Kirk from the front." (128-3)

During Shatner's absence, slating the start of filming on Day 4, scene 97, take 1 (Courtesy of Gerald Gurian)

While this was happening, Coon was busy doing his final rewrite, changing a pair of briefing room scenes to now play-out in Vandenberg's office. By not having to make a move from Stage 10 to Stage 9 and then back again, as the schedule had it planned, the company saved a few hours. The latest page revisions had "The Devil in the Dark" spend less time on board the

Enterprise than any other episode of *Star Trek* with the exception of the yet-to-be-made "All Our Yesterdays."

On Day 4, January 19, Pevney shot the remaining scenes that did not involve Kirk, and then cast and crew were excused. The production was now one day behind. On this night, NBC aired *Star Trek* for the 19th time, with "Arena."

Day 5, Friday, January 20. One day behind now became two. Desilu Stage 10 was dark. Cast and crew stayed home. Insurance paid the bill.

Shatner rejoins Nimoy for filming on Day 6
(Unaired film frame courtesy of Gerald Gurian)

Day 6, Monday, January 23. Shatner returned and production resumed. He would later admit that his father's death, the journey home for the funeral, the difficulties he was experiencing as a result of his failing marriage, and the exhausting work at *Star Trek*, had left him depressed. His acting, however, did not suffer.

Pevney said, "Shatner was very close to his father, and it really shook him up, but he managed. He was much better than I was when my wife died -- I was impossible." (141-2)

On the schedule this day: the portions of the scenes left unfinished from the week before, including Kirk's encounter with the Horta. More work in the caverns followed, as Pevney filmed 32 camera set-ups, covering 13 pages of script. Even at this pace, he failed to catch up and was a full day behind, not counting the lay-off day on Friday. Wrap time was 6:50 p.m.

"That was a very difficult show to do," Joseph Pevney said, "Janos Prohaska... he probably lost eight to ten pounds a day, just from moving around in the suit." (141-2)

Day 7, Tuesday, January 24. Still on Stage 10, the company moved onto the set for Vandenberg's office, filming all the exposition scenes, including the two that were originally planned for the briefing room on the Enterprise.

Day 8, Wednesday, January 25. The morning hours were spent finishing in Vandenberg's office, and then a move was made to Stage 9 for a pair of brief scenes on the ship's bridge, one with Kirk, Spock, and McCoy, the other with only Scotty (left in command while the three senior offices visit the planet).

Post-Production
Available for editing: January 26, 1967. Music score: tracked.

Fabien Tordjmann and Edit Team #3 did the cutting, including sneaking in those shots of Eddie Paskey's back, coupled with William Shatner's front, as Kirk encounters and interacts with the Horta.

The Westheimer Company handled the optical work, including materialization effects, phaser animation, and further animation needed when the Horta makes its first appearance by burning through solid rock.

With the extensive planet sets required, and delays due to Shatner's absence, "Devil" ran over *Star Trek*'s mandated six day shooting schedule and maximum budget of $185,000 per episode. The final tally: seven production days, one lay-off day, and $192,863 spent. The first season deficit was up to $83,980.

Release / Reaction
Premiere air date: 3/9/67. NBC repeat broadcast: 6/15/67.

Albert Whitlock painting used to open the coming attraction trailer, which aired only in 1967 (Courtesy of Gerald Gurian)

Star Trek made the cover of *TV Guide* the week "The Devil in the Dark" first aired on NBC.

Steven H. Scheuer reviewed "The Devil in the Dark" for his syndicated TV Key Preview column. Among papers to carry his column on March 9, 1967 was the *Milwaukee Journal*, in Milwaukee, Wisconsin. Scheuer wrote:

> *Star Trek* shines tonight with a truly ingenious space-age story of particular interest to serious science fiction fans. Captain Kirk and Mr. Spock encounter a monstrous creature of space, a strange looking and indestructible life form called the Horta, played by Janos Prohaska. The Horta has been stopping delivery of critical metals from a nearby planet. The creature is capable of burning people to a crisp and can readily bore tunnels through impassable walls, and the Enterprise is sent to investigate. The manner in which the monster's being is identified and then controlled, is a fascinating fictional tour-de-force.

Joan Crosby's *TV Scout* review appeared in, among other papers, the *Edwardsville Intelligencer*, in Edwardsville, Illinois. She wrote:

> This is a fine piece of science fiction about a planet filled with rich minerals and the sudden deaths of 50 people connected with a mining expedition. Just what is the monster that is lurking in those tunnels and burning his victims to a crisp? The climax of this story is actually quite moving as William Shatner comes face to tentacle [sic] with the creature and Leonard Nimoy manages to communicate through the agonizing -- for him -- means of telepathy.

With the cover of America's No. 1 selling magazine, and advance reviews such as these, *Star Trek* was ensured good ratings.

RATINGS / Nielsen National report, Thursday, March 9, 1967:

8:30 - 9 p.m.:		**Share:**	**Households:**
NBC:	*Star Trek* (first half)	no data	13,010,000
ABC:	***Bewitched***	no data	**13,830,000**
CBS:	*My Three Sons*	no data	11,530,000
9 - 9:30 P.M.:		**Share:**	**Households:**
NBC:	*Star Trek* (second half)	31.1%	no data
ABC:	*Love on a Rooftop*	26.8%	no data
CBS:	***Thursday Night Movie*** (start)	**38.2%**	no data
Independent stations:		3.9%	no data

Star Trek held second place for its entire broadcast with approximately 26 million people watching (an average of two per household). The movie on CBS: the television premiere of the 1961 drama *The Sins of Rachel Cade*, starring Angie Dickinson, Peter Finch, and Roger Moore.

One member of the viewing audience on March 9, Gene Roddenberry, was not fully happy with all he was seeing. He wrote to Gene Coon, beginning on a positive note.

> I want to congratulate you on an excellent show... full of suspense, jeopardy, all the things that help bring us a mass audience, (while) maintaining good science-fiction elements. The "monster" was treated very well and given beautiful and heart-warming characteristics toward the end. (GR26-1)

Roddenberry had placed quotation marks around the word "monster" for a reason. The word represented a pet peeve of his. His memo continued:

> We may have used the term "monster" a little too much at the beginning of the show. Would much prefer our people, highly trained astronauts of the future, well-acquainted with thousands of forms of alien life, use terms like "beings" or "creatures." (GR26-1)

In regard to the cavern floors, he wrote:

> This could have used some painting mottled effect, as it seemed awfully shiny and new and stage-surface-like for an underground mining installation. It took away from the reality, which the rough-blasted walls gave us. (GR26-1)

Bjo Trimble, who was visiting the set as Roddenberry's guest, explained that the floors were made smooth for the needs of the Horta. She said, "It would have been difficult for Janos [Prohaska] to navigate the rocky floor. He stood about six-four, but he could contort himself into the most amazing positions. He was down on his hands and knees, so they needed it to be a smooth floor; he was in a bad enough position as it was." (177-8)

Robert Justman concurred, saying, "That was a seven day production. We spent six of the seven days in those tunnels and catacombs. That meant the man in the Horta costume spent six of those seven days on his hands and knees. Correction: elbows and knees -- crawling, turning, pouncing, scurrying away. And we were fond of the man in the Horta costume. We hoped to see him be able to stand up and walk away from this job.... There were many other creatures scurrying about -- production people, camera operators, actors, each a potential lawsuit should one fall and break one's neck. And this is why stage floors are usually flat. You may recall that the Horta turned out not to be a beast after all. The real beast is the inherent short schedules of television production. If 'The Devil in the Dark' were a feature film, we would have been in those tunnels for several weeks instead of several days. Speaking only for myself, I was happy we were not in those tunnels for several weeks. It was not an easy production." (94-1)

In his long memo to Coon, Roddenberry also talked about casting, saying:

> Per NBC's continued reminder to us, one which I find myself agreeing with, we should make some more use of females as crew members in planet stories, or find some way to include females among groups and miners, who are here on a planet years at a time. Granted, this can get phony and unbelievable if not handled right, but let's keep in mind that we're in a century where women are granted equal status and responsibility with men. (GR26-1)

Others involved with the series were more taken by "The Devil in the Dark."

This was one of William Shatner's two favorites. "A terrific story," he said. "Exciting, thought-provoking, and intelligent." (156-8)

James Doohan picked this as a favorite, as well. Leonard Nimoy also listed it as one of his favorites, saying that the theme was "powerful," as it dealt with racism and "intercultural conflict," a fear of a person or thing that we do not know or understand. He remarked, "'The Devil in the Dark' illustrates beautifully how unreasoning fear begets violence -- and how an attempt at understanding can benefit both sides in a conflict." (128-3)

Entertainment Weekly chose "Devil" as Number Six in their Top Ten picks from the original series. *Cinefantastique* also listed "Devil" on its a Top Ten list.

From the Mailbag

Received after the premiere telecast of "The Devil in the Dark":

> Dear Gene: We've been watching *Star Trek* for some time. We tend to take science fiction very seriously, which gives us a perfectionist viewpoint; but we've found it generally enjoyable. When Mr. Spock turned up on the cover of *TV Guide*, we felt this was a very good sign indeed. But then came the evening of March 9. Gene, that show was a disaster. And all the worse because it must have attracted special attention after the fine *TV Guide* bit. The plot was a basically good idea, but it was realized in a very strained way. Your alien was not believable. The scene in which Spock makes contact with the alien was the low point, dragging on and on and pulling the show down with it. Some other points were unbelievable from an engineering viewpoint, which always detracts from the basic quality of the show. But we expect that. James Ashe, Editor, *Science Fiction Times*, N.Y., March 12, 1967.

In time, Gene Roddenberry ultimately went along with popular opinion and embraced the episode. However, immediately after its premiere, he had reservations, as indicated by this excerpt from his March 30 reply to Ashe:

Dear Jim: Whether or not the evening of March 9 was a disaster depends, of course, on whose viewpoint it is. It was not my favorite show either. On the other hand, we received not only one of our largest audience ratings but a considerable amount of complimentary mail from the upper level of our audience, even from many in Fandom. Yes, we've made episodes we wish we could forget, bury and hide. We can't. Each of these episodes costs something like $200,000 and the loss of a single one of them would result in a net loss for the entire year and neither television studios nor television networks nor their stockholders would permit that kind of loss.

Memories

Dorothy Fontana said, "That's the one that a lot of people remember very distinctly. The mother protecting her young. That's a great show; it's a great script." (64-2)

In 1995, the renowned science fiction author Arthur C. Clarke said of this episode, "It impressed me because it presented the idea, unusual in science fiction then *and* now, that something weird, and even dangerous, need not be malevolent. That is a lesson that many of today's politicians have yet to learn." (31B)

A Back Order of Three / "Errand of Mercy"

**Unaired film clip from "Errand of Mercy"
(Courtesy of Gerald Gurian)**

As "The Return of the Archons" filmed, NBC had yet to inform *Star Trek* whether any additional shows would be required beyond the delivery of 26. Robert Justman had been sweating out the wait. It was his job to make sure the scripts had gone through their breakdown and all aspects of the productions were properly prepared.

Weeks earlier, on November 13, NBC had coughed up $14,000 and authorized the writing of four additional scripts, just in case.

On December 8, with "Archons" in its third day of filming, Justman wrote Gene Coon:

> As you are aware, there is a definite likelihood of our being picked-up by the Network for four more shows this season. One of the conditions, or rather, the main condition of this pickup is that we will be able to keep delivering new shows to the Network without surcease through the 27th of April, 1967.... As of now, we have "Space Seed," which will follow the presently-in-production show and then likelihood that we can get "A Taste of Armageddon" sufficiently down to budget in order to enable us to follow "Space Seed." After that, we have *nothing*.

As had happened in October, 1966, when the mid-season pickup from NBC came and Roddenberry, Coon and Justman, with only days notice, had to be ready to put "Shore Leave" into production on the very day after "The Menagerie" finished filming, they now had to be ready with something/anything to put before the cameras should the network wish it.

With the script development money assured by NBC, Coon had been writing scripts of his own as well as rewriting those of others -- scripts that he knew might never see the light of a film set. He delivered a savagely pruned-down version of "A Taste of Armageddon" to Justman in time to follow on the heels of "Space Seed." And then, in sufficient time, he delivered his polish of D.C. Fontana's script for "This Side of Paradise," as well as his own script for "The Devil in the Dark." And this brought *Star Trek* to a total of 26 episodes. Beyond this, Coon had other scripts waiting in the wings ... or, at least, waiting near the wings.

Justman had been correct with his prediction that NBC would want four more shows. *Daily Variety* announced the news less than 24 hours later, on December 9, with the headline "*Star Trek* Given Another Hitch." Said the trade paper: "*Star Trek* yesterday received its second pickup of the season, to make for a firm 30 segs."

The network would scale this order back from four additional episodes to three, but, on December 9, Coon needed to get four more teleplays ready to go before the camera. He was still struggling to get a script for "The City on the Edge of Forever" that could actually be filmed somewhere close to budget, then dashed off a new one of his own, written in record time -- even for "the fastest typewriter in the west."

***

Episode 27: ERRAND OF MERCY

Written by Gene L. Coon
Directed by John Newland

John Abbott (second from right) in unaired film trim (Courtesy of Gerald Gurian)

From *TV Guide*, March 18, 1967:

A peace-loving race gives Captain Kirk a lesson in warfare. The inhabitants of the neutral planet Organia hesitate to interfere in a war between Kirk's federation and an invader -- until intervention becomes necessary.

Commander Kor, representing the Klingon Empire, wants Organia as a base. Kirk, representing the Earth-led United Federation of Planets, has the same desire. The Organians and their leader, Ayelborne, have a surprising idea of their own.

The theme, and hook, is a battle between the United States and the Communist Allies – or between Hawks and Doves -- circa 1967 ... with divine intervention ... on a distant alien world.

SOUND BITES

- *Kirk:* "Gentlemen, I've seen what the Klingons do to planets like yours. They are organized into vast slave labor camps. You'll have no freedoms whatsoever. Your goods will be confiscated. Hostages will be taken and killed. Your leaders will be confined. You'll be better off on a penal planet; infinitely better off." *Ayelborne:* "Captain, we see that your concern is genuine. We are moved. But we assure you that we are in absolutely no danger, and that there is no reason to concern yourself about us. If anyone is in danger, you are, and this troubles us greatly."

- *Kor, to the Organians:* "Where is your smile?... That stupid, idiotic smile everyone else seems to be wearing.... Smile, and smile. I don't trust men who smile too much."

- *Kirk, to Ayelborne:* "Even if you have some powers we don't understand, that doesn't give you the right to dictate to our Federation..." *Kor:* "...or our Empire ..." *Kirk:*

"...how we'll handle our inter-stellar relations! We have the right..." *Ayelborne, interrupting:* "To wage war, Captain? To kill millions of innocent people? To destroy life on a planetary scale? Is this what you are defending?" *Claymare:* "Your emotions are most discordant. We do not wish to seem inhospitable ... but really ... gentlemen ... you must go." *Ayelborne:* "Yes. The mere presence of beings like yourselves is intensely painful to us."

ASSESSMENT

Lifting a page from Jonathan Swift, *Star Trek* once again snuck a hot political debate onto prime time television by disguising the intent, changing the names and shifting the time period. Substitute the planet Organia for the divided nation of Vietnam, the Federation for the United States, and the Klingon Empire for Red China and its allies, North Vietnam and North Korea, and you can see Gene Coon's agenda for this topical material.

The problems are slight:

- There are a few questionable performances by minor characters, and a few awkwardly staged sequences -- but nothing out of the norm for a 1960s one-hour TV show shot in six days;

- We are again asked to accept the troublesome tendency of science fiction of this era to present stories on other worlds where everyone, planet natives as well as invaders, speak English, even when not in the presence of those who normally communicate in that language;

- And, for the benefit of the story, Kirk is portrayed as overtly macho and too quick to jump into a shoving match with the Klingons. Normally, the Captain is of a cooler head than this, and smarter.

While not a perfect episode, there are many special moments. The Klingons are first introduced here. Kor, portrayed by John Colicos, is a treasure. Coon did well in creating a worthy adversary for Kirk, as Paul Schneider had with the Romulan Commander in "Balance of Terror." Kor is not a one-dimensional character. His reaction to the news that he has the Captain of the Enterprise as a prisoner is delightful. It is clear Kor truly admires Kirk and craves his opponent's admiration in return. Beyond this, he is sad knowing that he must have Kirk executed in such an "inglorious" manner. He also detests having to order the killing of thousands of Organians. Of this, Coon wrote:

> The Klingon commander is sitting at his desk, hands over his face. He is, at this moment, an unhappy man. The fact is, he does not relish butchering unarmed civilians. He is a soldier, and a good one. He sits quietly, brooding.

Also effective: the eeriness, enhanced by the score, whenever members of this arrested civilization do something unexpected and profound, such as when Trefayne instinctively knows eight space ships have taken orbit around the planet, or that hundreds of armed men have appeared outside the gates of the city. Also, the clever surprise ending, that no one has died and the Organians are not as they appear. The best is saved for last: Kirk's realization that he's being a true horse's ass, catching himself making the very same argument as his sworn enemy -- to be free to wage war.

"Errand of Mercy" is a very worthwhile trek, even with a few bumps in the road.

THE STORY BEHIND THE STORY

Script Timeline:
Gene Coon's story outline, ST #45: mid December 1966.
Coon's 1st Draft teleplay: Late December 1966.

Coon's 2nd Draft script (Mimeo Department "Yellow Cover 1st Draft" teleplay):
January 3, 1967.
Coon's Final Draft teleplay: January 6, 1967.
Coon's Revised Final Draft teleplay: January 23, 1967.
Additional page revisions by Coon: January 26, 1967.

The title comes courtesy of Charles Dickens. A line from *The Life and Adventures of Nicholas Nickleby* reads, "It is an errand of mercy that brings me here. Pray, let me discharge it."

The quote applies to the writing of the story and script as much as to its theme. This was the 45th story assignment of the year. More assignments had been given out for *Star Trek*, and, therefore, more money spent developing stories than on any other series from this time. And too many of these treatments, outlines, and teleplays were not working out. It was not ego that prompted Gene Coon to stop rewriting scripts begun by others and, instead, with plenty of coffee and, according to secretary Ande Richardson-Kindryd, a few amphetamines, dash off three of his own ("Arena," "The Devil in the Dark" and, now, "Errand of Mercy"). Robert Justman was rightfully hollering for scripts that were ready to produce -- in six days, for $185,000. Of the assignments given out, of the stories and scripts in development, Coon had nothing remotely close to being ready to offer Justman. And so, on the very day he finished writing "The Devil in the Dark," Coon rolled a fresh sheet of paper into his typewriter, lit another cigarette, and began his third original *Star Trek* script.

"Errand of Mercy" sped through the process of story outline -- only one draft in the final week of December, 1966 -- to, days later, a First Draft script, then, mere days later, a Second Draft script.

Bob Justman told Coon:

> Perhaps we could clean up Kirk's orders to the Enterprise to skedaddle without waiting for him and Spock. Certainly, Kirk and Spock could be beamed up instantaneously upon receipt of news that the Enterprise is getting under attack; so, therefore, we need some other reason for them to remain behind. I certainly don't think that we should go for the excuse of a malfunction in the Transporter mechanism.... Why can't Kirk and Spock set their Phasers on heavy stun force in Scene 90? They could then dispose of the guards by tying them up and gagging them. Kirk seems much too bloodthirsty for my taste in this show anyhow. I feel that Kirk should never say "we cannot afford to fight fair". He should say "we must always try to fight fair".... Is it absolutely necessary that the Organians change into "pure energy... far too bright to be stared at"? If it is necessary, then please ring me up, as I have a suggestion as to how to achieve this Effect. (RJ27)

The Final Draft script came three days after that, on January 6. And then Coon stopped writing, for a week, anyway -- long enough to allow NBC time to respond.

Stan Robertson, at the network, was ecstatic. This was another action-adventure story that mostly took place on a planet and away from the confines of, as Robertson described it, the four walls of the Enterprise. Beyond this, the story had a message, but was not preachy. And production would clearly require both outdoor locations and a sizable cast -- so much so that many of the *Star Trek* stand-ins played their usual crewmen roles as well as appearing as either villagers or Klingons.

Coon's quick rewrite, factoring in the feedback from his colleagues, de Forest Research, and NBC -- his Revised Final Draft -- was finished on January 23, while Gene Roddenberry was out of the office and checked into the hospital. This time it wasn't exhaustion, at least as explained to *Daily Variety* for the trade's January 25 edition. Roddenberry claimed to have come down with rare illness -- silicosis. The trade explained, "A collector of precious stones, he was working on an opal, somehow absorbed silicote in the process. Back in his office, Roddenberry says this is the first case of silicosis since 1912."

Mary Black said, "Gene was too macho to wear a mask when he cut those stones – the former cop and all -- so he had been breathing all that stuff in. We had left the show by that time, but we heard about it. It seemed quite serious for a while there." (17a)

For his latest rewrite of "Errand of Mercy," Coon had been listening to Robert Justman, to the pleas and even threats regarding too many optical effects in the scripts. There were few in this one. The attack on the Enterprise from a Klingon scout ship was underplayed and written with an eye toward economy. Coon did not call for any shots showing the Enterprise being hit by the Klingon weapon blasts. Instead, he conveyed the hits the ship took by the shaking of the bridge. It was only after the budget projections came in low that the post house handling the effects was given instructions to visualize the attack. As for the Enterprise returning fire, the script reads, "ENTERPRISE FIRING PHASERS (STOCK) -- from 'Balance of Terror.'" And, regarding the phasers hitting their mark, Coon wrote, "ANGLE ON VIEWING SCREEN (STOCK) -- 'Balance of Terror'; as our phaser blasts explode among the stars." All other images of the Enterprise could, and would, be made up of stock shots. Only Kirk and Spock are shown beaming down and only from the "materialization" end. The transporter room is never even seen. And the Klingons are not seen materializing on Organia -- we hear about that through dialogue. We see no Klingon ships. And, for the finale, when two -- and only two -- of the Organians are seen changing from human form to "pure thought ... or energy," Coon wrote in suggestions as to how the effect could be handled without the expenditure of too much money (see Production Diary).

Other examples of an eye toward economy in Coon's script: McCoy is absent (the third and final time he was not present in the series). Scott misses out, too. We see little of the interior of the Enterprise (only the bridge, making room on Stage 9 for half the sets depicting the interior of rooms on Organia). And, counting his pennies, or lack of them, Coon wrote the village to match a standing outdoor set at Desilu 40 Acres.

Many extras were needed, and costumes, and animals, but the cost-cutting measures already implemented by Coon in his money-conscious screenplay allowed "Errand of Mercy" to be one of the less costly episodes of the season. NBC was getting what it wanted and Desilu's bank wasn't breaking as a result.

Three days after turning in his Revised Final Draft -- which was only the third draft of the script -- and on the day Pre-Production began, Coon delivered a handful of page revisions. Among other things, to make it possible to use the effects from "Balance of Terror," he changed Kirk's line about firing phasers to add that they should be set for wide dispersal, allowing the phasers to resemble photon torpedoes and erupt in space as they had in the episode from which these photographic effects were harvested from.

Few writers could churn out material as fast or as well as Gene Coon. Regarding his invention of *Star Trek*'s new villains, Dorothy Fontana revealed, "Gene Coon came up with the Klingons, though we never liked the name. We said, 'Gene, can't you come up with a different name than Klingon? We hate it.' It was odd sounding. You know, *Kling*-on -- as in clinging." (64-2)

There was no time to come up with something different. And time has since proven the name to be just fine.

Fontana, nonetheless, still amused, added, "Once we asked him, 'Where do Klingons come from? What's the name of their planet?' He said [laughing], 'Kling.'" (64-2)

What is quick and easy to write, however, is not always as quick and easy to make. Or, at least, so the pre-production phase revealed.

Pre-Production
January 16-20 & 23-25, 1967 (total 8 days prep).

Nearly every episode of the original *Star Trek* took six days to prepare, sometimes less. "Errand of Mercy" took eight. There were many new challenges here, including the hiring of a first time *Star Trek* director.

Joseph Pevney was the obvious choice to handle an action piece like "Errand of Mercy" but, while this episode was in its pre-production phase, Pevney was busy directing "The Devil in the Dark." Gene Coon had someone else in mind, someone he felt whose name would bring celebrity value to *Star Trek*.

John Newland had started his entertainment career as an actor. In 1950, before stepping behind the camera, he served as a regular cast member on *One Man's Family*, a primetime soap on NBC. Two years later, Newland received an Emmy nomination as Best Actor for his recurring work on *Robert Montgomery Presents*. It was there he first tried his hand at directing. He again served double duty, as an actor/director, on more than a dozen episodes of *The Loretta Young Show*.

**John Newland hosting *One Step Beyond*
(Courtesy of Gerald Gurian)**

In 1959, he began a three-year stint directing and hosting *Alcoa Presents*, a dramatic anthology series involving allegedly true stories of the supernatural. Initially named after its original sponsor, the series later became known as *One Step Beyond*.

Because of *One Step Beyond*, Newland had achieved celebrity status which brought further prestige to *Star Trek*. To baby boomers and sci-fi enthusiasts, Newland was thought of as the *other* Rod Serling. *One Step Beyond* actually beat *The Twilight Zone* to the airwaves by one year and Serling patterned his on-camera introductions after those by Newland.

Newland said, "I knew Rod... and he was a real supporter. He called me up and asked me to meet him for drinks. Well, once we were at the bar, Serling told me he was going to be producing and writing an anthology series of his own. He assured me that *The Twilight Zone* was going to be pure fantasy, with no discussion of proof or psychic powers.... [He did this] because he was a class act. He just wanted to let me know in person that he wasn't going to rip us off." (125-2)

Newland had worked with William Shatner before, giving him direction in "The Promise," an episode of *One Step Beyond*. He said of Shatner, "He's a charming actor, and a hard-working actor. I thought he was adorable, and he has been an excellent friend of mine." (125-2)

But Newland didn't know *Star Trek*. And, being a star director, he was provided with more prep time than the series' budget normally allowed for.

The first chore was casting. Because of the nature of the script, and the introduction of the Klingons, this was a longer and more involved process than usual.

As makeup artist Fred Phillips later recalled, "I had never heard of a Klingon before. And nothing in the script that I read told me what it was." (142-1)

Coon merely described them as hard-looking Asian-types. Fortunately, the actor hired to play the head Klingon had some ideas of his own.

John Colicos – the prototype Klingon
(Unaired film trim courtesy of Gerald Gurian)

John Colicos was recommended by Newland, who had worked with the actor on an episode of *One Step Beyond* and wanted him to play Kor, the Klingon commander. Colicos said, "We devised the makeup right there and then. [Fred Phillips] said, 'What do you want to look like?' I saw the script as a futuristic Russia and America at loggerheads over this peaceful little planet, so I said, 'Let's go back in the past and think Genghis Khan, because Kor is a military commander, ready to take over the entire universe with his hordes.' My hair happened to be very short and combed forward, so I said, 'Spray my hair, kink it up a bit and give me a vaguely Asian/Tartar appearance. Let's go for the brown-green makeup so I'm slightly not of this world,' and within two hours, this thing emerged and that was it." (33-1)

John Abbott, at 61, played Ayelborne, the leader of the Organian Council. He had over 100 acting credits in film and television. One year before this, he and Roger C. Carmel (Harry Mudd) were the prominent guest actors on "The Barter," an episode of *I Spy*. Between that time and this, Abbott was the featured guest player in "The Dream Merchant" on *Lost in Space*.

Peter Brocco, playing Claymare, Ayelborne's right hand man -- and he does sit to Ayelborne's right -- had over 200 credits in film and TV, which also included a recent episode of *Lost In Space* (he was the alien leader in that series episode "The Deadly Games of Gamma 6"). Brocco had also worked with Leonard Nimoy before, in *The Outer Limits*.

Victor Lundin, the Klingon Lieutenant, was no stranger to science fiction -- or to cult TV series of the 1960s. Of the former, he received second billing in Byron Haskin's 1964 cult classic *Robinson Crusoe on Mars*, as Friday, as well as appearances on *Voyage to the Bottom of the Sea* and *The Time Tunnel*. With "Errand of Mercy," he was the first Klingon to be seen on *Star Trek*. Lundin had also been in the running to be the first Vulcan. He said, "I had been called in when they were casting the role of Mr. Spock. I understood that it was between me, Leonard Nimoy and another actor as a distant third. Byron Haskin, who had directed *Robinson Crusoe on Mars* was working on *Star Trek*, and he tried to get me cast as Spock. But Gene Roddenberry and Nimoy had known each other since the 1950s, and Nimoy got the role." (109a)

Production Diary
Filmed January 26, 27, 30, 31 and February 1, & 2, 1967
(6 day production; cost: $175,527).

Principal photography began Thursday, January 26, 1967. This is the week that a fire in Apollo 1 resulted in the deaths of three astronauts -- Virgil "Gus" Grissom, Edward Higgins White, and Roger Chaffee. A treaty banning the use of military weapons in space was signed. The two big movies across America were *Hotel*, starring Rod Taylor, and *A Fistful of Dollars*, the first of Clint Eastwood's hit "spaghetti westerns." The new No. 2 song on radio stations, under The Monkees' "I'm a Believer," was "Tell It Like It Is" by Aaron Neville. There was no change on the best-selling record album lists – it was still *The Monkees*, followed by Herb Alpert and the Tijuana Brass with *S.R.O.* ("Standing Room Only"), as it had been for weeks. Diana Rigg and Patrick MacNee of *The Avengers* looked good on the cover of *TV Guide*. And a Chicago blizzard, dropping a record 23 inches of snow, caused 800 buses and 50,000 automobiles to be abandoned, claiming 26 lives. The weather in Los Angeles, however, was sunny and fair, making it possible for this episode to have a day of exterior production.

Filming began on Stage 9, for the scenes on the bridge that open and close the episode, plus the ones where Sulu takes command and, for the first time in the series, sits in the captain's chair.

Because many of the starship sets had been collapsed and pushed aside for "Devil in the Dark" and were not needed here, the interior of the dungeon on Organia, the hallways just outside, and the Council Chambers, were built on Stage 9. After finishing filming the bridge, Newland and company moved onto these new -- and temporary -- sets.

Meanwhile, in the precious few areas of Stage 10 not filled with sand, dirt and rock, Matt Jefferies and his crew were busy building Kor's office and the main corridors of the citadel.

John Newland with Shatner at Desilu 40 Acres
(Courtesy of Gerald Gurian)

Newland stepped into overtime on this first day, but wrapped in time to allow cast and crew to make it home for the 8:30 p.m. broadcast of "Tomorrow Is Yesterday," the 20th episode to air. According to A.C. Nielsen, *Star Trek* placed second during its first half-hour, then rose to first position from 9 to 9:30 p.m., with 32.2% of the television viewing audience tuning-in.

On Day 2, the company

Script Supervisor George A. Rutter in foreground, right,
while at 40 Acres (Courtesy of Gerald Gurian)

traveled to Culver City and Desilu 40 Acres for the third time in the series (the fourth, counting sequences filmed there from the first pilot film). This time, the Jerusalem city built in 1927 for Cecil B. DeMille's *King of Kings* was used as the Organian town square. The portion of the village just inside of the gate had been seen before on *Star Trek*, as an area of the castle on Rigel VII in "The Cage."

Care was taken and money spent for something that is barely noticeable: Look hard and you will see the livestock in the background as Kirk and Spock first enter into the Organian village. They are painted.

On Day 3, Monday, the company returned to Desilu Stage 9 for additional filming in the dungeon and the hallway outside. Newland then moved onto the Council Chamber set for the first of numerous sequences, including the lengthy scene from Act 1 where Kirk makes his argument to the Organian Elders to accept the help of the Federation against the Klingons.

On Day 4, Tuesday, the balance of the scenes in the Council Chamber on Stage 9 were filmed, taking the entire day. These included the scene that introduced John Colicos as Klingon Military Governor Kor.

Colicos said of Newland, "He was highly-intellectual; a highly-educated man. John was always reading a book. He was very professional, wasn't interested in any squabbles. If you didn't know all your lines, he would say, 'Well, when you're ready, I'll be ready,' and he would just sit and read his book. I think John always felt that television was just a notch beneath him." (33-1)

"There was no rehearsal time on *Star Trek*," Newland said. "You just went in and did it. But with guys like Shatner and Nimoy and the rest of the cast, it was easy. Good actors do very good things to begin with, so it's just a question of the director knowing how to put it all together." (125)

On Day 5, Wednesday, the company moved to Stage 10 and Kor's office in the citadel. The entire day was spent on this set.

On Day 6, the last of the scenes in Kor's office were filmed -- the climax and surprise ending of the story, as the Organians end the fighting. The sequences outside Kor's office (in the citadel corridor), were the final shots taken. Newland finished into overtime but otherwise on schedule and budget. Later that night, NBC aired "Court Martial," the 21st broadcast episode. As it had done the previous week, *Star Trek* came in at No. 2 from 8:30 to 9 p.m., and then climbed to first place from 9 to 9:30 p.m. A.C. Nielsen awarded the victory to ABC and *Bewitched* (now at an earlier time period) for that first half-hour, with a 32.9 audience share. *Star Trek* followed with a 27.7 share, and then *My Three Sons* with 25.1. During *Star Trek*'s second half-hour, it brought NBC a 29.4 audience share, besting the CBS movie (at 20.2) and ABC's new sitcom, *Love on a Rooftop*, starring Peter Duel, Judy Carne, and Rich Little, which trailed with 27.4% of the television audience.

John Newland later said he enjoyed his single directing assignment on *Star Trek*. He wanted to return but other commitments precluded his involvement.

Post-Production
Available for editing: February 3, 1967. Music score: tracked.

Bruce Schoengarth and Edit Team #2 did the cutting.

The Westheimer Company provided for the optical effects, including the Klingon weapons hitting the underside of the Enterprise, materialization effects, hand phaser animation, and the transformation of the Organians into the formless masses of light. Coon, in his script, described the effect this way:

> AYELBORNE AND CLAYMARE. They smile ... and they suddenly begin to change. They begin to glow ... brighter and brighter ... until at first they are an incredibly brilliant man-shaped object, glowing with the light of the sun ... and then they lose the man shape, and simply begin to glow, brighter and brighter, as if there were two suns in the room.... Two pulsating, incredibly brilliant masses of light. (SUGGESTION: PHOTOGRAPH THE SUN, DOUBLE IT, AND SUPERIMPOSE IT OVER THE FADING FIGURES OF THE TWO MEN.) Now they begin to fade, disappear. There is nothing left of them at all.

Child's play today. A tall order in 1967. Westheimer did a superb job in realizing Coon's vision.

As for the Citadel -- that looming fortress on a mountain top used by the Klingons as a home base -- the script merely says:

> The MATTE PAINTING should show something that looks rather like a ruined castle, or fortress, in the distance ... very old, decaying, but massive.

As it turned out, no matte painting was needed. What we see is a stock footage shot of Citadelle Laferriere in Haiti. The massive stone fortress was built in the early 1800s by the Haiti resistance fighters to safeguard the island and prevent the French from returning to reclaim their rule. The fortress stands to this day.

Even with the trip to Desilu 40 Acres, all the extras, livestock painted in strange colors, and all the Klingon uniforms and other costumes, "Errand of Mercy," at $175,527, came in under the studio per-episode allowance by $9,473, lowering the deficit to $74,507. They would need every dime of the savings. "The City on the Edge of Forever" was just around the corner.

Release / Reaction
Premiere air date: 3/23/67.

Steven H. Scheuer reviewed "Errand of Mercy" for his syndicated *TV Key Preview* column on March 23, 1967. Among newspapers to carry the review was the *Edwardsville Intelligencer*, in Edwardsville, Illinois. Scheuer wrote:

> Tonight this series makes the point that even a peace-loving man like Captain Kirk can be so carried away by a situation that he will find himself forcing war. He and Mr. Spock are on the planet Organia, trying to negotiate a treaty to keep the planet from falling to the Klingons, who occupy and enslave worlds. But the Klingons land during the negotiations and the Organians, who never stop smiling, first help our heroes and then turn them over to the enemy. John Colicos plays the Klingon leader.

A.C. Nielsen handled the nose counting.

RATINGS / Nielsen National report, Thursday, March 23, 1967:

8:30 - 9 p.m., 59.9% U.S. TVs in use.	Share:	Households:
NBC: *Star Trek* (first half)	No data	12,350,000
ABC: *Bewitched*	**No data**	**12,790,000**
CBS: *My Three Sons*	No data	11,090,000

9 - 9:30 p.m., 59.7% U.S. TVs in use.	Share:	Households:
NBC: *Star Trek* (second half)	30.0%	No further data
ABC: *Love on a Rooftop*	26.4%	No further data
CBS: ***Thursday Night Movie* (start)**	**32.6%**	**No further data**
Independent stations:	11.0%	No further data

Star Trek held second place for its entire hour. The CBS movie was the 1961 World War II era drama *The Counterfeit Traitor*, starring William Holden.

Robert Justman, the one at *Star Trek* given the chore of picking which episodes would repeat, passed this one by. It was surprising since this was the only first season episode to feature the Klingons and would be the catalyst for more episodes to come.

"I had an embarrassment of riches during that first season," Justman said. "And I felt we had episodes more-deserving of a second network airing. And we did." (94-1)

From the Mailbag

Received the week after NBC's airing of "Errand of Mercy":

> Dear Sirs... My wife and I consider *Star Trek* one of the most original and imaginative programs on television. The characterizations are interesting and unusually very consistent from program to program. However, on watching "An Errand of Mercy," [sic] we noticed the same foolish sequence that appeared on the program some time ago [about the Horta], namely, Mr. Spock's prediction of the odds against escape, "7826.7 to one." This is a most illogical thing for Spock to say, because such an accurate prediction requires an absolutely complete knowledge of the situation, with no room for deviation. This may seem like a small point, but it certainly annoys me, probably because I am a scientist.... I realize that the sequence is for laughs, but there is enough humor in the show without having to irritate what may be a large group of viewers. Tom S. (Stanford Research Institute).

Aftermath

"We never thought that they [the Klingons] were going to catch on the way they did," Dorothy Fontana said. "But let's face it, in production terms, Romulans and Vulcans were expensive to do because of the ears. You can hide some of it with headdresses and things like that, but you still had the eyebrows ... whereas the Klingons really just had facial hair and slightly darkened skin and that was pretty much it. You could go with that." (64-2)

The makeup choices, as designed by Colicos and Phillips, returned for "Friday's Child," "The Trouble with Tribbles," "A Private Little War," "Elaan of Troyius," "Day of the Dove," and "The Savage Curtain." It wasn't until 1979, and *Star Trek: The Motion Picture*, that the Klingons got a dramatic makeover. The explanation for the different look, given in a future episode of *Star Trek: The Next Generation*: like the Federation and Earth itself, the Klingon Empire included many different races.

As for the prototype, John Colicos was meant to return. His character was written into the early drafts for "The Trouble with Tribbles," "A Private Little War," and "Day of the Dove," but circumstances prevented his involvement. The character of Kor was next seen in "Time Trap," an episode of *Star Trek: The Animated Series* from 1974. James Doohan provided the voice. Colicos, as Kor, did eventually return to the *Star Trek* universe -- for three episodes of *Star Trek: Deep Space 9*.

The Prime Directive, first mentioned in "The Return of the Archons," and refined here by Gene Coon, was the central contention of many episodes to come and remained part of *Star Trek* from this time forward. The Organian Peace Treaty would return, as well, as the catalyst and subject of several future stories.

Memories

John Colicos said, "It was a great episode. It was wonderful because, in those days, it was basically the United States and Russia in the Cold War projected into the future. The dialog was phenomenal and we had our points of view and what I loved at the end of the thing is that we (Captain Kirk and Kor) turned into two stupid kids bickering, and the Organians said, 'Just hold it, you are not going anywhere with this war.'" (33-2)

Episode 28: THE CITY ON THE EDGE OF FOREVER
Written by Harlan Ellison
(with Gene Coon, Gene Roddenberry, and D.C. Fontana, uncredited)
(additional story elements by Steven Carabatsos, uncredited)
Directed by Joseph Pevney

From *TV Guide* CLOSE-UP listing, April 1, 1967:

8:30 ④⑳ STAR TREK—Adventure

'The City on the Edge of Forever'

[COLOR] Tonight's science-fiction drama is set in the past.

Under the influence of drugs, Dr. McCoy plunges through a time portal and into the New York City of the 1930's. Kirk and Spock follow him, fearing that the drugged medical officer might commit an act that will alter the course of history.

While trying to find McCoy, Kirk falls in love with Edith Keeler, a charity worker helping victims of the Depression. Kirk doesn't know exactly what McCoy is about to do, but he has learned that the doctor's actions could prove fatal to Edith.

Joseph Pevney directed from a script by Harlan Ellison. Kirk: William Shatner. Spock: Leonard Nimoy. McCoy: DeForest Kelley. Scott: James Doohan. Sulu: George Takei. (60 min.)

Guest Cast
Edith Keeler .... Joan Collins
Rodent .... John Harmon
Policeman .... Hal Baylor
Galloway .... David L. Ross

Joan Collins

SOUND BITES

- *Guardian of Forever:* "Since before your sun burned hot in space and before your race was born, I have awaited a question." *Kirk:* "Are you machine or being?" *Guardian of Forever:* "I am both and neither. I am my own beginning; my own ending."

- *Edith, to Kirk and Spock:* "You know as well as I how much you're out of place here." *Spock:* "Interesting. Where would you estimate we belong, Miss Keeler?" *Edith:* "You? At his side, as if you've always been there ... and always will."

- *Kirk:* "Peace *was* the way." *Spock:* "She was right. But at the wrong time.... Save her -- do as you heart tells you to do -- and millions will die who did not die before."

- *McCoy:* "You deliberately stopped me, Jim. I could have saved her! Do you know what you just did?" *Spock:* "He knows, doctor. He knows."

- *Guardian of Forever:* "Time has resumed its shape. All is as it was before." *Kirk:* "Let's get the hell out of here."

ASSESSMENT

This is more than *Star Trek* at its best; it is *television* at its best.

One of the central challenges of producing meaningful drama in a continuing series is that the lead characters must persevere. Whatever life-and-death situations the writers dream up, the audience has the foreknowledge that the series' leads will be back next week, unruffled. The future of the show depends on it. For a writer -- or a group of writers -- to come up with a story that challenges the recurring characters of a series and forces them to change or grow in some small way without derailing the entire series is rare. And that is the best way to describe "The City on the Edge of Forever" -- profoundly rare.

Gone With the Wind ... *Casablanca* ... *Love Story* ... *Somewhere in Time* ... and "The City on the Edge of Forever." They are among the greatest love stories ever depicted on the screen.

Get out your handkerchief.

THE STORY BEHIND THE STORY

Script Timeline
Assignment given: March 16, 1966.
Harlan Ellison's story outline / treatment, ST #7: March 21, 1966.
Ellison's revised story outline, gratis: May 1, 1966.
Ellison's 2nd Revised Story Outline, gratis: May 13, 1966.
Ellison's 1st Draft teleplay: June 3, 1966.
Ellison's Revised 1st Draft teleplay (designated by him as his Final Draft):
June 13, 1966.
Ellison's 2nd Draft teleplay, gratis (designated by him as his Rev. Final Draft):
August 12, 1966.
Steven Carabatsos' 1st Draft teleplay, based on Ellison's story: October, 1966.
Ellison's 2nd Rev. Final Draft teleplay, gratis:
December 1, 1966, not received until December 19.
Gene Coon's story outline, based on Ellison's story: December 29, 1966.
Coon's rewrite ("Rewrite 1st Draft"): January 9, 1967.
D.C. Fontana's rewrite ("Rewrite 2nd Draft"): January 18, 1967.
Fontana's script polish ("Rewrite Rev. 2nd Draft"): January 23, 1967.
Coon's script polish ("Shooting Script"): January 27, 1967.
Additional page revisions by Coon: January 30, 1967.
Gene Roddenberry's rewrite (Final Draft teleplay): February 1, 1967.
Additional page revisions by Coon & Roddenberry: February 2, 3, 8 & 9, 1967.

Note the lengthy sequence of drafts, redrafts, rewrites, polishes, and additions. Therein lies the tale behind the creation of this episode.

Harlan Ellison was one of the first writers Gene Roddenberry hired for *Star Trek*. Robert Justman said, "Gene was looking to find well-respected and highly-talented science-fiction writers. One of the most prestigious names on his list was Harlan Ellison." (94-4)

Ellison was 32 and, one year before this, had won the Writers Guild Award for "Demon with the Glass Hand," a 1964 episode of *The Outer Limits*. He also wrote scripts for *Route 66*, *Burke's Law*, *Alfred Hitchcock Presents*, and *The Man from U.N.C.L.E.* Another one of his pre-*Star Trek* jobs, *Voyage to the Bottom of the Sea*, resulted in Ellison using Cordwainer Bird for his screen credit. He said, "When I was just starting out, there was a science fiction writer named Cordwainer Smith. His real name was Paul Linebarger. He worked for the CIA, as did his wife, and he couldn't write fiction under his name, so he invented the name Cordwainer Smith. And he became a real icon in his field; he was a writer above the range of most writers. So when it came my turn to come up with a pseudonym, I wanted to pay homage to Cordwainer Smith, but I also wanted to give the bird to the person who had rewritten me – 'Here's the finger in your face!' So it's sort of a love/hate pseudonym. I've used it with some regularity. I used it on *Voyage to the Bottom of the Sea*. And I used it on *The Flying Nun*." (58)

Harlan Ellison, hard at work. "Let's face it, writing is an excruciating process." – Robert Justman

Recalling his inspiration for "The City on the Edge of Forever," Ellison said, "I had been reading a biography of the great evangelist Aimee Semple McPherson and I began toying with the idea of what would happen if Kirk fell in love with a woman like that… wouldn't it be interesting if they went back in time, and the woman who was so pure and good and decent, who Kirk is desperately in love with, had to die [in order] for time to be put right. And, if he was truly in love with her, how heart-wrenching that would be." (58-3)

Ellison pitched his idea to Roddenberry in March 1966. Contrary to the recollections of some, the treatment arrived quickly -- in less than a week.

Robert Justman said, "I can still remember reading it and thinking to myself, 'This is brilliant.'" (94-4)

The story *was* brilliant, but it was also very different than the episode it inspired. In this early version, it is not McCoy, in a drug induced state of madness, who flees to the dead world where the "time vortex" serves as a passageway to the past, but a depraved crewmember named Beckwith -- a drug dealer and murderer. The story, in fact, begins with Beckwith supplying a powerful narcotic -- the Jewels of Sound -- to a fellow crew member named LeBeque. The latter, the addict, wears "a look of almost orgasmic pleasure" after swallowing the pill and experiencing "the incredible music of the Jewels -- sounds from another time, another space, sounds that reach into LeBeque's head and strum the synapses of his brain, as lights collide and merge and swivel and twirl and dance in patterns of no-pattern... a man in the grip of an alien narcotic."

Ellison said, "I was one of the first writers that Roddenberry hired. It was so early in the history of *Star Trek* that Roddenberry really didn't know where he was going. The potential for me was wide open, so I was able to go and do what I wanted, and I was able to write the way I always write, which is from my own well of polluted instincts. I figured on a ship that size, with that many people thrown together, it would be like any military unit -- there would have to be some people who were just lawless." (58)

After LeBeque threatens to go to Kirk to turn Beckwith in, the drug dealer bludgeons the embittered addict to death. But there are witnesses to the crime. A court martial is conducted, Beckwith is found guilty and Kirk sentences him to be taken to the nearest uninhabited planet to be executed by firing squad. That planet, circling a dying sun, is the dead world of the time vortex.

Kirk and Spock, with a firing squad of 12, beam down with Beckwith. All wear "insulation suits" and "breatherpaks." Before they can carry out their task, their instruments register radiation coming from over the horizon. With Beckwith in tow, they follow the reading and soon find themselves on a mountaintop near a great city which appears to be uninhabited -- a city on the edge of forever. It is here they encounter "a group of men ... but such men as explorers from Earth have never known." Ellison described the nine-foot-tall men as, "Old as the chill and dying sun that casts only shadows on this empty planet."

These are the Guardians of Forever. They have been here, they say, "since before your sun burned hot in space, before your race came into being." They stand guard over "the time machine created by the Ancients."

Kirk is intrigued and asks to see an example of the history the gateway can reveal. He picks Earth as the subject and is shown scenes from his own world's past, up until the time of the great depression in the United States, circa 1930. At this point, Beckwith leaps through the vortex. In a blink, all has changed. Kirk is informed by the Guardians that history has been altered. He and the landing party immediately beam back to the ship to find out if their lives, and their Enterprise, have also been changed. They discover the starship is now a renegade vessel -- a pirate ship, in a sense -- manned by cutthroats. Kirk and his men are able to take control of the transporter room and lock the marauders out. He orders his men to stay and hold the transporter room while he and Spock beam back to the planet. Once there, the Guardians agree to send Kirk and Spock back to the time period to which Beckwith "invaded." The two men are told they will be seeking a young woman, "Edith Koestler" [the name used in this draft] who was to be run down by a moving van. Beckwith has somehow prevented Koestler from dying. In order to right time, they must stop him from doing this.

Therefore, in Ellison's story, Kirk falls in love with a woman he already knows must die. And he does this in a very short time span, since we do not meet Edith until just past the halfway point in the story. Also, it is not Kirk who makes the great personal sacrifice of allowing Edith to be run down by the truck; the Captain cannot bring himself to stop Beckwith from saving her. Spock must do it.

A heartbroken Kirk returns from the past with Spock and Beckwith. The latter is punished by the Guardians and sent back into the vortex to materialize "in the heart of a sun" and to experience his own death over and over throughout eternity.

Later, on the Enterprise, a saddened Kirk receives a visit from Spock, who tells his captain, "No woman was ever loved as much, Jim. Because no woman was ever offered the universe for love."

Even with such profound differences between this story and the one filmed, this "City on the Edge of Forever" was a startling and highly dramatic tale. But it was also clearly the blueprint to an expensive production. And there were things that were happening within the story -- things Kirk was doing -- that didn't fit the mold Roddenberry wanted for his series' lead. Ellison was asked to revise his story outline ... for free.

"The writing of the [revised] outline seemed to take a long time," Dorothy Fontana recalled. "Other stories came in. Then scripts. Weeks went by. No Ellison." (64-7)

It took five weeks, in fact, for Ellison to deliver his revised outline, and then another two to revise it again, the latter dated May 13. Of this, Fontana said, "It was delivered with glad cries of enthusiasm from Gene Roddenberry, Desilu, and NBC." (64-7)

The court martial was out. Instead, after killing LeBeque, Beckwith beams himself down to the planet. Kirk and Spock, with Yeoman Rand and a security detail, follow. At Roddenberry's request, to save money, Ellison removed any reference to environmental suits and breatherpaks. Another substantial change deals with the information given to Kirk and Spock by the Guardians. The giant, aged aliens do not name Edith in this version. They do not talk about specifics. Instead, they speak in generalities and parables.

In this version, Spock spots Edith (her last name now being Keeler) in the beginning of Act III where she leads a street corner revival. She speaks to the crowd of "disgruntled derelicts" about the "brotherhood of man; about the need to trust; the need to love." From here, the story progresses in much the same way as the previous drafts.

After reading the revised outline, Justman wrote to John D.F. Black:

> Don't ever tell Harlan ... but this outline is beautifully written. The fact that it may become rather difficult to achieve the effects that he has written into the story is another matter.... The time vortex is described as a shimmering pillar of light set between the grey-silver rocks. It would be nice if we could find a cheaper time vortex.... On page 10, the Earthmen reel back in astonishment as the behemoth bulk of a giant wooly mammoth bursts out of the foliage within the time vortex device. At the same moment, Bob Justman reels back in agony, as he does not believe that there is any color stock film available on mastodons bursting out of foliage. Or even giant wooly mammoths.... Plenty sets, plenty speaking parts, plenty extras, plenty locations, plenty shooting time, plenty money, plenty night-for-night shooting, plenty screams from management accompanied by dire threats and reflections upon our immediate ancestry. (RJ28-1)

It was now late May. The first episode to film, "The Corbomite Maneuver," was going before the cameras and, despite the frightful costs projections, Justman recalled how Roddenberry immediately put Ellison on assignment to go to script so that no more time would be lost. Roddenberry had done this before with Theodore Sturgeon ("Shore Leave") and Robert Bloch ("What Are Little Girls Made Of?").

The Writers Guild, at this time, allowed a freelance writer two weeks to deliver a First Draft teleplay. Producers almost always pushed to get the script sooner. Ellison took three weeks to deliver, not as long as some remembered but, nonetheless, late. Justman recalled, "We're in full production and rapidly running out of usable scripts and we still hadn't seen anything from Ellison. Because I'd worked with him in the past on *The Outer Limits*, I knew that he was a real procrastinator when it came to actually writing his scripts. He had trouble getting started because, let's face it… writing is an excruciating process." (94-4)

Mary Black said, "Harlan wasn't just a procrastinator; he was somebody who always had something more interesting to do." (17a),

"Harlan always had 40 things going," said John D.F. Black. "He was doing a book and he had this short story he had to get in, or whatever. At one point, Harlan was supposed to deliver, was supposed to deliver, was supposed to deliver ... and he was ill or he was this or he was that.... *The story just wasn't finished.*" (17-4)

Fontana remembered, "Harlan was going through an emotionally-intense and difficult period -- the breakup of one of the shortest marriages on record. On the other hand, we needed a script. Desperate measures were called for. Roddenberry set aside a desk in the assistant directors' room and asked Harlan to come in and work on the script in the studio. *Every day.*" (64-7)

John D.F. Black said, "Dear little Harlan. I like him. Even when we were going through all of that. He always wanted to be on the set. Always. First he wanted an office on the lot. So we got him one -- a little bitty office at the end of the hall, and he had it all to himself. Then he installed his portable record player so he could listen to his jazz records as he was writing -- or supposedly writing." (17a)

Ellison said, "They had me in my little office back in the wardrobe room on the first floor of the old building. It was like a closet. So I'd go to the set all the time and I got to be good close friends with Leonard Nimoy and Grace Lee Whitney." (58)

Black remembered, "Harlan would be in there with this rock and roll playing very loud, with the casting people trying to have readings and saying, 'Turn it down, Harlan!' I couldn't hear people in my office on the telephone and I'd tell him to 'Turn it down!' At one point, I guess the second or third day that he was there, I walked down the hall, because the [Rolling] Stones were playing -- *loud*. I knocked on the door and there wasn't any answer. I opened the door and Harlan wasn't there!" (17-4)

Nimoy, Ellison and Shatner take a break while filming "Mudd's Women" on Stage 10 (Courtesy of Harlan Ellison)

Black found Ellison on the set, having his picture taken. It was snapped during the filming of "Mudd's Women," with Ellison sandwiched between a grinning Kirk and Spock. Black recalled, "I said, 'Harlan, you're supposed to be writing. What are you doing here?' He said, 'I came over here for lunch with the company.' 'Harlan, it's 3:30 in the afternoon. The company has lunch at 2.' 'Well, I wanted to see what they were doing.' I said, 'Harlan, please go back to the office and finish the story.' So Harlan walked back with me, went into his office and the record goes on again.... When I went down to see how he was doing, the record was playing and Harlan wasn't there. He had gone out the window. Bobby Justman was of the mind that we should nail the door and the window shut." (17-4)

Again, in Ellison's defense, the total time period which all remembered as being both long and tortured was, in fact, only three weeks.

Fontana said, "Harlan did spend some time visiting the set, but that's considered necessary research for a writer. When a show hasn't been on the air yet, freelance writers must have an opportunity to study the actor's speech patterns and delivery, the little gestures and nuances each one brings to his or her role, and -- most of all -- the character relationships which are being built episode by episode." (64-7)

Mary Black added, "Okay. Fair enough. He was researching. But he really just liked to be in the middle of it; which is why he would always be on the set. When we had our long evenings catching-up, writing stuff, Harlan would show up. Sometimes he'd show up before Bob Justman left, and he would bump heads with Bob about whatever. Other times we'd go in there after Bob had left for the night. Bob's office had a bathroom, and a couch -- it was more comfortable than John's office. So the three of us would end up in there and Harlan would set up surprises for Bob Justman on his recording machine. I remember he opened the door to the john and had the microphone down into the depths of the toilet and repeatedly flushed it for Bob to hear when he came in the following morning. Harlan was always playing. He was constantly looking to have a good time. He was almost dodging the work. Bob would come in from lunch and find Harlan asleep on the couch in his office. He was a person who didn't have any boundaries." (17a)

Justman vividly recalled the day he came to work and, instead of flushing sounds on his tape machine, he found a finished First Draft teleplay. It was on June 7 (script dated June 3). He remembered thinking, "'I've got a script!' I'm smiling and I go to my office to give it a quick read. I stop smiling. Harlan's script is brilliantly written, but completely unusable. At first glance, I can tell it's going to be hugely expensive, and at the same time, his Enterprise characters are speaking incorrectly and, more importantly, behaving incorrectly." (94-4)

Case in point: When Kirk and Spock first arrive in New York City, 1930, they see "penniless men" listening to an "Orator" who is inciting them to riot. The Orator howls, "What kind of country is this, where men have to stand in bread lines just to fill their bellies? I'll tell you what kind -- a country run by the foreigners! All the scum we let in to take the food from our mouths, all the alien filth that pollutes our fine country." Hearing this, Spock says to Kirk, "Is this the heritage Earthmen brag about? This sickness?" Later, after Kirk and Spock flee an angry mob incited by the Orator, and take refuge in the basement of a building, Spock says, "Barbarian world!... As violent as any aboriginal world we ever landed on. My race never had this. We went to space in peace. Earthmen came with all of this behind them." Kirk fires back, "And that's why you hit space two hundred years after us!" Spock counters, "Try to tell me Earthmen uplifted my race. Tell me that, and use Beckwith as an example of nobility." An angry Kirk retorts, "I should have left you for the mob!"

The conflict was present, but the "voice" of *Star Trek* was not. Despite knowing there would have to be a sizable dialogue rewrite, Justman told John D.F. Black:

> Without a doubt, this is the best and most beautifully written screenplay we have gotten to date, and possibly we'll ever get this season. If you tell this to Harlan, I'll kill you. (RJ28-2)

But there was much bad news in Justman's memo. He warned:

> We cannot afford to make this show as it presently stands.... What we have to do is find a way to retain all the basic qualities contained within this screenplay and then make it economically feasible for us to photograph it. This is an eight-day show to my way of thinking. I would like to try for seven. (RJ28-2)

Ellison revised his script, begrudgingly. He later said, "You must understand that working in television can be a singularly crippling and brutalizing thing for the creative spirit, particularly if a writer perceives himself as something more than merely a hack or a creative typist who is helping to fill network airtime in order to sell new cars and deodorants. So a writer who cares about his work puts in small touches, special scenes, lines of enriching dialogue, that give him his reason for writing it. Almost all of those touches were excised in the name of straight action sequences. Their loss diminished the value of the script enormously. At least for me." (58-6).

Ellison was working faster now, taking only a week to submit his next draft. But he was not making all the changes the producers were asking for. A bemused John D.F. Black said, "Harlan didn't know anything about the production side. He knew half of what I knew, and *I* didn't know *anything*." (17-4)

Justman, writing a memo to Black, said:

> Cordwainer [Harlan] has made the oft-repeated statement that this show will cost 98 cents to shoot. Please keep him out of my office. I know that he will try to convince me that this show will cost 98 cents to shoot. I have been down this road before with Cordwainer. He did a segment of *The Outer Limits* entitled "The Glass Hand" [sic] which you may be aware of. Prior to the shooting of "The Glass Hand," Cordwainer was complaining that we were emasculating his handiwork. Emasculated or not, this show went on to win a Writers Guild Award and was also one of the best *Outer Limits* that we shot in two seasons. Tell Cordwainer that if he insists upon arguing budget with me, in the future I shall have to restrict him from my couch.... I will have him taken away by the "Civil People." (RJ28-2)

Mary Black said, "Bob and Harlan had a kind of running battle, because Harlan would write things that were absolutely beyond belief in terms of budget. And Harlan would always explain about how it would, of course, be possible for Bob to achieve it, and sometimes Harlan would show up before Bob went home and they would have a kind of mock battle. I remember Harlan standing on Bob's desk yelling at him. Not surprisingly, in the area of budget." (17a)

On August 15, after two months of what Justman remembered as "much telephonic prodding," Ellison turned in a second revised script -- the official 2nd Draft, dated August 12. Ellison typed "Revised *Final* Draft" on the cover page.

Justman immediately wrote a memo to Gene Coon, who was beginning his first week as producer, telling the new show-runner:

> As you may know, this property was first assigned March 16, 1966. We received this draft yesterday and today is August 16, 1966. Simple arithmetic gives us the information that it has been five months since the property was first assigned. As it presently stands, this latest draft is no more inexpensive to shoot, in my opinion, than the previous version. (RJ28-3)

There were other concerns. Justman's memo warned:

> Although Harlan's writing is beautiful, it is not *Star Trek* that he has written. It is a lovely story for an anthology television series or a feature.... I have been as frank as I possibly can be with regard to my comments on this version of the screenplay. I have not intended to be brutal in any way. It has been my experience in the past that somehow Cordwainer has gotten hold of my memos prior to my discussing them with him.... I would greatly appreciate it if Cordwainer could no longer obtain any of my memos with regard to his work in the future. (RJ28-3)

Roddenberry later said, "I think Harlan's a genius but he's not exactly the most disciplined writer in the world. He had my Scotty [sic] dealing in interplanetary drugs and things like that!" (145-1)

Ellison, still burning in the mid-1990s over this statement, fumed: "I gotcha Scotty right here, Gene. Anybody who ever read that script knows there's no Scotty selling drugs. Or any of the other horse puckey that has been spread for more than twenty-five years." (58-2)

The crew member dealing drugs was Beckwith, not Scotty. And Beckwith was a non-regular. Regardless, and even though no one had asked him at the time to take it out, it was Ellison's idea to make a member of the crew -- of *Gene Roddenberry's crew* -- a pusher.

Roddenberry complained, "Also, he wrote it so that it would have cost $200,000 more than I had to spend. He just wrote huge crowd scenes and all sorts of things. I tried to get him to change it and he wouldn't." (145-1)

Justman, on the side of management, said, "Gene tried to reason with Harlan. So did I, but we both struck out." (94-4)

According to William Shatner, he was sent to Ellison's home on Roddenberry's behalf to see if the famed writer was cooperating and making the changes that had been requested.

"I failed miserably," Shatner admitted. "I can remember getting inside the house and being yelled at throughout my visit. Harlan was very irate and within a rather short period of time he'd thrown me off his property, insane with anger at Justman, Roddenberry, and Coon. I was just the messenger, but he was out to kill me, too." (156-8)

Ellison said, "It all boiled down to Shatner not liking that Leonard had more and better lines than he did. He would count lines of dialogue, literally. He sat on the sofa in my living room and did that. And he would always give you some hyperbolic rationalization why Leonard should not have three lines on a page where he [Shatner] only had one. And it never made any sense at all, but you got the sense after a very short time that either you made the changes or he would go back and rat you out, which is what he did with Roddenberry. He went to Roddenberry and said, 'Well, it's an uneven script and I'm not getting my due and you'd better get in there and do some rewriting.' And Roddenberry chose Shatner over Nimoy, always. He didn't know where the gold laid in that show." (58)

At this point, Steve Carabatsos replaced John D.F. Black as Story Editor. Now it was his job to follow Gene Coon's instructions and fix the script.

Dorothy Fontana said, "The original script was a hell of a script. If it had been just an episode of *The Outer Limits*, it would have been fine. But it's not the best *Star Trek* script, because it doesn't involve the characters as deeply as they should be involved in an episode. The love story was there, but you didn't get to meet Edith Keeler until the third act. You might have seen her, but she never got to meet Kirk until Act Three. And that's too late. And the person who goes through to distort the time line was a crewman who was addicted to a narcotic, 'the Jewels of Sound.' You've never seen him before. You see him in the teaser and then he's gone. And then you pick him up later in the story, and they have to get him." (64-1)

In the Carabatsos version, the drug-dealing and drug using crew members were eliminated and, instead, McCoy became the catalyst who brings Kirk and party to the planet's surface for their encounter with the Guardian of Forever. As seen in the filmed episode, Sulu is injured on the bridge and McCoy is called to treat him. The ship shudders, and McCoy falls, hitting his head and being knocked unconscious. In sickbay, he is given an injection of adrenalin and suffers from "adrenalin poisoning." And this is why, in a maddened state, he beams himself to the planet.

In 1996, Ellison complained, "Carabatsos took a chain-saw to [my script] and screwed it up so badly that Gene [Roddenberry] asked me to come back and do yet *another* rewrite, for no money, of course." (58-2)

Ellison's "2nd Revised Final Draft" as he categorized it, dated December 1, arrived on December 19.

In a memo he sent to Roddenberry, one day after the arrival of the new version of the old script, Robert Justman said:

> I have just completed reading the "Second Revised Final Draft" of Harlan Ellison's script, which he has dated December 1, 1966, even though it was

delivered a hell of a lot later than that. I hear tell that there's a possibility that you, Mr. Roddenberry, will rewrite this draft to make it feasible for us to be able to photograph the story for this season's television viewers. (RJ28-4)

Among the notes:

- Would it be possible for McCoy to get infected in some other way [than a bite from an alien dog]? I am reminded of what we went through on a show entitled "THE MAN TRAP" [sic; it was "The Enemy Within"] in attempting to disguise a dog and make it look like a creature from some alien world. We ended up with a dog wearing a suit and a phony set of horns.
- Why establish that everybody is growing younger and that our chronometers are running backward? Does this fact improve the essential quality of Harlan's story? I submit to you that we have had the backward running chronometer bit several times during this season already. We had it in shows such as "THE NAKED TIME" and "TOMORROW IS YESTERDAY."
- On Page 3, Kirk has some words about a "parking orbit." Please explain.
- Again on Page 3, we have our ship rocking and bucking and everybody being thrown all over the place. This, as you no doubt know, is also a very familiar STAR TREK-type effect.
- The "red or crimson glow" effect is rather puzzling to me. How do we show this to the few people in America who don't have color sets? Why do we need this red or crimson glow?
- While I think of it, I am able to detect an approximate 58 pages to this version.... I do notice that there is still an extreme amount of description and direction to the Director and other people who are, or would be, involved in this project. This might have a tendency to reflect an even shorter page count than would at first be indicated here. Since the writer has also indicated how the film should be covered by the Director, insofar as the shots go, you might find an even greater disparity between the actual amount of pages and what is projected here. I am hinting that this is a 45-minute show [five minutes too short]. I will also hint, as I continue, that this show will still take about eight or nine days to shoot. I don't believe that much money has been saved in this version as compared with the previous versions. One does not write direction in a script about "a very small crowd of seven or eight people" and then give scene descriptions indicating a need for about 200 or 300 people.
- Why don't they just transport down to the area of the plateau [where the Guardians of forever are] immediately? Why do they have to transport down to an area on the planet that forces them to travel on foot for many miles? No wonder our Captain and Crew keep on getting into trouble all the time. They don't have enough sense to save shoe leather.
- How come they suddenly spot a City on the Edge of Forever? Why wasn't it spotted from the ship?
- Page 12A caused me to become exceedingly cruel to my wife and children the other night. And it is only one-eighth of a page!
- Scene 45 hurts me no end.
- I don't believe Scenes 46 through 55 at all [where a crowd turns on Kirk and Spock and chase them]. I hardly ever believed them in earlier versions and I am sorry to state that I have not changed my mind. Incidentally, this sequence is one of the instances wherein the writer

- has attempted to kid us by listing 7 or 8 extras and giving them business that should be handled by 200 or 300 people. I also don't believe the crowd turning on our people. The sequence is dramatic -- but unbelievable.
- Why don't you look at the beginning of Scene 62 and all the description contained therein and estimate to yourself how many extras you would have to hire to take care of the business indicated in the scene? Figure out how many people you would have to hire and how many people you would have to wardrobe... and how many cars... and how many special business [with] higher pay rate for extras who are given specific action to perform... and how many musicians and uniforms and car drivers and period [antique] cars and period trucks and set dressing in various windows... and lunches and suppers... and overtime and night penalty -- ten to twenty percent premium on hourly rates... and golden time -- 2 ½ times the hourly rate after twelve hours of "studio" work or fourteen hours of "nearby location" work... and so on and on and on... and you would find your pocketbook and your brains absolutely boggled by the enormity of it all.
- Gene, I have written many, many long memos to you on the subject of this story. As always, I feel that this is a fine story and was created by an extremely-talented writer. But we are in the sad position of being unfortunate enough not to be able to afford to make this story, even though it is of high-quality. I feel that we have gone as far as we can with Cordwainer and it must now devolve upon either you or Gene Coon to take this story in hand and make it shootable for us. If you don't, I fear that we must junk it. It would be immensely cheaper for us to throw away a complete screenplay of this sort than to attempt to film it. A very dear friend of mine used to have an expression which he used in times of stress and monetary troubles – "Your first loss is your best loss." Take your licking now and get out. It's cheaper in the long run. (RJ28-4)

It wasn't all negative. Justman made a creative suggestion for a change that would stick, and benefit the story. He told Roddenberry:

On Page 43, we have the staircase fall sequence. I feel that the author has missed an extremely dramatic opportunity here. Firstly, it would be damned difficult to stage this and have the sequence work correctly. By the time Kirk could make up his mind not to catch her, she could have fallen downstairs several times. What I would have done would have been to have him automatically, in reflex action, rescue her before she falls down all the way. Then, later, comes the extremely dramatic realization that he is probably going to be unable to prevent himself from interfering in any untoward fate which might befall the object of his affection. The verbalization of his feelings and his inability to keep his mitts off the girl could be brought out in the end of Scene 80 on Page 47 in his discussion with Mr. Spock. (RJ28-4)

The script clearly still needed a major overhaul. But Roddenberry had already suffered the slings and arrows of famed science fiction writers he'd rewritten on *Star Trek*. He was in no hurry to repeat the experience. So, Gene Coon ran the script through his typewriter over the Christmas and New Year's holidays, delivering it on January 9, 1967. Among the changes, he eliminated the subplot that takes place aboard the ship where, after the timeline has been disturbed, the Enterprise becomes a renegade ship. And then he found a few areas to add humor.

"The little touches of humor tend more to be Coon's than anyone else's," Fontana said, then added, with a laugh, "And Gene Coon's immortal line about Spock getting his head caught in a rice picker." (64-1)

Ellison is said to have hated it.

One day after delivery, Justman wrote Coon:

> This is pretty close to a shooting script... *finally*. There are certain areas within it, however, which I feel need some work before we can say that we can come anywhere close to budget on the show.... Just so that there is no misunderstanding, I want us to do this show. However... there is no doubt of it, and we should not kid ourselves, that we are going to get even close to a Series Budget on this particular segment. (RJ28-5)

Dorothy Fontana's turn came next. She was, after all, the brand new story editor.

"I reported to work the first day and walked right into a hornet's nest of trouble with 'The City on the Edge of Forever' at the heart of it," she said. "Gene Roddenberry and Gene Coon turned to me and said, 'You're it. You try a rewrite.' Talk about being tossed a live grenade!" (64-7)

Among the changes, Fontana invented cordrazine, the drug that puts McCoy into a temporary state of madness.

Ellison was not impressed. He preferred his own idea, from his rewrite of Steven Carabatsos' rewrite, using the venom of an animal bite to cause the madness, and argued, "Read my revised second draft, in which I gave Gene a *reasonable* way in which Dr. McCoy could have run amuck.... But no, Gene [Roddenberry] preferred having an accomplished ship's surgeon act in such a boneheaded manner that he injects himself with a deadly drug! Yeah, sure, you were a sensational plotter and writer, Gene, and you can schvitz roses with Lysol to make 'em grow!" (58-2)

Fontana wasn't about to tell Ellison that the cordrazine idea came from her. Years later, regarding another of her contributions, she said, "I tried to build the relationship of love between Edith and Kirk, gently and meaningfully, so her death would be the most-wrenching personal moment Kirk would ever know.... Harlan liked this draft a little better, but not much.... He thought Gene Coon wrote it. We kept our mouths shut." (64-2)

Of Fontana's rewrite, Justman wrote his colleagues:

> Although this latest version of Harlan's story comes closer to being producible than anything we have received to date, I would like to state that I feel there is hardly anything left of the beauty and mystery that was inherent in the screenplay as Harlan originally wrote it. It is very good *Star Trek* material now, but it certainly bears only structural resemblance at times to what Harlan originally delivered to us. It has none of his special magic any longer. Perhaps that is all for the best, but I for one, feel bad about it. I'm sure you'll be able to convince me that all of the things I liked best about Harlan's writing were unsuitable for good dramatic television entertainment.... But I still feel bad. I can't help it.... In closing, I would like to say that had this version of the script been turned in by some [other] writer, I am sure that we would all have been thrilled with it. My problem is that I read Harlan's original version and his various so-called re-workings of that version. (RJ28-6)

Justman warned that the script -- now Fontana's rewrite of Coon's rewrite of Carabatsos' rewrite of Ellison's story -- would still take at least seven days, and very probably eight, to film. He said:

> Sometimes I get the feeling the only way we could achieve a STAR TREK segment on budget would be to have 60 minutes of Mister Spock playing kazoo

solo as Captain Kirk holds him in his arms while standing in a telephone booth. (RJ28)

The work continued. Justman later said, "After several all-night sessions, Gene [Roddenberry] churned out his own revised final draft teleplay. His version is the one we began filming on the morning of February 3." (94-8)

Roddenberry's draft -- The "Final Draft" script, from February 1, with revised pages on February 2 and 3, retained much of the writing from Coon and Fontana. Ellison was livid. Thirty years later, he complained, "There are chunks of dialogue, [like the] speech Edith Keeler gives about how in the future everything will be wonderful because we'll have spaceships to feed the hungry people, which is precisely the kind of dopey Utopian bullshit Roddenberry loved. So I knew Gene had screwed around [with the script]. But I also knew he hadn't done the massive restructuring that was done to my story, although that expert liar told people from lecture platforms for the better part of a quarter of a century that it was *he* who rescued that brilliant script from the inept paws of the slacker Ellison ... when, in truth, Roddenberry had about as much writing ability as the lowest industry hack. A fact. Do with it what you will." (58-2)

Ellison later said, "If John D.F. Black rewrote you, you knew that either he would do a superlative job and you wouldn't have a beef about it or, if it was something that rankled you, you could talk him out of it or argue with him logically plot-wise so that you would arrive at the same place by different means. But Gene [Roddenberry], in terms of writing, was a very limited writer. He had three or four plots; they all showed up one way or another, most of which were man goes into space, man meets god, god is insane and man defeats him somehow. Or parallel planet stories. What I was doing was [famed evangelist] Aimee Semple McPherson as [Church of Scientology founder] L. Ron Hubbard, and that's who that character was. And when he altered her and made her what she was, I always thought it was just another mediocrity that he injected into my script, which Gene Coon just loved." (58)

On the day filming began, Robert Justman received a letter from Ellison's agent. It read:

> Mr. Ellison would like his credit on *Star Trek* episode "The City on the Edge of Forever," Production #6149-28, to read "Cordwainer Bird."

Ellison explained, "He threatened to get me blacklisted if I used Cordwainer Bird. I said I'm entitled, I've registered it and I've used the pseudonym before, and I don't want my name on this thing now." (58)

Regardless, Ellison's real name remained (as sole writer) when the screen credits were created during post-production. Justman explained, "After a lot of fussing and hemming and hawing and, finally, according to Harlan, an 'absolute threat' from Gene [Roddenberry] to keep him from ever working in Hollywood again, Cordwainer Bird was convinced to revert to being Harlan Ellison again, and his screen credit reflected that." (98-4)

Roddenberry did not take a screen credit for his contributions to the writing, as was the case with "The Corbomite Maneuver," "The Enemy Within," "What Are Little Girls Made Of?," and "Shore Leave." There's little doubt he would have liked credit -- *what writer wouldn't?* -- but, in his mind, the prestige these renowned science fiction authors brought to *Star Trek* was more important than the accolades he might receive as a script doctor, or even the bonus money and residuals which went along with the credit. Jerry Sohl, Richard Matheson, Robert Bloch, Theodore Sturgeon, and Harlan Ellison gave *Star Trek* that instant prestige.

Gene Coon also took no writing credit. He had already added his name to the scripts for "Space Seed" and "A Taste of Armageddon," thereby taking half the credit and half the residuals. But not here despite "City" being very-nearly a complete rewrite in regards to dialogue. Coon knew how important Harlan Ellison's name on *Star Trek* was to Roddenberry.

Roddenberry, in fact, believed he had an understanding with Ellison that neither of them, or any others on the *Star Trek* creative staff, would talk about the writing process of "The City on the Edge of Forever" to the public at large or the press, and Roddenberry later wrote to Ellison about this, when he felt that the latter had broken his word concerning their understanding. (More about this in "Release/Reaction.")

Pre-Production
January 26-27 & 30-31 & February 1 & 2, 1967 (total six days prep).

Joseph Pevney was hired to direct. He had more experience with feature films than any other *Star Trek* director and, in many ways, this episode was the closest thing to a feature film that *Star Trek* ever made. Pevney said, "Essentially, 'City on the Edge of Forever' was a motion picture. I treated it as a movie." (141-1)

Joan Collins was the most renowned guest star to appear on *Star Trek*. She was 33 and had worked in TV and films since the early 1950s. Collins was the female lead, opposite Ray Milland, in *The Girl in the Red Velvet Swing*. She was billed above Richard Egan for the lead in *Esther and the King*, above Richard Burton in *Sea Wife*, and was top girl in *Seven Thieves*, opposite Edward G. Robinson and Rod Steiger. She had also taken over for Dorothy Lamour as the girl-in-between Bob Hope and Bing Crosby in 1962's *The Road to Hong Kong*.

**Joan Collins on set
(Courtesy of Gerald Gurian)**

Joe D'Agosta said, "I think it was a bit of a surprise that Joan Collins was interested in doing a *Star Trek*. She was a very notorious actress. But, again, I think it was based on the allure of the show. There were two shows in town that everyone wanted to do -- *Mission: Impossible* and *Star Trek*. I say 'everyone,' meaning within certain limits. We couldn't get, say, John Wayne. Well, we actually *did* get John Wayne. He did a *Lucy*. But Lucy made that phone call." (43-4)

Joseph Pevney said, "Joan Collins was very good in it. She enjoyed working on that show, and Bill and Leonard were both very good to her.... Using her was a good choice." (141-2)

John Harman, who played Rodent, the milk thief who makes the mistake of also stealing McCoy's phaser, made over 200 appearances in movies and TV, from 1935 to 1983. He was 61 here, and returned to *Star Trek* for a prominent role in "A Piece of the Action."

Hal Baylor, the New York City Irish policeman, was a character actor in films and

TV with hundreds of roles under his belt. Before acting, he was a boxer, and often brought that talent into his work before the camera. Baylor returned to *Star Trek* for an appearance in "Elaan of Troyius."

It is Bart La Rue who provided the voice of the Guardian, not James Doohan, as some sources have claimed. La Rue was well liked at *Star Trek*. He returned, to be seen as well as heard, in "Bread and Circuses," and to provide more voiceovers in "The Gamesters of Triskelion," "Patterns of Force" and "The Savage Curtain."

David L. Ross, noticeable as a red-shirted security officer in "Miri," "The Return of the Archons," and "A Taste of Armageddon," is also noticeable here, playing security officer Galloway.

And John Winston, as Lt. Kyle, is present for his third appearance in the series. He gets knocked out by McCoy.

Production Diary
Filmed February 3, 6, 7, 8, 9, 10, 13 & 14 (1/2 day), 1967
(Planned as 6 day production; finishing 1½ days behind; total cost: $245,316).

Principal photography began on Friday, February 3, 1967. This was the week *The Smothers Brothers Comedy Hour* kicked-off on CBS-TV, with Ed Sullivan on hand to introduce the brothers, and guests Danny Thomas, James "Gomer Pyle" Nabors, Danny Thomas, and Jill St. John. And the Smothers won their time slot, beating NBC's top-show, *Bonanza*. A.C. Nielsen estimated that *The Smothers Brothers Comedy Hour* had 36.8% of the TV audience, compared to 24.3% for

Day 7, February 13, 1964, Bill McGovern on Stage 10
(Courtesy of Gerald Gurian)

Bonanza. The Monkees were on the cover of *TV Guide*, as well as having the top-selling record album in America (their debut disc, now in its thirteenth week at the summit). They also had the song getting the most radio action ("I'm a Believer"). Other performers had given up hope of hitting the top of the singles charts. The new song to be held off, at No. 2, was "Georgy Girl," by the New Seekers. *Dr. Zhivago* was the hottest movie ticket across the nation, having dethroned Don Knotts in *The Ghost and Mr. Chicken*. "Court Martial" had had its only NBC broadcast the night before, and *Star Trek* was now about to make its most-acclaimed episode.

Filming began at Desilu 40 Acres. This day, cast and crew assembled on the streets of Mayberry for the third time (following "Miri" and "The Return of the Archons").

Amazingly, Joseph Pevney was asked to get all the location work done in a single day, and to keep to the mandated six-day schedule. No one at *Star Trek* believed "The City on the Edge of Forever" could be shot in six days but, with a first season deficit of $74,507 on the books, and only two episodes left for Desilu to attempt to recoup (or at least reduce) this financial loss, the producers had to try ... or, at least, appear to be trying. Pevney fell behind immediately.

The work at 40 Acres was extensive. During the daylight hours, which only lasted until 5 p.m. during this time of year, the scene where Kirk and Spock arrive, literally leaping into an alleyway out of nowhere, was filmed. The two are spotted by the stunned crowds and hurry across a busy street. They enter a second alley where Kirk climbs a fire escape and steals clothing that has been hung out to dry. And then they are confronted by a policeman. Spock drops the cop with his "FSNP," then they flee, running down a second street, then into a third alleyway, then down the stairs and through a door which we will learn leads to the basement of the mission (the interior to be filmed later at the studio). More work was needed for the nighttime scenes. We see Kirk walking Edith home, having a conversation in front of Floyd's Barber Shop from *The Andy Griffith Show*, Floyd's name prominently displayed in the shop window; we see a deranged McCoy arrive in the dead of night, leaping into this world of the past and accosting a homeless man named Rodent; finally, there is the big finale, outside the mission, as Kirk and Spock are reunited with McCoy, and Edith is run down by a truck. All these scenes required numerous extras, with period costuming and period cars, all things guaranteed to complicate and slow down the business of filming.

With everyone but the studio bean-counters knowing that Pevney was not going to get it all done, that no director could, the immediate problem was when to finish ... and where? Desilu 40 Acres was bustling with activity. *Rango*, a western, needed the western street at 40 Acres, too close to the streets of Mayberry to allow both productions to film simultaneously. *Gomer Pyle* also had 40 Acres booked for its outdoor Marine Camp scenes, and *Hogan's Heroes* had a booking for the exterior of its POW camp. More of a problem in the coming week was *The Andy Griffith Show*, needing to get Mayberry back and shoot exteriors on the very streets *Star Trek* was using. Pevney and company had to wait several days before returning, well after dark.

On Day 2, Monday, production moved to Desilu Gower Stage 11, the home of *My Three Sons*. With that series on hiatus and its sets collapsed, Stage 11 was used for the interior Mission set and the back room where McCoy is bedridden and cared for by Edith.

DeForest Kelley shared, "During the filming, I became convinced that McCoy should also fall for the lovely Edith Keeler. I felt it would add to the intrigue, should McCoy as well as Kirk come under the spell of her decency, humanity, and beauty -- both inner and outer. I suggested it to Joe Pevney. I thought a good spot to indicate the attraction would be when Edith comes to McCoy's room where he's recuperating. Pevney shot it. It was never seen." (98-3)

On Day 3, Stage 10 was used for the interior Mission basement sequences, as well as the "flat" shared by Kirk and Spock.

Shooting on Day 4 was still on Stage 10, still filming scenes left unfinished from the previous day. The "Tenement Stairway" came next, where Spock witnesses Kirk saving Edith from tumbling down the stairs. With nightfall, the company moved outdoors behind Stage 10 and filmed the alleyway scenes where McCoy catches up with a fleeing Rodent, then collapses, allowing Rodent to find his phaser and accidentally disintegrate himself.

On Day 5, Stage 9 was used for all the scenes on the Enterprise bridge, including when McCoy, behaving like a madman, struggles with the Captain and other personnel.

John Stanley, a writer for *The San Francisco Examiner and Chronicle*, was visiting the set. In an article published in his paper's March 12, 1967, edition, he wrote:

> Shatner seems to be a fast-paced actor, his train of thought sharp, his speech fast-flowing. He is eager to compare his opinions of certain *Star Trek* episodes with those of others, and his interest perks up noticeably when his knowledge of science-fiction is called upon. "This is not a device of the future," began Shatner, pointing to a towel wrapped around one hand, its interiors crammed with ice cubes. "We were doing a fight sequence this morning and I think I sprained it. I'll have it x-rayed later today to find out. Isn't it marvelous the inventions man has today?"

This day was meant to be the only one spent on Stage 9, with the sequences in the ship's corridors and transporter room filmed, as well. But Pevney was unable to finish, now almost a full day behind.

Cast and crew were allowed to leave in time to make it home for the NBC premiere of "The Return of the Archons."

Day 6 began with catch-up work on Stage 9, finishing the leftover sequences from the day before, followed by a move to Stage 10 where building of the exterior planet set and the vortex had been completed.

Fontana recalled, "Harlan [in his script] had talked about this city, with 'rune' stones tumbled in the foreground, and then there was this time gate, which he really

Stage 10 – Bill McGovern slates a shot of the Guardian and the "rune stones" (Courtesy Gerald Gurian)

Shatner, Nimoy, Nichols, and Doohan step in where McGovern had stood seconds later (Unaired film trim courtesy of Gerald Gurian)

... and having a good laugh after a jump through the vortex (Courtesy of Gerald Gurian)

didn't describe very much. Matt Jefferies, who had great sensibilities, was out sick with the flu that particular week that it was to go into pre-production, and Rolland Brooks, who was the Art Department chair, took over to do that one. He had a couple martinis before dinner, before he read the script, and was confused about the description of 'rune stones.' He grabbed a dictionary and got to 'ruin' before he got to 'rune,' so there's these pieces of broken columns and things like this lying about, which had nothing to do with what the script said. And, of course, the time portal looked like this lopsided donut. And Matt Jefferies walked onto the set and said, '*What the hell is this?!*'" (64-1)

It was, nonetheless, an impressive set for a 1967 TV series.

Day 7. On Monday, work resumed on Stage 10, for the bulk of Act 1 on the planet set, with the hunt for McCoy, the encounter with the Guardian of Forever, and McCoy leaping through the time vortex.

On Day 8, Tuesday, February 14, Pevney continued working on the planet set. A cleaned-up McCoy returned from the past, along with Kirk and Spock, as the company filmed the last scene of the episode.

Pevney recalled, "Using 'hell' in the last line was something of a problem. Kirk said, 'Let's get the hell out of here,' and there were objections from the Network. Roddenberry had a meeting with them and said, 'There is no other word which conveys the emotion of the moment.' Of course, Bill [Shatner] fought for it, too. We all wanted it because it sounded so great. Finally, NBC said, 'What the *hell*, leave it in.'" (141-1)

Pevney turned the company over to director Herschel Daugherty at midday, for a move back to Stage 9 and the start of filming for "Operation: Annihilate!" Stage 10, not needed in this final episode of season one, went dark.

Post-Production
Available for editing: February 15, 1967. Music score: March 24, 1967.

James Ballas and Edit Team #1 did the superb editing. The montage of historical events, as seen through the time portal, was mostly made up of clips from the Paramount film library. The shot of the Brooklyn Bridge was stock footage.

The score for this episode was almost all tracked music. One exception is the song heard playing when Kirk strolls along a New York City street with Edith. "Good Night, Sweetheart" was first released in 1931, one year after this event supposedly takes place. It became a No. 1 hit in America for Guy Lombardo.

Film Effects of Hollywood provided the opticals and animation, including transporter effects, Rodent's disintegration, the impressive matte shots involving the time portal, and the equally impressive sequence when Kirk and Spock, and later McCoy, leap out of a brick wall in to 1930 New York City. Double-exposure techniques – a great challenge and expense in 1966 - were state-of-the-art for their time. Robert Justman, fretting over the costs, had written to Gene Roddenberry about it on December 20, 1966, forewarning:

> I am a bit at a loss to know what to do with the "time vortex." Certainly, if we intend to remain with the time vortex and the Optical Effects of various pieces of film MATTED into it, we must stage our sequences in such a way that we are not featuring the time vortex, except when we absolutely have to. Otherwise, we would be into the most complicated and expensive sequences we have ever attempted, believe it or not. STOCK FILM in color costs $10.00 per foot in ten-foot minimum cuts. Add to the cost of the STOCK FILM the cost of creating this composite effect, and the mind becomes boggled with the grandeur of it all.

(RJ28-4)

The solution: buy Black & White stock film footage.

Composer Fred Steiner provided a partial score for this episode. This was the sixth episode assigned to him.

Taking seven-and-a-half days to film, the $245,316 spent to produce "City" made it the most-costly episode of the original series, a staggering $60,316 over the per-episode allowance. This equates to $1.7 million in 2013, with overage of $420,000. The first season deficit nearly doubled, reaching $134,823.

Release / Reaction
Premiere air date: 4/6/67. NBC repeat broadcast: 8/31/67.

NBC publicity photo courtesy of Gerald Gurian

Joseph Pevney said, "Roddenberry was very happy with the end results of that.... He wrote me a letter which I'm very proud of -- I still have it -- congratulating me on my work and the extra special contributions he said I made to *Star Trek*." (141-2)

Joan Crosby reviewed "The City on the Edge of Forever" on April 5, 1967 for her syndicated column, *TV Scout*. Among the newspapers to carry the review was the *Edwardsville Intelligencer*, in Edwardsville, Illinois. Crosby wrote:

Star Trek takes a leaf from the *Time Tunnel*'s book and comes up with an interesting piece of science fiction. It also gives the show a new look as William Shatner and Leonard Nimoy spend most of their time tonight on Earth, circa 1930. They are there because Deforest Kelley went berserk from an accidental overdose of a powerful drug and then stepped through a time vortex, where he landed in the past and where he may change history's course and not for the better. This leads to an agonizing decision for Captain Kirk involving social worker Joan Collins, whom he has learned to love.

Steven H. Scheuer reviewed the episode the following day for his column, *TV Key Preview*. Among his newsprint carriers, the Toledo Blade, in Toledo, Ohio. Scheuer wrote:

Fans of this space-age series will get a surprise variation of *The Time Tunnel* theme tonight. The USS Enterprise gets all shaken up, its cool medico accidentally goes berserk, and ages of the past go hurtling by as Kirk and Spock brave a risky adventure by plunging into the 1930s. It's an absorbing tale, but it's a bit hard to take at times.

Time would prove this time-travel story to be a classic, but, in 1967, with sci-fi characters jumping from one period to another on *The Time Tunnel*, the appeal didn't seem as great ... at least, according to A.C. Nielsen.

RATINGS / Nielsen National report: Thursday, April 6, 1967:

8:30 - 9 p.m., 62.3% of U.S. TVs in use.	Share:	Households:
NBC: *Star Trek* (first half)	No data	11,640,000
ABC: *Bewitched*	**No data**	**15,040,000**
CBS: *My Three Sons*	No data	10,650,000

9 - 9:30 p.m., 61.6% of U.S. TVs in use.	Audience Share:	
NBC: *Star Trek* (second half)	28.4%	No further data
ABC: *Love on a Rooftop*	**32.1%**	**No further data**
CBS: *Thursday Night Movie* (start)	25.5%	No further data
Local independent stations:	14.0%	No further data

ABC stayed on top this night, with NBC and *Star Trek* in second position. The underperforming movie on CBS: *Branded*, a western starring Richard Widmark.

***

On June 20, 1967, Roddenberry sent a letter to Harlan Ellison. In part, it read:

Although we have a disagreement over that re-write, every evidence is that the show was highly-successful both from the mass audience aspect necessary to maintaining a show on the air, and from the critical audience as well... Never outside this office and particularly nowhere in sf or television circles have I ever mentioned that the script was anything but entirely yours. I have heard from a number of sources that you have been less than faithful to your side of this arrangement. I am told you do not hesitate to accept full praise and responsibility for the show, [and] go out of your way to say or suggest that I treated you badly, was dishonest in my dealings with you, and showed a lack of efficiency in my tasks which only your superior writing overcame. I further understand that you have stated you intend to say or intimate something of the same at Westercon 20 and possibly at the World Science-Fiction Convention in New York. While you are entitled to any honest opinions of me personally or professionally, you must understand that I will not permit any lies or misinformation to be circulated. At the risk of turning our currently honest disagreement into something more serious, I will fight such a thing with every weapon at my disposal. I never like to hurt a man, but no man should feel he can back me into a corner where my reputation, and therefore my livelihood and [that of] my family, is imperiled. (GR28-7)

Ellison and Roddenberry continued to fight one another with "every weapon at [their] disposal." Over the coming years, Roddenberry, feeling Ellison had broken the agreement to not speak in detail about the writing of the script, stepped forward and took credit for the version of the script that won a Hugo Award in 1968.

When interviewed by this author, Ellison said, "Roddenberry gave me very little choice. Every time he got in public, someone would ask him something and he would make up a lie. Or he would retell an older lie and then embellish it. I threatened him once that I would bust his nose so hard his great grandmother would bleed. He was not in awe of me by any means, at five foot five and he having the brawn of a dock-walloper. But he knew that I wasn't afraid of him and I wasn't afraid of anything that he could do. He knew he couldn't buy me and he couldn't scare me. Gene never missed an opportunity to retell the lies and engorge them, so that I'd look like a monster. I would go to a convention and draw in five to ten thousand people, and the fans, of course, not knowing any better and he being the Great Bird of the Galaxy, made it so I'd have to answer the same stupid questions about whether Gene Roddenberry saved my ass and on and on and on." (58)

Roddenberry, one year before his death, said, "He [Ellison] turned in an episode which was a brilliant piece of work -- if there had been no *Star Trek* pattern to follow. But, by the time of this episode, we had laid down who our people were, who Scotty was, and who the Doc was, and so on. Harlan treated it as though I had assigned him to do just a science-fiction episode. And I told him that wasn't satisfactory. So he futzed-around with a rewrite. But he just never solved the basic problem of why are we doing this series. Who is Kirk? Who is Spock? And so I rewrote it. Completely." (145-2)

"Harlan never forgave us for rewriting him," said Robert Justman, "and, out of spite, he submitted his original script to the Writers Guild, and he ended-up winning an award for this script that's never been produced." (94-4)

Star Trek had made a submission for the WGA award, as well -- the script for "The Return of the Archons."

Justman recalled, "Coon, Roddenberry, and I were all in attendance at the awards dinner, and as Ellison walked away from the podium with his award in one hand and his script in the other, he shook them at us, smirking, as if to say, 'There, that'll show you.' I looked at Gene, he looked at me and shrugged and said, 'Well, that's show biz.' So we just laughed it off. I mean, if the [script] hadn't been rewritten, the episode would never have been produced." (94-4)

Herb Solow was also present at the ceremony. He remembered Ellison's acceptance speech well. "Failing to mention *Star Trek* or even recognizing the two Genes or RJ, he quickly turned his attention to artistic integrity," said Solow. "Harlan berated the studio executive 'suits,' and the Executive Producers and Producers of television series, for 'interfering with the writing process.' ... The writer-dominated audience rose to their feet, *en masse*, and hailed this living hero who had the guts to publicly speak out against *them*!... Surprisingly, Gene Roddenberry seemed amused. He turned to us and shrugged." (161-3)

In 2013, Ellison said, "When I went to the awards, Gene Coon nearly choked on his dinner. He was sitting right down in front of me when I said what I said about the rewriting. Of course, nothing I've ever done in my 79 years has not in some way impaired my progress.

Whether I was working for Aaron Spelling, Darryl Zanuck, or Gene Roddenberry, I'm not afraid of anything, and that is a great flaw. It doesn't mean you're brave necessarily, it means you don't know when to turn and run when the snake is rattling." (58)

Mary Black recalled, "After all the awards had been given out and the awards area was shut down and people were just sort of milling, Harlan climbed over the tables that were between his table and our table – *on top of the tables and over the table* – to come over and yell, 'We won, we won!' to John." (17a)

"It really rankled me, because he won the Writers Guild prize," said Roddenberry. "And I made a complaint about that. I pointed out that...there are many excellent [first draft scripts] that could be submitted, but not fairly. Because it doesn't follow the pattern of what you guaranteed to write. And, we had a huge fight and [Harlan] was as near a thing as I ever had as an enemy. He was a very proud writer. And the very fact that I had rewritten it really upset him. But it was obvious why I had to rewrite it: I had to put *our* people in." (145-2)

As for the version that Roddenberry, Coon, and Fontana wrote, based on Ellison's story and as directed by Joseph Pevney, winning the International Hugo Award as Best Science Fiction Presentation of 1967, it would be 25 years before another television program received this honor -- *Star Trek: The Next Generation*, for the episode "The Inner Light."

Roddenberry always acknowledged "City" as one of his Top Ten favorite episodes from the original series. At the end of his life, for *The Last Conversation*, he picked it as his absolute favorite.

DeForest Kelley also picked "City" as his favorite. "I thought it was the best ensemble piece of work and that it captured a certain flavor and mood," he said. "I thought it was one of the most dramatic endings that I'd ever seen on a television show." (98-1)

William Shatner went back and forth between this episode and "The Devil in the Dark" as his favorite. On one occasion, in 1991, he said, "'City' is my favorite of the original *Star Trek* series because of the fact that it is a beautiful love story, well told." (156-10)

Leonard Nimoy picked "City" as *one* of his favorites.

Dorothy Fontana named it as one of her two favorite episodes (of the ones she was not the primary writer). The other was "The Trouble with Tribbles."

In 1994, *Entertainment Weekly* named "City" as #1 of all *Star Trek*s.

For its July 1, 1995, issue, *TV Guide* ranked "City" at #68 for their list of 100 Most Memorable Moments in TV History.

"The City on the Edge of Forever" got the short story treatment by James Blish for the February 1968 publication of *Star Trek 2*. Ellison sent Blish his version of the script in hopes that it would be adapted for the book instead of the Roddenberry/Coon/Fontana version. Blish, however, with all due apologies to Mr. Ellison, chose the latter as being a better candidate for this *Star Trek* paperback. He did, however, work in some elements of the Ellison version.

The Guardian of Forever returned in 1973 for "Yesteryear," an episode of *Star Trek: The Animated Series*, written by D.C. Fontana.

"Yesterday's Son," an original *Star Trek* novel by A.C. Crispin, which featured the Guardian of Forever, was published in 1983.

The Guardian returned again in a novel based on the characters of *Star Trek: The Next Generation*. *Imzadi*, by Peter David, was published in 1993.

The battle over the script for this episode was the subject of a book written by Harlan Ellison, called *The City on the Edge of Forever: The Original Teleplay That Became The*

Classic Star Trek Episode. It too was published in 1993.

From the Mailbag

Dear Sir: As corresponding secretary for the "New Box Canyon Indians," I speak in their behalf. Our tribe now numbers 27, all of whom became immovable 8:30 and 9:30 on Thursday nights. Robin J.

And from Roddenberry to Shatner:

Dear Bill [Shatner]: "The City on the Edge of Forever" is likely to be one of our best films of the year. NBC was particularly thrilled when they saw the intermediate cut of it and we had a number of calls from the Network congratulating us and asking that we congratulate you on the performance. The love story comes off magnificently and you were never better! You played it quietly with a dimensional intensity that is going to have the audience loving and then agonizing with you as they seldom do with an actor in a television drama. Congratulations. Gene Roddenberry.

Memories

Harlan Ellison said, "I loved Bobby Justman. He was always kind to me and he was in the true sense of the word a gentleman. And so was John Black and so were most of the people there. They all treated the writers with respect, not like they were only day workers. But everyone walked around Gene like the whole room was made of egg shell. He was half-loaded most of the time and fully-loaded the rest of the time." (58)

Gene Roddenberry's son, Rod, interviewed for this book in 2012, said, "Regardless of who is at fault there, I think that Harlan's mannerisms and personality in handling these things resulted in me having no respect for him at all. If he was a polite guy who said, 'You know what, Gene did this from my point of view, I disagree with it; it was his show, but I think he's wrong, and I won't forgive him for that.' If he just had that sort of subtle tone about it, I could respect him. But the manner in which he has conducted himself, and still does 45 years later, is really disgusting to me."

Dorothy Fontana said, "For 30 years I couldn't tell Harlan that I was one of the people who worked on that script. I was scared to death of him." (64-1)

Ellison said, "It was 20 years before I found out Dorothy did a lot of the rewriting. It practically broke my heart because I love Dorothy. And she was afraid to tell me she did that, *with cause*. Sometimes it's good to know when to be afraid." (50)

Joseph Pevney said, "It was a very honest episode and DeForest Kelly was so good in it. It was a pleasure working with the actors. They realized their full potential in that one." (141-1)

Dr. Laura Schlessinger, talk-show psychologist, author, and renowned *Star Trek* fan, said, "I remembered great moments like when Kirk goes back in time and has to let Edith Keeler die. I made my son watch 'City on the Edge of Forever' one night. He had never watched *Star Trek*, and I said 'Watch this one.' And, when it was over, he looked at me and said, 'That's powerful. He loved her. How did he have the courage to make that choice?' It made you think about things." (153)

DeForest Kelley said, "I had a feeling about that show. I knew it was going to be a winner, and I'm proud to have been a part of it. It's one of the few times I wished that I had been playing Kirk's role." (98-3)

Jerry Finnerman said, "That was a wonderful show.... I thought I lit it well; I thought

I had her [Joan Collins] looking good.... It was just good; it was a good script; it was good acting; Joan was a wonderful lady, very professional, and we enjoyed that... I enjoyed working with her." (63-3)

Joan Collins, in 1996, said, "To this day, people still want to talk about that episode; some remember me for that more than anything else I've done. I am amazed at the enduring popularity of *Star Trek* and particularly of that episode.... At the time, none of us would have predicted the longevity of the show. I couldn't be more pleased -- or more honored -- to be part of *Star Trek* history." (33a)

In another interview, Harlan Ellison said, "I've never loved that *Star Trek*. It's won awards and continues to be the most popular one ... my response is, 'You should'a seen the original." (58-1)

NBC publicity photo transforming a glamorous British star into a domesticated American immigrant (Courtesy of Gerald Gurian)

Episode 29: OPERATION: ANNIHILATE!
Written by Steven Carabatsos
(with Gene Roddenberry and Gene Coon, uncredited)
Directed by Herschel Daugherty

NBC's press release, issued March 22, 1967:

Screen capture from "Operation: Annihilate!" (CBS Studios, Inc.)

The USS Enterprise attempts to stem an epidemic of mass insanity that has already destroyed several planet colonies... in 'Operation-Annihilate' on the NBC Television Network's *Star Trek*.... Arriving on the planet Deneva, which appears to be in the path of the spreading malady, Captain Kirk (William Shatner) and Mr. Spock (Leonard Nimoy) find Kirk's sister-in-law, Aurelan, and his nephew, Peter, in a near-crazed condition, and learns that his brother, a biologist, has already died. When Mr. Spock contracts the disease [sic], Kirk appears to have no alternative but to annihilate the entire colony to prevent infection of the galaxy.

The creatures seem indestructible except in one regard -- a Denevan, piloting his space craft into that system's sun, was freed of the parasite seconds before he and his ship burned up. Something in the sun killed it, but tests with heat, radiation and gravity have been ineffective. Dr. McCoy believes light may be the answer -- light as bright as a sun. Spock, struggling against the creature that inhabits his body, is willing to be used as a guinea pig. The risk: the experiment could leave him blind.

Examined here: the human mind's ability to manage pain, the burden of command, and the consequences of living with a tragically-bad decision.

SOUND BITES

- *Spock:* "I am a Vulcan.... Pain is a thing of the mind. The mind can be controlled." *Kirk:* "You're only half Vulcan. What about the human half of you?" *Spock:* "It is proving to be an inconvenience."

- *McCoy:* "That man is sick! And don't give me any of that damnable logic about him being the only one for the job!" *Kirk:* "I don't have to, Bones. We both know he is."

- *Spock:* "The creature within me is gone. I am free of it ... and the pain. I am also quite blind. An equitable trade, Doctor. Thank you."

ASSESSMENT

The direction and the look of "Operation: Annihilate!" are above average. Many unique camera angles, especially on the bridge, add freshness. In addition, with the high stakes and the great personal battles waged, the performances are surprisingly reined-in. Much credit goes to first-time *Star Trek* director Herschel Daugherty.

Among the concepts that work are how the parasitic creatures have the ability to inject living tissue into the body of the host, which then invades the human nervous system, allowing the parasite to control its host with intense pain; and how each of these creatures are individual brain cells, interconnected through thought transmission, creating a life form with great intellect, but with no hands for building. Their survival depends on human slaves, to construct spaceships and allow "it" to travel the universe in search of new food sources.

This episode is also disturbing. It opens with a suicide. Then Kirk discovers his brother dead. Then his sister-in-law dies in excruciating pain. Their son -- Kirk's young nephew -- is near death and in a coma. Spock is in agony. Then he is blinded. Kirk blames McCoy. McCoy blames himself. Finally, Kirk must make a decision that may blind, or worse, kill a million people. Any of these elements could have carried a story. Combined, they leave this episode crowded and strangely unpleasant.

THE STORY BEHIND THE STORY

Script Timeline

Steven Carabatsos' story outline, ST #42, "Operation: Destroy!":
December 15, 1966.
Steven Carabatsos' revised story outline: late December 1966.
Carabatsos' 1st Draft teleplay: Early January 1967.
Carabatsos' 2nd Draft teleplay (Mimeo Department Writer's "Yellow Cover"
1st Draft teleplay, now "Operation: Annihilate!"): January 19, 1967.
D.C. Fontana's script polish (Final Draft teleplay): January 24, 1967.
Gene Coon's rewrite (Revised Final Draft teleplay): February 3, 1967.
Gene Roddenberry's rewrite (2nd Revised Final Draft): February 13, 1967.
Additional page revisions by Coon: February 14, 15 & 22, 1967.

In August 1966, when Steven Carabatsos was hired to serve as Story Editor, his contract also called for him to deliver one script of his own. With all the rewriting, including "Court Martial" for which he received a co-writing credit, Carabatsos had little time to begin an original script -- until early December when he was released from the in-house staff and replaced by Dorothy Fontana.

"'Operation: Annihilate!' was not really my original idea," Carabatsos later said. "Somebody gave me the idea -- Roddenberry, I believe." (28-1)

Actually, the original idea, or ideas, can be traced to three different sources. *Star Trek*'s 29th episode is in many ways reminiscent of Robert A. Heinlein's 1951 novel, *The Puppet Masters*. In Heinlein's story, people in the United States are being mentally-controlled by slug-like creatures that attach themselves to their hosts' backs. These aliens communicate with one another through "direct conference," whereby their hosts sit back-to-back and the slugs partially merge. The humans already inhabited by the aliens are being used to spread the invasion. Slugs are then sent through the mail, in search of more hosts.

The idea of controlling one's mind through pain was used in *Star Trek* before. Shimon Wincelberg came up with the notion for "Dagger of the Mind." What happens to Simon Van Gelder in that episode also happens to Aurelan Kirk here. McCoy talks to Kirk about his sister-in-law, Aurelan, saying, "When she answers questions -- any questions -- it's as though she has to fight to get the answers out; as though something is exerting pain to stop her." Just as it had been with Van Gelder.

The idea that these creatures are, in a sense, individual brain cells, all in communication with one another and combining to create a much larger entity, was taken from Jerry Sohl's script, "The Way of the Spores." Also in Sohl's original story, but cut from that episode, Sulu beamed aboard the Enterprise and tried to commandeer the ship -- much in the way Spock does here. The writing staff was taking elements cut from other scripts and placing them here.

Carabatsos turned in his 19-page story outline on December 15, 1966. It was far darker than the filmed episode. The people of Deneva are on the verge of complete self-annihilation. Carabatsos wrote:

> McCoy is concerned over the fact that the Denevans see death as the only escape from the pain incurred when taken over by the THINGS.

Even grimmer, the outline tells us:

> The people of the Enterprise may be about to witness the mass suicide of an entire planet, unless something is done, some formula arrived at, some treatment discovered.

In this early version of the story, as in the one filmed, Spock is a reluctant host for one of the creatures. But here, Kirk and McCoy worry that he, too, may commit suicide.

Carabatsos had Kirk agonize over the burden of his decision -- to kill all the men, women, and children on Deneva in order to stop these "things" from traveling to other worlds. Other than Spock, he does not have a personal stake in this -- his brother, sister-in-law and young nephew are not yet in the story. The weight on his shoulders, then, is his inner-conflict as to what action to take -- whether or not to kill millions of people. A line in the outline reads, "Kirk is seen to be walking down a darkened, deserted corridor, wrestling with his conscience." And then what would have been the most startling ending of any *Star Trek* episode -- Kirk uses the Enterprise's weapons to destroy all life on Deneva. McCoy supports this, and tells the Captain, "It had to be done, Jim. Someone had to make the decision. You had no choice." The outline ends, with Carabatsos writing, "And, as we fade out, we are left with the awful and vivid proportions involved in the terrible loneliness of command."

In "The Conscience of the King," Kirk had damned Karidian for coming to a decision such as this -- to kill some people so that others may live. The difference, of course, is that Karidian killed healthy people so that others could have food to eat; Kirk kills the inflected and suffering, all of whom will die anyway, to stop an invasion and keep this suffering from spreading beyond Deneva. Nonetheless, it was an ending that was not going to get approval from NBC ... or, for that matter, Gene Roddenberry, who suggested the premise to Carabatsos, sans the tragic ending.

Bob Justman was the first to respond, writing to Coon:

> Well, here I am at the end of the Story Treatment and I have discovered that Kirk has made the one and only decision he could possibly make. He destroys

the whole furschluggener planet. Has NBC read this Story Treatment yet? (RJ29-1)

The dark ending was taken out and replaced with something more in keeping with *Star Trek*. Kirk finds a way to destroy the creatures other than setting the surface of a populated planet ablaze with weapons fire. Regardless, in Carabatsos' script, the new ending was still very different from that eventually filmed. There are differences throughout the story.

The script begins as the filmed episode did, with the Enterprise tracking an epidemic of planetary scale madness which has been moving across a portion of the galaxy, and then encountering, and trying to prevent, a Denevan ship from flying into that planet's sun. Ship to ship contact is made. The Denevan pilot appears mad, but then proclaims that he is "free" before his ship burns up. In the last seconds of his life, he frantically searches for a way to save himself from his suicidal actions. On Deneva, Kirk and the landing party are attacked by a group of men with clubs, who shout at the Enterprise crew to get away, that they don't wish to hurt them. Next, we hear a woman scream, and the landing party runs to her aid. She is in the "communications center" -- a type of radio transmitting room -- with an unconscious man, trying to keep "it" out. She is hysterical. McCoy sedates her, and then returns to the ship with both her and the man. When Spock is struck down by one of the creatures, described as a "gelatinous mass" about the size of a football, and reminiscent of a jellyfish, Kirk does not pull it off his back. There is no need to. It has vanished on its own, as it penetrates Spock's skin and enters his body.

Back on the Enterprise, Kirk questions the two Denevans who were brought aboard. The woman is Aurelan; the man is her father, Menen. The Denevan who flew his ship into the sun and perished was Noban, Menen's son and brother of Aurelan. The father and daughter are the only two on Deneva who have not been taken over by the aliens. They were spared so that they will call for help, luring other ships to the planet so that the creatures could take over more humans and have more ships to use for further invasions throughout the universe.

Menen tells Kirk, "My son told me -- before he died -- that they need bodies the way we need tools. Arms and legs -- human beings. And once they take over, they can't be resisted. The people who tried to kill you in the street didn't want to hurt you. They wanted to help you. But the things ordered them to attack you, and they had no choice."

Aurelan adds, "My brother, Noban.... The creatures had him. He almost went mad from the pain. But he told us that Deneva is just a way-station for them. They mean to spread out. You see ... their hosts become useless after a while. They go mad. And then they need new hosts. More people. Planet after planet. They come, and they leave madness, and they go to the next ..."

Menen asks Kirk if Spock is important to him. Kirk says that Spock is more than a valued officer, but also one of his closet friends. Menen says, "In that case, kill him.... Now. Quickly. Because only endless agony lies ahead for him; agony that will end in madness. If you are his friend, be merciful."

Later, Spock, resisting the creature within, returns to the planet to capture a specimen and is attacked by a Denevan. Carabatsos' script continues to be very different from the one eventually filmed. In the final version, this encounter is not only brief, but seems to serve no purpose other than providing an Act break. In the Carabatsos script, however, this attack takes the plot in a whole different direction. The attacker, named Kartan, is being forced to go after Spock with an axe. But he is also pleading that Spock kill him. He shouts, "Run! Run! If you don't I'll have to kill you! You have a phaser! Kill me! Please kill me! Shoot! Shoot!"

This is a far more startling development than what we are given in the filmed episode. Further, after knocking Kartan out, Spock brings him to the ship for examination and we learn that he was to wed Aurelan before the invasion. She is horrified to see her fiancé like this and pleads that, if he cannot be saved, he be put out of his misery. She is also supportive of him being used in the experiments to find a way to destroy the creature. She sees it as Kartan's only chance to be spared from further agonizing pain ... and madness. Kartan is important to the story, because Spock is not a good candidate for the experimentation, being only half-human.

The ending to the Carabatsos script is nothing like that of his original story outline or the filmed episode yet to come. Spock, linked to the consciousness of the creature through that which lives within his body, is able to sense that it is a "composite organism" and that all its subparts are somehow connected and controlled by a "gigantic brain." Kirk, taking this a step further, comes up with the hypothesis that the individual cells are mindless, in fact almost lifeless, and that there is a central concentration of them somewhere. Spock, being in telepathic communication with the creature, is able to direct the Enterprise to the alien's home planet -- where the epidemic of madness first began hundreds of years earlier. Kirk orders Sulu to use the ship's weapons to set fire to the surface of that planet, not Deneva. The heat and the light created by the weapons destroy the central brain. The creature within Spock leaves the body of its host. It is weak and easily destroyed. And this happens a million times over on Deneva, too.

Carabatsos' Second Draft script from January 19, 1967, was sent to the Mimeo Department, and designated as the Yellow Cover First Draft. It was then sent to NBC.

Robert Justman still had issues, far too many to list. He did, however have one positive comment:

> Come to think of it, Gene, the thing I like best about this show is the fact that it is heavy in its emphasis upon Mister Spock. I know that can't do us any harm. (RJ29-2)

Stan Robertson was getting everything he usually asked for: a planet show, to be shot in part on location, and an interesting adversary/monster. What he wasn't getting was fast pacing. He wrote Gene Coon:

> This is an excellent dramatic script, certainly all of the important ingredients of action, adventure, jeopardy, conflict, suspense, characterizations, etc. However, in its "structure," as with the structures of a large number of the other scripts we've had this season, we have missed on a salient factor which is more apparent on the screen than it is on paper. And that is this -- we have not whetted the appetite of our viewers enough in the Teaser. (SR29)

In the teaser of the script Carabatsos had written, we get the back-story, telling us that madness has been spreading across this part of the galaxy and Deneva is the next planet in line. Kirk orders the Enterprise to proceed to Deneva. Fade down.

Recent audience research told Robertson that the show needed to open with a bang or that many in the viewing audience might switch channels to get their thrills on ABC or CBS. NBC was learning that if you don't catch them fast, you don't keep them.

For better or worse, Robertson was ahead of his time. He told Coon:

> I need not, I know, remind you that we are involved in a highly competitive visual medium in which the mass audience is, at best, fickle and approaching the

blasé after almost a decade and a half of network television as we know it. We must, I'm firmly convinced, so arouse their curiosity and interest in the shortest time possible after the NBC Peacock that they will be completely absorbed in what is to follow. We must "cheat" a little bit and offer a little of the dessert with the entree. (SR29)

Robertson cited a perfect example of a snappy *Star Trek* opening -- the one seen in the teaser for "Tomorrow Is Yesterday."

He continued:

As scripted, our story is written as a mystery and it is not until we are far along in it that we are presented with the actual visual confrontation of our "things". (SR29)

Since Robertson had made reference to a Dorothy Fontana script as a prime example of the type of writing -- and the type of teaser -- he wanted to see more of, Coon handed the script off to his new Story Editor for a sprucing-up.

Fontana's polish -- the January 24 Final Draft -- tightened the teaser and added in the action which, in the previous draft, didn't happen until the start of Act One -- the Enterprise encountering the Denevan ship which is racing toward that system's sun, and the ship's destruction. NBC now had a big bang to open with.

Fontana also introduced the creatures sooner than Carabatsos had, and eliminated the idea that the entire creature would invade the body of its intended host. Now, it would inject living tissue into the body of its host by means of a stinger. And Fontana added Nurse Chapel into the script, assisting McCoy during the surgery on Spock, and trying to keep the Vulcan from later leaving sickbay. A gripping dialogue scene, which did not last through all the rewriting, is present here. McCoy does not bring the specimen he removes from Spock to the bridge, as in the filmed version, but, instead, calls Kirk to his office. Of the "tendril" in the jar of clear fluid, McCoy says, "By itself, this tissue has no organs. And I'd guess the same for the individual creatures we saw on the surface. What I'm saying is that maybe all those separate creatures down there -- and this stuff here -- put together, make one entity."

The character of Menen was now seen but not heard, with Aurelan doing the talking and telling Kirk to kill Spock. Otherwise, the story structure remained very much the same.

The first person to make substantial changes was Gene Coon. With his rewrite, the February 3rd Revised Final Draft, the Fourth Act and the story's ending were retooled. It was here where the idea of having Spock experience blindness was added. And Spock would not be alone. Scotty clumsily knocks over a specimen case, freeing one of the creatures, and is attacked and inhabited by the creature. And he, too, is blinded in the effort to remove the alien from his body. Kirk, after wrestling with his conscience, makes the decision to blind all those on Deneva -- over a million people -- to free them from the aliens. It is McCoy, after the fact, who finds a way to surgically repair the eyes, allowing Spock and Scott to see again. Medics are then sent to Deneva to begin the process of corrective eye surgery on the million-plus inhabitants of the planet.

Justman commented:

Incidentally, since Engineer Scott has now been infected by the Creatures also, what have we done with him? Is he in Sickbay? Is he in another section of the Sickbay that we can't see? Has he died?... I am sure that you [Gene Coon] will agree with Mr. Roddenberry that I may not be the soul of tact, but I am extremely terrier-like in my determination to pursue a problem once I have fastened my teeth into it. As I have told the Great Bird of the Galaxy in the past,

I may disagree with his point of view, but I will fight to the death to preserve his right to be wrong. (RJ29-3)

Roddenberry did a rewrite next. Steven Carabatsos said, "[Roddenberry] had wanted to do an episode involving Captain Kirk's brother. Kind of a family connection." (28-1)

Roddenberry removed the character of Melen, adding in Sam Kirk, having Aurelan be Sam's wife, and giving them a son -- Peter (even though in "What Are Little Girls Made Of?" we are told Sam Kirk has two sons). The character of Kartan remained and still attacked Spock, but had so little significance, and was now in and out of the story so fast that his name is never even spoken. Roddenberry also took out the plot contrivance that had Scott being attacked and stung by one of the creatures. And he changed the ending. Spock loses his sight, but, before Kirk gives the order to blind all those on Deneva, McCoy discovers that only one spectrum of light need be used to kill the aliens -- one that is not harmful to the human eye. Lastly, Roddenberry added in a reasonable means for Spock to regain his sight -- due to that never-before-mentioned Vulcan inner eyelid.

Clearly, the script had been improved in many ways. But it had also become crowded. Good ideas do not always help a story -- not when there are too many of them.

Regardless, Roddenberry, Coon, and Fontana felt the script was now better. When James Blish, the science fiction author commissioned to turn the scripts into short story form for a series of Bantam paperback books, based his story on the Grey Cover Final Draft script and not on the 2nd Revised Final Draft, Fontana sent a memo to Roddenberry, complaining:

> This adapted story is not only *not* what we put on the air... [but] it lacks all the personal elements of urgency we placed in the story: the fact that the three people we find on the planet in the radio station are Kirk's brother Sam, his sister-in-law Aurelan, and nephew Peter; that the brother and sister-in-law die, etc." (DC29)

Roddenberry always believed that scripts got better with rewriting. At some point, however, too much writing leads to overwriting. And that is the case here.

Coon did more rewriting, with a series of minor page revisions on February 14, 15 and 22, as the episode was filming.

Pre-Production
February 3 & 6-10 & 13, 1967 (total 7 days prep).

Herschel Daugherty, 56, in TV since the early 1950s, was hired to direct. His resume included *Wagon Train* (nine episodes), *Alfred Hitchcock Presents* (15 episodes), and Boris Karloff's *Thriller* (16 assignments, including "The Grim Reaper," which starred William Shatner). He was also a frequent director for the anthology series *General Electric Theater*, where he won the Directors Guild award in 1957. Daugherty would return to *Star Trek* for "The Savage Curtain."

Because "The City on the Edge of Forever" ran one and a half days over, Daugherty got an extra day of prep.

Joan Swift played Aurelan Kirk, Captain Kirk's sister-in-law. Swift's work in TV had been in roles such as "Hatcheck Girl," "Saloon Girl," "Secretary," and "Stewardess." "Operation: Annihilate!" allowed her to scream, writhe in agony, have a hysterical fit, and then die.

Craig Hundley played Kirk's nephew, Peter. He was 12, and busy in television with guest spots on series such as *My Favorite Martian* and *Bewitched*. Immediately after

"Operation: Annihilate!," Hundley was added to the cast of *Days of Our Lives*. He returned for a bigger role on *Star Trek* in "And the Children Shall Lead."

Wah Chang designed the parasite creatures, which James Doohan called "flying omelets." Doohan said, "Those things went hurtling through the air on strings, and when the script called for one of them to smack Spock in the back, it nearly knocked him down." (52-1)

The moment was preserved for the year-end blooper reel shown at the company's wrap party.

Production Diary
Filmed February 14 (1/2 day), 15, 16, 17, 20, 21 & 22, 1967
(6 1/2 day production; cost: $196,780).

Principal photography began on Tuesday, February 14, 1967. This week: Mick Jagger, Keith Richards, and Marianne Faithfull were busted for procession of drugs. The Beatles released their new single: "Penny Lane," paired with "Strawberry Fields Forever." The top two films in the movie houses across America: *The Fox*, starring Sandy Dennis, and *Hurry Sundown*, starring Michael Caine, Jane Fonda, and Faye Dunaway. Steven Hill, Barbara Bain, and Martin Landau, the stars of *Star Trek*'s sister show, *Mission: Impossible*, had the cover of *TV Guide*. On television the night before the commencement of production on "Operation: Annihilate!," The Monkees performed "She" and "Sometime in the Morning" from their new album on their NBC series. Their self-titled debut album finally got knocked from the No. 1 spot in the record stores after a staggering 13 weeks at the top. It fell to No. 2 where it would sit for another month. The new top-selling album across the nation: *More of the Monkees*. Their "I'm a Believer" single was finally displaced as the most-played song on the radio and best-selling single, after seven weeks at the summit, now dropping to No. 2. The new 45 getting the most spins: "Kind of a Drag," by The Buckinghams.

Filming began at midday. "The City on the Edge of Forever" finally wrapped, making room for director Daugherty to get started. He wasn't complaining. Besides an extra day for preparation, he now had an extra half day to film.

Hamming for the camera, using phasers as electric shavers, while on location in Redondo Beach
(Courtesy of Gerald Gurian)

The original full-day schedule had planned to cover scenes in the transporter room, the briefing room, and Kirk's quarters. With only a half day to work, the expectations were now scaled back by 50%.

On Day 2, location filming took place at the TRW Defense and Space Group Campus, in Redondo Beach, California. This futuristic complex served as the Denevan city.

For Day 3, the company returned to Stage 9 to pick up where filming had left off on Tuesday, then moved onto the bridge set.

"Space Seed" aired for the first time on NBC this night.

The entirety of Day 4 was spent filming on the bridge, including the scripted ending of the episode, in which Kirk's nephew, Peter, now recovered and seeming happy, wears a mini Star Fleet uniform (gold shirt, like Kirk's) and sits in the captain's chair. In the dialogue, cut from the aired episode, Peter tells Kirk he wishes to stay on Deneva.

Day 5 was spent filming sequences in McCoy's office and sickbay. Shooting in sickbay continued on Day 6, including the dramatic scene in which McCoy admits to Kirk that he made a mistake in exposing Spock to the full spectrum of light.

Deleted "tag scene" with Craig Hundley
(from startrekhistory.com and startrekpropauthority.com)

The acting by the three leads -- Shatner, Nimoy, and Kelley -- and the gamut of emotions that passes among them brings forward a standout moment in this episode. Interviewed at this time, DeForest Kelley said, "I've been told that Dr. McCoy is the balancing rod between the two more extreme characters, Kirk and Spock.... Now, McCoy is merely human. At times he feels fear. At times he can perform really dangerous acts. But he's always just a man who feels and thinks and who searches. And, who makes mistakes. The audience reacts to each of us. They admire Captain Kirk for conquering the faults in our human natures. They are in awe of Mr. Spock. But they sympathize with and relate to Dr. McCoy." (98-13)

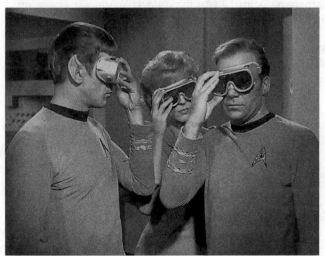

Day 6, as tests are run to see if bright light can kill the creature
(Unaired film trim courtesy of Gerald Gurian)

Day 7, February 22, 1967 -- the final shots were taken in-and-about the isolation booth.

After filming ended, the cast and crew hung around for a season-end wrap party. The following night, on Thursday, February 23, "A Taste of Armageddon" aired on NBC.

Post-Production
Available for editing: February 23, 1967. Music score: tracked.

Fabien Tordjmann and Edit Team #3 did the cutting, their eighth episode. The Westheimer Company provided the optical effects. The new shots of the Enterprise in space, however, came courtesy of Film Effects of Hollywood.

For the sounds made by the creature, Sound Editor Douglas H. Grindstaff said, "That was a kiss. I [recorded] about a hundred kisses and played with them. Only one of them worked out. It just pulsated with [the movements of the creature], and it fit real well. You had to use your imagination, and you had to be one step ahead of *them*. I would never tell anyone what I did.... They could ask me all day what I did, I wasn't going to tell them. You either liked it or you didn't. So, they finally quit asking." (76-1)

At $196,780, "Operation: Annihilate" came in $11,780 over its studio allocated budget. The first season ended $146,603 in the red. With *Mission: Impossible* also spending more than the studio had wished, Desilu was in danger of going out of business.

Release / Reaction:
Only NBC air date: 4/13/67.

Steven H. Scheuer reviewed "Operation: Annihilate!" for his April 13, 1967 *TV Key Preview* column. Among the newspapers to carry the review was the *Evening Independent*, in Florida. Scheuer wrote:

> *Star Trek* traces a mystery germ in this imaginative space-age story, which is an absorbing hour even if its variation on the theme of outer space horrors is not as meaningful as usual. Captain Kirk and Mr. Spock must solve the root cause of a paralyzing pain inflected on the inhabitants of a planet which drive the citizens into insanity and death.

Joan Crosby reviewed the episode for her syndicated column, *TV Scout*. Among the newspapers to carry Crosby's assessment on April 13 was the *Pulaski Southwest Times*, in Virginia. Crosby wrote:

> *Star Trek* has a hysterical and gory but very good piece of science fiction in its last new episode of the season. It seems that entire civilizations are being wiped out and the latest planet to be hit is where William Shatner's brother and wife live. But when Captain Kirk arrives, the disease has already taken his brother's life and now his widow and her son are seriously infected. The "Creature of the Evening" is a glob of brain-like cell matter which flies like a bat, adheres to a human and causes brain-searing pain.

The promise of "a glob of brain-like cell matter which flies like a bat" was too much to pass by, according to A.C. Nielsen.

RATINGS / Nielsen National report, Thursday, April 13, 1967:

8:30 - 9 p.m., 64.4% of U.S. TVs in use.		Households watching:
NBC:	*Star Trek* (first half)	12,300,000
ABC:	***Bewitched***	**15,150,000**
CBS:	*My Three Sons*	11,910,000

9 - 9:30 P.M.: 63.3% of U.S. TVs in use.		Audience Share:
NBC:	***Star Trek* (second half)**	**30.1 %**
ABC:	*Love on a Rooftop*	25.4%
CBS:	***Thursday Night Movie* (start)**	**30.5%**
Local independent stations:		14.0%

From 9:00-9:30 p.m., in a too-close-to-call race, *Star Trek* tied for No. 1 with the movie on CBS -- *About Miss Leslie*, starring Shirley Booth and Robert Ryan. In the April 24, 1967, edition of *Daily Variety*, the trade published the Top 40 list of the latest 30-City Nielsen survey. *Star Trek*, with this final first-run episode of the season, came in at a respectable No. 37 out of 90 prime time shows.

Robert Justman chose not to include it on his list of suggested summer repeats for NBC, even though it appeared to be everything the network had been asking for.

From the Mailbag

Received after the broadcast of "Operation: Annihilate!":

Dear Mr. Roddenberry: To begin with, let me say I enjoy your program *Star Trek*. I think it is one of the most sophisticated programs of its type on television. However, the purpose of this letter is to see if you can assist me in a problem which I have not been able to solve to date. I am an apartment complex builder in Santa Barbara and I continue to attempt to add amenities and upgrade my units as best I can. For some time, I have wanted to install in our new units an electronically controlled pocket panel door and I have done some research in this area. Our basic problem has been we can't get the doors to open and close fast enough. If, in effect, the sliding doors in the space craft in your *Star Trek* series are special effects rather than a function of building then, of course, you cannot be of any help to me. In short, how do you get the damn door to open and close so fast!.... Hoping to hear from you soon. I remain... Very Truly Yours. Marvin T. (Santa Barbara, California)

Received one-and-a-half weeks after the first airing of "Operation: Annihilate!":

Dear Gene, I just wanted to tell you how much I have enjoyed the *Star Trek* series this year. As a matter of fact, when I watched last night's "first episode" repeat ["Where No Man Has Gone Before"], I realized the enormous strides you and your group have made with this show since the shooting of that episode. My wife is probably the biggest fan you have. Sincerely, Mort Werner, President, NBC. (April 21, 1967)

Memories

Craig Hundley said, "I was a big fan of *Star Trek*, In fact, producer Gene Roddenberry wanted me as a regular on the series as Captain Kirk's nephew, Peter. Because of other commitments, I was unavailable. Gene did ask me back for the third season episode, 'And the Children Shall lead.'" (87-3)

38

Ratings, Reaction, Repeats, and Rewards

With the premiere of "The Man Trap," *Star Trek* received mixed reviews. Now, the critics were reappraising the series. TV columnists referred to it as "good science-fiction with great special effects" and "an exciting, futuristic adventure that keeps watchers on the edge of their seats." *TV Guide*'s Cleveland Amory, for that magazine's May 20, 1967, issue, wrote, "We would say that the show we most over-criticized was *Star Trek*... Lately we've enjoyed and admired much in the series."

During Season One, cast members of *Star Trek* appeared on the cover of *TV Guide*, *Ebony*, *TV Week*, *TV Showtime*, *TV Star Parade*, *TV Radio Mirror*, *The St. Louis Dispatch TV Magazine*, *The Boston Sunday Herald TV Magazine*, *Model Car & Science* magazine, and *TV Star Annual*, among others.

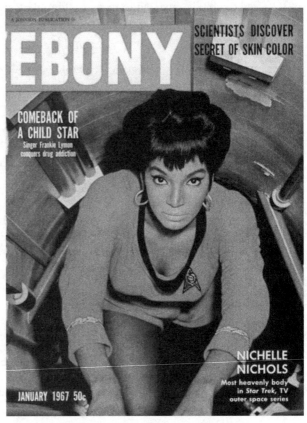

Nichelle Nichols, as Lt. Uhura, makes the cover of *Ebony* Magazine in January, 1967

By the time *Star Trek* was repeating the best episodes of its first season, the tabloids were picking up on the appeal of the series and its stars, prompting scores of articles in the likes of *16 Magazine* and *TV Movie Screen*. Shatner was either shown as macho, riding motorcycles and hunting with a bow and arrow, or as the image of the perfect dad, visiting an amusement park and going horseback riding with his three daughters, Leslie, Lisabeth, and Melanie, ages nine, six and two, respectively. Nimoy, sans the pointed ears but always with the Spock bangs, was shown reading poetry, or being analyzed in articles like, "How a Man with Pointed Ears Feels Deep Down ... When the Makeup Is Off." *Star Trek* was making good copy. And the flood gates had yet to open.

***

The *Star Trek* board game by Ideal Toys

Daily Variety, for its February 8, 1967 issue, reported that ABC Sales International, representing Desilu, had sold *Star Trek* to 28 foreign countries, and that the series had been dubbed into four languages … so far. This was a notable success for a series less than one year old. And this was just one of numerous revenue sources which were already paying into the studio and Roddenberry's Norway Productions. Another was merchandising. Just in time for Christmas, 1966, the first *Star Trek* tie-ins materialized on shelves in toy stores across the United States. Ideal Toys, one of the "Big Four" (the others being Marx, Mattel and Remco), had made its fortune off the Teddy Bear. Now it released the *Star Trek* board game. The packaging, featuring Kirk, Spock and Uhura on the bridge, was attractive. The game itself was pointless.

***Star Trek* coloring book, a deal at 29 cents**

Remco was doing well with their tie-in products based on television programs and popular singing groups, such as their Beatles' figures and the battery-driven, one-foot tall replica of the robot from *Lost in Space*. With *Star Trek*, the best Remco would do was the *Star Trek Astro Cruiser* "with movable cannon," the *Star Trek Astro Helmet* "with tinted visor," and the *Star Trek Astro Buzz Ray Gun* with, well, a buzzing sound. None of these items had anything to do with *Star Trek* as seen on TV. They merely exploited the name.

Hasbro, makers of 1952's Mr. Potato Head and 1964's G.I. Joe, went for the fast buck with the *Star Trek Paint by Numbers Kit*, with pictures of Kirk, Spock and the Enterprise.

Ray Line, the toy division of Ray Plastics, Inc., came up with the *Star Trek Tracer Gun*. It was pretty much the same disk-shooting tracer gun Ray Line already

AMT Enterprise model from 1967

marketed but now with the faces of Kirk and Spock and the name *Star Trek* on the cardboard packaging.

In early 1967, AMT took the lead with the crowning glory of all the various *Star Trek* merchandising ploys of the time. In the first six months alone, the model kit of the U.S.S. Enterprise sold a staggering 100,000 units.

In June 1967, Bantam published the first *Star Trek* paperback. Science fiction author James Blish (who had won a Hugo Award for 1959's *A Case of Conscience*) was hired to convert the series' screenplays into short story form. Since work of this nature was usually delegated to pulp fiction hacks, Roddenberry and staff believed they had struck literary gold. For the cover of the first collection: the striking illustration NBC had commissioned James Bama to draw for promoting the premiere of the series.

In the summer of 1967, Western Publishing, best known for its Gold Key Comics and Little Golden Books, introduced the *Star Trek* comic book line, with photographs of the

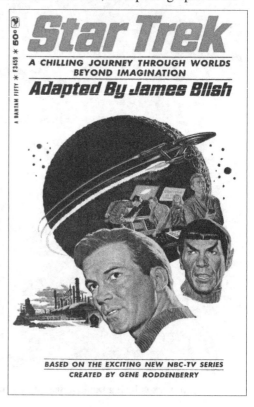

First Gold Key *Star Trek* comic, for 12 cents, and first Bantam *Star Trek* paperback, for 50 cents, both from early 1967

series' stars on front and back covers. The story concept in issue number one -- a planet populated by intelligent and carnivorous vegetation -- had been on the drawing board so long that it prominently featured Yeoman Rand.

All the merchandising meant good news for *Star Trek*'s lead cast members. Every time Kirk and Spock had their images printed on a toy package, a paperback book, or a comic, there was a royalty paid to Shatner and Nimoy. Desilu and Roddenberry, of course, made money too.

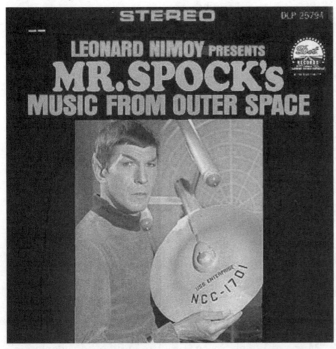

Nimoy's first Dot record album – a surprise hit in 1967

Another financial windfall came with the release of *Mr. Spock's Music from Outer Space*. In December 1966, Dot Records, a subsidiary of Paramount Pictures, approached Herb Solow with the idea of distributing a *Star Trek*-themed album. Solow immediately sent a memo to his colleagues, saying:

> I think we should pursue any record company that wants to do an outer space or Vulcan single record or album, be it straight dramatic music, weird music, Nichelle Nichols singing, Bill Shatner doing bird calls, or even the sound of Gene Roddenberry polishing a semi-precious stone on his grinder.

A deal was quickly struck and a music producer was chosen -- Charles Grean, a composer and arranger who had found success with disposable yet popular novelty fare, such as "I've Got a Lovely Bunch of Coconuts," by Merv Griffin, and "Quentin's Theme," the surprise radio hit from television's *Dark Shadows*. Grean was assigned the task of creating something on which the kids would squander $2.50 -- the going rate for an LP record. But Grean wasn't interested in Nichelle Nichols singing, Shatner doing bird calls, or Roddenberry and his grinder. He had his eye -- and his ear -- fixed on another member of the *Star Trek* family.

"Charles Grean has a teenage daughter who is a fan of Mr. Spock," Nimoy said in a 1968 interview. "She said, 'Well, if you're going to do an album of music from *Star Trek*, then Mr. Spock should be on that album.'"

Herb Solow expressed concern over Nimoy's involvement. In a December 14, 1966 memo to Roddenberry and the Desilu legal reps, he wrote:

> Regarding Leonard Nimoy, I imagine we have our standard deal with him and can convey it to Dot Records. If not, I would hope that we would have

some pressure on Alex Brewis [Nimoy's agent] not to dampen any interest in our deal by trying to price his client out of the Dot Records' business.

Brewis played ball. Nimoy signed on the Dot. It was good business all around.

Roddenberry wrote to Solow on December 19, 1966:

In the matter of the Leonard Nimoy album, since it will undoubtedly contain something of the *Star Trek* theme, I would expect to receive a lyric royalty. And, since "Mr. Spock" is a creation of mine -- maintained against some odds -- I would like to have some voice in the nature and direction of this album, nor do I feel that a special arrangement with myself and Norway Corporation on profits from the album would be at all out of order.

Publicity photo used in teen magazines promoting the music of Mr. Spock

"Norway Corporation" was another way of saying "Roddenberry."

The liner notes of the album Grean assembled, with Nimoy's enthusiastic support, described its content as "kicky, mod" arrangements of popular songs, like "Music to Watch Girls By," now given the new title "Music to Watch Space Girls By." And a "hip adaptation" of the "Theme to *Star Trek*." "Beyond Antares," William Hatch and Gene Coon's original song, which Uhura sang in "The Conscience of the King," was presented as a haunting and lovely instrumental. Nimoy talked his way through "Alien," a spoken-word piece explaining the nature of a Vulcan, and "Twinkle, Twinkle Little Earth," a somewhat amusing poem set to space-music, which he also co-wrote. Alexander Courage received the songwriting credit for "Where No Man Has Gone Before," a two-and-a-half minute track made-up of the music heard under Shatner's "Space, the final frontier..." narration. And then, yes, Nimoy sang. "You Are Not Alone," written for the album by a colleague of Grean's, was a perfect fit for the alienated Spock, with a lyric about watching stars in the sky and wondering if we are, indeed, not alone. The album closed with "A Visit to A Sad Planet," co-written by Grean. Set to suspenseful cinematic music, it was a spoken-word piece about the Enterprise coming across a dying planet, as documented by the ship's log. The people of this world had annihilated themselves through nuclear war. The not-so-surprising ending: The planet was known as Earth.

Pleased by the results, and even quite surprised, Charles Grean wrote to Ed Perlstein on March 2, 1967, admitting, "The Leonard Nimoy album turned-out much better than I expected!"

The music critic for *Variety* found the album to be better than expected, as well. The review for the April 19, 1967, edition, said:

> Leonard Nimoy, who plays Mr. Spock in the TV series *Star Trek*, is spotlighted here in a program of songs and readings mostly pegged to out-of-this world ideas. Nimoy's vocals on such numbers as "Where is Love," "You Are Not Alone" and "Lost in the Stars," are pleasantly rugged. He also registers nicely on his readings of tunes like "Twinkle, Twinkle Little Earth" and "A Visit to a Sad Planet," an ominous description of a post-atomic holocaust on Earth.

With Mr. Spock on the front cover, holding the three-foot long model of the Enterprise featured in "Tomorrow Is Yesterday," the record was not going to escape the attention of *Star Trek*'s growing legion of fans. It entered Billboard's album charts on June 10, 1967, and remained there for an impressive 25 weeks, selling steadily, well-through the Christmas buying season. Even the track selected as the album's single, "A Visit to A Sad Planet," made the charts. *Mr. Spock's Music from Outer Space* was intended to be a one-time event. However, before the end of the year, Dot was happy to sign Nimoy to a long-term contract.

The success of this latest *Star Trek* tie-in caused ill feelings between series' composer Alexander Courage and Gene Roddenberry. Courage wrote the music for the "Theme to *Star Trek*," featured on the album as an instrumental, but, to his way of thinking, had been forced into sharing credit and, more importantly, the royalty, with Roddenberry, who had dashed off a lyric for the song.

Justman said, "People are people. They have their good points and their bad points. And there were certain things that Gene did.... [He] was in financial need and he saw a way to get some money." (94-1)

Courage said, "I think I have the right to be bitter. It turns out there was a clause in my contract which had been supplied to Roddenberry by his attorney to the effect that if a lyric was ever written by Roddenberry to the theme I wrote, whether it was ever used or not, Roddenberry would share in my royalties.... So, Roddenberry wrote a lyric, presented it to me and announced that he would from then on participate in my royalties." (37-3)

On October 3, 1967, preparing for possible litigation, Roddenberry wrote a letter to Courage. It read, in part:

> In my old office, the small bungalow across the lot, you and I sat down one afternoon and discussed sharing the credits on the music. I recall very distinctly that you shook your head and stated you would naturally prefer not to split the money on the theme but, on the other hand, since this was the way it was and since we were working so closely together on the concept, you would go along with it.... I think you know it has never been my way or policy to be unfair. On the other hand, I have always considered handshake agreements not only to be as binding as written agreements but also more important.

Roddenberry won. Fifty percent of the royalties belonged to him. To add insult to injury, Courage disdained the lyric, which began:

> *Beyond the rim of the star-light,*
> *My love is wand'ring in star-flight.*
> *I know he'll find in star-clustered reaches,*
> *Lu-uv, strange love a star woman teaches.*

He complained, "Roddenberry's lyrics totally lacked musical practicality. He made two very serious errors in writing the lyrics. One, he changed the shape of the melody by adding extra beats, and two, he used a closed vowel with a z-z-z-z-z sound on the highest notes, something that gives great problems to singers."

Robert Justman added, "Owing to the 'royalty' issue, it's no wonder Sandy Courage lost all enthusiasm for the series and liking for Gene Roddenberry." (94-8)

Regardless, Courage would return. It was hard to ignore *Star Trek*.

***

Star Trek's first nod for its excellence in production came from an unlikely source: the January issue of the Count Dracula Society newsletter: "The society voted a science fiction program, NBC's *Star Trek*, as the best television program of the year, deserving the 1967 Television Award for its high quality of 'fantasy and imagination.'"

And it beat out *Dark Shadows*.

The second nod was not given for *Star Trek*'s scripts, or acting, or direction, or even for its optical effects, but for its sound -- a very deserving recognition. More than any other series on TV, the work that went into cleaning and enhancing the audio on each *Star Trek* episode was an immense chore. First, sounds had to be removed, such as the noise of wood dragging against wood whenever a door on the Enterprise slid open or shut (replaced by whooshes), and the creaks and moans from the bridge, along with footsteps, as the actors walked on the multi-leveled set of plywood and strained hinges that held each slice of the circular pie together. Second, the sounds of the ship had to be added. Each room had a constant and steady tone of its own, whether it was the blending of a hundred different electronic components on the bridge, or the low moan of the engines heard in the corridors, or the hydraulics of the turbo lifts, or the beeping of a heart monitoring device in sickbay. Call Kirk on his communicator, the Sound Editor had to add in a chirp. When Kirk flipped it open, dialed in a signal, and then flipped it shut -- three more sounds were needed. When the transporter was used, the Sound Editor faded-in the music cue from Alexander Courage that tinkled and hummed along with the effect. When the landing party materialized on an alien world, the Editor would cue the alien world atmospheric sound. There was also a phaser sound, the computer had a sound, and for the intercom, the boatswain whistle. You can rarely make it through more than 10 or 20 seconds of *Star Trek* without a sound effect being heard, often layers and layers of sound effects.

The nucleus of *Star Trek*'s sound department in 1966 and 1967 was Supervising Editor Jack Finlay, and sound editors Doug Grindstaff, Joseph Sorokin, and Tom Biggart. Finlay had been in charge of the audio enhancement on TV's *Combat!*, Grindstaff edited sound for a sci-fi movie called *Destination Inner Space*, Sorokin manipulated the soundtrack on Desilu's *The Untouchables*, and Biggart cut the audio together for the sitcom *Hazel*.

Finlay said, "Trying to get the work done on time was the big thing, because that's the name of the game in television -- deadlines. They didn't give us a lot of money to get the stuff together, but on one occasion I told Gene that I needed a full night on the sound stage to play back what I had, just to see what was there.... Joe [Sorokin] and I worked all through that night compositing everything I had, listening to it, changing it, eliminating some things and adding others." (62)

Sorokin said, "The bridge of the Enterprise was kind of a joint effort between Jack

Finlay and myself. We had about seven or eight loops going, perhaps as many as a dozen, and from that we made various combinations until we got it all down to one.... Originally, we tried to synchronize the sounds with all those flashing lights built onto the bridge, but that was a never-ending, totally ridiculous situation. So after a while we just got hold of a half-dozen to a dozen different loops of various sounds for the Enterprise bridge. Doug Grindstaff, I might say, is perhaps one of the most able, competent men in the business." (162)

Grindstaff said, "It was very tough, very hard work, and... we'd have to create a lot of stuff, spend hours working on it. Gene would come up to the cutting room, and I'd run something for him, and explain, 'This is what we're doing,' and he'd say, 'Yeah, that's it,' or 'Maybe you should take this direction.' I'd have three or four sounds that I'd developed to a certain point and then I'd have him come up to take a look at them and ask, 'Which way do you want to go?' Gene had a knack of pulling in people, creatively. All of a sudden you were just sucked into it, and you couldn't let go. It was a seven-day-a-week, total commitment. But it was just such a pleasure working with Roddenberry, Bob Justman, and Eddie Milkis. They were just great, the three of them." (76-2)

In recognition of their hard work, and singling-out the episode "Space Seed," *Star Trek*'s sound department received a nomination from MPSE -- the Motion Picture Sound Editors. On February, 16, 1967, Roddenberry sent a letter of congratulations to Douglas H. Grindstaff and Tom Biggart, the two contributors to that episode. He told them:

> Although I have congratulated you in person for your part in *Star Trek* being nominated for the Golden Reel Sound Award, I did want to put it in writing, too. *Star Trek* sound has been a challenging experience for all of us, to say the least. Without the craftsmanship and talent you brought, it could have been a frustrating and sad experience. Somehow, despite all the hard work, late hours and everything else, it was full of rewarding and pleased experiences. The part you played in all this should be recognized and I'm glad it has been recognized in this fashion. Whether we win the final Award or not is much less important than the fact that it was an excellent job done by a group of excellent people.

The Emmys could not ignore *Star Trek*, either. And that, in itself, was newsworthy. Science fiction had never been favored by the Academy of Television Arts and Sciences, *The Twilight Zone* being the only exception, nominated as Best Dramatic Series for one of its five seasons on CBS. Only one. Rod Serling also received two Emmys for Outstanding Writing, and was nominated for a third. But the other writers, including Richard Matheson, Jerry Sohl, and George Clayton Johnson, had been ignored. As were the directors. As were the composers. As were the set designers and makeup artists. As were the special effects technicians. As were the guest performers. As was the host. *The Outer Limits* was snubbed far worse. During its two-year run, the series garnered only one nomination at the Emmys: Jack Poplin was considered in the category of Best Art Direction. All else involved with this stylistic series were, in the eyes of the Academy, unworthy of recognition. But things were changing.

Leonard Nimoy recalled being at home with his wife on Monday, May 1, when he received a telegram from The Academy of Television Arts & Sciences. He was so surprised and overcome by the news that he joined his wife in doing a very *un*-Spock-like thing -- he cried. Nimoy, and Spock, had been nominated for an Emmy.

The actor later said, "I thought, 'Whoa. Wow. What a thrill.' Particularly because the nominations are done by your fellow actors, and I thought, 'They're getting it, they can see what I'm doing.' It just really moved me deeply." (128-18)

The press revealed the complete list of nominations the following day.

In the hybrid category of Individual Achievement in Art Direction and Allied Crafts, *Star Trek*'s Jim Rugg and his "Mechanical Special Effects" competed against those of *Voyage to the Bottom of the Sea*, the Makeup for "Mark Twain Tonight," the Makeup and Costume Design for "Alice Through the Looking Glass," as well as the Art Direction and Set Decoration for "Death of a Salesman." It was a strange mix of apples and oranges.

In the category of Cinematography, Jerry Finnerman's excellent work was ignored. In fact, only one Cinematographer was nominated, for the overly-bright lighting and run-of-the-mill camera work on *Bonanza*, and strangely, this was in competition against the Photographic Special Effects of L.B. Abbot for *The Time Tunnel* and *Voyage to the Bottom of the Sea*, and The Howard Anderson Company, for *Star Trek*.

In the category of Film and Sound Editing, Douglas H. Grindstaff was again acknowledged (as he had been by MPSE), and was pitted against a pair of film editors from *Mission: Impossible*, and a team of four sound editors who collaborated on *Voyage to the Bottom of the Sea*.

Nimoy's name showed-up in the category of Best Supporting Dramatic Actor, competing against Leo G. Carroll for *The Man from U.N.C.L.E.*, and Eli Wallach, for the dramatic special, "The Poppy Is Also a Flower." The character NBC had originally wanted off the series, the satanic-looking half-human that the network feared would alienate viewers in the South, was now acknowledged as a true contender.

The biggest surprise regarded the biggest trophy -- *Star Trek*, the most nominated science fiction series for a single year in the history of television, was being considered for the all-important category of Outstanding Dramatic Series, against *I Spy*, *Run for Your Life*, *The Avengers,* and *Mission: Impossible*. Win or lose, this was historic -- no science fiction program had ever been nominated, let alone perceived, as a Best Drama.

The 19th Annual Emmy Award ceremony took place on June 4, 1967. It was an important night for Desilu. *Star Trek* entered the room with its five nominations. *The Lucy Show* had garnered three, including one for the boss lady herself. *Mission: Impossible* had six. With these three shows, the little studio trying so hard to prove something to the industry had 14 nods from its peers.

Roddenberry, Coon, Justman, and Nimoy were there in their rented tuxedos, with their wives decked-out in recently-purchased gowns, all seated at the Desilu table. Herb Solow was also present, sitting close to the other nominees: Lucy and Gale Gordon from *The Lucy Show*, and members of the Impossible Missions Force, including creator Bruce Geller, producer Joe Gantman, and stars Martin Landau and Barbara Bain.

The technical awards came first. Jim Rugg, an apple in that apples and oranges category, lost to a pair of oranges, the prize being shared between Costume Design for "Alice Through the Looking Glass" and Makeup for "Mark Twain Tonight." The Howard Anderson Company lost to Irwin Allen's effects guru, for his work on *The Time Tunnel* and *Voyage to the Bottom of the Sea*. And Douglas Grindstaff gave it up to the team from *Voyage to the Bottom of the Sea*. There was little surprise when Leonard Nimoy and Leo G. Carroll watched Eli Wallach give the acceptance speech for Best Supporting Actor. As for Best Drama, even the *Star Trek* people were betting on *I Spy* or *Mission: Impossible*. The former, clearly the favorite for television's top prize, had won the Golden Globe award earlier in the year as Best Series on TV.

Even though *Star Trek* was not to go home a winner, this was nonetheless Desilu's night. *Mission: Impossible* was the big winner, not just as Outstanding Dramatic Series, but also for Outstanding Continued Performance by an Actress in a Leading Role in a Dramatic Series, Outstanding Writing Achievement in Drama, and Outstanding Achievements in Film and Sound Editing. No other show took home this many awards in 1967. And while *The Lucy Show* won only a single Emmy, it was the one that counted the most, at least to Lucy. She was crowned the funniest gal in television.

A big night for Lucy and Desilu – 14 nominations, 5 wins

Herb Solow remembered, "Bruce Geller, Barbara Bain, and *Mission* Producer Joe Gantman had already removed their dessert plates and proudly positioned their glistening gold Emmys before them. Roddenberry, Coon, and Justman, having little choice, continued trying to enjoy their desserts." (161-3)

***

It was unlikely that *Star Trek* was going to be able to deliver all four of the final first season episodes ordered by NBC, as announced by *Daily Variety* on December 9. "The City on the Edge of Forever" and "Operation: Annihilate!" -- episodes 28 and 29, respectively -- were both a week late in delivery to the network. "The Alternative Factor," the botched episode intended to be the final new show to air, had to be pulled forward on the broadcast list to No. 27. The scripts for Paul Schneider's "Tomorrow the Universe" and Theodore Sturgeon's "Amok Time," both commissioned in December, and D.C. Fontana's "Friday's Child," in development during January of 1967, were not going to be ready in time to keep Desilu Stages 9 and 10 from going dark for at least a couple weeks, thereby costing the studio substantial monetary losses. At the studio's request, NBC cut its order back to 29 episodes. That final episode ("Operation: Annihilate!") wrapped on February 22 and aired on April 13, 1967.

Robert Justman was delegated the task (or given the honor) of selecting which first season episodes would repeat on NBC. Of course, he took in consideration suggestions from Roddenberry, and from NBC, and from the fans, based on their letters to the show.

"The Man Trap," the first episode to air, was the first to *not* make the rerun list. According to A.C. Nielsen, more people had seen this *Star Trek* than any other, so, in Justman's mind, why watch it again? The mixed -- but mostly bad -- reviews "Man Trap" garnered after that much-watched premier also factored into Justman's decision.

"The Enemy Within," a well-received episode by fans and critics alike, was not in such great favor at the network, due to Captain Kirk's alter-ego's attempted rape of Yeoman

Rand. It also presented a continuity problem. Now that it was established that the Enterprise carried shuttlecraft, viewers might well wonder why one wasn't used to rescue Sulu and his landing party from the freezing planet. Despite this, the creative staff was proud of "Enemy" and it did make the first list of potential repeats Justman submitted to NBC in late March, 1967. A week later, on April 4, it was removed from the roster and replaced with "The Devil in the Dark," an episode that Roddenberry, at this time, did not care for, but which NBC regarded highly.

"Dagger of the Mind" was an episode the creative staff and the NBC programmers didn't seem to particularly like or dislike. It merely was. And, so, it was merely omitted.

"The Conscience of the King" was, for the most part, liked by the staff, but not by Stan Robertson at NBC, who found it completely lacking in action or adventure.

"The Galileo Seven" cost a good chunk of money to make, but many at *Star Trek*, Leonard Nimoy included, felt separating Kirk and Spock in the way this story did was, by and large, an experiment gone wrong.

"Court Martial," based on the fan mail, was well-liked. The staff, however, considered it a "dog."

"Errand of Mercy," which gave us our introduction to the Klingons, and the surprise ending involving the true nature of the Organians, was liked by many, but not by Justman. It didn't make the cut.

"The Alternative Factor," a rare case where creative staff, NBC, and the fans were in complete agreement, was the first season's one undeniable misfire. The gutting of the subplot -- the love story between white Lazarus and a black female engineering officer -- was one reason for the failure. The other, of course, was the last minute recasting caused by the sudden departure of John Drew Barrymore. All involved wanted to forget this *Trek*.

"Operation: Annihilate!" was the final dropout. It is certainly not a bad episode. But the creative staff had struggled with the cluttered script and never felt confident that they had worked all the bugs out.

Of the 21 episodes to repeat, Justman had his reasons for sequencing them as he did. In a memo to Roddenberry, he wrote, "Hopefully, it would be to our advantage to be able to schedule 'Miri' just after school vacation starts. And I believe that 'Arena' would be the right kind of show to schedule either just before or just after the Fourth of July Holiday."

With these two episodes, Justman was aiming toward a young audience. With others, he was vying for the *TV Guide* CLOSE-UP listing. Looking ahead at the other network's planned competition, and certain Thursday nights when it appeared ABC and CBS had little to brag about, he scheduled episodes he believed to be both excellent and highly promotable, hoping to catch the eye of the *TV Guide* critics and be regarded as the night's most outstanding program. He guessed wrong on the nights he scheduled "The Corbomite Maneuver," "The Naked Time," "The Menagerie, Part 1," and "Tomorrow Is Yesterday" -- all episodes he believed deserved to be singled-out. But *Star Trek* struck gold when the top-selling magazine in America put a spotlight on the repeats of "Shore Leave," "Balance of Terror," and "This Side of Paradise" as well as the late-season first run of "The City on the Edge of Forever." No other series snagged as many CLOSE-UP listings from *TV Guide* during the Spring and Summer months of 1967 than *Star Trek*.

The rerun season began as perhaps the first-run season should have, with the series' second pilot.

RATINGS / Nielsen 30-Market report for Thursday, April 20, 1967:
Repeat episode, "Where No Man Has Gone Before."

8:30 - 9 p.m., 58.9% households using TVs.	**Rating:**	**Share:**
NBC: *Star Trek* (first half)	17.1	29.0%
ABC: ***Bewitched***	**18.9**	**32.1%**
CBS: *My Three Sons*	14.6	24.8%
Independent stations:	10.3	14.1%
9 - 9:30 p.m., 60.1% households using TVs.	**Rating:**	**Share:**
NBC: ***Star Trek* (second half)**	**17.6**	**29.3%**
ABC: ***That Girl***	**17.6**	**29.3%**
CBS: *CBS Thursday Night Movie* (start)	17.0	28.3%
Independent stations:	10.0	13.1%

When first shown in September 1966, "Where No Man Has Gone Before" won its time slot. Now it came in second for the first half-hour, and tied at first place for the finale.

Of the competition, *Star Trek* had a new opponent at 9 p.m. On ABC, flip-flopping with *Love on a Rooftop* and now beginning 30 minutes earlier, was *That Girl*, a quirky sitcom about the exploits of aspiring actress Ann Marie (Marlo Thomas) and her New York City writer/boyfriend (Ted Bessell). On CBS was 1961's *A Raisin in the Sun*, starring Sidney Poitier.

But *Star Trek* remained a strong contender. Yet it was in danger of being cancelled.

In the early Summer of 1967, A.C. Nielsen compiled a Top 10 list of the highest-rated series with teenages between ages 12 and 17 (the most desirable demographic for sponsors), throughout for the month of April, during the network "sweeps" period. The shows ranked as follows:

1. *Bonanza* (NBC)
2. *The Beverly Hillbillies* (CBS)
3. *I Spy* (NBC)
4. *Gomer Pyle, U.S.M.C.* (CBS)
5. All Star Basketball (six-game playoff series) (ABC)
6. *Family Affair* (CBS)
7. *Thursday Night Movie* (CBS)
8. *The Avengers* (ABC)
9. *Star Trek* (NBC)
10. *Green Acres* (CBS)

One must wonder why a network would consider cancelling a Top 40 series (which was Top 10 with teens), that was almost always a solid second place entry in the ratings for its timeslot, and which often hit the No. 1 spot.

The answers and the most surprising *Star Trek* stories follow in the second volume of *These Are the Voyages*.

APPENDIX / SEASON ONE QUICK REFERENCE:

STAR TREK first season story assignments (in order given):

ST #	Title:	Writer:
1.	The Cage	Gene Roddenberry
2.	Where No Man Has Gone Before	Samuel A. Peeples
3.	The Omega Glory	Gene Roddenberry
4.	Warriors World	Stephen Kandel
4a.	Mudd's Women	Stephen Kandel; Roddenberry's story
5.	Dagger of the Mind	Shimon Wincelberg
6.	The Corbomite Maneuver	Jerry Sohl
7.	The City on the Edge of Forever	Harlan Ellison
8.	What Are Little Girls Made Of?	Robert Bloch
9.	The Naked Time	John D.F. Black
10.	The Machine That Went Too Far	A.E. van Vogt
11.	Chicago II	George C. Johnson; Roddenberry's idea
12.	Miri	Adrian Spies
13.	The Man Trap	Lee Erwin; reassigned to G.C. Johnson
14.	The Enemy Within	Richard Matheson
15.	Alien Spirit	Norman Katkov
16.	The Galileo Seven	Oliver Crawford
17.	The Conscience of the King	Barry Trivers
18.	Balance of Terror	Paul Schneider
19.	Untitled	Jack Guss
20.	Journey to Reolite	Alfred Brenner
21.	Charlie X	D.C. Fontana; Gene Roddenberry's story
22.	Return to Eden	Alvin Boretz
23.	Court Martial	Don Mankiewicz
24.	Shore Leave	Theodore Sturgeon; Roddenberry's idea
25.	Rites to Fertility	Robert Sheckley
1a.	From the First Day to the Last	John D.F. Black
1b.	The Menagerie	Gene Roddenberry
26.	This Side of Paradise	Jerry Soul
27.	Sisters in Space	Robert Sheckley
28.	Portrait of Black & White	Barry Trivers; Roddenberry's concept
29.	Rock-A-Bye Baby or Die!	George Clayton Johnson
30.	The Squire of Gothus	Paul Schneider
31.	The Squaw	Shimon Wincelberg
32.	Accident of Love	Allen Balter & William Woodfield
33.	The Return of the Archons	Boris Sobelman; Roddenberry's idea
34.	The Alternative Factor	Don Ingalls
35.	Botany Bay / Space Seed	Carey Wilbur
36.	A Taste of Armageddon	Robert Hammer
37.	Dreadnaught	Alf Harris & Jeeli Jacobs
38.	Tomorrow Is Yesterday	D.C. Fontana
39.	Arena	Gene L. Coon
40.	World of Warriors / Tomorrow the Universe	Paul Schneider
41.	Amok Time	Theodore Sturgeon; Roddenberry's idea
42.	Operation: Destroy / Operation: Annihilate!	Steven Carabatsos; Roddenberry's idea
43.	Friday's Child	D.C. Fontana
44.	The Devil in the Dark	Gene L. Coon
45.	Errand of Mercy	Gene L. Coon

STAR TREK first season episodes (in order filmed):

Prod #:	Title:	Director:	Days:
1.	The Cage	Robert Butler	
2.	Where No Man Has Gone Before	James Goldstone	8
3.	The Corbomite Maneuver	Joseph Sargent	6 ½
4.	Mudd's Women	Harvey Hart	7 ½
5.	The Enemy Within	Leo Penn	6 ¾
6.	The Man Trap	Marc Daniels	6
7.	The Naked Time	Marc Daniels	5 ¾
8.	Charlie X	Lawrence Dobkin	6 ½
9.	Balance of Terror	Vincent McEveety	6 ½
10.	What Are Little Girls Made Of?	James Goldstone	8
11.	Dagger of the Mind	Vincent McEveety	6 ½
12.	Miri	Vincent McEveety	7
13.	The Conscience of the King	Gerd Oswald	7
14.	The Galileo Seven	Robert Gist	7
15.	Court Martial	Marc Daniels	6 ½
16.	The Menagerie	Marc Daniels	5 ½
17.	Shore Leave	Robert Sparr	7
18.	The Squire of Gothos	Don McDougall	7
19.	Arena	Joseph Pevney	6
20.	The Alternative Factor	Gerd Oswald	7
21.	Tomorrow Is Yesterday	Michael O'Herlihy	6
22.	The Return of the Archons	Joseph Pevney	7
24.	Space Seed	Marc Daniels	6
23	A Taste of Armageddon	Joseph Pevney	6
25	This Side of Paradise	Ralph Senensky	7
26	The Devil in the Dark	Joseph Pevney	7
27	Errand of Mercy	John Newland	6
28	The City on the Edge of Forever	Joseph Pevney	7 ½
29.	Operation: Annihilate!	Herschel Daugherty	6 ½

STAR TREK first season broadcast schedule:

Air Date:	Title:
09/08/66	The Man Trap
09/15/66	Charlie X
09/22/66	Where No Man Has Gone Before
09/29/66	The Naked Time
10/06/66	The Enemy Within
10/13/66	Mudd's Women
10/20/66	What Are Little Girls Made Of?
10/27/66	Miri
11/03/66	Dagger of the Mind
11/10/66	The Corbomite Maneuver
11/17/66	The Menagerie, Part 1
11/24/66	The Menagerie, Part 2
12/01/66	(pre-emption) - Jack Benny Special
12/08/66	The Conscience of the King
12/15/66	Balance of Terror
12/22/66	(repeat) - What Are Little Girls Made Of?
12/29/66	Shore Leave
01/05/67	The Galileo Seven
01/12/67	The Squire of Gothos
01/19/67	Arena
01/26/67	Tomorrow Is Yesterday
02/02/67	Court Martial
02/09/67	The Return of the Archons
02/16/67	Space Seed
02/23/67	A Taste of Armageddon
03/09/67	This Side of Paradise
03/09/67	The Devil in the Dark
03/16/67	(pre-emption) – Ringling Brothers Circus Special
03/23/67	Errand of Mercy
03/30/67	The Alternative Factor
04/06/67	**The City on the Edge of Forever** (*TV Guide* CLOSE-UP listing)
04/13/67	Operation: Annihilate!
04/20/67	(repeat) – Where No Man Has Gone Before
04/27/67	(repeat) – The Naked Time
05/04/67	(repeat) – Mudd's Women
05/11/67	(repeat) – The Corbomite Maneuver
05/18/67	(repeat) – The Menagerie, Part 1
05/25/67	(repeat) – The Menagerie, Part 2
06/01/67	(repeat) – Charlie X
06/08/67	(repeat) – **Shore Leave** (*TV Guide* CLOSE-UP listing)
06/15/67	(repeat) – The Devil in the Dark
06/22/67	(repeat) – The Squire of Gothos
06/29/67	(repeat) – Miri
07/06/67	(repeat) – Arena
07/13/67	(repeat) – Tomorrow is Yesterday
07/20/67	(repeat) – A Taste of Armageddon
07/27/67	(repeat) – The Return of the Archons
08/03/67	(repeat) – **Balance of Terror** (*TV Guide* CLOSE-UP listing)
08/10/67	(repeat) – **This Side of Paradise** (*TV Guide* CLOSE-UP listing)
08/17/67	(pre-emption) – Music special: "An Evening at Tanglewood"
08/24/67	(repeat) – Space Seed
08/31/67	(repeat) – The City on the Edge of Forever
09/07/67	(pre-emption) – GE Theatre special: "Damn Yankees"

BIBLIOGRAPHY

WEBSITES:

www.startrekpropauthority.com
www.memorayalpha.com
www.startrek.com
www.startrekhistory.com
www.trekcore.com
orionpress/unseenelements

BOOKS:

Beam Me Up, Scotty, by James Doohan with Peter David (Pocket Books, December 1996).
Beyond Uhura: Star Trek and Other Memories, by Nichelle Nichols (G.P. Putnam's Sons, 1994).
Best of Enterprise Incidents, The, edited by James Van Hise (Pioneer Books, 1990).
Best of Trek, The, edited by Walter Irwin and G.B. Love (Signet Books, April 1978).
Best of Trek #2, The, edited by Walter Irwin and G.B. Love (Signet Books, March 1980).
Boarding the Enterprise, by David Gerrold and Robert J. Sawyer (Benbella Books, 2006).
Boldly Writing: A Trekker Fan and Zine History, 1967-1987, by Joan Marie Verba (FTL Publications, 1996).
Captains' Logs, by Edward Gross and Mark A. Altman (Little, Brown and Company, 1995).
City on the Edge of Forever, The, by Harlan Ellison (White Wolf Publishing, September 1996).
Desilu: The Story of Lucille Ball and Desi Arnaz, by Coyne Steven Sanders and Tom Gilbert (Quill / William Morris, 1993).
Encyclopedia of Trekkie Memorabilia, by Chris Gentry & Sally Gibson-Downs (Books Americana, 1988).
From Sawdust to Stardust: The Biography of DeForest Kelley, by Terry Lee Rioux (Pocket Books, February 2005).
Gene Roddenberry: The Last Conversation, by Yvonne Fern (University of California Press, 1994).
Gene Roddenberry: The Myth and the Man Behind Star Trek, by Joel Engel (Hyperion, 1994).
Great Birds of the Galaxy, by Edward Gross and Mark A. Altman (BoxTree Limited, 1994).
Greenberg's Guide to Star Trek Collectibles, by Christine Gentry and Sally Gibson-Downs (Greenberg Publishing, 1991).
I Am Not Spock, by Leonard Nimoy (Celestial Arts, November 1975).
I Am Spock, by Leonard Nimoy (Hyperion, 1996).
Inside Star Trek: The Real Story, by Herbert F. Solow and Robert H. Justman (Pocket Books, June 1996).
Longest Trek: My Tour of the Galaxy, The, by Grace Lee Whitney with Jim Denney (Quill Driver Books / World Dancer Press, 1998).
Making of Star Trek, The, by Stephen E. Whitfield and Gene Roddenberry (Ballantine Books, September 1968).
Music of Star Trek, The, by Jeff Bond (Lone Eagle Publishing, 1999).
On the Good Ship Enterprise: My 15 Years with Star Trek, by Bjo Trimble (The Donning Company / Publishers, 1983).
Shatner: Where No Man ..., by William Shatner, Sondra Marshak and Myrna Culbreath (Temp Star Books, 1979).
Starlog: Star Trek's Greatest Guest Stars, edited by David McDonnell (HarperCollins, January 1997).
Star Trek, adapted by James Blish (Bantam Books, January 1967).
Star Trek 2, adapted by James Blish (Bantam Books, February 1968).
Star Trek, No. 1: "K-G, Planet of Death" (Western Printing, 1967)
Star Trek: An Annotated Guide to Recourses on the Development, the Phenomenon, the People, the Television Series, the Films, the Novels and the Recordings, by Susan R. Gibberman (McFarland & Company, 1991).
Star Trek Compendium, The, by Allan Asherman (Pocket Books, 1986)
Star Trek Creator, by David Alexander (Roc Books / Penguin Group, June 1994).
Star Trek Fotonovel #1, City on the Edge of Forever, "Encounter with an Ellison," by Sandra Cawson (Bantam Books, November 1977).
Star Trek Interview Book, The, by Allan Asherman (Pocket Books, July 1988).
Star Trek Lives!, by Jaqueline Lichtenberg, Sondra Marshak and Joan Winston ((Bantam Books, July 1975).
Star Trek Memories, by William Shatner with Chris Kreski (HarperCollins, July 1994).
The Complete Directory to Prime Time Network TV Shows, by Tim Brooks and Earle Marsh (Ballantine Books, May 1979).
To the Stars: The Autobiography of George Takei, by George Takei (Pocket Books, October 1994).
Trek Classics, by Edward Gross (Image Publishing of New York, 1991).
Unauthorized History of Trek, The, by James Van Hise (HarperCollins, November 1995).
World of Star Trek, The, by David Gerrold (Ballantine Books, May 1973).

NEWSPAPER & MAGAZINE ARTICLES:

Weekly Variety, March 6, 1946, "Studio Contracts" -- Marc Daniels and DeForest Kelley.
Daily Variety, April 18, 1946, "35th P-T Feature" -- *Fear in the Night* starring DeForest Kelley.
Daily Variety, December 23, 1946, "*Variety Girl* Halts Until Friday" -- starring DeForest Kelley.
Daily Variety, December 26, 1946, "New Contracts" -- DeForest Kelley renewed by Paramount.
Weekly Variety, February 19, 1947, "Film Reviews: Fear in the Night," starring DeForest Kelley.
Variety, June 16, 1947; full page ad and sampling of reviews for *Fear in the City*, starring DeForest Kelley.
Weekly Variety, July 16, 1947, "Film Reviews: *Variety Girl*, co-starring DeForest Kelley.
Daily Variety, September 3, 1947, "Chatter" -- DeForest Kelley back from P.R. tour for Paramount.

Weekly Variety, October 20, 1947, Full page ad for *Variety Girl*," co-starring DeForest Kelley.
Daily Variety, June 22, 1948, "Film Reviews: *Canon City*," co-starring DeForest Kelley.
Daily Variety, April 17, 1952, "Film Preview: *Kid Monk Baroni*," co-starring Leonard Nimoy.
Daily Variety, June 19, 1953, "Television Reviews: *Favorite Story*: 'The Man Who Sold His Shadow,'" starring DeForest Kelley.
Daily Variety, July 17, 1953, "Ass't Directors to Air Their Prod'n Problems at Roundtable Parleys" -- Robert Justman.
Daily Variety, December 1, 1953, "Telepix Reviews: *Pepsi-Cola Playhouse*: 'Frozen Escape,'" co-starring DeForest Kelley.
Daily Variety, June 7, 1954, "Telepix Reviews: *Schlitz Playhouse of Stars*: 'Whale on the Beach,'" teleplay by Carey Wilbur.
Daily Variety, November 8, 1954, Telepix Reviews: *Inside Out*" – DeForest Kelley.
Dailey Variety, December 2, 1954, "Telpix Reviews: *Storm Signal*" – DeForest Kelley.
Daily Variety, May 19, 1955, "Telepix Reviews: *Science Fiction Theatre*: 'Y.O.R.D.,'" with DeForest Kelley.
Dailey Variety, February 2, 1956, "*Fox* at Bay" -- Robert Justman.
Daily Variety, March 6, 1956, "Kelley to Recreate OK Role for Hal Wallis."
Daily Variety, March 9, 1956, "Telepix Reviews: *Chevron Hall of Stars*: 'Secret Weapon of 117,'" teleplay by Robert Wesley (AKA Gene Roddenberry).
Daily Variety, May 18, 1956, "*Gunfight* Wounds Force Kelley from *Oklahoman*."
Weekly Variety, August 15, 1956, "Kidney Trouble Kayos Plummer, Shatner Subs."
Weekly Variety, October 10, 1956, "Television Reviews: *West Point*."
Daily Variety, November 23, 1956, "Telepix Reviews: *Stage for Tucson*."
Daily Variety, February 27, 1957, "Television Reviews: *Studio One*: 'The Defender'"; co-starring William Shatner.
Daily Variety, April 2, 1957, "'Eye' for Shatner," appearing on *Alfred Hitchcock*.
Weekly Variety, April 24, 1957, "Film Reviews: *The Girl in the Kremlin*"; screenplay by Gene L. Coon and Robert Hill.
Weekly Variety, May 1, 1957, "Legit Bits," William and Gloria Shatner quit Ontario play.
Daily Variety, May 7, 1957, "MGM Pacts Shatner."
Daily Variety, May 17, 1957, production date set for *The Brothers Karamazov*, co-staring Shatner.
Daily Variety, June 27, 1957, "Revue Pacts Coon."
Daily Variety, August 12, 1957, "Telepix Review: *Hands of the Enemy*" -- DeForest Kelley.
Daily Variety, August 13, 1957, "Telepix Reviews: *Kill and Run*" -- DeForest Kelley.
Weekly Variety, August 14, 1957, production continuing on *Brothers Karamazov* -- Shatner.
Daily Variety, September 16, 1957, "Telepix Reviews: *Have Gun, Will Travel*."
Daily Variety, September 23, 1957, "Telepix Reviews: *Schlitz Playhouse*: 'One Way Out'"; teleplay by Gene Coon.
Daily Variety, September 26, 1957, "Telepix Reviews: *Boots and Saddles*: 'The Gatling Gun'"; teleplay by Gene Roddenberry.
Weekly Variety, October 2, 1957, "Television Reviews: *Harbourmaster*: 'The Thievingest Dog,'" writer Carey Wilbur.
Daily Variety, October 4, 1957, "Telepix Reviews: *The Walter Winchell File*: 'Country Boy'"; teleplay by Adrian Spies.
Daily Variety, November 26, 1957, "Film Review: *Man in the Shadow*"; screenplay by Gene Coon.
Daily Variety, November 27, 1957, "Telepix Reviews: *Suspicion*: 'The Flight'"; teleplay by Halsted Welles and Gene Coon.
Daily Variety, December 16, 1957, "Telepix Reviews: *Jane Wyman Theatre*: 'The Perfect Alibi,'" teleplay by Roddenberry.
Daily Variety, January 9, 1958, "Light and Airy," by Jack Hellman, about "Sam Houston" pilot.
Daily Variety, January 13, 1958, "Telepix Reviews: *Schlitz Playhouse*: 'Guys Like O'Malley'"; teleplay by Gene Coon.
Daily Variety, February 6, 1958, "Light and Airy," by Jack Hellman, update Screen Gems' "Sam Houston" project.
Weekly Variety, February 19, 1958, "Film Reviews: *Brothers Karamazov*"; with William Shatner.
Daily Variety, April 14, 1958, "Telepix Reviews: *Shadow of a Dead Man*" -- DeForest Kelley.
Weekly Variety, June 4, 1958, "Film Reviews" -- *The Law and Jake Wade*, with DeForest Kelley.
Daily Variety, June 18, 1958, "Telepix Reviews: *Johnny Risk*" -- teleplay by Fred Freidberger, starring DeForest Kelley.
Daily Variety, June 23, 1958, "Television Reviews: *Playhouse 90*: 'A Town Has Turned to Dust'"; with Shatner.
Daily Variety, August 27, 1958, "15 Writers Set to do *Bat Masterson* Segs," including Roddenberry.
Daily Variety, September 12, 1958, "Legit Tryout: *The World of Suzie Wong*"; review for Shatner play.
Weekly Variety, October 1, 1958, "Television Reviews: *The Californians*: 'Dishonor for Matt Wayne,'" teleplay by Carey Wilbur.
Daily Variety, October 9, 1958, "Telepix Reviews: *Rescue 8*: 'The Ferris Wheel'"; teleplay by Gene Coon and Loren Dayle.
Daily Variety, October 13, 1958, "Telepix Reviews: *Cimarron City*: 'I, the People'" - teleplay by Gene Coon.
Weekly Variety, October 22, 1958, "Shows on Broadway: *The World of Suzie Wong*"; starring Shatner.
Daily Variety, November 11, 1958, "21 Teleplays Named for WGA Awards from shows since Axed"; includes nomination for Roddenberry.
Daily Variety, November 21, 1958, "West Downs East in Radio-TV Competition of Writers Guild" -- Gene Roddenberry wins for "Helen of Abajinian."
Daily Variety, March 3, 1959, "Short Shorts" -- son born to Robert Justman.
Weekly Variety, March 18, 1959, "ABC-TVs Complete Fall Lineup," includes "Big Walk," created by Roddenberry.
Weekly Variety, April 1, 1959, Film Reviews: *Warlock*" – with DeForest Kelley.
Daily Variety, April 27, 1959, "Light and Airy," by Jack Hellman; update on Roddenberry's "Big Walk."
Weekly Variety, May 6, 1959, "$7,000,000 in Pilots Down Drain; 200 Made But Only 35 Sold"; with update on "The Big Walk," by Roddenberry.
Daily Variety, May 25, 1959, Capra Named Prez at Anni SDG Meet" – Robert Justman voted V.P.
Daily Variety, June 2, 1959, "Sound and Picture," by Bob Chandler; status on Roddenberry deal with Screen Gems.

Weekly Variety, June 17, 1959, "Baptists' AM-TV Awards"; honoring Roddenberry.
Daily Variety, June 19, 1959, "Just for Variety," by Army Archerd, "TV 'heavy' DeForest Kelley." by Fred Freidberger and co-starring DeForest Kelley.
Daily Variety, August 4, 1959, "Geraghty to Rein Wrather Whiplash Skein in Australia"; Don Ingalls head writer and script supervisor.
Weekly Variety, October 7, 1959, "Syndication Reviews: *Lock Up*"; teleplay by Gene Coon.
Daily Variety, October 20, 1959, "Telepix Reviews: *General Electric Theater*: 'The Tallest Marine'"; teleplay by Gene Coon.
Daily Variety, October 30, 1959, Telepix Review: *The Four Just Men*: 'The Battle of the Bridge'"; teleplay by Gene Coon.
Daily Variety, November 2, 1959, "Telepix Review: *Desilu Playhouse*: 'So Tender, So Profane'"; teleplay by Adrian Spies.
Daily Variety, December 11, 1959, "Scribe Trio Joins Hal Hudson in New *Weapon* TV Oater"; Roddenberry deal.
Daily Variety, December 15, 1959, "Television Reviews: *Sunday Showcase*: 'The Indestructible Mr. Gore'"; starring Shatner.
Weekly Variety, December 16, 1959, "Screen Gems Loaded with Projects but Dozier Limits Pilots to 8 or 10"; includes update on Roddenberry's "The Big Walk."
Daily Variety, December 31, 1959, "Nimoy in Genet Legiter."
Daily Variety, January 15, 1960, "Gene Roddenberry Signs Exclusive Pact at SG."
Daily Variety, January 25, 1960, "Telepix Review: *Westinghouse Desilu Playhouse*: 'Meeting at Apalachin'"; teleplay by Adrian Spies.
Weekly Variety, January 27, 1960, "Tele Follow-Up comment: *Desilu Playhouse*."
Daily Variety, February 9, 1960, "Just for Variety," by Army Archerd"; update on "333 Montgomery Street."
Weekly Variety, March 23, 1960, "Film Reviews: *Thirteen Fighting Men*," co-screenplay by Robert Hamner.
Daily Variety, April 8, 1960, *Deathwatch* ad with reviews – Leonard Nimoy.
Daily Variety, May 16, 1960, "Television Reviews: *Westinghouse Desilu Playhouse*: 'City in Bondage'"; teleplay by Adrian Spies.
Weekly Variety, May 18, 1960, "Par TV in 2-Ply Sale; *Wrangler*, *Garland* All Set"; Roddenberry as writer and apprentice producer.
Daily Variety, June 15, 1960, "Television Reviews: *Alcoa Theatre*: '333 Montgomery'"; writer/producer Gene Roddenberry; co-starring DeForest Kelley.
Daily Variety, June 22, 1960, "Film Review: *House of Usher*," screenplay by Richard Matheson.
Weekly Variety, June 29, 1960. "*Wrangler*, *Diagnosis* Summer TV Entries Incept Pioneer Techniques," by Bob Chandler; concerning show involving Roddenberry.
Weekly Variety; June 30, 1960; review samplings for Shimon Wincelberg's *Kataki*.
Weekly Variety, July 6, 1960, "Par-TV *Wrangler* in Sponsor Jam"; series involving Roddenberry.
Weekly Variety, July 27, 1960, "*Wrangler* Gets Timid Go-Ahead"; Roddenberry involved in series.
Daily Variety, August 8, 1960, "Tele Review: *Wrangler*"; writer/producer Roddenberry.
Weekly Variety, August 10, 1960, Television Reviews: *Wrangler*"; writer/producer Roddenberry.
Daily Variety, September 6, 1960, "WGA 'Scabbing' Probe Still On"; Barry Trivers is WGA disciplinary committee chairman.
Daily Variety, September 12, 1960, "Telepix Reviews: The Tall Man," creator/writer/producer Samuel Peeples.
Weekly Variety, September 21, 1960, "Foreign Television Reviews: *Whiplash*"; teleplay by Roddenberry.
Variety, November 9, 1960, "Jeffrey Hunter Sees Playing Savior Start, Not End of Big Acting Roles."
Daily Variety, November 21, 1961, "150 Pilots Toe Prod'n Mark" -- Roddenberry's *Defiance County*.
Weekly Variety, November 22, 1961, "SG Gets TV Rights to *Farmer's Daughter*" - Roddenberry's *APO 923*.
Daily Variety, November 28, 1960, "*Tomorrow* for Culp," pilot written by Richard Matheson.
Daily Variety, December 15, 1960, "Justman TV Liaison" -- Robert Justman at MGM.
Daily Variety, February 3, 1961, "Film Review: *The Long Rope*," screenplay by Robert Hamner.
Daily Variety, March 22, 1961, "Shatner's 2-Bagger."
Daily Variety, April 26, 1961, "Film Reviews: *Master of the World*," screenplay by Richard Matheson.
Daily Variety, May 5, 1961, "Wind *Nuremberg* Shooting at Revue"; with Shatner.
Daily Variety, May 22, 1961, "Schnee Elected WGA-West Prez"; Barry Trivers is second V.P.
Daily Variety, June 8, 1961, "Television on Trial"; with Roddenberry as moderator.
Daily Variety, June 12, 1961, "Reveal New Crop of Sponsor Taboos as Writers Guild Puts 'TV on Trial,'" by Larry Tubelle; quoting Roddenberry.
Daily Variety, June 29, 1961, "Light and Airy," by Jack Hellman; quoting Gene Coon.
Daily Variety, July 28, 1961, *Meanwhile Back at the Front* ad with review samplings; book by Gene Coon.
Daily Variety, August 4, 1961, "Sam Peeples Preps New Revue Series."
Weekly Variety, August 9, 1961, "Film Reviews: *The Pit and the Pendulum*," screenplay by Richard Matheson.
Daily Variety, August 18, 1961, "Room for Shatner with Julie Harris"; Shatner into play.
Daily Variety, September 19, 1961, "Film Review: *Explosive Generation*," starring William Shatner.
Daily Variety, October 4, 1961, "Telepix Reviews: *Shannon*: 'The Embezzler's Daughter'"; teleplay by Roddenberry.
Weekly Variety, October 4, 1961, "Television Reviews: *Wagon Train*: 'The Captain Dan Brady Story'"; teleplay by Gene Coon; and "Shows Out of Town: *A Shot in the Dark*," starring Shatner.
Weekly Variety, October 11, 1961, "Film Reviews: *King of Kings*," starring Jeffrey Hunter.
Weekly Variety, October 18, 1961, "Film Reviews: *Judgment in Nuremberg*"; featuring Shatner.
Weekly Variety, October 25, 1961, Shows on Broadway: *A Shot in the Dark*"; starring Shatner.
Daily Variety, November 21, 1961, "On All Channels," by Dave Kaufman; concerning *Wrangler*, series Roddenberry worked on; "150 Pilots Toe Prod'n Mark," announcing "Defiance County" and "Douglass Selby."

Weekly Variety, November 22, 1961, "SG Gets TV Rights to Farmer's Daughter," plus update on Roddenberry's "APO 923."
Daily Variety, December 19, 1961, "CBS-TV Financing 2 More SG Pilots" -- Roddenberry's "APO 923" and "Defiance County"; also "On All channels," by Dave Kaufman, with update on "Douglass Selby."
Weekly Variety, December 20, 1961, "CBS-TV Practically All Set with '62-'63 Shows," including Roddenberry's "APO 923" and "Defiance County."
Daily Variety, December 27, 1961, "Four Screen Gems Pilots Will Roll Early Next Month," including Roddenberry's "APO 923" and "Defiance County."
Daily Variety, January 4, 1962, "ABC-TV Partnering Kovacs' New Series with Screen Gems"; status on "Defiance County" and "APO 923," both created by Roddenberry.
Daily Variety, January 5, 1962, "Bronson in Empire," with news that Roddenberry's "Defiance County" begins filming on January 8.
Daily Variety, February 2, 1967, "No CBS Shotgun on Shows," with Oscar Katz's word on Roddenberry's "APO 923."
Daily Variety, February 7, 1962, "Duning Tunes 'Defiance'"; update on Roddenberry pilot.
Daily Variety, February 26, 1962, "CBS-TV Adds Heft to Sat. Sked; Slots Jackie Gleason," bumping Roddenberry's "APO 923."
Daily Variety, March 1, 1962, "Light and Airy," by Jack Hellman, update on Roddenberry's "APO 923."
Daily Variety, April 27, 1962, "Light and Airy," by Jack Hellman; quoting Don Ingalls about *Have Gun, Will Travel*.
Daily Variety, May 9, 1962, "Shatner Exiting *Shot*."
Daily Variety, May 18, 1962, "7 Winners in Writers Guild B'casting Script Scramble" – Christopher Knopf, Barry Trivers, Shimon Wincelberg, Alvin Boretz.
Weekly Variety, May 23, 1962, "Film Reviews: *The Intruder*"; starring Shatner.
Weekly Variety, May 30, 1962, "Film Reviews: *Tales of Terror*," screenplay by Richard Matheson.
Daily Variety, August 9, 1962, "Light and Airy," by Jack Hellman; update on "Doug Selby" pilot.
Daily Variety, August 14, 1962, "On All Channels," by Dave Kaufman; update on "Doug Selby" pilot.
Daily Variety, August 27, 1962, "Light and Airy," by Jack Hellman – Don Ingalls on *Have Gun, Will Travel*.
Weekly Variety, October 3, 1962, "'4 Window Girl' as MGM Series," with news on Roddenberry's *The Lieutenant*.
Daily Variety, October 15, 1962, "Telepix Reviews: *McHale's Navy*: 'An Ensign for McHale'"; teleplay by Gene Coon.
Daily Variety, October 25, 1962, "Telepix Followup: *The Lloyd Bridges Show*: 'The Testing Ground,'" co-teleplay by Barry Trivers.
Daily Variety, November 23, 1962, "Telepix Folo-Ups: *The Eleventh Hour*: 'Hooray, Hooray, the Circus Is Coming to Town'"; teleplay by Gene Coon.
Daily Variety, December 11, 1962, "Roddenberry Reining Seg of *Virginian*."
Daily Variety, January 2, 1963, "Lockwood to Play Leatherneck *Lieutenant* for MGM-TV."
Daily Variety, January 9, 1963, "Legit Bits"; report on Leonard Nimoy Theater.
Daily Variety, January 21, 1963, "Susan Silo Harvests *Lieutenant* Role."
Daily Variety, January 31, 1963, "Film Reviews: *The Raven*," screenplay by Richard Matheson.
Daily Variety, February 1, 1963, "Vee's 1962 Gig Net Whee $194,000"; Bobby Vee training under Nimoy.
Daily Variety, February 7, 1963, "MGM's *Lieutenant* to NBC Next Fall"; Roddenberry creator/writer/producer.
Daily Variety, April 3, 1963, "MGM *Lieutenant* Musters 5 Scribes, Three Directors."
Daily Variety, April 24, 1963, "Record 64 Scribes Plotting MGM-TV Series for Fall" -- Art Wallace, Lee Erwin, Shimon Wincelberg.
Weekly Variety, July 24, 1963, "New York Sound Track," Jeffrey Hunter forced out of *The Long Flight*.
Daily Variety, June 26, 1963, "On All Channels: Marines Balk at *Lt.* Script," by Dave Kaufman; quoting Roddenberry.
Daily Variety, August 13, 1963, "On All Channels," by Dave Kaufman; quoting Roddenberry.
Daily Variety, September 16, 1963, "Telepix Reviews: *The Lieutenant*"; Roddenberry series.
Daily Variety, September 18, 1963, "Telepix Reviews: *Wagon Train*: 'The Molly Kincaid Story'"; teleplay by Gene Coon.
Weekly Variety, September 18, 1963, "Television Reviews: *The Lieutenant*," created and produced by Roddenberry.
Weekly Variety, September 25, 1963, "Television Reviews: *Temple Houston*," starring Jeffrey Hunter.
Daily Variety, October 7, 1963, "No Network Can dictate Artistic Policy to Ingalls; Quits *McPheeters*."
Daily Variety, October 17, 1963, "Henley for *Queens*"; production for Leonard Nimoy Theatre.
Daily Variety, October 24, 1963, "*Great* Roles for 4 More;" Shatner pilot project.
Daily Variety, October 25, 1963, "Telepix Follow-Up Reviews: *Channing*"; with Shatner.
Weekly Variety, October 23, 1963, "30 City Nielsen: ABC Swingin'" – *The Lieutenant*.
Daily Variety, November 6, 1963, "Don Ingalls Joins Revue Today as Staff Producer."
Daily Variety, November 8, 1963, "Ingalls on Revue's *Virginian* Series."
Daily Variety, November 12, 1963, "Not Enough Slices in TV Pie"; quoting Roddenberry; "*Temple Houston*'s Format Change Is Planned By Bluel"; series starring Jeffrey Hunter.
Daily Variety, November 26, 1963, "Shatner in *Sun*."
Daily Variety, December 11, 1963, "Chatter"; Vic Morrow to direct Nimoy in *Deathwatch* pic.
Daily Variety, December 16, 1963, "Telepix Follow-Up Reviews: *Temple Houston*," staring Jeffrey Hunter, teleplay by Carey Wilbur.
Daily Variety, December 18, 1963, "On All Channels," by Dave Kaufman; Don Ingalls creates fantasy pilot "Lucifer's Folly."
Weekly Variety, January 15, 1964, "Film Reviews: *The Man from Galveston*," starring Jeffrey Hunter.
Daily Variety, January 22, 1964, "Film Reviews: *The Comedy of Terror*," screenplay by Richard Matheson.
Daily Variety, February 3, 1964, "Janet Blair Cast as 'Lady' for *Destry*"; produced by Gene Coon.
Daily Variety, February 24, 1964, "Telepix Followup: *The Lieutenant*, 'To Set it Right'"; Roddenberry production; Lee Erwin script.
Daily Variety, February 26, 1964, "Screen Gems, Four Star Tie in WGA Nominations Tally" -- noms for Norman Katkov.

Weekly Variety, March 4, 1964, "Film Reviews: *Gunfight at Comanche Creek*," co-starring DeForest Kelley.
Daily Variety, March 10, 1964, "On All Channels: 'Point' Is Broken," by Dave Kaufman; quoting Roddenberry.
Daily Variety, March 20, 1964, "MGM-TV's *Lieutenant* at Ease After 'Kill'."
Daily Variety, May 13, 1964, "Roddenberry Reins Pilots for Desilu."
Weekly Variety, May 27, 1964: "Film Reviews: *The Killers*"; screenplay by Gene Coon.
Daily Variety, July 28, 1964, "On All Channels," by Dave Kaufman; D.C. Fontana script work.
Daily Variety, August 3, 1964, "Legit Reviews: *The Bald Soprano*," directed by Joseph Sargent.
Weekly Variety, August 12, 1964, "NBC-TV Yens Indie Product" ; Roddenberry created pilot "Assignment 100." And "Desilu and NBC-TV Setting Co-Prod'n *Assignment* Deal"; announcing *Star Trek* pilot.
Daily Variety, August 19, 1964, "Stockholders Given Roseate Desilu Report"; *Star Trek* plans.
Daily Variety, September 8, 1964, "Kandel, Avedon Plot Pilots at SG."
Daily Variety, September 21, 1964, "Telepix Reviews: *Kentucky Jones*," directed by Joseph Sargent.
Weekly Variety, September 30, 1964, "Shatner 'Project'-ed"; ; Shatner back at MGM; "Film Reviews: *The Outrage*"; featuring Shatner.
Daily Variety, October 6, 1964, "On All Channels," by Dave Kaufman; "Blood of the A.E.F." project for Roddenberry, as well as *Star Trek*, for Desilu.
Weekly Variety, October 14, 1964, "Film Reviews: Where Love Has Gone" -- with DeForest Kelley.
Daily Variety, October 19, 1964, "Television Reviews: *Bob Hope Chrysler Theatre*, 'Have Girls – Will Travel,' co-teleplay by Robert Hamner.
Daily Variety, November 11, 1964, "Len Nimoy Takes *Trek*"; first actor signed.
Daily Variety, November 19, 1964, "*Star Trek* Pilot for Jeff Hunter"; second actor signed.
Daily Variety, December 1, 1964, "Just for Variety," by Army Archerd; Susan Oliver third signed, called "Greenfinger" and "Bulgarian Pic Wins Peace Fest; Shatner ('Intruders') Best Actor."
Daily Variety, December 4, 1964, "John Hoyt Joins *Trek*"; fourth actor signed.
Daily Variety, December 16, 1964, "Desilu's 26-Week Net 424G, Un 6%" and "Telepic Followup: Voyage to the Bottom of the Sea: 'The Ghost of Moby Dick,'" teleplay by Robert Hamner.
Daily Variety, February 2, 1965, "Television Reviews: *For the People*"; Shatner series.
Weekly Variety, February 3, 1965, "Television Reviews: *For the People*"; 2nd review for Shatner series.
Daily Variety, February 24, 1965, "Congratulations on *For the People*"; review samplings.
Daily Variety, April 27, 1965, "Film Reviews: *Die! Die! My Darling!*," screenplay by Richard Matheson.
Daily Variety, May 4, 1965, "NBC-TV Taking 2nd Look at Desilu Pilot."
Weekly Variety, May 12, 1965, "'Definite Maybe' for Two Unsold Desilu Pilots."
TV Guide, May 29, 1965, "TV Teletype: Neil Hickey Reports."
Daily Variety, June 1, 1965, "All the Channels: Allen's 1997 Space Shot 1st Primetime Cliffhanger," by Dave Kaufman; quoting Irwin Allen.
Weekly Variety, June 23, 1965, "Desilu Plots 17 Series for '66."
The Milwaukee Journal, July 4, 1965, "Happy in Hollywood," by J.D. Spiro.
Daily Variety, July 9, 1965, "Ihnat Joins *Police*"; first actor signed.
Daily Variety, August 12, 1965, "NBC-TV to Decide Fate of 70 Future Projects Next Week."
Weekly Variety, August 18, 1965, "NBC-TV Sifting its Projects for '66-'67."
Daily Variety, September 9, 1965, "Desilu in ABC-TV Deal for *Savage*."
Daily Variety, September 15, 1965, "Another *Savage* TV Role for Bob Lansing."
The New York Times, September 16, 1965, review of *Lost in Space*, by Jack Gould.
Daily Variety, September 17, 1965, "Telepix Reviews: *Lost in Space*."
Daily Variety, September 20, 1965, "Telepix Reviews: *The Wild, Wild West*," teleplay by Gilbert Ralston.
Daily Variety, September 21, 1965, "Telepix Reviews: *Voyage to the Bottom of the Sea*: 'Jonah and the Whale.'"
Weekly Variety, September 29, 1965, "Television Review: *The Fugitive*" -- written by Robert Hamner.
Daily Variety, November 24, 1965, "Film Reviews: *Die, Monster, Die*," screenplay by Jerry Sohl.
Weekly Variety, December 1, 1965, ABC's 'Them Dogfaces,'" with update on "The Long Hunt for April Savage."
Daily Variety, December 24, 1965, "Majors Talk Young Blood but Don't Tap Any: Shatner."
Weekly Variety, September 29, 1965, "Television Reviews: *The Fugitive*: 'Middle of a Heat Wave,'" teleplay by Robert Hamner.
Daily Variety, "January 12, 1966, "On All Channels: Bob Conrad Wants the Job of His *Wild* Exec Producer," by Dave Kaufman.
Daily Variety, February 21, 1966, "Film Review: *Monster of Terror*," screenplay by Jerry Sohl.
Weekly Variety, February 23, 1966, "New Season at first Blush," with *Star Trek* and "April Savage" on schedules.
Daily Variety, March 1, 1966, "NBC Buys *Star Trek*, Desilu Sci-Fi Series."
Weekly Variety, March 2, 1966, "Next Season's Three Net Schedule -- First Round."
TV Guide, March 5, 1966, "For the Record," by Henry Harding.
Weekly Variety, March 9, 1966, "Oscar Katz Calls Quits at Desilu."
Weekly Variety, March 16, 1966, "Next Season's 3 Net Schedule -- 14th Round," with *Star Trek* and "April Savage" on slate.
Daily Variety, March 17, 1966, "Coon Scripts WB's *First to Fight*."
Daily Variety, "May 12, 1966, "Nine Directors on *Trek*."
Daily Variety, March 21, 1966, "Film Review: *Deathwatch*," starring Leonard Nimoy.
Daily Variety, March 24, 1966, "Lennart Wins WGA's Laurel" -- nom for Harlan Ellison.
Daily Variety, March 25, 1966, "Kandel *Iron* Producer."
Daily Variety, April 12, 1966, "Television Reviews: *Scalplock*," produced by Stephen Kandel, directed by James Goldstone, written by Kandel and Goldstone.
Daily Variety, May 23, 1966, "Two *Star* Aides Named."

Daily Variety, May 26, 1966, "Ingalls *High* Aide."
TV Guide, May 28, 1966, "TV Teletype: Joseph Finnigan Reports."
Daily Variety, June 7, 1966, "On All Channels: *Trek* into Future," by Dave Kaufman.
Daily Variety, June 9, 1966, "Just for *Variety*," by Army Archerd.
Oakland Tribune, June 19, 1966, "TV Enters the Space Race," by Bob MacKenzie.
Weekly Variety, July 13, 1966, "Desilu Posts a $15,000,000 Prod. Budget for '67-'68."
Daily Variety, July 13, 1966, "Film Review: *Frankenstein Conquers the World*," with screenplay by Jerry Sohl.
Daily Variety, July 15, 1966, "Just for *Variety*," by Army Archerd.
Indiana Evening Gazette, August 9, 1966, "Televisionese Tough Language," by Cynthia Lowary.
Daily Variety, August 9, 1966, "Coons [sic] *Trek* Producer."
TV Guide, August 13, 1966, "For the Record," by Henry Harding.
Weekly Variety, August 31, 1966, "Film Reviews: *Chamber of Horrors*," screenplay by Stephen Kandel.
The Indianapolis Star, TV Week, August 28, 1966, Grace Lee Whitney as Yeoman Janice Rand on cover, syndicated article, "*Star Trek* Resembles Space *Twilight Zone*," no author credited.
Daily Variety, September 1, 1966, article: "Roddenberry Talking Trek at Convention," no author credited.
TV Guide, September 3, 1966, program listing for "The Man Trap," Thursday, September 8, plus "Sneak a Peak at NBC Week" ad.
The Buffalo Evening News, September 3, 1966, "*Star Trek*: New Series Pits 400-Man Craft Against Space," by Charles Witbeck."
St. Louis Post-Dispatch TV Magazine, September 4, 1966, William Shatner as Captain Kirk on cover, plus NBC "Sneak Previews" ad.
Daily Variety, September 7, 1966, "On All Channels: Shatner's Heroic Switch," by Dave Kaufman.
Daily Variety, September 8, 1966, "Telepix Review: *Star Trek*," by Helm.
Indiana Evening Gazette, September 8, 1966, "TV Tonight."
The Times Recorder, September 8, 1966, "What's on the Air," by Naomi.
TV Guide, September 10, 1966, editor's preview of *Star Trek*, "Thursday on NBC" ad, "NBC Week is Here" ad, and program listing for "Charlie X," Thursday, September 15.
Daily Variety, September 12, 1966, "Telepix Reviews: *The Time Tunnel*: 'Rendezvous with Yesterday.'"
Daily Variety, September 13, 1966, "Telepix Reviews: *The Iron Horse*: 'The Rails Run West,'" written and produced by Stephen Kandel, directed by James Goldstone.
Weekly Variety, September 14, 1966, "Television Reviews: *Star Trek*" and "Television Off to the Races: Previews Reveal the Racial Mix," by Les Brown; "The Overnight Scores: Trendex & Arbitrons"; and *Star Trek* review by Trau, and *Time Tunnel* review.
The New York Times, September 16, 1966, "TV: Spies, Space and the Stagestruck," review of "Charlie X," by Jack Gould.
Daily Variety, September 16, 1966, "Telepix Reviews: *Lost in Space*."
TV Guide, September 17, 1966, NBC "The Blockbusters" ad, and program listing for "Where No Man Has Gone Before," Thursday, September 22 listing.
Broadcasting, September 19, 1966, "Critics' Views of Hits, Misses, sampling *Star Trek* reviews in *The Los Angeles Times*, by Hal Humphrey, *The Boston Globe*, by Percy Shain, *The New York Post*, by Bob Wilson, *The Philadelphia Inquirer*, by Harry Harris, *The Chicago American*, by Bill Irvin, and *The Washington Post*, by Lawrence Laurent.
Weekly Variety, September 21, 1966, "Television Reviews: *Voyage to the Bottom of the Sea*: 'Monster from the Inferno.'"
Daily Variety, September 23, 1966, "Telepix Folo-Up Reviews: *Bob Hope Chrysler Theatre*: 'Time of Flight,'" teleplay by Richard Matheson.
TV Guide, September 24, 1966, NBC "The Blockbusters!" ad, and program listing for "The Naked Time," Thursday, September 29.
Broadcasting, September 26, 1966, Trendix ratings for September 18 and 22.
Weekly Variety, September 28, 1966, "Television Reviews: *Lost in Space*."
TV Guide, October 1, 1966, program listing for "The Enemy Within," Thursday, October 6.
Broadcasting, October 3, 1966, "Trendex Top-40 Programs."
TV Guide, October 8, 1966, NBC "*Star Trek / The Hero*" ad, and program listing for "Mudd's Women," Thursday, October 13.
Broadcasting, October 10, 1966, *Star Trek* to be sponsored by Brown & Williamson.
Daily Variety, October 11, 1966, Nielsen Ratings, *Star Trek* at No. 33; "Eight New Shows in TvQ's Top 20," "*Star Trek* in Top 20."
Weekly Variety, October 12, 1966, "TV's New Top 40," *Star Trek* at No. 31, and "Eight New shows in TvQ's Top 20," which includes *Star Trek*.
TV Guide, October 15, 1966, "No One Ever Upsets the Star," by Michael Fessier, Jr., viewer letter by Judy Pugh, Seattle, program listing for "What Are Little Girls Made Of?," Thursday, October 20.
Syracuse Herald-American, October 16, 1966, "Shatner, Star of a Series, 'Hooked' on UFO Phenomenon," by J.E.V.
The New York Times, October 16, 1966, "How does Your Favorite Rate? Maybe Higher Than You Think," by Jack Gould.
Broadcasting, October 17, 1966, "The Ratings: A Photo Finish," *Star Trek* at No. 33.
TV Guide, October 22, 1966, program listing for "Miri," Thursday, October 27.
Boston Sunday Herald TV Magazine, October 23, 1966, Leonard Nimoy as Mr. Spock on cover, plus article "How TV Science Fiction Tries to Outshine Cape Kennedy," by Frank Judge.
Weekly Variety, October 26, 1966, "New Shows Have Male Appeal: TvQ," *Star Trek* at No. 2.
TV Guide, October 29, 1966, program listing for "Dagger of the Mind," Thursday, November 3.
Broadcasting, October 31, 1966, "NBC Leads Second Nielsen" and "Movies Are Viewer Favorites," TvQ placing *Star Trek* as favorite new show and No. 2 of 90 prime timers.
Weekly Variety, November 2, 1966, "Frisco Festival Reviews: *Incubus*"; starring Shatner.

TV Guide, November 5, 1966, viewer letter from Andrew Porter, and program listing for "The Corbomite Maneuver," Thursday, November 10, 1966.
TV Guide, November 12, 1966, NBC "Color Us Total" *Star Trek* ad, and program listing for "The Menagerie, Part 1," Thursday, November 17.
Broadcasting, November 14, 1966, "Two More Shows Axed," *Star Trek* in "Top Half" of ratings.
TV Guide, November 19, 1966, program listing for "The Menagerie, Part 2," Thursday, November 24.
TV Guide, November 26, 1966, "What Are a Few Galaxies Among Friends?," by Isaac Asimov, and program listing for "Jack Benny Special," Thursday, December 1, pre-empting *Star Trek*.
Broadcasting, November 28, 1966, "Agency Radio-TV Bill Soars Upward."
TV Guide, December 3, 1966, program listings for "The Conscience of the King," Thursday, December 8.
Broadcasting, December 5, 1966, "TvQ's Top-10 Programs By Age," *Star Trek* No. 5 out of 90 prime timers, all ages.
Daily Variety, December 9, 1966, "*Star Trek* Given Another Hitch."
TV Guide, December 10, 1966, program listing for "Balance of Terror," Thursday, December 15.
TV Guide, December 17, 1966, "Is This the Worst Season?," and program listing for repeat of "What Are Little Girls Made Of?," Thursday, December 22.
Boston Sunday Herald, December 18, 1966, "Shatner Catches a Big Wave," syndicated article from Hollywood, no author credited.
TV Guide, December 24, 1966, "Letters" by Samuel A. Peeples and response by Isaac Asimov, plus program listing for "Shore Leave," Thursday, December 29.
TV Guide, December 31, 1966, program listing for "The Galileo Seven," Thursday, January 6.
Ebony, January 1967, Nichelle Nichols as Lt. Uhura on cover, plus "A New Star in the TV Heavens" picture article, no author credited.
The Cleveland Press TV Showtime, January 6, 1967, with Leonard Nimoy as Mr. Spock on cover, plus article "New Breed of TV Hero," by Tom Weigel.
TV Guide, January 7, 1967, "The Doan Report: Happy NBC Plans Few Changes," plus "TV Teletype: Hollywood," by Joseph Finnigan, and program listing for "The Squire of Gothos," Thursday, January 7, 1967.
Jet, January 12, 1967, "Launch Write-In Drive to Save TV Series *Star Trek*," no author credited.
Syracuse Herald-Journal, January 12, 1967, "Dum De Dum Dum of *Dragnet* Returns," along with spot pick of "Squire of Gothos."
Valley Times TV Week, January 14, 1967, William Shatner as Captain Kirk on cover.
TV Guide, January 14, 1967, program listing for "Arena," Thursday, January 19.
Daily Variety, January 16, 1967, "John Drew Barrymore Reprimanded by SAG for Balking at *Star* Role," no author credited.
Daily Variety, January 19, 1967, "Who's Where."
TV Guide, January 21, 1967, "Letters," by Alice Richards, and program listing for "Tomorrow Is Yesterday," Thursday, January 26.
Broadcasting. January 23, 1967, Polaroid buys sponsorship of *Star Trek*.; "Second Season Loses to Movies," with Arbitron and Trendex ratings for "The Squire of Gothos."
Daily Variety, January 25, 1967, report on Roddenberry in hospital.
Weekly Variety, January 25, 1967, "Film Reviews: *First to Fight*," screenplay by Gene L. Coon.
TV Guide, January 28, 1967, program listing for "Court Martial," Thursday, February 2.
Chronicle-Telegram, February 2, 1967, "Television in Review," Thursday, February 2 planned airing of "The Alternative Factor."
TV Guide, February 4, 1967, program listing for "The Return of the Archons," Thursday, February 9.
Broadcasting, February 6, 1967, "A Profusion of Price Tags on Network Minutes."
Daily Variety, February 8, 1967, "Desilu *Mission* Complete Sellout in Latin America."
Oakland Tribune, February 10, 1967, "Bob MacKenzie on Television."
TV Guide, February 11, 1967, program listing for "Space Seed," Thursday, February 16.
Broadcasting, February 13, 1967, "No Deal Yet on Desilu."
Daily Variety, February 16, 1967, "Light and Airy," by Jack Hellman.
TV Guide, February 18, 1967, "Letters," by Mrs. Glen Tortorich, and program listing for "A Taste of Armageddon," Thursday, February 23.
Broadcasting, February 20, 1967, "Desilu, Famous Players to G & W." and "Annual Chess Game Stars: Networks Getting Set for Fall Season."
TV Guide, February 25, 1967, program listing for "This Side of Paradise," Thursday, March 2.
Broadcasting, February 27, 1967, "National Nielsens Give CBS Three in a Row."
Daily Variety, February 27, 1967, "How NBC and ABC Programs Shape Up (As of Now) for '68."
TV Guide, March 4, 1967, William Shatner as Captain Kirk and Leonard Nimoy as Mr. Spock on cover, with article "Product of Two Worlds," by Leslie Raddatz, plus program listing for "The Devil in the Dark," Thursday, March 4.
TV Guide, March 16, 1967, program listing for "Circus," Thursday, March 16, pre-empting *Star Trek*.
TV Guide, March 18, 1967, program listing for "Errand of Mercy," Thursday, March 23.
Syracuse Herald-Journal, March 23, 1967, "TV Tonight" spot pick for "Errand of Mercy."
TV Guide, March 25, 1967, "Review: *Star Trek*," by Cleveland Amory, and program listing for "The Alternative Factor," Thursday, March 30.
Daily Variety, March 28, 1967, "On All Channels: Herb Solow's Crystal Ball," by Dave Kaufman.
Weekly Variety, March 29, 1967, "Desilu's Budget Soars to Record $21-Mil for '67-'68."
TV Radio Mirror, April 1967, "Leonard Nimoy: Success Has Turned My Marriage Upside Down," by William Tusher.
Photo Screen, April 1968, "Leonard Nimoy: I Was a Teen-Age Wallflower."
TV Picture Life, April 1967, "William Shatner, Leonard Nimoy, DeForest Kelley: How Life Can Be Stranger Than Fiction."

16 Magazine, April 1967, "The Real Nimoy!"
TV Guide, April 1, 1967, Close Up listing for "The City on the Edge of Forever," Thursday, April 6.
Syracuse Herald-Tribune, April 6, 1967, "TV Tonight" spot pick for "The City on the Edge of Forever."
TV Guide, April 8, 1967, program listing for "Operation – Annihilate!," Thursday, April 13.
Los Angeles Herald-Examiner TV Weekly, April 16, 1967, "Spock, the Mysterious," by Charles Witbeck.
Weekly Variety, April 17, 1967, full-page ad for *Star Trek* from Desilu.
Weekly Variety, April 19, 1967, "Record Reviews: Leonard Nimoy: Mr. Spock's Music from Outer Space."
Daily Variety, April 24, 1967, "Oscarcast Runaway Leader of Latest 30-City Nielsen."
Daily Variety, April 26, 1967, "On All Channels: Seek a Filly for *Horse*," by Dave Kaufman.
Daily Variety, April 26, 1967, "Just for *Variety*," by Army Archerd.
Syracuse Herald-Journal, April 27, 1967, "TV Tonight" spot pick for repeat of "The Naked Time."
TV Guide, April 29, 1967, "Mr. Spock Is Dreamy," by Isaac Asimov.
Daily Variety, May 2, 1967, "CBS Wins Emmy Nominee Race" and "Barrier on *Trek*."
Daily Variety, May 12, 1967, full page "Thank You" from Howard A. Anderson Co. concerning Emmy nomination.
TV Guide, May 13, 1967, "Who Said TV Has to Make Sense?," by Stanley Frank, and "He Sees Beyond the Cameras."
Chronicle-Telegram, May 20, 1967, "Most Viewer Suggestions Go Into TV Wastebaskets.," by Gene Handsaker.
TV Guide, May 20, 1967, "Review by Cleveland Amory: Second Thoughts."
Weekly Variety, May 24, 1967, "TvQ Does Some Share-Cropping on New Season, and It Comes Up NBC," by Bill Greenley.
Daily Variety, May 31, 1967, "On All Channels," by Dave Kaufman.
TV Guide, June 3, 1967, CLOSE-UP listing for repeat of "Shore Leave," Thursday, June 8.
Daily Variety, June 9, 1967, Joseph D'Agosta casting for Desilu's *Star Trek*, *The Lucy Show*, *Mission: Impossible* and *Mannix*.
Weekly Variety, June 14, 1967, "Negro Employment in Network TV Extends to Seven Nights Next Fall," by Murray Horowitz.
Daily Variety, June 21, 1967, "On All Channels," by Dave Kaufman.
Daily Variety, June 28, 1967, "On All Channels," by Dave Kaufman.
Star Trek: K-G, Planet of Death, July 1967, Western Publishing.
TV Star Parade, July 1967, "Dressing Room Secrets of *Star Trek*."
16 Magazine, July 1967, "My Other Life," by Leonard Nimoy.
Silver Screen, July 1967, "Why Leonard Nimoy Hides His Two Children."
TV Guide, July 15, 1967, "Let Me Off at the Next Planet," no author credited.
TV Guide, July 22, 1967, Dot Records ad for "Leonard Nimoy Presents Mr. Spock's Music from Outer Space."
TV Week, July 23, 1967, "Jackrabbit Hunt on Motorcycle."
Daily Variety, July 28, 1967, "Just for *Variety*," by Army Archerd, *Star Trek* wins NAACP Image Award.
TV Guide, July 29, 1967, CLOSE-UP listing for repeat of "Balance of Terror," Thursday, August 3.
Modern Screen, August 1967, "How Leonard Nimoy Conquers His Earthly Problems."
TV Star Parade, August 1967, William Shatner as Captain Kirk and Leonard Nimoy as Mr. Spock on cover, plus articles "Leonard Nimoy's Deathwatch," by Susan Dennis, and "Bill Shatner's Triple Threat," by Lilyan Jones.
TV Radio Mirror, August 1967, Leonard Nimoy as Mr. Spock on cover, plus article "How a Man with Pointed Ears Feels – Deep Down – When the Makeup is Off," by Louise Almond.
TV Guide, August 5, 1967, CLOSE-UP listing for repeat of "This Side of Paradise," Thursday, August 10.
TV Guide, August 12, 1967, program listing for "An Evening at Tanglewood," pre-empting *Star Trek*.
Screen Stories, September 1967, "Leonard Nimoy and Bill Shatner: Their Topsy-Turvy Lives," by Dora Albert.
Castle of Frankenstein, No. 11, September 1967, Leonard Nimoy as Mr. Spock on cover, plus articles "The *Star Trek* Story," by Allan Asherman, and "Saucers Do Exist."
TV Picture Life, September 1967, "How Leonard Nimoy Tried to Save William Shatner's Marriage!"
TV Guide, September 2, 1967, program listing for "Police Story," Friday, September 7.
The Times Recorder, September 24, 1967, UPI article "*Star Trek*'s Nichelle Nichols Lives in Integrated Wilshire.," by Vernon Scott.
The News, September 28, 1967, "*Star Trek* Creator Wins Hugo Award."
Inside Star Trek, issue 2, August 1968, by D.C. Fontana; Fred Phillips interview,
Inside Star Trek, issue 3, September 1968, Dorothy C. Fontana interviewed by Ruth Berman; DeForest Kelley interviewed by Ruth Berman.
Inside Star Trek, issue 4, Oct. 1968, by Irving Feinberg; Walter Matt Jefferies interviewed by Dorothy Fontana.
Inside Star Trek, issue 6, December 1968, Leonard Nimoy interviewed by Ruth Berman; William Theiss interviewed by D.C. Fontana.
Inside Star Trek, issue 8, February 1968, George Takei interviewed by Ruth Berman.
Enterprise Incidents, #7, November 1979, Robert Bloch interview; Dorothy C. Fontana interviewed by Dennis Fischer.
Starlog #38, September 1980, DeForest Kelley interviewed by Karen E. Wilson.
Starlog #39, October 1980, Fred Freidberger interviewed by Mike Clark & Bill Cotter.
Starlog #41, Dec. 1980, letter from Dorothy Fontana; article by David Gerrold.
Starlog #42, January 1981, Mark Lenard interviewed by Alan Brender.
Fangoria #10, January 1981, Theodore Sturgeon interview.
Starlog #53, December 1981, Gene Winfield interviewed by James Van Hise.
Starlog #62, September 1982, Ricardo Montalban interviewed by Robert Greenberger; Bjo Trimble article.
Sensor Readings, April 1, 1984, David Gerrold interviewed by Don Hardin.
Starlog #105, April 1986, Grace Lee Whitney interviewed by Daniel Dickholtz.
Starlog #107, June 1986, Alexander Courage interviewed by Randy & Jean-Marc Lofficier.
Official Star Trek Fan Club #51, August 1986, Grace Lee Whitney interviewed by Dan Madsen.

Starlog #112, November 1986, Craig Huxley interview; Bruce Hyde by interviewed Frank Garcia.
Starlog #113, December 1986, Robert Bloch interviewed by Randy & Jean-Marc Lofficier; John Hoyt interviewed by Anthony Timpone; Sean Kenney interviewed by Frank Garcis.
Starlog #114, January. 1987, Marc Daniels interviewed by Edward Gross.
Starlog #115, February 1987, Ted Cassidy interviewed Joel Eisner.
Cinefantastique, Volume 17, No. 2, March 1987, Robert Bloch interviewed by Ben Herndon; Rolland Brooks interviewed by Ben Herndon; Alexander Courage interviewed by Hans Siden; Harlan Ellison interviewed by Ben Hernson; Gerald Perry Finnerman interviewed by Dennis Fischer; Dorothy C. Fontana interviewed by Ben Herndon; Walter Matt Jefferies interviewed by Ben Hernson; Fred Phillips interviewed by Ben Hernson; Gene Roddenberry interviewed by Ben Hernson; Jim Rugg interviewed by Ben Hernson.
Starlog #117, April 1987, Robert Butler interviewed by Edward Gross; Stephen Kandel interviewed; Carey Wilber interviewed by Edward Gross; Roger Perry interviewed by Mark Phillips; Meg Wyllie interviewed by Frank Garcia.
Starlog #118, May 1987, Dorothy C. Fontana interviewed by Edward Gross.
Starlog #119, June 1987, Barbara Anderson interviewed by Bill Warren.
Starlog #119, June 1987, Elisha Cook interviewed by Bill Warren.
Starlog #121, March 1988, Majel Barrett interviewed by Robert Greenberger.
Starlog #122, September 1987, Samuel Peeples interviewed by Edward Gross.
Starlog #124, November 1987, Gary Lockwood interviewed by Edward Gross.
Starlog #126, January 1988, Joseph Pevney interviewed by Edward Gross.
Starlog #127, February 1988, Roger C. Carmel interviewed by Dan Madsen,
Starlog #130, May 1988, Hagen Beggs interviewed by Frank Garcia; Arnold Moss interviewed by Diane Butler; John Newland interviewed by John McCarty; Adrian Spies interviewed by Edward Gross; Morgan Woodward, interviewed by Mark Phillips.
Starlog #131, June 1988, Michael O'Herlihy interviewed by Edward Gross.
Starlog #132, July 1988, Eddie Paskey interviewed by Kathleen M. Gooch.
Starlog #133, August 1988, Stewart Moss interviewed by Mark Phillips.
Starlog #135, October 1988, Susan Oliver interviewed by Frank Garcia; Jerry Sohl interviewed by Edward Gross.
Starlog #136, November 1988, Jerry Sohl interviewed by Edward Gross.
Starlog #138, January 1989, William Campbell interviewed by Steven H. Wilson.
Starlog #138, January 1989, John Colicos interviewed by Peter Bloch-Hansen.
Starlog #140, March 1989, Oliver Crawford interviewed by Edward Gross.
New York Times, April 29, 1989, Marc Daniels.
Starlog #144, July 1989, Vincent McEveety interviewed by Edward Gross.
Starlog #155, June 1990, Paul Carr interviewed by Bill & Jennifer Florence; Vic Perrin interviewed by Mike Clark & Mark Phillips.
Starlog #157, August 1990, Paul Comi interviewed by Mark Phillips.
Star Trek: The Official Fan Club Magazine #75, August 1990. Morgan Woodward interviewed by John S. Davis.
Starlog #159, October 1990, Shimon Wincelberg interviewed by Mike Clark.
Starlog #163, February 1991, Robert Brown interviewed by Duanne S. Arnott.
Starlog #168, July 1991, Steven Carabatsos interviewed by Edward Gross.
Starlog #169, August 1991, Gerald Fried interviewed by David Hirsch.
Starlog #172, November 1991, Ralph Senensky interviewed by Edward Gross.
Starlog #174, George Clayton Johnson interviewed by Bill Warren.
Starlog #177, April 1992, Don Mankiewicz interviewed by Bill Florence.
Starlog #179, June 1992, Don Ingalls interviewed by Lee Goldberg; Leo Penn interviewed by Pat Jankiewicz.
Starlog #190, May 1993, Malachi Throne interviewed by Joel Eisner.
Starlog #199, February 1994, Robert Hamner interviewed by Mark Phillips.
Entertainment Weekly, January 18, 1995, Bruce Hyde interview.
Star Trek Communicator, October 1995, John Colicos interviewed by Chris Roe.
Star Trek Communicator, June 1996, Leonard Nimoy interviewed by Chris Roe.
Cinefantastique, July 1996, Howard Anderson, Jr. interviews; Joe D'Agosta interview; Richard C. Datin; James Doohan; Linwood Dunn interview; James Goldstone interview; Douglass Grindstaff interview; Gerd Oswald interviewed; William Theiss interviewed; Greg Van der Veer interviewed; Albert Whitlock.
Starlog #236, June 1997, David Opatoshu interviewed by K.M. Drennan.
Star Trek Monthly, issue 26, April 1997, Dorothy C. Fontana.
Starlog #241, August 1997, Herbert F. Solow interviewed by Ian Spelling.
Star Trek Communicator, June 1998, by Dr. Laura Schlessinger.
Star Trek Communicator, December 1998, Craig Huxley interviewed by Kevin Dilmore.
Star Trek: The Magazine, December 1999, Fred Freidberger.

QUOTE INDEX:

1a.	Adler, Stretch	*Daily Variety*, November 21, 1961, by Dave Kaufman.
1b.	Allen, Irwin	*Daily Variety*, June 1, 1965, interviewed by Dave Kaufman.
1.	Anderson, Barbara	*Starlog #119*, interviewed by Bill Warren, June 1987.
1-1.	**Anderson, Barbara**	**Author interview, 2013.**
2-1.	Anderson, Howard	BBC interview, date unknown.
2-2.	Anderson, Howard	*Cinefantastique*, July 1996.
2a.	Anderson, Kay	*Star Trek Phile*, 1968.
6.	Arnaz, Desi	*Desilu*, interviewed by Coyne Sanders & Tom Gilbert (Harper, 1993).
7.	Babcock, Barbara	Sci Fi Channel, 1997.
8.	Ball, Fred	*Desilu*, interviewed by Coyne Sanders & Tom Gilbert (Harper, 1993).
9-1.	Ball, Lucille	*Desilu*, interviewed by Coyne Sanders & Tom Gilbert (Harper, 1993).
9-2.	Ball, Lucille	*Inside Star Trek: The Real Story*. Herb Solow & Robert Justman (Pocket Books, 1996)
9a.	**Banks, Emily**	**Author interview, 2012.**
10-1.	Barrett, Majel	BBC interview, date unknown.
10-2.	Barrett, Majel	Sci Fi Channel, 1997.
10-3.	Barrett, Majel	*Star Trek Memories*, interviewed by William Shatner and Chris Kreski (HarperCollins, 1993).
10-4.	Barrett, Majel	*Starlog #121*, interviewed by Robert Greenberger, March 1988.
12.	Beggs, Hagan	*Starlog #130*, interviewed by Frank Garcia, May 1988.
12-1.	**Beggs, Hagan**	**Author interview, 2013.**
17.	**Black, John D.F.**	**Author interview, 2013.**
17-1.	Black, John D.F.	*Gene Roddenberry: The Myth and the Man Behind Star Trek*, interviewed by Joel Engel (Hyperion, 1994).
17-2.	Black, John D.F.	*Star Trek: TOS Box Set*, Season 1.
17-3.	Black, John D.F.	StarTrek.com interview, date unknown.
17-4.	Black, John D.F.	*Trek Classics*, interviewed by Edward Gross (Image Publishing of New York, 1991).
17-5.	Black, John D.F.	*Starlog* Star Trek 25th Anniversary Special, 1991.
17a.	**Black, Mary Stowell**	**Author interview, 2013.**
17b.	**Blackburn, Bill**	**Author interview, 2008.**
18-1.	Bloch, Robert	*Cinefantastique*, interviewed by Ben Herndon, March 1987.
18-2.	Bloch, Robert	*Cinefantastique*, July 1996.
18-3.	Bloch, Robert	*Enterprise Incidents*, November 1979.
18-4.	Bloch, Robert	*Starlog #113*, interviewed by Randy & Jean-Marc Lofficier, December 1986.
22-1.	Brooks, Rolland	*Cinefantastique*, interviewed by Ben Herndon, March 1987.
22-2.	Brooks, Rolland	*Cinefantastique*, July 1996.
24.	Brown, Robert	*Starlog #163*, interviewed by Duanne S. Arnott, Feb. 1991.
24-1.	**Brown, Robert**	**Author interview, 2013.**
26-1.	Butler, Robert	*Starlog #117*, interviewed by Edward Gross, April 1987.
26-2.	Butler, Robert	*Star Trek Interview Book*, interviewed by Allan Asherman (Pocket Books, 1988).
26-3.	Butler, Robert	Archive of American Television, interviewed by Stephen Abranson, January 2004.

27-1.	Campbell, William	*From Sawdust to Stardust*, interviewed by Lee Rioux (Pocket Books, February 2005)
27-2.	Campbell, William	Sci Fi Channel, 1997.
27-3.	Campbell, William	*Starlog #138*, interviewed by Steven H. Wilson, Jan. 1989.
27-4.	Campbell, William	*Star Trek: TOS* Box Set, Season 1.
27-5.	Campbell, William	*Star Trek Greatest Guest Stars*, interviewed by Robert Greenberger & Ian Spelling (HarperPaperbacks, 1997)
27-6.	Campbell, William	*Star Trek Memories*, interviewed by William Shatner (1994, HarperPrism)
27-7.	Campbell, William	*The World of Star Trek*, interviewed by David Gerrold (Ballantine Books, 1973)
27-8.	Campbell, William	*Captains' Logs*, interviewed by Edward Gross & Mark A. Altman (Little Brown, 1995)
28-1.	Carabatsos, Steven	*Starlog #168*, interviewed by Edward Gross, July 1991.
28-2.	Carabatsos, Steven	*Trek Classics*, interviewed by Edward Gross (Image Publishing of New York, 1991)
29-1.	Carmel, Roger C.	*Trek Classics*, interviewed by Edward Gross, (Image Publishing of New York, 1991)
29-2.	Carmel, Roger C.	*Starlog #127*, interviewed by Dan Madsen, Feb. 1988.
29-3.	Carmel, Roger C.	*Star Trek's Greatest Guest Stars*, interviewed by Dan Madsen (HarperCollins, 1997)
30.	Carr, Paul	*Starlog #155*, interviewed by Bill & Jennifer Florence, June 1990.
31.	Cassidy, Ted	*Starlog #115*, interviewed Joel Eisner, February 1987.
31-1	Chambers, John	*Questar*, interviewed by Elaine Santangelo, December 1980.
31a.	Chapnick, Morris	*The Making of Star Trek*, interviewed by Stephen E. Whitfield (Ballantine Books, 1968)
31d.	Clark, Bobby	Roddenberry.com, interviewed by John and Ken, 2013.
33-1.	Colicos, John	*Starlog #138*, interviewed by Peter Bloch-Hansen, January 1989.
33-2	Colicos, John	*Star Trek Communicator*, interviewed by Chris Roe, October 1995.
33-3.	Colicos, John	*Star Trek's Greatest Guest Stars*, interviewed by Peter Bloch-Hansen (HarperCollins, 1997).
33a.	Collins, Joan	*TV Guide, Star Trek 30 Year Special Magazine*, 1996.
34.	Colodny, Lester	*Great Bird of the Galaxy*, by Edward Gross & Mark A. Altman (Boxtree Limited, 1994).
35.	Comi, Paul	*Starlog #157*, interviewed by Mark Phillips, Aug. 1990.
35-1.	**Comi, Paul**	**Author interview, 2013.**
36.	Cook, Elisha	*Starlog #119*, interviewed by Bill Warren, June 1987.
36aa.	Cook, Elisha	*Science Fiction Television Series: Episode Guides, Histories, and Cast s and Credits for 62 Prime-Time Shows, 1959 through 1989*, interviewed by Mark Phillips and Frank Garcia (McFarland & Co., 2006)
36a.	Coon, Gene	*The Making of Star Trek*, interviewed by Stephen E. Whitfield (Ballantine Books, 1968).
36b.	Coon, Gene	*The Trouble with Tribbles*, memos included in book by David Gerrold (Ballantine Books, 1973).
36c.	Coon, Gene	*The Trouble with Tribbles*, as told to David Gerrold (Ballantine Books, 1973).
36d.	Coon, Gene	*TV Guide*, July 15, 1967, "Let Me Off at the Next Planet."
37-1.	Courage, Alexander	*The Music of Star Trek*, interviewed by Jeff Bond (Lone Eagle Publishing, 1999).
37-2.	Courage, Alexander	*Starlog #107*, interviewed by Randy & Jean-Marc Lofficier, June 1986.
37-3.	Courage, Alexander	*Cinefantastique*, interviewed by Hans Siden, March 1987.
42-1.	Crawford, Oliver	*Great Bird of the Galaxy*, interviewed by Edward Gross

		(Boxtree Limited, 1994)
42-2.	Crawford, Oliver	*Starlog #140*, interviewed by Edward Gross, March 1989.
42-3.	Crawford, Oliver	*Trek Classics*, interviewed by Edward Gross, (Image Publishing of New York, 1991)
42-4.	Crawford, Oliver	imdb.com
43.	**D'Agosta, Joe**	**Author interview, 2010.**
43-1.	D'Agosta, Joe	*Cinefantastique*, July 1996.
43-2.	D'Agosta, Joe	*Star Trek Memories*, interviewed by William Shatner (HarperCollins, 1984)
43-3.	D'Agosta, Joe	*Inside Star Trek issue #7*, by Joe D'Agosta, 1968.
44-1.	Daniels, Marc	*Great Bird of the Galaxy*, interviewed by Edward Gross (Boxtree Limited, 1994).
44-2.	Daniels, Marc	*Starlog #114*, interviewed by Edward Gross, Jan. 1987.
44-3.	Daniels, Marc	*The Star Trek Interview Book*, interviewed by Allan Asherman (Pocket Books, 1988).
44-4.	Daniels, Marc	*Trek Classics*, interviewed by Edward Gross (Image Publishing of New York, 1991).
44-5.	Daniels, Marc	*Variety*, July 27, 1949, "Light Up the Drama," by Marc Daniels.
44-6.	Daniels, Marc	*Variety*, November 12, 1958, "TNT's Marc Daniels Believes TVs Closed-Circuit Show Biz Is Dynamite," interviewed by Jo Ranson.
44-7.	Daniels, Marc	*New York Times*, April 29, 1989.
45a.	Darby, Kim	popcultureaddict.com, "Truth and Grit," interviewed by Sam Tweedle, September 2010.
46.	Datin, Richard C.	*Cinefantastique*, July 1996.
47.	**De Lugo, Win**	**Author interview, 2010.**
49.	Dobkin, Lawrence	*The Star Trek Interview Book*, interviewed by Allan Asherman (Pocket Books, 1988).
52.	**Doohan, James**	**Author interview, 1992.**
52-1.	Doohan, James	*Beam Me Up, Scotty*, interviewed by Peter David (Pocket Books, 1996).
52-2.	Doohan, James	*The Best of Trek*, interviewed by Walter Irwin & G.B. Love (Signet Books, 1978).
52-3.	Doohan, James	*Cinefantastique*, July 1996.
52-4.	Doohan, James	Sci Fi Channel, 1997.
52-5.	Doohan, James	*Shatner: Where No Man ...*, interviewed by Sondra Marshak & Myrna Culbreath (Tempo Books, 1979).
52-6.	Doohan, James	*Star Trek Communicator*, interviewed by Dan Madsen, August 1999.
52-7.	Doohan, James	*The World of Star Trek*, interviewed by David Gerrold (Ballantine Books, 1973).
52-8.	Doohan, James	*Inside Star Trek issue #5*, interviewed by Ruth Berman, Nov. 1968.
53.	Dromm, Andrea	*Starlog Yearbook*, interviewed by Mark Phillips, Aug. 1998.
56.	Dunn, Linwood	*Cinefantastique*, July 1996.
57a.	Ehrlich, Jake	Telegram from Ehrlich, January 29, 1960, in the Kelley Home Archives, CA, Jake Ehrlich collection, cited in *From Sawdust to Stardust*, by Terry Lee Rioux (Pocket Books, February 2005)
57b.	Eitner, Don	*Science Fiction Television Series: Episode Guides, Histories, and Cast s and Credits for 62 Prime-Time Shows, 1959 through 1989*, interviewed by Mark Phillips and Frank Garcia (McFarland & Co., 2006)
58.	**Ellison, Harlan**	**Author interview, 2013.**
58-1.	Ellison, Harlan	*Cinefantastique, Volume 17, No. 2*, interviewed by Ben Hernson, March 1987.
58-2.	Ellison, Harlan	*The City on the Edge of Forever*, by Harlan Ellison (White Wolf Publishing, 1996).
58-3.	Ellison, Harlan	Sci Fi Channel, 1997.
58-4.	Ellison, Harlan	*Trek Classics*, interviewed by Edward Gross (Image Publishing of New York, 1991).
58-5.	Ellison, Harlan	*The Trouble with Tribbles*, interviewed by David Gerrold

		(Ballantine Books, 1973).
58-6.	Ellison, Harlan	*Star Trek Fotonovel #1*, interviewed by Sandra Cawson (Bantam Books, November 1977).
58a.	Felton, Norman	*Gene Roddenberry: The Myth and the Man Behind StarTrek*, interviewed by Joel Engel (Hyperion, 1994).
58b.	Feinberg, Irving	*Inside Star Trek, issue 4*, by Irving Feinberg, Oct. 1968.
58bb.	Felton, Norman	*Gene Roddenberry: The Myth and the Man Behind StarTrek*, by Joel Engel (Hyperion, 1994).
60.	Fernandez, Jackie	*Great Bird of the Galaxy*, interviewed by Edward Gross (Boxtree Limited, 1994).
62.	Finley, Jack	*The Star Trek Interview Book*, interviewed by Allan Asherman (Pocket, 1988).
63-1.	Finnerman, Gerald Perry	*Cinefantastique Vol. 17, No. 2*, interviewed by Dennis Fischer, March 1987.
63-2.	Finnerman, Gerald Perry	*Television: Companion to the PBS Series*, interviewed by Michael Winship, 1988.
63-3.	Finnerman, Gerald Perry	Archive of Television, interviewed by Karen Herman, Oct. 8, 2002.
64-1.	**Fontana, Dorothy C.**	**Author interview, 1994.**
64-2.	**Fontana, Dorothy C.**	**Author interview, 2007.**
64-3.	**Fontana, Dorothy C.**	**Author interview, 2007.**
64-4.	**Fontana, Dorothy C.**	**Author interview, 2007.**
64-4a.	**Fontana, Dorothy C.**	**Author's email interview, 2012.**
64-5.	Fontana, Dorothy C.	*Cinefantastique, Vol. 17, No. 2*, interviewed by Ben Herndon, March 1987.
64-6.	Fontana, Dorothy C.	*Cinefantastique*, July 1996.
64-7.	Fontana, Dorothy C.	*The City on the Edge of Forever*, interviewed by Harlan Ellison (White Wolf Publishing, 1996).
64-8.	Fontana, Dorothy C.	*Enterprise Incidents #7*, interviewed by Dennis Fischer, Nov. 1979.
64-9	Fontana, Dorothy C.	*From Sawdust to Stardust*, interviewed by Terry Lee Rioux (Pocket Books, 2005)
64-10.	Fontana, Dorothy C.	*Gene Roddenberry: The Myth and the Man Behind StarTrek*, from Foreword by D.C. Fontana and interview by Joel Engel (Hyperion, 1994).
64-11.	Fontana, Dorothy C.	*Great Bird of the Galaxy*, interviewed by Edward Gross (Boxtree Limited, 1994).
64-12	Fontana, Dorothy C.	*Starlog #41*, letter from Dorothy Fontana, Dec. 1980.
64-13.	Fontana, Dorothy C.	*Starlog #118*, interviewed by Edward Gross, May 1987.
64-14.	Fontana, Dorothy C.	*Star Trek: TOS* Box Set, Season 2.
64-15.	Fontana, Dorothy C.	*Star Trek Lives!*, by Jacqueline Lichtenberg, Sondra Marshak & Joan Winston (Bantam Books, 1973).
64-16.	Fontana, Dorothy C.	*Star Trek Memories*, interviewed by William Shatner (HarperCollins, 1994).
64-17.	Fontana, Dorothy C.	*Trek Classics*, interviewed by Edward Gross (Image Publishing of New York, 1991).
64-18.	Fontana, Dorothy C.	*The World of Star Trek*, interviewed by David Gerrold (Ballantine Books, 1973).
64-19.	Fontana, Dorothy C.	*Captain's Logs*, interviewed by Edward Gross (Little Brown, 1995).
64-20.	Fontana, Dorothy C.	*Inside Star Trek, issue 2*, by D.C. Fontana, August 1968.
64-21.	Fontana, Dorothy C.	*Inside Star Trek, issue 3*, interviewed by Ruth Berman, Sept. 1968.
64-22.	Fontana, Dorothy C.	*Star Trek Monthly*, issue 26, April 1997.
65.	**Forest, Michael**	**Author interview, 2011.**
67a.	**Freiberger, Ben**	**Author interview, 2011.**
68-1	Freiberger, Fred	*Starlog #39*, interviewed by Mike Clark & Bill Cotter, October 1980.
68-2.	Freiberger, Fred	*Star Trek Memories*, interviewed by William Shatner (HarperCollins, 1994)
68-3.	Freiberger, Fred	*The Star Trek Interview Book*, interviewed by Allan Asherman (Pocket Books, 1988).
68-4.	Freiberger, Fred	*Trek Classics*, interviewed by Edward Gross (Image Publishing of New York, 1991).
68-5.	Freiberger, Fred	*Great Bird of the Galaxy*, interviewed by Edward Gross

68-6.	Freiberger, Fred	(BoxTree Limited, 1994). Sci Fi Channel, 1997.
68-7.	Freiberger, Fred	*Star Trek: The Magazine*, December 1999.
68-8.	Freiberger, Fred	*Captain's Logs*, interviewed by Edward Gross (Little, Brown, 1995).
68a.	**Freiberger, Lisa**	**Author interview, 2011.**
69-1.	Fried, Gerald	*The Music of Star Trek*, by Jeff Bond (Lone Eagle, 1999).
69-2.	Fried, Gerald	*Starlog #169*, interviewed by David Hirsch, Aug. 1991.
69-3.	Fried, Gerald	*The Star Trek Interview Book*, interviewed by Allan Asherman (Pocket Books, 1988).
64-4.	Fried, Gerald	Archive of American Television.
69-5.	**Fried, Gerald**	**Author interview, 2011.**
70.	Furia, Jr., John	*Great Bird of the Galaxy*, interviewed by Edward Gross (BoxTree Limited, 1994).
70a.	Gardner, Erle Stanley	*Star Trek Creator*, by David Alexander, letters from the Estate of Erle Stanley Gardner (Penguin Books, 1994).
73-1.	**Gerrold, David**	**Author interview, 2007.**
73-2.	Gerrold, David	BBC interview, unknown date.
73-3.	Gerrold, David	*Gene Roddenberry: The Myth and the Man Behind StarTrek*, interviewed by Joel Engel (Hyperion, 1994).
73-4.	Gerrold, David	*Great Bird of the Galaxy*, interviewed by Edward Gross (BoxTree Limited, 1994).
73-5	Gerrold, David	*Starlog #41*, by David Gerrold, December 1980.
73-6.	Gerrold, David	*The Trouble with Tribbles*, by David Gerrold (Ballantine 1973).
73-7.	Gerrold, David	*The World of Star Trek*, by David Gerrold (Ballantine, 1973).
73-8.	Gerrold, David	*Cinefantastique*, July 1996.
73-9.	Gerrold, David	*Captain's Logs*, interviewed by Edward Gross (Little Brown, 1995).
73-10.	Gerrold, David	*Sensor Readings*, interviewed by Don Hardin, April 1, 1984.
73a.	Gillis, Jackson	*Star Trek Creator*, by David Alexander (Penguin Books, 1994).
74.	Goldberg, Whoopi	*Star Trek's Greatest Guest Stars*, interviews by Marc Shapiro & Ian Spelling (HarperCollins, 1997).
75-1.	Goldstone, James	*Cinefantastique*, July 1996.
75-2.	Goldstone, James	*The Star Trek Interview Book*, interviewed by Allan Asherman (Pocket Books, 1988).
75-3.	Goldstone, James	*Trek Classics*, interviewed by Edward Gross (Image Publishing of New York, 1991).
76-1.	Grindstaff, Douglass	*Cinefantastique*, July 1996.
76-2.	Grindstaff, Douglass	*The Star Trek Interview Book*, interviewed by Allan Asherman (Pocket Books, 1988).
77.	Halsey, Dorris	*Great Bird of the Galaxy*, interviewed by Edward Gross (BoxTree Limited, 1994).
78.	Hammer, Robert	*Starlog #199*, interviewed by Mark Phillips, Feb. 1994.
78a.	Held, Karl	*Science Fiction Television Series: Episode Guides, Histories, and Cast s and Credits for 62 Prime-Time Shows, 1959 through 1989*, interviewed by Mark Phillips and Frank Garcia (McFarland & Co., 2006)
84.	Holly, Ed	*Desilu*, by Coyne Steven Sanders & Tom Gilbert (William Morrow and Company, 1993).
85.	**Howard, Clint**	**Author interview, 2010.**
86.	Hoyt, John	*Starlog #113*, interviewed by Anthony Timpone, Dec. 1986.
86a.	Hunter, Jeffrey	*Milwaukee Journal*, July 4, 1965, "Happy in Hollywood," interviewed by J.D. Spiro.
86b.	Hunter, Jeffrey	*Los Angeles Citizen News*, January 30, 1965, interviewed by Joan Schmitt.

87-1.	Huxley, Craig	*Starlog #112*, November 1986.
87-2.	Huxley, Craig	*Star Trek Communicator*, interviewed by Kevin Dilmore, Dec. 1998.
87-3..	Huxley, Craig	*Science Fiction Television Series: Episode Guides, Histories, and Cast s and Credits for 62 Prime-Time Shows, 1959 through 1989*, interviewed by Mark Phillips and Frank Garcia (McFarland & Co., 2006)
88-1.	Hyde, Bruce	*Entertainment Weekly*, January 18, 1995.
88-2.	Hyde, Bruce	*Starlog #112*, by interviewed Frank Garcia, Nov. 1986.
88-3.	Hyde, Bruce	StarTrekHistory.com
88-4	**Hyde, Bruce**	**Author interview, 2010.**
89.	Ingalls, Don	*Starlog #179*, interviewed by Lee Goldberg, June 1992.
90.	Jackson, Sherry	Sci Fi Channel, 1997.
90-1.	**Jackson, Sherry**	**Author's interview, 2013.**
91-1.	Jefferies, Walter Matt	BBC interview, date unknown.
91-2.	Jefferies, Walter Matt	*Cinefantastique*, interviewed by Ben Hernson, March 1987.
91-3.	Jefferies, Walter Matt	*Gene Roddenberry: The Myth and the Man Behind Star Trek*, interviewed by Joel Engel (Hyperion, 1994).
91-4.	Jefferies, Walter Matt	*The Making of Star Trek*, interviewed by Stephen E. Whitfield (Ballantine, 1968).
91-5.	Jefferies, Walter Matt	*Star Trek: TOS* Box Set, Season 2.
91-6.	Jefferies, Walter Matt	startrek.com
91-7.	Jefferies, Walter Matt	*The Star Trek Interview Book*, interviewed by Allan Asherman (Pocket Books, 1988).
91-8.	Jefferies, Walter Matt	*Star Trek Memories*, interviewed by William Shatner (HarperCollins 1994).
91-9.	Jefferies, Walter Matt	*Inside Star Trek, issue 4*, interviewed by Dorothy Fontana, Oct. 1968.
91-10.	Jefferies, Walter Matt	*Inside Star Trek, issue 12*, by Matt Jefferies.
93-1	**Johnson, George Clayton**	**Author interview, 2007.**
93-2.	Johnson, George Clayton	*Cinefantastique*, July 1996.
93-3	Johnson, George Clayton	*Starlog #174*, interviewed by Bill Warren, January 1992.
93-4.	Johnson, George Clayton	*The Star Trek Interview Book*, interviewed by Allan Asherman (Pocket Books, 1988).
93-5.	Johnson, George Clayton	*Trek Classics*, interviewed by Allan Asherman (Image Publishing of New York, 1991).
94-1.	**Justman, Robert H.**	**Author interview, 2007.**
94-2.	Justman, Robert H.	BBC interview, date unknown.
94-3.	Justman, Robert H.	*From Sawdust to Stardust*, interviewed by Terry Lee Rioux (Pocket Books, 2005).
94-4.	Justman, Robert H.	*Star Trek Memories*, interviewed by William Shatner (HarperCollins, 1994).
94-5.	Justman, Robert H.	*Gene Roddenberry: The Man and the Myth Behind StarTrek*, interviewed by Joel Engel (Hyperion, 1994).
94-6..	Justman, Robert H.	*Gene Roddenberry: The Last Conversation*, interviewed by Yvonne Fern (University of California Press, 1994).
94-7.	Justman, Robert H.	*Great Bird of the Galaxy*, interviewed by Edward Gross (BoxTree Limited, 1994).
94-8.	Justman, Robert H.	*Inside Star Trek: The Real Story*, specific text written by Robert Justman (Pocket Books, 1996).
94-9.	Justman, Robert H.	*The Music of Star Trek*, interviewed by Jeff Bond (Lone Eagle, 1999).
94-10.	Justman, Robert H.	Sci Fi Channel, 1997.
94-11.	Justman, Robert H.	*Star Trek: TOS* Box Set, Season 1.
94-12.	Justman, Robert H.	*Star Trek: TOS* Box Set, Season 2.
94-13.	Justman, Robert H.	*Star Trek: TOS* Box Set, Season 3.
94-14.	Justman, Robert H.	*Trek Classics*, interviewed by Edward Gross (Image Publishing of New York, 1991).
94-15.	Justman, Robert H.	*The World of Star Trek*, interviewed by David Gerrold (Ballantine Books, 1973).
94-16.	Justman, Robert H.	*Captain's Logs*, interviewed by Edward Gross (Little Brown, 1995).
94-17.	Justman, Robert H.	*The Star Trek Interview Book*, interviewed by Allan Asherman (Pocket Books, 1988).
94-20.	Justman, Robert H.	Letter written, December 12, 2001.

95-1.	**Kandel, Stephen**	**Author interview, 2007.**
95-2.	Kandel, Stephen	*Starlog #117*, interviewed by Edward Gross, April 1987.
95-3.	Kandel, Stephen	*The Star Trek Interview Book*, interviewed by Allan Asherman (Pocket Books, 1988).
95-4.	Kandel, Stephen	*Trek Classics*, interviewed by Edward Gross (Image Publishing of New York, 1991).
95-5	Kandel, Stephen	**Author interview, 2010.**
96-1.	Katz, Oscar	*Star Trek Creator*, interviewed by David Alexander (Penguin Books, 1994).
96-2.	Katz, Oscar	*Captain's Logs*, by Edward Gross and Mark A. Altman (Little Brown.1995)
97-1.	Kellerman, Sally	Sci Fi Channel, 1997.
97-2.	Kellerman, Sally	startrek.com, staff interview, September 16, 2010.
98-1.	Kelley, DeForest	*From Sawdust to Stardust*, interviewed by Terry Lee Rioux (Pocket Books, 2005).
98-1a.	Kelley, Deforest	*A Harvest of Memories*, working ms. by Kristine Smith, Kelly Home Archives, CA, cited in *From Sawdust to Stardust*, by Terry Lee Rioux (Pocket Books, 2005).
98-1b.	Kelley, Deforest	Correspondence from Denver Kelley, as printed in *From Sawdust to Stardust*, by Terry Lee Rioux (Pocket Books, 2005).
98-1c.	Kelley, DeForest	Speech given at St. Petersburg, Florida, November 1991 by Kelley; cited in *From Sawdust to Stardust*, by Terry Lee Rioux (Pocket Books, 2005).
98-2.	Kelley, DeForest	*History of Trek*, interviewed by Joseph Gulick (Pioneer Books, 1991).
98-3.	Kelley, DeForest	Sci Fi Channel, 1997/
98-4.	Kelley, DeForest	*Shatner: Where No Man …* . William Shatner, Sondra Marshak and Myrna Culbreath (Tempo Books, 1979).
98-5	Kelley, De Forest	*Starlog #38*, interviewed by Karen E. Wilson, Sept. 1980.
98-6.	Kelley, DeForest	*The Star Trek Interview Book*, interviewed by Allan Asherman (Pocket Books, 1988).
98-7.	Kelley, DeForest	*Star Trek Memories*, interviewed by William Shatner (HarperCollins, 1994).
98-8.	Kelley, DeForest	*The World of Star Trek*, interviewed by David Gerrold (Ballantine Books, 1973).
98-9.	Kelley, DeForest	*Inside Star Trek, issue 3*, interviewed by Ruth Berman, Sept. 1968.
98-10.	Kelley, DeForest	*Sunday Herald Traveler*, March 31, 1968, "Is There a Doctor in the House?," interviewed by Vernon Scott.
98-11.	Kelley, DeForest	*TV Star Parade*, November 1967, "DeForest Kelley is Out of This World," interviewed by Jane Harrol.
98-12.	Kelley, DeForest	imdb.com.
98-13.	Kelley, DeForest	*TV Picture Life*, March 1968, "I'll Never Forgive Nimoy and Shatner," interviewed by Seli Groves.
98-14.	Kelley, DeForest	DeForest Kelley file, Academy of Motion Pictures Arts and Sciences, Los Angeles California, as told to Paramount Publicist A.C. Lyles.
98-15.	Kelley, DeForest	*TV Guide*, August 24, 1968, "Where is the Welcome Mat?" interviewed by staff writer.
99.	Kendall, Wanda	*Star Trek Creator*, interviewed by David Alexander (Penguin Books, 1994).
100-1.	Kenney, Sean	*Starlog #113*, interviewed by Frank Garcis, Dec. 1986.
100-2.	**Kenney, Sean**	**Author interview, 2010.**
101a.	Knopf, Christopher	*Gene Roddenberry: The Myth and the Man Behind StarTrek*, interviewed by Joel Engel (Hyperion, 1994).
104a.	**Landau, Martin**	**Author interview, 2006.**
106.	Larson, Glen	Great Bird of the Galaxy, by Edward Gross and Mark A.Altman (BoxTree Limited, 1994).
107-1.	Lenard, Mark	*Cinefantastique*, July 1996.
107-2.	Lenard, Mark	*Starlog #42*, interviewed by Alan Brender, Jan. 1981.
107-3.	Lenard, Mark	*Star Trek's Greatest Guest Stars*, by Robert Greenberger and David McDonnell (HarperCollins, 1997).

109	**Lockwood, Gary**	Author interview, 2011.
109-1	Lockwood, Gary	*Starlog #124*, interviewed by Edward Gross, Nov. 1987.
109-2.	Lockwood, Gary	*Trek Classics*, interviewed by Edward Gross (Image Publishing of New York, 1991).
109a.	Lundin, Vic	*Science Fiction Television Series: Episode Guides, Histories, and Cast s and Credits for 62 Prime-Time Shows, 1959 through 1989*, interviewed by Mark Phillips and Frank Garcia (McFarland & Co., 2006)
112.	Mailer, Lev	StarTrekHistory.com
113-1	Mankiewicz, Don	*Starlog #177*, interviewed by Bill Florence, April 1992.
113-2.	Mankiewicz, Don	classictvhistory.com, interviewed by Steven W. Bowie, 2007.
113-3	**Mankiewicz, Don**	Author interview, 2011.
113a	**Mars, Bruce**	Author interview, 2013.
113b.	**Marshall, Don**	Author interview, 2011.
116a.	Matheson, Richard	Archive of American Television, interviewed by Karen Haman, April 16, 2006.
116b.	**Matheson, Richard**	Author interview, 2011.
117-1.	McEveety, Vincent	*Starlog #144*, interviewed by Edward Gross, July 1989.
117-2.	McEveety, Vincent	*Trek Classics*, interviewed by Edward Gross (Image Publishing of New York, 1991).
117-3.	McEveety, Vincent	*Captain's Logs*, interviewed by Edward Gross (Little Brown, 1995).
117-4.	**McEveety, Vincent**	Author interview, 2011.
117a.	Menhoff, George	*Inside Star Trek, issue 12*, by George Menhoff, 1969.
119-1.	Milkis, Eddie	*Cinefantastique*, July 1996.
119-2.	Milkis, Eddie	*Star Trek Memories*, interviewed by William Shatner and/or Chris Kreski (HarperCillins, 1994).
119aa.	Mines, Stephen	*Starlog* #283, interviewed by Mark Phillips, February 2001.
119a.	**Montaigne, Lawrence**	Author interview, 2011.
120-1	Montalban, Ricardo	*Starlog #62*, interviewed by Robert Greenberger, September 1982.
120-2.	Montalban, Ricardo	*Star Trek: TOS* Box Set, Season 1.
120-3.	Montalban, Ricardo	*Star Trek's Greatest Guest Stars*, interviewed by Robert Greenberger (HarperCollins, 1997).
120a.	Moore, Ronald D.	Memory Alpha internet interview, June 24, 1997.
120b.	**Morgan, Sean**	Author interview, 2010.
121.	Moss, Arnold	*Starlog #130*, interviewed by Diane Butler, May 1988.
122-1.	Moss, Stewart	Sci Fi Channel, 1997.
122-2.	Moss, Stewart	*Starlog #133*, interviewed by Mark Phillips, Aug. 1988.
122-3.	**Moss, Stewart**	Author interview, 2011.
125-1.	Newland, John	*Starlog #130*, interviewed by John McCarty, May 1988.
125-2.	Newland, John	Blog interview by John Kenneth Muir, 1999.
127-1.	Nichols, Nichelle	BBC interview, date unknown.
127-2.	Nichols, Nichelle	*Beyond Uhura*, by Nichelle Nichols (G.P. Putnam's Sons, 1994).
127-3.	Nichols, Nichelle	*Cinefantastique*, July 1996.
127-4.	Nichols, Nichelle	Sci Fi Channel, 1997.
127-5.	Nichols, Nichelle	*Shatner: Where No Man ...* , byWilliam Shatner, Sondra Marshak and Myrna Culbreath (Tempo Books, 1979).
127-6.	Nichols, Nichelle	*Star Trek: TOS* Box Set, Season 2.
127-7.	Nichols, Nichelle	*Star Trek: TOS* Box Set, Season 3.
127-8.	Nichols, Nichelle	*The Star Trek Interview Book*, interviewed by Allan Asherman (Pocket Books, 1988).

127-9.	Nichols, Nichelle	*Star Trek Memories*, interviewed by William Shatner and/or Chris Kreski (HarperCollins, 1994).
127-10.	Nichols, Nichelle	*The World of Star Trek*, interviewed by David Gerrold (Ballantine Books, 1973).
127-11.	Nichols, Nichelle	*StarTrek*.com, staff interview, October 19, 2010.
127-12.	Nichols, Nichelle	*TV Guide*, July 15, 1967, "Let Me Off at the Next Planet."
128.	**Nimoy, Leonard**	**Author interview, 2013.**
128-1.	Nimoy, Leonard	*Gene Roddenberry: The Myth and the Man Behind Star Trek*, interviewed by Joel Engel (Hyperion, 1994).
128-2.	Nimoy, Leonard	*Great Bird of the Galaxy*, interviewed by Edward Gross and/or Mark A. Altman (BoxTree Limited, 1994).
128-3.	Nimoy, Leonard	*I Am Spock*, by Leonard Nimoy (Hyperion, 1996).
128-3a.	Nimoy, Leonard	*I Am Not Spock*, by Leonard Nimoy (Celestial Arts, November 1975)
128-4.	Nimoy, Leonard	Sci Fi Channel, 1997.
128-5.	Nimoy, Leonard	*Shatner: Where No Man ...*, byWilliam Shatner, Sondra Marshak and Myrna Culbreath (Tempo Books, 1979).
128-6.	Nimoy, Leonard	*Star Trek: TOS* Box Set, Season 1.
128-7.	Nimoy, Leonard	*Star Trek: TOS* Box Set, Season 2.
128-8.	Nimoy, Leonard	*Star Trek: TOS* Box Set, Season 3.
128-9.	Nimoy, Leonard	*Star Trek Communicator*, interviewed by Chris Roe, June 1996.
128-10.	Nimoy, Leonard	*Star Trek Communicator*, August 1999.
128-11.	Nimoy, Leonard	*The Star Trek Interview Book*, interviewed by Allan Asherman (Pocket Books, 1988).
128-12.	Nimoy, Leonard	*Star Trek Lives!*, by Jacqueline Lichtenberg, Sondra Marshak and Joan Winston (Bantam Books, 1975).
128-13.	Nimoy, Leonard	*Star Trek Memories*, interviewed by William Shatner and/or Chris Kreski (HarperCollins, 1994).
128-14.	Nimoy, Leonard	*Trek Classics*, by Edward Gross (Image Publishing of New York, 1991).
128-15.	Nimoy, Leonard	*The World of Star Trek*, interviewed by David Gerrold (Ballantine, 1973).
128-16.	Nimoy, Leonard	*Inside Star Trek, issue 6*, interviewed by Ruth Berman, Dec. 1968.
128-17.	Nimoy, Leonard	*New York Times*, "Girls All Want to Touch the Ears," interviewed by Digby Diehl, August 25, 1968.
128-18.	Nimoy, Leonard	*Archive of American Television*, interviewed by Karen Herman, November 2, 2002.
128-19.	Nimoy, Leonard	*Photo TV Land*, December 1967, "Outer Space's Inside Battle," interviewed by Rhonda Green.
128-20.	Nimoy, Leonard	*Screen Stories*, September 1967, "Leonard Nimoy and Bill Shatner: Their Topsy-Turvy Lives," interviewed by Dora Albert.
128-21.	Nimoy, Leonard	*TV Guide*, March 4, 1967, "Product of Two Worlds," interviewed by Leslie Raddatz.
128-22.	Nimoy, Leonard	*Los Angeles Herald-Examiner TV Weekly*, "Spock, the Mysterious," interviewed by Charles Witbeck.
128-23.	Nimoy, Leonard	*TV Star Parade*, August 1967, "Leonard Nimoy's *Deathwatch*," interviewed by Susan Dennis.
128-24.	Nimoy, Leonard	ontd-startrek.livejournal.com, "Company of Angels Turns 50 (And celebrates with its first director, Leonard Nimoy)," interviewed by Steven Leigh Morris.
128-25.	Nimoy, Leonard	*Monsters of the Movies*, August 1975. Interviewed by Mike Harrison and Jeff Gelb.
128-26.	Nimoy, Leonard	BBC 1, 1971. Interviewed by Michael Aspel.
128a.	Nimoy, Sandra	*TV Guide*, March 4, 1967, "Product of Two Worlds," interviewed by Leslie Raddatz.
129-1.	**Nuyen, France**	**Author interview, 2012.**
130.	O'Connell, William	Sci Fi Channel, 1997.
131.	O'Herlihy, Michael	*Starlog #131*, interviewed by Edward Gross, June 1988.
132,	Oliver, Susan	*Starlog #135*, interviewed by Frank Garcia, Oct. 1988.
133.	Opatoshu, David	*Starlog #236*, interviewed by K.M. Drennan, June 1997.
134.	Oswald, Gerd	*Cinefantastique*, July 1996.
135-1.	Paskey, Eddie	*Starlog #132*, interviewed by Kathleen M. Gooch, July 1988.

135-2.	**Paskey, Eddie**	**Author interview, 2011.**
136-1.	Peeples, Samuel	*Gene Roddenberry: The Myth and the Man Behind Star Trek*, by Joel Engel (Hyperion, 1994).
136-2.	Peeples, Samuel	*Starlog #122*, interviewed by Edward Gross, Sept. 1987.
136-3.	Peeples, Samuel	*The Star Trek Interview Book*, interviewed by Allan Asherman (Pocket, 1988).
137.	Penn, Leo	*Starlog #179*, interviewed by Pat Jankiewicz, June 1992.
138.	Perrin, Vic	*Starlog #155*, interviewed by Mike Clark & Mark Phillips, June 1990.
139.	Perry, Roger	*Starlog #117*, interviewed by Mark Phillips, April 1987.
139-1.	**Perry, Roger**	**Author interview, 2013.**
141-1.	Pevney, Joseph	*Starlog #126*, interviewed by Edward Gross, Jan. 1988.
141-2.	Pevney, Joseph	*The Star Trek Interview Book*, interviewed by Allan Asherman (Pocket Books, 1988).
141-3	Pevney, Joseph	*Trek Classics*, by Edward Gross (Image Publishing of New York, 1991).
142-1	Phillips, Fred	*Cinefantastique*, interviewed by Ben Hernson, March 1987.
142-2.	Phillips, Fred	*The Making of Star Trek*, interviewed by Stephen E. Whitfield (Ballantine, 1968).
143-4.	Phillips, Fred	*Inside Star Trek, issue 2*.
143-4.	Phillips, Fred	*Inside Star Trek, issue 3*, interviewed by Fred Phillips, August 1968.
141a.	Raff, Robert	*The Star Trek Interview Book*, interviewed by Allan Asherman (Pocket Books, 1988).
144a.	Riegler, Hank	*Inside Star Trek: The Real Story*, interviewed by Robert Justman and/or Herb Solow (Pocket Books, 1996).
144b.	**Richardson-Kindryd, Ande**	**Author's interview.**
145	**Roddenberry, Gene**	**Author interview, 1982.**
145-1	Roddenberry, Gene	*Cinefantastique*, interviewed by Ben Hernson, March 1987.
145-2	Roddenberry, Gene	*Gene Roddenberry: The Last Conversation*, interviewed by Yvonne Fern (University of California Press, 1994).
145-3	Roddenberry, Gene	*Great Bird of the Galaxy*, by Edward Gross and Mark Altman (BoxTree Limited, 1994).
145-4	Roddenberry, Gene	*The Making of Star Trek*, interviewed by Stephen E. Whitfield (Ballantine, 1968).
145-5	Roddenberry, Gene	*Shatner: Where No Man ...* , byWilliam Shatner, Sondra Marshak and Myrna Culbreath (Tempo Books, 1979).
145-6	Roddenberry, Gene	*Star Trek: TOS* Box Set, Season 1.
145-7	Roddenberry, Gene	*Star Trek Creator*, by David Alexander (Penguin, 1994).
145-8	Roddenberry, Gene	*Star Trek Lives!*, by Jacqueline Lichtenberg, Sondra Marshak and Joan Winston (Bantam Books, 1975).
145-9	Roddenberry, Gene	*The Star Trek Interview Book*, interviewed by Allan Asherman (Pocket Books, 1988).
145-10	Roddenberry, Gene	*The World of Star Trek*, by David Gerrold (Ballantine, 1973).
145-11	Roddenberry, Gene	*Trek Classics*, by Edward Gross (Image Publishing of New York, 1991).
145-12	**Roddenberry, Gene**	**Author interview, 1990.**
145-13	Roddenberry, Gene	*Inside Star Trek, issue 1*, by Gene Roddenberry, 1968.
145-14.	Roddenberry, Gene	*Daily Variety*, June 7, 1966, interviewed by Dave Kaufman.
145-15.	Roddenberry, Gene	*Daily Variety*, July 15, 1966, "Just for Variety," interviewed by Army Archerd.
145-16.	Roddenberry, Gene	*Daily Variety*, January 16, 1967, "John Drew Barrymore Reprimanded by SAG for Balking at *Star* Role."
145-17.	Roddenberry, Gene	*Daily Variety*, February 9, 1967, "Seek 'Star' Femme Regular to do *Trek* at Desilu."
145-18.	Roddenberry, Gene	*Daily Variety*, February 16, 1967, "Light and Airy," interviewed by Jack Hellman.
145-19.	Roddenberry, Gene	*Daily Variety*, June 21, 1967, "On All Channels," interviewed by Dave Kaufman.
145-20.	Roddenberry, Gene	*Daily Variety*, June 28, 1967, "On All Channels," interviewed by Dave Kaufman.

145-21.	Roddenberry, Gene	*TV Guide*, July 15, 1967, "Let Me Off at the Next Planet."
145-22.	Roddenberry, Gene	*TV Guide*, March 4, 1967, "Product of Two Worlds," interviewed by Leslie Raddatz.
145-23.	Roddenberry, Gene	*The Humanists*, March/April 1991, interviewed by David Alexander.
145-24.	Roddenberry, Gene	*Gene Roddenberry: The Myth and the Man Behind StarTrek*, by Joel Engel.
145a.	**Rod Roddenberry**	**Author interview, 2012.**
146.	Rolfe, Sam	*Gene Roddenberry: The Myth and the Man Behind Star Trek*, interviewed by Joel Engel (Hyperion, 1994).
147.	Rugg, Jim	*Cinefantastique*, interviewed by Ben Hernson, March 1987.
151.	**Sargent, Joseph**	**Author interview, 2010.**
153.	Schlessinger, Dr. Laura	*Star Trek Communicator*, by Dr. Laura Schlessinger, June 1998.
153a.	Schlosser, Herbert	*Inside Star Trek: The Real Story*, interviewed by Robert Justman and/or Herb Solow (Pocket Books, 1996)
154.	Schneider, Paul	*Trek Classics*, interviewed by Edward Gross (Image Publishing of New York, 1991).
155-1	Senensky, Ralph	*Great Bird of the Galaxy*, interviewed by Edward Gross (BoxTree Limited, 1994).
155-2.	Senensky, Ralph	*Starlog #172*, interviewed by Edward Gross, Nov. 1991.
155-3.	Senensky, Ralph	*The Star Trek Interview Book*, interviewed by Allan Asherman (Pocket Books, 1988).
155-4.	Senensky, Ralph	*Trek Classics*, interviewed by Edward Gross (Image Publishing of New York, 1991).
155-5.	Senensky, Ralph	webpage blog, 2010.
155-6.	**Senensky, Ralph**	**Author interview, 2011.**
155a-1.	Shatner, Lisabeth	*Captain's Log, William Shatner's Personal Account of the Making of Star Trek V: The Final Frontier*, by William Shatner (*Star Trek* Publishing, 1989).
155a-2.	Shatner, Lisabeth	Personal blog.
166-1.	Shatner, William	*Great Bird of the Galaxy*, by Edward Gross and Mark Altman (BoxTree Limited, 1994).
166-2.	Shatner, William	Sci Fi Channel, 1997.
166-3.	Shatner, William	*Shatner: Where No Man …* , byWilliam Shatner, Sondra Marshak and Myrna Culbreath (Tempo Books, 1979).
166-4.	Shatner, William	*Star Trek: TOS* Box Set, Season 1.
166-5.	Shatner, William	*Star Trek: TOS* Box Set, Season 2.
166-6.	Shatner, William	*Star Trek Communicator*, August 1999.
166-7.	Shatner, William	*The Star Trek Interview Book*, interviewed by Allan Asherman (Pocket Books, 1988).
166-8.	Shatner, William	*Star Trek Memories*, by William Shatner and Chris Kreski (HarperCollins, 1994).
166-9.	Shatner, William	*The World of Star Trek*, interviewed by David Gerrold (Ballantine, 1973).
166-10.	Shatner, William	*Trek Classics*, by Edward Gross (Image Publishing of New York, 1991).
166-11.	Shatner, William	*TV Week*, August 28, 1966, "*Star Trek* Resembles Space *Twilight Zone*."
166-12.	Shatner, William	*Daily Variety*, September 7, 1966, "Shatner's Heroic Shift," interviewed by Dave Kaufman.
166-13.	Shatner, William	*Daily Variety*, July 15, 1966, "Just for Variety," interviewed by Army Archerd.
166-14.	Shatner, William	*TV Guide*, October 15, 1966, "No One Ever Upsets the STAR," interviewed by Michael Fessier, Jr.
166-15.	Shatner, William	*Syracuse Herald-American*, October 16, 1966, "Shatner, Star of TV Series, 'Hooked' on UFO Phenomenon."
166-16.	Shatner, William	*Boston Sunday Herald*, December 18, 1966, "Shatner Catches a Big Wave."
166-17.	Shatner, William	*Victoria Daily Times*, October 28, 1967, "Canada's First Man in Space," interviewed by Walter Roessing.
166-18.	Shatner, William	*Photo TV Land*, December 1967, "Outer Space's Inside Battle,"

166-19.	Shatner, William	interviewed by Rhonda Green. *Screen Stories*, Sept. 1967, "Leonard Nimoy and Bill Shatner: Their Topsy-Turvy Lives," interviewed by Dora Albert.
158a.	**Sloman, Peter**	**Author's interview, 2013.**
160-1.	Sohl, Jerry	*Gene Roddenberry: The Myth and the Man Behind Star Trek*, interviewed by Joel Engel (Hyperion, 1994).
160-2.	Sohl, Jerry	*Starlog #135*, interviewed by Edward Gross, October 1988.
160-3.	Sohl, Jerry	*Starlog #136*, interviewed by Edward Gross, November 1988.
160-4.	Sohl, Jerry	*Trek Classics*, interviewed by Edward Gross (Image Publishing of New York, 1991).
161-1.	Solow, Herbert F.	CJAD AM, interviewed by Peter Anthony Holder, Sept. 1996.
162-2.	Solow, Herbert F.	*Gene Roddenberry: The Myth and the Man Behind Star Trek*, interviewed by Joel Engel (Hyperion, 1994).
162-3.	Solow, Herbert F.	*Inside Star Trek: The Real Story*, by Herb Solow and Robert Justman (Pocket Books, 1996).
162-4.	Solow, Herbert F.	Sci Fi Channel, 1997.
161-5.	Solow, Herbert F.	*Starlog #241*, interviewed by Ian Spelling, August 1997.
161-6.	Solow, Herbert F.	*Star Trek Communicator, issue #107*, interviewed by Dan Madsen, June 1996.
161-7.	Solow, Herbert F.	*Daily Variety*, March 28, 1967, "On All Channels: Herb Solow's Crystal Ball," interviewed by Dave Kaufman.
162.	Sorokin, Joseph	*The Star Trek Interview Book*, interviewed by Allan Asherman (Pocket Books, 1988).
164-1.	Spies, Adrian	*Starlog #130*, interviewed by Edward Gross, May 1988.
164-2.	Spies, Adrian	*Trek Classics*, interviewed by Edward Gross (Image Publishing of New York, 1991).
166.	Stanley, Jerry	*Gene Roddenberry: The Myth and the Man Behind StarTrek*, interviewed by Joel Engel (Hyperion, 1994).
167.	Unnamed Series Insider	*Great Bird of the Galaxy*, by Edward Gross and Mark Altman (BoxTree Limited, 1994).
168.	Steiner, Fred	*The Music of Star Trek*, interviewed by Jeff Bond (Lone Eagle, 1999).
169a.	Stowell-Black, Mary	*Gene Roddenberry: The Myth and the Man Behind StarTrek*, interviewed by Joel Engel (Hyperion, 1994).
169b.	Sturgeon, Theodore	*Fangoria #10*, January 1981.
171-1	Takei, George	*Cinefantastique*, July 1996.
171-2	Takei, George	Sci Fi Channel, 1997.
171-3	Takei, George	*Star Trek: TOS* Box Set, Season 2.
171-4	Takei, George	*To the Stars*, by George Takei (Pocket Books, 1994).
171-5	Takei, George	*The World of Star Trek*, interviewed by David Gerrold (Ballantine Books, 1973).
171-6	Takei, George	*Inside Star Trek, issue 8*, interviewed by Ruth Berman, 1968.
171-7	Takei, George	*TV Guide Star Trek 25th Anniversary Special*, 1991.
172-1.	Theiss, William	*Cinefantastique*, July 1996.
172-2.	Theiss, William	startrekpropauthority.com, interviewed by James Magna, 1988.
172-3.	Theiss, William	*Inside Star Trek, issue 6*, interviewed by D.C. Fontana, Dec. 1968.
172-4.	Theiss, William	*Inside Star Trek, issue 7*, interviewed by D.C. Fontana, 1968.
173-1.	Throne, Malachi	*Starlog #190*, interviewed by Joel Eisner, May 1993.
173-2.	**Throne, Malachi**	**Author interview, 2011.**
174.	Tinker, Grant	*Gene Roddenberry: The Myth and the Man Behind Star Trek*, interviewed by Joel Engel (Hyperion, 1994).
176.	Tordjmann, Fabien	*The Star Trek Interview Book*, interviewed by Allan Asherman (Pocket Books, 1988).
177-1.	Trimble, Bjo	*On the Good Ship Enterprise*, by Bjo Trimble (Donning Company/Publishers, 1983).

177-2	Trimble, Bjo	*Starlog #62*, by Bjo Trimble, September 1982.
177-3	Trimble, Bjo	*Star Trek: TOS* Box Set, Season 2.
177-4	Trimble, Bjo	*Star Trek: TOS* Box Set, Season 3.
177-5	Trimble, Bjo	*Star Trek Creator*, interviewed by David Alexander (Penguin Books, 1994).
177-6	Trimble, Bjo	*Star Trek Memories*, interviewed by William Shatner and/or Chris Kreski ((HarperCollins, 1994).
177-7	Trimble, Bjo	*The World of Star Trek*, interviewed by David Gerrold (Ballantine Books, 1973).
177-8	**Trimble, Bjo**	**Author interview, 2012.**
177a.	Trimble, John	*Gene Roddenberry: The Myth and the Man Behind Star Trek*, interviewed by Joel Engel (Hyperion, 1994).
178.	Van der Veer, Greg	*Cinefantastique*, July 1996.
180a.	**Weaver, Andrea**	**Author interview, 2011.**
181.	Whitfield, Stephen E.	*The Making of Star Trek*, by Stephen E. Whitfield (Ballantine Books, 1968).
182.	Whitlock, Albert	*Cinefantastique*, July 1996.
183-1.	Whitney, Grace Lee	*Cinefantastique*, July 1996.
183-2.	Whitney, Grace Lee	*The Longest Trek*, by Grace Lee Whitney (Quill Driven Books, 1998).
183-3.	Whitney, Grace Lee	Sci Fi Channel, 1997.
183-4.	Whitney, Grace Lee	*Starlog #105*, interviewed by Daniel Dickholtz, April 1986.
183-5.	Whitney, Grace Lee	*The Star Trek Interview Book*, interviewed by Allan Asherman (Pocket Books, 1988).
183-6.	**Whitney, Grace Lee**	**Author interview, 2010.**
183-7.	Whitney, Grace Lee	*Official Star Trek Fan Club #51*, interviewed by Dan Madsen, August 1986.
184-1.	Wilber, Carey	*Starlog #117*, interviewed by Edward Gross, April 1987.
184-2.	Wilber, Carey	*Trek Classics*, interviewed by Edward Gross (Image Publishing of New York, 1991).
186.	Wincelberg, Shimon	*Starlog #159*, interviewed by Mike Clark, October 1990.
187	**Windom, William**	**Author interview, 2011.**
188	Winfield, Gene	*Starlog #53*, interviewed by James Van Hise, Dec. 1981.
189a.	**Winston, John**	**Author interview, 2010.**
192-1.	Woodward, Morgan	*Starlog #130*, interviewed by Mark Phillips, May 1988.
192-2.	Woodward, Morgan	*Star Trek: The Official Fan Club Magazine #75*, interviewed by John S. Davis, August 1990.
195.	Wyllie, Meg	*Starlog #117*, interviewed by Frank Garcia, April 1987.
197.	Ziv, Fred	*Star Trek Creator*, by David Alexander (Penguin, 1994).

MEMOS / LETTERS INDEX:

1. WHERE NO MAN HAS GONE BEFORE
Gene Roddenberry	GR1-1, date unknown / GR1-2, date unknown / GR1-3, 6/11/66 / GR1-4, 4/11/66 / GR1-5, 4/11/66
James Goldstone	JG1-1, Mid June / JG1-2, 6/16/65
Broadcast Standards	BS1, 6/15/66

2. THE CORBOMITE MANEUVER
Matt Jefferies	MJ2, 4/12/66
Robert Justman	RJ2-1, 4/4/66 / RJ2-2, 4/21/66
Stan Robertson	SR2-1, 4/12/66 / SR2-2, 5/2/66 / SR2-3, 5/17/66
Gene Roddenberry	GR2, Late May '66
Bill Theiss	BT2, 4/25/66

3. MUDD'S WOMEN
Jack Guss	JG3, 3/28/66
Robert Justman	RJ3-1, 4/20/66 / RJ3-2, 5/18/66 / RJ3-3, 5/24/66
Stan Robertson	SR3, 6/2/66
Gene Roddenberry	GR3-1, 4/18/66 / GR3-2, 5/13/66 / GR3-3, 5/19/66

4. THE ENEMY WITHIN
John D.F. Black	JB4-1, 4/25/66 / JB4-2, 5/24/66
Robert Justman	RJ4-1, 4/8/66 / RJ4-2, 4/22/66 / RJ4-3, 5/23/66 / RJ4-4, 6/1/66
Jon Kubichan	JK4, 4/28/66
Leonard Nimoy	LN4, 6/8/66
Stan Robertson	SR4-1, 4/25/66 / SR4-2, 6/10/66
Gene Roddenberry	GR4-1, Early April '66 / GR4-2, 4/26/66 / GR4-3, 5/23/66 / GR4-4, 5/24/66 / GR4-5, 9/14/66
Bill Theiss	BT4, 4/26/66

5. THE MAN TRAP
George C. Johnson	GCJ5, 6/13/66
Robert Justman	RJ5-1, 4/8/66 / RJ5-2, 4/15/66 / RJ5-3, 5/24/66 / RJ5-4, 6/2/66 / RJ5-5, 6/10/66 / RJ5-6, 6/14/66 / RJ5-7, 8/10/66 / RJ5-8, 11/3/66
Gene Roddenberry	GR5-1, 4/15/66 / GR5-2, 6/2/66 / GR5-3, 8/24/66
Stan Robertson	SR5-1, 4/19/66 / SR5-2, 6/21/66

6. THE NAKED TIME
No memos available.

7. CHARLIE X
John D.F. Black	JB7, 6/7/66
Robert Justman	RJ7-1, 4/28/66 / RJ7-2, 5/11/66 / RJ7-3, 6/7/66
Stan Robertson	SR7-1, 4/22/66 / SR7-2, 7/6/66 / SR7-3, 9/12/66
Gene Roddenberry	GR7-1, 4/22/66 / GR7-2, 6/13/66 / GR7-3, 6/30/66

8. BALANCE OF TERROR
Robert Justman	RJ8-1, 4/26/66 / RJ8-2, 5/24/66 / RJ8-3, 6/7/66
Stan Robertson	SR8-1, 5/4/66 / SR8-2, 6/30/66
Gene Roddenberry	GR8-1, no date / GR8-2, 4/18/66 / GR8-3, 5/28/66 / GR8-4, 6/15/66
Paul Schneider	PS8, 4/14/66

9. WHAT ARE LITTLE GIRLS MADE OF?
John D.F. Black	JDFB9, 5/3/66
Robert Bloch	RB9-1, 3/19/66 / RB9-2, 4/26/66
Kellam De Forest	KDF9, 5/26/66
Robert Justman	RJ9-1, 4/14/66 / RJ9-2, 4/27/66 / RJ9-3, 5/6/66 / RJ9-4, 9/1/66
Broadcast Standards	BS9-1, 5/2/66 / BS9-2, 7/29/66 / BS9-3, 8/2/66
Stan Robertson	SR9-1, 4/8/66 / SR9-2, 5/5/66 / SR9-3, 5/31/66
Gene Roddenberry	GR9-1, 3/29/66 / GR9-2, 3/31/66 / GR9-3, 4/15/66 / GR9-4, 4/20/66 / GR9-5, 5/20/66 / GR9-6, 7/28/66
Herb Solow	HS9, 5/24/66

10. DAGGER OF THE MIND
Shimon Wincelberg SW10-1, 6/15/66 / SW10-2, date unknown
John D.F. Black JDFB10, 6/16/66
Robert Justman RJ10-1, 4/4/66 / RJ10-2, 6/28/66
Gene Roddenberry GR10, 4/14/66
Stan Robertson SR10, 5/19/66

Broadcast Standards BS10-1, 5/20/66 / BS10-2, 7/22/66
Ed Perlstein EP10, 9/12/66

11. MIRI
Robert Justman RJ11-1, 4/7/66 / RJ11-2, 5/16/66 / RJ11-3, 6/13/66 / RJ11-4, 8/11/66
Gene Roddenberry GR11-1, 4/19/66 / GR11-2, 5/19/66 / GR11-3, 6/12/66 / GR11-4, June '66 / GR11-5, 6/24/66 / GR11-6, 8/15/66 / GR11-7, 10/28/66
John D.F. Black JB11, 5/18/66
Stan Robertson SR11, 4/15/66
Broadcast Standards BS11, 8/16/66

12. THE CONSCIENCE OF THE KING
Robert Justman RJ12-1, 4/14/66 / RJ12-2, 5/9/66 / RJ12-3, 6/13/66 / RJ12-4, 8/4/66 / RJ12-5, 8/15/66
Gene Roddenberry GR12-1, 4/15/66 / GR12-2, 6/13/66 / GR12-3, 6/14/66 / GR12-4, 8/15/66 / GR12-5, 9/2/66 / GR12-6, 9/29/66
John D.F. Black JB12-1, 5/12/66 / JB12-2, 8/3/66
Stan Robertson SR12, 4/26/66
Broadcast Standards BS12-1, 8/23/66 / BS12-2, 8/25/66

13. THE GALILEO SEVEN
Matt Jefferies MJ13, 4/12/66
Gene Roddenberry GR13-1, March '66 / GR13-2, 4/14/66 / GR13-3, 8/24/66 / GR13-4, 8/29/66 / GR13-5, 9/1/66
Robert Justman RJ13-1, 4/4/66 / RJ13-2, 4/26/66 / RJ13-3, 5/25/66 / RJ13-4, 8/23/66
Stan Robertson SR13-1, 4/12/66 / SR13-2, 9/13/66
Broadcast Standards BS13-1, 9/14/66
Ed Perlstein EP13-1, 9/26/66

14. COURT MARTIAL
Don Mankiewicz DM14, 6/26/66
Gene Roddenberry GR14-1, 4/22/66 / GR14-2, 5/6/66 / GR14-3, 9/12/66 / GR14-4, 9/16/66 / GR14-5, date unknown
Robert Justman RJ14-1, 5/5/66 / RJ14-2, 8/16/66 / RJ14-3, 9/7/66
John D.F. Black JB14-1, 5/6/66 / JB14-2, July '66
Gene Coon GC14, 8/11/66
Stan Robertson SR14, 9/28/66
De Forest Research DFR14, 9/26/66
Greg Peters GR14, 9/29/66

15 & 16. THE MENAGERIE
Robert Justman RJ15-1, 9/14/66 / RJ15-2, 10/20/66
Gene Roddenberry GR15-1, 10/7/66 / GR15-2, date unknown
Stan Robertson SR15, 10/5/66
Isaac Asimov IA15, 11/31/66
Herb Solow HS15, 10/7/66

17. SHORE LEAVE
Theodore Sturgeon TS17-1, June '66 / TS17-2, 6/20/66
Gene Roddenberry GR17-1, 5/20/66 / GR17-2, 6/2/66 / GR17-3, 6/8/66 / GR17-4, 6/21/66 / GR17-5, 7/5/66 / GR17-6, 10/19/66 / GR17-7, 10/25/66
Robert Justman RJ17-1, 5/17/66 / RJ17-2, 5/18/66 / RJ17-3, 6/9/66 / RJ17-4, 6/22/66 / RJ17-5, 9/14/66
Gene Coon GC17, 9/15/66
Stan Robertson SR17, 6/1/66
De Forest Research DFR17, 10/14/66

18. THE SQUIRE OF GOTHOS
Paul Schneider PS18, date unknown
Gene Roddenberry GR18-1, 8/16/66 / GR18-2, 10/12/66
Robert Justman RJ18-1, 8/15/66 / RJ18-2, 10/13/66 / RJ18-3, 10/27/66
Staff Staff18, 10/11/66
Stan Robertson SR18, 10/25/66

19. ARENA
Gene Roddenberry   GR19, 10/24/66
Robert Justman   RJ19, 10/27/66
Stan Robertson   SR19, 10/14/66
De Forest Research   DFR19-1, 10/14/66 / DFR19, 11/2/66
Broadcast Standards   BS19, 10/25/66

20. THE ALTERNATIVE FACTOR
Gene Roddenberry   GR20-1, 8/29/66 / GR20-2, Sept '66 / GR20-3, 11/3/66
Robert Justman   RJ20-1, 9/6/66 / RJ20-2, 9/22/66 / RJ20-3, 10/19/66 / RJ20-4, 11/9/66
Gene Coon   GC20, 9//2/66
Joe D'Agosta   JDA20, 11/18/66
Stan Robertson   SR20-1, 9/21/66 / SR20-2, 11/16/66
Herb Solow   HB20, 11/21/66

21. TOMORROW IS YESTERDAY
Gene Roddenberry   GR21, 1/31/67
Robert Justman   RJ21-1, 10/17/66 / RJ21-2, 11/3/66 / RJ21-3, 11/11/66 / RJ21-4, 11/17/66
Stan Robertson   SR21, 10/10/66

22. THE RETURN OF THE ARCHONS
Gene Roddenberry   GR22-1, 8/24/66 / GR22-2, 11/29/66
Robert Justman   RJ22-1, 8/23/66 / RJ22-2, 9/2/66 / RJ22-3, 10/14/66 / RJ22-4, 11/3/66
Gene Coon   GC22, 9/6/66
Stan Robertson   SR22, 9/8/66
Broadcast Standards   BS22, 11/14/66

23. SPACE SEED
Gene Roddenberry   GR23, 12/6/66
Robert Justman   RJ23-1, 9/6/66 / RJ23-2, 11/1/66 / RJ23-3, 12/13/66
Gene Coon   GC23-1, 9/2/66 / GC23-2, 9/7/66 / GC23-3, 9/7/66 / GC23-4, 11/1/66
D.C. Fontana   DCF23, 10/27/66
Stan Robertson   SR23, 9/12/66
Marc Daniels   MD23, 1/23/67

24. A TASTE OF ARMAGEDDON
Robert Justman   RJ24-1, 9/22/66 / RJ24-2, 10/28/66 / RJ24-3, 11/28/66 / RJ24-4, 12/7/66
Gene Coon   GC24, 9/15/66
D.C. Fontana   DCF24, 10/21/66
Stan Robertson   SR24, 9/29/66

25. THIS SIDE OF PARADISE
Jerry Sohl   JS25-1, 3/1/67 / JS25-2, 2/19/68
Gene Roddenberry   GR25-1, 9/1/66 / GR25-2, 10/12/66
Robert Justman   RJ25-1, 6/17/66 / RJ25-2, Date unknown / RJ25-3, 8/15/66 / RJ25-4, 12/15/66 / RJ25-5, 12/25/66
Stan Robertson   SR25, 8/15/66
De Forest Research   DFR25, 12/16/66

26. THE DEVIL IN THE DARK
Gene Roddenberry   GR26-1, 3/23/67 / GR26-2, 3/30/67
Robert Justman   RJ26, 11/30/66
Stan Robertson   SR26, 12/7/66
De Forest Research   DFR26, 12/22/66

27. ERRAND OF MERCY
Robert Justman   RJ27, 1/4/67

28. THE CITY ON THE EDGE OF FOREVER
Robert Justman   RJ28, 12/20/66

29. OPERATION: ANNIHILATE!
Robert Justman   RJ29, Date unknown
Stan Robertson   SR29, 1/23/67

**NBC promotional photo for Season Two timeslot change
(Courtesy of Gerald Gurian)**

Stay tuned …

LSTR 14/15
WITHDRAWN